EUROPE

TOURIST and MOTORING ATLAS
ATLAS ROUTIER et TOURISTIQUE
STRASSEN- und REISEATLAS
TOERISTISCHE WEGENATLAS
ATLANTE STRADALE e TURISTICO
ATLAS DE CARRETERAS y TURÍSTICO

II

Sommaire / Contents / Inhaltsübersicht / Inhoud

Sommaire / Contents / Inhaltsübersicht / Inhoud

60-71

1 : 1 500 000
1 cm = 15 km

Scandinavie
Scandinavia

Skandinavien
Scandinavië

72-87

1 : 500 000
1 cm = 5 km

Pays Baltes
Baltic Countries

Baltische Länder
Baltische Landen

88-99

1 : 700 000
1 cm = 7 km

Pologne
Poland

Polen
Polen

100-111

1 : 700 000
1 cm = 7 km

Grèce
Greece

Griechenland
Griekenland

112-113

1 : 450 000
1 cm = 4.5 km

Chypre
Cyprus

Zypern
Cyprus

114-117

Europe
1 : 3 330 000

Europa
1 cm = 33 km

118-186

Index

Register

Plans de ville / Town plans / Stadtpläne / Stadsplattegronden
Piante di città / Planos de ciudades / Plantas de Cidade

118	Amsterdam	129	Budapest	139	Hamburg	155	Manchester	172	Salzburg
119	Antwerpen	130	Dijon	140	Hannover	155	Marseille	172	Sevilla
118	Athína	130	Dresden	140	Helsinki	156	Milano	173	Stockholm
122	Barcelona	131	Dublin	141	Istanbul	158	Monaco	174	Strasbourg
122	Basel	130	Dubrovnik	143	Köln	157	München	175	Stuttgart
123	Belfast	131	Düsseldorf	141	København	158	Nantes	176	Torino
123	Berlin	134	Edinburgh	146	Lausanne	159	Napoli	177	Toulouse
124	Bern	134	Essen	147	Leipzig	160	Nice	180	València
124	Birmingham	135	Firenze	146	Liège	160	Nürnberg	177	Valletta
125	Bologna	135	Frankfurt a. Main	147	Lille	164	Oslo	180	Venezia
126	Bonn	136	Genève	148	Lisboa	165	Palermo	181	Warszawa
126	Bordeaux	137	Genova	148	Liverpool	162	Paris	182	Wien
127	Bratislava	137	Gent	150	London	166	Porto	183	Zagreb
127	Bremen	138	Glasgow	154	Luxembourg	167	Praha	184	Zürich
128	Brugge	138	Göteborg	152	Lyon	168	Roma		
128	Bruxelles	139	Den Haag	154	Madrid	169	Rotterdam		

IV

Europe des 27
27 EU Member States
Europa der 27
Het Europa van de 27

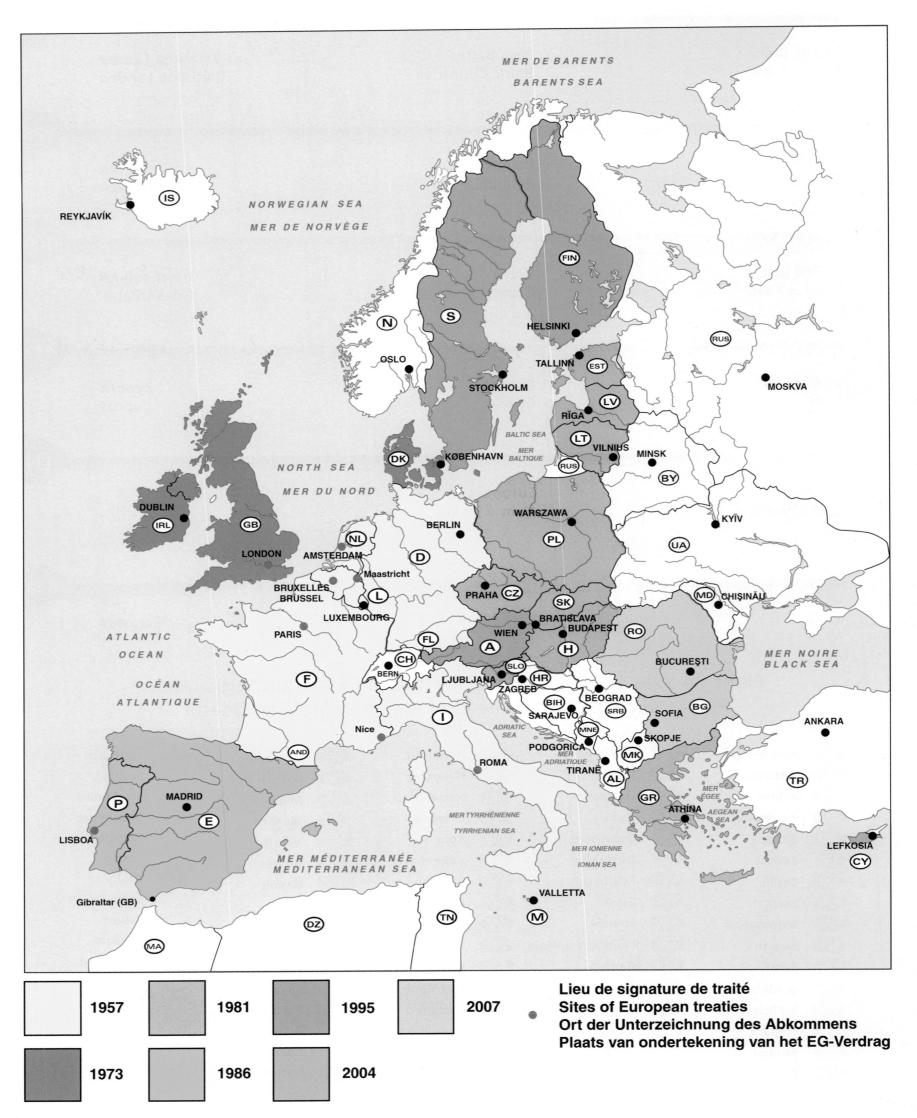

	1957		1981		1995		2007
	1973		1986		2004		

Lieu de signature de traité
Sites of European treaties
Ort der Unterzeichnung des Abkommens
Plaats van ondertekening van het EG-Verdrag

Schengen

Espace de libre circulation des personnes
Area of free movement between member states
Abschaffung der Binnengrenzkontrollen
Ruimte voor vrij verkeer van personen
Area di libera circolazione delle persone
Espacio de libre circulación de personas
Espaço de livre circulação de pessoas

(EU) + Schengen

(EU) + Schengen

(EU) + Schengen

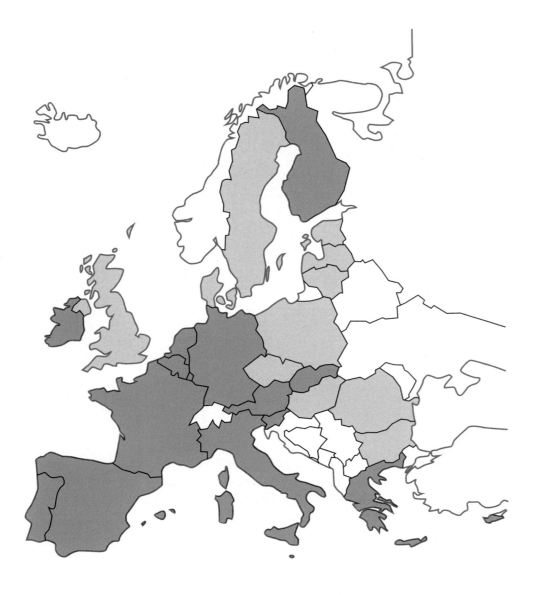

Euro : €

(EU) + €

(EU) + €

Pays de l'UE
EU states
EU-Staaten
(EU) EU-lidstaten
Paesi dell'UE
Países de la UE
Países da UE

	NOM FRANÇAIS	NOM LOCAL	(x1000)	hab/km²	km²	(Capitale)	(Adhésion UE)	(Monnaie)	(1 000 000 000 €)	(en €)	(GMT)	RÉGIME POLITIQUE	FÊTE NATIONALE
D	ALLEMAGNE	Deutschland	82 422,3	231	357 046	Berlin	25 mars 1957	€	603,6	7 333	+1 (hiver) +2 (été)	République fédérale	03/10
A	AUTRICHE	Österreich	8 192,8	98	83 858	Wien (Vienne)	1 janvier 1995	€	67,9	8 182	+1 (hiver) +2 (été)	République fédérale	26/10
B	BELGIQUE	België, Belgique	10 472,8	343	30 528	Brussel/Bruxelles	25 mars 1957	€	81,7	7 773	+1 (hiver) +2 (été)	Monarchie constitutionnelle et parlementaire	21/07
BG	BULGARIE	Balgarija	7 385,3	67	110 912	Sofia	1 janvier 2007	Leva (BGN)	-	-	+2 (hiver) +3 (été)	République	03/03
CY	CHYPRE	Kýpros, Kibris	778,5	84	9 251	Lefkosia (Nicosie)	1 mai 2004	Livre chypriote (CYP)	3,8	4 881	+2 (hiver) +3 (été)	République	01/10
DK	DANEMARK	Danmark	5 450,6	126	43 093	København (Copenhague)	1 janvier 1973	Danske Krone (DKK)	56,3	10 336	+1 (hiver) +2 (été)	Monarchie parlementaire	16/04
E	ESPAGNE	España	45 116,8	89	506 030	Madrid	1 janvier 1986	€	261,0	5 869	+1 (hiver) +2 (été)	Royaume (Monarchie parlementaire)	12/10
EST	ESTONIE	Eesti	1 342,4	30	45 228	Tallin	1 mai 2004	Eesti Kroon (EEK)	3,8	2 831	+2 (hiver) +3 (été)	République	24/02
FIN	FINLANDE	Suomi, Finland	5 231,4	15	338 145	Helsinki/Helsingfors	1 janvier 1995	€	43,9	8 319	+2 (hiver) +3 (été)	République	06/12
F	FRANCE	France	64 471,4	119	543 965	Paris	25 mars 1957	€	462,9	7 302	+1 (hiver) +2 (été)	République	14/07
GR	GRÈCE	Ellada	11 043,8	84	131 957	Athína (Athènes)	1 janvier 1981	€	47,5	4 252	+2 (hiver) +3 (été)	République	25/03
H	HONGRIE	Magyarország	9 981,3	106	93 966	Budapest	1 mai 2004	Forint (HUF)	25,3	2 514	+1 (hiver) +2 (été)	République	20/08
IRL	IRLANDE	Ireland, Éire	4 062,2	58	70 273	Dublin	1 janvier 1973	€	46,3	11 000	GMT (hiver) +1 (été)	République	17/03
I	ITALIE	Italia	58 133,5	193	301 323	Roma (Rome)	25 mars 1957	€	383,7	6 489	+1 (hiver) +2 (été)	République	02/06
LV	LETTONIE	Latvija	2 281,3	35	64 856	Riga	1 mai 2004	Lats (LVL)	4,9	2 148	+2 (hiver) +3 (été)	République	18/11
LT	LITUANIE	Lietuva	3 585,9	55	65 300	Vilnius	1 mai 2004	Litas (LTL)	6,8	2 009	+2 (hiver) +3 (été)	République	16/02
L	LUXEMBOURG	Luxembourg, Lëtzebuerg	474,4	183	2 586	Luxembourg	25 mars 1957	€	9,0	19 587	+1 (hiver) +2 (été)	Monarchie constitutionnelle	23/06
M	MALTE	Malta	400,2	1 266	316	Valletta (La Valette)	1 mai 2004	Maltese Lira (MTL)	1,3	3 202	+1 (hiver) +2 (été)	République	21/09
NL	PAYS-BAS	Nederland	16 335,7	438	37 330	Amsterdam	25 mars 1957	€	138,1	8 442	+1 (hiver) +2 (été)	Monarchie constitutionnelle et parlementaire	30/04
PL	POLOGNE	Polska	38 518,2	123	312 685	Warszawa (Varsovie)	1 mai 2004	Zloty (PLN)	75,6	1 983	+1 (hiver) +2 (été)	République	03/05
P	PORTUGAL	Portugal	10 605,9	115	91 906	Lisboa (Lisbonne)	1 janvier 1986	€	40,4	3 812	+1 (hiver) +2 (été)	République	10/06
R	ROUMANIE	România	22 303,5	94	238 391	Bucuresti (Bucarest)	1 janvier 2007	Leu (RON)	-	-	+2 (hiver) +3 (été)	République	01/12
GB	ROYAUME-UNI	United Kingdom of Great Britain & Northern Ireland	59 911,6	246	243 305	London (Londres)	1 janvier 1973	Pound Sterling (GBP)	50,7	834	GMT (hiver) +1 (été)	Monarchie constitutionnelle	13/06
SK	SLOVAQUIE, République	Slovenská Republika	5 439,5	111	49 034	Bratislava	1 mai 2004	Slovenská Koruna (SKK)	13,2	2 447	+1 (hiver) +2 (été)	République	01/09
SLO	SLOVÉNIE	Slovenija	2 010,3	99	20 273	Ljubljana	1 mai 2004	€	8,2	4 079	+1 (hiver) +2 (été)	République	01/07
S	SUÈDE	Sverige	9 042,6	20	449 963	Stockholm	1 janvier 1995	Svensk Krona (SEK)	-	-	+1 (hiver) +2 (été)	Monarchie parlementaire	06/06
CZ	TCHÈQUE, République	Česká Republika	10 235,4	130	78 866	Praha (Prague)	1 mai 2004	Koruna Česká (CZK)	30,9	3 004	+1 (hiver) +2 (été)	République	28/10

Sources :
Eurostat 2008

Climat      Climate      Klima      Klimaat

Températures (Moyenne mensuelle)
16 max. quotidien
8 min. quotidien

Average daily temperature
16 maximum
8 minimum

Temperaturen (Monatlicher Durchschnitt)
16 maximale Tagestemperatur
8 minimale Tagestemperatur

Temperaturen (Maandgemiddelde)
16 maximum
8 minimum

Précipitations (Moyenne mensuelle) — **Average monthly rainfall** — **Nierderschlagsmengen (Monatlicher Durchschnitt)** — **Gemiddelde maandelijkse neerslag**

☐ 0-20mm	☐ 20-50mm	☐ 50-100mm	■ + 100mm	☐ 0-20mm

Températures — cities (left column)

City		1	2	3	4	5	6	7	8	9	10	11	12
Amsterdam	NL	5 / 1	4 / 0	7 / 2	10 / 5	14 / 8	18 / 11	20 / 13	20 / 14	18 / 12	14 / 8	9 / 5	6 / 2
Andorra la Vella	AND	6 / -1	7 / -1	12 / 2	14 / 4	17 / 6	23 / 10	26 / 12	24 / 12	22 / 10	16 / 6	10 / 2	6 / -1
Athína	GR	13 / 6	14 / 7	16 / 8	20 / 11	25 / 16	30 / 20	33 / 23	33 / 23	29 / 19	24 / 15	19 / 12	15 / 8
Beograd	SER	3 / -3	5 / -2	11 / 2	18 / 7	23 / 12	26 / 15	28 / 17	28 / 17	24 / 13	18 / 8	11 / 4	5 / 0
Bergen	N	3 / -1	3 / -1	6 / 0	9 / 3	14 / 7	16 / 10	19 / 12	19 / 12	15 / 10	11 / 6	8 / 3	5 / 1
Berlin	D	2 / -3	3 / -3	8 / 0	13 / 4	19 / 8	22 / 12	24 / 14	23 / 14	20 / 10	13 / 6	7 / 2	3 / -1
Bern	CH	2 / -4	4 / -3	9 / 1	14 / 4	18 / 8	21 / 11	23 / 13	22 / 13	19 / 10	13 / 5	7 / 1	3 / -2
Bordeaux	F	9 / 2	11 / 2	15 / 4	17 / 6	20 / 9	24 / 12	25 / 14	26 / 14	23 / 12	18 / 8	13 / 5	9 / 3
Bratislava	SK	2 / -3	4 / -2	10 / 1	16 / 6	21 / 11	24 / 14	26 / 16	26 / 16	22 / 12	15 / 7	8 / 3	4 / 0
Bremen	D	3 / -2	4 / -2	8 / 0	13 / 4	18 / 7	21 / 11	22 / 13	22 / 12	19 / 10	13 / 6	8 / 3	4 / 0
Brno	CZ	2 / -5	3 / -5	8 / -1	15 / 4	20 / 9	23 / 12	25 / 14	25 / 13	21 / 9	14 / 4	7 / 2	3 / -1
Bruxelles / Brussel	B	4 / -1	7 / 0	10 / 2	14 / 5	18 / 8	22 / 11	23 / 12	22 / 12	21 / 11	16 / 7	9 / 3	6 / 0
Bucureşti	RO	1 / -7	4 / -5	10 / -1	18 / 5	23 / 10	27 / 14	30 / 16	30 / 15	25 / 11	18 / 6	10 / 2	4 / -3
Budapest	H	1 / -4	4 / -2	10 / 2	17 / 7	22 / 11	26 / 15	28 / 16	27 / 16	23 / 12	16 / 7	8 / 3	4 / -1
Cagliari	I	14 / 7	15 / 7	17 / 9	19 / 11	23 / 14	27 / 18	30 / 21	30 / 21	27 / 19	23 / 15	19 / 11	16 / 9
Chişinău	MD	-1 / -8	1 / -5	6 / -2	16 / 6	23 / 11	26 / 14	27 / 16	27 / 15	23 / 11	17 / 7	10 / 3	2 / -4
Cork	IRL	8 / 2	9 / 3	11 / 4	13 / 5	16 / 7	19 / 10	20 / 12	20 / 12	18 / 10	14 / 7	11 / 4	9 / 3
Dresden	D	2 / -4	3 / -3	8 / 0	14 / 4	19 / 8	22 / 11	24 / 13	24 / 13	20 / 10	13 / 5	8 / 2	3 / -2
Dublin	IRL	8 / 2	8 / 2	10 / 3	12 / 5	14 / 7	18 / 10	19 / 11	19 / 11	17 / 10	14 / 7	10 / 4	8 / 3
Dubrovnik	HR	12 / 6	13 / 6	14 / 8	17 / 11	21 / 14	25 / 18	29 / 21	28 / 21	25 / 18	21 / 14	17 / 10	14 / 8
Edinburgh	GB	6 / 1	6 / 1	8 / 2	11 / 4	14 / 6	17 / 9	18 / 11	18 / 11	16 / 9	13 / 7	9 / 4	7 / 2
Gibraltar	GB	16 / 9	16 / 9	18 / 11	20 / 11	23 / 14	27 / 17	29 / 19	29 / 20	27 / 19	24 / 15	20 / 12	17 / 9
Göteborg	S	1 / -3	1 / -4	4 / -2	9 / 2	16 / 7	19 / 12	21 / 14	20 / 14	16 / 10	11 / 6	6 / 3	4 / 0
Graz	A	1 / -5	4 / -4	9 / 0	15 / 5	19 / 9	23 / 13	25 / 14	24 / 14	20 / 10	14 / 5	7 / 1	2 / -2
Helsinki	FIN	-3 / -9	-4 / -9	0 / -7	6 / -1	14 / 4	19 / 9	22 / 13	20 / 12	15 / 8	8 / 3	3 / -1	-1 / -5
Iráklio	GR	16 / 9	16 / 9	17 / 10	20 / 12	23 / 15	27 / 19	29 / 22	29 / 22	27 / 19	24 / 17	21 / 14	18 / 11
Istanbul	TR	8 / 3	9 / 3	11 / 3	16 / 7	21 / 12	25 / 16	28 / 18	28 / 18	24 / 16	20 / 13	15 / 9	11 / 6
Kérkira	GR	14 / 6	15 / 6	16 / 8	19 / 10	23 / 13	28 / 17	31 / 19	32 / 19	28 / 17	23 / 14	19 / 11	16 / 8
København	DK	2 / -2	2 / -3	5 / -1	10 / 3	16 / 8	19 / 11	22 / 14	21 / 14	18 / 11	12 / 7	7 / 3	4 / 1
Kyïv	UA	-4 / -10	-2 / -8	3 / -4	14 / 5	21 / 11	24 / 14	25 / 15	24 / 14	19 / 9	13 / 6	5 / 0	-1 / -6
Lisboa	P	14 / 8	15 / 8	17 / 10	20 / 12	21 / 13	25 / 15	27 / 17	28 / 17	26 / 17	22 / 14	17 / 11	15 / 9
Ljubljana	SLO	2 / -4	5 / -3	10 / 0	15 / 4	20 / 9	24 / 12	26 / 14	25 / 13	22 / 10	15 / 6	8 / 2	4 / 0
London	GB	6 / 2	7 / 2	10 / 3	13 / 6	17 / 8	20 / 12	22 / 14	21 / 13	19 / 11	14 / 8	10 / 5	7 / 3
Luxembourg	L	3 / -1	4 / -1	10 / 1	14 / 4	18 / 8	21 / 11	23 / 13	22 / 13	19 / 10	13 / 6	7 / 3	4 / 0
Lyon	F	6 / -1	7 / 0	13 / 3	16 / 6	20 / 10	24 / 13	27 / 16	26 / 15	23 / 12	16 / 7	10 / 4	6 / 0
Madrid	E	9 / 2	11 / 2	15 / 5	18 / 7	21 / 10	27 / 15	31 / 17	30 / 17	25 / 14	19 / 10	13 / 5	9 / 2
Marseille	F	10 / 2	12 / 2	15 / 5	18 / 8	22 / 11	26 / 15	29 / 18	28 / 18	25 / 15	20 / 11	15 / 7	11 / 4
Milano	I	5 / 0	8 / 2	14 / 6	18 / 10	23 / 14	27 / 18	29 / 20	28 / 19	24 / 16	17 / 11	10 / 6	6 / 2
Minsk	BY	-4 / -13	-4 / -11	1 / -7	11 / 2	18 / 8	21 / 12	22 / 12	21 / 12	15 / 8	9 / 4	2 / -1	-3 / -8

Températures — cities (right column)

City		1	2	3	4	5	6	7	8	9	10	11	12
Monaco / Monte-Carlo	MC	12 / 8	13 / 8	14 / 10	16 / 12	19 / 15	23 / 19	26 / 22	26 / 22	24 / 20	20 / 16	16 / 12	14 / 10
Moskva	RUS	-9 / -16	-6 / -14	0 / -8	10 / 1	19 / 8	21 / 11	23 / 13	22 / 12	16 / 7	9 / 3	2 / -3	-5 / -10
Napoli	I	12 / 4	13 / 5	15 / 6	18 / 9	22 / 12	26 / 16	29 / 18	29 / 18	26 / 16	22 / 12	17 / 9	13 / 6
Odense	DK	2 / -2	2 / -3	5 / -1	11 / 2	16 / 6	19 / 9	21 / 12	21 / 12	17 / 9	12 / 5	7 / 3	4 / 1
Oslo	N	-2 / -7	-1 / -7	4 / -4	10 / 1	16 / 6	20 / 10	22 / 13	21 / 12	16 / 8	9 / 3	3 / -1	0 / -4
Oulu	FIN	-6 / -13	-6 / -14	-1 / -11	4 / -4	11 / 2	17 / 8	21 / 12	19 / 10	13 / 6	5 / 0	0 / -5	-5 / -9
Palermo	I	16 / 8	16 / 8	17 / 9	20 / 11	24 / 14	27 / 18	30 / 21	30 / 21	28 / 19	25 / 16	21 / 12	18 / 10
Paris	F	6 / 1	7 / 1	12 / 4	16 / 6	20 / 9	23 / 13	25 / 15	24 / 14	21 / 12	16 / 8	10 / 5	7 / 2
Plymouth	GB	8 / 4	8 / 4	10 / 5	12 / 6	15 / 8	18 / 11	19 / 13	19 / 13	17 / 12	14 / 9	11 / 6	9 / 5
Porto	P	13 / 5	14 / 5	16 / 8	18 / 9	20 / 11	23 / 13	25 / 15	25 / 15	24 / 14	21 / 11	17 / 8	14 / 5
Praha	CZ	0 / -5	3 / -4	8 / -1	13 / 2	18 / 7	21 / 10	23 / 12	23 / 12	19 / 9	13 / 4	6 / 0	2 / -3
Rennes	F	8 / 2	9 / 2	13 / 4	15 / 5	18 / 8	22 / 11	23 / 13	23 / 13	21 / 11	16 / 8	11 / 5	8 / 3
Reykjavík	IS	2 / -2	3 / -2	4 / -1	6 / 1	10 / 4	12 / 7	14 / 9	14 / 8	11 / 6	7 / 3	4 / 0	2 / -2
Riga	LV	-4 / -10	-3 / -10	2 / -7	10 / 1	16 / 6	21 / 11	22 / 13	21 / 12	16 / 8	10 / 4	4 / -1	-2 / -7
Roma	I	11 / 5	13 / 5	15 / 7	18 / 10	23 / 13	28 / 17	30 / 20	30 / 19	27 / 17	22 / 13	16 / 9	13 / 6
Salzburg	A	1 / -6	3 / -5	9 / -1	14 / 4	19 / 8	22 / 11	24 / 13	23 / 13	20 / 10	14 / 5	8 / 0	3 / -3
Sarajevo	BIH	3 / -4	5 / -3	10 / 0	15 / 5	20 / 8	24 / 12	26 / 13	26 / 13	22 / 10	16 / 6	9 / 2	5 / -1
Sevilla	E	15 / 6	17 / 7	20 / 9	24 / 11	27 / 13	32 / 17	36 / 20	36 / 20	32 / 18	26 / 14	20 / 10	16 / 7
Skopje	MK	5 / -3	8 / -1	12 / 3	19 / 7	23 / 10	28 / 13	31 / 15	31 / 14	26 / 11	19 / 6	12 / 3	6 / -1
Sofia	BG	2 / -4	4 / -3	10 / 1	16 / 5	21 / 9	24 / 13	27 / 14	26 / 15	22 / 11	16 / 6	9 / 3	4 / -1
Stockholm	S	-1 / -5	-1 / -5	3 / -4	8 / 1	16 / 6	20 / 11	22 / 14	20 / 13	15 / 9	9 / 5	5 / 2	1 / -2
Strasbourg	F	3 / -2	5 / -2	10 / 1	14 / 4	19 / 8	22 / 11	24 / 13	23 / 13	20 / 10	14 / 6	8 / 2	4 / 0
Stuttgart	D	3 / -3	5 / -2	10 / 1	14 / 4	19 / 8	22 / 11	24 / 13	23 / 13	20 / 10	14 / 6	8 / 2	4 / -2
Szczecin	PL	2 / -3	2 / -3	7 / -1	12 / 2	18 / 7	22 / 11	23 / 13	23 / 12	18 / 9	13 / 5	7 / 1	3 / -1
Tallinn	EST	-4 / -10	-4 / -11	0 / -7	8 / 0	14 / 5	19 / 10	20 / 13	20 / 12	15 / 8	9 / 4	3 / -1	-1 / -6
Thessaloníki	GR	9 / 2	12 / 3	14 / 5	20 / 10	25 / 14	29 / 18	32 / 21	32 / 21	27 / 17	22 / 13	16 / 9	11 / 4
Tiranë	AL	12 / 2	12 / 2	15 / 5	18 / 8	23 / 12	28 / 16	31 / 17	31 / 17	27 / 14	23 / 10	17 / 8	14 / 5
Tromsø	N	-2 / -6	-2 / -6	0 / -5	3 / -2	7 / 1	12 / 6	16 / 9	15 / 8	10 / 5	5 / 1	2 / -2	0 / -4
Umeå	S	-4 / -12	-4 / -12	0 / -9	5 / -3	12 / 2	18 / 9	20 / 12	18 / 10	13 / 5	7 / 0	2 / -4	-2 / -9
Vaasa	FIN	-4 / -11	-5 / -11	0 / -10	5 / -3	12 / 3	18 / 9	20 / 13	18 / 11	13 / 6	7 / 1	2 / -3	-2 / -7
València	E	15 / 6	16 / 7	18 / 9	20 / 11	23 / 13	26 / 17	29 / 20	29 / 20	27 / 18	23 / 13	19 / 10	16 / 7
Valladolid	E	8 / 0	10 / 0	14 / 3	16 / 5	20 / 8	26 / 12	29 / 14	29 / 14	25 / 12	19 / 7	12 / 3	8 / 1
Valletta	M	14 / 10	15 / 10	16 / 11	18 / 13	22 / 16	26 / 19	29 / 22	29 / 22	27 / 19	24 / 16	20 / 12	16 /
Venezia	I	6 / 1	8 / 2	12 / 5	16 / 10	20 / 14	24 / 18	27 / 20	27 / 19	24 / 16	18 / 11	12 / 7	7 / 3
Vilnius	LT	-5 / -11	-3 / -10	2 / -7	12 / 1	18 / 7	21 / 11	23 / 14	22 / 12	16 / 8	10 / 4	3 / -1	-2 / -7
Warszawa	PL	0 / -6	0 / -6	6 / -2	12 / 3	20 / 9	23 / 12	24 / 15	23 / 14	19 / 10	13 / 5	5 / 1	2 / -3
Wien	A	1 / -4	3 / -3	8 / -1	15 / 6	19 / 10	23 / 14	25 / 15	24 / 15	19 / 11	13 / 7	7 / 3	3 / 0
Zagreb	HR	3 / -2	6 / -1	11 / 3	17 / 7	22 / 11	26 / 14	28 / 15	27 / 15	23 / 12	16 / 7	9 / 3	4 / 0
Zürich	CH	2 / -3	5 / -2	10 / 1	15 / 4	19 / 8	23 / 11	25 / 13	24 / 13	20 / 11	14 / 6	7 / 2	3 / -2

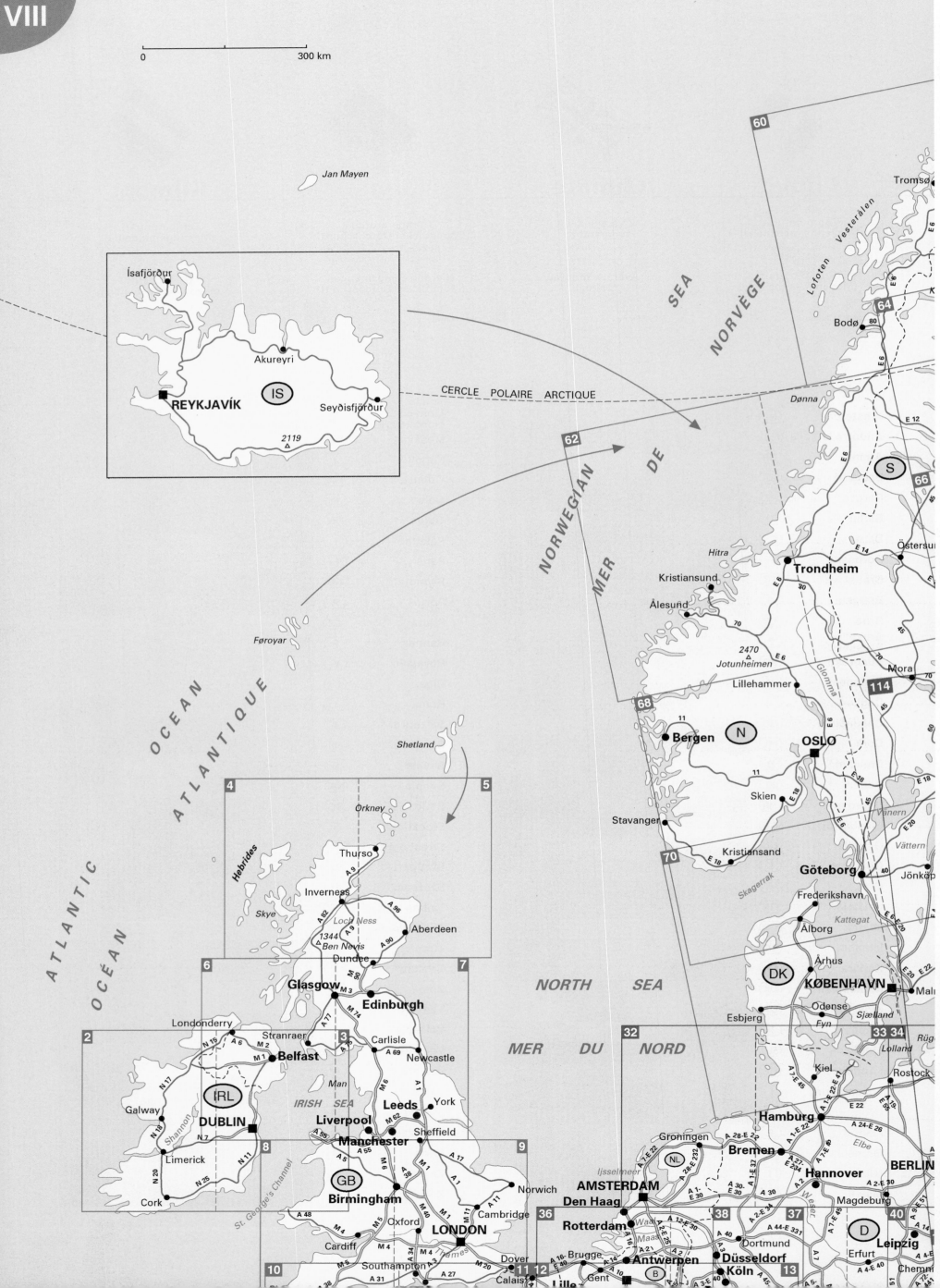

VIII

0 300 km

Jan Mayen

Ísafjörður

Akureyri

REYKJAVÍK IS

Seyðisfjörður

2119

CERCLE POLAIRE ARCTIQUE

Føroyar

OCEAN ATLANTIQUE

ATLANTIC OCÉAN

Shetland

Orkney

Thurso

Hebrides

Inverness

Skye *Loch Ness*

1344 Ben Nevis

Dundee

Glasgow

Edinburgh

Londonderry

Stranraer Carlisle

Belfast Newcastle

IRL

Galway

DUBLIN

Man

IRISH SEA

Leeds York

Liverpool

Manchester Sheffield

Limerick

GB

Cork

Birmingham

Norwich

Oxford Cambridge

LONDON

Cardiff

Southampton Dover

Calais

SEA NORVÈGE

Tromsø

Lofoten Vesterålen

Bodø 80

64

E 6

Dønna

E 12

S

Östersun

Hitra

Kristiansund

Trondheim

Ålesund

2470 Jotunheimen

Mora

Lillehammer

114

68

Bergen N OSLO

Skien

Stavanger

Kristiansand

Göteborg Jönköp

Vänern

Vättern

Skagerrak

Frederikshavn

Ålborg Kattegat

Århus

DK KØBENHAVN Mal

NORTH SEA

Odense Sjælland

Esbjerg Fyn

33 34

Lolland Rüg

32 MER DU NORD

Kiel

Rostock

Groningen

Hamburg

NL Bremen

AMSTERDAM Hannover BERLIN

Den Haag

36 Magdeburg

Rotterdam 38 37 40

Dortmund D Leipzig

Brugge Düsseldorf Erfurt Chem

Antwerpen Köln 13

Gent B Lille

IX

MER DE BARENTS

BARENTS SEA

Nordkapp
61
Kirkenes
Murmansk
Koľskij Poluostrov
Mezen'
ARCTIC CIRCLE
Ivalo
Usogorsk
L
A
P
L
A
N
D
Kousomen'
MER BLANCHE SEA
65
Kiruna
MER WHITE SEA
Archangeľsk
2111
ebnekaise
Kem'
Malmberget
Kuùsamo
Severnaja Dvina
Kotlôs
Rovaniemi
Kemi
Luleå
Oulu
Oulujärvi
67
FIN
Pielinen
Petrozavodsk
Onežkoje Oz.
Vologda
Umeå
Kuopio
Joensuu
Vaasa
Saimaa
Ładozskoje Oz.
Čerepovec
Sundsvall
Päijänne
115
Tampere
Rybinskoje Vdchr.
Rybinsk
69
Nižnij Novgor
Gävle
Lahti
St. Peterburg
FINLAND FINLANDE
73
Novgorod
Tver'
Turku
HELSINKI
72
Uppsala
74
75
TALLINN
Čudskoje Oz.
MOSKVA
STOCKHOLM
EST
79
Pskov
Saaremaa
77
Tver'
71
78
LV
RUS
76
RĪGA
83
80
81
82
Vicebsk
Smolensk
Gotland
LT
87
Or'ol
Kalmar
Öland
Klaipéda
85
Br'ansk
84
91
86
VILNIUS
Mahiëŭ
Kaunas
Kaliningrad
89
90
35
MINSK
Bornholm
BY
Homeľ
Charkiv
88
Gdańsk
95
Čerhihiv
Poltava
93
94
Brest
KYÏV
Szczecin
WARSZAWA
92
Poznań
Žytomir
Kremenčuc'ke Vodoschovyšče
117
Łódź
Lublin
Dnipropetrovs'k
PL
99
Wrocław
UA
39
41
97
L'viv
Vinnycja
116
96
98
Kryvyj Rih
Dresden
Kraków

MER BALTIQUE BALTIC SEA
GULF OF BOTHNIA GOLFE DE BOTNIE

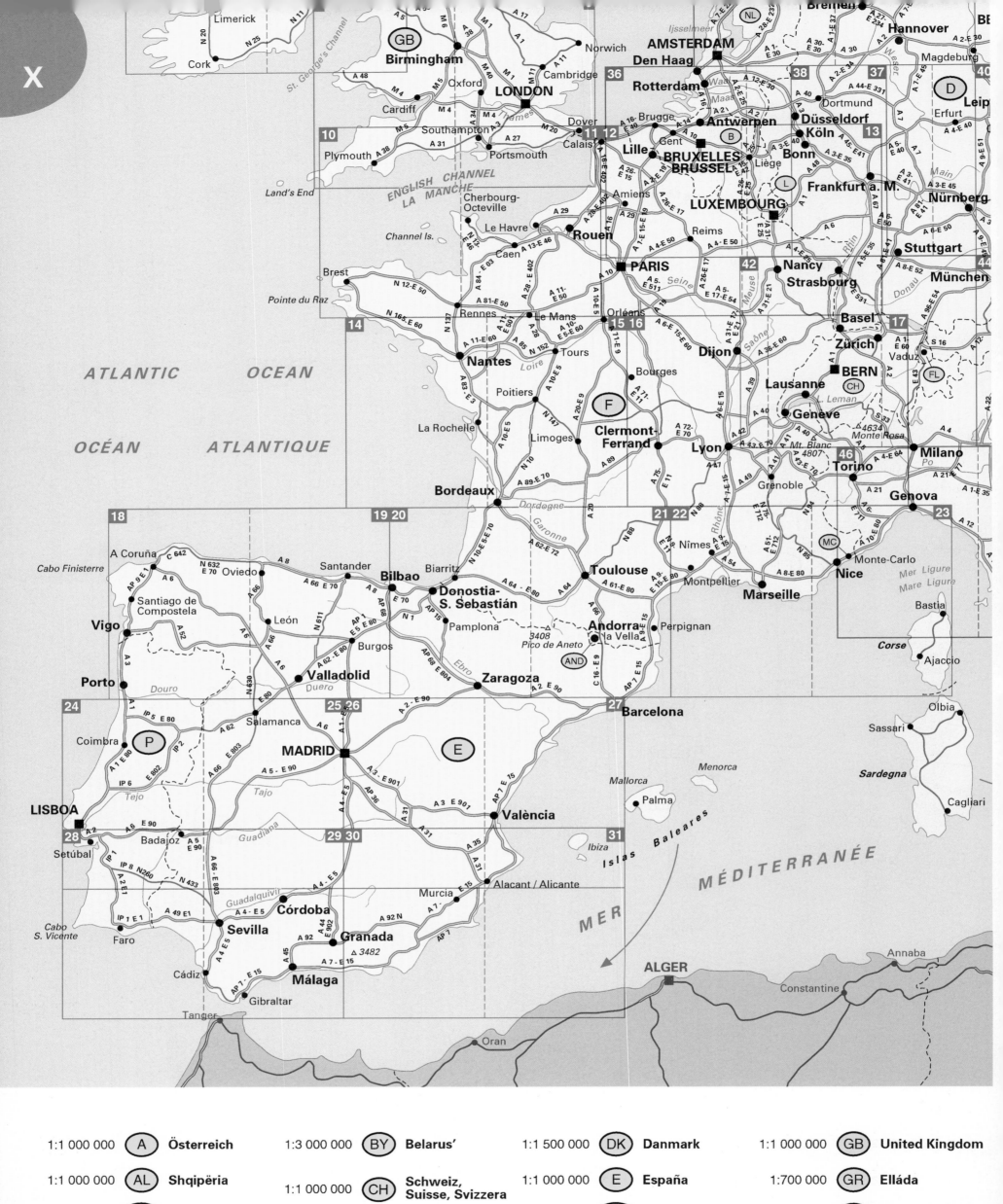

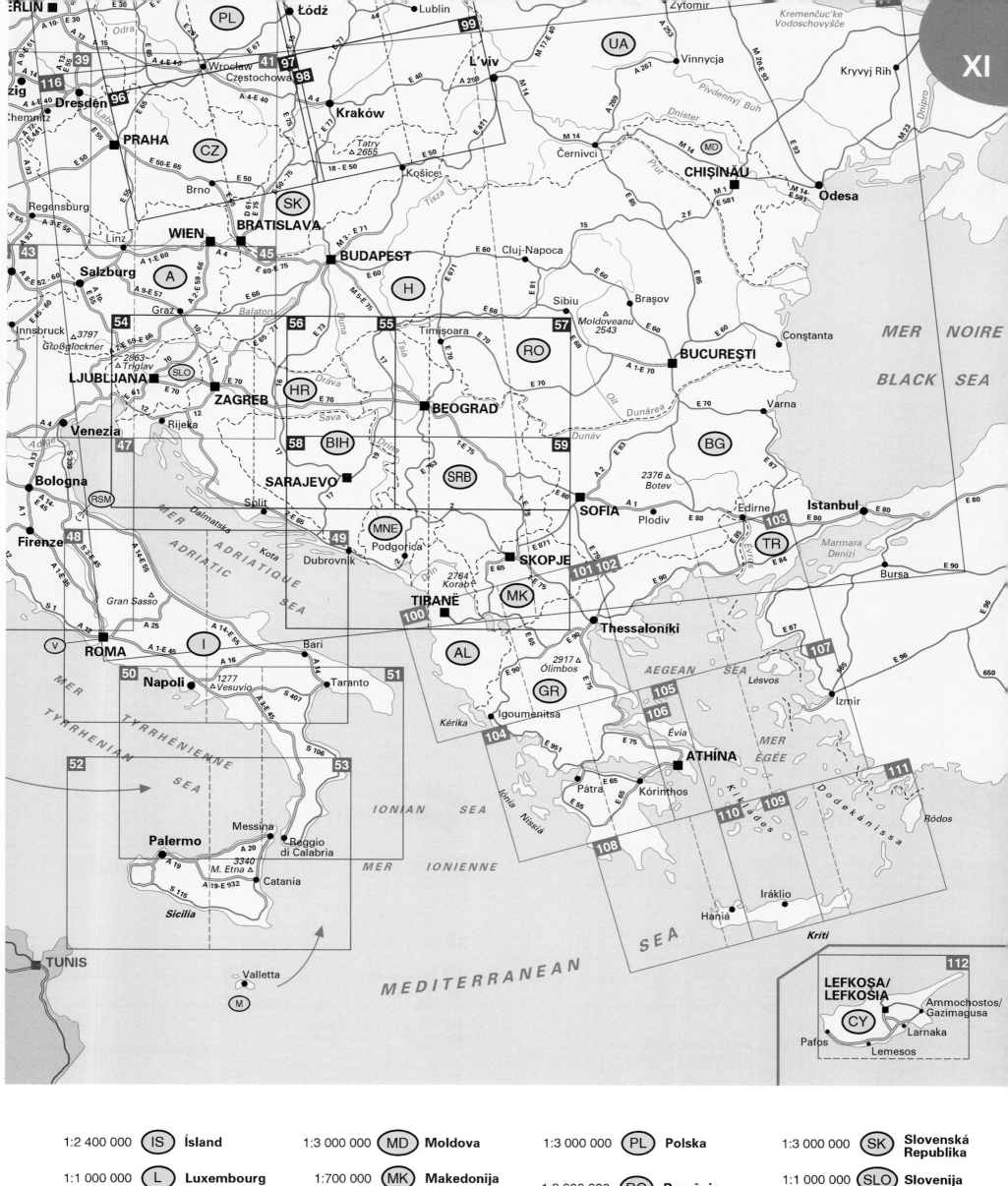

1:2 400 000	IS	Ísland	1:3 000 000	MD	Moldova	
1:1 000 000	L	Luxembourg	1:700 000	MK	Makedonija	
1:3 000 000	LT	Lietuva	1:1 000 000	MNE	Crna Gora	
1:3 000 000	LV	Latvija	1:1 500 000	N	Norge	
1:500 000	M	Malta	1:1 000 000	NL	Nederland	
1:1 000 000	MC	Monaco	1:1 000 000	P	Portugal	

1:3 000 000	PL	Polska
1:3 000 000	RO	România
1:1 000 000	RSM	San Marino
1:3 000 000	RUS	Rossija
1:1 500 000	S	Sverige

1:3 000 000	SK	Slovenská Republika
1:1 000 000	SLO	Slovenija
1:1 000 000	SRB	Srbija
1:3 000 000	TR	Türkiye
1:3 000 000	UA	Ukraïna
1:1 000 000	V	Vaticano

Conduire en Europe

Les tableaux d'information suivants indiquent les principaux règlements routiers communiqués au moment de la rédaction de cet atlas (17.06.08) ; la signification des symboles est indiquée ci-dessous, ainsi que quelques notes supplémentaires.

- Limitations de vitesse en kilomètres/heure s'appliquant aux :
- autoroutes
- routes à une seule chaussée
- routes à chaussées séparées
- agglomérations urbaines
- Péage sur les autoroutes ou toute autre partie du réseau routier
- Jeu d'ampoules de rechange
- Taux maximum d'alcool toléré dans le sang. On ne doit pas considérer ceci comme acceptable ; il n'est JAMAIS raisonnable de boire et de conduire.
- Age minimum du conducteur
- Port de la ceinture de sécurité à l'avant
- Age minimum des enfants admis à l'avant.
- Port de la ceinture de sécurité à l'avant et à l'arrière
- Gilet de sécurité
- Câble de remorquage
- Triangle de présignalisation
- Port du casque pour les motocyclistes et les passagers
- Trousse de premiers secours
- Allumage des codes jour et nuit
- Extincteur
- Pneus cloutés

Documents nécessaires obligatoires à tous les pays : certificat d'immatriculation du véhicule ou certificat de location, assurance responsabilité civile, plaque d'identification nationale.

Driving in Europe

The information panels which follow give the principal motoring regulations in force when this atlas was prepared for press (17.06.08). An explanation of the symbols is given below, together with some additional notes.

- Speed restrictions in kilometres per hour applying to:
- motorways
- single carriageways
- dual carriageways
- urban areas
- Whether tolls are payable on motorways and/or other parts of the road network.
- Whether a spare bulb set must be carried
- Maximum permitted level of alcohol in the bloodstream. This should not be taken as an acceptable level - it is NEVER sensible to drink and drive.
- Minimum age for drivers
- Whether seatbelts must be worn by the driver and front seat passenger
- Minimum age for children to sit in the front passenger seat.
- Whether seatbelts are compulsory for the driver and all passengers in both front and back seats
- Reflective jacket
- Tow rope
- Whether a warning triangle must be carried.
- Whether crash helmets are compulsory for both motorcyclists and their passengers
- Whether a first aid kit must be carried
- Whether headlights must be on at all time
- Whether a fire extinguisher must be carried
- Studded tyres

Documents required for all countries: vehicle registration document or vehicle on hire certificate, third party insurance cover, national vehicle indentification plate. You are strongly advised to contact the national Automobile Club for full details of local regulations.

Autofahren in Europa

Die nachfolgenden Tabellen geben Auskunft über die wichtigsten Verkehrsbestimmungen in den einzelnen Ländern dieses Atlasses (Stand 17.06.08); die Erklärung der Symbole sowie einige ergänzende Anmerkungen finden Sie im Anschluß an diesen Text.

- Geschwindigkeitsbegrenzungen in km/h bezogen auf:
- Autobahnen
- Straßen mit einer Fahrbahn
- Schnellstraßen mit getrennten Fahrbahnen
- geschlossene Ortschaften
- Autobahn-, Straßen- oder Brückenbenutzungsgebühren
- Mitführen eines Satzes von Glühbirnen als Reserve
- Promillegrenze: Es sei darauf hingewiesen, daß auch die kleinste Menge Alkohol am Steuer das Fahrvermögen beeinträchtigt
- Mindestalter für Kfz-Führer
- Anschnallpflicht vorne
- Mindestalter, ab welchem Kinder vorne sitzen dürfen.
- Anschnallpficht vorne und hinten
- Sicherheitsweste
- Abschleppseil
- Mitführen eines Warndreiecks
- Helmpflicht für Motorradfahrer und Beifahrer
- Mitführen eines Verbandkastens
- Abblendlicht vorgeschrieben (Tag und Nacht)
- Mitführen eines Feuerlöschers
- Spikereifen

Notwendige und vorgeschriebene Dokumente in allen Staaten: Fahrzeugschein oder Mietwagenbescheinigun, Internationale grüne Versicherungskarte, Nationlitätskennzeichen. Es empfiehlt sich, genauere Infomationen bei den jeweiligen Automobilclubs einzuholen.

Autorijden in Europa

In de tabellen hierna staan de voornaamste verkeersregels medegedeeld bij het opstellen van deze Atlas (17.06.08); de betekenis van de symbolen is hieronder beschreven met enkele toelichtingen.

- Snelheidsbeperkingen in km/uur op:
- autosnelwegen
- wegen met één rijbaan
- wegen met gescheiden rijbanen
- binnen de bebouwde kom
- Tol op de autosnelwegen of op een ander gedeelte van het wegennet
- Reservelampen verplicht
- Maximum toegestaan alcoholgehalte in het bloed. Dit dient niet beschouwd te worden als een aanvaardbaar gehalte; het is NOOIT verstandig om te rijden na gebruik van alcohol.
- Minimumleeftijd bestuurder
- Autogordel verplicht voor bestuurder en passagier voorin
- Minimum leeftijd voor kinderen voorin het voertuig.
- Autogordel, verplicht voor- en achterin
- Reflecterend vest
- Sleepkabel
- Gevarendriehoek verplicht
- Valhelm verplicht voor motorrijders en passagiers
- EHBO-pakket verplicht
- Dimlichten verplicht zowel 's nachts als overdag
- Brandblusapparaat
- Spijkerbanden

Vereiste documenten in alle landen: kentekenbewijs van het voertuig of huurcertificaat, verzekering burgerlijke aansprakelijkheid, plaat land van herkomst. Het verdient aanbeveling informatie in te winnen bij de automobielclub.

Code	Country	🛣	🛣 (2)	Road	Built-up area	Alcohol ‰	(a)	(b)	(c)	Child age	Warning triangle	First-aid kit	Fire extinguisher	Spare bulbs	(d)	Min. age	(e)	Period 1	Period 2	(f)
A	ÖSTERREICH	130		100	50	0,05	●		●	14	●	●	○			18	●	●	1/10-1/5		●
AL	SHQIPËRIA			80	40	0,00					○	○	○			18	●	●			○
AND	ANDORRA			90	50	0,05			●	10	●	○	○	●		18	●		1/11-15/5		○
B	BELGIQUE, BELGIË	120	120	90	50	0,05		●		12	●	●	●			18	●		1/11-31/3		●
BG	BALGARIJA	130		90	50	0,05	●		●	10	●	●	●			18	●	1/11-1/3		●	●
BIH	BOSNA I HERCEGOVINA	120	100	80	60	0,03		●		12	●	●	○	●	●	18	●	●			○
BY	BELARUS'			90	60	0,00	●		●	12						18					○
CH	SCHWEIZ, SUISSE, SVIZZERA	120	100	80	50	0,05	●		●		●	○	○			18	●		24/10-30/4		○
CY	KÝPROS, KIBRIS	100		80	50	0,05			●	12	●x2	○	○			18	●				○
CZ	CESKÁ REPUBLIKA	130		90	50	0,00	●		●		●	●	○	●		18	●	●			○
D	DEUTSCHLAND			100	50	0,05			●		●	●	○			16				●	○
DK	DANMARK	130		80	50	0,05			●		●	○	○			18	●		1/11-15/4		○
E	ESPAÑA	120		90	50	0,05	●		●		●x2	○	○	●		18	●				●
EST	EESTI	110		90	50	0,00			●		●	●	●			18	●		16/10-15/4		○
F	FRANCE	130	110	90	50	0,05	●		●	10	●	○	○	○		18	●		15/11-31/3		●
FIN	SUOMI, FINLAND	120		80	50	0,05			●	3	●	○	○			18	●		1/11-20/4		○
FL	LIECHTENSTEIN			80	50	0,08										18			1/11-30/4		○
GB	UNITED KINGDOM	112	112	96	48	0,08			●		○	○	○			17	●				○
GR	ELLÁDA	120		90	50	0,05	●		●	12	●	●				18	●				
H	MAGYARORSZÁG	130	110	90	50	0,00	●		●	12	●	●	○	●		17	●	●	●		○
HR	HRVATSKA	130	110	90	50	0,00	●		●	12	●	●	○			18	●	●	●		●
I	ITALIA	130		90	50	0,05	●		●	12	●	●	○	○		18	●		15/11-15/3		●
IRL	IRELAND	120		80	50	0,08			●		○	○	○			17	●				○
IS	ÍSLAND			90	50	0,05			●	14	●	○	○			17	●		15/11-15/4		○
L	LUXEMBOURG	130		90	50	0,05			●	11	●	○	○			18	●		1/12-31/3		○
LT	LIETUVA	130	110	90	50	0,04			●	12	●	●	●			16	●		1/11-1/4		●
LV	LATVIJA	110		90	50	0,05			●		●	●	●			18	●		1/10-30/4		
M	MALTA			80	50	0,08			●	11	○	○	○			18	●				○
MC	MONACO				50	0,05				10	○	○	○			18	●			●	○
MD	MOLDOVA			90	60	0,00			●	12	●	●	●			18	●				○
MK	MAKEDONIJA	120		80	60	0,05			●	12	●	●	○	●	●	18	●				○
MNE	CRNA GORA	120		80	50	0,05			●	12	●	○	○			18	●			●	●
N	NORGE	90		80	50	0,02	●		●		●	○	○			18	●		1/11-20/4		●
NL	NEDERLAND	120	100	80	50	0,05			●	12	●	○	○			18	●				●
P	PORTUGAL	120		90	50	0,49	●		●		●	●	○			18	●			●	●
PL	POLSKA	130	110	90	50	0,02			●		●	○	●			18	●				○
RO	ROMÂNIA	130		90	50	0,00	●		●	12	●	●	○			18	●				○
RSM	SAN MARINO			70	50	0,08			●	12	○	○	○			18	●		1/1-31/12		○
RUS	ROSSIJA	110		90	60	0,00			●	12	●	●	●			18	●				○
S	SVERIGE	110		70	50	0,02			●		●	○	○			18	●		1/10-30/4		○
SK	SLOVENSKÁ RÉPUBLIKA	130		90	60	0,00	●		●	12	●	●	○	●	●	18	●				○
SLO	SLOVENIJA	130	100	90	50	0,05			●	12	●	●	○			18	●				●
SRB	SRBIJA	120	100	80	60	0,05			●	12	●	●	●			18				●	○
TR	TÜRKIYE	120		90	50	0,05			●	10	●	●	○			18	●			●	○
UA	UKRAÏNA	130		90	60	0,00	●		●	12	●	●	●			18	●	22/12-20/3	1/11-31/12		○

Obligatoire ● Vorgeschrieben   Recommandé ○ Empfohlen   Interdit ● Verboten   Période d'autorisation 1/11-30/4 Genehmigungsdauer   Renseignement non communiqué ✳ Keine Auskunft erhalten
Compulsory   Verplicht   Recommanded   Aanbevolen   Prohibited   Verboden   Period of regulation enforcement   Toegelaten periode   No information currently available   Informatie niet meegedeeld

A Österreich

ÖAMTC
Schubertring 1-3,
1010 WIEN
☎ : +43 (0) 1 711 990
Fax : +43 (0) 1 713 18 07
http:// www.oeamtc.at
e-mail : office@oeamtc.at

ARBÖ
Mariahilfer Straße 180,
1150 WIEN
☎ : +43 1 891 217
Fax : +43 1 891 21 236
http:// www.arboe.or.at/
e-mail : id@arboe.or.at

AND Andorra

Automòbil Club d'Andorra (ACA)
Carrer Babot Camp 13,
ANDORRA la VELLA
☎ : +376 803 400
Fax : +376 822 560
http:// www.aca.ad

B Belgique, België

R.A.C.B
Rue d'Arlon 53 bte 3 / Aarlenstraat 53
bus 3
1040 BRUXELLES / BRUSSEL
☎ : +32 2 287 09 11
Fax : +32 2 230 75 84
http://www.racb.com
e-mail : autoclub@racb.com

Touring Club Belgium (TCB)
Rue de la Loi 44 / Wetstraat 44,
1040 BRUXELLES / BRUSSEL
☎ : +32 2 233 22 02
Fax : +32 2 286 33 23
http://www.touring.be
e-mail :presid@touring.be

BG Balgarija

**Union des Automobilistes
Bulgares (UAB)**
Place Pozitano 3
1090 SOFIA
☎ : +359 2 935 79 35
Fax : +359 2 981 61 51
http://www.uab.org
e-mail :sba@uab.org

BIH Bosna Hercegovina

BIHAMK
Skenderija 23
71000 SARAJEVO
☎ : +387 33 212 772
Fax : +387 33 213 668
 http:// www.bihamk.ba
e-mail : info@bihamk.ba

BY Belarus'

**Belorusskij Klub
Avtomototurizma (BKA)**
ul. Zaharova, 55
22 0088 MINSK
☎ : +375 17 222 06 66
Fax : +375 17 233 90 45
http://www.bka.by
e-mail : info@bka.by

CH Schweiz, Suisse, Svizzera

**Touring Club Suisse / Schweiz /
Svizzero (TCS)**
Case postale 820
1214 VERNIER

☎ : +41 22 417 27 27
Fax : +41 22 417 20 20
http://www.tcs.ch
e-mail : irtge@tcs.ch

**Automobil Club der Schweiz
Automobile Club de Suisse
(ACS)**
Wasserwerkgasse 39
3000 BERN 13
☎ : +41 31 328 31 11
Fax : +41 31 311 03 10
http://www.acs.ch
e-mail : acszv@acs.ch

CY Kýpros, Kibris

**Cyprus Automobile Association
(CAA)**
PO Box 22279
1519 LEFKOSIA
☎ : +357 22 313 233
Fax : +357 22 313 482
http://www.caa.com.cy
e-mail : info@caa.com.cy

CZ Ceská Republika

**Ústrední automotoklub Ceské
republiky (UAMK)**
Na Strzi 9,
14002 PRAHA 4
☎ : +420 2 611 04 242
Fax : +420 2 611 04 235
http://www.uamk-cr.cz
e-mail : sekretar@uamk-cr.cz

**Autoklub Ceské republiky
(ACCR)**
Opletalova 29,
11000 PRAHA 1
☎ : +420 224 210 266
Fax : +420 222 246 275
http://www.autoklub.cz
e-mail : inet@autoklub.cz

D Deutschland

ADAC
Am Westpark 8,
81373 MÜNCHEN
☎ : +49 89 76 76 0
Fax : +49 89 76 76 25 00
http://www.adac.de
e-mail : adac@adac.de

**Automobilclub von Deutschland
(AVD)**
Lyoner Str. 16
60528 FRANKFURT am MAIN
☎ : +49 69 660 60
Fax : +49 69 660 67 89
http://www.avd.de
e-mail : avd@avd.de

DK Danmark

**Forenede Danske Motorejere
(FDM)**
Postboks 500
2800 KGS. LYNGBY
☎ : +45 45 27 07 07
Fax : +45 45 27 09 93http://www.fdm.dk
e-mail : fdm@fdm.dk

E España

**Real Automóvil Club de España
(RACE)**
c/ Isaac Newton, 4
28760 - Tres Cantos MADRID
☎ : +34 91 594 72 75
Fax : +34 91 594 75 36
http://www.race.es
e-mail : presidencia@race.es

**Real Federación Española de
Automovilismo (RFE de A)**
c/ Escultor Peresejo, 68bis
28023 MADRID
☎ : +34 91 729 94 30
Fax : +34 91 357 02 03
http://www.rfeda.es
e-mail : rfeda@rfeda.es

EST Eesti

Eesti Autoklubi (EAK)
Laki 11
12915 TALLINN
☎ : +372 979 188
Fax : +372 979 110
http://www.autoclub.ee
e-mail : eak@autoclub.ee

Eesti Autosporti Liit (EAL)
Vabaduse pst 13,
12214 TALLINN
☎ : +372 6398 666
Fax : +372 6398 553
http://www.autosport.ee
e-mail : eal@sport.ee

F France

Automobile Club de France
6, Place de la Concorde
75008 PARIS
☎ : +33 1 43 12 43 12
Fax : +33 1 43 12 43 43

**Fédération Française des
Automobiles Clubs et Usagers
de la Route**
76 Avenue Marceau
75008 PARIS
☎ : +33 1 56 89 20 70
Fax : +33 1 47 20 37 23
http://www.automobileclub.org
e-mail : ffac.presse1@wanadoo.fr

FIN Suomi, Finlande

Autoliitto (AL)
Hämeentie 105 A
00550 HELSINKI
☎ : +358 9 72 58 44 00
Fax : +358 9 72 58 44 60
http://www.autoliitto.fi
e-mail : autoliitto@autoliitto.fi

FL Liechtenstein

**Automobilclub des Fürstentums
Liechtenstein (ACFL)**
Pflugstrasse 20, Post Fach 934,
9490 VADUZ
☎ : +423 237 67 67
Fax : +423 233 30 50

GB United Kingdom

Automobile Association (AA)
Basing View
RG21 4DA BASINGSTOKE
☎ : +44 870 600 0371
Fax : +44 191 235 5111
http:// www.theaa.com
e-mail : customer-services@theaa.com

Green Flag Motoring Assistance
Cote Lane, Pudsey
LS28 5GF LEEDS
☎ : +44 (0)141 221 38 50
Fax : + 44 (0)845 246 15 57

http://www.greenflag.com
e-mail : member-queries@greenflag.com

GR Elláda

**Automobile and Touring Club of
Greece (ELPA)**
L. Messogion 395
153 43 - ATHINA
☎ : +30 210 606 8800
Fax : +30 210 606 8981
http://www.elpa.gr
e-mail : info@elpa.gr

H Magyarország

Magyar Autóklub (MAK)
Rómer Flóris u. 4/a
1024 BUDAPEST
☎ : +36 1 345 1 800
Fax : +36 1 345 1 801
http://www.autoklub.hu
e-mail : info@ autoklub.hu

HR Hrvatska

Hrvatski Autoklub (HAK)
Avenija Dubrovnik 44,
10020 ZAGREB
☎ : +385 1 66 11 999
Fax : +385 1 66 23 111
http://www.hak.hr
e-mail : borse@hak.hr

I Italia

Automobile Club d'Italia (ACI)
B.P 2839,
00185 ROMA
☎ : +39 6 499 81
Fax : +39 6 499 827 23
http://www.aci.it
e-mail : info@aci.it

Touring Club Italiano (TCI)
Corso Italia 10,
20122 MILANO
☎ : +39 2 85 261
Fax : +39 2 852 63 20
http://www.touringclub.it
e-mail : ufficio.comunicazione@touring-
club.it

IRL Ireland

**Royal Irish Automobile Club
(RIAC)**
34, Dawson Street,
DUBLIN 2
☎ : +353 1 677 51 41
Fax : +353 1 671 55 51
http://www.motorsportireland.com
e-mail : info@motorsportireland.com

**The Automobile Association
Ireland Limited**
56, Dury Street,
DUBLIN 2
☎ : +353 1 617 99 99
Fax : +353 1 617 94 00
http://www.aaireland.ie
e-mail : aa@aaireland.ie

IS Ísland

**Félag Islenskra Bifreidaeigenda
(FIB)**
Borgartúni 33,
105 REYKJAVIK
☎ : +354 414 99 99
Fax : +354 414 99 98
http://www.fib.is
e-mail : fib@fib.is

Icelandic Motorsport Association (LIA)
Engjavegur 6,
130 REYKJAVIK
☎ : +354 58 89 100
Fax : +354 58 89 102
http://www.centrum.is/lia
e-mail : lia@centrum.is

 **Luxembourg**

Automobile Club du Grand Duché de Luxembourg (ACL)
54 Route de Longwy,
8007 BERTRANGE
☎ : +352 45 00 45
Fax : +352 45 04 55
http://www.acl.lu
e-mail : acl@acl.lu

 Lietuvia

Lietuvos Automobilininku Sajunga (LAS)
Antakalnio 28,
10305 VILNIUS
☎ : +370 5 210 44 33
Fax : +370 5 270 95 92
http://www.las.lt
e-mail : info@las.lt

Lietuvos Automobiliu Sporto Federacija (LASF)
Draugystes 19-344, - 51230 KAUNAS
☎ : +370 37 350 106
Fax : +370 37 350 106
http://www.lasf.lt
e-mail : lasf@lasf.lt

 Latvija

Latvijas Automoto Biedriba (LAMB)
Raunas 16b,
1039 RIGA
☎ : +37 1 6756 6222
Fax : +37 1 6751 3678
http://www.lamb.lv
e-mail : lamb@lamb.lv

Latvijas Automobilu Federacija (LAF)
Brivibas Gatve 266-107,
1006 RIGA
☎ : +37 1 701 22 09
Fax : +37 1 755 14 65
http://www.laf.lv
e-mail : laf@latnet.lv

 Malte

Touring Club (TCM)
P.O. Box 16
MSD 01 – MSIDA
☎ : +356 7900 0116
Fax : +356 2123 8226

 Monaco

Automobile Club de Monaco (ACM)
23 Boulevard Albert 1er, BP 464
98012 MONACO
☎ : +377 93 15 26 00
Fax : +377 93 25 80 08
http://www.acm.mc
e-mail : info@acm.mc

MD Moldava

Automobil Club din Moldova (ACM)
str. Armeneasca 33/1

2012 CHISINAU
☎ : +373 22 29 27 03
Fax : +373 22 20 22 24
http://www.acm.md
e-mail : office@acm.md

MK Makedonija

Avto Moto Sojuz na Makedonija
Ivo Ribar Lola br. 51- 1000 SKOPJE
☎ : +389 2 318 11 81
Fax : +389 2 318 11 89
http://www.amsm.com.mk
e-mail : amsm@amsm.com.mk

MNE Crna Gora

Auto moto Savez Crne Gore
Cetinjski put b.b.
81000 PODGORICA
☎ : +381 81 234 467
Fax : +381 81 234 467
http://www.amscg.cg.yu
e-mail : amscgsistem@cg.yu

 **Norge**

Kongelig Norsk Automobilklub (KNA)
Postboks 2425 Solli
0201 OSLO
☎ : +47 21 60 49 00
Fax : +47 21 60 49 01
http://www.kna.no
e-mail : kna@kna.no

Norges Automobil-Forbund (NAF)
Postboks 6682 Etterstad
0609 OSLO
☎ : +47 22 34 14 00
Fax : +47 22 33 13 72
http://www.naf.no
e-mail : medlemsservice@naf.no

NL Nederland

Koninklijke Nederlandse Toeristenbond (ANWB)
Wassenaarseweg 220
2509 BA - DEN HAAG
☎ : +31 70 314 71 47
Fax : +31 70 314 69 69
http://www.anwb.nl
e-mail : info@anwb.nl

Koninklijke Nederlandse Automobiel Club (KNAC)
Postbus 93114
2509 AC - DEN HAAG
☎ : +31 70 383 16 12
Fax : +31 70 383 19 06
http://www.knac.nl
e-mail : ledenservice@knac.nl

 Portugal

Automóvel Club de Portugal (ACP)
Rua Rosa Araújo 24-26,
1250-195 LISBOA
☎ : +351 21 318 02 02
Fax : +351 21 318 02 27
http://www.acp.pt
e-mail : info@acp.pt

PL Polska

Polski Zwiazek Motorowy (PZM)
Ul. Kazimierzowska 66

02-518 WARSZAWA
☎ : +48 22 849 93 61
Fax : +48 22 848 19 51
http://www.pzm.pl
e-mail : office@pzm.pl

Polskie Towarzystwo Turystyczno-Krajoznawcze (PTTK)
ul. Senatorska 11
00-075 WARSZAWA
☎ : +48 22 826 57 35
Fax : +48 22 826 25 05
http://www.pttk.pl
e-mail : poczta@pttk.pl

RO România

Automobil Clubul Român (ACR)
str. Tache Ionescu 27, Sector 1
010353 BUCURESTI
☎ : +40 21 222 22 22
Fax : +40 21 222 15 52
http://www.acr.ro
e-mail : acr@acr.ro

RUS Rossija

Russian Automobile Society (VOA)
Leotjevskij per., 23
125009 MOSKVA
☎ : +7 495 747 66 66
http://www.voa.ru
e-mail : voa@voa.ru

Avtoclub assistance Rus (ACAR)
Krasnogo Mayaka 26
117570 - MOSKVA
☎ : +7 095 105 50 00
Fax : +7 095 105 50 96
e-mail : acar@acarus.ru

RSM San Marino

Automobile Club San Marino (ACS)
Via A. Giangi, 66
47 891 DOGANA
☎ : +378 549 90 88 60
Fax : +378 549 97 29 26
http:// www.automobileclub.sm
e-mail : info@automobileclub.sm

SRB Srbija

Auto-Moto Savez Srbije (AMSS)
Kneginje Zorke 58
11000 BEOGRAD
☎ : +381 11 333 12 00
http://www.amss.org.yu
e-mail : info@amss.org.yu

 Sverige

Kungl Automobil Klubben
Södra Blasieholmshamnen 6
11148 STOCKHOLM
☎ : +46 8 678 00 55
Fax : +46 8 678 00 68
http://www.kak.se
e-mail : info@kak.se

Svenska Bilsportförbundet (SBF)
Bergkällavägen 31 A
192 79 SOLLENTUNA
☎ : +46 8 626 33 00
Fax : +46 8 626 33 22
http://www.sbf.se
e-mail : mailbox@sbf.se

Motormännens Riksförbund (M)
Box 49163
100 29 STOCKHOLM

☎ : +46 8 690 38 00
Fax : +46 8 690 38 24
http://www.motormannen.se
e-mail : service@motormannen.se

SK Slovenská Republika

Autoklub Slovenskej Republiky (AKSR)
na Holícskej 30
851 01 BRATISLAVA
☎ : +421 2 638 346 78
Fax : +421 2 638 345 67
http://www.aksr.sk
e-mail : autoklub@autoklubsr.sk

Slovensky Autoturist Klub (SATC)
Bosákova 3
851 04 BRATISLAVA
☎ : +421 2 682 492 11
http://www.satc.sk
e-mail : dispecing@satc.sk

SLO Slovenija

Avto-Moto Zveza Slovenije (AMZS)
Dunajska 128a
1000 LJUBLJANA
☎ : +386 1 530 53 00
Fax : +386 1 530 54 10
http://www.amzs.si
e-mail : info.center@amzs.si

TR Türkiye

Türkiye Otomobil Sporlari Federasyonu (TOSFED)
Göksuevleri Kartopu Cad. B168/A
Anadoluhisari - Beykoz
ISTANBUL
☎ : +90 216 465 11 55
Fax : +90 216 465 11 57
http://www.tosfed.org.tr
e-mail : ik@tosfed.org.tr

Türkiye Turing ve Otomobil Kurumu (TTOK)
1. Otosanayi Sitesi yani - 4. Levent
ISTANBUL
☎ : +90 212 282 81 40
Fax : +90 212 282 80 42
http://www.turing.org.tr
e-mail : turing@turing.org.tr

UA Ukraïna

Fédération Automobile d'Ukraine (FAU)
P.O. Box 10697,
79000 LVIV
☎ : +380 322 97 06 41
Fax : +380 322 97 06 41
e-mail : office@fau.ua

112UA
bul. Ak. Pidstrigacha, 6
79060 LVIV
☎ : +380 32 29 70 112
Fax : +380 32 29 71 112
http://www.112ua.com
e-mail : office@112ua.com

Distances / Distances / Entfernungen / Afstandstabel

Les distances sont comptées à partir du centre-ville et par la route la plus pratique, c'est à dire celle qui offre les meilleures conditions de roulage, mais qui n'est pas nécessairement la plus courte.

Distances are calculated from town-centres and using the best roads from a motoring point of view - not necessarily the shortest.

Die Entfernungen gelten ab Stadtmitte unter Berücksichtigung der günstigsten (nicht immer kürzesten) Strecke.

De afstanden zijn in km berekend van centrum tot centrum langs de geschickste, dus niet noodzakelijkerwijze de kortste route.

2208 km

Amsterdam
Athína
Barcelona
Basel
Beograd
Bergen
Berlin
Bilbao
Bordeaux
Bratislava
Bruxelles/Brussel
Bucureşti
Budapest
Calais
Cherbourg
Clermont-Ferrand
Dublin
Dubrovnik
Firenze
Frankfurt-am-Main
Genève
Genova
Göteborg
Hamburg
Helsinki
İstanbul
København
Köln
Kraków
Kyїv
Lille
Lisboa
Ljubljana
London
Luxembourg
Lyon
Madrid
Málaga
Marseille
Milano
Minsk
Moskva
München
Nantes
Napoli
Oslo
Palermo
Paris
Porto
Praha
Riga
Roma
Rotterdam
Salzburg
Sarajevo
Sevilla
Skopje
Sofia
St. Peterburg
Stockholm
Strasbourg
Tallinn
Thessaloniki
Toulouse
Tromsø
Valencia
Venezia
Vilnius
Warszawa
Wien
Zagreb
Zürich

Légende / Key / Zeichenerklärung / Verklaring van de tekens

Routes / Roads / Straßen / Wegen

Français		Key	Deutsch		Nederlands
Autoroute		Motorway	Autobahn		Autosnelweg
Échangeurs : complet, partiels, sans précision		Interchanges : complete, limited, not specified	Anschlussstellen : Voll - bzw. Teilanschluss, ohne Angabe		Aansluitingen : volledig, gedeeltelijk, zonder aanduiding
Numéros d'échangeurs		Interchange numbers	Anschlussstellennummern		Afritnummers
Double chaussée de type autoroutier		Dual carriageway with motorway characteristics	Schnellstraße mit getrennten Fahrbahnen		Gescheiden rijbanen van het type autosnelweg
Route de liaison internationale ou nationale		International and national road network	Internationale bzw.nationale Hauptverkehrsstraße		Internationale of nationale verbindingsweg
Route de liaison interrégionale ou de dégagement		Interregional and less congested road	Überregionale Verbindungsstraße oder Umleitungsstrecke		Interregionale verbindingsweg
Autre route		Other road	Sonstige Straße		Andere weg
Route revêtue		Road surfaced	Straße mit Belag		Verharde weg
Non revêtue		Unsurfaced	Ohne Belag		Onverharde weg
Route en mauvais état		Road in bad condition	In schlechtem Zustand		Weg in slechte staat
Chemin d'exploitation - Sentier		Rough track - Footpath	Wirtschaftsweg - Pfad		Landbouwweg - Pad
Autoroute, route en construction		Motorway, road under construction	Autobahn, Straße im Bau		Autosnelweg, weg in aanleg
(le cas échéant: date de mise en service prévue)		(when available : with scheduled opening date)	(ggf. voraussichtliches Datum der Verkehrsfreigabe)		(indien bekend : datum openstelling)

Largeur des routes / Road widths / Straßenbreiten / Breedte van de wegen

Français		Key	Deutsch		Nederlands
Chaussées séparées		Dual carriageway	Getrennte Fahrbahnen		Gescheiden rijbanen
4 voies		4 lanes	4 Fahrspuren		4 rijstroken
3 voies		3 lanes	3 Fahrspuren		3 rijstroken
2 voies larges		2 wide lanes	2 breite Fahrspuren		2 brede rijstroken
2 voies		2 lanes	2 Fahrspuren		2 rijstroken
1 voie		1 lane	1 Fahrspur		1 rijstrook

Distances (totalisées et partielles) / Distances (total and intermediate) / Straßenentfernungen (Gesamt- und Teilentfernungen) / Afstanden (totaal en gedeeltelijk)

Français		Key	Deutsch		Nederlands
Sur autoroute { section à péage		Toll roads } on motorway	auf der Autobahn { Mautstrecke		gedeelte met tol } op autosnelwegen
section libre		Toll-free section	mautfreie Strecke		tolvrij gedeelte
GB et IRL 39 en kilomètres, 24 en miles		GB , IRL 39 in kilometers, 24 in miles	GB / IRL 39 in Kilometern, 24 in Meilen		GB , IRL 39 in kilometers, 24 in mijlen

Numérotation - Signalisation / Numbering - Signs / Nummerierung - Wegweisung / Wegnummers - Bewegwijzering

Français		Key	Deutsch		Nederlands
Route européenne, autoroute, autre route	E 10 A 6 N 51	European route, motorway, other road	Europastraße, Autobahn, sonstige Straße	E 10 A 6 N 51	Europaweg, autosnelweg, andere weg
GB : itinéraire principal (Primary route) IRL : itinéraire principal (National primary et secondary route)	A 40 A 68	GB : Primary route IRL : National primary and secondary route	GB : Empfohlene Fernverkehrsstraße (Primary route) IRL : Empfohlene Fernverkehrsstraße (National primary und secondary route)	A 40 A 68	GB : Hoofdweg (Primary route) IRL : Hoofdweg (National primary en secondary route)
Ville signalée par un panneau vert sur les grandes liaisons routières	YORK Wells	Town name is shown on a green sign on major routes	Grün beschilderte Ortsdurchfahrt an Fernverkehrsstrecken	YORK Wells	Stad aangegeven met een groen bord op de grote verbindingswegen

Obstacles / Obstacles / Verkehrshindernisse / Hindernissen

Français		Key	Deutsch		Nederlands
Forte déclivité (flèches dans le sens de la montée)		Steep hill (ascent in direction of the arrow)	Starke Steigung (Steigung in Pfeilrichtung)		Steile helling (pijlen in de richting van de helling)
En Écosse : route très étroite avec emplacements pour croisement (passing places)		In Scotland: narrow road with passing places	In Schottland: sehr schmale Straße mit Ausweichstellen (passing places)		In Schotland : smalle weg met uitwijkplaatsen
Enneigement : période probable de fermeture	11-6	Snowbound, impassable road during the period shown	Eingeschneite Straße : voraussichtl. Wintersperre	11-6	Sneeuw : vermoedelijke sluitingsperiode
Barrière de péage		Toll barrier	Mautstelle		Tol
Localité percevant un octroi (Norvège)	(‡)	Town having a toll (Norway only)	Ort, in dem eine Gebühr erhoben wird (Norwegen)	(‡)	Plaats waar tol geheven wordt (Noorwegen)

Transports / Transportation / Verkehrsmittel / Vervoer

Français		Key	Deutsch		Nederlands
Voie ferrée - Auto/Train		Railway - Motorail	Bahnlinie - Autoreisezug		Spoorweg - Autotrein
Bac pour autos		Car ferry	Autofähre		Veerpont voor auto's
Liaison maritime: permanente - saisonnière		Ferry lines: year-round - seasonal	Schiffsverbindungen: ganzjährig - saisonbedingte Verbindung		Ferry: het hele jaar - tijdens het seizoen
Aéroport		Airport	Flughafen		Luchthaven

Hébergement - Administration / Accommodation - Administration / Unterkunft - Verwaltung / Verblijf - Administratie

Français		Key	Deutsch		Nederlands
Localité ayant des ressources hôtelières		Place with at least one hotel	Ort mit Übernachtungsmöglichkeiten		Plaats met hotel
Refuge de montagne - Camping		Mountain refuge hut - Camping site	Schutzhütte - Campingplatz		Berghut - Kampeerterrein
Espagne: Parador - Portugal: Pousada	P	Spain: Parador, Portugal: Pousada	Spanien: Parador - Portugal: Pousada	P	Spanje: Parador, Portugal: Pousada
Capitale de division administrative	A L P	Administrative district seat	Verwaltungshauptstadt	A L P	Hoofdplaats van administratief gebied
Limite administrative		Administrative boundary	Verwaltungsgrenze		Administratieve grens
Frontière: Douane principale - Douane avec restriction	+++++++++	National boundary: Principal customs post - Secondary customs post	Staatsgrenze - Zollstation mit Einschränkungen	+++++++++	Staatsgrens: Hoofddouanekantoor - Douanekantoor met beperkte bevoegdheden
Zone interdite aux étrangers		Restricted area for foreigners	Sperrgebiet für Ausländer		Terrein verboden voor buitenlanders

Curiosités / Sights / Sehenswürdigkeiten / Bezienswaardigheden

Français		Key	Deutsch		Nederlands
Édifice religieux - Château		Religious building - Historic house, castle	Sakral-Bau - Schloss, Burg		Kerkelijk gebouw - Kasteel
Pierre runique - Grotte		Rune stone - Cave	Runenstein - Höhle		Runensteen - Grot
Église en bois debout - Ruines		Stave church - Ruins	Stabkirche - Ruine		Stavkirke (houten kerk) - Ruïne
Gravure rupestre - Monument mégalithique		Rock carving - Prehistoric monument	Felsbilder - Vorgeschichtliches Steindenkmal		Rotstekening - Megaliet
Monastère - Site antique		Monastery - Antiquities	Kloster - Antike Fundstätte		Klooster - Overblijfsel uit de Oudheid
Parcours pittoresque		Scenic route	Landschaftlich schöne Strecke		Schilderachtig traject
Parc national		National park	Nationalpark		Nationaal park
Autre curiosité		Other place of interest	Sonstige Sehenswürdigkeit		Andere bezienswaardigheid

Signes particuliers aux plans de ville / Main signs on town plans / Signaturen in Stadtplan / Bijzondere tekens op de stadsplattegronden

Français		Key	Deutsch		Nederlands
Hôtel de ville - Police	H POL	Town hall - Police station	Rathaus - Polizeirevier	H POL	Stadhuis - Politie
Bureau de poste - Université	U	Post office - University	Postamt - Universität	U	Postkantoor - Universiteit
Office de tourisme		Tourist information centre	Stadtinformation		Informatie voor toeristen
Cimetière - Marché couvert		Cemetery - Covered market	Friedhof - Markthalle		Begraafplaats - Overdekte markt
Parking		Car park	Parkplatz		Parkeerplaats
Hôpital		Hospital	Krankenhaus		Hospitaal
Musée - Parc animalier, zoo	M	Museum - Safari park, zoo	Museum - Tierpark, Zoo	M	Museum - Safaripark, dierentuin
Parc de loisirs - Jardin botanique		Recreation ground - Botanical gardens	Erholungspark - Botanischer Garten		Recreatiepark - Plantentuin
Château		Historic house, castle	Schloss, Burg		Kasteel
Monument		Monument	Denkmal		Monument
Moulin à vent - Hippodrome		Windmill - Horse racetrack	Windmühle - Pferderennbahn		Molen - Renbaan
Golf		Golf course	Golfplatz		Golfterrein
Stade		Stadium	Stadion		Stadion

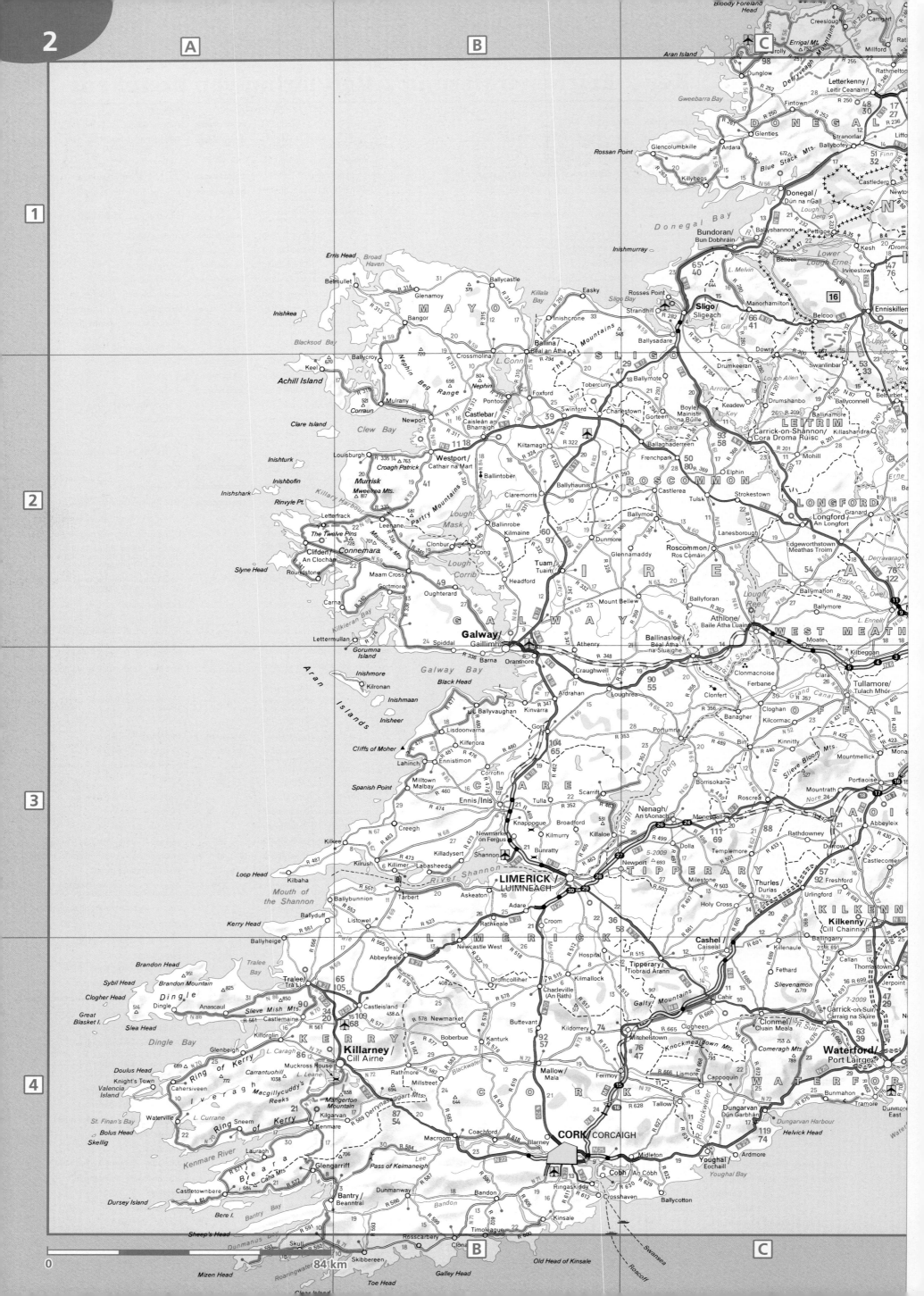

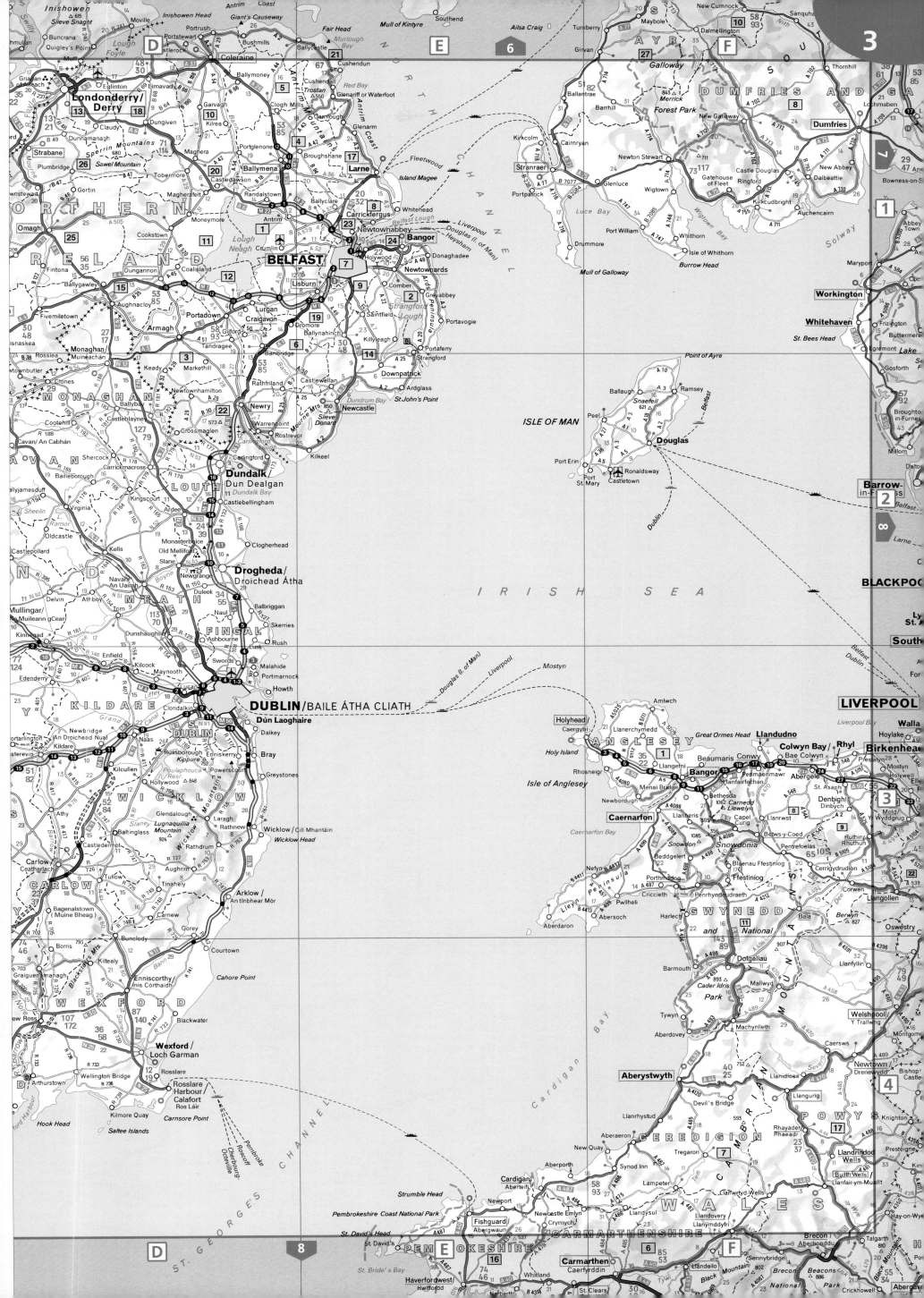

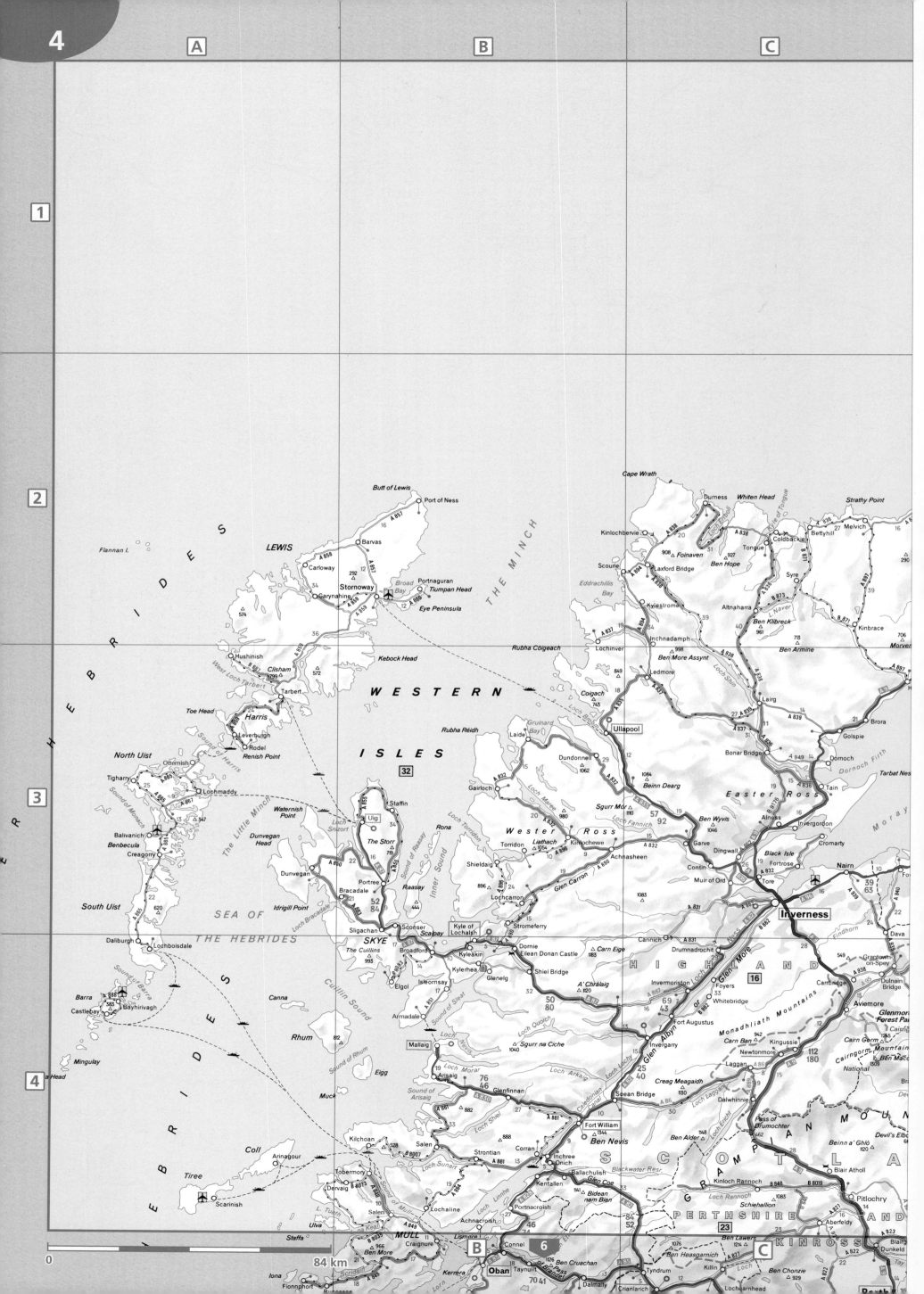

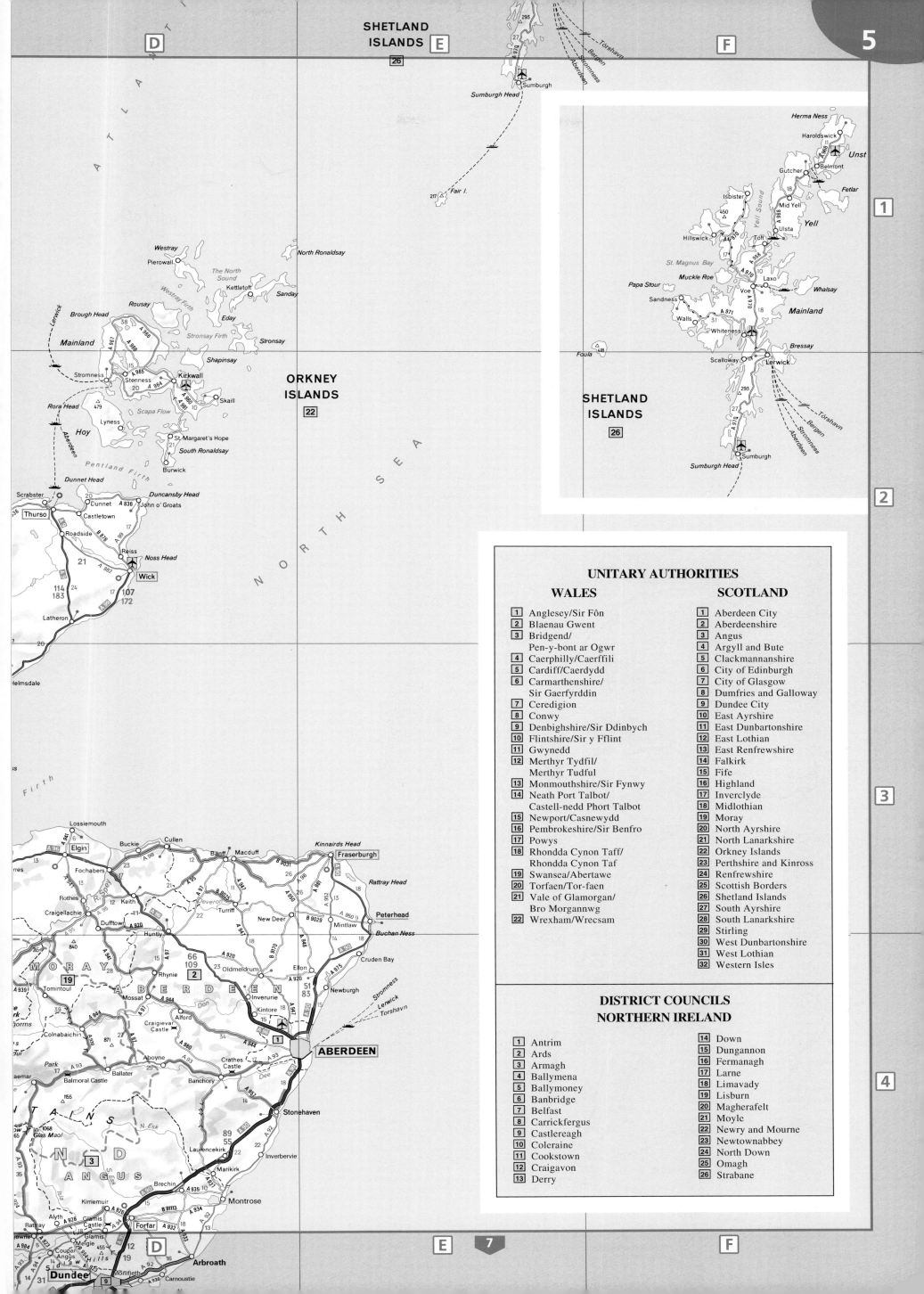

SHETLAND ISLANDS E 26

ORKNEY ISLANDS 22

SHETLAND ISLANDS 26

UNITARY AUTHORITIES

WALES

1 Anglesey/Sir Fôn
2 Blaenau Gwent
3 Bridgend/
   Pen-y-bont ar Ogwr
4 Caerphilly/Caerffili
5 Cardiff/Caerdydd
6 Carmarthenshire/
   Sir Gaerfyrddin
7 Ceredigion
8 Conwy
9 Denbighshire/Sir Ddinbych
10 Flintshire/Sir y Fflint
11 Gwynedd
12 Merthyr Tydfil/
   Merthyr Tudful
13 Monmouthshire/Sir Fynwy
14 Neath Port Talbot/
   Castell-nedd Phort Talbot
15 Newport/Casnewydd
16 Pembrokeshire/Sir Benfro
17 Powys
18 Rhondda Cynon Taff/
   Rhondda Cynon Taf
19 Swansea/Abertawe
20 Torfaen/Tor-faen
21 Vale of Glamorgan/
   Bro Morgannwg
22 Wrexham/Wrecsam

SCOTLAND

1 Aberdeen City
2 Aberdeenshire
3 Angus
4 Argyll and Bute
5 Clackmannanshire
6 City of Edinburgh
7 City of Glasgow
8 Dumfries and Galloway
9 Dundee City
10 East Ayrshire
11 East Dunbartonshire
12 East Lothian
13 East Renfrewshire
14 Falkirk
15 Fife
16 Highland
17 Inverclyde
18 Midlothian
19 Moray
20 North Ayrshire
21 North Lanarkshire
22 Orkney Islands
23 Perthshire and Kinross
24 Renfrewshire
25 Scottish Borders
26 Shetland Islands
27 South Ayrshire
28 South Lanarkshire
29 Stirling
30 West Dunbartonshire
31 West Lothian
32 Western Isles

DISTRICT COUNCILS
NORTHERN IRELAND

1 Antrim
2 Ards
3 Armagh
4 Ballymena
5 Ballymoney
6 Banbridge
7 Belfast
8 Carrickfergus
9 Castlereagh
10 Coleraine
11 Cookstown
12 Craigavon
13 Derry
14 Down
15 Dungannon
16 Fermanagh
17 Larne
18 Limavady
19 Lisburn
20 Magherafelt
21 Moyle
22 Newry and Mourne
23 Newtownabbey
24 North Down
25 Omagh
26 Strabane

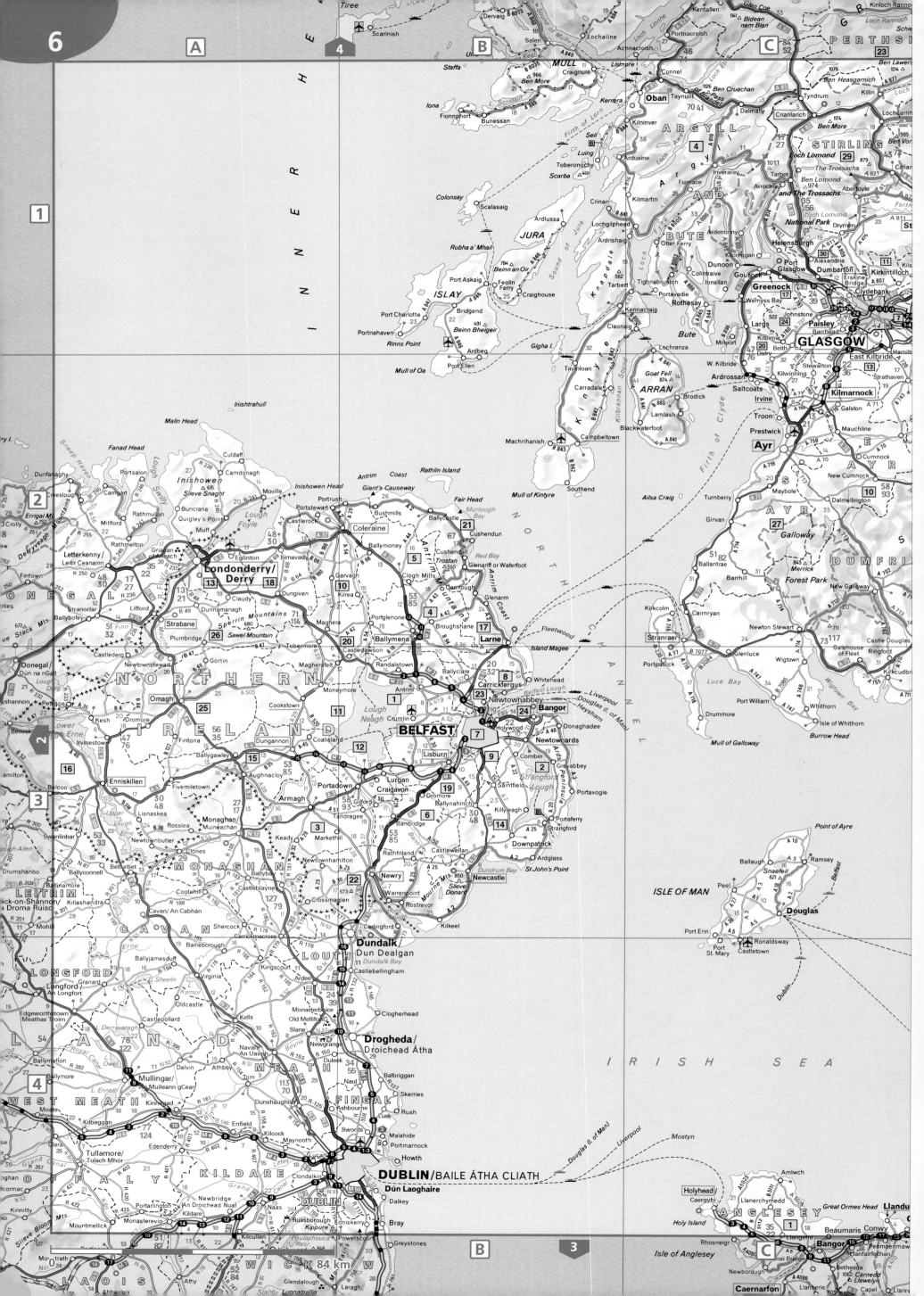

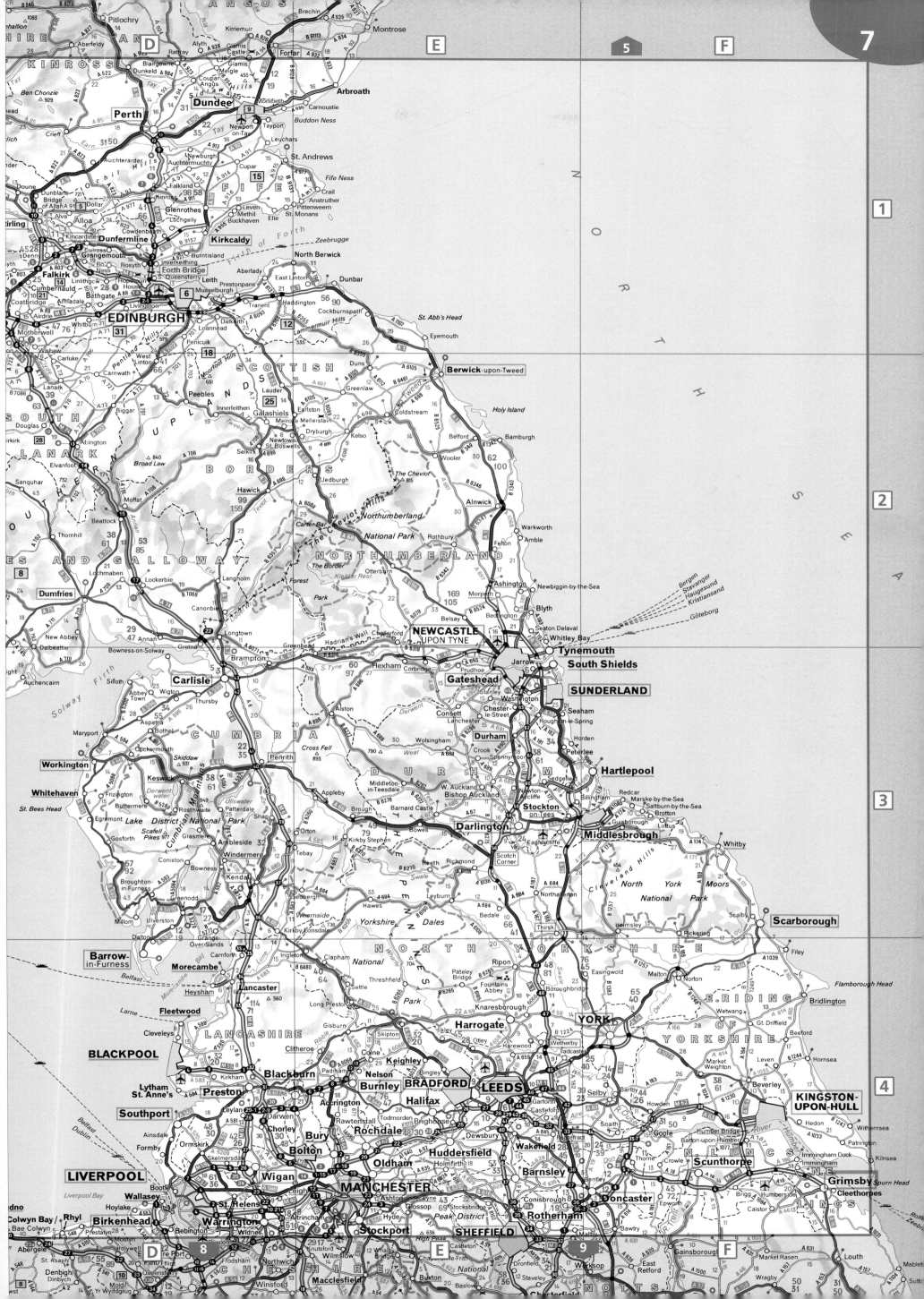

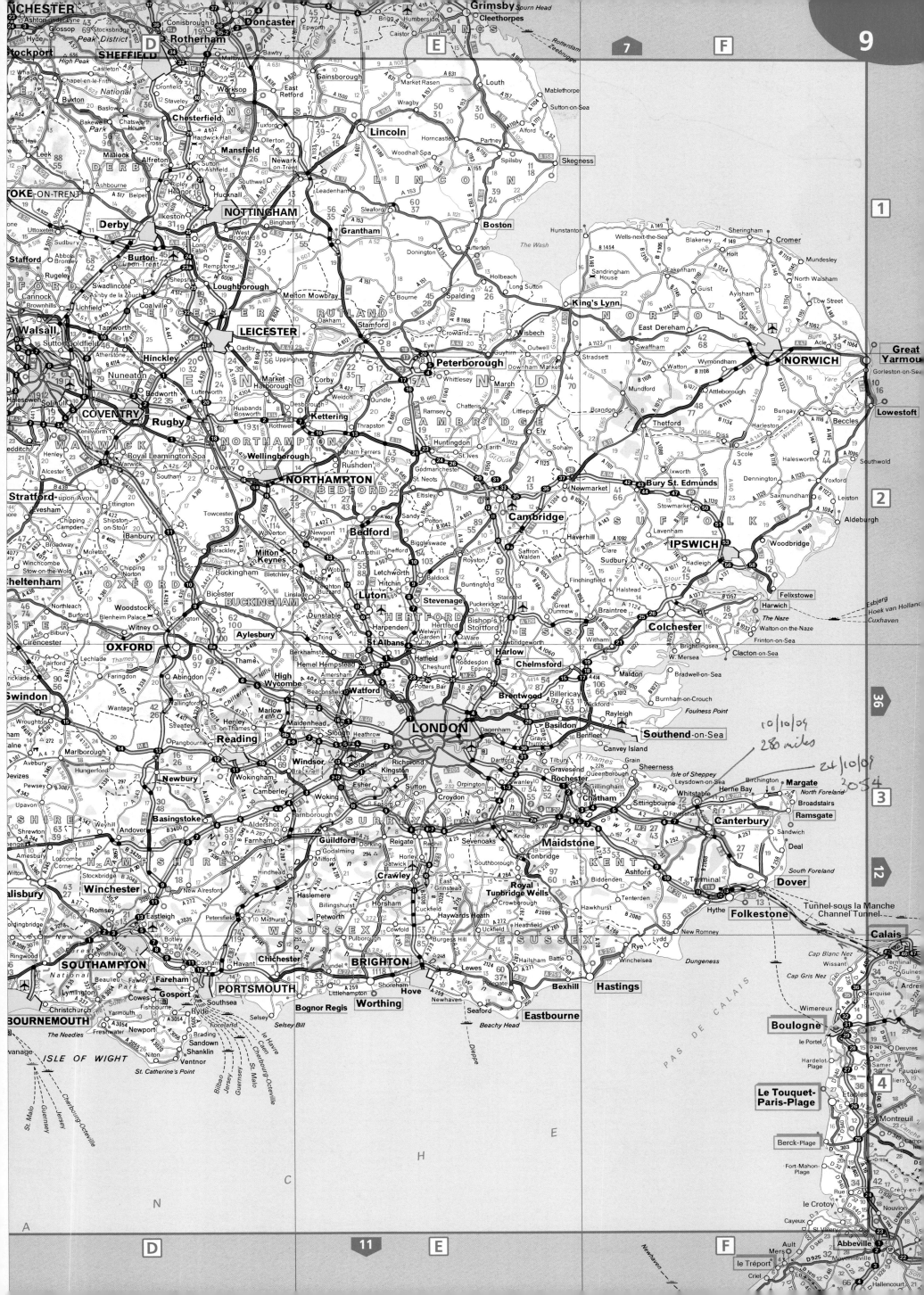

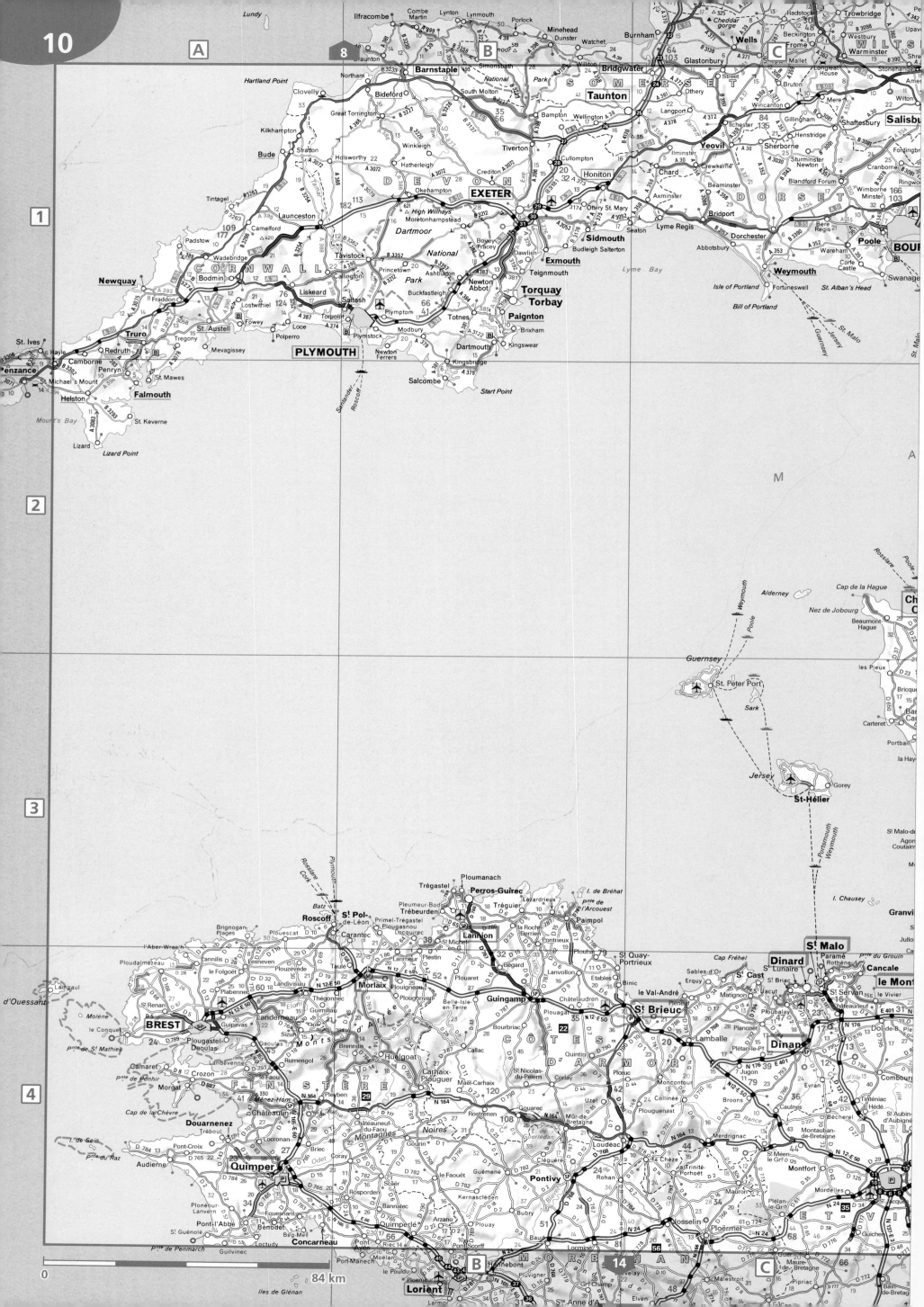

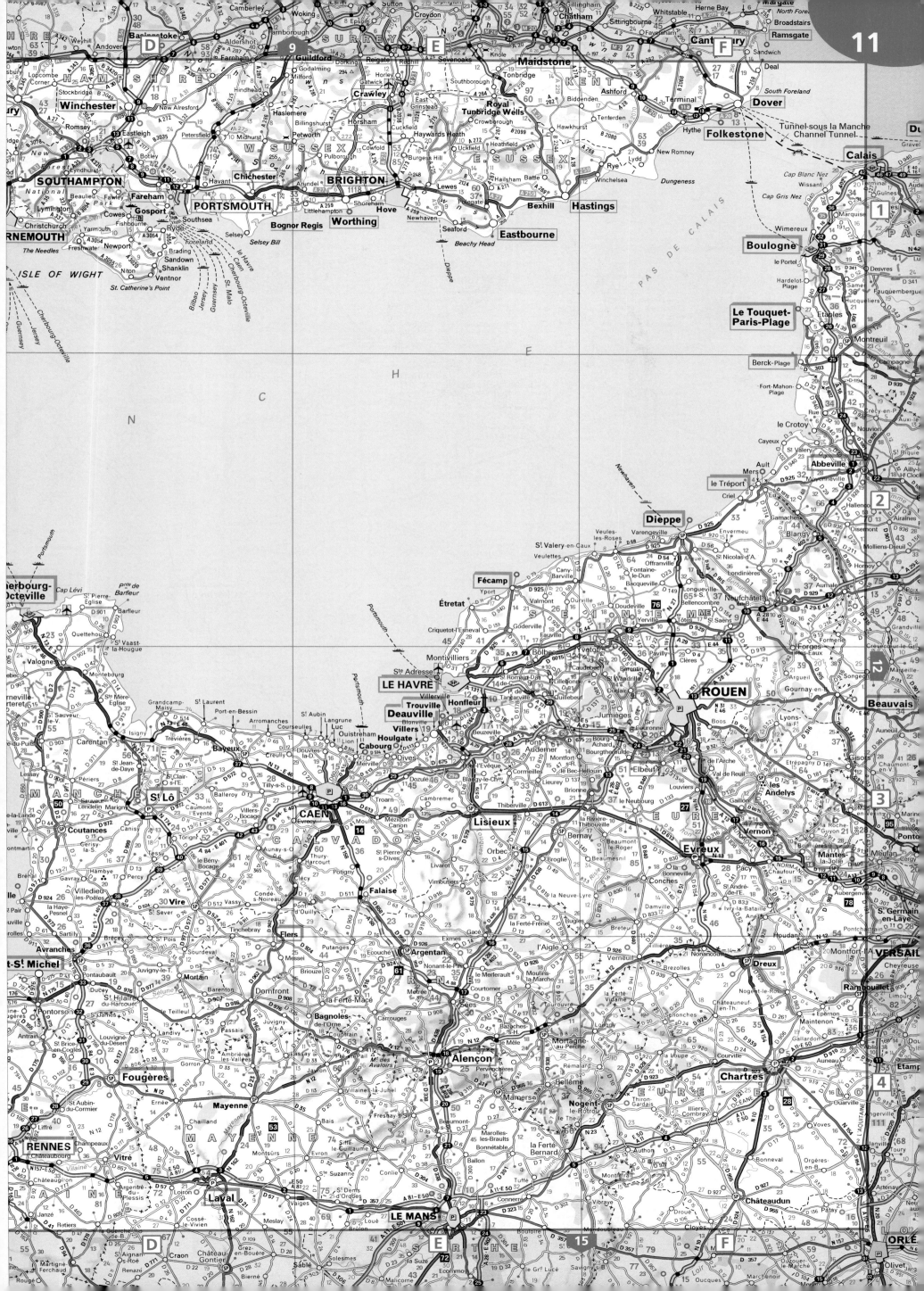

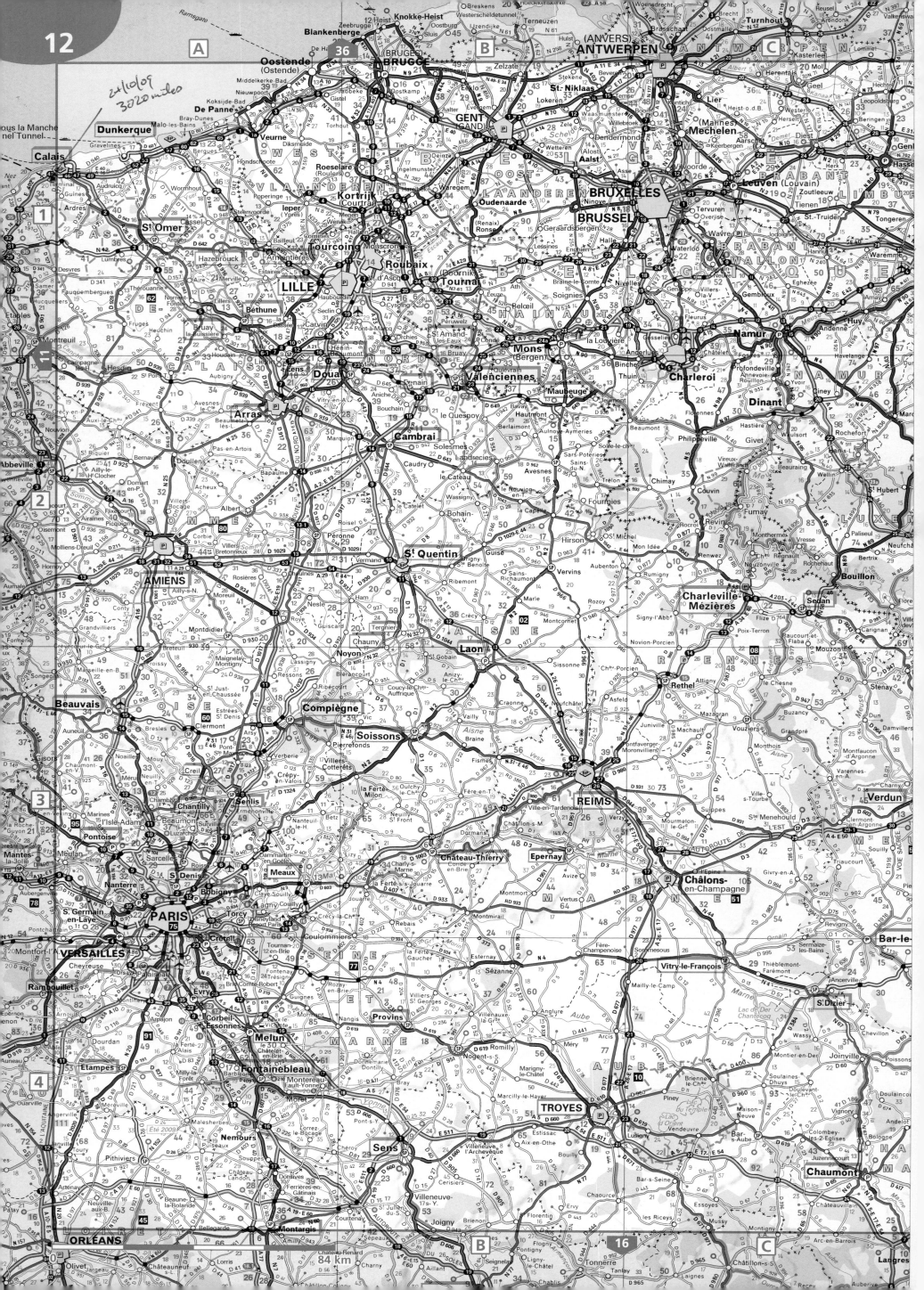

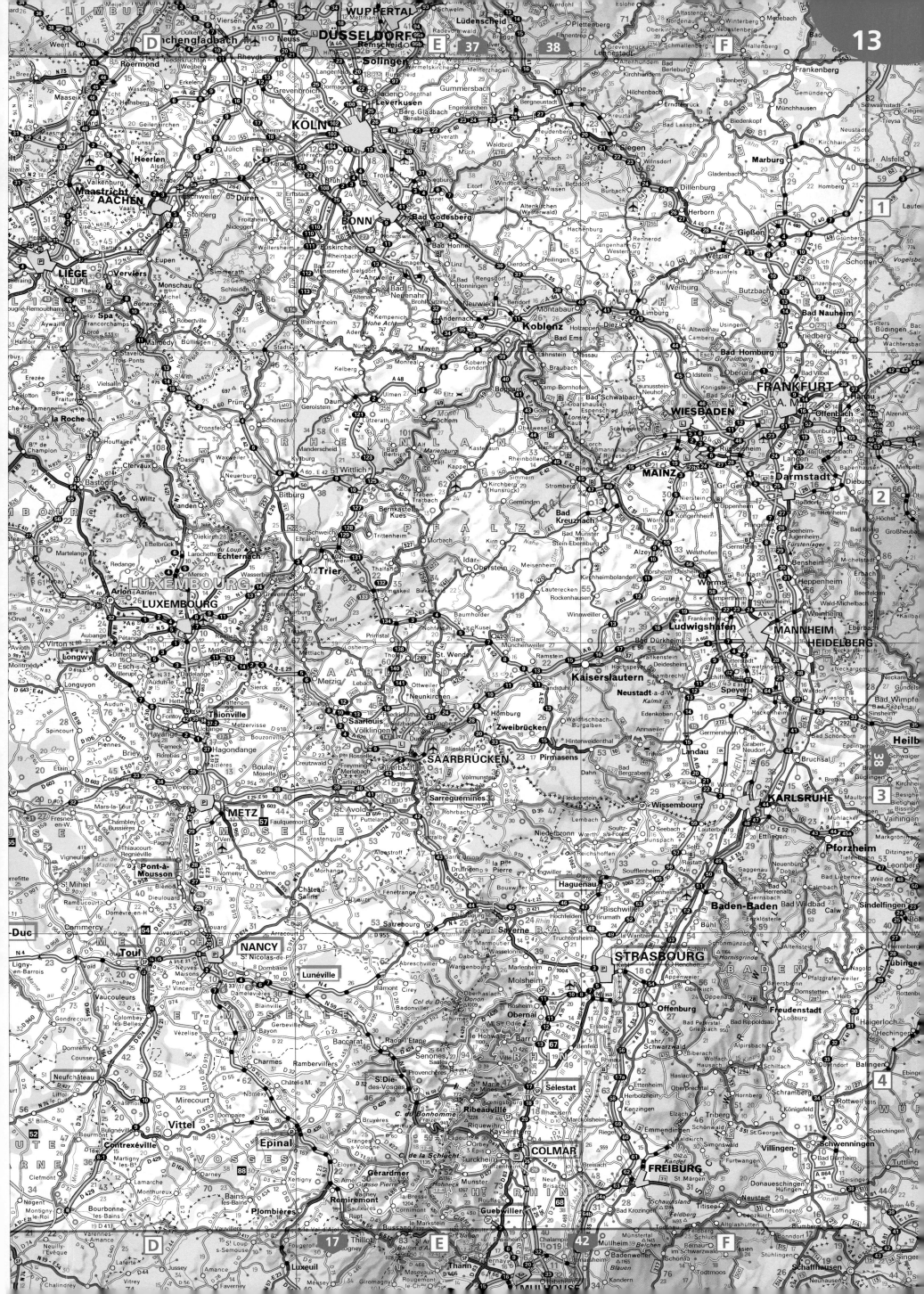

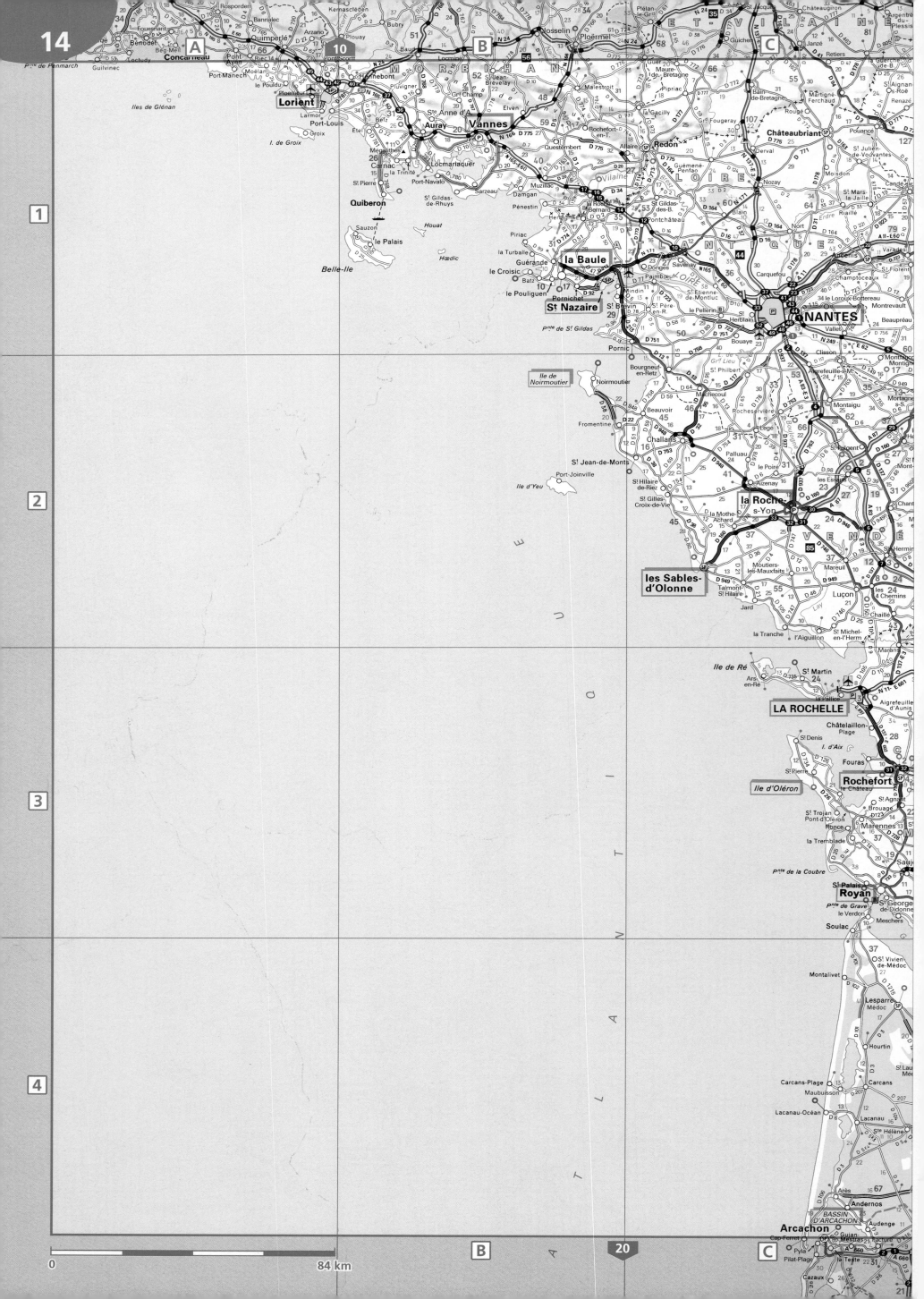

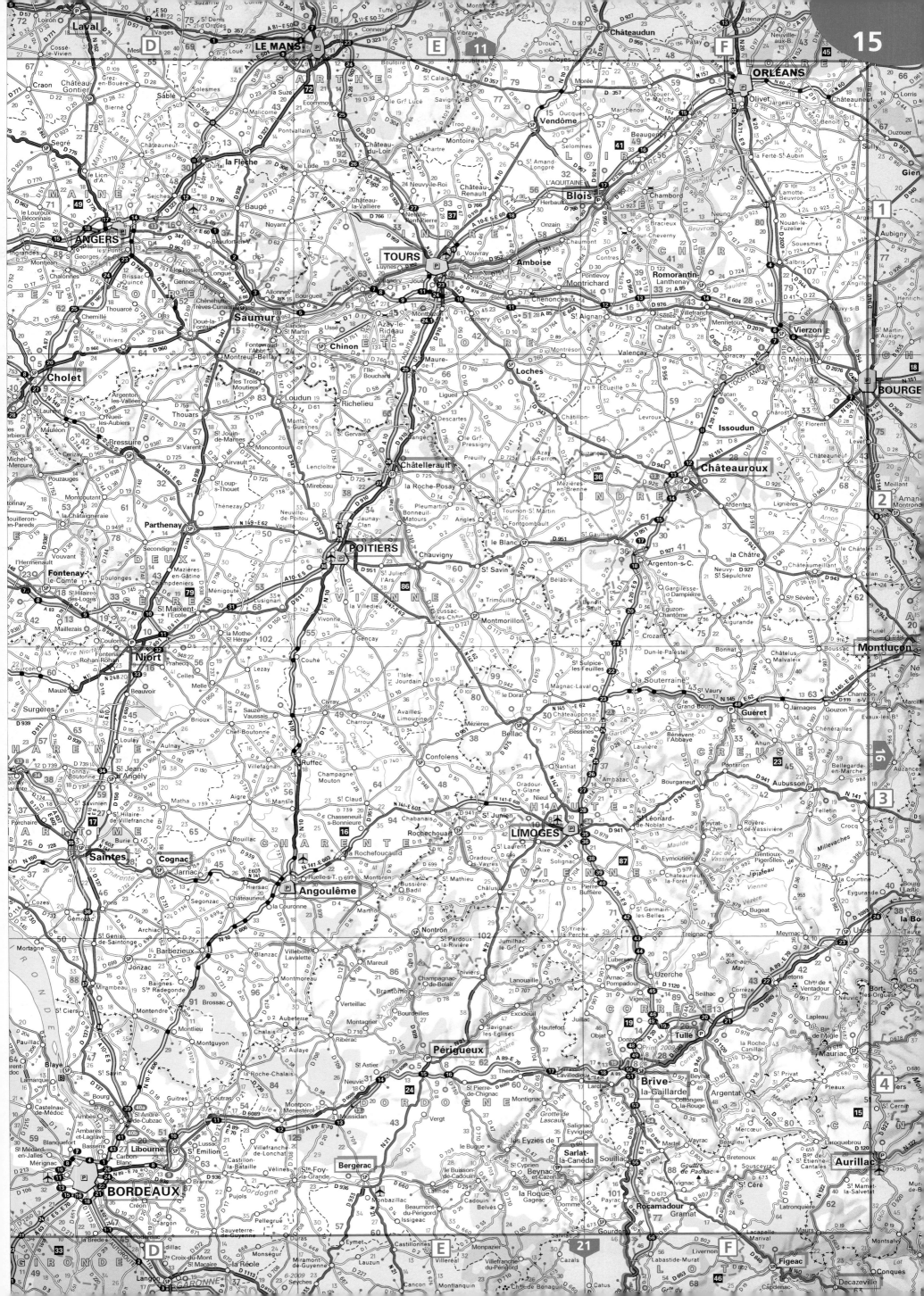

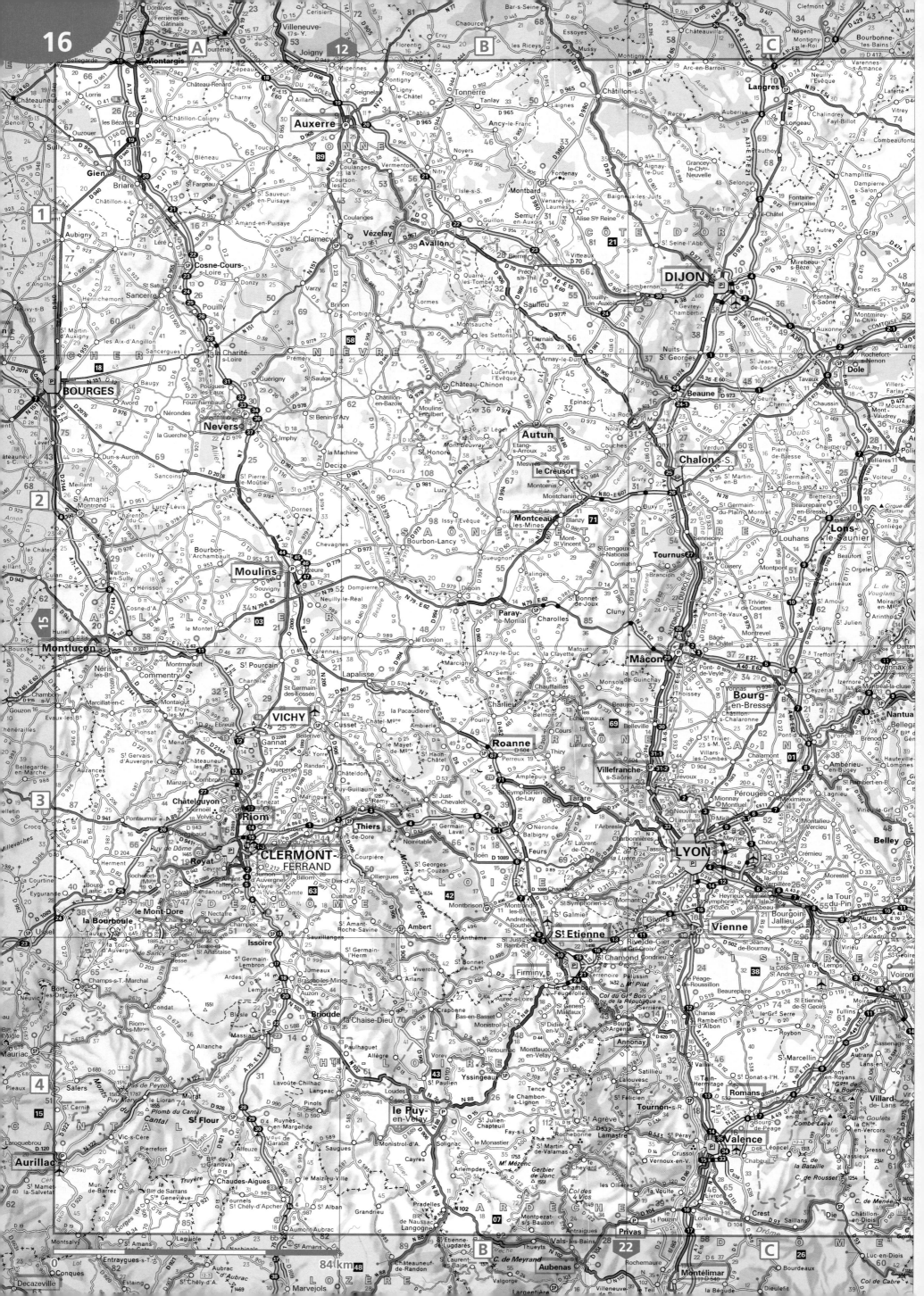

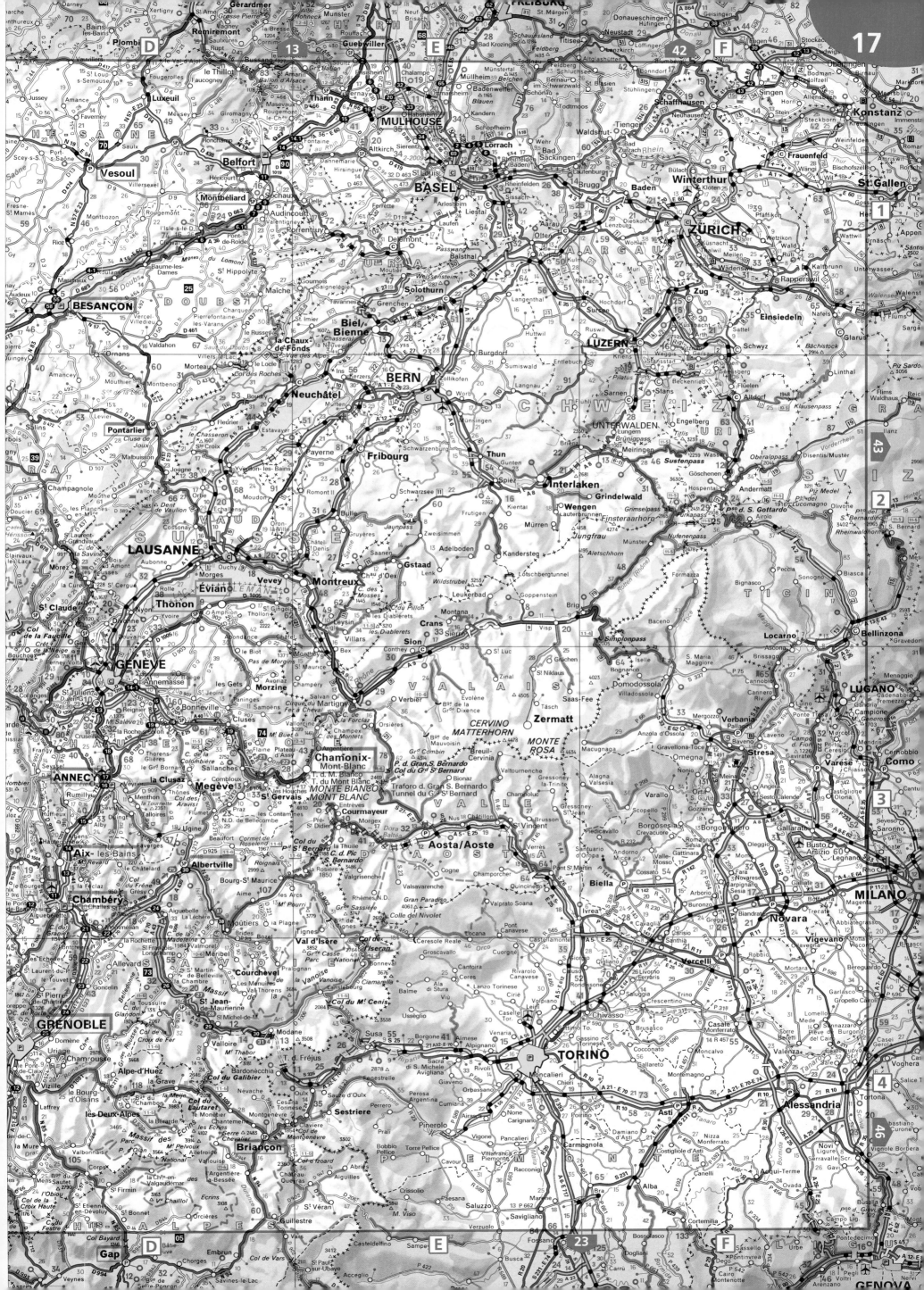

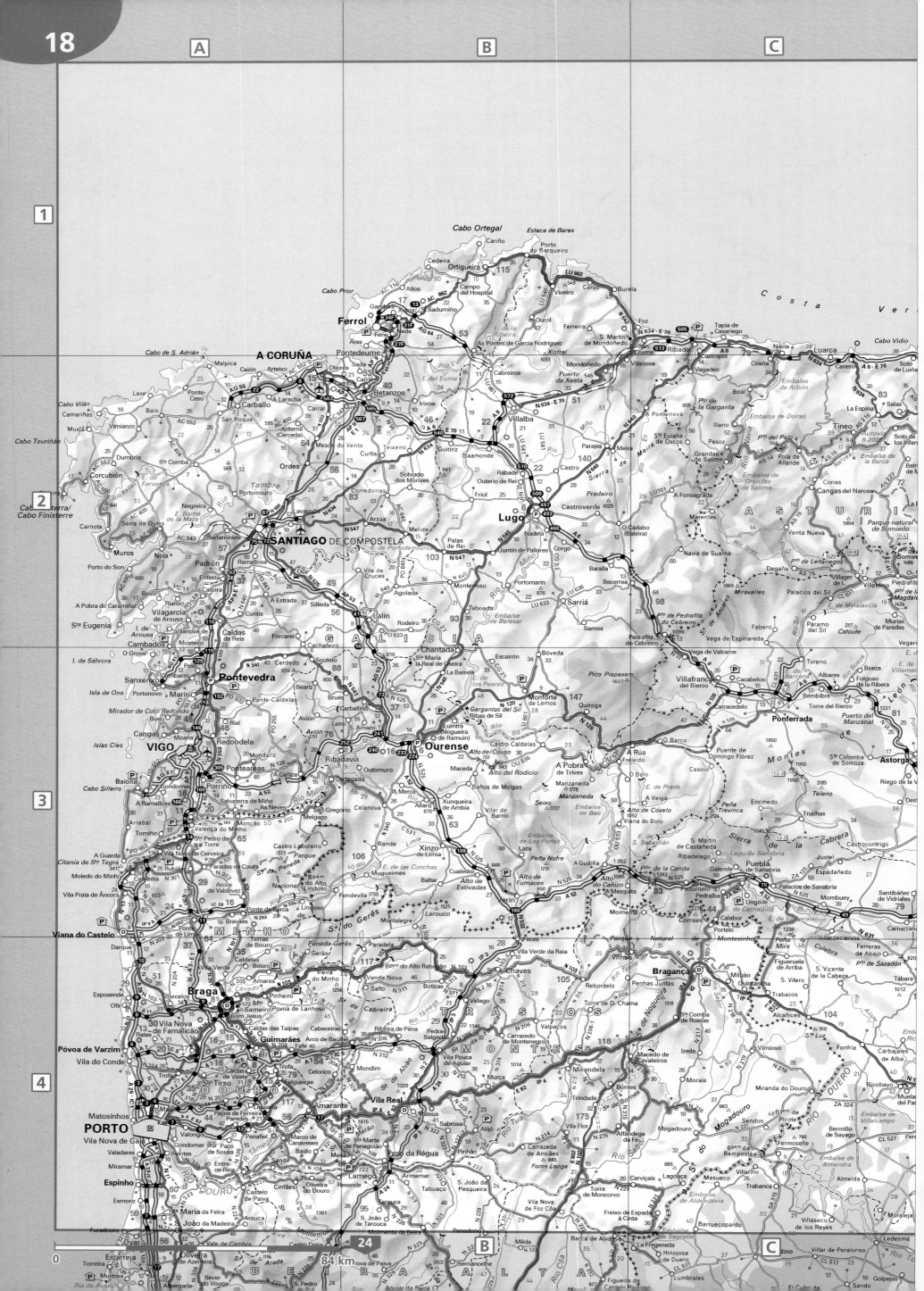

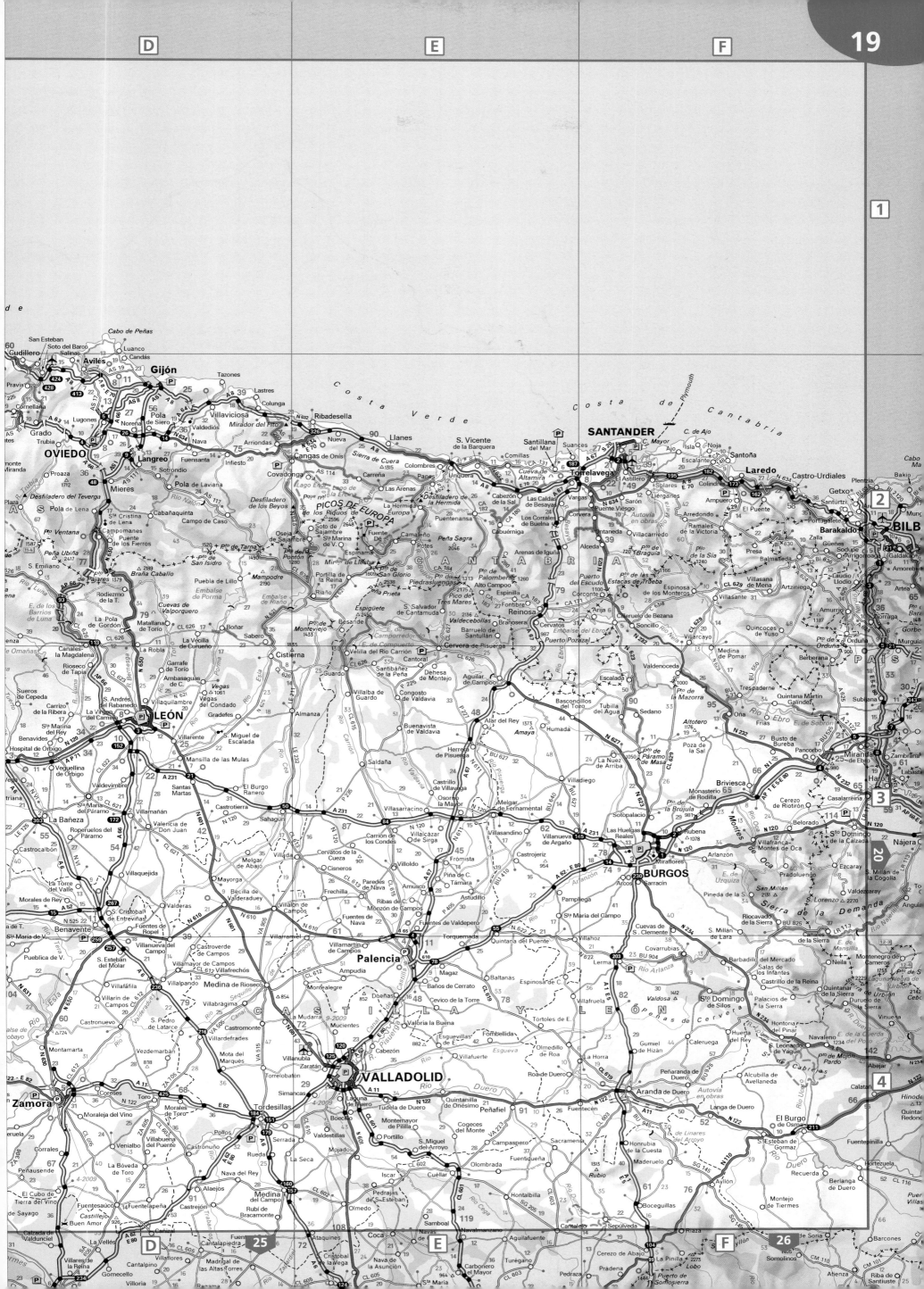

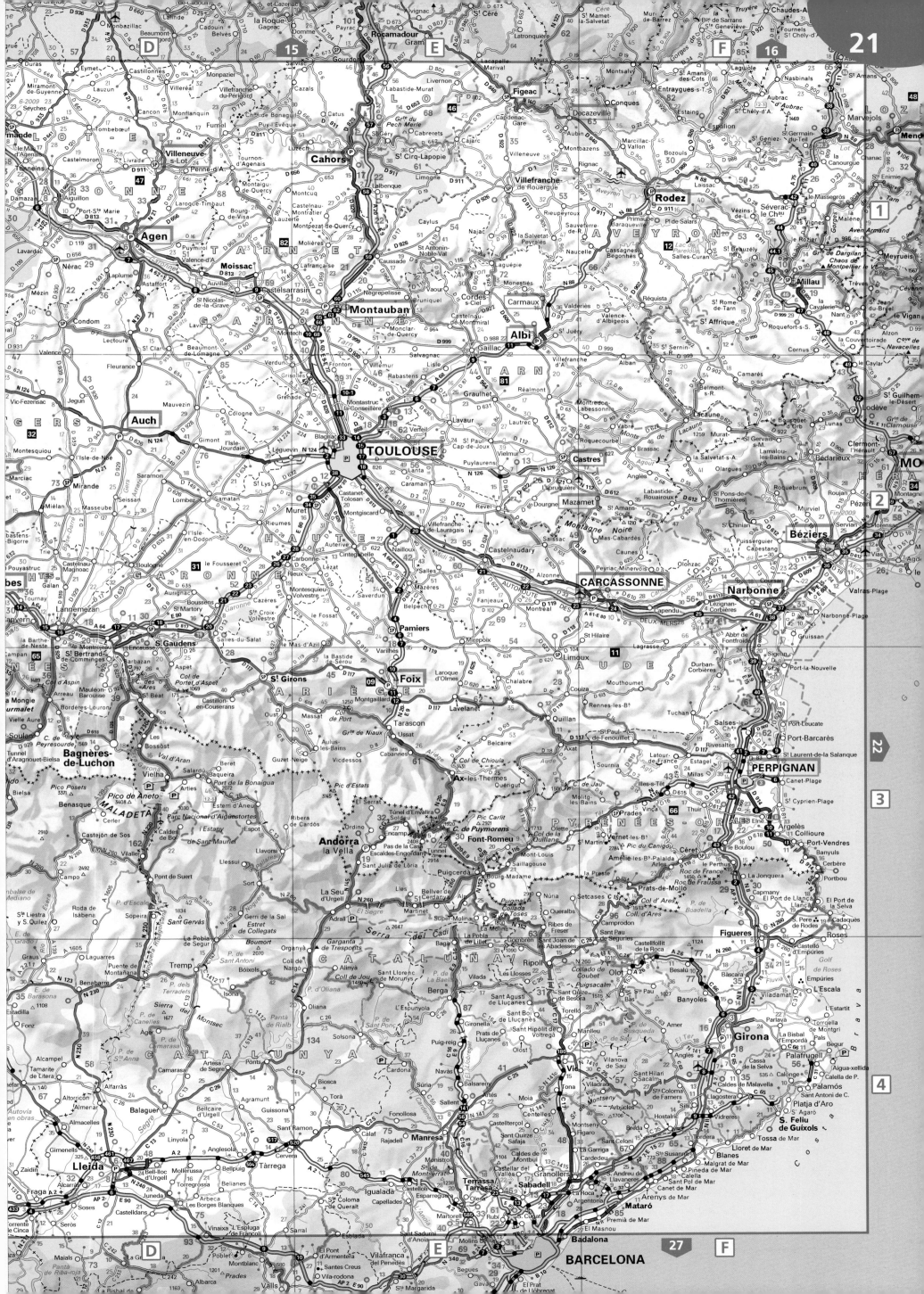

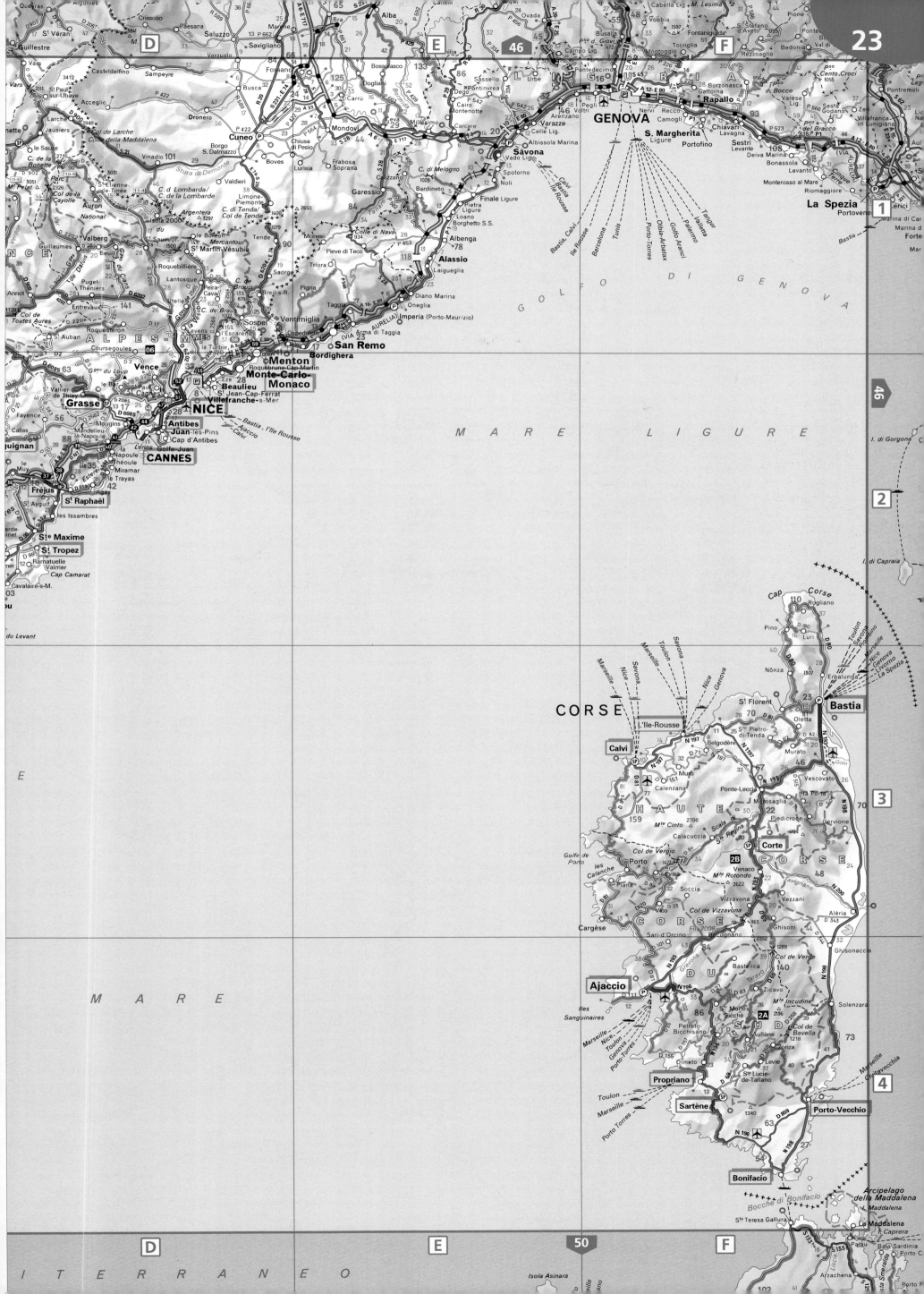

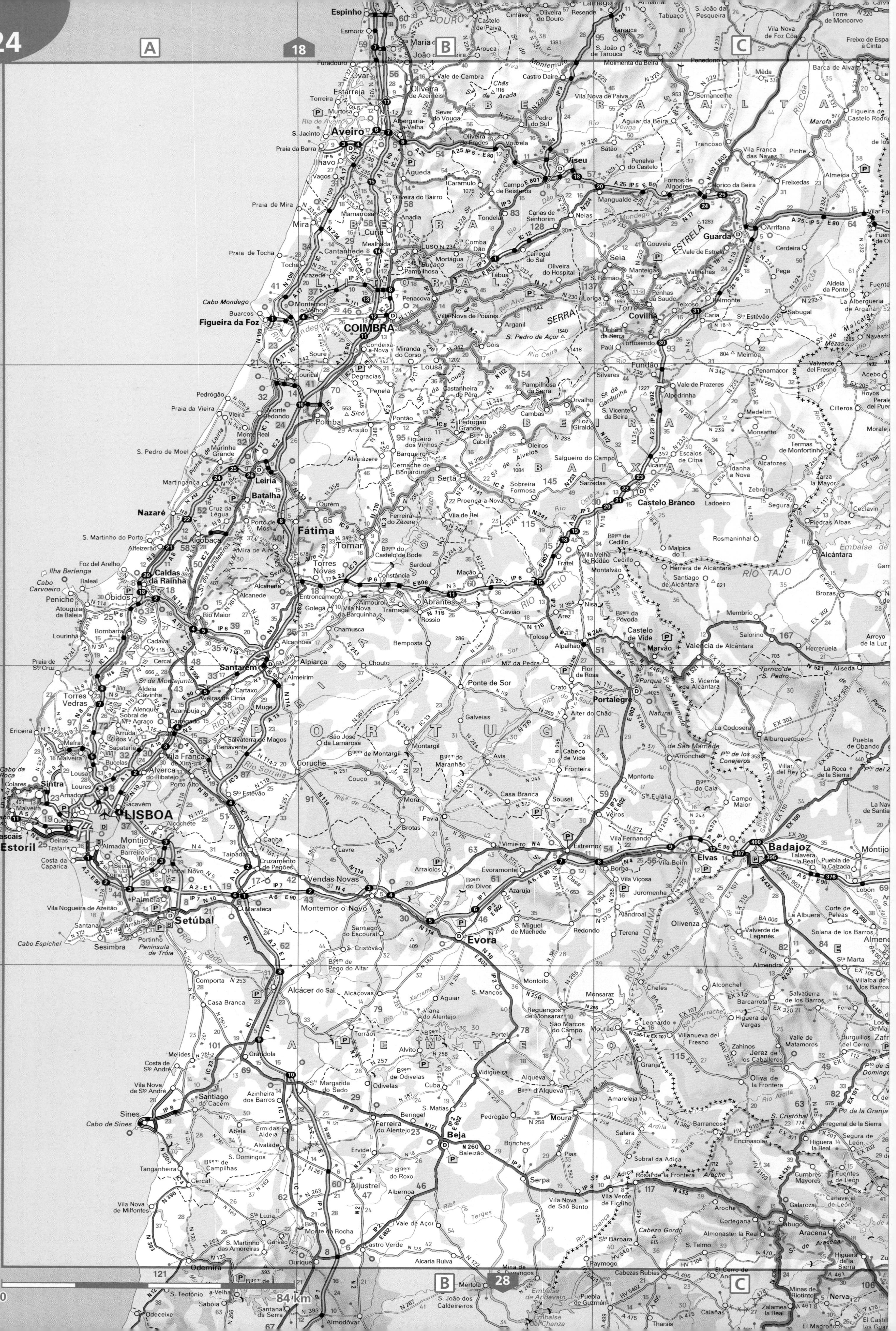
A
B
C
18
28
1
2
3
4
Espinho
Ovar
Aveiro
Viseu
Guarda
Coimbra
Figueira da Foz
Covilhã
Fundão
Castelo Branco
Leiria
Batalha
Nazaré
Fátima
Tomar
Caldas da Rainha
Peniche
Óbidos
Abrantes
Santarém
Portalegre
Torres Vedras
Sintra
LISBOA
Cascais
Estoril
Setúbal
Évora
Elvas
Badajoz
Estremoz
Beja
Serpa
Sines
Odemira
Ourique
Mértola
Moura
Grândola
Alcácer do Sal
Montemor-o-Novo
Vendas Novas
Ponte de Sor
Marvão
Valencia de Alcántara
Alcántara
Olivenza
Jerez de los Caballeros
Aracena
Nerva
Zafra
Rio Tejo
Rio Mondego
Rio Guadiana
Serra da Estrela
BEIRA ALTA
BEIRA BAIXA
BEIRA LITORAL
ALENTEJO
PORTUGAL
Cabo Mondego
Cabo Carvoeiro
Ilha Berlenga
Cabo da Roca
Cabo Espichel
Cabo de Sines
0
84 km

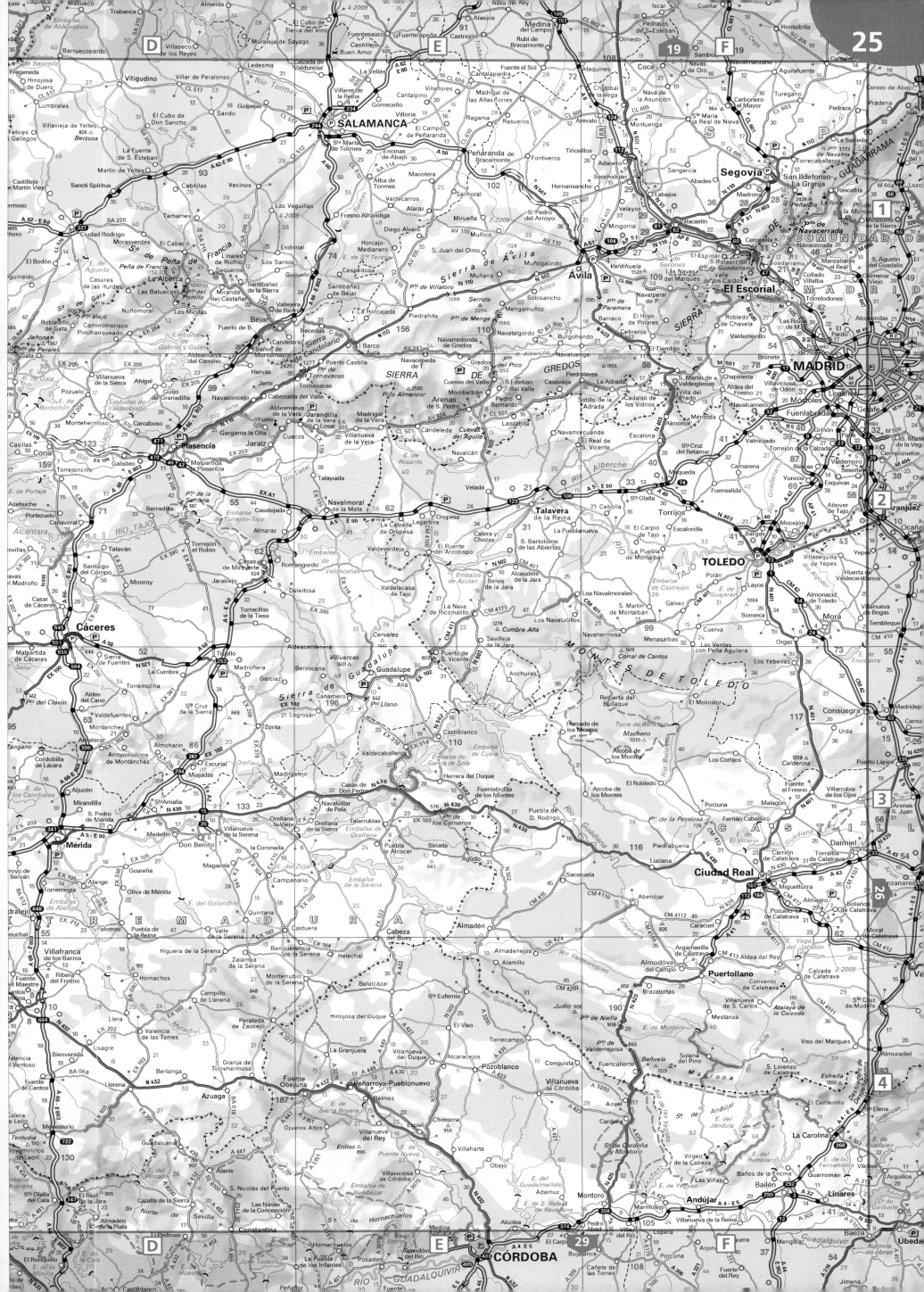

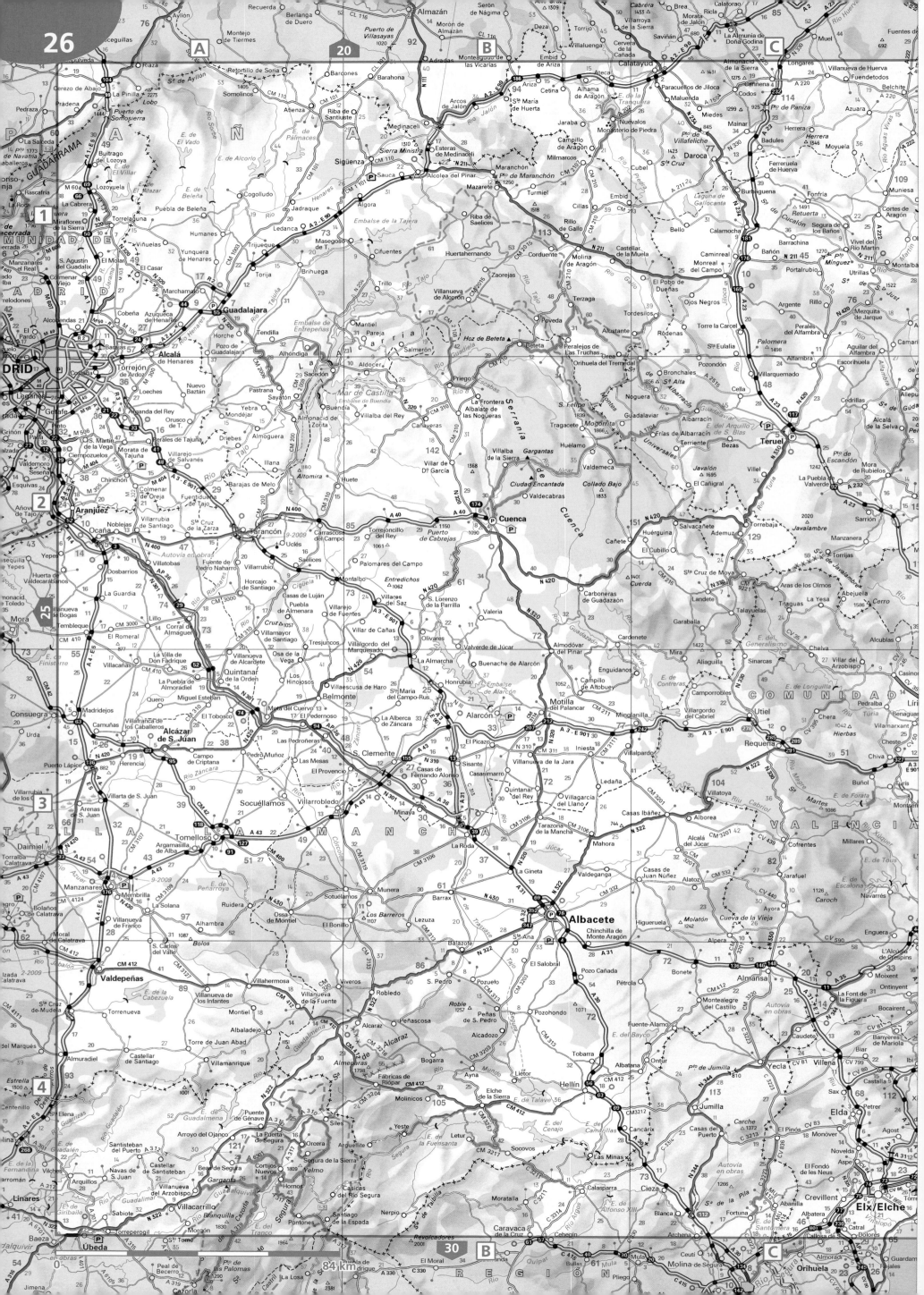

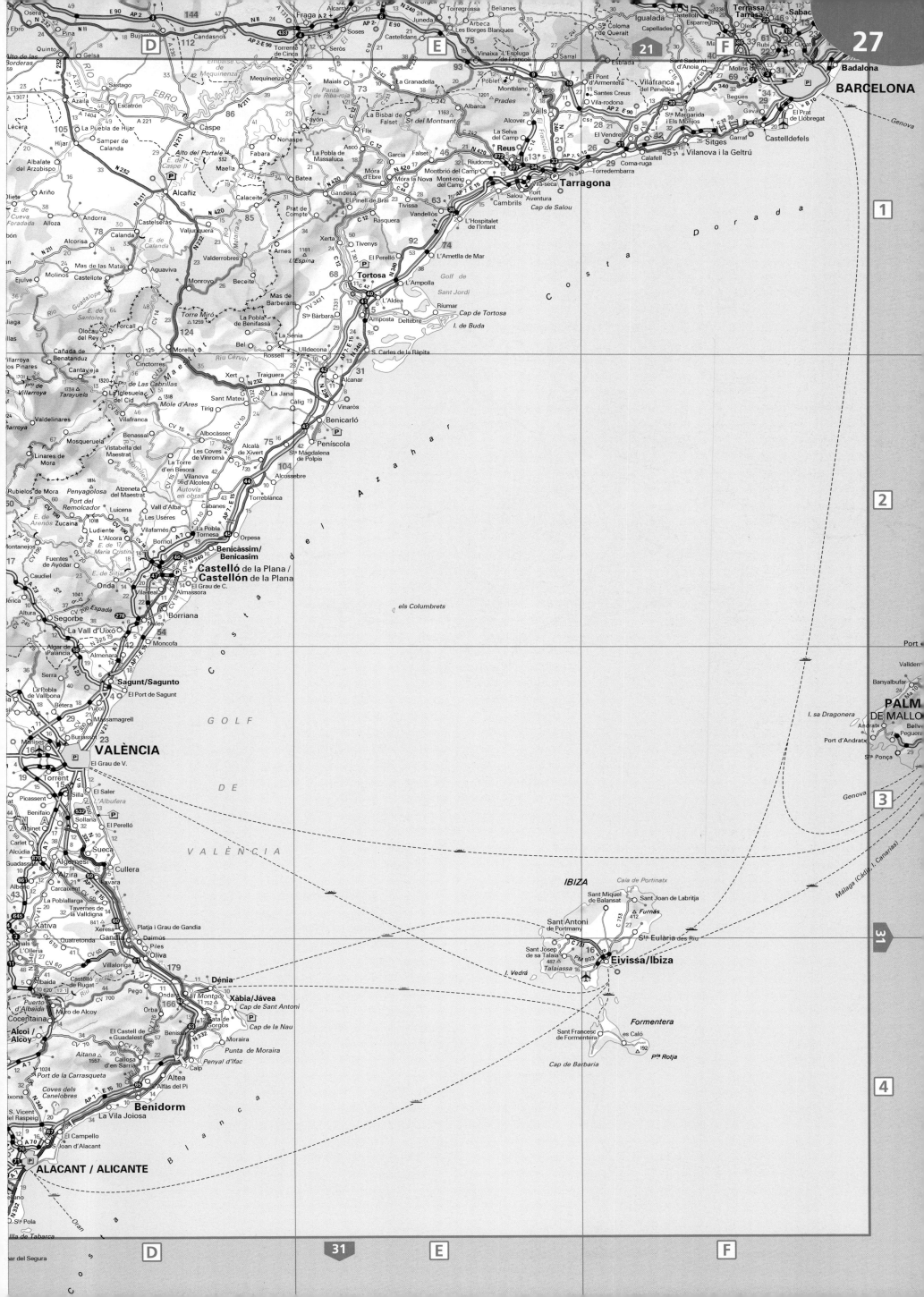

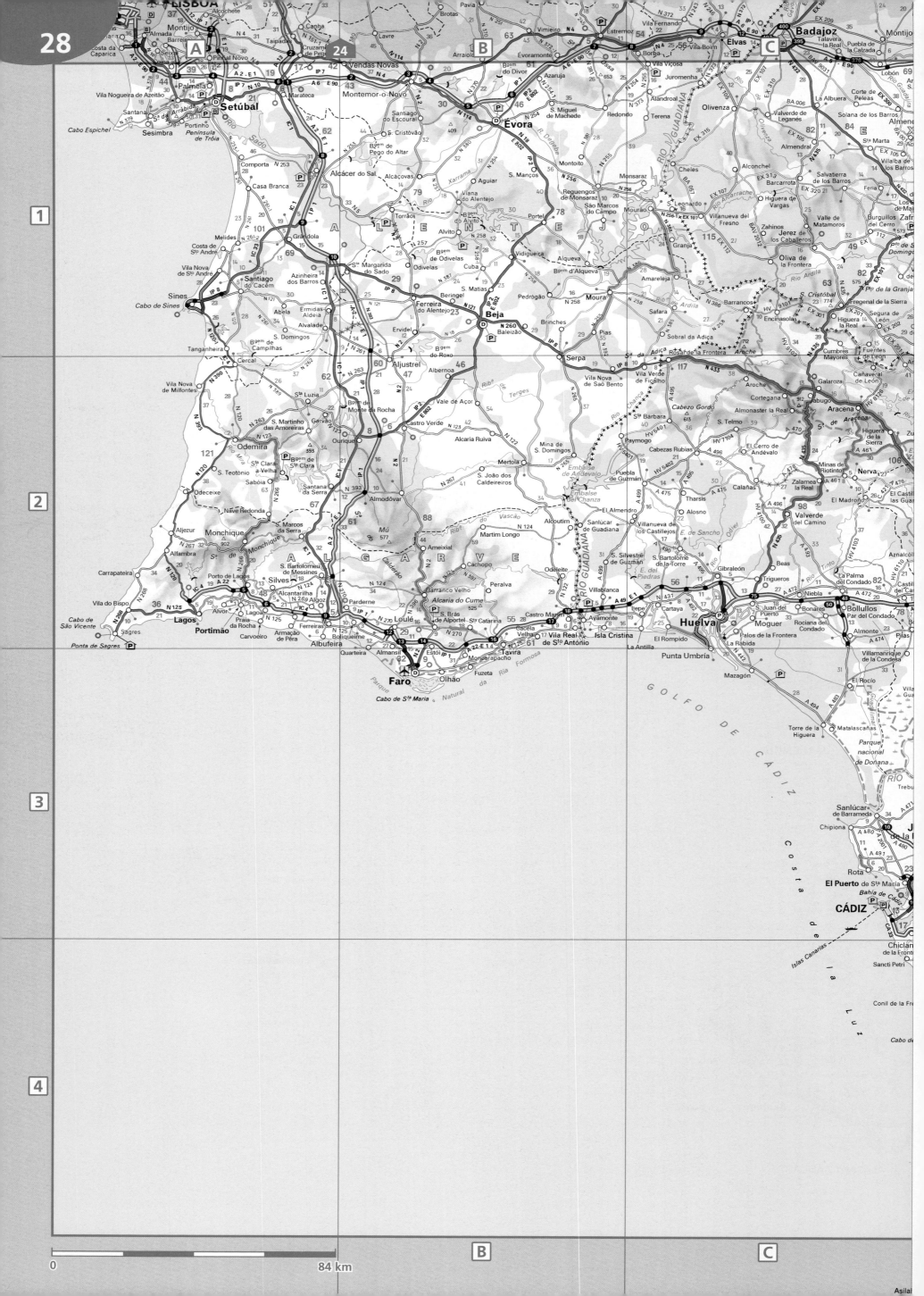

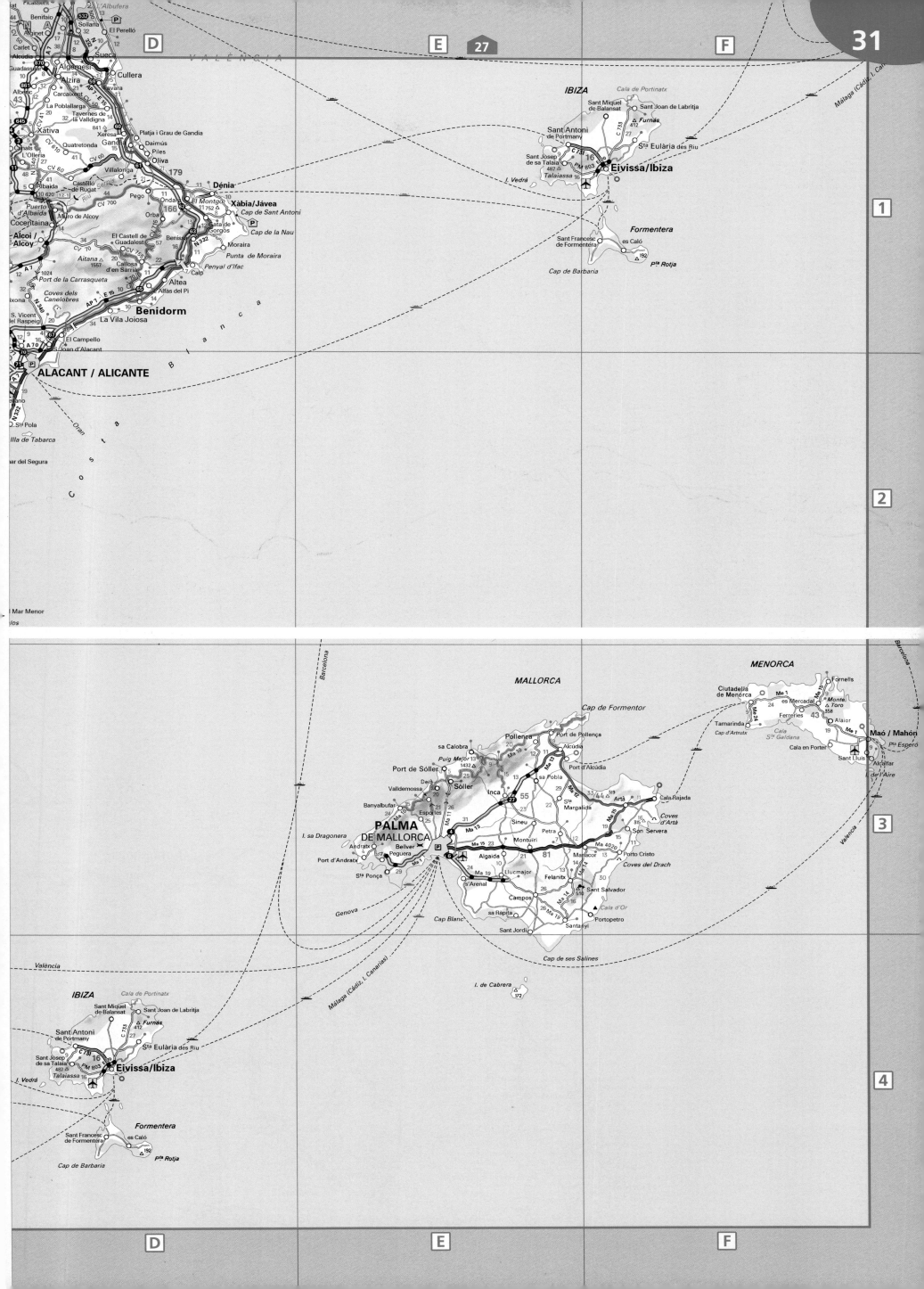

Top map

VALÈNCIA

D · **E** · **27** · **F**

L'Albufera
Picassent
Benifaió
Sollana
El Perelló
Carlet
Sueca
Alginet
Algemesi
Guadassuar
Cullera
Alberic
Alzira
Carcaixent
La Poblallarga
Xàtiva
Gandia
Tavernes de la Valldigna
Platja i Grau de Gandia
L'Olleria
Quatretonda
Daimús
Piles
Xeresa
Oliva
Albaida
Villalonga
Muro de Alcoy
Pego
Orba
Castelló de Rugat
Dénia
Puerto d'Albaida
Cocentaina
El Montgó
Xàbia/Jávea
Cap de Sant Antoni
Alcoi / Alcoy
El Castell de Guadalest
Benissa
Gata de Gorgós
Cap de la Nau
Aitana
Moraira
Port de la Carrasqueta
Callosa d'en Sarrià
Punta de Moraira
Penyal d'Ifac
Calp
S. Vicent del Raspeig
Altea
Alfàs del Pi
Coves dels Canelobres
Benidorm
La Vila Joiosa
El Campello
Sant Joan d'Alacant
ALACANT / ALICANTE
Sta Pola
Illa de Tabarca
Mar del Segura
Mar Menor

IBIZA
Cala de Portinatx
Sant Miquel de Balansat
Sant Joan de Labritja
Furnàs
Sant Antoni de Portmany
Sta Eulària des Riu
Sant Josep de sa Talaia
Talaiassa
Eivissa/Ibiza
I. Vedrà
Formentera
Sant Francesc de Formentera
es Caló
Pta Rotja
Cap de Barbaria

Málaga (Cádiz, I. Can...)

1

2

Bottom map

Barcelona
MALLORCA
Cap de Formentor
MENORCA
Ciutadella de Menórca
Fornells
es Mercadal
Monte Toro
Ferreries
Alaior
Tamarinda
Cap d'Artrutx
Cala Sta Galdana
Maó / Mahón
Pta Esperó
Cala en Porter
Sant Lluís
Alcaufar
de l'Aire
Pollença
Port de Pollença
sa Calobra
Alcúdia
Puig Major
Port d'Alcúdia
Port de Sóller
sa Pobla
Artà
Cala Rajada
Deià
Sóller
Inca
Coves d'Artà
Valldemossa
Sta Margalida
Banyalbufar
Son Servera
Esporles
Sineu
Porto Cristo
I. sa Dragonera
PALMA DE MALLORCA
Petra
Coves del Drach
Bellver
Peguera
Algaida
Montuiri
Manacor
Andratx
Santanyí
Port d'Andratx
Llucmajor
Felanitx
Cala d'Or
Sta Ponça
s'Arenal
Sant Salvador
Portopetro
Genova
Campos
sa Ràpita
Cap Blanc
Sant Jordi
Cap de ses Salines
València
Málaga (Cádiz, I. Canarias)
I. de Cabrera

3

València
IBIZA
Cala de Portinatx
Sant Miquel de Balansat
Sant Joan de Labritja
Furnàs
Sant Antoni de Portmany
Sta Eulària des Riu
Sant Josep de sa Talaia
Talaiassa
Eivissa/Ibiza
I. Vedrà
Formentera
Sant Francesc de Formentera
es Caló
Pta Rotja
Cap de Barbaria

4

D · **E** · **F**

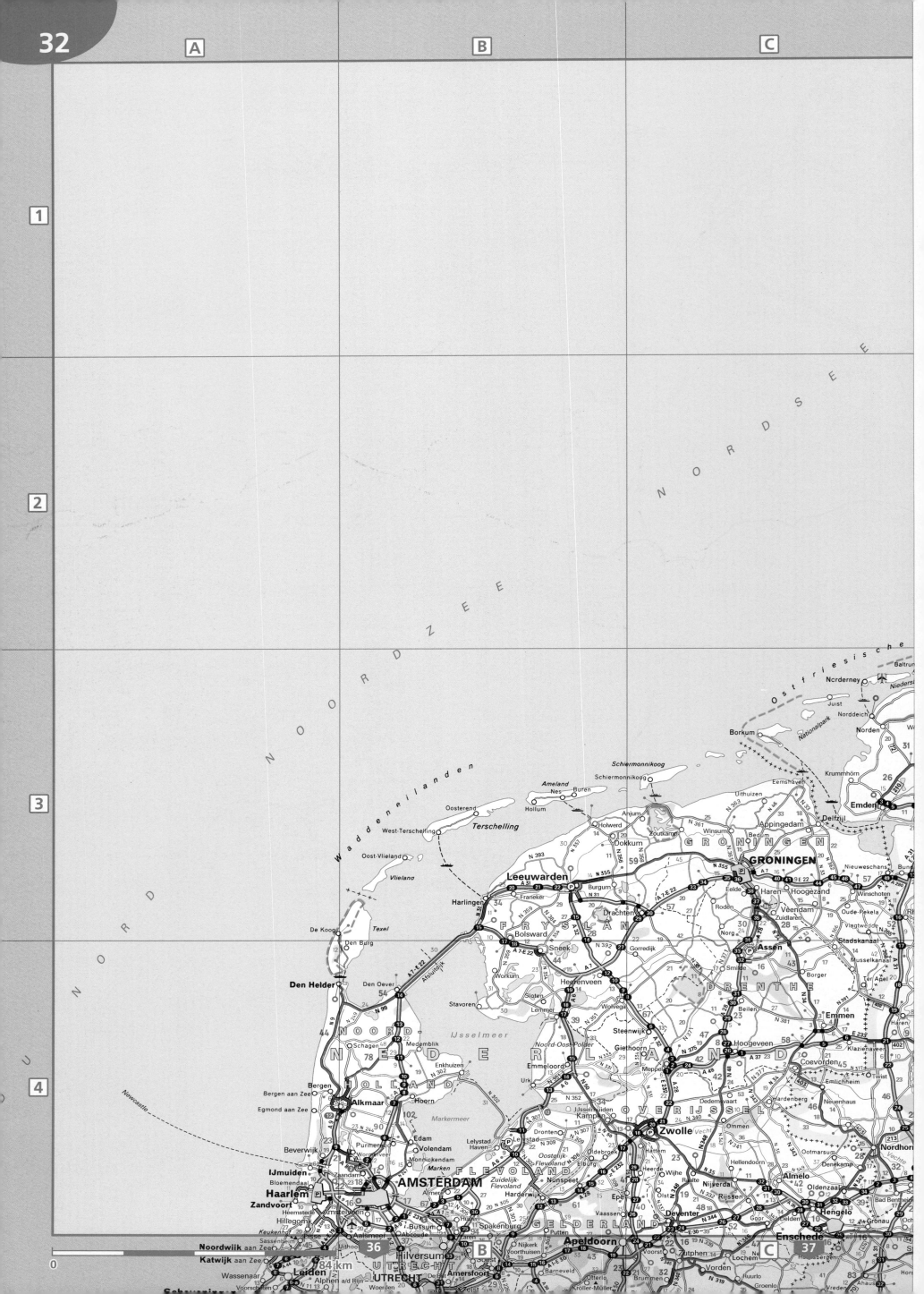

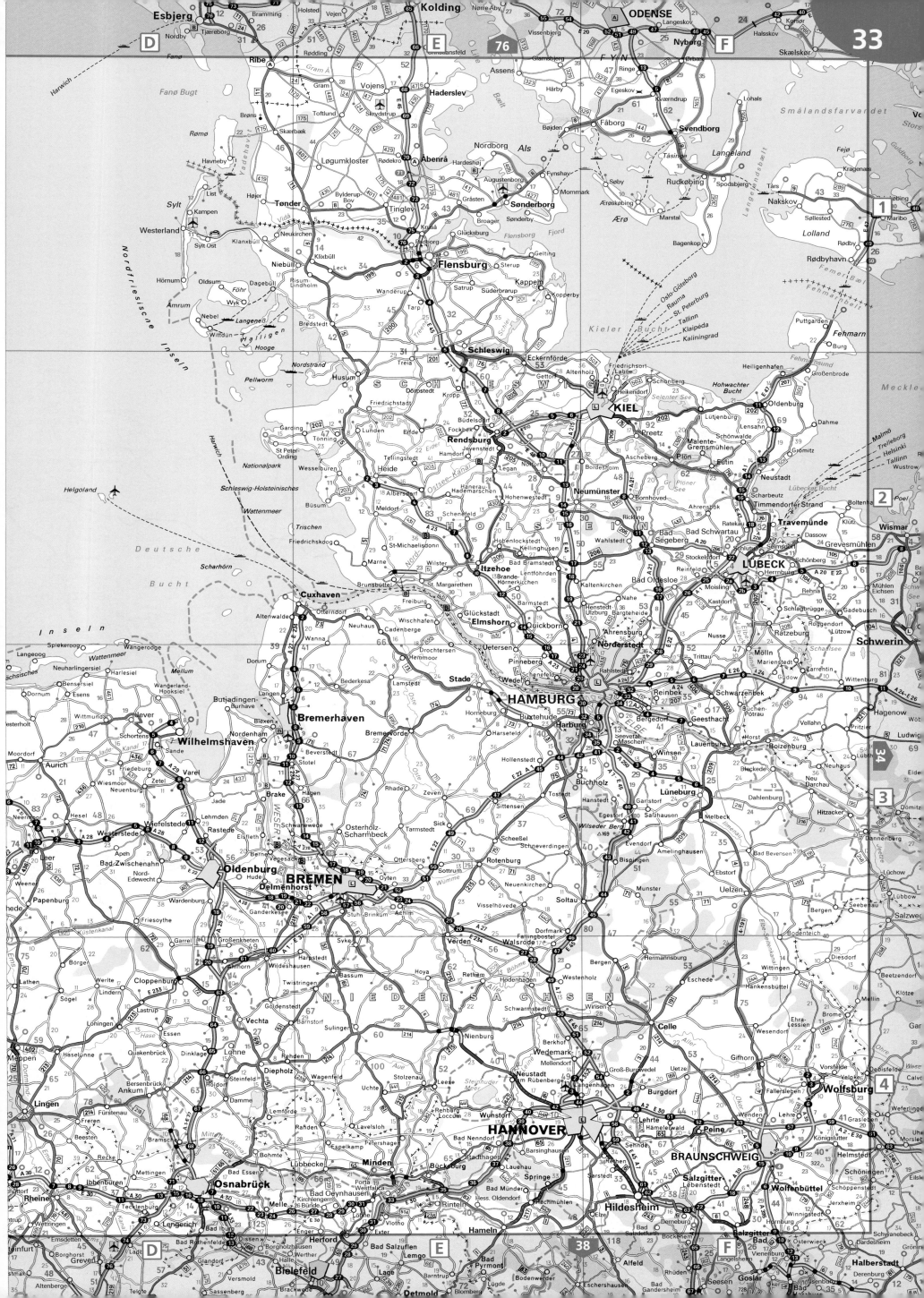

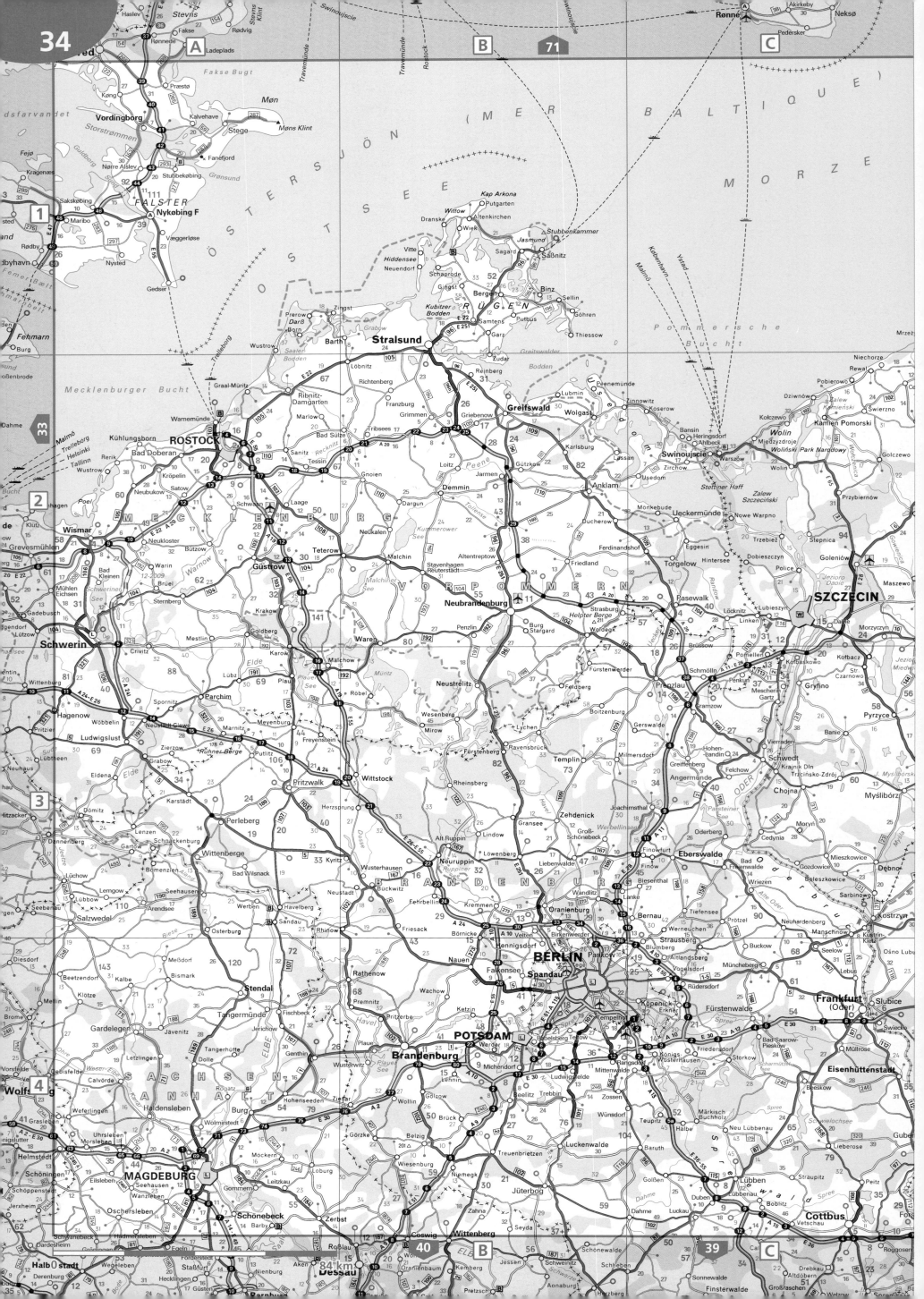

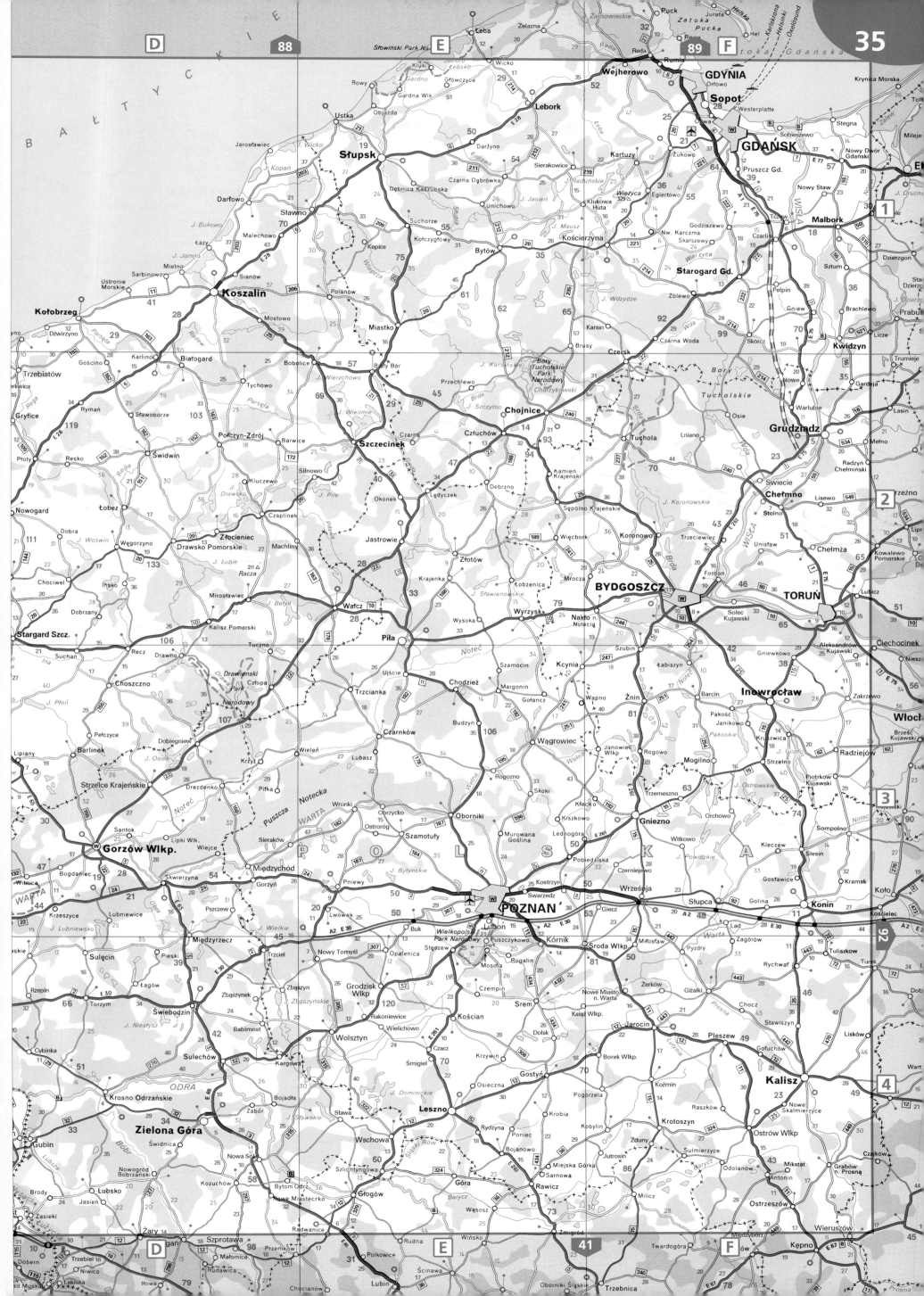

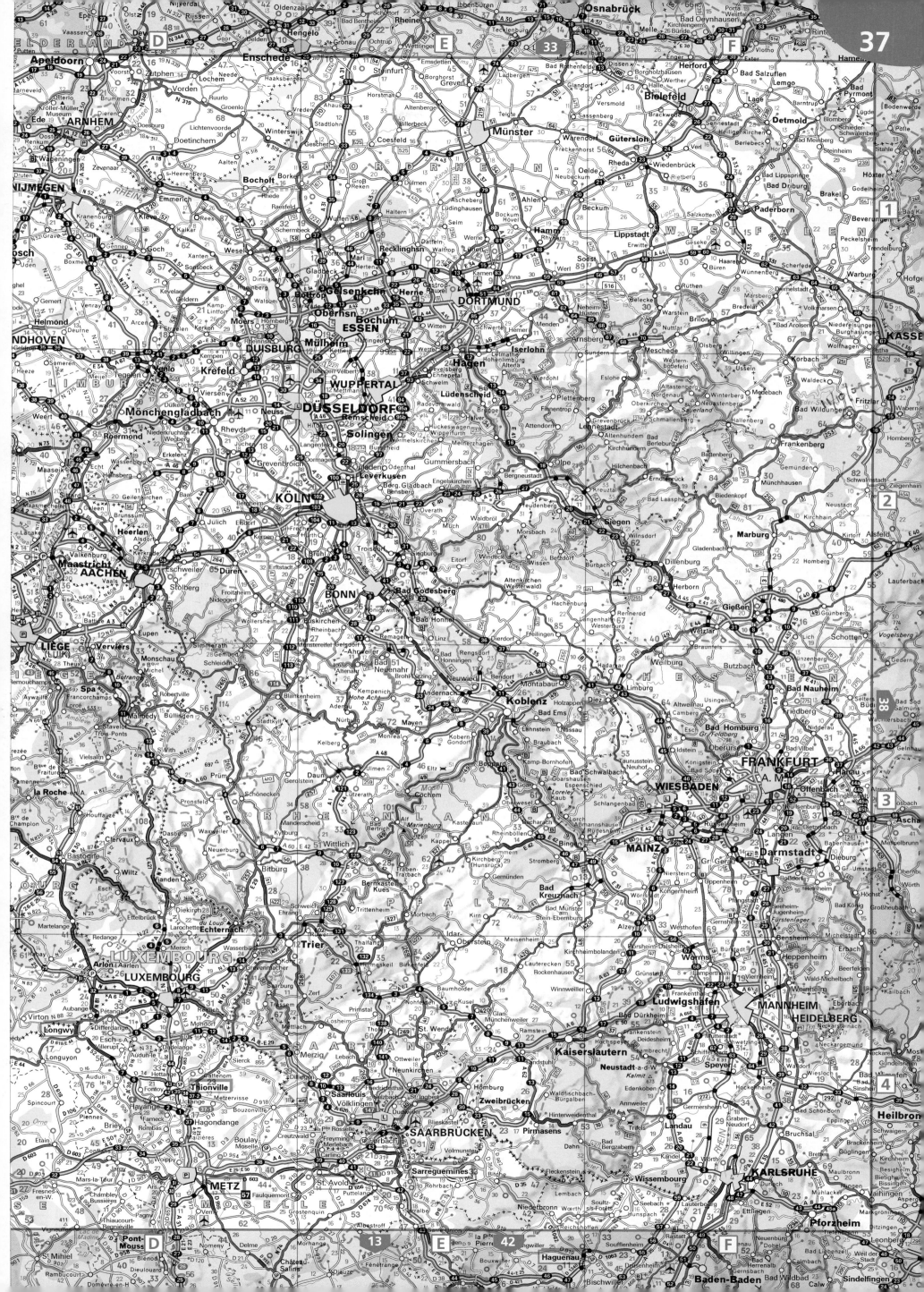

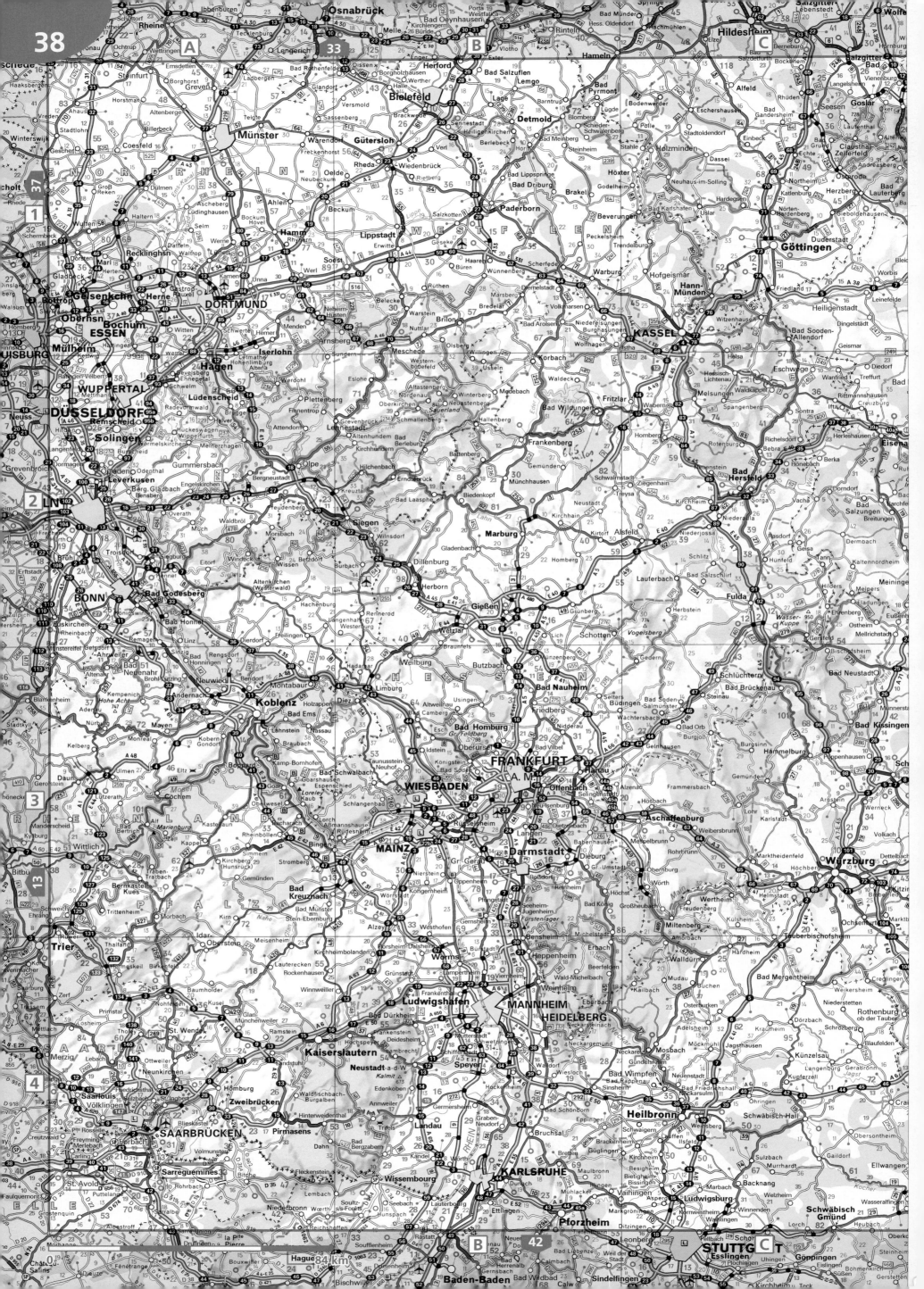

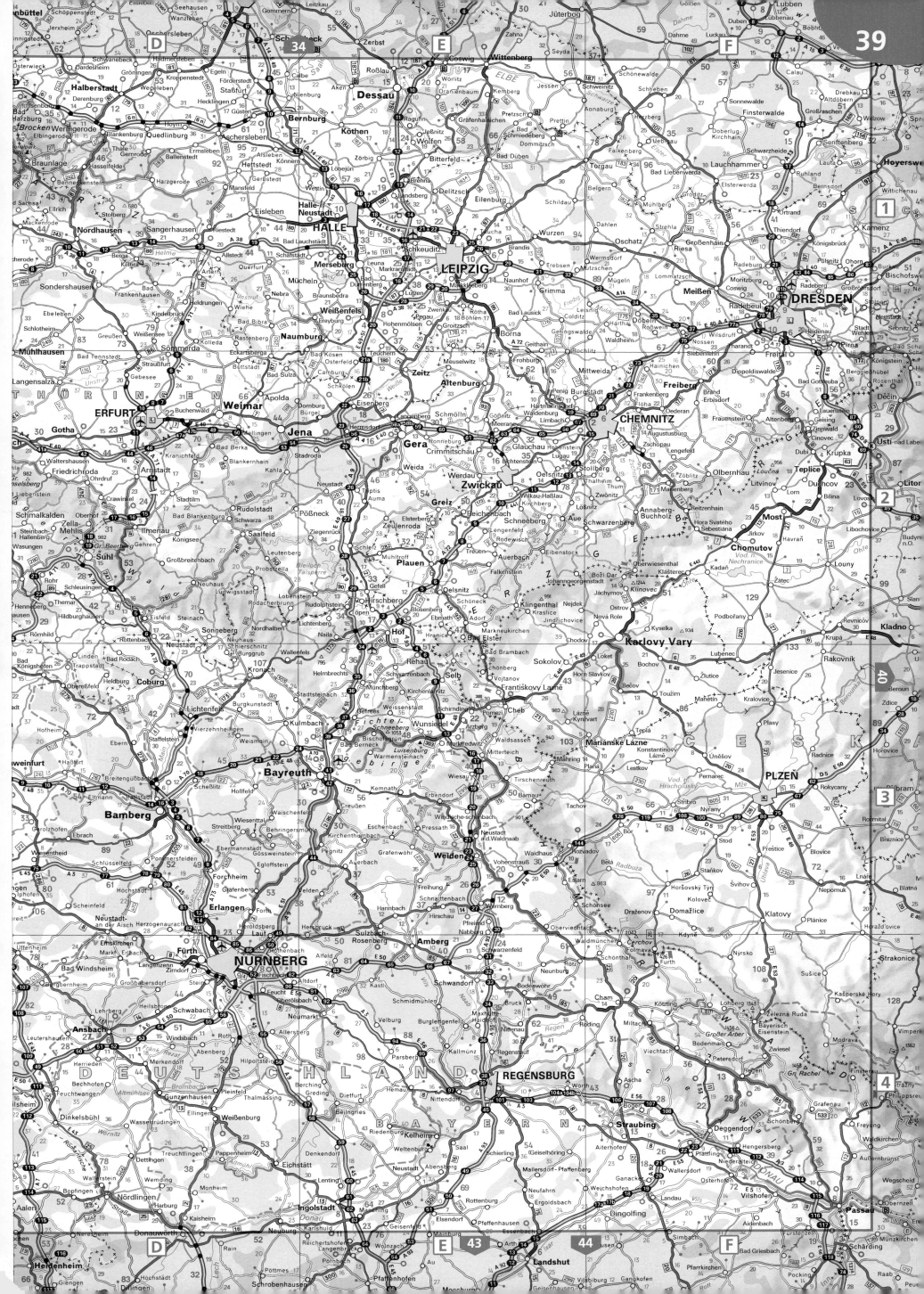

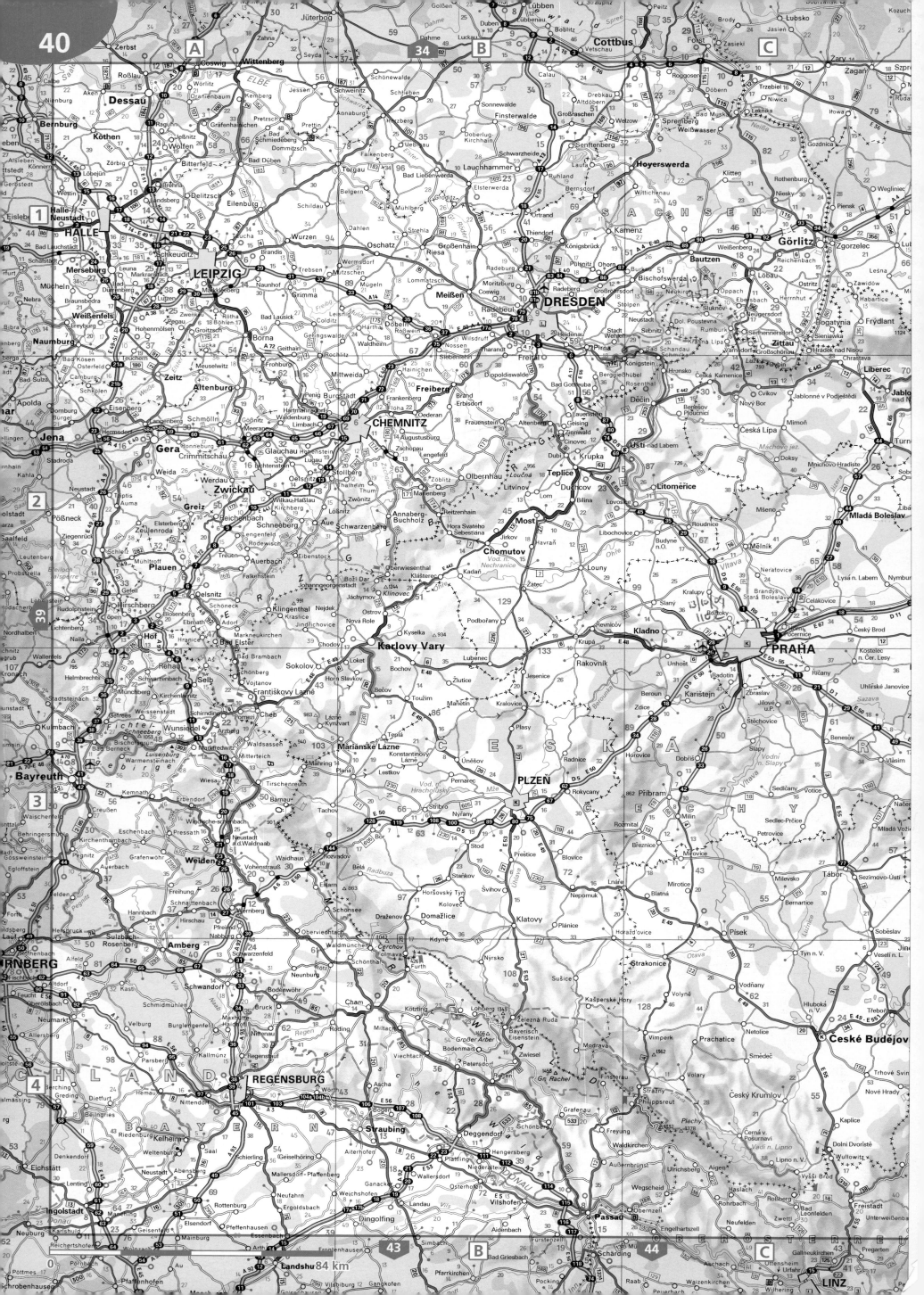

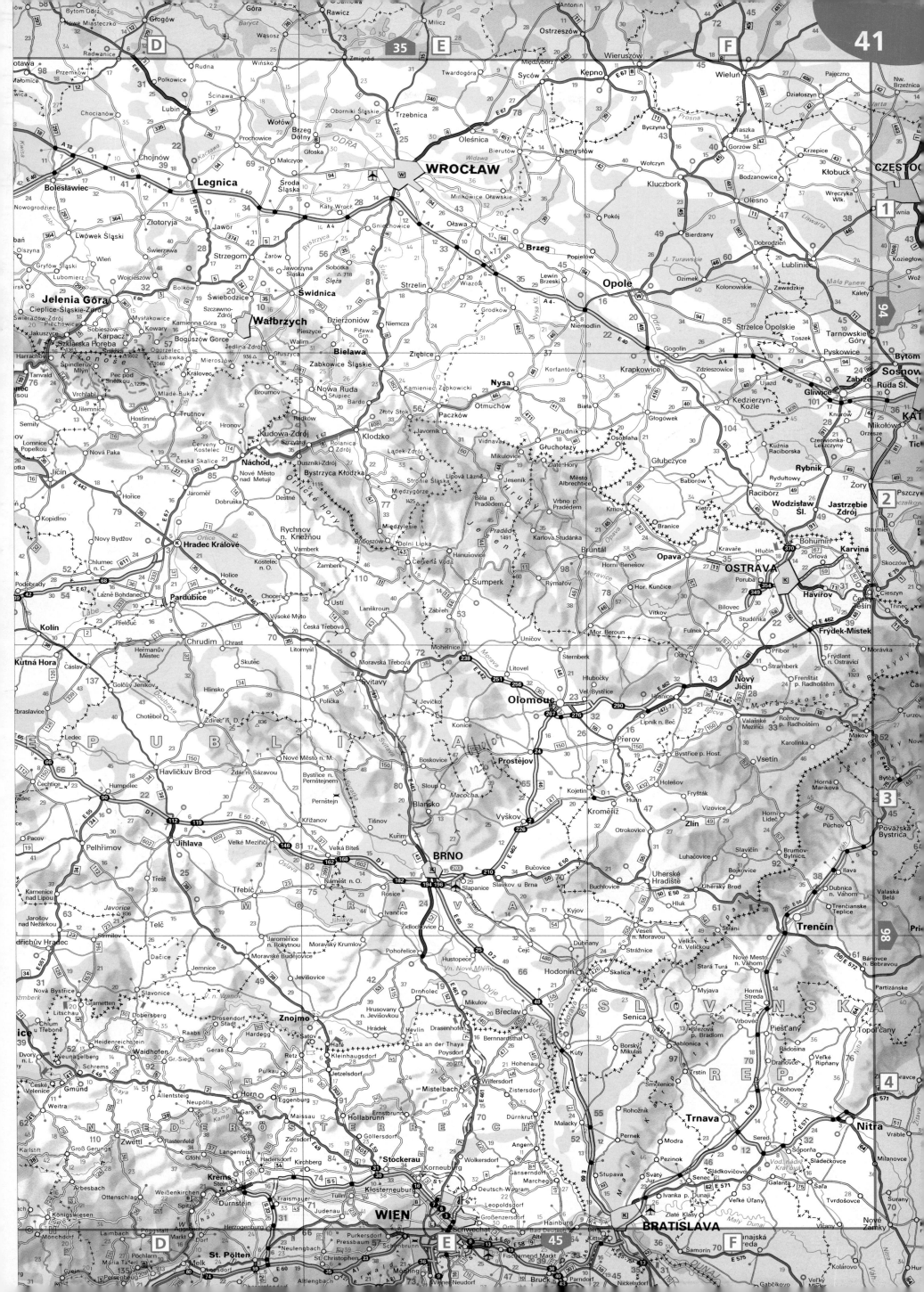

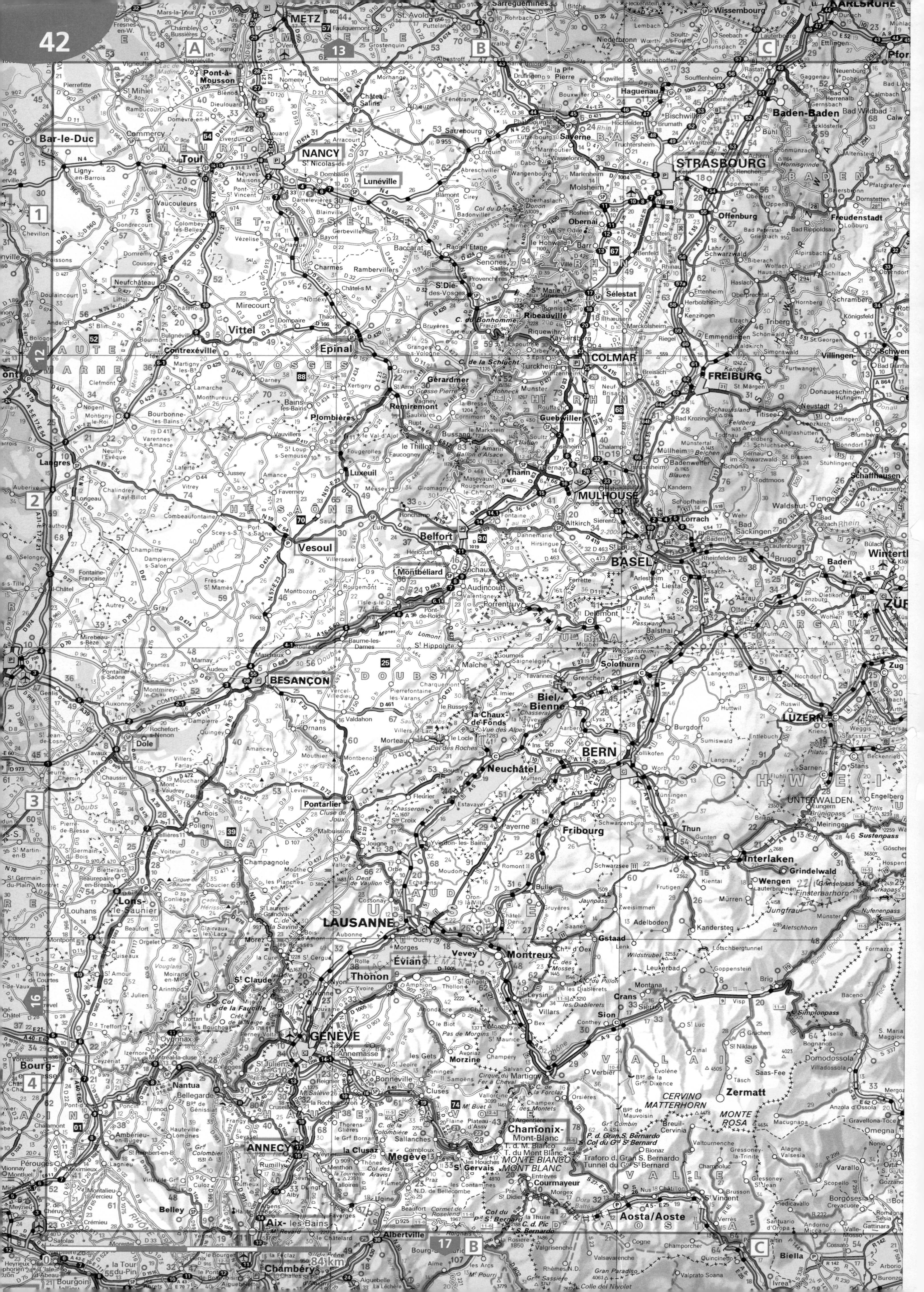

METZ
NANCY
Lunéville
Bar-le-Duc
Toul
Pont-à-Mousson
St. Mihiel
Commercy
Sarrebourg
Saverne
Haguenau
STRASBOURG
Baden-Baden
Offenburg
Freudenstadt
Obernai
Sélestat
Ribeauvillé
COLMAR
FREIBURG
St. Dié-des-Vosges
Epinal
Vittel
Contrexéville
Neufchâtel
Langres
Gérardmer
Remiremont
Plombières
Luxeuil
Guebwiller
Thann
MULHOUSE
Lorrach
BASEL
Belfort
Montbéliard
Vesoul
BESANÇON
Dole
Pontarlier
Lons-le-Saunier
Delémont
Solothurn
Biel/Bienne
La Chaux-de-Fonds
Neuchâtel
BERN
Fribourg
LUZERN
Thun
Interlaken
Grindelwald
LAUSANNE
Vevey
Montreux
Evian
Thonon
GENÈVE
St. Claude
Bourg-en-Bresse
Nantua
ANNECY
Aix-les-Bains
Chambéry
Albertville
Megève
Chamonix-Mont-Blanc
MONTE BIANCO
MONT BLANC
Courmayeur
Aosta/Aoste
Sion
Crans
Zermatt
CERVINO
MATTERHORN
MONTE ROSA
Gstaad
Domodossola
Biella
Belley
Zürich
Winterthur
Baden
Aarau
Zug
Schaffhausen
MOSELLE
MEURTHE-ET-MOSELLE
VOSGES
HTE-SAÔNE
DOUBS
JURA
HAUTE-SAVOIE
SUISSE
VALAIS
AARGAU
SCHWEIZ
BADEN
BAS-RHIN
HT-RHIN
AOSTA
84 km

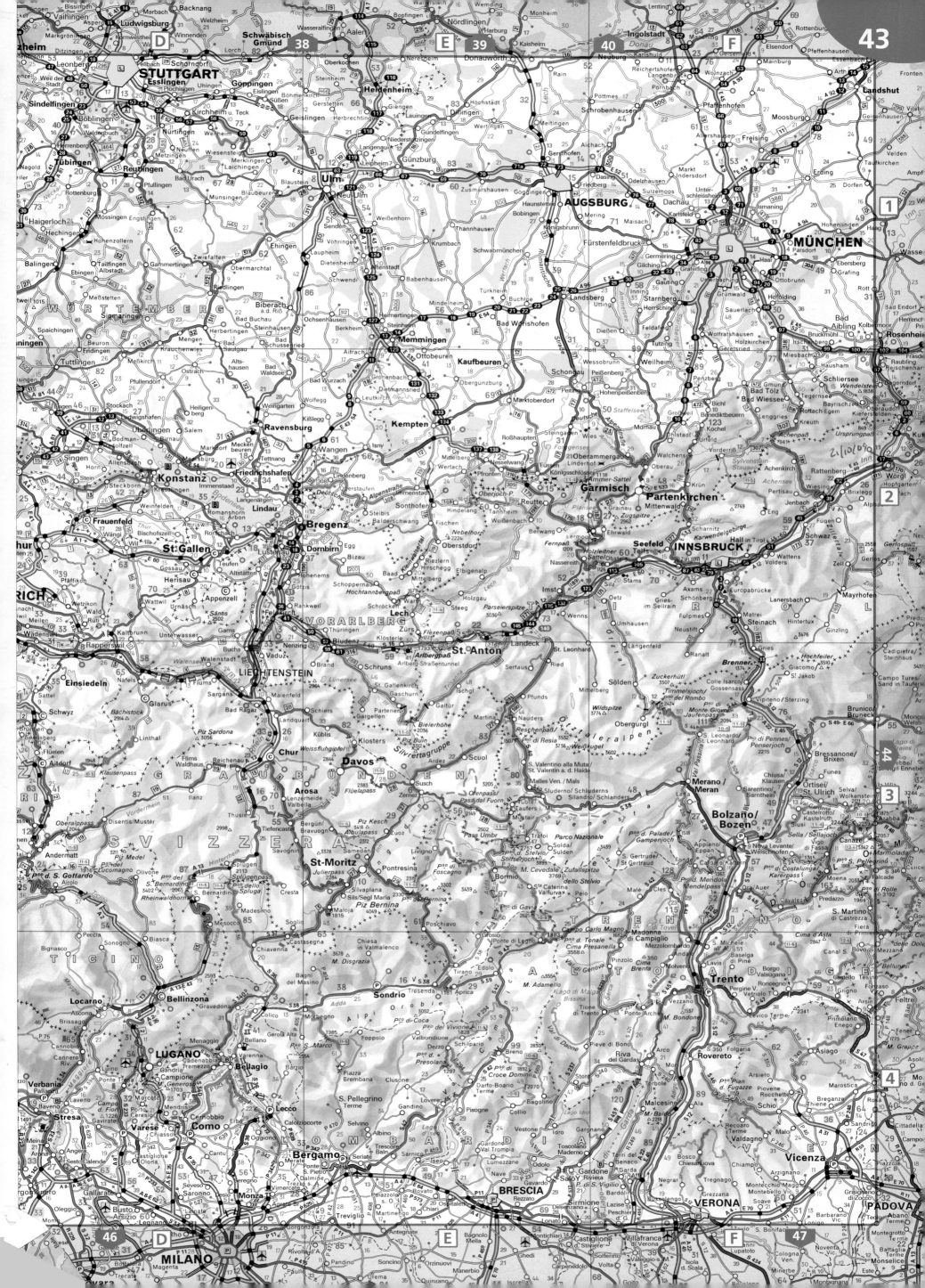

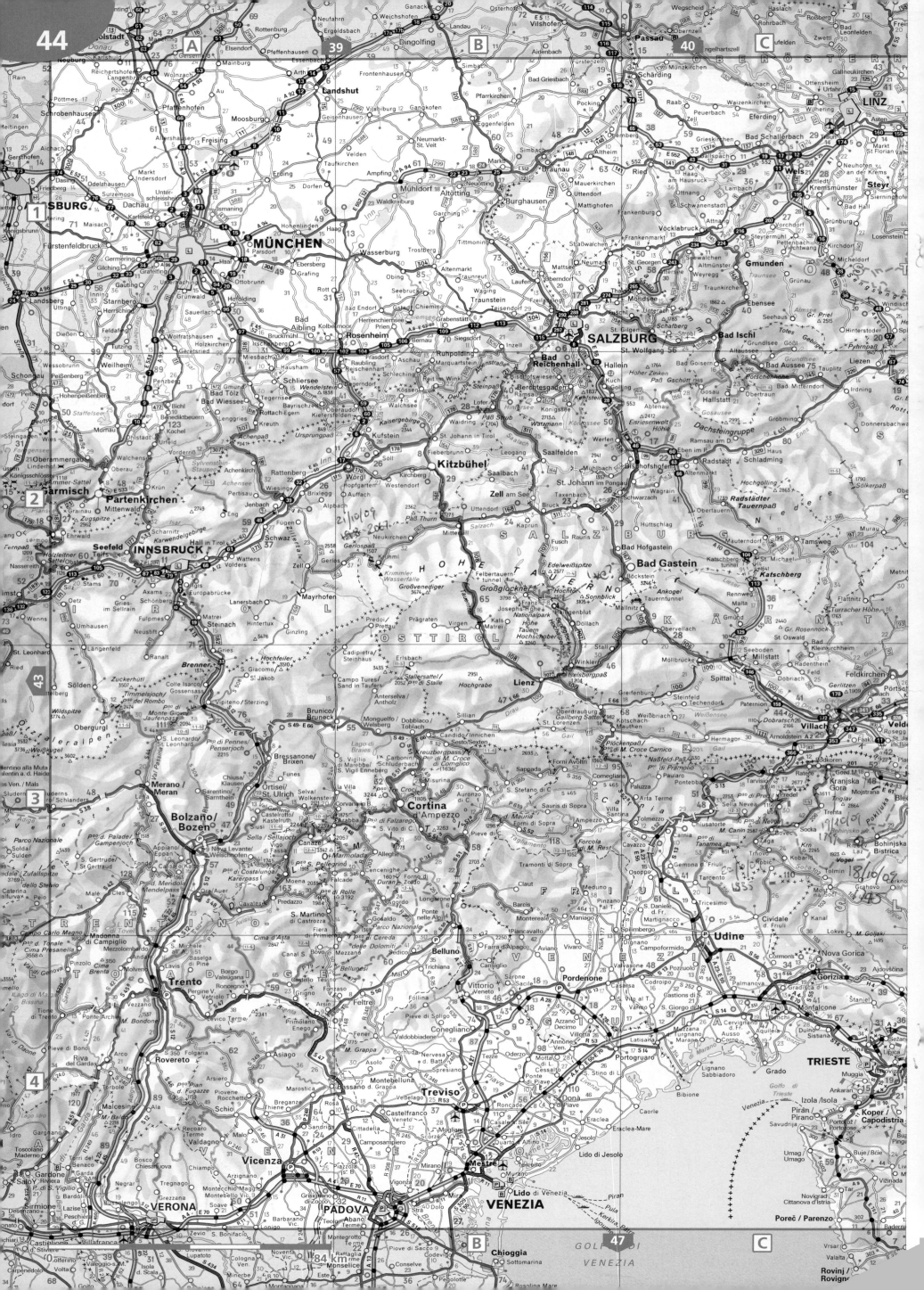

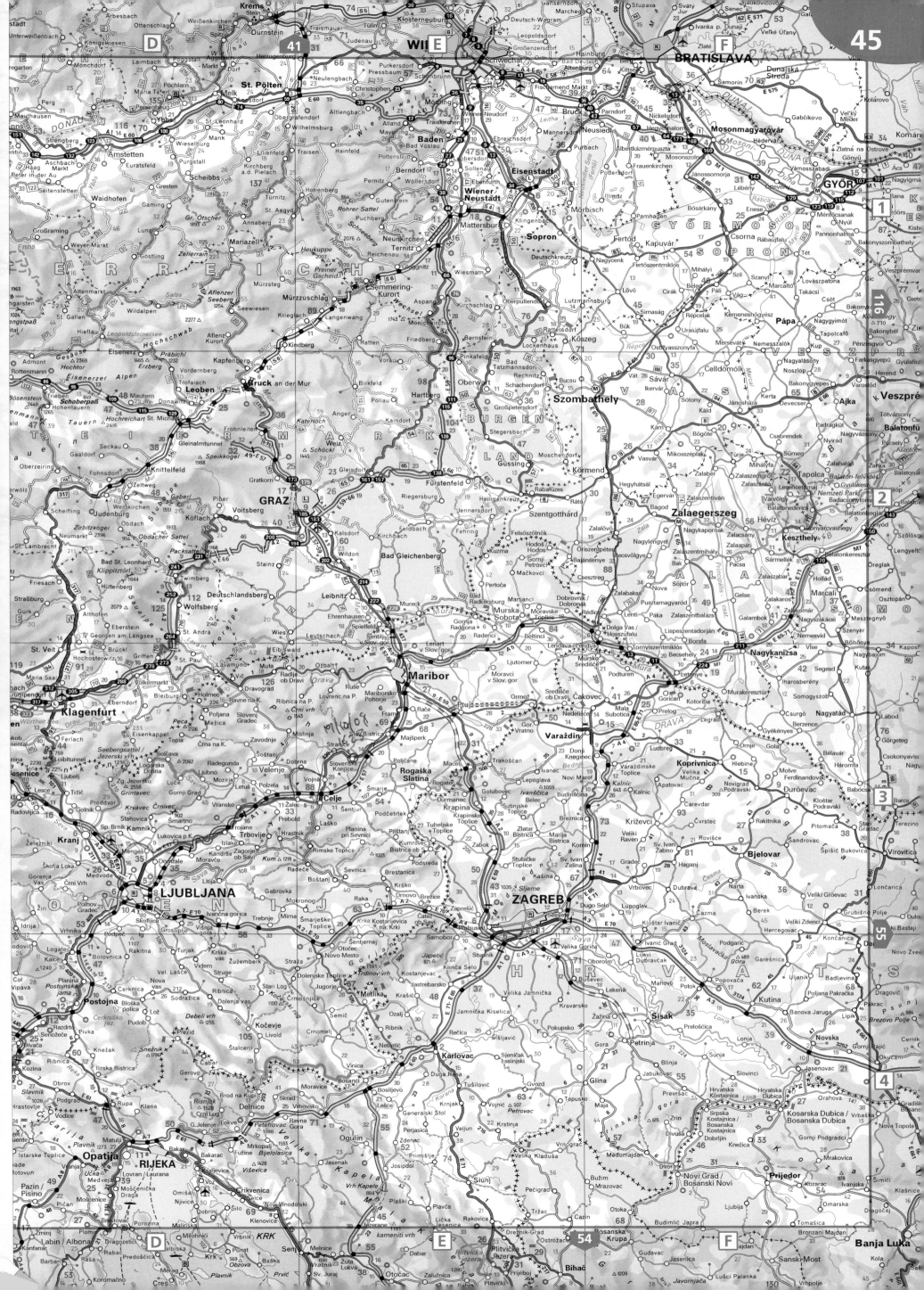

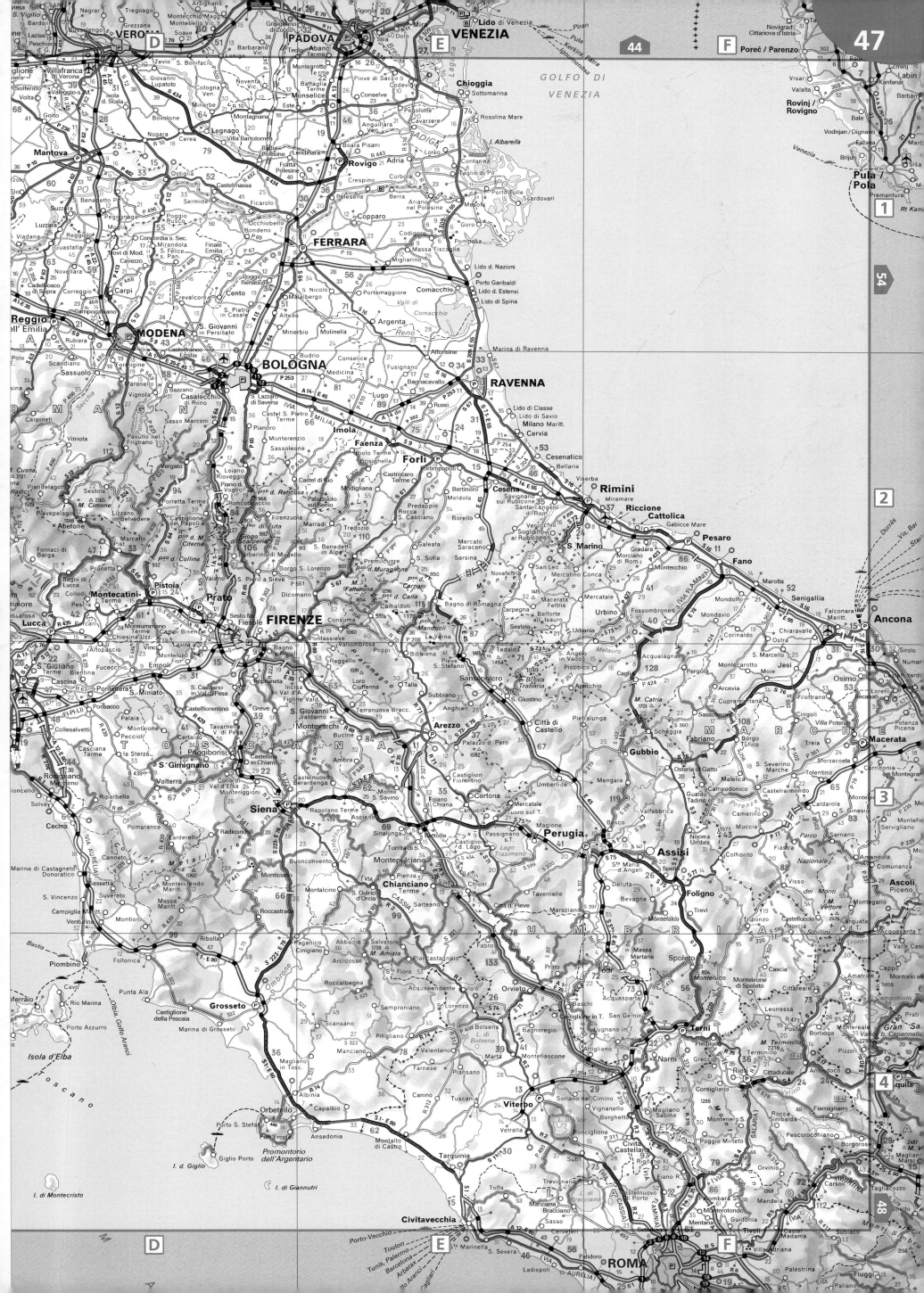

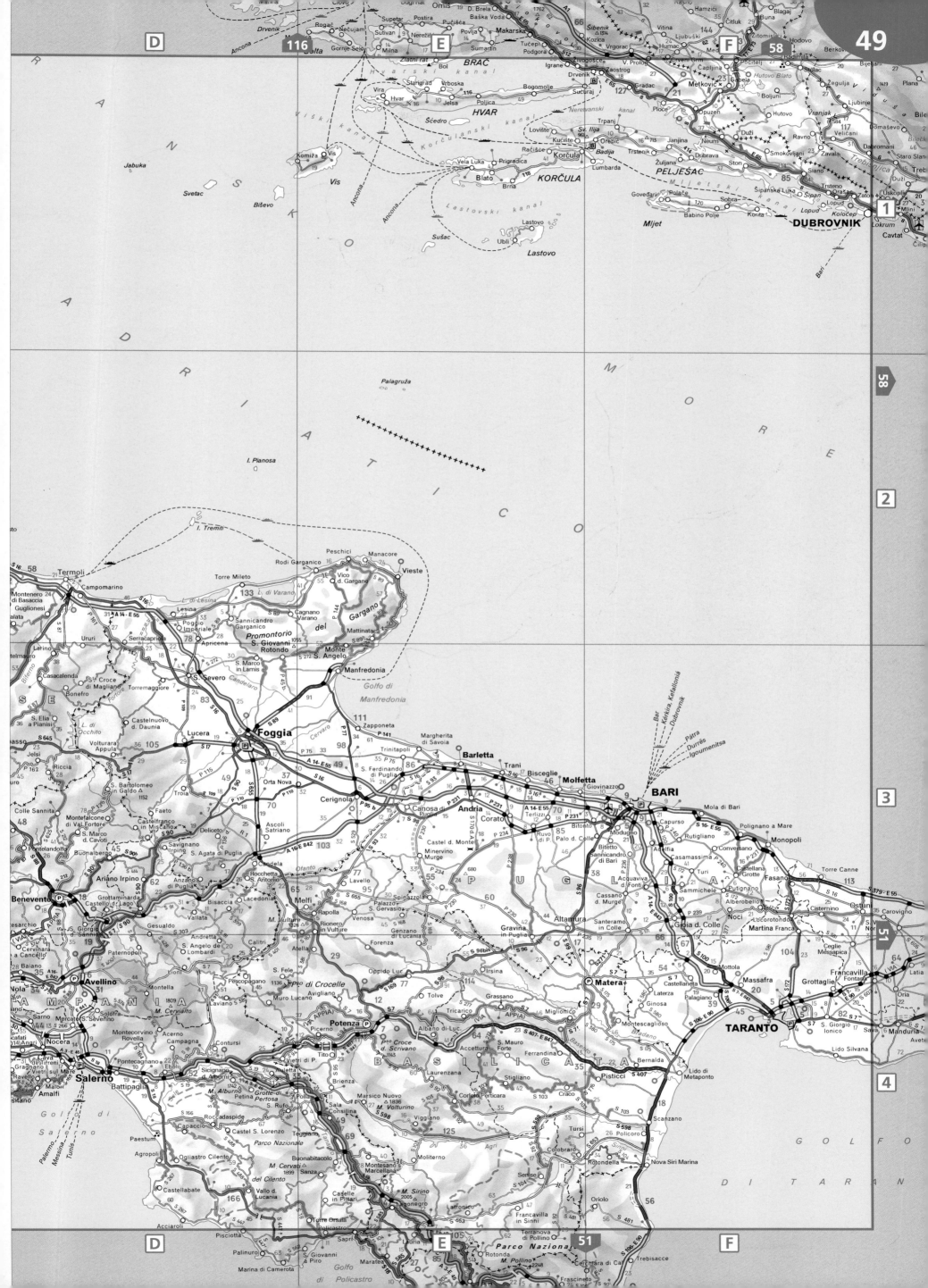

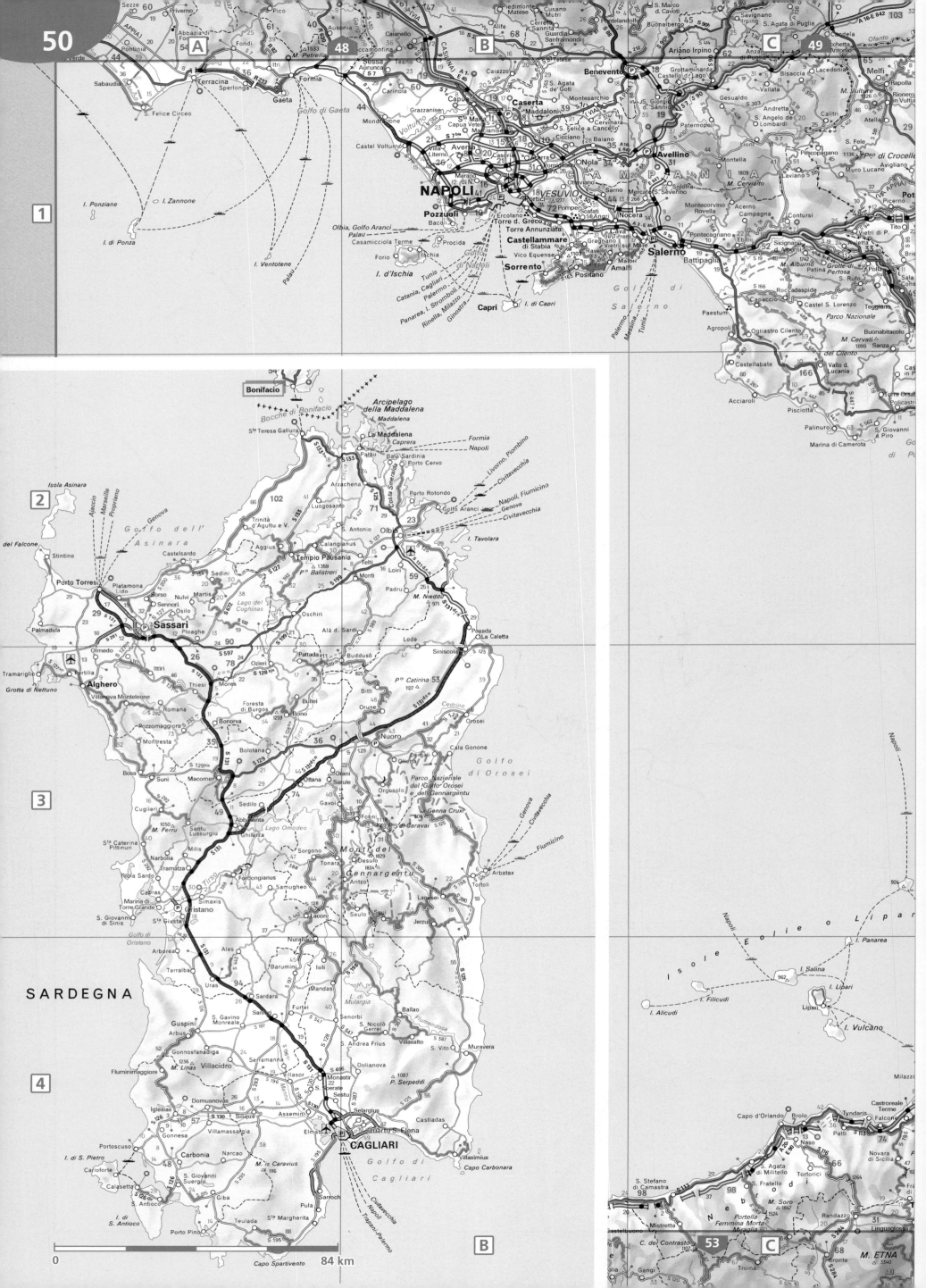

A   B   50   C

1

2

I. di Ustica

MARE TIRRE

Livorno
Tunis
Genova
Cagliari
Civitavecchia

Napoli
Salerno

SICILIA

Capo Gallo
Sferracavallo   Mondello
Punta Raisi   6 30   M. Pellegrino
                    606   PALERMO   Cefalù
                 S 113   Solunto
S. Vito lo Capo   Torre d. Impiso   Cinisi   Carini   Bagheria   Casteldaccia   S 115
Golfo di   44   Monreale   Termini
Castellammare   29   44   S 118   Misilmeri   Altavilla   113 54 Imerese S 19 E 90
                        53   Trabia
Cagliari   Castellammare   26   S 186   Partinico   Piana   S 121   Caccamo   Buonfornello   P.o Carbo.
                d. Golfo   34   d. Albanesi   47   197
Trapani   Erice   S 113   32   Alcamo   S 113   Marineo   S. Cipirello   58   Villafrati   Montemaggiore Belsito   Collesano
        Paceco   S 187   Fulgatore   12   15   S 118   R.ca Busambra   Belsito   36   Caltavuturo   66
Isole   I. Levanzo   Segesta   21   24   1613   S 121   Roccapalumba   50   Alia   A 11
Egadi   42   Calatafimi   43   624   Corleone   27   Prizzi   18   126   Resuttano
I-Maréttimo   Birgi   10   A 29 dir   53   S 118   155   28   S 188   126   S 121   23   S.a Caterina
I. Favignana   50   38   41   S 188   Lercara   Villarmosa
I. di Pantelleria   36   Salemi   S 118   57   Chiusa Sclafani   Friddi   Mussomeli   Caltanisse
Marsala   S 188   S.a Ninfa   Partanna   S.a Margherita   Sclafani   53   S. Stefano   41   S. Cataldo
        19   8   di Belice   31   Sambuca   Quisquina   Serradifalco
Castelvetrano   S 115   188   di Sicilia   S. Biagio Platani   Montedoro
        22   A 29   21   17   44   Caltabellotta   Alessandria   83   58   Delia
Mazara d. Vallo   E 931   18   Menfi   S 188   Aragona   Canicatti
        Campobello   Selinunte   20   94   Ribera   Platani   Naro   S 122
        di Mazara   Marinella   16   Sciacca   Raffadali   S 123   Favara   Campobello
                        S 115   S 118   Agrigento   576   di Licata
MARE   E 931   Porto Empedocle   6   Naro   410   43
                                Palma   72
                                di Montechiaro

3

Trapani

Pantelleria   Tracino
              836
I. di Pantelleria

I. di Linosa

Isole
Pelagie

Porto Empedocle

I. di Lampedusa
Lampedusa

MEDITERR

4

0   84 km

B   C

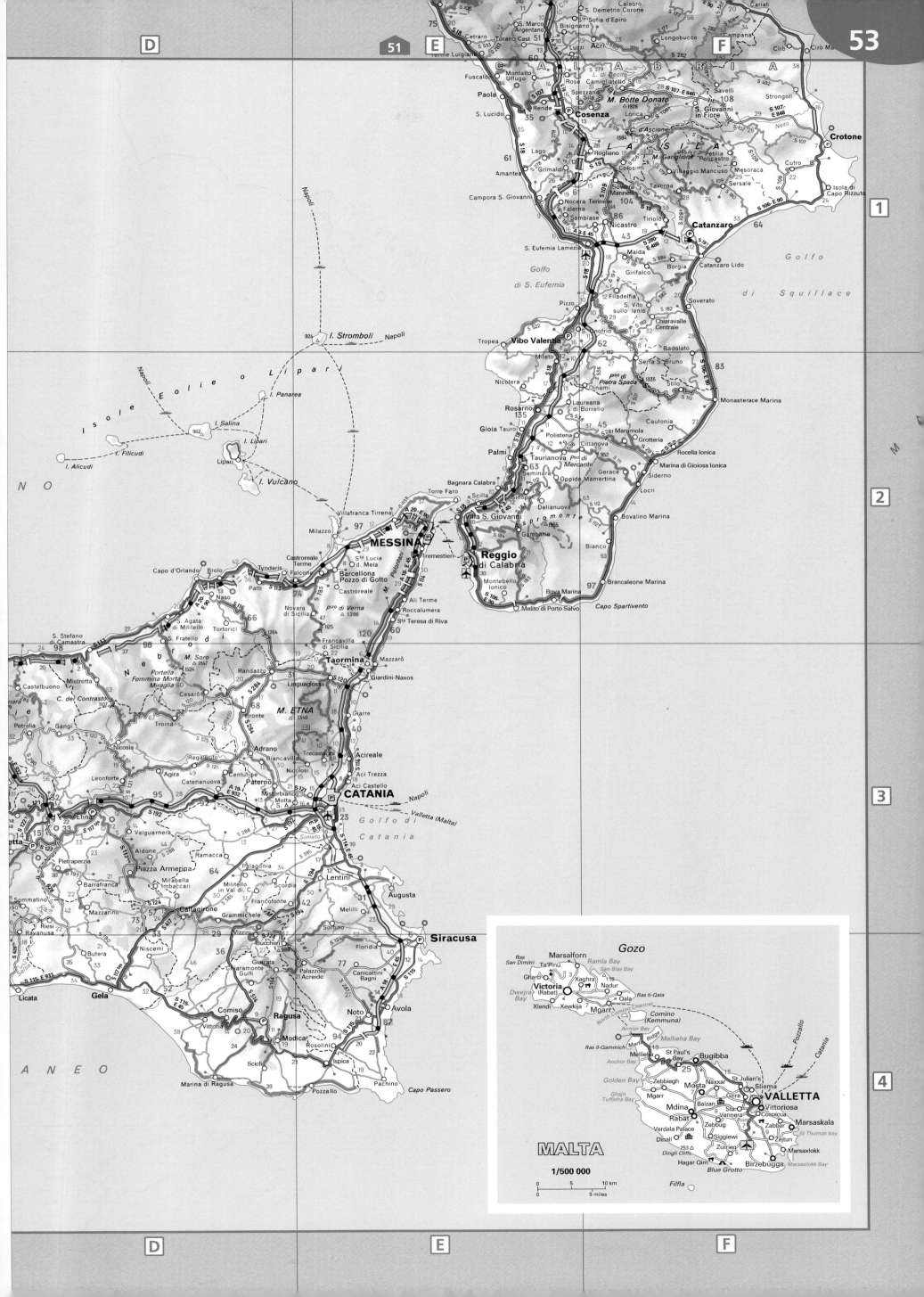

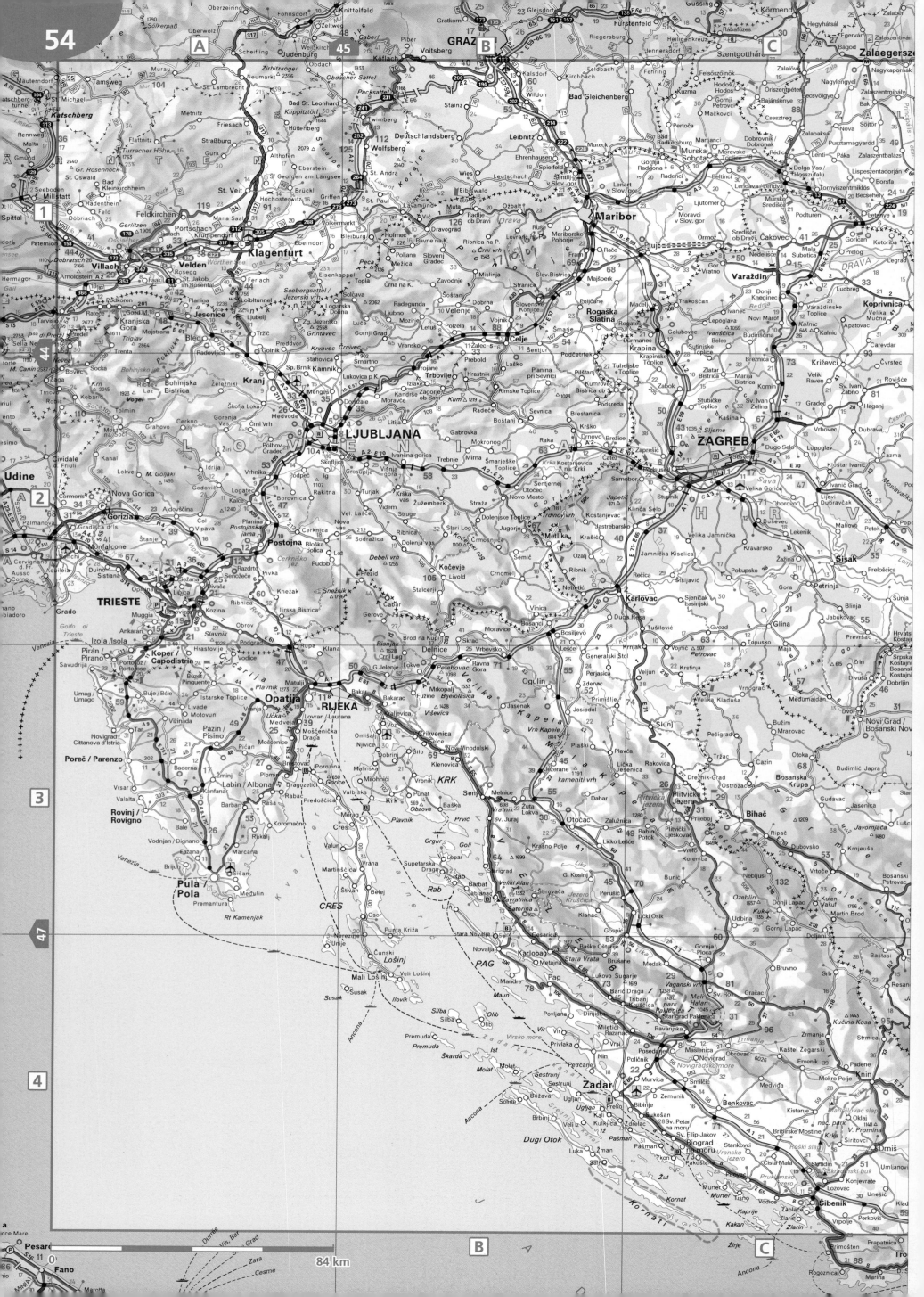

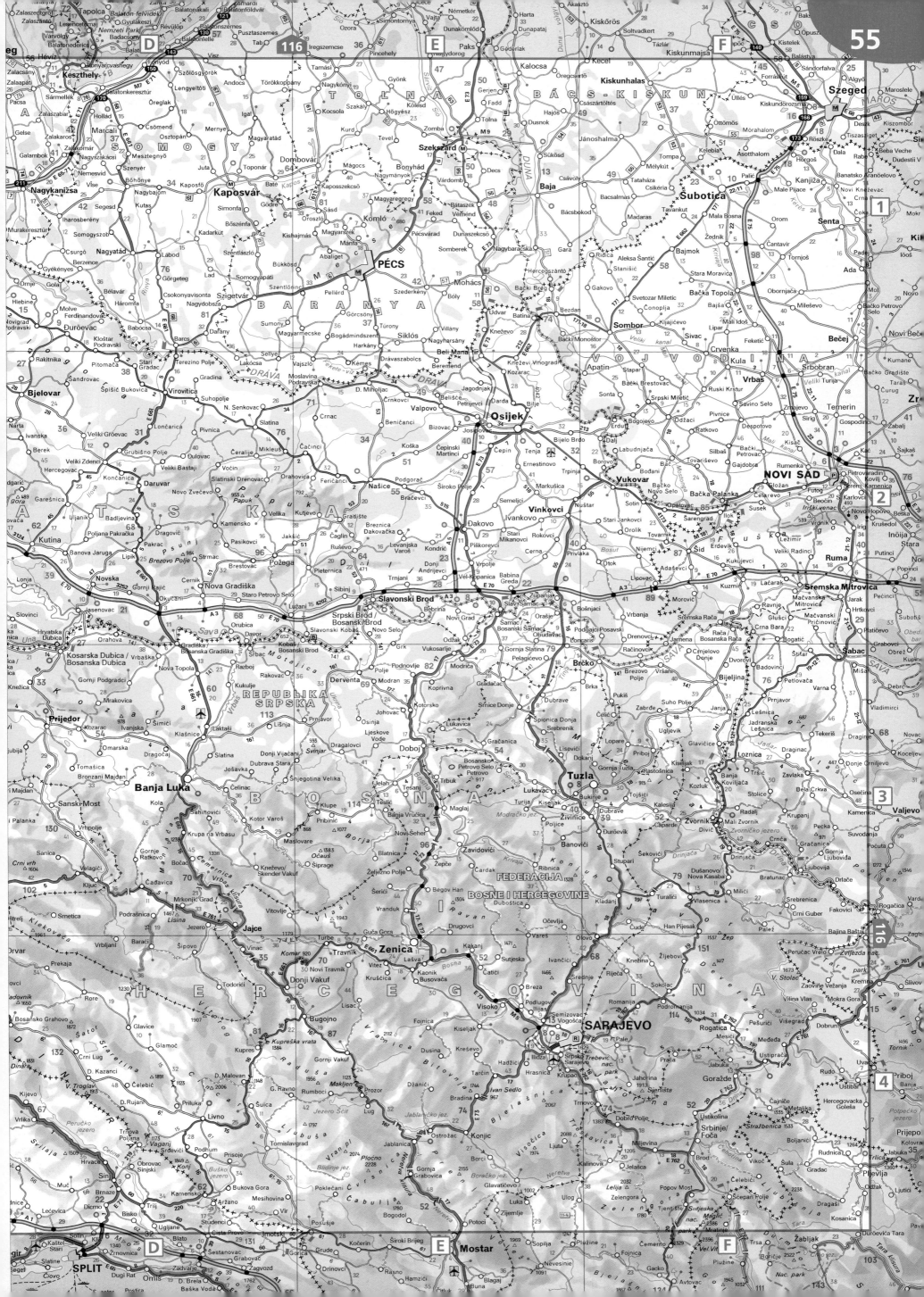

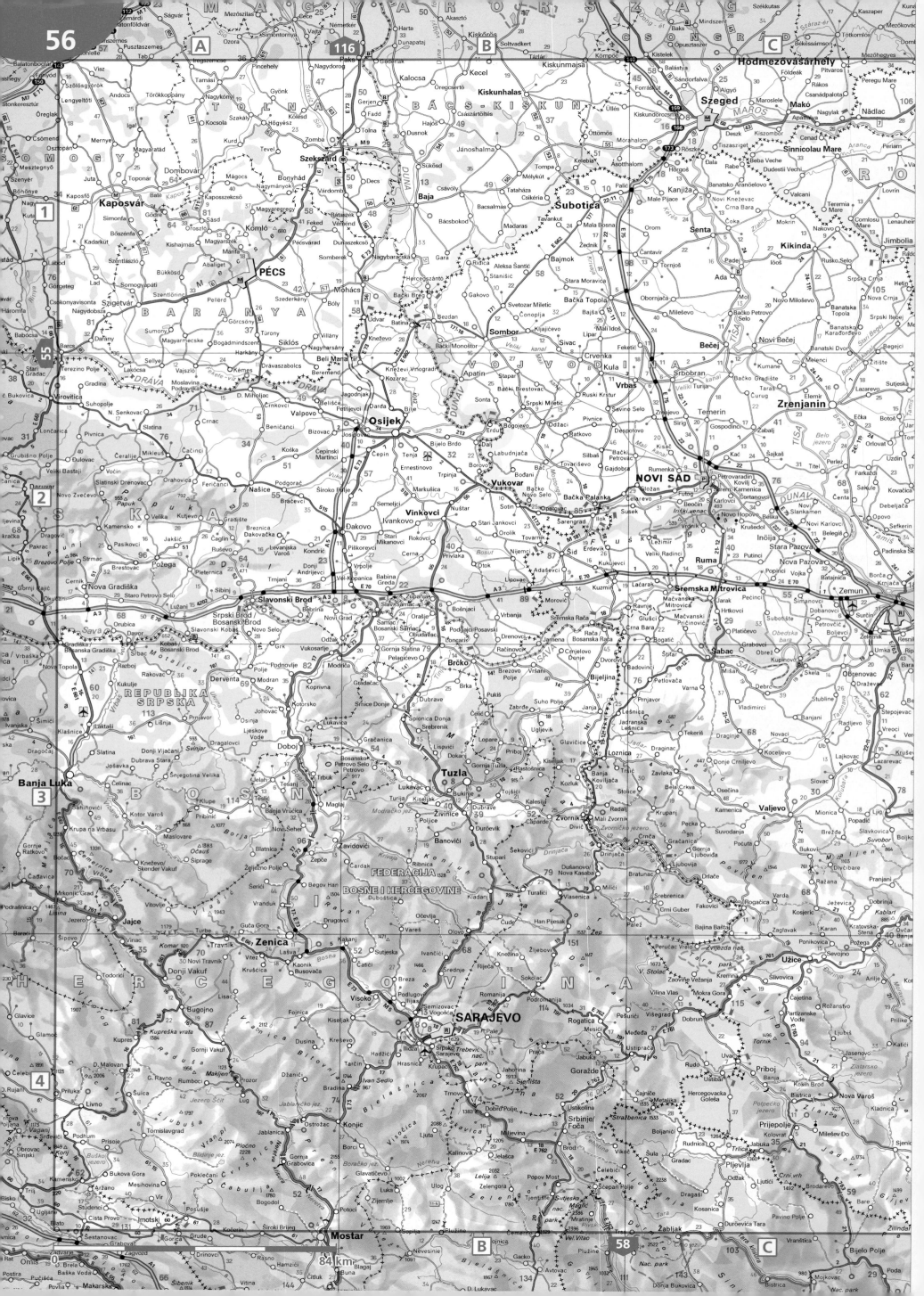

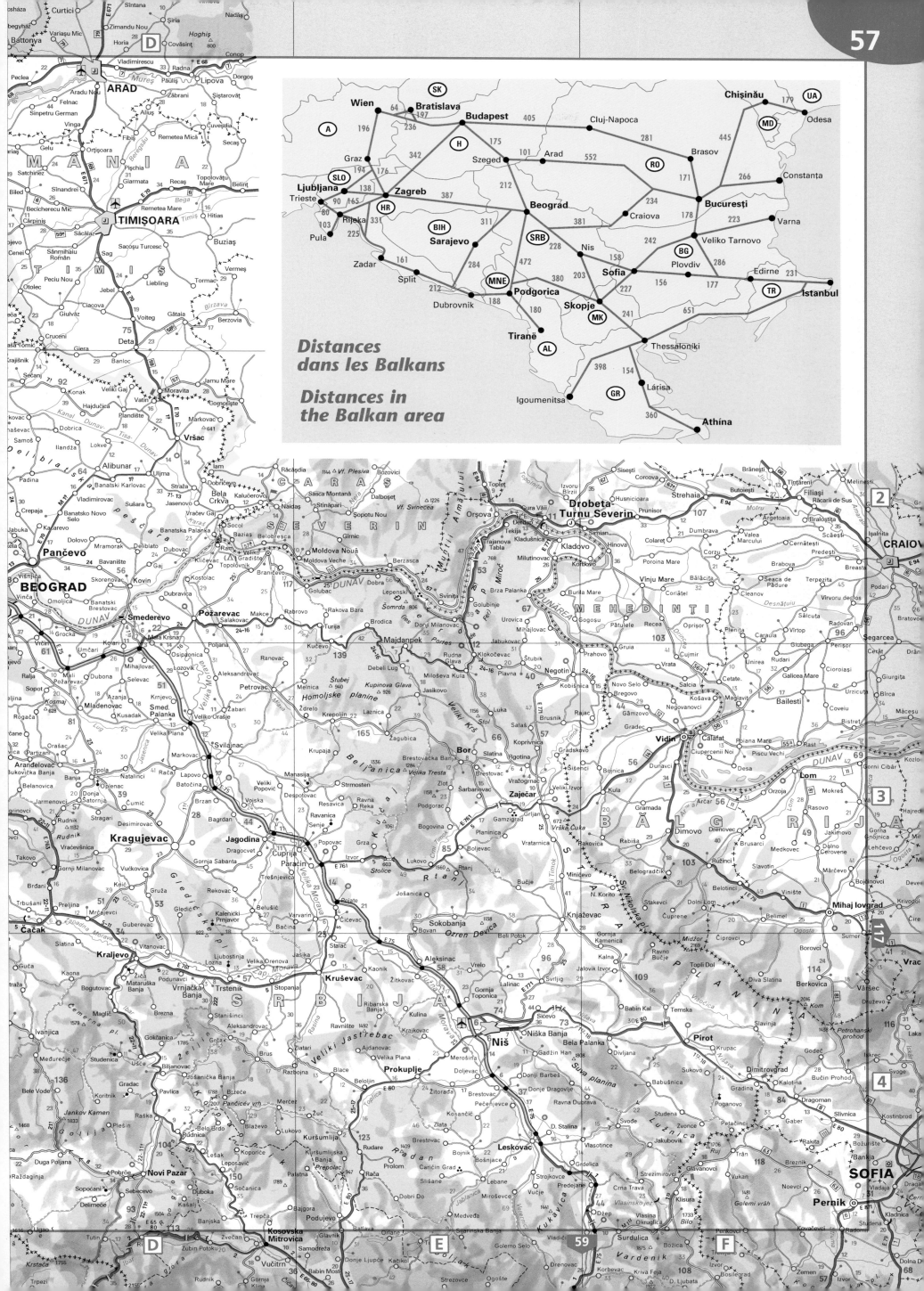

Distances dans les Balkans

Distances in the Balkan area

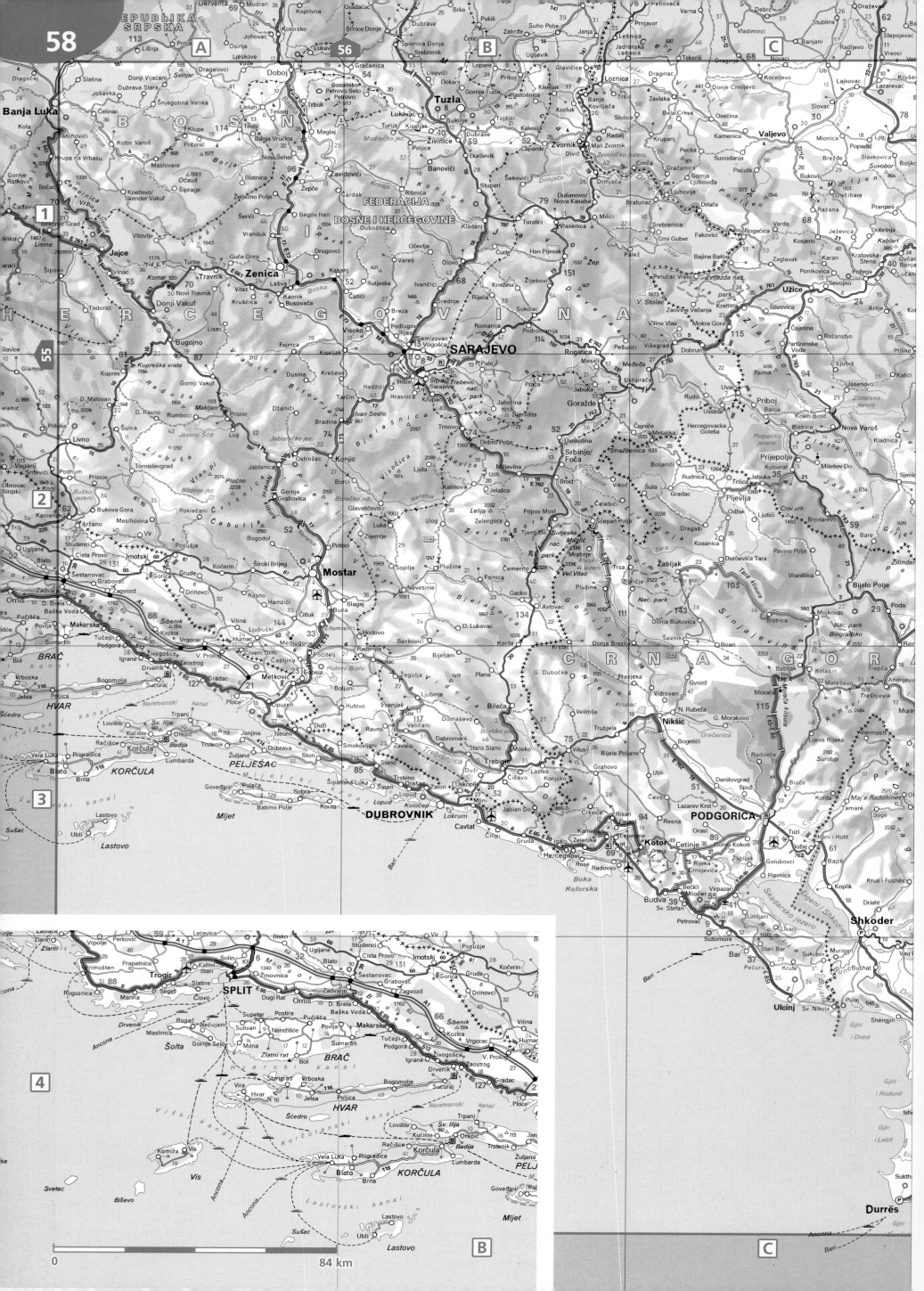

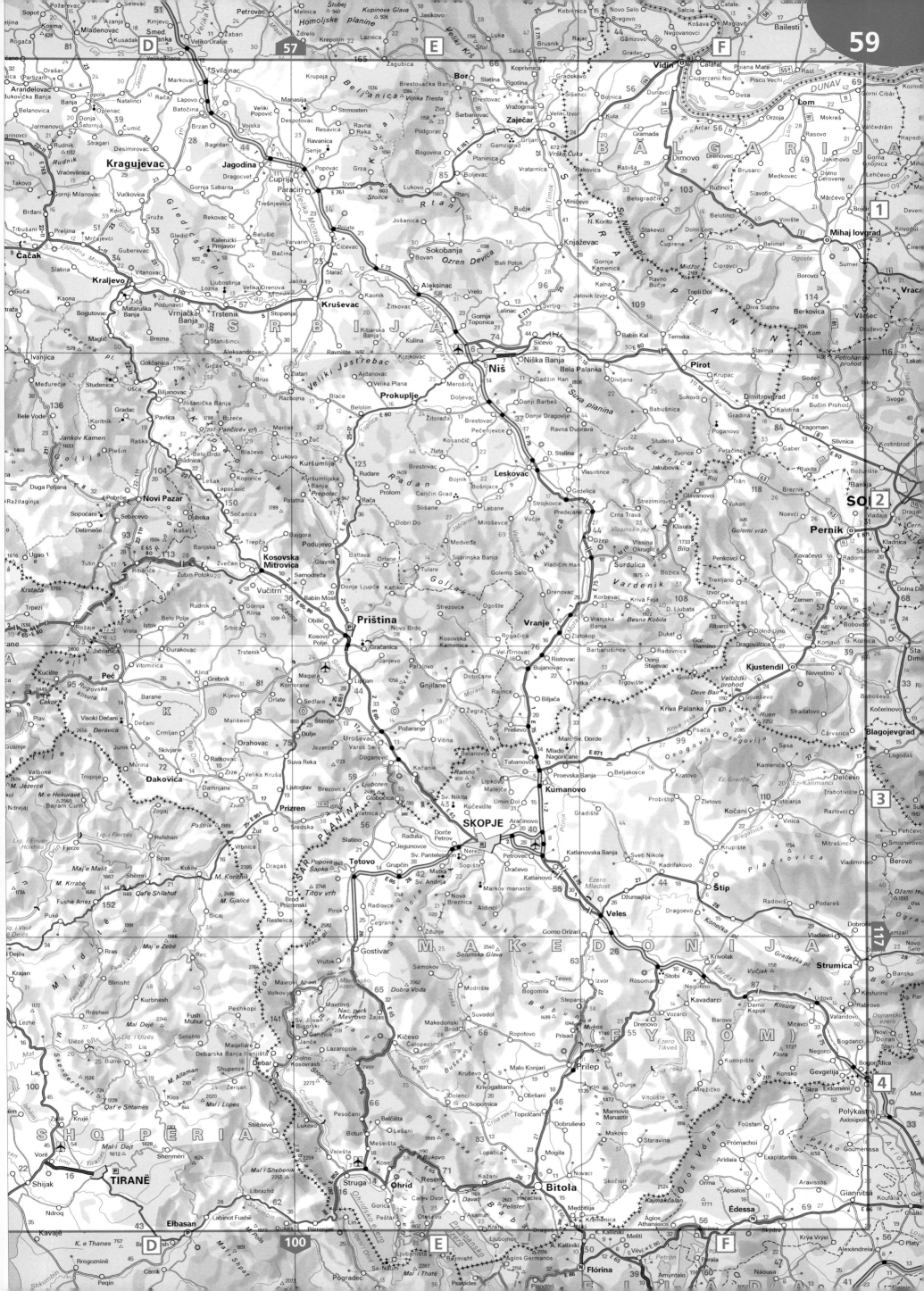

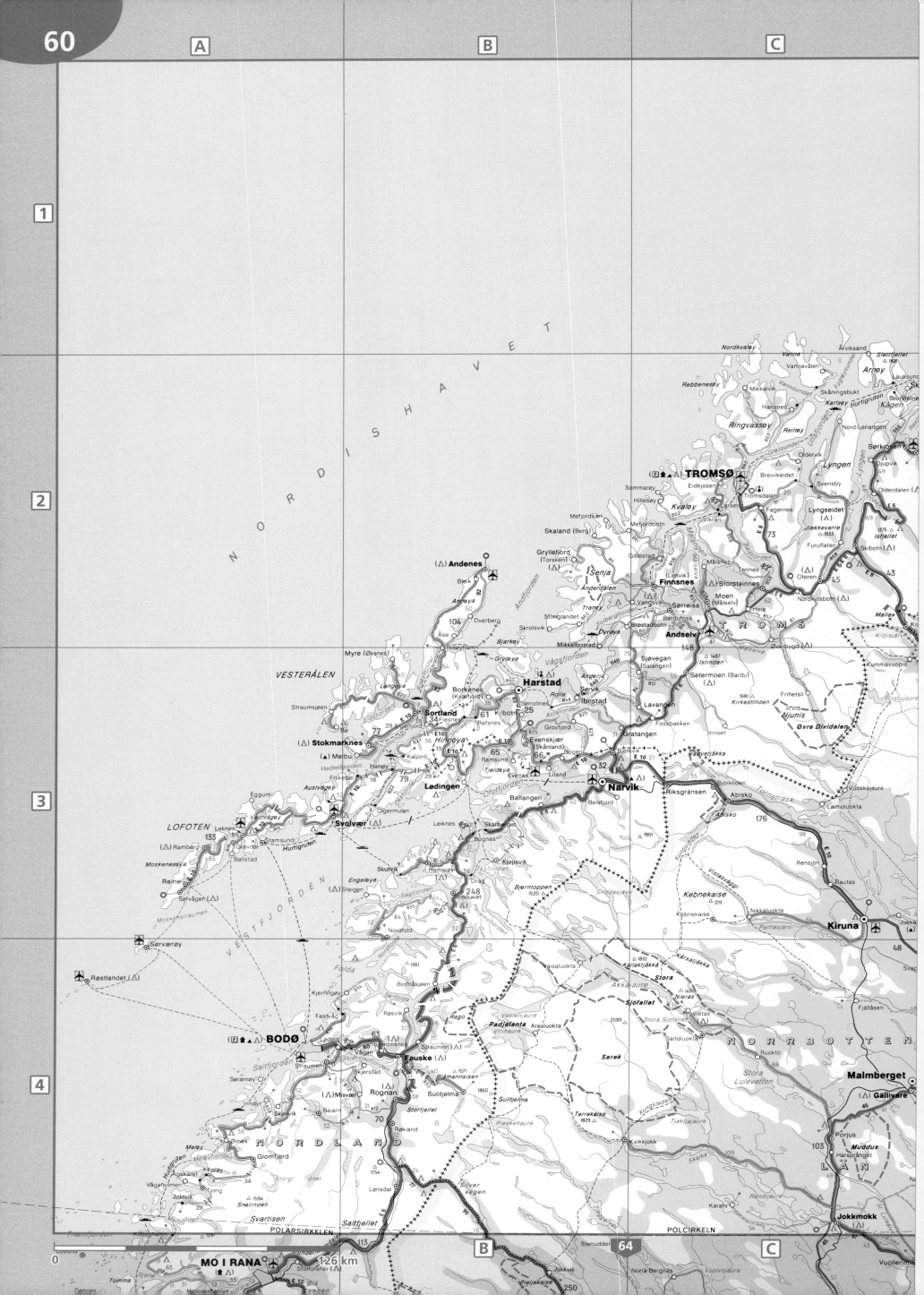

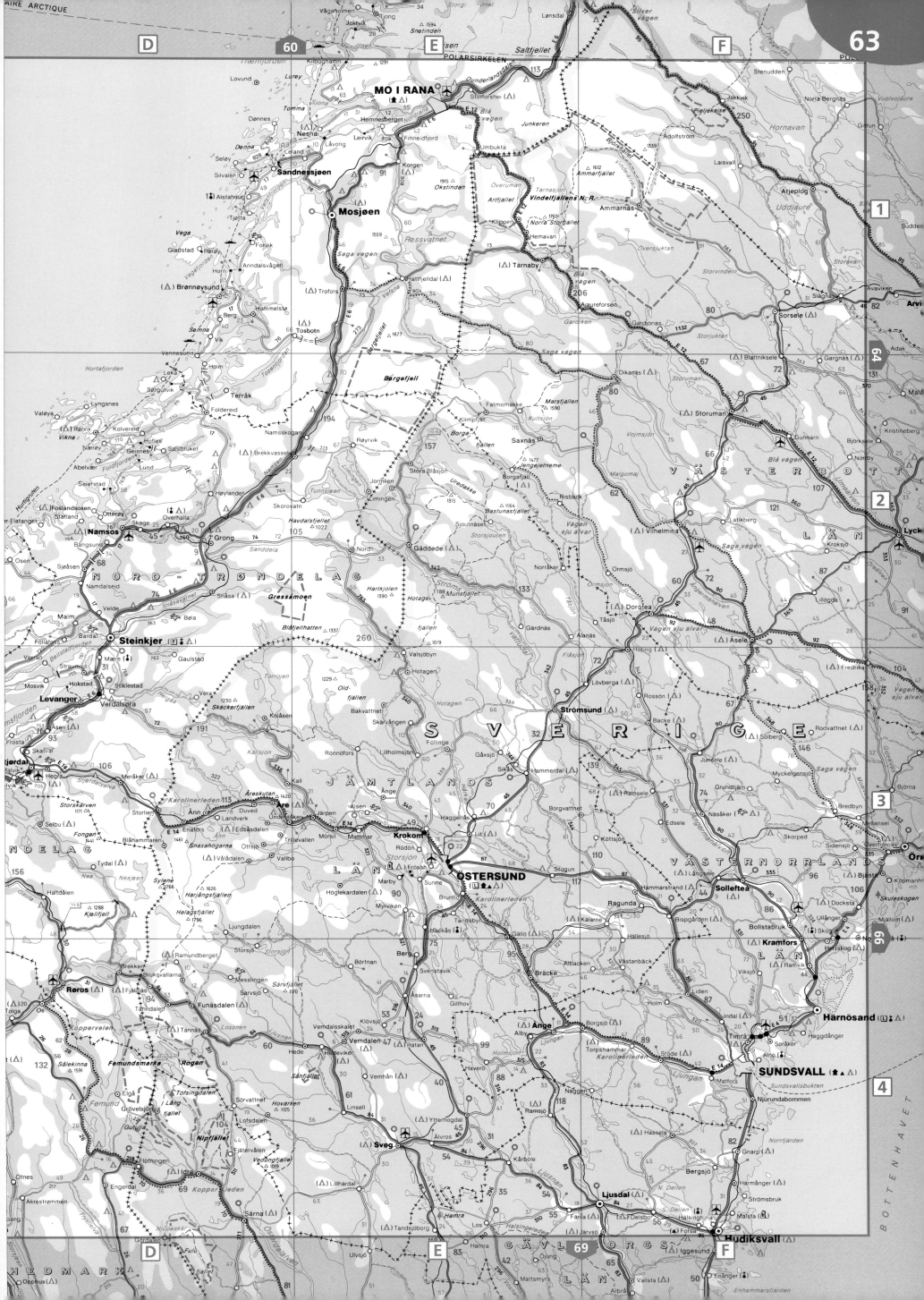

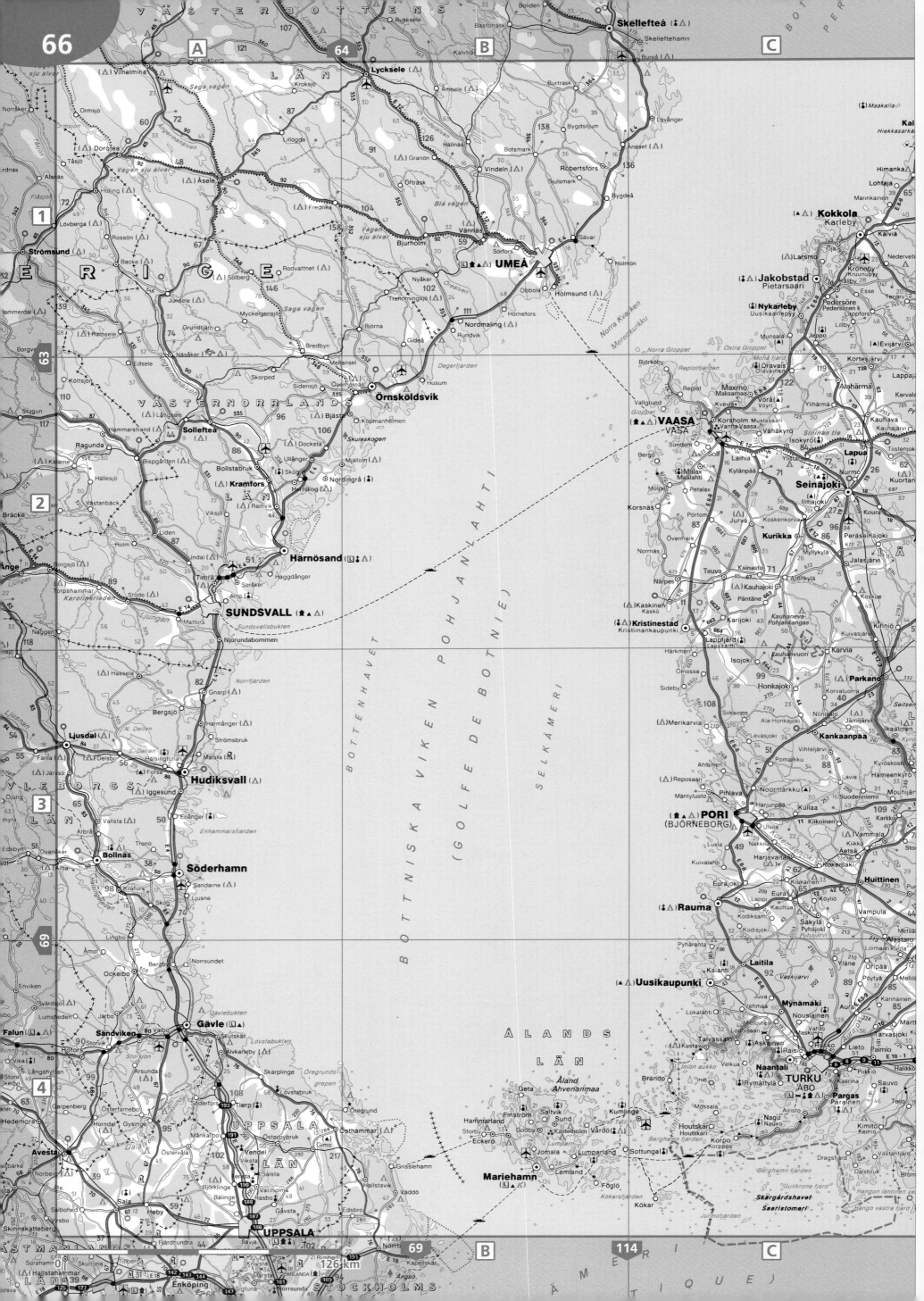

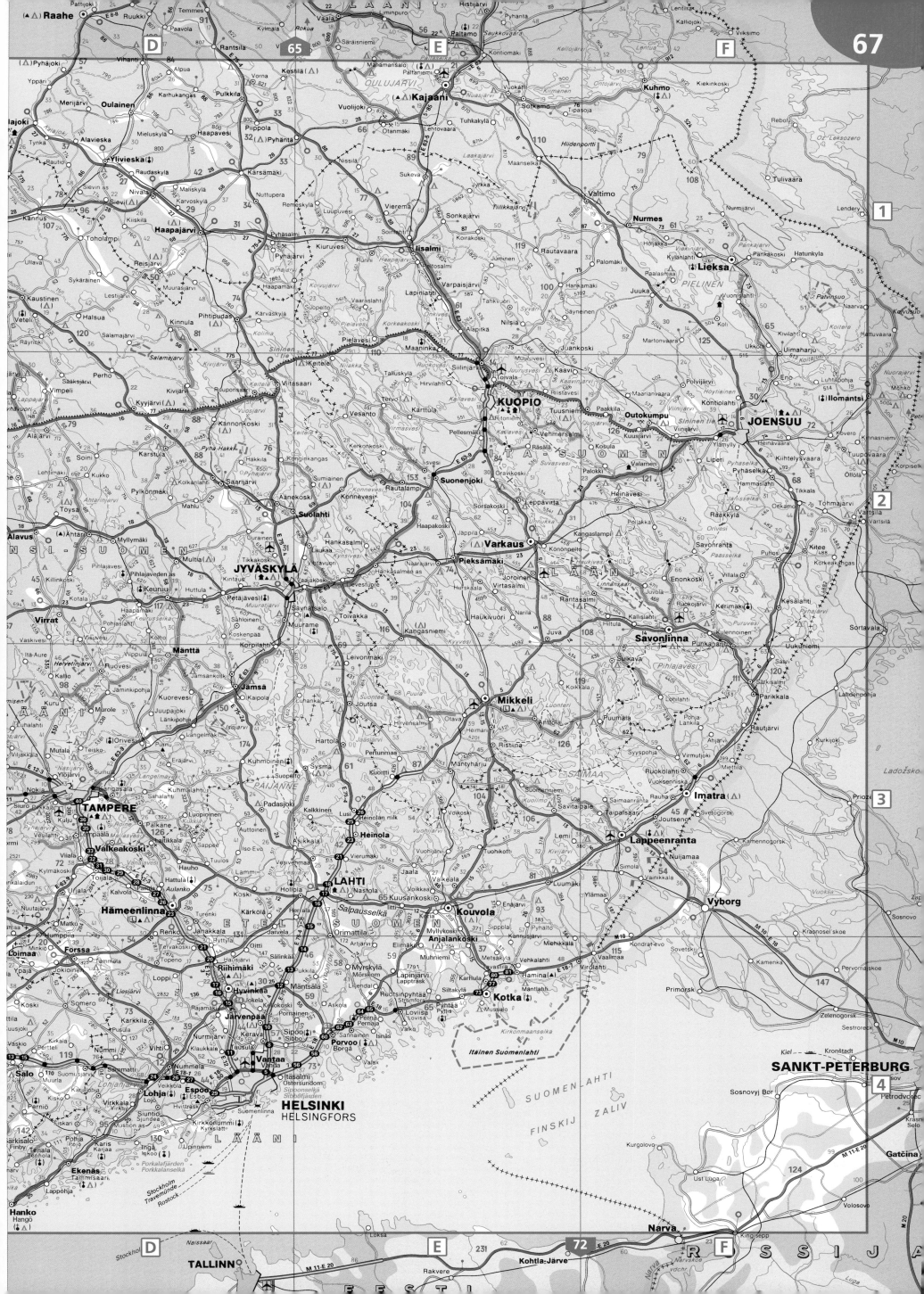

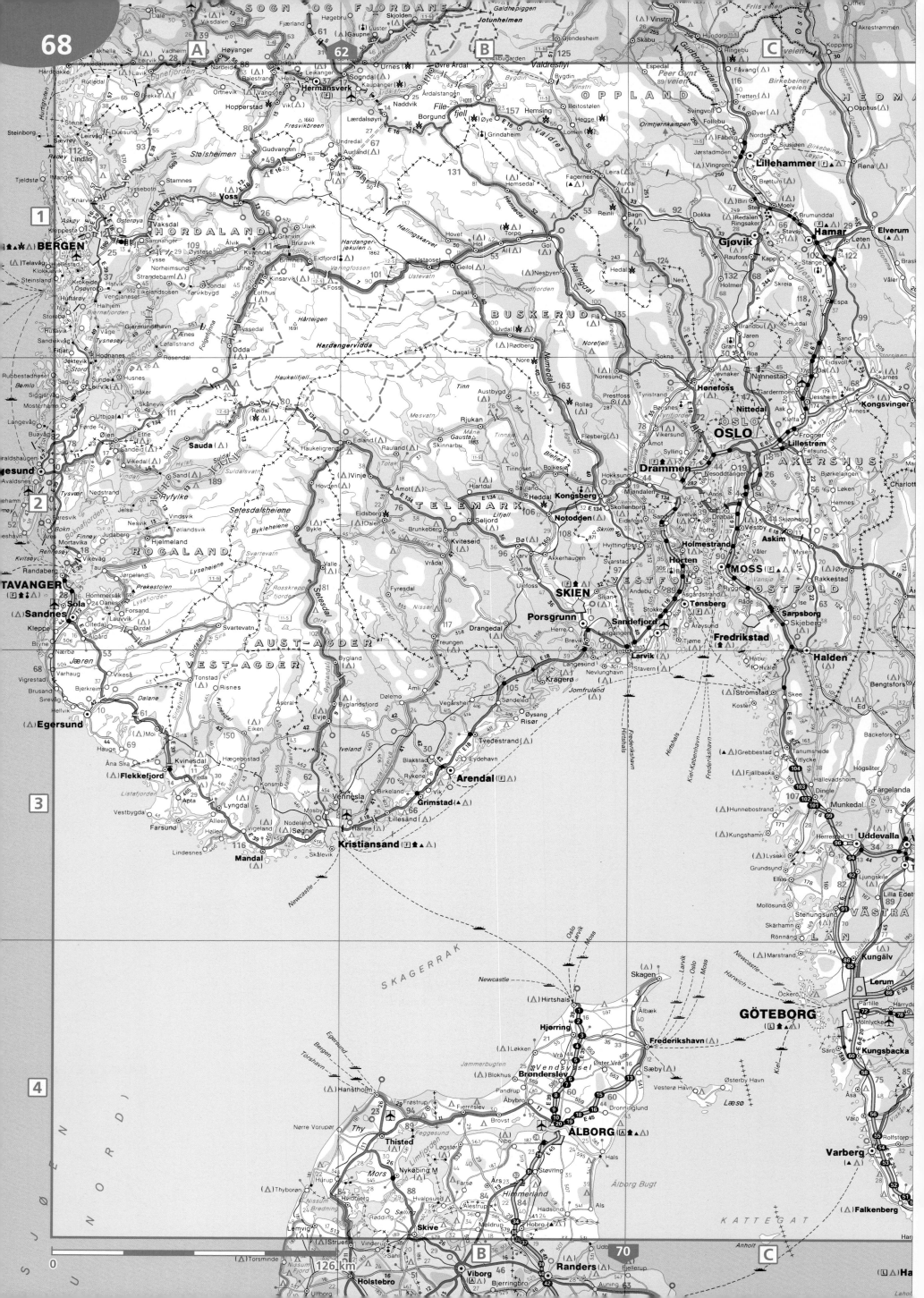

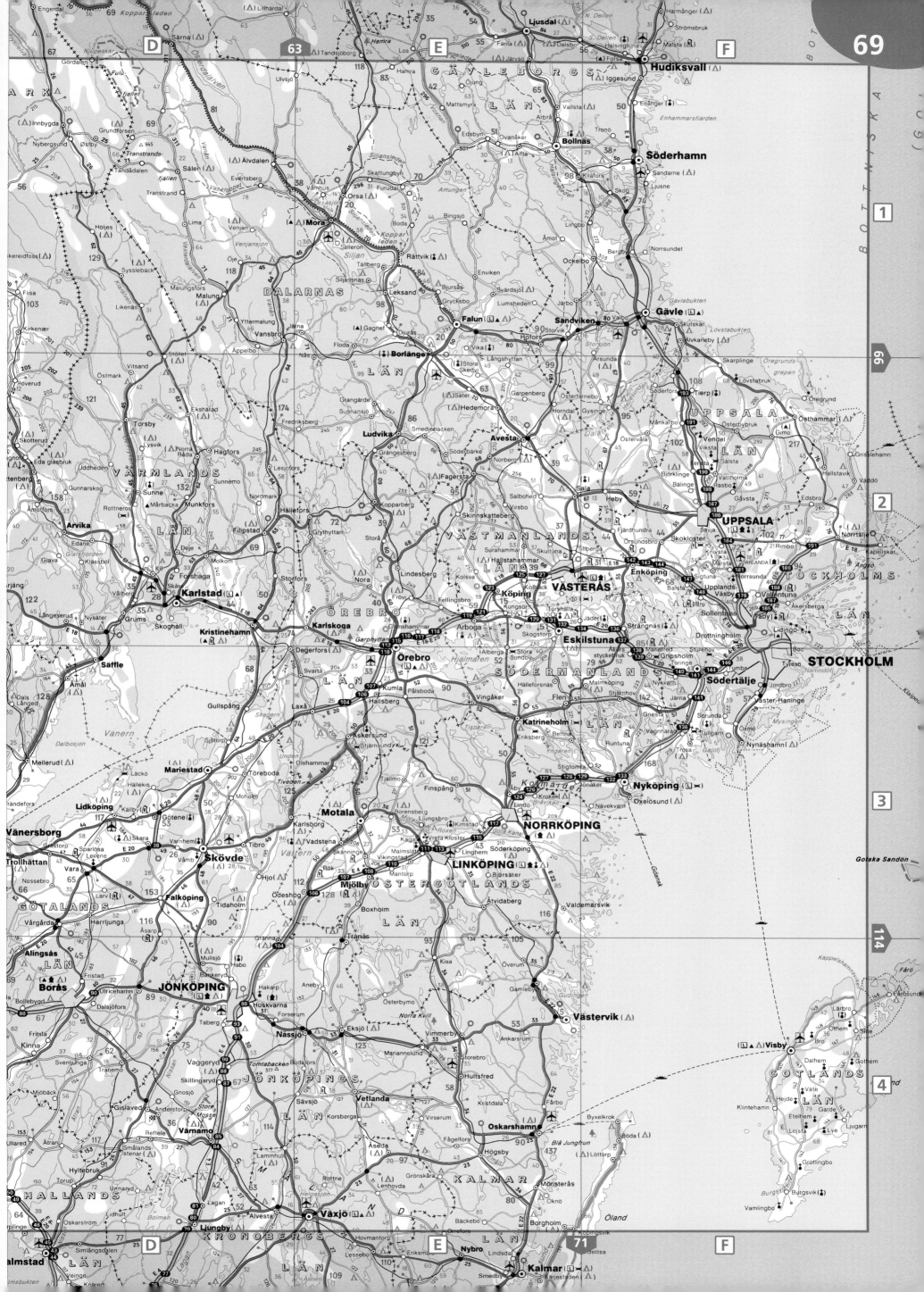

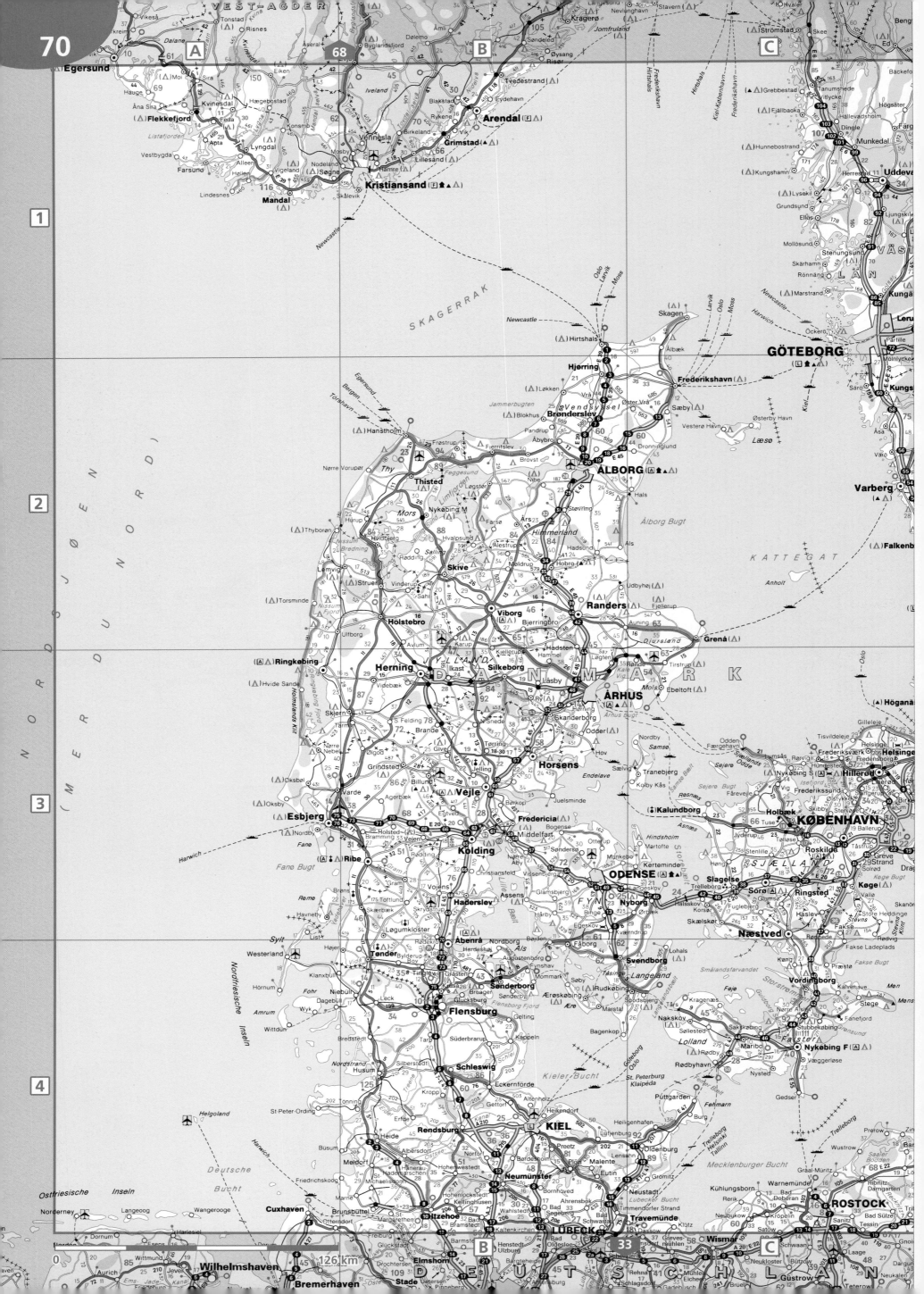

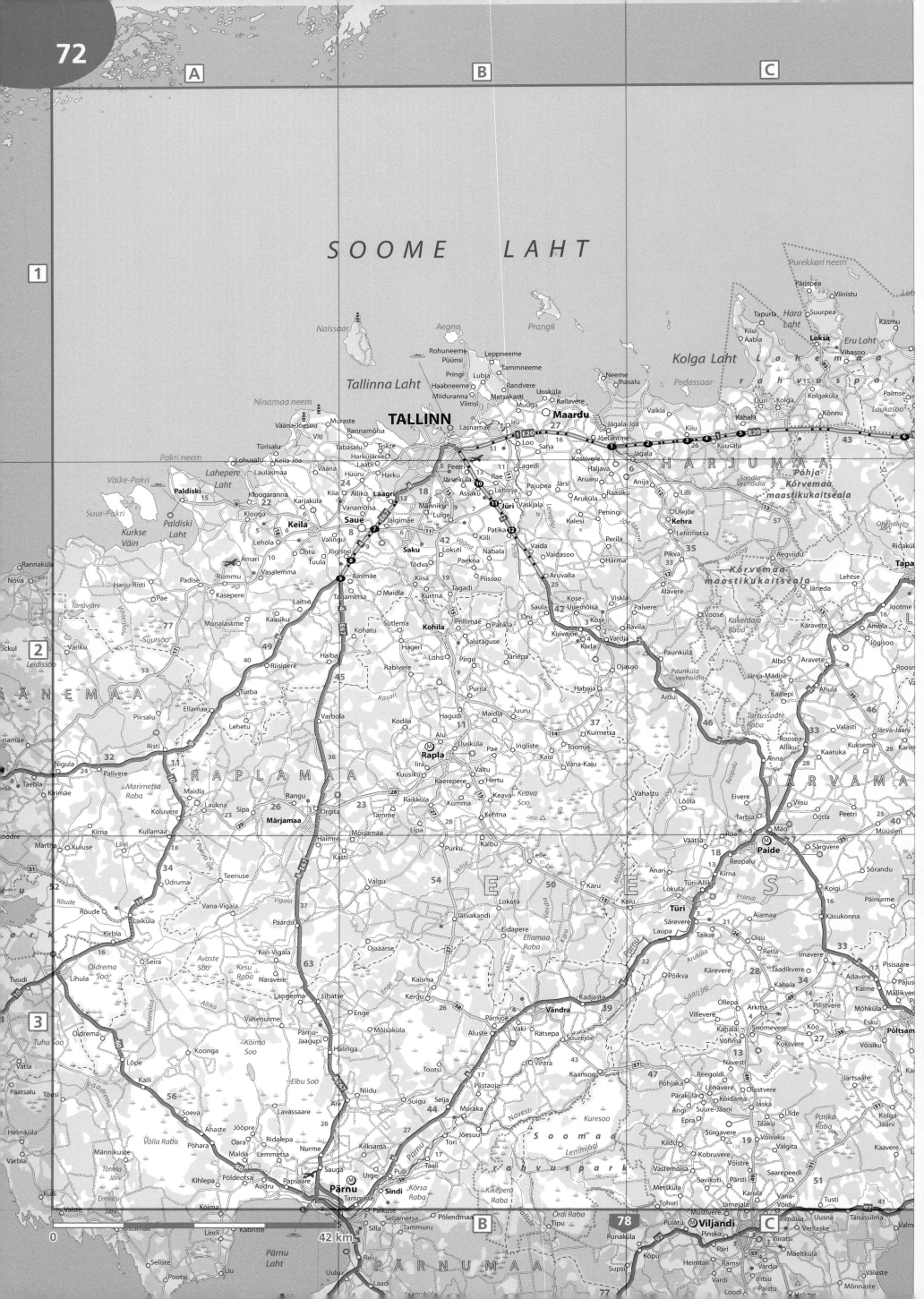

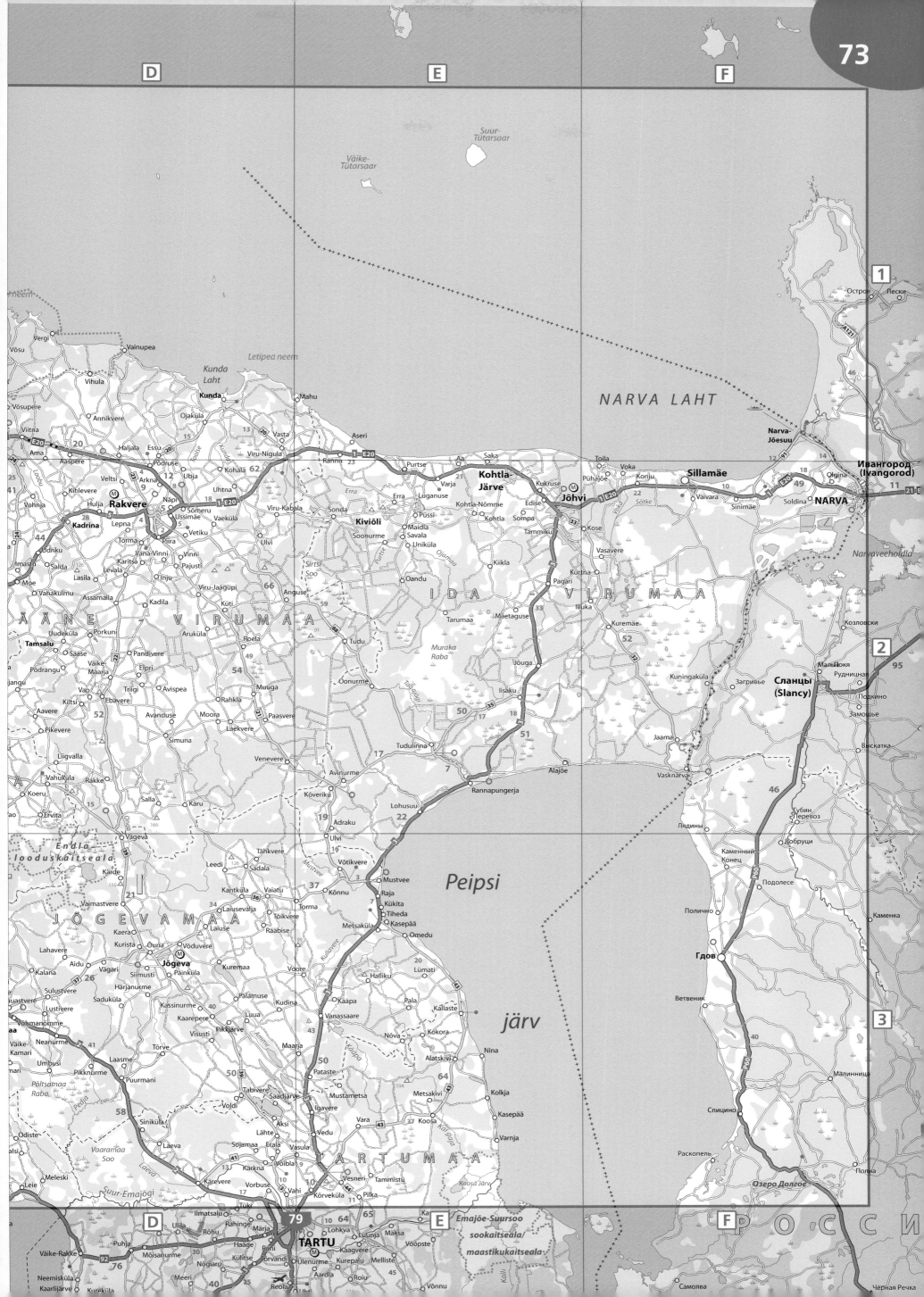

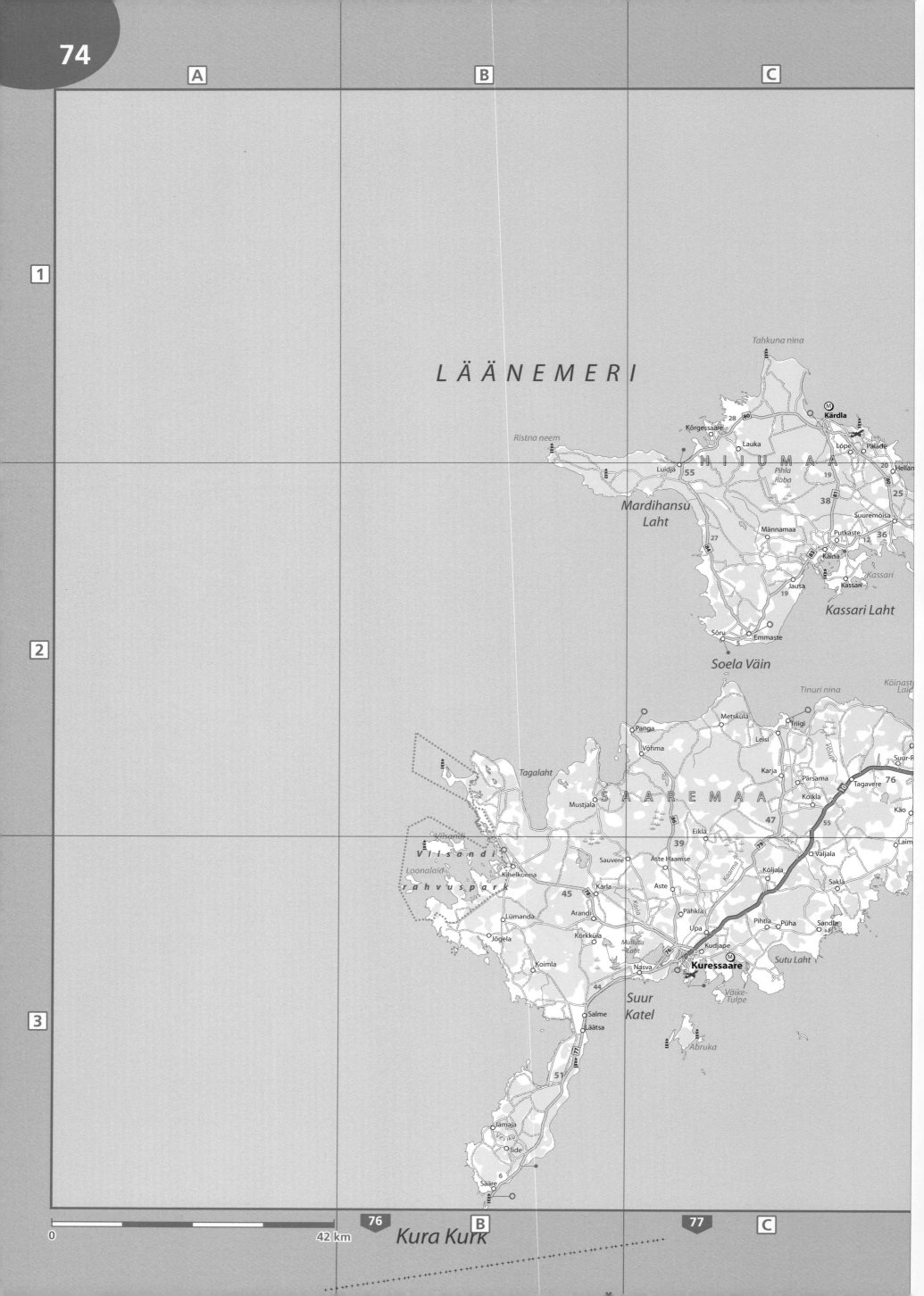

A   B   C

1

2

3

L Ä Ä N E M E R I

Tahkuna nina

Kõrgessaare
28 80
Kärdla
Ristna neem
Lauka
Lõpe Palade
Luidja 55
H I I U M A A
Hellam
Pihla Raba
19 20
Mardihansu Laht
38 25
Männamaa
Suuremõisa
27
Putkaste 36
12
Kaina
Kassari
Jausa
19 Kassari *Kassari Laht*
Sõru
5 Emmaste

Soela Väin

Tinuri nina *Kõinastu Laid*

Metsküla Triigi
Panga Leisi *Võlupe*
Võhma Suur-R
Karja
Tagalaht Pärsama 76
S A A R E M A A Tagavere
Mustjala Koikla 55
86 47 Käo
39 Eikla Laim
Viisandi Sauvere Aste Haamse 79 Väljala
V i i s a n d i Kõljala Sakla
Loonalaid Kihelkonna Aste
r a h v u s p a r k 45 Kärla Pähkla
Arandi Pihtla Püha
Lümanda Kõrkküla Upa Sandla
Jõgela *Mullutu Laht* Kudjape
Koimla Nasva **Kuressaare**
Väike-Tulpe
44 *Suur Katel* *Sutu Laht*
Salme
Läätsa *Abruka*
77
51
Jämaja
Vesiku Iide
6 Sääre

0   42 km
B   C

Kura Kurk

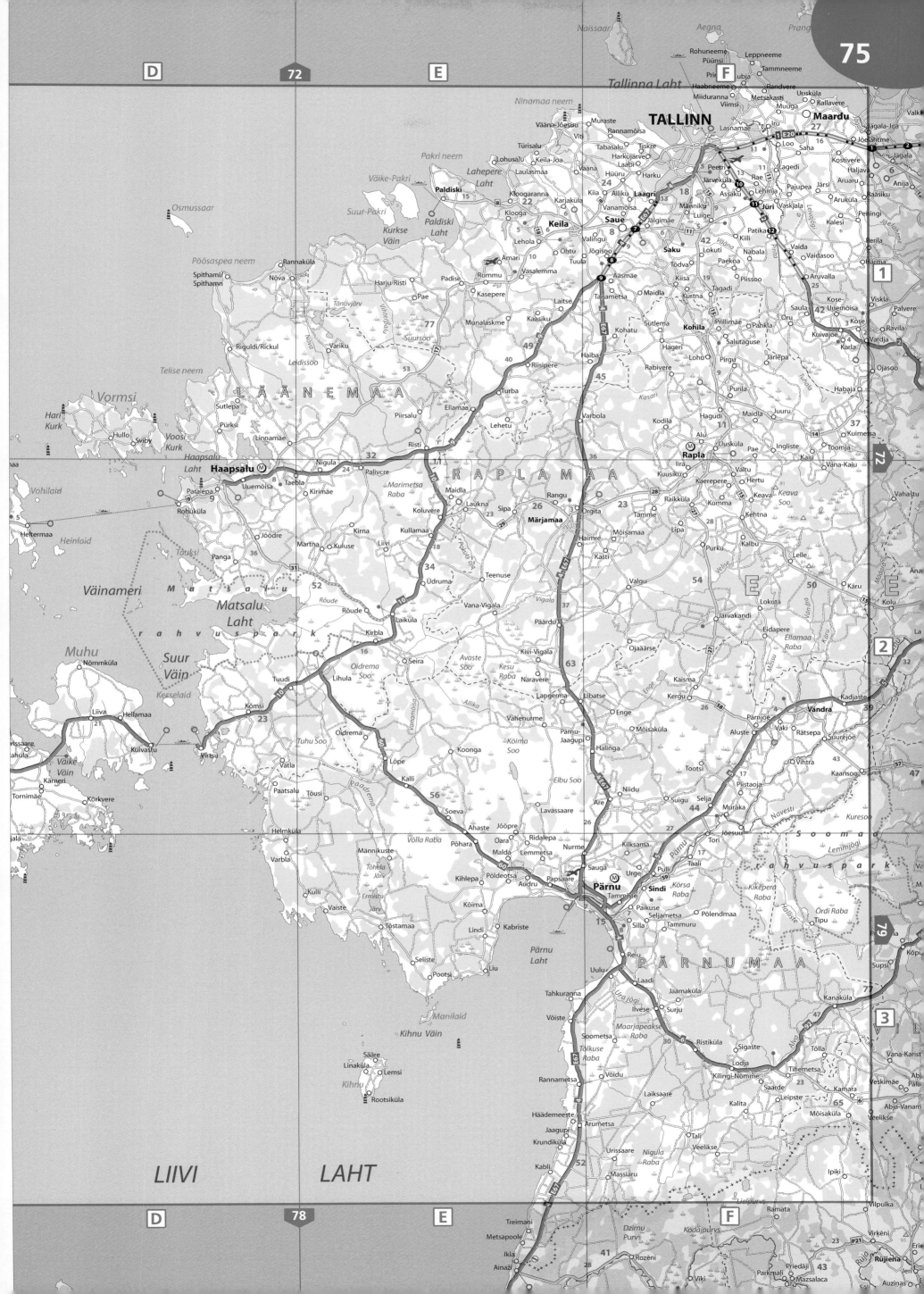

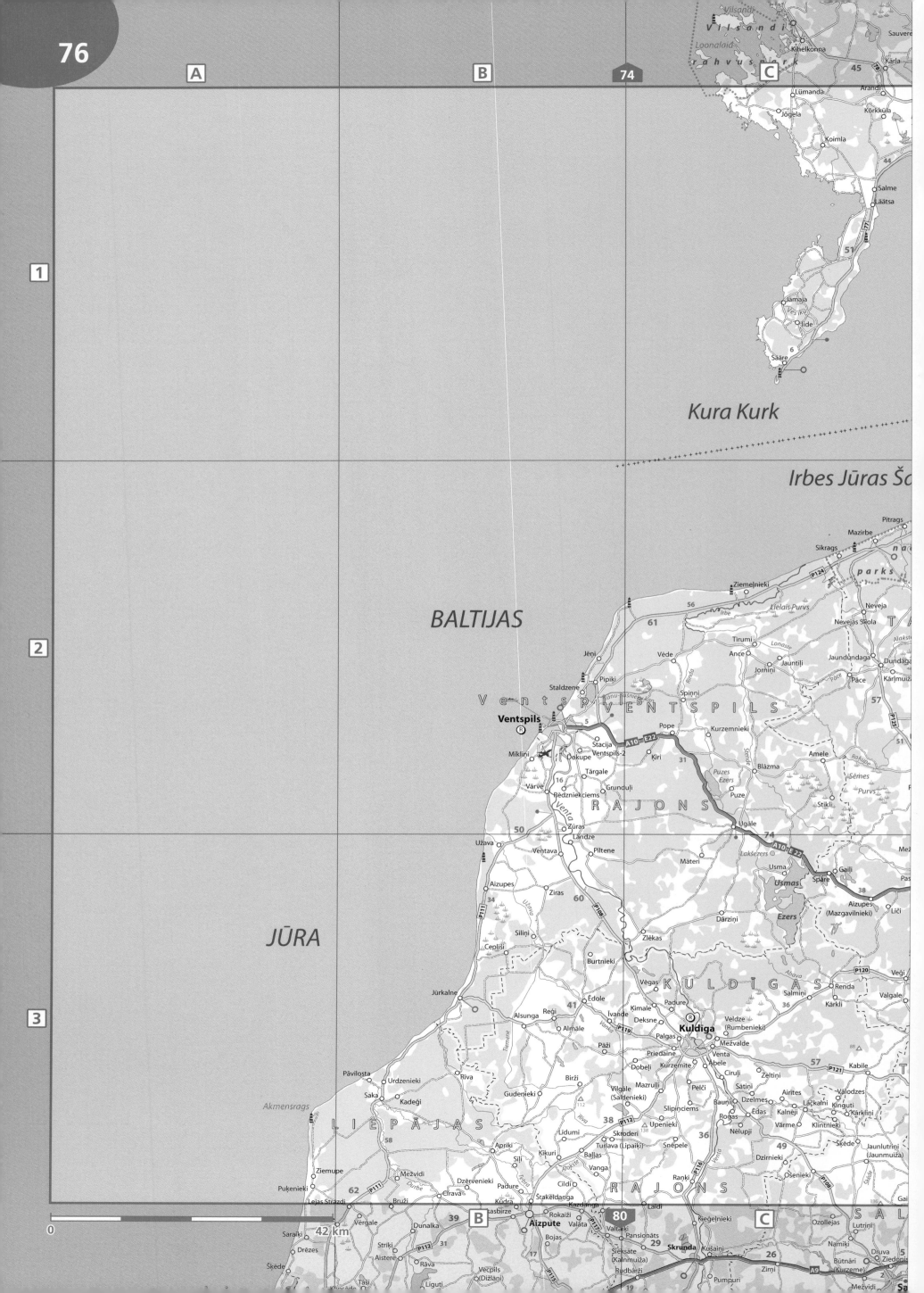

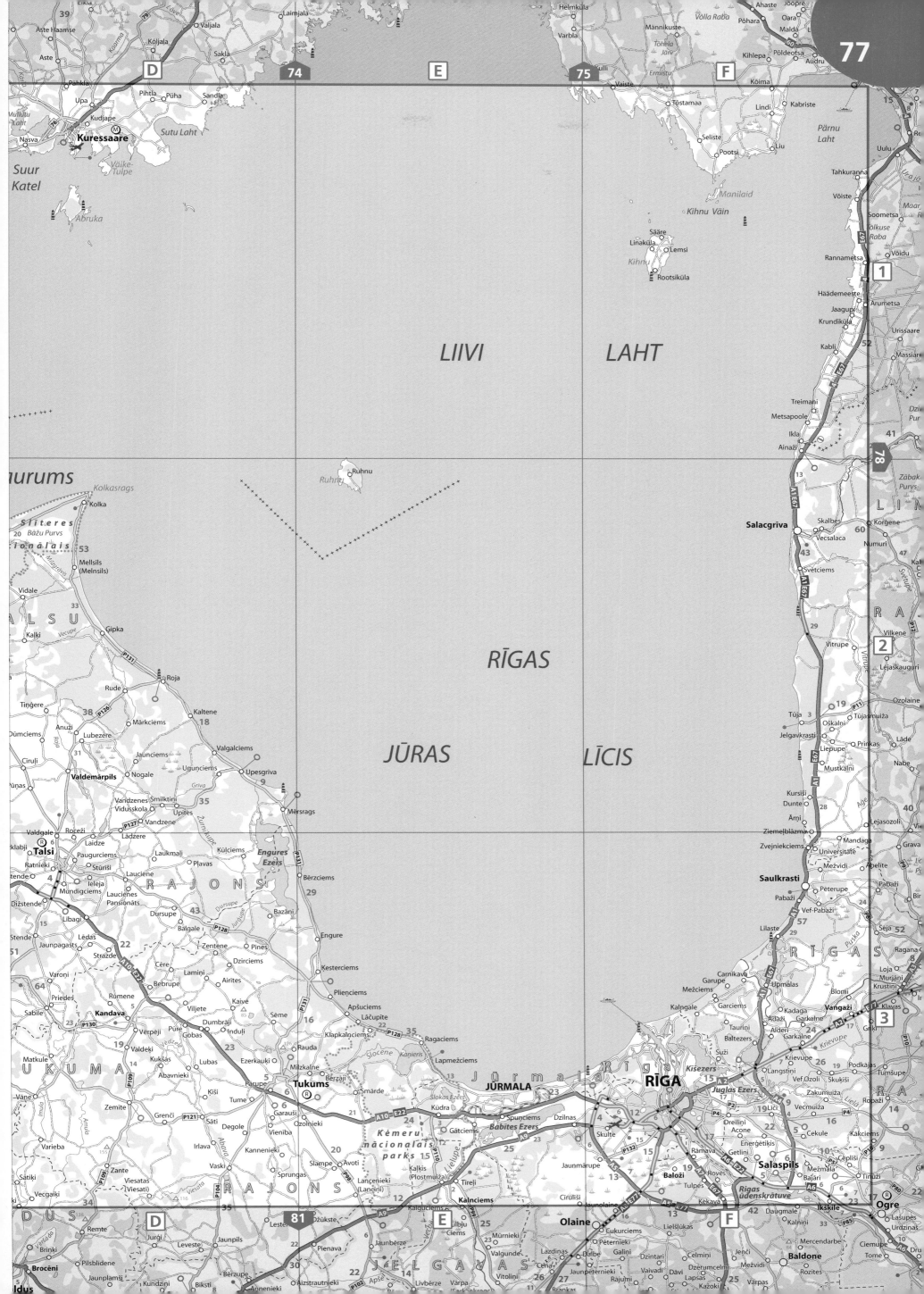

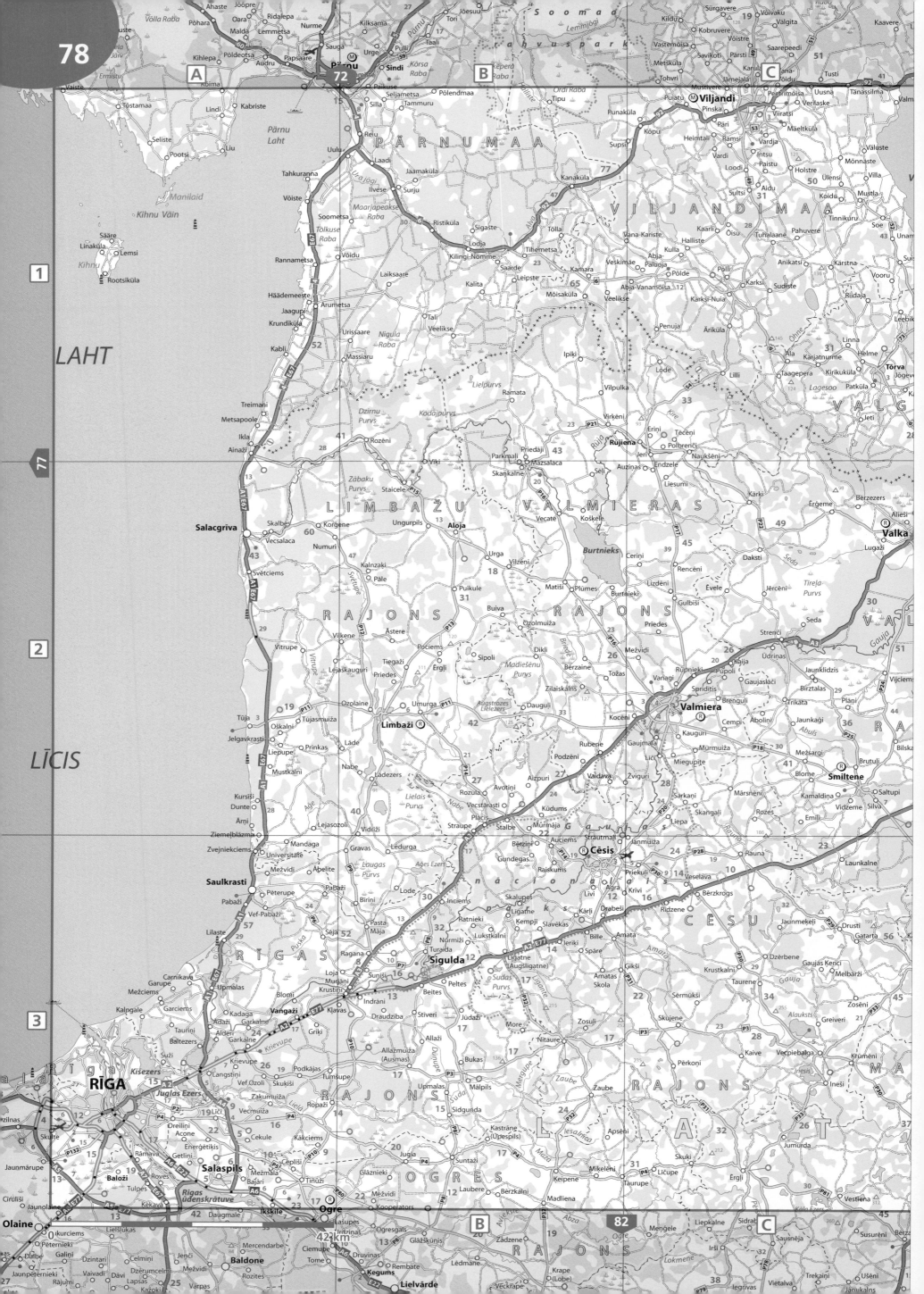

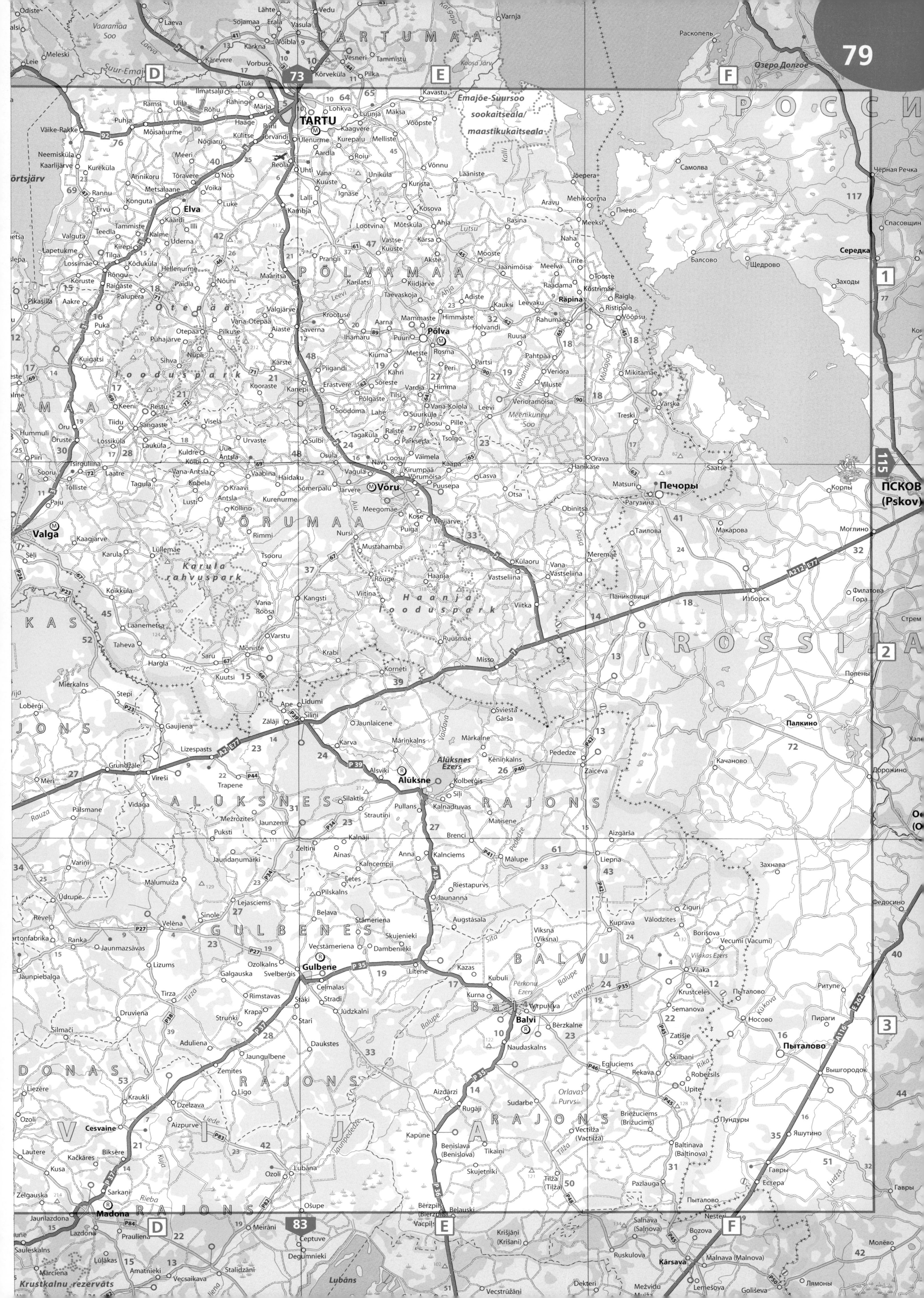

РОССИЯ / ROSSIJA

TARTUMAA

PÕLVAMAA

VÕRUMAA

ALŪKSNES RAJONS

GULBENES RAJONS

BALVU RAJONS

MADONAS RAJONS

VILJANDIMAA

Otepää looduspark

Karula rahvuspark

Haanja looduspark

Krustkalnu rezervāts

TARTU

Elva

Valga

Võru

Põlva

Räpina

Печоры

ПСКОВ (Pskov)

Alūksne

Gulbene

Balvi

Madona

Cesvaine

Kārsava

Пыталово

Озеро Долгое

Чёрная Речка

Середка

Самолва

Lähte, Vedu, Varnja, Sojamaa, Erala, Vasula, Kärkna, Võibla, Kärevere, Vorbuse, Tüki, Kõrveküla, Pilka, Ilmatsalu, Ramsi, Ülila, Rõhu, Rahinge, Märja, Haage, Büni, Lohkva, Lüünja, Kavastu, Kaagvere, Vesneri, Tammistu, Mäksa, Võõpste, Mõisanurme, Nõgiaru, Meeri, Jõrvandi, Külitse, Kurepalu, Melliste, Väike-Rakke, Puhja, Neemisküla, Kurekūla, Annikoru, Metsalaane, Tõravere, Nõo, Voika, Luke, Kambja, Ülenurme, Aardla, Roiu, Vana-Kuuste, Ignase, Unikūla, Kurista, Kosova, Võnnu, Lääniste, Aravu, Mehikoorma, Meeksi, Пнёво, Naha, Rasina

P/RVA, Kiidjärve, Karilatsi, Leevi, Vastse-Kuuste, Kiuma, Prangli, Mõtsküla, Akste, Adiste, Kauksi, Meelva, Raadama, Kõstrimäe, Raigla, Ristipalo, Võõpsu, Mammaste, Himmaste, Holvandi, Ruusa, Pahtpää, Veriora, Viluste, Mikitamäe, Värska, Treski, Saatse

Valga, Kaagjärve, Karula, Lüllemäe, Tsooru, Rimmi, Nursi, Puiga, Mustahamba, Rõuge, Haanja, Vastseliina, Viitka, Külaoru, Vana-Vastseliina, Meremäe, Obinitsa, Tailova, Паниковичи, Изборск, Палкино

Valka, Mārkalne, Sviesta, Gārša, Pededze, Kēniņkalns, Zaiceva, Качаново, Kolberģis, Sili, Kalnadruvas, Pullans, Matisene, Brenci, Aizgārša, Liepna, Захнава, Зигури

Gulbene, Litene, Kazas, Kubuli, Kurna, Vārpulēva, Balvi, Bērzkalne, Naudaskalns, Egleciems, Rekava, Robežsils, Upīte, Krustceles, Semanova, Hosovo, Пираги, Пыталово

Cesvaine, Kraukļi, Dzelzava, Aizpurve, Ozoli, Ļubāna, Kapūne, Beņislava (Benislova), Tikaini, Skujetnīki, Tilža, Rugāji, Sudarbe, Aizdziri

Madona, Jaunlazdona, Lazdona, Prauliena, Meirāni, Ceptuve, Degumnieki, Stalidzāni, Krišjāņi (Krišani), Ruskulova, Salnava (Salnava), Bozova, Kārsava, Малнава (Malnova)

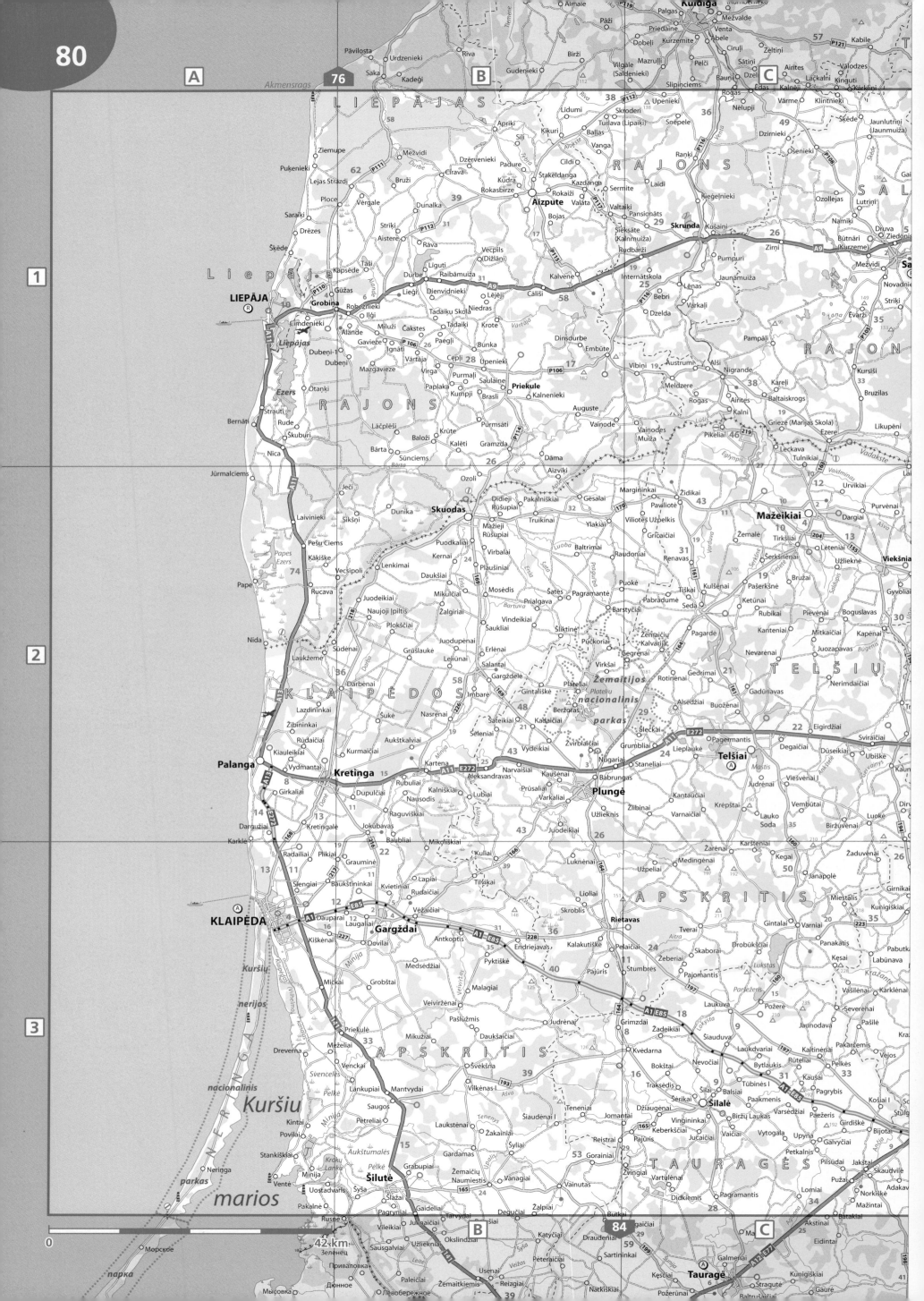

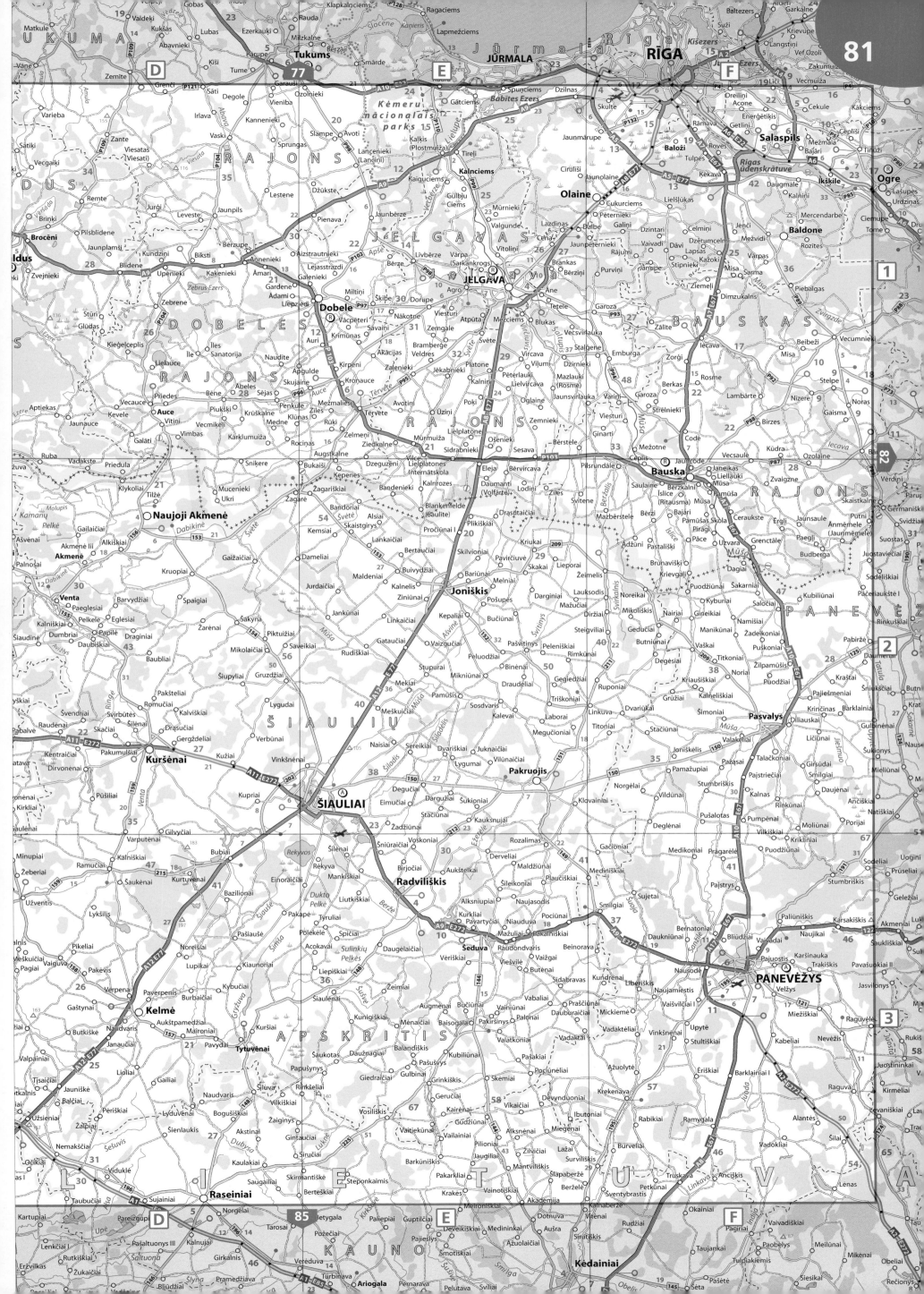

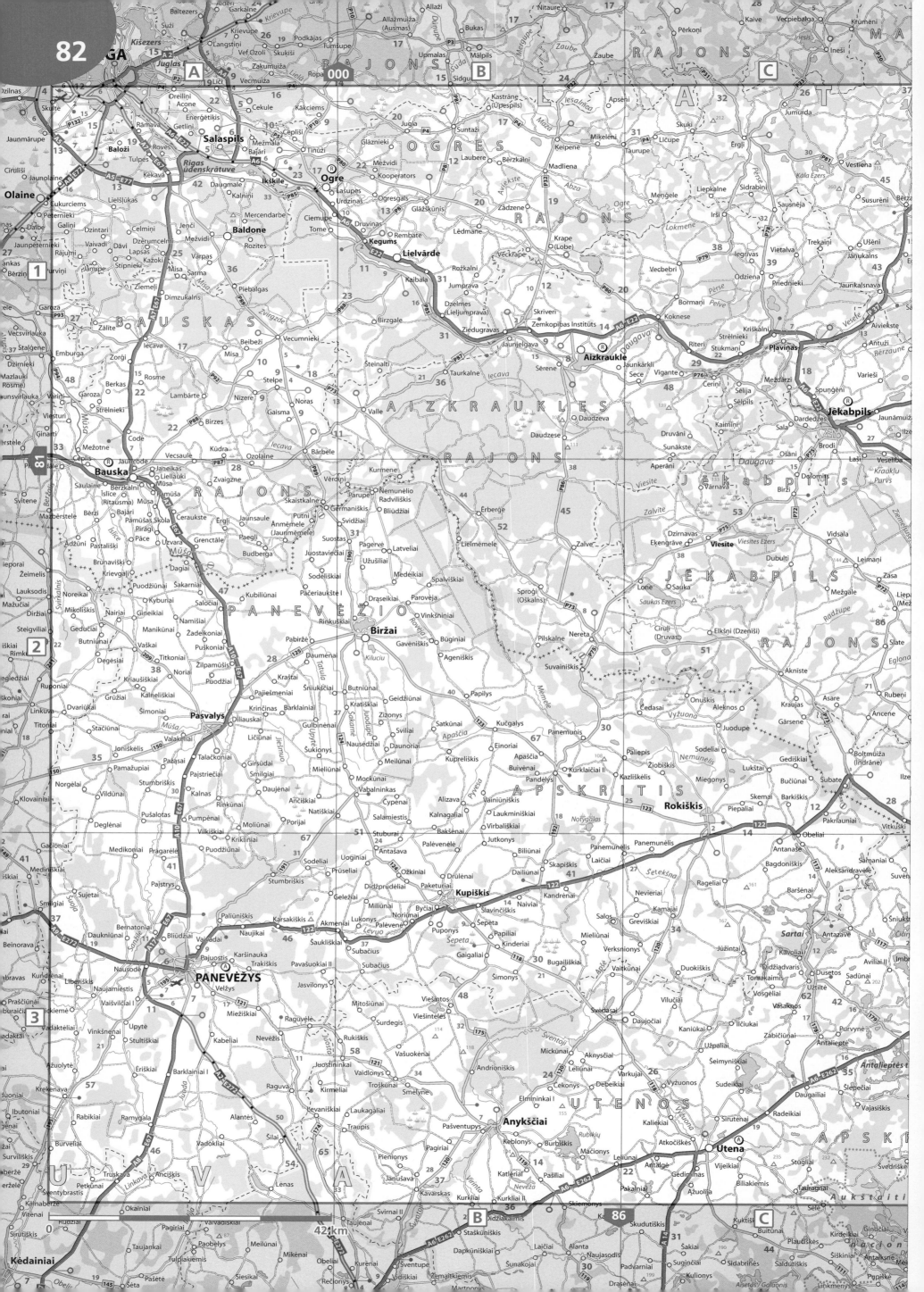

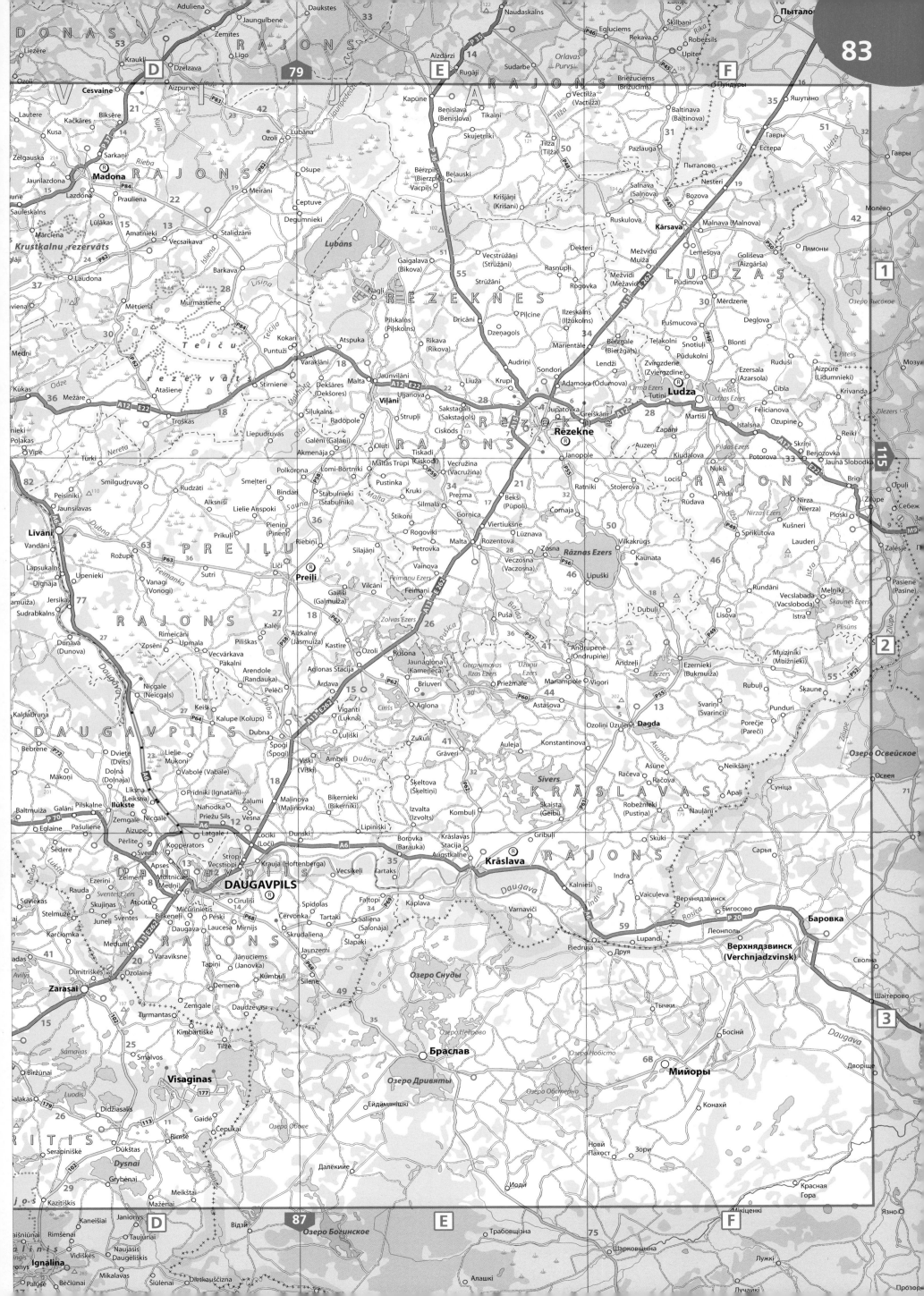

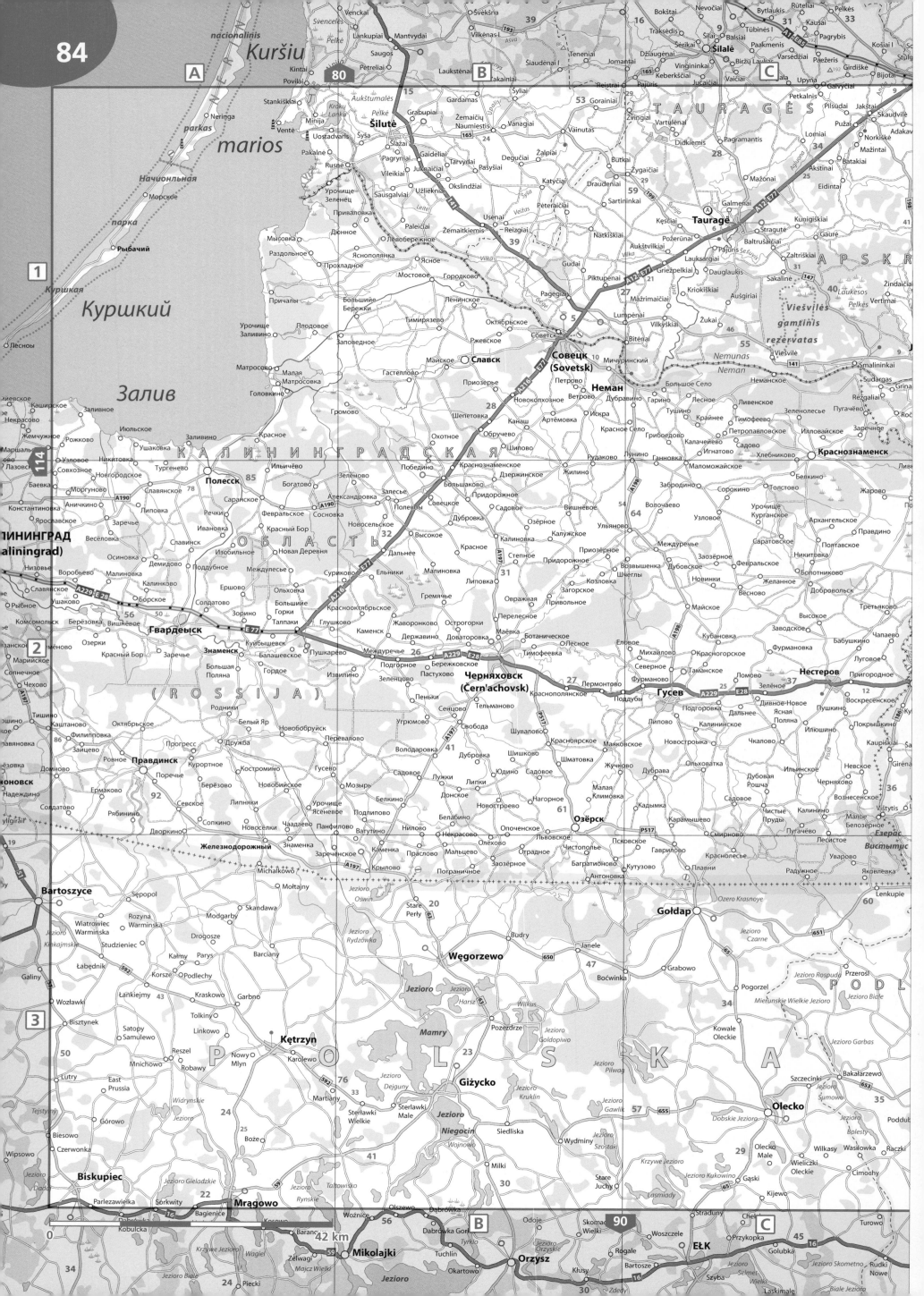

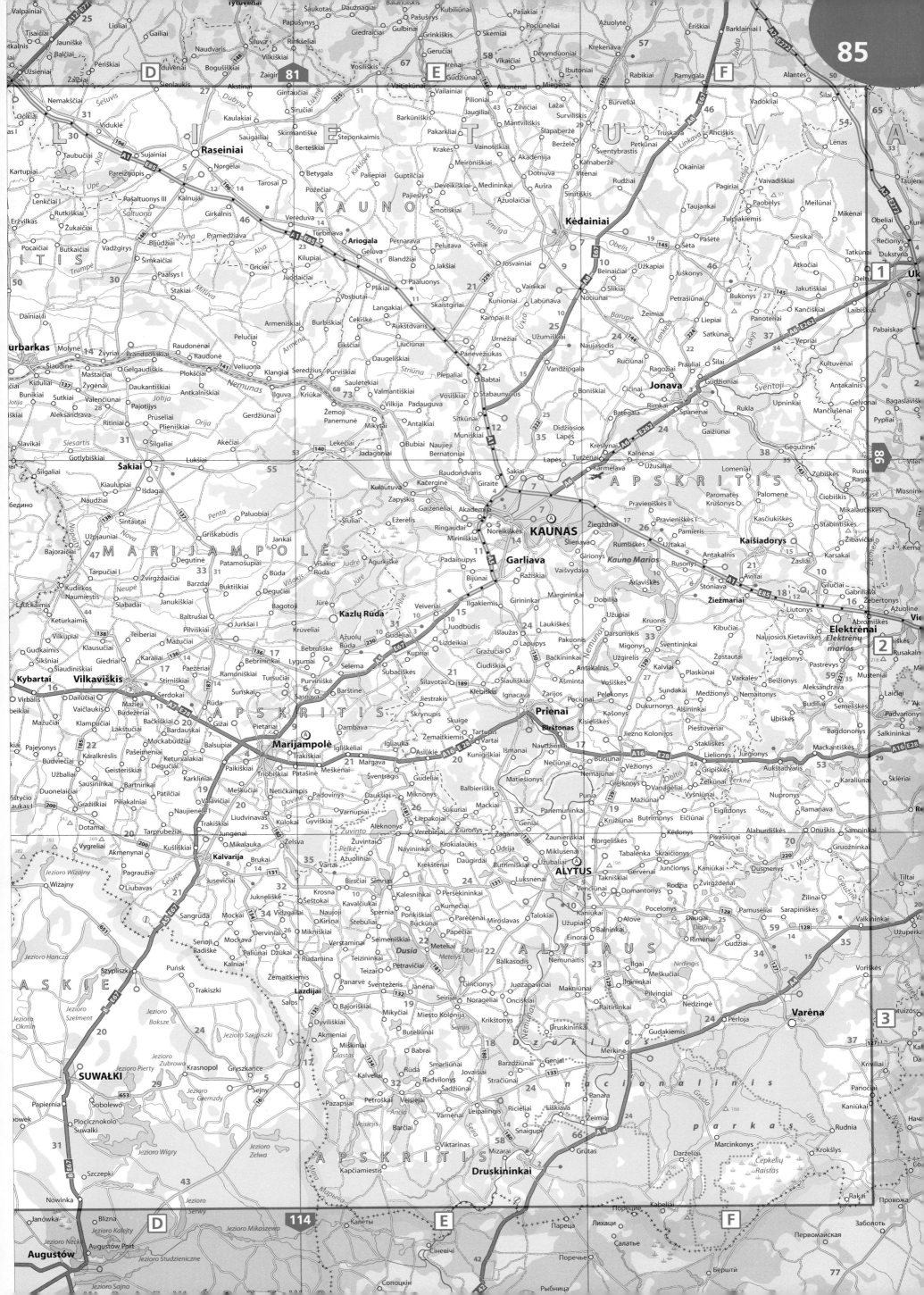

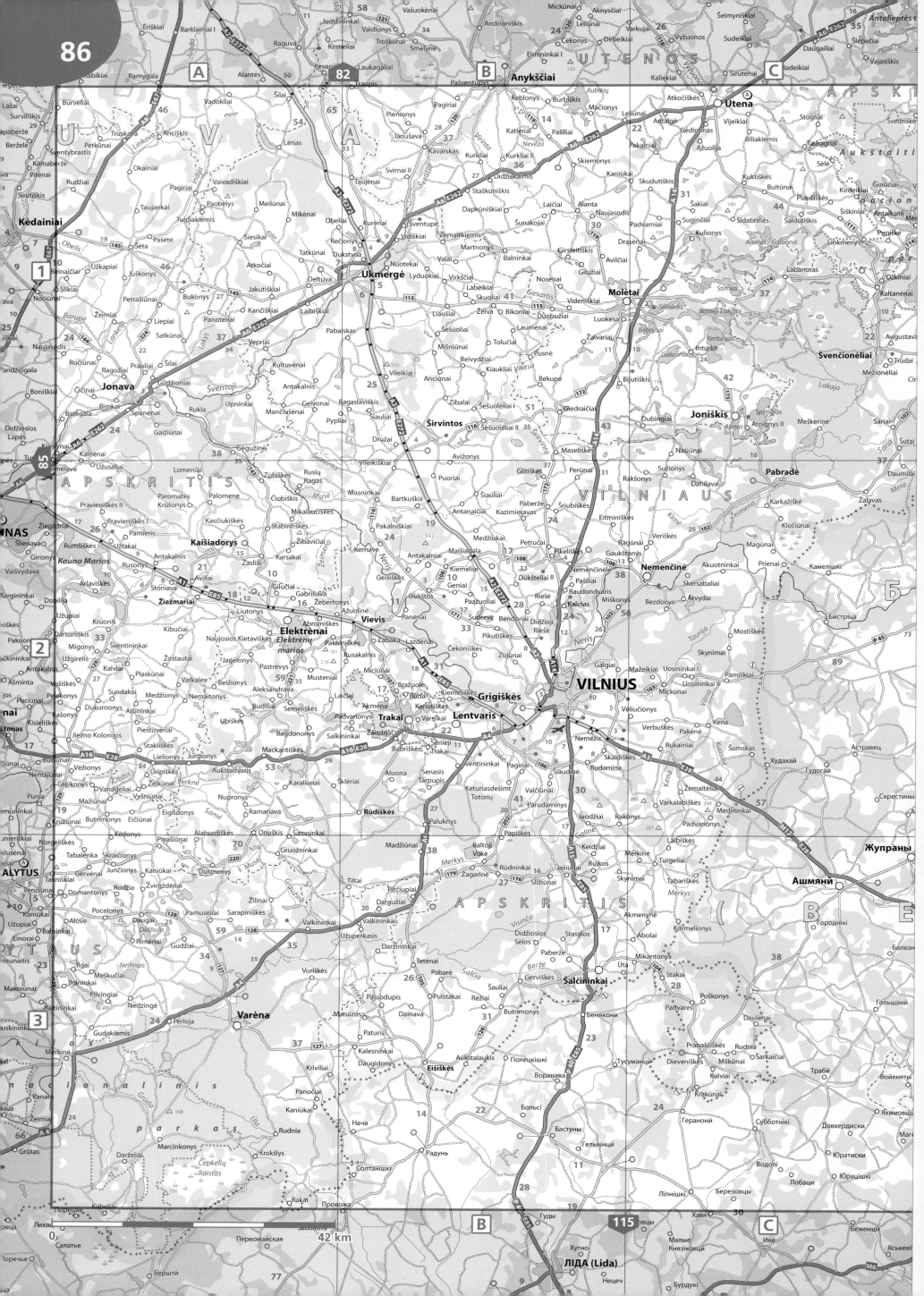

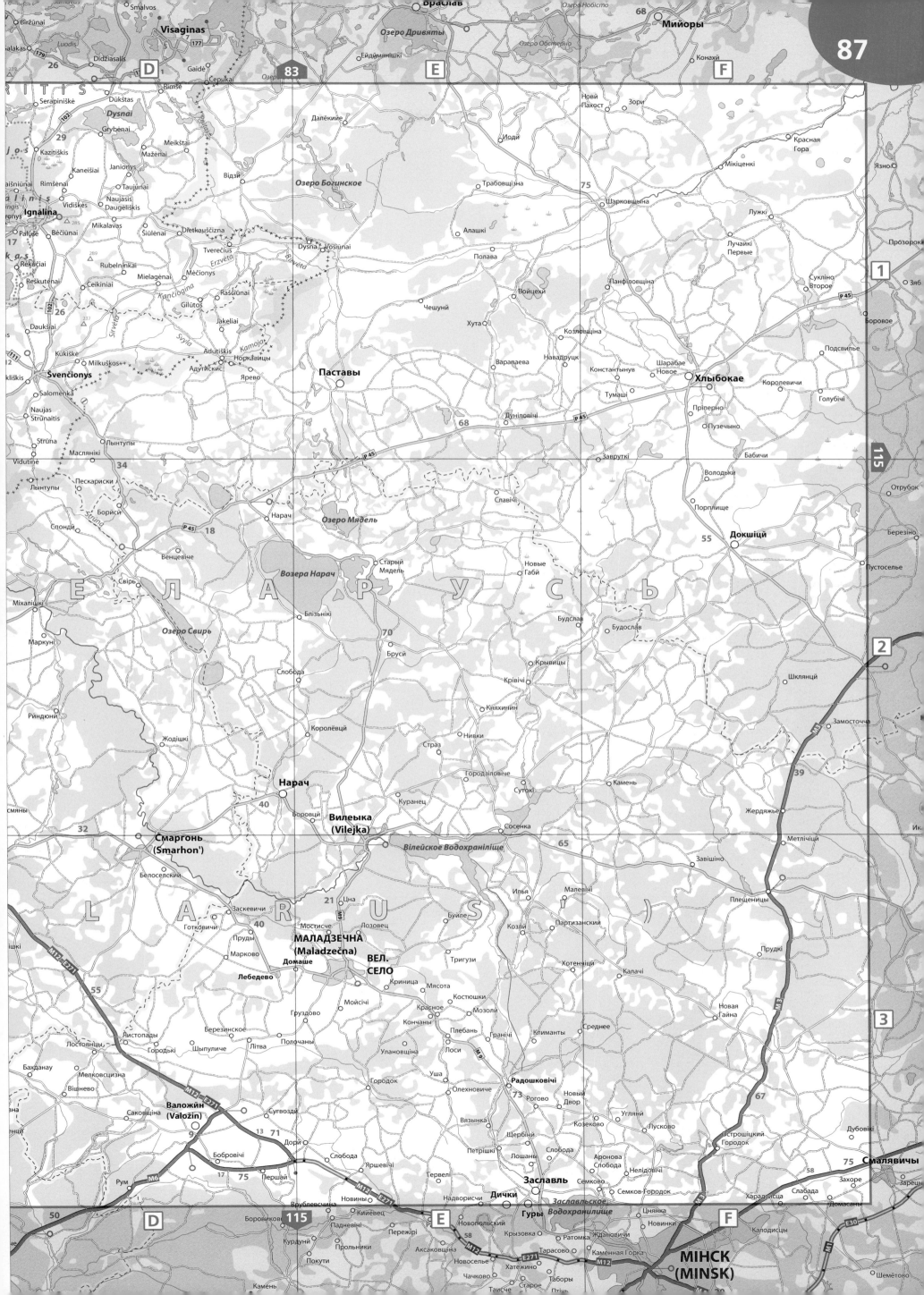

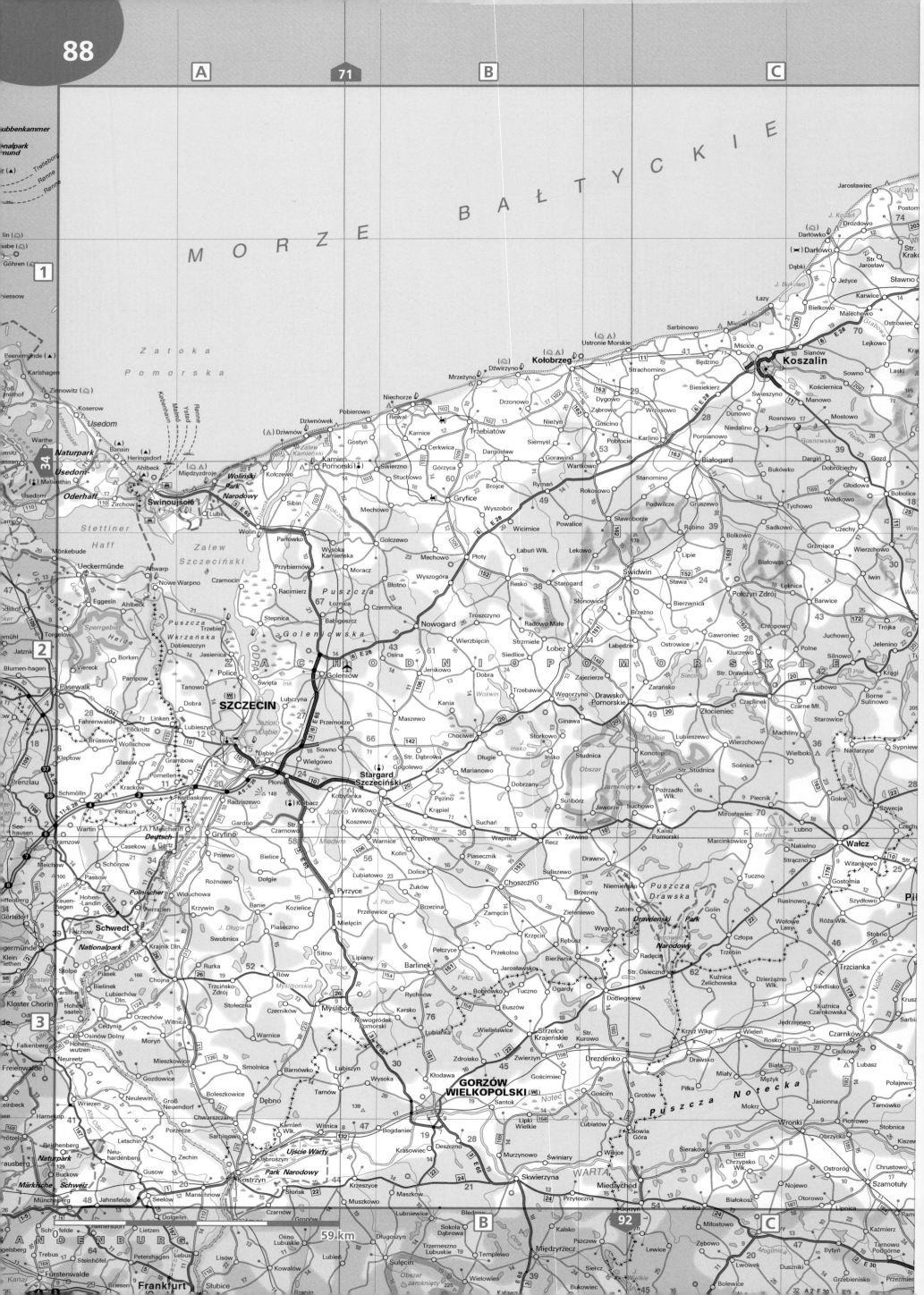

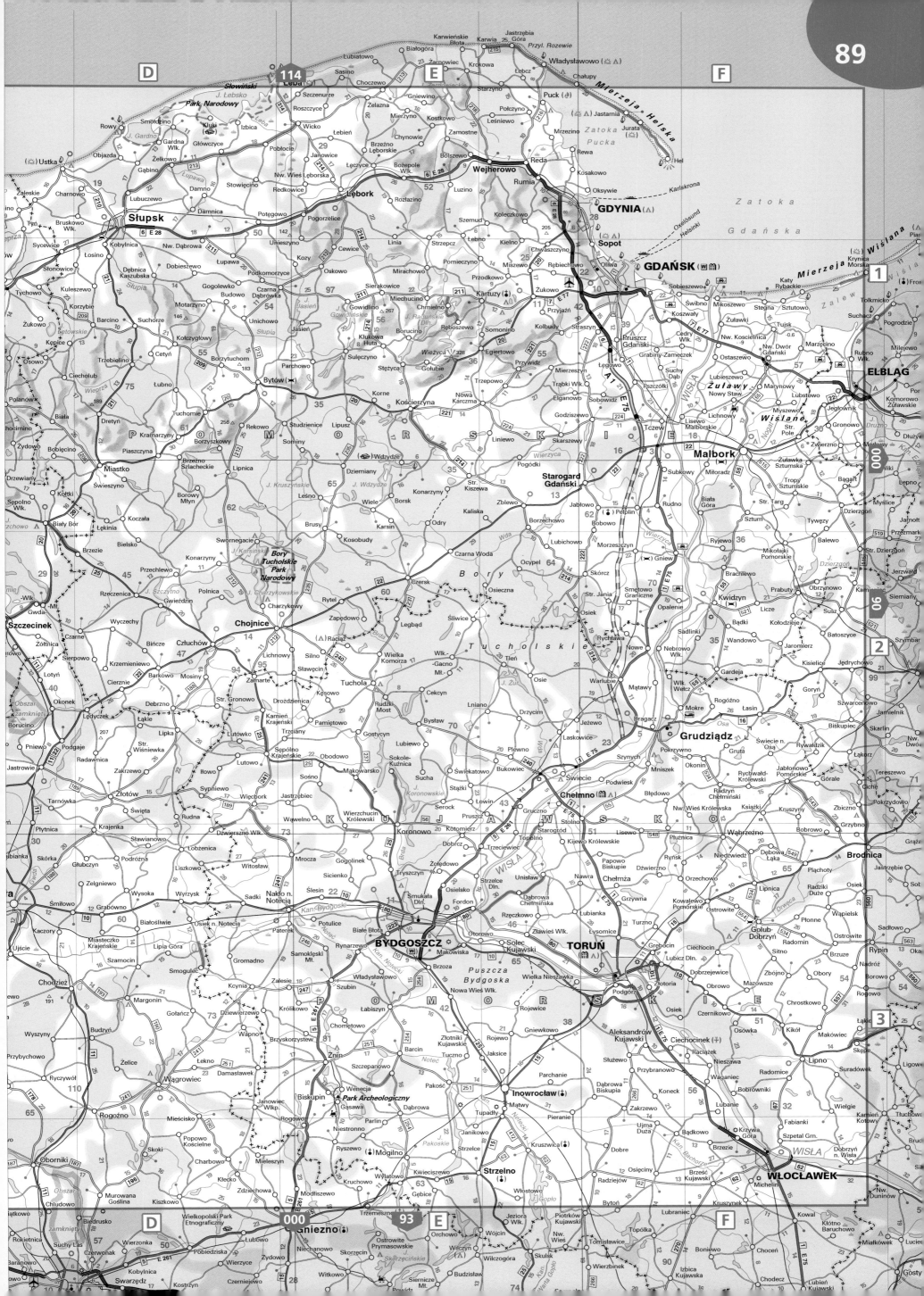

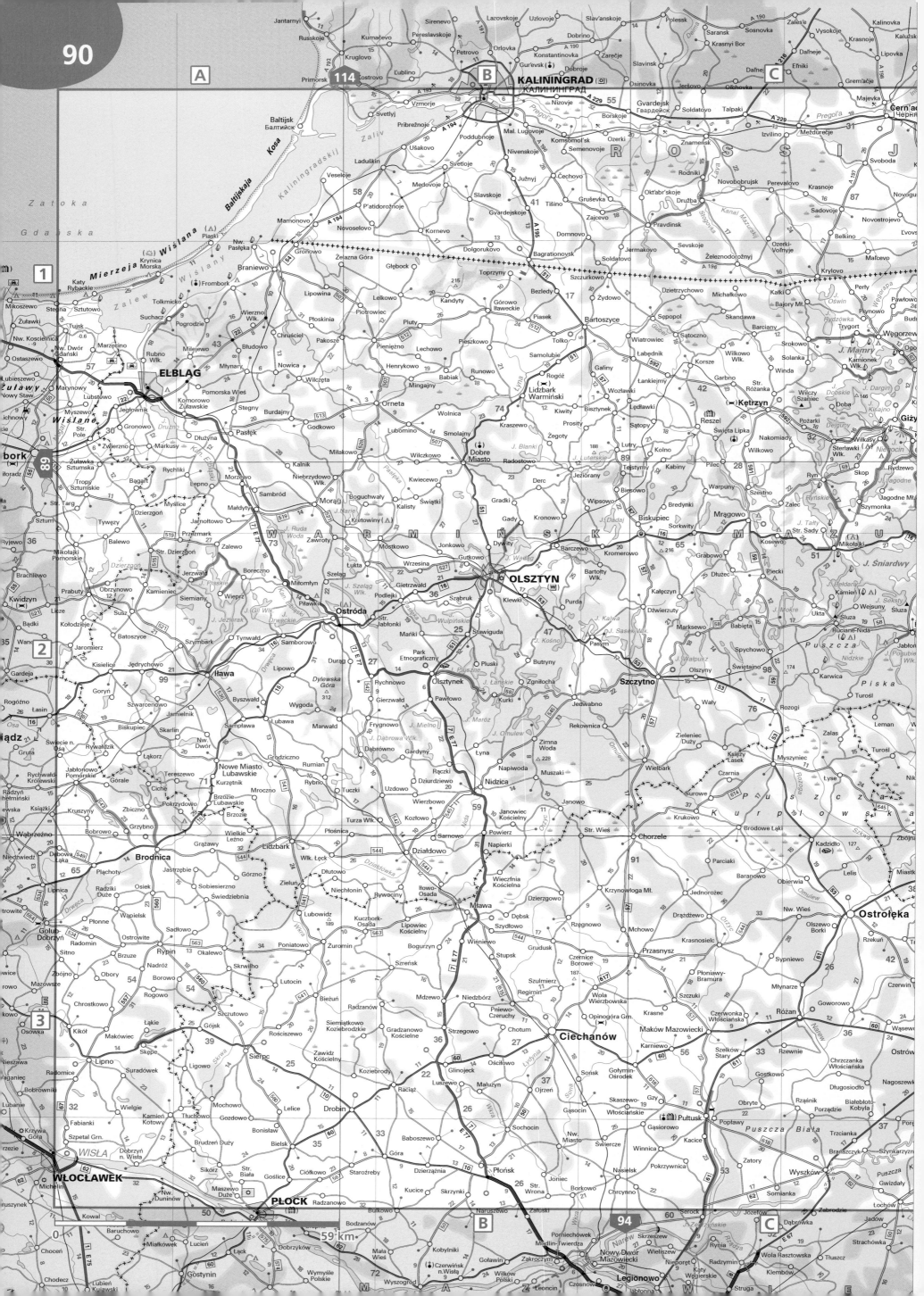

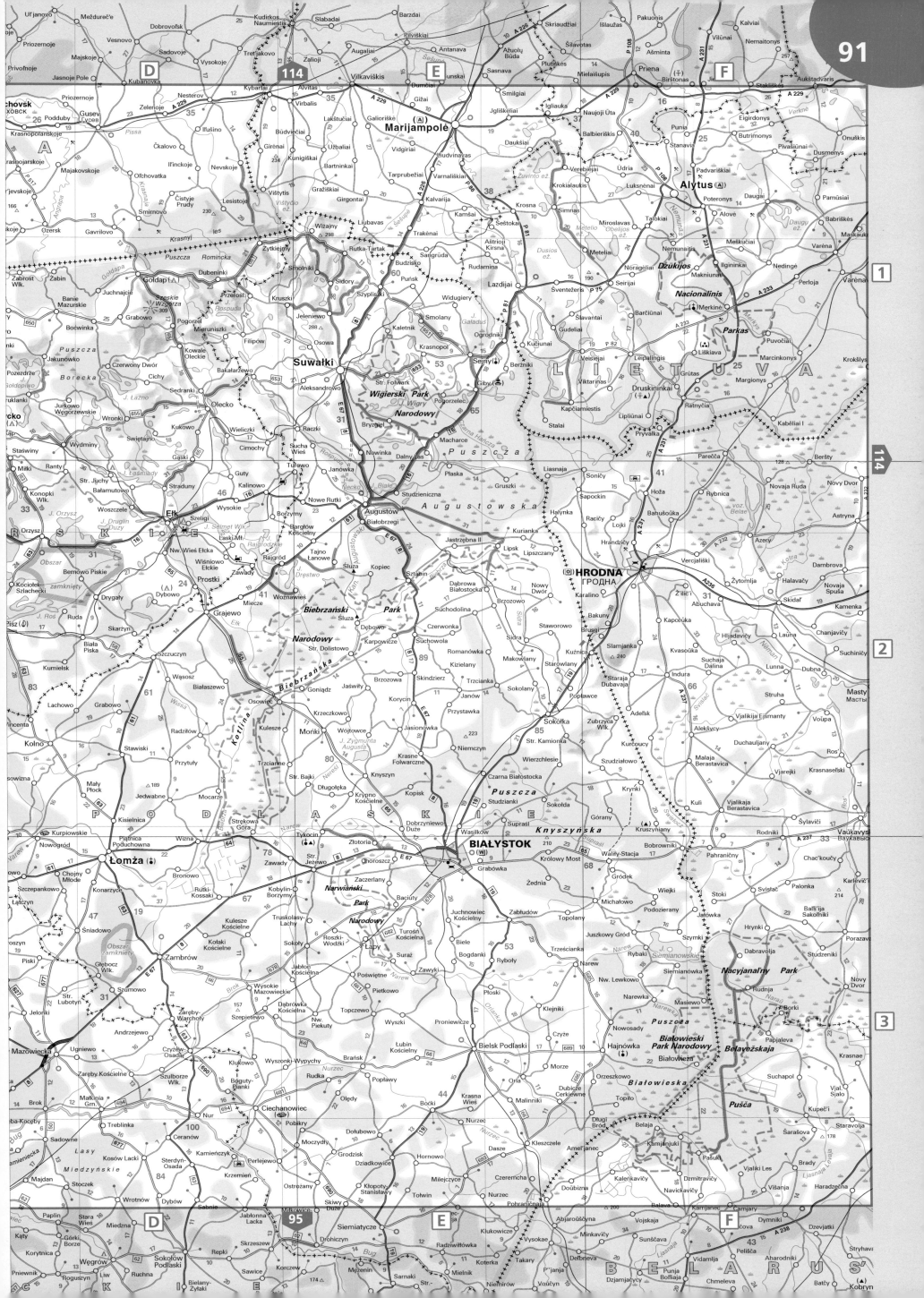

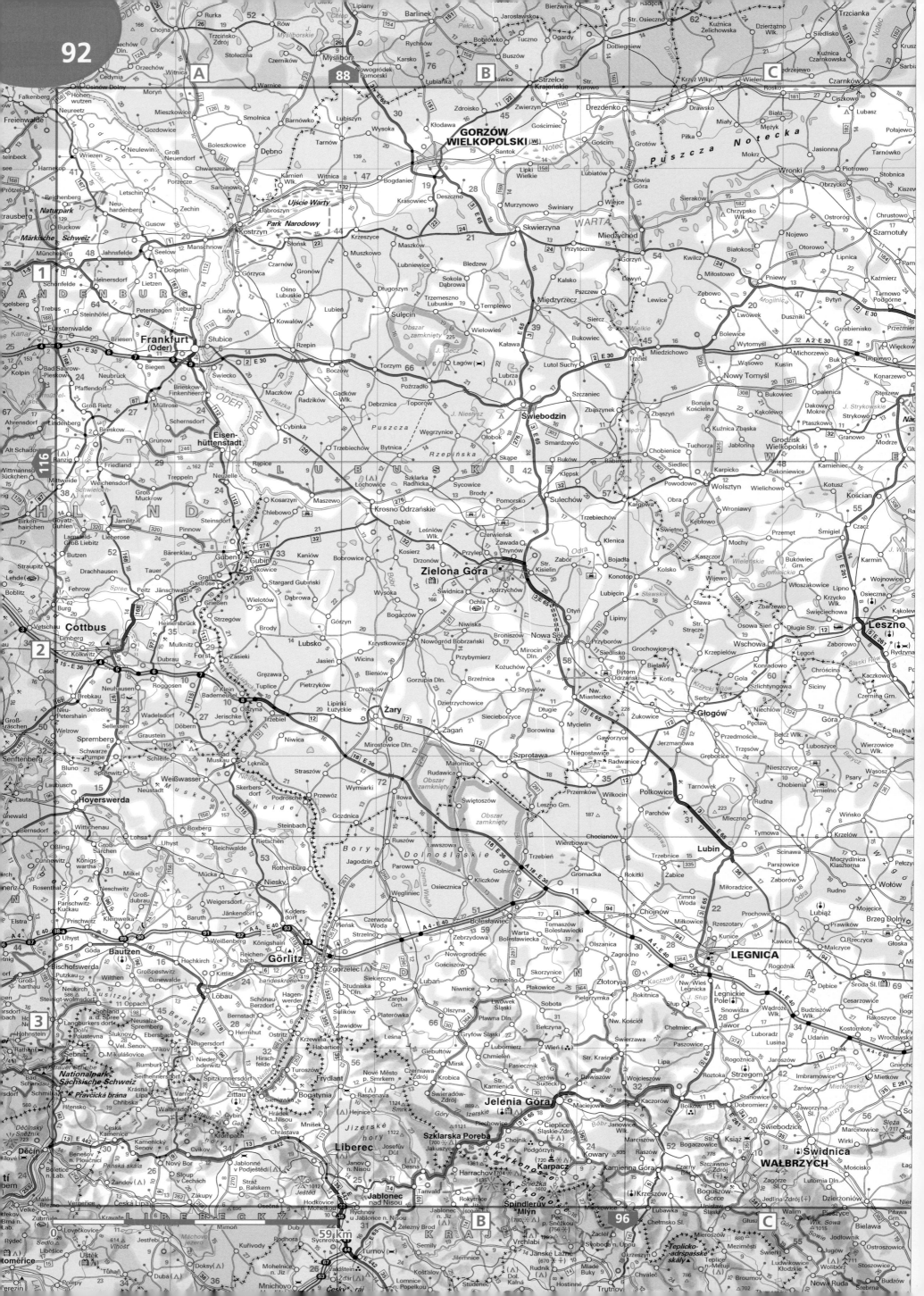

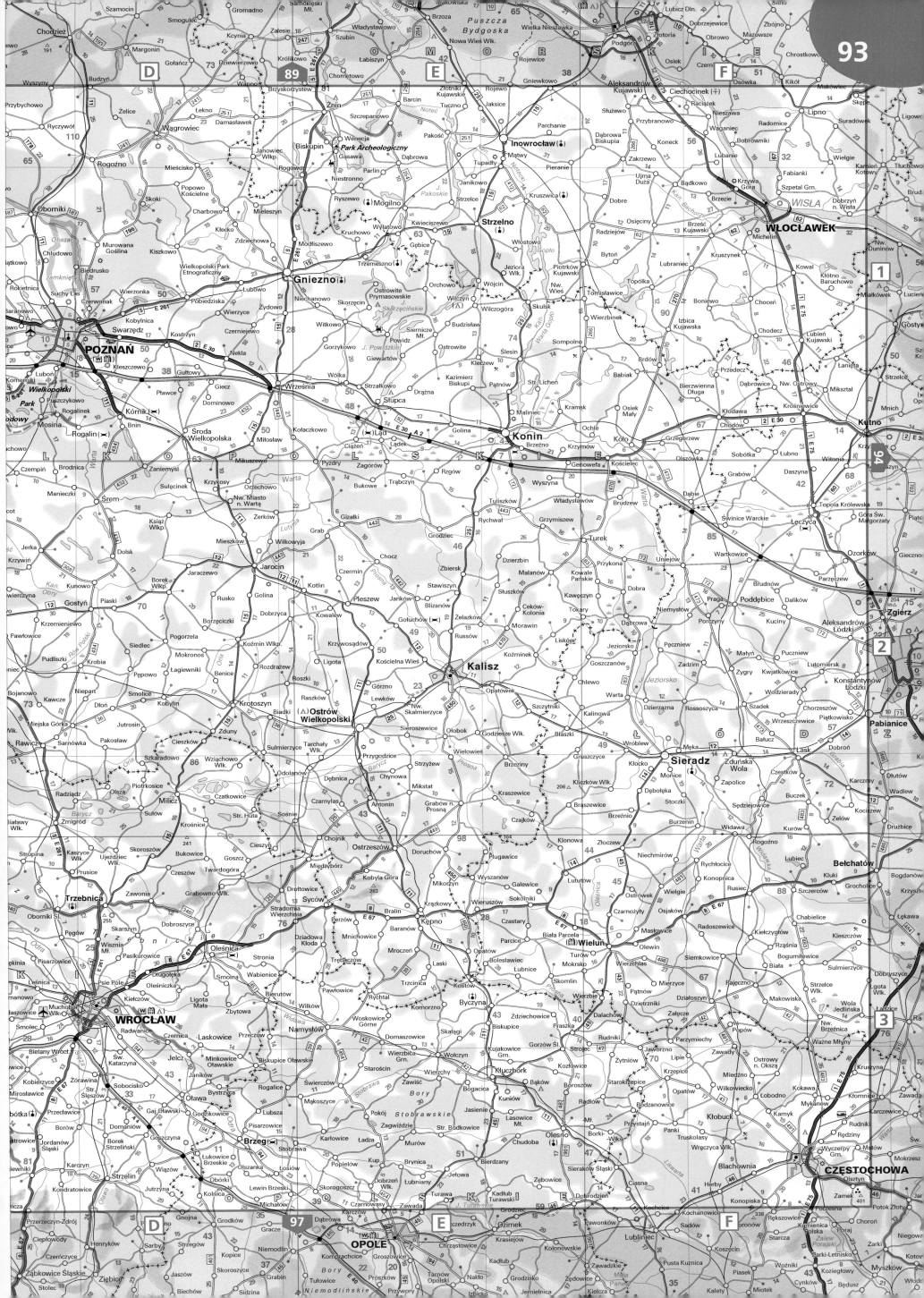

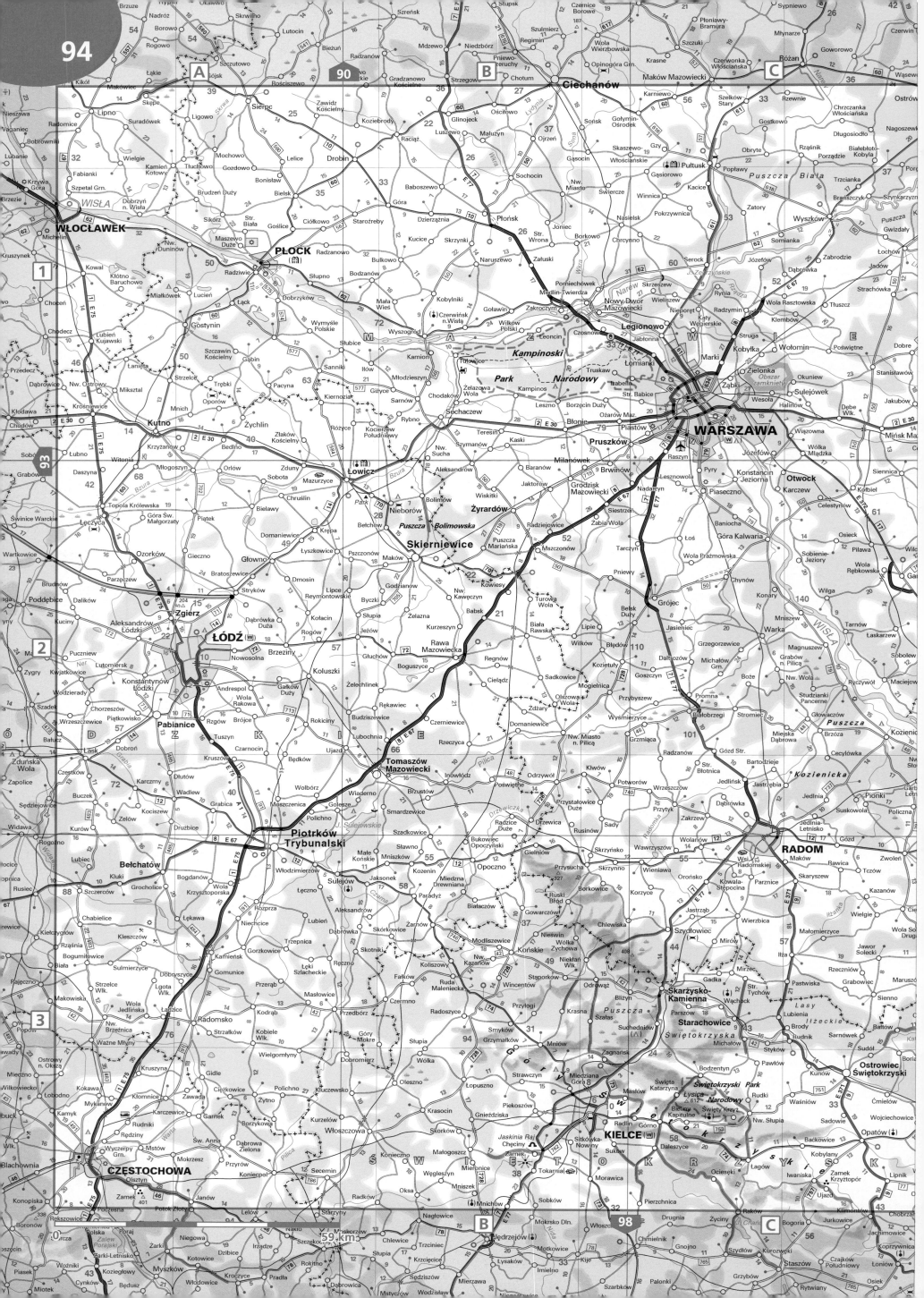

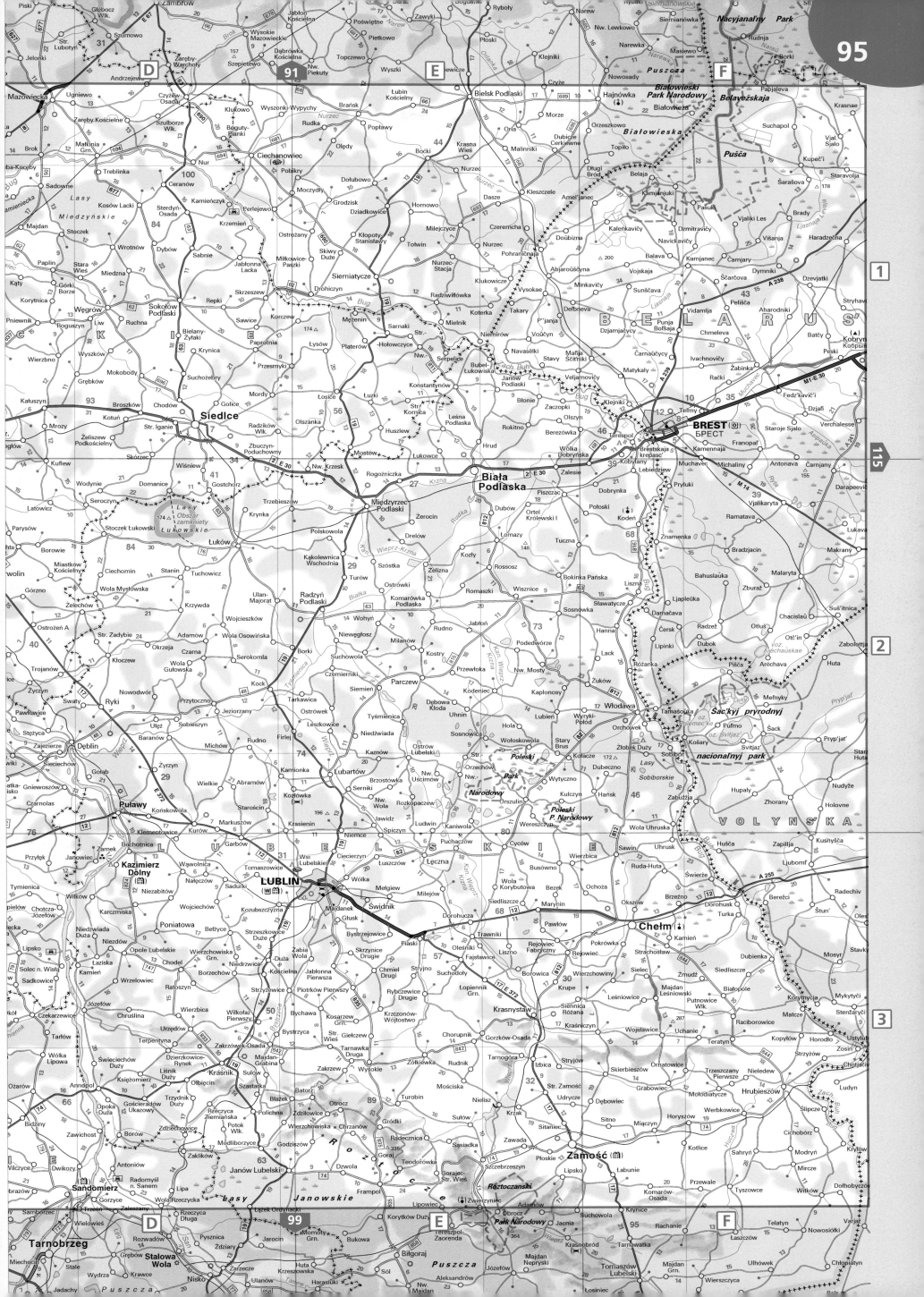

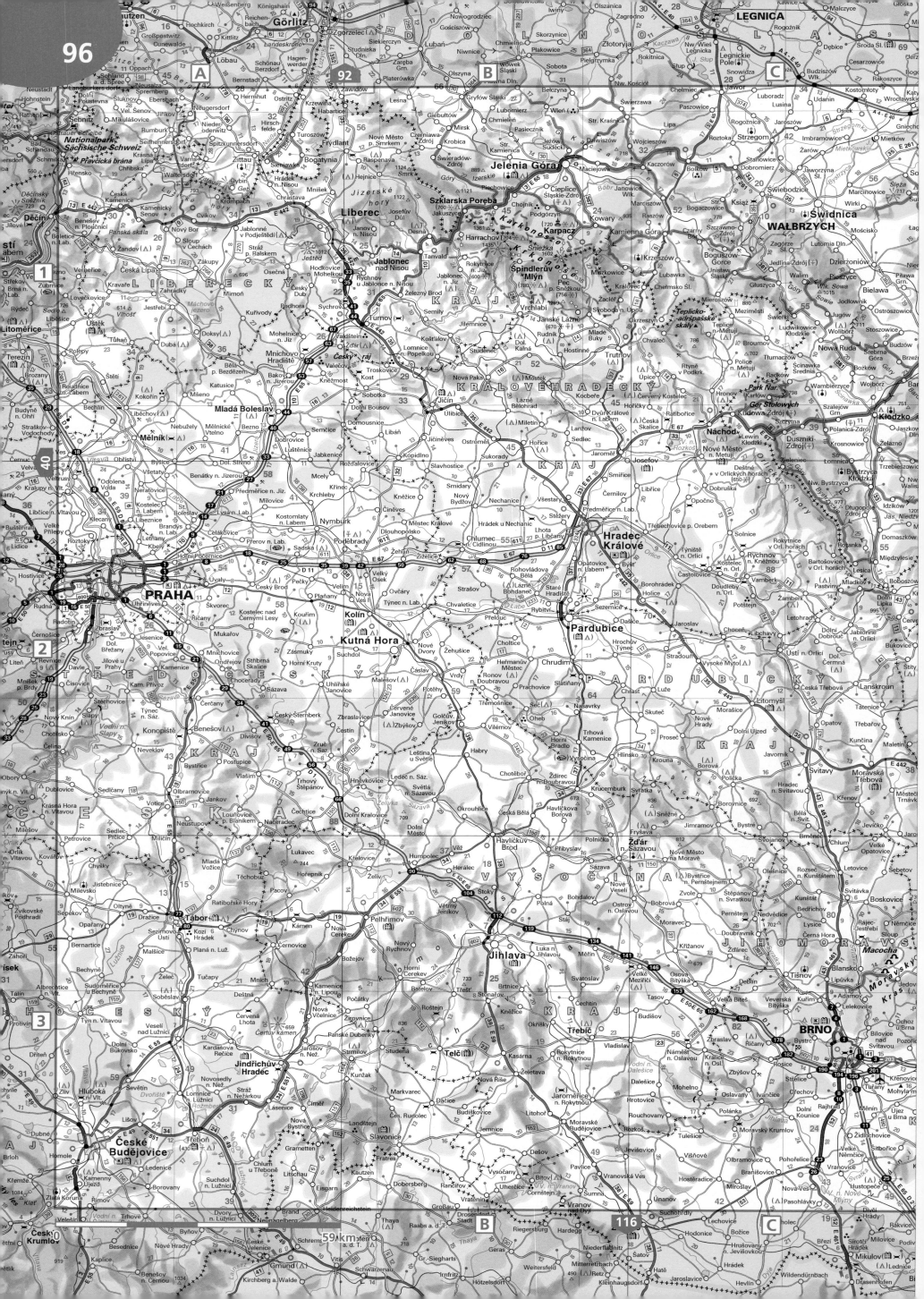

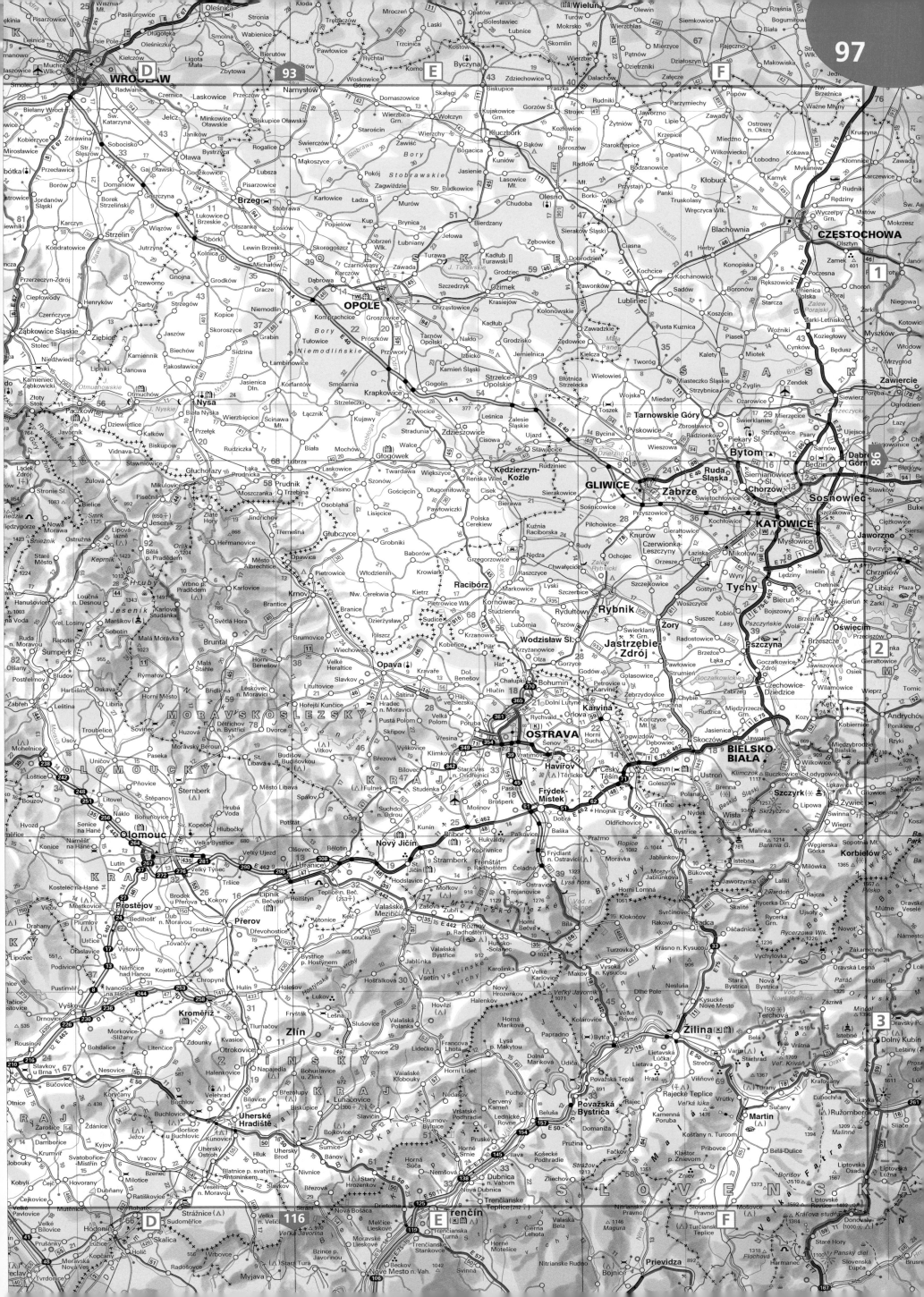

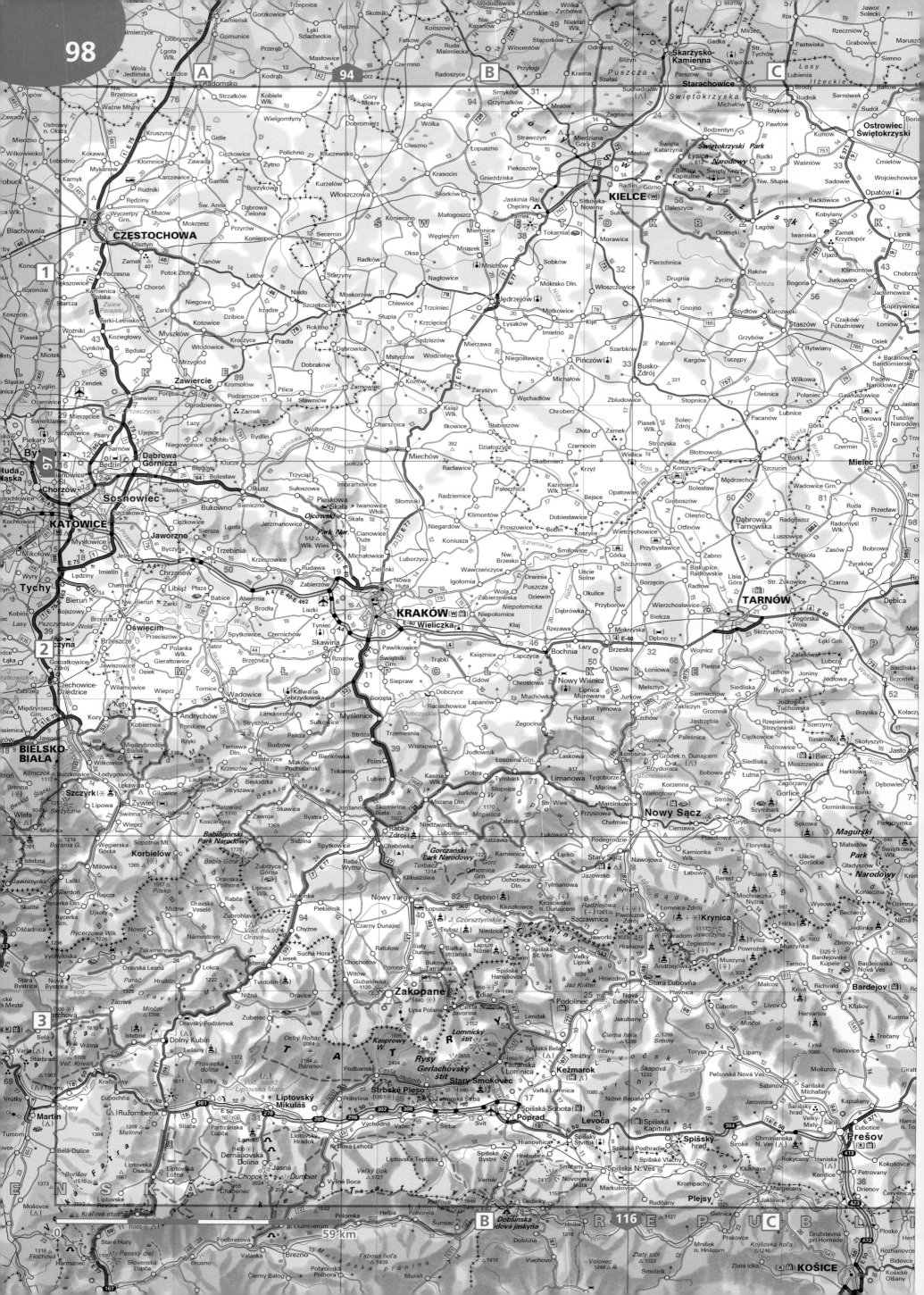

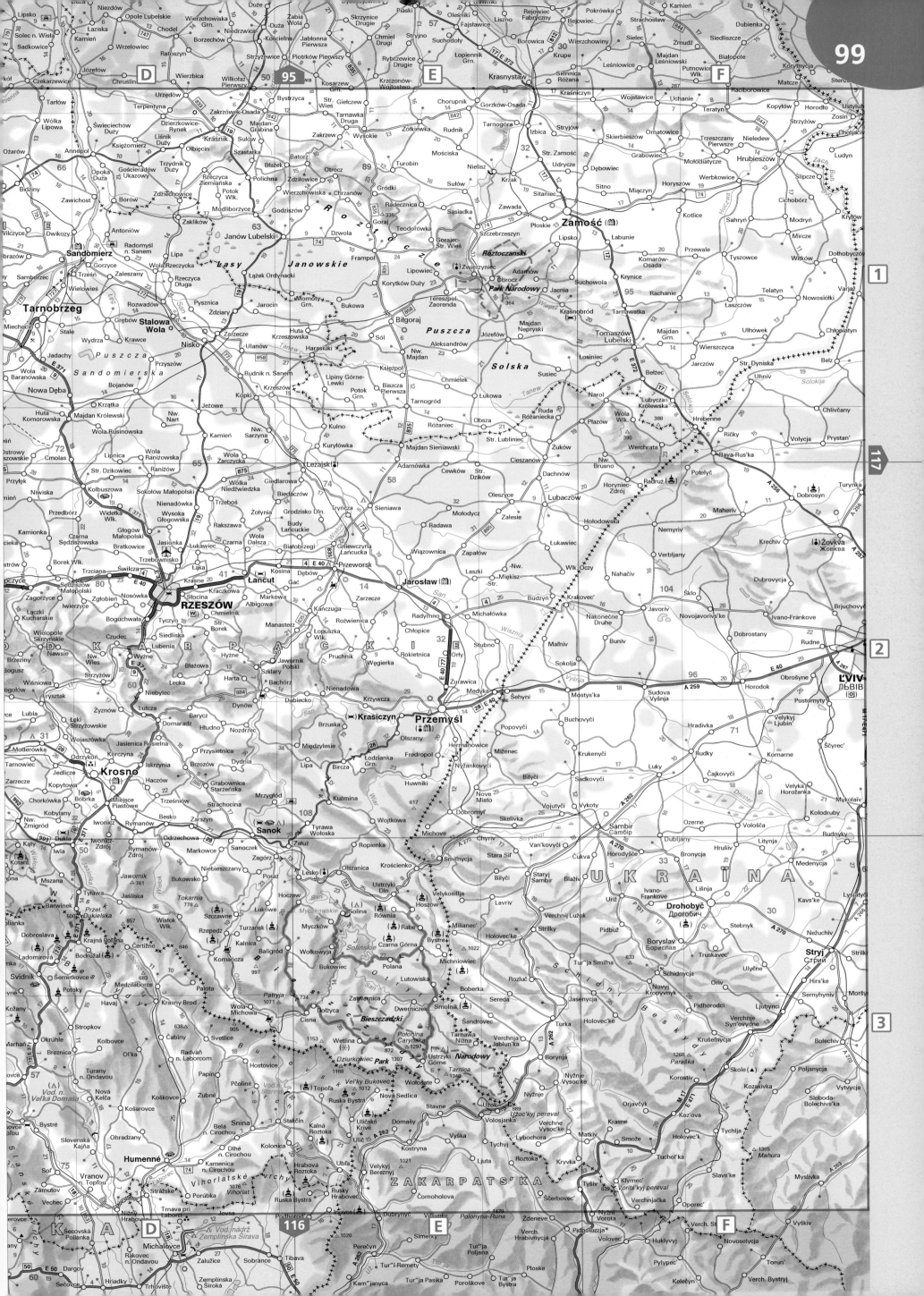

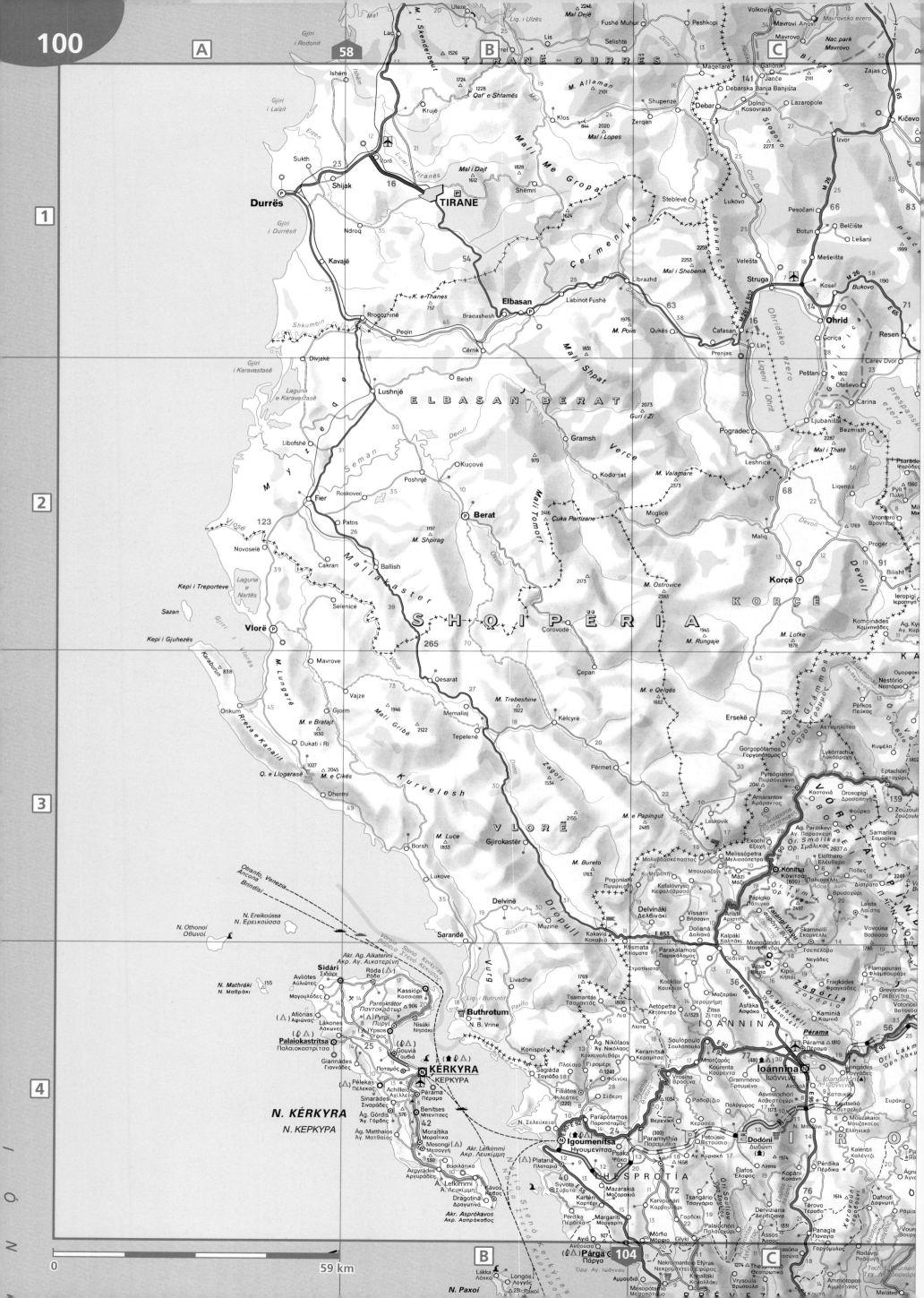

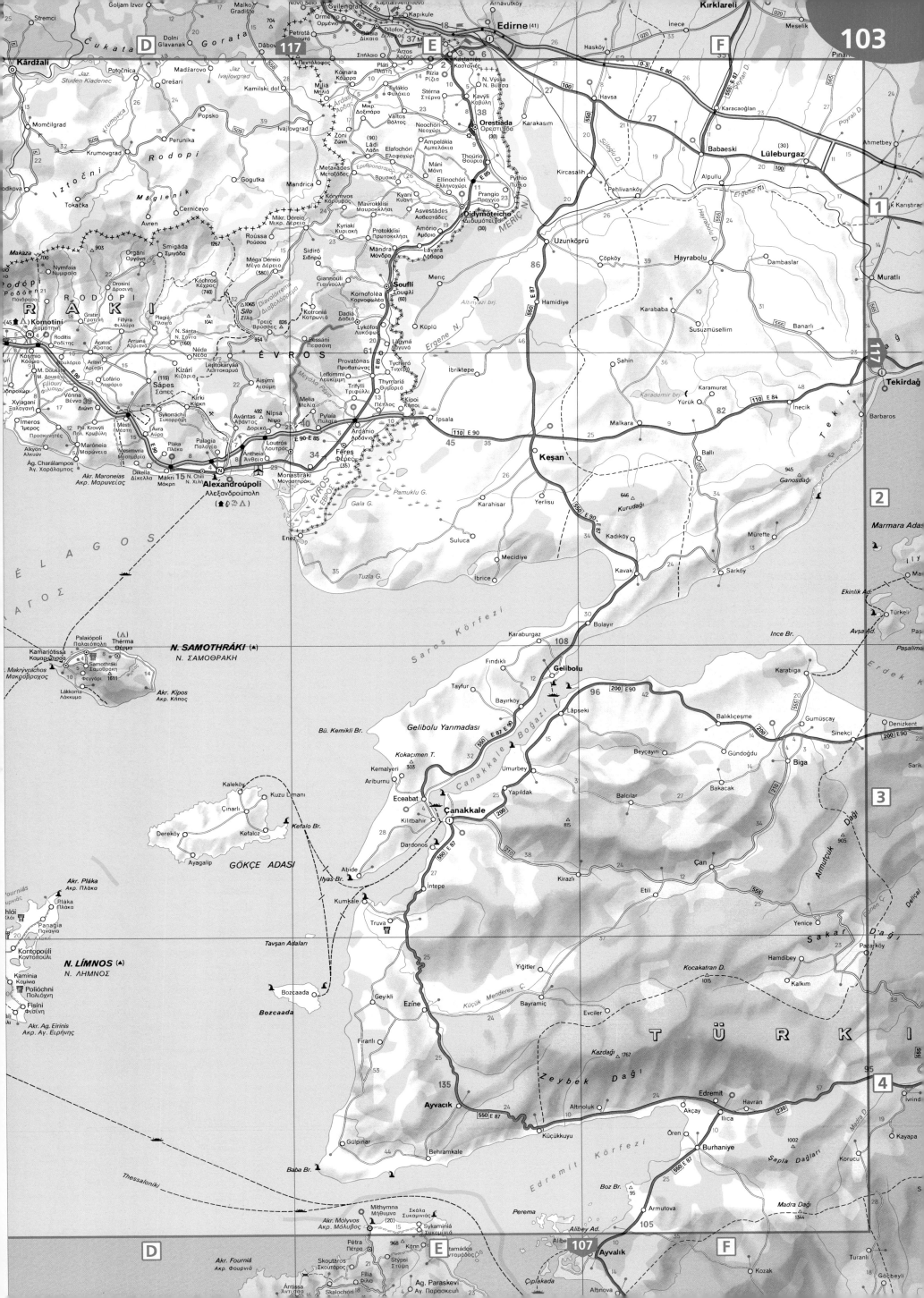

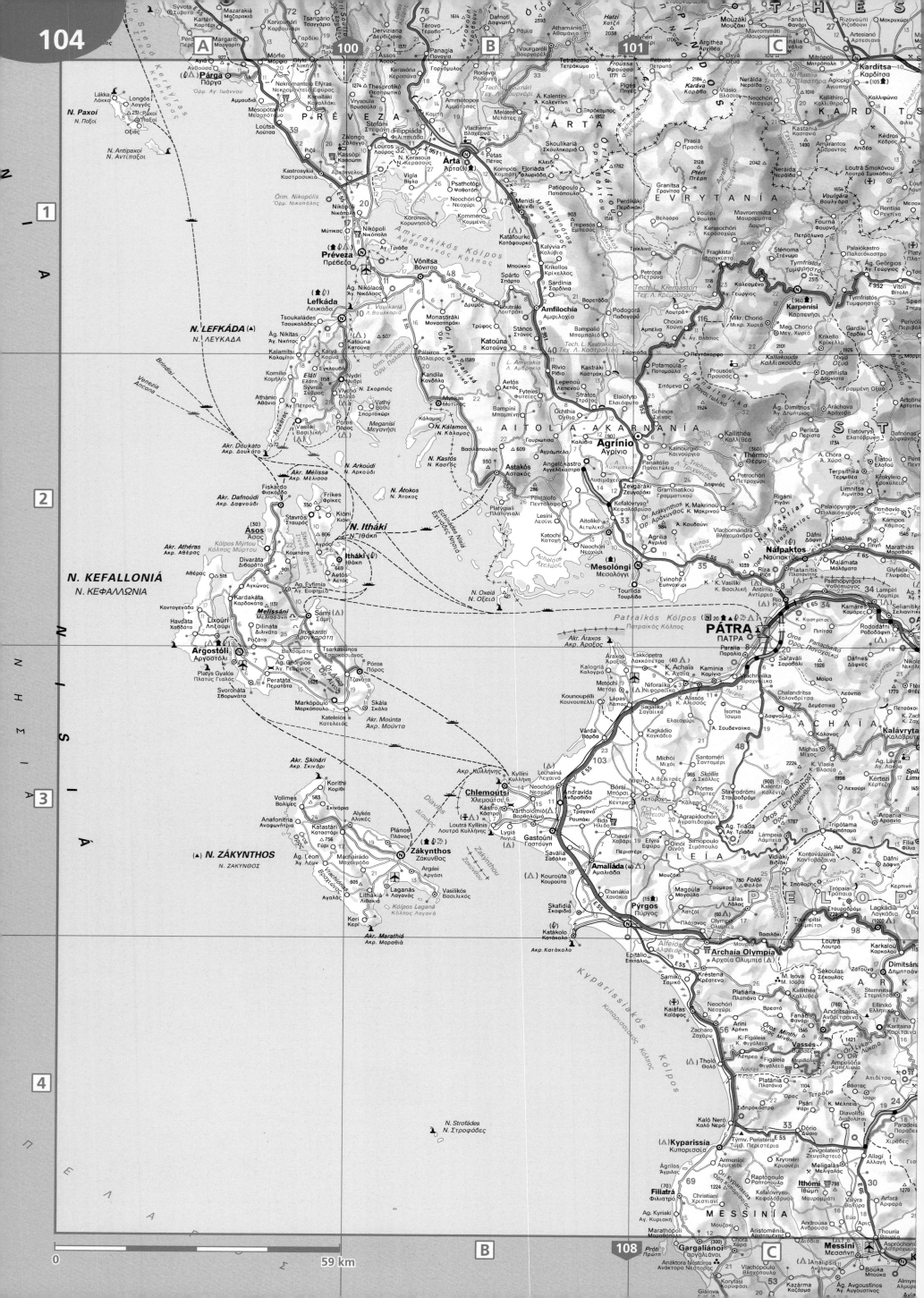

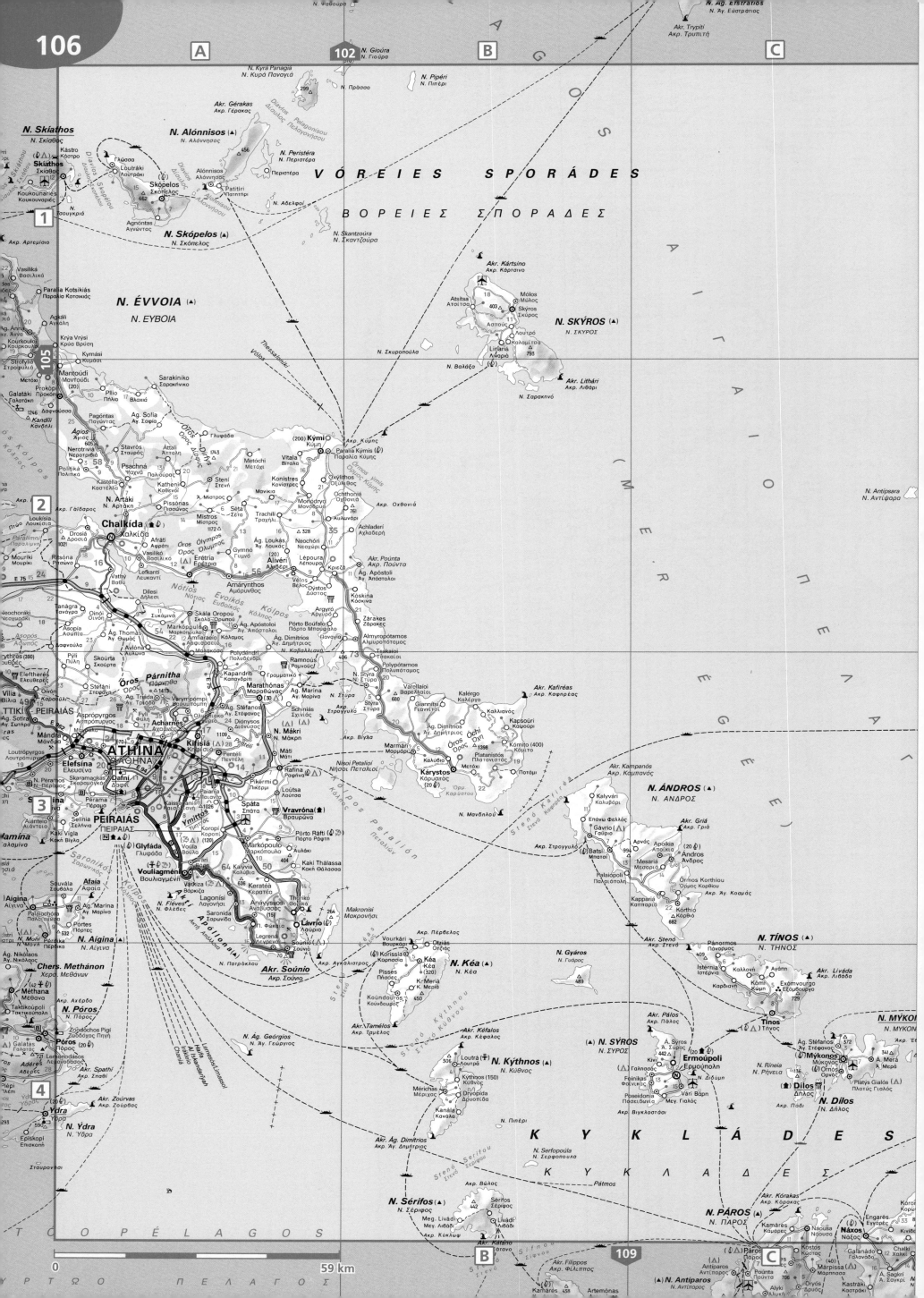

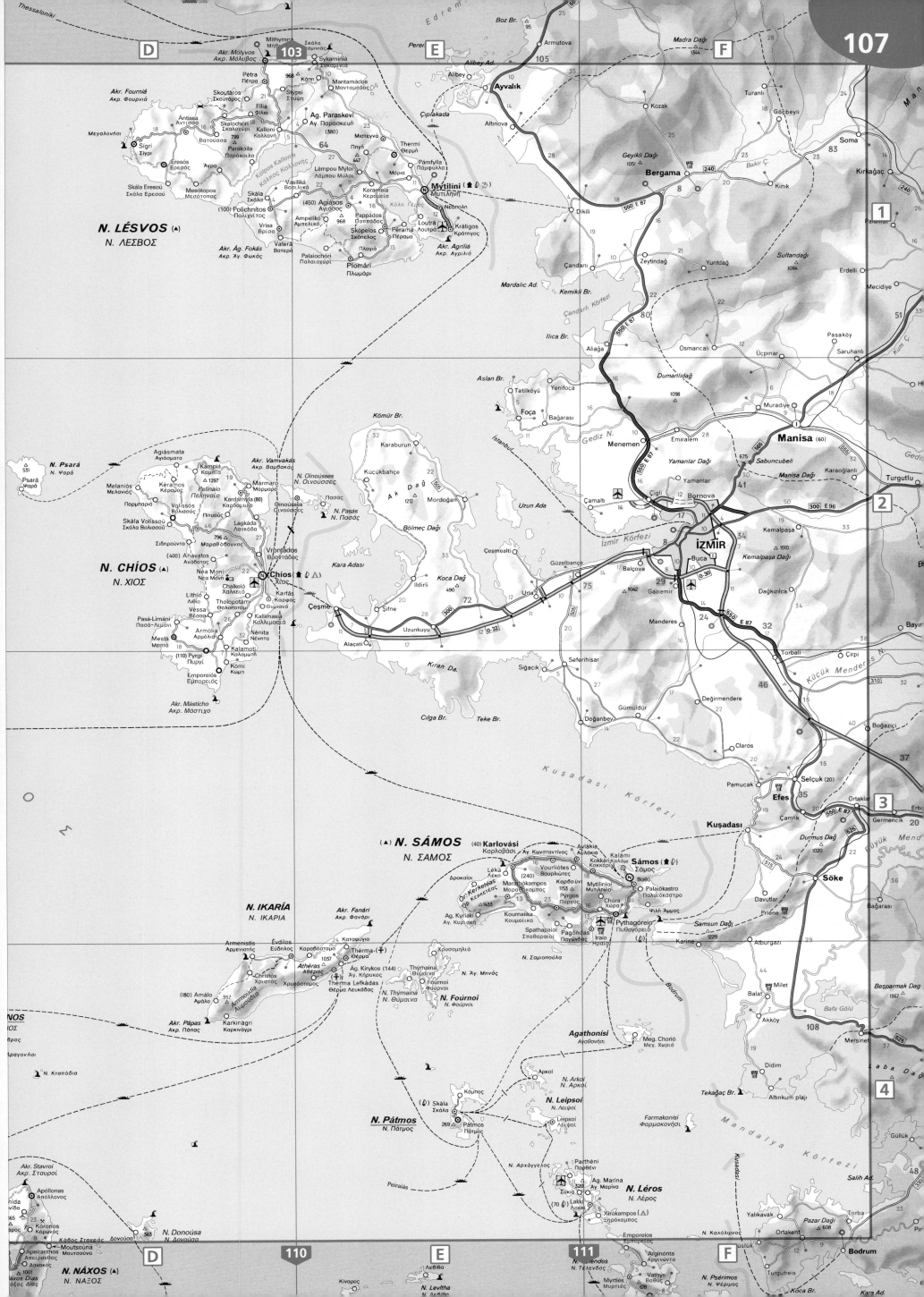

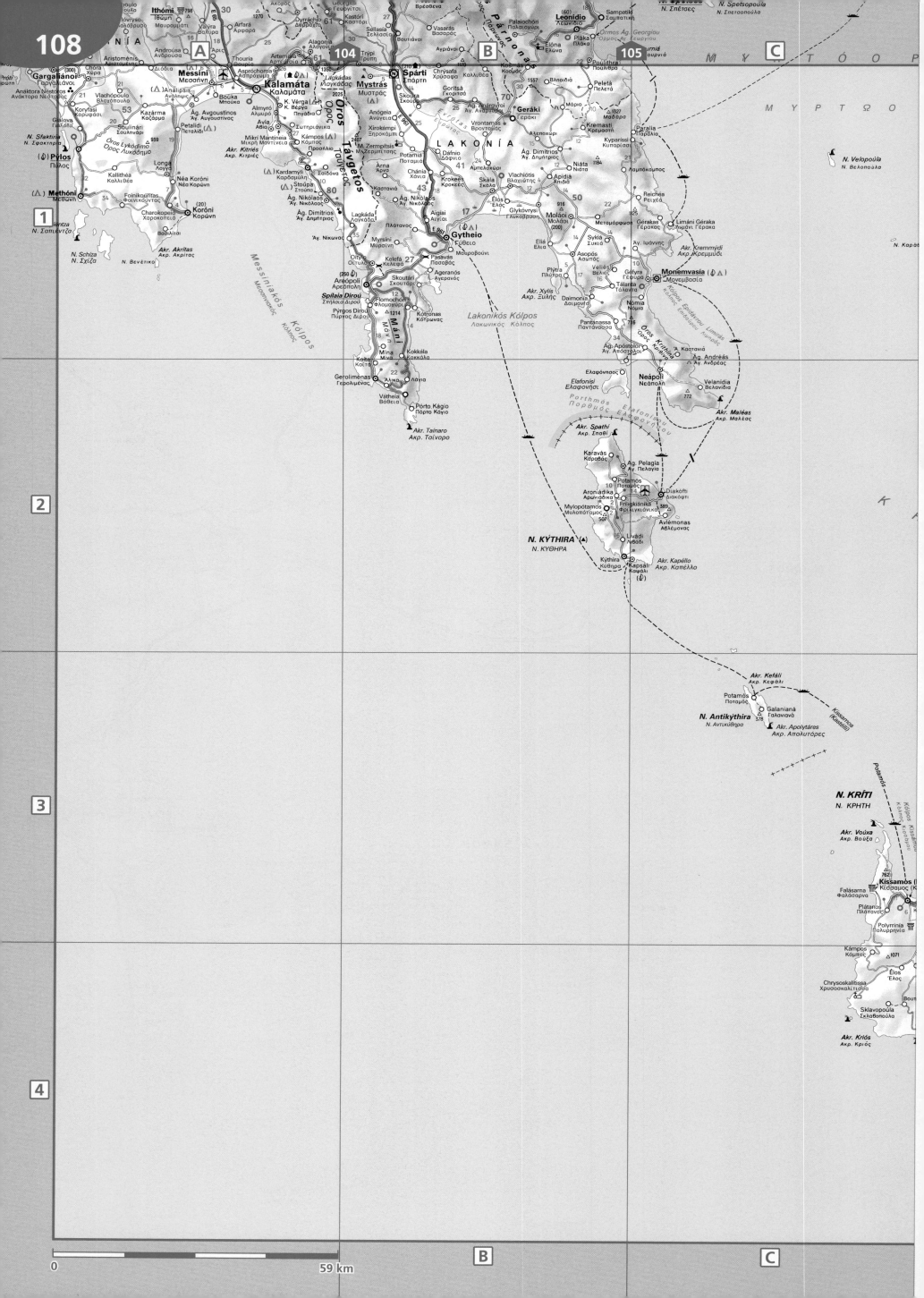

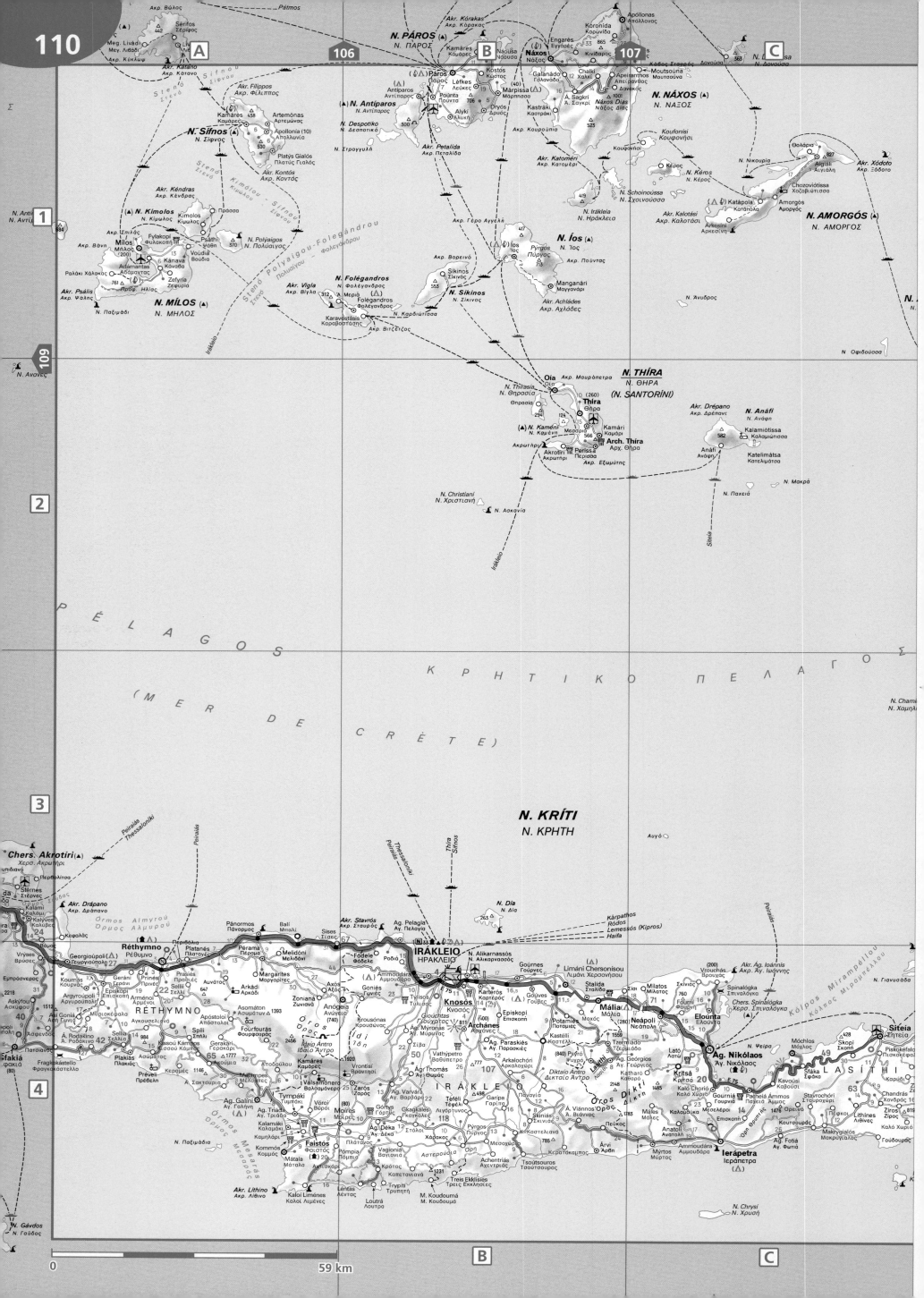

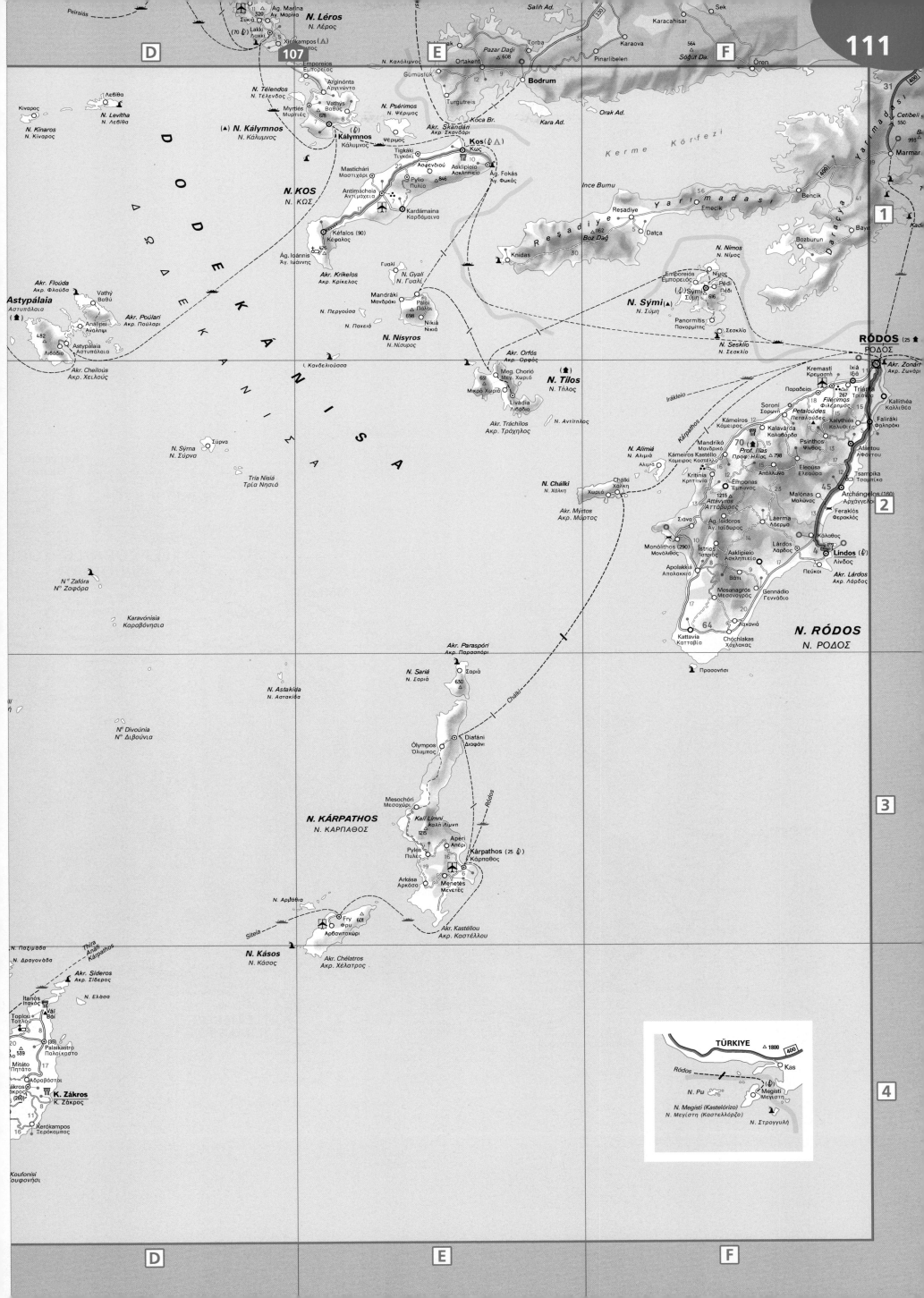

D 107

N. Léros
Ν. Λέρος

Peiraiás

Ag. Marina
Αγ. Μαρίνα
Sükiá
Lakki
Λακκί
320
(70)
Xirókampos
Ξηρόκαμπος

Emporeiós
Εμπορειός
Arginónta
Αργινώντα
N. Télendos
Ν. Τέλενδος
Arginónta
Vathýs
Βαθύς
Myrtiés
Μυρτιές
(Δ) N. Kálymnos
Ν. Κάλυμνος
Kálymnos
Κάλυμνος
Mastichári
Μαστιχάρι

Pazar Dağı
△ 608
Torba

Karacahisar

Sek

Karaova

Pinarlibelen

Soğut Da.

Ören

Bodrum

Gümüşlük

Ortakent

Turgutreis

Koca Br.

Kara Ad.

Orak Ad.

N. Psérimos
Ν. Ψέριμος
Psérimos
Ψέριμος
Akr. Skándári
Ακρ. Σκάνδάρι

Kerme Körfezi

Reşadiye Yarımadası

Ince Burnu

Boz Dağ
△

Reşadiye
Emecik
Bencik
Datça
Bozburun

Knidas

N. KOS
Ν. ΚΩΣ
Tigkáki
Τιγκάκι
Kos
Κως
Asfendioú
Ασφενδιού
Asklipieío
Ασκληπιείο
Ag. Fokás
Αγ. Φωκάς
Pylio
Πυλιό
846 △
Antimácheia
Αντιμάχεια
Kardámaina
Καρδάμαινα

Kéfalos (90)
Κέφαλος
Ag. Ioánnis
Αγ. Ιωάννης
Akr. Kríkelos
Ακρ. Κρίκελος

Gyalí
N. Gyalí
Ν. Γυαλί
Mandráki
Μανδράκι
Páloi
Πάλοι
Nikiá
Νικιά
N. Nisyros
Ν. Νίσυρος

N. Nímos
Ν. Νίμος
Emporeiós
Εμπορειός
N. Sými (Δ)
Ν. Σύμη
Sými
Σύμη
Pédi
Πέδι
Panormítis
Πανορμίτης

RÓDOS (25)
ΡΟΔΟΣ
Akr. Zonári
Ακρ. Ζωνάρι

N. Seskíio
Ν. Σεσκλίο

Astypálaia
Αστυπάλαια
Akr. Floúda
Ακρ. Φλούδα
Vathý
Βαθύ
Análipsi
Ανάληψη
Akr. Poúlari
Ακρ. Πούλαρι
Astypálaia
Αστυπάλαια
482
Livádio
Λιβάδιο
Akr. Cheiloús
Ακρ. Χειλούς

DODEKANISA
ΔΩΔΕΚΑΝΗΣΑ

Akr. Orfós
Ακρ. Ορφός

N. Tílos
Ν. Τήλος
Meg. Chorió
Μεγ. Χωριό
651
Mikró Chorió
Μικρό Χωριό
Livádia
Λιβάδια
Akr. Tráchilos
Ακρ. Τράχηλος
N. Antítplos
Ν. Αντίτηλος

ı. Kandelioússa
ı. Κανδελιούσσα

Kremasti
Κρεμαστή
Ixiá
Ιξιά
Triánta
Τριάντα
267
Filérimos
Φιλέριμος
Soroní
Σορωνή
Petaloúdes
Πεταλούδες
Paradeísi
Παραδείσι
Kalythiés
Καλυθιές
Faliráki
Φαλιράκι
Kallithéa
Καλλιθέα

Irákleio
Ηράκλειο

N. Alimiá
Ν. Αλιμιά
N. Chálki
Ν. Χάλκη
Chálki
Χάλκη
Akr. Mýrtos
Ακρ. Μύρτος

N. Syrna
Ν. Σύρνα
Sýrna
Σύρνα

Tría Nisiá
Τρία Νησιά

Kámeiros
Κάμειρος
Kalavárda
Καλαβάρδα
Mandrikó
Μανδρικό
Psinthos
Ψίνθος
Prof. Ilías
Προφ. Ηλίας
△ 798
Kámeiros Kastéllo
Κάμειρος Καστέλλο
Kritinía
Κρητηνία
Émponas
Έμπωνας
Attávyros
Αττάβυρος
1215 △
Apóllona
Απόλλωνα
Eleoúsa
Ελεούσα
Afántou
Αφάντου
Tsampíka
Τσαμπίκα
Malónas
Μαλώνας
45
Archángelos (160)
Αρχάγγελος
Siána
Σιάνα
Ag. Isídoros
Αγ. Ισίδωρος
Laérma
Λαέρμα
Feraklós
Φεράκλος
Monólithos (290)
Μονόλιθος
Istrios
Ιστριός
Asklipieío
Ασκληπιείο
Lárdos
Λάρδος
Kálathos
Κάλαθος
Apolakkiá
Απολακκιά
Váti
Βάτι
Líndos
Λίνδος
Peúkoi
Πεύκοι
Mesanagrós
Μεσαναγρός
Gennádio
Γεννάδιο
Akr. Lárdos
Ακρ. Λάρδος
64
Kattaviá
Καττάβια
Chóchlakas
Χόχλακας
Sáchania
Σαχανιά

N. RÓDOS
Ν. ΡΟΔΟΣ

Prasonísi
Πρασονήσι

Akr. Paraspóri
Ακρ. Παρασπόρι

N. Saría
Ν. Σαριά
Saría
Σαριά
630 △

N. Astakída
Ν. Αστακίδα

Nσ Divoúnia
Νσ Διβούνια

Diafáni
Διαφάνι
Ólympos
Όλυμπος

Nσ Zafóra
Νσ Ζαφόρα

Karavónisia
Καραβόνησια

Mesochóri
Μεσοχώρι
Kalí Limni
Καλή Λίμνη
1215
Apéri
Απέρι
N. KÁRPATHOS
Ν. ΚΑΡΠΑΘΟΣ
Pylés
Πυλές
Kárpathos (25)
Κάρπαθος
Arkása
Αρκάσα
Menetés
Μενετές

N. Arlidúa
Ν. Αρλιάδα
Fry
Φρυ
601
Ardanitóchári
Αρδανιτόχάρι
Siteía
Σιτεία
Akr. Kastéllou
Ακρ. Καστέλλου

Thíra
Θήρα
Anáfi
Ανάφι
Kárpathos
Κάρπαθος
N. Paximáda
Ν. Παξιμάδα
N. Kásos
Ν. Κάσος
Akr. Chélatros
Ακρ. Χέλατρος
Akr. Síderos
Ακρ. Σίδερος
N. Elássa
Ν. Ελάσσα
Itanós
Ιτανός
Vái
Βάι
Toploú
Τοπλού
Palaíkastro
Παλαίκαστρο
539 △
Mítato
Μήτατο
K. Zákros
Κ. Ζάκρος
Xerókampos
Ξερόκαμπος
Koufonísi
Κουφονήσι

TÜRKIYE
△ 1800

Ródos
Ρόδος
Kas

N. Ro
Ν. Ρω

N. Megísti (Kastelórizo)
Ν. Μεγίστη (Καστελλόριζο)
Megísti
Μεγίστη
N. Stroggylí
Ν. Στρογγυλή

D   E   F

1

Cape Apostolos Andreas

136 △
✝ Apostolos
Andreas

191 △

Rizokarpaso

241 △

Aigialousa

383 △

Agios
Andronikos

K A R P A S I A

Leonarisso   Vothylakas

Eptakomi   166 △

330 △   Koma
Davlos   Komi   toú Gialou

724 △   Patriki   **64**

Akanthou

Agios
Amvrosios   740 △   Agios Théodoros

Kalograia   Cape Elaia

819 △
Charkeia

30 △ 740   91 △
Trikomo   2

Lefkoníko   Gypsou   Lapathos

Kythrea   Milia   *Kastros*
Neo Chorio   *Kalamoullis*   AMMOCHOSTOS BAY
Trachoni   Peristérona
Exo   Limnia   Agios Sergios
Metochi   *Gerokolympos*
Palaikythro   Genagra   Limnia   Salamis
Angastina   Prastio   Styllói   Egkomi
Pediaios   **61**   Apostolos
Afanteia   47   Varnavas
Askeia   **Vatili**   Acheritou   **AMMOCHOSTOS / GAZIMAĞUSA**
Tymvou   140 △   **(FAMAGUSTA)**
Gialias   **Lysi**   Kalopsida   **Deryneia**
186 △   Tremetousia   Kontea   **45**
Geri   Arsos   Makrasyka   E 903   Frenaros
Potamia   Achna   **28**   Avgorou   **Paralimni**
Athienou   Troulloi   20   Sotira
350 △   *Dhekelia*   Pyla   Liopetri   174 △
Lympia   *Base*   Xylotymvou   Agia Napa
32   *Sovereign*   Ormideia   25
A 2   **Area**
20   Voroklini   17   Xylofagou
B 2   **A 3**   **B 3**   Cape Gkreko
Aradippou   19   **48**
Tremithos   Livadia   Agia Napa
29   **72**   **6**   LARNAKA BAY   Cape Pyla   3
yrga   Kalo Chorio   **B 5**
Hala Sultan   Cape Pyla
Tekkesi   *Salt Lake*
33   **LARNAKA**
A 5
(688)   **32**   **B 5**
Dromolaxia
Anglisides   Larnaka International Airport
Anafotida   Kiti
Perivolia
Mazotos   Cape Kiti

M E D I T E R R A N E A N   S E A

━━━ Ligne de démarcation - Green Line

⬥ Passage contrôlé - Check point

0 ━━━━━━━━━━ 20 km

4

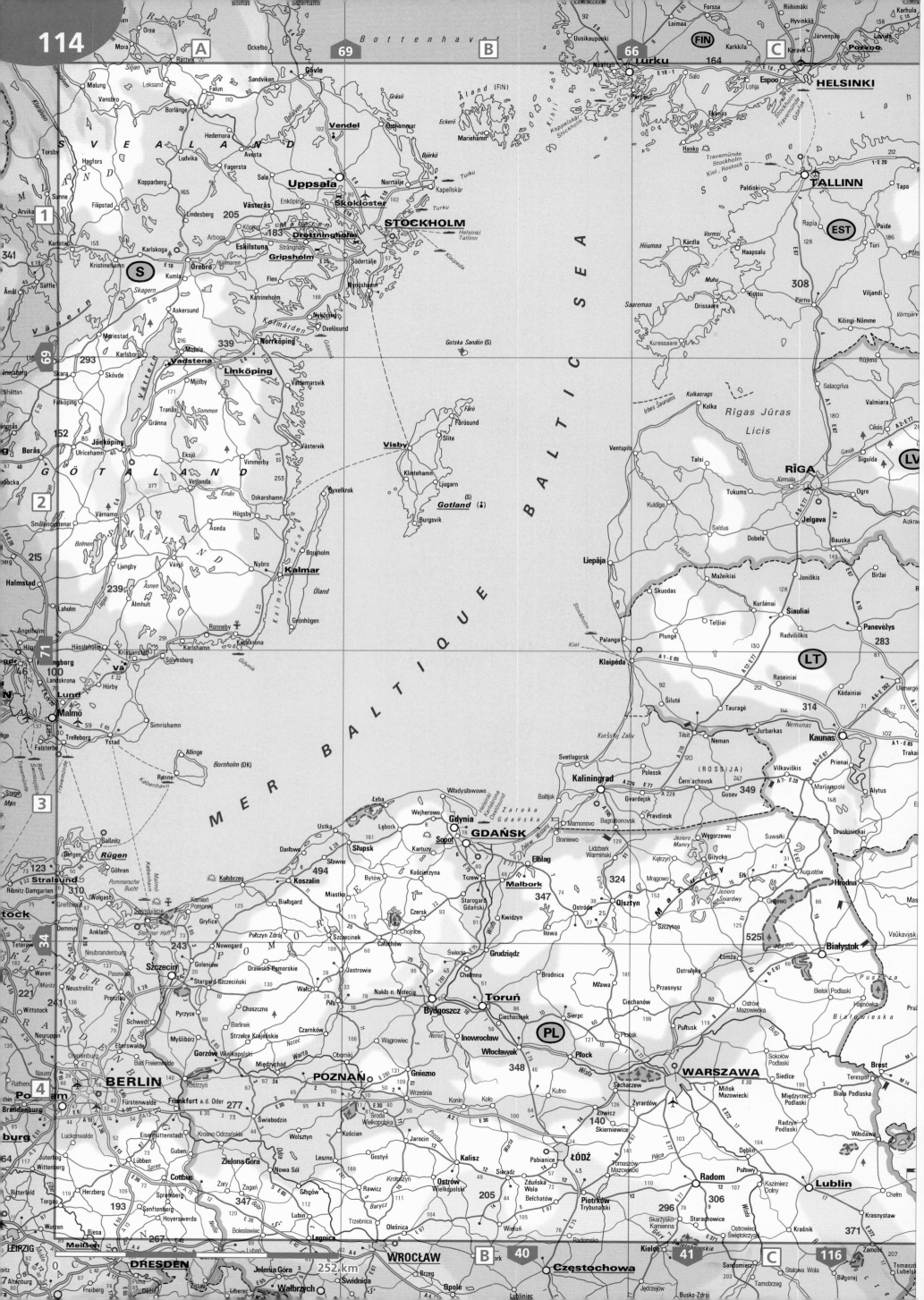

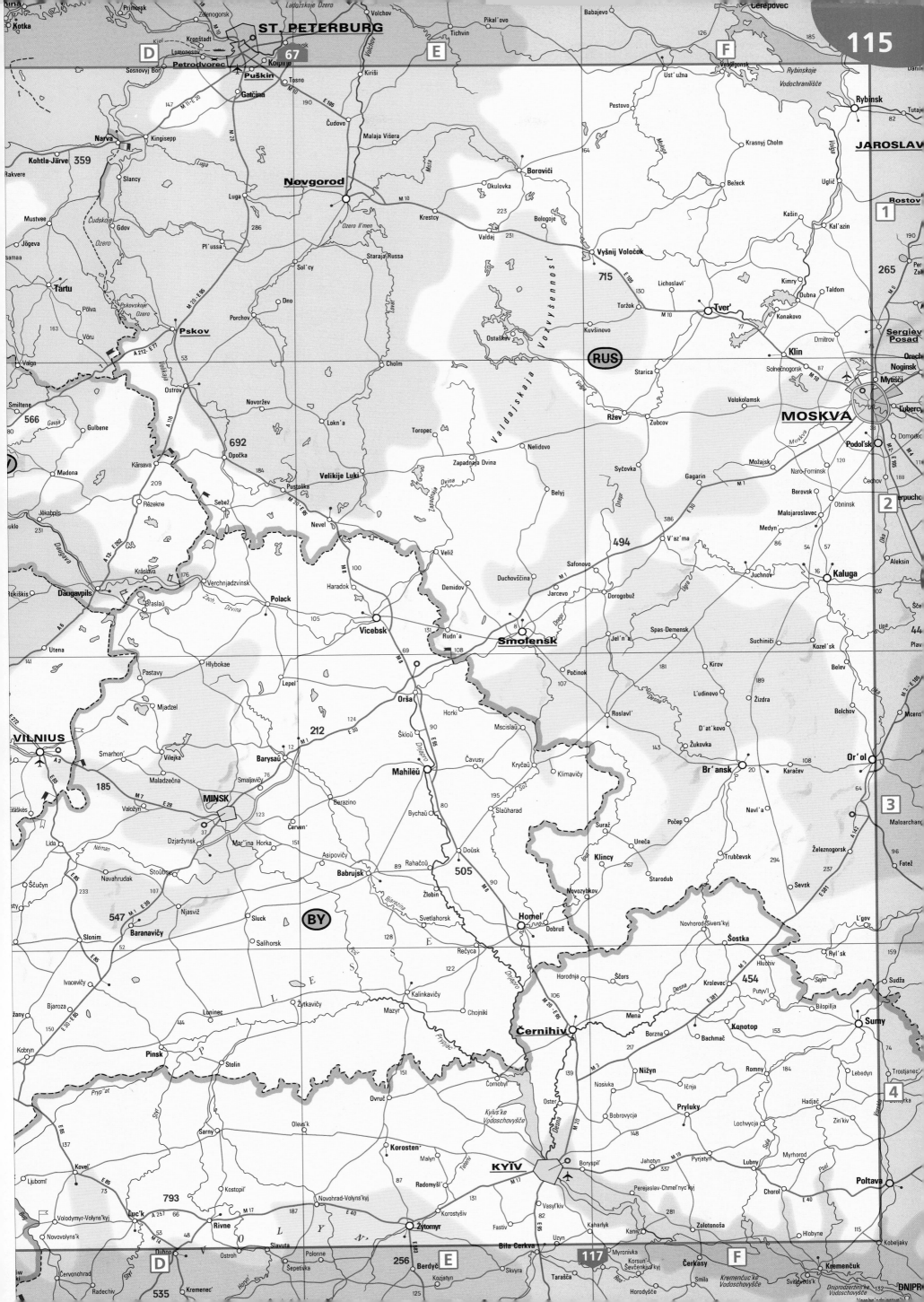

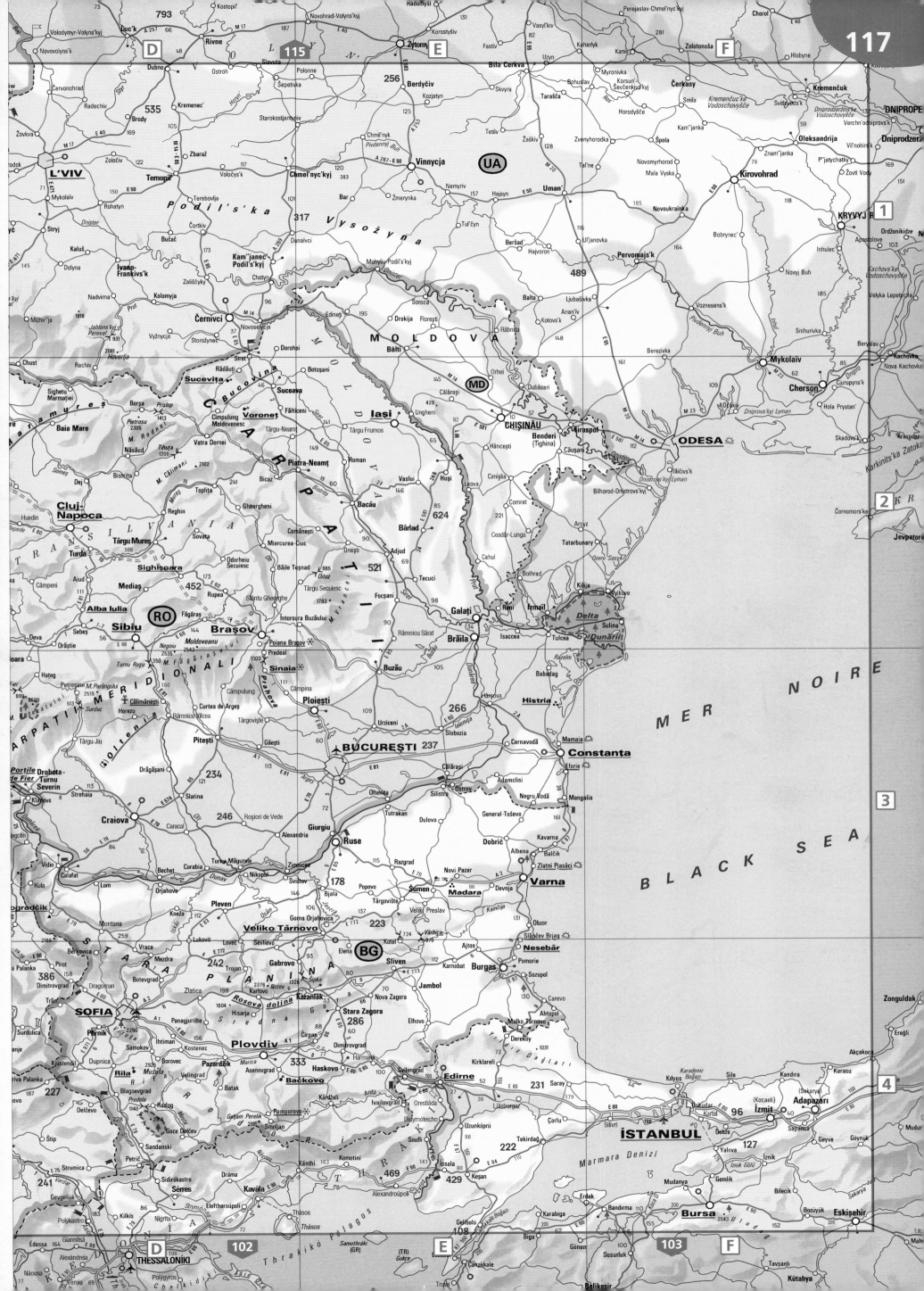

A

A Baiuca *E*	18	A2
A Cañiza *E*	18	A3
A Coruña *E*	18	A2
A. Drossiní *GR*	103	D1
A Estrada *E*	18	A2
A Fonsagrada *E*	18	C2
A Guarda *E*	18	A3
A Gudiña *E*	18	B3
Á. Hóra *GR*	104	C2
Á. Kalendíni *GR*	104	B1
Á. Kaliníki *GR*	101	D2
Á. Laracha *E*	18	A2
Á. Lefkími *GR*	100	A4
Á. Melás *GR*	101	D2
Á. Merá *GR*	106	C4
A Merca *E*	18	B3
A Mezquita *E*	18	B3
A Pobra do Caraminâl *E*	18	A2
Á. Polidéndri *GR*	101	F4
A. Pontenova *E*	18	C2
A. Poróia *GR*	101	F1
A Ramallosa *E*	18	A3
Á. Rodákino *GR*	109	D4
A Rúa *E*	18	C3
Á. Sangrí *GR*	109	F1
Á. Síros *GR*	106	C4
A Veiga *E*	18	C3
Á. Viános *GR*	109	F4
Á. Vrondoú *GR*	102	A1
Á. Zervohóri *GR*	101	E2
Aa *EE*	73	E2
Aachen *D*	13	D1
Aakre *EE*	79	D1
Aalen *D*	38	C4
Aalsmeer *NL*	32	B4
Aalst *B*	12	B1
Aalten *NL*	37	D1
Aalter *B*	12	B1
Äänekoski *FIN*	69	D2
Aapajärvi *FIN*	65	D1
Aarau *CH*	17	E1
Aarberg *CH*	17	E2
Aarburg *CH*	17	E1
Aardla *EE*	79	E1
Aarna *EE*	79	E1
Aarschot *B*	12	C1
Ääsmäe *EE*	72	B2
Aaspere *EE*	73	D1
Aavasaksa *FIN*	64	C2
Aavere *EE*	73	D2
Abades *E*	25	F1
Abadiño *E*	20	A2
Abanilla *E*	26	C4
Abano Terme *I*	47	E1
Abavnieki *LV*	77	D3
Abbadia S. Salvatore *I*	47	E4
Abbasanta *I*	50	A3
Abbeville *F*	11	F2
Abbey Town *GB*	7	D3
Abbeyfeale *IRL*	2	B4
Abbeyleix / Mainistir Laoise *IRL*	2	C3
Abbiategrasso *I*	17	F3
Abborrträsk *S*	64	B2
Abbots Bromley *GB*	9	D1
Abbotsbury *GB*	8	C4
Abcoude *NL*	32	B4
Abejar *E*	20	A4
Abejuela *E*	26	C2
Abela *P*	24	A4
Åbele *LV*	76	D1
Åbeles *LV*	81	D1
Åbelite *LV*	77	F3
Abelvær *N*	63	D2
Abenberg *D*	39	D4
Abenójar *E*	25	F3
Åbenrå *DK*	70	B3
Abensberg *D*.	39	E4
Aberaeron *GB*	3	F4
Aberdare / Aberdâr *GB*	8	C2
Aberdaron *GB*	3	E3
Aberdeen *GB*	5	F1
Aberdovey / Aberdyfi *GB*	3	F4
Aberfeldy *GB*	4	C4
Aberfoyle *GB*	6	C1
Abergavenny / Y-Fenni *GB*	8	C2
Abergele *GB*	3	F3
Aberlady *GB*	7	D1
Abermaw / Barmouth *GB*	3	F4
Aberporth *GB*	3	E4
Abersoch *GB*	3	F3
Abertillery *GB*	8	C2
Aberystwyth *GB*	3	F4
Abetone *I*	47	D2
Abiego *E*	20	C4
Abingdon *GB*	9	D3
Abington *GB*	7	D2
Abisko *S*	60	C3
Abja-Paluoja *EE*	78	C1
Abja-Vanamõisa *EE*	78	C1
Abla *E*	30	A3
Ablis *F*	11	F4
Abolai *LT*	86	C3
Åboliņi *LV*	78	C2
Abondance *F*	17	D2
Abony *H*	116	C2
Aboyne *GB*	5	D4
Abrantes *P*	24	B2
Abreschviller *F*	13	E4

Abriès *F*	17	E4
Abromiškes *LT*	85	F2
Abtenau *A*	44	C2
Åby *S*	67	E3
Åbybro *DK*	70	B2
Acceglio *I*	23	D1
Accettura *I*	49	E4
Acciaroli *I*	49	D4
Accous *F*	20	C3
Accrington *GB*	7	E4
Acebo *E*	24	C2
Acedo *E*	20	A3
Acehúche *E*	25	D2
Acerno *I*	49	D4
Acerra *I*	48	C3
Aceuchal *E*	25	D3
Achenkirch *A*	43	F2
Achern *D*	13	F4
Acheux-en-Amiénois *F*	11	A2
Achim *D*	33	E3
Achnacroish *GB*	4	B4
Achnasheen *GB*	4	B3
Aci Castello *I*	53	E4
Aci Trezza *I*	53	E4
Acireale *I*	53	E4
Acle *GB*	9	F1
Acokavai *LT*	81	E3
Acone *LV*	77	F3
Acqualagna *I*	47	F3
Acquapendente *I*	47	E4
Acquasanta Terme *I*	48	B2
Acquasparta *I*	47	F4
Acquaviva delle Fonti *I*	49	E3
Acqui Terme *I*	17	F4
Acri *I*	51	D2
Ada *SRB*	56	C1
Adak *S*	64	B2
Adakavas *LT*	80	C3
Adámandas *GR*	109	E1
Adamclisi *RO*	117	E1
Ādami *LV*	81	D1
Adamova (Odumova) *LV*	83	E1
Adamów (Lubelskie) *PL*	99	F1
Adamówka *PL*	99	E2
Adamuz *E*	25	E4
Adanero *E*	25	F1
Adapazarı *TR*	117	F4
Adare *IRL*	2	B3
Adaševci *SRB*	55	F3
Adavere *EE*	72	C3
Adaži *LV*	77	F3
Adelboden *CH*	17	E2
Adelfia *I*	49	F3
Adelsheim *D*	38	C4
Ademuz *E*	26	C2
Adenau *D*	13	E1
Adendro *GR*	101	F2
Adiste *EE*	79	E1
Adjud *RO*	117	E2
Admont *A*	45	D2
Adolfsström *S*	64	A2
Adorf *D*	39	E2
Adra *E*	30	A3
Adradas *E*	20	A4
Adraku *EE*	73	E3
Adrall *E*	21	E3
Adrano *I*	53	D3
Adria *I*	47	E1
Aduliena *LV*	79	D3
Adutiškis *LT*	87	D1
Ādžūni *LV*	81	F2
Aegviidu *EE*	72	C2
Ænes *N*	66	A1
Aerinó *GR*	105	D1
Ærøskøbing *DK*	70	B4
Aetópetra *GR*	100	C4
Aetós *GR*	101	D2
Aetós (Etolía-Akarnanía) *GR*	104	B2

Aetós (Kefaloniá) *GR*	104	A2
Äetsä *FIN*	68	C3
Afándou *GR*	111	F2
Åfarnes *N*	62	B3
Aféa *GR*	105	F3
Affi *I*	43	F4
Afiónas *GR*	100	A4
Áfissos *GR*	105	E1
Áfitos *GR*	102	A3
Afjord *N*	62	C2
Aflenz Kurort *A*	45	D1
Afráti *GR*	105	E1
Ag. Ána *GR*	105	E1
Ag. Ána *GR*	105	E2
Ág. Anárgiri *GR*	101	E4
Ág. Andónios *GR*	101	F2
Ág. Andréas *GR*	105	D4
Ág. Apóstoli *GR*	106	A2
Ág. Apóstoli *GR*	105	F2
Ág. Apóstoli *GR*	108	C1
Ág. Athanássios *GR*	102	B2
Ág. Athanássios *GR*	101	D2
Ág. Avgoustínos *GR*	108	A1
Ág. Déka *GR*	109	E4
Ág. Dimítrios *GR*	101	E3
Ág. Dimítrios *GR*	104	C2
Ág. Dimítrios *GR*	108	B1
Ág. Efimía *GR*	104	A2
Ág. Efstrátios (Nissí) *GR*	102	C4
Ág. Efthímía *GR*	105	D2
Ág. Fokás *GR*	111	E1
Ág. Fotiá *GR*	110	C4
Ág. Galíni *GR*	109	E4
Ág. Geórgios *GR*	105	E1
Ág. Geórgios *GR*	104	A3
Ág. Geórgios *GR*	109	F4

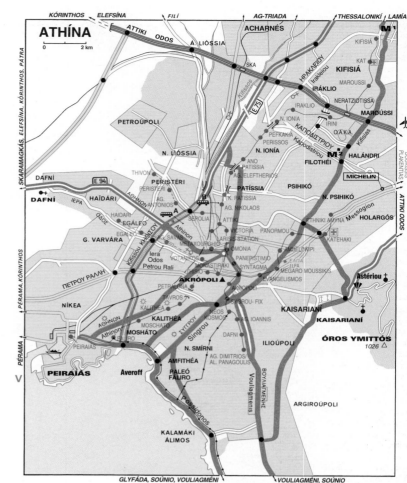

ATHÍNA

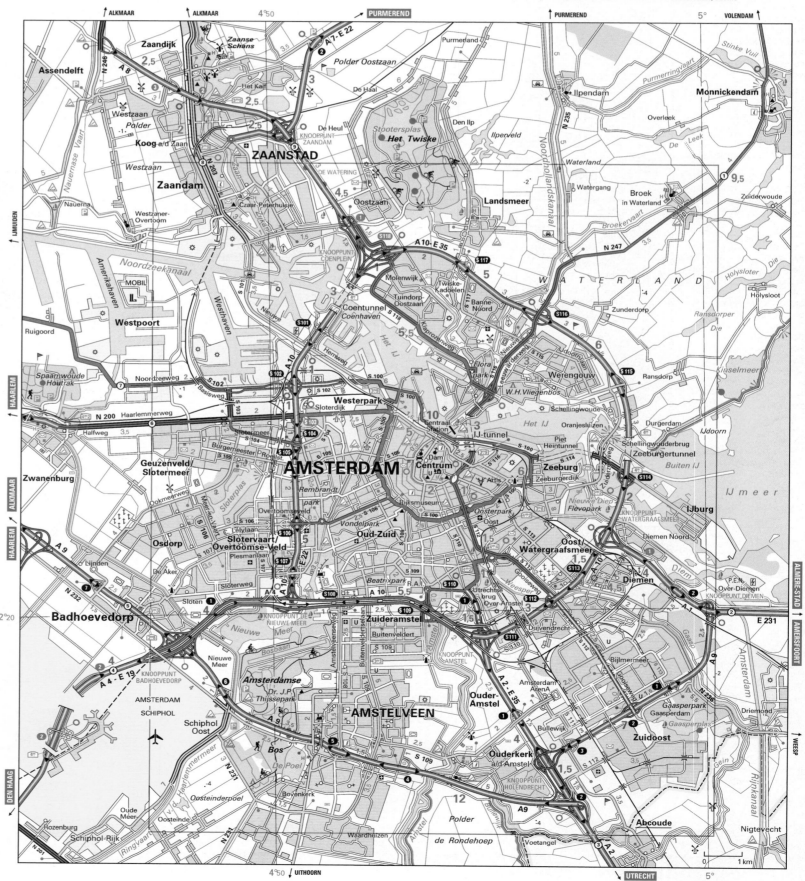

AMSTERDAM

Ág. Geórgios (Fthiótida) GR....104 C2
Ág. Geórgios (Nissí) GR....105 F4
Ág. Germanós GR....101 D2
Ág. Górdis GR....100 B4
Ág. Harálambos GR....103 D2
Ág. Ioánis GR....101 F4
Ág. Ioánis GR....109 D4
Ág. Ioánis (Korinthía) GR....105 E3
Ág. Ioánis (Magnissía) GR....105 E1
Ág. Ioánis (Viotía) GR....105 E3
Ág. Issídoros GR....111 F3
Ag. Kiriakí GR....101 D2
Ag. Kiriakí GR....107 E3
Ag. Kiriakí GR....104 C4
Ag. Kírikos GR....107 E4
Ág. Konstandínos GR....101 E4
Ág. Konstandínos GR....105 E2
Ág. Kosmás GR....102 C2
Ág. Kosmás GR....101 D3
Ág. Léon GR....104 A3
Ág. Loukás GR....105 F2
Ág. Mámas GR....102 A3
Ág. Marína GR....107 F4
Ág. Marína GR....109 D3
Ág. Marína (Attikí-Piréas) GR....105 F3
Ag. Marína (Fthiótida) GR....105 D1
Ag. Marína (N. Égina) GR....105 F3
Ág. Márkos GR....101 F1
Ág. Mathéos GR....100 B4
Ág. Mironas GR....109 F4
Ág. Nikítas GR....104 A1
Ág. Nikólaos GR....102 A3
Ág. Nikólaos GR....100 B4
Ág. Nikólaos GR....104 B1
Ág. Nikólaos GR....108 B1
Ág. Nikólaos GR....108 A1
Ág. Nikólaos GR....110 C4
Ág. Nikólaos (Atikí-Piréas) GR....105 E4
Ág. Nikólaos (Fokída) GR....105 D2
Ág. Nikólaos (Fthiótida) GR....105 E2
Ág. Pandeleímonas GR....101 D2
Ag. Paraskeví GR....101 F1
Ag. Paraskeví GR....102 B2
Ag. Paraskeví GR....100 C3
Ag. Paraskeví GR....107 E1
Ag. Paraskiés GR....109 F4
Ág. Pávlos GR....101 F3
Ág. Pelagía GR....108 B2
Ág. Pelagía GR....109 F4
Ág. Pétros GR....105 D4
Ág. Pnévma GR....102 A1
Ág. Pródromos GR....102 A3
Ág. Rouméli GR....109 D4
Ag. Sofía (Arkadía) GR....105 D4
Ág. Sofía (Évia) GR....105 F2
Ág. Sóstis GR....105 D1
Ág. Sotíra GR....105 E3
Ág. Stéfanos GR....105 F3
Ág. Stéfanos GR....106 C4
Ág. Theódori GR....101 D3
Ág. Theódori (Korinthía) GR....105 E3
Ág. Theódori (Magnissía) GR....105 E1
Ág. Thomás GR....105 F2
Ág. Thomás GR....109 F4
Ág. Triáda GR....101 F3
Ág. Triáda GR....105 F3
Ág. Triáda GR....104 C3
Ág. Varvára GR....109 F4
Ág. Vassílios GR....101 F2
Ág. Vassílios GR....105 E3
Ág. Vissários GR....105 D1
Agathoníssi GR....107 F4
Agay F....23 D2
Agazzano I....46 C1
Agde F....22 A2
Agen F....21 D1
Ageníškis LT....82 B2
Áger E....21 D4
Ageranós GR....108 B1
Agerbæk DK....70 B3
Aggius I....50 A2
Aggsbach A....45 D1
Agiá GR....101 F4
Agía Lávra GR....104 C3
Agía Triáda GR....109 E4
Agíasma GR....102 C2
Agiásmata GR....107 D2
Agiássos GR....107 E1
Ágio Óros GR....102 B3
Agiófilo GR....101 D4
Agiókambos GR....101 F4
Agiókambos GR....105 E1
Agionóri GR....105 E3
Agiopigí GR....104 C1
Agira I....53 D3
Aglona LV....83 E2
Aglonas Stacija LV....83 E2
Ágnanda GR....100 C4
Agnanderó GR....101 E4
Agnandi GR....105 E2
Agnóndas GR....105 F1
Agnone I....48 C3

Agolada E....18 B2
Agon-Coutainville F....11 D3
Agorá GR....102 B1
Agordo I....44 B3
Agost E....26 C4
Agra LV....78 B3
Agramunt E....21 D4
Agrate Brianza I....43 D4
Ágreda E....20 A4
Agreliá GR....101 E4
Agriá GR....105 E1
Agrigento I....52 C3
Agriliá GR....104 C2
Agrínio GR....104 C2
Agriovótano GR....105 E3
Agro LV....81 E1
Agropoli I....49 D4
Ágskaret N....60 A4
Aguadulce E....29 E3
Aguadulce E....30 A3
Aguaviva E....27 D1
Agudo E....25 E3
Águeda P....24 B1
Aguiar P....24 B4
Aguiar da Beira P....24 C1
Aguilafuente E....25 F1
Aguilar de Campóo E....19 E3
Aguilar de la Frontera E....29 E2
Aguilar del Alfambra E....26 C1
Águilas E....30 B3
Agurkiške LT....85 E2
Aharnés GR....105 F3
Ahaste EE....72 A3

Ahaus D....37 E1
Åheim N....62 A4
Ahendriás GR....109 F4
Ahigal E....25 D2
Ahílio GR....100 B4
Ahílio GR....101 F4
Ahinós GR....102 A2
Ahja EE....79 E1
Ahladerí GR....106 B2
Ahladohóri GR....102 A1
Ahlainen FIN....68 C3
Ahlbeck D....34 C2
Ahlen D....37 E1
Ahlhorn D....33 D4
Ahrensbök D....33 F2
Ahrensburg D....33 F2
Ahrweiler D....13 E4
Ähtäri FIN....69 D2
Ahtopol BG....117 E4
Ahula EE....72 C2
Ahun F....15 F3
Åhus S....71 D3
Ahvenselkä FIN....65 E1
Aidenbach D....39 F4
Aidone I....53 D3
Aidonia GR....105 D3
Aidu (Jõgeva) EE....73 D3
Aidu (Viljandi) EE....78 C1
Aigen im Mühlkreis A....40 C4
Aigle CH....17 E2

Aignan F....20 C2
Aignay-le-Duc F....16 C1
Aigre F....15 D3
Aigrefeuille-d'Aunis F....14 C3
Aigrefeuille-sur-Maine F....14 C2
Aigua Blava E....21 F4
Aiguebelette-le-Lac F....17 D3
Aiguebelle F....17 E3
Aigueperse F....16 A3
Aigues-Mortes F....22 A2
Aiguilles F....17 E4
Aiguillon F....21 D1
Aigurande F....15 F2
Ailefroide F....17 D4
Aillant-sur-Tholon F....16 A1
Ailly-le-Haut-Clocher F....12 A2
Ailly-sur-Noye F....12 A2
Aime F....17 D3
Ainaži LV....79 E3
Ainaži LV....77 F1
Ainhoa F....28 B2
Aínsa E....20 C3
Ainsdale GB....7 D4
Ainzón E....20 B4
Airaines F....12 A2
Airasca I....17 E4
Airdrie GB....7 D1
Aire-sur-la-Lys F....12 A1
Aire-sur-l'Adour F....20 C2
Airisto FIN....68 C4
Aïrites (Kuldigas) LV....76 C3
Aïrites (Saldus) LV....80 C1

Aïrites (Tukuma) LV....77 D3
Airolo CH....17 F2
Airvault F....15 D2
Aistere LV....80 B1
Aiterhofen D....39 F4
Aitrach D....43 E2
Aiud RO....117 D2
Aiviekste LV....82 C1
Aix-en-Othe F....12 B4
Aix-en-Provence F....22 B2
Aix-les-Bains F....17 D3
Aixe-sur-Vienne F....15 E3
Aizdzírži LV....79 E3
Aizenay F....14 C2
Aizgārša LV....79 F3
Aizkalne (Jāsmuiža) LV....83 E2
Aizkraukle LV....82 B1
Aizpūre (Lidumnieki) LV....83 F1
Aizpuri LV....78 B2
Aizpurve LV....79 D3
Aizpute LV....80 B1
Aizstrautnieki LV....81 D1
Aizupe LV....83 D3
Aizupes LV....76 B3
Aizupes (Mazgavilnieki) LV....76 C3
Aizviki LV....80 B2
Ajaccio F....23 F4
Ajaureforsen S....63 F1
Ajdanovac SRB....57 E4
Ajdovščina SLO....54 A2
Ajka H....116 B2
Ajo E....19 F2

Ajos FIN....65 D2
Ajtos BG....117 E4
Akācijas LV....81 E1
Akademija (Kaunas) LT....85 D2
Akademija (Kėdainiai) LT....85 E1
Äkäsjokisuu FIN....64 C1
Äkäslompolo FIN....64 C1
Akçakoca TR....117 F4
Akečiai LT....85 D1
Aken D....39 E1
Åkers styckebruk S....67 F3
Åkirkeby DK....71 E4
Akkerhaugen N....66 B2
Akmenäja LV....83 E2
Akmene LT....85 D2
Akmene III LT....81 D2
Akmeniai (Alytaus) LT....85 E3
Akmeniai (Panevėžio) LT....82 B3
Akmenynai LT....85 D2
Akmenyne LT....86 C3
Akniste LV....82 C2
Aknysčiai LT....85 D1
Akranes IS....62 A2
Akráta GR....105 D3
Akréfnio GR....105 E2
Akrestrømmen N....63 D4
Akrítas GR....101 D3

Akrogiáli GR....102 A2
Akropótamos GR....102 B2
Akrotíri GR....109 F2
Akrotíri (Hers.) GR....109 F4
Akrovoúni GR....102 B2
Äksi EE....73 D2
Akste EE....79 E1
Akstinai (Kauno) LT....81 D3
Akstinai (Taurages) LT....84 C1
Akujärvi FIN....61 F3
Akureyri IS....62 B1
Akuotninkai LT....86 C2
Ål N....66 B1
Ala EE....78 C1
Ala I....43 F4
Alà dei Sardi I....50 B2
Ala di Stura I....17 E4
Ala-Honkajoki FIN....68 C2
Ala-Vuokki FIN....65 F3
Alaburdiškes LT....85 F3
Alacant / Alicante E....27 D4
Alaejos E....19 E4
Alagí GR....104 C4
Alagna Valsesia I....17 E3
Alagón E....20 B4
Alagonía GR....105 D4
Alahärmä FIN....68 C2
Alaior E....31 F3
Alajõe EE....73 F2
Alakylä FIN....65 D1
Alalkomenés GR....105 E2
Alameda E....29 E3
Alamillo E....25 E4

Alanás S....63 E2
Ålande LV....80 B1
Alandroal P....24 C3
Alange E....25 D4
Alanís E....25 D4
Alanta LT....86 B1
Alantes LT....81 E3
Alapitka FIN....69 E1
Alar del Rey E....19 E3
Alaraz E....25 E1
Alarcón E....26 B3
Alassio I....23 F2
Alastaro FIN....68 C3
Alatoz E....26 C3
Alatri I....48 B3
Alatskivi EE....73 E3
Alaverre EE....72 C2
Alavieska FIN....65 D3
Alavus / Alavo FIN....69 D2
Alba I....17 F4
Alba Adriatica I....48 B1
Alba de Tormes E....25 E1
Alba Iulia RO....117 D2
Albacete E....26 B3
Albacken S....68 A2
Álbæk DK....70 C1
Albaida E....27 D4
Albaladejo E....26 A4
Albalate de Cinca E....20 C4
Albalate de las Nogueras E....26 B2
Albalate del Arzobispo E....27 D1
Alban F....21 F2

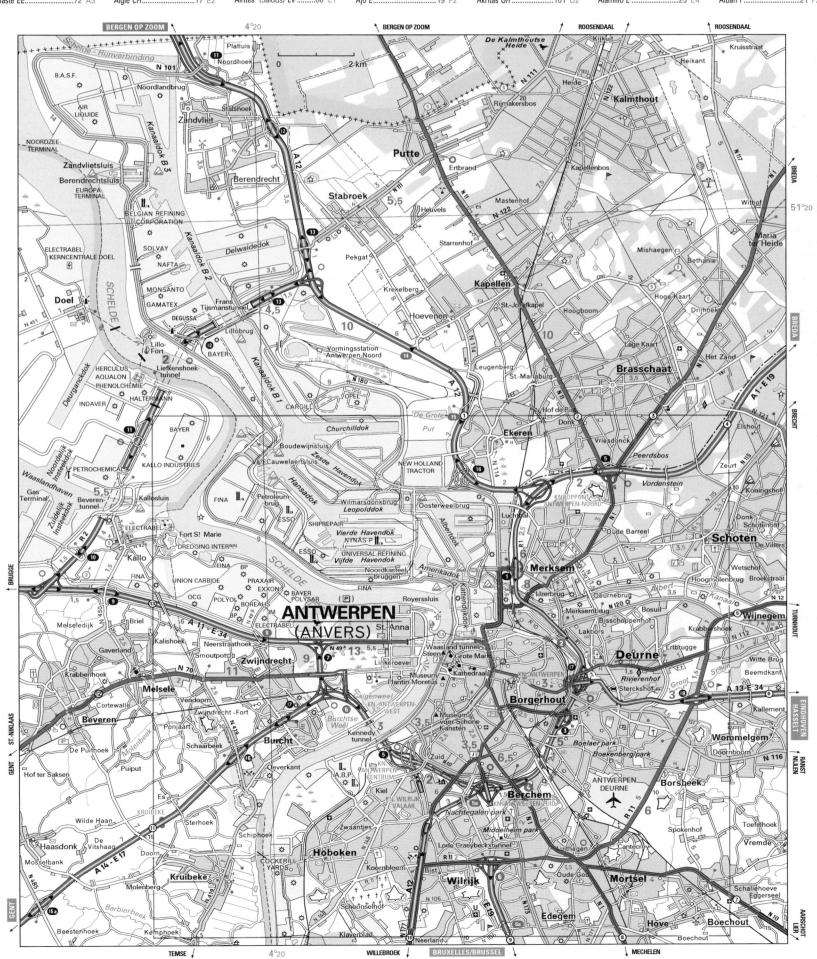

Albánchez *E* 30 B3
Albano di Lucania *I* 49 E4
Albano Laziale *I* 48 A3
Albarca *E* 27 E1
Albares de la Ribera *E* 18 C3
Albarracín *E* 26 C2
Albatana *E* 26 C4
Albatera *E* 26 C4
Albena *BG* 117 E3
Albenga *I* 23 E1
Albens *F* 17 D3
Alberga *S* 67 E3
Albergaria-a-Velha *P* 24 B1
Alberic *E* 27 D3
Albernoa *P* 24 B4
Alberobello *I* 49 F3
Albersdorf *D* 33 E2
Albert *F* 12 A2
Albertville *F* 17 D3
Albestroff *F* 13 E3
Albi *F* 21 E1
Albiano d'Ivrea *I* 17 D4
Albinia *I* 47 D4
Albino *I* 43 E4
Albissola Marina *I* 23 E1
Albocàsser *E* 27 D2
Alboloduy *E* 30 A3
Albolote *E* 29 F3
Alborea *E* 26 C4
Ålborg *DK* 70 B2
Albox *E* 30 B3
Albstadt *D* 43 D1
Albu *EE* 72 C2
Albufeira *P* 28 A2
Albujón *E* 30 C2
Albuñol *E* 30 A3
Alburquerque *E* 24 C3
Alby *S* 63 E4
Alby-sur-Chéran *F* 17 D3
Alcácer do Sal *P* 24 A4
Alçácovas *P* 24 A4
Alcadozo *E* 26 B4
Alcafozes *P* 24 C2
Alcains *P* 24 C2
Alcalá de Guadaira *E* 29 D2
Alcalá de Henares *E* 26 A1
Alcalá de la Selva *E* 26 C2
Alcalá de los Gazules *E* 29 D4
Alcalá de Xivert *E* 27 D2
Alcalá del Júcar *E* 26 C4
Alcalá del Río *E* 29 D2
Alcalá la Real *E* 29 F2
Alcalfar *E* 31 F3
Alcamo *I* 52 B3
Alcampel *E* 21 D4
Alcanar *E* 27 E2
Alcanede *P* 24 A2
Alcanena *P* 24 A2
Alcanhões *P* 24 A2
Alcañices *E* 18 C4
Alcañiz *E* 27 D1
Alcántara *E* 24 C2
Alcantarilha *P* 28 A2
Alcantarilla *E* 30 C2
Alcaracejos *E* 25 E4
Alcaraz *E* 26 B4
Alcaria Ruiva *P* 24 B4
Alcarràs *E* 21 D4
Alcaudete *E* 29 F2
Alcaudete de la Jara *E* 25 F3
Alcázar de San Juan *E* 26 A3
Alceda *E* 19 F2
Alcester *GB* 9 D2
Alcoba de los Montes *E* 25 F3
Alcobaça *P* 24 A2
Alcobendas *E* 26 A1
Alcocer *E* 26 B2
Alcochete *P* 24 A3
Alcoi / Alcoy *E* 27 D4
Alcolea *E* 29 E2
Alcolea de Cinca *E* 20 C4
Alcolea del Pinar *E* 26 B1
Alcolea del Río *E* 29 D2
Alconchel *E* 24 C4
Alcorisa *E* 27 D1
Alcossebre *E* 27 D2
Alcoutim *P* 28 B2
Alcover *E* 27 E1
Alcoy / Alcoi *E* 27 D4
Alcubierre *E* 20 C4
Alcubilla de Avellaneda *E* 19 F4
Alcublas *E* 26 C2
Alcúdia *E* 31 F3
Alcudia de Guadix *E* 30 A3
Alcuéscar *E* 25 D3
Aldea del Cano *E* 25 D3
Aldea del Fresno *E* 25 F2
Aldea del Rey *E* 26 A4
Aldea Quintana *E* 29 E2
Aldeacentenera *E* 25 D2
Aldeanueva de Ebro *E* 20 A3
Aldeanueva de la Vera *E* 25 D2
Aldeanueva del Camino *E* 25 D2
Aldeburgh *GB* 9 F2
Aldeia da Ponte *P* 24 C1
Aldeia Gavinha *P* 24 A3
Alderi *LV* 77 F3
Aldershot *GB* 9 D3
Aldinci *MK* 59 E3
Aledo *E* 30 B2
Aleknonys *LT* 85 E3
Aleknos *LT* 82 C2

Aleksa Šantić *SRB* 55 F1
Aleksandrava (Marijampoles) *LT* 85 D1
Aleksandrava (Vilniaus) *LT* 85 F2
Aleksandravas *LT* 80 B2
Aleksandravele *LT* 82 C3
Aleksandrov *RUS* 115 F1
Aleksandrovac (Kruševac) *SRB* 57 D4
Aleksandrovac (Požarevac) *SRB* 57 D3
Aleksandrów (Łódzkie) *PL* 94 B3
Aleksandrów (Lubelskie) *PL* 99 E1
Aleksandrów Kujawski *PL* 89 F3
Aleksandrów Łódzki *PL* 94 A2
Aleksin *RUS* 115 F2
Aleksinac *SRB* 57 E4
Alençon *F* 11 E4
Alenquer *P* 24 A3
Alepohóri (Arkadía) *GR* 105 D4
Alepohóri (Attikí-Piréas) *GR* 105 E3
Aléria *I* 23 F3
Alès *F* 22 A1
Ales *I* 50 A4
Aleşd *RO* 116 C2
Alessandria *I* 17 F4
Alessandria della Rocca *I* 52 C3
Ålestrup *DK* 70 B2
Ålesund *N* 62 B3
Alexandria *GB* 6 C1
Alexándria *GR* 101 E2
Alexandria *RO* 117 D3
Alexandroúpoli *GR* 103 D2
Alf *D* 13 E2
Alfajarín *E* 20 C4
Alfambra *E* 26 C2
Alfambra *P* 28 A2
Alfândega da Fé *P* 18 B4
Alfaro *E* 20 B4
Alfarràs *E* 21 D4
Alfedena *I* 48 C3
Alfeizerão *P* 24 A2
Alfeld *D* 38 C1
Alfeld *D* 39 E4
Alfiós *GR* 104 C4
Alfonsine *I* 47 E2
Alford *GB* 5 D4
Alfreton *GB* 9 D1
Alfta *S* 67 E1
Algaida *E* 31 E3
Algar *E* 29 D3
Algar de Palància *E* 27 D2
Älgård *N* 66 A2
Algarinejo *E* 29 F3
Algarrobo *E* 29 F3
Algatocín *E* 29 D3
Algeciras *E* 29 D4
Algemesí *E* 27 D3
Alghero *I* 50 A3
Alginet *E* 27 D3
Algodonales *E* 29 D3
Algorta *E* 26 B1
Algoz *P* 28 A2
Alhama de Almería *E* 30 A3
Alhama de Aragón *E* 26 B1
Alhama de Granada *E* 29 F3
Alhama de Murcia *E* 30 C2
Alhambra *E* 26 A3
Alhaurín el Grande *E* 29 E3
Alhóndiga *E* 26 A1
Ali Terme *I* 51 D4
Alía *E* 25 E3
Alía *I* 52 C3
Aliaga *E* 26 C1
Aliaguilla *E* 26 C3
Aliartos *GR* 105 D2
Alibunar *SRB* 57 D2
Alicante / Alacant *E* 27 D4
Alicún de Ortega *E* 30 A2
Alieši *LV* 78 C2
Alife *I* 48 C3
Alijó *P* 18 B4
Alikés *GR* 104 B3
Alikí (N. Páros) *GR* 109 F1
Alikianós *GR* 109 D3
Alimiá (Nissí) *GR* 111 F2
Alingsås *S* 67 E4
Alinyà *E* 21 E4
Alise-Ste-Reine *F* 16 B1
Aliseda *E* 24 C2
Alistráti *GR* 102 B2
Alivéri *GR* 105 F2
Alizava *LT* 82 B2
Aljezur *P* 28 A2
Aljucén *E* 25 D3
Aljustrel *P* 24 B4
Alkión *GR* 103 D2
Alkiškiai *LT* 81 D2
Alkmaar *NL* 32 A4
Alksnenai *LT* 81 E3
Alksniši *LV* 83 D2
Alksniupiai *LT* 81 E3
Allaire *F* 14 B1
Alland *A* 45 E1
Allariz *E* 18 B3
Allaži *LV* 78 B3

Allažmuiža (Ausmas) *LV* 78 B3
Alleen *N* 66 A3
Alleghe *I* 44 B3
Allègre *F* 16 B4
Alledo *E* 47 D1
Allensbach *D* 17 F1
Allentsteig *A* 41 D4
Allepuz *E* 26 C2
Allersberg *D* 39 D4
Allershausen *D* 43 F1
Alleuze *F* 16 A4
Allevard *F* 17 D4
Alliku *EE* 72 B2
Allinge Sandvig *DK* 71 E4
Allo *E* 20 A3
Alloa *GB* 7 D1
Allones *F* 15 D1
Allonnes *F* 15 D1
Allos *F* 17 E4
Allstedt *D* 39 D1
Almacelles *E* 21 D4
Almáchar *E* 29 F3
Almada *P* 24 A3
Almadén *E* 25 E3
Almadén de la Plata *E* 25 D4
Almadenejos *E* 25 E4
Almagro *E* 25 F3
Almajano *E* 20 A4
Almále *LV* 76 B3
Almancil *P* 28 B3
Almansa *E* 26 C4
Almanza *E* 19 E3
Almaraz *E* 25 D2
Almargen *E* 29 E3
Almarza *E* 20 A4
Almassora *E* 27 D2
Almazán *E* 20 A4
Almedinilla *E* 29 F2
Almeida *P* 18 C4
Almeirim *P* 24 C1
Almeirim *P* 24 A2
Almelo *NL* 32 C4
Almenar *E* 21 D4
Almenar de Soria *E* 20 A4
Almenara *E* 27 D3
Almendral *E* 24 C3
Almendralejo *E* 25 D3
Almere-Stad *NL* 32 B4
Almería *E* 30 A3
Almerimar *E* 30 A3
Almese *I* 17 E4
Älmhult *S* 71 D2
Almiri *GR* 105 E3
Almiró *GR* 108 A1
Almiró *GR* 104 C4
Almiropótamos *GR* 106 B2
Almirós *GR* 105 D1
Almodôvar *P* 28 B2
Almodóvar del Campo *E* 25 F4
Almodóvar del Pinar *E* 26 B3
Almodóvar del Río *E* 29 E2
Almogía *E* 29 F3
Almoguera *E* 26 A2
Almoharín *E* 25 D3
Almonacid de la Sierra *E* 20 B4
Almonacid de Toledo *E* 25 F2
Almonacid de Zorita *E* 26 A2
Almonaster la Real *E* 24 C4
Almonte *E* 28 C2
Almoradí *E* 30 C2
Almorox *E* 25 F2
Almudévar *E* 20 C4
Almuñécar *E* 29 F3
Almuradiel *E* 26 A4
Alness *GB* 4 C3
Alnø *S* 68 A2
Alnwick *GB* 7 E2
Aloja *LV* 78 B2
Alónia *GR* 101 F3
Alónnisos *GR* 105 F1
Alónnissos (Nissí) *GR* 105 F1
Álora *E* 29 E3
Alosno *E* 28 C2
Alove *LT* 85 F3
Alozaina *E* 29 E3
Alp *E* 21 E3
Alpalhão *P* 24 B2
Älpari *EE* 25 E3
Alpbach *A* 43 F2
Alpe-d'Huez *F* 17 D4
Alpedrinha *P* 24 C2
Alpera *E* 26 C3
Alphen aan den Rijn *NL* 36 C1
Alpiarça *P* 24 A2
Alpignano *I* 17 E4
Alpirsbach *D* 13 F4
Alpua *FIN* 65 D3
Alqueva *P* 28 B2
Als *DK* 70 B2
Alsasua / Altsasu *E* 20 A3
Alsdorf *D* 13 D1
Alsedžiai *LT* 80 C2
Alsen *S* 63 E3
Alsfeld *D* 38 C2
Alsike *LV* 80 C1
Alši *LV* 80 C1
Alsiai *LT* 81 E2
Alšininkai *LT* 85 F2
Alsleben *D* 39 D1
Alstahaug *N* 63 D1
Alston *GB* 7 D2
Alsunga *LV* 76 B3
Alsviki *LV* 79 E2
Alt Ruppin *D* 34 B3
Alta *N* 61 D2
Altamura *I* 49 E3
Altastenberg *D* 37 F2
Altaussee *A* 44 C2

Altavilla Milicia *I* 50 B4
Altdöbern *D* 39 F1
Altdorf *CH* 17 F2
Altdorf b. Nürnberg *D* 39 D4
Altea *E* 27 D4
Altedo *I* 47 D1
Altena *D* 37 F2
Altenahr *D* 13 E1
Altenau *D* 38 C1
Altenberg *D* 39 F2
Altenberge *D* 37 E1
Altenburg *D* 39 E2
Altenholz *D* 33 F2
Altenhundem *D* 13 F1
Altenkirchen *D* 34 B1
Altenkirchen i. Westerwald *D* 13 E1
Altenmarkt *A* 44 C2
Altenmarkt a. d. Alz *D* 44 B1
Altenmarkt bei Sankt Gallen *A* 45 D1
Altenstadt *D* 43 F1
Altensteig *D* 13 F4
Altentreptow *D* 34 B2
Altenwalde *D* 33 D2
Alter do Chão *P* 24 B3
Altglashütten *D* 13 F4
Altheim *A* 44 B1
Altkirch *F* 17 E1
Altlandsberg *D* 34 C4
Altlengbach *A* 45 E1
Altmünster *A* 44 C1
Altnaharra *GB* 4 C2
Alton *GB* 9 D3
Altopascio *I* 44 A4
Altorricón *E* 21 D4
Altötting *D* 44 B1
Altrincham *GB* 7 D3
Altsasu / Alsasua *E* 20 A3
Altshausen *D* 43 D2
Altstätten *CH* 43 D2
Altura *E* 27 D2
Altweilnau *D* 13 F1
Altzola *E* 20 A2
Alu *EE* 72 B2
Alüksne *LV* 79 E2
Aluona *LT* 86 B2
Alustante *E* 26 C1
Aluste *EE* 72 B3
Alva *GB* 7 D1
Alvaiázere *P* 24 A2
Alvalade *P* 24 A4
Alvdal *N* 62 C4
Alverca do Ribatejo *P* 24 A3
Alvesta *S* 71 E2
Alvignac *F* 15 F4
Alvito *P* 24 B4
Älvkarleby *S* 67 F1
Alvor *P* 28 A2
Älvros *S* 63 E4
Älvsbyn *S* 63 E4
Alwernia *PL* 98 A2
Alyth *GB* 5 D4
Alytus *LT* 85 E3
Alzenau *D* 37 F3
Alzey *D* 13 F2
Alzira *E* 27 D3
Alzon *F* 22 A1
Alzonne *F* 21 E2
Ama *EE* 73 D2
Amadora *P* 24 A3
Åmål *S* 67 D3
Amalfi *I* 49 D4
Amaliáda *GR* 104 B3
Amaliápoli *GR* 105 E1
Amálo *GR* 107 D4
Amance *F* 17 D1
Amancey *F* 17 D2
Amandola *I* 47 F3
Amantea *I* 51 D3
Amárandos *GR* 100 C3
Amárandos *GR* 104 C1
Amarante *P* 18 A4
Amareleja *P* 24 C4
Amares *P* 18 A4
Ämari *EE* 72 C2
Amári *LV* 81 D1
Amárinthos *GR* 105 F2
Amata *LV* 78 C3
Amatas Skola *LV* 78 B3
Amatnieki *LV* 83 D1
Amatrice *I* 47 F4
Amay *B* 12 C1
Ambarès-et-Lagrave *F* 15 D4
Ambasaguas *E* 19 D3
Ambazac *F* 15 F3
Ambelákia *GR* 103 E4
Ambelákia *GR* 101 F4
Ambeli *LV* 83 E2
Ambelía *GR* 105 D1
Ambelikó *GR* 107 E1
Ambelióna *GR* 104 C4
Ambelónas *GR* 101 E4
Amberg *D* 39 E4
Ambérieu-en-Bugey *F* 16 C3
Ambert *F* 16 B3
Ambès *F* 15 D4
Ambierle *F* 16 B3
Amble *GB* 7 E2
Ambleside *GB* 7 D2
Amboise *F* 15 E1
Ambra *I* 47 D3
Ambrières-les-Vallées *F* 11 D4

Ameixial *P* 28 B2
Amele *LV* 76 C2
Amelia *I* 47 F4
Amélie-les-Bains-Palalda *F* 21 F3
Amelinghausen *D* 33 F3
Amer *E* 21 F4
Amerongen *NL* 36 C1
Amersfoort *NL* 36 C1
Amersham *GB* 9 E3
Amesbury *GB* 9 D3
Amfiaraío *GR* 105 F2
Amfiklia *GR* 105 D2
Amfilohía *GR* 104 B1
Amfípoli *GR* 102 C2
Amfissa *GR* 105 D2
Amigdaleónas *GR* 102 B2
Amigdaliá *GR* 105 D2
Amilly *F* 16 A1
Amíndeo *GR* 101 D2
Åmli *N* 66 C2
Amlwch *GB* 3 F3
Ammanford / Rhydaman *GB* 8 B2
Ämmänsaari *FIN* 65 E3
Ammarnäs *S* 64 A2
Amohóri *GR* 101 D2
Amolianí *GR* 102 B3
Amolianí (Nissí) *GR* 102 B3
Amorbach *D* 38 C4
Amorebieta *E* 20 A2
Amorgós *GR* 110 C1
Amorgós (Nissí) *GR* 110 C1
Amório *GR* 103 E1
Åmot *N* 66 C2
Åmot *N* 66 B2
Åmot *S* 67 E1
Åmotfors *S* 67 D2
Amótopos *GR* 104 B1
Amou *F* 20 C2
Amoudára *GR* 109 F4
Amoudára *GR* 110 C4
Ampezzo *I* 44 B3
Ampfing *D* 44 B1
Amphion-les-Bains *F* 17 D2
Amplepuis *F* 16 B3
Amposta *E* 27 E1
Ampthill *GB* 9 E2
Ampudia *E* 19 E4
Ampuero *E* 19 F2
Amriswil *CH* 43 D2
Amsele *S* 64 B3
Amstelveen *NL* 32 B4
Amsterdam *NL* 32 B4
Amstetten *A* 45 D1
Amurrio *E* 19 F2
Amusco *E* 19 E3
Amvrossía *GR* 102 C1
Åna Sira *N* 66 A3
Anadia *P* 24 B1
Anáfi *GR* 110 C2
Anáfi (Nissí) *GR* 110 C2
Anafonítria *GR* 104 A3
Anagni *I* 48 B3
Análipsi *GR* 105 E2
Análipsi *GR* 111 D1
Análipsis *GR* 108 A1
Anan'īv *UA* 117 E1
Anaráhi *GR* 101 D3
Anárgiri *GR* 101 D3
Ánari *EE* 72 C3
Anascaul *IRL* 2 A4
Ånäset *S* 64 B3
Anatoli *GR* 101 F4
Anatolí *GR* 110 C4
Anatolikó *GR* 101 D2
Anávatos *GR* 107 D2
Anávissos *GR* 105 F3
Anávra (Kardítsa) *GR* 105 D1
Anávra (Magnissía) *GR* 105 D1
Ance *LV* 76 C2
Ancene *LV* 82 C2
Ancenis *F* 14 C1
Ancerville *F* 12 C4
Anchuras *E* 25 E3
Ančiškiai *LT* 82 A2
Anciškis *LT* 81 E1
Anciūnai *LT* 86 B1
Ancona *I* 47 F2
Ancy-le-Franc *F* 16 B1
Anda *N* 62 A4
Andalo *I* 43 F3
Åndalsnes *N* 62 B3
Andartikó *GR* 101 D2
Andebu *N* 66 C2
Andelot *F* 12 C4
Andenes *N* 60 B2
Andenne *B* 12 C1
Andermatt *CH* 17 F2
Andernach *D* 13 E1
Andernos-les-Bains *F* 14 C4
Andigonos *GR* 101 D2
Andikira *GR* 105 D2
Andikíthira (Nissí) *GR* 108 A1
Andímahia *GR* 111 E1
Andímilos (Nissí) *GR* 109 D1
Andíparos *GR* 109 F1
Andíparos (Nissí) *GR* 109 F1
Andípaxi (Nissí) *GR* 104 A1
Andípsara (Nissí) *GR* 106 C2
Andírio *GR* 104 C2
Ándissa *GR* 107 D1

Andoain *E* 20 A2
Andorno Micca *I* 17 F3
Andorra *E* 27 D1
Andosilla *E* 20 A3
Andover *GB* 9 D3
Andratx *E* 31 E3
Andravída *GR* 104 B3
Andrespol *PL* 94 A2
Andretta *I* 49 D4
Andrézieux-Bouthéon *F* 16 B3
Andria *I* 49 E3
Andrijevica *MNE* 58 C3
Andrioniškis *LT* 82 B3
Andritsena *GR* 104 C4
Ándros *GR* 106 C3
Ándros (Nissí) *GR* 106 C3
Andrússa *GR* 104 C4
Andrupene (Ondrupine) *LV* 83 E2
Andrychów *PL* 98 A2
Andselv *N* 60 A2
Andújar *E* 25 F4
Anduze *F* 22 A1
Andzeli *LV* 83 F2
Åne *LV* 81 E1
Aneby *S* 67 E4
Anet *F* 11 F3
Ånge (Jämtland) *S* 63 E3
Ångelholm *S* 71 D3
Angeli *FIN* 61 E2
Angelohóri *GR* 101 E2
Angelókastro *GR* 104 B2
Angelókastro *GR* 105 E3
Anger *A* 45 E2
Angera *I* 17 F3
Angermünde *D* 34 C3
Angern a. d. March *A* 41 E4
Angers *F* 15 D1
Angerville *F* 12 A4
Anghiari *I* 44 B3
Ångi *EE* 72 C3
Angístri *GR* 105 E3
Angístri (Nissí) *GR* 105 E3
Angistro *GR* 102 A1
Angitis *GR* 102 B1
Anglès *E* 21 F2
Anglès *F* 21 F2
Angles-sur-l'Anglin *F* 15 E2
Anglesola *E* 21 D4
Anglet *F* 20 B2
Anglure *F* 12 B4
Angoulême *F* 15 D3
Angri *I* 49 D4
Angués *E* 20 C4
Anguiano *E* 20 A3
Anguillara Veneta *I* 47 E1
Anguse *EE* 73 D2
Aniane *F* 22 A2
Aniche *F* 12 B2
Anija *EE* 72 C2
Anikatsi *EE* 78 C1
Ánixi *GR* 101 D4
Anjony-le-Château *F* 12 B4
Anjalankoski *FIN* 69 E3
Anjum *NL* 32 C3
Ankaran *SLO* 54 A2
Ankarsrum *S* 67 E4
Anklam *D* 34 B2
Ankum *D* 33 D4
Änmele (Jaunmēmele) *LV* 81 F2
Ånn *S* 63 D3
Anna *E* 27 D3
Anna *LV* 79 E3
Annaberg-Buchholz *D* 39 F2
Annaberg im Lammertal *A* 45 D1
Annaburg *D* 39 F1
Annan *GB* 7 D2
Anndalsvågen *N* 63 D1
Annecy *F* 17 D3
Annemasse *F* 17 D3
Annenieki *LV* 81 D1
Annikoru *EE* 79 D1
Annivere *EE* 73 D1
Annonay *F* 16 C4
Annone Veneto *I* 44 B3
Annopol *PL* 95 D3
Annot *F* 17 E4
Annweiler *D* 13 F3
Anógia *GR* 108 B1
Anógia *GR* 109 E4
Anópoli *GR* 109 D4
Añover de Tajo *E* 25 F2
Ansbach *D* 39 D4
Anse *F* 16 C3
Ansedónia *I* 47 D4
Ansião *P* 24 A1
Ansnes *N* 63 D1
Ansó *E* 20 C3
Anstruther *GB* 7 D1
Antakalnis *LT* 86 B2
Antalieptė *LT* 82 C3
Antalkiai *LT* 85 C1
Antanaičiai *LT* 86 B2
Antanašė *LT* 82 C3

Antas *E* 30 B3
Antašava *LT* 82 B3
Antazave *LT* 82 C3
Antegnate *I* 46 C1
Antemil *E* 18 A2
Antequera *E* 29 E3
Anterselva di Mezzo / Antholz Mittertal *I* 44 B3
Anthí *GR* 102 A2
Anthili *GR* 105 D1
Anthótopos *GR* 105 D1
Antibes *F* 23 E2
Antkalniškiai *LT* 85 D1
Antkoptis *LT* 80 B3
Antnäs *S* 64 C2
Antonin *PL* 93 E2
Antraigues-sur-Volane *F* 16 B4
Antrain *F* 11 D4
Antrim *GB* 3 D1
Antrodoco *I* 47 F4
Antsla *EE* 79 D2
Anttola *FIN* 69 E3
Antuži *LV* 82 C1
Antwerpen *B* 12 C1
Anuži *LV* 77 D2
Anykščiai *LT* 82 B3
Anzano di Puglia *I* 49 D3
Anzio *I* 48 B3
Anzola d'Ossola *I* 17 F3
Anzy-le-Duc *F* 16 B3
Aoiz / Agoitz *E* 20 B3
Aosta / Aoste *I* 17 E3
Apali *LV* 83 E1
Apášcia *LT* 82 B2
Apatin *SRB* 55 F1
Apatovac *HR* 54 C1
Ape *LV* 79 D2
Apecchio *I* 47 E3
Apeldoorn *NL* 37 D1
Apen *D* 33 D3
Aperäni *LV* 82 C2
Apéri *GR* 111 E3
Apgulde *LV* 81 E1
Apidiá *GR* 108 B1
Apikia *GR* 106 C3
Apíranthos *GR* 109 F1
Apolakiá *GR* 111 F2
Apolda *D* 39 D2
Apólonas *GR* 107 D4
Apolonía *GR* 102 A2
Apolonía *GR* 109 E1
Apóstoli *GR* 109 E4
Apóstolove *UA* 117 F1
Appelbo *S* 67 D1
Appenweier *D* 13 F4
Appenzell *CH* 43 D2
Appiano s. str. d. vino / Eppan *I* 43 F3
Appingedam *NL* 32 C3
Appleby *GB* 7 D2
Aprica *I* 43 E4
Apricena *I* 49 D2
Apriki *LV* 76 B3
Aprilia *I* 48 B3
Ápsalos *GR* 101 E2
Apšeni *LV* 78 B3
Apses *LV* 83 D3
Apšuciems *LV* 77 E3
Apt *F* 22 B1
Apta *N* 66 A3
Áptera *GR* 109 D3
Aptiekas *LV* 81 D1
Aquileia *I* 44 C4
Arabba *I* 43 F3
Aracena *E* 24 C4
Aračinovo *MK* 59 E3
Arad *RO* 116 C2
Aradena *GR* 109 D4
Aragona *I* 52 C3
Aráhova *GR* 104 C2
Aráhova *GR* 105 D2
Aramits *F* 20 C3
Aranda de Duero *E* 19 F4
Aranđelovac *SRB* 57 D3
Arandi *EE* 74 B3
Aranjuez *E* 26 A2
Arantzazu *E* 20 A3
Aras de los Olmos *E* 26 C2
Arasluokta *S* 64 A1
Áratos *GR* 103 D1
Aravaca *E* 25 F1
Aravete *EE* 79 D1
Aravu *EE* 79 E1
Arazede *P* 24 B1
Arbatax *I* 50 B3
Arbeca *E* 21 D4
Arbesbach *A* 44 C1
Arbois *F* 17 D2
Arbon *CH* 43 D2
Arborea (Località) *I* 50 A4
Arborio *I* 17 F3
Arbrå *S* 67 E1
Arbroath *GB* 7 E1
Arbúcies *E* 21 F4
Arbus *I* 50 A4
Arc-en-Barrois *F* 16 C1
Arcachon *F* 14 C4
Arce *I* 48 B3
Arcen *NL* 37 D1
Arcevia *I* 47 F3
Archena *E* 30 C2
Archiac *F* 15 D3
Archidona *E* 29 E3
Arcidosso *I* 47 D4
Arcis-sur-Aube *F* 12 B4
Arco *I* 43 F4
Arco de Baúlhe *P* 18 A4
Arcos *E* 19 F3
Arcos de Jalón *E* 26 B1
Arcos de la Frontera *E* 29 D3
Arcos de Valdevez *P* 18 A3
Arcusa *E* 20 C3
Arcyz *UA* 117 E2
Ardales *E* 29 E3
Árdalstangen *N* 66 B1
Ardánio *GR* 103 E2
Ardara *IRL* 2 C1
Árdava *LV* 83 E2
Ardberg *GB* 6 B1
Ardee / Baile Átha Fhirdhia *IRL* 3 D2
Ardentes *F* 15 F2
Ardentinny *GB* 6 C1
Ardez *CH* 43 E3
Ardglass *GB* 3 E2
Ardisa *E* 20 C4
Ardlussa *GB* 6 B1
Ardmore / Aird Mhór *IRL* 2 C4
Ardrahan *IRL* 2 B3
Ardres *F* 12 A1
Ardrishaig *GB* 6 C1
Ardrossan *GB* 6 C2
Ardu *EE* 72 C2
Arduaíne *GB* 6 B1
Ardvasar *GB* 4 B4
Are *EE* 72 B3
Åre *S* 63 D3
Areeta *E* 20 A2
Arenas de Cabrales *E* 19 E2
Arenas de Iguña *E* 19 E2
Arenas de San Juan *E* 26 A3
Arenas de San Pedro *E* 25 E2
Arendal *N* 66 B3
Arendole (Randauka) *LV* 83 D2
Arendonk *B* 36 C2
Arendsee *D* 34 A3
Arenys de Mar *E* 21 F4
Arenzano *I* 23 E1
Areópoli *GR* 108 B1
Ares *E* 18 B1
Arès *F* 14 C4
Aréthoussa *GR* 102 A2
Areti *GR* 102 A2
Arévalo *E* 25 F1
Arez *P* 24 B2
Arezzo *I* 47 E3
Argalastí *GR* 105 E1
Argamasilla de Alba *E* 26 A3
Argamasilla de Calatrava *E* 25 F4
Arganda del Rey *E* 26 A2
Arganil *P* 24 B1
Argássi *GR* 104 B3
Argelès-Gazost *F* 20 C3
Argelès-sur-Mer *F* 21 F3
Argent-sur-Sauldre *F* 16 A1
Argenta *I* 47 E1
Argentan *F* 11 E4
Argentat *F* 15 F4
Argente *E* 26 C1
Argentière *F* 17 E3
Argenton-Château *F* 15 D2
Argenton-sur-Creuse *F* 15 F2
Argentona *E* 21 F4
Argentré-du-Plessis *F* 11 D4
Argiádes *GR* 100 B4
Arginónda *GR* 111 E1
Argiropoúlio *GR* 101 E4
Argiroúpoli *GR* 109 D4
Argithéa *GR* 101 D4
Árgos *GR* 105 D3
Árgos Orestikó *GR* 101 D3
Argostóli *GR* 104 A3
Arguedas *E* 20 B4
Arguellite *E* 26 B4
Arguis *E* 20 C3
Arh. Kleonés *GR* 105 D3
Arh. Neméa *GR* 105 D3
Arhánes *GR* 109 E4
Arhángelos *GR* 101 E2
Árhangelos *GR* 111 F2
Arhéa Epídavros *GR* 105 E3
Arhéa Kórinthos *GR* 105 D3
Arhéa Olympía *GR* 104 C4
Arhéa Thíra *GR* 109 F2
Århus *DK* 70 B3
Ariá *GR* 103 D1
Ariano Irpino *I* 49 D3
Ariano nel Polesine *I* 47 E1
Aribe *E* 20 B3
Aridéa *GR* 101 E2
Arija *E* 19 F2
Ärikülä *EE* 78 C1
Arild *S* 71 D3
Arilje *SRB* 56 C4
Arinagour *GB* 6 A4
Ariní *GR* 104 C4
Ariño *E* 27 D1
Arinthod *F* 16 C2
Ariogala *LT* 85 E1

Arisaig GB....4 B4
Aristi GR....100 C3
Aristoménis GR....108 A1
Arísvi GR....103 D2
Aritzo I....50 B3
Ariza E....26 B1
Ärjäng S....66 C2
Arjeplog S....64 A2
Arjona E....29 F2
Arkádi GR....109 E4
Arkadia PL....94 B2
Arkalohóri GR....109 F4
Arkássa GR....111 E3
Arkessíni GR....110 C1
Arkí (Nissí) GR....107 E4
Arkitsa GR....105 E2
Arklow / An tInbhear
  Mór IRL....3 D3
Arkma EE....72 C3
Arkna EE....73 D2
Arkoúdi (Nissí) GR....104 A2
Arlanc F....16 B4
Arlanda S....67 E4
Arlanzón E....19 F3
Arlaviškes LT....85 F2
Arlempdes F....16 B4
Arles F....22 B2
Arles-sur-Tech F....21 F3
Arlesheim CH....17 E1
Arlon B....13 D2
Arma di Taggia I....23 E1
Armação de Pêra P....28 A2
Armadale GB....3 D1
Armamar P....18 B4
Arméni GR....109 E4
Armenií GR....104 C4
Armeniškiai LT....85 E1
Armenistis GR....107 D4
Armentières F....12 A1
Armilla E....29 F3
Armólia GR....107 D2
Árna GR....108 B1
Arnac-Pompadour F....15 F4
Arnay-le-Duc F....16 B2
Arnéa GR....102 A3
Arneburg D....34 A4
Arnedillo E....20 A3
Arnedo E....20 A3
Arnés E....27 D1
Árnes N....66 C2
Árni E....46 C2
Árni LV....77 F2
Arnionys II LT....86 C1
Árnissa GR....101 E2
Arnoldstein A....44 C3
Arnsberg D....37 F1
Arnstadt D....39 D2
Arnstein D....38 C3
Aroania GR....104 C3
Aroche E....24 C4
Arogí GR....102 C2
Arona I....17 F3
Aroniádika GR....108 A3
Aronkylä FIN....68 C2
Åros N....66 C2
Arosa CH....43 E3
Arouca P....18 A4
Árøysund N....66 C2
Arpajon F....12 A4
Arpela FIN....68 C2
Arquata del Tronto I....47 F3
Arques F....12 A1
Arques-la-Bataille F....11 F2
Arquillos E....26 A4
Arrabal E....18 A3
Arracourt F....13 E4
Arraiolos P....24 B3
Arras F....12 A2
Arrasate /
  Mondragón E....20 A2
Arreau F....21 D3
Arredondo E....19 F2
Arrens-Marsous F....20 C3
Arrifana F....24 C1
Arrigorriaga E....20 A2
Arriondas E....19 D2
Arroba de
  los Montes E....25 F3
Arrochar GB....6 C1
Arromanches-les-
  Bains F....11 D3
Arronches P....24 C2
Arroyo de la Luz E....25 D2
Arroyo de
  San Serván E....25 D3
Arroyo del Ojanco E....26 A4
Arroyomolinos de
  Léon E....24 C4
Arroyomolinos de
  Montánchez E....25 D2
Arruda dos Vinhos P....24 A3
Års DK....70 B2
Ars-en-Ré F....14 C3
Ars-sur-Moselle F....13 D3
Arsié I....43 F4
Arsiero I....43 F4
Arskógssandur IS....62 B1
Årsunda S....67 F1
Arsy F....12 A3
Artà E....31 F3
Árta GR....104 B1
Arta Terme I....44 A3
Artajona E....20 B3
Artea E....20 A2
Artemíssia GR....105 D4

Artemíssio GR....105 E1
Artemónas GR....109 E1
Artena I....48 B3
Artenay F....12 A4
Artern D....39 D1
Artés E....21 E4
Artesa de Segre E....21 D4
Artessianó E....101 E4
Arth CH....17 F1
Arth D....43 F1
Arthurstown IRL....3 D4
Arties E....21 D3
Artjärvi FIN....69 E3
Artotína GR....104 C2
Artziniega E....19 F2
Arudy F....20 C2
Arukäla (Harju) EE....72 B2
Arukäla
  (Lääne-Viru) EE....73 D2
Arumetsa EE....75 E3
Arundel GB....9 E4
Aruvalla EE....72 B2
Árvi GR....109 F4
Arvidsjaur S....64 B2
Arvik N....62 A4
Arvika S....67 D2
Årvíksand N....60 C1
Arvydai LT....86 C2
Arzachena I....50 B2
Arzacq-Arraziguet F....20 C2
Arzano F....10 B4
Arzberg D....39 E3
Arzignano I....43 F4
Árzos GR....103 E1
Arzúa E....18 B2
As B....13 D1
Aš CZ....40 A3
As Neves E....18 A3
As Pontes de García
  Rodríguez E....18 B1
Åsa S....66 C4
Asamati MK....59 E4
Asare LV....82 C2
Åsarna S....63 E4
Åsarp S....67 D3
Ascain F....20 B2
Ascha D....39 F4
Aschach an der
  Donau A....44 C1
Aschaffenburg D....38 C3
Aschau i. Chiemgau D....44 B2
Aschbach-Markt A....45 D1
Ascheberg D....33 F2
Ascheberg D....37 E1
Aschendorf (Ems) D....33 D3
Aschersleben D....39 D1
Asciano I....47 E3
Ascó E....27 E1
Asco F....23 F3
Ascoli Piceno I....48 B1
Ascoli Satriano I....49 D3
Ascona CH....17 F3
Åse N....60 B2
Åseda S....71 E2
Åsele S....64 A3
Åsen N....63 D3
Asenovgrad BG....117 D4
Åseral N....66 A3
Aseri EE....73 E1
Asfáka GR....100 C4
Asfeld F....12 B3
Åsgårdstrand N....66 C2
Ashbourne GB....9 D1
Ashbourne IRL....3 D3
Ashburton GB....8 B4
Ashby de la Zouch GB....9 D1
Ashford GB....9 F3
Ashington GB....7 E1
Ashton-under-Lyne GB....7 E4
Asiago I....43 F4
Asikkala FIN....69 E3
Asín E....20 B3
Asipovíč BY....115 E3
Asiūkle LT....85 E2
Ask N....66 C2
Askainen FIN....68 C4
Askeaton IRL....2 B3
Askersund S....67 E3
Askifou GR....109 D4
Askim N....66 C2
Asklipiío GR....111 E1
Asklipió GR....111 F2
Askola FIN....69 E4
Askós GR....102 A2
Askvoll N....62 A4
Ašminta LT....85 E2
Asmunti FIN....65 D2
Asola I....46 C1
Asolo I....44 A4
Asopía GR....105 E3
Aspang Markt A....45 E1
Aspatria GB....7 D1
Aspe E....26 C4
Asperg D....38 C4
Aspet F....21 D3
Aspróhoma GR....108 A1
Asprópirgos GR....105 F3
Asproválta GR....102 A3
Assaku EE....72 B2
Assamalla EE....73 D2
Asse B....12 B1
Assemini I....50 A4
Assen NL....32 C4
Assens DK....70 B3
Assergi I....48 B2

Assíni GR....105 E4
Assisi I....47 F3
Assmannshausen D....13 F2
Assópia GR....105 F2
Assopós GR....108 B1
Ássos GR....100 C4
Ássos GR....104 A2
Astaffort F....21 D1
Astakída (Nissí) GR....111 D3
Astakós GR....104 B2
Astašova LV....83 E2
Aste EE....74 C1
Aste Haamse EE....74 C3
Åstere LV....78 B2
Asti I....17 F4
Astipálea GR....111 D1
Astipálea (Nissí) GR....111 D1
Astorga E....19 D3
Åstorp S....71 D3
Aštrioji Kirsna LT....85 D3
Ástros GR....105 D4
Astudillo E....19 E3
Asúne LV....83 F2
Ašvenai LT....81 D2
Asvestádes GR....103 E1
Asvestohóri GR....100 C4
Asvestópetra GR....101 D3
Atalándi GR....105 E2
Átali GR....105 F2
Ataquines E....25 E1
Atarfe E....29 F3
Atašiene LV....83 D1
Ateca E....26 B1
Atella I....49 E4
Atessa I....48 C2
Ath B....12 B1
Athamánio GR....101 D4
Athánio GR....104 A2
Athboy IRL....3 D2
Athenry / Baile Átha
  an Rí IRL....2 C3
Atherstone GB....9 D1
Athína GR....105 F3
Áthira GR....101 F2
Athlone / Baile Átha
  Luain IRL....2 C3
Áthos GR....102 B3
Athy / Baile Átha Í IRL....3 D3
Atienza E....26 A1
Atina I....48 C3
Atios E....18 B1
Atkočiai LT....85 F1
Atkočiškes LT....82 C3
Átokos (Nissí) GR....104 A2
Atptūa
  (Daugavpils) LV....83 D3
Atptūa (Jelgavas) LV....81 E1
Ätran S....71 D2
Atri I....48 C2
Atsiki GR....102 C3
Atsitsa GR....106 B1
Atspuka LV....83 E1
Attendorn D....37 E2
Attigliano I....47 E4
Attigny F....12 C3
Attleborough GB....9 F2
Attnang-Puchheim A....44 C1
Åtvidaberg S....67 E3
Atzeneta del
  Maestrat E....27 D2
Au D....43 F1
Aub D....38 C4
Aubagne F....22 C2
Aubange B....13 D2
Aubenas F....22 A1
Aubenton F....12 B2
Aubergenville F....12 A3
Auberive F....16 C1
Aubeterre-sur-
  Dronne F....15 D4
Aubigny-sur-Nère F....16 A1
Aubin F....21 E1
Aubonne CH....17 D2
Aubrac F....21 F1
Aubusson F....15 F3
Auce LV....81 D1
Auch F....21 D2
Auchencairn GB....3 F1
Auchterarder GB....7 D1
Auchtermuchty GB....7 D1
Auciems LV....78 B3
Audenge F....14 C4
Audierne F....10 A4
Audincourt F....17 E1
Audlem GB....8 C1
Audru EE....72 A4
Audruicq F....12 A1
Audun-le-Roman F....13 D3
Audun-le-Tiche F....13 D3
Aue D....39 E2
Auerbach D....39 E2
Auerbach i. d.
  Oberpfalz D....39 E3
Auffach A....44 B2
Aughnacloy GB....3 D1
Aughrim IRL....3 D3
Augmenai LT....81 E2
Augsburg D....43 F1
Augstásala L....79 D3
Augstkalne
  (Dobeles) LV....81 E2

Augstkalne
  (Krāslavas) LV....83 E3
Augusta I....53 E3
Augustavas LT....86 C1
Auguste LV....80 B1
Augustenborg DK....70 B4
Augustenborg DK....70 B4
Augustow PL....91 E2
Augustowska
  (Puszcza) PL....91 E1
Augustusburg D....39 F2
Aukan N....62 B3
Aukra N....62 B3
Aukštadvaris LT....85 F2
Aukštalaukis LT....86 B3
Aukštdvaris LT....85 E1
Aukštelkai LT....81 E3
Aukštkalviai LT....80 B2
Aukštpamedžiai LT....81 D3
Aukštvilkiai LT....84 C1
Auleja LV....83 E2
Auletta I....49 D4
Aulla I....46 C2
Aullène F....23 F4
Aulnay F....15 D3
Aulnoye-Aymeries F....12 B2
Ault F....11 F2
Aulus-les-Bains F....21 E3
Auma D....39 D2
Aumale F....11 F2
Aumetz F....13 D3
Aumont-Aubrac F....16 A4
Aunay-sur-Odon F....11 D3
Auneau F....11 F4
Auneuil F....12 A3
Auning DK....70 B2
Aups F....23 D2
Aura FIN....68 C4
Auray F....14 B1
Aurdal N....66 B1
Aure N....62 C3
Aurec-sur-Loire F....16 B4
Auri LV....81 E1
Aurich D....33 D3
Aurignac F....21 D2
Aurillac F....16 A4
Auritz / Burguete E....20 B3
Aurland N....66 B1
Auron F....23 D1
Auronzo di Cadore I....44 B3
Aurora E....20 C1
Auschwitz =
  Oświęcim PL....97 F2
Aušgiriai LT....84 C1
Ausonia I....48 C3
Aušra LT....85 E1
Aussa-Corno I....44 C4
Außernbrünst D....39 F4
Austbygd N....66 B2
Austrumi LV....80 C1
Auterive F....21 E2
Authon-du-Perche F....11 F4
Autol E....20 A3
Autrans F....16 C4
Autrey-lès-Gray F....16 C1
Autti FIN....65 E1
Auttoinen FIN....69 D3
Autun F....16 B2
Auvillar F....21 D1
Auxerre F....16 B1
Auxi-le-Château F....12 A2
Auxonne F....16 C1
Auzances F....16 A3
Auzeni LV....83 F1
Auzinas LV....78 C2
Auzon F....16 A4
Availles-Limouzine F....15 E3
Avaldsnes N....66 A2
Avallon F....16 B1
Avándas GR....103 D1
Avavira GR....102 C2
Aváviken S....64 B2
Ávdira GR....102 C2
Aveiras de Cima P....24 A3
Aveiro P....24 B1
Avellino I....49 D4
Aversa I....48 C4
Avesnes-le-Comte F....12 A2
Avesnes-sur-Helpe F....12 B2
Avesta S....67 E2
Avetrana I....51 F1
Avezzano I....48 B2
Avgerinós GR....101 D3
Avia GR....108 A1
Aviano I....44 B4
Aviemore GB....4 C4
Avigliana I....17 E4
Avigliano I....49 E4
Avignon F....22 B1
Ávila E....25 F1
Avilés E....19 D2
Avilés LT....86 B1
Aviliai LT....85 F2
Avilii II LT....82 C3
Avintes P....18 A4
Avinurme EE....73 D2
Avión E....18 A3
Avioth F....13 D3
Avis P....24 B3
Avispea EE....73 D2
Avize F....12 B3
Avižonys LT....86 B2
Avlákia GR....107 D4
Avlémonas GR....108 C2
Avli LT....85 F2
Avliótes GR....100 A4

Avlóna GR....105 F2
Avlum DK....70 B2
Avola I....53 E4
Avonmouth GB....8 C3
Avord F....16 A2
Avoriaz F....17 D3
Avoti LV....77 E3
Avotini (Cēsu) LV....78 B2
Avotini (Jelgavas) LV....81 E1
Åvra GR....103 D2
Avranches F....11 D4
Avtovac BIH....58 B2
Ax-les-Thermes F....21 E3
Axams A....43 F2
Axat F....21 E3
Axiohóri GR....101 F2
Axióupoli GR....101 F2
Axminster GB....8 C4
Axós GR....109 E4
Ay F....12 B3
Ayamonte E....28 B2
Ayerbe E....20 C3
Aylesbury GB....9 D2
Ayllón E....19 F4
Aylsham GB....9 F2
Ayna E....26 B4
Ayora E....26 C3
Ayr GB....3 F1
Aywaille B....13 D1
Azaila E....27 D1
Azambuja P....24 A3
Azanja SRB....57 D3
Azaruja P....24 B3
Azay-le-Ferron F....15 E2
Azay-le-Rideau F....15 E1
Azinheira dos
  Barros P....24 A4
Azkoitia E....20 A2
Aznalcázar E....29 D2
Aznalcóllar E....29 D2
Azpeitia E....20 A2
Azuaga E....25 D4
Azuara E....26 C1
Azuel E....25 F4
Ažuolaičiai LT....85 E1
Ažuolija E....82 C3
Ažuoline LT....86 A2
Ažuoliniai LT....85 E3
Ažuolu Būda LT....85 E2
Ažuolyte LT....85 F2
Azuqueca de Henares E....26 A1
Azzano Decimo I....44 B4

B

Baad A....43 E2
Baal D....13 D1
Baamonde E....18 B2
Baarle-Nassau NL....36 C1
Baarn NL....36 C1
Babadag RO....117 E3
Babajevo RUS....115 F1
Babelsberg D....34 B4
Babenhausen D....38 C3
Babenhausen D....43 E1
Babia Góra PL....98 A3
Babiak
  (Wielkopolskie) PL....93 F1
Babice PL....98 A2
Babimost PL....92 C2
Babin Kal SRB....57 F4
Babin Most SRB....59 E2
Babin Potok HR....54 C3
Babina Greda HR....55 E2
Babino Polje HR....58 A3
Babiogórski Park
  Narodowy PL....98 A3
Babljak MNE....58 C3
Baborów PL....97 E2
Baboszewo PL....90 B3
Babrai LT....86 B2
Babriškes LT....86 B2
Babrujsk BY....115 E3
Babrungas LT....80 B2
Babtai LT....85 E1
Babušnica SRB....57 F4
Bač SRB....55 F2
Bacău RO....117 E2
Baccarat F....13 D4
Baceno I....17 F2
Bacharach D....13 F2
Bachmač UA....115 F3
Bačina SRB....57 E3
Bačka Palanka SRB....55 F1
Bačka Topola SRB....55 F1
Bäckaskog S....71 D3
Backe S....68 A1
Bäckebo S....71 E2
Bäckefors S....66 C3
Bački Bred SRB....55 F2
Bački Monoštor SRB....55 E1
Bačkininkai LT....85 E2
Bačkiškiai LT....85 D2
Backnang D....38 C4
Bačko Gradište SRB....56 C2
Bačko Novo Selo SRB....55 F2
Bačko Petrovo
  Selo SRB....56 C1
Baćkowice PL....94 C3
Bacoli I....48 C4
Bacqueville-en-Caux F....11 F2
Bad Aibling D....43 F1
Bad Arolsen D....37 F1

Bad Aussee A....44 C2
Bad Bentheim D....32 C4
Bad Bergzabern D....13 F3
Bad Berka D....39 D2
Bad Berleburg D....13 F1
Bad Berneck D....39 D3
Bad Bevensen D....33 E4
Bad Bibra D....39 D1
Bad Blankenburg D....39 D2
Bad Brambach D....39 E2
Bad Bramstedt D....33 D2
Bad Brückenau D....38 C3
Bad Buchau D....42 A2
Bad Camberg D....13 F1
Bad Deutsch
  Altenburg A....45 F1
Bad Doberan D....34 A2
Bad Driburg D....37 F1
Bad Düben D....39 E1
Bad Dürkheim D....13 F3
Bad Dürrenberg D....39 E1
Bad Dürrheim D....13 F4
Bad Elster D....39 E2
Bad Ems D....13 E1
Bad Endorf D....44 B1
Bad Essen D....33 D4
Bad Frankenhausen D....39 D1
Bad Freienwalde D....34 C3
Bad Friedrichshall D....38 C1
Bad Gandersheim D....38 C1
Bad Gastein A....44 C2
Bad Gleichenberg A....45 E2
Bad Godesberg D....13 E1
Bad Goisern A....44 C2
Bad Gottleuba D....39 F2
Bad Griesbach i.
  Rottal D....44 B1
Bad Grund D....38 C1
Bad Hall A....44 C1
Bad Harzburg D....38 C1
Bad Herrenalb D....13 F3
Bad Hersfeld D....38 C2
Bad Hofgastein A....44 C2
Bad Homburg D....13 F2
Bad Honnef D....13 E1
Bad Hönningen D....13 E1
Bad Iburg D....33 D4
Bad Ischl A....44 C2
Bad Karlshafen D....38 C1
Bad Kissingen D....38 C3
Bad Kleinen D....34 A2
Bad Kleinkirchheim A....44 C3
Bad König D....37 F3
Bad Königshofen D....39 D3
Bad Kösen D....39 E1
Bad Kreuznach D....13 F2
Bad Krozingen D....13 F4
Bad Laasphe D....13 F1
Bad Langensalza D....39 D2
Bad Lauchstädt D....39 E1
Bad Lausick D....39 E1
Bad Lauterberg D....38 C1
Bad Leonfelden A....40 C4
Bad Liebenstein D....38 C2
Bad Liebenwerda D....39 F1
Bad Liebenzell D....13 F3
Bad Lippspringe D....37 F1
Bad Meinberg D....37 F1
Bad Mergentheim D....38 C4
Bad Mitterndorf A....44 C2
Bad Münder D....33 F4
Bad Münster a.
  Stein D....13 F2
Bad Münstereifel D....13 E1
Bad Muskau D....40 C1
Bad Nauheim D....13 F1
Bad Nenndorf D....33 E4
Bad Neuenahr D....13 E1
Bad Neustadt D....38 C3
Bad Oeynhausen D....33 E4
Bad Oldesloe D....33 F2
Bad Orb D....38 C3
Bad Peterstal D....13 F4
Bad Pyrmont D....37 F1
Bad Radkersburg A....45 E2
Bad Rappenau D....38 C3
Bad Reichenhall D....44 B2
Bad Rippoldsau D....42 A1
Bad Rodach D....39 D3
Bad Rothenfelde D....37 E1
Bad Saarow D....34 C4
Bad Sachsa D....39 D1
Bad Säckingen D....17 E1
Bad Salzdetfurth D....38 C1
Bad Salzschlirf D....38 C2
Bad Salzuflen D....37 F1
Bad Salzungen D....38 C2
Bad Saulgau D....42 A2
Bad Schallerbach A....44 C1
Bad Schandau D....40 C2
Bad Schmiedeberg D....39 E1
Bad Schönborn D....13 F3
Bad Schussenried D....43 D1
Bad Schwalbach D....13 F2
Bad Schwartau D....33 F2
Bad Segeberg D....33 F2
Bad Soden D....38 C3
Bad Soden am
  Taunus D....13 F1
Bad Sooden-
  Allendorf D....38 C1
Bad St Leonhard im
  Lavanttal A....45 D2
Bad Sulza D....39 D2
Bad Sülze D....34 B2
Bad Tatzmannsdorf A....45 E2

Bad Tennstedt D....39 D2
Bad Tölz D....43 F2
Bad Urach D....43 D1
Bad Vilbel D....13 F2
Bad Vöslau A....45 E1
Bad Waldsee D....43 D2
Bad Wiessee D....43 F2
Bad Wildungen D....37 F2
Bad Wilsnack D....34 A3
Bad Wimpfen D....38 C4
Bad Windsheim D....39 D4
Bad Wörishofen D....43 E1
Bad Wurzach D....43 D2
Bad Zurzach CH....17 F1
Bad Zwischenahn D....33 D3
Badajoz E....24 C3
Badalona E....21 E4
Baden A....45 E1
Baden CH....17 F1
Baden-Baden D....13 F3
Badenweiler D....17 E1
Baderna HR....54 A3
Badia Polesine I....47 D1
Badia Tedalda I....47 E2
Bądki PL....89 F2
Bądkowo PL....89 F3
Badljevina HR....55 D2
Badolato I....51 E3
Badolatosa E....29 E3
Badonviller F....13 E4
Badovinci SRB....55 F3
Badules E....26 C1
Baena E....29 F2
Baeza E....30 A2
Bàga E....21 E4
Bagaslaviškis LT....86 B1
Bagdoniškis LT....82 C3
Bagdononys LT....85 F2
Bagenalstown / Muine Bheag
  IRL....3 D3
Bagenkop DK....70 B4
Bagheria I....50 B4
Bagn N....66 B1
Bagnacavallo I....47 E2
Bagnara Calabra I....51 D4
Bagnères-de-Bigorre F....20 C2
Bagnères-de-Luchon F....21 D3
Bagni del Masino I....43 D3
Bagni di Lucca I....47 D2
Bagno a Ripoli I....47 D3
Bagno di Romagna I....47 E2
Bagnoles-de-l'Orne F....11 E4
Bagnolo Mella I....43 D4
Bagnols-les-Bains F....22 A1
Bagnols-sur-Cèze F....22 B1
Bagnoregio I....47 E4
Bagolino I....43 E4
Bagotoji LT....85 D2
Bagrationovsk RUS....114 B3
Bagrdan SRB....57 D3
Baia Mare RO....117 D2
Baia Sardinia I....50 B2
Baiano I....49 D4
Baião P....18 B4
Baiersbronn D....13 F4
Baignes-Ste-
  Radegonde F....15 D4
Baigneux-les-Juifs F....16 B1
Bäile Herculane RO....116 C2
Băile tuşnad RO....117 D2
Bailén E....25 F4
Bailieborough / Coill an
  Chollaigh IRL....3 D2
Bailleul F....12 A1
Bain-de-Bretagne F....14 C1
Bains-les-Bains F....13 D4
Baio E....18 A2
Baiona E....18 A3
Bais F....11 E4
Baisogala LT....81 E3
Bajári (Bauskas) LV....81 F2
Bajári (Rigas) LV....78 C2
Bajgora SRB....57 D4
Bajina Bašta SRB....56 C4
Bajmok SRB....55 E1
Bajoraičiai LT....85 D2
Bajoriškiai LT....85 E3
Bajša SRB....55 E1
Bakałarzewo PL....91 D2
Bakar HR....54 B3
Bakarac HR....54 B3
Bakewell GB....9 D1
Bakio E....20 A1
Bakkafjörður IS....62 B1
Bakkejord N....60 B1
Bakšėnai LT....82 B4
Bakšiai LT....85 E2
Bakšuri A....44 C1
Bala GB....8 B1
Balaguer E....21 D4
Balandiškis LT....82 C4
Balanegra E....30 A4
Balaruc-les-Bains F....22 A2
Balassagyarmat H....116 B2
Balatonfüred H....116 B2
Balatonlelle H....116 B2
Balatonszemes H....116 B2
Balbieriškis LT....85 E2
Balbigny F....16 B3
Balbriggan /
  Baile Brigín IRL....3 D2
Balčik BG....117 E3
Balderschwang D....43 D2
Baldock GB....9 E2
Baldone LV....81 F1

Bale HR....54 A3
Baleal P....24 A2
Baleizão P....24 B4
Balerma E....30 A4
Balestrand N....66 A1
Balgale LV....77 D3
Bali GR....109 E3
Baligród PL....99 E3
Balikesir TR....117 F4
Bálinge S....67 F2
Balingen D....43 D1
Balivanich GB....4 A3
Balkasodis LT....85 E3
Balkaluish GB....4 B4
Ballaghaderreen / Bealach an
  Doirín IRL....2 C2
Ballangen N....60 B3
Ballantrae GB....3 E1
Ballao I....50 B4
Ballas LV....76 B3
Ballater GB....5 D4
Ballaugh GB....3 F2
Balleastedt D....39 D1
Balleroy F....11 D3
Ballerup DK....70 C3
Ballina / Béal an
  Átha IRL....2 B1
Ballinamore / Béal an Átha
  Mhóir IRL....2 C2
Ballinasloe / Béal Átha na
  Sluaighe IRL....2 C3
Ballingarry IRL....2 C4
Ballinrobe / Baile an
  Róba IRL....2 B2
Ballintubber IRL....2 B2
Ballobar E....20 C4
Ballon F....11 E4
Ballstad N....60 A3
Ballybay IRL....3 D2
Ballybofey / Bealach
  Féich IRL....2 C1
Ballybunnion IRL....2 B3
Ballycastle GB....6 B2
Ballycastle IRL....2 B1
Ballyclare GB....3 E1
Ballyconnell IRL....2 C2
Ballycotton IRL....2 C4
Ballycroy IRL....2 A2
Ballyduff IRL....2 A3
Ballyfarnon IRL....2 C2
Ballygawley GB....3 D1
Ballyhaunis / Béal Átha
  hAmhnais IRL....2 B2
Ballyheige IRL....2 A4
Ballyjamesduff IRL....3 D2
Ballymahon / Baile Uí
  Mhatháin IRL....2 C2
Ballymena GB....3 D1
Ballymoe IRL....2 C2
Ballymoney GB....3 D1
Ballymote / Baile an
  Mhóta IRL....2 C2
Ballynahinch GB....3 E1
Ballysadare IRL....2 C2
Ballyshannon / Béal Átha
  Seanaidh IRL....2 B2
Ballyvaughan IRL....2 B3
Balmaseda E....19 F2
Balme I....17 E4
Balneario de
  Panticosa E....20 C3
Balninkai (Alytaus) LT....85 F3
Balninkai (Utenos) LT....86 B1
Baloži (Liepājas) LV....77 D3
Baloži (Rigas) LV....77 E3
Balsareny E....21 E4
Balsiai LT....80 C2
Balsicas E....30 C2
Balsorano I....48 B3
Bålsta S....67 F2
Balsthal CH....17 E1
Balsupiai LT....85 D2
Balta UA....117 E1
Baltaiskrogs LV....80 C1
Baltanás E....19 E4
Baltar E....18 B3
Baltezers LV....77 F3
Bâlţi MD....117 E1
Baltijsk RUS....114 B3
Baltinava
  (Baltinova) LV....79 F3
Baltinglass / Bealach
  Conglais IRL....3 D3
Baltmuiža LV....83 D2
Baltoji Voke LT....86 B3
Baltów PL....94 C3
Balšėnai LT....82 B3
Baltrimai LT....80 B2
Bakvattnet S....63 F3
Bala E....21 E4
Baltrušaičiai LT....84 C1
Baltrušiai LT....85 E2
Balvi LV....79 E3
Balvu Stacija LV....79 D3
Bambalió GR....104 B1
Bamberg D....39 D3
Bambini GR....104 B1
Bamburgh Castle GB....7 E1
Bampton GB....8 B4
Banagher IRL....2 C3
Banatska Palanka SRB....57 E2
Banatska Topola SRB....56 C1
Banatski
  Brestovac SRB....57 D2
Banatski Dvor SRB....56 C2
Banatski Karlovac SRB....57 D2
Banatsko
  Aranđelovo SRB....56 C1

Banatsko
Karađorđevo SRB ...56 C1
Banatsko Novo
Selo SRB ...57 D2
Banbridge GB ...3 D1
Banbury GB ...9 D2
Banchory GB ...5 D4
Bande F ...18 B3
Bandenieki LV ...81 E2
Bandırma TR ...117 F4
Bandol F ...22 C2
Bandon / Droichead na
Bandan IRL ...2 B4
Bandoriai LT ...81 E2
Banff GB ...5 D3
Bangor IRL ...2 B1
Bangor
(Gwynedd) GB ...3 F3
Bangor
(North-Down) GB ...3 E1
Bangsund N ...63 D2
Banie PL ...88 A3
Banie Mazurskie PL ...91 D1
Banja
(Kragujevac) SRB ...57 D3
Banja (Užice) SRB ...56 C4
Banja Koviljača SRB ...55 F3
Banja Luka BIH ...55 E3
Banjani SRB ...56 C3
Banjska SRB ...59 D2
Bankeryd S ...67 D4
Bannalec F ...10 B4
Bañon E ...26 C1
Banon F ...22 C1
Baños de Cerrato E ...19 E4
Baños de la Encina E ...25 E4
Baños de la
Fuensanta E ...30 B2
Baños de Molgas E ...18 B3
Baños de
Montemayor E ...25 D1
Banova Jaruga HR ...55 D2
Banovići BIH ...55 E3
Bansin D ...34 C2
Banská Bystrica SK ...116 B1
Banská Štiavnica SK ...116 B2
Bansko MK ...59 F4
Bantry / Beanntraí IRL ...2 A4
Banyalbufar E ...31 E3
Banyeres de Mariola E ...26 C4
Banyoles E ...21 F4
Banyuls-sur-Mer F ...21 E3
Bapaume F ...12 A2
Baqueira E ...21 D3
Bar MNE ...58 C4
Bar UA ...117 E1
Bar-le-Duc F ...12 C3
Bar-sur-Aube F ...12 C4
Bar-sur-Seine F ...12 C4
Baraći BIH ...55 D4

Barahona E ...26 B1
Barajas E ...26 A1
Barajas de Melo E ...26 A2
Barajevo SRB ...56 C3
Barakaldo E ...20 A2
Baralla E ...18 B2
Barane SRB ...59 D3
Baranavičy BY ...115 D3
Baranów (Wielkopolskie)
PL ...93 E3
Baranów
Sandomierski PL ...99 D1
Baranowo
(Wielkopolskie) PL ...93 D1
Baraque-de-Fraiture B ...13 D2
Baraque-Michel B ...13 D1
Baraqueville F ...21 F1
Barbadillo del
Mercado E ...19 F4
Barban HR ...54 A3
Barbarano Vicentino I ...43 F4
Barbarušince SRB ...59 F2
Barbastro E ...20 C4
Barbat HR ...54 B3
Barbate E ...29 D4
Barbazan F ...21 D3
Barberino di Mugello I ...47 D2
Barbezieux F ...15 D4
Barbizon F ...12 A4
Barbotan-les-
Thermes F ...20 C1
Barby D ...34 A4
Barca de Alva P ...24 C1
Barcarrota E ...24 C4
Barcellona Pozzo di
Gotto I ...51 E4
Barcelona E ...27 F1
Barcelonnette F ...23 D1
Barcelos P ...18 A4
Barchfeld D ...38 C2
Barči LT ...85 E3
Barciany PL ...90 C1
Barcin PL ...89 E3
Barcis I ...44 B3
Barcones E ...26 A1
Barcs H ...116 B3
Barczewo PL ...90 B2
Bardal N ...63 D2
Bardauskai LT ...85 D2
Bardi I ...46 C2
Bardineto I ...23 E1
Bardo PL ...96 C1
Bardolino I ...43 F4
Bardonecchia I ...27 D4
Bardufoss N ...60 C2
Bare SRB ...58 C2
Barèges F ...20 C3
Barentin F ...11 F3

Barenton F ...11 D4
Barfleur F ...11 D2
Bargas E ...25 F2
Bargłów Kościelny PL ...91 E2
Bargoed GB ...8 C2
Bargteheide D ...33 F2
Bari I ...49 F3
Barić Draga HR ...54 B4
Barisciano I ...48 B2
Bariūnai LT ...81 E2
Barjac F ...22 A1
Barjols F ...22 C2
Barkava LV ...83 D1
Barkiškis LT ...82 C2
Barklainiai LT ...81 E1
Barklainiai I LT ...81 F3
Barkūniškis LT ...81 E3
Bârlad RO ...117 E2
Barlby GB ...7 F4
Barletta I ...49 E3
Barlinek PL ...88 B3
Barmouth /
Abermaw GB ...3 F4
Barmstedt D ...33 E2
Barna / Bearna IRL ...2 B3
Barnard Castle GB ...7 E3
Bärnau D ...39 E3
Barneveld NL ...36 C1
Barneville-Carteret F ...10 C3
Barnsley GB ...7 E4
Barnstaple GB ...8 B3
Barnstorf D ...33 D4
Barntrup D ...37 F1
Barovo MK ...59 F4
Barqueiro P ...24 B2
Barr F ...13 E4
Barracas E ...26 C2
Barracchia E ...26 C1
Barraco E ...25 F1
Barrafranca I ...53 D3
Barranco Velho P ...28 B2
Barrancos P ...24 C4
Barranda E ...30 B2
Barrax E ...26 B3
Barre-des-Cévennes F ...22 A1
Barrea I ...48 C3
Barreiro P ...24 A3
Barrême F ...22 C1
Barrhead GB ...6 C1
Barrhill GB ...3 F1
Barrière-de-
Champlon B ...13 D2
Barrow-in-Furness GB ...7 D4
Barruecopardo E ...18 C4
Barruelo de
Santullán E ...19 E2
Barry / Barri GB ...8 B3
Barše SRB ...58 C2
Baršėnai LT ...82 C3
Barsinghausen D ...33 E4
Barštine LT ...85 E2

Barstyčiai LT ...80 B2
Bärta LV ...80 B1
Barth D ...34 B1
Bartkuškis LT ...86 B2
Bartninkai LT ...85 D2
Barton-upon-
Humber GB ...7 F4
Bartoszyce PL ...90 B1
Barumini I ...50 A4
Baruth D ...34 C4
Barvas GB ...4 B2
Barvydžiai LT ...81 D2
Baryčaū BY ...115 D3
Barzdai LT ...85 D2
Barzdžiūnai LT ...85 E3
Barzio I ...43 D4
Bas-en-Basset F ...16 B4

Bašaid SRB ...56 C1
Bàscara E ...21 F4
Baschi I ...47 E4
Basconcillos del
Tozo E ...19 F3
Basel CH ...17 E1
Baselga di Pinè I ...43 F4
Basildon GB ...9 E3
Basingstoke GB ...9 D3
Baška HR ...54 B3
Baška Voda HR ...58 A2
Baške Oštarje HR ...54 B4
Baslow GB ...9 D1
Basovizza I ...44 B4
Bassano del Grappa I ...43 F4
Bassens F ...15 D4
Bassum D ...33 E4
Båstad S ...71 D3
Bastasi BIH ...54 C4

Bastelica F ...23 F4
Bastia F ...23 F3
Bastogne B ...13 D2
Bastuträsk S ...64 B3
Batajnica SRB ...56 C2
Batak BG ...117 D3
Batakiai LT ...84 C1
Batalha P ...24 A2
Batea E ...27 D1
Bategala LT ...85 F1
Bath GB ...9 D3
Bathgate GB ...7 D1
Batina HR ...55 E1
Batlava SRB ...57 D3
Batočina SRB ...57 D2
Batsí GR ...106 B3
Battaglia Terme I ...47 E1
Battenberg D ...13 F1

Battice B ...13 D1
Battipaglia I ...49 D4
Battle GB ...9 E4
Batuecas
(Monasterio Las) E ...25 D1
Batz-sur-Mer F ...14 B1
Baubliai
(Klaipedos) LT ...80 B2
Baubliai (Šiauliu) LT ...81 D2
Baud F ...10 B4
Baugé F ...15 D1
Baugy F ...16 A2
Baukštininkai LT ...80 A3
Baume-les-Dames F ...17 D1
Baumholder D ...13 E2
Bauni LV ...76 C3
Bauska LV ...81 F2
Bautzen D ...40 C1
Bavanište SRB ...57 D2

Bavay F ...12 B2
Baveno I ...17 F3
Bawtry GB ...7 F4
Bayerisch Eisenstein D ...39 F4
Bayeux F ...11 D3
Bayhirivagh GB ...4 A4
Bayon F ...13 D4
Bayonne F ...20 B2
Bayreuth D ...39 E3
Bayrischzell D ...43 F2
Baza E ...30 A3
Bažāni LV ...77 D3
Bazas F ...20 C1
Bazilionai LT ...81 D3
Bazoches-sur-Hoëne F ...11 E4
Bazzano I ...47 D2
Beaconsfield GB ...9 E3
Beaminster GB ...8 C4
Beariz E ...18 A3
Beas E ...28 C2
Beas de Segura E ...26 A4
Beasain E ...20 A2
Beattock GB ...7 D2
Beaucaire F ...22 B2
Beaufort F ...16 C2
Beaufort F ...17 D3
Beaufort-en-Vallée F ...15 D1
Beaugency F ...15 F1
Beaujeu F ...16 B3
Beaulieu GB ...9 D4
Beaulieu-sur-
Dordogne F ...15 F4
Beaulieu-sur-Mer F ...23 D2
Beaumaris GB ...3 F3
Beaumesnil F ...11 F3
Beaumetz-lès-Loges F ...12 A2
Beaumont B ...12 C2
Beaumont-de-
Lomagne F ...21 D2
Beaumont-du-
Périgord F ...15 E4
Beaumont-Hague F ...10 C2
Beaumont-le-Roger F ...11 F3
Beaumont-sur-Oise F ...12 A3
Beaumont-sur-
Sarthe F ...11 E4
Beaune F ...16 C2
Beaune-la-Rolande F ...12 A4
Beaupréau F ...14 C1
Beauraing B ...12 C2
Beaurepaire F ...16 C4
Beaurepaire-en-
Bresse F ...16 C2
Beauvais F ...12 A3
Beauvoir-sur-Mer F ...14 C2
Beauvoir-sur-Niort F ...15 D3
Bebington GB ...7 D4
Bebra D ...38 C2
Bebrene LV ...83 D2
Bebri LV ...80 C1
Bebrina HR ...55 E2
Bebrininkai LT ...85 D2
Bebruliške LT ...85 E2
Bebrupe LV ...77 D3
Beccles GB ...9 F2
Becedas E ...25 E1
Beceite E ...27 E1
Bečej SRB ...56 C1
Becerreá E ...18 C2
Bécherel F ...10 C4
Bechet RO ...117 D3
Bechhofen D ...39 D4
Bečić Miločer MNE ...58 C4
Becilla de
Valderaduey E ...19 D3
Bečiūnai LT ...87 D3
Beckenried CH ...17 F2

BARCELONA

Arnau d'Oms ... CS 4
Berlin ... BT 12
Bisbe Català ... AT 13
Bonanova (Pas. de la) ... BT 16
Borbó (Av. de) ... CS 17
Carles III (Gran Via de) ... BT 38
Constitució ... BT 50
Creu Coberta ... BT 53
Dalt (Travessera de) ... CS 56
Doctor Pi i Molist ... CS 65
Entença ... BT 71
Estadi (Av. de l') ... BCT 75
Fabra i Puig (Pas. de) ... CS 77
Gavà ... BT 84
Gran de Sant Andreu ... CS 88

Guinardó (Ronda del) ... CS 90
Josep Tarradellas (Av. de) ... BT 102
Manuel Girona (Pas. de) ... BT 112
Mare de Déu de Montserrat (Av. de la) ... CS 113
Marina ... CT 114
Marquès de Comillas (Av. del) ... BT 115
Miramar (Av. de) ... CT 119
Numància ... BT 136
Piferrer ... CS 136
Pi i Margall ... CS 138
Poblenou (Rambla del) ... DT 141
Príncep d'Astúries (Av. del) ... BT 144
Pujades (Pas. de) ... CT 145
Ramiro de Maeztu ... CS 146

Ramon Albó ... CS 147
Reina Elisenda de Montcada (Pas. de la) ... BT 151
Reina Maria Cristina (Av. de la) ... BT 152
Ribes (Carret.) ... CS 154
Rio de Janeiro (Av. de) ... CS 156
Santa Coloma (Av. de) ... CS 186
Sant Antoni Maria Claret ... CT 162
Sant Antoni (Ronda de) ... CT 160
Sant Gervasi (Pas. de) ... BS 164
Sant Pau (Ronda de) ... CT 174
Sardenya ... CT 191
Tarragona ... BT 194
Tibidabo (Av. del) ... BS 196
Universitari (Pl. de la) ... CT 198
Verdun (Pas. de) ... CS 200

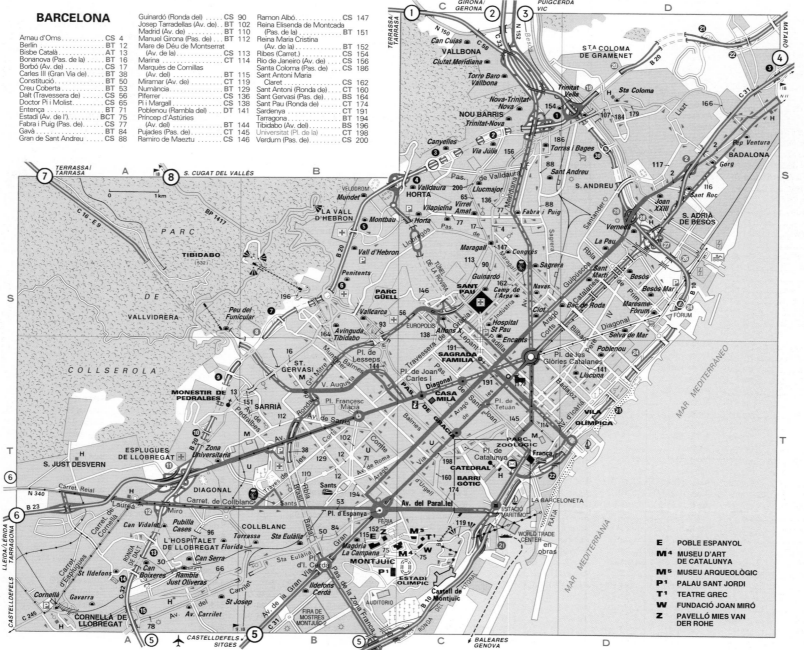

E — POBLE ESPANYOL
M4 — MUSEU D'ART DE CATALUNYA
M5 — MUSEU ARQUEOLÒGIC
P1 — PALAU SANT JORDI
T1 — TEATRE GREC
W — FUNDACIÓ JOAN MIRÓ
Z — PAVELLÓ MIES VAN DER ROHE

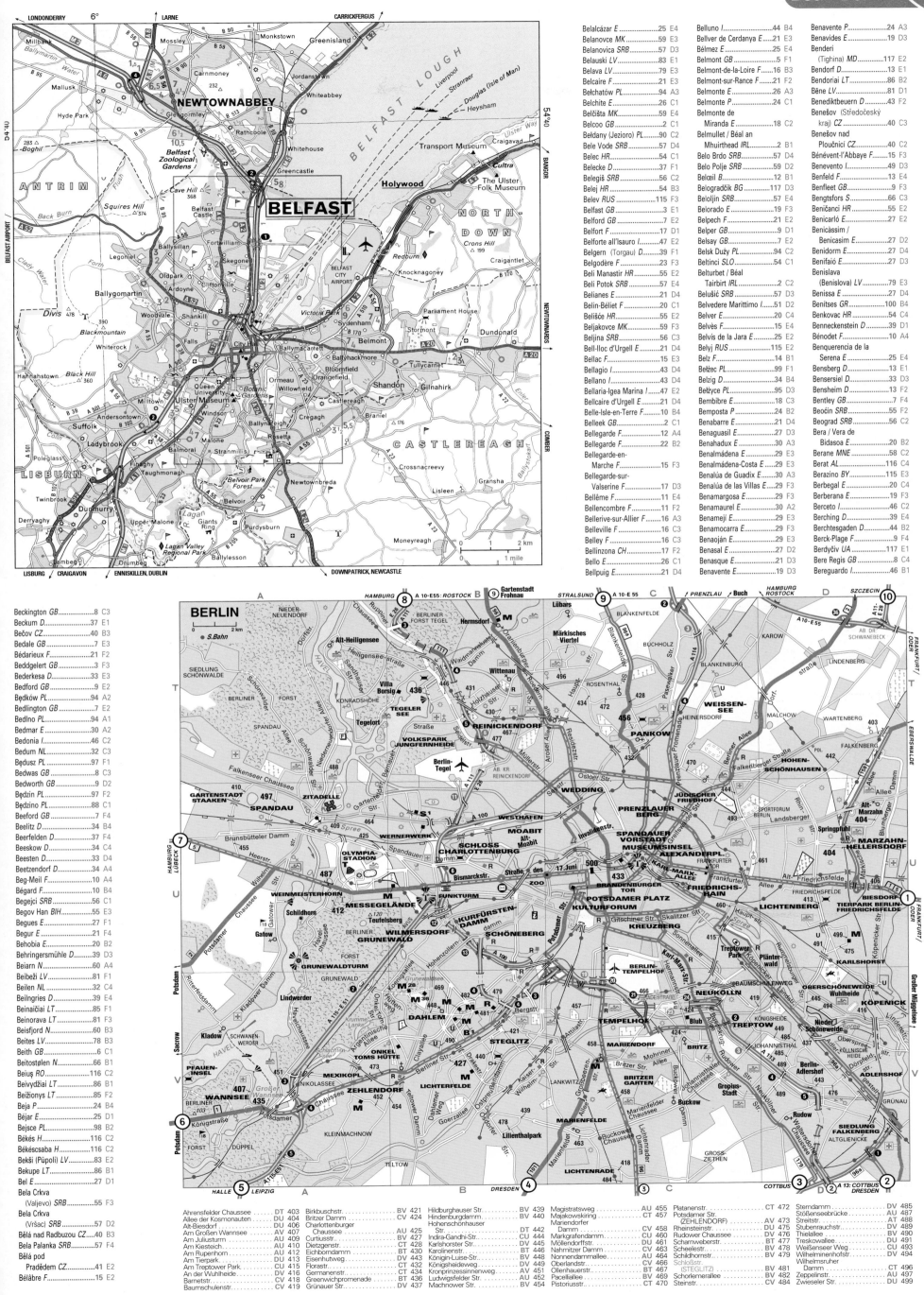

Belalcázar E.....25 E4
Belanovce MK.....59 E3
Belanovica SRB.....57 D3
Belauski LV.....83 E1
Belava LV.....79 E3
Belcaire F.....21 E3
Belchatów PL.....94 A3
Belchite E.....26 C1
Belčišta MK.....59 E3
Belcoo GB.....2 C1
Bełdany (Jezioro) PL.....90 C2
Bele Vode SRB.....57 D4
Belec HR.....54 C1
Belecke D.....37 F1
Belegiš SRB.....56 C2
Belej HR.....54 B3
Belev RUS.....115 F2
Belfast GB.....3 E1
Belford GB.....7 E2
Belfort F.....17 D1
Belforte all'Isauro I.....47 E2
Belgern (Torgau) D.....39 F1
Belgodère F.....23 E3
Beli Manastir HR.....55 E2
Beli Potok SRB.....57 E4
Belianes E.....21 D4
Belin-Béliet F.....20 C1
Belišće HR.....55 E2
Beljakovce MK.....59 E3
Beljina SRB.....56 C2
Bell-lloc d'Urgell E.....21 D4
Bellac F.....15 E3
Bellagio I.....43 D4
Bellano I.....43 D4
Bellaria-Igea Marina I.....47 E2
Bellcaire d'Urgell E.....21 D4
Belleek GB.....2 C1
Bellegarde F.....12 A4
Bellegarde F.....22 B2
Bellegarde-en-Marche F.....15 F3
Bellegarde-sur-Valserine F.....17 D3
Bellême F.....11 E4
Bellencombre F.....11 E2
Bellerive-sur-Allier F.....16 A3
Belleville F.....16 C3
Belley F.....16 C3
Bellinzona CH.....17 F2
Bello E.....26 C1
Bellpuig E.....21 D4

Belluno I.....44 B4
Bellver de Cerdanya E.....21 E3
Bélmez E.....25 E4
Belmont GB.....5 F1
Belmont-de-la-Loire F.....16 B3
Belmont-sur-Rance F.....21 F2
Belmonte E.....26 A3
Belmonte P.....24 C1
Belmonte de Miranda E.....18 C2
Belmullet / Béal an Mhuirthead IRL.....2 B1
Belo Brdo SRB.....57 D4
Belo Polje SRB.....59 D2
Belœil B.....12 B1
Belogradčik BG.....117 D3
Beloljin SRB.....57 D4
Belorado E.....19 F3
Belpech F.....21 E3
Belper GB.....9 D1
Belsay GB.....7 E2
Belsk Duży PL.....94 C2
Beltinci SLO.....54 C1
Belturbet / Béal Tairbirt IRL.....2 C1
Belušić SRB.....57 D3
Belvedere Marittimo I.....51 D2
Belver E.....20 C4
Belvès F.....15 E4
Belvís de la Jara E.....25 E2
Belyj RUS.....115 E2
Belz F.....14 B1
Belžec PL.....99 F1
Belzig D.....34 B4
Betżyce PL.....95 D3
Bembibre E.....18 C3
Bemposta P.....24 B2
Benabarre E.....21 D4
Benaguasil E.....27 D3
Benahadux E.....30 A3
Benalmádena E.....29 E3
Benalmádena-Costa E.....29 E3
Benalúa de Guadix E.....30 A3
Benalúa de las Villas E.....29 D3
Benamargosa E.....29 E3
Benamaurel E.....30 A2
Benamejí E.....29 E3
Benamocarra E.....29 E3
Benaoján E.....29 E3
Benasal E.....27 D2
Benasque E.....21 D3
Benavente E.....19 D3

Benavente P.....24 A3
Benavides E.....19 D3
Benderi (Tighina) MD.....117 E2
Bendorf D.....13 E1
Bendoriai LT.....86 B2
Bēne LV.....81 D1
Benediktbeuern D.....43 F2
Benešov (Středočeský kraj) CZ.....40 C3
Benešov nad Ploučnicí CZ.....40 C3
Bénévent-l'Abbaye F.....15 F3
Benevento I.....49 D3
Benfeld F.....13 E4
Benfleet GB.....9 F3
Bengtsfors S.....66 C3
Beničanci HR.....55 E2
Benicarló E.....27 E2
Benicàssim / Benicasim E.....27 D2
Benidorm E.....27 D4
Benifaió E.....27 D3
Benislava (Benislova) LV.....79 E3
Benissa E.....27 D4
Benitses GR.....100 B4
Benkovac HR.....54 C4
Benneckenstein D.....39 D1
Bénodet F.....10 A4
Benquerencia de la Serena E.....25 E4
Bensberg D.....13 E1
Bensersiel D.....33 E1
Bensheim D.....13 F2
Bentley GB.....7 F4
Beočin SRB.....55 F2
Beograd SRB.....56 C2
Bera / Vera de Bidasoa E.....20 B2
Berane MNE.....58 C2
Berat AL.....116 C4
Berazino BY.....115 E3
Berbegal E.....20 C4
Berberana E.....19 F3
Berceto I.....46 C2
Berching D.....39 E4
Berchtesgaden D.....44 B2
Berck-Plage F.....9 F4
Berdyčiv UA.....117 E1
Bere Regis GB.....8 C4
Bereguardo I.....46 B1

Beckington GB.....8 C3
Beckum D.....37 E1
Bečov CZ.....40 B3
Bedale GB.....7 E3
Bédarieux F.....21 F2
Beddgelert GB.....3 F3
Bederkesa D.....33 E3
Bedford GB.....9 E2
Będków PL.....94 A2
Bedlington GB.....7 E2
Bedlno PL.....94 A1
Bedmar E.....30 A2
Bedonia I.....46 C2
Bedum NL.....32 C3
Będusz PL.....97 F1
Bedwas GB.....8 C3
Bedworth GB.....9 D2
Będzin PL.....97 F2
Będzino PL.....88 C1
Beeford GB.....7 F4
Beelitz D.....34 B4
Beerfelden D.....37 F4
Beeskow D.....34 C4
Beesten D.....33 D4
Beetzendorf D.....34 A4
Beg-Meil F.....10 A4
Bégard F.....10 B4
Begejci SRB.....56 C1
Begues E.....27 F1
Begur E.....21 F4
Behobia E.....20 B2
Behringersmühle D.....39 D3
Beiarn N.....60 A4
Beibeži LV.....81 F1
Beilen NL.....32 C4
Beilngries D.....39 E4
Beinašiai LT.....85 F1
Beinorava LT.....81 F3
Beisfjord N.....60 B3
Beites LV.....78 B3
Beith GB.....6 C1
Beitostølen N.....66 B1
Beiuş RO.....116 C2
Beivydžiai LT.....86 B1
Beižionys LT.....85 F2
Beja P.....24 B4
Béjar E.....25 E2
Bejsce PL.....98 B2
Békés H.....116 C2
Békéscsaba H.....116 C2
Bekši (Pūpoli) LV.....83 E2
Bekupe LT.....86 B1
Bel E.....27 D1
Bela Crkva (Valjevo) SRB.....55 F3
Bela Crkva (Vršac) SRB.....57 D2
Bela Palanka SRB.....57 F4
Bělá nad Radbuzou CZ.....40 B3
Bělá pod Pradědem CZ.....41 E2
Bélâbre F.....15 E2

BERLIN

Ahrensfelder Chaussee.....DT 403
Allee der Kosmonauten.....DU 404
Alt-Biesdorf.....DV 406
Am Großen Wannsee.....AV 407
Am Juliusturm.....AU 409
Am Kiesteich.....AU 410
Am Ruperhorn.....AT 412
Am Tierpark.....CU 413
Am Treptower Park.....CV 415
An der Wuhlheide.....DV 416
Barnetstr..... CV 418
Baumschulenstr..... DV 419

Birkbuschstr..... BV 421
Britzer Damm.....BV 424
Charlottenburger Chaussee.....AU 425
Curtiusstr..... BV 427
Dietzgenstr..... CT 428
Eichborndamm.....BT 430
Eisenhutweg.....DV 432
Florastr..... CT 433
Germanenstr..... CT 434
Greenwichpromenade.....AT 436
Grünauer Str..... DV 437

Hildburghauser Str..... BV 439
Hindenburgdamm.....BV 440
Hohenschönhauser Str..... DT 442
Indira-Gandhi-Str..... CU 444
Karlshorster Str..... BT 446
Karolinenstr..... BT 446
Königin-Luise-Str..... AU 448
Königsheideweg.....CV 449
Kronprinzessinnenweg.....AV 451
Ludwigsfelder Str..... AV 452
Machnower Str..... CV 454

Magistratsweg.....AU 455
Majakowskiring.....CT 457
Mariendorfer Damm.....BV 458
Markgrafendamm.....CU 460
Möllendorffstr..... DU 461
Nahmitzer Damm.....AV 463
Nonnendammallee.....AU 464
Oberlandstr..... CV 466
Ollenhauerstr..... BT 467
Pacelliallee.....AU 469
Pistoriusstr..... CT 470

Platanenstr..... CT 472
Potsdamer Str. (ZEHLENDORF).....AV 473
Rheinsteinstr..... CV 475
Rudower Chaussee.....DV 476
Scharnweberstr..... BT 477
Scheelestr..... AV 478
Schildhornstr..... BV 479
Schloßstr. (STEGLITZ).....BV 481
Schorlemerallee.....BV 482
Steinstr..... CV 484

Sterndamm.....DV 485
Stößenseebrücke.....AU 487
Streitstr..... AT 488
Stubenrauchstr..... AU 489
Thielallee.....BV 490
Treskowallee.....BV 491
Weißenseer Weg.....CU 493
Wilhelminenhofstr..... CV 494
Wilhelmsruher Damm.....CT 496
Zeppelinstr..... AU 497
Zwieseler Str..... DU 499

Berehove UA	116 C2	Berlaimont F	12 B2
Berek HR	55 D2	Berlanga E	25 D4
Berest PL	98 C3	Berlanga de Duero E	19 F4
Beret E	21 D3	Berlebeck D	37 F1
Berettyóújfalu H	116 C2	Berlevåg N	61 F1
Berezivka UA	117 F2	Berlin D	34 B4
Berg A	45 F1	Bermeo E	20 A2
Berg N	63 D1	Bermillo de Sayago E	18 C4
Berg S	63 E4	Bern CH	17 E2
Berga D	39 D1	Bernalda I	49 F4
Berga E	21 E4	Bernartice (Jihočeský	
Bergamo I	43 E4	kraj) CZ	40 C3
Bergara E	20 A2	Bernáti LV	80 A1
Bergby S	67 E3	Bernatoniai LT	81 F3
Bergedorf		Bernau D	34 B3
(Hamburg-) D	33 F3	Bernau i.	
Bergen D	34 B1	Schwarzwald D	17 E3
Bergen D	33 F4	Bernaville F	12 A1
Bergen N	66 A1	Bernay F	11 E3
Bergen NL	32 A4	Bernburg D	39 D1
Bergen (Dumme) D	33 F3	Berndorf A	45 E1
Bergen aan Zee NL	32 A4	Berne D	33 D1
Bergen op Zoom NL	36 B1	Bernhardsthal A	41 E4
Bergerac F	15 E4	Bernkastel-Kues D	13 E2
Berggießhübel D	39 F2	Bernsdorf D	39 F1
Bergheim D	13 D1	Bernstein A	45 E1
Bergisch Gladbach D	13 E1	Beroun CZ	40 C3
Bergnäset S	64 C2	Berovo MK	59 F3
Bergneustadt D	13 E1	Berra I	47 E1
Bergö FIN	68 C2	Berre-l'Étang F	22 B2
Bergsjö S	68 A3	Beršad' UA	117 E1
Bergsviken S	114 C3	Beršstele LV	81 E1
Bergues F	12 A1	Bersenbrück D	33 D4
Bergün / Bravuogn CH	43 E3	Bertamiráns E	18 A2
Beringel P	24 B4	Bertaučiai LT	81 E2
Beringen B	12 C1	Berteškiai LT	81 E1
Berja E	30 A3	Bertinoro I	47 E2
Berjozovka LV	83 F2	Bertrix B	12 C2
Berka D	38 C2	Bērvircava LV	81 E2
Berkåk N	62 C3	Berwang A	43 E2
Berkas LV	81 F1	Berwick-upon-	
Berkhamsted GB	9 E3	Tweed GB	7 E2
Berkheim D	43 E1	Beryslav UA	117 F1
Berkhof D	33 E4	Bērzaine LV	78 B2
Berkovica BG	117 D4	Bērzaune LV	82 C1
Berkovići BIH	58 B2	Bērzāji LV	77 E3
Bērzciems LV	77 E3	Béznar E	29 F3
Bērze LV	81 E1	Biała (Opolskie) PL	89 D1
Bērzele LT	81 F3	Biała Parcela PL	93 F3
Bērzezers LV	78 C2	Biała Piska PL	91 D2
Bērzgale (Bieržgals) LV	83 F1	Biała Podlaska PL	95 E2
Bērzi LV	81 F2	Biała Rawska PL	94 B2
Bērzini (Cēsu) LV	78 B3	Białe Błota PL	89 D3
Bērzini (Jelgavas) LV	81 E2	Białka PL	95 E2
Bērzkalne LV	79 E3	Białobrzegi	
Bērzkalni		(Mazowieckie) PL	91 E3
(Bauskas) LV	81 F2	Białobrzegi	
Bērzkalni (Ogres) LV	78 B3	(Podkarpackie) PL	99 D2
Bērzkrogs LV	78 C3	Białogard PL	88 C2
Berzocana E	25 C3	Białopole PL	95 F2
Beržoras LT	80 B2	Białośliwie PL	89 D3
Bērzpils (Bierzpils) LV	83 E1	Białowieski Park	
Bērzupe LV	81 D1	Narodowy PL	91 F3
Besalú E	21 F4	Białowieża PL	91 F3
Besande E	19 E2	Biały Bór PL	89 D2
Besançon F	17 D1	Biały Dunajec PL	98 D3
Besenyszög D	38 C4	Białystok PL	91 E3
Besigheim D	38 C4	Biancavilla I	53 D3
Beška SRB	56 C2	Bianco I	51 D4
Besko PL	99 D2	Biandrate I	17 F3
Besse-et-St-		Biar E	26 C4
Anastaise F	16 A4	Biarritz F	20 B2
Besse-sur-Issole F	22 C2	Biasca CH	17 F2
Bessèges F	22 A1	Biasteri E	20 A3
Bessines-sur-		Bibbiena I	47 E3
Gartempe F	15 F3	Biberach an der Riß D	43 D1
Betanzos E	18 B2	Biberach i. Kinzigtal D	13 F4
Betelu E	20 A2	Bibinje HR	54 C4
Bétera E	27 D3	Bibione I	44 C4
Beteta E	26 B1	Bibury GB	9 D2
Bethesda GB	3 F3	Bicaz RO	117 D2
Béthune F	12 A1	Bicester GB	9 D2
Bettna S	67 E3	Bichl D	43 F2
Bettola I	46 C1	Bidache F	20 B2
Bettolle I	47 E3	Bidart F	20 B2
Bettyhill GB	4 C1	Biddenden GB	9 F3
Betws-y-Coed GB	3 F3	Bideford GB	8 B3
Betygala LT	85 E1	Biebelried D	38 C3
Betz F	12 A3	Biebrza PL	91 E2
Betzdorf D	13 E1	Biebrzanska	
Beuil F	23 D1	(Kotlina) PL	91 E2
Beura-Cardezza I	17 F3	Biebrzański Park	
Beuron D	43 D1	Narodowy PL	91 E2
Beuzeville F	11 E3	Biecz PL	98 C2
Bevagna I	47 F3	Biedenkopf D	13 F1
Beveren B	12 B1	Biedrusko PL	93 D1
Beverley GB	7 F4	Biel / Bienne CH	17 E1
Beverstedt D	33 E3	Bielany-Żyłaki PL	95 D1
Beverungen D	38 C1	Bielawa PL	96 C1
Beverwijk NL	32 A4	Bielawy	
Bewdley GB	8 C2	(Łodzkie) PL	94 A2
Bex CH	17 E2	Bielefeld D	37 F1
Bexhill GB	9 E4	Bielice (Zachodniopo-	
Beynac-et-Cazenac F	15 E4	morskie) PL	88 A3
Beynat F	16 A4	Bieliny Kapitulne PL	94 C3
Bezas E	26 C2	Biella I	17 F3
Bezdan SRB	55 E1	Bielsa E	21 D3
Bezdonys LT	86 C2	Bielsk PL	90 C4
Bežeck RUS	115 F1	Bielsk Podlaski PL	91 E3
Béziers F	21 F2	Bielsko-Biała PL	97 F2
		Bieniów PL	92 B2
		Bienne / Biel CH	17 E1
		Bientina I	47 D3
		Bienvenida E	25 D4
		Bierawa PL	97 E2
		Bierné F	15 D1
		Bierre-lès-Semur F	16 B1
		Bieruń PL	97 F2
		Bierutów PL	93 E3
		Bierzwnik PL	88 B3
		Biescas E	20 C3
		Biesenthal D	34 C2
		Biesiekierz PL	88 C1
		Bieszczady PL	99 D3
		Bieszczadzki Park	
		Narodowy PL	99 E3
		Bietigheim D	38 C4
		Bieżuń PL	90 A3
		Biga TR	117 E4
		Biggar GB	7 D2
		Biggleswade GB	9 E2
		Bignasco CH	17 F2
		Bihać BIH	54 C3
		Bijele Poljane MNE	58 C3
		Bijeljani BIH	58 B3
		Bijeljina BIH	55 E2
		Bijelo Brdo HR	55 F3
		Bijelo Polje MNE	58 C2
		Bijotai LT	80 C3
		Bijūnai LT	85 E3
		Bijutiškis LT	86 C2
		Bikernieki	
		(Bikerniki) LV	83 E3

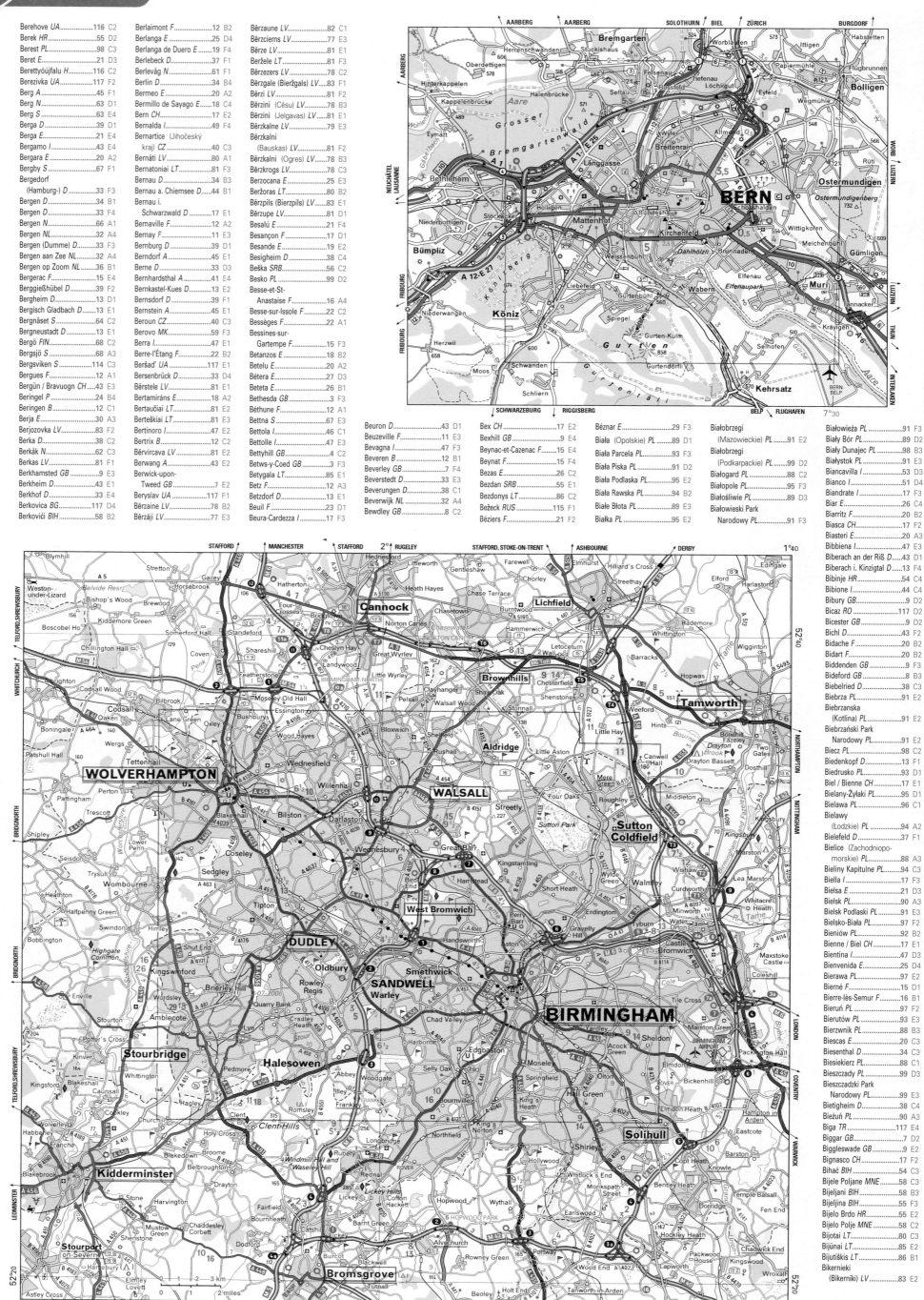

BOLOGNA

Amaseo (V. R.) .... GU 6
Arno (V.) .... HV 9
Artigiano (V. d.) .... GU 10
Bandiera (V. I.) .... FV 12
Barbieri (V. F.) .... GU 13
Barca (V. d.) .... FV 15

Battaglia (V. d.) .... HU 16
Bentivogli (V. G.) .... GV 19
Beverara (V. della) .... FU 20
Cadriano (V.) .... GHU 21
Castiglione (V.) .... HU 25
Cavazzoni (V. F.) .... HV 27
Codivilla (V.) .... GV 31
Colombo (V. C.) .... FU 34
Coubertin (V. de) .... FV 36

Dagnini (V. G.) .... GV 39
Firenze (V.) .... HV 42
Foscherara (V. d.) .... GV 43
Gagarin (V. Y.) .... FU 45
Gandhi (Viale M. K.) .... FU 49
Marconi (V.) .... EV 61

Marco Polo (V.) .... FU 60
Mario (V. A.) .... GV 63

Martelli (V. T.) .... HV 66
Matteotti (V.) .... GU 67
Mazzini (V.) .... GV 69
Mezzofanti (V. G.) .... GV 70
Montefiorino (V.) .... FV 73
Ospedaletto (V. d.) .... EU 79
Palagi (V. P.) .... GV 81
Panigale (V.) .... GV 82

Persicetana Vecchia (V.) .... EU 85
Persicetana (V.) .... EU 84
Pietra (V. d.) .... EU 88
Pirandello (V. L.) .... HU 90
Porrettana (V.) .... FVE 91
Putti (V. V.) .... GV 96
Sabbioni (V. d.) .... GV 100
Saffi (V. A.) .... FU 103

Sigonio (V. C.) .... GV 111
Sturzo (V. Don L.) .... FV 112
S. Barbara (V.) .... GV 105
S. Mamolo (V.) .... FU 108
Timavo (V.) .... FU 115
Tolmino (V.) .... FV 117
Tosarelli (V. B.) .... HU 118

Bikoniai LT 86 B1
Bikšėre LV 79 D3
Biksti LV 81 D1
Bila Cerkva UA 117 E1
Bilbao E 20 A2
Bildudalur IS 62 A1
Bile HR 55 E2
Bileća BIH 58 B3
Bilecik TR 117 F4
Biłgoraj PL 99 E1
Bilhorod-Dnistrovs'kyj UA 117 E1
Biliakiemis LT 82 C3
Bilina CZ 40 B2
Biliūnai LT 82 B3
Biljača SRB 59 E3
Biljanovac SRB 57 D4
Bille LV 78 B3
Billerbeck D 37 E1
Billericay GB 9 E3
Billingham GB 7 E1
Billingshurst GB 9 E3
Billom F 16 A3
Billund DK 70 B3
Bilopillja UA 115 F4
Bilovec CZ 41 F2
Bilska UA 78 C2
Bilto N 61 D2
Bilzen B 13 D1
Binaced E 20 C4
Binarowa PL 98 C3
Binasco I 46 B1
Binche B 12 B2
Bindari LV 83 D2
Binéfar E 21 D4
Binenai LT 81 E2
Bingen D 13 F2
Bingham GB 9 D1
Bingley GB 7 E1
Bingsjö S 67 E1
Binic F 10 B4
Binz D 34 B4
Bioče MNE 58 C3
Biograd na moru HR 54 C4
Bionaz I 17 E3
Birchington GB 9 F3
Bircza PL 99 E2
Biri N 66 C1
Birini LV 78 B3
Birjoučiai LT 81 E3
Birkeland N 66 B3
Birkeneli LV 83 D3
Birkenfeld D 13 E2
Birkenhead GB 7 D4
Birkenwerder D 34 B3
Birkerød DK 70 C3
Birkfeld A 45 E2
Birmingham GB 9 D2
Birnau D 17 F1
Birr / Biorra IRL 2 C3
Birščiai LT 85 E3
Birštonas LT 85 E3
Biržai LT 82 B2
Birzebbuga M 53 F4
Birzes LV 81 F1
Birzgale LV 78 B3
Birži (Jēkabpils) LV 82 C2
Birži (Kuldīgas) LV 76 B3
Birztalas LV 78 C2

Biržūnai LT 83 D3
Biržuvenai LT 80 C2
Biržu Laukas LT 80 C3
Bisaccia I 49 D3
Biscarrosse F 20 B1
Biscarrosse-Plage F 20 B1
Bisceglie I 49 E3
Bischofsgrün D 39 D3
Bischofsheim an der Rhön (Kreis Rhön-Grabfeld) D 38 C3
Bischofshofen A 44 C2
Bischofswerda D 40 C1
Bischofswiesen D 44 B2
Bischwiller F 13 F3
Bisenti I 48 B2
Biševo HR 58 A4
Bishop Auckland GB 7 E3
Bishop's Castle GB 8 C2
Bishop's Stortford GB 9 E3
Bisignano I 51 D2
Bisko HR 55 D4
Biskupiec (Kujawsko-Pomorskie) PL 89 F2
Biskupiec (Warmińsko-Mazurskie) PL 90 C2
Biskupin PL 89 E3
Bismark D 34 A4
Bismo N 62 B4
Bispgården S 68 A2
Bispingen D 33 F3
Bistrica (Prijepolje) SRB 56 C4
Bistrica (Žabljak) MNE 58 C2
Bistrica ob S. SLO 54 B2
Bistrița RO 117 D2
Bisztynek PL 90 C1
Bitburg D 13 D2
Bitche F 13 E3
Bitetto I 49 F3
Bitola MK 59 D3
Bitonto I 49 F3
Bitterfeld D 39 E1
Bitti I 50 B3
Bizau A 43 E2
Bizovac HR 55 E2
Bjala BG 117 D2
Bjaroza BY 115 D1
Bjärkreim N 66 A3
Bjärnum S 71 E3
Bjelovar HR 55 D2
Bjerkreim N 66 A3
Bjerkvik N 60 B3
Bjerringbro DK 70 B2
Bjørkelangen N 66 C2
Björketorp S 71 E3
Björkliden S 60 C3
Björkö FIN 67 F2
Björköby FIN 67 F2
Björksele S 64 B3
Bjorli N 62 B4
Björna S 68 B3
Bjørnevatn N 61 F2
Bjørsäter S 72 B1
Bjurholm S 68 B1
Bjursås S 67 E1
Bjuv S 71 D3

Blace SRB 57 E4
Blachownia PL 93 F3
Blackburn GB 7 D4
Blackpool GB 7 D4
Blackwater IRL 3 D4
Blackwaterfoot GB 6 C2
Blaenau Ffestiniog GB 3 F3
Blaenavon GB 8 C2
Blagaj BIH 58 B2
Blagnac F 21 E2
Blagoevgrad BG 117 D4
Bláhammaren S 63 D3
Blain F 14 C1
Blainville-sur-l'Eau F 13 D4
Blair Atholl GB 4 C4
Blairgowrie GB 7 D1
Blakeney GB 9 F1
Blakstad N 66 B3
Blámont F 13 E4
Blanca E 26 C4
Blandford Forum GB 8 C4
Blandžiai LT 85 E1
Blanes E 21 F4
Blangy-le-Château F 11 E3
Blangy-sur-Bresle F 11 F2
Blankenberge B 36 B2
Blankenburg D 39 D1
Blankenfelde (Saulite) LV 81 E2
Blankenhain D 39 D2
Blankenheim D 13 D1
Blanquefort F 15 D4
Blansko CZ 41 E3
Blanzac F 15 D4
Blanzy F 16 B2
Blarney IRL 2 B4
Błaszki PL 93 F2
Blatná CZ 40 C3
Blatnica BIH 55 E3
Blato HR 58 A4
Blattniksele S 64 A3
Blaubeuren D 43 D1
Blaufelden D 38 C4
Blaustein D 43 E1
Blaye F 15 D4
Blaževo SRB 57 D4
Blažma LV 76 C2
Błażowa PL 99 D2
Bleckede D 33 F3
Bled SLO 54 A2
Błędów (Śląskie) PL 98 A2
Bledzew PL 92 B1
Bleiburg A 45 D2
Bleicherode D 39 D1
Bleik N 60 B2
Bléneau F 16 A1
Blénod-lès-Pont-à-Mousson F 13 D3
Blérancourt F 12 B3
Bléré F 15 E1
Blesle F 16 A4
Bletchley GB 9 E2
Bletterans F 16 C2
Blexen D 33 D3
Blidene LV 81 D1
Blieskastel D 13 E3
Bligny-sur-Ouche F 16 C2
Blīnja HR 54 C2

Bliūdžiai (Biržai) LT 82 B2
Bliūdžiai (Kauno) LT 85 D1
Bliūdžiai (Panevėžys) LT 81 F3
Blizanów PL 93 F2
Bližyn PL 94 C3
Bloemendaal NL 32 A4
Blois F 15 F1
Blokhus DK 70 B1
Blomberg D 37 F1
Blome LV 78 C2
Blomi LV 77 F2
Blönduós IS 62 A1
Błonie (Mazowieckie) PL 94 B1
Blonti LV 83 F1
Blonville-sur-Mer F 11 E3
Blosenberg D 39 E2
Bloška polica SLO 54 B2
Blovice CZ 40 B3
Bludenz A 43 E3
Blukas LV 81 E1
Blumberg D 34 C4
Blumberg D 13 F4
Blyth GB 7 E2
Bnin PL 93 D1
Bø (Telemark) N 66 B2
Bo' Ness GB 7 D1
Boal E 18 C2
Boan MNE 58 C2
Boara Pisani I 47 E1
Bobbio I 46 B1
Bobbio Pellice I 17 E4
Bobigny F 12 A3
Bobingen D 43 D1
Böblingen D 38 C4
Boblitz D 34 C4
Bobolice PL 88 C2
Boboszów PL 96 C2
Bobowa PL 98 C2
Bóbr PL 92 C1
Bóbrka PL 99 D2
Bobrovycja UA 115 F4
Bobrowice PL 92 B2
Bobrowniki (Podkarpackie) PL 91 F3
Bobrynec' UA 117 F1
Bočac BIH 55 D3
Bocairent E 26 C4
Boceguillas E 19 F4
Bochnia PL 98 B2
Bocholt B 13 D1
Bochov CZ 40 B3
Bochum D 37 E1
Bockenem D 38 C1
Boćki PL 91 E3
Böckstein A 44 C2
Bockum-Hövel D 37 E1
Bocognano F 23 F3
Boda S 67 E1
Böda S 71 F2
Bodafors S 67 E4
Boďani SRB 55 F2
Bodegraven NL 36 C1
Boden S 64 C1
Bodenmais D 39 F4
Bodenteich D 33 F4
Bodenwerder D 38 C1
Bodenwöhr D 39 E4

Bodman D 43 D2
Bodmin GB 8 A4
Bodø N 60 A4
Bodzentyn PL 94 C3
Boecillo E 19 E4
Boège F 17 D3
Boën F 16 B3
Boeza E 18 C3
Boffalora sopra Ticino I 17 F3
Bogarra E 26 B4
Bogatić SRB 55 F2
Bogatynia PL 92 B3
Bogdanci MK 59 E3
Bogdaniec PL 88 B3
Bogen D 39 F4
Bogen N 60 B3
Bogense DK 70 B3
Bogetići MNE 58 C3
Bognanco I 27 F4
Bognes N 60 B3
Bognor Regis GB 9 E4
Bogodol BIH 58 B2
Bogojevo SRB 55 F2
Bogomila MK 59 D3
Bogomolje HR 58 A3
Bogoria PL 98 C1
Bogorodica MK 59 F4
Bogovina SRB 57 E3
Boguchwała PL 99 D2
Bogušišikiai LT 81 D3
Boguslavas LT 80 C2
Boguszów Gorce PL 92 C3
Bogutovac SRB 57 D3
Boguty-Pianki PL 91 D3
Bohain-en-Vermandois F 12 B2
Boherboy IRL 2 B4
Bohinjska Bistrica SLO 54 A2
Böhlen D 39 E1
Böhmenkirch D 43 E1
Bohmte D 33 D4
Bohoduchiv UA 115 F4
Böhönye H 116 B2
Bohumín CZ 41 F2
Bohuslav UA 117 F1
Boiro E 18 A2
Bois-d'Amont F 17 D2
Boitzenburg D 34 B3
Bóixols E 21 D4
Bojadła PL 92 C2
Bojano I 48 C3
Bojanów PL 99 D2
Bojanowo PL 93 D2
Bojas LV 80 B1
Bøjden DK 70 B3
Bojkovice CZ 41 F3
Bojnik SRB 57 E4
Bojszowy PL 98 B2
Bokštai LT 80 C3
Bol HR 58 A4
Bolaños de Calatrava E 25 F3
Bolbec F 11 E3
Bolchov RUS 115 F3
Bolesław (Małopolskie) PL 98 A2

Bolesławiec (Dolnośląskie) PL 92 B3
Bolesławiec (Łódzkie) PL 93 E3
Boleszkowice PL 88 A3
Bolhrad UA 117 E2
Boliden S 64 B3
Bolimów PL 94 B2
Bolimowska (Puszcza) PL 94 B2
Boliqueime P 28 B2
Boljanići MNE 55 F4
Boljevac SRB 57 E3
Boljevci SRB 56 C2
Boljuni BIH 58 B3
Bolkesjø N 66 B2
Bolków PL 92 C3
Bollebygd S 67 D4
Bollène F 22 B1
Bollnäs S 67 F1
Bollstabruk S 68 A2
Bollullos de la Mitación E 29 D2
Bollullos Par del Condado E 28 C2
Bolochovo RUS 115 F2
Bologna I 47 D2
Bologne F 12 C4
Bologoje RUS 115 E1
Bolotana I 50 A3
Bolsena I 47 E4
Bolsward NL 32 B3
Boltaña E 20 C3
Boltenhagen D 33 F2
Boltimuiža (Indrāne) LV 82 C2
Bolton GB 7 E4
Bolungarvík IS 62 A1
Bolzano / Bozen I 43 F3
Bom Jesus do Monte P 18 A4
Bombarral P 24 A2
Bomenzien D 33 A4
Boñar E 19 D2
Bonares E 28 C2
Bonassola I 23 F1
Bondeno I 47 D1
Bonefro I 48 C3
Bonete E 26 C4
Bonifacio F 23 F4
Boniškiai LT 85 E1
Bonn D 13 E1
Bonnåsjøen N 60 B4
Bonnat F 15 F3
Bonndorf (Kreis Waldshut) D 17 F1
Bonnétable F 11 E4
Bonneuil-Matours F 15 E2
Bonneval F 11 F4
Bonneville F 17 D3
Bonnières-sur-Seine F 11 F3
Bonnieux F 22 B2
Bono I 50 A3
Bonorva I 50 A3
Boo S 67 F3
Boos F 11 F3
Bootle GB 7 D4

Bopfingen D 39 D4
Boppard D 13 E2
Bor CZ 40 B3
Bor SRB 57 E3
Borås S 67 D4
Borba P 24 C3
Borbona I 47 F4
Borča SRB 56 C2
Borci BIH 55 E4
Bordeaux F 15 D4
Bordères-Louron F 21 D3
Bordesholm D 33 E2
Bordighera I 23 E1
Bore I 46 C1
Borek Wielkopolski PL 93 D2
Borello I 47 E2
Borensberg S 67 E3
Borgafjäll S 63 E2
Borgarfjörður IS 62 C1
Borgarnes IS 62 A1
Börger D 33 D4
Borger NL 32 C4
Borghetto I 47 E4
Borghetto Santo Spirito I 23 E1
Borgholm S 71 F2
Borgholzhausen D 37 F1
Borghorst D 37 E1
Borgia I 51 E3
Borgo S. Dalmazzo I 23 D1
Borgo S. Lorenzo I 47 D3
Borgo Tufico I 47 F3
Borgo Val di Taro I 46 C2
Borgo Valsugana I 43 F3
Borgomanero I 17 F3
Borgone Susa I 17 E4
Borgonovo Val Tidone I 46 C1
Borgorose I 47 F4
Borgosesia I 17 F3
Borgsjö S 68 A3
Borgvattnet S 63 F3
Boričie MNE 58 C2
Borisova LV 79 F3
Borja E 20 B4
Borken D 37 E1
Borkenes / Kvæfjord N 60 B3
Borki (Lubelskie) PL 95 E2
Børkop DK 70 B3
Borkowice PL 94 B3
Borkum D 32 C2
Borlänge S 67 E1
Bormani LV 82 C2
Bormes-les-Mimosas F 22 C2
Bormio I 43 F2
Born am Darß (Kreis Nordvorpommern) D 34 A1
Borna (Kreis Leipziger Land) D 39 E2
Borne Sulinowo PL 88 C2
Bornes P 18 B4
Bornhöved D 33 F2
Börnicke (Kreis Havelland) D 34 B3

Borovnica SLO 54 A2
Borovo HR 55 F2
Borovsk RUS 115 F2
Borów (Dolnośląskie) PL 93 D3
Borowa PL 98 C1
Borowie PL 95 D2
Borre N 66 C2
Borriana / Burriana E 27 D2
Borriol E 27 D2
Borris IRL 3 D4
Borrisokane / Buiríos Uí Chéin IRL 2 C3
Borşa RO 117 D2
Børselv N 61 E1
Börsi GR 104 C3
Bort-les-Orgues F 16 A4
Börtnan S 63 E4
Boryspil' UA 115 E4
Borzechowo PL 89 E2
Borzęcin PL 98 C2
Borzna UA 115 F4
Borzonasca I 23 F1
Borzytuchom PL 89 D1
Bosa I 50 A3
Bosanci HR 54 B2
Bosanska Dubica / Kosarska Dubica BIH 55 D3
Bosanska Gradiška BIH 55 D2
Bosanska Gradiška / Gradiška BIH 55 D2
Bosanska Kostajnica / Srpska Kostajnica BIH 54 C3
Bosanska Krupa BIH 54 C3
Bosanska Rača / Rača BIH 55 F2
Bosanski Brod / Srpski Brod BIH 55 E2
Bosanski Kobaš / Kobaš BIH 55 E2
Bosanski Novi / Novi Grad BIH 54 C3
Bosanski Petrovac BIH 54 C3
Bosanski Šamac / Šamac BIH 55 E2
Bosansko Grahovo BIH 55 D4
Bosansko Petrovo Selo / Petrovo BIH 55 E3
Bosco I 47 F3
Bosco Chiesanuova I 43 F4
Boscoreale I 48 C4
Bosilegrad SRB 59 F2
Bosiljevo HR 54 B2
Bosjökloster S 71 D3
Bošnjace SRB 57 E4
Bošnjaci HR 55 E2
Bossolasco I 23 E1
Bossòst E 21 D3
Boštanj SLO 54 B2
Boston GB 9 E1
Botevgrad BG 117 D4
Bothel GB 7 D3
Boticas P 18 B4
Botley GB 9 D4
Botngård N 62 C3
Botoš SRB 56 C2
Botoşani RO 117 E2
Botsmark S 64 B3
Bottrop D 37 E1
Botun MK 59 E4
Bouaye F 14 C1
Boucau F 20 B2
Bouchain F 12 B2
Boudry CH 17 D2
Bouillon B 12 C2
Bouilly F 12 B4
Boúka GR 108 A3
Boulay-Moselle F 13 D3
Boulogne-sur-Gesse F 21 D2
Boulogne-sur-Mer F 9 F4
Bouloire F 11 E4
Bourbon-Lancy F 16 B2
Bourbon-l'Archambault F 16 A2
Bourbonne-les-Bains F 13 D4
Bourbourg F 12 A1
Bourbriac F 10 B4
Bourdeaux F 22 B1
Bourdeilles F 15 E4
Bourg F 15 D4
Bourg-Achard F 11 E3
Bourg-Argental F 16 B4
Bourg-de-Péage F 16 C4
Bourg-de-Visa F 21 D1
Bourg-en-Bresse F 16 C3
Bourg-Lastic F 16 A3
Bourg-Madame F 21 E3
Bourg-St-Andéol F 22 B1
Bourg-St-Maurice F 17 D3
Bourganeuf F 15 F3
Bourges F 15 F2
Bourgneuf-en-Retz F 14 C2
Bourgoin-Jallieu F 16 C3
Bourgtheroulde-Infreville F 11 F3
Bourgueil F 15 E1
Bourmont F 13 D4
Bourne GB 9 E1
Bournemouth GB 9 D4
Bouro P 18 A4
Boussac F 15 F2
Boussens F 21 D2
Bouxwiller F 13 E3

Bouzonville F.................13 D3
Bova Marina I.................51 D4
Bovalino Marina I.............51 E4
Bovan SRB....................57 E3
Bovec SLO....................43 F3
Bóveda (Lugo) E..............18 B3
Bøverdal N...................62 B4
Boves F......................12 A2
Boves I......................23 D1
Bovey Tracey GB...............8 B4
Bovolone I...................47 D1
Bowes GB.....................7 E3
Bowness GB...................7 D3
Bowness-on-Solway GB.........7 D3
Boxholm S....................67 E3
Boxmeer NL...................37 D1
Boxtel NL....................36 C1
Boyle / Mainistir na
   Búille IRL................2 C2
Božaj MNE....................58 C3
Božavar HR...................54 B4
Bozel F......................17 D3
Bozen / Bolzano I............43 F3
Boži Dar CZ..................40 B2
Božica SRB...................59 F2
Bozouls F....................21 F1
Bozova LV....................83 F1
Bozüyük TR..................117 F4
Bozzolo I....................46 C1
Bra I........................17 F4
Brač (Otok) HR...............58 A4
Bracadale GB..................4 A3
Bracciano I..................47 E4
Bračevci HR..................55 E2
Bracieux F...................15 F1
Bräcke S.....................63 E4
Brackenheim D................38 C4
Brackley GB...................9 D2
Bracknell GB.................9 D3
Brackwede D..................37 F1
Brad RO.....................117 D2
Bradford GB...................7 E4
Bradford-on-Avon GB..........8 C3
Bradina BIH..................55 E4
Brading GB....................9 D4
Bradwell-on-Sea GB...........9 F3
Braemar GB....................5 D4
Braga P......................18 A4
Bragança P...................18 C4
Brăila RO...................117 D2
Braine F.....................12 B3
Braine-le-Comte B............12 B1
Braintree GB..................9 F2
Brake (Unterweser) (Kreis
   Wesermarsch) D............33 D3
Brakel D.....................37 F1
Bräkne-Hoby S................71 E3
Bralin PL....................97 F2
Brallo di Pregola I..........46 B1
Brálos GR...................105 D2
Bramberge LV.................81 E1
Bramming DK..................70 B3
Brampton GB...................7 D3
Bramsche D...................33 D4
Brancaleone Marina I.........51 D4
Brancion F...................16 C2
Brand A......................43 E3
Brand-Erbisdorf D............39 F2
Brandbu N....................66 C1
Brande DK....................70 B3
Brande-
   Hörnerkirchen D..........33 E2
Brandenburg D................34 B4
Brandis
   (Muldentalkreis) D.......39 E1
Brändö FIN...................68 C4
Brandon GB....................9 F2
Branduoliškiai LT............85 D1
Branice PL...................97 F2
Braničevo SRB................57 D2
Braniewo PL..................90 A1
Brankas LV...................81 E1
Branne F.....................15 D4
Brañosera E..................19 E2
Brańsk PL....................91 E3
Br'ansk RUS.................115 F3
Brantôme F...................15 E4
Braskereidfoss N.............66 C1
Braslaŭ BY.................115 D2
Brasli LV....................80 B1
Brașov RO...................117 D2
Brassac F....................21 F2
Brassac-les-Mines F..........4 A4
Brasschaat B.................36 C2
Bratislava SK...............116 B1
Brattvåg N...................62 B3
Bratunac BIH.................55 F3
Braubach D...................13 E2
Braunau A....................44 B1
Braunfels D..................13 F1
Braunlage D..................39 D1
Braunsbedra D................39 E1
Braunschweig D...............33 F4
Braunton GB...................8 B3
Bravães P....................18 A3
Bray / Bré IRL...............3 D3
Bray-Dunes F.................12 A1
Bray-sur-Seine F.............12 A3
Bray-sur-Somme F.............12 A2
Brazatortas E................25 F4
Bražuole LT..................86 B2
Brbinj HR....................54 B4
Brčko BIH....................55 F3
Brđani SRB...................57 D3
Brea E.......................20 B4
Brécey F.....................11 D4
Brechin GB....................5 D4

Brecht B.....................36 C2
Břeclav CZ...................41 E4
Brecon /
   Aberhonddu GB.............8 B2
Breda E......................21 F4
Breda NL.....................36 C1
Bredbyn S....................68 A1
Bredelar D...................37 F1
Bredstedt D..................33 E1
Bree B.......................13 D1
Breganze I...................43 F4
Bregenz A....................43 D2
Bréhal F.....................11 D3
Brehna D.....................39 E1
Breiðdalsvík IS..............62 C1
Breil-sur-Roya F.............23 D1
Breisach D...................13 E4
Breitengüßbach D.............39 D3
Breitungen D.................38 C2
Breivikbotn N................61 D1
Breivikeidet N...............60 C2
Brekken N....................63 D4
Brekkvasselv N...............63 E3
Brekstad N...................62 C3
Bremen
   (Kreis Bremen) D.........33 E3
Bremerhaven D................33 D3
Bremervörde D................33 E3
Bremsnes N...................62 B3
Brenci LV....................79 E3
Brenes E.....................29 E3
Brenguli LV..................78 C2
Brenna PL....................97 F2
Brennilis F..................10 B4
Breno I......................43 E4
Brénod F.....................16 C3
Brentwood GB..................9 E3
Brescia I....................43 E4
Breskens NL..................36 B2
Bresles F....................12 A3
Bressanone / Brixen I........43 F3
Bressuire F..................15 D2
Brest BY....................114 C4
Brest F......................10 A4
Brestanica SLO...............54 B2
Brestova HR..................55 D2
Brestovac (Bor) SRB..........57 E3

Brestovac
   (Leskovac) SRB...........57 E4
Brestovac
   (Prokuplje) SRB..........57 E4
Brestovac (Rijeka) HR........54 A3
Brestovac
   (Slavonski Brod) HR......54 A3
Brestovačka
   Banja SRB................57 E3
Bretenoux F..................15 F4
Breteuil F...................12 A2
Breteuil-sur-Iton F..........11 F3
Bretten D....................13 F3
Breuil Cervinia I............17 E3
Breza SRB....................56 C3
Brežđe SRB...................56 C2
Brežice SLO..................54 B2
Brezna SRB...................57 D4
Breznica HR..................54 C2
Đakovačka HR.................55 E2
Březnice CZ..................40 C3
Brezno SK...................116 B1
Brézolles F..................11 F4
Brezovica SRB................59 E3
Brezovo Polje BIH............55 F3
Briançon F...................17 D4
Briare F.....................16 A1
Brenci LV....................79 E3
Bribirske Mostine HR.........54 C4
Bricquebec F.................11 D3
Brides-les-Bains F...........17 D3
Bridge of Allan GB...........7 D1
Bridgend F....................8 B3
Bridgend /
   Pen-y-bont GB............8 B3
Bridgnorth GB................8 C1
Bridgwater GB................8 C3
Bridlington GB...............7 F4
Bridport GB..................8 C4
Brie-Comte-Robert F..........12 A3
Briec F......................10 A4
Brielle NL...................36 B1
Brienne-le-Château F.........12 C4
Brienon-sur-
   Armançon F...............12 B4
Brienz CH....................17 E2
Brienza I....................49 E4

Briey F......................13 D3
Briežuciems
   (Brīžucims) LV...........79 F3
Brig CH......................17 F2
Brigg GB......................7 F4
Brighouse GB..................7 E4
Brightlingsea GB.............9 F2
Brighton GB..................9 E4
Brigi LV.....................83 F2
Brignogan-Plages F...........10 A3
Brignoles F..................22 C2
Brihuega E...................26 A1
Brijuni / Brioni
   (Otoci) HR...............54 A3
Briksdal N...................62 B3
Brilon D.....................37 F1
Brimnes N....................66 A1
Brinches P...................24 B4
Brindisi I...................51 F1
Brinki LV....................81 D1
Brinon-sur-Beuvron F.........16 A1
Brioni HR....................54 A3
Brioni / Brijuni
   (Otoci) HR...............54 A3
Brionne F....................11 F3
Brioude F....................16 A4
Brioux-sur-Boutonne F........15 D3
Briouze F....................11 E4
Brisighella I................47 E2
Brissac-Quincé F.............15 D1
Brissago CH..................17 F3
Bristol GB....................8 C3
Briuveri LV..................83 E2
Brive-la-Gaillarde F.........15 F4
Briviesca E..................19 F3
Brixham GB....................8 B4
Brixlegg A...................43 F2
Brjanslækur IS...............62 A1
Brka BIH.....................55 F3
Brna HR......................58 A3
Brnaze HR....................55 D4
Brno CZ......................41 E3
Bro (Gotland) S..............67 F4
Bro
   (Stockholms län) S.......67 F2
Broadford BIH................55 F4
Broadford IRL................2 B3
Broadstairs GB...............9 F3

Broadway GB..................9 D2
Broager DK...................70 B4
Broby S......................71 D3
Brocēni LV...................81 D1
Brod BIH.....................55 F4
Brod na Kupi HR..............54 B2
Brodnica (Kujawsko-
   Pomorskie) PL............90 A3

Brodarevo SRB................56 C4
Brodi LV.....................82 C1
Brodica SRB..................57 E2
Brodick GB....................6 C2
Brodnica
   (Wielkopolskie) PL.......93 D2
Brody UA....................117 D1
Brody (Lubuskie) PL..........92 B2
Broglie F....................11 E3
Brohl Lützing D..............13 E1
Brojce PL....................88 B2

Brok PL......................91 D3
Brolo I......................50 C4
Bromary FIN..................69 D4
Brome D......................33 F4
Bromölla S...................71 D3
Bromsgrove GB................8 C2
Bromyard GB..................8 C2

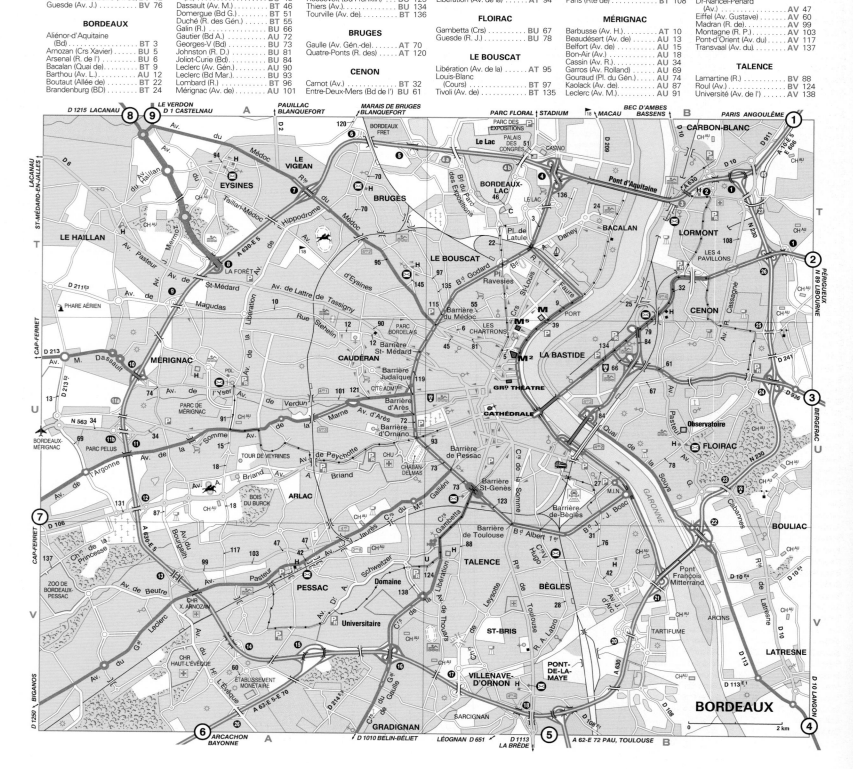

BONN

An der Josefshöhe............AV 5
Augustusring.................AV 6

Friedrich-Breuer-Str.........AV 13
Friedrich-Ebert-Allee........AX 14
Hausdorffstr.................AX 17
Heinrich-Böll-Ring...........AX 18
Hermann-Wandersleb-Ring......AX 18

Kaiser-Karl-Ring.............AV 19
Meckenheimer Allee...........AX 25
Poppelsdorfer Allee..........AX 32
Provinzialstr................AX 35
St. Augustiner Str...........AV 42

BÈGLES

Buisson (R. F.)..............BV 28
Capelle (Av. A.).............BV 31
Chevalier-de-la-Barre (R. du)BV 42
Guesde (Av. J.)..............BV 76

BORDEAUX

Aliénor-d'Aquitaine
   (Bd)......................BT 3
Arnozan (Crs Xavier).........BU 5
Arsenal (R. de l')...........BU 6
Bacalan (Quai de)............BT 9
Barthou (Av. L.).............BT 15
Boutaut (Allée de)...........BT 22
Brandenburg (BD).............BT 24

Brazza (Quai de).............BT 25
Brienne (Quai de)............BU 27
Chartrons (Quai des).........BTU 39
Croix-de-Seguey
   (R.).....................BU 45
Dassault (Av. M.)............BT 46
Domergue (Bd G.).............BT 51
Duché (R. des Gén.)..........BT 55
Galin (R.)...................BU 66
Gautier (Bd A.)..............AU 72
Georges-V (Bd)...............AU 73
Johnston (R. D.).............BU 81
Joliot-Curie (Bd)............BU 84
Leclerc (Av. Gén.)...........AU 90
Leclerc (Bd Mar.)............BU 93
Lombard (R.).................BT 96
Mérignac (Av. de)............AU 101

Pierre-1er (Bd)..............BT 115
Président-Wilson
   (Bd).....................AU 119
République (Av. de la).......AU 121
Roosevelt (Bd Franklin)......BU 123
Thiers (Av.).................BU 134
Tourville (Av. de)...........BU 136

BRUGES

Gaulle (Av. Gén.-de.)........AT 70
Quatre-Ponts (R.)............AT 120

CENON

Carnot (Av.).................BT 32
Entre-Deux-Mers (Av. de).....BU 61

Jean-Jaurès (Av.)............BU 79

EYSINES

Libération (Av. de la).......AT 94

FLOIRAC

Gambetta (Crs)...............BU 67
Guesde (R. J.)...............BU 78

LE BOUSCAT

Libération (Av. de la).......AU 95
Louis-Blanc
   (Cours)..................BT 97
Tivoli (Av. de)..............BT 135

Zola (R. Émile)..............AT 145

LORMONT

Paris (Rte de)...............BT 108

MÉRIGNAC

Barbusse (Av. H.)............AT 10
Beaudésert (Av. de)..........AU 13
Belfort (Av. de).............AU 15
Bon-Air (Av.)................AU 18
Cassin (Av. R.)..............AU 24
Garros (Av. Rolland).........AU 69
Gouraud (Pl. du Gén.)........AU 74
Kaolack (Av. de).............AU 87
Leclerc (Av. M.).............AU 91

Souvenir (Av. du)............AU 131

PESSAC

Dr-Nancel-Pénard
   (Av.)....................AV 47
Eiffel (Av. Gustave).........AV 60
Madran (R. de)...............AV 99
Montagne (R. P.).............AV 103
Pont-d'Orient (Av. du).......AV 117
Transval (Av. du)............AV 137

TALENCE

Lamartine (R.)...............BV 88
Roul (Av.)...................BV 124
Université (Av. de l').......AV 138

BORDEAUX

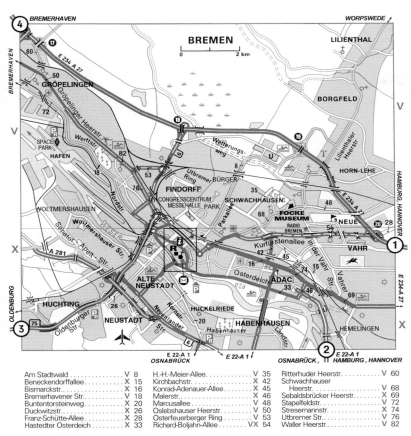

BREMEN

Am Stadtwald . . . . V 8
Beneckendorffallee . . . . X 15
Bismarckstr. . . . . X 16
Bremerhavener Str. . . . . V 18
Buntentorsteinweg . . . . X 20
Duckwitzstr. . . . . X 26
Franz-Schütte-Allee . . . . X 28
Hastedter Osterdeich . . . . VX 33
H.-H.-Meier-Allee . . . . V 35
Kirchbachstr. . . . . X 42
Konrad-Adenauer-Allee. . . . . X 45
Malerstr. . . . . X 46
Marcusallee . . . . V 48
Oslebshauser Heerstr. . . . . V 50
Osterfeuerberger Ring . . . . V 53
Richard-Boljahn-Allee. . . . . VX 54
Ritterhuder Heerstr. . . . . V 60
Schwachhauser Heerstr. . . . . V 68
Sebaldsbrücker Heerstr. . . . . X 69
Stapelfeldstr. . . . . X 72
Stresemannstr. . . . . X 74
Utbremer Str. . . . . X 76
Waller Heerstr. . . . . V 82

Buiva LV....78 B2
Buivenai LT....82 B2
Buivydžiai LT....81 E2
Bujalance E....29 F2
Bujanovac SRB....59 E3
Bujaraloz E....20 C4
Buje HR....54 A3
Buk PL....93 D1
Bukaiši LV....81 E2
Bukas LV....78 B3
Bukinje BIH....55 E3
Bukonys LT....85 F1
Bukova Gora BIH....55 D4
Bukovi SRB....56 C3
Bukowiec (Kujawsko-Pomorskie) PL....89 E2
Bukowina Tatrzańska PL..98 B3
Bukowno PL....98 A2
Bukowsko PL....99 D3
Buktiškiai LT....85 D2
Bülach CH....17 F1
Bulgnéville F....13 D4
Bullas E....30 B2
Bulle CH....17 E2
Büllingen B....13 D4
Bully-les-Mines F....12 A1
Bultei I....50 A3
Buna BIH....58 A2
Bunclody IRL....3 D4
Buncrana / Bun Cranncha IRL....6 A2
Bunde D....32 C3
Bünde D....33 E4
Bundoran / Bun Dobhráin IRL....2 C1
Bunessan GB....6 B1
Bungay GB....9 F2
Bunić HR....54 C3
Bunikiai LT....85 D1
Bunka LV....80 B1
Bunmahon IRL....2 C4
Buñol E....26 C3
Buntingford GB....9 E2
Buñuel E....20 B4
Buonabitàcolo I....49 E4
Buonalbergo I....49 D3
Buonconvento I....47 E3
Buonfornello I....52 C3
Buoženai LT....80 C2
Burbach D....13 F1
Burbáguena E....26 C1
Burbaičiai LT....81 D3
Burbiškiai LT....85 E1
Burbiškis LT....82 B3
Bureå S....64 C3
Burela E....18 B1
Buren NL....32 B3
Büren (Kreis Paderborn) D....37 F1

Burg auf Fehmarn (Kreis Ostholstein) D....33 F1
Burg b. Magdeburg D....34 A4
Burg Stargard (Kreis Mecklenburg-Strelitz) D....34 B2
Burgas BG....117 E4
Burgau (Kreis Günzburg) D....43 E1
Burgbernheim D....39 D4
Burgdorf CH....17 E1
Burgdorf D....33 F4
Bürgel (Saale-Holzland-Kreis) D....39 E2
Burgess Hill GB....9 E4
Burggrub D....39 D3
Burghasungen D....38 C1
Burghausen (Kreis Altötting) D....44 B1
Burgjoß D....38 C3
Burgkunstadt D....39 D3
Burglengenfeld D....39 E4
Burgohondo E....25 E1
Burgos E....19 F3
Burgsinn D....38 C3
Burgstädt (Kreis Mittweida) D....39 F3
Burgsvik S....67 F4
Burgui/Burgi E....20 B3
Burguillos del Cerro E....24 C4
Burgum NL....32 B3
Burgwedel D....33 F4
Burhave D....33 D3
Burie F....15 D3
Burjassot E....27 D3
Burkau D....40 C1
Burnham-on-Crouch GB....9 F3
Burnham-on-Sea GB....8 C3
Burnley GB....7 E4
Burntisland GB....7 D1
Buronzo I....17 F3
Burrel AL....116 C4
Burry Port / Porth Tywyn GB....8 B2
Bursa TR....117 F4
Burscheid D....13 E1
Bürstadt D....13 F2
Burtnieki (Kuldīgas) LV....76 B3
Burtnieki (Valmieras) LV....78 B2
Burton-upon-Trent GB....11 D3
Burträsk S....64 B3
Burveliai LT....81 F3
Burwick GB....5 D2
Bury GB....7 D4
Bury St Edmunds GB....9 F2
Burzenin PL....93 F3
Busalla I....46 B2
Busca I....23 D1
Buševac HR....54 C2

Bushmills GB....6 B2
Busko-Zdrój PL....98 C1
Busovača BIH....55 E4
Bussang F....17 D1
Busseto I....46 C1
Bussière-Badil F....15 E3
Bussolengo I....43 F4
Bussum NL....32 B4
Busto Arsízio I....17 F3
Busto de Bureba E....19 F3
Büsum D....33 E2
Buteliūnai LT....85 E3
Butenai LT....81 E3
Butera I....53 D4
Butkai LT....84 B1
Butkaičiai LT....85 D1
Butkiške LT....81 D3
Bütnāri (Kurzeme) LV....80 C1
Butniūnai (Panevežio) LT....82 B2
Butniūnai (Šiauliu) LT....81 F1
Butrimiškiai LT....85 E3
Butrimonys (Alytaus) LT....85 F2
Butrimonys (Vilniaus) LT....86 B3
Buttermere GB....7 D3
Buttevant IRL....2 B4
Buttstädt D....39 D2
Butzbach D....13 F1
Bützow (Kreis Güstrow) D....34 A2
Buxtehude D....33 E3
Buxton GB....9 D1
Buxy F....16 C2
Buzançais F....15 F2
Buzancy F....12 C3
Bužău RO....117 E1
Buzet HR....54 A3
Bužim BIH....54 C3
Bychaŭ BY....115 D3
Bychawa PL....95 E3
Byčiai LT....82 B3
Byczyna (Opolskie) PL....93 E3
Byczyna (Śląskie) PL....98 A2
Bydgoski (Kanał) PL....89 E3
Bydgoszcz PL....89 E3
Bygdeå S....68 B1
Bygland N....66 A3
Byglandsfjord N....66 A3
Bykle N....66 A2
Bylderup-Bov DK....70 B4
Byrkjelo N....62 B4
Byske S....64 C3
Bystra PL....98 A2
Bystre PL....99 E3
Bystřice nad Pernštejnem CZ....41 E3

Bystřice pod Hostýnem CZ....41 F3
Bystrzyca Kłodzka PL....96 C2
Bytlaukis LT....80 C3
Bytom PL....97 F2
Bytom Odrzański PL....92 C2
Bytoń PL....93 F1
Bytów PL....89 D1
Byxelkrok S....71 F2

C
Cabañaquinta E....19 D2
Cabanes E....27 D2
Čabar HR....54 B2
Cabeceiras de Basto P....18 B4
Cabeço de Vide P....24 B3
Cabella Ligure I....46 B2
Cabeza del Buey E....25 E4
Cabezas Rubias E....28 C2
Cabezón E....19 E4
Cabezón de la Sal E....19 E2
Cabezuela del Valle E....25 D2
Cabo de Gata E....30 B3
Cabo de Palos E....30 C2
Cabourg F....11 E3
Cabras E....29 E2
Cabra del Santo Cristo E....30 A2
Cabras I....50 A3
Cabreiros E....18 B2
Cabrerets F....21 E1
Cabrillas E....25 D1
Caburniga E....19 E2
Cacabelos E....18 C3
Čačak SRB....57 D3
Caccamo I....52 C3
Cacela Velha P....28 B2
Cáceres E....25 D2
Cachafeiro E....18 A2
Cachopo P....28 B2
Čačinci HR....55 E2
Cadalso de los Vidrios E....25 F2
Cadaqués E....21 F3
Cadaval P....24 A2
Čađavica BIH....55 D3
Čadca SK....116 B1
Cadelbosco di Sopra I....47 D1
Cadenabbia I....43 D4
Cadenberge D....33 E2
Cadenet F....22 B2
Cádiar E....30 A3
Cadillac F....20 C1
Cadipietra / Steinhaus I....44 B3
Cádiz E....28 C3
Cadouin F....15 E4

Bronchales E....26 C2
Brønderslev DK....70 B2
Broni I....46 B1
Brønnøysund N....63 D1
Brøns DK....70 B3
Bronte I....53 D3
Bronzani Majdan BIH....55 D3
Broons F....10 C4
Brora GB....4 C3
Brósarp S....71 D3
Brossac F....15 D4
Brøstadbotn N....60 B2
Broszków PL....95 D1
Brotas P....24 B3
Broto E....20 C3
Brotton GB....7 F3
Brøttum N....66 C1
Brou F....11 F4
Brou F....16 C3
Brouage F....14 C3
Brough GB....7 E3
Broughshane GB....3 D1
Broughton-in-Furness GB....7 D3
Broumov CZ....41 D2
Brovst DK....70 B2
Brownhills GB....9 D1
Brozas E....24 C2
Bruay-la-Buissière F....12 A1
Bruay-sur-l'Escaut F....12 B2
Bruchsal D....13 F3
Brück (Kreis Potsdam-Mittelmark) D....34 B4
Bruck an der Großglockner-straße A....44 B2
Bruck an der Leitha A....45 E1
Bruck an der Mur A....45 D2
Bruck i. d. Oberpfalz (Kreis Schwandorf) D....39 E4
Brückl A....45 D3
Bruckmühl D....43 F1
Brudzeń Duży PL....90 A3
Brudzew PL....93 F2
Brüel D....34 A2
Brués E....18 B3
Brugg CH....17 F1
Brugge B....12 B1
Brügge D....37 E2
Brühl (Erftkreis) D....13 E1
Brukai LT....85 D3
Bruksvallarna S....63 D4
Brûlon F....11 E4
Brumath F....13 F3
Brummen NL....37 D1
Brumov-Bylnice CZ....41 F3
Brumunddal N....66 C1
Brunaviški LV....81 F2
Brunete E....25 F2
Brunflo S....63 E3
Brunico / Bruneck I....44 B3
Bruniquel F....21 E1
Brunkeberg N....66 B3
Brunnen CH....17 F1
Brunsbüttel D....33 E2
Brunssum NL....13 D1
Bruntál CZ....41 E2
Bruravik N....66 A1
Brus SRB....57 D4
Brusand N....66 A3
Brušane HR....54 B4
Brusasco I....17 F4
Brusnik SRB....57 E3
Brusson I....17 E3
Brüssow D....34 C2
Brusy PL....89 E2
Bruton GB....8 C3
Brutuli LV....78 C2
Bruvno HR....54 C4
Bruxelles / Brussel B....12 C1

Bruyères F....13 E4
Bružai LT....80 C2
Bruži LT....80 B1
Bruzilas LV....80 C1
Brwinów PL....94 B2
Bryne N....71 A2
Brynmawr GB....8 C2
Brza Palanka SRB....57 E2
Brzan SRB....57 D3
Brzeće SRB....57 D4
Brzeg PL....93 E3
Brzeg Dolny PL....93 D3
Brześć Kujawski PL....89 F3
Brzesko PL....98 B2
Brzeszcze PL....97 F2
Brzeźce PL....97 F2
Brzezie (Pomorskie) PL....89 D2
Brzezinka PL....97 F2
Brzeziny (Łódzkie) PL....94 A2
Brzeziny (Wielkopolskie) PL....93 F2
Brzeźnica (Małopolskie) PL....98 A2
Brzeźnio PL....93 F2
Brzeźno (Wielkopolskie) PL....93 F1
Brzeźno (Zachodniopomorskie) PL....88 C2
Brzeźno Lęborskie PL....89 E1
Brzostek PL....98 C2
Brzozów PL....99 D2
Brzuze PL....89 F3
Brzyska PL....98 C2
Buarcos P....24 A1
Buavåg N....66 A2
Bubiai (Kauno) LT....85 E1
Bubiai (Šiauliu) LT....81 D3
Bubry F....10 B4
Bučač UA....117 D1
Buçaco P....24 B1
Buccheri I....53 D4
Bucchianico I....48 C4
Bucelas P....24 A3
Buchen D....38 C4
Büchen (Kreis Herzogtum Lauenburg) D....33 F3
Büchen-Pötrau D....33 F3
Buchenwald D....39 D2
Buchholz i. d. Nordheide (Kreis Harburg) D....33 E3
Buchloe D....43 E1
Buchlovice CZ....41 F3
Buchs CH....43 D3
Buchy F....11 F3
Bucine I....47 E3
Bučiūnai (Joniškis) LT....81 E2
Bučiūnai (Kauno) LT....85 F2
Bučiūnai (Panevežio) LT....82 C2
Bučiūnai (Šeduva) LT....81 E3
Bučje SRB....57 E3
Bückeburg D....33 E4
Buckfastleigh GB....8 B4
Buckhaven GB....7 D1
Buckie GB....5 D3
Buckingham GB....9 D2
Buckow (Kreis Märkisch-Oderland) D....34 C4
Buckūnai LT....85 E3
Bückwitz D....34 B3
Bučovice CZ....41 E3
Bucureşti RO....117 E3
Buczek PL....94 A2
Buczkowice PL....97 F2
Bud N....62 B3
Büda (Marijampoles) LT....85 D2

Büda (Vilniaus) LT....86 B2
Budapest H....116 B2
Búðardalur IS....62 A1
Budberga LV....81 F2
Buddusò I....50 B3
Bude GB....8 A3
Büdelsdorf D....33 E2
Budiliai LT....85 F2
Büdingen (Wetteraukreis) D....37 F3
Budinščina HR....54 C1
Budleigh Salterton GB....8 B4
Budrio I....47 D2
Budry PL....91 D1
Budva MNE....58 C3
Büdvietiai LT....85 D2
Budy Łancuckie PL....99 E2
Budynê nad Ohří CZ....40 C2
Budzisko PL....91 E1
Budziszewice PL....94 B2
Budzisczów Wielki PL....92 C3
Budzów (Dolnośląskie) PL....96 C1
Budzów (Małopolskie) PL....98 A2
Buenache de Alarcón E....26 B3
Buenavista de Valdavia E....19 E3
Buendía E....26 A2
Bueu E....18 A3
Bugailiškiai LT....82 B3
Bugeat F....15 F3
Büginiai LT....85 F3
Bugojno BIH....55 E4
Bugøynes N....61 F1
Bühl (Baden) (Kreis Rastatt) D....13 F3
Buikos LT....86 B3
Builth Wells / Llanfair-ym-Muallt GB....3 F4
Buis-les-Baronnies F....22 B1
Buitrago del Lozoya E....26 A1
Buitūnai LT....86 C1

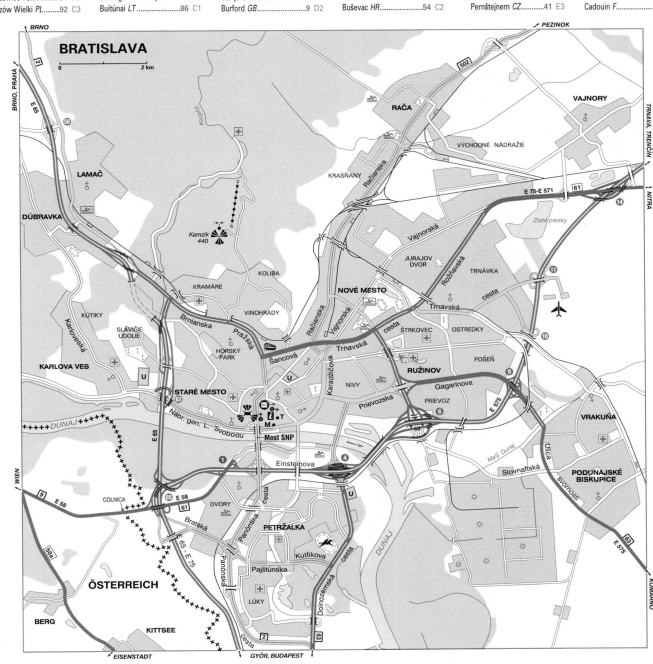

BRATISLAVA

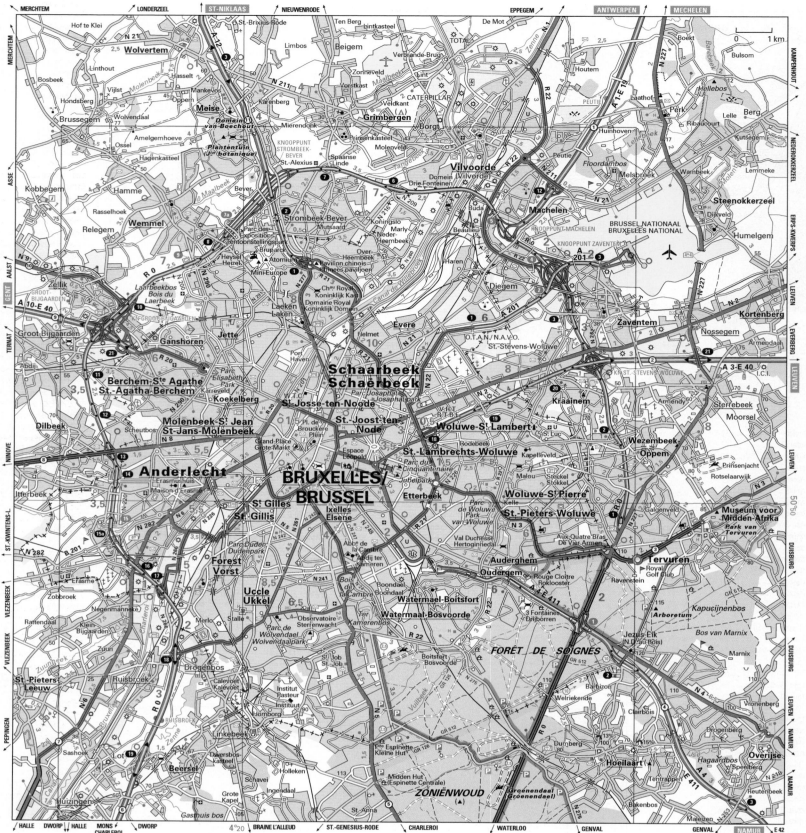

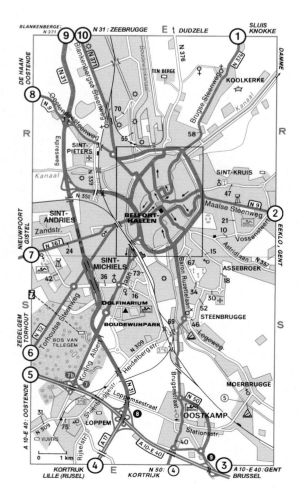

BRUGGE

Bossuytlaan	ER	10
Daverlostr.	ERS	15
Dorpsstr.	ES	16
Dries	ES	18
Fortuinstr.	ER	21
Gistelse Steenweg	ER	24
Kongostr.	ES	34
Koningin Astridlaan	ES	36
Leopold III laan	ES	42
Meulestree	ER	46
Moerkerkse Steenweg	ER	47
Odegemstr.	ES	52
Pathoekeweg	ER	55
Sint-Katarinastr.	ERS	67
Sint-Michielstr.	ER	69
Sint-Pieterskerklaan	ER	70
Spoorwegstr.	ER	73
s Heer Boudewijnsburg	ER	30
van Praetstr.	ER	58

OOSTKAMP

Kortrijkstr.	ES	40

ZEDELGEM

Heidelbergstr.	ES	31
Stationstr.	ES	75

Caen F	11	E3
Caernarfon GB	3	F3
Caerphilly / Caerffili GB	8	C3
Caersws GB	3	F4
Cagli I	47	F3
Cagliari I	50	B4
Čaglin HR	55	E2
Cagnano Varano I	49	D2
Cagnes-sur-Mer F	23	D2
Caher / An Chathair IRL	2	C4
Cahersiveen / Cathair Saidhbhín IRL	2	A4
Cahors F	21	E1
Cahul MD	117	E2
Caianello I	48	C3
Caiazzo I	48	C3
Caión E	18	A2
Cairnryan GB	3	E1
Cairo Montenotte I	23	E1
Caistor GB	7	F4
Caivano I	48	C4
Cajarc F	21	E1
Čajetina SRB	56	C4
Čajniče BIH	55	E4
Čakovec HR	54	C1
Čakštes LV	80	B1
Cala en Porter E	31	F3
Cala Gonone I	50	B3
Cala Rajada E	31	F3
Calabor E	18	C3
Calacéite E	27	D1
Calacuccia F	23	F3
Calaf E	21	E4
Calafat RO	117	D3
Calafell E	27	F1
Calahonda E	29	F3
Calahorra E	20	A3
Calais F	12	A1
Calamocha E	26	C1
Calañas E	28	C2
Calanda E	27	D1
Calangianus I	50	A2
Călărași MD	117	E2
Călărași RO	117	E3
Calasetta I	50	A4
Calasparra E	26	B4
Calatafimi I	52	B3
Calatañazor E	20	A4
Calatayud E	26	C1
Calatorao E	20	B4
Calau D	39	F1
Calbe D	39	D1
Calcena E	20	B4
Caldaro s. str. d. Vino / Kaltern a. d. W. I	43	F3
Caldarola I	47	F3
Caldas da Rainha P	24	A2
Caldas das Taipas P	18	A4
Caldas de Reis E	18	A2
Caldas de Vizela P	18	A4
Caldelas P	18	A4
Caldes de Boí E	21	D3
Caldes de Malavella E	21	F4
Caldes de Montbui E	21	E4
Caldirola I	46	B2
Calella E	21	F4
Calella de Palafrugell E	21	F4
Calenzana F	23	F3
Calera de León E	25	D4
Calera y Chozas E	25	E3
Calería E	27	E2
Caleruega E	19	F4
Caletta I	21	F4
Călimănești RO	117	D3
Cališi LV	80	B1
Calitri I	49	D3
Calizzano I	23	E1
Callac F	10	B4
Callan / Callainn IRL	2	C4
Callander GB	6	C1
Callas F	22	C2
Callington GB	8	B4
Callosa de Segura E	30	C2
Callosa d'en Sarrià E	27	D4
Calmazzo I	47	F2
Calmbach D	13	F3
Calne GB	8	C3
Calolziocorte I	43	D4
Calonge E	21	F4
Calp E	27	D4
Caltabellotta I	52	C3
Caltagirone I	53	D3
Caltanissetta I	53	D3
Caltavuturo I	52	C3
Caluso I	17	F4
Calvi F	23	F3
Calvörde D	34	A4
Calw D	13	F3
Calzada de Calatrava E	25	F4
Calzada de Valdunciel E	25	E1
Camaiore I	46	C2
Camaldoli (Convento) I	47	D2
Cámaleño E	19	E2
Camarasa E	21	D4
Camarena E	25	F2
Camarès F	21	F2
Camaret-sur-Mer F	10	A4
Camariñas E	18	A1
Camarzana de Tera E	18	C3
Camas E	29	D2
Cambados E	18	A3
Cambas P	24	B2
Camberley GB	9	D3
Cambil E	29	F2
Cambo-les-Bains F	20	B2
Camborne GB	8	A4
Cambrai F	12	B2
Cambremer F	11	D3
Cambridge GB	9	F2
Cambrils E	27	E1
Camburg D	39	E2
Camelford GB	8	A4
Camerino I	47	F3
Camigliatello Silano I	51	E2
Caminha P	18	A3
Caminomorisco E	25	C1
Caminreal E	26	C1
Camogli I	23	F3
Campagna I	49	D4
Campagne-lès-Hesdin F	12	A2
Campan F	20	C3
Campana I	51	E2
Campanario E	25	D3
Campanas E	20	B3
Campaspero E	19	E4
Campbeltown GB	6	B2
Campi Bisenzio I	47	D2
Campi Salentina I	51	E3
Campiglia Marittima I	47	D3
Campillo de Altobuey E	26	B3
Campillo de Aragón E	26	B1
Campillo de Arenas E	29	E3
Campillo de Llerena E	25	C3
Campillos E	29	E3
Campitello Matese I	48	B3
Campli I	48	B2
Campo E	21	D3
Campo de Besteiros P	24	B1
Campo de Caso E	19	D2
Campo de Criptana E	26	A3
Campo del Hospital E	18	B1
Campo di Giove I	48	C2
Campo Ligure I	17	F4
Campo Maior P	24	C3
Campo Tures / Sand in Taufers I	43	F3
Campobasso I	48	C3
Campobello di Licata I	52	C4
Campobello di Mazara I	52	B3
Campodonico I	47	F3
Campoformido I	44	C4
Campogalliano I	47	D1
Campomanes E	19	D2
Campomarino I	49	D2
Campóo (Alto) E	19	E2
Campora S. Giovanni I	51	E3
Camporrobles E	26	C3
Campos E	31	E3
Camposampiero I	44	B4
Camprodon E	21	F3
Camucia I	47	E3
Camuñas E	26	A3
Cañada de Benatanduz E	27	D2
Çanakkale TR	117	E4
Canal S. Bovo I	43	F4
Canales E	19	F3
Canals E	27	D3
Cañamero E	25	D3
Canas de Senhorim P	24	B1
Cañaveral E	25	D2
Cañaveral de León E	24	C4
Cañaveras E	26	B2
Canazei I	43	F3
Cancale F	10	C4
Cancarix E	26	B4
Cancon F	21	D1
Candanchú E	20	C3
Candás E	19	D2
Candasnos E	20	C4
Candé F	14	C1
Candela I	49	D3
Candelario E	25	D2
Candeleda E	25	E2
Candes-St-Martin F	15	D1
Canelli I	17	F4
Canero E	18	C2
Canet de Mar E	21	F4
Canet-Plage F	21	F3
Cañete E	26	C2
Cañete de las Torres E	29	F3
Cañete la Real E	29	E3
Canfranc-Estación E	20	C3
Cangas E	18	A3
Cangas de Onís E	19	E2
Cangas del Narcea E	18	C2
Canha P	24	A3
Canicatti I	52	C3
Canicattini Bagni I	53	E4
Caniles E	30	A3
Canino I	47	E4
Canisy F	11	D3
Cañizal E	25	E1
Canjáyar E	30	A3
Cannero Riviera I	17	F3
Cannes F	23	D2
Cannich GB	4	C3
Cannobio I	17	F3
Cannock GB	9	D1
Canonbie GB	7	D2
Canosa di Puglia I	49	E3
Cansano I	48	C2
Cantalapiedra E	25	E1
Cantalejo E	25	F1
Cantalpino E	25	E1
Cantanhede P	24	B1
Cantavieja E	27	D2
Čantavir SRB	55	F1
Canterbury GB	9	F3
Cantillana E	29	D2
Cantoira I	17	E4
Cantoral E	19	E3
Cantoria E	30	B3

BUDAPEST

Árpád Fejedelem útja . . . . . . CY 3
Bem József tér . . . . CY 7
Bogdáni út . . . . CY 12
Egressy út . . . . DY 20
Erzsébet krt . . . . CZ 22

Fehérvári út . . . . CZ 24
Felsö Zöldmáli út . . . . BCY 25
Ferenc krt . . . . CZ 28
Göncöl u. . . . . DY 40
Irinyi József u. . . . . CZ 54

Karinthy Frigyes út . . . . CZ 60
Karolina út . . . . BCZ 62
Kárpát u. . . . . CZ 72
Királyok útja . . . . CY 72
Lágymányosi híd . . . . CZ 80
Lajos u. . . . . CY 82

Margit krt. . . . . CY 91
Nagyszölös u. . . . . BCZ 97
Nánási út . . . . CY 99
Pacsirtamezö u. . . . . CY 105
Pusztaszeri út . . . . BCY 110

Röppentyü u. . . . . DY 118
Schönherz Zoltán u. . . . . . . CY 124
Szentendrei út . . . . CY 133
Szépvölgyi út . . . . BCY 138
Szt. István krt . . . . CY 146

Vajda Péter u. . . . . DZ 158
Viharhegyi út . . . . BY 166
Vihar u. . . . . CY 164
Vörösvári út . . . . CY 170

Cantù I......43 D4
Canvey Island GB......9 F3
Cany-Barville F......11 E2
Caorle I......44 C4
Caorso I......46 C1
Cap-Ferret F......20 B1
Capaccio I......49 D4
Capaci I......50 B4
Capalbio I......47 E4
Caparde BIH......55 F3
Caparroso E......20 B3
Capbreton F......20 B2
Capdenac-Gare F......21 E1
Capel Curig GB......3 E1
Capellades E......21 E4
Capendu F......21 F2
Capestang F......21 F2
Capestrano I......48 B2
Capileira E......30 A3
Capistrello I......48 B3
Čapljina BIH......58 F1
Capmany E......21 F3
Capo d'Orlando I......53 D4
Cappelle sul Tavo I......48 C2
Cappoquin / Ceapach Choinn IRL......2 C1
Capracotta I......48 C3
Capri I......48 C4
Capriati a Volturno I......48 C3
Captieux F......20 C1
Capua I......48 C3
Capurso I......49 F3
Capvern F......21 D2
Caracal RO......117 D3
Caracuel de Calatrava E......25 C3
Caraman F......21 E2

Caramanico Terme I......48 C2
Caramulo P......24 B1
Caransebeş RO......116 C3
Carantec F......10 B4
Caravaca de la Cruz E......26 B4
Carbajales de Alba E......18 C4
Carballiño E......18 B3
Carballo E......18 A2
Carbon-Blanc F......15 D4
Carboneras E......30 B3
Carboneras de Guadazaón E......26 B2
Carbonero el Mayor E......25 F1
Carbonia I......50 A4
Carbonin / Schluderbach I......44 B3
Carbonne F......21 D2
Carcaboso E......25 D2
Carcabuey E......29 F2
Carcaixent E......27 D3
Carcans F......14 C4
Carcans-Plage F......14 C4
Carcassonne F......21 F2
Carcastillo E......20 B3
Carcès F......22 C2
Cardedeu E......21 E4
Cardeña E......25 F4
Cardenete E......26 B2
Cardiff / Caerdydd GB......8 C3
Cardigan / Aberteifi GB......7 D4
Cardona E......21 E4
Carei RO......116 C2
Carentan F......11 D4
Carev Dvor MK......59 E4
Carevdar HR......54 C1

Carevo BG......117 E4
Cargèse F......23 F3
Carhaix-Plouguer F......10 B4
Caria P......24 C1
Cariati I......51 E2
Carignan F......12 C2
Carignano I......17 E4
Carina MK......59 E4
Cariñena E......26 C1
Carini I......50 A4
Cariño E......18 B1
Carinola I......48 C3
Carisio I......17 F3
Carlet E......27 D3
Carling F......13 E3
Carlingford IRL......3 D2
Carlisle GB......7 D1
Carloforte I......50 A4
Carlow / Ceatharlach IRL......3 D2
Carloway GB......4 A2
Carluke GB......7 D2
Carmagnola I......17 E4
Carmarthen / Caerfyrddin GB......3 D1
Carmaux F......21 E1
Carmona E......29 D2
Carna IRL......2 B2
Carnac F......14 B1
Carndonagh / Carn Domhnach IRL......6 A2
Carnew IRL......3 D3
Carnforth GB......7 D4
Carnia I......44 C3
Carnikava LV......77 E3
Carnlough GB......3 E1
Carnon-Plage F......22 A2

Carnota E......18 A2
Carnoustie GB......7 E1
Carnwath GB......7 D2
Carolles F......11 D3
Carovigno I......51 E1
Carpaneto Piacentino I......46 C1
Carpenedolo I......46 C1
Carpentras F......22 B1
Carpi I......47 D1
Carpignano Sesia I......17 F3
Carpineti I......47 D2
Carpineto Romano I......48 B3
Carpinone I......48 C3
Carquefou F......14 C1
Carqueiranne F......22 C2
Carracedelo E......18 C3
Carradale GB......6 B2
Carral E......18 A2
Carrapateira P......24 A3
Carrara I......46 C2
Carrascosa del Campo E......26 A2
Carrazeda de Ansiães P......18 B4
Carrazedo de Montenegro P......18 B4
Carrbridge GB......4 C3
Carregado P......24 A3
Carregal do Sal P......24 B1
Carreña E......19 D3
Carrenza E......19 F2
Carrick-on-Shannon-Cora Droma Rúisc IRL......2 C2
Carrick-on-Suir / Carraig na Siúire IRL......2 C4
Carrickfergus GB......3 E1

Carrickmacross / Carraig Mhachaire Rois IRL......3 D2
Carrigart / Carraig Airt IRL......6 A2
Carrió E......18 B2
Carrión de Calatrava E......25 F3
Carrión de los Condes E......19 E3
Carrizo de la Ribera E......19 D3
Carro F......22 B2
Carrouges F......11 E4
Carru I......23 E1
Carry-le-Rouet F......22 B2
Carsoli I......47 F4
Cartagena E......30 C2
Cártama E......29 E3
Cartaxo P......24 A3
Cartaya E......28 C2
Carteret F......10 C3
Carviçais P......18 C4
Carvin F......12 A1
Carvoeiro P......24 A3
Casa Branca P......24 B3
Casa Branca P......24 B3
Casabermeja E......29 E3
Casacalenda I......49 D3
Casaio E......18 C3
Casal di Principe I......48 C4
Casalarreina E......20 A3
Casalbordino I......48 C2
Casalbuttano ed Uniti I......46 C1
Casale Monferrato I......17 F4
Casale sul Sile I......44 B4
Casalecchio di Reno I......47 D2
Casalmaggiore I......46 C1
Casalpusterlengo I......46 C1

Casamari (Abbazia di) I......48 B3
Casamassima I......49 F3
Casamicciola Terme I......48 C4
Casar de Cáceres E......25 D2
Casarabonela E......29 E3
Casarano I......51 F1
Casares E......29 D4
Casares de las Hurdes E......25 D1
Casariche E......29 E3
Casarsa della Delízia I......44 B4
Casas de Don Pedro E......25 E3
Casas de Fernando Alonso E......26 B3
Casas de Juan Núñez E......26 C3
Casas de Luján E......26 A2
Casas de Miravete E......25 E2
Casas del Puerto E......26 C4
Casas Ibáñez E......26 C3
Casas Nuevas E......30 C2
Casasimarro E......26 C3
Casatejada E......25 D2
Casavieja E......25 F2
Cascais P......24 A3
Cascante E......20 C3
Cascia I......47 F4
Casciana Terme I......47 D3
Cascina I......47 D3
Casei Gerola I......17 F4
Caselle in Pittari I......49 F4
Caselle Torinese I......17 E4
Caserta I......48 C3
Caserta Vecchia I......48 C3
Casetas E......20 B4
Cashel / Caiseal IRL......2 C4

Casicas del Río Segura E......26 A4
Casillas de Coria E......25 D2
Casina I......47 D2
Casinos E......26 C3
Časlav CZ......41 D3
Casltepollard IRL......6 A4
Casola in Lunigiana I......46 C2
Casoli I......48 C2
Casoria I......48 C4
Caspe E......27 D1
Cassà de la Selva E......21 F4
Cassagnes-Bégonhès F......21 F1
Cassano allo Ionio I......51 D2
Cassano delle Murge I......49 F3
Cassel F......12 A1
Cassino I......48 C3
Cassis F......22 C2
Castalla E......26 C4
Castanet-Tolosan F......21 E2
Castanheira de Pêra P......24 B2
Castasegna CH......43 D4
Casteggio I......46 B1
Castejón de Monegros E......20 C4
Castejón de Sos E......21 D3
Castejón de Valdejasa E......20 B4
Castel del Monte I......48 B2
Castel del Monte I......49 E3
Castel del Rio I......47 E2
Castel di Sangro I......48 C3
Castel Gandolfo I......48 A3
Castel Madama I......47 F4
Castel S. Giovanni I......46 B1

Castel S. Lorenzo I......49 D4
Castel S. Pietro Terme I......47 E2
Castel Volturno I......48 C4
Castelbuono I......53 D3
Casteldaccia I......50 B4
Casteldelfino I......23 D1
Castelfidardo I......48 B1
Castelfiorentino I......47 D2
Castelfranco Emilia I......47 D2
Castelfranco in Miscano I......49 D3
Castelfranco Veneto I......44 B4
Casteljaloux F......20 C1
Castell de Ferro E......30 A3
Castellabate I......49 D4
Castellammare del Golfo I......52 B3
Castellammare di Stabia I......48 C4
Castellamonte I......17 E4
Castellana Grotte I......49 F3
Castellane F......22 C1
Castellaneta I......49 F4
Castellar de la Muela E......26 B1
Castellar de Santiago E......26 A4
Castellar de Santisteban E......26 A4
Castellar del Vallès E......21 E4
Castell'Arquato I......46 C1
Castelldans E......21 D4
Castelldefels E......21 E4
Castelleone I......46 C1
Castellfollit de la Roca E......21 F4
Castellina in Chianti I......47 D3
Castelló de la Plana / Castellón de la Plana I......27 D2
Castelló de Rugat E......27 D4
Castelló d'Empúries E......21 F4
Castello di Lago I......43 F4
Castellolí E......21 E4
Castellón de la Plana / Castelló de la Plana I......27 D2
Castellote I......27 D1
Castellterçol E......21 E4
Castelluccio I......47 F3
Castelmassa I......47 D1
Castelmauro I......48 C3
Castelmoron-sur-Lot F......21 D1
Castelnau-de-Médoc F......15 D4
Castelnau-de-Montmiral F......21 E1
Castelnau-Magnoac F......21 E1
Castelnau-Montratier F......21 E1
Castelnau-Rivière-Basse F......20 C2
Castelnaudary F......21 E2
Castelnovo ne' Monti I......46 C2
Castelnuovo Berardenga I......47 E3
Castelnuovo Bocca d'Adda I......46 C1
Castelnuovo della Daunia I......49 D3
Castelnuovo di Garfagnana I......47 D2
Castelnuovo di Porto I......47 F4
Castelnuovo Scrivia I......17 F4
Castelo Branco P......24 C2
Castelo de Paiva P......18 A4
Castelo de Vide P......24 C2
Castelraimondo I......47 F3
Castelrotto / Kastelruth I......43 F4
Castelsardo I......50 A2
Castelsarrasin F......21 D1
Castelserás E......27 D1
Casteltermini I......52 C3
Castelvecchio Subequo I......48 B2
Castelvetrano I......52 B3
Castets F......20 B1
Castiadas I......50 B4
Castiglion Fiorentino I......47 E3
Castiglioncello I......47 D3
Castiglione d'Adda I......46 C1
Castiglione dei Pepoli I......47 D2
Castiglione del Lago I......47 E3
Castiglione della Pescaia I......47 D4
Castiglione delle Stiviere I......46 C1
Castiglione in Teverina I......47 E4
Castiglione Messer Marino I......48 C3
Castiglione Olona I......17 F3
Castilblanco E......25 E3
Castilblanco de los Arroyos E......29 D2
Castilléjar E......30 A2
Castillejo de Martín Viejo E......25 D1
Castillo de Locubín E......29 F2
Castillon-en-Couserans F......21 D3
Castillon-la-Bataille F......15 D4
Castillonnès F......21 D1
Castilruiz E......20 A4
Castions di Strada I......44 C4
Castle Douglas GB......3 F1

DIJON

Aiguillottes (Bd des)	A 2	Concorde (Av. de la)	B 28	Moulin (R. Jean)	B 63
Allobroges (Bd des)	A 3	Einstein (Av. Albert)	A 36	Nation (Rd-Pt de la)	B 66
Bachelard (Bd Gaston)	A 4	Europe (Bd de l')	B 38	Orfèvres (R. des)	A 68
Bellevue (R. de)	A 5	Europe (Rd-Pt de l')	B 40	Ouest (Bd de l')	A 69
Bertin (Av. J.B.)	B 6	Fauconnet (R. Gén.)	AB 42	Parc (Cours du)	B 70
Briand (Av. A.)	B 8	Fontaine-les-Suisses (Bd)	B 44	Poincaré (Av. R.)	B 71
Camus (Av. Albert)	B 12	Fontaine-lès-Dijon (R.)	A 43	Pompidou (Rd-Pt Georges)	B 72
Castel (Bd du)	A 13	France-Libre (Pl. de la)	AB 45	Pompon (Bd F.)	A 73
Champollion (Av.)	B 14	Gabriel (Bd)	B 46	Prat (Av. du Colonel)	B 75
Chanoine-Bardy (Imp.)	B 16	Gallieni (Bd Mar.)	AB 48	Rembrandt (Bd)	B 78
Chanoine-Kir (Bd)	A 17	Gaulle (Crs Gén-de)	B 50	Rolin (Q. Nicolas)	A 79
Chateaubriand (R. de)	B 19	Gorgets (Bd des)	A 52	Roosevelt (Av. F. D.)	B 80
Chèvre-Morte (Bd de)	A 20	Jeanne-d'Arc (Bd)	B 55	Saint-Exupéry (Pl.)	B 85
Churchill (Bd W.)	A 22	Kennedy (Bd J.)	A 56	Schuman (Bd Robert)	B 88
Clomiers (Bd des)	A 26	Magenta (R.)	B 58	Strasbourg (Bd de)	B 90
		Maillard (Bd)	A 60	Trimolet (Bd)	B 91
		Mansart (Bd)	A 62	8-Mai-1945 (Rd-Pt du)	B 96
		Mont-Blanc (Av. du)	B 65	26e-Dragons (R. du)	B 98

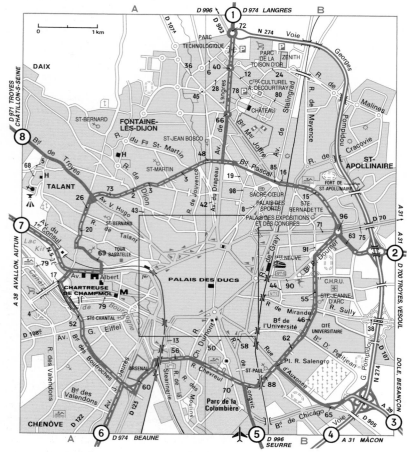

DRESDEN

Alttolkewitz	V 57	Fritz-Löffler-Str.	V 62	Naumannstr.	V 78
Borsbergstr.	V 58	Gerhart-Hauptmann-Str.	V 63	Nossener Brücke	V 71
Emerich-Ambros-Ufer	U 60	Hamburger Str.	V 64	Nürnberger Str.	V 72
Flügelwegbrücke	UV 61	Innsbrucker Straße	V 84	Washingtonstr.	U 75
		Lommatzscher Str.	U 69	Wehlener Str.	V 81
		Moritzburger Landstr.	V 74	Zellescher Weg	V 83
		Moritzburger Weg	U 75		

Cena LV	81 E1	Cêre LV	77 D3	Černivci UA	117 D1	Cesenatico I	47 E2
Cencenighe Agordino I	44 B3	Cerea I	47 D1	Cernobbio I	43 D4	Cēsis LV	78 B3
Cenicero E	20 A3	Čerepovec RUS	115 F1	Cerreto Sannita I	48 C3	Česká Kamenice CZ	40 C2
Čenta SRB	56 C2	Ceres I	17 E4	Cerrigydrudion GB	3 F3	Česká Lípa CZ	40 C2
Centelles E	21 E4	Ceresole Reale I	17 E3	Certaldo I	47 D3	Česká Skalice CZ	41 D2
Cento I	47 D1	Céret F	21 E3	Cervatos E	19 E2	Česká Třebová CZ	41 D2
Centuripe I	53 D3	Cerezo de Abajo E	26 A1	Cervatos de la Cueza E	19 E3	České Budějovice CZ	40 C4
Cepagatti I	48 C2	Cerezo de Riotirón E	19 F3	Červen' BY	7 D2	České Velenice CZ	41 D4
Čepin HR	55 E2	Cergy F	12 A3	Cerignola I	49 E3	Český Brod CZ	40 C3
Čepinski Martinci HR	55 E2	Cerignola I	49 E3	Červená Voda CZ	41 E2	Český Krumlov CZ	40 C4
Cepli LV	80 B1	Cérilly F	16 A2	Červený Kostelec CZ	41 D2	Český Těšín CZ	41 F2
Ceplis LV	81 F2	Cerini		Cervera I	21 E4	Cespedosa E	25 E1
Cepliši (Ogres) LV	77 F3	(Aizkraukles) LV	82 C1	Cervera de la Cañada E	20 B4	Cessalto I	44 B4
Cepliši (Ventspils) LV	76 B3	Cerini (Valmieras) LV	78 C2	Cervera de Pisuerga E	19 E3	Cesvaine LV	79 D3
Ceppo di Rocca Santa		Cerisiers F	12 B4	Cervera del Río		Cetina E	26 B1
Maria I	48 B2	Cerisy-la-Salle F	11 D3	Alhama E	20 A4	Cetinje MNE	58 C3
Ceprano I	48 B3	Cerizay F	48 A3	Cerveteri I	47 E2	Cetraro I	51 D2
Ceptuve LV	83 D1	Čerkasy UA	117 F1	Cervia I	47 E2	Ceuta E	29 D4
Čepukai LT	83 D3	Čerkaly UA	117 F1	Cervignano del Friuli I	44 C4	Ceuti E	30 C2
Čeralije HR	55 D2	Cerler E	21 D3	Cervinara I	49 D4	Ceva I	23 E1
Ceranów PL	91 D3	Cerna HR	55 E2	Cervione F	23 F3	Cevico de la Torre E	19 E4
Ceraukste LV	81 E2	Černá v Pošumaví CZ	40 C4	Cervo E	18 B1	Čevo MNE	58 C3
Celmini LV	81 F1	Cernache de		Červonka LV	83 E3	Cewice PL	89 E1
Cercal E	24 A2	Bonjardim P	24 B2	Červonohrad UA	117 D1	Ceyrat F	16 A3
Cercal E	24 A4	Čern'achovsk RUS	114 C3	Cervera del Río		Ceyzériat F	16 C3
Cercedilla E	25 F1	Cernavodă RO	117 E3	Cesana Torinese I	17 E4	Chabanais F	16 A3
Cerchiara di Calabria I	51 D2	Cernay F	17 E1	Cesarò I	53 D3	Chabeuil F	16 C4
Cerdedo E	18 A3	Černihiv UA	115 E4	Cesarzowice PL	93 D3	Chablis F	16 B1
Cerdeira P	24 C1	Černivci UA	78 C2	Cesena I	47 E2	Chabówka PL	98 B3

Castlebar / Caisleán an		Catoira E	18 A2	Čejč CZ	41 E4
Bharraigh IRL	2 B2	Catral E	26 C4	Cekcyn PL	89 E2
Castlebay GB	4 A4	Cattenom F	13 D3	Čekiške LT	85 E1
Castlebellingham IRL	3 D2	Cattolica I	47 F2	Čekoniškes LT	86 B2
Castleblayney / Baile na		Catus F	21 E1	Čekonys LT	82 B3
Lorgan IRL	3 D2	Caudebec-en-Caux F	11 F3	Ceków-Kolonia PL	93 F2
Castlecomer / Caisleán an		Caudete E	26 C4	Cekule LV	77 F3
Chomair IRL	2 C3	Caudiel E	27 D2	Čelákovice CZ	40 C2
Castledawson GB	3 D1	Caudry F	12 B2	Celano I	48 B2
Castlederg GB	2 C1	Caulnes F	10 C4	Celanova E	18 B3
Castledermot IRL	3 D3	Caulonia I	51 E4	Celararevo SRB	55 F2
Castleford GB	7 E4	Caumont-l'Éventé F	11 D3	Čelebić BIH	55 D4
Castleisland / Oileán		Caunes-Minervois F	21 E1	Čelebići BIH	55 D4
Ciarraí IRL	2 B4	Căuşani MD	117 E2		
Castlemaine IRL	2 A4	Caussade F	21 E1	Čelić BIH	55 F3
Castlerea / An Caisleán		Cauterets F	20 C3	Čelinac BIH	55 D3
Riabhach IRL	2 C2	Cava de' Tirreni I	49 D4	Celje SLO	54 B1
Castlerock GB	6 A2	Cavaglià I	17 F3	Cella E	26 C2
Castleton GB	9 D1	Cavaillon F	22 B2	Celle D	33 F4
Castletown GB	5 D2	Cavalaire-sur-Mer F	23 D2	Celle Ligure I	23 E1
Castletown		Cavalese I	43 F3	Celles-sur-Belle F	15 D3
(Isle of Man) GB	3 F2	Cavalière F	22 C2	Celmalas E	79 E3
Castletownbere IRL	2 A4	Cavan / An Cabhán IRL	6 A3	Celmini LV	81 F1
Castlewellan GB	3 D2	Cavarzere I	47 E1	Čelopeci MK	59 E4
Castrejón E	19 D4	Cavazzo Carnico I	44 C3	Celorico da Beira P	24 C1
Castres F	21 E2	Cavezzo I	47 D1	Celorico de Basto P	18 A4
Castries F	22 A2	Cavo I	47 D4	Čemerno BIH	58 B2
Castril E	30 A2	Cavour I	17 E4	Cempi LV	78 C2
Castrillo de la Reina E	19 F4	Cavtat HR	58 B3		
Castrillo de		Cayeux-sur-Mer F	9 F4		
Villavega E	19 E3	Caylus F	21 E1		
Castro E	18 B2	Cayres F	16 B4		
Castro Caldelas E	18 B3	Cazalla de la Sierra E	25 D4		
Castro Daire P	24 B1	Cazals F	21 E1		
Castro del Río E	29 E2	Cazaubon F	20 C1		
Castro Laboreiro P	18 A3	Cazaux F	20 B1		
Castro Marim P	28 B2	Cazères F	21 D2		
Castro Verde P	24 B4	Cazin BIH	54 C3		
Castrocalbón E	19 D3	Čazma HR	54 C2		
Castrocaro Terme I	47 E2	Cazorla E	30 A2		
Castrocontrigo E	18 C3	Cea E	18 B3		
Castrojeriz E	19 E3	Ceadir-Lunga MD	117 E2		
Castromonte E	19 E3	Ceanannus Mór (Kells) /			
Castronuño E	19 D4	Ceanannas IRL	3 D2		
Castrop-Rauxel D	37 E1	Cebolla E	25 F2		
Castropol E	18 C1	Cebreros E	25 F1		
Castroreale I	51 D4	Ceccano I	48 B3		
Castroreale Terme I	50 C4	Cece H	116 B2		
Castroverde E	19 D3	Čechov RUS	115 F2		
Castroverde de		Čechtice CZ	41 D3		
Campos E	19 D4	Ceclavín E	24 C2		
Castrovillari I	51 E2	Čedasai LT	82 C2		
Castuera E	25 D3	Cedillo E	24 C2		
Catania I	53 E3	Cedrillas E	26 C2		
Catanzaro I	51 E3	Cedynia PL	88 A3		
Catanzaro Lido I	51 E3	Cefalù I	50 B4		
Catarroja E	27 D3	Ceglèd H	116 C2		
Catenanuova I	53 D3	Ceglie Messapica I	49 F4		
Čatež ob Savi SLO	54 B2	Čegrane MK	59 E3		
Čatići BIH	55 E4	Cehegín E	30 B2		
Catignano I	48 C2	Ceikiniai LT	87 D1		

Bana Josipa Jelačića .	BYZ 4	Dr. Roka Mišetića	AZ 15	Od Svetog Mihajla . . . . BY 50
Čingrije (Pera)	BZ 10	Kranjčevića		Od Tabakarije . . . . CZ 52
Dr. Ante Starčevića .	BCZ 12	(Silvija Strahimira) .	BY 31	Petra Krešimira
Dr. Ante Sercera . . .	AYZ 13	Nazora (Vladimira) . . BCZ 43		IV. . . . . CZ 56

DUBROVNIK

Îles Élaphites, Lopud / RIJEKA, MLJET / TRSTENO / PELJEŠAC, SPLIT

Chabris F 15 F1
Chagny F 16 C2
Chailland F 14 D4
Chaillé-les-Marais F 14 C2
Chalabre F 21 E3
Chalais F 15 D4
Chalamont F 16 C3
Chalampé F 17 E1
Chalindrey F 16 C1
Chalkis GR 105 F2
Challans F 14 C2
Challes-les-Eaux F 17 D3
Chalon-sur-Saône F 16 C2
Chalonnes-sur-Loire F 15 D1
Châlons-en-Champagne F 12 C3
Chałupki PL 97 E2
Chałupy PL 89 E1
Châlus F 15 E3
Cham D 39 F4
Chambéry F 17 D3
Chambley-Bussières F 13 D3
Chambly F 12 A3
Chambon-sur-Lac F 16 A3
Chambon-sur-Voueize F 16 A3
Chambord F 15 F1
Chamonix-Mont-Blanc F 17 E3
Champagnac-de-Belair F 15 E4
Champagne-Mouton F 15 D3
Champagnole F 17 D2
Champdeniers-Saint-Denis F 15 D2
Champeaux F 11 D4
Champeix F 16 A3
Champéry CH 17 E3
Champex CH 17 E3
Champlitte-et-le-Prélot F 16 C1
Champoluc I 17 E3
Champorcher I 17 E3
Champs-sur-Tarentaine F 16 A4
Champtoceaux F 14 C1
Chamrousse F 17 D3
Chamusca P 24 B2
Chanac F 21 F1
Chanas F 16 C4
Chantada E 18 B3
Chantelle F 16 A3
Chantemerle F 17 D4
Chantilly F 12 A3
Chantonnay F 14 C2
Chaource F 13 D4
Chapel-en-le-Frith GB 9 D1
Chapinería E 25 F2
Charbonnières-les-Bains F 16 C3
Charbowo PL 89 D3
Chard GB 8 C3
Charenton-du-Cher F 16 A2
Charleroi B 12 C4
Charlestown IRL 2 B2
Charleville / An Ràth IRL 2 B4
Charleville-Mézières F 12 C2
Charlieu F 16 B3
Charlottenberg S 67 D2
Charly-sur-Marne F 12 B3
Charmes F 13 D4
Charny F 16 A1
Charny-sur-Meuse F 12 C3
Charolles F 16 B2
Chârost F 15 F2
Charquemont F 17 D1
Charroux F 15 D3
Chartres F 11 F4
Charzykowy PL 89 D2
Chasseneuil-sur-Bonnieure F 15 E3
Château-Arnoux-St-Auban F 22 C1
Château-Chinon F 16 B2
Château-d'Oex CH 17 E2
Château-du-Loir F 15 E1
Château-Gontier F 15 D1
Château-la-Vallière F 15 E1
Château-Landon F 12 A4
Château-Porcien F 12 C3
Château-Queyras F 17 E4
Château-Regnault F 12 C2
Château-Renard F 16 A1
Château-Renault F 15 E1
Château-Salins F 13 D3
Château-Thierry F 12 B3
Châteaubourg F 11 D4
Châteaubriant F 14 C1
Châteaudun F 11 F4
Châteaugiron F 11 D4
Châteaulin F 10 A4
Châteaumeillant F 15 F2
Châteauneuf-de-Randon F 22 A1
Châteauneuf-d'Ille-et-Vilaine F 10 C4
Châteauneuf-du-Faou F 10 B4
Châteauneuf-du-Pape F 22 B1
Châteauneuf-en-Thymerais F 11 F4
Châteauneuf-la-Forêt F 15 F3
Châteauneuf-les-Bains F 16 A3

Châteauneuf-sur-Charente F 15 D3
Châteauneuf-sur-Cher F 15 F2
Châteauneuf-sur-Loire F 15 F1
Châteauneuf-sur-Sarthe F 15 D1
Châteauponsac F 15 E3
Châteaurenard F 22 B1
Châteauroux F 15 F2
Châteauvillain F 12 C4
Châtel F 17 D2
Châtel-Montagne F 16 B3
Châtel-St Denis CH 17 E2
Châtel-sur-Moselle F 13 D4
Châtelaillon-Plage F 14 C3
Châtelaudren F 10 B4
Châteldon F 16 B3
Châtelet B 12 C2
Châtelguyon F 16 A3
Châtellerault F 15 E2
Châtelus-Malvaleix F 15 F3
Châtenois F 13 D4
Chatham GB 9 F3
Châtillon F 17 E3
Châtillon-Coligny F 16 A1
Châtillon-en-Bazois F 16 B2
Châtillon-en-Diois F 16 C4
Châtillon-sur-Chalaronne F 16 C3
Châtillon-sur-Indre F 15 E2
Châtillon-sur-Loire F 16 A1
Châtillon-sur-Marne F 12 B3
Châtillon-sur-Seine F 16 B1
Chatteris GB 9 E2
Chaudes-Aigues F 16 A4
Chauffailles F 16 B3
Chaufour-lès-Bonnières F 11 F3
Chaulnes F 12 A2
Chaumergy F 16 C2
Chaumont F 12 C4
Chaumont-en-Vexin F 12 A3
Chaumont-sur-Loire F 15 E1
Chauny F 12 B2
Chaussin F 16 C2
Chauvigny F 15 E2
Chaves P 18 B4
Chazelles-sur-Lyon F 16 B3
Cheb CZ 40 A3
Chęciny PL 94 B3
Chef-Boutonne F 15 D3
Cheles E 24 C4
Chełm PL 95 F3
Chełmek PL 97 F2
Chełmiec (Małopolskie) PL 98 C2
Chełmno PL 89 E2
Chelmsford GB 9 E3
Chełmża PL 89 F3
Cheltenham GB 8 C2
Chelva E 26 C3
Chemillé F 15 D1

Chemin F 16 C2
Chemnitz (Kreis Chemnitz Stadt) D 39 F2
Chénérailles F 15 F3
Chenonceaux F 15 E1
Chepstow / Cas-Gwent GB 8 C3
Chera E 26 C3
Cherbourg-Octeville F 11 D2
Chéroy F 12 A4
Cherson UA 117 F2
Cheshunt GB 9 E3
Cheste E 26 C3
Chester GB 8 C1
Chester-le-Street GB 7 E3
Chesterfield GB 9 D1
Chevagnes F 16 B3
Chevillon F 12 C4
Chevreuse F 12 A4
Chiampo I 72 A3
Chianciano Terme I 47 E3
Chiaramonte Gulfi I 53 D4
Chiaravalle I 47 D3
Chiaravalle Centrale I 51 E3
Chiari I 43 E4
Chiasso CH 17 F3
Chiavari I 23 F1
Chiavenna I 43 D4
Chichester GB 9 D4
Chiclana de la Frontera E 29 D4
Chieming D 44 B1
Chieri I 17 E4
Chiesa in Valmalenco I 43 E4
Chiesina Uzzanese I 47 D2
Chieti I 48 C2
Chimay B 12 C2
Chinchilla de Monte Aragón E 26 B3
Chinchón E 26 A2
Chinon F 15 E1
Chioggia I 47 E1
Chipiona E 28 C3
Chippenham GB 8 C3
Chipping Campden GB 9 D2
Chipping Norton GB 9 D2
Chipping Sodbury GB 8 C3
Chirivel E 30 B2
Chișinău MD 117 E2
Chişinău-Criş RO 116 C2
Chiusa / Klausen I 43 F3
Chiusa di Pesio I 23 D1
Chiusa Sclafani I 52 C3
Chiusaforte I 44 C3
Chiusi I 47 E3
Chiva E 26 C3
Chivasso I 17 F4
Chlewiska PL 94 C3
Chlum u Třeboně CZ 41 D4
Chlumec nad Cidlinou CZ 41 D2
Chmel'nyc'kyj UA 117 D1
Chmielnik PL 99 D2

Am Schönenkamp T 2
Arnulfstr. T 3
Benderstr. T 4
Bernburger Str. T 5
Brehmstr. S 10
Corneliusstr. T 14
Danziger Str. S 16
Deutzer Str. T 17
Düsseldorfer Str. ST 18
Eckenerstr. S 20
Fahnburgstr. S 26
Grafenberger Allee T 35
Graf-Adolf-Str. T 34
Graf-Recke-Str. S 36
Hamborner Str. S 37
Heerdter Landstr. T 40
Heidelberger Str. T 41
In den Kötten T 48
Kaiserswerther Str. T 54
Kalkumer Str. S 56
Klein-Eller T 57
Königsberger Str. T 58
Krefelder Str. T 61
Lindemannstr. T 63
Ludenberger Str. S 65
Luegallee T 66
Lütticher Str. S 67
Merowingerstr. T 69
Münchener Str. T 72
Münsterstr. S 75
Niederlöricker Str. S 76
Niederrheinstr. S 78
Oberkasseler Brücke T 82
Oberlöricker Str. S 83
Oberrather Str. S 84
Pariser Str. T 85
Pöhlerweg T 86
Rather Broich S 87
Reichswaldallee S 89
Reisholzer Str. T 90
Rennbahnstr. S 91
Rheinkniebrücke T 116
Sandtragerweg S 92
Südlicher Zubringer T 99
Ulmenstr. S 102
Unterrather Str. S 103
Vennhauser Allee T 106
Werdener Str. T 110
Werstener Str. T 110
Westfalenstr. S 112

Chmielno (Pomorskie) PL 89 E1
Chmil'nyk UA 117 D1
Chobienice PL 92 C2
Choceń CZ 41 D2
Choceń PL 93 F1
Chochołów PL 98 B3
Chocianów PL 92 C3
Chociwel PL 88 B3
Chocz PL 93 E2
Choczewo PL 89 E1
Chodaków PL 94 B1
Chodecz PL 93 F1
Chodel PL 95 D3
Chodov (Sokolov) CZ 40 A2
Chodów PL 95 D1
Chodzież PL 89 D3
Chojna PL 88 A3
Chojnice PL 89 D2
Chojnik (zamek) PL 92 B3
Chojniki BY 115 E4
Chojnów PL 92 C3
Cholet F 15 D2
Chollerford GB 7 E2
Chołm RUS 115 E2
Chomutov CZ 40 B2
Chomutov CZ 116 A1
Chorges F 22 C1
Chorkówka PL 99 D2

Chorley GB 7 D4
Chorol UA 115 F4
Choroszcz PL 91 E3
Chorzele PL 90 C3
Chorzów PL 97 F2
Choszczno PL 88 B3
Chotěboř CZ 41 D3
Chotyn UA 117 D1
Chouto P 24 B3
Chrast CZ 41 D3
Chrastava CZ 40 C2
Christchurch GB 9 D4
Christiansfeld DK 70 B3
Chrostkowo PL 89 F3
Chrzanów (Małopolskie) PL 98 A2
Chrząstowice PL 97 E1
Chrzypsko Wielkie PL 88 C3
Chuchelná CZ 41 D2
Chur CH 23 F1
Church Stretton GB 8 C1
Chust UA 117 D2
Chwałęcice PL 7 E2
Chwarszczany PL 88 A3
Chwaszczyno PL 89 E1
Chybie PL 97 F2
Chynów (Lubuskie) PL 92 B3

Chynów (Mazowieckie) PL 94 C2
Chyżne PL 98 A3
Ciasna PL 93 F3
Cibla LV 83 F1
Cicciano I 48 C4
Čićevac SRB 57 E3
Čićevo BIH 58 B3
Čičinai LT 85 F1
Cidones E 20 A4
Ciechanów PL 90 B3
Ciechanowiec PL 91 D3
Ciechocinek PL 89 F3
Cieladz PL 94 B2
Ciemupe LV 82 B1
Ciepielów PL 94 C3
Cieplice PL 92 B3
Ciepłowody PL 97 D1
Cieszanów PL 99 E2
Cieszków PL 93 D3
Cieszyn (Śląskie) PL 97 F2
Cieza E 26 C4
Ciężkowice (Małopolskie) PL 98 C2
Ciężkowice (Śląskie) PL 98 A2
Cifuentes E 26 B1
Cigliano I 17 F4

Cilavegna I 17 F4
Cildi LV 76 B3
Cilla LV 83 F1
Cillas E 26 B1
Cilleros E 24 C2
Cilleruelo de Bezana E 19 F2
Cimadevilla E 80 A1
Cimdenieki LV 80 A1
Cimişlia MD 117 E2
Cîmpeni RO 117 D2
Cîmpina RO 117 D3
Cîmpulung RO 117 D3
Cîmpulung Moldovenesc RO 117 D2
Cinctorres E 27 D2
Ciney B 12 C2
Cinfães P 18 A4
Cingoli I 47 F3
Cinigiano I 47 E4
Cinisi I 50 A4
Cínovec CZ 40 B2
Cintegabelle F 21 E2
Cintruénigo E 20 B4
Ciovo (Otok) HR 58 A4
Cirava LV 76 B3
Cirencester GB 9 D3
Cirey-sur-Vezouze F 13 D4
Ciria E 20 A4
Cirié I 17 E4

Cîrkliškis LT 87 D1
Cirò I 51 E2
Cirò Marina I 51 E2
Čirpan BG 117 E4
Ciruli (Kuldīgas) LV 76 C3
Ciruli (Talsu) LV 77 D2
Ciruli (Druvas) LV 82 C2
Cirulīši (Daugavpils) LV 83 D3
Cirulīši (Rigas) LV 81 E1
Cisek PL 97 E2
Ciskods LV 83 E1
Cisna PL 99 E3
Cisneros E 19 E3
Cisowa PL 97 E1
Čista Mala HR 54 C4
Cista Provo HR 58 A2
Cisterna di Latina I 48 B3
Cisternino I 49 F3
Cistierna E 19 D3
Citluk BIH 58 A2
Città della Pieve I 47 E3
Città di Castello I 47 E3
Città S. Angelo I 48 C2
Cittadella I 44 B4
Cittaducale I 47 F4
Cittanova I 51 D4
Cittareale I 47 F4
Ciudad Real E 25 F3

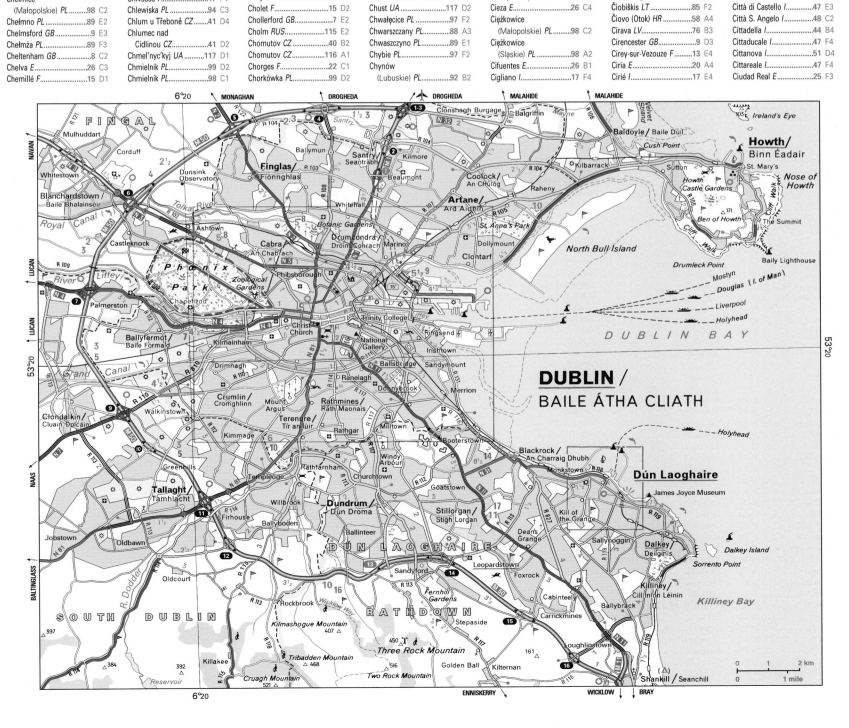

Ciudad Rodrigo E....25 D1
Čiudiškiai LT....85 E2
Ciutadella de Menorca E....31 F3
Cividale del Friuli I....44 C3
Civita Castellana I....47 F4
Civitanova Marche I....48 B1
Civitavecchia I....47 E4
Civitella del Tronto I....48 B2
Civitella Roveto I....48 B3
Civray F....15 E3
Cjurupyns'k UA....117 F2
Clacton-on-Sea GB....9 F2
Clairvaux-les-Lacs F....16 A1
Clamecy F....16 A1
Claonaig GB....6 C1
Clapham GB....7 E4
Clara / Clóirtheach IRL....2 C3
Clare GB....9 F2
Claremorris / Clár Chlainne Mhuiris IRL....2 B2
Claudy GB....3 D1
Clausthal-Zellerfeld D....38 C1
Claut I....44 B3
Clavière I....17 D4
Clay Cross GB....9 D1
Claye-Souilly F....12 A3
Clécy F....11 E3
Cleethorpes GB....7 F4
Clefmont F....13 D4
Cléguérec F....10 B4
Clelles F....16 C4
Clères F....11 F3
Clermont F....12 A3
Clermont-en-Argonne F....12 C3
Clermont-Ferrand F....16 A3
Clermont-l'Hérault F....22 A2
Clerval F....17 D1
Clervaux F....13 D1
Cléry-St-André F....15 F1
Cles I....43 F3
Clevedon GB....8 C3
Cleveleys GB....7 D4
Clifden / An Clochán IRL....2 A2
Clisson F....14 C2
Clitheroe GB....7 E4
Clogh Mills GB....3 D1
Cloghan IRL....2 C4
Clogheen IRL....2 C4
Clogherhead IRL....3 D2
Clonakilty / Cloich na Coillte IRL....2 B4
Clonbur / An Fhairche IRL....2 B2
Clondalkin IRL....3 D3
Clones / Cluain Eois IRL....3 D2
Clonmel / Cluain Meala IRL....2 C4
Cloppenburg D....33 D4
Clovelly GB....8 B3
Cloyes-sur-le-Loir F....11 F4
Cluj-Napoca RO....117 D2
Clun GB....8 C2
Cluny F....16 C2
Cluses F....17 D3
Clusone I....43 E4
Clydebank GB....6 C1
Ćmielów PL....94 C3
Cmolas PL....99 D2
Coachford IRL....2 B4
Coalisland GB....3 D1
Coalville GB....9 D1
Coaña E....18 C2
Coatbridge GB....6 C2
Cobeña E....26 A1
Cobh / An Cóbh IRL....2 B4
Coburg D....39 D3
Coca E....25 F1
Cocconato I....17 F4
Cocentaina E....27 D4
Cochem D....13 E2
Cockburnspath GB....7 E1
Cockermouth GB....7 D3
Code LV....81 F1
Codevigo I....47 E1
Codigoro I....47 E1
Codogno I....46 C1
Codos E....26 C1
Codroipo I....44 C4
Coesfeld D....33 D4
Coevorden NL....32 C4
Cofrentes E....26 C3
Cognac F....15 D3
Cogne I....17 E3
Cogolin F....23 D2
Cogolludo E....26 A1
Coimbra P....24 B1
Coín E....29 D3
Coina P....24 A3
Čoka SRB....55 F1
Col SLO....54 A2
Colares E....24 A3
Cölbe D....13 F1
Colchester GB....9 F2
Coldbackie GB....4 C2
Colditz D....39 E1
Coldstream GB....7 E1
Coleford GB....8 C2
Coleraine GB....6 B2
Colfiorito I....47 E4
Colico I....43 D4
Coligny F....16 C2
Colinas E....29 D3
Colindres E....19 F2
Colintraive GB....6 C1
Coll de Nargó E....21 E4

Colle di Val d'Elsa I....47 D3
Colle Isarco / Gossensaß I....43 F3
Colle Sannita I....49 D3
Collecchio I....46 C1
Colleferro I....48 B3
Collesalvetti I....47 D3
Collesano I....52 C3
Colli a Volturno I....48 C3
Collinée F....10 C4
Collio I....43 E4
Collioure F....21 F3
Collodi I....47 D2
Collonges F....17 D3
Collonges-la-Rouge F....15 F4
Colmar F....13 E4
Colmars F....23 D1
Colmenar E....29 E3
Colmenar de Oreja E....26 A2
Colmenar Viejo E....25 F1
Colnabaichín GB....5 D4
Colne GB....7 E4
Colobraro I....49 E4
Cologna Veneta I....47 D1
Cologne F....21 D2
Colombey-les-Belles F....13 D4
Colombey-les-Deux-Églises F....12 C4
Colombres E....19 E2
Colomera E....29 F3
Colorno I....46 C1
Colosimi I....51 E3
Colunga E....19 D2
Colwyn Bay / Bae Colwyn GB....3 F3
Coma-ruga E....21 F1
Comacchio I....47 E1
Comănești RO....117 E2
Combarro E....18 A3
Combe Martin GB....8 B3
Combeaufontaine F....17 D1
Comber GB....3 E1
Combloux F....17 D3
Combourg F....10 C4
Combronde F....16 A3
Comeglians I....44 B3
Comillas E....19 E2
Comines B....12 A1
Comines F....12 A1
Comiso I....53 D4
Commentry F....16 A3
Commercy F....13 D3
Como I....43 D4
Cómpeta E....29 F3
Compiègne F....12 A3
Comporta P....24 A4
Comps-sur-Artuby F....22 C2
Comrat MD....117 E2
Comunanza I....47 F3
Concarneau F....10 A3
Conches-en-Ouche F....11 F3
Concordia sulla Secchia I....47 D1
Condat F....16 A4
Condé-en-Brie F....12 B4
Condé-sur-l'Escaut F....12 B1
Condé-sur-Noireau F....11 D3
Condeixa-a-Nova P....24 B1
Condom F....21 D1
Condrieu F....16 C4
Conegliano I....44 B4
Conflans-en-Jarnisy F....13 D3
Confolens F....15 E3
Cong / Conga IRL....2 B2
Conga / Cong IRL....2 B2
Congleton GB....8 C1
Congosto de Valdavia E....19 D3
Congresbury GB....8 C3
Conil de la Frontera E....29 D4
Conisbrough GB....7 E4
Coniston GB....7 D3
Conlie F....11 E4
Conliège F....16 C2
Connel GB....6 C1
Connerré F....11 E4
Čonoplja SRB....55 F1
Conques F....21 F1
Conquista E....25 E4
Conselice I....47 E1
Conselve I....47 E1
Consett GB....7 D3
Constância P....24 B2
Constanța RO....117 E3
Constantina E....29 D2
Consuegra E....26 A3
Consuma I....47 E2
Contarina I....47 E1
Conthey CH....17 E3
Contigliano I....47 F4
Contin GB....5 E3
Contres F....15 F1
Contrexéville F....13 D4
Contursi Terme I....49 D4
Conty F....12 A2
Conversano I....49 F3
Conwy GB....3 F3
Cookstown GB....3 D1
Cootehill / Muinchille IRL....3 D2
Čop UA....116 C1
Cope E....30 C3
Copertino I....51 F1
Copparo I....47 E1
Corabia RO....117 D3
Corato I....49 E3

Coray F....10 B4
Corbeil-Essonnes F....12 A4
Corbie F....12 A2
Corbigny F....16 B1
Corbola I....47 E1
Corbridge GB....7 E3
Corby GB....9 E2
Corcieux F....13 E4
Corconte E....19 F2
Corcubión E....18 A2
Cordes-sur-Ciel F....21 E1
Córdoba E....29 E2
Cordobilla de Lácara E....25 D3
Corduente E....26 B1
Corella E....20 B4
Coreses E....19 D4
Corfe Castle GB....8 C4
Corgo E....18 B2
Cori I....48 B3
Coria E....25 D2
Coria del Río E....29 D2
Corias E....18 C2
Corigliano Calabro I....51 E2
Corinaldo I....47 F2
Coripe E....29 D3
Cork / Corcaigh IRL....2 B4
Corlay F....10 B4
Corleone I....52 C3
Corleto Perticara I....49 E4
Çormatin F....16 C2
Cormeilles F....11 E3
Cormery F....15 E1
Cormons I....44 C4
Cornago E....20 A4
Cornellana E....19 D2
Corniglio I....46 C2
Cornimont F....13 E4
Čornobyl' UA....115 E4
Čornomors'ke UA....117 F3
Cornuda I....44 B4
Cornus F....21 F1
Corps F....17 D4
Corral de Almaguer E....26 A2
Corrales del Vino E....19 D4
Corran GB....4 B1
Corredoiras E....18 B2
Correggio I....47 D1
Corrèze F....15 F4
Corridonia I....48 B1
Corrofin IRL....2 B3
Corsham GB....8 C3
Čortanovci SRB....56 C2
Corte F....23 F3
Corte de Peleas E....24 C3
Cortegada E....18 A3
Cortegana E....24 C4
Cortemaggiore I....46 C1
Cortemilia I....17 F4
Corteolona I....46 B1
Cortes E....20 B4
Cortes de Aragón E....26 C1
Cortes de Baza E....30 A2
Cortes de la Frontera E....29 D3
Cortijos Nuevos E....26 A4
Cortina d'Ampezzo I....44 B3
Čortkiv UA....117 D1
Cortona I....47 E3
Coruche P....24 A3
Corvara in Badia I....43 F3
Corvera E....30 C2
Corvera de Toranzo E....19 F2
Corwen GB....3 F3
Cosenza I....51 E3
Cosham GB....9 D4
Cosne-d'Allier F....16 A2
Cosne-sur-Loire F....16 A1
Cossato I....17 F3
Cossé-le-Vivien F....11 D4
Cossonay CH....17 D2
Costa de Caparica P....24 A3
Costa de Santo André P....24 A4
Costigliole d'Asti I....17 F4
Coswig D....39 E1
Coswig D....39 F1
Cotignac F....22 C2
Cottbus D....34 C4
Couches F....16 B2
Couço P....24 B3
Coucy-le-Château-Auffrique F....12 B3
Couhé F....15 E3
Couilly-Pont-aux-Dames F....12 A3
Couiza F....21 E3
Coulanges-la-Vineuse F....16 B1
Coulanges-sur-Yonne F....16 A1
Coulommiers F....12 B3
Coulon F....15 D2
Coulonges-sur-l'Autize F....15 D2
Coupar Angus GB....7 D1
Couptrain F....11 E4
Cour-Cheverny F....15 F1
Courçon F....15 D3
Courmayeur I....17 E3
Cournon-d'Auvergne F....16 A3
Courpière F....16 B3
Cours F....16 B3
Coursan F....21 F2
Coursegoules F....23 D1
Courseulles-sur-Mer F....11 E3

Courson-les-Carrières F....16 A1
Courtenay F....12 B4
Courthézon F....22 B1
Courtomer F....11 E4
Courtown IRL....3 D4
Courville-sur-Eure F....11 F4
Coussey F....13 D4
Coutances F....11 D3
Coutras F....15 D4
Couvin B....12 C2
Cova da Iria P....24 A2
Covadonga E....19 D2
Covarrubias E....19 F4
Coventry GB....9 D2
Covilhã P....24 C1
Cowbridge / Bont-faen GB....8 B3
Cowdenbeath GB....7 D1
Cowes (Isle of Wight) GB....9 D4
Cowfold GB....9 E3
Cozes F....15 D3
Craco I....49 E4
Craigavon GB....3 D1
Craigellachie GB....5 D3
Craighouse GB....6 B1
Craignure GB....6 B1
Crail GB....7 E1
Crailsheim D....38 C4
Craiova RO....117 D3
Cranborne GB....10 C1
Cranbrook GB....9 E3
Crans-sur-Sierre CH....17 E2
Craon F....15 D1
Craonne F....12 B3
Craponne-sur-Arzon F....16 B4
Crato P....24 B3
Craughwell IRL....2 B3
Craven Arms GB....8 C2
Crawinkel D....39 D2
Crawley GB....9 E3
Creagorry GB....4 A3
Crécy-en-Ponthieu F....12 A2
Crécy-la-Chapelle F....12 A3
Crécy-sur-Serre F....12 B3
Crediton GB....8 B4
Creegh IRL....2 B3
Creeslough IRL....6 A2
Creglingen D....38 C4
Creil F....12 A3
Crema I....46 C1
Crémieu F....16 C3
Cremona I....46 C1
Créon F....15 D4
Crepaja SRB....57 D2
Crépy-en-Valois F....12 A3
Cres HR....54 B4
Cres HR....54 B3
Crescentino I....17 F4
Crespino I....47 E1
Crest F....16 C4
Cresta CH....43 D3
Créteil F....12 A4
Creully F....11 D3
Creußen D....39 E3
Creutzwald F....13 E3
Crevacuore I....17 F3
Crevalcore I....46 C1
Crèvecœur-le-Grand F....12 A3
Crevillent E....26 C4
Crewe GB....8 C1
Crewkerne GB....8 C3
Crianlarich GB....6 C1
Criccieth GB....8 A1
Crickhowell GB....8 C2
Cricklade GB....9 D3
Crieff GB....7 D1
Criel-sur-Mer F....11 F2
Crikvenica HR....54 B3
Crimmitschau D....39 E2
Crinan GB....6 B1
Criquetot-l'Esneval F....11 E2
Crissolo I....17 E4
Crivitz D....34 A3
Crljenovo Donje BIH....55 F3
Crni Guber BIH....55 F3
Crni Lug BIH....55 D4
Crni Lug HR....54 B3
Črni Vrh SLO....54 A2
Črnkovci HR....55 F2
Crnomelj SLO....54 B2
Crocq F....15 F3
Crolly / Croithlí IRL....2 C1
Cromarty GB....4 C3
Cromer GB....9 F1
Crook GB....7 D3
Croom IRL....2 B3
Cross Hands GB....8 B2
Crosshaven IRL....2 B4
Crossmaglen GB....3 D2
Crossmolina / Crois Mhaoilíona IRL....2 B1
Crotone I....51 E3
Crowborough GB....9 E3
Crowland GB....9 E1
Crowle GB....7 F4
Croyde GB....8 B3
Croydon GB....9 E3
Crozant F....15 F2

Crozon F....10 A4
Cruden Bay GB....5 E4
Crudgington GB....8 C1
Crumlin GB....3 D1
Cruseilles F....17 D3
Cruz da Légua P....24 A2
Cruzamento de Pegões P....24 A3
Crveni Grm BIH....58 A3
Crvenka SRB....55 F2
Csongrád H....116 C2
Csorna H....116 B2
Cuacos de Yuste E....25 D2
Cualedro E....18 B3
Cuba E....24 B4
Cubel E....26 C1
Cuckfield GB....9 E3
Čude BIH....55 F3
Cudillero E....19 D2
Čudovo RUS....115 E1
Cuéllar E....19 E4
Cuenca (Cuenca) E....26 B2
Cuers F....22 C2
Cuerva E....25 F2
Cuevas de San Clemente E....19 F3
Cuevas de San Marcos E....29 E3
Cuevas del Almanzora E....30 B3
Cuevas del Becerro E....29 E3
Cuevas del Campo E....30 A2
Cuevas del Valle E....25 E2
Cuglieri I....50 A3
Cuijk NL....37 D1
Cuiseaux F....16 C2
Cuisery F....16 C2
Cukurciems LV....81 F1
Culan F....15 F2
Culdaff IRL....6 A2
Culemborg NL....36 C1
Cúllar Baza E....30 A2
Cullen GB....5 D3
Cullera E....27 D3
Cullompton GB....8 B4
Culoz F....17 D3
Culross GB....7 D1
Cumbernauld GB....7 D1
Cumbres Mayores E....24 C4
Cumiana I....17 E4
Čumić SRB....57 D3
Cumnock GB....6 C2
Cunault F....15 E1
Cuneo I....23 E1
Cunlhat F....16 B3
Čunski HR....54 B4
Cuntis E....18 A2
Cuorgnè I....17 E4
Cupar GB....7 D1
Cupello I....48 C2
Cupramontana I....47 F3
Čuprija SRB....57 E3
Curia P....24 B1
Curtea de Argeș RO....117 D3
Curtis E....18 B2
Cusano Mutri I....48 C3
Cushendall GB....3 E1
Cushendun GB....3 E1
Cusset F....16 A3
Cutro I....51 E3
Cuxhaven D....33 E2
Cvikov CZ....40 C2
Čvrstec HR....54 C2
Cwmbrân GB....8 C3
Čybinka PL....92 B1
Cyców PL....95 E3
Čypenai LT....82 B2
Cysoing F....12 B1
Czacz PL....93 D2
Czaplinek PL....88 C2
Czarna (Podkarpackie) PL....99 D2
Czarna Białostocka PL....91 E2
Czarna Dąbrówka PL....89 D1
Czarna Górna PL....99 E3
Czarne PL....88 C2
Czarnków PL....88 C3
Czarnocin (Łódzkie) PL....94 A2
Czarnożyły PL....93 F3
Czarny Bór PL....92 C3
Czarny Dunajec PL....98 B3
Czastary PL....93 F3
Czchów PL....98 C2
Czechowice-Dziedzice PL....97 F2
Czechy PL....93 D2
Czemierniki PL....95 E3
Czempiń PL....93 D2
Czeremcha PL....91 E2
Czermin (Wielkopolskie) PL....93 E2
Czerniawa-Zdrój PL....92 B3
Czernica PL....93 D3
Czernice Borowe PL....90 B3
Czerniejewo PL....93 E1
Czerniewice PL....94 B2
Czernikowo PL....89 F3
Czersk PL....89 E2
Czerwieńsk PL....92 B1
Czerwin PL....91 D3
Czerwińsk nad Wisłą PL....94 B1
Czerwionka-Leszczyny PL....97 F2
Czerwonak PL....93 D1

Częstochowa PL....94 A3
Człopa PL....88 C3
Człuchów PL....89 D2
Czosnów PL....94 B1
Czudec PL....99 D2
Czyżew-Osada PL....91 D3

D

D. Brela HR....58 A2
D. Kazanci BIH....55 D4
D. Ljubata SRB....59 F2
D. Lukavac BIH....58 B2
D. Malovan BIH....55 D4
D. Rujani BIH....55 D4
D. Seget HR....58 A4
D. Stalina SRB....57 E4
D. Zemunik HR....54 C4
Dabar HR....54 B3
Dąbie (Lubuskie) PL....92 B1
Dąbie (Wielkopolskie) PL....93 F2
Dąbie (Zachodniopomorskie) PL....88 A2
Dąbie (Jezioro) PL....88 A2
Dąbie (Jezioro) PL....90 C1
Dabilje MK....59 F4
Dabo F....13 E4
Dabromani BIH....58 B3
Dąbroszyn PL....88 A3
Dąbrowa (Kujawsko-Pomorskie) PL....89 E3
Dąbrowa (Opolskie) PL....97 E1
Dąbrowa (Wielkopolskie) PL....93 F2
Dąbrowa Białostocka PL....91 E2
Dąbrowa Biskupia PL....89 F3
Dąbrowa Chełmińska PL....89 E2
Dąbrowa Górnicza PL....97 F2
Dąbrowa Tarnowska PL....98 C2
Dąbrowa Zielona PL....94 A3
Dąbrówno PL....90 B2
Dachau D....43 F1
Dačice CZ....41 D4
Dadiá GR....103 E1
Dáfnes GR....104 C3
Dáfni GR....104 C3
Dáfni I....105 F3
Dáfni (Ágio Óros) GR....102 C2
Dáfni (Etolia-Akarnanía) GR....104 C2
Dáfni (Lésvos) GR....102 C4
Dáfnio GR....108 B1
Dáfnónas GR....102 C1
Dafnónas GR....101 D1
Dafnotí GR....100 C4
Dagali N....66 B1
Dagda LV....83 F2
Dagebüll D....33 D1
Dagenham GB....9 E3
Dagiai LT....81 F2
Dahlen D....39 F1
Dahlenburg D....33 F3
Dahme (Kreis Ostholstein) D....33 F2
Dahme (Kreis Teltow-Fläming) D....34 C4
Dahn D....13 F3
Dailiūnai LT....81 E1
Dailučiai LT....85 D2
Daimiel E....25 F3
Daimús E....27 D4
Dainava LT....86 B3
Dainiai II LT....85 D1
Daksti LV....81 E1
Dal N....66 C2
Đala SRB....55 F1
Dalbe LV....81 E1
Dalbeattie GB....3 F1
Dalby S....71 D3
Dale N....62 A4
Dale N....66 A1
Dalen N....66 B2
Daleszyce PL....94 C3
Dalhem S....67 F4
Dalías E....30 A3
Daliburgh GB....4 A3
Dalkeith GB....7 D1
Dalkey IRL....3 D3
Dalmally GB....6 C1
Dalmellington GB....6 C2
Dalmine I....43 E4
Dalry GB....6 C2
Dals Långed S....66 D3
Dalsbruk FIN....76 B3
Dalsjöfors S....67 D4
Dalton in Furness GB....7 D3
Dalvík IS....84 C1
Dalwhinnie GB....4 C4
Däma LV....80 D1
Damaskiná GR....101 D1
Damasławek PL....89 D3
Damássi GR....101 D2
Damazan F....21 D1
Dambava LT....85 D2
Dambenieki LV....79 E3
Damelevières F....13 D4

Dameliai LT....81 E2
Damgan F....14 B1
Damianó GR....101 E2
Dammartin-en-Goële F....12 A3
Damme (Kreis Vechta) D....33 D4
Damnjane SRB....59 D3
Dampierre F....16 C1
Dampierre-sur-Salon F....16 C1
Damville F....11 F3
Damvillers F....13 D3
Dangé-St-Romain F....15 E2
Danilava LT....86 C2
Danilov RUS....115 F1
Danilovgrad MNE....58 C3
Dannemarie F....17 E1
Dannenberg (Elbe) (Kreis Lüchow-Dannengerg) D....33 F3
Daoulas F....10 A4
Dapkūniškiai LT....86 B1
Darbenai LT....80 B2
Darda HR....55 E2
Dardedzes LV....82 C1
Dardesheim D....39 D1
Darfo-Boario Terme I....43 E4
Degaña E....18 C2
Dargai LT....80 C2
Dargin (Jezioro) PL....90 C1
Darginiai LT....81 E2
Dargun D....34 B2
Dargužiai (Alytaus) LT....86 B3
Dargužiai (Klaipedos) LT....80 A2
Dargužiai (Šiauliu) LT....81 E2
Darlington GB....7 E3
Darłówko PL....88 C1
Darłowo PL....88 C1
Darmstadt D....13 F2
Darney F....13 D4
Daroca E....26 C1
Darque P....18 A4
Darsūniškis LT....85 F2
Dartford GB....9 E3
Dartmouth GB....8 B4
Daruvar HR....55 D2
Darwen GB....7 E4
Darželiai LT....85 F3
Daržininkai LT....86 B3
Dasburg D....13 D2
Dasing D....43 F1
Dassel D....38 C1
Dassohóri GR....102 C2
Dassow D....33 F2
Dasze PL....91 E3
Daszyna PL....94 A2
D'at'kovo RUS....115 F3
Datteln D....37 E1
Daubiškiai LT....81 D2
Dauburačiai LT....80 C3
Daudzese LV....82 B1
Daudzevas LV....83 D3
Daugai LT....85 F3
Daugava LT....80 A2
Daugavpils LV....83 D3
Daugeliškiai LT....81 E1
Daugirdai LT....83 D3
Daugleikis LT....84 C1
Daugmale LT....81 F1
Dauguli LV....78 B2
Daujenai LT....81 E2
Daujočiai LT....82 C3
Daukantiškiai LT....85 D2
Daukniūnai LT....81 D3
Daukšaičiai LT....80 B3
Daukšiai (Klaipedos) LT....80 D2
Daukšiai (Marijampoles) LT....85 E2
Daukšiai (Vilniaus) LT....87 D1
Daukstes LV....79 E3
Daulenai LT....86 C3
Daumantai (Volfärte) LV....81 E2
Daumenai LT....81 E2
Daumilai LT....86 C2
Daun D....13 E2
Daunoriai LT....82 B3
Dauparai LT....80 B3
Daužnagiai LT....82 B3
Dava S....4 C3
Daventry GB....9 D2
Dāvi LV....81 F1
Dávia GR....105 D4
Dávlia GR....105 D2
Davor HR....55 D2
Davos CH....43 E3
Dawlish GB....8 B4
Dax F....20 B2
De Bilt NL....36 C1
De Haan B....12 A1
De Koog NL....32 A3
De Panne B....12 A1
Deal GB....9 F3
Deauville F....11 E3
Deba E....20 A3
Debar MK....59 D4
Debarska Banja Banjišta MK....59 D4
Dębe Wielkie PL....94 C1
Debeikiai LT....82 B3
Debeli Lug SRB....57 E3
Debeljača SRB....57 D2

Dębica PL....98 C2
Dęblin PL....95 D2
Dębnica Kaszubska PL....89 D1
Dębno (Nowy Targ) PL....98 B3
Dębno (Tarnów) PL....98 C2
Dębno (Zachodniopomorskie) PL....88 A3
Dębołęka PL....93 F2
Dębów PL....99 D2
Dębowa Kłoda PL....95 E2
Dębowa Łąka PL....89 F3
Dębowiec PL....98 C2
Dębowiec (Śląskie) PL....97 F2
Dębowo PL....91 D2
Debrc SRB....56 C3
Debrecen H....116 C2
Debrzno PL....89 D2
Dečani SRB....59 D3
Decazeville F....21 E1
Děčín CZ....40 C2
Decize F....16 A2
Dedemsvaart NL....32 C4
Degaña E....18 C2
Degerfors S....67 D3
Degerndorf a. Inn D....44 A3
Degesiai LT....81 F2
Deggendorf D....39 F4
Deglenai LT....81 F2
Deglova LV....83 F1
Dego I....23 E1
Degole LV....77 D3
Degracias P....24 B2
Degučiai (Büda) LT....85 D2
Degučiai (Karkliniai) LT....85 D2
Degučiai (Klaipedos) LT....84 C1
Degučiai (Šiauliu) LT....81 E2
Degumnieki LV....83 E1
Degutine LT....85 D2
Dehesa de Montejo E....19 E3
Deidesheim D....13 F3
Deinze B....12 B1
Deiva Marina I....23 F1
Dej RO....117 D2
Deje S....67 D3
Deksne LV....76 C3
Dekteri LV....83 F1
Delčevo MK....59 F4
Delden NL....32 C4
Deleitosa E....25 D2
Delémont CH....17 E1
Deléria GR....101 E4
Delfi GR....105 D2
Delft NL....36 B1
Delfzijl NL....32 C3
Delia I....52 C3
Delianuova I....51 D4
Deliblato SRB....57 D2
Deliceto I....49 E3
Delimeđe SRB....57 D4
Delitzsch D....39 E1
Delle F....17 E1
Delme F....13 D3
Delmenhorst D....33 E3
Delnice HR....54 B3
Delsbo S....68 A3
Deltebre E....27 E1
Deltuva LT....85 F1
Delvin IRL....3 D2
Delvináki GR....100 C3
Demene LV....83 D3
Demidov RUS....115 E3
Demir Kapija MK....59 F4
Demmin D....34 B2
Demonía GR....108 C3
Den Burg NL....32 B3
Den Haag = 's-Gravenhage NL....36 B1
Den Helder NL....32 B3
Den Oever NL....32 B4
Denain F....12 B2
Denbigh / Dinbych GB....3 F3
Dendermonde B....12 B1
Dendrohóri GR....101 D2
Denekamp NL....32 C4
Dénia E....27 D4
Denkendorf D....39 E4
Dennington GB....9 F2
Denny GB....7 D1
Derby GB....9 D1
Dereköy TR....117 E4
Derenburg D....39 D1
Dermbach (Wartburgkreis) D....38 C2
Derneburg D....33 F4
Deruta I....47 F3
Dervaig GB....4 B4
Derval F....14 C1
Dervéni GR....105 D3
Derventa BIH....55 E3
Derviniai LT....85 D3
Dervíziana GR....100 C4
Desborough GB....9 D2
Descartes F....15 E2
Desenzano del Garda I....43 E4
Desfina GR....105 D2
Desimirovac SRB....57 D3
Desio I....43 D4
Deskáti GR....101 D4
Despotikó (Nissi) GR....109 E1
Despotovac SRB....57 E3
Despotovo SRB....55 F2

Dessau (Kreis Dessau Stadt) *D* 39 E1
Deštné v Orlických horach *CZ* 41 D2
Destriana *E* 18 C3
Desulo *I* 50 B3
Desvres *F* 12 A1
Deszczno *PL* 88 B3
Deta *RO* 116 C3
Detmold *D* 37 F1
Dettelbach *D* 38 C3
Deurne *NL* 37 D1
Deutsch Wagram *A* 41 E4
Deutschkreutz *A* 45 E1
Deutschlandsberg *A* 45 D2
Deva *RO* 117 D2
Deveikiškiai *LT* 85 E1
Deventer *NL* 32 C4
Devil's Bridge / Pontarfynach *GB* 3 F4
Devizes *GB* 8 C3
Devnja *BG* 117 E3
Devynduoniai *LT* 81 E3
Dewsbury *GB* 7 E4
Deyá *E* 31 E3
Deza *E* 20 A4
Dezzo *I* 43 E4
Día (Nissi) *GR* 109 F3
Diafáni *GR* 111 E3
Diakófti *GR* 108 C2
Diakoftó *GR* 105 D3
Diamante *I* 51 E2
Diano Marina *I* 23 E1
Diápora Nissiá *GR* 105 E3
Diavatá *GR* 101 F2
Diavolitsi *GR* 104 C4
Dibbersen (Kreis Harburg) *D* 33 E3
Dicmo *HR* 55 D4
Dicomano *I* 47 E2
Didieji Rūšupiai *LT* 80 B2
Dídima *GR* 105 E4
Didimótiho *GR* 103 F1
Didkiemis *LT* 80 C3
Didžiadvaris *LT* 82 C3
Didžiakaimis *LT* 86 B1
Didžiasalis *LT* 83 D3
Didžioji Riešė *LT* 86 B2
Didžiosios Lapes *LT* 85 E1
Didžiosios Selos *LT* 86 B3
Didžprūdėliai *LT* 82 B3
Die *F* 16 C4
Dieburg *D* 13 F2
Diedorf (Unstrut-Hainich-Kreis) *D* 38 C2
Diego Álvaro *E* 25 E1
Diekirch *L* 13 D2
Diemelstadt *D* 37 F1
Dienvidnieki *LV* 80 B1
Diepholz *D* 33 D4
Dieppe *F* 11 F2
Dierdorf *D* 13 E1
Dieren *NL* 37 D1
Diesdorf (Altmarkkreis Salzwedel) *D* 33 F4
Dießen a. Ammersee (Kreis Landsberg a. Lech) *D* 43 F1
Diest *B* 12 C4
Dietenheim *D* 43 E1
Dietfurt a. d. Altmühl (Kreis Neumarkt i. d. OPf.) *D* 39 E4
Dietikon *CH* 17 F1
Dietkauščizna *LT* 87 D1
Dietmannsried *D* 43 E2
Dietzenbach *D* 38 B3
Dieulefit *F* 22 B1
Dieulouard *F* 13 D2
Dieuze *F* 13 E3
Dieveniškes *LT* 86 C3
Diez *D* 13 F1
Diezma *E* 30 A3
Differdange *L* 13 D3
Digermulen *N* 60 B3
Dignája *LV* 83 D2
Dignano *I* 44 C4
Digne-les-Bains *F* 22 C1
Digoin *F* 16 B2
Dijon *F* 16 C1
Dikanäs *S* 64 A3
Díkea *GR* 103 E1
Dikela *GR* 103 E3
Dikli *LV* 78 B2
Diksmuide *B* 12 A1
Dílesi *GR* 105 F2
Diliauskai *LT* 81 F2
Dilináta *GR* 104 A2
Dillenburg *D* 13 F1
Dillingen (Saar) (Kreis Saarlouis) *D* 13 E3
Dillingen an der Donau (Kreis Dillingen) *D* 43 E1
Dilofos *GR* 103 E1
Dílos (Nissi) *GR* 106 C4
Dímena *GR* 105 E3
Dimitra *GR* 101 F4
Dimitríes *LT* 83 D3
Dimitritsí *GR* 102 A4
Dimitsána *GR* 104 C4
Dimzukalns *LV* 81 F1
Dínali *M* 53 F4
Dínami *I* 51 D3
Dinan *F* 10 C4
Dinant *B* 12 C2

Dinard *F* 10 C4
Dingelstädt *D* 38 C1
Dingle *S* 66 C3
Dingle / An Daingean *IRL* 2 A4
Dingolfing *D* 39 F4
Dingwall *GB* 4 C3
Dinjiška *HR* 54 B4
Dinkelsbühl *D* 39 D4
Dinklage *D* 33 D4
Dinsdurbe *LV* 80 B1
Dinslaken *D* 37 D1
Dío *GR* 101 E3
Diónissos *GR* 105 F3
Dipótama *GR* 102 B3
Dippoldiswalde *D* 39 F2
Diráhio *GR* 105 D4
Dirdal *N* 66 A2
Diroú (Spílea) *GR* 108 B1
Dirvonenai (Šiauliu) *LT* 81 D2
Dirvonenai (Telšiu) *LT* 80 C2
Diržiai *LT* 81 F2
Disentis / Mustér *CH* 17 F2
Dispilio *GR* 101 D3
Diss *GB* 9 F2
Dissen (Kreis Osnabrück) *D* 37 F1
Dístomo *GR* 105 D3
Dístos *GR* 105 F2
Ditzingen *D* 43 D1
Divača *SLO* 54 A2
Divaráta *GR* 104 A2
Divčibare *SRB* 56 C3
Dives-sur-Mer *F* 11 E3
Divié *BIH* 55 F3
Divljana *SRB* 57 F4
Divonne-les-Bains *F* 17 D2
Divoúnia (Nissi) *GR* 111 D3
Divri *GR* 105 D1
Divuša *HR* 54 C3
Dižstende *LT* 77 D3
Djúpivogur *IS* 62 C1
Djupvik *N* 60 C2
Djurås *S* 67 E1
Długołęka (Dolnośląskie) *PL* 93 D3
Dłutów *PL* 94 A2
Dmitrov *RUS* 115 F1
Dniprodzeržyns'k *UA* 117 F1
Dnipropetrovs'k *UA* 117 F1
Dno *RUS* 115 D1
Dobanovci *SRB* 56 C2
Dobbiaco / Toblach *I* 44 B3
Dobczyce *PL* 98 B2
Dobel *D* 13 F3
Dobele *LV* 81 E1
Dobelí *LV* 76 C3
Döbeln *D* 39 F1
Döbern (Kreis Spree-Neiße) *D* 40 C1
Dobersberg *A* 41 D4
Dobiegniew *PL* 88 B3
Dobilija *LT* 85 F2
Doboj *BIH* 55 E3
Dobosnica *BIH* 55 E3
Dobra *SRB* 57 E2
Dobra (Małopolskie) *PL* 98 B2
Dobra (Nowogard) *PL* 88 B2
Dobra (Szczecin) *PL* 88 A2
Dobra (Wielkopolskie) *PL* 93 F2
Dobrčane *SRB* 59 E3
Dobrcz *PL* 89 E3
Dobre (Kujawsko-Pomorskie) *PL* 89 F3
Dobre Miasto *PL* 90 B2
Dobri Do *SRB* 57 E4
Döbriach *A* 44 C3
Dobrič *BG* 117 E3
Dobrica *SRB* 57 D2
Dobričevo *SRB* 57 D2
Dobrinj *HR* 54 B3
Dobrinja *SRB* 56 C3
Dobříš *CZ* 40 C3
Dobrljin *BIH* 54 C3
Dobrna *SLO* 54 B1
Dobrodzień *PL* 97 E1
Dobro Polje *BIH* 55 F4
Dobromierz (Dolnośląskie) *PL* 92 C3
Dobromyśl *PL* 94 A2
Dobrošinci *MK* 59 F4
Dobroszyce *PL* 93 D3
Dobrovnik *SLO* 54 C1
Dobruň *BIH* 55 F3
Dobruška *CZ* 41 D2
Dobrzany *PL* 88 B3
Dobrzeń Wielki *PL* 93 E3
Dobrzyń nad Wisłą *PL* 89 F3
Docksta *S* 68 A2
Dodóni *GR* 100 C4
Doesburg *NL* 37 D1
Doetinchem *NL* 37 D1
Doganović *SRB* 59 E3
Dogliani *I* 23 E1
Doïráni *GR* 101 E3
Dojani *BIH* 55 F3
Dokka *N* 66 C1
Dokkum *NL* 32 B3
Dokós (Nissi) *GR* 105 D4

Doksy *CZ* 40 C2
Dokupe *LV* 76 B2
Dol-de-Bretagne *F* 10 C4
Dole *F* 16 C2
Dølemo *N* 66 B3
Dolenci *MK* 59 E4
Dolenjavas *SLO* 54 B2
Dolenjske Toplice *SLO* 54 B2
Dolgas Vas *SLO* 54 C1
Dolgellau *GB* 3 F4
Dolgie *PL* 88 A3
Dołhobyczów *PL* 95 F3
Doliana *GR* 100 C3
Dolianova *I* 50 B4
Dolice *PL* 88 B3
Dolíhi *GR* 101 E3
Doljani *MK* 59 E4
Doljevac *SRB* 57 E4
Dolla *IRL* 2 C3
Döllach *A* 44 B2
Dollar *GB* 7 D1
Dolle *D* 34 A4
Dolná (Dolnaja) *LV* 83 D2
Dolní Dvořiště *CZ* 40 C4
Dolní Lipka *CZ* 41 D2
Dolní Poustevna *CZ* 40 C1
Dolno Kosovrasti *MK* 59 D4
Dolo *I* 44 B4
Dolomîts *LV* 82 C2
Dolores *E* 26 C4
Dolovo *SRB* 57 D2
Dolsk *PL* 93 D2
Dolyna *UA* 117 D1
Dołżyca *PL* 99 E3
Domanice *PL* 95 D2
Domaniewice (Łodzkie) *PL* 94 A2
Domaniów *PL* 93 D3
Domantonys *LT* 85 D2
Domaradz *PL* 99 D2
Domašovo *BIH* 58 B3
Domaszowice *PL* 93 E3
Domažlice *CZ* 40 B3
Dombás *N* 62 C4
Dombasle-sur-Meurthe *F* 13 D4
Dombóvár *H* 116 B2
Domburg *NL* 36 B1
Domène *F* 17 D4
Doméniko *GR* 101 E4
Domèvre-en-Haye *F* 13 D3
Domfront *F* 11 D4
Dominikowice *PL* 98 C2
Dömitz *D* 34 A3
Domme *F* 15 E4
Dommitzsch *D* 39 E1
Domnísta *GR* 104 C2
Domodedovo *RUS* 115 F2
Domodossola *I* 17 F3
Domokós *GR* 105 D1
Dompaire *F* 13 D4
Dompierre-sur-Besbre *F* 16 B2
Domrémy-la-Pucelle *F* 13 D4
Domusnovas *I* 50 A4
Domvréna *GR* 105 E2
Domžale *SLO* 54 A2
Don Benito *E* 25 D3
Doña María Ocaña *E* 30 A3
Doña Mencía *E* 29 F2
Donaghadee *GB* 3 E1
Donaueschingen *D* 13 F4
Donauwörth *D* 43 E1
Donawitz *A* 45 D2
Doncaster *GB* 7 E4
Donegal / Dún na nGall *IRL* 2 C1
Donetzebe / Santesteban *E* 20 B2
Dongen *NL* 36 C1
Donges *F* 14 C1
Donington *GB* 9 E1
Donja Brezna *MNE* 58 C2
Donja Bukovica *MNE* 58 C2
Donja Šatornja *SRB* 57 D3
Donje Crniljevo *SRB* 55 F3
Donje Dragovlje *SRB* 57 E4
Donje Ljupče *SRB* 59 E2
Donji Andrijevci *HR* 55 E2
Donji Barbeš *SRB* 57 E4
Donji Kneginec *HR* 54 C3
Donji Lapac *HR* 54 C4
Donji Miholjac *HR* 55 E2
Donji Milanovac *SRB* 57 E2
Donji Stajovce *SRB* 59 E3
Donji Vakuf *BIH* 55 E3
Donji Vijačani *BIH* 55 E3
Donnemarie-Dontilly *F* 12 B4
Donnersbachwald *A* 44 C2
Dønnes *N* 63 D1
Donostia-San Sebastián *E* 20 A4
Donoússa (Nissi) *GR* 107 D4
Donzenac *F* 15 F4
Donzère *F* 22 B1
Donzy *F* 16 A1
Đorče Petrov *MK* 59 E3
Dorchester *GB* 8 C4
Dordives *F* 12 A4
Dordrecht *NL* 36 C1
Dorfen (Kreis Erding) *D* 43 F1
Dorfmark *D* 33 E3
Dorgali *I* 50 B3
Dório *GR* 104 C4

Dorkáda *GR* 101 F2
Dorking *GB* 9 E3
Dormagen *D* 13 E1
Dormans *F* 12 B3
Dornbirn *A* 43 D2
Dornburg (Saale-Holzland-Kreis) *D* 39 D2
Dorndorf (Wartburgkreis) *D* 38 C2
Dornes *F* 16 A2
Dornie *GB* 4 B4
Dornoch *GB* 4 C3
Dornstetten *D* 13 F4
Dornum *D* 33 D3
Dorog *H* 116 B2
Dorogobuž *RUS* 115 F2
Dorohoi *RO* 117 D1
Dorohusk *PL* 95 F3
Dorotea *S* 64 A3
Dörpstedt *D* 37 E1
Dorsten *D* 37 E1
Dortan *F* 17 D2
Dortmund *D* 37 E1
Doruchów *PL* 93 E3
Dorum *D* 33 D3
Dorupe *LV* 81 E1
Douai *F* 12 B2
Douarnenez *F* 10 A4
Doucier *F* 17 D2
Doudeville *F* 11 F2
Doué-la-Fontaine *F* 15 D1
Douglas *GB* 3 F2
Douglas *GB* 3 F2
Doulaincourt *F* 12 C4
Doulevant-le-Château *F* 12 C4
Doullens *F* 12 A2
Doune *GB* 8 D1
Dourdan *F* 12 A4
Dourgne *F* 21 E2
Doúsk *BY* 115 E3
Douvaine *F* 17 D2
Douvres-la-Délivrande *F* 11 E3
Dover *GB* 9 F3
Dovilai *LT* 80 B3
Dovre *N* 62 C4
Downham Market *GB* 9 F2
Downpatrick *GB* 3 E2
Dowra *IRL* 2 C1
Doxarás *GR* 101 E4
Doxáto *GR* 102 B2
Dozulé *F* 11 E3
Drabeši *LV* 78 B3
Dračevo *MK* 59 E3
Dragalovci *BIH* 55 E3
Dragacz *PL* 94 A2
Drăgăşani *RO* 117 D3
Dragaši *MNE* 55 F4
Draginac *SRB* 56 B3
Draginiai *LT* 81 D2
Draginje *SRB* 56 C2
Dragočaj *BIH* 55 D3
Dragoevo *MK* 59 F3
Dragoman *BG* 59 F1
Dragoní *I* 48 C3
Dragør *DK* 71 D3
Dragoš *MK* 59 E4
Dragosvet *SRB* 57 D3
Dragotiná *GR* 100 B4
Dragović *HR* 54 C3
Dragozetići *HR* 54 A3
Dragsfjärd *FIN* 76 C1
Dragsvik *N* 66 A1
Draguignan *F* 22 C2
Dráma *GR* 101 F4
Drammen *N* 66 C2
Drangedal *N* 66 B2
Dranske *D* 34 B1
Draseikiai *LT* 82 B2
Drásenai *LT* 86 C1
Drasenhofen *A* 41 E4
Drąsutaičiai *LT* 81 E2
Draudeliai *LT* 84 B1
Draudeniai *LT* 84 B1
Draudzība *LV* 78 B3
Dravograd *SLO* 54 B1
Drawa *PL* 88 C2
Drawienski Park Narodowy *PL* 88 C3
Drawno *PL* 88 B3
Drawsko *PL* 88 C3
Drawsko Pomorskie *PL* 88 C2
Draženov *CZ* 40 B3
Draževac *SRB* 56 C2
Drebkau *D* 39 F1
Dreilini *LV* 77 F3
Drelów *PL* 95 E2
Drenovci *HR* 55 F2
Drenovo *MK* 59 F4
Drépano *GR* 101 E3
Drépano *GR* 105 E4
Dresden *D* 39 F1
Dreux *F* 11 F4
Dreverna *LT* 80 A3
Drezdenko *PL* 88 B3
Drežnica *HR* 54 B3
Drežnik Grad *HR* 54 C3
Dricāni *LV* 83 E1

Driebergen-Rijsenburg *NL* 36 C1
Driebes *E* 26 A2
Driméa *GR* 105 D2
Drimós *GR* 101 F2
Drinjača *BIH* 55 F3
Drinovci *BIH* 58 A2
Driopída *GR* 106 A3
Driós *GR* 109 F1
Drlače *SRB* 55 F3
Drnholec *CZ* 41 E4
Drniš *HR* 54 C4
Drnje *HR* 55 D1
Drnovo *SLO* 54 B2
Drøbak *N* 66 C2
Drobeta-Turnu Severin *RO* 117 D3
Drobin *PL* 90 A3
Drobukščiai *LT* 80 C3
Drochtersen *D* 33 E3
Drogheda / Droichead Átha *IRL* 3 D2
Drohiczyn *PL* 95 E1
Drohobyč *UA* 117 D1
Droitwich *GB* 9 D2
Drokija *MD* 117 E1
Dromcolliher *IRL* 2 B4
Dromore *GB* 6 A3
Dromore *GB* 3 D1
Dronero *I* 23 D1
Dronfield *GB* 9 E1
Drongaráti *GR* 104 A2
Dronninglund *DK* 70 C2
Dronten *NL* 32 B4
Drosendorf Stadt *A* 41 D4
Drossáto *GR* 101 F1
Drosseró *GR* 101 E2
Drossiá *GR* 105 F2
Drossohóri *GR* 105 D2
Drossopigí *GR* 100 C3
Drossopigí (Flórina) *GR* 101 D3
Drottningholm *S* 67 F2
Droué *F* 11 F4
Drozdowo *PL* 88 C1
Drúlenai *LT* 82 B3
Drulingen *F* 13 E3
Drumkeeran *IRL* 2 C2
Drummore *GB* 3 E1
Drumnadrochit *GB* 4 C4
Drumshanbo *IRL* 2 C2
Drusenheim *D* 13 F3
Druskininkai *LT* 85 E3
Druskininkai (miestas) *LT* 85 E3
Drusti *LV* 78 C3
Druten *NL* 36 C1
Druva *LV* 80 C1
Druvāni *LV* 82 C1
Druviena *LV* 79 D3
Druvinas *LT* 82 B1
Družai *LT* 86 B1
Družba *PL* 94 A2
Drvar *BIH* 54 C4
Drvenik *HR* 58 A3
Drvenik (Otok) *HR* 58 A4
Drwęca *PL* 90 A2
Drwęckie (Jezioro) *PL* 90 B2
Drwinia *PL* 98 B2
Dryburgh Abbey *GB* 7 E2
Drymen *GB* 6 C1
Drzewica *PL* 94 B2
Drzycim *PL* 89 E3
Dubăsari *MD* 117 E2
Dubci *HR* 58 A4
Dubí *CZ* 40 A2
Dubica Cerkiewne *PL* 91 E3
Dubiecko *PL* 99 E2
Dubienka *PL* 95 F3
Dubingiai *LT* 86 C1
Dublin / Baile Átha Cliath *IRL* 3 D3
Dubna *LV* 83 D2
Dubna *RUS* 115 F1
Dubňany *CZ* 41 E4
Dubno *UA* 117 D1
Duboka *SRB* 57 D4
Dubona *SRB* 57 D2
Duboštica *BIH* 55 E3
Dubovac *SRB* 57 D2
Dubovsko *BIH* 54 C4
Dubów *PL* 95 E2
Dubrava (Peljesac Otok) *HR* 58 A3
Dubrava (Zagreb) *HR* 54 C2
Dubrava Stara *SRB* 57 D2
Dubrave (Brčko) *BIH* 55 E3
Dubrave (Tuzla) *BIH* 55 E3
Dubravica *BIH* 55 E3
Dubrovnik *HR* 58 B3
Dubuli *LV* 83 F2
Dubulti *LV* 82 C2
Ducey *F* 11 D4
Duchcov *CZ* 40 A2
Ducherow *D* 34 B2
Duchovščina *RUS* 115 E2
Duclair *F* 11 F2
Dudelange *L* 13 D3
Duderstadt *D* 38 C1
Dudweiler *D* 13 E3
Dueñas *E* 19 E4
Duesund *N* 66 A1
Dufftown *GB* 5 D3

Duga Poljana *SRB* 57 D4
Duga Reka *HR* 54 B2
Dugi Otok (Otok) *HR* 54 B4
Dugi Rat *HR* 58 A4
Dugi Selo *HR* 54 C2
Duingt *F* 17 D3
Duino-Aurisina *I* 44 C4
Duisburg *D* 37 D1
Dukat *SRB* 59 F2
Dukielska (Przełęcz) *PL* 99 D3
Dukla *PL* 99 D3
Dūkštas *LT* 83 D3
Dūkštai *LT* 86 B2
Dūkštos *LT* 86 B2
Dukstyna *LT* 86 B1
Dukurnonys *LT* 85 E1
Duleek *IRL* 3 D2
Dulje *SRB* 59 D3
Dülken *D* 37 D2
Dülmen *D* 37 E1
Dulnain Bridge *GB* 4 C4
Đulovac *HR* 55 D2
Dulovo *BG* 117 E3
Dumbarton *GB* 6 C1
Dumbría *E* 18 A2
Dumbriai *LT* 81 D2
Dūmciems *LV* 77 E1
Dumfries *GB* 3 F1
Dun Laoghaire *IRL* 3 D3
Dun-le-Palestel *F* 15 F2
Dun-sur-Auron *F* 16 A2
Dunaföldvár *H* 116 B2
Dunaïvci *UA* 117 D1
Dunajec *PL* 98 B3
Dunalka *LV* 80 B1
Dunaújváros *H* 116 B2
Dunava (Dunova) *LV* 83 D2
Dunavci *BG* 117 D3
Dunbar *GB* 7 E1
Dunblane *GB* 7 D1
Dundaga *LV* 76 C2
Dundalk / Dún Dealgan *IRL* 3 D2
Dundee *GB* 7 E1
Dundonnell *GB* 4 B3
Dunfanaghy *IRL* 6 A2
Dunfermline *GB* 7 D1
Dungannon *GB* 3 D1
Dungarvan / Dún Garbhán *IRL* 2 C4
Dungiven *GB* 3 D1
Dunglow / An Clochán Liath *IRL* 2 C1
Dunika *LV* 80 B2
Dunje *MK* 59 F4
Dunkeld *GB* 7 D1
Dunkerque *F* 12 A1
Dunmanway / Dún Mánmhaí *IRL* 2 B4
Dunmore / Dún Mór *IRL* 2 B2
Dunmore East *IRL* 3 D4
Dunnamanagh *GB* 3 D1
Dunnet *GB* 5 D2
Dunoon *GB* 6 C1
Duns *GB* 7 E2
Dunshaughlin *IRL* 3 D2
Dunski *LT* 83 E3
Dunstable *GB* 9 E2
Dunster *GB* 8 C3
Dunte *LV* 77 F2
Dunvegan *GB* 4 A3
Duobužiai *LT* 86 B1
Duokiškis *LT* 82 C3
Duonelaičiai *LT* 85 D2
Dupnica *BG* 117 D4
Dupuličiai *LT* 80 B2
Đurakovac *SRB* 59 D3
Durango *E* 20 A3
Duras *F* 14 C4
Durban-Corbières *F* 21 F2
Durbe *LV* 80 B1
Đurđevac *HR* 55 D2
Đurđević *BIH* 55 F4
Đurđevića Tara *MNE* 58 C2
Đurđevik *BIH* 55 E3
Düren *D* 13 E1
Durham *GB* 7 E3
Durlach *D* 13 F3
Đurmanec *HR* 54 C1
Durness *GB* 4 C2
Dürnkrut *A* 41 E4
Dürnstein *A* 41 D4
Durrës *AL* 116 C4
Durrow *IRL* 3 D3
Dursley *GB* 8 C3
Durtal *F* 15 D1
Duruelo *E* 19 E4
Dušanovo *BIH* 58 C3
Dūseikiai *LT* 80 C2
Dusetos *LT* 82 C3
Dusina *BIH* 55 E3
Dusmenys *LT* 85 F3
Düsseldorf *D* 37 D2
Duszniki *PL* 92 C1
Duszniki-Zdrój *PL* 96 C1
Duved *S* 68 B4
Düzce *TR* 117 F4
Duži (Mostar) *BIH* 58 A3
Duži (Trebinje) *BIH* 58 B3
Dvariškiai *LT* 81 E2
Dvariūkai *LT* 81 F3
Dverberg *N* 60 C2
Dviete (Dvīts) *LV* 83 D2
Dvor *HR* 54 C3
Dvorovi *BIH* 55 F3

Dvory nad Lužnicí *CZ* 41 D4
Dvůr Králové nad Labem *CZ* 41 D2
Dwikozy *PL* 95 D2
Dybowo *PL* 91 D2
Dydnia *PL* 99 D2
Dygowo *PL* 88 C1
Dynów *PL* 99 D2
Dyrnes *N* 62 B3
Dysna *LT* 87 E1
Dyviškiai *LT* 85 E3
Dywity *PL* 90 B2
Džaniči *BIH* 55 E4
Dzegužkrēvi *LT* 81 E2
Dzelda *LV* 80 C1
Dzelmes *LV* 76 C3
Dzelmes (Lieljumprava) *LV* 82 B1
Dzelzava *LV* 79 D3
Dzenagols *LV* 83 E1
Džepi *SRB* 57 F4
Dzērbene *LV* 78 C3
Dzērumcelmi *LV* 81 F1
Dzērvenieki *LV* 76 B3
Dziadkowice *PL* 91 E3
Dziadowa Kłoda *PL* 93 D3
Działdowo *PL* 90 B3
Działoszyce *PL* 98 B1
Działoszyn *PL* 93 F3
Dziemiany *PL* 89 D2
Dzierzążnia *PL* 90 B3
Dzierzgoń *PL* 89 F2
Dzierżoniów *PL* 96 C1
Dzilnas *LV* 77 E3
Dzintari *LV* 81 F1
Dzirciems *LV* 77 D3
Dzirnavas *LV* 82 C2
Dzirnieki (Jelgavas) *LV* 81 E1
Dzirnieki (Kuldīgas) *LV* 76 C3
Dziwiszów *PL* 92 C3
Dziwnów *PL* 88 A1
Dziwnówek *PL* 88 A1
Dzjaržynsk *BY* 115 D3
Dzūkai *LT* 85 D3
Džūkste *LV* 81 E1
Džumajlija *MK* 59 F3
Dźwierzuty *PL* 90 C2
Dzwola *PL* 95 E3

E

Eaglescliffe *GB* 7 E3
Eándio *GR* 105 E3
Eani *GR* 101 E3
Earith *GB* 9 E2
Earlston *GB* 7 E2
Easingwold *GB* 7 E3
Easky *IRL* 2 B2
East Dereham *GB* 9 F1
East Grinstead *GB* 9 E3
East Kilbride *GB* 6 C1
East Linton *GB* 7 E1
Eastbourne *GB* 9 F3
Eastleigh *GB* 9 D3
Eaux-Bonnes *F* 20 C3
Eauze *F* 20 C2
Ebavere *EE* 73 D1
Ebbw Vale / Glyn Ebwy *GB* 8 C2
Ebeleben *D* 39 D1
Ebeltoft *DK* 70 C3
Eben im Pongau *A* 44 C2
Ebenfurth *A* 45 E1
Ebensee *A* 44 C2
Eberbach (Rhein-Neckar-Kreis) *D* 37 F4
Ebersberg *D* 43 D1
Ebersberg *A* 44 C2
Eberstein *A* 45 D2
Eberswalde *D* 34 C4
Ebmath *D* 39 E2
Eboli *I* 49 D4
Ebrach *D* 38 C3
Ébreuil *F* 16 A3
Eccleshall *GB* 8 C1
Eceabat *TR* 117 E4
Echallens *CH* 27 E1
Echt *NL* 37 D2
Echte *D* 38 C1
Echternach *L* 13 E2
Écija *E* 29 E2
Eckartsberga *D* 39 D1
Eckernförde *D* 33 E1
Eckerö *FIN* 68 B4
Écommoy *F* 15 E1
Écos *F* 11 F3
Ecseny *H* 116 B2
Écueillé *F* 15 F1
Ed *S* 66 C3
Eda glasbruk *S* 67 D2
Edam *NL* 32 B4
Edane *S* 66 C2
Edas *LV* 76 C3

Ede *NL* 37 D1
Edelény *H* 116 C2
Édenderry / Éadan Doire *IRL* 3 D3
Edenkoben *D* 13 E3
Édessa *GR* 101 E2
Edgeworthstown / Meathas Troim *IRL* 2 C2
Edinburgh *GB* 7 D1
Edineţi *MD* 117 E1
Edipsós *GR* 105 E1
Edirne *TR* 117 E4
Edise *EE* 73 E2
Edland *N* 66 B2
Edole *LV* 76 B3
Edoya *N* 62 B3
Edsåsdalen *S* 63 D3
Edsbro *S* 67 F1
Edsbyn *S* 67 E1
Edsele *S* 68 A1
Eeklo *B* 12 B1
Eelde *NL* 32 C3
Eemshaven *NL* 32 C3
Eferding *A* 44 C1
Efira *GR* 104 C3
Efkarpía *GR* 101 F2
Efkarpía *GR* 102 A2
Eforie *RO* 117 E3
Efxinoúpoli *GR* 105 D1
Egeln *D* 39 D1
Eger *H* 116 C2
Egersund *N* 66 A3
Egeskov *DK* 70 B3
Egestorf (Kreis Harburg) *D* 33 F3
Egg *A* 43 F3
Eggenburg *A* 41 D4
Eggenfelden *D* 44 B1
Eggesin *D* 34 C2
Eggum *N* 60 A3
Eghezée *B* 12 C1
Égiáli *GR* 110 C1
Egíe *GR* 108 B1
Egiertowo *PL* 89 E1
Egilsstaðir *IS* 62 C1
Égina *GR* 105 E3
Égina (Nissi) *GR* 105 E3
Egínio *GR* 101 F3
Égira *GR* 105 D3
Eglaine *LV* 83 D3
Egláji *LV* 82 C1
Eglésiai *I* 81 E2
Égletons *F* 15 F4
Eglinton *GB* 3 D1
Égloffstein *D* 39 D3
Egluciems *LV* 79 F3
Egmond aan Zee *NL* 32 B4
Egósthena *GR* 105 E3
Egremont *GB* 3 F1
Egtved *DK* 70 B3
Egüés *E* 20 B3
Éguzon *F* 15 F2
Ehináades Nissiá *GR* 104 C3
Ehingen (Donau-Kreis) *D* 43 D1
Ehínos *GR* 102 C1
Ehra-Lessien *D* 33 F4
Ehrang *D* 13 E2
Ehrenberg (Kreis Fulda) *D* 38 C2
Ehrenhausen *A* 45 D2
Ehrwald *A* 43 F2
Eibar *E* 20 A3
Eibenstock *D* 39 E2
Eibiswald *A* 45 D3
Eichstätt *D* 39 D4
Eičiūnai *LT* 85 F2
Eidapere *EE* 72 B2
Eiðar *IS* 62 C1
Eide *N* 62 B3
Eidfjord *N* 66 B1
Eidi *DK* 62 A2
Eidintai *LT* 84 C1
Eidkjosen *N* 60 C2
Eidsbugarden *N* 66 B1
Eidsdal *N* 62 B4
Eidsfoss *N* 66 C2
Eidsvåg *N* 62 B3
Eidsvoll *N* 66 C1
Eigirdonys *LT* 85 F2
Eigirdžiai *LT* 80 C2
Eikelandsosen *N* 66 A1
Eiken *N* 66 B3
Eikesdalen *N* 62 B4
Eikla *EE* 74 C3
Eikšiai *LT* 85 E1
Eilenburg *D* 39 E1
Eimučiai *LT* 81 E3
Einbeck *D* 38 C1
Eindhoven *NL* 36 C2
Einorai *LT* 85 E3
Einoraičiai *LT* 81 E3
Einoriai *LT* 82 B2
Einsiedeln *CH* 17 F1
Eipri *EE* 73 D2
Eisenach (Kreis Eisenach) *D* 38 C2
Eisenberg (Saale-Holzland-Kreis) *D* 39 E2
Eisenerz *A* 45 D2
Eisenhüttenstadt *D* 34 C4
Eisenkappel *A* 45 D3
Eisenstadt *A* 45 E1

EDINBURGH

Eisfeld D.....39 D2
Eišiškes LT.....86 B3
Eisleben Lutherstadt D.....39 D1
Eislingen D.....43 D1
Eitminiškes LT.....86 B2
Eitorf D.....13 E1
Eivere EE.....72 C2
Eivissa / Ibiza E.....31 D4
Ejea de los Caballeros E.....20 B4
Ejulve E.....27 D1
Ekára GR.....105 D1
Ekenäs / Tammisaari FIN.....69 D4
Ekengräve LV.....82 C2
Eksharad S.....67 D2
Eksjö S.....67 E4
El Algar E.....30 C2
El Almendro E.....28 C2
El Alquián E.....30 B3
El Arahal E.....29 D3
El Astillero E.....19 F2
El Barco de Ávila E.....25 E1
El Bodón E.....25 D1
El Bonillo E.....25 F1
El Bosque E.....29 D3
El Burgo E.....29 E3
El Burgo de Osma E.....19 F4
El Burgo Ranero E.....19 D3
El Cabaco E.....25 D1
El Campello E.....27 D4
El Campo de Peñaranda E.....25 E1
El Cañigral E.....26 C2
El Carpio E.....29 E2
El Carpio de Tajo E.....25 F2
El Casar E.....26 A1
El Castell de Guadalest E.....27 D4
El Castillo de las Guardas E.....29 D2
El Centenillo E.....25 F4
El Cerro de Andévalo E.....28 C2
El Coronil E.....29 D3
El Cubillo E.....26 C2
El Cubo de Don Sancho E.....25 D1
El Cubo de Tierra del Vino E.....19 D4
El Cuervo E.....29 D3
El Ejido E.....30 A3
El Escorial E.....25 F1
El Espinar E.....25 F1
El Figaró E.....21 E4
El fondó de les Neus E.....26 C4
El Formigal E.....20 C3
El Grado E.....20 C4
El Grau de València E.....27 D3
El Hoyo de Pinares E.....25 F1
El Madroño E.....28 C2
El Masnou E.....21 F4
El Molar E.....26 A1
El Molinillo E.....25 F3
El Moral E.....30 B2
El Pardo E.....25 F1
El Paular E.....25 F1
El Pedernoso E.....26 A3
El Pedroso E.....29 D2
El Perelló E.....27 E1
El Perelló E.....27 E3
El Picazo E.....26 B3
El Pinell de Brai E.....27 E1
El Pobo de Dueñas E.....26 C1
El Pont d'Armentera E.....27 F1
El Port de la Selva E.....21 F3
El Port de Llançà E.....21 F3

El Port de Sagunt E.....27 D3
El Portal E.....29 D3
El Portet de Morella E.....27 D4
El Prat de Llobregat E.....27 F1
El Provencio E.....26 B3
El Puente E.....19 F2
El Puente del Arzobispo E.....25 E2
El Puerto de Santa María E.....28 C3
El Real de la Jara E.....25 D4
El Real de San Vicente E.....25 E2
El Robledo E.....25 F3
El Rocío E.....28 C3
El Romeral E.....26 A2
El Rompido E.....28 C3
El Ronquillo E.....29 D2
El Royo E.....20 A4
El Rubio E.....29 E3
El Saler E.....27 D3
El Salobral E.....26 B4
El Saucejo E.....29 E3
El Tiemblo E.....25 F1
El Toboso E.....26 A3
El Vendrell E.....27 F1
El Villar de Arnedo E.....20 A3
El Viso E.....25 E4
El Viso del Alcor E.....29 D3
Elafohóri GR.....103 E1
Elafoníssi GR.....108 B2
Élafos GR.....100 C4
Elassóna GR.....101 E4
Eláti GR.....101 D4
Elátia GR.....105 D2
Elatohóri GR.....101 E3
Elatoú GR.....104 C2
Elatóvrissi GR.....104 C2
Elbasan AL.....116 C4
Elbeuf F.....11 F3
Elbigenalp A.....43 E2
Elbingerode (Harz) (Kreis Wernigerode) D.....39 D1
Elbląg PL.....90 A1
Elbląski (Kanal) PL.....90 A1
Elburg NL.....32 B4
Elche / Elx E.....26 C4
Elche de la Sierra E.....26 B4
Elda E.....26 C4
Eldena (Kreis Ludwigslust) D.....34 A3
Elefsína GR.....105 F3
Eleftherés GR.....102 C2
Eleftherés GR.....101 E4
Eleftherés GR.....105 E3
Eléftheron GR.....100 C3
Eleftherohóri GR.....101 D3
Eleftheroúpoli GR.....102 B2
Eleja LV.....81 E2
Elektrenai LT.....85 E2
Elemir SRB.....56 C2
Elena BG.....117 E4
Eleófito GR.....104 B2
Eleohória GR.....102 B2
Eleónas GR.....105 D2
Eleoússa GR.....111 F2
Elgå N.....63 D4
Elganowo PL.....89 E1
Elgin GB.....5 D3
Elgoibar E.....20 A2
Elgol GB.....4 B4
Elhovo BG.....117 E4

Eliniko GR.....104 C4
Elinohóri GR.....103 E1
Elizondo E.....20 B2
Ełk PL.....91 D2
Ełksni (Dzenīši) LV.....82 C2
Ellamaa EE.....72 A2
Ellesmere GB.....8 C3
Ellesmere Port GB.....8 C1
Ellingen (Kreis Weißenburg-Gunzenhausen) D.....39 D4
Ellon GB.....5 E4
Ellös S.....66 C3
Ellrich D.....39 D1
Ellwangen (Ostalbkreis) D.....39 D4
Elmas I.....50 A4
Elmininkai I LT.....82 B3
Elmshorn D.....33 E2
Elne F.....21 F3
Elnesvågen N.....62 B3
Elóna GR.....105 D4
Elopía GR.....105 E2
Elorrio E.....20 A2
Élos (Haniá) GR.....108 C4
Élos (Lakonía) GR.....108 B1
Eloúnda GR.....110 C4
Éloyes F.....13 E4
Elphin IRL.....2 C3
Elsdorf (Erftkreis) D.....13 D1
Elsendorf (Kreis Kelheim) D.....39 E4
Elsfleth D.....33 D3
Elsterberg D.....39 E2
Elsterwerda D.....39 F1
Eltisley GB.....9 E2
Elva EE.....79 D1
Elvanfoot GB.....7 D2
Elvas P.....24 C3
Elvekrok N.....62 B4
Elven F.....14 B1
Elverum N.....66 C1
Elx / Elche E.....26 C4
Ely GB.....9 E2
Elzach (Kreis Emmendingen) D.....13 F4
Elze (Kreis Hildesheim) D.....33 F4
Em. Papás GR.....102 A2
Embessós GR.....104 B1
Embid E.....26 C1
Embid de Ariza E.....20 A4
Émbonas GR.....111 F2
Emborió GR.....107 D3
Emboriós GR.....111 E1
Emboriós GR.....111 F1
Embrun F.....17 E4
Emburga LV.....81 E1
Embúte LV.....80 B1
Emden (Kreis Emden) D.....32 C3
Emili LV.....78 C2
Emlichheim D.....32 C4
Emmaboda S.....71 E2
Emmaste EE.....74 C2
Emmeloord NL.....32 B4
Emmen NL.....32 C4
Emmendingen D.....13 F4
Emmerich D.....37 D1
Empoli I.....47 D3
Emsdetten D.....33 D4
Emskirchen D.....39 D4
Enafors S.....63 D3
Enäjärvi FIN.....69 D3
Encausse-les-Thermes F.....21 D3
Encinas de Abajo E.....25 E1

Encinasola E.....24 C4
Encinedo E.....18 C3
Endriejavas LT.....80 B3
Endrinal E.....25 D1
Endzele LV.....78 C2
Enego I.....43 F4
Energetikis LV.....77 F3
Enfesta E.....18 A2
Eng A.....43 F2
Engarés GR.....106 C4
Enge E.....72 B3
Engelberg CH.....17 F2
Engelhartszell A.....40 C4
Engelsdorf D.....39 E1
Engelskirchen D.....13 E1
Engen D.....43 D2
Engerdal N.....63 D4
Enghien B.....12 B1
Engstingen D.....43 D1
Enguera E.....26 C4
Enguídanos E.....26 C3
Engure LV.....77 E3
Enkhuizen NL.....32 B4
Enköping S.....67 F2
Enna I.....53 D3
Ennepetal D.....37 E2
Ennezat F.....16 A3
Ennis / Inis IRL.....2 B4
Enniscorthy / Inis Córthaidh IRL.....3 D4
Enniskerry IRL.....3 D3
Enniskillen GB.....2 C1
Ennistimon / Inis Díomáin IRL.....2 B3
Enns A.....44 C1
Eno FIN.....69 F2
Enonkoski FIN.....69 F2
Enontekiö FIN.....61 D3
Enschede NL.....32 C4
Ensisheim F.....17 E1
Ense / Elche E.....26 C4
Entlebuch CH.....17 F2
Entraygues-sur-Truyère F.....21 F1
Entre-os-Rios P.....18 A4
Entrevaux F.....23 D1
Entrèves I.....17 E3
Entroncamento P.....24 B2
Envermeu F.....11 F2
Enviken S.....67 E1
Enzklösterle D.....13 F3
Epanomí GR.....101 F3
Epe NL.....32 B4
Épernay F.....12 B3
Épernon F.....11 F4
Épila E.....20 B4
Épinac F.....16 B2
Épinal F.....13 E4
Episkopí GR.....105 E2
Episkopí GR.....105 D2
Episkopí (Iráklio) GR.....109 F4
Episkopi (Réthimno) GR.....109 E4
Epitálio GR.....104 C4
Epping GB.....9 E3
Eppingen D.....37 F4
Epra EE.....72 C2
Epsom GB.....9 E3
Eptahóri GR.....100 C3
Eptálofos GR.....105 D2
Epworth GB.....7 F4
Eraclea I.....44 B4
Eraclea Mare I.....44 B4
Eräjärvi FIN.....69 D3
Erala EE.....73 D3
Erastvere EE.....79 E1

Eratiní GR.....105 D2
Eratinó GR.....102 C2
Erátira GR.....101 D3
Erba I.....43 D4
Erbach i. Odenwald D.....37 F4
Erbalunga F.....23 F3
Erbendorf D.....39 E3
Erberge LV.....82 B2
Ercolano I.....48 C4
Érd H.....116 B2
Erdek TR.....117 E4
Erdevik SRB.....55 F2
Erding D.....43 F1
Erdut HR.....55 F2
Ereğli TR.....117 F4
Eresfjord N.....62 B3
Eressós GR.....107 D1
Erétria GR.....105 F2
Erezée B.....13 D2
Erfde D.....33 E2
Erftstadt D.....13 E1
Erfurt D.....39 D2
Ergeme LV.....78 C2
Ergli (Bauskas) LV.....81 F2
Ergli (Limbažu) LV.....78 B2

Ergli (Madonas) LV.....78 C3
Ergoldsbach D.....39 E4
Erice I.....52 B3
Ericeira P.....24 A3
Erikoússa (Nissí) GR.....100 A3
Eriksberg S.....67 E3
Eriksmåle S.....71 E2
Erini LV.....78 C1
Eriškiai LT.....81 F3
Erithrés GR.....105 E3
Erkelenz D.....13 D1
Erkner D.....34 C4
Erla E.....20 B4
Erlangen D.....39 D3
Erlenai LT.....80 B2
Erlsbach A.....44 B3
Ermenonville F.....12 A3
Ermidas-Aldeia P.....24 A4
Ermióni GR.....105 E4
Ermoúpoli GR.....106 C4
Ermsleben D.....39 D1
Erndtebrück D.....13 F1
Ernée F.....11 D4
Ernestinovo HR.....55 E2
Ernstbrunn A.....41 E4
Erquy F.....10 C4
Erra EE.....73 E2
Erratzu E.....20 B2
Erstein F.....13 F4
Ervenik HR.....54 C4
Ervidel P.....24 B4
Ervita EE.....73 D2
Ervu EE.....79 D1
Ervy-le-Châtel F.....12 B4
Erwitte D.....37 F1
Erzberg A.....45 D2
Eržvilkas LT.....85 D2
Es Caló E.....31 D4
es Mercadal E.....31 F3
Esbjerg DK.....70 A3
Esblada E.....21 E4
Escairón E.....18 B3
Escalada E.....19 F3
Escalante E.....19 F2
Escalona E.....25 F2
Escalonilla E.....25 F2
Escalos de Cima P.....24 C2
Escatrón E.....21 D2
Esch (Waldems-) (Rheingau-Taunus-Kreis) D.....13 F2
Esch-sur-Alzette L.....13 D2
Esch-sur-Sûre L.....13 D2
Eschede D.....33 F4
Eschenbach i. d. Oberpfalz (Kreis Neustadt a. d. Waldnaab) D.....39 E3
Eschershausen (Kreis Holzminden) D.....38 C1
Eschwege D.....38 C2
Eschweiler (Kreis Aachen) D.....13 D1
Escombreras E.....30 C2
Escorihuela E.....26 C2
Escos F.....20 B4
Escucha E.....27 D2
Escurial E.....25 D3
Esens D.....33 D3

Esguevillas de Esgueva E.....19 E4
Esher GB.....9 E3
Eskifjörður IS.....62 C1
Eskilstuna S.....67 F2
Eskişehir TR.....117 F4
Eskoriatza E.....20 A2
Esku EE.....72 C3
Eslarn D.....39 E3
Eslohe D.....37 F2
Eslöv S.....71 D3
Esmoriz P.....18 A4
Espa N.....66 C1
Espadañedo E.....18 B3
Espalion F.....21 F1
Esparreguera E.....21 E4
Espedal N.....66 C1
Espejo E.....29 E2
Espelette F.....20 B2
Espelkamp D.....33 E4
Espenschied D.....13 F2
Espera E.....29 D3
Espiel E.....25 E4
Espinama E.....19 E2
Espinho P.....18 A4
Espinilla E.....19 E2
Espinosa de Cerrato E.....19 E4
Espinosa de los Monteros E.....19 F2
Espoo / Esbo FIN.....69 D4
Esporles E.....31 E3
Esposende P.....18 A4
Espot E.....21 D3
Espunyola E.....21 E3
Esquedas E.....20 C4
Esquivias E.....25 F2
Esse FIN.....68 C1
Essen (Kreis Cloppenburg) D.....33 D4
Essen (Kreis Essen) D.....37 E1
Essenbach D.....43 F1
Essimi GR.....103 D2
Esslingen D.....43 D1
Essoyes F.....12 C4
Essu EE.....73 D2
Estación de Salinas E.....29 F3
Estadilla E.....21 D3
Estagel F.....21 F3
Estaing F.....21 F1
Estaires F.....12 A1
Estarreja P.....18 A4
Estavayer-le-Lac CH.....17 D2
Este I.....47 D1
Estella / Lizarra E.....20 A3
Estepa E.....29 E3
Estepona E.....29 E4
Esteras de Medinaceli E.....26 B1
Esternay F.....12 B4
Esterri d'Àneu E.....21 D3
Estissac F.....12 B4
Estói P.....28 B3
Estoril P.....24 A3
Estrées-St-Denis F.....12 A3
Estremoz P.....24 B3
Esztergom H.....116 B2

Étables-sur-Mer F.....10 B4
Étain F.....13 D3
Étampes F.....12 A4
Étang-sur-Arroux F.....16 B2
Étaples F.....9 F4
Étel F.....14 B1
Etelhem S.....67 E4
Etne N.....66 A2
Etoliko GR.....104 B2
Étréchy F.....11 F3
Étrépagny F.....11 F3
Étretat F.....11 E2
Ettelbruck L.....13 D2
Etten-Leur NL.....36 C1
Ettenheim D.....13 E4
Ettington GB.....9 E1
Ettlingen D.....13 E3
Ettlingenweier D.....13 F3
Etxarri-Aranatz E.....20 A3
Eu F.....11 F2
Eugénie-les-Bains F.....20 C2
Eupen B.....13 D1
Eura FIN.....68 C3
Eurajoki FIN.....68 C3
Euratsfeld A.....45 D3
Europoort NL.....36 B1
Euskirchen D.....13 E1
Eußenhausen D.....38 C2
Eutin D.....33 F2
Evangelismós GR.....101 E4
Evangelístria GR.....105 E3
Evarži LV.....80 C1
Évaux-les-Bains F.....16 A2
Évdilos GR.....107 D3
Evele LV.....78 C2
Evendorf D.....33 F3
Evenes N.....60 B3
Evenskjær / Skånland N.....60 B3
Evergem B.....12 B1
Everöd S.....71 D3
Evertsberg S.....67 D1
Evesham GB.....9 D2
Évia (Nissí) GR.....105 F1
Évian-les-Bains F.....17 D2
Evijärvi FIN.....68 C1
Evinohóri GR.....104 C2
Évisa F.....23 F3
Evje N.....66 A3
Évlalo GR.....102 C2
Evolène CH.....17 E3
Évora P.....24 B3
Évoramonte P.....24 B3
Évran F.....10 C4
Évrecy F.....11 D3
Évreux F.....11 F3
Évron F.....11 D4
Evropós GR.....101 F2
Evrostína GR.....105 D3
Évry F.....12 A4
Evzoni GR.....101 F1
Exaplátanos GR.....101 E2
Éxarhos GR.....105 E2
Excideuil F.....15 E4
Exeter GB.....8 B4
Exmes F.....11 E4
Exmouth GB.....8 B4

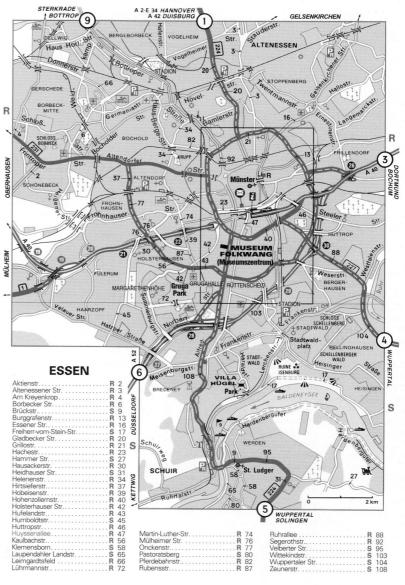

ESSEN

Aktienstr.....R 2
Altenessener Str.....R 3
Am Kreyenkrop.....R 5
Borbecker Str.....R 6
Brückstr.....R 9
Burggrafenstr.....R 13
Essener Str.....R 16
Freiherr-vom-Stein-Str.....R 17
Gladbecker Str.....R 21
Grillostr.....R 21
Hachestr.....R 23
Hammer Str.....S 27
Hausackerstr.....R 30
Heidhauser Str.....S 31
Helenenstr.....R 34
Hirtsieferstr.....R 38
Hobeisenstr.....R 39
Hohenzollernstr.....R 40
Holsterhauser Str.....R 42
Hufelandstr.....R 43
Humboldtstr.....R 44
Huyssenallee.....R 47
Kaulbachstr.....R 56
Klemensborn.....S 58
Laupendahler Landstr.....S 66
Leimgardtsfeld.....S 66
Lührmannstr.....R 72
Martin-Luther-Str.....R 74
Mülheimer Str.....R 76
Onckenstr.....R 77
Pastoratsberg.....S 80
Pferdebahnstr.....R 82
Rubensstr.....R 87
Ruhrallee.....R 88
Segerothstr.....R 92
Velberter Str.....S 95
Wittekindstr.....S 103
Wuppertaler Str.....S 104
Zeunerstr.....S 108

FIRENZE

Agnelli (V. Giovanni) . . . . BS 4
Alberti (Pza L. B.) . . . . BS 6
Aretina (V.) . . . . BS 13
Chiantigiana (V.) . . . . BS 36
Colombo (Lungarno C.) . . . . BS 37
D'Annunzio (V. G.) . . . . BS 41
De Amicis (Viale E.) . . . . BS 45
Europa (Viale) . . . . BS 49
Giannotti (Viale D.) . . . . BS 58
Guidoni (Viale A.) . . . . AR 67
Mariti (V. G. F.) . . . . BR 81
Novoli (V. di) . . . . AR 91
Panche (V. delle) . . . . BR 100
Paoli (V.) . . . . AS 103
Paoli (Viale Pasquale) . . . . . BS 105
Pietro Leopoldo (Pza) . . . . . BR 114
Poggio Imperiale (Viale del) . BS 118
Pollaiuolo (V. A. del) . . . . . . AS 121
Salviati (V.) . . . . BR 144
S. Domenico (V.) . . . . BR 147
Villamagna (V. di) . . . . BS 196

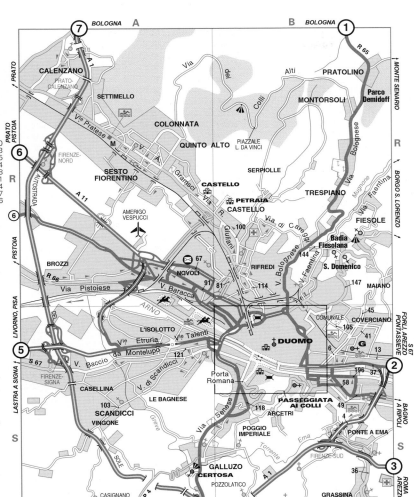

Exohí GR 102 A1
Exohí GR 102 C2
Exohí GR 101 E3
Exohí GR 100 C3
Exómvourgo GR 106 C4
Exter D 33 E4
Eydehavn N 66 B3
Eye GB 9 E1
Eyemouth GB 7 E1
Eyguières F 22 B2
Eygurande F 16 A3
Eymet F 21 D1
Eymoutiers F 15 F3
Ezcaray E 19 F3
Eczároz/Ezkaroze E 20 B3
Èze F 23 D2
Ezere LV 80 C1
Eželeris LT 85 E2
Ezerini LV 83 D3
Ezerkauki LV 77 D3
Ezernieki
  (Bukmuiža) LV 83 F2
Ezersala (Azarsola) LV .. 83 F1

F

Faak A 44 C3
Fabara E 27 D1
Fåberg N 66 C1
Fabero E 18 C2
Fåborg DK 70 B4
Fabriano I 47 F3
Fábricas de Riópar E ... 26 B4
Fabro I 47 E4
Facinas E 29 D4
Facture F 20 B1
Faenza I 47 E2
Faeto I 49 D3
Fafe P 18 A4
Făgăraş RO 117 D2
Fågelfors S 71 E2
Fagernes N 60 C2
Fagernes N 66 B1
Fagersta S 67 E2
Fagurhólsmýri IS 62 B2
Fairford GB 9 D3
Fajsławice PL 95 E3
Fakenham GB 9 F1
Fakovići BIH 55 F3
Fakse DK 70 C3
Fakse Ladeplads DK 70 C3
Falaise F 11 E3
Falakró GR 102 B1
Falåssarna GR 108 C3
Falcade I 44 B3
Falces E 20 B3
Falconara Marittima I .. 47 F2
Falcone I 50 C4
Falerna I 51 D3
Faliráki GR 111 F2
Falkenberg S 71 D2
Falkenberg (Kreis Elbe-
  Elster) D 39 F1
Falkensee D 34 B4
Falkenstein
  (Vogtlandkreis) D 39 E2
Falkirk GB 7 D1
Falkland GB 7 D1

Falkonéra (Nissí) GR ... 109 D1
Falköping S 67 D3
Falków PL 94 B3
Fallersleben D 33 F4
Fällfors S 64 B3
Fallingbostel D 33 E4
Falmouth GB 8 A4
Falset E 27 E1
Fálticeni RO 117 D2
Faltopi LV 83 E3
Falun S 67 E1
Famjin
  (Færøerne) DK 62 A3
Fanári GR 102 C2
Fanári GR 101 D4
Fanári GR 105 E4
Fanári GR 104 C4
Fanefjord DK 70 C4
Fanjeaux F 21 E2
Fano I 47 F2
Fanós GR 101 E2
Fara Novarese I 17 F3
Fårbo S 67 E4
Fareham GB 9 D4
Fårevejle DK 70 C3
Färgelanda S 66 C3
Färila S 63 E4
Farindola I 48 B2
Faringdon GB 9 D3
Farini I 46 C1
Färjestaden S 71 E2
Farkadóna GR 101 E4
Farkaždin SRB 56 C2
Farlete E 20 C4
Farmakoníssi GR 107 F4
Farnborough GB 9 D3
Farnese I 47 E4
Farnham GB 9 D3
Faro P 28 B3
Fårösund S 67 F4
Farra d'Alpago I 44 B3
Farsø DK 70 B2
Farsund N 66 A3
Farum DK 70 C3
Fasano I 49 F3
Fáskrúðsfjörður IS 62 C1
Fastiv UA 115 E4
Fastov RUS 115 E4
Fátima P 24 A2
Fatmomakke S 63 E2
Faucogney-et-la-Mer F .. 17 D1
Faulquemont F 13 E3
Fauquembergues F 12 A1
Fauske N 60 B4
Fauville-en-Caux F 11 E2
Fåvang N 66 C1
Favara E 27 D3
Favara I 52 C3
Faverges F 17 D3
Faverney F 17 D1
Faversham GB 9 E3
Fawley GB 9 D4
Fay-sur-Lignon F 16 B4
Fayence F 23 D2
Fayl-Billot F 16 C1
Fayón E 27 E1
Fažana HR 54 A1
Fécamp F 11 E2
Feces de Abaixo E 18 B4
Feda N 66 A3

Fehmarn (Insel) (Kreis
  Ostholstein) D 33 F2
Fehrbellin D 34 B3
Fehring A 45 E2
Feimani LV 83 E2
Feketić SRB 55 F1
Felanitx E 31 E3
Feld am See A 44 C3
Feldafing D 43 F1
Feldbach A 45 E2
Feldberg (Kreis
  Breisgau-Hochschwarzwald)
  D 13 F4
Feldberg (Kreis Mecklenburg-
  Strelitz) D 34 B3
Feldkirch A 43 D2
Feldkirchen in
  Kärnten A 44 C3
Felgueiras P 18 A4
Felgueras E 19 D2
Felicianova LV 83 F1
Felixstowe GB 9 F2
Fellabær IS 62 C1
Fellbach D 43 D1
Felletin F 15 F3
Fellingsbro S 67 E2
Felton GB 7 E2

Feria E 24 C4
Feričanci HR 55 E2
Ferlach A 45 D2
Fermo I 48 B1
Fermoselle E 18 C4
Fermoy / Mainistir Fhear
  Mai IRL 2 C4
Fernán Caballero E 25 F3
Fernán Núñez E 29 E2
Ferney-Voltaire F 17 D3
Ferrandina I 49 E4
Ferrara I 47 E1
Ferreira E 18 B1
Ferreira do Alentejo P .. 24 B4
Ferreira do Zêzere P 24 B2
Ferreiras P 28 A2
Ferreras de Abajo E 18 C4
Ferreries E 31 F3
Ferreruela de
  Huerva E 26 C1
Ferrette F 17 E1
Ferriere I 46 C2
Ferrières-en-Gâtinais F .. 12 A4
Ferrol E 18 B1
Fertilia I 50 A3
Festós GR 109 E4
Festvåg N 60 B4
Fethard / Fiodh Ard IRL .. 2 C4
Fetsund N 66 C2
Feucht D 39 D4
Feuchtwangen D 39 D4
Feurs F 16 B3
Feyzin F 16 C3
Ffestiniog GB 6 B3
Fiamignano I 47 F4
Fiano Romano I 47 F4
Fiastra I 47 F3
Ficarolo I 47 D1
Fidenza I 46 C1
Fieberbrunn A 44 B2
Fier AL 116 C4
Fiera di Primiero I 44 B3
Fiesole I 47 D3
Figeac F 21 E1
Figline Valdarno I 47 E3
Figueira da Foz P 24 A1
Figueira de Castelo
  Rodrigo P 24 C1
Figueiró dos Vinhos P .. 24 B2
Figueres E 21 F3
Figueruela de Arriba E .. 18 C4
Fihtio GR 105 D3
Filadelfia I 51 D3
Filadélfio GR 102 A2
Filáki GR 105 D1
Filákio GR 103 E1
Filakopí GR 109 E1
Filérimos GR 111 F2
Fiţjar N 66 A1
Filí GR 105 F2

Filia GR 107 D1
Filia GR 104 C3
Filiátes GR 100 B4
Filipi GR 104 C4
Filipi (P) GR 102 B2
Filipiáda GR 104 B3
Filipów PL 91 D1
Filipstad S 67 D2
Fíra GR 103 D1
Fillan N 62 C3
Filo GR 101 E4
Filótas GR 101 D2
Filottrano I 47 F3
Finale Emilia I 47 D1
Finale Ligure I 23 E1
Fiñana E 30 A3
Finchingfield GB 9 E2
Finikas GR 106 C4
Finikoúndas GR 108 A1
Finja S 71 D3
Finneidfjord N 63 E1
Finnentrop D 37 E2
Finnsnes / Lenvik N 60 C2
Finow
  (Kreis Barnim) D 34 C3
Finowfurt
  (Kreis Barnim) D 34 C3
Finspång S 67 E3
Finsterau D 39 F4
Finsterwalde D 39 F1
Finström FIN 68 B4
Fintona I 3 D1
Fintown / Baile na
  Finne IRL 2 C1
Fionnphort GB 6 B1
Fiorenzuola d'Arda I 46 C1
Firenze I 47 D3
Firenzuola I 47 D2
Fidenza I 46 C1
Firlej PL 95 E2
Firminy F 16 B4
Firmo I 51 D2
Fischamend Markt A 45 E1
Fischbach (Kreis Nürnberger
  Land) D 39 D4
Fischbeck
  (Kreis Stendal) D 34 A4
Fischen i. Allgäu D 43 E2
Fishbourne GB 9 D4
Fishguard /
  Abergwaun GB 3 E4
Fiskárdo GR 104 A2
Fiskari FIN 69 D4
Fiskebøl N 60 B3
Fismes F 12 B3
Fissini GR 103 D4
Fisterra E 18 A2
Fitero E 20 A4
Fities GR 104 B2
Fivizzano I 46 C2

Fiumicino I 48 A3
Fivemiletown GB 3 D1
Fivizzano I 46 C2
Fjærland N 62 B4
Fjällåsen S 64 B1
Fjällbacka S 66 C3
Fjällnäs S 63 D4
Fjärdhundra S 67 F2
Fjätervålen S 63 D4
Fjelie S 71 D3
Fjellerup DK 70 C2
Fjerritslev DK 70 B2
Flå N 66 B1
Fladungen D 38 C2
Flaine F 17 D3
Flakk N 62 C3
Flåm N 66 A1
Flambourári GR 100 C4
Flámbouro GR 102 A2
Flámbouro GR 101 D2
Flamouriá GR 101 E2
Flattnitz A 44 C2
Flatval N 62 C3
Fleetwood GB 7 D4
Flekkefjord N 66 A3
Flen S 67 E3
Flensburg D 33 E1
Flers F 11 D4
Flesberg N 66 B2
Flesnes N 60 B3
Fleurance F 21 D2
Fleurier CH 17 D2
Fleurus B 12 C1
Fleury-en-Bière F 12 A4
Fleury-sur-Andelle F 11 E3
Fléves (Nissí) GR 105 F3
Flims-Waldhaus CH 43 D3
Flint / Fflint GB 8 C1
Flintsbach D 44 B2
Flisa N 67 D1
Flix E 27 E1
Flixecourt F 12 A2
Flize F 12 C1
Floda S 67 D1
Flogny-la-Chapelle F ... 16 B1
Flöha D 39 F2
Flomohóri GR 108 B1
Flor da Rosa P 24 B3
Florac F 22 A1
Florennes B 12 C2
Florensac F 22 A2
Florenville B 12 C2
Floreşti MD 117 E1
Floriáda GR 104 B3
Floridia I 53 E4
Flórina GR 101 D2
Flörsheim-Dalsheim D .. 13 F2
Flötningen S 63 D4
Fluðir IS 62 A2
Flüelen CH 17 F2

FRANKFURT AM MAIN

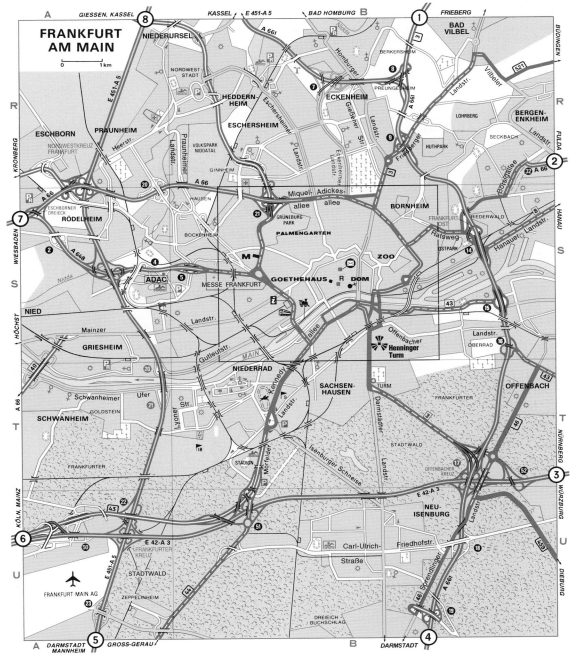

Flühli CH...............17 E2
Flumet F...............17 D3
Fluminimaggiore I...............50 A4
Flums CH...............43 D3
Foca / Srbinje BIH...............55 F4
Foce Verde I...............48 B3
Fochabers GB...............5 D3
Fockbek D...............33 E2
Focşani RO...............117 E2
Fódele GR...............109 E4
Foggia I...............49 D3
Föglö FIN...............68 B4
Fohnsdorf A...............45 D2
Foiano della Chiana I...............47 E3
Foix F...............21 E3
Fojnica (Mostar) BIH...............58 B2
Fojnica (Zenica) BIH...............55 F4
Foldereid N...............63 D2
Foleá GR...............102 B2
Folégandros GR...............109 E1
Folégandros
(Nissi) GR...............109 E1
Folgaria I...............43 F4
Folgoso de la Ribera E...............18 C3
Foligno I...............47 F3
Folkestad N...............62 A4
Folkestone GB...............9 F3
Follafoss N...............63 D2
Folldal N...............62 C4
Follebu N...............66 C1
Follina I...............44 B4
Föllinge S...............63 E3
Follonica I...............47 D4
Folmava CZ...............40 B4
Fombellida E...............19 E4
Fondevila E...............18 A3
Fondi I...............48 B3
Fondo I...............43 F3
Fonfría E...............26 C1
Fonn N...............62 B4
Fonni I...............50 B3
Fonollosa E...............21 E4
Font-Romeu-Odeillo-
Via F...............21 E3
Fontaine F...............17 E1
Fontaine-de-
Vaucluse F...............22 B1
Fontaine-Française F...............16 C1
Fontaine-le-Dun F...............11 F2
Fontainebleau F...............12 A4
Fontanigorda I...............46 B2
Fontenay-le-Comte F...............15 D2
Fontenay-Trésigny F...............12 A4
Fontevraud-l'Abbaye F...............15 D1
Fontgombault F...............15 E2
Fontibre E...............19 E2
Fontoy F...............13 D3
Fontvieille F...............22 B2
Fonz E...............21 D4
Fonzaso I...............43 F4
Foppolo I...............43 E4
Forbach F...............13 E3
Forcall E...............27 D1
Forcalquier F...............22 C1
Forcarei E...............18 A2
Forchheim (Kreis
Forchheim) D...............39 D3
Førde N...............62 A4
Førde N...............66 A2
Förderstedt D...............39 D1
Fordingbridge GB...............9 D4
Fordon PL...............89 E3
Fordongianus I...............50 A3
Forenza I...............49 E4
Foresta di Burgos I...............50 A3
Føresvik N...............66 A2
Forfar GB...............5 D4
Forges-les-Eaux F...............11 F3
Forio I...............48 C4
Forli I...............47 E2
Forli del Sannio I...............48 C3
Forlimpopoli I...............47 E2
Formazza I...............17 F2
Formby Point GB...............7 D4
Formentor (Cap de) E...............31 F3
Formerie F...............11 F2
Formia I...............48 B3
Formigine I...............47 D2
Fornaci di Barga I...............47 D2
Fornells E...............31 F3
Forni Avoltri I...............44 B3
Forni di Sopra I...............44 B3
Forno di Zoldo I...............44 B3
Fornos de Algodres P...............24 C1
Fornovo di Taro I...............46 C1
Forøy N...............60 A4
Forres GB...............4 C3
Forsa S...............63 D4
Forserum S...............67 D4
Forshaga S...............67 D2
Forsnes N...............62 C2
Forssa FIN...............69 D4
Forst (Kreis Spree-
Neiße) D...............35 D4
Fort Augustus GB...............4 C4
Fort-Mahon-Plage F...............9 F4
Fort William GB...............4 B4
Forte dei Marmi I...............46 C2
Forth D...............39 D3
Fortrose GB...............4 C3
Fortuna E...............26 C4
Forvik N...............63 D1
Fos F...............21 D3
Fos-sur-Mer F...............22 B2
Foslandsosen N...............63 D2
Fosnavåg N...............62 A4

Fossacesia I...............48 C2
Fossano I...............23 E1
Fossanova
(Abbazia di) I...............48 B3
Fossbakken N...............60 C3
Fosses-la-Ville B...............12 C2
Fossombrone I...............47 F2
Fotiná GR...............101 E3
Fotolívos GR...............102 B2
Fouesnant F...............10 A4
Foug F...............13 D4
Fougères F...............11 D4
Fougerolles F...............17 D1
Fouras F...............14 C3
Fourchambault F...............16 A2
Fourfourás GR...............109 E4
Fourmies F...............12 B2
Fourná GR...............104 C1
Fournels F...............16 A4
Fournés GR...............109 D3
Fóurni GR...............107 E4
Foúrni GR...............105 E4
Foúrni GR...............110 C4
Foúrni (Nissi) GR...............107 E4
Fours F...............16 B2
Foústani GR...............101 E2
Fowey GB...............8 C4
Foxford IRL...............2 B3
Foyers GB...............4 C4
Foz E...............18 C1
Foz do Arelho P...............24 A2
Foz Giraldo P...............24 B2
Frabosa Soprana I...............23 E1
Fraddon GB...............8 A4
Fraga E...............21 D4
Frailes E...............29 F2
Fraize F...............13 E4
Fram SLO...............54 B1
Frammersbach D...............38 C3
Frampol PL...............95 E3
Francavilla al Mare I...............48 C2
Francavilla di Sicilia I...............51 D4
Francavilla Fontana I...............51 E1
Francavilla in Sinni I...............49 E4
Francofonte I...............53 D3
Francorchamps B...............13 D1
Frändefors S...............66 C3
Franeker NL...............32 B3
Frangista GR...............104 C1
Frangokástelo GR...............109 D4
Frangy F...............17 D3
Frankenberg (Kreis
Mittweida) D...............39 F2
Frankenberg (Kreis Waldeck-
Frankenberg) D...............13 F1
Frankenburg A...............44 C1
Frankenmarkt A...............44 C1
Frankenstein
(Kreis Kaiserslautern
Land) D...............13 F3
Frankenthal (Kreis Frankenthal
Pfalz) D...............13 F2
Frankfurt a. Main
(Kreis Frankfurt am
Main) D...............13 F2
Frankfurt an der Oder (Kreis
Frankfurt Oder) D...............34 C4
Františkovy Lázně CZ...............40 A3
Franz Josephs-Höhe A...............44 B2
Franzburg D...............34 B2
Frascati I...............48 B3
Frascineto I...............51 D2
Fraserburgh GB...............5 E3
Fraserburg GB...............5 E3
Frasne F...............17 D2
Frýdek-Místek CZ...............41 F2
Frýdlant CZ...............40 C1
Frýdlant nad
Ostravicí CZ...............41 F3
Frygnowo PL...............90 B2
Fryšták CZ...............41 F3
Frysztak PL...............99 D2
Fteliá GR...............102 B2
Ftéri GR...............101 E3
Ftéri GR...............104 C1
Fucecchio I...............47 D3
Fuencaliente E...............25 F4
Fuendejalón E...............20 B4
Fuendetodos E...............26 C1
Fuengirola E...............29 E4
Fuenlabrada E...............25 F4
Fuenlabrada de los
Montes E...............25 E3
Fuenmayor E...............20 A3
Fuensalida E...............25 F2
Fuensanta E...............19 D2
Fuensanta de Martos E...............29 F2
Fuente Álamo E...............26 C4
Fuente Álamo E...............30 C2
Fuente Dé E...............19 E2
Fuente de Cantos E...............25 D4
Fuente de Pedro
Naharro E...............26 A2
Fuente de Piedra E...............29 E3
Fuente del Maestre E...............25 D3
Fuente el Fresno E...............25 F3
Fuente Obejuna E...............25 E4
Fuente Palmera E...............29 E1
Fuentecén E...............19 F4
Fuenteguinaldo E...............25 D1
Fuentelapeña E...............19 D4
Fuentepinilla E...............20 A4
Fuentes de
Andalucía E...............29 E2
Fuentes de Ayódar E...............27 D2
Fuentes de Ebro E...............20 C4
Fuentes de León E...............24 C4
Fuentes de Nava E...............19 E3

Fresne-St-Mamès F...............17 D1
Fresnes-en-Woëvre F...............13 D3
Fresno Alhándiga E...............25 E1
Fuentes de Oñoro E...............24 C1
Fuentes de Ropel E...............19 D3
Fuentes de
Valdepero E...............19 E3
Fuentesaúco E...............19 D4
Fuentidueña E...............19 F4
Fuentidueña de Tajo E...............26 A2
Fuerte del Rey E...............29 F2
Fügen A...............43 F2
Fuglebjerg DK...............70 C3
Fulda D...............38 C2
Fulgatore I...............52 B3
Fulnek CZ...............41 F2
Fulpmes A...............43 F2
Fumay F...............12 C2
Fumel F...............21 D1
Funäsdalen S...............63 D4
Fundão P...............24 C2
Funes / Villnöß I...............43 F3
Furadouro P...............24 B1
Furci I...............48 C2
Furnace GB...............6 C1
Fürstenau D...............33 D4
Fürstenberg D...............34 B3
Fürstenfeld A...............45 E2
Fürstenfeldbruck D...............43 F1
Fürstenwalde D...............34 C4
Fürstenwerder D...............34 B3
Fürstenzell D...............44 B1
Furta H...............50 A4
Fürth D...............39 D4
Furth i. Wald D...............39 F4
Furtwangen D...............13 F4
Furudal S...............67 E1
Furuflaten N...............60 C2
Fuscaldo I...............51 D3
Fusch a. d. Großglockner-
straße A...............44 B2
Fuschl A...............44 C1
Fusignano I...............47 E2
Füssen D...............43 E2
Fustiñana E...............20 B4
Futog ( ) SRB...............55 F2
Fuzeta P...............28 B3
Fužine HR...............54 B3
Fynshav DK...............70 B4

G

G. Duboćke MNE...............58 B3
G. Kosinj HR...............54 B3
G. Morakovo MNE...............58 C3
G. Ravno BIH...............55 D4
Gaaldorf A...............45 D2
Gabarret F...............20 C1
Gabela BIH...............58 A3
Gabia la Grande E...............29 F3
Gabicce Mare I...............47 F2
Gąbin PL...............94 A1
Gabriliava LT...............85 F2
Gabrovka SLO...............54 B2
Gabrovo BG...............117 D4
Gacé F...............11 E3
Gačioniai LT...............81 F3
Gacko BIH...............58 B2
Gäddede S...............63 E2
Gadebusch D...............33 F2
Gádor E...............30 A3

Gadūnavas LT...............80 C2
Gaður IS...............62 A2
Gadžin Han SRB...............57 E4
Găeşti RO...............117 D3
Gaeta I...............48 B3
Gagarin RUS...............115 F2
Gaggenau D...............13 F3
Gagliano del Capo I...............51 F2
Gagnef S...............67 E1
Gaide D...............83 D3
Gaideliai LT...............84 B1
Gaigalava (Bikova) LV...............83 E1
Gaigaliai LT...............82 B3
Gaiki LT...............81 D1
Gailaičiai LT...............81 D2
Gaildorf D...............38 C4
Gailey GB...............8 C1
Gaili LV...............76 C3
Gailiai LT...............81 D3
Gailiši (Galmuiža) LV...............83 E2
Gaillac F...............21 E1
Gaillon F...............11 F3
Gaisma LV...............81 F1
Gaišiūnai LT...............81 D2
Gaiženeliai LT...............85 E2
Gaižiūnai LT...............85 F1
Gaj SRB...............57 D2
Gajdobra SRB...............55 F2
Gakovo SRB...............55 F1
Galan F...............21 D2
Galanádo GR...............109 F1
Galáni LV...............83 D2
Galanianá GR...............108 C3
Galanta SK...............116 B2
Galapagar E...............25 F1
Galaroza E...............24 C4
Galarinós GR...............101 F3
Galárbow PL...............95 D2
Galashiels GB...............7 D2
Galatádes GR...............101 E2
Galatás
(Attikí-Piréas) GR...............105 E4
Galatás
(Korinthía) GR...............105 D3
Galáti LV...............81 D1
Galaţi RO...............117 E2
Galatina I...............51 F1
Galatiní GR...............101 D3
Galátista GR...............102 A3
Galatone I...............51 F1
Galáxidi GR...............105 D2
Galdakao E...............20 A2
Galeata I...............47 E2
Galende E...............18 C3
Galéni (Galáni) LV...............83 E1
Galenieki LV...............81 E1
Galera E...............30 A2
Galewice PL...............93 F3
Galgauska LV...............79 D3
Galgiai LT...............86 B2
Galičnik MK...............59 E4
Galini LV...............81 F1
Galipsós GR...............102 B2
Galisteo E...............25 D2
Gallarate I...............17 F3
Gallardon F...............11 F4
Gallareto I...............17 F4
Gallargues-le-
Montueux F...............22 A2
Galliate I...............17 F3

Gallipoli I...............51 F1
Gällivare S...............64 B1
Gallneukirchen A...............44 C1
Gällö S...............63 E3
Gallsbach A...............44 C1
Gallur E...............20 B4
Galmenai LT...............84 C1
Galston GB...............6 C2
Galtür A...............43 E3
Galveias P...............24 B3
Gálvez E...............25 F2
Galvyčiai LT...............80 C2
Galway / Gaillimh IRL...............2 B3
Gamaches F...............11 F2
Gambarie I...............51 D4
Gamingen A...............45 D1
Gamleby S...............67 E4
Gammelstaden S...............64 C2
Gammertingen D...............43 D1
Gams D...............63 D3
Gamvik N...............61 E1
Ganacker D...............39 F4
Gándara E...............18 B1
Ganderkesee D...............33 D3
Gandesa E...............27 E1
Gandia E...............27 D4
Gandino I...............43 E4
Gandria CH...............17 F3
Gángáles GR...............109 F4
Ganges F...............22 A1
Gangi I...............53 D3
Gangkofen D...............44 B1
Gannat F...............16 A3
Gänserndorf A...............41 E4
Gañuelas E...............30 C2
Gap F...............22 C1
Garaušī LV...............77 D3
Garbatka-Letnisko PL...............95 D2
Garbów PL...............95 D2
Garching a. d. Alz D...............44 B1
Garcia E...............27 E1
Garciaz E...............25 E2
Garciems LV...............77 F3
Garda I...............43 F4
Gardamas LT...............80 B3
Gardanne F...............22 B2
Gårdby S...............71 F2
Garde S...............67 F4
Gardeja PL...............89 F2
Gardelegen D...............34 A4
Garding D...............33 E2
Gardjönäs S...............64 A2
Gårdnäs S...............63 E2
Gardone Riviera I...............43 E4
Gardone Val Trompia I...............43 E4
Gårdslösa S...............71 F2
Garešnica HR...............55 D2
Garessio I...............23 E1
Garforth GB...............7 E4
Gargaliáni GR...............108 A1
Garganta la Olla E...............25 D2
Gargellen A...............43 D3
Gargilesse-
Dampierre F...............15 F2
Gargnano I...............43 F4
Gargnäs S...............64 A3
Gargždai LT...............80 B3
Gargždele LT...............80 B2

Garípa GR...............109 F4
Garkalne LV...............77 F3
Garlasco I...............23 F1
Garliava LT...............85 E2
Garlin F...............20 C2
Garlstorf
(Kreis Harburg) D...............33 F3
Garmisch-
Partenkirchen D...............43 F2
Garnek PL...............94 A3
Garoza (Bauskas) LV...............81 F1
Garoza (Jelgavas) LV...............81 F1
Garpenberg S...............67 E2
Garraf E...............21 F1
Garrafe de Torío E...............19 D3
Garray E...............20 A4
Garrel D...............33 D4
Garrovillas de
Alconétar E...............25 D2
Garrucha E...............30 B3
Gars am Kamp A...............41 D4
Gärsene LV...............82 C2
Gartow (Kreis Lüchow-
Dannenberg) D...............34 A3
Gartz D...............34 C3
Garupe LV...............77 F3
Garvagh GB...............3 D1
Garvão P...............24 A4
Garve GB...............4 C3
Garwolin PL...............94 C2
Garynahine GB...............4 A2
Garz D...............34 B1
Gąsawa PL...............89 E3
Gaschurn A...............43 E3
Gassino Torinese I...............17 E4
Gastoúni GR...............104 B3
Gaštynai LT...............81 D3
Gata E...............25 D2
Gata de Gorgos E...............27 D4
Gatarta LT...............78 C3
Gataučiai LT...............81 E2
Gātciems LV...............77 D3
Gatčina RUS...............115 D1
Gatehouse of Fleet GB...............3 F1
Gateshead GB...............7 E3
Gattinara I...............17 F3
Gattorna I...............23 F2
Gaucín E...............29 D4
Gaujas Kenci LV...............78 C3
Gaujaslāči LV...............78 C3
Gaujiena LV...............79 D2
Gaujmala LV...............78 C2
Gaukštonys LT...............86 C2
Gaulenai LT...............84 C1
Gaulstad N...............63 D3
Gaure LT...............84 C1
Gautegiz-Arteaga E...............20 A2
Gauting D...............43 F1
Gavá E...............21 F1
Gavardo I...............43 E4
Gavarnie F...............20 C2
Gavdopoúla
(Nissi) GR...............109 D4
Gávdos (Nissi) GR...............109 D4
Gaveniškis LT...............82 B2
Gavi I...............17 F4
Gavião P...............24 B2
Gavieze LV...............80 B1
Gavirate I...............17 F3
Gävle S...............67 E2
Gavoi I...............50 A3

Gavray F...............11 D3
Gavrilov-Jam RUS...............115 F1
Gávrio GR...............106 B3
Gävsta S...............67 F2
Gawozryce PL...............92 C2
Gäxsjö S...............63 E3
Gazzuolo I...............47 D1
Gdańsk PL...............89 F1
Gdov RUS...............115 D1
Gdów PL...............98 B2
Gdynia PL...............89 F1
Geaune F...............20 C2
Gebesee D...............39 D2
Gebice PL...............89 E3
Gebze TR...............117 F4
Gedern D...............38 C2
Gediminas LT...............82 C3
Gediškiai LT...............80 C2
Gedrimai LT...............80 C2
Gedser DK...............70 C4
Gedučiai LT...............81 F2
Geel B...............12 C1
Geertruidenberg NL...............36 C1
Geesthacht D...............33 F3
Gefell D...............39 E2
Géfira GR...............101 F2
Géfira GR...............108 C1
Gefíria GR...............105 D1
Gefrees D...............39 E3
Gegiedžiai LT...............81 E2
Gegrenai LT...............80 C2
Gegužine LT...............85 F1
Gehren (Ilm-Kreis) D...............39 D2
Geidžiūnai LT...............82 B2
Geilenkirchen D...............13 D1
Geilo N...............66 B1
Geiranger N...............62 B3
Geisa D...............38 C2
Geiselhöring D...............39 E4
Geisenfeld D...............39 E4
Geisenhausen D...............44 B1
Geising D...............39 F2
Geisingen (Kreis
Tuttlingen) D...............13 F4
Geisleben S...............86 B2
Geislingen a. d.
Steige D...............43 D1
Geismar (Kreis
Eichsfeld) D...............38 C2
Geisnes N...............63 D2
Geisteriškiai LT...............85 D2
Geithain D...............39 E1
Gela I...............53 D4
Geldern D...............37 D1
Geležiai LT...............82 A3
Gelgaudiškis LT...............85 D1
Gelibolu TR...............117 E4
Gelnhausen D...............38 C3
Gelsa E...............27 D1
Gelsdorf D...............13 E1
Gelsenkirchen D...............37 E1
Gelting D...............33 E1
Geluva LT...............85 E1
Gelvonai LT...............85 F1
Gembloux B...............12 C1
Gemeaux F...............16 C1
Gémenos F...............22 C2
Gemert NL...............37 D1
Gemlik TR...............117 F4

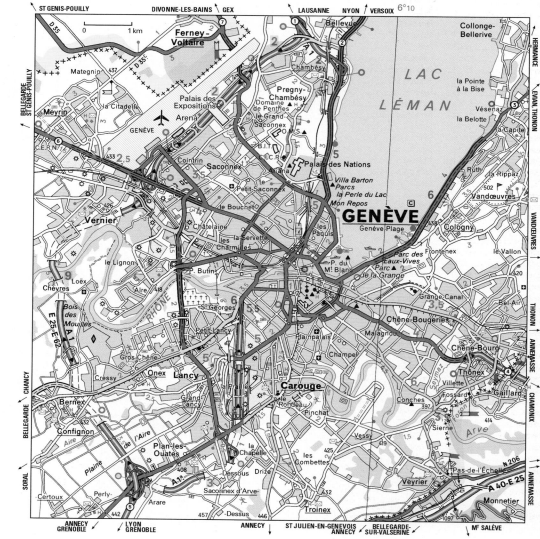

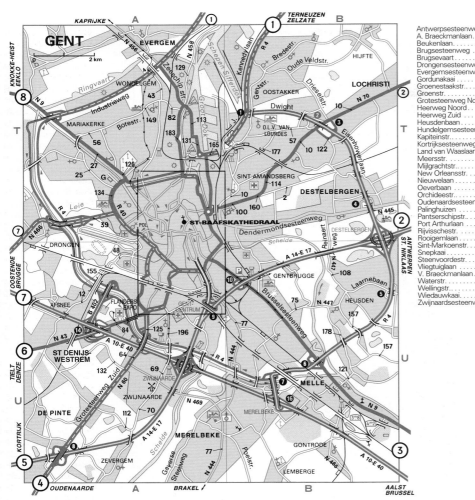

GENT

Antwerpsesteenweg . . . . BT 10
A. Braeckmanlaan . . . . BT 2
Beukenlaan . . . . AU 12
Brugsesteenweg . . . . AT 25
Brugsevaart . . . . AT 27
Drongensesteenweg . . . . AT 39
Evergemsesteenweg . . . . AT 43
Gordunakaai . . . . AU 48
Groenestaakstr. . . . . AT 56
Groenstr. . . . . BT 57
Grotesteenweg Noord . . . . AU 64
Heerweg Noord . . . . AU 69
Heerweg Zuid . . . . AU 70
Heusdenbaan . . . . BU 75
Hundelgemsesteenweg . . . . . ABU 77
Kapiteinstr. . . . . AT 82
Kortrijksesteenweg . . . . AU 84
Land van Waaslaan . . . . BT 100
Meersstr. . . . . AU 108
Mijlgrachtstr. . . . . AU 112
New Orleansstr. . . . . AT 113
Nieuwelaan . . . . AT 114
Oeverbaan . . . . BU 121
Orchideestr. . . . . BT 122
Oudenaardsesteenweg . . . . . . AU 125
Palinghuizen . . . . AT 126
Pantserschipstr. . . . . AT 129
Port Arthurlaan . . . . AT 131
Rijvisschestr. . . . . AT 132
Rooigemlaan . . . . AT 134
Sint-Markoenstr. . . . . AT 149
Snepkaai . . . . AU 155
Steenvoordestr. . . . . BU 157
Vliegtuiglaan . . . . AT 165
V. Braeckmanlaan . . . . BT 160
Waterstr. . . . . BT 177
Wellingstr. . . . . AT 178
Wiedauwkaai . . . . AT 183
Zwijnaardsesteenweg . . . . . . AU 196

Giżycko PL 90 C1
Gjendesheim N 62 C4
Gjermundshavn N 66 A1
Gjesvær N 61 E1
Gjov (Færøerne) DK . . .62 A2
Gjøvik N 66 C1
Gla GR 105 E2
Gladbeck D 37 E1
Gladenbach D 13 F1
Gladstad N 63 D1
Glamis GB 5 D4
Glamoč BIH 55 D4
Glamsbjerg DK 70 B3
Glan-Münchweiler D . . .13 E3
Glandorf D 37 E1
Glanshammar S 67 F2
Glarus CH 17 F1
Glasgow GB 6 C1
Glastonbury GB 8 D3
Glauchau D 39 E2
Glavatičevo BIH 55 E4
Glavice BIH 55 D4
Glavičice BIH 55 F3
Glavnik SRB 59 D4
Glāznieki LV 78 B3
Glāžškūnis LV 82 B1
Gledić SRB 57 D3
Gleisdorf A 45 E2
Glenamoy / Gleann na
 Muaidhe IRL 2 B1
Glenariff or
 Waterfoot GB 3 E1
Glenarm GB 3 E1
Glenbeigh IRL 2 A4
Glencolumbkille / Gleann Cholm
 Cille IRL 2 C1
Glendalough IRL 3 D3
Glenelg GB 4 B4
Glenfinnan GB 4 B4
Glengarriff / An Gleann
 Garbh IRL 2 A4
Glenluce GB 3 F1
Glennamaddy IRL 2 C2
Glenrothes GB 7 D1
Glenties IRL 2 C1
Glifa GR 105 E2
Glifáda GR 104 C2
Glifáda GR 105 F3
Gliki GR 104 C2
Glikóvrissi GR 108 B1
Glina HR 54 C2
Glinojeck PL 90 B3
Glitiškes LT 86 B2
Gliwice PL 97 F2
Głogów PL 92 C2
Głogów Małopolski PL . .99 D2
Głogówek PL 97 E2
Glomfjord N 60 A4
Glommersträsk S 64 B3
Glossop GB 7 E4
Głowaczów PL 94 C2
Głowno PL 94 A2
Głubczyce PL 97 E2
Głuchołazy PL 97 E2
Głuchów PL 94 B2
Glücksburg D 33 E1
Glückstadt D 33 E2
Glūdas LV 81 D1
Glumsø DK 70 C4

Glušci SRB 55 F2
Głusk PL 95 E3
Głuszyca PL 96 C1
Gmünd A 41 D4
Gmünd A 44 C2
Gmund D 43 F2
Gmunden A 44 C1
Gnarp S 68 A3
Gnesta S 67 F3
Gniew PL 89 F2
Gniewczyna
 Łańcucka PL 99 E2
Gniewkowo PL 89 E3
Gniewoszów PL 95 D2
Gniezno PL 93 E1
Gnjilane SRB 59 E1
Gnoien D 34 B2
Gnojno PL 98 C1
Gnosjö S 67 D4
Gobas LV 77 D3
Goce Delčev BG 117 D4
Goch D 37 D1
Goczałkowice-Zdrój PL . .97 F2
Goczałkowickie
 (Jezioro) PL 97 F2
Godalming GB 9 E3
Godby FIN 68 B4
Godelheim D 38 C1
Goderville F 11 E2
Godkowo PL 90 A1
Godmanchester GB 9 E2
Godovič SLO 54 A2
Godów PL 97 F2
Godzieszze Wielkie PL . .93 E2
Godziszewo PL 89 F1
Goes NL 36 B1
Göggingen (Kreis Augsburg
 Stadt) D 43 E1
Gogolin PL 97 E1
Göhren (Kreis
 Rügen) D 34 B1
Goirle NL 36 C1
Góis P 24 B1
Goito I 47 D1
Gójsk PL 90 A3
Gökcanica SRB 57 D4
Gola HR 55 D1
Gołąb PL 95 D2
Gołańcz PL 89 D3
Golčův Jeníkov CZ 41 D3
Golcza PL 98 B2
Golczewo PL 88 B2
Gołdap PL 91 D1
Goldbach (Kreis
 Aschaffenburg) D 38 C3
Goldberg (Kreis
 Parchim) D 34 A2
Gloggnitz A 45 E1
Goldenstedt D 33 D4
Golegã P 24 B2
Golemo Selo SRB 59 E2
Goleniów PL 88 A2
Goleszów PL 97 F2
Golfe-Juan F 23 D2
Golfo Aranci I 50 B2
Goli (Otok) HR 54 B3
Golina
 (Wielkopolskie) PL . . .93 E1
Gološeva (Aizgārša) LV . .83 F1
Göllersdorf A 41 E4
Golling A 44 B2
Golnik SLO 54 A2
Golpejas E 25 D1
Golspie GB 4 C1
Golßen D 34 C4

Golub-Dobrzyń PL 89 F3
Golubac SRB 57 E2
Golubinje SRB 57 E2
Golubovci MNE 58 C3
Golubovec HR 54 C1
Gołuchów PL 93 E2
Golymin-Ośrodek PL 90 C3
Golzow (Kreis Potsdam-
 Mittelmark) D 34 B4
Gómara E 20 A4
Gomáti GR 102 A3
Gombrèn E 21 E4
Gomecello E 25 E1
Gómfi GR 101 D2
Gommern D 34 A4
Gomunice PL 94 A3
Goncelin F 17 D4
Gondomar E 18 A3
Gondomar P 18 A4
Gondrecourt-le-
 Château F 13 D4
Gönen TR 117 E4
Góni GR 101 E4
Gonia GR 109 D3
Goniądz PL 91 E2
Goniés GR 109 E4
Gonnesa I 50 A4
Gonnosfanadiga I 50 A4
Goole GB 7 F4
Goor NL 32 C4
Goppenstein CH 17 E2
Göppingen D 43 D1
Gór Stołowych (Park
 Narodowy) PL 88 C3
Gor. Tlamino SRB 59 F3
Gor. Vratno HR 54 C1
Gora A 54 C2
Góra
 (Dolnośląskie) PL 93 D2
Góra
 (Mazowieckie) PL 90 B3
Góra Kalwaria PL 94 C2
Góra Swiętej
 Małgorzaty PL 94 A2
Gorainiai LT 80 B3
Goraj PL 95 E3
Górale PL 89 F2
Goražde BIH 55 F4
Gorczański Park
 Narodowy PL 98 B3
Gördalen S 67 D1
Gordes F 22 B1
Gorenja Vas SLO 54 A2
Gorey / Guaire IRL 3 D4
Gorgonzola I 46 B1
Gorgopótamos GR 100 C3
Gorica BIH 58 A2
Gorica MK 59 E4
Goričan HR 54 C1
Gorinchem NL 36 C1
Goritsá GR 108 B1
Gorizia I 44 C4
Gorlice PL 98 C2
Görlitz D 40 C1
Gorna Orjahovica BG . .117 D3
Gorni Kokoti MNE 58 C3
Gornica LV 83 E2
Gornja Grabovica BIH . . .55 E4
Gornja Kamenica SRB . .57 E4
Gornja Klina SRB 59 D2
Gornja Ljubovida SRB . .55 F3
Gornja Ploča HR 54 C4
Gornja Radgona SLO . . .54 C1
Gornja Sabanta SRB . . .57 D3
Gornja Slatina BIH 55 E3

Gemona del Friuli I 44 C3
Gémozac F 15 D3
Gemünd (Eifel) D 13 D1
Gemünden D 13 E2
Gemünden (Wohra) D . . .13 F1
Gemünden a. Main D . . .38 C3
Genádio I 111 F2
Genaralski Stol HR 54 B3
Gençay F 15 E2
General-Toševo BG 117 F1
Genève CH 17 D2
Geniai (Alytus) LT 85 E3
Geniai (Merkinė) LT 86 E3
Geniai (Vilniaus) LT 86 B1
Genisséa GR 102 C2
Genk B 13 D1
Genlis F 16 C1
Gennep NL 37 D1
Gennes F 15 D1
Génolhac F 22 A1
Genova I 23 F1
Gent B 12 B1
Genthin D 34 A4
Gentioux F 15 E3
Genzano di Lucania I . . .49 E4
Genzano di Roma I 48 B4
Georgiani GR 101 E3
Georgioúpoli GR 109 D4
Georgitsi GR 105 D4
Georgsmarienhütte D . . .33 D4
Gera D 39 E2
Geraardsbergen B 12 B1
Gerabronn D 38 C4
Gerace I 51 E4
Gerakári GR 101 F1
Gerakári GR 109 E4
Gerakaroú GR 102 A2
Gérakas GR 108 C1
Geráki GR 108 B1
Gerakiní GR 102 A3
Geráni GR 109 E4
Gérardmer F 13 E4
Geras A 41 D4
Gerbéviller F 13 E4
Gerbini I 53 D3
Gerbstedt D 39 D1
Gerdžiūnai LT 85 D1
Gerena E 29 D2
Gerès P 18 A4
Geretsried D 43 F2
Gérgal E 30 A3
Gergždeliai LT 81 D2
Geringswalde D 39 F1
Gerlos A 44 A3
Germaniškis LT 82 A2
Gérmas GR 101 D3
Germering D 43 F1
Germersheim D 13 F3
Gernika-Lumo E 20 A2
Gernrode (Kreis
 Quedlinburg) D 39 D1
Gernsheim D 13 F2
Gerola Alta I 43 D4
Geroliménas GR 108 B2
Gerolstein D 13 E2
Gerolzhofen D 39 D3
Geroplátanos GR 102 A3
Gerovo HR 54 B2
Gerri de la Sal E 21 D3
Gersau CH 17 F2
Gersfeld D 38 C2
Gerstetten D 43 E1
Gersthofen D 43 E1
Gerswalde D 34 C3

Geručiai LT 81 E3
Gervenai LT 85 F3
Gerviškes LT 86 B3
Gesalai LT 80 B2
Gescher D 37 E1
Geseke D 37 F1
Gesualdo I 49 D3
Geta FIN 68 B4
Getafe E 25 F2
Getelini LV 77 F3
Gettorf D 33 E2
Getxo E 20 A2
Gevelsberg D 37 E2
Gevgelija MK 59 F4
Gevrey-Chambertin F . . .16 C1
Gex F 17 D2
Geyve TR 117 F4
Gföhl A 41 D4
Ghedi I 46 C1
Gheorgheni RO 117 D2
Ghilarza I 50 A3
Ghisonaccia F 23 F4
Ghisoni F 23 F3
Giáli (Nissi) GR 111 E1
Giálova GR 108 A1
Giáltra GR 105 E1
Gianitsá GR 101 E2
Gianitsi GR 106 B3
Giannádes GR 100 B4
Giannoúli GR 103 E1
Giardini-Naxos I 51 D4
Giáros (Nissi) GR 106 B4

Giarratana I 53 D4
Giarre I 53 E3
Giat F 16 A3
Giaveno I 17 E4
Giba I 50 A4
Gibostad N 60 C2
Gibraleón E 28 C2
Gibraltar GB 29 D4
Gilučiai LT 85 F2
Giby PL 91 E1
Gideå S 68 B1
Gidle PL 94 A3
Gieboldehausen D 38 C1
Giedraičiai
 (Šiauliu) LT 81 E3
Giedraičiai
 (Utenos) LT 86 B1
Giedriai LT 85 D2
Giełczew PL 95 E3
Gielniów PL 94 B3
Gien F 16 A1
Giengen a. d. Brenz D . . .43 E1
Giens F 22 C2
Gierałtowice
 (Śląskie) PL 97 F2
Gierzwałd PL 90 B2
Gießen D 13 F1
Giethoorn NL 32 C4
Gietrzwałd PL 90 B2
Gifhorn D 33 F4
Giglio Porto I 47 D4
Gignac F 22 A2
Gijón E 19 D2

Gikši LV 78 B3
Gilching D 43 F1
Gilford GB 3 D1
Gilleleje DK 70 C3
Gillhov S 63 E4
Gillingham GB 9 F3
Gillingham GB 9 D3
Gilučiai LT 85 F2
Gilužiai LT 86 B1
Gilvyčiai LT 81 D3
Gilze NL 36 C1
Gimenells E 21 D4
Gimnó GR 105 F2
Gimo S 67 F2
Gimont F 21 D2
Ginarti LV 81 F1
Ginčionys LT 85 E3
Gineikiai LT 81 F2
Gingst D 34 B1
Ginosa I 49 F3
Gintalai LT 80 C3
Gintališke LT 80 B2
Gintaučiai LT 80 C3
Ginučiai LT 86 C1
Ginzling A 43 F2
Gioia del Colle I 49 F3
Gioia Tauro I 51 D4
Gioúra (Nissi) GR 102 B4
Giovinazzo I 49 E3
Gipka LV 77 D2
Giraite LT 85 E2

Girdiške LT 80 C3
Girenai LT 84 C2
Girifalco I 51 E3
Girininkai LT 85 E2
Girionys LT 85 E2
Girkaliai LT 80 C3
Girkalnis LT 85 D1
Girnikai LT 81 D3
Giromagny F 17 D1
Girona E 21 F4
Gironella E 21 E4
Girsteitiškis LT 86 B1
Girsūdai LT 81 D3
Girvan GB 6 C2
Gisburn GB 7 E4
Gislaved S 71 D2
Gisors F 11 F3
Gistel B 12 A1
Gíthio GR 108 B1
Gittun S 64 B2
Giugliano in
 Campania I 48 C4
Giulianova Lido I 48 C2
Giurgiu RO 117 E3
Give DK 70 B3
Givet F 12 C2
Givors F 16 C3
Givry F 16 C2
Givry-en-Argonne F 12 C3
Gižai LT 85 D2
Gizalki PL 93 E2
Gizéla GR 102 C2

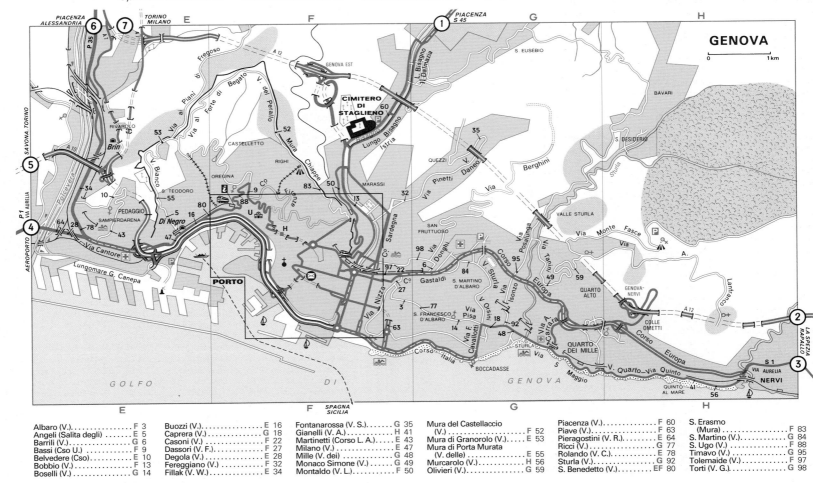

GENOVA

Albaro (V.) . . . . F 3
Angeli (Salita degli) . . . . E 5
Barrili (V.) . . . . G 6
Bassi (Cso U.) . . . . F 9
Belvedere (Cso) . . . . .E 10
Bobbio (V.) . . . . .F 13
Boselli (V.) . . . . .G 14
Buozzi (V.) . . . . .E 16
Caprera (V.) . . . . .G 18
Casoni (V.) . . . . .F 22
Dassori (V.) . . . . .F 25
Degola (V.) . . . . .E 28
Fereggiano (V.) . . . . .F 32
Fillak (V. W.) . . . . .E 34
Fontanarossa (V. S.) . . . . . .G 35
Ganelli (V. A.) . . . . .H 41
Martinetti (Corso L. A.) . . . .E 43
Milano (V.) . . . . .E 47
Mille (V. dei) . . . . .G 48
Monaco Simone (V.) . . . . . .G 49
Montaldo (V. L.) . . . . .F 50
Mura del Castellaccio
 (V.) . . . . .F 52
Mura di Granorolo (V.) . . . . .E 53
Mura di Porta Murata
 (V. delle) . . . . .E 55
Murcarolo (V.) . . . . .H 56
Olivieri (V.) . . . . .G 59
Piacenza (V.) . . . . .F 60
Piave (V.) . . . . .F 63
Pieragostini (V. R.) . . . . . . .E 64
Ricci (V.) . . . . .G 77
Rolando (V. C.) . . . . .E 78
Sturla (V.) . . . . .G 92
S. Benedetto (V.) . . . . .EF 80
S. Erasmo
 (Mura) . . . . .F 83
S. Martino (V.) . . . . .G 84
S. Ugo (V.) . . . . .F 88
Timavo (V.) . . . . .G 95
Tolemaide (V.) . . . . .F 97
Torti (V. G.) . . . . .G 98

Gornja Toponica SRB....57 E4
Gornja Tuzla BIH....55 F3
Gornje Jelenje HR....54 B3
Gornje Ratkovo BIH....55 D3
Gornje Selo HR....58 A4
Gornji Grad SLO....54 B1
Gornji Kneginec HR....54 C1
Gornji Lapac HR....54 C3
Gornji Milanovac SRB....57 D3
Gornji Petrovci SLO....54 C1
Gornji Podgradci BIH....55 D3
Gornji Rajić HR....55 D2
Gornji Vakuf BIH....55 E4
Górno PL....90 B1
Gorno Orizari MK....59 F3
Goro I....47 E1
Górowo Iławeckie PL....90 B1
Gorredijk NL....32 C4
Gorron F....11 D4
Gorsleston-on-Sea GB....9 F2
Gort / An Gort IRL....2 B3
Gorteen IRL....2 C2
Gortin GB....3 D1
Górtis GR....109 E4
Gortmore / An Gort
  Mór IRL....2 B2
Goryń PL....89 F2
Görzke D....34 B4
Gorzków-Osada PL....95 E3
Gorzkowice PL....94 A3
Górzno (Kujawsko-
  Pomorskie) PL....90 A3
Górzno
  (Mazowieckie) PL....95 D2
Gorzów Śląski PL....93 F3
Gorzów
  Wielkopolski PL....88 B3
Górzyca
  (Lubuskie) PL....92 A1

Górzyca (Zachodniopomorskie)
  PL....88 B2
Gorzyce
  (Podkarpackie) PL....99 D1
Gorzyce (Śląskie) PL....97 E2
Gosaldo I....44 B3
Gosau A....44 C2
Göschenen CH....17 F2
Gościeradów
  Ukazowy PL....95 D3
Gościno PL....88 B1
Gosforth GB....7 D3
Goslar D....38 C1
Gościce PL....90 A3
Gospić HR....54 C3
Gospođinci SRB....56 C2
Gosport GB....9 D4
Gossau CH....43 D2
Gosselies B....12 C1
Gößnitz D....39 E2
Gößweinstein D....39 D3
Gostivar MK....59 E4
Göstling A....45 D1
Gostycyn PL....89 E2
Gostyń (Śląskie) PL....97 E2
Gostyń
  (Wielkopolskie) PL....93 D2
Gostynin PL....94 A1
Goszczanów PL....93 F2
Grabów PL....93 F2
Grabow (Kreis
  Ludwigslust) D....34 A3
Grabów nad Pilicą PL....94 C2
Grabów nad
  Prosna PL....93 E2
Grabowiec
  (Lubelskie) PL....95 F3
Grabupiai LT....80 B2
Gračac HR....54 C3
Gračanica BIH....55 E3

Goumois F....17 E1
Goúra GR....105 D3
Gourdon F....15 F4
Gourin F....10 B4
Gournes GR....109 F4
Gournia GR....110 C4
Gouveia P....24 C1
Goúves GR....109 F4
Gouviá GR....100 B4
Gouzon F....15 F3
Govedari HR....58 A3
Gowarczów PL....94 B3
Gowidlino PL....89 E1
Göynük TR....117 F4
Gozd PL....94 C3
Gozd. M. SLO....54 A1
Gozdnica PL....92 B2
Gozdowo PL....90 A3
Gozzano I....17 F3
Graal-Müritz D....34 A2
Graben-Neudorf D....13 F3
Grabenstätt D....44 B1
Grabica PL....94 A2
Grabiny-Zameczek PL....89 F1
Grabovac HR....58 A2
Grabovci SRB....56 C3
Grabów PL....93 F2
Grabowiec
  (Lubelskie) PL....95 F3
Grabupiai LT....80 B2
Gračac HR....54 C3
Gračanica BIH....55 E3

Gračanica
  (Priština) SRB....59 E3
Gračanica
  (Valjevo) SRB....55 F3
Graçay F....15 F2
Grächen CH....17 E3
Gradac HR....58 A3
Gradac MNE....55 F4
Gradac SRB....57 D4
Gradačac BIH....55 E3
Gradara I....47 F2
Gradec HR....54 C2
Gradefes E....19 D3
Gradina HR....55 D2
Gradina SRB....57 F4
Gradisca d'Isonzo I....44 C4
Gradište HR....55 E2
Gradište MK....59 F3
Grado E....19 D2
Grado I....44 C4
Gradsko MK....59 F4
Gradskovo SRB....57 E3
Gräfelfing D....43 F1
Grafenau (Kreis Freyung-
  Grafenau) D....39 F4
Gräfenberg (Kreis
  Forchheim) D....39 D3
Gräfenhainichen D....39 E1
Grafenwöhr D....39 D3
Grafing D....43 F1
Gragnano I....48 C4
Grahovo MNE....58 B3
Grahovo SLO....54 A2
Graiguenamanagh / Gráig na
  Manach IRL....3 D4
Grain GB....9 F3
Grainau D....43 F2
Grajewo PL....91 D2
Grajvoron RUS....115 F4

Gram DK....70 B3
Gramat F....15 F4
Gramatikó GR....105 D1
Gramatikoú GR....104 C2
Graméni GR....102 A1
Graméno GR....100 C4
Grametten A....41 D4
Grammichele I....53 D3
Gramzda LV....80 B1
Gramzow (Kreis
  Uckermark) D....34 C3
Gran N....66 C1
Granada E....29 F3
Gránard / Granard IRL....2 C3
Grancey-le-Château F....16 C1
Grand-Champ F....14 B1
Grand-Couronne F....11 F3
Grand-Fougeray F....14 C1
Grandas de Salime E....18 C2
Grandcamp-Maisy F....11 D3
Grândola P....24 A4
Grandpré F....12 C3
Grandrieu F....16 B4
Grandvilliers F....12 A2
Grañén E....20 C4
Grängärde S....67 E2
Grange-over-Sands GB....7 D3
Grangemouth GB....7 D1
Granges-sur-
  Vologne F....13 E4
Grängesberg S....67 E2
Granitis GR....102 B1
Granitsa GR....104 C1
Granja P....24 C4
Granja de
  Torrehermosa E....25 D4
Gränna S....67 D3
Granollers E....21 E4
Granön S....66 C2
Granowo PL....93 D1
Gransee D....34 B3
Grantham GB....9 E1
Grantown-on-Spey GB....4 C4
Granville F....11 D3
Granvin N....66 A1
Grasleben D....34 A4
Grasmere GB....7 D3
Grassano I....49 D1
Grasse F....23 D2
Gråsten DK....70 B4
Gråstorp S....67 D2
Gratangen N....60 B3
Gratiní GR....103 D1
Gratkorn A....45 D1
Grau de Castelló E....27 D2
Graulhet F....21 E2
Graumine LT....80 B3
Graus E....21 D4
Grávalos E....20 A4
Gravas LV....78 B3
Gravdal N....60 A3
Grave NL....37 D1
Gravedona I....43 D4
Gravelines F....12 A1
Gravellona Toce I....17 F3
Gräveri LV....83 E2
Gravesend GB....9 E3
Graviá GR....105 D2
Gravina in Puglia I....49 E3
Gravoúna GR....102 C2

Gray F....16 C1
Grays Thurrock GB....9 E3
Graz A....45 E2
Grazalema E....29 D3
Grążawy PL....90 A3
Grażiškiai LT....85 D2
Gražučiai LT....85 E2
Grazzanise I....48 C4
Gramzda LV....80 B1
Grčak SRB....57 D4
Grdelica SRB....57 E4
Great Driffield GB....7 F4
Great Dunmow GB....9 E2
Great Malvern GB....8 C2
Great Torrington GB....8 C3
Great Yarmouth GB....9 F1
Grebbestad S....66 C3
Grebków PL....95 D1
Grebnik SRB....59 D3
Grębów PL....99 D1
Greccio I....47 D4
Greding D....39 E4
Greenhead GB....7 E3
Greenlaw GB....7 D2
Greenock GB....6 C1
Greenodd GB....7 D3
Greggio I....43 E4
Gregolímano GR....105 E1
Greifenburg A....44 C3
Greiffenberg D....34 C3
Greifswald D....34 B2
Greikonys LT....85 F2
Grein A....45 D1
Greiškāni LV....83 E1
Greiveri LV....78 C3
Greiz D....39 E2
Grenå DK....70 C2
Grenade F....21 D2
Grenade-sur-l'Adour F....20 C2
Grenchen CH....17 E1
Grenči LV....77 D3
Grenctāle LV....81 F2
Grenoble F....17 D4
Grense Jakobselv N....61 F1
Gréoux-les-Bains F....22 C2
Gresse-en-Vercors F....16 C4
Gressoney-la Trinité I....17 E3
Gressoney-St Jean I....17 E3
Gresten A....45 D1
Grésy-sur-Isère F....17 D3
Greußen D....39 D1
Greve in Chianti I....47 D3
Greve Strand DK....70 C3
Greven D....37 E1
Grevená GR....101 D2
Grevenbroich D....13 D1
Grevenbrück D....37 F2
Grevenitío GR....100 C4
Grevenmacher L....13 D2
Grevesmühlen D....33 F2
Greviškiai LT....82 C3
Grey Abbey GB....3 E1
Greystones / Na Clocha
  Liatha IRL....3 D3
Grez-en-Bouère F....11 D4
Grezzana I....43 F4
Grgur (Otok) HR....54 B3
Gribuli LV....83 E3
Gricaičiai LT....80 C2
Griciai LT....85 D1
Griebenow D....34 B2

Gries am Brenner A....43 F3
Gries im Sellrain A....43 F2
Grieskirchen A....44 C1
Grieze (Marijas
  Skola) LV....80 C1
Grießpelkiai I LT....84 C1
Griffen A....45 D3
Grigišķes LT....86 B2
Grignan F....22 B1
Grigno I....43 F4
Grignols F....20 C1
Griki LV....78 A3
Grimaldi I....51 D3
Grimaud F....23 D2
Grimma D....39 E1
Grimmen D....34 B2
Grimsby GB....7 F4
Grimstad N....66 B3
Grimzdai LT....81 F2
Griniačiai LT....84 C1
Grindaheim N....66 B1
Grindavík IS....62 A2
Grindelwald CH....17 F2
Grindsted DK....70 B3
Grinkiškis LT....81 E3
Griñón E....25 F2
Gripiškes LT....85 D2
Gripsholm S....67 F3
Grisignano di Zocco I....43 F4
Grisolles F....21 E2
Grisslehamn S....67 F2
Gritsa GR....101 E2
Gríva GR....101 E2
Grizáno GR....101 D2
Grk BIH....55 E3
Grljan SRB....57 E3
Grnča SRB....55 F3
Grøa N....62 C2
Grobina LV....80 B1
Gröbming A....44 C2
Grobštai LT....80 B3
Grocholice PL....94 A3
Grocka SRB....57 D2
Gródek nad
  Dunajcem PL....98 C2
Gröditz D....39 F1
Gródki PL....95 E3
Grodków PL....97 D1
Grodziczno PL....90 A3
Grodziec
  (Wielkopolskie) PL....93 E2
Grodzisk PL....91 E3
Grodzisk
  Mazowiecki PL....94 B2
Grodzisk
  Wielkopolski PL....92 C1
Groenlo NL....37 D1
Groitzsch D....39 E1
Groix F....14 A1
Grójec PL....94 C2
Grömitz D....33 F2
Gromnik PL....98 C2
Gronau (Westfalen) D....37 E1
Grong N....63 D2
Grönhögen S....71 E3
Gröningen D....39 D1
Groningen NL....32 C3

Gronowo PL....90 A1
Gronowo PL....89 F1
Grönskåra S....71 E2
Gropello Cairoli I....46 B1
Groscavallo I....17 E4
Grosio I....43 E4
Groß-Gerau D....13 F2
Groß Gerungs A....41 D4
Groß Schönebeck D....34 B3
Groß-Siegharts A....41 D4
Groß-Umstadt D....13 D2
Großbreitenbach D....39 D2
Großenbrode D....33 F2
Großenhain D....39 F1
Großenkneten D....33 D4
Großenzersdorf A....41 E4
Grosseto I....46 C2
Großhabersdorf D....38 D3
Großheubach D....38 C3
Großpetersdorf A....45 E2
Großraming A....45 D1
Großraschen D....39 F1
Großreken D....37 E1
Großröhrsdorf D....39 F1
Großschönau D....40 C1
Großweil D....43 F2
Großwitzeetze D....34 A3
Grostenquin F....13 E3
Grosuplje SLO....54 B2
Groszowice PL....97 E1
Grötlingbo S....67 F4
Grottaglie I....49 F4
Grottaminarda I....49 D3
Grottammare I....48 B1
Grotteria I....51 E4
Grövelsjön S....63 D3
Grovfjord N....60 B3
Grubišno Polje HR....55 D2
Gruda HR....58 B3
Grude BIH....58 A2
Grudusk PL....90 B3
Grudziądz PL....89 F2
Gruissan F....21 F2
Grumbliai LT....80 C1
Grums S....67 D2
Grünau im Almtal A....44 C1
Grünberg D....13 F1
Grundarfjörður IS....62 A1
Grundforsen S....67 D1
Grundlsee A....44 C2
Grundsund S....66 C3
Grundtjärn S....68 A1
Grunduli LT....76 B2
Grundzāle LV....79 D2
Grünstadt D....13 F2
Grünwald D....43 F1
Gruočninkai LT....85 F3
Grupčin MK....59 E3
Gruślauke LT....80 B2
Gruta PL....89 F2
Grūtas LT....85 E3
Gruyères CH....17 E2
Gruž SRB....57 D4
Gruzdžiai LT....81 D2
Gružiai LT....81 F2
Grybenai LT....83 D3
Grybów PL....98 C2
Grycksbo S....67 E2
Gryfino PL....88 A2
Gryfów Śląski PL....92 B3
Gryllefjord / Torsken N....60 B2
Grythyttan S....67 E2
Grza SRB....57 E3
Grzebienisko PL....93 D1
Grzegorzew PL....93 F1
Grzmiąca (Zachodniopomorskie)
  PL....88 C2
Grzybno PL....89 F3
Gstaad CH....17 E2
Gstadt D....44 B1
Guadahortuna E....30 A2
Guadalajara E....26 A1
Guadalaviar E....26 B2
Guadalcanal E....25 D4
Guadalupe E....25 E3
Guadarrama E....25 F1
Guadassuar E....27 D3
Guadiana E....29 D4
Guadix E....30 A3
Gualdo Tadino I....47 E3
Guarda P....24 C1
Guadamar del
  Segura E....30 C2
Guardia Sanframondi I....48 C3
Guardiagrele I....48 C2
Guardo E....19 E3
Guareña E....25 E4
Guarromán E....25 F4
Guastalla I....47 D1
Gubbio I....47 E3
Guben D....35 D4
Guberevac SRB....57 D3
Gubin PL....92 A1
Guča SRB....57 D4
Guča Gora BIH....55 E4
Gudai LT....84 B1
Gudavac BIH....54 C3
Gudeliai (Kazlu
  Rūda) LT....85 E2
Gudeliai
  (Šventragis) LT....85 E2
Gudenieki LV....76 B3
Gudhjem DK....71 E4
Gudkaimis LT....85 D2
Gudow D....33 F3

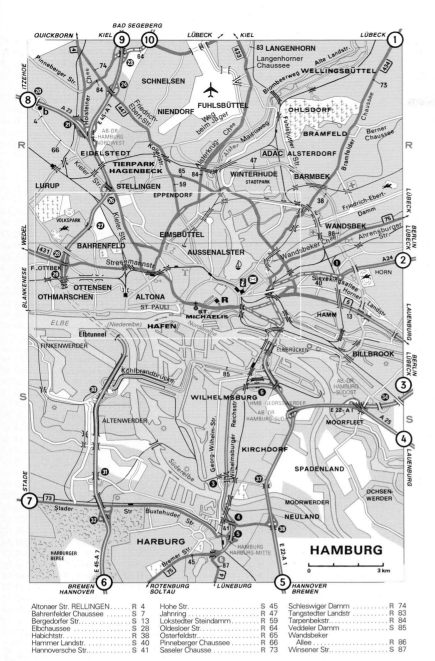

HAMBURG

0   3 km

Altonaer Str. RELLINGEN	R 4	
Bahrenfelder Chaussee	S 7	
Bergedorfer Str.	S 13	
Elbchaussee	S 28	
Habichtstr.	R 38	
Hammer Landstr.	S 40	
Hannoversche Str.	S 41	
Hohe Str.	S 45	
Jahrring	R 47	
Lokstedter Steindamm	R 59	
Oldesloer Str.	R 64	
Osterfeldstr.	R 65	
Pinneberger Chaussee	R 66	
Saseler Chausse	R 73	
Schlesiwger Damm	R 74	
Tangstedter Landstr	R 83	
Tarpenbekstr.	R 84	
Veddeler Damm	S 85	
Wandsbeker Allee	R 86	
Winsener Str.	S 87	

Gudvangen N......66 A1
Gudžiai LT......85 F3
Gudžioniai LT......85 F1
Gudžiūnai LT......81 E3
Guebwiller F......13 E4
Guémené-Penfao F......14 C1
Guémené-sur-Scorff F......10 B4
Güeñes E......19 F2
Guer F......10 C4
Guérande F......14 B1
Guéret F......15 F3
Guérigny F......16 A2
Guéthary F......20 B2
Gueugnon F......16 B2
Güglingen D......38 C4
Guglionesi I......49 D2
Guichen F......10 C4
Guidonia I......47 F4
Guignes F......12 A4
Guijo de Granadilla E......25 D2
Guijuelo E......25 E1
Guildford GB......9 E3
Guillaumes F......23 D1
Guillena E......29 E4
Guillestre F......17 D4
Guillon F......16 B1
Guilvinec F......10 A3
Guimarães P......18 A4
Guimiliau F......10 A4
Guînes F......12 A1
Guingamp F......10 B4
Guipavas F......10 A4
Guisborough GB......7 F3
Guiscard F......12 B2
Guise F......12 B2
Guissona E......21 E3
Guist GB......9 F1
Guitiriz E......18 B2
Guitres F......15 D4
Gujan-Mestras F......20 B1
Gulbene LV......79 E3
Gulbinai LT......81 E3
Gulbinenai LT......82 A2
Gulbiši LV......78 C2
Gulbju Ciems LV......81 E3
Gullspång S......67 D2
Gumiel de Hizán E......19 F4
Gummersbach D......13 E1
Gundegas LV......78 B3
Gundelfingen a.d.
Donau A......43 E1
Gundelsheim D......38 C4
Gunnarn S......64 A3
Gunnarsbyn S......64 C2
Gunnarskog S......67 D2
Gunten CH......17 E2
Günterode D......38 C1
Guntín de Pallares E......18 B2
Günzburg D......43 E1
Gunzenhausen D......39 D4

Guptilčiai LT......85 E1
Gurk A......45 D2
Gurrea de Gállego E......20 C4
Gusev RUS......114 C3
Gusinje MNE......58 C3
Guspini I......50 A4
Güssing A......45 E2
Güssten D......39 D1
Güstrow D......34 A2
Gutcher GB......5 F1
Gutenstein A......45 E1
Gütersloh D......37 F1
Gützkow D......34 B2
Guyhirn GB......9 E1
Gūžas LV......80 A1
Guzet-Neige F......21 E3
Gvardejsk RUS......114 C3
Gvarv N......66 B2
Gvozd MNE......58 C3
Gvozdmost HR......54 C2
Gwda Mała PL......89 D2
Gwda Wielka PL......89 D2
Gwizdały PL......90 C3
Gy F......16 C1
Gyöngyös H......116 C2
Győr H......116 B2
Gysinge S......67 E4
Gyula H......116 C2
Gyviškiai LT......85 E2
Gyvoliai LT......80 C2

H

H. E. erdap SRB......57 E2
Haabneeme EE......72 B1
Haag A......45 D1
Haag am Hausruck A......44 C1
Haag i. Oberbayern D......44 B1
Haage EE......79 D1
Haaksbergen NL......37 D1
Haamstede NL......36 B1
Haanja EE......79 E2
Haapajärvi FIN......69 D1
Haapakoski FIN......69 D2
Haapamäki (Keski-
Suomi) FIN......69 D2
Haapamäki
(Oulu) FIN......69 D1
Haapavesi FIN......65 D3
Haapsalu EE......75 D3
Haar D......43 F1
Haaren D......37 F1
Haarlem NL......32 A4
Habaja EE......72 B2
Habartice CZ......40 C1
Habay-la-Neuve B......13 D2
Habo S......67 D4

Habsheim F......17 E1
Håbu N......66 C3
Hachenburg D......13 E1
Hachmühlen D......33 E3
Hackås S......63 E4
Hadamar D......13 F1
Haddington GB......7 D1
Hadersdorf am
Kamp A......41 D4
Haderslev DK......70 B3
Hadjač UA......115 F4
Hadleigh GB......9 F2
Hadmersleben D......34 A4
Hadsten DK......70 B2
Hadsund DK......70 B2
Hadžići BIH......55 E4

Hægebostad N......66 A3
Haganj HR......54 C2
Hagen D......37 E2
Hagen i. Bremischen D......33 E3
Hagenow D......33 F3
Hageri EE......72 B2
Hagetmau F......20 C2
Hagfors S......67 D2
Häggdånger S......68 A2
Haggenås S......63 E3
Hagondange F......13 D3
Hagudi EE......72 B2
Haguenau F......13 F3
Hahnbach D......39 E3
Haiba EE......72 A2
Haidaku EE......79 D2

Haigerloch D......43 D1
Hailsham GB......9 E4
Hailuoto FIN......65 -D3
Haimre EE......72 A3
Hainburg a. d.
Donau A......45 F1
Hainfeld A......45 E1
Hainichen D......39 F2
Hajdúböszörmény H......116 C2
Hajdučica SRB......57 D2
Hajdúszoboszló H......116 C2
Hajnówka PL......91 F3
Hajsyn UA......117 E1
Hajvoron UA......117 E1
Hakarp S......67 D4
Hakkas S......64 C1
Häkkilä FIN......69 D2
Halandritsa GR......104 C3
Halbe D......34 C4
Halberstadt D......39 D1
Halden N......66 C2
Haldensleben D......34 A4
Halesowen GB......9 D2
Halesworth GB......9 F2
Halhjem N......66 A1
Halifax GB......7 F2
Halikko FIN......69 D4
Halinga EE......72 A3
Halinów PL......94 C1
Haljala EE......73 D2
Haljava EE......72 B2
Halkeró GR......102 B2
Hálki GR......101 F4
Hálki GR......109 F1
Hálki GR......111 E2
Hálki (Nissi) GR......111 E4
Halkiádes GR......101 E4
Halkidóna GR......101 F2
Halkió GR......107 D2
Hall in Tirol A......43 F2
Halle B......12 B1
Halle D......37 F1
Halle D......39 E1
Halle-Neustadt D......39 E1
Hällefors S......67 E2
Hälleforsnäs S......67 E3
Hallein A......44 B2
Hällekis S......67 D3
Hallenberg D......37 F2
Hallencourt F......12 A2
Hällesjö S......68 A2
Halliku EE......73 E3
Halliste EE......78 C1
Hällnäs S......64 B3
Hallörmsstaður IS......62 B1
Hallsberg S......67 E3
Hallstadt D......39 D3
Hallstahammar S......67 E2
Hallstatt A......44 C2
Hallstavik S......67 F2
Halluin F......12 B1
Halmstad S......70 D2
Hals DK......70 C2
Halsa N......62 B3
Hälsingtuna S......68 A3
Halsskov DK......70 C3
Halstead GB......9 F2
Halsteren NL......36 B1
Haltdålen N......63 D3
Haltern (Kreis
Recklinghausen) D......37 E1

Halver D......37 E2
Ham F......12 B2
Hamar N......66 C1
Hamarøy N......60 B3
Hamburg D......33 F3
Hamdorf (Kreis Rendsburg-
Eckernförde) D......33 E2
Hämeenkyrö FIN......68 C3
Hämeenlinna FIN......69 D3
Hämelerwald D......33 F4
Hameln D......33 E4
Hamersleben D......34 A4
Hamili (Nissi) GR......111 D3
Hamilton GB......7 D1
Hamina FIN......69 E4
Hamm (Westfalen) D......37 E1
Hammarland FIN......68 B4
Hammarstrand S......68 A2
Hammaslahti FIN......69 F2
Hammel DK......70 B3
Hammelburg D......38 C3
Hammerdal S......63 E3
Hammerfest N......61 D1
Hammershus DK......71 E4
Hamminkeln D......37 E1
Hamoir B......13 D1
Hamra S......67 E1
Hamre N......66 B3
Hamzali MK......59 F3
Hamzići BIH......58 A2
Han Pijesak BIH......55 F3
Han-sur-Lesse B......12 C2
Hanákia GR......104 B3
Hanau D......13 F2
Hăncești MD......117 E2
Handrás GR......110 C4
Hanerau-
Hademarschen D......33 E2
Hánia GR......101 F4
Hánia GR......108 B1
Haniá GR......109 D3
Hanikase EE......79 E2
Haniótis GR......102 A3
Harta PL......99 D2
Hartberg A......45 E2
Hartha (Kreis
Döbeln) D......39 F1
Hartlepool GB......7 F3
Hartmannsdorf D......39 E2
Hartola FIN......69 D3
Harwich GB......9 F2
Harzgerode D......39 D1
Haselünne D......33 D4
Haskovo BG......117 E4
Haslach an der Mühl A......40 C4
Haslach i. Kinzigtal D......13 F4
Hasle DK......71 E4
Haslemere GB......9 D3
Haslev DK......70 C3
Hasparren F......20 B2
Hassela S......68 A3
Hasselfelde D......39 D1
Hasselt B......12 C1
Haßfurt D......39 D3
Hässleholm S......71 D3
Hastière-Lavaux B......12 C2
Hastings GB......9 F4
Hasvik N......61 D1
Hatě CZ......41 E4
Hațeg RO......117 D3
Hatfield GB......9 E3
Hatherleigh GB......8 B4
Hattem NL......32 C4
Hattfjelldal N......63 E1

Hardenberg NL......32 C4
Harderwijk NL......32 B4
Hardeshøj DK......70 B4
Hardheim D......38 C4
Hareid N......62 B4
Harelbeke B......12 B1
Haren D......32 C4
Haren NL......32 C3
Harewood GB......7 E4
Hargla E......79 D2
Haritoméni GR......102 A1
Harjavalta FIN......68 C3
Harjunpää FIN......68 C3
Harju-Risti EE......72 A2
Harklowa PL......98 C2
Harku EE......72 B2
Härkmeri FIN......68 C2
Harkjärve EE......72 B2
Harlech GB......3 F3
Harlesien D......33 D3
Harleston GB......9 F2
Harlingen NL......32 B3
Harlow GB......9 E3
Harmånger S......68 A3
Harmanli BG......117 E4
Härnösand S......68 A2
Haro E......20 A3
Harokopió GR......108 A1
Haroldswick GB......5 F1
Haroué F......13 D4
Harpenden GB......9 E2
Harplinge S......71 D2
Harpstedt D......33 E4
Harrachov CZ......41 D2
Harrislee D......33 E1
Harrogate GB......7 E4
Härryda S......66 C4
Harsefeld D......33 E3
Harsprånget S......64 B1
Harstad N......60 B3
Harsvik N......62 C2
Harta PL......99 D2
Hartberg A......45 E2

Hattingen (Ennepe-Rhur-
Kreis) D......37 E1
Hattula FIN......69 D3
Hattuvaara
(Ilomantsi) FIN......69 F2
Hatunkyla
(Lieksa) FIN......69 F1
Hatvan H......116 C2
Hatvik N......66 A1
Haubourdin F......12 A1
Hauge N......66 A2
Haugesund N......66 A2
Hauho FIN......69 D3
Haukeligrend N......66 A2
Haukipudas FIN......65 D2
Haukivuori FIN......69 E2
Haunstetten (Kreis Augsburg
Stadt) D......43 E1
Haus A......44 C2
Hausach D......13 F4
Hausham D......43 F2
Hausjärvi FIN......69 D4
Hautajärvi FIN......65 E1
Hautefort F......15 E4
Hauteville-Lompnes F......16 C3
Hautmont F......12 B2
Havant GB......9 D4
Havári EE......104 B3
Havdáta GR......104 A1
Havelange B......12 C2
Havelberg D......34 A3
Haverfordwest /
Hwlffordd GB......8 A2
Haverhill GB......9 E2
Haverö S......63 E4
Havířov CZ......41 F2
Havlíčkův Brod CZ......41 D3
Havneby DK......70 A3
Havøysund N......61 D1
Havraň CZ......40 B2
Hawes GB......7 E3
Hawick GB......7 D2
Hawkhurst GB......9 E3
Hay-on-Wye GB......8 C2
Hayange F......13 D3
Hayle GB......8 A4
Haywards Heath GB......9 E3
Hazebrouck F......12 A1
Headford / Áth Cinn IRL......2 B2
Heanor GB......9 D1
Héas F......20 C3
Heathfield GB......9 E4
Heby S......67 F2
Hechingen D......43 D1
Hecho E......20 C3
Hechtel B......12 C1
Hecklingen D......39 D1
Hédé F......10 C4
Hede S......63 E4
Hedemora S......67 E2
Hedenäset S......64 C2
Hedeviken S......63 E4
Hedon GB......7 F4
Heemstede NL......32 A4
Heerde NL......32 C4
Heerenveen NL......32 B4
Heerlen NL......13 D1
Heeze NL......36 C2
Hegge N......66 B1
Hegra N......63 D3
Heia N......60 C2
Heide D......33 E2
Heidelberg D......13 F3

0   2 km

NOORDZEE

SCHEVENINGEN

('S-GRAVENHAGE)
DEN HAAG

DELFT

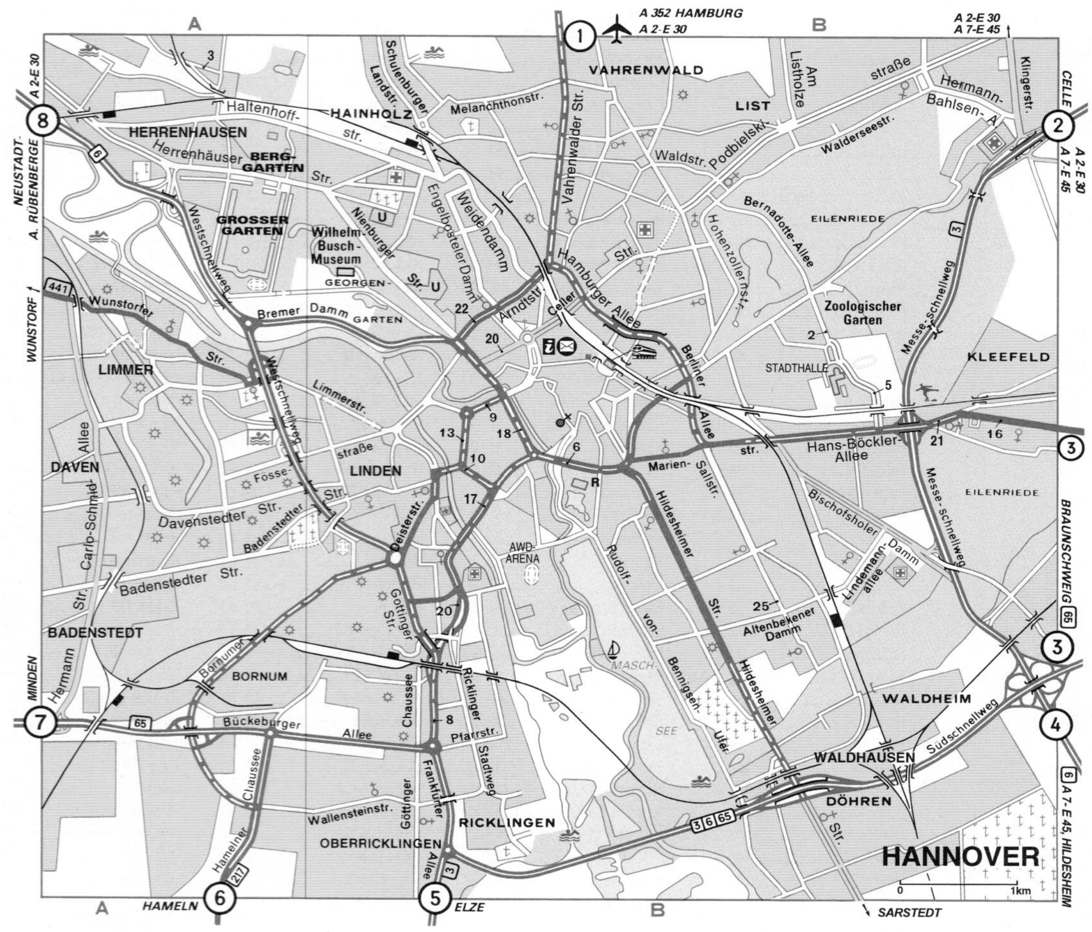

Adenauerallee . . . . B 2
Altenauer Weg . . . A 3
Clausewitzstr. . . . . B 5
Friedrichswall . . . . B 6
Friedrich-Ebert-Str. B 8
Goethestr. . . . . B 9
Gustav-Bratke-Allee . . . . B 10
Humboldtstr. . . . . . B 13
Kirchröder Str. . . . . B 16
Lavesallee . . . . B 17
Leibnizufer . . . . . . B 18
Ritter-Brüning-Str. . B 20
Scheidestr. . . . . . . B 21
Schloßwender St. . B 22
Stöckner Str. . . . . A 23
Stresemannallee . B 25

Heidenau *D* 39 F1
Heidenheim a. d. Brenz *D* 43 E1
Heidenreichstein *A* 41 D4
Heikendorf *D* 33 F2
Heikkila *FIN* 65 E2
Heilbronn *D* 38 C4
Heiligenberg *D* 43 D2
Heiligenblut *A* 44 B2
Heiligenhafen *D* 33 F2
Heiligenkirchen *D* 37 F1
Heiligenkreuz im Lafnitztal *A* 45 E2
Heiligenstadt *D* 38 C1
Heilsbronn *D* 39 D4
Heimari *FIN* 69 E3
Heimdal *N* 62 C3
Heimertingen *D* 43 E1
Heimtali *EE* 78 C1
Heinävaara *FIN* 69 F2
Heinävesi *FIN* 69 F2
Heinola *FIN* 69 E3
Heinolan mlk *FIN* 69 E3
Heinsberg *D* 13 D1
Heist *B* 36 B2
Heist-op-den-Berg *B* 12 C1
Hejde *S* 67 F4
Hel *PL* 89 F1
Heldburg *D* 39 D3
Heldrungen *D* 39 D1
Helechal *E* 25 E4
Helensburgh *GB* 6 C1
Hella *IS* 62 A2
Hella *N* 66 A1
Hellamaa (Hiiu) *EE* 74 C2
Hellamaa (Saare) *EE* 75 D2
Hellendoorn *NL* 32 C4
Hellenurme *EE* 79 D1
Hellesylt *N* 62 B4
Hellevoetsluis *NL* 36 B1
Hellín *E* 26 B4
Hellvik *N* 66 A3
Helmbrechts (Kreis Hof) *D* 39 E3
Helme *EE* 78 C1
Helmküla *EE* 75 D3
Helmond *NL* 37 D1
Helmsdale *GB* 5 D3
Helmsley *GB* 7 F3
Helmstadt *D* 38 C3
Helmstedt *D* 34 A4
Helsa *D* 38 C2
Helsingborg *S* 71 D3
Helsinge *DK* 70 C3
Helsingør *DK* 71 D3
Helsinki / Helsingfors *FIN* 69 D4
Helska (Mierzeja) *PL* 89 F1
Helston *GB* 8 A4
Heltermaa *EE* 75 D2
Hemau *D* 39 E4
Hemavan *S* 63 E1
Hemel Hempstead *GB* 9 E3
Hemer *D* 37 E1
Hemnes *N* 66 C2
Hemnesberget *N* 63 E1
Hemsedal *N* 66 B1
Hemsing *N* 66 B1
Hendaye *F* 20 B2
Hengelo *NL* 32 C4
Hengersberg *D* 39 F4
Hénin-Beaumont *F* 12 A2
Henley *GB* 9 D2
Henley-on-Thames *GB* 9 D3
Henneberg *D* 38 C2
Hennebont *F* 14 B1
Hennef *D* 13 E1
Hennigsdorf *D* 34 B4
Hennset *N* 62 C3
Henrichemont *F* 16 A1
Henrykowo *PL* 90 B1
Henstedt-Ulzburg *D* 33 F2
Henstridge *GB* 8 C3
Heppenheim a. d. Weise (Kreis Worms) *D* 13 F2
Heraklea *MK* 59 E4
Herbault *F* 15 E1
Herbertingen *D* 43 D1
Herbignac *F* 14 B1
Herbolzheim (Kreis Emmendingen) *D* 13 F4
Herborn *D* 13 F1
Herbrechtingen *D* 43 E1
Herbstein *D* 38 C2
Herby *PL* 93 F3
Hercegnovi *MNE* 58 B3
Hercegovac *HR* 55 D2
Hercegovacka Goleša *SRB* 56 C4
Hereford *GB* 8 C2
Herencia *E* 26 A3
Herentals *B* 12 C1
Herford *D* 37 F1
Héricourt *F* 17 D1
Heringsdorf (Kreis Ostvorpommern) *D* 34 C2
Herisau *CH* 43 D2
Hérisson *F* 16 A2
Herk-de-Stad *B* 12 C1
Herleshausen *D* 38 C2
Hermagor *A* 44 C3
Hermannsburg *D* 33 F4
Hermansverk *N* 66 A1
Heřmanův Městec *CZ* 41 D2
Herment *F* 16 A3
Hermeskeil *D* 13 E2
Hermsdorf (Saale-Holzland-Kreis) *D* 39 E2
Hernani *E* 20 A2
Hernansancho *E* 25 F1
Herne *D* 37 E1
Herne Bay *GB* 9 F3
Herning *DK* 70 B3
Heroldsberg *D* 39 D3
Herónia *GR* 105 E2
Herrala *FIN* 69 E3
Herre *N* 66 B2
Herrenberg *D* 43 D1
Herrera *E* 29 E3
Herrera de Alcántara *E* 24 C2
Herrera de los Navarros *E* 26 C1
Herrera de Pisuerga *E* 19 E3
Herrera del Duque *E* 25 E3
Herreruela *E* 24 C2
Herrestad *S* 66 C3
Herrieden *D* 39 D4
Herrljunga *S* 67 D3
Herrnburg *D* 33 F2
Herrnhut *D* 40 C1
Herrsching *D* 43 F1
Herrskog *S* 68 A2
Hersbruck (Kreis Nürnberger Land) *D* 39 E3
Herselt *B* 12 C1
Hérso *GR* 101 F1
Herstal *B* 13 D1
Herten *D* 37 E1
Hertford *GB* 9 E2
Hertu *EE* 72 B2
Hervás *E* 25 D2
Herzberg *D* 38 C1
Herzberg (Kreis Elbe-Elster) *D* 39 F1
Herzogenaurach *D* 39 D3
Herzogenburg *A* 45 E1
Herzsprung (Kreis Ostprignitz-Ruppin) *D* 34 B3
Hesdin *F* 12 A2
Hesel *D* 33 D3
Hesseng *N* 61 F2
Hessisch Lichtenau *D* 38 C2
Hessisch Oldendorf *D* 33 E4
Hetekylä *FIN* 65 E2
Hetin *SRB* 57 D1
Hettange-Grande *F* 13 D3
Hettstedt (Kreis Mansfelder Land) *D* 39 D1
Heubach (Ostalbkreis) *D* 38 C4
Heuchin *F* 12 A1
Hexham *GB* 7 E3
Heyrieux *F* 16 C3
Heysham *GB* 7 D4
Hiddensee (Insel) (Kreis Rügen) *D* 34 B1
Hieflau *A* 45 D1
Hiersac *F* 15 D3
Hietaniemi *FIN* 65 E1
High Wycombe *GB* 9 D3
Higham Ferrers *GB* 9 E2
Higuera de la Serena *E* 25 D4
Higuera de la Sierra *E* 24 C4
Higuera de Vargas *E* 24 C4
Higuera la Real *E* 24 C4
Higueruela *E* 26 C3
Híjar *E* 27 D1
Hilchenbach *D* 13 F1
Hildburghausen *D* 39 D2
Hilden *D* 37 E2
Hilders *D* 38 C2
Hildesheim *D* 33 F4
Hiliomódi *GR* 105 E3
Hillegom *NL* 32 A4
Hillerød *DK* 70 C3
Hillesøy *N* 60 C2
Hillswick *GB* 5 F1
Hilpoltstein *D* 39 D4
Hiltula *FIN* 69 F2
Hilvarenbeek *NL* 36 C1
Hilversum *NL* 36 C1
Himanka *FIN* 64 C3
Hímaros *GR* 102 A1
Himma *EE* 79 E1
Himmaste *EE* 79 E1
Hinckley *GB* 9 D2
Hindelang *D* 43 E2
Hindhead *GB* 9 D3
Hinojares *E* 30 A2
Hinojosa de Duero *E* 25 D1
Hinojosa del Duque *E* 25 E4
Hintersee *D* 34 C2
Hinterstoder *A* 44 C1
Hintertux *A* 43 F2
Hinterweidenthal *D* 13 F3
Híos *GR* 107 D2
Híos (Nissí) *GR* 107 D2
Hirschau (Kreis Amberg-Sulzbach) *D* 39 E3
Hirschberg (Saale-Orla-Kreis) *D* 39 E2
Hirschegg *A* 43 E2
Hirsingue *F* 17 E1
Hirson *F* 12 B2
Hîrşova *RO* 117 E3
Hirtshals *DK* 70 B1
Hirvasvaara *FIN* 65 E1
Hirvensalmi *FIN* 69 E3
Hirvilahti *FIN* 69 E2
Hirwaun *GB* 8 B2
Hisarja *BG* 117 D4
Histria *RO* 117 E3
Hitchin *GB* 9 E2
Hitzacker *D* 33 F3
Hjartdal *N* 66 B2
Hjellestad *N* 66 A1
Hjelmeland *N* 66 A2
Hjo *S* 67 D3
Hjørring *DK* 70 B2
Hlebine *HR* 55 D1
Hlemoútsi *GR* 104 B3
Hlinsko *CZ* 41 D3
Hlobyne *UA* 115 F4
Hlubočky *CZ* 41 F3
Hluboká *CZ* 40 C4
Hluchiv *UA* 115 F4
Hlučín *CZ* 41 F2
Hłudno *PL* 99 D2
Hluk *CZ* 41 F3
Hlybokae *BY* 115 D3
Hobro *DK* 70 B2
Höchberg *D* 38 C3
Hochdorf *CH* 17 F1
Hochfelden *F* 13 E3
Hochosterwitz *A* 45 D3
Hochspeyer *D* 13 F3
Höchst i. Odenwald (Odenwaldkreis) *D* 37 F3
Höchstadt a. d. Aisch (Kreis Erlangen-Höchstadt) *D* 39 D3
Höchstädt a. d. Donau (Kreis Dillingen a. d. Donau) *D* 43 E1
Hockenheim *D* 13 F3
Hoddesdon *GB* 9 E3
Hodenhagen *D* 33 E4
Hódmezővásárhely *H* 116 C2
Hodnanes *N* 66 A2
Hodnet *GB* 8 C1
Hodonín *CZ* 41 E4
Hodoš *SLO* 54 C1
Hodovo *BIH* 58 B2
Hoedekenskerke *NL* 36 B2
Hoek van Holland *NL* 36 B1
Hoemsbu *N* 62 B4
Hof *D* 39 E2
Hofgeismar *D* 38 C1
Hofheim *D* 39 D3
Hofles *N* 63 D2
Höfn *IS* 62 B2
Hofolding *D* 43 F1
Hofors *S* 67 E1
Hofsós *IS* 62 A1
Höganäs *S* 71 D3
Høgebru *N* 66 B1
Höglekardalen *S* 63 E3
Högsäter *S* 66 C3
Högsby *S* 71 E2
Hohenau *A* 41 E4
Hohenberg *A* 45 E1
Hohenems *A* 43 D2
Hohengandern *D* 38 C1
Hohenlimburg *D* 37 E2
Hohenlinden *D* 43 F1
Hohenlockstedt *D* 33 E2
Hohenmölsen *D* 39 E1
Hohenpeißenberg *D* 43 F2
Hohenseeden *D* 34 A4
Hohenstein *D* 39 E2
Hohentauern *A* 45 D2
Hohenwestedt *D* 33 E2
Hóhlakas *GR* 111 F2
Højer *DK* 70 B4
Hokksund *N* 66 C2
Hokstad *N* 63 D3
Hol *N* 66 B1
Hola Prystan' *UA* 117 F2
Holbæk *DK* 70 C3
Holbeach *GB* 9 E1
Holdorf *D* 33 D4
Holešov *CZ* 41 F3
Holice *CZ* 41 D2
Höljäkkä *FIN* 69 F1
Höljes *S* 67 D1
Hollabrunn *A* 41 E4
Høllen *N* 66 A3
Hollenstedt (Kreis Harburg) *D* 33 E3
Hollfeld *D* 39 D3
Hollingsholm *N* 62 B3
Hollola *FIN* 69 E3
Hollum *NL* 32 B3
Hollywood *IRL* 3 D3
Holm *N* 63 D2
Holm *S* 68 A2
Hólmavik *IS* 62 A1
Holmen *N* 66 C1
Holmestrand *N* 66 C2
Holmön *S* 68 B1
Holmsund *S* 68 B1
Holstebro *DK* 70 B2
Holsted *DK* 70 B3
Holstre *EE* 78 C1
Holsworthy *GB* 8 B3
Holt *GB* 9 F1
Holvandi *EE* 79 E1
Holwerd *NL* 32 B3
Holy Cross *IRL* 2 C3
Holyhead / Caergybi *GB* 3 E3
Holywell / Treffynnon *GB* 8 C1
Holywood *GB* 3 E1
Holzappel *D* 13 F1
Holzgau *A* 43 E2
Holzkirchen (Kreis Miesbach) *D* 43 F1
Holzminden *D* 38 C1
Homberg (Efze) (Schwalm-Eder-Kreis) *D* 38 C2
Homberg (Niederrhein) (Kreis Duisburg) *D* 37 D1
Homberg (Ohm) (Vogelsbergkreis) *D* 13 F1
Homburg *D* 13 E3
Homec *SLO* 54 B1
Homel' *BY* 115 E3
Hommelstø *N* 63 D1
Hommelvik *N* 63 D3
Hommersåk *N* 66 A2
Hondarribia / Fuenterrabía *E* 20 B2
Hondschoote *F* 12 A1
Hönebach *D* 38 C2
Hønefoss *N* 66 C2
Honfleur *F* 11 E3
Høng *DK* 70 C3
Hónikas *GR* 105 D3
Honiton *GB* 8 B4
Honkajoki *FIN* 68 C3
Honningsvåg *N* 61 E1
Honrubia *E* 26 B3
Honrubia de la Cuesta *E* 19 F4
Hontalbilla *E* 19 E4
Hontoria del Pinar *E* 19 F4
Hoogeveen *NL* 32 C4
Hoogezand Sappemeer *NL* 32 C3
Hoogstraten *B* 36 C2
Höör *S* 71 D3
Hoorn *NL* 32 B4
Hopfgarten *A* 44 B2
Hóra *GR* 107 F3
Hóra *GR* 108 A1
Hora Svatého Šebestiána *CZ* 40 B2
Horažďovice *CZ* 40 B3
Horb *D* 13 F4
Hörby *S* 71 D3
Horcajo de los Montes *E* 25 E3
Horcajo de Santiago *E* 26 A2
Horcajo Medianero *E* 25 E1
Horche *E* 26 A1
Horden *GB* 7 E3
Horeftó *GR* 101 F4
Hořejší Kunčice *CZ* 41 F2
Horezu *RO* 117 D3
Horgen *CH* 17 F1
Horgoš *SRB* 55 F1
Hořice *CZ* 41 D2
Horki *BY* 115 E3
Horley *GB* 9 E3
Horn *A* 41 D4
Horn *D* 37 F1
Horn *D* 17 F1
Horn *N* 63 D1
Hornachos *E* 25 D4
Hornachuelos *E* 29 E2
Hornberg *D* 13 F4
Hornburg (Kreis Wolfenbüttel) *D* 33 F4
Horncastle *GB* 9 E1
Horndal *S* 67 E2
Horneburg *D* 33 E3
Hörnefors *S* 68 B1
Horní Benešov *CZ* 41 F2
Horní Lideč *CZ* 41 F3
Horní Počernice *CZ* 40 C2
Horní Slavkov *CZ* 40 B3
Hornindal *N* 62 B4
Hørning *DK* 70 B3
Hornos *E* 26 A4
Hornoy *F* 12 A2
Hornsea *GB* 7 F4
Hörnum *D* 33 D1
Horodło *PL* 95 F3
Horodnja *UA* 115 E4
Horodok *UA* 117 D1
Horodyšče *UA* 117 F1
Hořovice *CZ* 40 C3
Horsens *DK* 70 B3
Horsham *GB* 9 E3
Hørsholm *DK* 70 C3
Horšovský Týn *CZ* 40 B3
Horst (Kreis Ludwigslust) *D* 33 F3
Horstmar *D* 37 E1
Horten *N* 66 C2
Hortezuela *E* 19 F4
Hortiátis *GR* 101 F2
Horyniec *PL* 99 F2
Hösbach *D* 38 C3
Hospental *CH* 17 F2
Hospital *IRL* 2 B4
Hospital de Órbigo *E* 19 D3
Hossa *FIN* 65 F2
Hossegor *F* 20 B2
Hostalric *E* 21 F4
Hostinné *CZ* 41 D2
Hoszów *PL* 99 E3
Hotagen *S* 63 E3
Hoting *S* 68 A1
Hotton *B* 13 D2
Houdain *F* 12 A1
Houdan *F* 11 F4
Houeillès *F* 20 C1
Houffalize *B* 13 D2
Houghton-le-Spring *GB* 7 E3
Houlgate *F* 11 E3
Houmnikó *GR* 102 A2
Hoúni *GR* 104 C1
Hourtin *F* 14 C4
Houtskär / Houtskari *FIN* 68 C4
Hov *DK* 70 B3
Hovden *N* 66 A2
Hove *GB* 9 E4
Hovet *N* 66 B1
Hovmantorp *S* 71 E2
Høvringen *N* 62 C4
Howden *GB* 7 F4
Howth / Binn Éadair *IRL* 3 D3
Höxter *D* 38 C1
Hoya *D* 33 E4
Høyanger *N* 62 A4
Hoyerswerda *D* 40 C1
Hoylake *GB* 7 D4
Høylandet *N* 63 D2
Hoym *D* 39 D1
Hoyos *E* 24 C2
Hozoviótissa *GR* 110 C1
Hradec Králové *CZ* 41 D2
Hrádek (Znojmo) *CZ* 41 E4
Hrádek nad Nisou *CZ* 40 C1
Hrafnagil *IS* 62 B1
Hranice *CZ* 41 F3
Hranice (Karlovarský kraj) *CZ* 40 A2
Hrasnica *BIH* 55 E4
Hrastnik *SLO* 54 B2
Hrastovlje *SLO* 54 A3
Hrebenne *PL* 99 F1
Hřensko *CZ* 40 C2
Hríssafa *GR* 108 B1
Hrissí (Nissí) *GR* 110 C4
Hrissí Aktí *GR* 102 C2
Hrissí Amoúdia *F* 102 C2
Hrissó *GR* 102 A2
Hrissoúpoli *GR* 102 C2
Hrissovítsi *GR* 105 D4
Hristianí *GR* 104 C4
Hristianí (Nissí) *GR* 109 F2
Hristós *GR* 107 D4
Hrodna *BY* 114 C3
Hrómio *GR* 101 E3
Hronov *CZ* 41 D2

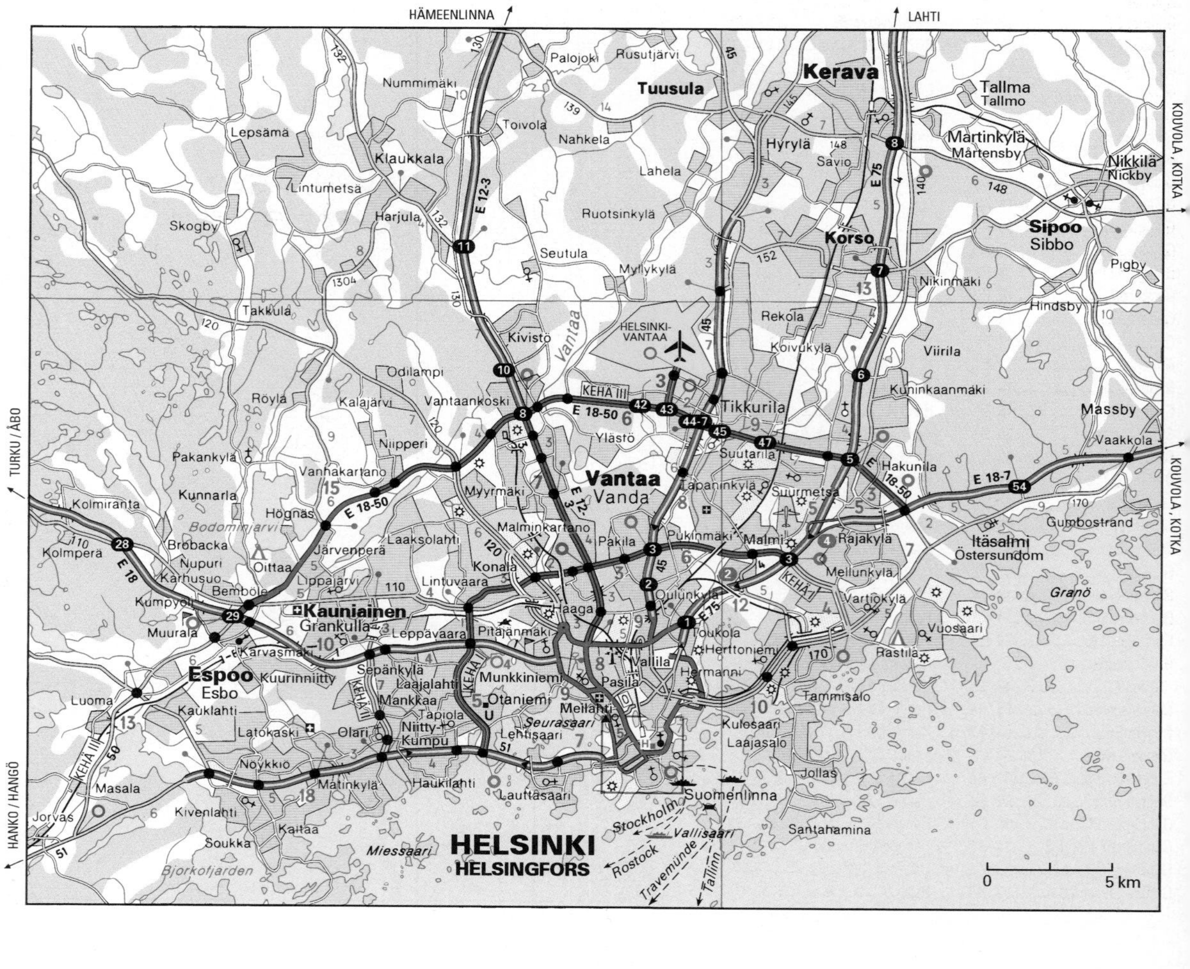

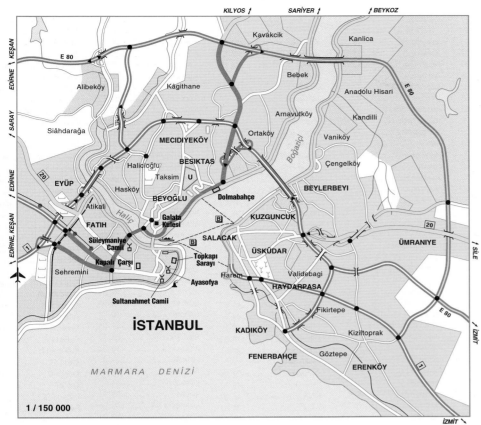

İSTANBUL
1 / 150 000

Hrtkovci SRB.........55 F2
Hrubieszów PL........95 F3
Hrušovany nad
  Jevišovkou CZ......41 E4
Hrvatska Dubica HR...55 D2
Hrvatska Kostajnica HR...54 C3
Hückeswagen D........37 E2
Hucknall GB..........9 D1
Hucqueliers F........12 A1
Huddersfield GB......7 E4
Hude D...............33 D3
Hudiksvall S.........68 A3
Huedin RO...........117 D2
Huélago E............30 A3
Huélamo E............26 B2
Huelgas (Real Monasterio de
  las) E.............19 F3
Huelgoat F...........10 B4
Huelma E.............29 F2
Huelva E.............28 C2
Huércal Overa E......30 B3
Huérguina E..........26 C2
Huerta de
  Valdecarábanos E...26 A2
Huerta del Rey E.....19 F4
Huertahernando E.....26 B1
Huerto E.............20 C4
Huesa E..............30 A2
Huesca E.............20 C4
Huéscar E............30 A2
Huete E..............26 A2
Huétor Santillán E...29 F3
Huétor Tájar E.......29 F3
Hüfingen D...........13 F4
Huftarøy N...........66 A1
Huittinen FIN........68 C3
Huizen NL............32 B4
Hulín CZ.............41 F3
Hulja EE.............73 D2
Hullo EE.............75 D1
Hulst NL.............36 B2
Hultsfred S..........67 E4
Humac BIH............58 A2
Humada E.............19 E3
Humanes E............26 A1
Humenné SK..........116 C1
Hummuli EE...........78 C1
Humpolec CZ..........41 D3
Humppila FIN.........69 D3
Hundested DK.........70 C3
Hundorp N............62 C4
Hunedoara RO........117 D3
Hünfeld D............38 C2
Hungerford GB........9 D3
Hunnebostrand S......66 C3
Hunspach F...........13 F3
Hunstanton GB........9 F1
Huntingdon GB........9 D2
Huntly GB............5 D3
Hurdal N.............66 C1
Huriel F.............16 A2
Hurskaala FIN........69 E2
Hürth D..............13 E1
Hurup DK.............70 B2
Húsafell IS..........62 A1
Husavik N............66 A1
Husbands Bosworth GB...9 D2
Hushinish GB.........4 A3
Huşi RO.............117 E2
Huskvarna S..........67 D4
Husnes N.............66 A2
Hustopeče CZ.........41 E4
Husum S..............68 B2
Husum (Kreis
  Nordfriesland) D...33 E2
Hutovo BIH...........58 A3
Hüttenberg A.........45 D2
Hüttschlag A.........44 C2
Huttula FIN..........69 D2
Huttwil CH...........17 E1

Huy B...............12 C1
Hvalba (Færøerne) DK..62 A3
Hvalpsund DK.........70 B2
Hvalvík (Færøerne) DK..62 A3
Hvammstangi IS.......62 A1
Hvar HR..............58 A4
Hvar (Otok) HR.......58 A4
Hveragerdi IS........62 A2
Hvidbjerg DK.........70 B2
Hvide Sande DK.......70 A3
Hvittingfoss N.......66 C2
Hvitträsk FIN........69 D4
Hvolsvöllur IS.......62 A2
Hüüru EE.............72 B2
Härjanurme EE........73 D3
Härma EE.............72 B2
Häädemeeste EE.......75 E3
Hyaler N.............66 C3
Hyde GB..............7 E4
Hyen N...............62 A4
Hyères F.............22 C2
Hyltebruk S..........71 D2
Hyrynsalmi FIN.......65 E3
Hythe GB.............9 F3
Hyvinkää FIN.........69 D4
Hyypiö FIN...........65 D1
Hyżne PL.............99 D2

I

Ía GR..............109 F2
Iaşi RO............117 E2
Íasmos GR..........102 C1
Ibbenbüren D........33 D4
Ibestad N...........60 B3

Ibi E...............27 D4
Ibiza / Eivissa E...31 D4
Ibutoniai LT........81 E3
Ičnja UA...........115 F4
Idanha-a-Nova P.....24 C2
Idar-Oberstein D....13 E2
Idoméni GR.........101 F1
Iđoš SRB............56 C1
Ídra GR............105 E4
Ídra (Nissí) GR....105 E4
Idre S..............63 D4
Idrija SLO..........54 A2
Idro I..............43 E4
Idstein D...........13 F2
Idzików PL..........96 C2
Iecava LV...........81 F1
Iegrivas LV.........82 C1
Ieleja LV...........77 D3
Ieper B.............12 A1
Ierápetra GR.......110 C4
Ieriki LV...........78 B3
Ierissós GR........102 A3
Ieropigí GR........100 C2
Ifestía GR.........102 C1
Ifjord N............61 E1
Ifta D..............38 C2
Ig SLO..............54 A2
Iga vas SLO.........54 A2
Igalo MNE...........58 B3
Igavere EE..........73 E3
Iggesund S..........67 F1
Iglesias I..........50 A4
Igliauka LT.........85 E2
Igliškeliai LT......85 E2
Igls A..............43 F2
Ignacava LT.........85 E2
Ignalina LT.........87 D1
Ignase EE...........79 E1

Ignāti LV...........80 B1
Igoumenitsa GR.....100 B4
Igrane HR...........58 A3
Igualada E..........21 E4
Ihamaru EE..........79 E1
Ihasalu EE..........72 B1
Ihtiman BG.........117 D4
Ii FIN..............65 D2
Iide EE.............74 B3
Iira EE.............72 B2
Iisaku EE...........73 E2
Iisalmi FIN.........69 E1
Iisvesi FIN.........69 E2
IJmuiden NL.........32 A4
IJsselmuiden NL.....32 B4
IJzendijke NL.......36 B2
Ikaalinen FIN.......68 C3
Ikaría (Nissí) GR..107 D4
Ikast DK............70 B3
Ikla EE.............77 F1
Ikšķile LV..........77 F3
Ilandža SRB.........57 D2
Ilanz CH............43 D3
Iława PL............90 A2
Ilche E.............20 C4
Ilchester GB........8 C3
Ilčiukai LT.........82 C3
Île LV..............81 D1
Īles Sanatorija LV..81 D1
Ilfracombe GB.......8 B3
Ilgai LT............85 F3
Ilgakiemis LT.......85 E2
Ilgi LT.............80 B1
Ilgininkai LT.......85 D1
Ilguva LT...........85 D1
Ilía GR............105 E1
Ílida GR...........104 C3

Ilidža *BIH* ...55 E4
Ilijas *BIH* ...55 E4
Iliki *GR* ...105 E2
Iliókastro *GR* ...105 E4
Ilirska Bistrica *SLO* ...54 A2
Ilkeston *GB* ...9 D1
Ilkley *GB* ...7 E4
Illana *E* ...26 A2
Illano *E* ...18 C2
Illar *E* ...30 A3
Ille-sur-Têt *F* ...21 F3
Illertissen *F* ...43 E1
Illescas *E* ...25 F2
Illhaeusern *F* ...13 D4
Illi *EE* ...79 D1
Illičivs'k *UA* ...117 F2
Illiers-Combray *F* ...11 F4
Illingen *D* ...37 F3
Illmitz *A* ...45 F1
Illora *E* ...29 F3
Illueca *E* ...20 B4
Illuka *EE* ...73 F2
Ilmajoki *FIN* ...68 C2
Ilmatsalu *EE* ...79 D1
Ilmenau *D* ...39 D2
Ilminster *GB* ...8 C3
Ilok *HR* ...55 F2
Ilomantsi *FIN* ...69 E1
Ilovik (Otok) *HR* ...54 B4
Iłów *PL* ...94 B1
Iłowa *PL* ...90 B3
Iłowo-Osada *PL* ...90 B3
Ilsenburg *D* ...39 D1
Ilsfeld *D* ...38 C4
Ilūkste *LV* ...83 D2
Ilvese *EE* ...75 F3
Ilža *PL* ...94 C3
Ilze *LV* ...83 D2
Ilzenieki *LV* ...82 C1
Ilzeskalns
  (Ilžukolns) *LV* ...83 E1
Imastu *EE* ...73 D2
Imatra *FIN* ...69 F3
Imavere *EE* ...72 C3
Imbare *LT* ...80 B2
Imbradas *LT* ...83 D3
Imeros *GR* ...103 D2
Imielin *PL* ...97 F2
Imielno *PL* ...98 B1
Imitós *GR* ...105 F3
Immenstaad *D* ...43 D2
Immenstadt *D* ...43 E2
Immingham *GB* ...7 F4
Immingham Dock *GB* ...7 F4
Imola *I* ...47 C2
Imotski *HR* ...58 A2
Imperia *I* ...23 E1
Imphy *F* ...16 A2
Impruneta *I* ...47 D3
Imst *A* ...43 E2
Inari *FIN* ...65 F1
Inca *E* ...31 E3
Inchnadamph *GB* ...4 C2
Inchree *GB* ...4 B4
Inciems *LV* ...78 C3
Incisa in Val d'Arno *I* ...47 C3
Indal *S* ...68 A2
Indija *SRB* ...56 C2
Indra *LV* ...83 E2
Indrāni *LV* ...78 B3
Induli *LV* ...77 D3
Ineši *LV* ...78 C3
Infiesto *E* ...19 D2
Ingå / Inkoo *FIN* ...69 D4
Ingelmunster *B* ...12 B1
Ingleton *GB* ...7 E4
Ingliste *D* ...39 E4
Ingolstadt *D* ...39 E4
Ingrandes *F* ...15 D1
Ingwiller *F* ...13 D3
Inhulec' *UA* ...117 F1
Iniö *FIN* ...68 C4
Inió *GR* ...105 F3
Inoússes *GR* ...107 E2
Inoússes (Nissi) *GR* ...107 E2
Inowłódz *PL* ...94 B2
Inowrocław *PL* ...89 E3
Ins *CH* ...17 E2
Iñsko *PL* ...88 B2
Interlaken *CH* ...17 E2
Internātskola *LV* ...80 C1
Íntorsura
  Buzăului *RO* ...117 D1
Intsu *EE* ...78 C1
Inturke *LT* ...86 C1
Inverbervie *GB* ...5 D4
Inveraray *GB* ...6 C1
Invergarry *GB* ...4 C3
Invergordon *GB* ...4 C3
Inverkeithing *GB* ...7 D1
Invermoriston *GB* ...4 C4

Inverness *GB* ...4 C3
Inverurie *GB* ...5 D4
Inzell *D* ...44 B1
Ioánina (L.) *GR* ...100 C4
Ioánina *GR* ...100 C4
Íos *GR* ...109 F1
Íos (Nissi) *GR* ...109 F1
Ipáti *GR* ...105 D1
Ipéria *GR* ...101 E4
Iphofen *D* ...39 D3
Ipiki *LV* ...75 F3
Ipsala *TR* ...117 E4
Ipsilí Ráhi *GR* ...102 B1
Ípsos *GR* ...100 B4
Ipswich *GB* ...9 F2
Irákleia *GR* ...105 D1
Irákleia (Nissi) *GR* ...109 F1
Iráklio *GR* ...109 F4
Irdning *A* ...44 C2
Iréo *GR* ...105 D3
Iréo *GR* ...107 F3
Iréo (Akr.) *GR* ...105 E4
Íria *GR* ...105 E4
Irig *SRB* ...55 F2
Irixoa *E* ...18 B2
Irlava *LV* ...77 D3
Iron-Bridge *GB* ...8 C1
Irschenberg *D* ...43 F1
Irši *LV* ...82 C1
Irsina *I* ...49 E4
Iru *EE* ...72 B1
Irún *E* ...20 B2
Irurtzun *E* ...20 B3
Irvine *GB* ...6 C2
Irvinestown *GB* ...2 C1
Irxleben *D* ...34 A4
Is-sur-Tille *F* ...16 C1
Isaba/Izaba *E* ...20 B3
Isaccea *RO* ...117 E2
Ísafjörður *IS* ...62 A1
Isane *N* ...62 A4
Isbister *GB* ...5 F1
Iscar *E* ...19 E4
Ischgl *A* ...43 E3
Ischia *I* ...48 C4
Išdagai *LT* ...85 D2
Ise *N* ...66 C2
Iselle *I* ...17 F2
Iselsberg *A* ...44 B3
Iseo *I* ...43 E4
Iserlohn *D* ...37 E1
Isernia *I* ...48 C3
Isfjorden *N* ...62 B3
Isili *I* ...50 A4
Isla *E* ...19 F2
Isla Cristina *E* ...28 B2
Išlaužas *LT* ...85 E2
Isle of Whithorn *GB* ...3 F1
Isleornsay *GB* ...4 B4
Íslice (Ritausma) *LV* ...81 F2
Išmanai *LT* ...85 E2
Ismaning *D* ...43 F1
Isnäs *FIN* ...69 E4
Isny *D* ...43 E2
Iso-Evo *FIN* ...69 D3
Isojoki *FIN* ...68 C2
Isokylä *FIN* ...65 D1
Isokyrö *FIN* ...68 C1
Isola 2000 *F* ...23 D1
Isola del Gran Sasso
  d'Italia *I* ...48 B2
Isola del Liri *I* ...48 B3
Isola della Scala *I* ...47 D1
Isola di Capo Rizzuto *I* ...51 E3
Isona *E* ...21 D4
Isorella *I* ...46 C1
Ispica *I* ...53 E4
Issigeac *F* ...15 E4
Issoire *F* ...16 A3
Íssoma *GR* ...104 C3
Issoudun *F* ...15 F2
Issóva (M) *GR* ...104 C4
Issy-l'Évêque *F* ...16 B2
Ist (Otok) *HR* ...54 B4
Istalsna *LV* ...83 F1
Istán *E* ...29 E3
Istanbul *TR* ...117 F4
Istarske Toplice *HR* ...54 A3
Istebna *PL* ...97 F3
Istérnia *GR* ...106 C4
Istha *D* ...37 F1
Isthmía *GR* ...105 E3
Istibanja *MK* ...59 F3
Istiéa *GR* ...105 E1
Istok *SRB* ...59 D2
Istra *LV* ...83 F2
Istres *F* ...22 B2
Ístrios *GR* ...111 F2
Itä-Aure *FIN* ...69 D3
Itäsalmi /
  Östersundom *FIN* ...69 D4
Itéa *GR* ...101 D2
Itéa *GR* ...101 D3
Itéa (Fokida) *GR* ...105 D2
Itéa (Karditsa) *GR* ...105 E4
Itháki *GR* ...104 A2
Itháki (Nissi) *GR* ...104 A2
Ithómi *GR* ...104 C4
Íti *GR* ...105 D1
Itri *I* ...48 B3
Itti *GR* ...69 E3
Ittiri *I* ...50 A3
Itzehoe *D* ...33 F2
Ivacevičy *BY* ...115 D4
Ivajlovgrad *BG* ...117 E4

Ivalo *FIN* ...61 F3
Ivančice *CZ* ...41 E3
Ivančići *BIH* ...55 F4
Ivančna gorica *SLO* ...54 B2
Ívande *LV* ...76 B3
Ivanec *MK* ...54 C1
Ivanić Grad *HR* ...54 C2
Ivanjica *SRB* ...57 D4
Ivāneda *EE* ...72 C2
Ivano-Frankivs'k *UA* ...117 D1
Ivanska *HR* ...55 D2
Ívira *GR* ...102 A2
Ivrea *I* ...17 E3
Ivry-la-Bataille *F* ...11 F3
Iwaniska *PL* ...94 C3
Iwanowice
  Włościański *PL* ...98 B2
Iwierzyce *PL* ...99 D2
Iwonicz-Zdrój *PL* ...99 D3
Ixiá *GR* ...111 F2
Ixworth *GB* ...9 F2
Izbica (Lubelskie) *PL* ...95 E3
Izbica Kujawska *PL* ...93 F1
Izbicko *PL* ...97 E1
Izeda *P* ...18 C4
Izegem *B* ...12 B1
Iznernore *F* ...16 C3
Izlake *SLO* ...54 B2
Izmaïl *UA* ...117 E2
Izmit (Kocaeli) *TR* ...117 F4
Iznájar *E* ...29 F3
Iznalloz *E* ...29 F3
Iznik *TR* ...117 F4
Izola *SLO* ...54 A3
Izvalta (Izvolts) *LV* ...83 E2
Izvor (Jagodina) *SRB* ...57 E3
Izvor (Kičevo) *MK* ...59 E4
Izvor (Veles) *MK* ...59 F4
Izvor (Vranje) *SRB* ...57 D3

J

Jaagupi *EE* ...75 E3
Jaala *FIN* ...69 E3
Jaama *EE* ...73 F2
Jaamaküla *EE* ...75 F3
Jaanimõisa *EE* ...79 E1
Jabbeke *B* ...12 B1
Jablan Do *BIH* ...58 B3
Jablanac *HR* ...54 B3
Jablanica *BIH* ...55 E4
Jabłoń (Lubelskie) *PL* ...95 E2
Jablonec nad
  Nisou *CZ* ...40 C2
Jabłonka *PL* ...98 A3
Jabłonna
  (Mazowieckie) *PL* ...94 C1
Jabłonna Lacka *PL* ...95 D1
Jabłonna Pierwsza *PL* ...95 E3
Jablonné v
  Podještědí *CZ* ...40 C2
Jabłonowo
  Pomorskie *PL* ...89 F2
Jabłowo *PL* ...89 F2
Jablunkov *CZ* ...41 F2
Jabugo *E* ...24 C4
Jabuka *BIH* ...55 F4
Jabuka
  (Beograd) *SRB* ...57 D2
Jabuka
  (Prijepolje) *SRB* ...56 C4
Jabuka (Otok) *HR* ...58 A4
Jabukovac *HR* ...54 C2
Jabukovac *SRB* ...57 E2
Jaca *E* ...20 C3
Jáchymov *CZ* ...40 B2
Jadagoniai *LT* ...85 E1
Jäder *S* ...67 E2
Jaderberg *D* ...33 D3
Jadów *PL* ...94 C1
Jadranska
  Lešnica *SRB* ...55 F3
Jadraque *E* ...26 A1
Jaén *E* ...29 F2
Jägala *EE* ...72 C2
Jägala-Joa *EE* ...72 B1
Jagelonys *LT* ...85 F2
Jagodina *SRB* ...57 E3
Jagodnjak *HR* ...55 E2
Jagsthausen *D* ...38 C4
Jahotyn *UA* ...115 F4
Jajce *BIH* ...55 D3
Jakeliai *LT* ...87 D1
Jäkkvik *S* ...64 A2
Jakobstad /
  Pietarsaari *FIN* ...68 C1
Jakovlev Izvor *SRB* ...57 F4
Jaktorów *PL* ...94 B2
Jakubovik *SRB* ...57 F4
Jakuszyce *PL* ...92 B3
Jakutiškiai *LT* ...85 F1
Jalasjärvi *FIN* ...68 C2
Jälgimäe *EE* ...72 B2
Jaligny-sur-Besbre *F* ...16 B2
Jambol *BG* ...117 E4
Jämaja *EE* ...74 B3
Jämejala *EE* ...78 C1
Jamena *SRB* ...55 F2
Jämijärvi *FIN* ...68 C3
Jäminkipohja *FIN* ...69 D3

Jämjö *S* ...71 E3
Jämsä *FIN* ...69 D3
Jämsänkoski *FIN* ...69 D3
Janakkala *FIN* ...69 D3
Janapole *LV* ...80 C3
Janaučiai *LT* ...81 D2
Jančе *MK* ...59 E4
Jāneda *EE* ...72 C2
Janeikas *LV* ...81 F2
Janenai *LT* ...85 E3
Janikowo *PL* ...89 E3
Janionys *LT* ...87 D1
Janja *BIH* ...55 F3
Janjevo *SRB* ...59 E3
Janjina *HR* ...58 A3
Jankai *LT* ...85 D2
Jankūnai *LT* ...81 E2
Jänmuiža *LV* ...78 C3
Janopole *LV* ...83 E2
Janów (Podlaskie) *PL* ...91 E2
Janów (Śląskie) *PL* ...98 A1
Janów Lubelski *PL* ...95 D3
Janów Podlaski *PL* ...95 E1
Janowiec *PL* ...94 C3
Janowiec
  Wielkopolski *PL* ...89 D3
Janowskie (Lasy) *PL* ...99 D1
Jānuciems
  (Janovka) *LV* ...83 D3
Jānukalns *LV* ...82 C1
Janukiškiai *LT* ...85 D2
Jānupe *LV* ...81 F1
Janušava *LT* ...82 B3
Janville *F* ...12 A4
Janzé *F* ...11 D4
Jäppilä *FIN* ...69 E2
Jaraba *E* ...26 B1
Jaraczewo *PL* ...93 D2
Jarafuel *E* ...26 C3
Jaraicejo *E* ...25 D2
Jaraiz de la Vera *E* ...25 D2
Jarak *SRB* ...55 F2
Jarandilla de la Vera *E* ...25 E2
Järbo *S* ...67 E1
Jarcevo *RUS* ...115 E2
Jard-sur-Mer *F* ...14 C2
Jaren *N* ...66 C1
Jargeau *F* ...15 F1
Jarkovac *SRB* ...57 D2
Järlepa *EE* ...72 B2
Jarmen *D* ...34 B2
Jarmenovci *SRB* ...57 D3
Järna *S* ...67 F1
Järna *S* ...67 F3
Jarnages *F* ...15 F3
Jarny *F* ...13 D3
Jarocin
  (Wielkopolskie) *PL* ...93 E2
Jaroměř *CZ* ...41 D2
Jaroměřice nad
  Rokytnou *CZ* ...41 D3
Jaroslavl' *RUS* ...115 F1
Jarosław *PL* ...99 E2
Järpen *S* ...63 E3
Jarrow *GB* ...7 E3
Järsi *EE* ...72 B2
Järtsaare *EE* ...72 C3
Järva-Jaani *EE* ...72 C2
Järvakandi *EE* ...72 B3
Järva-Madise *EE* ...72 C2
Järve *EE* ...73 E2
Järvelä *EE* ...69 D3
Järveküla *EE* ...72 B2
Järvenpää *FIN* ...69 D3
Järvere *EE* ...79 E2
Järvsö *S* ...68 A2
Jaša Tomić *SRB* ...57 D2
Jasenak *HR* ...54 B3
Jasenica *BIH* ...54 C3
Jasenovac *HR* ...55 D2
Jasenovo
  (Užice) *SRB* ...56 C4
Jasenovo
  (Vršac) *SRB* ...57 D2
Jasień (Lubuskie) *PL* ...92 B2
Jasień
  (Pomorskie) *PL* ...89 E1
Jasienica (Śląskie) *PL* ...97 F2
Jasienica (Zachodniopomorskie)
  PL ...88 A2
Jasieniec *PL* ...94 C2
Jasika *SRB* ...57 E4
Jasikovo *SRB* ...57 E3
Jasionka *PL* ...99 D2
Jasionówka *PL* ...91 E2
Jašiūnai *LT* ...86 B3
Jaska *EE* ...72 C3
Jaśliai *LT* ...85 E1
Jasło *PL* ...98 C2
Jastarnia *PL* ...89 F1
Jastrebarsko *HR* ...54 C2
Jastrowie *PL* ...89 D2
Jastrząb *PL* ...94 C2
Jastrzębia
  (Mazowieckie) *PL* ...94 C2
Jastrzębia Góra *PL* ...89 E1
Jastrzębie-Zdrój *PL* ...97 F2
Jasvilonys *LT* ...82 A3
Jaświły *PL* ...91 E2

Jaunāmuiža
  (Kuldīgas) *LV* ...80 C1
Jaunanna *LV* ...79 E3
Jaunauce *LV* ...81 D2
Jaunciems *LV* ...77 D2
Jaunbērze *LV* ...81 E1
Jaunciems *LV* ...81 F2
Jaundanumārki *LV* ...79 D3
Jaundundaga *LV* ...76 C2
Jaungulbene *LV* ...79 D3
Jauniske *LT* ...81 D3
Jaunjelgava *LV* ...82 B1
Jaunkagi *LV* ...78 C2
Jaunkalsnava *LV* ...82 C1
Jaunkārkli *LV* ...82 B1
Jaunklidzis *LV* ...78 C2
Jaunlaicene *LV* ...79 D3
Jaunlazdona *LV* ...83 D1
Jaunlutrini
  (Jaunmuiža) *LV* ...76 C3
Jaunmārupe *LV* ...77 F3
Jaunmazsāvas *LV* ...79 D3
Jaunmekeli *LV* ...78 C3
Jaunodava *LT* ...80 C3
Jaunolaine *LV* ...81 F3
Jaunpagasts *LV* ...77 D3
Jaunpēternieki *LV* ...81 F1
Jaunpiebalga *LV* ...79 D3
Jaunpils *LV* ...81 D1
Jaunplamši *LV* ...81 D1
Jaunsaule *LV* ...81 F2
Jaunsilavas *LV* ...83 D2
Jaunsvirlauka *LV* ...81 F1
Jauntīli *LV* ...76 C2
Jaunvilāni *LV* ...83 E1
Jaunzemi
  (Alūksnes) *LV* ...79 D2
Jaunzemi
  (Daugavpils) *LV* ...83 E3
Jausa *EE* ...74 C2
Jausiers *F* ...23 D1
Jávea / Xàbia *E* ...27 D4
Jävenitz *D* ...34 A4
Jávorív *UA* ...116 C1
Javornik (Olomoucký
  kraj) *CZ* ...41 E2
Jävre *S* ...64 C3
Javron *F* ...11 E4
Jawor *PL* ...92 C3
Jaworki *PL* ...98 B3
Jaworzno (Śląskie) *PL* ...97 F2
Jaworzyna *PL* ...98 C3
Jaworzyna Śląska *PL* ...92 C3
Ječi *LV* ...80 B2
Jedburgh *GB* ...7 E2
Jedlicze *PL* ...99 D2
Jedlina-Zdrój *PL* ...96 C1
Jedlińsk *PL* ...94 C2
Jedlnia-Letnisko *PL* ...94 C2
Jędrychowo *PL* ...89 F2
Jędrychów *PL* ...92 B2
Jedwabne *PL* ...91 D2
Jedwabno *PL* ...90 C2
Jeesiö *FIN* ...65 D1
Jegun *F* ...21 D2
Jegunovce *MK* ...59 E3
Jēkabnieki *LV* ...81 E1
Jēkabpils *LV* ...82 C1
Jektevik *N* ...66 A2
Jektvik *N* ...60 A4
Jelah *BIH* ...55 E3
Jelašca *BIH* ...55 F4
Jelcz-Laskowice *PL* ...93 D3
Jeleń *PL* ...97 F2
Jelenia Góra *PL* ...92 B3
Jeleniewo *PL* ...91 E1
Jeleśnia *PL* ...98 A2
Jelgava *LV* ...81 E1
Jelgavkrasti *LV* ...77 F2
Jelling *DK* ...70 B3
Jel'n'a *RUS* ...115 F2
Jelsa *HR* ...58 A4
Jelsa *N* ...66 A2
Jelsi *I* ...49 D3
Jemielnica *PL* ...97 E1
Jemielno *PL* ...92 C2
Jemnice *CZ* ...41 D4
Jena *D* ...39 D2
Jenbach *D* ...43 F2
Jenči *LV* ...81 F1
Jēni *LV* ...76 B2
Jennersdorf *A* ...45 E2
Jeppo *FIN* ...68 C1
Jērčēni *LV* ...78 C2
Jerez de la Frontera *E* ...29 D3
Jerez de los
  Caballeros *E* ...24 C4
Jeri *LV* ...78 C1
Jérica *E* ...27 D2
Jerichow *D* ...34 A4
Jerjersika *LV* ...83 D2
Jerte *E* ...25 D2
Jerxheim *D* ...33 F4
Jerzmanowa *PL* ...92 C2
Jerzu *I* ...50 B4
Jesenice *SLO* ...54 A1
Jesenice
  (Rakovník) *CZ* ...40 B3
Jeseník *CZ* ...41 E2
Jesi *I* ...47 F3
Jesolo *I* ...48 A1
Jessen *D* ...39 E1
Jessheim *N* ...66 C2
Jeßnitz *D* ...39 E1

Jeti *EE* ...78 C1
Jetzelsdorf *A* ...41 E4
Jeumont *F* ...12 B2
Jevenstedt *D* ...33 E2
Jever *D* ...33 D3
Jevičko *CZ* ...41 E3
Jevíšovice *CZ* ...41 D4
Jevnaker *N* ...66 C2
Jezerane *HR* ...54 B3
Jezerce *SRB* ...59 E3
Ježevica *SRB* ...56 C3
Jezewo *PL* ...89 F2
Jeziorany *PL* ...90 B2
Jeziorsko *PL* ...93 F2
Jeziorzany *PL* ...95 D2
Jeżów *PL* ...94 B2
Jeżów Sudecki *PL* ...92 C3
Jeżowe *PL* ...99 D1
Jičín *CZ* ...41 D2
Jiestrakis *LT* ...85 E2
Jieznas *LT* ...85 E2
Jiezno Kolonijos *LT* ...85 F2
Jihlava *CZ* ...116 A1
Jihlava (Sídla) *CZ* ...41 D3
Jílemnice *CZ* ...41 D2
Jílové u Prahy *CZ* ...40 C3
Jimbolia *RO* ...116 C3
Jimena *E* ...29 F2
Jimena de la
  Frontera *E* ...29 D4
Jindřichovice *CZ* ...40 A2
Jindřichův Hradec *CZ* ...41 D4
Jirkov *CZ* ...40 B2
Joachimsthal *D* ...34 C3
Jockfall *S* ...64 C1
Jódar *E* ...30 A2
Jodłowa *PL* ...98 C2
Jodoigne *B* ...12 C2
Jõelähtme *EE* ...72 B1
Joensuu *FIN* ...69 F2
Jõepera *EE* ...79 E1
Jõesuu *EE* ...72 B3
Jõgela *EE* ...74 B3
Jõgeva *EE* ...73 D3
Jõgeveste *EE* ...79 D1
Jõgisoo (Harju) *EE* ...72 B2
Jõgisoo (Järva) *EE* ...72 C2
Johanngeorgenstadt *D* ...39 E2
John o' Groats *GB* ...5 D2
Johnstone *GB* ...6 C1
Johovac *BIH* ...55 E3
Joigny *F* ...12 B4
Joinville *F* ...12 C4
Jokela *FIN* ...69 D4
Jokijärvi *FIN* ...65 E2
Jokikylä *FIN* ...65 E3
Jokioinen *FIN* ...69 D3
Jokkmokk *S* ...64 B1
Jokūbavas *LT* ...80 B2
Joloskylä *FIN* ...65 D2
Jomala *FIN* ...68 B4
Jomantai *LT* ...80 C2
Jönåker *S* ...67 E3
Jonava *LT* ...85 F1
Joniec *PL* ...90 C3
Joniškėlis *LT* ...81 F2
Joniškis (Šiauliu) *LT* ...81 E2
Joniškis (Utenos) *LT* ...86 C1
Jönköping *S* ...67 D4
Jonzac *F* ...15 D4
Jõõdre *EE* ...75 D2
Jõõpre *EE* ...72 A3
Joosu *EE* ...79 E1
Jootme *EE* ...72 C2
Jordanów *PL* ...98 B2
Jordbro *S* ...67 F3
Jormlien *S* ...63 E2
Jörn *S* ...64 B3
Jornini *LV* ...76 C2
Joroinen *FIN* ...69 E2
Jørpeland *N* ...66 A2
Jørstadmoen *N* ...66 C1
Jošanica *SRB* ...57 E3
Jošanička Banja *SRB* ...57 D4
Jošavka *BIH* ...55 D3
Josipdol *HR* ...54 B3
Josipovac *HR* ...55 E2
Josselin *F* ...10 C4
Josvainiai *LT* ...85 E1
Jouarre *F* ...12 B3
Joué-lès-Tours *F* ...15 E1
Jõuga *EE* ...73 E2
Jougne *F* ...17 D2
Joukokylä *FIN* ...65 E3
Joutsa *FIN* ...69 E3
Joutseno *FIN* ...69 F3
Joutsijärvi *FIN* ...65 E1
Jovaišai *LT* ...85 E3
Joyeuse *F* ...17 D4
Józefów (Lublin) *PL* ...95 D3
Józefów
  (Mazowieckie) *PL* ...94 C2
Józefów (Zamość) *PL* ...99 E1
Juan-les-Pins *F* ...23 D2
Juankoski *FIN* ...69 E1
Jucaičiai *LT* ...80 C3
Jüchen *D* ...13 D1
Juchnajcie *PL* ...91 D1
Juchnov *RUS* ...115 F2
Judaberg *N* ...66 A2
Jūdaži *LV* ...78 B3
Judenau *A* ...41 E4
Judenburg *A* ...45 D2

Judrenai
  (Klaipėdos) *LT* ...80 B3
Judrenai (Telšiu) *LT* ...80 C2
Jūdzkalni *LV* ...79 E2
Jugla *LV* ...77 F3
Jugon-les-Lacs *F* ...10 C4
Jugorje *SLO* ...54 B2
Juillac *F* ...15 F4
Juist *D* ...32 C3
Jukkasjärvi *S* ...60 C3
Juknaičiai
  (Klaipėdos) *LT* ...84 B1
Juknaičiai (Šiauliu) *LT* ...81 E2
Jukneliške *LT* ...85 D2
Jülich *D* ...13 D1
Jullouville *F* ...11 D3
Jumaliskylä *FIN* ...65 E3
Jumeaux *F* ...16 A4
Jumièges *F* ...11 E3
Jumilhac-le-Grand *F* ...15 E4
Jumilla *E* ...26 C4
Juminen *FIN* ...69 E1
Jumisko *FIN* ...65 E1
Jumprava *LV* ...82 B1
Jumurda *LV* ...78 C3
Junčionys *LT* ...85 F3
Juneda *E* ...21 D4
Juneli *LV* ...83 D3
Jungenai *LT* ...85 D3
Junik *SRB* ...59 D2
Juniville *F* ...12 C3
Junosuando *S* ...64 C1
Junsele *S* ...68 A1
Juntusranta *FIN* ...65 F2
Juodaičiai *LT* ...85 D1
Juodbūdis *LT* ...85 E2
Juodeikiai
  (Klaipėdos) *LT* ...80 B2
Juodeikiai (Telšiu) *LT* ...80 B2
Juodupe *LT* ...82 C2
Juodupenai *LT* ...80 C2
Juodžiai *LT* ...86 B2
Juoksenki *FIN* ...64 C1
Juorkuna *FIN* ...65 E2
Juostaviečiai *LT* ...81 F2
Juostininkai *LT* ...82 B3
Juozapavas *LT* ...85 E3
Juozapavičiai *LT* ...85 E3
Jupatowka *LV* ...83 E1
Jurata *PL* ...89 F1
Jurbarkas *LT* ...85 D1
Jurdaičiai *LT* ...81 E2
Jūre *LT* ...85 E2
Jurgi *LV* ...81 D1
Jurgionys *LT* ...85 E3
Jūri *EE* ...72 B2
Jūrkalne *LV* ...76 B3
Jurkšai I *LT* ...85 D2
Jūrmala *LV* ...77 E3
Jūrmalciems *LV* ...80 A2
Jurmu *FIN* ...65 E2
Juromenha *P* ...24 C3
Jurva *FIN* ...68 C2
Jusevičiai *LT* ...85 D3
Juškonys *LT* ...85 F3
Jussey *F* ...17 D1
Justel *E* ...18 C3
Jüterbog *D* ...34 B4
Jutkonys *LT* ...85 F3
Jutrosin *PL* ...93 D2
Juuka *FIN* ...69 F1
Juuma *FIN* ...65 F1
Juupajoki *FIN* ...69 D3
Juuru *EE* ...72 B2
Juva *FIN* ...69 E2
Juva (Åland) *FIN* ...68 C4
Juvigny-le-Tertre *F* ...11 D4
Juvigny-sous-
  Andaine *F* ...11 D4
Juvola *FIN* ...69 E2
Juzennecourt *F* ...12 C4
Jūžintai *LT* ...82 C2
Jyderup *DK* ...70 C3
Jyrkkä *FIN* ...69 E1
Jyväskylä *FIN* ...69 D2

K

K. Ahaïa *GR* ...104 C3
K. Alissós *GR* ...104 C3
K. Asséa *GR* ...105 D4
K. Doliána *GR* ...105 D4
K. Figália *GR* ...104 C4
K. Gadzéa *GR* ...105 E1
K. Kamíla *GR* ...102 A1
K. Klinés *GR* ...101 D2
K. Makrinoú *GR* ...104 C2
K. Meriá *GR* ...106 B4
K. Moussounitsa *GR* ...105 D2
K. Nevrokópi *GR* ...102 A1
K. Tithoréa *GR* ...105 D2
K. Vassiliki *GR* ...104 C2
K. Vérga *GR* ...108 A1
K. Vérmio *GR* ...101 E2
K. Zahloroú *GR* ...105 D3
Kaagjärve *EE* ...79 D1
Kaagvere *EE* ...79 E1
Kaakamo *FIN* ...65 D2
Kaalepi *EE* ...72 C2
Kaamanen *FIN* ...61 E2
Kaansoo *EE* ...72 B3
Kääpa (Jõgeva) *EE* ...73 E3

Kääpa (Võru) *EE* ...79 E2
Käärdi *EE* ...79 D1
Kaarepere *EE* ...73 D3
Kaaresuvanto *FIN* ...61 D3
Kaarina *FIN* ...68 C4
Kaarli *EE* ...78 C1
Kaarlijärve *EE* ...79 E1
Kaaruka *EE* ...72 C2
Kaasiku *EE* ...72 A2
Kaatsheuvel *NL* ...36 C1
Kaavere *EE* ...72 C3
Kaavi *FIN* ...69 E2
Kabala *EE* ...72 C3
Kābdalis *S* ...64 B2
Kabeliai (Alytaus) *LT* ...86 A3
Kabeliai
  (Panevežio) *LT* ...81 F3
Kabile *EE* ...75 E3
Kabli *EE* ...75 E3
Kabriste *EE* ...75 E3
Kać *SRB* ...55 F2
Kačanik *SRB* ...59 E3
Kačarevo *SRB* ...57 D2
Kačergine *LT* ...85 E2
Kachovka *UA* ...117 F1
Kačkol *SRB* ...59 D2
Kačkāres *LV* ...79 D3
Kaczorów *PL* ...92 C3
Kadaga *LV* ...77 F3
Kadaičiai *LT* ...80 B2
Kadaň *CZ* ...40 B2
Kadegi *LV* ...76 B3
Kadila *EE* ...73 D2
Kadjaste *EE* ...72 B3
Kadrifakovo *MK* ...59 F3
Kadrina *EE* ...73 D2
Kadziidło *PL* ...90 C3
Kaera *EE* ...73 D3
Kaerepere *EE* ...72 B2
Káfjord *N* ...61 E1
Käge *S* ...64 B3
Kahala (Harju) *EE* ...72 C1
Kahala (Järva) *EE* ...72 C3
Kaharlyk *UA* ...115 E4
Kahla (Jena) *D* ...39 D2
Kähri *EE* ...79 E1
Kaiáfas *GR* ...104 C4
Kaibala *LV* ...82 B1
Kaiguciems *LV* ...81 E1
Kaija *LV* ...78 C2
Kailbach *D* ...38 C4
Kaimini *LV* ...82 C1
Käina *EE* ...74 C2
Kainasto *FIN* ...68 C2
Kaindorf *A* ...45 E2
Kaipola *FIN* ...69 D3
Kairala *FIN* ...65 E1
Kairenai *LT* ...81 E3
Kaiserslautern *D* ...13 E3
Kaisheim *D* ...39 D4
Kaišiadorys *LT* ...85 F2
Kaisma *EE* ...72 B3
Kaiu *EE* ...72 B2
Kaive (Cēsu) *LV* ...78 C3
Kaive (Tukuma) *LV* ...77 D3
Kajaani *FIN* ...65 E3
Kakan (Otok) *HR* ...54 C4
Kakanj *BIH* ...55 E3
Kakavía *GR* ...100 B3
Käkciems *LV* ...78 A3
Kakenieki *LV* ...81 D1
Kakí Thálassa *GR* ...105 F3
Kakí Vígla *GR* ...105 F3
Kakléške *LV* ...80 A2
Kąkolewnica
  Wschodnia *PL* ...95 E2
Kakslauttanen *FIN* ...61 F3
Kalá Nerá *GR* ...105 E1
Kalá Nissiá *GR* ...105 E3
Kalajoki *FIN* ...65 D3
Kalak *N* ...61 E1
Kalakutiškė *LT* ...80 B3
Kalamáki *GR* ...101 F4
Kalamáki *GR* ...105 E1
Kalamáta *GR* ...108 A1
Kalambáka *GR* ...101 D4
Kalambáki *GR* ...102 B2
Kalámi *GR* ...107 F3
Kalámi *GR* ...109 D3
Kalamitsi *GR* ...102 B3
Kalamitsi *GR* ...104 C2
Kálamos (Nissi) *GR* ...104 A2
Kalamoti *GR* ...107 D2
Kalamotó *GR* ...102 A2
Kalana *EE* ...73 D3
Kalándra *GR* ...102 A3
Kalanti *FIN* ...68 C4
Kalapódi *GR* ...105 E2
Kalárne *S* ...68 A2
Kalávryta *GR* ...105 D3
Kalawa *PL* ...92 B1
Kal'azin *RUS* ...115 F1
Kalbe *D* ...34 A3
Kalce *SLO* ...54 A2
Kaldabruna *LV* ...83 D2
Kalēji *LV* ...83 D3
Kaléndzi *GR* ...100 C4
Kaléndzi *GR* ...104 C3
Kalérgo *GR* ...106 B3
Kalesija *BIH* ...55 F3
Kalesninkai
  (Alytaus) *LT* ...85 E3

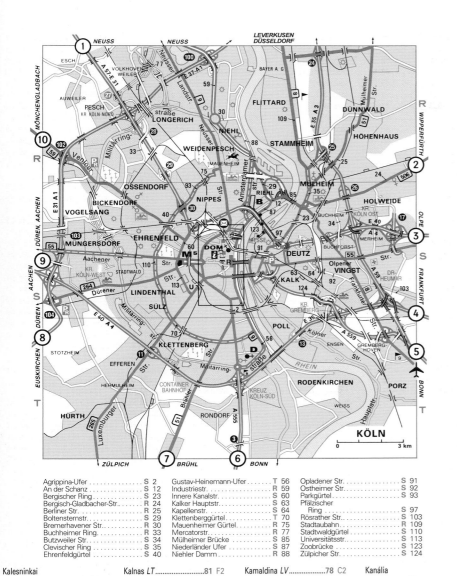

Agrippina-Ufer . . . . S 2
An der Schanz . . . . S 12
Bergischer Ring . . . . S 23
Bergisch-Gladbacher-Str. . . R 24
Berliner Str. . . . . R 25
Boltensternstr. . . . . S 29
Bremerhavener Str. . . . . R 30
Buchheimer Ring . . . . R 33
Butzweiler Str. . . . . S 34
Clevischer Ring . . . . S 35
Ehrenfeldgürtel . . . . S 40

Gustav-Heinemann-Ufer . . . T 56
Industriestr. . . . . R 59
Innere Kanalstr. . . . . S 60
Kalker Hauptstr. . . . . S 63
Kapellenstr. . . . . S 64
Klettenbergürtel . . . . T 70
Mauenheimer Gürtel . . . . . . R 75
Mercatorstr. . . . . R 77
Mülheimer Brücke . . . . S 85
Niederländer Ufer . . . . S 87
Niehler Damm . . . . R 88

Opladener Str. . . . . S 91
Ostheimer Str. . . . . S 92
Parkgürtel . . . . S 93
Pfälzischer Ring . . . . S 97
Rösrather Str. . . . . R 103
Stadtautobahn . . . . R 109
Stadtwaldgürtel . . . . S 110
Universitätsstr. . . . . S 113
Zoobrücke . . . . S 123
Zülpicher Str. . . . . S 124

Kalesninkai (Vilniaus) LT 86 B3
Kaléti LV 80 B1
Kaletnik PL 91 E1
Kalety PL 97 F1
Kalevai LT 81 E2
Kali HR 54 B4
Kalí Liménes GR 109 E4
Kaliáni GR 105 D3
Kaliekiai LT 82 C3
Kalifitos GR 102 B1
Kalimassiá GR 107 D2
Kálimnos GR 111 E1
Kálimnos (Nissí) GR 111 E1
Kalinas LT 86 B2
Kaliningrad RUS 114 B3
Kalinkavičy BY 115 E4
Kalinovnik BIH 55 F4
Kalinowo PL 91 D2
Kalipéfki GR 101 E3
Kaliráhi GR 101 D3
Kaliráhi GR 102 B3
Kalisz PL 93 E2
Kalisz Pomorski PL 88 C2
Kalita EE 75 F3
Kalithéa GR 108 A1
Kalithéa GR 111 F2
Kalithéa (Dráma) GR 102 B1
Kalithéa (Etolia-Akarnanía) GR 104 C2
Kalithéa (Halkidikí) GR 102 A3
Kalithéa (Ilia) GR 104 C4
Kalithiés GR 111 F2
Kalithiro GR 104 C1
Kaliváry GR 106 B3
Kalíves GR 109 D3
Kalívia GR 104 B1
Kalívia (Ahaïa) GR 105 D3
Kalívia (Attikí-Piréas) GR 105 F3
Kalívia (Korinthía) GR 105 D3
Kalívia Varikoú GR 101 F3
Kalix S 64 C2
Kaljord N 60 B3
Kalkar D 37 D1
Kalki LV 77 D2
Kalkis (Plostmuiža) LV 77 E3
Kalkkinen FIN 69 E3
Kall S 63 D3
Kallaste EE 73 E4
Kallavere EE 72 B1
Källby FIN 68 C1
Källby S 67 D3
Kalli EE 72 A3
Kallinge S 71 E3
Kallio FIN 69 D3
Kalliojoki FIN 65 F3
Kalliojärvi FIN 69 F2
Kallmünz D 39 E4
Kalmar S 71 E2
Kalme (Jõgeva) EE 72 C2
Kalme (Tartu) EE 79 D1
Kalme (Valga) EE 79 D2
Kalna SRB 57 F4
Kalnaberže LT 85 E1
Kalnadruvas LV 79 E2
Kalnagaliai LT 82 B2
Kalnāji LV 79 E3

Kalnas LT 81 F2
Kalncempji LV 79 E3
Kalnciems (Alūksnes) LV 79 E3
Kalnciems (Jelgavas) LV 81 E1
Kalnēji LV 76 C3
Kalnelis LT 81 E2
Kalneliškiai LT 81 F2
Kalnenai LT 85 F2
Kalnenieki LV 80 B1
Kalngale LV 77 F3
Kalni LV 80 C1
Kalni LV 85 D3
Kalnieši LV 83 E3
Kalnik HR 54 C1
Kalnini (Jelgavas) LV 81 E1
Kalnini (Rigas) LV 81 F1
Kalniškiai (Klaipedos) LT 80 B2
Kalniškiai (Ramučiai) LT 81 D3
Kalniškiai (Venta) LT 81 D2
Kalnrozes LV 81 E2
Kalnujai LT 85 D1
Kalnzaki LV 78 B2
Kaló Horió GR 110 C4
Kaló Neró GR 104 C4
Kalocsa H 116 B2
Kalogriá GR 104 B3
Kalohóri GR 101 D4
Kalókastro GR 102 A2
Kaloní GR 107 D1
Kaloní GR 105 E4
Kaloskopí GR 105 D1
Kalpáki GR 100 C4
Kals A 44 B2
Kalsdorf A 45 E2
Kaltanenai LT 86 C1
Kaltenkirchen D 33 E2
Kaltennordheim D 38 C2
Kaltezés GR 105 D4
Kaltinenai LT 80 C3
Kaluđerovo SRB 57 D2
Kaluga RUS 115 F2
Kalundborg DK 70 C3
Kalupe (Kolups) LV 83 D2
Kaluš UA 117 D1
Kałuszyn PL 95 D1
Kalvåg N 62 A4
Kalvarija LT 85 D3
Kalvehave DK 70 C4
Kalveliai LT 85 E3
Kälviä FIN 68 C1
Kalviai (Kauno) LT 85 F2
Kalviai (Vilniaus) LT 85 F3
Kalviškiai LT 81 D2
Kalvola FIN 69 D3
Kalvträsk S 64 B3
Kalwaria Zebrzydowska PL 98 A2
Kam'janec'-Podil's'kyj UA 117 D1
Kam''janka UA 117 F1
Kam''janka Dniprovs'ka UA 117 F3
Kamajai LT 82 C3

Kamaldina LV 78 C2
Kamara EE 75 F3
Kamáres GR 104 C2
Kamáres GR 106 C4
Kamáres (Iráklio) GR 109 E4
Kamáres (N. Sífnos) GR 109 E1
Kamari EE 73 D3
Kamári GR 109 D3
Kamariótissa GR 103 D3
Kambánis GR 101 F2
Kambiá GR 107 D2
Kambja EE 79 D1
Kambohóri GR 101 E2
Kámbos GR 104 C2
Kámbos (Haniá) GR 108 C3
Kámbos (Messinía) GR 108 A1
Kamen D 37 E1
Kaména Voúrla GR 105 E2
Kamenari MNE 58 B3
Kaméni (Nissí) GR 109 F2
Kamenica MK 59 F3
Kamenica SRB 56 C3
Kamenice nad Lipou CZ 41 D3
Kamensko (Daruvar) HR 55 D2
Kamensko (Split) HR 55 D4
Kamenz D 39 F1
Kamień (Chełm) PL 95 F3
Kamień (Lublin) PL 99 D1
Kamień (Podkarpackie) PL 99 D1
Kamień (Warmińsko-Mazurskie) PL 90 C2
Kamień Krajeński PL 89 D2
Kamień Pomorski PL 88 A2
Kamienica PL 98 B3
Kamieniec (Warmińsko-Mazurskie) PL 89 F2
Kamieniec (Wielkopolskie) PL 92 C2
Kamieniec Ząbkowicki PL 97 D1
Kamienna Góra PL 92 C3
Kamiennik PL 97 D1
Kamieńsk PL 94 A3
Kamieński (Zalew) PL 88 A1
Kamínia GR 103 D4
Kamínia GR 100 C4
Kamínia GR 104 C3
Kamionek Wielki PL 90 C1
Kamionka Wielka PL 98 C3
Kámiros GR 111 F2
Kámiros Kastélo GR 111 F2
Kamnik SLO 54 A2
Kamp Bornhofen D 13 E2
Kamp-Lintfort D 37 D1
Kampai II LT 81 E1
Kaplava LV 83 E3
Kampen NL 32 B4
Kampen (Sylt) D 33 D1
Kampinos PL 94 B1
Kampinoski Park Narodowy PL 94 B1
Kanakália LT 75 E3
Kanal SLO 54 A1
Kanála GR 106 B4
Kanaláki GR 104 A1

Kanália (Karditsa) GR 101 D4
Kanália (Magnissía) GR 101 F4
Kanatádika GR 105 E1
Kánava GR 109 E1
Kančiškiai LT 85 F1
Kańczuga PL 99 E2
Kándanos GR 108 B3
Kandava LV 77 D3
Kandel D 13 F3
Kandern D 17 E1
Kandersteg CH 17 E2
Kándia GR 105 E4
Kandíla GR 104 B2
Kandíla GR 105 D3
Kandra TR 117 F4
Kandrenai LT 82 B3
Kandrše SLO 54 B2
Kaneišiai LT 87 D1
Kanepi EE 79 E1
Kanestraum N 62 B3
Kanfanar HR 54 A3
Kangádio GR 104 C3
Kangasala FIN 69 D2
Kangaslampi FIN 69 E2
Kangasniemi FIN 69 E2
Kangosjärvi FIN 61 D3
Kangsti EE 79 D2
Kaniükai (Alytus) LT 85 F3
Kaniükai (Panočiai) LT 86 A3
Kaniükai (Skudutiškis) LT 86 C1
Kaniükai (Užpaliai) LT 82 C3
Kaniv UA 115 F4
Kaniwola PL 95 E2
Kanjiža SRB 55 F1
Kankaanpää FIN 68 C3
Kannenieki LV 77 D3
Kannonkoski FIN 69 D2
Kannus FIN 68 C1
Kannusjärvi FIN 69 E3
Kantaučiai LT 80 C2
Kanteniai LT 80 C3
Kantküla EE 73 D3
Kanturk / Ceann Toirc IRL 2 B4
Käo EE 74 C2
Kaona SRB 56 B4
Kaonik BIH 55 E4
Kaonik SRB 57 E4
Kap PL 91 D1
Kapandríti GR 105 F3
Kaparéli GR 105 E2
Kapariá GR 105 E4
Kapčiamiestis LT 85 E3
Kapellskär S 67 F2
Kapenai LT 81 D2
Kapfenberg A 45 D2
Kaplava LV 83 E3
Kaplice CZ 40 C4
Kapninos PL 94 B1
Kápp N 66 C1
Kappel D 13 E2
Kappeln D 33 E1
Kappl A 43 F1
Kapríje (Otok) HR 54 C4
Kaprun A 44 B2
Kapsáli GR 108 C2
Kápsas GR 105 D4

Kapsēde LV 80 A1
Kapsoúri GR 106 B3
Kapūne LV 79 E3
Kapuvár H 116 B2
Karabiga TR 117 E4
Karačev RUS 115 F3
Karaliai LT 85 D2
Karaliünai LT 85 F2
Karalkreslis LT 85 D2
Karan SRB 56 C4
Karasjok N 61 E2
Karasu TR 117 F4
Karats S 64 B1
Karavás S 108 B2
Käravete EE 72 C2
Karavómilos GR 105 D1
Karavónissia (Nissiá) GR 111 D2
Karavostássis GR 109 E1
Kárböle S 63 E4
Karcag H 116 C2
Karčiomka LT 83 D3
Karczew PL 94 C2
Karczmiska PL 95 D3
Karczmy PL 94 A2
Kardakáta GR 104 A2
Kardámena GR 111 E1
Kardámila GR 107 D2
Kardamíli GR 108 A1
Kärde EE 73 D3
Kardiá GR 101 F3
Karditsa GR 101 E4
Kárdla EE 74 C1
Kardžali BG 117 E4
Kareli LV 80 C1
Karesuando S 61 D3
Kärevere (Järva) EE 72 C3
Kärevere (Tartu) EE 73 D3
Karfás GR 107 D2
Kargowa PL 92 C2
Karhukangas FIN 65 D3
Karhula FIN 69 E4
Kariá GR 101 E3
Kariá GR 104 A1
Kariá (Árgolida) GR 105 D4
Kariá (Fthiótida) GR 105 D2
Kariani GR 102 B2
Kariés GR 102 B3
Kariés (Fthiótida) GR 105 D1
Kariés (Lakonía) GR 105 D4
Karigasniemi FIN 61 E2
Karijoki FIN 68 C2
Karilatsi EE 79 E1
Karinainen FIN 68 C4
Karinu EE 72 C2
Kariotiškes LT 86 B2
Kariótissa GR 101 E2
Karis / Karjaa FIN 69 D4
Káristos GR 106 B3
Karitena GR 104 C4
Karitsa EE 73 D2
Karja EE 74 C2
Karjaküla EE 72 A2
Karjalohja FIN 69 D4
Karjatnurme EE 78 C1
Karkaloú GR 104 C4
Karkažiške LT 86 C2
Kärki LV 78 C2
Karkinágri GR 107 D4
Karkkila FIN 69 D4
Karkku FIN 68 C3
Karkle LT 80 A3
Karklenai LT 80 C3
Kárkli LV 76 C3
Karklini LV 76 C3
Karkliniai LT 85 D3
Kärklumuiža LV 81 D1
Kärkna EE 73 D3
Kärkölä FIN 69 D3
Karkonosze PL 92 B3
Karksi EE 78 C1
Karksi-Nuia EE 78 C1
Karla EE 72 B2
Kärla EE 74 B3
Kárlas (L.) GR 101 F4
Karlevi EE 71 E3
Kärli LV 78 B3
Karlino PL 88 C1
Karlivka UA 115 F4
Kärlmuiža LV 76 C2
Karlobag HR 54 B4
Karlovac HR 54 B3
Karlovássi GR 107 E3
Karlovo BG 117 D4
Karlovy Vary CZ 40 B2
Kárłow PL 96 C1
Karlsborg S 67 D3
Karlsburg D 43 F1
Karlsfeld D 43 F1
Karlshamn S 71 E3
Karlshuld D 43 F1
Karlskoga S 67 E2
Karlskrona S 71 E3
Karlstad S 67 D2
Karlstadt D 38 C3
Karlštejn CZ 40 C3
Karlstift A 40 C4
Karmelava LT 85 F2
Kärneri LT 75 D2
Karnezéika GR 105 E4
Karnice PL 88 B1
Karniewo PL 90 C3
Karnobat BG 117 E4
Karolinka CZ 41 F3

Karow (Kreis Parchim) D 34 A2
Karpacz PL 92 C3
Kärpänkylä FIN 65 F2
Karpathos GR 111 E3
Kárpathos (Nissí) GR 111 E3
Karpeníssi GR 104 C1
Karperí GR 102 A1
Karperó GR 101 D3
Karpicko PL 92 C2
Kärsa EE 79 E1
Karsakai LT 85 F2
Karsakiškis LT 81 F3
Kärsämäki FIN 65 D3
Kärsava LV 83 F1
Karsko PL 88 B3
Karstädt (Kreis Prignitz) D 34 A3
Karste EE 79 D1
Karšteniai LT 80 C3
Kärstna EE 78 C1
Karstula FIN 69 E2
Kartal TR 117 F4
Kartena LT 80 B2
Kartéri GR 100 B4
Kartéri GR 105 D3
Karterós GR 109 C4
Kartonfabrika LV 79 D3
Karttula FIN 69 E2
Kartuzy PL 89 E1
Käru (Lääne-Viru) EE 73 D2
Käru (Rapla) EE 72 B3
Karula (Valga) EE 79 D2
Karula (Viljandi) EE 72 C3
Karungi S 64 C2
Karunki FIN 64 C2
Karup DK 70 B2
Karva FIN 79 E2
Karvala FIN 69 D1
Kärväskylä FIN 69 D1
Karvia FIN 68 C2
Karviná CZ 41 F2
Karvounári GR 100 C4
Karwia PL 89 E1
Kašalj SRB 57 D4
Kasčiukiškes LT 85 F2
Kasepere EE 72 A2
Kasepää (Jõgeva) EE 73 E3
Kasepää (Tartu) EE 73 E3
Kašin RUS 115 F1
Kašina HR 54 C2
Kašira RUS 115 F2
Kaskinen / Kaskö FIN 68 B2
Käsmu EE 72 C1
Kašonys LT 85 F2
Kašpakas GR 102 C4
Kašperské Hory CZ 40 B4
Kasprowy Wierch PL 98 B3
Kassándra GR 102 A3
Kassándria GR 102 A3
Kassari EE 74 C2
Kassel D 38 C1
Kassinurme EE 73 D3
Kássos (Nissí) GR 111 E3
Kassiópi GR 104 A1
Kastania GR 104 C1
Kastaniá GR 105 D3
Kastaniá (Imathía) GR 101 E3
Kastaniá (Trikala) GR 101 D4
Kastaniés GR 103 E1
Kastaniótissa GR 105 E1
Kaštel Stari HR 58 A4
Kaštel Žegarski HR 54 C4
Kastéla GR 105 F2
Kastélholm FIN 68 B4
Kastéli GR 109 F4
Kastellaun D 13 E2
Kasterlee B 36 C2
Kasti EE 72 B3
Kastíre LV 83 E2
Kastl (Kreis Amberg-Sulzbach) D 39 E4
Kastorf (Kreis Herzogtum Lauenburg) D 33 F2
Kastóri GR 105 D4
Kastoriá GR 101 D2
Kastós (Nissí) GR 104 B2
Kastráki GR 101 D4
Kastráki GR 104 B2
Kastráki GR 109 F1
Kastráki (Etolia-Akarnanía) GR 104 B2
Kastrí (Arkadía) GR 105 D4
Kastrí (Fthiótida) GR 104 B2
Kástro GR 104 B2
Kástro (Magnissía) GR 105 F1
Kástro (Viotía) GR 105 E2
Kastrossikiá GR 104 A1
Kaszaona EE 72 C3
Kaszyce Wielkie PL 93 D3
Katáfigio GR 101 E2
Katáfito GR 102 A1
Katáfourko GR 104 B1
Katahás GR 101 E3
Katákolo GR 104 B3
Katálako GR 102 C4
Katápola GR 110 C1
Katastári GR 104 A3
Katavía GR 111 F3
Kateliós GR 104 B3

Katerini GR 101 F3
Katharó GR 109 F4
Kathení GR 105 F2
Katići SRB 56 C4
Kätkäsuvanto FIN 61 D3
Katlanovo MK 59 E3
Katlanovska Banja MK 59 E3
Katlenburg-Lindau D 38 C1
Katleriai LT 82 B3
Káto Zákros GR 111 D4
Katohí GR 104 B2
Katoúna (Etolia-Akarnanía) GR 104 B1
Katoúna (Lefkáda) GR 104 A1
Katowice PL 97 F2
Katrineholm S 67 E3
Katwijk aan Zee NL 36 C1
Katy Rybackie PL 89 F1
Katyčiai LT 84 B2
Kaub D 13 E2
Kaufbeuren D 43 E2
Kauguri LV 78 C2
Kauhajärvi FIN 68 C2
Kauhajoki FIN 68 C2
Kauhava FIN 68 C2
Kaukonen FIN 65 D1
Kauksi EE 79 E1
Kauksnujai LT 81 E2
Kaulakiai LT 81 D3
Kaunas LT 85 E2
Kaunata LV 83 F2
Kaunatava LT 80 C2
Kaupanger N 66 B1
Kaupiškiai LT 84 C2
Kaušai LT 80 C3
Kaušenai LT 80 B2
Kaustinen FIN 68 C1
Kautokeino N 61 D2
Kauttua FIN 68 C3
Kavadarci MK 59 F4
Kavajë AL 116 C4
Kavála GR 102 B2
Kavalčiukai LT 85 E3
Kavarna BG 117 F3
Kavarskas LT 82 B3
Kavili GR 103 E1
Kavírio-Hlói GR 103 D3
Kävlinge S 71 D3
Kavoliai LT 82 C3
Kávos GR 100 B3
Kavoússi GR 110 C4
Kawęczyn PL 93 F2
Käylä FIN 65 E1
Kaysersberg F 13 E4
Kažani MK 59 E4
Kazanlák BG 117 E4
Kazanów PL 94 C3
Kazárma GR 108 A1
Kazas LT 79 E3
Kazdanga LV 80 B3
Kazimieravas LT 86 B2
Kazimierz Biskupi PL 93 E1
Kazimierz Dolny PL 95 D3
Kazimierza Wielka PL 98 B2
Kazincbarcika H 116 C2
Kazitiškis LT 83 D3
Kazliškelis LT 82 B2
Kazlu Rūda LT 85 E2
Kaźmierz PL 93 D1
Kažoki LV 81 F1
Kcynia PL 89 D3
Kdyně CZ 40 B3
Kéa GR 106 B4
Kéa (Nissí) GR 106 B4
Keadew IRL 2 C2
Keady GB 3 D2
Keava EE 72 B2
Keberkščiai LT 80 C3
Keblonys LT 82 B3
Kebnekaise S 60 C2
Kecskemét H 116 C2
Kedainiai LT 85 E1
Kedonys LT 85 F3
Kédros GR 104 C1
Kędzierzyn-Koźle PL 97 E2
Keel IRL 2 A2
Keeni EE 79 D1
Keerbergen B 12 C1
Kefalári GR 105 D4
Kefaloniá (Nissí) GR 104 A2
Kéfalos GR 111 E1
Kefalóvrisso GR 100 C3
Kefalóvrisso GR 101 E4
Kefalóvrisso (Etolia-Akarnanía) GR 104 B2
Kefalóvrisso (Messinía) GR 104 C4
Keflavík IS 62 A1
Kegai LT 80 C3
Kegums LV 82 B1
Kehl D 13 F4
Kehra EE 72 C2
Kehrókambos GR 102 C1
Kéhros GR 103 D1
Kehtna EE 72 B2
Keidžiai LT 86 B3
Keighley GB 7 D1
Keila EE 72 A2
Keila-Joa EE 72 A2
Keipene LV 78 B3
Keiši LV 83 D2
Keitele FIN 69 E1
Keith GB 5 D1
Kekava LV 81 F1
Kelankylä FIN 65 E2
Kelberg D 13 E2
Kelbra D 39 D1
Kelčyrë AL 100 B3
Kelefá GR 108 B1
Kelheim D 39 E4
Kellinghusen D 33 E2
Kellokoski FIN 69 D4
Kelme LT 81 D3
Kelso GB 7 E2
Kelujärvi FIN 65 E1
Kemberg D 39 E1
Kembs F 17 E1
Kemi FIN 65 D2
Kemijärvi FIN 65 E1
Keminmaa FIN 65 D2
Kemnath D 39 E3
Kempele FIN 65 D3
Kempen (Kreis Viersen) D 37 D2
Kempenich D 13 E1
Kempji LT 78 B3
Kempten D 43 E2
Kemsiai LT 81 E2
Kena LT 86 C2
Kendal GB 7 D3
Kendrikó GR 101 F1
Kenilworth GB 9 D2
Kéninkalns LV 79 E2
Kenmare / Neidín IRL 2 A4
Kennacraig GB 6 B1
Kenoúrgio GR 104 C2
Kentallen GB 4 B2
Kentraičiai LT 81 D2
Kenzingen D 13 F4
Kepaliai LT 81 E2
Kepenes LT 81 E2
Kepi i Gjuhezës AL 100 A2
Kępçce PL 89 D1
Kępno PL 93 E3
Keramía GR 107 E1
Keramídi GR 101 F4
Keramítsa GR 100 C4
Kéramos GR 107 D2
Keramotí GR 102 C2
Kerassiá GR 101 F4
Kerassiá GR 105 E1
Kerassiés GR 101 E2
Kerassohóri GR 104 C1
Kerassóna GR 104 B1
Keratéa GR 105 F3
Kerava FIN 69 D4
Kergu EE 72 B3
Kerí GR 104 B3
Kerimäki FIN 69 F2
Kerken D 37 D1
Kérkira GR 100 B4
Kérkira (Nissí) GR 100 B4
Kerkonkoski FIN 69 E2
Kerkrade NL 13 D1
Kernai LT 80 B2
Kernascléden F 10 B4
Kernave LT 86 B2
Kéros (Nissí) GR 109 F1
Kerpen (Erftkreis) D 13 E1
Kertemide DK 70 C3
Kértezi GR 104 C3
Kerzers CH 17 E2
Kesälahti FIN 69 F2
Keşan TR 117 E4
Kesh GB 2 C1
Kęsowo PL 89 E2
Kessariáni GR 105 F3
Kesteren LV 77 E3
Kestilä FIN 65 D3
Keswick GB 7 D3
Keszthely H 116 B2
Kętrzyn PL 90 C1
Kettering GB 9 E2
Kettletoft GB 5 D1
Kettwig D 37 E2
Ketūnai LT 80 C2
Keturiasdešimt Totoriu LT 86 B2
Keturkaimis LT 85 D2
Keturvalakiai LT 85 D2
Kęty PL 97 F2
Ketzin D 34 B4
Keuruu FIN 69 D2
Kevelaer D 37 D1
Kevele LT 81 D1
Kevo FIN 61 E2
Keynsham GB 8 C3
Kežmarok SK 116 C1
Keşai LT 80 C3
Keşčiai LT 84 C1
Kiani GR 103 E1
Kiáto GR 105 D3
Kiaukliai LT 86 B1
Kiaulakiai LT 80 A2
Kiaulupiai LT 85 D2
Kiaunoriai LT 81 D3
Kiberg N 61 F1
Kibučiai LT 81 E1
Kičevo MK 59 E4
Kidderminster GB 8 C2
Kidlington GB 9 D2
Kidsgrove GB 8 C1
Kiduliai LT 85 D1
Kidwelly / Cydweli GB 8 B2
Kiefersfelden D 44 B2
Kiegelceplis LV 81 D1
Kiegelnieki LV 80 C1
Kiekinkoski FIN 65 F3
Kiel D 33 F2
Kielce PL 94 B3
Kiełczygłów PL 93 F3

Kielno *PL* 89 E1
Kiemeliai *LT* 86 B2
Kiemeliškes *LT* 86 B2
Kiental *CH* 17 E2
Kierinki *FIN* 65 D1
Kiernozia *PL* 94 A1
Kietrz *PL* 97 E2
Kietz *D* 34 C3
Kifissiá *GR* 105 F3
Kifjord *N* 61 E1
Kihelkonna *EE* 74 B3
Kihlanki *FIN* 64 C1
Kihlepa *EE* 72 A3
Kihlevere *EE* 73 D2
Kihniö *FIN* 68 C2
Kiia *EE* 72 B2
Kiidjärve *EE* 79 E1
Kiihtelysvaara *FIN* 69 F2
Kiikala *FIN* 69 D4
Kiikka *FIN* 68 C3
Kiikla *EE* 73 E2
Kiikoinen *FIN* 68 C3
Kiili *EE* 72 B2
Kiiminki *FIN* 65 D3
Kiisa *EE* 72 B2
Kiiskilä *FIN* 69 D1
Kiistala *FIN* 61 E3
Kiiu *EE* 72 C1
Kiiu-Aabla *EE* 72 C1
Kije *PL* 98 B1
Kijevo *FIN* 55 D4
Kijevo *SRB* 59 D3
Kikinda *SRB* 56 C1
Kikół *PL* 89 F3
Kikuri *LV* 76 B3
Kil *S* 57 D2
Kíla *GR* 101 D3
Kiláda *GR* 101 E3
Kiláda *GR* 105 E4
Kilafors *S* 67 F1
Kilbaha *IRL* 2 A3
Kilbeggan *IRL* 2 C3
Kilbirnie *GB* 6 C1
Kilboghamn *N* 63 E1
Kilbotn *N* 60 B3
Kilchoan *GB* 4 B4
Kilcock *IRL* 3 D3
Kilcormac *IRL* 2 C3
Kilcreggan *GB* 6 C1
Kilcullen *IRL* 3 D3
Kildare / Cill Dara *IRL* 3 D3
Kildorrery *IRL* 2 B4
Kildu *EE* 72 C3
Kilelér *GR* 101 F4
Kilfenora *IRL* 2 B3
Kilgarvan *IRL* 2 B4
Kilija *UA* 117 E2
Kilingi-Nõmme *EE* 75 F3
Kilini *GR* 104 B3
Kilkee / Cill Chaoi *IRL* 2 B3
Kilkeel *GB* 3 E2
Kilkenny / Cill Chainnigh *IRL* 2 C3
Kilkhampton *GB* 8 B4
Kilkís *GR* 101 F2
Kilksama *FIN* 72 A3
Killadysert *IRL* 2 B3
Killaloe / Cill Dalua *IRL* 2 B3
Killarney / Cill Airne *IRL* 2 B4
Killashandra *IRL* 2 C3
Killenaule *IRL* 2 C4
Killimer *IRL* 2 B3
Killin *GB* 6 C1
Killinkoski *FIN* 69 D2
Killorglin / Cill Orglan *IRL* 2 A4
Killybegs / Na Cealla Beaga *IRL* 2 C2
Killyleagh *GB* 3 E1
Kilmaine *IRL* 2 B2
Kilmallock / Cill Mocheallóg *IRL* 2 B4
Kilmarnock *GB* 6 C2
Kilmartin *GB* 6 C1
Kilmore Quay *IRL* 3 D4
Kilmurry *IRL* 2 B3
Kilninver *GB* 6 C1
Kilnsea *GB* 7 F4
Kilpisjärvi *FIN* 60 C2
Kilrea *GB* 3 D1
Kilronan / Cill Rónáin *IRL* 2 B3
Kilrush / Cill Rois *IRL* 2 B3
Kilsyth *GB* 7 D1
Kiltealy *IRL* 3 D4
Kiltimagh *IRL* 2 B2
Kiltsi *EE* 73 D2
Kilupiai *LT* 85 E1
Kilwinning *GB* 6 C2
Kilyos *TR* 117 F4
Kimale *LV* 76 C3
Kimássi *GR* 105 F1
Kimbartiške *LT* 83 D3
Kiméria *GR* 102 C1
Kimi *GR* 105 F2
Kimísseos Theotókou *GR* 105 D3
Kimito / Kemiö *FIN* 68 C2
Kímolos *GR* 109 E1
Kímolos (Nissí) *GR* 109 E1
Kimry *RUS* 115 F1
Kimstad *S* 67 E3
Kinaros (Nissí) *GR* 111 D1
Kinbrace *GB* 4 C2
Kincardine *GB* 7 D1
Kindberg *A* 45 D1
Kindelbrück *D* 39 D1

Kinderiai *LT* 82 B3
Kinéta *GR* 105 E3
Kingisepp *RUS* 115 D1
King's Lynn *GB* 9 E1
Kingsbridge *GB* 8 B4
Kingscourt *IRL* 3 D2
Kingston-upon-Hull *GB* 7 F4
Kingston-upon-Thames *GB* 9 E3
Kingswear *GB* 8 B4
Kington *GB* 8 C2
Kingussie *GB* 4 C4
Kinguti *LV* 76 C3
Kinira *GR* 102 C2
Kinloch Rannoch *GB* 4 C4
Kinlochbervie *GB* 4 C2
Kinlochewe *GB* 4 B4
Kinna *S* 67 D4
Kinnasniemi *FIN* 69 F2
Kinnegad *IRL* 3 D2
Kinnitty *IRL* 2 C3
Kinnula *FIN* 69 D1
Kinross *GB* 7 D1
Kinsale / Cionn tSáile *IRL* 2 B4
Kinsarvik *N* 66 A1
Kintai *LT* 80 A3
Kintaus *FIN* 69 D2
Kintore *GB* 5 D4
Kinvarra *IRL* 2 B3
Kióni *GR* 104 A2
Kiparíssi *GR* 108 B1
Kiparissia *GR* 104 C4
Kipárissos *GR* 101 E4
Kipi *GR* 103 E2
Kípi *GR* 100 C4
Kipinä *FIN* 65 D2
Kipourió *GR* 101 D3
Kirá Panagiá (Nissí) *GR* 105 F1
Kirbla *EE* 72 A3
Kirchbach in Steiermark *A* 45 E2
Kirchberg *A* 44 B2
Kirchberg (Kreis Zwickauer Land) *D* 39 F2
Kirchberg (Hunsrück) (Rhein-Hunsrück-Kreis) *D* 13 E2
Kirchberg am Wagram *A* 41 D4
Kirchberg an der Pielach *A* 45 D1
Kirchdorf an der Krems *A* 44 C1
Kirchenlamitz *D* 39 E3
Kirchenthumbach *D* 39 E3
Kirchhain *D* 13 F1
Kirchheim (Kreis Hersfeld-Rotenburg) *D* 38 C2
Kirchheim a. Neckar *D* 38 C4
Kirchheimbolanden *D* 13 F3
Kirchhundem *D* 13 F1
Kirchlengern *D* 33 E4
Kirchmöser *D* 34 B4
Kirchschlag in der Bucklingen Welt *A* 45 E1
Kirdeikiai *LT* 86 C1
Kirepi *EE* 79 D1
Kiri *LV* 76 C2
Kiriaki *GR* 103 E1
Kiriáki *GR* 105 E2
Kirikuküla *EE* 78 C1
Kirimäe *EE* 75 E2
Kiriši *RUS* 115 E1
Kirkby Lonsdale *GB* 7 D3
Kirkby Stephen *GB* 7 D3
Kirkcaldy *GB* 7 D1
Kirkcolm *GB* 3 E1
Kirkcudbright *GB* 3 F1
Kirkenær *N* 66 B1
Kirkenes *N* 61 F2
Kirkham *GB* 7 D4
Kirki *GR* 103 D2
Kirkintilloch *GB* 6 C1
Kirkjubæjarklaustur *IS* 62 B2
Kirkjubøur (Færøerne) *DK* 62 A3
Kirkkonummi / Kyrkslätt *FIN* 69 D4
Kirklareli *TR* 117 E4
Kirkliai *LT* 80 C2
Kirkwall *GB* 5 D2
Kirmeliai *LT* 82 A3
Kirn *D* 13 E2
Kirna (Järva) *EE* 72 C3
Kirna (Lääne) *EE* 72 A2
Kirov *RUS* 115 F3
Kirovohrad *UA* 117 E1
Kirovsk *RUS* 115 D1
Kirpēni *LV* 81 E1
Kirriemuir *GB* 7 D1
Kirtorf *D* 13 F1
Kirumpäe *EE* 79 E2
Kiruna *S* 60 B3
Kiržač *RUS* 115 F1
Kisa *S* 67 E4
Kisajno (Jezioro) *PL* 90 C1
Kiseljak (Sarajevo) *BIH* 55 F3
Kiseljak (Tuzla) *BIH* 55 F3
Kiši *LV* 77 D3
Kisielice *PL* 89 E2
Kisieliškes *LT* 85 F2
Kiškenai *LT* 80 A3
Kisko *FIN* 69 D4
Kisköros *H* 116 B2
Kiskunfélegyháza *H* 116 C2

Kiskunhalas *H* 116 C2
Kíssamos (Kastéli) *GR* 108 C3
Kisslegg *D* 43 E2
Kissoú Kámbos *GR* 109 E4
Kistanje *HR* 54 C4
Kisújszállás *H* 116 C2
Kisvárda *H* 116 C2
Kiszkowo *PL* 89 D3
Kita *GR* 108 B2
Kitee *FIN* 69 F2
Kíthira *GR* 108 B2
Kíthira (Nissí) *GR* 108 B2
Kíthnos *GR* 106 B4
Kíthnos (Nissí) *GR* 106 B4
Kitka *FIN* 65 E1
Kitróni *GR* 105 E2
Kittilä *FIN* 61 E3
Kitzbühel *A* 44 B2
Kitzingen *D* 38 C3
Kiudalova *LV* 83 F2
Kiukainen *FIN* 69 D1
Kiuma *EE* 79 E1
Kiuruvesi *FIN* 69 E1
Kivéri *GR* 105 D4
Kivijärvi *FIN* 69 D2
Kivilahti *FIN* 69 F2
Kivitaipale *FIN* 69 E1
Kivi-Vigala *EE* 72 A3
Kivióli *EE* 73 E2
Kivotós *GR* 101 D3
Kiwity *PL* 90 B1
Kizário *GR* 103 D2
Kjellerup *DK* 70 B2
Kjerringøy *N* 60 B4
Kjerringvåg *N* 62 C3
Kjøllefjord *N* 61 E1
Kjøpsvik *N* 60 B3
Kjustendil *BG* 117 D4
Kladanj *BIH* 55 F3
Kladnica *SRB* 57 E2
Kladnice *SRB* 55 D4
Kladno *CZ* 40 C2
Kladovo *SRB* 57 E2
Klæbu *N* 60 B3
Klagenfurt *A* 45 D3
Klaipeda *LT* 80 A3
Klaksvik (Færøerne) *DK* 62 A3
Klampučiai *LT* 85 D2
Klana *HR* 54 A3
Klanac *HR* 54 B3
Klangiai *LT* 85 D1
Klanxbüll *D* 33 D1
Klapkalnciems *LV* 77 E3
Klášnice *BIH* 55 D3
Klässbol *S* 67 D2
Klášterec nad Ohří *CZ* 40 B2
Klatovy *CZ* 40 B3
Klaukkala *FIN* 69 D4
Klausučiai *LT* 85 D2
Klavas *LV* 78 B3
Klazienaveen *NL* 32 C4
Klebiškis *LT* 85 E2
Klecko *PL* 89 D3
Kleczew *PL* 93 E1
Kleinhaugsdorf *A* 41 E4
Klembów *PL* 94 C1
Klenovica *HR* 54 B3
Kleppe *N* 66 A2
Kleppestø *N* 66 A1
Kleszczele *PL* 91 E3
Kleszczewo *PL* 93 D1
Kleszczów *PL* 94 A3
Kleve *D* 37 D1
Klewki *PL* 90 B2
Kličevac *SRB* 57 D2
Klimavičy *BY* 115 E3
Klimontów (Świętokrzyskie) *PL* 98 C1
Klimpfjäll *S* 63 E2
Klin *RUS* 115 F1
Klina *HR* 59 D3
Klinča Selo *HR* 54 C2
Klincy *RUS* 115 F3
Klingenbach *A* 45 E1
Klingenthal *D* 39 F2
Klintehamn *S* 67 F4
Klippan *S* 71 D3
Klippen *S* 63 E1
Klis *HR* 58 A4
Klissoúra *GR* 101 D2
Klisura *SRB* 57 F4
Klitoría *GR* 105 D3
Klitten *D* 40 C1
Klixbüll *D* 33 D1
Kljajićevo *SRB* 55 F1
Ključ *BIH* 55 D3
Klobuck *PL* 93 F3
Kločiūnai *LT* 86 C2
Kłocko *PL* 93 F2
Kłodawa (Lubuskie) *PL* 88 B3
Kłodawa (Wielkopolskie) *PL* 93 F1
Kłodzko *PL* 96 C1
Kløfta *N* 66 C2
Klokkarvik *N* 66 A1
Klokočevac *SRB* 57 E2
Kloniniai Mijaugonys *LT* 85 F2
Klonowa *PL* 93 F3
Klooga *EE* 72 A2
Kloogaranna *EE* 72 A2
Kloštar Ivanić *HR* 54 C2

Kloštar Podravski *HR* 55 D1
Klösterle *A* 43 E3
Klosterneuburg *A* 41 E4
Klosters *CH* 43 E3
Kloten *CH* 17 F1
Kłótno Baruchowo *PL* 94 A1
Klötze *D* 34 A4
Klovainiai *LT* 81 E2
Klöverträsk *S* 64 C3
Klövsjö *S* 63 E4
Kluczbork *PL* 93 E3
Klucze *PL* 98 A2
Kluczewsko *PL* 94 B3
Kluki (Łodzkie) *PL* 94 A3
Kluki (Pomorskie) *PL* 89 E1
Klukowa Huta *PL* 89 E1
Klukowicze *PL* 91 E3
Klünas *LV* 81 E1
Klupe *BIH* 55 E3
Klütz *D* 33 F2
Klwów *PL* 94 B3
Klykoliai *LT* 81 D2
Knäred *S* 71 D2
Knaresborough *GB* 7 E4
Knarvik *N* 66 A1
Kneža *BG* 117 D3
Knežak *SLO* 54 A2
Kneževi Vinogradi *HR* 55 E1
Kneževo *HR* 55 E1
Kneževo / Skender Vakuf *BIH* 55 D3
Knežica *BIH* 55 D3
Knežina *BIH* 55 F4
Knić *SRB* 57 D3
Knidi *GR* 101 D3
Knighton / Trefyclawdd *GB* 8 C2
Knight's Town *IRL* 2 A4
Knin *HR* 54 C4
Knittelfeld *A* 45 D2
Knivsta *S* 67 D2
Knjaževac *SRB* 57 E3
Knokke-Heist *B* 36 B2
Knossós *GR* 109 F4
Knurów *PL* 97 F2
Knutsford *GB* 8 C1
Knyszyn *PL* 91 E2
Knyszyńska (Puszcza) *PL* 91 E2
Kobarid *SLO* 54 A2
Kobaš / Bosanski Kobaš *BIH* 55 E2
Kobela *EE* 79 D2
Kobeljaky *UA* 117 F1
København *DK* 70 C3
Kobern-Gondorf *D* 13 E2
Kobierzyce *PL* 93 D3
Kobiór *PL* 97 F2
Kobišnica *SRB* 57 F3
Koblenz *D* 13 E1
Kobruvere *EE* 72 C3
Kobryn *BY* 115 D4
Kobyla Góra *PL* 93 E3
Kobylanka *PL* 88 A2
Kobylin *PL* 93 D2
Kobylin-Borzymy *PL* 91 E3
Kobyłka *PL* 94 C1
Kobylnica (Pomorskie) *PL* 89 D1
Kočani *MK* 59 F3
Koceljevo *SRB* 56 C3
Kočeni *LT* 78 C2
Kočerin *BIH* 58 A2
Kočevje *SLO* 54 B2
Kochanowice *PL* 97 F1
Kochel a. See *D* 43 F2
Kochłowice *PL* 97 F2
Kock *PL* 95 D2
Koczała *PL* 89 D2
Kodeń *PL* 95 F2
Kodiksami *FIN* 68 C3
Kodila *EE* 72 B2
Kodisjoki *FIN* 68 C3
Kodrąb *PL* 94 A3
Kõdukÿla *EE* 79 D1
Koeru *EE* 72 C2
Kőflach *A* 45 D2
Køge *DK* 70 C3
Kohala *EE* 73 D2
Kohatu *EE* 72 B2
Kohila *EE* 72 B2
Kohtla *EE* 73 E2
Kohtla-Järve *EE* 73 E2
Kohtla-Nõmme *EE* 73 E2
Kõidama *EE* 72 C3
Koidu *EE* 78 C1
Koigi *EE* 72 C3
Koikkala *FIN* 69 E3
Koikküla *EE* 79 D2
Koikla *EE* 74 C2
Kõima *EE* 72 A3
Koimla *EE* 74 B3
Koirakoski *FIN* 69 E1
Koivu *FIN* 65 D2
Kojetín (Olomoucký kraj) *CZ* 41 E3
Kokála *GR* 108 B3
Kokári *GR* 107 F3
Kokari *LV* 83 E1
Kokemäki *FIN* 68 C3
Kokin Brod *SRB* 56 C4
Kókino Neró *GR* 101 F4
Kokkola / Karleby *FIN* 68 C1
Koknese *LV* 82 C1
Kokora *EE* 73 E3
Kokoti *GR* 105 D1

Koksijde-Bad *B* 12 A1
Koksvere *EE* 72 C3
Kola *BIH* 55 D3
Kołaczkowo *PL* 93 E1
Kołaczyce *PL* 98 C3
Kałaki Kościelne *PL* 91 D3
Kolari *FIN* 64 C1
Kolari *SRB* 57 D3
Kolásen *S* 63 D3
Kolašin *MNE* 58 C3
Kolbäck *S* 67 D2
Kołbacz *PL* 88 A2
Kolbermoor *D* 43 F1
Kolbergis *LV* 79 D2
Kołbiel *PL* 94 C1
Kolbudy *PL* 89 E1
Kolbuszowa *PL* 99 D2
Kolby Kås *DK* 70 C3
Kołczygłowy *PL* 89 D1
Kolding *DK* 70 B3
Kolga *EE* 72 C1
Kolga-Jaani *EE* 72 C3
Kolgakülä *EE* 72 C1
Kolho *FIN* 69 D2
Koli *FIN* 69 F1
Kolimvári *GR* 109 D3
Kolín *CZ* 41 D2
Kolín *CZ* 116 A1
Kolindrós *GR* 101 E3
Kolines *GR* 105 D4
Kóljala *EE* 74 C3
Kolka *LV* 77 D2
Kolkanlahti *FIN* 69 D2
Kolkja *EE* 73 E3
Kólleda *D* 39 D1
Kollino *EE* 79 D2
Köln *D* 13 E1
Kolnica *PL* 95 D2
Kolno (Podlaskie) *PL* 91 D2
Koło *PL* 93 F1
Kołobrzeg *PL* 88 B1
Koločep (Otok) *HR* 58 B3
Kołodzieje *PL* 89 F2
Kolomyja *UA* 117 D1
Kolonowskie *PL* 97 E1
Koloveč *CZ* 40 B3
Kolovrat *SRB* 56 C4
Kolpino *RUS* 115 D1
Kolsko *PL* 92 C2
Kolsva *S* 67 E2
Kolu *EE* 72 C3
Koluszki *PL* 94 A2
Koluvere *EE* 72 A2
Kolvereid *N* 63 D2
Komagfjord *N* 61 D1
Komańcza *PL* 99 D3
Kómanos *GR* 101 D3
Kómara *GR* 108 B1
Komarówka Podlaska *PL* 95 E2
Kombóti *GR* 104 B1
Kombuli *LV* 83 E2
Koméno *GR* 104 B1
Kómi *GR* 107 D3
Kómi *GR* 106 C4
Komília *GR* 104 A2
Komin *HR* 58 B2
Kómito *GR* 106 B3
Komiža *HR* 58 A3
Komló *H* 116 B2
Komniná *GR* 102 C1
Komniná *GR* 101 D3
Komnináde *GR* 100 C2
Komorane *SRB* 59 D3
Komornik *PL* 93 D1
Komorowo Żuławskie *PL* 90 A1
Komotiní *GR* 103 D1
Komprachcice *PL* 97 E1
Kömsi *EE* 75 D2
Konak *SRB* 57 D1
Konakovo *RUS* 115 F1
Konarzyce *PL* 91 D3
Konarzyny (Pomorskie) *PL* 89 D2
Končanica *HR* 55 D2
Kondiás *GR* 105 E1
Kondopoúli *GR* 103 D4
Kondovázena *GR* 104 C3
Kondratowice *PL* 93 D3
Koneck *PL* 89 F3
Kong *DK* 70 C4
Köngernheim *D* 13 F2
Konginkangas *FIN* 69 D2
Kongsberg *N* 66 B2
Kongsfjord *N* 61 F1
Kongsvinger *N* 66 C1
Konguta *EE* 72 C3
Konice *CZ* 41 E3
Koniecpol *PL* 94 A3
Königs Wusterhausen *D* 34 C4
Königsbrück *D* 39 F1
Königsbrunn *D* 43 E1
Königsee *D* 39 D2
Königsfeld i. Schwarzwald *D* 13 F4
Königslutter *D* 34 A4
Königssee *D* 44 B2
Königstein *D* 13 F2
Königstein *D* 40 B1
Königswiesen *A* 41 D4
Königswinter *D* 13 E1
Konin *PL* 93 F1
Koniskós *GR* 101 D4
Konistres *GR* 105 F2
Kónitsa *GR* 100 C3
Konjevrate *HR* 54 C4
Konjic *BIH* 58 B1
Konjsko *BIH* 58 B3
Konju *EE* 73 F2
Könnern *D* 39 D1
Konnevesi *FIN* 69 E2
Könnu (Harju) *EE* 72 C1
Könnu (Jõgeva) *EE* 73 E2
Könönpelto *FIN* 69 E2
Konopiska *PL* 97 F1
Konopnica *PL* 93 F3
Konotop (Lubuskie) *PL* 92 C2
Konotop *UA* 115 F2
Końskie *PL* 94 C2
Konsko *MK* 59 F4
Końskowola *PL* 95 D2
Konsmo *N* 66 A3
Konstancin-Jeziorna *PL* 94 C2
Konstantinova *LV* 83 F2
Konstantinovy Lázně *CZ* 40 B3
Konstantynów *PL* 95 E1
Konstantynów Łódzki *PL* 94 A2
Konstanz *D* 17 F1
Kontich *B* 12 C1
Kontiolahti *FIN* 69 F2
Kontiomäki *FIN* 65 E3
Konttajärvi *FIN* 65 D2
Konz *D* 13 D2
Köö *EE* 72 C2
Koonga *EE* 72 A3
Kooperators (Daugavpils) *LV* 83 D3
Kooperators (Ogres) *LV* 82 B1
Kooraste *EE* 79 D1
Koosa *EE* 73 E3
Kopań (Jezioro) *PL* 88 C1
Kopáni *GR* 100 C3
Kopanós *GR* 101 E2
Koparnes *N* 62 A4
Kópasker *IS* 61 D2
Köpenick *D* 34 C4
Kopervik *N* 66 A2
Kopidlno *CZ* 41 D2
Köping *S* 67 E2
Köpingsvik *S* 71 F2
Köpmanholmen *S* 68 B2
Koporiče *SRB* 59 E2
Koppang *N* 66 C1
Kopparberg *S* 67 E2
Kopperby *D* 33 E1
Koprivna *BIH* 55 E3
Koprivnica *BIH* 55 E3
Koprivnica *SRB* 57 F2
Koprzywnica *PL* 99 D1
Köpu *EE* 78 C1
Korbach *D* 37 F2
Korbevac *SRB* 59 F2
Korbielów *PL* 98 A3
Korbovo *SRB* 57 F2
Korçë *AL* 116 C4
Korčula *HR* 58 B3
Korčula (Otok) *HR* 58 A3
Korczew *PL* 95 E1
Korczyna *PL* 99 D2
Korenica *HR* 54 C3
Korfantów *PL* 97 D1
Kórfos *GR* 105 E3
Korgen *N* 63 E1
Korgene *LV* 78 A2
Körgessaare *EE* 74 B2
Koria *FIN* 69 E3
Korifássi *GR* 108 A1
Korikío Ándro *GR* 105 D2
Korinós *GR* 101 E3
Korínthio (Dióriga) *GR* 105 E3
Korissía *GR* 106 B4
Korita *BIH* 58 B2
Korita *HR* 58 A3
Korita *MNE* 59 D3
Korithi *GR* 104 A3
Koritnik *SRB* 57 D4
Körkküla *EE* 74 B3
Körkvere *EE* 74 B3
Körmend *H* 116 B2
Kornat (Otok) *HR* 54 C4
Korneti *LV* 117 E3
Korneuburg *A* 41 E4
Kórnik *PL* 93 D1
Kornofoléa *GR* 103 E1
Kornwestheim *D* 38 C4
Koróna *GR* 101 F2
Koróni *GR* 108 A1
Korónia *GR* 105 E2
Koronída *GR* 107 D2
Koronissía *GR* 104 B1
Kóronos *GR* 107 D2
Koronoúda *GR* 101 F2
Koronowo *PL* 89 E2

Koropí *GR* 105 F3
Korosten' *UA* 115 E4
Korostyšiv *UA* 115 E1
Korpilahti *FIN* 69 D2
Korpilombolo *S* 64 C1
Korpo / Korppoo *FIN* 68 C4
Korsberga *S* 71 E2
Korsholm / Mustasaari *FIN* 68 C2
Korsnäs *FIN* 68 C2
Korsør *DK* 70 C3
Korsun'-Ševčenkivs'kyj *UA* 117 F1
Korsze *PL* 90 C1
Kortesjärvi *FIN* 69 D2
Kórthio *GR* 106 C3
Kortrijk *B* 12 B1
Kortteenperä *FIN* 65 D2
Koruste *EE* 79 D1
Korvala *FIN* 65 D1
Korvaluoma *FIN* 68 C2
Kõrveküla *EE* 73 E3
Korycin *PL* 91 E2
Korytków Duży *PL* 99 E1
Kos *GR* 111 E1
Kos (Nissí) *GR* 111 E1
Kosančić *SRB* 57 E4
Kosanica *MNE* 58 C2
Kosarska Dubica / Bosanska Dubica *BIH* 55 D3
Koscian *PL* 93 D1
Kościelec *PL* 93 F2
Kościerzyna *PL* 89 E1
Kose (Harju) *EE* 72 C2
Kose (Ida-Viru) *EE* 73 E2
Kose (Võru) *EE* 79 E2
Kosel *MK* 59 E4
Kosewo *EE* 79 D1
Koserow *S* 34 C2
Kose-Uuemõisa *EE* 72 B2
Kosewo *PL* 95 D3
Košiai I *LT* 80 C3
Košice *SK* 116 C1
Kosina *PL* 99 E2
Kosjerić *SRB* 56 C3
Koška *HR* 55 E1
Koškele *S* 78 B2
Koskenkorva *FIN* 68 C2
Koskenpää *FIN* 69 D2
Koski (Hämeen lääni) *FIN* 69 D3
Koski (Turun ja Porin lääni) *FIN* 69 D4
Koskue *FIN* 68 C2
Kosmás *GR* 108 B1
Kósmio *GR* 103 D1
Kosova *GR* 79 E1
Kosovo Polje *SRB* 59 E2
Kosovska Kamenica *SRB* 59 E2
Kosovska Mitrovica *SRB* 59 D2
Kosów Lacki *PL* 91 D3
Kössen *A* 44 B2
Kósta *S* 105 E4
Kostanjevac *HR* 54 B2
Kostanjevica na K. *SLO* 54 B2
Kostelec nad Černými Lesy *CZ* 40 C3
Kostelec nad Orlicí *CZ* 41 D2
Kostenec *BG* 117 D3
Kostivere *EE* 72 B1
Kostolac *SRB* 57 D2
Kostopil' *UA* 115 D4
Kóstos *GR* 109 F1
Köstrimãe *EE* 79 E1
Kostrzyn (Lubuskie) *PL* 88 A3
Kostrzyn (Wielkopolskie) *PL* 93 D1
Kosturino *MK* 59 F4
Kosula *FIN* 69 E1
Koszalin *PL* 88 C1
Koszęcin *PL* 97 F1
Kőszeg *H* 116 B2
Koszyce *PL* 98 B2
Kotala (Häme) *FIN* 65 E1
Kotala (Lappi) *FIN* 65 E1
Kotan *FIN* 99 D3
Kótronas *GR* 108 B1
Kotel *BG* 117 E3
Koterka *PL* 95 F1
Koteļ *LV* 92 C2
Kotlin *PL* 93 E2
Kotor *MNE* 58 C3
Kotor Varoš *BIH* 55 D3
Kotoriba *HR* 54 C1
Kotorsko *BIH* 55 D3
Kotovs'k *UA* 117 E1
Kotraža *SRB* 57 D4
Kotronas *GR* 108 B1
Kotel *BG* 117 E3
Koufália *GR* 101 F2
Koufonissi *GR* 110 C4
Koufós *GR* 102 A3
Koukkala / Karleby *FIN* 68 C1
Koukounariés *GR* 105 F1
Kouméika *GR* 107 E3
Koúndouros *GR* 106 B4
Kounoupéli *GR* 104 B3

Koura *FIN* 68 C2
Koúrenda *GR* 100 C4
Kourkouli *GR* 105 F1
Kournás *GR* 109 D3
Kouroúta *GR* 104 B3
Koutselió *GR* 100 C4
Koutsó *GR* 102 C2
Koutsóhero *GR* 101 E4
Kouvola *FIN* 69 E3
Kovačica *SRB* 56 C2
Kovel' *UA* 115 C3
Kõveriku *EE* 73 E2
Kovero *FIN* 69 F2
Kovilj *SRB* 56 C2
Kovin *SRB* 57 D2
Kowal *PL* 94 A1
Kowala-Stępocina *PL* 94 C2
Kowale Oleckie *PL* 91 D1
Kowalewo Pomorskie *PL* 89 F3
Kowary *PL* 96 B1
Kowiesy *PL* 94 B2
Kõylió *FIN* 68 C3
Kozáni *GR* 101 D3
Kozarac *BIH* 55 D3
Kozarac *HR* 55 E2
Kozica *HR* 58 B2
Kozięgłowy *PL* 97 F1
Kozienice *PL* 94 C2
Kozienicka (Puszcza) *PL* 94 C2
Kozina *SLO* 54 A2
Kozjatyn *UA* 117 E1
Kozłówka *PL* 95 E2
Kozłowo *PL* 90 B2
Kozluk *BIH* 55 F3
Koźmin *PL* 93 E2
Koźminek *PL* 93 E2
Kozubszczyzna *PL* 95 D3
Kožuchów *PL* 92 B2
Kozy (Śląskie) *PL* 97 F2
Kraavi *EE* 79 E1
Krabi *EE* 79 E2
Krąg *PL* 89 D1
Kragenæs *DK* 70 C4
Kragerø *N* 66 B3
Kragujevac *SRB* 57 D3
Krajenka *PL* 89 D3
Krajišnik *SRB* 56 C2
Krajkovac *SRB* 57 E4
Krajnik Dolny *PL* 88 A3
Krakes *LT* 85 E1
Krakhella *N* 62 A4
Krakow *D* 34 A2
Kraków *PL* 98 B2
Krakūnai *LT* 86 C3
Kraljevica *HR* 54 B3
Kraljevo *SRB* 57 D4
Královec *CZ* 41 D2
Kralovice *CZ* 40 B2
Kralupy nad Vltavou *CZ* 40 C2
Kramarzyny *PL* 89 D1
Kramfors *S* 68 A2
Kramsk *PL* 93 F1
Kranenburg *D* 37 D1
Krani *MK* 59 E4
Kraniá (Grevená) *GR* 101 D3
Kraniá (Trikala) *GR* 101 D3
Kraniá Elassónas *GR* 101 E3
Kranichfeld *D* 39 D2
Kranidi *GR* 105 E4
Kranj *SLO* 54 A2
Kranjska Gora *SLO* 54 A1
Krápa *LV* 79 D3
Krape (Lobe) *LV* 82 B1
Krapina *HR* 54 C1
Krapinske Toplice *HR* 54 C1
Krapkowice *PL* 97 E1
Krašić *HR* 54 B2
Krasiczyn *PL* 99 E2
Krāslava *LV* 83 F2
Kräslavas Stacija *LV* 83 E3
Kraslice *CZ* 40 A2
Krásná Lípa *CZ* 40 C1
Krasne (Podkarpackie) *PL* 95 D3
Kraśnik *PL* 95 D3
Krasno Polje *HR* 54 B3
Krasnobród *PL* 99 F1
Krasnohrad *UA* 115 F2
Krasnoperekops'k *UA* 117 F2
Krasnopol *PL* 90 C1
Krasnosielc *PL* 90 C2
Krasnystaw *PL* 99 F1
Krasocin *PL* 94 B3
Krašiai *LT* 81 F2
Kraszewice *PL* 93 E2
Krátigos *GR* 107 F3
Kratiškiai *LT* 82 B2
Kratovo *MK* 59 F3
Kratovska Stena *SRB* 56 C4
Krauchenwies *D* 43 D1
Krauja (Hoftenberga) *LV* 83 D3
Kraujas *LV* 82 C2
Kraukli *LV* 79 D3
Krautheim *D* 38 C4
Kravaře (Moravskoslezský kraj) *CZ* 41 F2
Kravarsko *HR* 54 C2
Kražiai *LT* 81 D2

Krążkowy PL ...93 E3
Krefeld D ...37 D2
Krekenava LT ...81 F3
Krekštenai LT ...85 E3
Kremasti GR ...108 B1
Kremasti GR ...111 F2
Kremastón (Teh. L.) GR ...104 C1
Kremenčúk UA ...117 F2
Kremenec' UA ...117 E1
Kremenica MK ...59 F4
Kremmen D ...34 B3
Kremna SRB ...56 C4
Kremnica SK ...116 B1
Krems a. d. Donau A ...41 D4
Kremsmünster A ...44 C4
Krepoljin SRB ...57 E3
Krepštai LT ...80 C2
Kreševo BIH ...55 E4
Kreslynai LT ...85 F1
Krestcy RUS ...115 F4
Kréstena GR ...104 C4
Kretinga LT ...80 A2
Kretingale LT ...80 A2
Kretowiny PL ...90 B2
Kreuth D ...43 F2
Kreuzlingen CH ...17 F1
Kreuztal D ...13 F1
Kría Vríssi GR ...101 E2
Kria Vríssi GR ...105 F1
Kriaušiškiai LT ...81 F2
Krieglach A ...45 E1
Kriens CH ...17 F1
Krievgali LV ...81 F2
Krievupe LV ...77 F3
Kríkelo GR ...104 C1
Krikelos GR ...104 B1
Krikliniai LT ...81 F3
Krikštonys LT ...85 E3
Krimml A ...44 B2
Krimpen aan den IJssel NL ...36 C1
Krimūnas LV ...81 E1
Krinčinas LT ...81 F2
Krinídes GR ...102 B2
Kriokiškiai LT ...84 C1
Krionéri GR ...102 A2
Krionéri GR ...104 C2
Krionéri GR ...105 D3
Krionéri GR ...104 C4
Kriopigí GR ...102 A3
Krišjáni (Krišani) LV ...83 E1
Kriškalni LV ...82 C1
Kristalopigí GR ...101 D2
Kristdala S ...67 E4
Kristiansand N ...66 A3
Kristianstad S ...71 D3
Kristineberg S ...64 B3
Kristinehamn S ...67 D3
Kristinehov S ...71 D3
Kristinestad / Kristiinan- kaupunki FIN ...68 C2
Krithéa GR ...101 F2
Kríti (Nissí) GR ...109 F4
Kritinía GR ...111 F2
Kritsá GR ...110 C4
Kriúkai LT ...85 E1
Kriukai LT ...81 E2
Kriva Feja SRB ...57 F2
Kriva Palanka MK ...59 F3
Krivanda LV ...83 F1
Krivi LV ...78 B3
Kriviliai LT ...86 A3
Krivogaštani MK ...59 E4
Krivolak MK ...59 F4
Křížanov CZ ...41 D3
Križevci HR ...54 C2
Krk HR ...54 B3
Krk (Otok) HR ...54 B3
Krnjača SRB ...56 C2
Krnjak HR ...54 C3
Krnjeuša BIH ...54 C4
Krnjevo SRB ...57 D3
Krnov CZ ...41 F2
Krobia PL ...93 D2
Krobica PL ...92 B3
Kroczyce PL ...98 A1
Krokeés GR ...108 B1
Krokeide N ...66 A1
Krokek S ...67 E3
Krokialaukis LT ...85 E3
Krokílio GR ...104 C2
Krokom S ...63 E3
Krókos GR ...101 E3
Krokowa PL ...89 E1
Kroksjö S ...64 A3
Krokślys LT ...85 F3
Krolevec' UA ...115 F4
Królikowo PL ...89 E3
Kroměříž CZ ...41 F3
Kromlów PL ...98 A1
Kronach D ...39 D3
Kronauce LV ...81 E1
Kronoby / Kruunupyy FIN ...68 C1
Kronshagen D ...33 F2
Kronštadt RUS ...115 D1
Krootuse EE ...79 E1
Kröpelin D ...34 A2
Kroppenstedt D ...39 D1
Krościenko nad Dunajcem PL ...98 B3
Krośnice PL ...93 D2
Krośniewice PL ...94 A1

Krosno PL ...99 D2
Krosno Odrzańskie PL ...92 B2
Krote LV ...80 B1
Krotoszyn PL ...93 E2
Kroussónas GR ...109 E4
Krška vas SLO ...54 B2
Krško SLO ...54 B2
Krstac MNE ...58 B2
Krstinja HR ...54 C3
Kruiningen NL ...36 B2
Krujë AL ...116 C4
Kruki LV ...83 E2
Kruklanki PL ...91 D1
Krumbach (Schwaben) D ...43 E1
Krūmēni LV ...78 C3
Krummhörn D ...32 C3
Krumpendorf A ...45 D3
Krün D ...43 F2
Krundikūla EE ...75 E3
Kruonis LT ...85 F2
Krupá CZ ...40 B2
Krupa na Vrbasu BIH ...55 D3
Krupac BIH ...55 E4
Krupac SRB ...57 F4
Krupaja SRB ...57 E3
Krupanj SRB ...55 F3
Krupe PL ...95 E3
Krupi LV ...83 E1
Krupište MK ...59 F3
Krupka CZ ...40 B2
Kruså DK ...70 B4
Kruščica BIH ...55 E4
Kruševac SRB ...57 E4
Kruševica SRB ...57 D3
Kruševo MK ...59 E4
Krūškalne LV ...81 D1
Krustceles LV ...79 F3
Krustini LV ...78 B3
Krustkalni LV ...78 C3
Kruszwica PL ...89 E3
Kruszyna PL ...94 A3
Kruszyniany PL ...91 F2
Krūte LV ...80 B1
Krute MNE ...58 C4
Kruveliai LT ...85 E2
Kružiūnai LT ...85 F2
Kryčaŭ BY ...115 E3
Krynica (Małopolskie) PL ...98 C3
Krynica Morska PL ...90 A1
Krynice PL ...99 F1
Krynki (Podlaskie) PL ...91 F2
Krypno Kościelne PL ...91 E2
Kryvyj Rih UA ...117 F1
Krywosądów PL ...93 E2
Krzanowice PL ...97 E2
Krzcin PL ...88 B3
Krzelów PL ...93 D3
Krzemieniewo (Wielkopolskie) PL ...93 D2
Krzepice PL ...93 F3
Krzeszów (Dolnośląskie) PL ...92 C3
Krzeszów (Podkarpackie) PL ...99 D1
Krzeszowice PL ...98 A2
Krzeszyce PL ...88 B3
Krzykosy PL ...93 E2
Krzynowłoga Mała PL ...90 B3
Krzywa Góra PL ...89 F3
Krzywcza PL ...99 E2
Krzywiń PL ...93 D2
Krzywin PL ...88 B3
Krzyż (Wielkopolskie) PL ...88 C3
Krzyżanowice PL ...97 E2
Krzyżtopór (Zamek) PL ...94 C3
Książ PL ...92 C3
Książ Wielki PL ...98 B1
Książ Wielkopolski PL ...93 D2
Ktísmata GR ...100 D3
Kubiliūnai (Panevėžio) LT ...81 F2
Kubiliūnai (Šiauliu) LT ...81 E3
Kublis CH ...43 E3
Kubuli LT ...79 E3
Kučevo SRB ...57 E2
Kuchl A ...44 B2
Kuciny PL ...94 A2
Kučište HR ...58 A3
Kučkailiai LT ...82 B2
Kuczbork-Osada PL ...90 B3
Kudina EE ...73 D3
Kudirkos Naumiestis LT ...85 D2
Kudjape EE ...74 C3
Kudowa-Zdrój PL ...96 C1
Kūdra (Bauskas) LV ...81 F2
Kūdra (Rīgas) LV ...80 B1
Kūdums LV ...78 B2
Kufstein A ...44 B2
Kühlungsborn D ...34 A2
Kuhmalahti FIN ...69 D2
Kuhmo FIN ...65 F3
Kuhmoinen FIN ...69 D2
Kuigatsi EE ...79 D1
Kuivajärvi FIN ...65 F3
Kuivaniemi FIN ...65 D1
Kuivasjärvi FIN ...68 C2

Kuivastu EE ...75 D2
Kūkas LV ...83 D1
Kukës AL ...116 C4
Kukiške LT ...87 D1
Kukko FIN ...69 D2
Kukruse EE ...73 E2
Kukšas LV ...77 D3
Kuksema EE ...72 C2
Kuktiškes LT ...86 C1
Kukujevci SRB ...55 F2
Kukulje BIH ...55 D3
Kula BG ...117 D3
Kula SRB ...55 F2
Kulaini LV ...80 C1
Kulautuva LT ...85 E2
Külciems LV ...77 D3
Kuldiga LV ...76 C3
Kuldre EE ...79 D1
Kulen Vakuf BIH ...54 C3
Kulennoinen FIN ...69 F2
Kulesze Kościelne PL ...91 D3
Kuliai LT ...80 B3
Kulina SRB ...57 E4
Kulionys LT ...86 C1
Kūlitse EE ...79 D1
Kulju FIN ...69 D3
Kulkjica HR ...54 B4
Kulla EE ...78 C1
Kullaa FIN ...68 C3
Kullamaa EE ...72 A3
Külli EE ...75 E3
Kulmbach D ...39 D3
Kuloharju FIN ...65 E2
Külökai LT ...85 D2
Kulšenai LT ...80 C2
Külsheim D ...38 C3
Kultakero FIN ...65 D1
Kultuvenai LT ...85 F1
Kuluse EE ...72 A3
Kumane SRB ...56 C2
Kumanovo MK ...59 E3
Kumbuli LV ...83 D3
Kumečiai LT ...85 E3
Kumla S ...67 E3
Kumlinge FIN ...68 B4
Kumma EE ...72 B2
Kummavuopio S ...60 C3
Kumpji LV ...80 B1
Kumrovec HR ...54 B2
Kunda EE ...73 D1
Kundrenai LT ...81 F3
Kundzini LV ...81 D1
Kungälv S ...66 C4
Kungsbacka S ...66 C4
Kungshamn S ...66 C3
Kungsör S ...67 E2
Kunice PL ...92 C3
Kunigiškiai (Kauno) LT ...85 E2
Kunigiškiai (Šiaulenai) LT ...81 E3
Kunigiškiai (Taurages) LT ...84 C1
Kunigiškiai (Užventis) LT ...80 C3
Kuningaküla EE ...73 F2
Kunioniai LT ...85 E1
Kunów PL ...94 C3
Kunowo PL ...93 D2
Kunrau D ...33 F4
Kunszentmárton H ...116 C2
Künzelsau D ...38 C4
Kuolio FIN ...65 E2
Kuopio FIN ...69 E2
Kuorevesi FIN ...69 D3
Kuortane FIN ...69 D3
Kuortti FIN ...69 E3
Kupa HR ...54 B2
Kupferzell D ...38 C4
Kupiškis LT ...82 B3
Kuprava LV ...79 F3
Kupreliškis LT ...82 B2
Kupres BIH ...55 D4
Kupriai (Kauno) LT ...85 E2
Kupriai (Šiauliu) LT ...81 D2
Kūrėkūla EE ...79 D1
Kuremaa EE ...73 D3
Kuremäe EE ...73 F2
Kurenai LT ...86 B1
Kurenurme EE ...79 E1
Kurepalu EE ...79 E1
Kuressaare EE ...74 C3
Kurikka FIN ...68 C2
Kuřim CZ ...41 E3
Kurista (Jõgeva) EE ...73 D3
Kurista (Tartu) EE ...79 E1
Kurklaičiai II LT ...82 B2
Kurkliai (Šiauliu) LT ...81 E3
Kurkliai (Utenos) LT ...86 B1
Kurkliai II LT ...82 B3
Kurmelionys LT ...86 C3
Kurmene LV ...82 B2
Kurna LV ...80 B2
Kurów (Lubelskie) PL ...95 D3
Kurpiowskie PL ...91 D2
Kurplowska (Puszcza) PL ...90 C2
Kuršėnai LT ...81 D2
Kuršiai LT ...81 D3
Kurši (Limbažu) LV ...77 F2
Kurši (Saldus) LV ...80 C1
Kursk RUS ...115 F3
Kursu FIN ...65 E1
Kuršumlija SRB ...57 E4

Kuršumlíjska Banja SRB ...57 E4
Kurtakko FIN ...64 C1
Kurtna (Harju) EE ...72 B2
Kurtna (Ida-Viru) EE ...73 F2
Kurtuvenai LT ...81 D2
Kuru FIN ...69 D3
Kuryłówka PL ...99 E1
Kurzemite LV ...76 C3
Kurzennieki LV ...76 C2
Kurzętnik PL ...90 A2
Kusa LV ...79 D3
Kusadak SRB ...57 D3
Kušaini LV ...80 C1
Kusel D ...13 E2
Kušliškiai LT ...85 D3
Küsnacht CH ...17 F1
Kušneri LV ...83 F2
Küssnacht CH ...17 F1
Kustavi FIN ...68 C3
Kütahya TR ...117 F4
Küti EE ...73 D2
Kutina HR ...55 D2
Kutjevo HR ...55 E2
Kutná Hora CZ ...41 D3
Kutno PL ...94 A1
Kuttanen FIN ...61 D3
Kuttura FIN ...61 E3
Kuumu FIN ...65 F3
Kuusalu EE ...72 C1
Kuusamo FIN ...65 E2
Kuusankoski FIN ...69 E3
Kuusiku EE ...72 B2
Kuusjärvi FIN ...69 E2
Kuusjoki FIN ...69 D4
Kuutsi EE ...79 D2
Kuvšinovo RUS ...115 F1
Kužiai LT ...81 D2
Kuzma SLO ...54 C1
Kuzmin SRB ...55 F2
Kuźnia Raciborska PL ...97 E2
Kuźnica PL ...91 F2
Kværnangsbotn N ...61 D2
Kværndrup DK ...70 B3
Kvalsund N ...61 D1
Kvam N ...62 C4
Kvanne N ...66 A1
Kvanndal N ...66 A1
Kvedarna LT ...80 C2
Kvernes N ...62 B3
Kvevlax FIN ...68 C2
Kvietiniai LT ...80 B3
Kvikkjokk S ...60 B4
Kvikne N ...62 C4
Kvinesdal N ...66 A3
Kviteseid N ...66 B2
Kwidzyn PL ...89 F2
Kwilcz PL ...92 C1
Kybartai LT ...85 D2
Kybeikiai LT ...84 C2
Kybučiai LT ...81 D3
Kyburiai LT ...81 F2
Kyïv UA ...115 E4
Kyjov CZ ...41 E4
Kylänlahti FIN ...69 F1
Kylänpää FIN ...68 C2
Kyle of Lochalsh GB ...4 B4
Kyleakin GB ...4 B4
Kylerhea GB ...4 B4
Kylestrome GB ...4 C2
Kyllburg D ...13 D2
Kylmäkoski FIN ...69 D3
Kylmälä FIN ...65 D3
Kyritz D ...34 B3
Kyrksæterøra / Hemme N ...62 C3
Kyröskoski FIN ...68 C3
Kyselka CZ ...40 B2
Kyyjärvi FIN ...69 D2

L

La Adrada E ...25 F2
La Alberca E ...25 D1
La Alberca de Záncara E ...26 B3
La Albergueria de Argañán E ...24 C1
La Albuera E ...29 D2
La Algaba E ...29 D2
La Almarcha E ...26 B3
La Almunia de Doña Godina E ...20 B4
La Antilla E ...28 C2
La Azohía E ...30 C3
La Bañeza E ...19 D3
La Barca de la Florida E ...29 D3
La Barrela E ...18 B3
La Barthe-de-Neste F ...21 D2
La Bassée F ...12 A1
La Bastide-Clairence F ...20 B2
La Bastide-de-Sérou F ...21 E3
La Bâtie-Neuve F ...22 C1
La Baule F ...14 B1
La Bégude-de-Mazenc F ...22 B1
La Bérarde F ...17 D4
La Bisbal de Falset E ...27 E1
La Bisbal d'Empordà E ...21 F4
La Bonneville-sur-Iton F ...11 F3
La Bourboule F ...16 A3
La Bóveda de Toro E ...19 D4

La Brède F ...15 D4
La Bresse F ...13 E4
La Cabrera E ...25 D3
La Calahorra E ...30 A3
La Caletta I ...50 B2
La Calzada de Oropesa E ...25 E2
La Campana E ...29 D2
La Canourgue F ...21 F1
La Capelle F ...12 B2
La Carlota E ...29 E2
La Carolina E ...25 F4
La Cava E ...27 E1
La Cavalerie F ...21 F2
La Chaise-Dieu F ...16 B4
La Chambre F ...17 D4
La Chapelle-d'Angillon F ...16 A1
La Chapelle-de-Guinchay F ...16 C3
La Chapelle-en-Valgaudémar F ...17 D4
La Chapelle-en-Vercors F ...16 C4
La Charité-sur-Loire F ...16 A1
La Chartre-sur-le-Loir F ...15 E1
La Châtaigneraie F ...15 D2
La Châtre F ...15 F2
La Chaux-de-Fonds CH ...17 D1
La Chèze F ...10 C4
La Ciotat F ...22 C2
La Clayette F ...16 B3
La Clusaz F ...17 D3
La Codosera E ...24 C3
La Coronada E ...25 D3
La Côte-St-André F ...16 C4
La Couronne F ...15 D3
La Courtine F ...15 F3
La Couvertoirade F ...21 F1
La Crau F ...22 C2
La Croix-Valmer F ...23 D2
La Cumbre E ...25 D3
La Cure F ...17 D2
La Espina E ...19 D2
La Féclaz F ...17 D3
La Fère F ...12 B2
La Ferté-Alais F ...12 A4
La Ferté-Bernard F ...11 E4
La Ferté-Frênel F ...11 E3
La Ferté-Gaucher F ...12 B4
La Ferté-Macé F ...11 E4
La Ferté-Milon F ...12 B3
La Ferté-sous-Jouarre F ...12 B3
La Ferté-St-Aubin F ...15 F1
La Ferté-Vidame F ...11 F4
La Flèche F ...15 D1
La Font de la Figuera E ...26 C4
La Franca E ...19 E2
La Fregeneda E ...24 C1
La Frontera E ...26 B2
La Fuente de San Esteban E ...25 D1
La Gacilly F ...14 C1
La Garde-Freinet F ...22 C2
La Garriga E ...21 E4
La Gineta E ...26 B3
La Granadella E ...27 E1
La Grand-Combe F ...22 A1
La Grand-Croix F ...16 B3
La Grande-Motte F ...22 A2
La Granjuela E ...25 E4
La Grave F ...17 D4
La Guardia E ...26 A2
La Guardia de Jaén E ...29 F2
La Guerche-de-Bretagne F ...11 D4
La Guerche-sur-l'Aubois F ...16 A2
La Haye-du-Puits F ...11 D3
La Haye-Pesnel F ...11 D3
La Hermida E ...19 E2
La Herradura E ...29 F3
La Horcajada E ...25 E2
La Horra E ...19 F4
La Iglesuela del Cid E ...27 D2
La Jana E ...27 E2
La Javie F ...22 C1
La Jonquera E ...21 F3
La Lantejuela E ...29 D2
La Léchère F ...17 D3
La Línea de la Concepción E ...29 D4
La Losa E ...30 A2
La Loupe F ...11 F4
La Louvière B ...12 B1
La Luisiana E ...29 D2
La Machine F ...16 B2
La Maddalena I ...50 B2
La Magdalena E ...19 D3
La Malène F ...21 F1
La Manga del Mar Menor E ...30 C2
La Mesa Roldán E ...30 B3
La Molina E ...21 E3
La Mothe-Achard F ...14 C2
La Mothe-St-Héray F ...15 D2
La Motte-Chalancon F ...22 B1
La Motte-du-Caire F ...22 C1
La Mudarra E ...19 E4
La Muela E ...20 B4
La Mure F ...17 D4
La Napoule F ...23 D2
La Nava de Ricomalillo E ...25 E2

La Nava de Santiago E ...25 D3
La Neuve-Lyre F ...11 F3
La Neuveville CH ...17 E1
La Nuez de Arriba E ...19 F3
La Paca E ...30 B2
La Pacaudière F ...16 B3
La Pallice F ...14 C2
La Palma del Condado E ...28 C2
La Petite-Pierre F ...13 E3
La Pinilla E ...26 A1
La Plagne F ...17 D3
La Plaza E ...19 D2
La Pobla de Benifassà E ...27 D1
La Pobla de Lillet E ...21 E3
La Pobla de Massaluca E ...27 E1
La Pobla de Segur E ...21 D4
La Pobla de Vallbona E ...27 D3
La Pobla Llarga E ...27 D3
La Pobla Tornesa E ...27 D2
La Pola de Gordón E ...19 D2
La Porta F ...23 F3
La Preste F ...21 F3
La Primaube F ...21 F1
La Puebla de Almoradiel E ...26 A3
La Puebla de Cazalla E ...29 D3
La Puebla de Híjar E ...27 D1
La Puebla de los Infantes E ...29 E2
La Puebla de Montalbán E ...25 F2
La Puebla del Río E ...29 D3
La Pueblanueva E ...25 E2
La Puerta de Segura E ...26 A4
La Rábita E ...30 A3
La Rambla E ...29 E2
La Réole F ...15 D4
La Rinconada E ...29 D2
La Rivière-Thibouville F ...11 F3
La Robla E ...19 D2
La Roca de la Sierra E ...24 C3
La Roca del Vallès E ...21 F4
La Roche-Bernard F ...14 B1
La Roche-Canillac F ...15 F4
La Roche-Chalais F ...15 D4
La Roche-Derrien F ...10 B3
La Roche-en-Ardenne B ...13 D2
La Roche-Guyon F ...11 F3
La Roche-Posay F ...15 E2
La Roche-sur-Foron F ...17 D3
La Roche-sur-Yon F ...14 C2
La Rochefoucauld F ...15 E3
La Rochelle F ...14 C2
La Rochepot F ...16 C2
La Rochette F ...17 D4
La Roda E ...26 B3
La Roda de Andalucía E ...29 E3
La Roque-Gageac F ...15 E4
La Roquebrussanne F ...22 C2
La Rosière-1850 F ...17 D3
La Salceda E ...25 F1
La Salvetat-Peyralès F ...21 E1
La Salvetat-sur-Agout F ...21 F2
La Seca E ...19 D4
La Selva del Camp E ...27 E1
La Sénia E ...27 D1
La Seu d'Urgell / Seo de Urgel E ...21 E3
La Seyne-sur-Mer F ...22 C2
La Solana E ...26 A3
La Souterraine F ...15 F3
La Spezia I ...46 C2
La Sterza I ...47 D3
La Suze-sur-Sarthe F ...15 D1
La Teste-de-Buch F ...20 B1
La Thuile I ...17 E3
La Torre del Valle E ...19 D3
La Torre d'en Besora E ...27 D2
La Tour-d'Auvergne F ...16 A3
La Tour-du-Pin F ...16 C4
La Tour-Fondue F ...22 C2
La Toussuire F ...17 D4
La Tranche-sur-Mer F ...14 C2
La Tremblade F ...14 C3
La Trimouille F ...15 E2
La Trinité-Porhoët F ...10 C4
La Trinité-sur-Mer F ...14 B1
La Turballe F ...14 B1
La Turbie F ...23 D2
La Unión E ...30 C2
La Vall d'Uixó E ...27 D2
La Vecilla E ...19 D2
La Vellés E ...25 E1
La Verna I ...47 D2
La Verpillière F ...16 C4
La Vila Joiosa / Villajoyosa E ...27 D4
La Villa / Stern I ...44 B3
La Villa de Don Fadrique E ...26 A3
La Villedieu-du-Clain F ...15 E2
La Virgen del Camino E ...19 D3
La Voulte-sur-Rhône F ...16 C4

La Wantzenau F ...13 F4
La Yesa E ...26 C2
Laa an der Thaya A ...41 E4
Laabi EE ...72 B2
Laadi EE ...75 D3
Laage D ...34 A2
Laagri EE ...72 B2
Laanemetsa EE ...79 D2
Lääniste EE ...73 D3
Laasme EE ...73 D3
Laatre EE ...79 D2
Laatsa EE ...74 B3
Labacolla E ...18 A3
Labajos E ...25 F1
Labanoras LT ...86 C1
Labasheeda IRL ...2 B3
Labastida E ...20 A3
Labastide-Murat F ...21 E1
Labastide-Rouairoux F ...21 F2
Labeikiai LT ...86 B1
L'Aber-Wrac'h F ...10 A3
Labin HR ...54 A3
Łabiszyn PL ...89 E3
Laboe D ...33 F2
Laborai LT ...81 E2
Labouheyre F ...20 C1
Labowa PL ...98 C3
Labrit F ...20 C1
Labruguière F ...21 E2
Labudnjaca SRB ...55 F2
Labūnava (Kauno) LT ...85 E1
Labūnava (Šiauliu) LT ...80 C3
Łabunie PL ...95 F3
Lacanau F ...14 C4
Lacanau-Océan F ...14 C4
Lacapelle-Marival F ...15 F4
Láčarak SRB ...55 F2
Lacaune F ...21 F2
Lacco Ameno I ...48 C4
Lacedonia I ...49 D3
Łąck PL ...94 A1
Lačkalni LV ...76 C3
Łącko PL ...98 B3
Läckö S ...67 D3
Laconi I ...50 A3
Lāčplēši LV ...80 B1
Lacq F ...20 C2
Lāčupīte LV ...77 F3
Ląd PL ...93 E1
Ladbergen D ...37 E1
Läde EE ...78 B2
Lądek PL ...93 E1
Lądek-Zdrój PL ...97 D2
Lādezers LV ...78 B2
Ládi GR ...103 E1
Ladispoli I ...48 A3
Ladoeiro P ...24 C2
Lādzere LV ...77 D3
Laekvere EE ...73 D2
Lǽrma GR ...111 F2
Laeva EE ...73 D3
Laferté-sur-Amance F ...16 C1
Laffrey F ...17 D4
Láfka GR ...105 D3
Láfkos GR ...105 E1
Lafrançaise F ...21 E1
Lagan S ...71 D2
Laganás GR ...104 B3
Lagartera E ...25 E2
Lage (Kreis Lippe) D ...37 F1
Lagedi EE ...72 C2
Laggan GB ...4 C4
Łagiewniki (Dolnośląskie) PL ...93 D3
Laginá GR ...103 E2
Laginá GR ...101 E2
Lágos GR ...102 C2
Lagoa P ...18 A4
Lagoaça P ...18 C4
Lagonegro I ...49 E4
Lagónissi GR ...105 F3

Laigueglia I ...23 E1
L'Aiguillon-sur-Mer F ...14 C2
Laihia FIN ...68 C2
Laiksaare EE ...75 F3
Laikūla EE ...72 A3
Laïliás GR ...102 A1
Laimbach A ...45 D1
Laimjala EE ...74 C3
Laimoluokta S ...60 C3
Lainate I ...43 D4
Lairg GB ...4 C3
Laissac F ...21 F1
Laísta GR ...100 C3
Laisvall S ...64 A2
Laitikkala FIN ...69 D3
Laitila FIN ...68 C4
Laitse EE ...72 A2
Laiuse EE ...73 D3
Laiusevälja EE ...73 D3
Laižuva LT ...81 D2
Lajkovac SRB ...56 C3
Laka GR ...104 A1
Łąka (Śląskie) PL ...97 F2
Lakavica MK ...59 F3
Lakí GR ...107 E4
Láki GR ...109 D3
Łąka (Kujawsko-Pomorskie) PL ...89 F3
Łąkie (Wielkopolskie) PL ...89 D3
Lákoma GR ...103 D3
Lákones GR ...100 A4
Lakópetra GR ...104 C3
Lakselv N ...61 E2
Lakštučiai LT ...85 D2
Laktaši BIH ...55 D3
Lálas GR ...104 C3
Lalbenque F ...21 E1
L'Alcora E ...27 D2
L'Alcúdia E ...27 D3
L'Alcúdia de Crespins E ...27 D3
L'Aldea E ...27 E1
L'Alfàs del Pi E ...27 D4
Lalín E ...18 B3
Lalinac SRB ...57 F4
Lalinde F ...15 E4
Laliótis GR ...105 D3
Lall EE ...79 E1
Lalm N ...62 C4
Lalouvesc F ...16 B4
Lalueza E ...20 C3
Lam D ...39 F4
Lama dei Peligni I ...48 C2
Lamalou-les-Bains F ...21 F2
Lamarche F ...13 D4
Lamastre F ...16 B4
Lambach A ...44 C1
Lamballe F ...10 C4
Lambārte LV ...81 F1
Lambesc F ...22 B2
Lámbia GR ...104 C3
Łambinowice PL ...97 D1
Lambiri GR ...104 C2
Lambou Míli GR ...107 F2
Lambrecht D ...13 F3
Lamego P ...18 B4
L'Ametlla de Mar E ...27 E1
Lamía GR ...105 D1
Lamini LV ...77 D3
Lamlash GB ...6 C1
Lammhult S ...71 E2
Lammi FIN ...69 D3
Lamotte-Beuvron F ...15 F1
Lampaul F ...10 A4
Lampedusa I ...52 A4
Lampertheim D ...13 F2
Lampeter / Llanbedr Pont Steffan GB ...3 F1
L'Ampolla E ...27 E1
Lamstedt D ...33 E3
Lamure-sur-Azergues F ...16 B3
Lana I ...43 F3
Lanaja E ...20 C4
Lanaken B ...13 D1
Lanark GB ...7 D4
Lancaster GB ...7 D4
Lancenieki (Lancini) LV ...77 E3
Lanchester GB ...7 E3
Lanciano I ...48 C2
Łańcut PL ...99 D2
Landau a. d. Isar (Kreis Dingolfing-Landau) D ...39 F4
Landau i. d. Pfalz (Kr. Landau i. d. Pfalz) D ...13 F3
Landeck A ...43 E2
Landerneau F ...10 A4
Landete E ...26 C2
Landévennec F ...10 A4
Landivisiau F ...10 A4
Landivy F ...11 D4
Landquart CH ...43 D3
Landrecies F ...12 B2
Landriano I ...46 B1
Landsberg D (Saalkreis) ...39 E1
Landsberg a. Lech D ...43 E1
Landshut D ...44 B1
Landskrona S ...71 D3
Landstuhl D ...13 E3
Landverk S ...63 D3

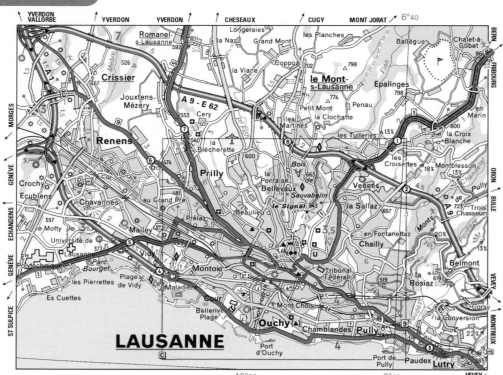

LAUSANNE

Landze LV 76 B3
Lanersbach A 43 F2
Lanesborough IRL 2 C2
Langa de Duero E 19 F4
Langáda GR 107 D2
Langáda GR 108 B1
Langadás GR 101 F2
Langádia GR 104 C3
Langadíkia GR 102 A2
Langakiai LT 85 E1
Langangen N 66 B2
Langeac F 16 A4
Langeais F 15 E1
Längelmäki FIN 69 D3
Langelsheim D 38 C1
Langen D 33 D3
Langen (Kreis
  Offenbach) D 13 F2
Langenargen D 43 D2
Langenau D 43 E1
Langenberg (Stadtkreis
  Gera) D 39 E2
Langenbruck D 43 F1
Langenburg D 38 C4
Längenfeld A 43 F2
Langenfeld D 13 E1
Langenhagen D 33 E4
Langenhahn D 13 F1
Langenlois A 41 D4
Langenthal CH 17 E1
Langenwang A 45 E1
Langenzenn D 39 D4
Langeoog D 33 D3
Langerma EE 72 A3
Långeserud S 67 D2
Langeskov DK 70 C3
Langesund N 66 B3
Langevåg N 66 A2
Langevågen N 62 B3
Langfjord N 61 D2
Langhirano I 46 C2
Langholm GB 7 D2
Langnau
  im Emmental CH 17 E2
Langogne F 16 B4
Langon F 20 C1
Langport GB 8 C3
Langres F 16 C1
Langrune-sur-Mer F ...11 E3
Långsele S 68 A2
Langstini LV 77 F3
Långträsk S 64 B2
Łanięta PL 94 A1
Lanjarón E 29 F3
Lankaičiai LT 81 E2
Lanke D 34 B3
Länkipohja FIN 69 D3
Lankupiai LT 80 D3
Lanmeur F 10 B4
Lannemezan F 21 D2
Lannilis F 10 A4
Lannion F 10 B3
Lanouaille F 15 E4
Lans-en-Vercors F 16 C4
Lanškroun CZ 41 E1
Lanslebourg-
  Mont-Cenis F 17 E4
Lanta F 21 E2
Lantosque F 23 D1
Lanusei I 50 B3
Lanvollon F 10 B4
Lanzahíta E 25 E2
Lanzo Torinese I 17 E4
Laon F 12 B3
Lapalisse F 16 B3
Łapanów PL 98 B2
Lápas GR 104 B3
Laperdiguera E 20 C4
Lapes LT 85 E2
Lapetukme EE 79 D1
Lapiai LT 80 B3
Lapinjärvi /
  Lappträsk FIN 69 E4
Lapinlahti FIN 69 E1

Lapleau F 15 F4
Laplume F 21 D1
Lapmežciems LV 77 E3
Lapovo SRB 57 D3
Lappajärvi FIN 69 D2
Lappalaisten-
  Kesätuvat FIN 61 D3
Lappea FIN 64 C1
Lappeenranta FIN 69 F3
Lappfjärd /
  Lapväärtti FIN 68 C2
Lappfors FIN 68 C1
Lappi FIN 68 C3
Lapsas LV 81 E1
Lapsukalns LV 83 D2
Łapsze Niżne PL 98 B3
Lapua FIN 68 C2
Lapupys LT 80 D3
Łapy PL 91 E3
L'Aquila I 48 B2
Laragh IRL 3 D3
Laragne-Montéglin F ...22 C1
L'Arbresle F 16 B3
Lärbro S 67 F4
Larche F 15 E4
Larche F 23 D1
Larderello I 47 D3
Lárdos GR 111 F2
Laredo E 19 F2
Laren NL 32 B4
Largentière F 22 A1
L'Argentière-
  la-Bessée F 17 D4
Largs GB 6 C1
Lárimna GR 105 E2
Larino I 49 D3
Lárissa GR 101 E4
Larmor-Plage F 14 A1
Larne GB 3 E1
Larochette L 13 D2
Laroles E 30 A3
Laroque-d'Olmes F 21 E3
Laroque-Timbaut F 21 D1
Laroquebrou F 15 F4
Larraga E 20 B3
Larseng N 60 C2
Larsmo FIN 68 C1
Laruns F 20 C3
Larv S 67 D3
Larvik N 66 C3
Las Cabezas
  de San Juan E 29 D3
Las Caldas
  de Besayas E 19 E2
Las Mesas E 26 A3
Las Minas E 26 B4
Las Navas
  de la Concepción E ...25 D4
Las Navas
  del Marqués E 25 F1
Las Negras E 30 B3
Las Pajanosas E 29 D3
Las Pedroñeras E 26 A3
Las Pedrosas E 20 B4
Las Rozas
  de Madrid E 25 F1
Las Veguillas E 25 D1
Las Vertientes E 30 B2
Las Viñas E 25 F4
Lasalle F 22 A1
Lasarte-Oria E 20 A2
Laši LV 82 C2
Lasila EE 73 D2
Łasin PL 89 F2
Łask PL 94 A3
Łaskarzew PL 94 A2
Laško SLO 54 B2
Laskowa PL 98 B3
Laskowice (Jelcz-) PL ..93 D2
Lasnamäe EE 72 B1
Lasovice Małe PL 93 F3
Lassan D 34 B4

Lassay-les-Châteaux F ..11 D4
Lassigny F 12 A3
Lassíthi GR 109 F4
Lastovo HR 58 A3
Lastovo (Otok) HR 58 A3
Lastra a Signa I 47 D3
Lastres E 19 D2
Lastrup D 33 D4
Lastva BIH 58 B3
Lašupes LV 82 A1
Lašva BIH 55 E4
Lasva EE 79 E2
Łaszczów PL 99 F1
Laterza I 49 E4
Lathen D 33 D4
Latheron GB 5 D2
Latiano I 51 E3
Latikberg S 64 A3
Latina I 48 B3
Latisana I 44 C4
Lató GR 110 C4

Latour-de-France F 21 F3
Latowicz PL 95 D2
Latronico I 49 E4
Latronquière F 15 F4
Latveliai LT 82 B2
Laubere LV 78 B3
Laucesa LV 83 D3
Lauchhammer D 39 F1
Lastva BIH 58 B3
Lauciene LV 77 D3
Laucienes
  Pansionāts LV 77 D3
Lauckaimis LT 85 D2
Lauder GB 7 D2
Lauderi LV 83 F2
Laudona LV 83 D1
Lauenau
  (Hannover) D 33 E4
Lauenburg D 33 F3
Lauenstein
  (Weißeritzkreis) D 39 F2
Lauf a. d. Pegnitz D 39 D4
Laufen CH 17 E1

Laufen (Kreis
  Berchtesgadener
  Land) D 44 B1
Laufenburg CH 17 E1
Laufenburg D 17 E1
Lauffen a. Neckar D 38 C4
Laugaliai LT 80 B3
Laugar IS 62 A1
Laugarbakki IS 62 A1
Laugarvatn IS 62 A2
Lauingen (Kr. Dillingen
  a.d.Donau) D 43 E1
Laujar de Andarax E ...30 A3
Lauka EE 74 C1
Laukaa FIN 69 E2
Laukagaliai LT 82 B3
Laukdvariai LT 80 C3
Laukiškes LT 85 E2
Laukmalī F 77 D3
Laukna EE 72 A2
Lauko Soda LT 80 C2

Lavre P 24 B3
Lávrio GR 105 F3
Ławszowa PL 92 B3
Laxá S 67 E3
Laxe E 18 A2
Laxford Bridge GB 4 C2
Laxo GB 5 F1
Layos E 25 F2
Laza E 18 B3
Lažai LT 81 E3
Lazarev Krst MNE 58 C3
Lazarevac SRB 56 C3
Lazarevo SRB 56 C2
Lazaropole MK 59 D3
Lazdenai LT 86 B2
Lazdijai LT 85 E3
Lazdinas LV 81 E1
Lazdininkai LT 80 C2
Lazdona LV 83 D1
Lazise I 43 F4
Łaziska PL 95 D3
Łaziska Górne PL 97 F2
Lázně Bohdaneč CZ 41 D2
Lázně Kynžvart CZ 40 A3
Laznica SRB 57 E3
Łazy (Śląskie) PL 98 A1
Łazy (Zachodnio-
  pomorskie) PL 88 C1
Le Bar-sur-Loup F 23 D2
Le Beausset F 22 C2
Le Bec-Hellouin F 11 F3
Le Bény-Bocage F 11 D3
Le Biot F 17 D2
Le Blanc F 15 E2
Le Bleymard F 22 A1
Le Boréon F 23 D1
Le Boulou F 21 F3
Le Bourg-d'Oisans F ...17 D4
Le Bourget-du-Lac F ...17 D3
Le Bousquet-d'Orb F ...21 F2
Le Bugue F 15 E4
Le Buisson-
  de-Cadouin F 15 E4
Le Cap-d'Agde F 22 A2
Le Cateau-
  Cambrésis F 12 B2
Le Catelet F 12 B2
Le Caylar F 21 F2
Le Chambon-
  Feugerolles F 16 B4
Le Chambon-
  sur-Lignon F 16 B4
Le Château-d'Oléron F ..14 C3
Le Châtelard F 17 D3

Le Châtelet F 15 F2
Le Châtelet-en-Brie F ..12 A4
Le Chesne F 12 C3
Le Cheylard F 16 B4
Le Conquet F 10 A4
Le Creusot F 16 B2
Le Croisic F 14 B1
Le Crotoy F 9 F4
Le Donjon F 16 B3
Le Dorat F 15 E3
Le Faou F 10 A4
Le Faouët F 10 B4
Le Folgoët F 10 A4
Le Fossat F 21 E2
Le Fousseret F 21 D2
Le Grand-Bornand F ...17 D3
Le Grand-Bourg F 15 F3
Le Grand-Lemps F 16 C4
Le Grand-Lucé F 15 E1
Le Grand-Pressigny F ..15 E2
Le Grand-Serre F 16 C4
Le Grau-du-Roi F 22 A2
Le Havre F 11 E3
Le Hohwald F 13 E4
Le Lauzet-Ubaye F 22 C1
Le Lavandou F 22 C2
Le Lion-d'Angers F 15 D1
Le Lioran F 16 A4
Le Locle CH 17 E1
Le Loroux-Bottereau F ..14 C1
Le Louroux-
  Béconnais F 15 D1
Le Luc F 22 C2
Le Lude F 15 E1
Le Malzieu-Ville F 16 A4
Le Mans F 11 E4
Le Markstein F 13 E4
Le Mas-d'Agenais F 21 D1
Le Mas-d'Azil F 21 E3
Le Massegros F 21 F1
Le Mayet-
  de-Montagne F 16 B3
Le Mêle-sur-Sarthe F ..11 E4
Le Merlerault F 11 E4
Le Monastier-
  sur-Gazeille F 21 F1
Le Monêtier-
  les-Bains F 17 D4
Le Mont-Dore F 16 A3
Le Mont-St-Michel F ...11 D4
Le Montet F 16 A3
Le Muy F 23 D2
Le Neubourg F 11 F3

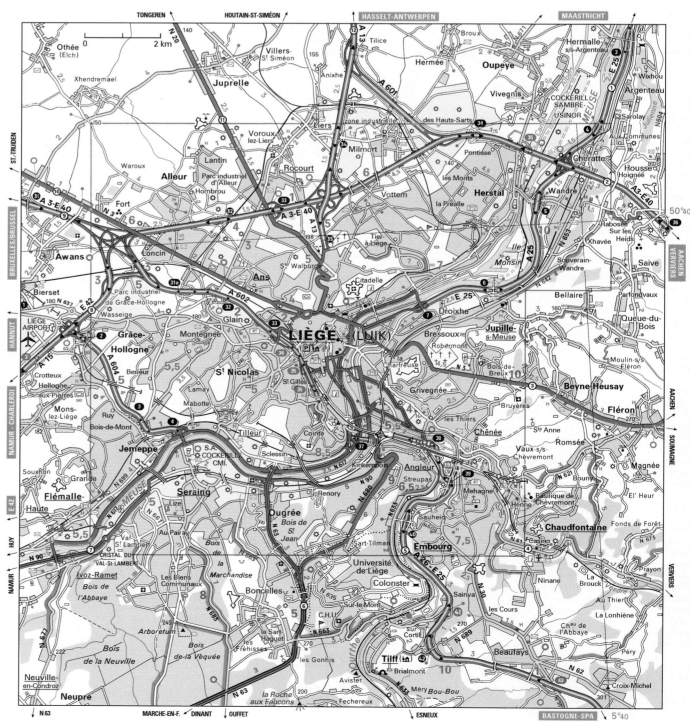

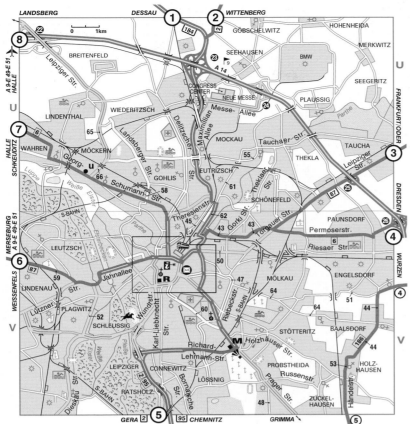

LEIPZIG

Adenauerallee .... V 43
Baalsdorfer Str. ..... V 44
Berliner Str. .... V 45
Breite Str. .... V 47
Chemnitzer Str. ...... V 48
Eisenbahnstr. .... V 50
Hauptstr. .... V 53
Kieler Str. .... U 55
Lindenthaler Str. .... U 58
Louise-Otto-Peters-Allee ..... U 65
Merseburger Str. ..... U 59
Mockauer Str. .... U 61
Philipp-Rosenthal-Str. .... U 60
Rackwitzer Str. ...... U 62
Slevogtstr. .... U 66
Zschochersche Str. ... V 63
Zweinaundorfer Str. .. V 64

Leirbotn N 61 D2
Leiria P 24 A2
Leiro E 18 B3
Leirpollskogen N 61 F1
Leirvåg N 66 A1
Leirvik N 63 E1
Leirvik (Færøerne) DK 62 A3
Leirvik (Hordaland) N 66 A2
Leirvik (Sogn og Fjordane) N 66 A1
Leisi EE 74 C2
Leisnig D 39 F1
Leiston GB 9 F2
Leith GB 7 D1
Leitza E 20 B2
Leitzkau D 34 A4
Leivonmäki FIN 69 E3
Lejas Strazdi LV 80 B1
Lejasciems LV 79 D3
Lejaskauguri LV 78 A2
Lejasozoli LV 77 F2
Lejasstrazdi LV 81 E1
Lêjêji LV 80 B1
Léka GR 107 E3
Leka N 63 D2
Lekáni GR 102 B1
Łękawa PL 94 A3
Łękawica PL 97 F2
Lekečiai LT 85 E1
Lekeitio E 20 A2
Lekenik HR 54 C2
Leknes N 60 A3
Leknes (Møre og Romsdal) N 62 B4
Łęknica (Lubuskie) PL 92 A2
Leksand S 67 E1
Leksvik N 62 C3
Lekunberri E 20 B3
Leland N 63 E1

Lemgo D 37 F1
Lemi FIN 69 E3
Lemland FIN 68 B4
Lemmenjoki FIN 61 E1
Lemmer NL 32 B4
Lemmetsa EE 72 A3
Lemonodásos GR 105 E4
Lempäälä FIN 69 D3
Lempdes-sur-Allagnon F 16 A2
Lemsi EE 75 E3
Lemvig DK 70 B2
Lenart-v-Slov.-gor SLO 54 B1
Lenas LT 81 F3
Lênas LV 80 C1
Lencloître F 15 C2
Lend A 44 B2
Léndas GR 109 E4
Lendava SLO 54 C1
Lendinara I 47 D1
Lendži LV 83 F1
Lengefeld (Mittlerer Erzgebirgskreis) D 39 F2
Lengenfeld D 39 E2
Lengerich D 33 D4
Lenggries D 43 F2
Lenhovda S 71 E2
Lenk CH 17 E2
Lenkčiai I LT 85 E1
Lenkimai LT 80 B2
Lennestadt D 37 F2
Lens F 12 A1
Lensahn D 33 F2
Lentföhrden D 33 E2
Lenti H 116 B2
Lentiira FIN 65 F3
Lenting D 39 E4
Lentini I 53 E3
Lentvaris LT 86 B2
Lenzburg CH 17 F1
Lenzen (Kreis Prignitz) D 34 A3
Lenzerheide / Lai CH 43 F3
Lenzkirch D 13 F4
Leoben A 45 D2
Leobersdorf A 45 E1
Leogang A 44 B2
Leominster GB 8 C2
León E 19 D3
Léon F 20 B1
Leonberg D 43 D1
Léoncel F 16 C4
Leondári (Arkadía) GR 105 D4

Leondári (Kardítsa) GR 105 D1
Leóndio GR 105 D3
Leonessa I 47 F4
Leonforte I 53 D3
Leonídio GR 105 E4
Leopoldsburg B 12 C1
Leopoldsdorf im Marchfelde A 41 E4
Leova MD 117 E2
Lepe E 28 C2
Lepel' BY 115 D2
Lepenoú GR 104 C2
Lepetane MNE 58 B3
L'Épine F 12 C3
Lepna EE 73 D2
Lepoglava HR 54 C1
Leposavić SRB 57 D4
Lépoura GR 105 F2
Leppäjärvi FIN 61 D3
Leppävirta FIN 69 E2
Leppneeme EE 72 B1
Leptokariá GR 103 D2
Leptokariá GR 101 F3
Lercara Friddi I 52 C3
Léré F 16 A1
Lerici I 46 C2
Lerín E 20 A3
Lerma E 19 F4
Lermoos A 43 E2
Léros (Nissí) GR ... 107 F4
Lerum S 66 C4
Lerwick GB 5 F2
Les E 21 D3
Les Abrets F 16 C3
Les Aix-d'Angillon F 16 A1
Les Andelys F 11 E3
Les Arcs F 17 D3
Les Arcs F 22 C2
Les Baux-de-Provence F 22 B2
Les Bézards F 16 A1
Les Borges Blanques E 21 D4
Les Bouchoux F 17 D2
Les Cabannes F 21 E3
Les Contamines-Montjoie F 17 D3
Les Coves de Vonromà E 27 D4
Les Deux-Alpes F 17 D4
Les Diablerets CH ... 17 E2
Les Écharmeaux F 16 B3

Le Nouvion-en-Thiérache F 12 B2
Le Palais F 14 B1
Le Péage-de-Roussillon F 16 C4
Le Pellerin F 14 C1
Le Perthus F 21 F3
Le Poiré-sur-Vie F .. 14 C2
Le Pont-de-Beauvoisin F 16 C3
Le Pont-de-Claix F .. 17 D4
Le Pont-de-Montvert F 22 A1
Le Pontet F 22 B1
Le Portel F 9 F4
Le Pouldu F 14 A1
Le Pouliguen F 14 B1
Le Pouzin F 16 C4
Le Puy-en-Velay F ... 16 B4
Le Quesnoy F 12 B2
Le Rozier F 21 F1
Le Russey F 17 D1
Le Sauze F 23 D1
Le Teil F 22 B1
Le Teilleul F 11 D4
Le Theil F 11 E4
Le Thillot F 17 D1
Le Touquet-Paris-Plage F 9 F4
Le Touvet F 17 D4
Le Trayas F 23 D2
Le Tréport F 11 F2
Le Val-André F 10 C4
Le Val-d'Ajol F 13 E4
Le Verdon-sur-Mer F . 14 C3
Le Vigan F 22 A1
Le Vivier-sur-Mer F . 10 C4
Leadenham GB 9 E1
Łeba PL 89 D1
Lebach D 13 E3
Lebane SRB 57 F4
Lebedyn UA 115 F4
Lebenstedt D 33 F4
Lebesby N 61 E1
Łebno PL 89 E1
Łebork PL 89 E1
Lebrija E 29 D3
Łebsko (Jezioro) PL . 89 E1
Lebus D 34 C4
Lecce I 51 F1
Lecco I 43 D4
Lécera E 26 C1
Lečevica HR 55 D4
Lech A 43 E2
Lechlade GB 9 D3
Leciñena E 20 C4
Leck D 33 E1
Leckava LT 80 C1
Lectoure F 21 D1
Łęczna PL 95 E3
Łęczyca PL 94 A2
Ledaña E 26 A4
Ledanca E 26 A1
Lêdas LV 77 D3
Ledbury GB 9 D2
Ledeč nad Sázavou CZ 41 D3
Ledesma E 25 D1
Lédignan F 22 A1
Lédmane LV 82 B1
Ledmore GB 4 C3
Ledurga LV 78 B3
Lędziny PL 97 F2
Leebiku EE 78 C1
Leedi EE 73 D3
Leeds GB 7 E4
Leek GB 9 D1
Leenane IRL 2 B2
Leer D 33 D3
Leerdam NL 36 C1

Leese D 33 E4
Leeuwarden NL 32 B3
Leevaku EE 79 E1
Leevi EE 79 E1
Lefkáda GR 104 A1
Lefkáda (Nissí) GR . 104 A1
Lefkádia GR 101 E2
Lefkaditi GR 105 D2
Lefkandi GR 105 F2
Léfkara GR 101 E3
Léfkes GR 109 F1
Lefkími GR 103 E2
Lefkógia GR 102 A1
Lefkópigi GR 101 D3
Lehená GR 104 B3
Lehetu EE 72 A2

Łęg PL 99 D1
Legan D 33 E2
Leganés E 25 F2
Legé F 14 C2
Legionowo PL 94 C1
Legnago I 47 D1
Legnano I 17 F3
Legnica PL 92 C3
Legnickie Pole PL ... 92 C3
Legrad HR 54 C1
Legrená GR 105 F3
Léguevin F 21 D2
Legutiano E 20 A1
Lehená GR 104 B3
Lehetu EE 72 A2

Lehmden D 33 D3
Lehmja EE 72 B2
Lehnin D 34 B4
Lehola EE 72 A2
Léhovo GR 101 D2
Lehrberg D 39 D4
Lehre D 33 F4
Lehrte D 33 E4
Lehtimäki FIN 69 D2
Lehtmetsa EE 72 C2
Lehtovaara (Lapin Lääni) FIN 65 D1
Lehtovaara (Oulun Lääni) FIN 65 E3
Lehtse EE 72 C2

Leibnitz A 45 E2
Leicester GB 9 D1
Leiden NL 36 C1
Leie EE 73 D3
Leighton Buzzard GB .. 9 E3
Leikanger N 66 A1
Leimani LV 82 C2
Leinefelde D 38 C1
Leinì I 17 E4
Leipalingis LT 85 E3
Leipheim D 43 E1
Leipste EE 75 F3
Leipzig D 39 E1
Leira N 66 B1
Leira N 66 B1

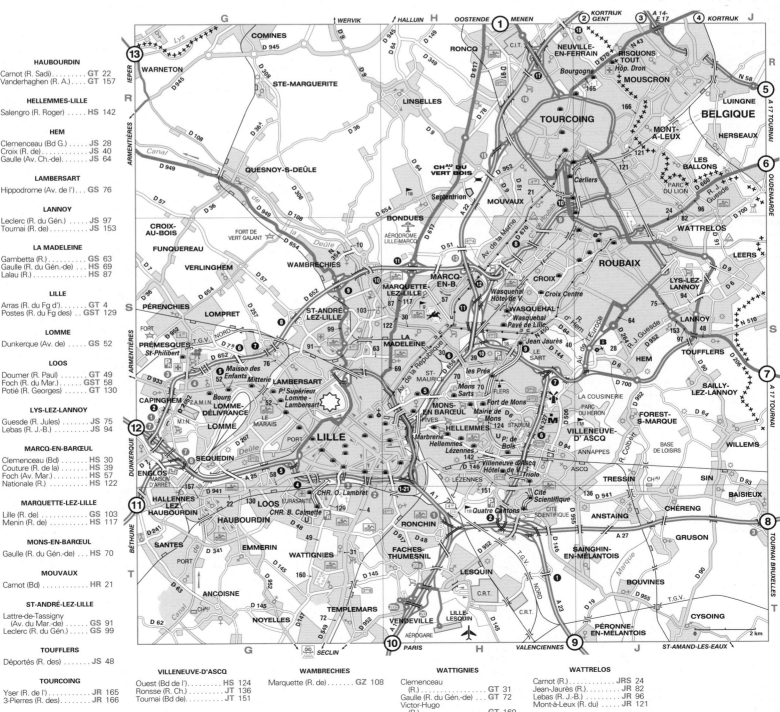

HAUBOURDIN
Carnot (R. Sadi) .... GT 22
Vanderhaghen (R. A.) ..... GT 157

HELLEMMES-LILLE
Salengro (R. Roger) ..... HS 142

HEM
Clemenceau (Bd G.) .... JS 28
Croix (R. de) .... JS 40
Gaulle (Av. Ch.-de) ...... JS 64

LAMBERSART
Hippodrome (Av. de l') ... GS 76

LANNOY
Leclerc (R. du Gén.) ..... JS 97
Tournai (R. de) .... JS 153

LA MADELEINE
Gambetta (R.) .... GS 63
Gaulle (R. du Gén.-de) ... HS 69
Lalau (R.) .... HS 87

LILLE
Arras (R. du Fg d') ...... GT 4
Postes (R. du Fg des) .... GST 129

LOMME
Dunkerque (Av. de) .... GS 52

LOOS
Doumer (R. Paul) .... GT 49
Foch (R. du Mar.) .... GST 58
Potié (R. Georges) .... GT 130

LYS-LEZ-LANNOY
Guesde (R. Jules) .... JS 75
Lebas (R. J.-B.) .... JS 94

MARCQ-EN-BARŒUL
Clemenceau (Bd) .... HS 30
Couture (R. de la) .... HS 39
Foch (Av. Mar.) .... HS 57
Nationale (R.) .... HS 122

MARQUETTE-LEZ-LILLE
Lille (R. de) .... HS 103
Menin (R. de) .... HS 117

MONS-EN-BARŒUL
Gaulle (R. du Gén.-de) ... HS 70

MOUVAUX
Carnot (Bd) .... HR 21

ST-ANDRÉ-LEZ-LILLE
Lattre-de-Tassigny (Av. du Mar.-de) ... GS 91
Leclerc (R. du Gén.) ..... GS 99

TOUFFLERS
Déportés (R. des) .... JS 48

TOURCOING
Yser (R. de l') .... JR 165
3-Pierres (R. des) .... JR 166

VILLENEUVE-D'ASCQ
Ouest (Bd de l') .... HS 124
Ronsse (R. Ch.) .... JT 136
Tournai (Bd de) .... JT 151

WAMBRECHIES
Marquette (R. de) .... GZ 108

WATTIGNIES
Clemenceau (R.) .... GT 31
Gaulle (R. du Gén.-de) ... GT 72
Victor-Hugo (R.) .... GT 160

WATTRELOS
Carnot (R.) .... JRS 24
Jean-Jaurès (R.) .... JR 82
Lebas (R. J.-B.) .... JR 96
Mont-à-Leux (R. du) ...... JR 121

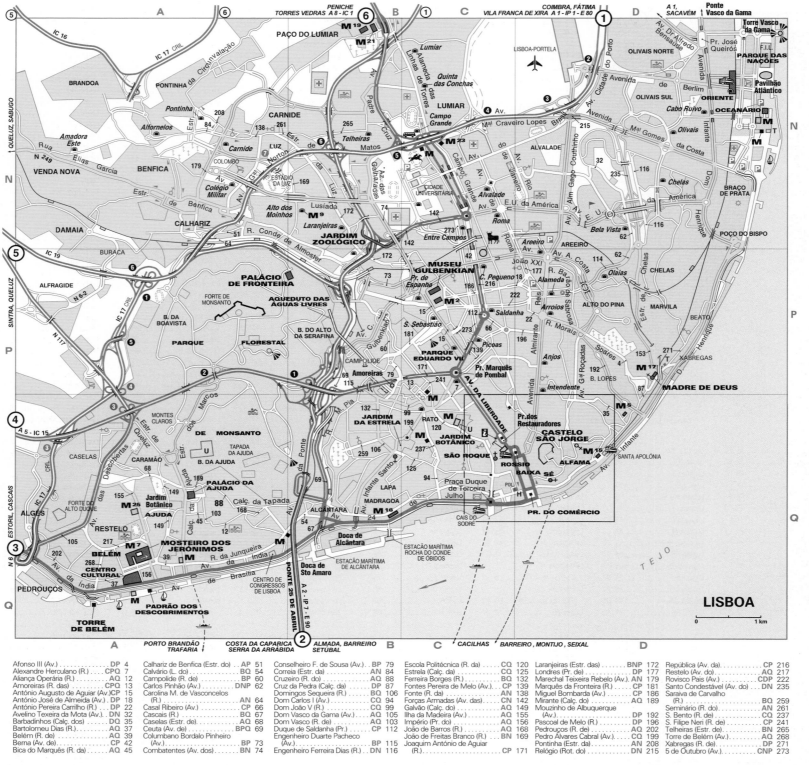

LISBOA

0   1 km

L'Espluga de Francolí E 27 E1
L'Espunyola E 21 E4
Lessay F 11 D3
Lessebo S 71 E2
Lessines B 12 B1
Lessíni GR 104 B2
L'Estartit E 21 F4
Lestelle-Bétharram F 20 C2
Lestene LV 81 D1
Lestijärvi FIN 69 D3
Lestkov CZ 40 A3
Lésvos (Nissí) GR 107 D1
Leszno
    (Mazowieckie) PL 94 B1
Leszno
    (Wielkopolskie) PL 93 D2
Lesznowola PL 94 C2
Letchworth GB 9 C2
Leteniai LT 80 C2
Letenye H 116 B2
Letes LV 79 E1
Letino I 48 C3
Letmathe D 37 E2
Letterfrack IRL 2 A2
Letterkenny /
    Leitir Ceanainn IRL 2 C1
Lettermullan /
    Leitir Mealláin IRL 2 B2
Letur E 26 A2
Letuš SLO 54 B1
Letzlingen D 34 A4
Leuchars GB 7 D1
Leukerbad CH 17 E2
Leuna D 39 E1
Leutenberg D 39 E3
Leutershausen D 39 D4
Leutkirch D 43 E3
Leutschach A 45 E1
Leuven B 12 C1
Leuze-en-Hainaut B 12 A1
Levajok N 61 E2
Levala EE 73 F2
Levanger N 63 D3
Leveniškiai LT 82 A3
Levanjska Varoš HR 55 E2
Levanto I 23 E1
Leväsjoki FIN 68 C3
Leven GB 7 D1
Leven GB 7 F4
Levene S 66 D3
Levens F 23 D1
Leverano I 51 F1
Leverburgh GB 4 A3
Leverkusen D 13 E1
Leveste LV 81 D1
Levet F 16 A2
Levice SK 116 B2
Levico Terme I 43 F4
Levidi GR 108 A3
Levie F 23 F4
Levier F 17 D2
Levitha (Nissí) GR 111 C1
Levoča SK 116 C1
Levroux F 15 F2
Lewes GB 9 C4
Lewin Brzeski PL 93 E3
Lewin Kłodzki PL 96 C1

Afonso III (Av.) .... DP 4
Alexandre Herculano (R.) ... CPQ 7
Aliança Operária (R.) .... AQ 12
Amoreiras (R. das) .... CPQ 13
António Augusto de Aguiar (Av.)CP 15
António José de Almeida (Av.) DP 18
António Pereira Carrilho (R.) . DP 22
Avelino Teixeira da Mota (Av.) . DN 32
Barbadinhos (Calç. dos) ..... DQ 35
Bartolomeu Dias (R.) .... AQ 37
Belém (R. de) .... AQ 39
Berna (Av. de) .... CP 42
Bica do Marquês (R. da) ..... AQ 45
Calhariz de Benfica (Estr. do) . AP 51
Calvário (L. do) .... BQ 54
Campolide (R. de) .... BP 60
Carlos Pinhão (R.) .... DNP 62
Carolina M. de Vasconcelos
    (R.) .... AN 64
Casal Ribeiro (Av.) .... CP 66
Cascais (R. de) .... BQ 67
Caselas (Estr. de) .... AQ 68
Ceuta (Av. de) .... BPQ 69
Columbano Bordalo Pinheiro
    (Av.) .... BP 73
Combatentes (Av. dos) .... BN 74
Conselheiro F. de Sousa (Av.) . BP 79
Correia (Estr. da) .... AN 84
Cruzeiro (R. do) .... AQ 88
Cruz da Pedra (Calç. da) .... DP 87
Domingos Sequeira (R.) ...... BQ 106
Dom Carlos I (Av.) .... CQ 94
Dom João V (R.) .... CQ 99
Dom Vasco da Gama (Av.) ..... AQ 105
Duque de Saldanha (Pr.) ..... CP 112
Engenheiro Duarte Pacheco
    (Av.) .... BN 115
Engenheiro Ferreira Dias (R.) . DN 116
Escola Politécnica (R. da) .. CQ 120
Estrela (Calç. da) .... AN 125
Ferreira Borges (R.) .... BQ 132
Fontes Pereira de Melo (Av.) . CP 139
Fonte (R. da) .... AN 138
Forças Armadas (Av. das) .... CN 142
Galvão (Calç. do) .... AQ 149
Ilha da Madeira (Av.) .... AQ 105
Império (Pr. do) .... AQ 156
João de Barros (R.) .... AQ 168
João de Freitas Branco (R.) . BN 169
Joaquim António de Aguiar
    (R.) .... CP 171
Laranjeiras (Estr. das) ..... BNP 172
Londres (Pr. de) .... DP 177
Marechal Teixeira Rebelo (Av.) AN 179
Marquês da Fronteira (R.) ... CP 181
Miguel Bombarda (Av.) .... CP 186
Mirante (Calç. do) .... AQ 189
Mouzinho de Albuquerque
    (Av.) .... DP 192
Pascoal de Melo (R.) .... DP 196
Pedrouços (R. de) .... AQ 202
Pedro Alvares Cabral (Av.) .. CQ 199
Pontinha (Estr. da) .... AN 208
Relógio (Rot. do) .... DN 215
República (Av. da) .... CP 216
Restelo (R. do) .... AQ 217
Rovisco Pais (Av.) .... CDP 222
Santo Condestável (Av. do) .. DN 235
Saraiva de Carvalho
    (R.) .... BQ 259
Seminário (R. do) .... AN 261
S. Bento (R. de) .... CQ 237
S. Filipe Neri (R. de) ...... CP 241
Telheiras (Estr. de) .... BN 265
Torre de Belém (Av.) .... AQ 268
Xabregas (R. de) .... DP 271
5 de Outubro (Av.) .... CNP 273

Les Échelles F 17 D4
Les Essarts F 14 C2
Les Eyzies-de-Tayac F 15 E4
Les Gets F 17 D3
Les Herbiers F 14 C2
Les Houches F 17 D3
Les Issambres F 23 D2
Les Lecques F 22 C2
Les Llosses E 21 E4
Les Matelles F 22 A2
Les Mées F 22 C1
Les Menuires F 17 D4
Les Ollières-
    sur-Eyrieux F 16 C4
Les Pieux F 10 C3
Les Planches-
    en-Montagne F 17 D2
Les Ponts-de-Cé F 15 D1
Les Quatre Chemins F 14 C2
Les Riceys F 12 C4
Les Rosiers-sur-Loire F ...15 D1
Les Rousses F 17 D2
Les Sables-d'Olonne F 14 C2
Les Settons F 16 B1
Les Trois-Épis F 13 E4
Les Trois-Moutiers F 15 D2
Les Useres E 27 D2
Les Vans F 22 A1
Les Vignes F 21 F1
Lešak SRB 57 D4
Lešani MK 59 E4
Lešć HR 54 B3
L'Escala / La Escala E 21 F4
Lescar F 20 C2
L'Escarène F 23 D2
Lesce SLO 54 A1
Lescun F 20 C3
Lesina I 49 D2
Lesja N 62 C4
Lesjöfors S 67 D2
Lesko PL 99 E3
Leskovac SRB 57 E4
Leśna PL 92 B3
Lesneven F 10 A4
Lešnica SRB 55 F3
Leśnica
    (Dolnośląskie) PL 93 D3
Leśnica (Opolskie) PL 97 E1
Leśniowice PL 95 F3
Lesparre-Médoc F 14 C4

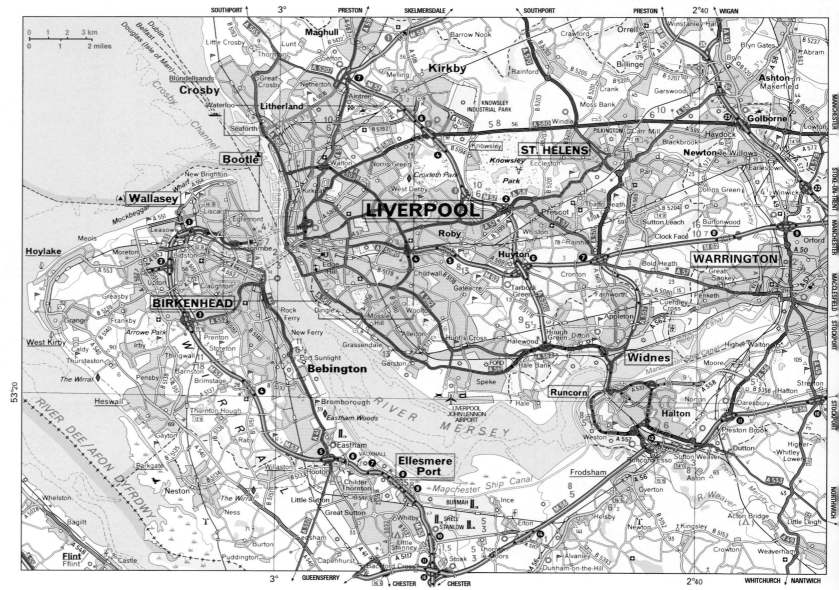

Leyburn GB....7 E3
Leyland GB....7 D4
Leysdown-on-Sea GB....9 F3
Leysin CH....17 E2
Leżajsk PL....99 D1
Lézardrieux F....10 B3
Lézat-sur-Lèze F....21 E4
Lezay F....15 D3
Lezhë AL....116 C4
Lézignan-Corbières F....21 E4
Lezoux F....16 A3
Lezuza E....26 B3
Lgota Wielka PL....94 A3
L'gov RUS....115 F3
L'Hermenault F....15 D2
L'Hospitalet
  de l'Infant E....27 E1
Liabygda N....62 B4
Lianokládi GR....105 D1
Liaušiai LT....86 B1
Líbáň CZ....41 D2
Libatse EE....72 A3
Liberec CZ....40 C2
Liberec CZ....116 A1
Liberiškis LT....81 F3
Libiąż PL....98 A2
Libochovice CZ....40 C2
Libourne F....15 D4
Librilla E....30 C2
Licata I....53 D4
Licciana Nardi I....46 C2
Lich D....13 F1
Lichfield GB....9 D1
Lichoslavl' RUS....115 F1
Lichtenberg D....39 E2
Lichtenfels D....39 E2
Lichtenstein D....39 E2
Lichtenvoorde NL....37 D1
Liči (Preiłu) LV....83 D2
Liči (Rigas) LV....77 F3
Liči (Talsu) LV....76 C3
Liči (Valmieras) LV....78 C2
Ličiūnai LT....81 F2
Lička Jesenica HR....54 B3
Lički Osik HR....54 C3
Ličko Lešće HR....54 B3
Ličupe LV....78 C3
Lida BY....115 D3
Liden S....68 A2
Lidhult S....71 D2
Lidingö S....67 F2
Lidköping S....67 E3
Lido degli Estensi I....47 E1
Lido delle Nazioni I....47 E1
Lido di Camaiore I....46 C2
Lido di Classe I....47 E2
Lido di Jesolo I....44 B4
Lido di Metaponto I....49 F4
Lido di Ostia I....48 A3
Lido di Savio I....47 E2
Lido di Spina I....47 E1
Lido di Torre Mileto I....49 F3
Lido di Venezia I....44 B4
Lido Silvana I....49 F4
Lidoriki GR....105 D2
Lidumi (Alūksnes) LV....79 E2
Lidumi (Kuldigas) LV....76 B3
Lidzbark PL....90 B4
Lidzbark Warmiński PL....90 B3
Liebenwalde D....34 B4
Lieberose D....34 C4
Liechtenstein FL....43 D3
Liège B....13 D1
Liegi LV....80 B1
Lieksa FIN....69 F1
Lielauce LV....81 D1
Lielie Anspoki LV....83 D2
Lielie Mukoni LV....83 D2
Lielionys LT....85 F2
Liellauki LV....81 F2
Lielmēmele LV....82 B2
Lielplatone LV....81 E1
Lielplatones
  Internātskola LV....81 E2
Lielšļūkas LV....81 F1
Lielvārde LV....82 B1
Lielvircava LV....81 E1
Lienz A....44 B3
Liepa LV....78 C2
Liepāja LV....80 A1
Liepakojai LT....85 E2
Liepas
  (Mežamuiža) LV....82 C2
Liepiai LT....85 F1
Liepiškiai LT....81 E1
Liepkalne LV....82 C1
Liepkalne LV....80 C2
Liepna LV....79 F3
Lieporai LT....81 E1
Liepudruvas LV....83 D1
Liepupe LV....77 F2
Liepziedi LV....81 E1
Lier B....12 C1
Liérganes E....19 F2
Liernais F....16 B1
Liestal CH....17 E1
Liesumi LV....78 C2
Lieto FIN....68 C4
Liétor E....26 B4
Lieurey F....11 E3
Lievestuore FIN....69 E3
Liévin F....12 A2
Liezen A....44 B2
Liezère LV....79 D2
Liffol-le-Grand F....13 D4

Lifford IRL....6 A2
Liffré F....11 D4
Ligatne LV....78 B3
Ligatne
  (Augšligatne) LV....78 B3
Ligiá GR....104 B3
Lignano Pineta I....44 C4
Lignano Sabbiadoro I....44 C4
Lignières F....15 F2
Ligny-en-Barrois F....12 C4
Ligny-le-Châtel F....16 B1
Ligourió GR....105 E4
Ligowo PL....90 A3
Ligueil F....15 E2
Liháda GR....105 E1
Lihula EE....72 A3
Liigvalla EE....73 D2
Liikasenvaara FIN....65 F1
Liiva EE....75 D2
Liivi EE....72 A3
Lijeva Rijeka MNE....58 C3
Lijevi Dubravčak HR....54 C2
Likėnas S....67 D1
Likófos GR....103 E1
Likoporiá GR....105 D3
Likórahi GR....100 C3
Likóstomo GR....102 B2
Likouría GR....105 D3
Liksna (Leiksna) LV....83 D2
Likupėni LV....80 C1
Liland N....60 B3
Lilaste LV....77 F3
L'Ile-Bouchard F....15 E2
L'Ile-Rousse F....23 F3
Lilea GR....105 D2
Lilienfeld A....45 D1
Liljendal FIN....69 E4
Lilla Edet S....66 C3
Lillby FIN....68 C1
Lille F....12 B1
Lillebonne F....11 E3
Lillehammer N....66 C1
Lillerød DK....70 C3
Lillers F....12 A1
Lillesand N....66 B3
Lillestrøm N....66 C2
Lillhärdal S....63 E4
Lillholmsjön S....63 E3
Lilli (Harju) EE....72 C2
Lilli (Viljandi) EE....78 C1
Lillo E....26 A2
Lillögda S....64 A3
Lima S....67 D1
Limáni Géraka GR....108 C1
Limáni
  Hersoníssou GR....109 F4
Limanowa PL....98 B2
Limavady GB....3 D1
Limbach D....39 E2
Limbaži LV....78 B2
Limburg a. d. Lahn D....13 F1
Limenária GR....102 B2
Limerick /
  Luimneach IRL....2 B3
Limingen N....63 E2
Liminka FIN....65 D3
Liminpuro FIN....65 E3
Limljani MNE....58 C3
Límnes GR....105 E3
Límni GR....105 E2
Limnítsa GR....102 B2
Límnos GR....104 C2
Limoges F....15 E3
Limogne-en-Quercy F....21 E1
Limone Piemonte I....23 D1
Limonest F....16 C2
Limours-en-Hurepoix F....12 A4
Limoux F....21 E3
Linaküla EE....75 E3
Linares E....26 A4
Linares de Mora E....27 D2
Linares de Riofrío E....25 D1
Linariá GR....106 B3
Lincoln GB....9 E1
Lindås N....66 A1
Lindau i. Bodensee
  (Kreis Lindau-
  Bodensee) D....43 D2
Lindern D....33 D4
Lindesberg S....67 E2
Lindesnes N....66 A3
Lindi EE....75 E3
Lindö S....67 E3
Lindos GR....111 F2
Lindoso E....18 A3
Lindow D....34 B3
Lindsdal S....71 E2
Lingbo S....67 F1
Linge N....62 B4
Lingen D....33 D4
Linghem S....67 E3
Linguaglossa I....51 D4
Linkaičiai LT....81 E2
Linken D....34 C2
Linkmenys LT....86 C1
Linkuva LT....81 F2
Linlithgow GB....7 D1
Linna EE....78 C1
Linnamäe EE....75 D1

Linsell S....63 E4
Linslade GB....9 E2
Linte EE....79 F1
Linthal CH....17 F2
Linyola E....21 D4
Linz A....44 C1
Linz a. Rhein D....13 F1
Lioliai (Šiaulių) LT....81 D3
Lioliai (Telšių) LT....80 B3
Lion-sur-Mer F....11 E3
Lioni I....49 D4
Lióprasso GR....101 E4
Lipa EE....72 B2
Lipa
  (Dolnośląskie) PL....92 C3
Lipar SRB....55 F1
Liperi FIN....69 F2
Lipiany PL....88 B3
Lipica SLO....54 A2
Lipie (Śląskie) PL....98 B3
Lipik HR....55 D2
Lipiński LV....83 E3
Lipinki PL....98 C2
Lipinki łużyckie PL....92 B2
Lipka PL....89 D2
Lipko LV....83 E3
Lipkovo MK....59 E4
Lipljan SRB....59 E3
Lipnica (Kujawsko-
  Pomorskie) PL....89 F3
Lipnica
  (Pomorskie) PL....89 D2
Lipnica
  (Wielkopolskie) PL....88 C3
Lipnica Murowana PL....98 B2
Lipnica Wielka PL....98 A3
Lipnik PL....94 C3
Lipník nad Bečvou CZ....41 F3
Lipno (Kujawsko-
  Pomorskie) PL....89 F3
Lipno
  (Wielkopolskie) PL....93 D2
Lipno nad Vltavou CZ....40 C4
Lipová-lázně CZ....41 E2
Lipovac HR....55 F2
Lipová PL....97 F2
Lipowiec Kościelny PL....90 B3
Lipowo PL....90 A2
Lippstadt D....37 F1
Lipsi I....107 E4
Lipsi (Nissi) I....107 E4
Lipsk PL....91 E2
Lipsko
  (Mazowieckie) PL....95 D3
Liptovský Mikuláš SK....116 B1
Lipuški LV....83 F2
Lirkia GR....105 D3
Lisac BIH....55 E4
Lisboa P....24 A3
Lisburn GB....2 C3
Lisdoonvarna / Lios Dúin
  Bhearna IRL....2 B3
Lisewo (Kujawsko-
  Pomorskie) PL....89 F3
Lisia Góra PL....98 C2
Lisieux F....11 E3
Liskeard GB....8 A4
Liškiava LT....85 E3
Lisków PL....93 F2
L'Isle-Adam F....12 A3
L'Isle-d'Abeau F....16 C3
L'Isle-de-Noé F....21 D2
L'Isle-en-Dodon F....21 D2
L'Isle-Jourdain F....15 E3
L'Isle-Jourdain F....21 D2
L'Isle-sur-la-Sorgue F....22 B1
L'Isle-sur-le-Doubs F....17 D1
L'Isle-sur-Serein F....16 B1
Lisle-sur-Tarn F....21 E2
Lismore / Lios Mór IRL....2 C4
Lisnaskea GB....6 A3
Lišnja BIH....55 D3
Lisova E....83 F2
Lisovići BIH....55 E3
Lit S....63 E3
Lit-et-Mixe F....20 B1
Litene LV....79 E3
Lithakiá GR....104 B3
Lithínes GR....110 C4
Lithio GR....107 D2
Liti GR....101 F2
Litija SLO....54 B2
Litóhoro GR....101 E3
Litoměřice CZ....40 C2
Litomyšl CZ....41 E2
Litovel CZ....41 E3
Litschau A....41 D4
Lóbón E....24 C3
Littlehampton GB....9 E4
Littleport GB....9 E2
Litvínov CZ....40 B2
Liu EE....75 E3
Liubavas LT....85 D3
Liučiūnai LT....85 E1
Liudvinavas LT....85 D2
Liutkiškiai LT....81 E3
Liutonys LT....85 F2
Liuža LT....83 E1
Livade HR....54 A3
Livaderó GR....102 B1
Livaderó GR....101 E3
Livádi GR....102 B3
Livádi GR....101 E3

Livádi GR....106 B4
Livádi GR....108 B2
Livadiá GR....105 E2
Livádia GR....111 E2
Livaditis GR....102 C1
Livadohóri GR....102 C4
Livanátes GR....105 E2
Līvāni LV....83 D2
Livari MNE....58 C3
Livarot F....11 E3
Livbērze LV....81 E1
Liverá GR....101 D3
Liverdun F....13 D3
Livernon F....21 E1
Liverpool GB....7 D4
Līvi LV....78 B3
Livigno I....43 E3
Livingston GB....7 D1
Livno BIH....55 D4
Livo FIN....65 E2
Livold SLO....54 B2
Livorno I....46 C3
Livorno Ferraris I....17 F4
Livron-sur-Drôme F....16 C4
Liw PL....95 D1
Lixoúri GR....104 A2
Lizard GB....8 A4
Lizdeikiai LT....85 E2
Lizdēni LV....78 C2
Līzespasts LV....79 D2
Lizums LV....79 D2
Lizy-sur-Ourcq F....12 A3
Lizzano in Belvedere I....47 D2
Ljeskove Vode BIH....55 E3
Ljig SRB....56 C3
Ljubaništa MK....59 E4
Ljubaševka UA....117 F1
Ljubija BIH....55 D3
Ljubinje BIH....58 B3
Ljubiš SRB....56 C4
Ljubljana SLO....54 A2
Ljubno SLO....54 B1
Ljubojno MK....59 E4
Ljuboml' UA....115 D4
Ljubovija SRB....56 B3
Ljubuški BIH....58 A2
Ljugarn S....67 F4
Ljungby S....71 D2
Ljungbyhed S....71 D3
Ljungdalen S....63 D3
Ljungsbro S....67 E3
Ljungskile S....66 C3
Ljusdal S....67 F1
Ljusne S....67 F1
Ljuta BIH....55 E4
Ljutići MNE....56 B4
Ljutoglav SRB....59 D3
Ljutomer SLO....54 C1
Llagostera F....21 F4
Llanberis GB....3 F3
Llançà E....21 F3
Llandeilo GB....8 B2
Llandovery /
  Llanymddyfri GB....8 B2
Llandrindod Wells GB....3 F4
Llandudno GB....3 F3
Llandysul GB....8 B1
Llanelli GB....8 B2
Llanerchymedd GB....3 F3
Llanes E....19 E2
Llanfairfechan GB....3 F3
Llanfyllin GB....3 F4
Llangadog GB....8 B2
Llangefni GB....3 F3
Llangollen GB....8 C1
Llangurig GB....3 F4
Llanidloes GB....3 F4
Llanrhystud GB....3 F4
Llanrwst GB....3 F3
Llanwrtyd Wells GB....3 F4
Llavorsí E....21 D3
Lleida E....21 D4
Llera E....25 D4
Llerena E....25 D4
Lles de Cerdanya E....21 E3
Llessui E....21 D3
Llíria E....27 D3
Llodio / Laudio E....20 A2
Lloret de Mar E....21 F4
Llucena E....27 D2
Llucmajor E....31 E3
Llutxent E....27 E4
Lniano PL....89 E2
Löbau D....40 C1
Lobenstein D....39 E1
Löberöd S....71 D3
Łobez PL....88 B2
Łobżenica PL....89 D3
Loburg D....34 A4
Łobżenica PL....89 D3
Locana I....17 E3
Ločarica HR....55 D2
Locarno CH....17 F2
Lochaline GB....4 B1
Lochcarron GB....4 B3
Lochearnhead GB....6 C1
Lochem NL....37 D1
Loches F....15 E2
Lochgelly GB....7 D1
Lochgilphead GB....6 C1
Lochinver GB....4 B2
Lochmaben GB....7 D2

Lochmaddy GB....4 A3
Łochów PL....91 D3
Łochowice PL....92 B2
Lochranza GB....6 C1
Lochvycja UA....115 F4
Loçki (Loči) LV....83 D3
Locīši LV....83 F2
Lockenhaus A....45 E1
Lockerbie GB....7 D2
Löcknitz D....34 C2
Locmariaquer F....14 B4
Locminé F....10 B4
Locorotondo I....49 F3
Locquirec F....10 B3
Locri I....51 E4
Locronan F....10 A4
Loctudy F....10 A4
Lodë I....50 B2
Lode (Limbažu) LV....78 B3
Lode (Valmieras) LV....78 C1
Lodève F....21 F2
Lodi I....46 C1
Loding N....60 B3
Lödingen N....60 B3
Lödini LV....81 E2
Lodja EE....75 F3
Lodosa E....20 A3
Łódź PL....94 A2
Loeches E....26 A2
Loen N....62 B4
Løfallstrand N....66 A1
Lofário GR....103 D2
Lofer A....44 B2
Löffingen D....13 F4
Lofsdalen S....63 D4
Lofthus N....66 A1
Log SLO....54 A1
Logarska dolina SLO....54 A1
Logatec SLO....54 A2
Logroño E....20 A3
Logrosán E....25 E3
Løgstør DK....70 B3
Løgten DK....70 B3
Løgumkloster DK....70 B3
Lohals DK....70 C4
Lohberg D....39 F4
Lohilahti FIN....69 F3
Lohiniva FIN....65 D1
Lohja / Lojo FIN....69 D4
Lohkva EE....79 E1
Löhne D....33 E4
Lohne (Oldenburg) D....33 D4
Lohr a. Main D....38 C3
Lohtaja FIN....68 C1
Lohu EE....72 B2
Lohusalu EE....72 B2
Lohusuu EE....73 E2
Loiano I....47 D2
Loimaa FIN....69 C4
Loimaan kunta FIN....68 C4
Loiri I....48 C2
Loiron F....11 D4
Loitz D....34 B2
Loja E....30 C2
Lojsta S....67 F4
Lokalahti FIN....68 B4
Løken N....66 C2
Lokeren B....12 B1
Loket CZ....39 F2
Lokka FIN....61 F3
Løkken DK....70 B2
Løkken N....62 C3
Lokn'a RUS....115 E2
Lokrum (Otok) HR....58 C3
Loksa EE....72 C1
Lokuta (Järva) EE....72 C3
Lokuta (Rapla) EE....72 B2
Lokuti EE....72 B2
Lokve HR....54 B3
Lokve SLO....54 A2
Lokve SRB....57 D2
L'Olleria E....27 D3
Lom BG....117 D3
Lom N....62 B4
Lom
  (Ústecký kraj) CZ....40 B2
Łomazy PL....95 E2
Lomazzo I....17 F3
Lombez F....21 D2
Lomello I....17 F4
Łomianki PL....89 E2
Lomen N....66 B1
Lomeniai LT....85 F2
Lomiai LT....80 C3
Łomianki PL....94 C1
Lomi-Bortniki LV....79 D2
Lomma S....71 D3
Lommatzsch D....39 F1
Lommel B....36 C1
Lomnice
  nad Popelkou CZ....41 D2
Lomonosov RUS....115 D1
Łompolo FIN....61 D2
Łomża PL....91 D3
Lonato I....46 C1
Lončari BIH....55 E3
Londinières F....11 F2
London GB....9 E3
Londonderry GB....3 D1
Lone LV....82 C1
Long Eaton GB....9 D1
Long Preston GB....7 E3
Long Sutton GB....9 E1
Longá GR....108 A1

Longádes GR....100 C4
Longaníkos GR....105 D4
Longares E....20 B4
Longarone I....44 B3
Longeau F....16 C1
Longford /
  An Longfort IRL....2 C2
Longny-au-Perche F....11 F4
Longobucco I....51 E2
Longós GR....104 A1
Longtown GB....7 D2
Longué F....15 D2
Longueville-sur-Scie F....11 F2
Longuyon F....13 D2
Longwy F....13 D2
Lonigo I....47 D1
Löningen D....33 D4
Łoniów PL....98 C1
Lonja HR....55 D2
Lons-le-Saunier F....16 C2
Lönsboda S....71 D3
Lønstad N....60 B4
Loo EE....72 B1
Loodi EE....78 C1
Lööla EE....72 C2
Loosdorf A....45 D1
Loosu EE....79 E2
Lootvina EE....79 E2
Lopar HR....54 B3
Lopare BIH....55 F3
Lopatica MK....59 E4
Lopcombe Corner GB....9 D3
Lôpe (Hiiu) EE....74 C1
Lôpe (Pärnu) EE....72 A3
Lopera E....29 F2
Łopiennik Górny PL....95 E3
Loppa N....61 D1
Loppi FIN....69 D4
Lopud (Otok) HR....58 B3
Łopuszna PL....98 B3
Łopuszno PL....94 B3
Lora N....62 C4
Lora del Río E....29 D2
Lorca E....30 C2
Lorcé B....13 D1
Loreo I....47 E1
Loreto I....48 A4
Loreto Aprutino I....48 C2
Lorgues F....22 C2
Lorica I....51 E3
Lorient F....14 A1
Loriol-sur-Drôme F....16 C4
Lormes F....16 B1
Loro Ciuffenna I....47 E3
Lorquin F....13 E4
Lörrach D....17 D1
Lorrez-le-Bocage F....12 A4
Lorris F....16 A1
Los S....63 E4
Los Alcázares E....30 C2
Los Arcos E....20 A3
Los Baños de Guardias
  Viejas E....30 A3
Los Barrios E....29 D4
Los Corrales
  de Buelna E....19 E2
Los Cortijos
  de Abajo E....25 F3
Los Dolores E....30 C2
Los Gallardos E....30 B3
Los Hinojosos E....26 A3
Los Lobos E....30 C3
Los Navalmorales E....25 F3
Los Navalucillos E....25 E2
Los Palacios
  y Villafranca E....29 D3
Los Santos E....25 D1
Los Santos
  de Maimona E....25 D4
Los Villares E....29 F2
Los Yébenes E....25 F2
Losar de la Vera E....25 E2
Losenstein A....44 C1
Losheim D....13 E3
Łosice PL....95 E1
Lošinj HR....54 B4
Lossémae EE....39 E2
Lössnitz D....39 E2
Lostwithiel GB....8 A4
Lote N....62 A4
Løten N....66 C1
Löttorp S....71 F2
Loudéac F....10 C4
Loudes F....16 B4
Loudias GR....101 F2
Loudun F....15 D2
Loué F....11 E4
Loughborough GB....9 D1
Loughrea /
  Baile Locha Riach IRL....2 B3
Louhans F....16 C2
Louisaari FIN....68 C4
Louisburgh IRL....2 B2
Loukissia GR....105 E2
Loulay F....15 D3
Loulé P....24 B4
Louny CZ....40 B2
Lourdes F....20 C2
Loures P....24 A3

Louriçal P....24 A2
Lourinhã P....24 A2
Loúros GR....104 B1
Lousã P....24 B1
Lousa P....24 A3
Lousada P....18 A4
Louth GB....9 E1
Loutrá E....102 A1
Loutrá GR....107 E1
Loutrá GR....109 E4
Loutrá GR....104 C4
Loutrá GR....106 B4
Loutrá Aridéas GR....101 E2
Loutrá Edipsoú GR....105 E1
Loutrá Elefterón GR....102 B2
Loutrá Ipátis GR....105 D1
Loutrá Kaitsas GR....105 D1
Loutrá Kilinis GR....104 B3
Loutrá Langadá GR....101 F2
Loutrá Smokóvou GR....104 C1
Loutrá Vólvis GR....102 A2
Loutráki GR....104 B1
Loutráki
  (Korinthía) GR....105 E3
Loutráki
  (Magnissía) GR....105 E1
Loutró GR....109 D4
Loutró Elénis GR....105 E3
Loutrópigi GR....104 C1
Loutrópirgos GR....105 E3
Loutrós GR....103 D2
Loútsa GR....104 A1
Loútsa GR....105 E3
Louvain-la-Neuve B....12 C1
Louviers F....11 F3
Louvigné-du-Désert F....11 D4
Lövånger S....64 C3
Lövberga S....68 A1
Lovere I....43 E4
Loviisa / Lovisa FIN....69 E4
Loviště HR....58 A3
Lovosice CZ....40 C2
Lovran HR....54 A3
Lövstabruk S....67 F2
Lovund N....63 D1
Low Street GB....9 F1
Löwenberg D....34 B3
Lowestoft GB....9 F2
Łowicz PL....94 B2
Łowyń PL....92 C1
Loż SLO....54 A2
Lozna SRB....57 D4
Loznica SRB....55 F3
Lozovac HR....54 C4
Lozovik SRB....57 D3
Lozoyuela E....26 A1
Luanco E....19 D1
Luarca E....18 C2
Lubaczów PL....99 E2
Lubań PL....92 B3
Lubāna LV....79 D3
Lübars D....34 A4
Lubartów PL....95 E2
Lubas LV....77 D3
Lubasz PL....88 C3
Lubawa PL....90 A4
Lubawka PL....96 C1
Lübbecke D....33 E4
Lübben D....34 C4
Lübbenau D....34 C4
Lübbow D....34 A3
Lubczyna PL....88 B2
Lübeck D....33 F2
Lubenec CZ....40 B2
Lubenia PL....99 D2
L'ubercy RUS....115 F2
Lüberersac F....15 F4
Lubezere LV....77 D2
Lubiąż PL....92 C3
Lubiatowo PL....89 E2
Lubichowo PL....89 E2
Lubicz Dolny PL....89 F3
Lubień
  (Małopolskie) PL....98 B2
Lubień Kujawski PL....94 A1
Lubieszyn PL....88 A2
Lubiewo PL....89 E2
Lubin
  (Dolnośląskie) PL....92 C3
Lubja EE....79 E2
Lublin PL....95 E2
Lubliniec PL....97 F1
Lubmin D....34 B2
Łubniany PL....93 D3
Łubnice (Łódzkie) PL....93 F3
Łubnice
  (Świętokrzyskie) PL....98 C1
Lubniewice PL....92 B1
Lubny UA....115 F4
Lubochnia PL....94 B2
Lubomia PL....97 D2
Lubomierz
  (Dolnośląskie) PL....92 B3
Lubomino PL....90 B3
Luboń PL....93 D1
Lubowidz PL....90 A3
Łubowo PL....89 F4
Lubraniec PL....93 F1
Lubrín E....30 B3
Lubrza (Lubuskie) PL....92 B1
Lubrza (Opolskie) PL....97 D1
Lubsko PL....92 B2
Lubsza PL....93 E3

Lübtheen D....33 F3
Lubycza Królewska PL....99 F1
Lübz D....34 A3
Luc-en-Diois F....22 B1
Luc-sur-Mer F....11 E3
Lucainena
  de las Torres E....30 B3
Lucan IRL....3 D3
Lučani SRB....56 C4
Lucca I....47 D3
Luče SLO....54 B1
Lucena E....29 E2
Lucenay-l'Évêque F....16 B2
Lučenec SK....116 B2
Luceni E....20 B4
Lucera I....49 D3
Lúchov D....34 A3
Luciana E....25 F3
Lucito I....48 C3
Luc'k UA....115 D4
Lucka D....39 E1
Luckau D....34 C4
Luckenwalde D....34 B4
Luçon F....14 C2
Ludbreg HR....54 C1
Lüdenscheid D....37 E2
Ludiente E....27 D2
Lüdinghausen D....37 E1
L'udinovo RUS....115 F3
Ludlow GB....8 C2
Ludvika S....67 E2
Ludwigsburg D....38 C4
Ludwigsfelde D....34 B4
Ludwigshafen D....13 F2
Ludwigshafen D....43 D2
Ludwigslust D....34 A3
Ludwigstadt D....39 D2
Ludza LV....83 F1
Lug HR....55 E4
Luga RUS....115 D1
Lugagnano
  Val d'Arda I....46 C1
Lugano CH....17 F3
Lüganuse EE....73 E2
Lugau D....39 E2
Lugaži LV....78 C2
Lügde D....37 F1
Lugnano in Teverina I....47 F4
Lugo E....18 B2
Lugo I....47 E2
Lugoj RO....116 C3
Lugones E....19 D2
Luhačovice CZ....41 F3
Luhalahti FIN....69 D3
Luhanka FIN....69 E3
Luhtapohja FIN....69 F2
Luidja EE....74 C2
Luige EE....72 B2
Luino I....17 F3
Luka BIH....55 E4
Luka HR....54 B4
Luka SRB....57 E3
Luke EE....79 D1
Luknainen LT....80 B3
Lukonys LT....82 B3
Lukovica-p-K. SLO....54 B2
Lukovit BG....117 D3
Lukovo MK....59 E4
Lukovo SRB....57 E3
Lukovo SRB....57 D3
Lukovo Šugarje HR....54 B4
Łuków PL....95 D2
Łukowa PL....99 E1
Łukowica PL....98 B2
Lukšiai LT....85 D2
Luksnenai LT....85 E3
Lukstkalni LV....78 B3
Łukta PL....90 A2
Lūlākas LV....83 D1
Luleå S....64 C2
Lüleburgaz TR....117 E4
Luliški LV....83 E2
Lüllemäe EE....79 D2
Lümanda EE....74 B3
Lümati EE....73 E3
Lumbarda HR....58 A3
Lumbier E....20 B3
Lumbrales E....25 D1
Lumbres F....12 A1
Lumezzane I....43 E4
Lumijoki FIN....65 D3
Lumparland FIN....68 B4
Lumpenai LT....84 C1
Lumsås DK....70 C3
Lumsheden S....67 E1
Luna E....20 B3
Lund N....63 D2
Lund S....71 D3
Lunde N....66 B2
Lunden D....33 E2
Lüneburg D....33 F3
Lunel F....22 A2
Lünen D....37 E1
Lunéville F....13 D4
Lungern CH....17 F2
Lungro I....51 D2
Luninec BY....115 D3
Lunz A....45 D1
Luogosanto I....50 A2
Luoke LT....80 C3
Luokesa LT....86 B1
Luopioinen FIN....69 D3

Luosto FIN 65 D1
Lupandi LV 83 F3
Lupikai LT 81 D3
Lupoglav HR 54 C2
Luque E 29 F2
Lurbe-St-Christau F 20 C2
Lurcy-Lévis F 16 A2
Lure F 17 D1
Lurgan GB 3 D1
Luri F 23 F2
Lurisia I 23 E1
Lury-sur-Arnon F 15 F2
Lušci Palanka BIH 54 C3
Lushnjë AL 116 C4
Lusi FIN 69 E3
Lusignan F 15 D2
Lusigny-sur-Barse F 12 C4
Lusina PL 92 C3
Lusk IRL 3 D2
Luso P 24 B1
Lussac F 15 D4
Lussac-les-Châteaux F 15 E2
Lussan F 22 A1
Lustenau A 43 D2
Luster N 62 B4
Lusti EE 79 D2
Lustivere EE 73 D3
Lütjenburg D 33 F2
Lutomiersk PL 94 A2
Luton GB 9 E2
Lutowiska PL 99 E3
Lutrini LV 80 C1
Lutterberg D 38 C1
Lutterworth GB 9 D2
Lututów PL 93 F3
Lutzelbourg F 13 E3
Lützen D 39 E1
Lutzerath D 13 E2
Lutzmannsburg A 45 E1
Lützow D 33 F2
Luua EE 73 D3
Luumäki FIN 69 E3
Luunja EE 79 E1
Luupuvesi FIN 69 E1
Luusua FIN 65 E1
Luvia FIN 68 C3
Luxembourg L 13 D2
Luxeuil-les-Bains F 17 D1
Luynes F 15 E1
Luz-St-Sauveur F 20 C3
Luzaide / Valcarlos E 20 B2
Lužani HR 55 D2
Luzarches F 12 A3
Luzech F 21 E1
Luzern CH 17 F1
Łużna PL 98 C2
Lūznava LV 83 E2
Luzy F 16 B2
Luzzara I 47 D1
Luzzi I 51 D2
L'viv UA 117 D1
Lwówek PL 92 C1
Lwówek Sląski PL 92 B3
Lychen D 34 B3
Lycksele S 64 B3
Lydd GB 9 F4
Lydney GB 8 C2
Lyduokiai LT 86 B1
Lyduvenai LT 81 D3
Łydynia PL 90 B3
Lye S 67 F4
Lygudai LT 81 D2
Lygumai (Marijampoles) LT 85 E2
Lygumai (Šiauliu) LT 81 E2
Lykšilis LT 81 D3
Lyme Regis GB 8 C4
Lymington GB 9 D4
Lyndhurst GB 9 D4
Lyness GB 5 D2
Lyngdal N 66 A3
Lyngseidet N 60 C2
Lyngsnes N 63 D2
Lynmouth GB 8 B3
Lynton GB 8 B3
Lyon F 16 C3
Lyons-la-Forêt F 11 F3
Lysá nad Labem CZ 40 C2
Łysa Polana PL 98 B3
Łyse PL 90 C2
Lysekil S 66 C3
Lyski PL 97 E2
Łysomice PL 89 F3
Łysów PL 95 E1
Lyss CH 17 E1
Lysvik S 67 D2
Łyszkowice PL 94 A2
Lytham St Anne's GB 7 D4

M

M. Doukáto GR 103 D2
Maam Cross / An Teach Dóite IRL 2 B2
Maaninka FIN 69 E1
Maaninkavaara FIN 65 E1
Maanselkä FIN 65 E3
Maardu EE 72 B1
Maarianvaara FIN 69 F2
Maaritsa EE 79 D1
Maarja EE 73 E3
Maaseik B 13 D1
Maasmechelen B 13 D1
Maassluis NL 36 B1
Maastricht NL 13 D1
Maastricht NL 13 D1
Määttälänvaara FIN 65 E2
Mablethorpe GB 9 E1
Macael E 30 B3
Mação P 24 B2
Macclesfield GB 8 C1
Macduff GB 5 D3
Maceda E 18 B3
Macedo de Cavaleiros P 18 C4
Macelj HR 54 C1
Macerata I 47 F3
Macerata Feltria I 47 E2
Machault F 12 C3
Machecoul F 14 C2
Machrihanish GB 6 B2
Machynlleth GB 3 F4
Maciejowa PL 92 C3
Maciejowice PL 94 C2
Mačionys LT 82 B3
Mackantiškes LT 85 F2
Mackenrode D 39 D1
Mackiai LT 85 E2
Mačkovci SLO 54 C1
Macomer I 50 A3
Mâcon F 16 C3
Macotera E 25 E1
Macroom / Maigh Chromtha IRL 2 B4
Macugnaga I 17 F3
Mačvanski Pričinović SRB 55 F2
Maddaloni I 48 C4
Maderuelo E 19 F4
Madesimo I 43 D3
Madliena LV 78 B3
Madona LV 79 D3
Madonna di Campiglio I 43 F4
Madrid E 26 A2
Madridejos E 26 A3
Madrigal de la Vera E 25 E2
Madrigal de las Altas Torres E 25 E1
Madrigalejo E 25 D3
Madrona E 25 F1
Madroñera E 25 D3
Madžiūnai LT 86 B3
Maël-Carhaix F 10 B4
Maella E 27 D1
Mäeltküla EE 78 C1
Mære N 63 D3
Maesteg GB 8 B3
Mäetaguse EE 73 E2
Mafra P 24 A3
Magacela E 25 D3
Magallón E 20 B4
Magaña E 20 A4
Magaz E 19 E4
Magdeburg D 34 A4
Magenta I 17 F3
Maghera GB 3 D1
Magherafelt GB 3 D1
Magione I 47 E3
Maglaj BIH 55 E3
Magliano de' Marsi I 48 B2
Magliano in Toscana I 47 E4
Magliano Sabina I 47 F4
Maglič SRB 57 D4
Maglie I 51 F1
Magnac-Laval F 15 E3
Magnor N 67 D2
Magnuszew PL 94 C2
Magny-en-Vexin F 11 F3
Magoúla GR 104 C3
Magūnai LT 86 C2
Magura SRB 59 E3
Maherádo GR 104 B3
Mahilëŭ BY 115 E3
Mahlu FIN 69 D2
Mahmudiye TR 117 F4
Mahora E 26 B3
Mahovo HR 54 C2
Mähring D 39 E3
Mahu EE 73 E1
Maia P 18 A4
Maials E 27 E1
Maîche F 17 D1
Maida I 51 E3
Maidenhead GB 9 D3
Maidla (Harju) EE 72 B2
Maidla (Ida-Viru) EE 73 E2
Maidla (Rapla) EE 72 B2
Maidla (Rapla) EE 72 A2
Maidstone GB 9 F3
Maienfeld CH 43 D3
Maignelay-Montigny F 12 A3
Maijanen FIN 65 D1
Maillezais F 15 D2
Mailly-le-Camp F 12 C4
Mainar E 26 C1
Mainburg D 43 F1
Maintenon F 11 F4
Mainz D 13 F2
Maiori I 49 D4
Mairena del Alcor E 29 D2
Maironiai LT 81 D3
Maisach D 43 F1
Maišiagala LT 86 B2
Maison-Neuve F 12 C4
Maissau A 41 D4
Maizières-lès-Metz F 13 D3
Maja HR 54 C3
Majdan Królewski PL 99 D1
Majdanek PL 95 E3
Majdanpek SRB 57 E3

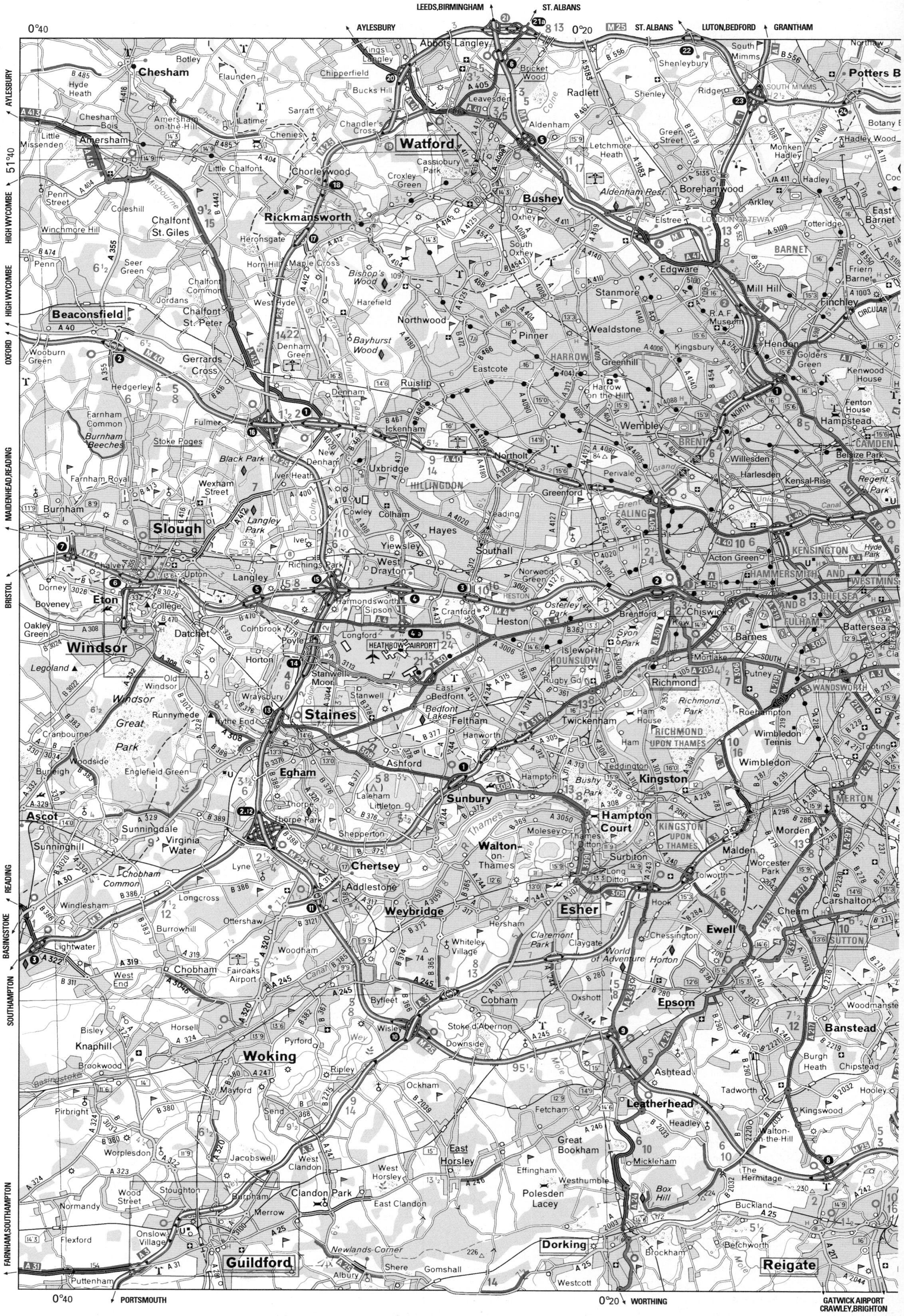
LEEDS,BIRMINGHAM
ST. ALBANS
AYLESBURY
LUTON,BEDFORD
GRANTHAM
0°40
0°20
51°40
HIGH WYCOMBE
OXFORD
MAIDENHEAD,READING
BRISTOL
READING
BASINGSTOKE
SOUTHAMPTON
FARNHAM,SOUTHAMPTON
PORTSMOUTH
WORTHING
GATWICK AIRPORT
CRAWLEY,BRIGHTON
Chesham
Amersham
Watford
Rickmansworth
Bushey
Beaconsfield
Slough
Windsor
Eton
Staines
Egham
Ascot
Sunbury
Chertsey
Weybridge
Esher
Walton-on-Thames
Kingston
Richmond
Epsom
Banstead
Woking
Leatherhead
Guildford
Dorking
Reigate
Heathrow Airport

Majšperk SLO 54 B1
Makarska HR 58 A3
Makce SRB 57 D2
Makedonski Brod MK 59 E4
Makniūnai LT 85 E3
Makó H 116 C2
Mākoni LV 83 D2
Makovo MK 59 F4
Maków (Łodzkie) PL 94 B2
Maków (Mazowieckie) PL 94 C3
Maków Mazowiecki PL 90 C3
Maków Podhalański PL 98 A2
Makowlany PL 91 E2
Makrahómi GR 105 D1
Mákri GR 103 D2
Makríamos GR 102 C2
Makrígialos GR 101 F3
Makrigialós GR 110 C4
Makrihóri GR 102 B2
Makrihóri GR 101 E4
Makrinítsa GR 101 F4
Makriplágio GR 102 B1
Makriráhi GR 105 D1
Makrohóri GR 101 E2
Makronissi (Nissí) GR 105 F3
Mäksa EE 79 E1
Maksniemi FIN 65 D2
Malå S 64 B3
Mala Bosna SRB 55 F1
Mala Krsna SRB 57 D2
Mala Subotica HR 54 C1
Mala Vyska UA 117 F1
Maladzečna BY 115 D3
Málaga E 29 E3
Malagiai LT 80 B3
Malagón E 25 F3
Malahide / Mullach Íde IRL 3 D3
Malaja Višera RUS 115 E1
Malalbergo I 47 D1
Malámata GR 104 C2
Malandríno GR 105 D2
Malanów PL 93 F2
Malaucène F 22 B1
Malax / Maalahti FIN 68 C2
Malbork PL 89 F1
Malbuisson F 17 D2
Malcesine I 43 F4
Malchin D 34 B2
Malchow D 34 A3
Malczyce PL 92 C3
Malda EE 72 A3
Maldegem B 12 B1
Maldeniai LT 81 E2
Maldon GB 9 F3
Małdyty PL 90 A2
Maldžiūnai LT 81 E3
Malé I 43 F3
Małe Gacno PL 89 E2
Male Pijace SRB 55 F1
Malechowo PL 88 C1
Máleme GR 109 D3
Malente D 33 F2
Máles GR 109 F4
Malesherbes F 12 A4
Malessína GR 105 E2
Malestroit F 14 B1
Malgrat de Mar E 21 F4
Mali Iđoš SRB 55 F1
Mali Lošinj HR 54 B4
Mali Požarevac SRB 57 D3
Mali Zvornik SRB 55 F3
Mália GR 109 F4
Malicorne-sur-Sarthe F 15 D1
Maliniec PL 93 F1
Malinka PL 97 F3
Malinova (Malinovka) LV 83 D2
Malinska HR 54 B3
Mališevo SRB 59 D3
Maliskylä FIN 69 D1
Małkinia Górna PL 91 D3
Malko Tarnovo BG 117 E4
Mallaig GB 4 B4
Mallén E 20 B4
Mallersdorf D 39 E4
Malles Venosta / Mals I 43 E3
Mällikvere EE 72 C3
Mallnitz A 44 C2
Mallow / Mala IRL 2 B4
Mallwyd GB 3 F4
Malm N 63 D2
Malmberget S 64 B1
Malmédy B 13 D1
Malmesbury GB 8 C3
Malmköping S 67 F3
Malmö S 71 D3
Malmö-Sturup (Flygplats) S 71 D3
Malmslätt S 67 E3
Malnava (Malnova) LV 83 F1
Malo I 43 F4
Malo Konjari MK 59 E4
Malo-les-Bains F 12 A1
Maloarchangel'sk RUS 115 F3
Małogoszcz PL 94 B3
Maloja CH 43 E3
Malojaroslavec RUS 115 F2
Małomice PL 92 B2
Malónas GR 111 F2
Måløy N 62 A4
Malpartida de Cáceres E 25 D2
Malpartida de Plasencia E 25 D2
Malpica de Bergantiños E 18 A2
Malpica do Tejo P 24 C2
Mālpils LV 78 B3
Målsnes N 60 C2
Malsta S 68 A3
Malta A 44 C2
Malta (Rozentova) LV 83 E2
Malta (Vilāni) LV 83 E1
Maltas Trūpi LV 83 E2
Maltby GB 7 E4
Malton GB 7 F4
Maluenda E 26 C1
Mālumuiža LV 79 D3
Malung S 67 D1
Malungsfors S 67 D1
Mālupe LV 79 E3
Malveira P 24 A3
Malveira P 24 A3
Malvik N 62 C3
Mały Płock PL 91 D2
Malyn UA 115 E4
Mamaia RO 117 E3
Mamarrosa P 24 B1
Mamers F 11 E4
Mammaste EE 79 E1
Mammola I 51 E4
Mamonovo RUS 114 F3
Mamry (Jezioro) PL 90 C1
Manacor E 31 F3
Manacore I 49 E2
Manamansalo FIN 65 E3
Mancha Real E 29 F2
Manchester GB 7 E4
Manching D 39 E4
Manciano I 47 E4
Mančiušenai LT 85 F1
Mandaga LV 77 F3
Mandal N 66 A3

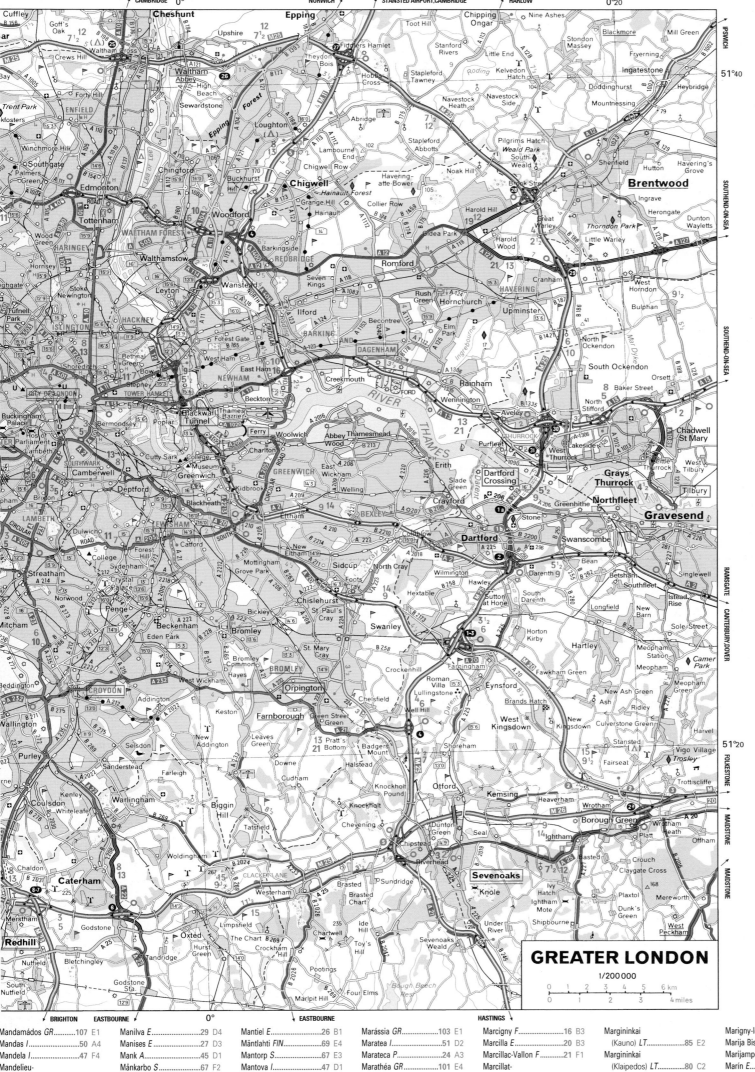

Marinkainen FIN........68 C1
Mārinkalns LV..........79 E2
Marino I................48 A3
Märja EE................79 E1
Märjamaa EE.............72 A2
Marjaniemi FIN.........65 D3
Märkalne LV.............79 E1
Markaryd S..............71 D3
Märkciems LV...........77 D2
Markdorf D.............43 E3
Market Drayton GB.......8 C1
Market Harborough GB....9 E1
Market Rasen GB.........9 E1
Market Weighton GB......7 D1
Markethill GB...........3 C1
Markgröningen D........38 C4
Marki PL...............94 C1
Markina E..............20 A2
Märkisch Buchholz D....34 C4
Markkleeberg D.........39 E1
Markneukirchen
 (Hof) D...............39 E2
Markópoulo GR.........104 A3
Markópoulo GR.........105 F3
Markópoulo
 (Oropoú) GR..........105 F2
Markovac SRB...........57 D2
Markowice PL...........97 C2
Markranstädt D.........39 E1
Markt Erlbach D........39 D4
Markt Indersdorf D.....43 F1
Markt St Florian A.....44 C1
Marktbreit D...........38 C3
Marktheidenfeld D......38 C3
Marktl D...............44 B1
Marktoberdorf D........43 E3
Marktredwitz D.........39 E3
Markušica HR...........55 E2
Markusy PL.............89 F1
Markuszów PL...........95 D3
Marl D.................37 E1
Marlborough GB.........9 D3
Marle F................12 B2
Marlow D...............34 A2
Marlow GB..............9 D3
Marmande F.............21 D1
Marmári GR............106 B3
Mármaro GR...........107 F1
Marmolejo E............25 F4
Marmoutier F...........13 E4
Marnay F...............16 C1
Marne D................33 E2
Marnitz D..............34 A3
Marnovo Manastir MK....59 D4
Marolles-les-Braults F..11 E4
Marónia GR............103 D2
Marostica I............47 F2
Marotta I..............47 F2
Márpissa GR...........109 F1
Marquartstein D........44 B2
Marquion F.............12 B2
Marquise F..............9 F4
Marradi I..............47 E2
Marraskoski FIN........65 C1
Mars-la-Tour F.........13 D3
Marsaglia I............46 B2
Marsala I..............52 B3
Marsberg D.............37 F1
Marsciano I............47 E3
Marseillan F...........22 A2
Marseille F............22 B2
Marseille-
 en-Beauvaisis F.......12 A3
Marsico Nuovo I........49 E4
Marske-by-the-Sea GB....7 F3
Mārsnēni LV............78 C2
Märsta S...............67 F2
Marstal DK.............70 B4
Marstrand S............64 C4
Marta I................47 E4
Martano I..............51 F4
Martel F...............15 F4
Martelange B...........13 D2
Marthon F..............15 E3
Martignacco I..........44 C3
Martigné-Ferchaud F....14 C1
Martigny CH............17 E3
Martigny-les-Bains F...13 D4
Martigues F............22 B2
Martim Longo P........28 B2
Martin SK.............116 B1
Martin Brod BIH........54 C3
Martín de la Jara E....29 E3
Martin de Yeltes E.....25 D1
Martina CH.............43 E3
Martina Franca I.......49 F3
Martinengo I...........43 E4
Martinet E.............21 E3
Martingança P..........24 A2
Martinniemi FIN........65 D2
Martino GR............105 E2
Martinšćica HR.........54 B3
Martis I...............50 A2
Martiši LV.............83 C1
Martjanci SLO..........54 C1
Martna EE..............72 A3
Martnonys LT...........86 B1
Martofte DK............70 C3
Martonvaara FIN........69 F1
Martorell E............21 E4
Martos E...............29 F2
Martti FIN.............61 F3
Marttila FIN...........68 C4
Marvão P...............24 C2
Marvejols F............21 F1
Marykirk GB.............5 D4
Marynin PL.............95 E3

Mandamádos GR.........107 E1
Mandas I...............50 A4
Mandela I..............47 F4
Mandelieu-
 la-Napoule F..........23 D2
Manderscheid D.........13 E2
Mandínia GR...........105 D4
Mandoúdi GR...........105 F2
Mándra GR.............103 D4
Mándra GR.............105 F3
Mandráki GR...........111 E4
Mandre HR..............54 B4
Mandriko GR...........111 F2
Manduria I.............51 E1
Manerbio I.............46 C1
Manětín CZ.............40 B3
Manfredonia I..........49 E3
Mangalia RO...........117 E3
Mángana GR............102 C2
Manganári GR..........109 F1
Manger N...............66 A1
Mangualde P............24 C1
Máni GR...............103 E1
Máni GR...............108 C3
Maniago I..............44 B3
Manikūnai LT...........81 F2

Manilva E..............29 D4
Manises E..............27 D3
Mank A.................45 D1
Mankborka S............67 F2
Mankiškiai LT..........81 E3
Manlleu E..............21 E4
Männamaa EE............74 C2
Mannersdorf
 am Leithagebirge A....45 E1
Mannheim D.............13 F2
Männiku EE.............72 B2
Männikuste EE..........72 A3
Manoppello I...........48 C2
Manorhamilton /
 Cluainín IRL...........2 C1
Manosque F.............22 C2
Manowo PL..............88 C1
Manresa E..............21 E4
Manschnow D............34 C3
Mansfield GB............9 D1
Mansilla
 de las Mulas E........19 D3
Mansle F...............15 D3
Manteigas P............24 C1
Mantes-la-Jolie F......11 F3

Mantiel E..............26 B1
Mäntlahti FIN..........69 E4
Mantorp S..............67 E3
Mantova I..............47 D1
Mäntsälä FIN...........69 D2
Mantsiás GR...........104 C2
Mänttä FIN.............69 D2
Mantviliškiai LT.......81 E3
Mantvydai LT...........80 B3
Mäntyharju FIN.........69 D2
Mäntyjärvi FIN.........65 E2
Mäntyluoto FIN.........68 B2
Manzanares E...........26 A3
Manzanares el Real E...25 F1
Manzaneda E............18 B3
Manzanera E............26 C2
Manzat F...............16 A3
Marchamalo E...........26 A4
Manziana I.............47 E4
Maó E..................45 F3
Mão EE.................72 C3
Maqueda E..............25 F2
Mar'ina Horka BY.....115 D3
Maranchón E............26 B1
Maranello I............47 D2
Marano di Napoli I.....48 C4
Marano Lagunare I......44 C4
Marans F...............14 C2

Marássia GR...........103 E1
Maratea I..............51 D2
Marateca P.............24 A3
Marathéa GR...........101 E4
Marathiás GR..........104 C2
Marathókambos GR......107 D3
Marathónas GR.........105 F3
Marathópoli GR........108 A1
Márathos GR...........105 E1
Marbach a. Neckar D....38 C4
Mårbacka S.............67 D3
Marbella E.............29 E4
Marburg D..............13 F1
Marby S................63 E3
Marčana HR.............54 A3
March GB................9 E2
Marciana E.............47 E4
Marche-en-Famenne B....12 C2
Marchegg A.............41 E4
Marchena E.............29 D2
Marchenoir F...........15 F1
Marchiennes F..........12 B2
Marciac F..............20 C2
Marciana I.............48 C4
Marcianise I...........48 C4
Märciena LV............83 D1

Marcigny F.............16 B3
Marcilla E.............20 B3
Marcillac-Vallon F.....21 F1
Marcillat-
 en-Combraille F.......16 A3
Marcilly-le-Hayer F....12 B4
Marcinkonys LT.........85 F3
Marcinkowice
 (Małopolskie) PL.....98 B2
Marcinkowice (Zachodnio-
 pomorskie) PL.........88 C3
Marcinowice PL.........93 D3
Marciszów PL...........92 C3
Marckolsheim F.........13 E4
Marco de Canaveses P...18 A4
Marcoule F.............22 B1
Marene I...............17 E4
Marennes F.............14 C3
Marentes E.............18 C2
Mareuil F..............15 E4
Mareuil-sur-Lay F......14 C2
Margarites GR.........109 E4
Margariti GR..........100 C4
Margate GB..............9 F3
Margava LT.............85 E2
Margherita di Savoia I..49 E3

Marcigny F.............16 B3
Marcilla E.............20 B3
Margininkai
 (Kauno) LT............85 E2
Margininkai
 (Klaipėdos) LT........80 C2
Margonin PL............89 D3
Marguerittes F.........22 B2
Maria E................30 B2
Maria Saal A...........45 D1
Maria Taferl A.........45 D1
Mariampole LV..........83 E2
Mariannelund S.........67 E4
Mariánské Lázně CZ.....40 B3
Mariazell A............45 D1
Maribo DK..............70 C4
Maribor SLO............54 B1
Mariborsko
 Pohorje SLO...........54 B1
Mariefred S............67 F3
Mariehamn FIN..........68 B4
Marienberg D...........39 F2
Marienborn D...........34 A3
Marienstedt D..........33 F3
Mariental LV...........83 F1
Marieux F..............12 A2
Marignane F............22 B2
Marigny F..............11 D3

Marigny-le-Châtel F....12 B4
Marija Bistrica HR.....54 C2
Marijampole LT.........85 D2
Marín E................18 A3
Marina HR..............58 A4
Marina di Camerota I...50 C2
Marina di Campo I......47 D4
Marina di Carrara I....46 C2
Marina di Castagneto-
 Donoratico I..........47 D3
Marina di Gioiosa
 Ionica I..............51 E4
Marina di Grosseto I...47 D4
Marina di Leuca I......51 F2
Marina di Massa I......46 C2
Marina di Pietrasanta I.46 C2
Marina di Pisa I.......46 C2
Marina di Ragusa I.....53 D4
Marina di Ravenna I....47 E2
Marina di Torre
 Grande I..............50 A3
Marinella I............52 B3
Marineo I..............52 C3
Marines F..............12 A3
Maringues F............16 A3
Marinha Grande P......24 A2

BRON
Mendès-France (Av. P.) . . . DR 103
Roosevelt (Av. F.) . . . . DQR 143
8 Mai 1945 (R. du) . . . . . . DQ 188

ÉCULLY
Champagne (Rte de) . . . . AP 25
Dr-Terver (Av. du) . . . . AP 38
Marietton (R.) . . . . AP 99
Roosevelt (Av. F.) . . . . AP 142

LA MULATIÈRE
Mulatière (Pont de la) . . . . BQ 111

LYON
Bourgogne (R. de) . . . . BP 14
Chambaud-de-la-Bruyère (Bd) . . . . BR 23
Mulatière (Pont de la) . . . . BQ 111
Pasteur (Bd) . . . . BQ 115
Rockefeller (Av.) . . . . CQ 138
St-Simon (R.) . . . . APB 153

OULLINS
Perron (R. du) . . . . BR 119

PIERRE-BÉNITE
Europe (Bd de l') . . . . BR 43

STE-FOY-LÈS-LYON
Fonts (Ch. des) . . . . AQ 55

Thomas (Crs A.) . . . . CQ 168

ST-FONS
Jean-Jaurès (Av.) . . . . CR 79
Semard (Bd P.) . . . . BR 159
Sembat (R. M.) . . . . BR 161

ST-PRIEST
Herriot (Bd E.) . . . . DR 77
Maréchal (R. H.) . . . . DP 97

Franche-Comté (R. de) . . . . BQ 59

TASSIN-LA-DEMI-LUNE
Foch (Av. Mar.) . . . . AQ 53
République (Av.) . . . . DR 134
Victor-Hugo (Av.) . . . . . . APQ 175

VAULX-EN-VELIN
Allende (Av. S.) . . . . DP 3

Rostand (R. E.) . . . . DR 145
Gaulle (Av. Ch.-de) . . . . . . DP 67

VÉNISSIEUX
Cachin (Av. M.) . . . . CR 18
Frères L. et E.
Bertrand (R. des) . . . . CR 61

VILLEURBANNE
Chirat (R. F.) . . . . CQ 29
Jean-Jaurès (R.) . . . . CQ 80

Menen B 12 B1
Menesjärvi FIN 61 E3
Menetés GR 111 E3
Ménez-Hom F 10 A4
Menfi I 52 B3
Mengamuñoz E 25 E1
Mengara I 47 E3
Mengele LV 82 C1
Mengen D 43 D1
Mengeš SLO 54 A2
Mengíbar E 29 F2
Menidi GR 104 B1
Ménigoute F 15 D2
Mennetou-sur-Cher F 15 F1
Mens F 17 D4
Mentana I 47 F4
Menthon-St-Bernard F 17 D3
Menton F 23 D1
Méntrida E 32 C4
Meppel NL 32 C4
Meppen D 33 D4
Mequinenza E 27 D1
Mer F 15 F1
Merag HR 54 B3
Meråker N 63 D3
Meran / Merano I 43 E3
Merano / Meran I 43 E3
Merate I 43 D4
Mercatale I 47 E3
Mercatale I 47 E3
Mercatino Conca I 47 E3
Mercato S. Severino I 49 D4
Mercato Saraceno I 47 E2
Mercendarbe LV 81 F1
Mercéz SRB 57 E2
Mercœur F 15 F4
Merdrignac F 10 A4
Mërdzene LV 83 F2
Mere GB 8 C3
Meremäe EE 79 E2
Méréville F 12 A4
Mergozzo I 17 F3
Méri LV 79 D2
Méribel F 17 D4
Mérida E 25 D3
Mérignac F 15 D4
Mérihas GR 106 B4
Merijärvi FIN 65 D3
Merikarvia FIN 68 C3
Mering D 43 E1
Merkendorf D 39 D4
Merkine (Alytaus) LT 85 F1
Merkine (Vilniaus) LT 86 C3
Merklingen D 43 D1
Merošina SRB 57 E4
Mers-les-Bains F 11 F2
Mersch L 13 D2
Merseburg D 39 E1
Mërsrags LV 77 D2
Merthyr Tydfil GB 8 C3
Mértola P 28 B2
Méru F 12 A3
Merville F 12 A1
Merville-
Franceville-Plage F 11 D1
Méry-sur-Seine F 12 B4
Merzig D 13 E3
Mesagne I 51 F1
Mesão Frio P 18 B4
Meschede D 37 F1
Meschers-
sur-Gironde F 14 C3
Mešeišta MK 59 E4
Mesići BIH 55 F4
Mesihovina BIH 55 D4
Meškenai LT 85 E2
Meškerine LT 86 C1
Meškučiai
(Alytaus) LT 85 F3
Meškučiai
(Marijampoles) LT 85 E3
Meškučiai
(Mekiai) LT 81 E2
Meškuičiai
(Pabutkalnis) LT 81 D3
Meslay-du-Maine F 11 D4
Mesocco CH 43 D3
Mesola I 47 E1
Mesón do Vento E 18 A2
Mesoraca I 51 E3
Mespelbrunn D 38 C3
Messanagrós GR 111 E3
Messara GR 106 C3
Meßdorf D 34 A4
Messei F 11 D4
Mëssi GR 102 C2
Messiméri GR 101 F3
Messimvría GR 103 D2
Messina I 51 D4
Messini GR 108 A1
Meßkirch D 43 D2
Messlingen S 7 F1
Messohóra GR 101 D4
Messohóri GR 101 E4
Messohóri GR 111 E3
Messolónghi GR 104 C2
Messongí GR 100 B4
Messopótamo GR 104 A1
Messótopos GR 107 D1
Meßstetten D 43 D1
Mestá GR 107 D2
Mestanza E 25 F4
Mésti GR 103 D2
Mestlin D 34 A4
Město Albrechtice CZ 41 F2
Mestre I 44 B4

Maryport GB 7 D3
Mas-Cabardès F 21 F2
Mas de Barberáns E 27 E1
Mas de las Matas E 27 D1
Masegoso de Tajuña E 26 B1
Maselíškes LT 86 B1
Masevaux F 17 E1
Masi N 61 D2
Masku FIN 68 C4
Maslenica HR 54 C4
Maslinica HR 58 A4
Maslovare BIH 55 D3
Masłów PL 94 C3
Masłowice
(Lodzkie) PL 93 F3
Massa I 46 C2
Massa Fiscaglia I 47 E1
Massa Marittima I 46 C2
Massa Martana I 47 F4
Massafra I 49 F4
Massamagrell E 27 D3
Massarosa I 46 C2
Massat F 21 D2
Masseube F 21 D2
Massiac F 16 A4
Massiaru EE 75 F3
Maštaičiai LT 85 D1
Mastihári GR 111 E1
Masty BY 115 D3
Masueco E 18 C4
Maszewo
(Lubuskie) PL 92 B2
Maszewo (Zachodnio-
pomorskie) PL 88 B2
Mátala GR 109 E4
Matalascañas E 28 C3
Matalebreras E 20 A4
Matallana de Torío E 19 D2
Mataró E 21 F4
Mataruška Banja SRB 57 D4
Mateševo MNE 58 C3
Matejče MK 59 E3
Matelica I 47 E3
Matera I 49 F4
Máteri LV 76 C3
Matészalka H 116 C2
Mateus P 18 B4
Matfors S 68 A2

Matha F 15 D3
Mathráki (Nissi) GR 100 A4
Máti GR 105 F3
Matiešionys LT 85 E2
Matignon F 10 C4
Matisene LV 79 E2
Matíši LV 78 B2
Matka MK 59 E3
Matku FIN 69 D3
Matkule LV 77 D3
Matlock GB 9 D1
Matosinhos P 18 A4
Matour F 16 B3
Matrei am Brenner A 43 F2
Matrei in Osttirol A 44 B2
Matsuri EE 79 E2
Mattersburg A 45 E1
Mattighofen A 44 B1
Mattinata I 49 E2
Mattmar S 67 E4
Mattsee A 44 B1
Mattsmyra S 67 E1
Matuizos LT 86 B3
Matulji HR 54 A3
Mątwy PL 89 E2
Maubeuge F 12 C2
Maubourguet F 20 C2
Maubuisson F 14 C4
Mauchline GB 6 C2
Mauerkirchen A 44 B1
Mauguio F 22 A2
Maula FIN 65 D2
Maulbronn D 13 F3
Mauléon F 20 B2
Mauléon-Licharre F 20 B2
Maun (Otok) HR 54 B4
Maure-de-Bretagne F 11 D4
Mauriac F 15 F4
Mauron F 10 C4
Maurs F 21 F4
Mautern A 45 D2
Mauterndorf A 44 C2
Mauthausen A 44 C1
Mauthen A 44 B3
Mauvezin F 21 D2
Mauzé-
sur-le-Mignon F 15 D3
Mavrohóri GR 101 D2
Mavroklíssi GR 103 E4

Mavroléfki GR 102 B2
Mavromáta GR 104 C1
Mavromáti GR 101 D4
Mavroúda GR 102 A2
Mavrovi Anovi MK 59 E4
Mavrovo MK 59 E4
Mavrovoúni
(Lárissa) GR 101 E1
Mavrovoúni
(Péla) GR 101 D2
Maxhütte-Haidhof D 39 E4
Maxmo /
Maksamaa FIN 68 C2
Maybole GB 6 C2
Mayen D 13 E2
Mayenne F 11 D4
Mayerling A 45 D1
Mayet F 15 E1
Maynooth /
Maigh Nuad IRL 3 D3
Mayorga E 19 D3
Mayrhofen A 43 F2
Mazagón E 28 C3
Mazagran F 12 C3
Mazamet F 21 F2
Mazara del Vallo I 52 B3
Mazarakiá GR 100 B4
Mazarete E 26 B1
Mazarrón E 30 C2
Mazeikiai (Telšiu) LT 80 C2
Mažeikiai (Vilniaus) LT 86 C2
Mažėnai LT 83 D3
Mazères F 21 E2
Mazgavieze LV 80 C3
Mázi GR 100 C3
Mažieji Büdežerai LT 85 D2
Mažieji Rūšupiai LT 80 B2
Mazières-en-Gâtine F 15 D2
Mažintai LT 85 D1
Mazirbe LV 76 C2
Mažiūnai LT 85 F2
Mazlauki (Rosme) LV 81 E1
Mažonai LT 84 C1
Mažrimaičiai LT 84 C1
Mazrulli LV 76 C3
Mazsalaca LV 78 B2

Mažučiai
(Pilviškiai) LT 85 D2
Mažučiai (Šiauliu) LT 81 E2
Mažučiai (Virbalis) LT 85 D2
Mažuliai LT 81 E3
Mazurzyce PL 94 A2
Mazyr BY 115 D4
Medyn' RUS 115 F2
Medžionys LT 85 F2
Medžitlija MK 59 E4
Mcensk RUS 115 F2
Mealhada P 24 B1
Meaux F 12 A3
Mechelen B 12 C1
Mečionys LT 87 D1
Meckenbeuren D 43 D2
Mêda P 24 C1
Medak HR 54 C4
Mede I 17 F4
Medebach D 37 F2
Medeđa BIH 55 F4
Medelim P 24 C2
Medellín E 25 D3
Medemblik NL 32 B4
Mediaş RO 117 D2
Medicina I 47 E2
Medikoniai LT 81 F3
Medina Azahara E 29 E2
Medina de Pomar E 19 F3
Medina de Rioseco E 19 D4
Medina del Campo E 19 E4
Medina-Sidonia E 29 D4
Medinaceli E 26 B1
Medingenai LT 80 C3
Medininkai
(Kauno) LT 85 E1
Medininkai
(Vilniaus) LT 86 C2
Medkiai LT 81 F3
Medjugorje BIH 58 A2
Medne LV 81 D1
Medni LV 83 D1
Médoussa GR 102 C1
Medsėdžiai LT 80 B3
Medulin HR 54 A3
Medumajdam HR 54 C3
Medumi LV 83 D3
Meduno I 44 B3

Meðurečje SRB 57 D4
Medveda SRB 57 D4
Medveja HR 54 A3
Medvida HR 54 C4
Medvode SLO 54 A2
Medyka PL 99 E2
Medžiukai LT 86 B2
Meegomäe EE 79 E2
Meeksi EE 79 E1
Meelva EE 79 E1
Meerane D 39 E2
Meeri EE 79 D1
Meersburg D 17 D1
Mefjordbotn N 60 B2
Mefjordvær N 60 B2
Meg. Horió GR 104 C1
Meg. Horió GR 107 F4
Meg. Horió GR 111 E2
Meg. Livádi GR 106 B4
Meg. Monastíri GR 101 E1
Meg. Panagía GR 102 A3
Meg. Vólvi GR 102 A2
Méga Dério GR 103 D1
Méga Spíleo GR 105 D3
Megalóhori GR 101 D4
Megalópoli GR 105 D4
Meganíssi GR 104 B2
Megaplátanos GR 105 E2
Mégara GR 105 D3
Megárhi GR 101 D4
Mégisti GR 111 F4
Megísti (Kastelórizo)
(Nissi) GR 111 F4
Megučioniai LT 81 E2
Mehamn N 61 E1
Mehedeby S 68 A4
Mehikoorma EE 79 F1
Mehun-sur-Yèvre F 15 F2
Meigle GB 7 D1
Meijel NL 37 D1
Meikštai LT 83 D1
Meilen CH 17 F1
Meillant F 16 A2
Meilūnai
(Panevežio) LT 82 B2

Meilūnai (Vilniaus) LT 85 F1
Meimoa P 24 C1
Meina I 17 F3
Meinerzhagen D 13 E1
Meiningen D 39 D2
Meira E 18 B2
Meirâni LV 83 D1
Meiringen CH 17 F2
Meironiškiai LT 85 E1
Meironys LT 87 D1
Meisenheim D 13 E3
Meißen D 39 F1
Meitingen D 43 E1
Mekiai LT 81 E2
Mel I 44 B4
Melalahti FIN 65 E3
Mélambes GR 109 E4
Melaniós GR 107 D2
Melánthio GR 101 D3
Melátes GR 104 B1
Melbârži LV 78 C3
Melbeck D 33 F3
Melbu N 60 B3
Meldal N 62 C3
Meldola I 47 E2
Meldorf D 33 D2
Meldzere LV 80 C1
Melegnano I 46 B1
Melenci SRB 56 B2
Melendugno I 51 F1
Meleski EE 73 D3
Melfi I 49 E3
Melgaço P 18 A3
Melgar de Abajo E 19 E3
Melgar de Fernamental E 19 F3
Melhus N 62 C3
Meliá GR 101 E2
Melía GR 103 E2
Melide E 18 B2
Melides P 24 A4
Melidóni GR 109 D4
Meligalás GR 104 C4
Melíki GR 101 E2
Melilli I 53 E3
Mélisey F 17 D1
Melíssa GR 102 C2
Melissáni GR 104 A2
Melíssi GR 105 D3
Melissohóri GR 105 E2

Melissópetra GR 100 C3
Melissourgós GR 102 A2
Melito Porto Salvo I 51 D4
Melívia GR 102 C1
Melívia GR 101 F4
Melk A 45 D1
Melksham GB 8 C3
Mellansel S 68 A1
Melle D 33 D4
Melle F 15 D3
Mellendorf D 33 E4
Mellerud S 67 D3
Mellieha M 53 F4
Mellilä FIN 68 C4
Mellín D 33 F4
Mellingen D 39 D2
Melliste EE 79 E1
Mellrichstadt D 38 C2
Mellsils (Melnsils) LV 77 D2
Melnai LT 81 E2
Melnica SRB 57 E3
Melnik HR 54 B3
Mélnik CZ 40 C2
Melniki LV 83 F2
Melpers D 38 C2
Melrose GB 7 D2
Melsungen D 38 C2
Meltaus FIN 65 D1
Melton Mowbray GB 9 D1
Meltosjärvi FIN 65 D1
Melun F 12 A4
Melvich GB 4 C2
Membrilla E 26 A3
Membrío E 24 C2
Memmingen D 43 E1
Mena UA 115 F1
Menaggio I 43 D3
Menai Bridge /
Porthaethwy GB 3 D4
Menasalbas E 25 F3
Menat F 16 A3
Mendavia E 20 A3
Mende F 22 A1
Menden (Sauerland) D 37 E1
Mendenitsa GR 105 E2
Mendig D 13 E1
Mendrisio CH 17 F3

Mesvres *F* 16 B2
Metajna *HR* 54 B4
Metaliko *GR* 101 F2
Metalio *GR* 105 D4
Metaljka *BIH* 55 F4
Metamórfossi *GR* 101 F1
Metamórfossi *GR* 102 A3
Metangitsi *GR* 102 A3
Metaxádes *GR* 103 E1
Meteliai *LT* 85 E3
Metéora *GR* 101 D4
Méthana *GR* 105 D4
Methil *GB* 7 D1
Methóni *GR* 101 F3
Methóni *GR* 108 A1
Metković *HR* 58 A3
Metlika *SLO* 54 B2
Metnitz *A* 44 C2
Metóhi *GR* 104 B3
Metóhi (Árgolida) *GR* 105 E4
Metóhi (Évia) *GR* 105 F2
Metóhi (Magnissía) *GR* 105 E1
Mètriena *LV* 83 D1
Metsakasti *EE* 72 B1
Metsakivi *EE* 73 E3
Metsäküla *EE* 73 E3
Metsäkylä *FIN* 65 E2
Metsäkylä *FIN* 69 E4
Metsalaane *EE* 79 D1
Metsämaa *FIN* 69 D3
Metsapoole *EE* 77 F1
Metsküla (Saare) *EE* 74 C2
Metsküla (Viljandi) *EE* 72 C3
Métsovo *GR* 101 D4
Metste *EE* 79 E1
Mettingen *D* 33 D4
Mettlach *D* 13 E3
Mettmann *D* 37 E2
Metz *F* 13 D3
Metzervisse *F* 13 D3
Metzingen *D* 43 D1
Meulan *F* 12 A1
Meung-sur-Loire *F* 15 F1
Meursault *F* 16 C2
Meuselwitz *D* 39 E2
Mevagissey *GB* 8 A4
Meximieux *F* 16 C1
Meyenburg *D* 34 A3
Meymac *F* 15 F3
Meyrueis *F* 22 A1
Meyzieu *F* 16 C3
Mežåre *LV* 83 D1
Mežciems (Jelgavas) *LV* 81 E1
Mežciems (Rigas) *LV* 77 F3
Meždārzi *LV* 82 C1
Mezdra *BG* 117 D4
Mèze *F* 22 A2
Mézel *F* 22 C1
Meželiai *LT* 80 D4
Mežgale *LV* 82 C2
Mežica *SLO* 54 B1
Mézidon *F* 11 E3
Mézières-en-Brenne *F* 15 E2
Mézières-sur-Issoire *F* 15 E3
Mézin *F* 21 D1
Mežioneliai *LT* 86 C1
Mežklabji *LV* 77 D3
Mežmala *LV* 77 F3
Mežmaliešì *LV* 81 E1
Mežőberény *H* 116 C2
Mezőkövesd *H* 116 C2
Mežotne *LV* 81 F1
Mežotúr *H* 116 C2
Mezquita de Jarque *E* 26 C1
Mežrozites *LV* 79 D2
Mežsargi *LV* 78 C2
Mežvalde *LV* 76 C2
Mežvidi (Baldone) *LV* 81 F1
Mežvidi (Liepājas) *LV* 76 B3
Mežvidi (Ogres) *LV* 82 B1
Mežvidi (Saldus) *LV* 80 C1
Mežvidi (Saulkrasti) *LV* 77 F3
Mežvidi (Valmieras) *LV* 78 C2
Mežvidi (Mežavidi) *LV* 83 F1
Mežvidu Muiža *LV* 83 F1
Mezzano *I* 43 F4
Mezzolombardo *I* 43 F4
Mgarr *M* 53 F4
Miączyn *PL* 95 F3
Miajadas *E* 25 D3
Miałkówek *PL* 94 A1
Miasteczko Krajeńskie *PL* 89 D3
Miasteczko Śląskie *PL* 97 F1
Miastko *PL* 89 D2
Miastkowo *PL* 91 D3
Michałkowo *PL* 90 C1
Michalovce *SK* 116 C1
Michałów (Świętokrzyskie) *PL* 98 B1
Michałowice *PL* 98 B2
Michałowo *PL* 91 F3
Micheldorf *A* 48 A1
Michelin *PL* 89 F3
Michelstadt *D* 37 D3
Michendorf *D* 34 A4
Michorzewo *PL* 92 C1
Michów *PL* 95 D2
Miciūnai *LT* 86 B2
Mickai *LT* 80 A3
Mickieme *LT* 81 F3
Mickūnai (Utenos) *LT* 82 B3

Mickūnai (Vilniaus) *LT* 86 C2
Mičurinietis *LV* 83 D3
Mikrópoli *GR* 102 A1
Mid Yell *GB* 5 F1
Middelburg *NL* 36 B1
Middelfart *DK* 70 B3
Middelharnis *NL* 36 B1
Middelkerke-Bad *B* 12 A1
Middlesbrough *GB* 7 F3
Middleton-in-Teesdale *GB* 7 E3
Middlewich *GB* 8 C1
Midhurst *GB* 9 D3
Midleton / Mainistir na Corann *IRL* 2 C4
Midsund *N* 62 B3
Miechów *PL* 98 B1
Miechucino *PL* 99 D1
Miedes *E* 26 C1
Miedwie (Jezioro) *PL* 88 A2
Miedziana Góra *PL* 94 B3
Miedzichowo *PL* 92 C1
Miedzna *PL* 95 D1
Miedźno *PL* 93 F3
Międzybórz *PL* 93 E3
Międzybrodzie Bialskie *PL* 97 F2
Miedzychód *PL* 88 C3
Międzygórze *PL* 96 C2
Międzylesie (Dolnośląskie) *PL* 96 C2
Międzyrzec Podlaski *PL* 95 E2
Międzyrzecz *PL* 92 B1
Międzyrzecze Górne *PL* 97 F2
Międzyzdroje *PL* 88 A2
Miegenai *LT* 81 E3
Miegonys *LT* 82 C2
Miegupite *LV* 78 C2
Miehikkälä *FIN* 69 E3
Miejsce Piastowe *PL* 99 D2
Miejska Górka *PL* 93 D2
Mękinia *PL* 93 D3
Mielagenai *LT* 87 D1
Mielan *F* 21 D2
Mielec *PL* 98 C2
Mielęcin *PL* 88 A3
Mieleszyn *PL* 89 D3
Mieliūnai (Bugailiškiai) *LT* 82 B3
Mieliūnai (Mockūnai) *LT* 82 B2
Mielno *PL* 88 C1
Mieluskylä *FIN* 65 D3
Miercurea-Ciuc *RO* 117 D2
Mieres *E* 19 D2
Mierkalns *LV* 79 D2
Mieroszów *PL* 96 C1
Mierzęcice *PL* 97 F1
Miesbach *D* 43 F2
Mieścisko *PL* 89 D3
Miestalis *LT* 80 C3
Miesto Kolonija *LT* 85 E3
Mieszków *PL* 93 E2
Mieszkowice *PL* 88 A3
Mietków *PL* 93 D3
Mietoinen *FIN* 68 C4
Miettila *FIN* 69 F3
Mieżiškiai *LT* 81 F3
Migennes *F* 16 A1
Migliarino *I* 47 E1
Miglionico *I* 49 E4
Migonys *LT* 85 F2
Miguel Esteban *E* 26 A3
Miguelturra *E* 25 F3
Mihajlovac (Negotin) *SRB* 57 D3
Mihajlovac (Smederevo) *SRB* 57 E2
Mihas *GR* 104 C3
Mihói *GR* 104 C3
Miidurranna *EE* 72 B1
Mijas *E* 29 E3
Mijoux *F* 17 D2
Mikalaučiškes *LT* 85 F2
Mikalauka *LT* 85 D3
Mikalavas *LT* 87 D1
Mikantonys *LT* 86 C3
Mikenai *LT* 85 F1
Miki *GR* 102 C1
Mikitamäe *EE* 79 F1
Mikkelbostad *N* 60 B2
Mikkeli *FIN* 69 E2
Mikkelvik *N* 60 C2
Mikleuš *HR* 55 D2
Miklini *LV* 76 B2
Miklusenai *LT* 85 E3
Mikniškiai *LT* 85 E3
Miknonys *LT* 85 E2
Mikolaičiai *LT* 81 D2
Mikołajki *PL* 90 C2
Mikołajki Pomorskie *PL* 89 F2
Mikoliškis *LT* 86 B3
Mikoliškis *LT* 81 F2
Mikołów *PL* 97 F2
Mikonos *GR* 106 C4
Mikonos (Nissi) *GR* 106 C4
Mikr. Dério *GR* 103 E1
Mikr. Eleftherohóri *GR* 101 E3
Mikr. Horió *GR* 104 C1
Mikrí Mandínia *GR* 108 A1
Mikrí Préspa *GR* 101 D2
Mikrókambos *GR* 101 F2
Mikroklissoúra *GR* 102 B1

Mikrolímni *GR* 101 D2
Mikromiliá *GR* 102 B1
Mikrópoli *GR* 102 A1
Mikstat *PL* 93 E2
Mikulčiai *LT* 80 B2
Mikulov *CZ* 41 E4
Mikulovice (Olomoucký kraj) *CZ* 41 E2
Mikuszewo *PL* 93 E2
Mikužiai *LT* 80 B3
Mikyčiai *LT* 85 E3
Mikytai *LT* 85 E1
Milagro *E* 20 B3
Milano *I* 46 B1
Milano Marittima *I* 47 E2
Milanówek *PL* 94 B2
Milatos *GR* 109 F4
Milazzo *I* 51 D4
Milejczyce *PL* 91 E3
Milejewo *PL* 90 A1
Milejów *PL* 95 E3
Mileševo Dol *SRB* 56 C4
Mileševo *SRB* 55 F1
Milestone *IRL* 2 C3
Miletići *HR* 54 B4
Mileto *I* 51 D3
Milevsko *CZ* 40 C3
Milford *GB* 9 E3
Milford Haven / Aberdaugleddau *GB* 8 A2
Milhão *P* 18 C4
Mili *GR* 105 D4
Miliá *GR* 103 E1
Miliá *GR* 101 D3
Miliá *GR* 105 D4
Milići *BIH* 55 F3
Milicz *PL* 93 D2
Miliés *GR* 105 E1
Milín *CZ* 40 C3
Milína *GR* 105 E1
Milis *I* 50 A3
Militello in Val di Catania *I* 53 D3
Miliūnai *LT* 82 B3
Miljevina *BIH* 55 F4
Miłki *PL* 91 D2
Miłkowice *PL* 92 C3
Milkūnai *LT* 86 C3
Milkuškos *LT* 87 D1
Millares *E* 26 C3
Millas *F* 21 F3
Millau *F* 21 F1
Millesimo *I* 23 E1
Millford *IRL* 6 A2
Millom *GB* 6 C3
Millport *GB* 6 C1
Millstatt *A* 44 C3
Millstreet *IRL* 2 B4
Milltown Malbay / Sráid na Cathrach *IRL* 2 B3
Milly-la-Forêt *F* 12 A4
Milmarcos *E* 26 B1
Milmersdorf *D* 34 B3
Milna *HR* 58 A4
Milohnići *HR* 54 B3
Miłomłyn *PL* 90 A2
Milopótamos *GR* 108 B2
Milos *GR* 109 E1
Miloševa Kula *SRB* 57 E3
Miłosław *PL* 93 E1
Miltach *D* 39 F4
Miltenberg *D* 38 C3
Miltini *LV* 81 E1
Milton Keynes *GB* 9 E2
Milutinovic *SRB* 57 E2
Miłuž *LV* 80 B1
Milzkalne *LV* 77 E3
Mimizan *F* 20 B1
Mimizan-Plage *F* 20 B1
Mimoň *CZ* 40 C2
Mina *GR* 108 B1
Mina de São Domingos *P* 28 B2
Minas de Riotinto *E* 28 C2
Minaya *E* 26 B3
Mindelheim *D* 43 E1
Minden *D* 33 E4
Mindin *F* 14 B1
Minehead *GB* 8 B3
Minerbe *I* 47 D1
Minerbio *I* 47 D1
Minervino Murge *I* 49 E3
Minglanilla *E* 26 C3
Mingorría *E* 25 F1
Miničevo *SRB* 57 F3
Minija *LT* 80 A3
Minkió *FIN* 69 D3
Minsk *BY* 115 D3
Mińsk Mazowiecki *PL* 94 C1
Minsterley *GB* 8 C1
Mintlaw *GB* 5 E3
Minupiai *LT* 86 C3
Mionica *SRB* 56 C3
Mionnay *F* 16 C3
Míos (Nissí) *GR* 109 E1
Miotek *PL* 97 F1
Mira *E* 26 C3
Mira *I* 44 B4
Mira *P* 24 B1
Mira de Aire *P* 24 A2
Mirabella Imbaccari *I* 53 D3
Mirachowo *PL* 89 E1
Miraflores *E* 19 F3
Miraflores de la Sierra *E* 25 F1
Miramar *E* 23 D2

Miramar *P* 18 A4
Miramare *I* 47 F2
Miramas *F* 22 B2
Mirambeau *F* 15 D4
Miramont-de-Guyenne *F* 21 D1
Miranda de Ebro *E* 20 A3
Miranda del Castañar *E* 25 D1
Miranda do Corvo *P* 24 B1
Miranda do Douro *P* 18 C4
Mirande *F* 21 D2
Mirandela *P* 18 B4
Mirandola *I* 47 D1
Mirano *I* 44 B4
Miravci *MK* 59 F4
Mircze *PL* 95 F3
Mirebeau *F* 15 E2
Mirebeau-sur-Bèze *F* 16 C1
Mirecourt *F* 13 D4
Mirepoix *F* 21 E2
Míres *GR* 109 E4
Miribel *F* 16 C3
Mírina *GR* 102 C4
Mirințkiai *LT* 80 B3
Mirna *SLO* 54 B2
Miroševce *SRB* 57 E4
Miroslavas *LT* 85 E3
Miroslawiec *PL* 88 C2
Mirotice *CZ* 40 C3
Mirovice *CZ* 40 C3
Mirow *D* 34 B3
Mirsíni *GR* 108 B1
Mirsk *PL* 92 B3
Mirtiés *GR* 111 E1
Mirtos *GR* 109 F4
Mirueña de los Infanzones *E* 25 E1
Mirzec *PL* 94 C3
Misa (Bauskas) *LV* 81 F1
Misa (Rigas) *LV* 81 F1
Mišar *SRB* 55 F3
Misi *FIN* 65 D1
Misilmeri *I* 50 B4
Miskolc *H* 116 C2
Miškonys *LT* 86 B2
Mislinja *SLO* 54 B1
Mišniūnai *LT* 86 B1
Misso *EE* 79 E2
Mistelbach *A* 41 E4
Misterbianco *I* 53 D3
Mistretta *I* 50 C4
Mistros *GR* 105 F2
Misurina *I* 44 B3
Misvær *N* 60 B4
Miszewo *PL* 89 E1
Miszkowice *PL* 96 B1
Mitchelstown / Baile Mhistéala *IRL* 2 C4
Míthimna *GR* 103 E4
Mítikas *GR* 104 B2
Mitilíni *GR* 107 E1
Mitilinii *GR* 107 F3
Mitkaičiai *LT* 80 C2
Mitošiūnai *LT* 82 B3
Mitrašinci *MK* 59 F3
Mitrópoli *GR* 104 C1
Mittelberg *A* 43 E2
Mittelberg *A* 43 F2
Mittenwald *D* 43 F2
Mittenwalde *D* 34 C4
Mitterteich *D* 39 E3
Mittweida *D* 39 F2
Mizarai *LT* 85 E3
Mižhir"ja *UA* 117 D2
Mjadzel *BY* 115 D3
Mjällom *S* 67 D4
Mjöbäck *S* 67 D4
Mjölby *S* 67 E3
Mjøndalen *N* 66 C2
Mladá Boleslav *CZ* 40 C2
Mladá Boleslav *CZ* 116 A1
Mladá Vožice *CZ* 40 C3
Mladé Buky *CZ* 41 D2
Mladenovac *SRB* 57 D3
Mlado Nagoričane *MK* 59 E3
Mława *PL* 90 B3
Mlini *HR* 58 B3
Mljet (Otok) *HR* 58 A3
Młodzieszyn *PL* 94 B1
Młogoszyn *PL* 94 B2
Młynary *PL* 90 A1
Mnichovo Hradiště *CZ* 40 C2
Mnichów *PL* 98 B1
Mnichowice *PL* 93 E3
Mniów *PL* 94 B3
Mniszek (Kujawsko-Pomorskie) *PL* 89 F2
Mniszków *PL* 94 B3
Mo i Rana *N* 63 E1
Moaña *E* 18 A3
Moate / An Móta *IRL* 2 C3
Mocejón *E* 25 F2
Mochnaczka Nyżna *PL* 98 C3
Mochów *PL* 93 E4
Mochowo *PL* 90 A3
Mockbüdžiai *LT* 85 D2
Mockai *LT* 85 D3
Mockava *LT* 85 D3
Möckern *D* 34 A4
Möckmühl *D* 38 C3
Mockūnai *LT* 82 B3
Moclín *E* 29 F2
Modane *F* 17 D4

Modbury *GB* 8 B4
Modena *I* 47 D1
Módi *GR* 105 D2
Modica *I* 53 D4
Modigliana *I* 47 E2
Modliborzyce *PL* 95 D3
Mödling *A* 41 E4
Modran *BIH* 55 E3
Modrava *CZ* 40 B4
Modrica *BIH* 55 E3
Modrište *MK* 59 E4
Moe *EE* 73 D2
Moëlan-sur-Mer *F* 14 A1
Moelv *N* 66 C1
Moena *I* 43 F3
Moers *D* 37 D1
Moffat *GB* 7 D2
Mogadouro *P* 18 C4
Mogielnica *PL* 94 B2
Mogila *MK* 59 E4
Mogilany *PL* 98 B2
Mogilno *PL* 89 E3
Moglia *I* 47 D1
Mogliano Veneto *I* 44 B4
Mogón *E* 26 A4
Moguer *E* 28 C2
Mohács *H* 116 B3
Mohelnice *CZ* 41 E3
Mohill / Maothail *IRL* 2 C2
Möhkö *FIN* 69 F2
Mohós *GR* 110 C4
Moholm *S* 67 D3
Mohyliv-Podil's'kyj *UA* 117 E1
Moi *N* 66 A3
Moià *E* 21 E4
Moie *I* 47 F3
Moimenta *P* 18 C3
Moimenta da Beira *P* 24 C1
Moirans *F* 16 C4
Moirans-en-Montagne *F* 16 C2
Mõisaküla (Pärnu) *EE* 72 B3
Mõisaküla (Viljandi) *EE* 75 F3
Moisaküla *EE* 72 B3
Mõisanurme *EE* 79 D1
Moisdon-la-Rivière *F* 14 C1
Moisiovaara *FIN* 65 E3
Moisling *D* 33 F2
Moissac *F* 21 D1
Moita *P* 24 A3
Moixent *E* 26 C4
Mojácar *E* 30 B3
Mojados *E* 19 E4
Mojkovac *MNE* 58 C2
Mokobody *PL* 95 D1
Mokolai *LT* 85 D2
Mokra Gora *SRB* 56 C4
Mokre *PL* 89 F2
Mokrin *SRB* 56 C1
Mokro Polje *HR* 54 C4
Mokronog *SLO* 54 B2
Mokrsko *PL* 93 E4
Mokrzesz *PL* 94 A3
Mol *B* 12 C1
Mol *SRB* 56 C1
Mola di Bari *I* 49 F3
Molái *GR* 108 B1
Molat *I* 47 D1
Molat (Otok) *HR* 54 B4
Mold / Yr Wyddgrug *GB* 8 C1
Molde *N* 62 B3
Moldova Nouă *RO* 116 C3
Møldrup *DK* 70 B2
Moledo do Minho *P* 18 A3
Moletai *LT* 86 C1
Molfetta *I* 49 E3
Molières *F* 21 E1
Molina de Aragón *E* 26 B1
Molina de Segura *E* 30 C2
Molinella *I* 47 E1
Molinicos *E* 26 B4
Molinos *E* 26 C1
Molins de Rei *E* 27 F1
Moliterno *I* 49 E4
Molitg-les-Bains *F* 21 F3
Moliūnai *LT* 81 F3
Molkom *S* 67 D2
Möllbrücke *A* 44 C3
Mollerussa *E* 21 E4
Molliens-Dreuil *F* 12 A2
Mollina *E* 29 E2
Mölln *D* 33 F3
Mollösund *S* 66 C4
Mólos *GR* 105 D1
Mólos *GR* 105 D1
Molpe *FIN* 68 C2
Molsheim *F* 13 E4
Molve *HR* 54 C1
Molveno *I* 43 F3
Molyne *LT* 85 D1
Mombeltrán *E* 25 D2
Mombuey *E* 18 C3
Mommark *DK* 70 B4
Momo *I* 43 E4
Mon Idée *F* 12 C2
Monaco (Principauté de) *MC* 23 D2
Monaghan / Muineachán *IRL* 3 D2

Monasterevin *IRL* 3 D3
Monasterio de Rodilla *E* 19 F3
Monastir *I* 50 A4
Monastiráki *GR* 103 E2
Monastiráki *GR* 104 B1
Monbazillac *F* 15 E4
Moncalieri *I* 17 E4
Moncalvo *I* 17 E4
Monção *P* 18 A3
Moncarapacho *P* 28 B3
Mönchdorf *A* 45 D1
Mönchengladbach *D* 37 D2
Monchique *P* 28 A2
Monclar-de-Quercy *F* 21 E1
Moncontour *F* 10 C4
Moncontour *F* 15 D2
Moncoutant *F* 15 D2
Monda *E* 29 E3
Mondariz *E* 18 A3
Mondavio *I* 47 F3
Mondéjar *E* 26 A2
Mondim de Basto *P* 18 B4
Mondolfo *I* 47 F3
Mondoñedo *E* 18 B2
Mondorf-les-Bains *L* 13 D3
Mondoubleau *F* 11 F4
Mondovì *I* 23 E1
Mondragon *F* 22 B1
Mondragone *I* 48 C3
Monein *F* 20 C2
Monemvassía *GR* 108 C1
Mónesi di Triora *I* 23 E1
Monestier-de-Clermont *F* 16 C4
Monestiés *F* 21 E1
Moneygall *IRL* 2 C3
Moneymore *GB* 3 D1
Monfalcone *I* 44 C4
Monflanquin *F* 21 D1
Monforte *P* 24 C2
Monforte de Lemos *E* 18 B3
Monghidoro *I* 47 D2
Monguelfo-Welsberg *I* 44 B4
Moní (Nissí) *GR* 105 E3
Monice *PL* 93 F2
Mönichkirchen *A* 45 E2
Monifieth *GB* 7 D1
Möniste *EE* 79 F3
Monistrol-d'Allier *F* 16 B4
Monistrol de Montserrat *E* 21 E4
Monistrol-sur-Loire *F* 16 B4
Mönkebude *D* 34 C2
Mönki *PL* 91 D2
Monmouth / Trefynwy *GB* 8 C2
Mönnaste *EE* 78 C1
Monnickendam *NL* 32 B4
Monodéndri *GR* 100 C4
Monódrio *GR* 105 F2
Monólithos *GR* 111 F2
Monopoli *I* 49 F3
Monor *H* 116 B2
Monòver *E* 26 C4
Monpazier *F* 21 D1
Monreal *E* 20 C3
Monreal del Campo *E* 26 C1
Monreale *I* 50 B4
Monroy *E* 25 D2
Monroyo *E* 27 D1
Mons *B* 12 B2
Monsanto *P* 24 C2
Monsaraz *P* 24 C3
Monschau *D* 13 D1
Monségur *F* 20 C1
Monselice *I* 47 E1
Monsols *F* 16 B3
Mönsterås *S* 71 E2
Monsummano Terme *I* 47 D2
Mont-de-Marsan *F* 20 C2
Mont-Louis *F* 21 E3
Mont-roig del Camp *E* 27 F1
Mont-sous-Vaudrey *F* 16 C2
Mont-St-Vincent *F* 16 B2
Montabaur *D* 13 E1
Montagnac *F* 22 A2
Montagnana *I* 47 D1
Montagrier *F* 15 E4
Montaigu *F* 14 C2
Montaigu-de-Quercy *F* 21 E1
Montaigut *F* 16 A3
Montaione *I* 47 D3
Montalbán *E* 26 C1
Montalbo *E* 26 A2
Montalcino *I* 47 D3
Montalegre *P* 18 B3
Montalieu-Vercieu *F* 16 D3
Montalivet-les-Bains *F* 14 B4
Montalto di Castro *I* 47 E4
Montalto di Marche *I* 48 B1
Montalto Uffugo *I* 51 D2
Montalvão *P* 24 C2
Montamarta *E* 19 D4
Montana *BG* 117 D3
Montana *CH* 17 E2
Montañana *E* 20 B4
Montánchez *E* 25 D2
Montanejos *E* 27 D2
Montargil *P* 24 B3
Montargis *F* 12 A4

Montastruc-la-Conseillère *F* 21 E2
Montauban *F* 21 E1
Montauban-de-Bretagne *F* 10 C4
Montbard *F* 16 B1
Montbazens *F* 21 E1
Montbazon *F* 15 E1
Montbéliard *F* 17 D1
Montbenoît *F* 17 D2
Montblanc *F* 27 E1
Montbozon *F* 17 D1
Montbrió del Camp *E* 27 E1
Montbrison *F* 16 B3
Montbron *F* 15 E3
Montceau-les-Mines *F* 16 B2
Montcenis *F* 16 B2
Montchanin *F* 16 B2
Montcornet *F* 12 C3
Montcuq *F* 21 D1
Montdidier *F* 12 A3
Monte da Pedra *P* 24 B2
Monte Real *P* 24 A2
Monte Redondo *P* 24 A2
Monte S. Angelo *I* 49 E3
Monte S. Savino *I* 47 D3
Monteagudo de las Vicarías *E* 20 A4
Montealegre *E* 19 E4
Montealegre del Castillo *E* 26 C4
Montebello Ionico *I* 51 D4
Montebello Vicentino *I* 43 F4
Montebelluna *I* 44 B4
Montebourg *F* 11 D3
Montecarotto *I* 47 F3
Montecassino (Abbazia di) *I* 48 C3
Montecatini Terme *I* 47 D2
Montecchio *I* 47 F2
Montecchio Maggiore *I* 43 F4
Montech *F* 21 D1
Montechiaro *I* 46 B2
Montecorvino Rovella *I* 49 D4
Montederamo *E* 52 C3
Montefalco *I* 47 F3
Montefalcone di Val Fortore *I* 49 D3
Montefalcone nel Sannio *I* 48 C2
Montefiascone *I* 47 E4
Montefiore dell'Aso *I* 48 B1
Montefiorino *I* 47 D2
Montefrío *E* 29 F2
Montegallo *I* 47 F3
Montegiorgio *I* 48 B1
Montegranaro *I* 48 B1
Montegrotto Terme *I* 47 E1
Montehermoso *E* 25 D2
Montejicar *E* 29 F2
Montejo de Tiermes *E* 19 F4
Monteleone di Spoleto *I* 47 F4
Montélimar *F* 22 B1
Montella *I* 49 D4
Montellano *E* 29 D3
Montelupo Fiorentino *I* 47 D3
Montemaggiore Belsito *I* 52 C3
Montemagno *I* 17 F4
Montemayor *E* 29 E2
Montemayor de Pililla *E* 19 E4
Montemor-o-Novo *P* 24 A3
Montemor-o-Velho *P* 24 A1
Montendre *F* 15 D4
Montenegro de Cameros *E* 20 A4
Montenero di Bisaccia *I* 48 C2
Montenero Sabino *I* 47 F4
Montepulciano *I* 47 E3
Montereale *I* 47 F4
Montereale Valcellina *I* 44 B3
Montereau-Fault-Yonne *F* 12 A4
Monterenzio *I* 47 D2
Monteriggioni *I* 47 D3
Monteroni di Lecce *I* 51 F1
Monterosso al Mare *I* 23 F1
Monterotondo *I* 47 E4
Monterotondo Marittimo *I* 47 D3
Monterroso *E* 18 B3
Monterrubio de la Serena *E* 25 E4
Monterubbiano *I* 48 B1
Montesa *E* 26 C4
Montesano sulla Marcellana *I* 49 D4
Montesarchio *I* 49 D3
Montescaglioso *I* 49 E4
Montesilvano Marina *I* 48 C1
Montesquieu-Volvestre *F* 21 D2
Montesquiou *F* 21 D2
Montevarchi *I* 47 E1
Montfaucon *F* 16 B4
Montfaucon-d'Argonne *F* 12 C3
Montfaucon-en-Velay *F* 16 B4
Montfort-en-Chalosse *F* 20 C2
Montfort-l'Amaury *F* 11 F4
Montfort-sur-Meu *F* 10 C4
Montfort-sur-Risle *F* 11 E3
Montgaillard *F* 21 E3

Montgenèvre *F* 17 D4
Montgiscard *F* 21 E2
Montgomery / Trefaldwyn *GB* 8 C1
Montguyon *F* 15 D4
Monthermé *F* 12 C2
Monthois *F* 12 C3
Monthey *CH* 17 E2
Monthureux-sur-Saône *F* 13 D4
Monti *I* 50 B2
Montichiari *I* 46 C1
Monticiano *I* 47 D3
Montiel *E* 26 A4
Montier-en-Der *F* 12 C4
Montignac *F* 15 E4
Montigny-le-Roi *F* 13 D4
Montigny-sur-Aube *F* 16 C1
Montijo *E* 24 C3
Montijo *P* 24 A3
Montilla *E* 29 E2
Montioni *I* 47 D3
Montivilliers *F* 11 E3
Montjean-sur-Loire *F* 15 D1
Montlhéry *F* 12 A4
Montlieu-la-Garde *F* 15 D4
Montlouis-sur-Loire *F* 15 E1
Montluçon *F* 16 A2
Montluel *F* 16 C3
Montmarault *F* 16 A3
Montmartin-sur-Mer *F* 11 D3
Montmédy *F* 12 C3
Montmélian *F* 17 D3
Montmirail *F* 12 B3
Montmirail *F* 11 F4
Montmoreau-St-Cybard *F* 15 D4
Montmorillon *F* 15 E2
Montmort *F* 12 B3
Montoggio *I* 46 B2
Montoire-sur-le-Loir *F* 15 E1
Montoito *P* 24 B4
Montorio al Vomano *I* 48 B1
Montoro *E* 25 F4
Montpellier *F* 22 A2
Montpezat-de-Quercy *F* 21 E1
Montpezat-sous-Bauzon *F* 16 B4
Montpon-Ménestérol *F* 15 D4
Montpont-en-Bresse *F* 16 C2
Montréal *F* 21 D1
Montréal-la-Cluse *F* 16 C3
Montredon-Labessonnié *F* 21 E2
Montréjeau *F* 21 D2
Montrésor *F* 15 E1
Montresta *I* 50 A3
Montret *F* 16 C2
Montreuil *F* 11 F1
Montreuil-Bellay *F* 15 D1
Montreux *CH* 17 E2
Montrevault *F* 14 C1
Montrevel-en-Bresse *F* 16 C2
Montrichard *F* 15 E1
Montrond-les-Bains *F* 16 B3
Montrose *GB* 5 D4
Monts-sur-Guesnes *F* 15 E2
Montsalvy *F* 16 A4
Montsauche-les-Settons *F* 16 B1
Montseny *E* 21 F4
Montserrat *E* 27 D3
Montserrat (Monestir) *E* 21 E4
Montsúrs *F* 11 D4
Montuenga *E* 25 F1
Montuïri *E* 31 E3
Monza *I* 43 D4
Monzón *E* 20 C4
Monzón de Campos *E* 19 E3
Moora *EE* 73 D2
Moordorf *D* 33 D3
Moosburg a. d. Isar *D* 43 F1
Mór *H* 116 B2
Mora *E* 25 F2
Mora *P* 24 B3
Mora de Rubielos *E* 26 C2
Móra d'Ebre *E* 27 E1
Móra la Nova *E* 27 E1
Morąg *PL* 90 A2
Morais *P* 18 C4
Moraitika *GR* 100 B4
Moral de Calatrava *E* 25 F4
Moraleda de Zafayona *E* 29 F3
Moraleja *E* 24 C2
Moraleja de Sayago *E* 18 C4
Moraleja del Vino *E* 19 D4
Morales de Rey *E* 19 D3
Morales de Toro *E* 19 D4
Morano Calabro *I* 51 D2
Mörarp *S* 71 D3
Morasverdes *E* 25 D1
Morata de Jalón *E* 20 B4
Morata de Tajuña *E* 26 A2
Moratalla *E* 26 B4
Moravče *SLO* 54 B2
Moravci v-Slov.-gor *SLO* 54 C1
Moravice *HR* 54 B2
Morávka *CZ* 41 F3

LUXEMBOURG

Auguste-Charles (R.) .. BX 10
Carrefours (R. des) .... AV 18
Cents (R.) .... BV 19
Cimetière (R. du)...... BX 25
Eich (R. d') .... ABV 36
Guillaume (Av.) ...... AV 55
Hespérange (R. d') .... BX 61
Merl (R. de) .... AX 76
Mulhenbach (R. de) ... AV 79
Patton (Bd du Général) . BV 86
Rollingergrund (R. de). AV 102
Strassen (R. de) ...... AV 112
10-Septembre (Av. du) . AV 127

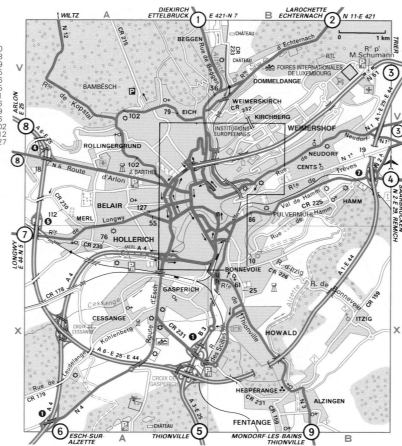

Motala S 67 E3
Motherwell GB 7 D1
Motilla del Palancar E .26 B3
Motovun HR 54 A3
Motril E 29 F3
Mötsküla EE 79 E1
Motta di Livenza I 44 B4
Motta S. Anastasia I ...53 E3
Motta Visconti I 46 B1
Mottola I 49 F4
Mouchard F 17 D2
Moudon CH 17 D2
Moúdros GR 102 C4
Mougins F 23 D2
Mouhijärvi FIN 68 C3
Mouilleron-en-Pareds F .15 D2
Moulins F 16 A2
Moulins-Engilbert F 16 B2
Moulins-la-Marche F 11 E4
Moult F 11 E3
Mount Bellew /
 An Creagán IRL 2 C2
Mountain Ash /
 Aberpennar GB 8 B2
Mountmellick /
 Móinteach Mílic IRL ...2 C3
Mountrath IRL...........2 C3
Moura P 24 B4
Mourão P 24 C4
Mourenx F 20 C2
Mouríki GR 105 D3
Mourmelon-le-Grand F ..12 C3
Mourniés GR 109 D3
Mourujärvi FIN 65 E1
Mouscron B 12 B1
Moustiers-Ste-Marie F .22 C1
Mouthe F 17 D2
Mouthier-
 Haute-Pierre F 17 D2
Mouthoumet F 21 F3
Moutier CH 17 E1
Moûtiers F 17 D3
Moutiers-
 les-Mauxfaits F 14 C2
Moutsoúna GR 109 F1
Mouy F 12 A3
Mouzáki GR 100 C4
Mouzáki GR 101 D4
Mouzon F 12 C2
Moville /
 Bun an Phobail IRL ...6 A2
Moyenneville F 11 F2
Moyuela E 26 C1
Možajsk RUS 115 F2
Mozirje SLO 54 B1
Mrągowo PL 90 C2
Mrakovica BIH 55 D3
Mramorak SRB 57 D2
Mratinje MNE 58 B2
Mrazovac BIH 54 C3

Mrčajevci SRB 57 D3
Mrežičko MK 59 F4
Mrkonjić Grad BIH 55 D3
Mrkopalj HR 54 B3
Mrocza PL 89 E3
Mrzeżyno PL 88 B1
Mrzygłód (Śląskie) PL .98 A1
Mscislaŭ BY 115 E3
Mšeno CZ 40 C2
Mstów PL 94 A3
Mszana PL 99 D3
Mszana Dolna PL 98 B2
Mszczonów PL 94 B2
Muć HR 55 D4
Muccia I 47 E3
Much D 13 E1
Much Wenlock GB 8 C1
Mücheln D 39 E2
Mucientes E 19 E4
Mudanya TR 117 F4
Mudau D 38 C4
Mudurnu TR 117 F4
Muel E 20 B4
Muelas del Pan E 18 C4
Muff IRL 6 A2
Muge P 24 A3
Mügeln D 39 F1
Muggia I 44 B4
Mugron F 20 C2
Mugueimes E 18 B3
Mühlacker D 13 F3
Mühlbach am Hochkönig A44
 B2
Mühlberg D 39 F1
Mühldorf D 44 B1
Mühlen Eichsen D 33 F2
Mühlhausen D 38 C2
Mühltroff D 39 E2
Muhniemi FIN 69 E4
Muhos FIN 65 D3
Muir of Ord GB 4 C3
Muirkirk GB 6 C1
Muitnica (Medni) LV ...83 E3
Muizniki (Muižnieki) LV .83 F1
Mukačeve UA 116 C1
Mula E 30 C2
Mülheim a. d. Ruhr D ..37 E1
Mulhouse F 17 E1
Müllheim D 17 E1
Mullingar / An Muileann
 gCearr IRL 2 C2
Mullrose D 34 C4
Mullsjö S 67 D4
Mulrany / An Mhala
 Raithní IRL 2 B2
Multia FIN 69 D2
Mumbles (The) GB 8 B3
Munalaskme EE 72 A2
Muñana E 25 E1

Münchberg D 39 E3
Müncheberg D 34 C4
München D 43 F1
Münchhausen D 13 F1
Mundesley GB 9 F1
Mundford GB 9 F2
Mundigciems LV 77 D3
Munera E 26 B3
Mungia E 20 A2
Muñico E 25 E1
Muniesa E 26 C1
Muniškiai LT 85 E1
Munkebo DK 70 B3
Munkedal S 66 C3
Munkfors S 66 C2
Münnerstadt D 38 C1
Muñogalindo E 25 E1
Munsala FIN 68 C1
Münsingen CH 17 E2
Münsingen D 43 D1
Münster CH 17 F2
Munster F 33 F3
Munster F 13 E4
Münster (Westfalen) D .37 F1
Münstertal D 13 F4
Münzenberg D 13 F1
Münzkirchen A 44 C1
Muodoslompolo S 61 D3
Muonio FIN 61 D3
Mur-de-Barrez F 16 A4
Mur-de-Bretagne F 10 B4
Muraka EE 72 B3
Murano I 44 B4
Muraste EE 72 A1
Murat F 16 A4
Murat-sur-Vèbre F 21 F2
Murato F 23 F3
Murau A 44 C2
Muravera I 50 B4
Murça P 18 B3
Murchante E 20 B4
Murcia E 30 C2
Mureck A 45 E2
Muret F 21 E2
Murgia E 20 A3
Muri CH 17 F1
Murias de Paredes E ...18 C2
Murino MNE 59 D3
Murjāni LV 78 B3
Murjek S 64 B2
Mürmāja LV 78 B2
Mürmuiža
 (Jelgavas) LV 81 E1
Mürmuiža
 (Valmieras) LV 78 C2
Murnau D 43 F2
Mürnieki LV 81 E1
Muro F 23 F3
Muro de Alcoy E 27 D4

Moravská Třebová CZ ...41 E3
Moravské
 Budějovice CZ 41 D4
Moravske Toplice SLO ..54 C1
Moravský Beroun CZ ...41 F2
Moravský Krumlov CZ ..41 E4
Morawica PL 94 B3
Morbach D 13 E2
Morbegno I 43 D4
Mörbisch A 45 E1
Mörbylånga S 71 E3
Morcenx F 20 B1
Morciano
 di Romagna I 47 F2
Morcone I 48 C3
Morcote CH 17 F3
Mordelles F 10 C4
Mordy PL 95 D1
More LV 78 B3
Morecambe GB 7 D4
Moreda E 30 A3

Morée F 15 E1
Morella E 27 D1
Mores I 50 A3
Morestel F 16 C3
Moret-sur-Loing F 12 A4
Moreton-in-Marsh GB ...9 D2
Moretonhampstead GB ...8 B4
Moreuil F 12 A2
Morez F 17 D2
Morfasso I 46 C1
Mórfio GR 104 A1
Morgat F 10 A2
Morges CH 17 D2
Morgex I 17 E2
Morhange F 13 E3
Mori I 43 F4
Morina SRB 59 D3
Moritzburg D 39 F1
Morjärv S 64 C2
Morlaàs F 20 C2
Morlaix F 10 B4

Mormanno I 51 D2
Mormant F 12 A4
Mormoiron F 22 B1
Mornant F 16 C3
Morón de Almazán E ...20 A4
Morón
 de la Frontera E 29 D3
Morosaglia I 23 F3
Morović SRB 55 E2
Morpeth GB 7 E2
Mörrum S 71 E3
Morsbach D 13 E1
Morsleben D 34 A4
Mortagne-au-Perche F .11 D4
Mortagne-
 sur-Gironde F 15 D3
Mortagne-sur-Sèvre F ..15 D2
Mortain F 11 D4
Mortara I 17 F4
Morteau F 17 D2

Mortrée F 11 E4
Moryń PL 88 A3
Morzeszczyn PL 89 F2
Morzewo PL 90 A2
Morzine F 17 D3
Mosbach D 38 C4
Mosby N 66 A3
Mošćenice HR 54 A3
Mošćenička Draga HR ..54 A3
Moschendorf A 45 E2
Mosedis LT 80 B2
Moshokariá GR 105 D3
Moshopótamos GR 101 E3
Mosina PL 93 D1
Mosjøen N 63 E1
Mosko BIH 58 B3
Moskorzew PL 98 B1
Moskosel S 64 B2
Moskva RUS 115 F2
Moslavina HR 55 E2

Mosqueruela E 27 D2
Moss N 66 C2
Mossala FIN 68 C4
Mossat GB 5 D4
Mössingen D 43 D1
Most CZ 40 B2
Most na Soči SLO 54 A2
Mosta M 53 F4
Mostar BIH 58 A4
Mosteiro E 18 A3
Mosterhamn N 66 A2
Móstoles E 25 F2
Mostys'ka UA 116 C1
Mosvik N 63 D3
Moszczenica
 (Łódzkie) PL 94 A2
Moszczenica
 (Małopolskie) PL 98 C2
Mota del Cuervo E 26 A3
Mota del Marqués E ...19 D4

MADRID

Andalucía (Av. de) ....BM 12
Andes (Av. de los) ....CL 13
Atocha (R. del) ....BM 22
Ciudad de Barcelona
 (Av. de la) ....BM 46
Complutense (Av.) ....AL 51
Delicias (Pas. de las) .....BM 66
Estación de Hortaleza
 (Carret. a la) ....CL 89
Florida (Pas. de la) ....BM 100
General Ricardos ....BM 110
Ginzo de Limia ....BL 113
Infanta Isabel (Pas. de la) .BL 119
Isla de Oza ....BL 120
Manzanares (Av. del) ......BM 142
Mar de Cristal (Gta del) ...CL 144
Miraflores (Av. de) ....AL 161
Monforte de Lemos (Av. de) .BL 165
Raimundo Fernández
 Villaverde ....BT 195
Reina Cristina (Pas. de la) .BM 198
Reina Victoria (Av. de la) ..BL 200
Reyes Católicos (Av. de los) .BL 204
Ribera del Sena ....CL 205
Santa María de la Cabeza
 (Pas. de) ....BM 229
San Francisco de Sales
 (Pas. de) ....BL 216
San Luis (Av. de) ....CL 223
Toledo (Ronda de) ....BM 235
Valdetorres de Jarama .....CL 241
Valladolid (Av. de) ....CL 244
Veinticinco de Septiembre
 (Av. del) ....CL 247

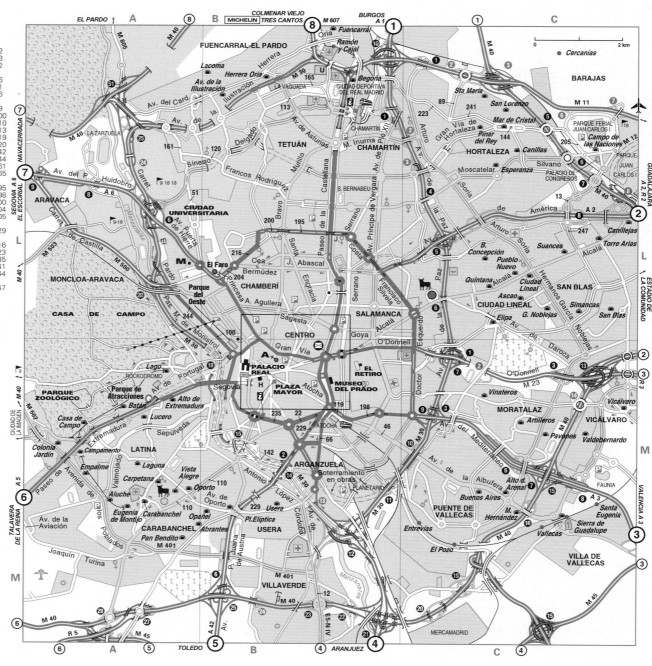

Muro Lucano I 49 D4
Murol F 16 A3
Murole FIN 69 D3
Muros E 18 A2
Murowana Goślina PL 89 D3
Mürren CH 17 E2
Murrhardt D 38 C4
Murska Sobota SLO 54 C1
Mursko Središče HR 54 C1
Murten CH 17 E2
Murter HR 54 C4
Murter (Otok) HR 54 C4
Murtosa P 24 B1
Murtovaara FIN 65 E2
Murvica HR 54 C4
Murviel-lès-Béziers F 21 F2
Mürzsteg A 45 D1
Mürzzuschlag A 45 E1
Mûsa LV 81 F2
Musninkai LT 86 B2
Mussalo FIN 69 E4
Musselburgh GB 7 D1
Mussidan F 15 E4
Mussomeli I 52 C3
Mussy-sur-Seine F 12 C4
Mustahamba EE 79 E2
Mustametsa EE 73 E3
Mustasaari FIN 85 E3
Mustion as FIN 69 D4
Mustivere EE 78 C1
Mustjala EE 74 C2
Mustkalni LV 77 F2
Mustla EE 78 C1
Mustvee EE 73 E3
Muszyna PL 98 C3
Muszynka PL 98 C3
Muta SLO 54 B1
Mutala FIN 69 D3
Mutterstadt D 13 F3
Mutzschen D 39 E1
Muuga (Harju) EE 72 B1
Muuga
  (Lääne-Viru) EE 73 D2
Muurame FIN 69 D2
Muurasjärvi FIN 69 D1
Muurla FIN 68 D4
Muurola FIN 65 D2
Muuruvesi FIN 69 E1
Müüsleri EE 72 C2
Muxia E 18 A2
Muzillac F 14 B1
Muzzana
  del Turgnano I 44 C4
Myckelgensjö S 68 A1
Myczkowskie
  (Jezioro) PL 99 E3

MARSEILLE

Aix (R. d') ....BY
Briançon (Bd de) ....BX 13
Canebière (La) ....BY
Catalans (R. des) ....AY 16
Chartreux (Av. des) ....CY 17
Guesde (Pl. Jules) ....BY 35
Guigou (Bd) ....BX 36
Lesseps (Bd Ferdinand de) ....AX 40
Moulin (Bd Jean) ....CY 47
Paradis (R.) ....BYZ
Pologne (Pl. de) ....CY 51
Pompidou (Prom. Georges) .....BZ 52
Sartre (Av. Jean-Paul) ....CX 59
Strasbourg (Bd) ....BX 61
Verdun (R. de) ....CY 70

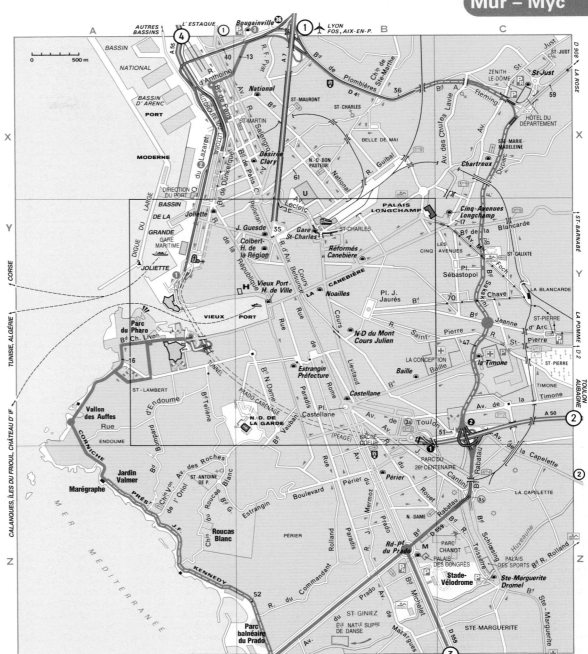

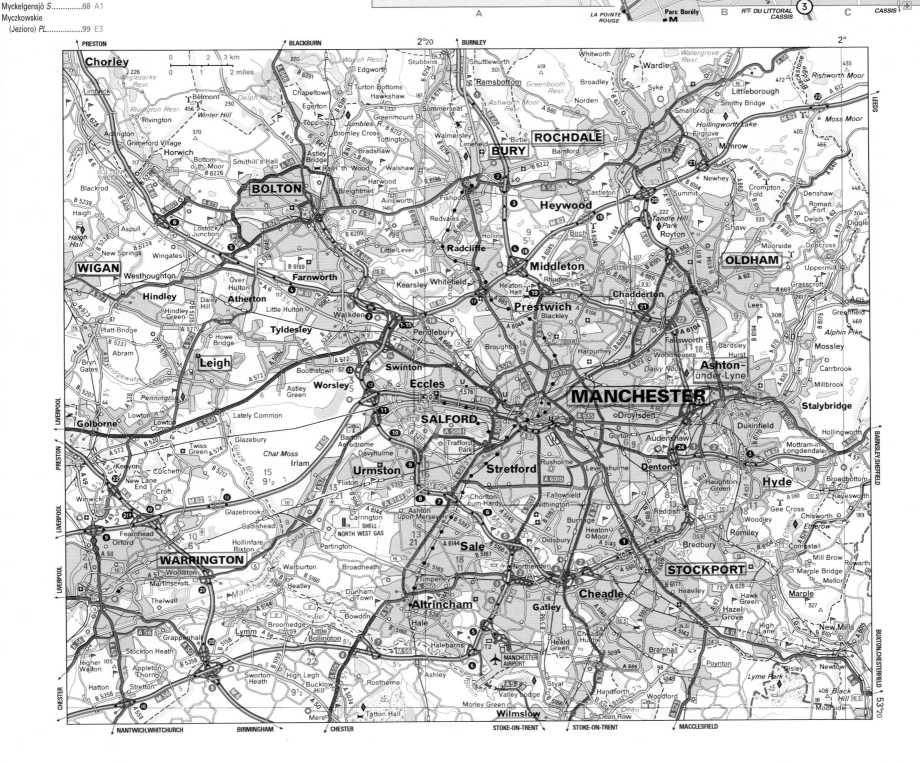

Mykanów PL 94 A3
Mykines (Færøerne) DK 62 A3
Mykolaïv UA 117 F2
Mykolaïv UA 117 D1
Myllykoski FIN 69 E3
Myllykylä FIN 68 C2
Myllymäki FIN 69 D2
Mynämäki FIN 68 C4
Myre / Øksnes N 60 B3
Myrhorod UA 115 F4
Myronivka UA 117 F1
Myrskylä / Mörskom FIN 69 E4
Myrviken S 63 E3
Mysen N 66 C2
Myślenice PL 98 B2
Myślibórz PL 88 A3
Mysłowice PL 97 F2
Myszków PL 98 A1
Myszyniec PL 90 C2
Mytišči RUS 115 F2

N

N. Agathoúpoli GR 101 F3
N. Alikarnassós GR 109 F4
N. Anhíalos GR 105 E1
N. Apolonía GR 102 A2
N. Artáki GR 105 F2
N. Éfessos GR 101 E3
N. Erásmio GR 102 C2
N. Fókea GR 102 A3
N. Hilí GR 103 D2
N. Iraklítsa GR 102 B2
N. Kalikrátia GR 101 F3
N. Kariá GR 102 C2
N. Karváli GR 102 B2
N. Kerassoús GR 104 B1
N. Kerdília GR 102 A2
N. Kios GR 105 D4
N. Korito SRB 57 F3
N. Mákri GR 105 F3
N. Málgara GR 101 F2
N. Marmarás GR 102 A3
N. Messángala GR 101 F3
N. Mihanióna GR 101 F3
N. Monastíri GR 105 D1
N. Moudaniá GR 102 A3
N. Pagassés GR 105 E1
N. Péla GR 101 F2
N. Péramos GR 102 B2
N. Péramos GR 105 E3
N. Perivóli GR 101 F4
N. Petrítsi GR 102 A1
N. Potídea GR 102 A3
N. Róda GR 102 B3
N. Rubeži MNE 58 C3
N. Sánda GR 103 D1
N. Sánda GR 101 F2
N. Senkovac HR 55 D2
N. Silata GR 101 F3
N. Skióni GR 102 A3
N. Skopós GR 102 A2
N. Stíra GR 106 B3
N. Tríglia GR 101 F3
N. Víssa GR 103 E1
N. Zíhni GR 102 A2
N. Zoí GR 101 E2
Naamijoki FIN 64 C1
Naantali FIN 68 C4
Naarajärvi FIN 69 E2
Naarva FIN 69 F1
Naas / An Nás IRL 3 D3
Nabala EE 72 B2
Nabburg D 39 E4
Nabe LV 78 B2
Načeradec CZ 40 C3
Náchod CZ 41 D2
Nadarzyn PL 94 C2
Naddvik N 66 B1
Nadela E 18 B2
Nădlac RO 116 C2
Nadróż PL 89 F3
Nadur M 53 F4
Nadvirna UA 117 D1
Nærbø N 66 A3
Nærøy N 63 D2
Næstved DK 70 C3
Näfels CH 17 F1
Náfpaktos GR 104 C2
Náfplio GR 105 E4
Naggen S 68 A2
Nagli LV 83 E1
Nagłowice PL 98 B1
Nagold D 13 F4
Nagu / Nauvo FIN 68 C4
Nagyatád H 116 B2
Nagykálló H 116 C2
Nagykanizsa H 116 B2
Nagykőrös H 116 C2
Naha EE 79 E1
Nahe D 33 F2
Nahodka LV 83 D2
Naila D 39 E2
Nailloux F 21 E2
Nailsworth GB 8 C3
Nairiai LT 81 F2
Nairn GB 4 C3
Naisiai LT 81 E2
Naiviai LT 82 B3
Najac F 21 E1
Nájera E 20 A3
Nakkila FIN 68 C3
Nakło (Opolskie) PL 97 E1
Nakło nad Notecią PL 89 E3
Näkotne LV 81 E1
Nakovo SRB 56 C1
Nakskov DK 70 C4
Nałęczów PL 95 D3
Näljänkä FIN 65 E2
Naltijärvi FIN 61 E3
Namdalseid N 63 D2
Náměšť nad Oslavou CZ 41 E3
Namiki LV 80 C1
Namišiai LT 81 F2
Namsos N 63 D2
Namsskogan N 63 E2
Namur B 12 C1
Namysłów PL 93 E3
Nancy F 13 D4
Nangis F 12 B4
Nannestad N 66 C2
Nant F 21 F1
Nanterre F 12 A3
Nantes F 14 C1
Nanteuil-le-Haudouin F 12 A3
Nantiat F 15 E3
Nantua F 16 C3
Nantwich GB 8 C1
Náoussa GR 101 E2
Náoussa GR 106 C4
Napoli I 48 C4
Naravere EE 72 A3
Narberth / Arberth GB 8 A3
Narbolia I 50 A3
Narbonne F 21 F2
Narbonne-Plage F 21 F2
Narcao I 50 A4
Nardo I 51 F1
Narewka PL 91 F3
Narila FIN 69 E2
Narkaus FIN 65 D2
Narni I 47 F4
Naro I 52 C3
Naro-Fominsk RUS 115 F2
Narol PL 99 F1
Närpes FIN 68 C2
Narta HR 55 D2
Narthäki GR 105 D1
Naruszewo PL 94 B1
Narva EE 73 F2
Narvaišiai LT 80 B2
Narva-Jõesuu EE 73 F1
Narvik N 60 B3
Narwiański Park Narodowy PL 91 E3
Nås S 67 E2
Nåsåker S 68 A1
Năsăud RO 117 D2
Nasbinals F 21 F1
Našice HR 55 E2
Nasielsk PL 90 B3
Našiūnai LT 86 C1
Naso I 50 C4
Nasrenai LT 80 B2
Nassau D 13 E1
Nassereith A 43 E2
Nässjo S 67 E4
Nastola FIN 69 E3
Nasva EE 74 C3
Natalinci SRB 57 D3
Natiškiai LT 82 B2
Natkiškiai LT 84 B1
Nattavaara S 64 B1
Nättraby S 71 E3
Naucelle F 21 F1
Naudaskalns LV 79 E3
Nauders A 43 E3
Naudīte LV 81 D1
Naudvaris (Kauno) LT 81 D3
Naudvaris (Šiauliu) LT 81 D3
Naudžiai LT 85 D2
Naudžiūnai LT 85 E2
Nauen D 34 B4
Naujamiestis LT 81 F3
Naujas Strūnaitis LT 87 D1
Naujasis Daugeliškis LT 87 D1
Naujasodis (Kauno) LT 85 F1
Naujasodis (Šiauliu) LT 81 E3
Naujasodis (Utenos) LT 86 B1
Naujieji Bernatoniai LT 85 E2
Naujienele I LT 85 D2
Naujikai LT 81 F3
Naujoji Akmene LT 81 D2
Naujoji Ipiltis LT 80 B2
Naujoji Kirsna LT 85 E3
Naujosios Kietaviškes LT 85 F2
Naukšēni LV 78 C1
Naul IRL 3 D2
Naulāni LV 83 F2
Naumburg D 39 E1
Naunhof D 39 E1
Nausedžiai LT 82 B2
Nausode LT 81 F3
Nausodis LT 80 B2
Naustdal N 62 A4
Nava E 18 C1
Nava de la Asunción E 25 F1
Nava del Rey E 19 D4
Navacepeda de Tormes E 25 E1
Navacerrada E 25 F1
Navaconcejo E 25 D2
Navahermosa E 25 F2
Navahrudak BY 115 D3
Navalcán E 25 E2
Navalcarnero E 25 F2
Navaleno E 19 F4
Navalmanzano E 25 F1
Navalmoral de la Mata E 25 E2
Navalperal de Pinares E 25 F1
Navaluenga E 25 F1
Navalvillar de Pela E 25 E3
Navamorcuende E 25 E2
Navan / An Uaimh IRL 3 D2
Navarredonda de Gredos E 25 E2
Navarrenx F 20 C2
Navarrés E 26 C3
Navarrete E 20 A3
Navàs E 21 E4
Navas de Oro E 25 F1
Navas de San Juan E 26 A4
Navas del Madroño E 24 C2
Navascués E 20 B3
Navasfrias E 24 C1
Navatalgordo E 25 E1
Nave I 43 E4
Nave Redonda P 28 A2
Nävekvarn S 67 F3
Navelli I 48 B2
Naveros E 29 D4
Navesti EE 72 C3
Navi EE 79 E2
Navia E 18 C1
Navia de Suarna E 18 C2
Navininkai LT 85 E3
Navl'a RUS 115 F3
Nawojowa PL 98 C3
Náxos GR 106 C4
Náxos (Nissí) GR 106 C4
Nay F 20 C2
Nazaré P 24 A2
Néa Epídavros GR 105 E3
Néa Kíos B 105 D4
Néa Koróni GR 108 A1
Néa Moní GR 107 D2
Neanurme EE 73 D3
Neápoli GR 101 D3
Neápoli GR 108 C2
Neápoli GR 109 F4
Neath / Castell-nedd GB 8 B2
Nebel D 33 D1
Nebljusi HR 54 C3
Nebra D 39 D1
Nečiūnai LT 85 E2
Neckarelz D 38 C4
Neckargemünd D 13 F3
Neckarsteinach D 13 F3
Neckarsulm D 38 C4
Nečujam HR 58 A4
Neda E 18 B1
Néda GR 103 D2
Nedelišće HR 54 C1
Nedervetil FIN 68 C1
Nedstrand N 66 A2
Nędza PL 97 E2
Nedzinge LT 85 F3
Neede NL 37 D1
Neeme EE 72 B1
Neemisküla EE 79 D1
Neermoor D 33 D3
Nefyn GB 3 F3
Negorci MK 59 F4
Negotin SRB 57 E3
Negotino MK 59 F4
Negrar I 43 F4
Negreira E 18 A2
Nègrepelisse F 21 E1
Negru Vodă RO 117 E3
Neheim-Hüsten D 37 E1
Neiden N 61 F2
Neikšāni LV 83 F2
Neila E 19 F4
Nejdek CZ 40 A2
Nekla PL 93 E1
Nekromandío Efíras GR 104 A1
Neksø DK 71 E4
Nelas P 24 B1
Nelidovo RUS 115 E2
Nellim FIN 61 F2
Nelson GB 7 E4
Nēlupji LV 76 C3
Nemaitonys LT 85 F2
Nemajūnai LT 85 F2
Nemakščiai LT 81 D3
Neman RUS 114 C3
Neméa GR 105 D3
Nemenčine LT 86 C2
Nemenčinele LT 86 B2
Nemežis LT 86 B2
Nemours F 12 A4
Nemunaitis LT 85 E3
Nemunelio Radviliškis LT 82 B2
Nemyriv UA 117 E1
Nenagh / An tAonach IRL 2 C3
Nénita GR 107 D2
Nenzing A 43 D2
Neohoráki GR 105 E2
Neohóri GR 103 E1
Neohóri GR 101 E4
Neohóri (Árta) GR 104 B1
Neohóri (Etolía-Akarnanía) GR 104 B2
Neohóri (Évia) GR 105 F2
Neohóri (Fthiótida) GR 105 D2
Neohóri (Ilía) GR 104 C4
Neohóri (Kardítsa) GR 104 C1
Neohóri (Magnissía) GR 105 E1
Nepomuk CZ 40 B3
Nérac F 21 D1
Neráida GR 104 C1
Neratovice CZ 40 C2
Nerdvika N 62 B3
Neresheim D 43 E1
Nereta LV 82 B2
Nereto I 48 B1
Nerezi MK 59 E3
Nerezine HR 54 B4
Nerežišća HR 58 A4
Nerimdaičiai LT 80 C2
Neringa LT 80 A3
Néris-les-Bains F 16 A3
Nerja E 29 F3
Néronde F 16 B3
Nérondes F 16 A2
Nerotriviá GR 105 F2
Nerpio E 26 B4
Nerva E 28 C2
Nervesa d. Battaglia I 44 B4
Nervi I 23 F1
Nes N 66 C1
Nes NL 32 B3
Nesbyen N 66 B1
Nesebăr BG 117 E4
Nesjahverfi IS 62 B1
Neskaupstaður IS 62 C1
Nesle F 12 A2
Nesna N 63 E1
Nesoddtangen N 66 C2
Nesseby N 61 F1
Nesselwang D 43 E2
Nestáni GR 105 D4
Nesteri LV 83 F1
Nestório GR 100 C3
Néstoros (Anáktora) GR 108 A1
Nesvik N 66 A2
Netičkampis LT 85 D2
Netolice CZ 40 C4
Netretić HR 54 B2
Nettetal D 37 D2
Nettuno I 48 B3
Neu Darchau D 33 F3
Neu-Isenburg D 13 F2
Neu Lübbenau D 34 C4
Neu Ulm D 43 E1
Neuastenberg D 37 F2
Neubeckum D 37 E1
Neubrandenburg D 34 B2
Neubukow D 34 A2
Neuburg a. d. Donau D 39 D4
Neuchâtel CH 17 E2
Neuenburg D 33 D3
Neuenburg D 13 F3
Neuendorf D 34 B1
Neuendorf (b. Hiddensee) D 34 B1
Neuenhaus D 32 C4
Neuenkirchen D 33 E3
Neuenstadt D 38 C4
Neuenstein D 38 C2
Neuerburg D 13 D2
Neuf-Brisach F 13 E4
Neufahrn D 39 E4
Neufchâteau B 13 D2
Neufchâteau F 13 D4
Neufchâtel-en-Bray F 11 F2
Neufchâtel-sur-Aisne F 12 B3
Neufelden A 40 C4
Neuffen D 43 D1
Neugersdorf D 40 C1
Neuhardenberg D 34 C3
Neuharlingersiel D 33 D3
Neuhaus D 33 F3
Neuhaus D 39 D2
Neuhaus (Oste) D 33 E2
Neuhaus i. Solling D 38 C1
Neuhaus-Schierschnitz D 39 D3
Neuhausen CH 17 F1
Neuhofen an der Krems A 44 C1
Neuillé-Pont-Pierre F 15 E1
Neuilly-en-Thelle F 12 A3
Neuilly-le-Réal F 16 A2
Neuilly-l'Évêque F 16 C1
Neuilly-St-Front F 12 B3
Neukalen D 34 B2
Neukirch (Kreis Bautzen) D 40 C1
Neukirchen D 33 D1
Neukirchen am Großvenediger A 44 B2
Neukloster D 34 A2
Neuleugbach A 45 E1
Neum BIH 58 A3
Neumarkt A 44 B1
Neumarkt i. d. Oberpfalz D 39 E4
Neumarkt in Steiermark A 45 D2
Neumarkt-St Veit D 44 B1
Neumünster D 33 E2
Neunagelberg A 41 D4
Neunburg v. Wald D 39 E4
Neung-sur-Beuvron F 15 F1
Neunkirchen A 45 E1
Neunkirchen (Saar) D 13 E3
Neuötting D 44 B1
Neupölla A 41 D4
Neuruppin D 34 B3
Neusiedl am See A 45 F1
Neuss D 37 D2
Neustadt D 34 B3
Neustadt D 40 C1
Neustadt D 34 B1
Neustadt (Titisee-) D 13 F4
Neustadt (Hessen) D 13 F1
Neustadt a. d. Aisch D 39 D3
Neustadt a. d. Donau D 39 E4
Neustadt a. d. Waldnaab D 39 E3
Neustadt a. d. Weinstraße D 13 F3
Neustadt a. Rübenberge D 33 E4
Neustadt b. Coburg D 39 D3
Neustadt-Glewe (Kreis Ludwigslust) D 34 A3
Neustadt i. Holstein D 33 F2
Neustift im Stubaital A 43 F2
Neustrelitz D 34 B3
Neuves-Maisons F 13 D4
Neuvic F 15 F4
Neuvic F 15 E4
Neuville-aux-Bois F 12 A4
Neuville-de-Poitou F 15 E2
Neuville-sur-Saône F 16 C3
Neuvy-le-Roi F 15 E1
Neuvy-St-Sépulchre F 15 F2
Neuvy-sur-Barangeon F 15 F1
Neuwied D 13 E1
Névache F 17 D4
Nevarenai LT 80 C2
Neveja LV 76 C2
Nevejas Skola LV 76 C2
Nevel RUS 115 E2
Nevers F 16 A2
Nevesinje BIH 58 B2
Nevėžis LT 81 F3
Nevieriai LT 82 C3
Nevlunghavn N 66 B3
Nevočiai LT 80 C3
New Abbey GB 3 F1
New Alresford GB 9 D3
New Cumnock GB 6 C2
New Deer GB 5 D3
New Galloway GB 3 F1
New Quay / Ceinewydd GB 3 F4
New Romney GB 9 F4
New Ross / Ros Mhic Thriúin IRL 3 D4
Newark-on-Trent GB 9 E1
Newbiggin-by-the-Sea GB 7 E2
Newborough GB 3 F3
Newbridge / An Droichead Nua IRL 3 D3
Newburgh GB 5 E4
Newburgh GB 7 D1
Newbury GB 9 D3
Newcastle GB 3 E2
Newcastle Emlyn / Castell Newydd Emlyn GB 3 E4
Newcastle-under-Lyme GB 8 C1
Newcastle-upon-Tyne GB 7 E3

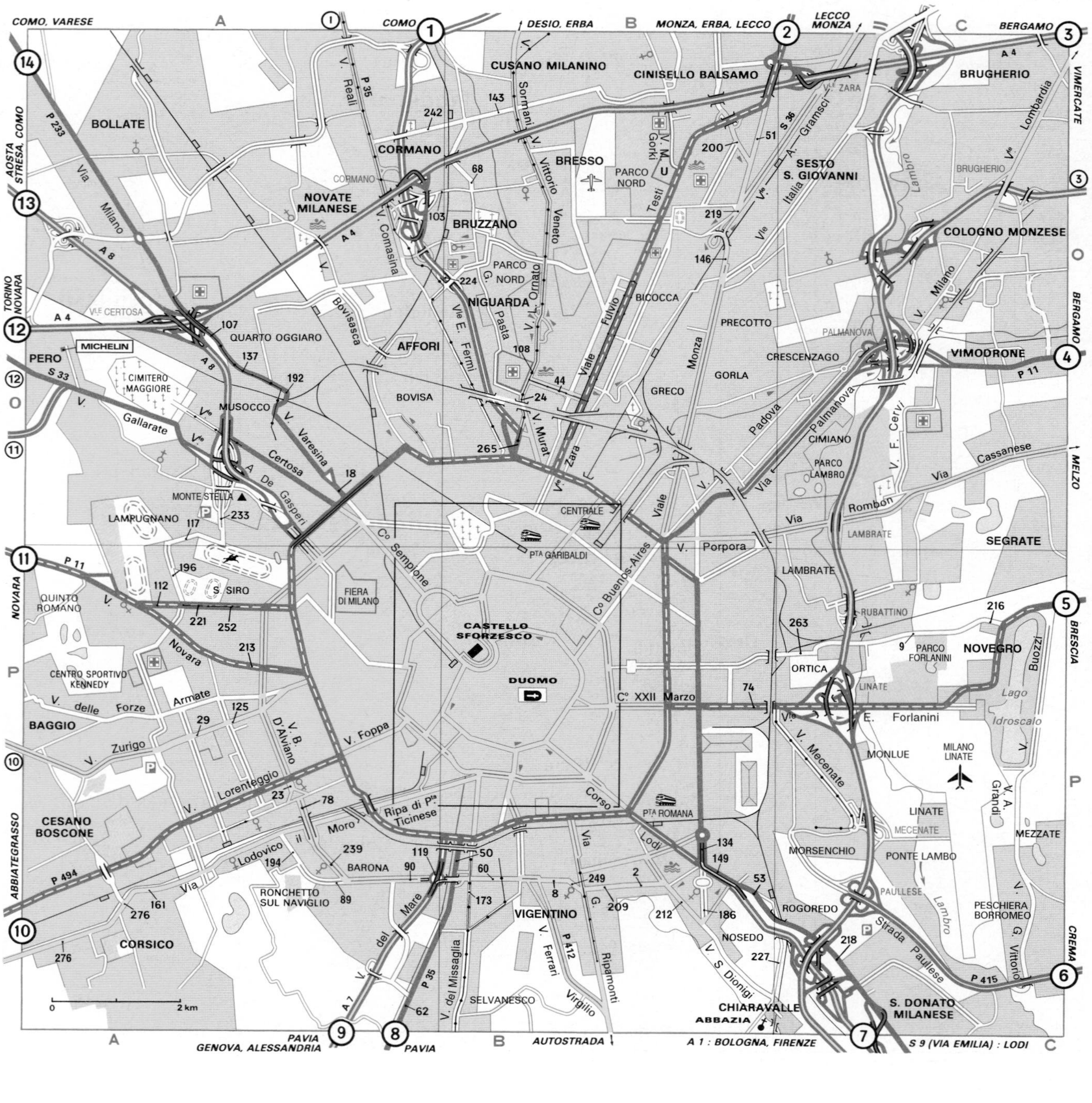

MILANO

Agrate (V. M. d') BP 2
Antonini (V. G.) BP 8
Arcangelo Corelli (V.) CP 9
Bartolini (V.) AO 18
Bellini (V. G.) AP 23
Benefattori dell' Ospedale (V.) BO 24
Berna (V.) AP 29
Cardinale A. Sforza (V.) BP 50
Casiraghi (Vle F.) BO 51
Cassinis (V. G. B.) BP 53
Cà Granda (Viale) BO 44
Cermenate (V. G. da) BP 60
Chiesa Rossa (V.) AP 62
Comasinella (V.) BO 68
Corsica (Viale) BP 74
Don L. Milani (Cavalcavia) AP 78
Faenza (Viale) AP 89
Famagosta (Viale) AP 90
Girardengo (V.) AO 103
Grassi (V. G. B.) AO 107
Graziano Imperatore BO 108
Harar (V.) AP 112
Ippodromo (V.) AOP 117
La Spezia (V.) AP 119
Legioni Romane (Viale) AP 125
Lucania (Viale) BP 134
Mambretti (V.) AO 137
Marconi (V. G.) BO 143
Marelli (Vle) BO 146
Marochetti (V.) BP 149
Milano (V.) AP 161
Montegani (V.) BP 173
Omero (Viale) BP 186
Palizzi (V.) AO 192
Parenzo (V.) AP 194
Patroclo (V.) AP 196
Picardi (V. F.) BO 200
Quaranta (V. B.) BP 209
Ravenna (V.) BP 212
Rembrandt (V.) AP 213
Rivoltana (Strada) CP 216
Rogoredo (V.) CP 218
Roma (V.) BO 219
Rospigliosi (V. dei) AP 221
Rubicone (Viale) BO 224
Sàuro (V. N.) AO 242
Solaroli (V.) BP 249
Stratico (V. S.) AP 252
S. Arialdo (V.) CP 227
S. Elia (V. A.) AO 233
S. Rita da Cascia (V.) AP 239
Tucidide (V.) CP 263
Valassina (V.) BO 265
Vittorio Emanuele (V.) AP 276

Newcastle West /
An Caisleán Nua IRL......2 B4
Newhaven GB......9 E4
Newmarket GB......9 E2
Newmarket IRL......2 B4
Newmarket
on Fergus IRL......2 B3
Newnham GB......8 C2
Newport GB......8 C1
Newport GB......3 E4
Newport GB......9 D4
Newport IRL......2 C1
Newport / Baile
Uí Fhiacháin IRL......2 B2
Newport /
Casnewydd GB......8 C3
Newport-on-Tay GB......7 D1
Newport Pagnell GB......9 D2
Newquay GB......8 A4
Newry GB......3 D2
Newton Abbot GB......8 B2
Newton-Aycliffe GB......7 D1
Newton Ferrers GB......8 B2
Newton Stewart GB......3 F1
Newtonmore GB......4 C4
Newtown GB......8 C2
Newtown /
Drenewydd GB......3 F4
Newtown
St Boswells GB......7 E2
Newtownabbey GB......3 E1
Newtownards GB......3 E1
Newtownbutler GB......6 A3
Newtownhamilton GB......3 D2
Newtownstewart GB......3 D1
Nexon F......15 E3
Neyland GB......8 A2
Niáta GR......108 B1
Niauduva LT......81 E3
Nibe DK......70 B2
Nica LV......80 A1
Nicastro I......51 D3
Nice F......23 D2
Nicgale LV......83 D2
Nicgale (Neicgals) LV......83 D2
Nickelsdorf A......45 F1
Nicolosi I......53 E3
Nicosia I......53 D3
Nicotera I......51 D3
Nida LV......80 A2
Nidderau D......13 F2
Nideggen D......13 D1
Nidri GR......104 A2
Nidzica PL......90 B2
Niebla E......28 C2
Nieborów PL......94 B2

Niebüll D......33 E1
Niebylec PL......99 D2
Niechanowo PL......93 E1
Niechlów PL......92 C2
Niechmirów PL......93 F3
Niechorze PL......88 B1
Niederalteich D......39 F4
Niederaula D......38 C2
Niederbronn-
les-Bains F......13 E3
Niederelsungen D......37 F1
Niederjossa D......38 C2
Niederkrüchten D......37 D2
Niederstetten D......38 C4
Niederstotzingen D......43 E1
Niedras LV......80 B1
Niedrzwica Duża PL......95 D3
Niedzica PL......98 B3
Niedźwiada PL......95 E2
Niedźwiedź
(Małopolskie) PL......98 B2
Niedźwiedzia
(Jaskinia) PL......97 D2
Niegocin (Jezioro) PL......90 C1
Niegosławice
(Lubuskie) PL......92 C2
Niegowa PL......98 A1
Niegripp D......34 A4
Nielisz PL......95 E3
Niemce PL......95 E3
Niemcza PL......97 D1
Niemegk D......34 B4
Niemisel S......64 C2
Niemodlin PL......99 D1
Nienadówka PL......99 D2
Nienburg D......33 E4
Nienburg D......39 D1
Niepołomice PL......98 B2
Nieporęt PL......94 C1
Niersten D......13 F2
Niesky D......40 C1
Niestronno PL......89 E3
Niesawa PL......89 F3
Nieul F......15 E3
Nieuweschans NL......32 C3
Nieuwpoort-Bad B......12 A1
Niforéka GR......104 C3
Nigrande LV......80 C1
Nigrita GR......102 A2
Nigula EE......72 A2
Niilo EE......72 B3
Ninisalo FIN......68 C3
Nijar E......30 B3
Njemci HR......55 F2
Nijkerk NL......36 C1
Nijmegen NL......37 D1

Nijverdal NL......32 C4
Níkea GR......101 E4
Niki NL......101 D2
Nikiá GR......111 E1
Nikissiani GR......102 B1
Nikitas GR......102 A3
Nikkaluokta S......60 C3
Nikoléika GR......105 D3
Nikopol BG......117 D3
Nikopol' UA......117 F1
Nikópoli GR......104 B1
Nikópoli GR......104 B1
Nikšić MNE......58 C3
Nilivaara S......64 C1
Nilsiä FIN......69 E1
Nîmes F......22 A2
Nimféa GR......103 D1
Nimféo GR......101 D2
Nímos (Nissi) GR......111 F1
Nin HR......54 B4
Nina EE......73 E3
Ninove B......12 B1
Niort F......15 D2
Nipsa GR......103 D2
Nirza (Nierza) LV......83 F2
Niš SRB......57 E4
Niscemi I......53 D4
Niška Banja SRB......57 E4
Nisko PL......99 D1
Nissáki GR......100 B4
Nissilä FIN......65 E3
Nissiros (Nissi) GR......111 E1
Nitaure LV......78 B3
Niton GB......9 D4
Nitra SK......116 B2
Nitry F......16 B1
Nittedal N......66 C2
Nittenau D......39 E4
Nittendorf D......39 E4
Nivala FIN......69 D1
Nivelles B......12 C1
Niwiska
(Podkarpackie) PL......99 D2
Nizza Monferrato I......17 F4
Njasviž BY......115 D3
Njivice HR......54 B3
Njurundabommen S......68 A2
Noailles F......12 A3
Noáin E......20 B3
Noblejas E......26 A2
Nocera Inferiore I......49 D4
Nocera Terinese I......51 D3

Nocera Umbra I......47 F3
Noceto I......46 C1
Noci I......49 F3
Nociūnai LT......85 F1
Nodeland N......66 A3
Nœux-les-Mines F......12 A1
Nogale LV......77 D2
Nogara I......47 D1
Nogaro F......13 D4
Nogent F......13 D4
Nogent-le-Roi F......11 F4
Nogent-le-Rotrou F......11 F4
Nogent-sur-Seine F......12 B4
Noginsk RUS......115 F2
Nogueira de Ramuín E......18 B3
Noguera E......26 C2
Nohfelden D......13 E2
Noia E......18 A2
Noirétable F......16 B3
Noirmoutier-en-l'Île F......14 B2
Noja E......19 F2
Nokia FIN......69 D3
Nola I......48 C4
Nolay F......16 B2
Noli I......23 E1
Nomeny F......13 D4
Nomexy F......13 D4
Nómia GR......108 C1
Nonancourt F......11 F4
Nonant-le-Pin F......11 E4
Nonaspe E......27 D1
None I......23 E1
Nonio I......17 F3
Nontron F......15 D3
Nonza F......23 F3
Noordwijk aan Zee NL......36 C1
Noormarkku FIN......68 C3
Nora S......67 E2
Norageliai LT......85 E3
Noras S......81 F1
Nord Edewecht D......33 D3
Nord-Lenangen N......60 C2
Nordborg DK......70 B4
Nordby (Århus) DK......70 C4
Nordby (Ribe) DK......70 A3
Norddeich D......32 C3
Nordeide N......66 A1
Norden D......32 C3
Nordenau D......37 F2
Nordenham D......33 D2
Norderney D......32 C3
Norderstedt D......33 F2
Nordfjordeid N......62 A4
Nordfold N......60 B3

Nordhalben D......39 D2
Nordhausen D......39 D1
Nordhorn D......32 C4
Nordingrå S......68 A2
Nordkjosbotn N......60 C2
Nordli N......63 E2
Nördlingen D......39 D4
Nordmaling S......68 B1
Nordmark S......67 D2
Nordseter N......66 C1
Norðurfjörður IS......62 A1
Nore N......66 B2
Noreikiai LT......81 F2
Noreikiškes LT......85 E2
Noreišiai LT......81 D3
Noresund N......66 B2
Norg NL......32 C3
Norgelai (Kauno) LT......85 D1
Norgelai
(Panevėžio) LT......81 F2
Norgeliškes LT......85 F3
Norheimsund N......66 A1
Noriai LT......81 F2
Noriūnai LT......82 B3
Norkiške LT......85 D3
Norra Bergnäs S......64 A2
Norra Råda S......67 D2
Norråker S......63 E2
Norrby S......64 A3
Norrby DK......70 C4
Norrköping S......67 E3
Norrnäs FIN......68 C2
Norrsunda S......67 F2
Norrsundet S......67 F1
Norrtälje S......67 F2
Norrviken S......71 D3
Norsjö S......64 B3
Nort-sur-Erdre F......14 C1
Nörten-Hardenberg D......38 C1
North Berwick GB......7 E1
North Walsham GB......9 F1
Northallerton GB......7 E3
Northam GB......8 B3
Northampton GB......9 D2
Northeim D......38 C1
Northleach GB......8 C1
Northwich GB......8 C1
Norton GB......7 F4
Nortorf D......33 E1
Norwich GB......9 F1
Nosenai LT......86 B1

Nosivka UA......115 F4
Nossebro S......67 D3
Nossen D......39 F1
Noteć PL......89 E3
Notecka (Puszcza) PL......88 C3
Nótia GR......101 E1
Noto I......53 E4
Notodden N......66 B2
Notre-Dame-
de-Bellecombe F......17 D3
Nottingham GB......9 D1
Nouan-le-Fuzelier F......15 F1
Nousiainen FIN......68 C3
Nouvion-en-Ponthieu F......12 A1
Nouzonville F......12 C2
Nova Breznica MK......59 E3
Nová Bystřice CZ......41 D4
Nova Crnja SRB......56 C1
Nova Gorica SLO......54 A2
Nova Gradiška HR......55 D2
Nova Kachovka UA......117 F2
Nova Levante /
Welschnofen I......43 F3
Nová Paka CZ......41 D2
Nova Pazova SRB......56 C2
Nova Role CZ......40 B2
Nova Siri Marina I......49 F3
Nova Topola BIH......55 D3
Nova Varoš SRB......56 C4
Nova Vas SLO......54 A2
Nova Zagora BG......117 E2
Novaci MK......59 E3
Novaci SRB......56 C2
Novadneki LV......80 C1
Novafeltria I......47 E2
Novales F......20 C4
Novalja HR......54 B4
Novara I......17 F3
Novara di Sicilia I......50 C4
Nové Město
na Moravě CZ......41 D3
Nové Město
nad Metují CZ......41 D2
Nové Město
nad Váhom SK......116 B1
Nové Zámky SK......116 B2
Novelda E......26 C4
Novellara I......46 C1
Noventa Vicentina I......47 D1
Noves F......22 B1
Novgorod RUS......115 E1
Novhorod-
Sivers'kyj UA......115 F3
Novi Bečej SRB......56 C1
Novi di Modena I......47 D1
Novi Dojran MK......59 F4

Novi Grad (Brčko) BIH......55 E2
Novi Grad /
Bosanski Novi BIH......54 C3
Novi Karlovci SRB......56 C2
Novi Kneževac SRB......55 F1
Novi Ligure I......17 F2
Novi Marof HR......54 C1
Novi Pazar BG......117 E2
Novi Pazar SRB......57 D4
Novi Sad SRB......56 C2
Novi Šeher BIH......55 E3
Novi Slankamen SRB......56 C2
Novi Travnik BIH......55 E3
Novi Vinodolski HR......54 B3
Novigrad (Poreč) HR......54 A3
Novigrad (Zadar) HR......54 C4
Novigrad
Podravski HR......55 D1
Novion-Porcien F......12 C2
Novo Brdo SRB......59 E2
Novo mesto SLO......54 B2
Novo Miloševo SRB......56 C1
Novo Selo BIH......55 D2
Novo Selo MK......59 F4
Novo Zvečevo HR......55 D2
Novohrad-
Volyns'kyj UA......115 D3
Novomyrhorod UA......117 F1
Novoržev RUS......115 D1
Novoselycja UA......117 D1
Novosil' RUS......115 F3
Novoukraïnka UA......117 F1
Novovolyns'k UA......115 D3
Novozybkov RUS......115 D3
Novska HR......55 D2
Nový Bor CZ......40 C2
Nový Bydžov CZ......41 D2
Nový Jičín CZ......41 F3
Novyj Buh UA......117 F1
Nowa Brzeźnica PL......94 A3
Nowa Dęba PL......99 D1
Nowa Huta PL......98 B2
Nowa Karczma PL......89 E1
Nowa Morawa PL......97 D2
Nowa Pasłęka PL......90 B1
Nowa Ruda PL......96 C1
Nowa Sarzyna PL......99 D1
Nowa Słupia PL......94 C3
Nowa Sól PL......92 C2
Nowa Sucha PL......94 B2
Nowa Wieś Ełcka PL......91 D2
Nowa Wieś
Lęborska PL......89 E1
Nowa Wieś Wielka PL......89 E3
Nowe PL......89 F2
Nowe Brzesko PL......98 B2

Nowe Miasteczko PL......92 C2
Nowe Miasto PL......90 B3
Nowe Miasto
Lubawskie PL......90 A2
Nowe Miasto
nad Pilicą PL......94 B2
Nowe Miasto
nad Wartą PL......93 E2
Nowe Ostrowy PL......94 A1
Nowe Skalmierzyce PL......93 E2
Nowe Warpno PL......88 A2
Nowinka PL......91 E1
Nowogard PL......88 B2
Nowogród PL......91 D1
Nowogród
Bobrzański PL......92 B2
Nowogrodziec PL......92 B3
Nowosolna PL......94 A2
Nowy Bieruń PL......97 F2
Nowy Duninów PL......90 A3
Nowy Dwór
Gdański PL......89 F1
Nowy Dwór
Mazowiecki PL......94 B1
Nowy Kawęczyn PL......94 B2
Nowy Korczyn PL......98 C2
Nowy Sącz PL......98 C2
Nowy Staw PL......89 F1
Nowy Targ PL......98 B3
Nowy Tomyśl PL......92 C1
Nowy Waliszów PL......96 C1
Nowy Wiśnicz PL......98 B2
Nowy Żmigród PL......99 D2
Noyant F......15 D1
Noyers F......16 B1
Noyers-sur-Jabron F......22 C1
Noyon F......12 A3
Nozay F......14 C1
Nozdrzec PL......99 D2
Nueva E......19 E2
Nueva Carteya E......29 E2
Nuévalos E......26 A1
Nuevo Baztán E......26 A2
Nugariai LT......80 B2
Nuijamaa FIN......69 F3
Nuits-St-Georges F......16 C1
Nukši LV......83 F2
Nules E......27 D2
Nulvi I......50 A2
Numana I......48 B1
Numancia E......20 A4
Nummela FIN......69 D4
Nummi FIN......69 D4
Numuri LV......78 A2
Nuneaton GB......9 D2
Nunnanen FIN......61 E2
Nuñomoral E......25 D2
Nunspeet NL......32 B4
Nuorgam FIN......61 F1
Nuotekai LT......86 B1
Nupronys LT......85 F2
Nur PL......91 D3
Nurallao I......50 A4
Nürburg D......13 E2
Núria E......21 E3
Nurme EE......72 A3
Nurmes FIN......69 F1
Nurmijärvi FIN......69 D4
Nurmijärvi
(Pohjois-Karjala) FIN......69 F1
Nurmiži LV......78 B3
Nurmo FIN......68 C2
Nürnberg D......39 D3
Nürnberg D......39 D4
Nursi EE......79 E2
Nürtingen D......43 D1
Nus I......17 E3
Nusse D......33 F2
Nuštar HR......55 E2
Nuttlar D......37 F1
Nuttupera FIN......69 E1
Nuutajärvi FIN......69 D3
Nõgiaru EE......79 D1
Nõmmküla EE......75 D2
Nõo EE......79 D1
Nüpli EE......79 D1
Nõuni EE......79 D1
Nõva (Jõgeva) EE......73 E3
Nõva (Lääne) EE......75 D1
Näpi EE......73 D2
Nyåker S......68 B1
Nyborg DK......70 C3
Nybro S......71 E2
Nyírbátor H......116 C2
Nyíregyháza H......116 C2
Nykarleby /
Uusikaarlepyy FIN......68 C1
Nykøbing F DK......70 C4
Nykøbing M DK......70 B2
Nyköping S......67 F3
Nykvarn S......67 F3
Nymburk CZ......40 C2
Nynäshamn S......67 F3
Nyon CH......17 D2
Nyons F......22 B1
Nýřany CZ......40 B3
Nýrsko CZ......40 B4
Nyrud N......61 F2
Nysa PL......97 D1
Nysäter S......67 D2
Nyseter N......62 C3
Nyskie (Jezioro) PL......97 D1
Nysted DK......70 C4
Nyvoll N......61 D1

Albert-Roßhaupter-Str......BT 2
Aschheimer Str......DS 9
Berg-am-Laim-Str......DS 23
Brudermühlstr......CT 29
Candidstr......CT 31
Englschalkinger Str......DS 47
Georg-Brauchle-Ring......BCR 57
Hanauer Str......CR 66
Handsastr......CS 68
Heckenstallerstr......BT 70
Johanneskirchner Str......DS 80
Leuchtenbergring......DS 104
Melchiorstr......DT 131
Meyerbeerstr......AS 136
Münchner Str......DR 142
Murnauer Str......BT 145
Neubiberger Str......DT 146
Offenbachstr......AS 153
Ottobrunner Str......DT 158
Plinganserstr......CT 166
Schäftlarnstr......CT 187
Siemensallee......BT 197
Südl.
Auffahrtsallee......BS 205
Tierparkstr......CT 209
Triebstr......CR 212
Tübinger Str......BCS 217
Waldfriedhofstr......BT 226
Wendl-Dietrich-
Str......BS 229

MÜNCHEN (city map)

Map edge references: KARLSFELD · E 53-A 92 · DACHAU · INGOLSTADT · REGENSBURG NÜRNBERG E 45-A 9 · LANDSHUT · ERDING · STUTTGART, AUGSBURG E 52 · A 99 · KR. MÜNCHEN-WEST · LINDAU, AUGSBURG · E 54-A 96 · GERMERING · STARNBERG · PASSAU · WASSERBURG · EBERSBERG · E 552 · A 94 · A 995 · GARMISCH-PARTENKIRCHEN A 952: STARNBERG · INNSBRUCK · Bavaria-Filmstadt · BAD-TÖLZ GRÜNWALD · SALZBURG, INNSBRUCK · E 45-52-A 8 · BAD-TÖLZ · E 45-52 SALZBURG

Map labels: Langwieder See · DR. MÜNCHEN-ALLACH · ALLACH · FASANERIE NORD · Lerchenauer See · Ludwigsfelder Str · Harthof · Am Hart · Kieferngarten · Heidemann Str · Blütenanger · Am Blütenanger · UNTERFÖHRING · Frankfurter Ring · ADAC · MOOSACH · MILBERTSHOFEN · Milbertshfn. · Freimann · FREIMANN · Petuelring · Olympia-park · Museum BMW · Studenten-Stadt · Halle Heide · Olympia-turm · STADION · HIRSCHAU · SCHWABING · Englischer Garten · UNTERMENZING · OBER-MENZING · Verdistr · Menzinger Str · DTC · NYMPHENBURG · Gern · ALTE PINAKOTHEK · OBERFÖHRING · ENGLSCHALKING · BOGENHAUSEN · Böhmerw. pl. · Arabellapark · DENNING · AUBING · PIPPING · NEUHAUSEN · Nymphenburger Str · HIRSCHGARTEN · BAYERISCHES NATIONALMUSEUM · RESIDENZ · FRAUENKIRCHE · ASAMKIRCHE · Heimeranpl. · LAIM · THERESIEN WIESE · DEUTSCHES MUSEUM · BERG AM LAIM · TRUDERING · NEUAUBING · LOCHHAM · GRÄFELFING · Würmtalstr · BLUMENAU · SPORT HALLE · Kolumbus-pl. · Silberhornstr · Kari-Preis-Pl. · Michaelibad · RAMERSDORF · OSTPARK · MARTINSRIED · Klinikum GROSSHADERN · KLEINHADERN · Haderner Stern · Holzapfelkreuth · Partnachpl. · Implerstr · Harras · GIESING · Giesing · Untersberg str · Wetterst. Pl. · St-Quirin-Pl. · PERLACH · NEU PERLACH · NEURIED · Forstenrieder Allee · Machtlfinger Str · OBERSENDLING · MITTER SENDLING · Thalkirchen · TIERPARK HELLABRUNN · HARLACHING · Grünwalder str · FASANGARTEN · Neuperlach-Süd · FÜRSTENRIEDER WALD · Fürstenried-West · FORSTENRIED · SOLLN · Wolfratshauser str · UNTERBIBERG · FORST KASTEN · STOCKDORF · FORSTENRIEDER PARK · PERLACHER FORST · Th.-Giehse-Allee

O

O Barco E...............18 C3
O Bolo E................18 B3
O Cádabo E............18 B2
O Grove E.............18 A3
Oadby GB...............9 D1
Oakham GB..............9 E1
Oandu EE...............73 E2
Oanes N................66 A2
Oara EE................72 A3
Óassi GR.............105 D3
Oban GB................6 C1
Obbola S...............68 B1
Obdach A..............45 D2
Obejo E................25 E4
Obeliai
  (Panevežio) LT......82 C3
Obeliai (Vilniaus) LT..86 B1
Oberammergau D........43 F2
Oberau D...............43 F2
Oberaudorf D..........44 B2
Oberdrauburg A........44 A3
Obereßfeld D..........39 D3
Obergrafendorf A......45 D1
Obergünzburg D........43 F3
Obergurgl A...........43 F3
Oberhaslach F.........13 E4
Oberhausen (Kreis
  Oberhausen) D.......37 E1
Oberhof
  (Kreis Schmalkalden-
  Meiningen) D........39 D2
Oberkirch
  (Ortenaukreis) D....13 F4
Oberkirchen D.........37 F2
Oberkochen D..........39 D4
Obermarchtal D........43 D1
Obernai F.............13 E4
Obernberg am Inn A....44 A1
Obernburg D...........38 C3
Oberndorf a. Neckar
  (Kreis Freiburg) D...13 F4
Oberndorf bei Salzburg A..44 B1
Obernzell D...........40 C4
Oberölsbach D.........39 E4
Oberprechtal D........13 F4
Oberpullendorf A......45 E1
Obersontheim D........38 C4
Oberstaufen
  (Kreis Oberallgäu) D..43 E2
Oberstdorf D..........43 E2
Obertauern A..........44 C2
Obertraun A...........44 C2
Oberursel D...........13 F2
Obervellach A.........44 C2
Oberviechtach D.......39 E3
Oberwart A............45 E1
Oberwesel D...........13 E2
Oberwiesenthal D......39 F2
Oberwölz A............44 C2
Oberzeiring A.........45 D2
Óbidos P..............24 A2
Obilić SRB............59 E2
Obing D...............44 B1
Obinitsa EE...........79 E2
Objat F...............15 F4
Obninsk RUS..........115 F2
Obojan' RUS..........115 F4
Obón E................26 C1
Oborniki PL...........89 D3
Oborniki Śląskie PL...93 D3
Obornjača SRB.........55 F1
Oborovo HR............54 C2
Obrazów PL............95 D3
Obrenovac SRB.........56 C3
Obrež SRB.............56 C3
Obrov SLO.............54 A2
Obrovac HR............54 A2
Obrovac Sinjski HR....55 D4
Obrowo PL.............89 F3
Obršani MK............59 E4
Obrzycko PL...........88 C3
Obsteig A.............43 F2
Obsza PL..............99 F2
Obudavac BIH..........55 E3
Obzor BG.............117 E3
Očakiv UA............117 F3
Ocaña E...............26 A2
Occhiobello I.........47 D1
Očevlja BIH...........55 E3
Ochagavía E...........20 B3
Ochla PL..............92 B2
Ochsenfurt D..........38 C3
Ochsenhausen D........43 E1
Ochtrup D.............32 C4
Ochtyrka UA..........115 F4
Očikiai LT............81 D3
Ockelbo S.............67 F1
Öckerö S..............66 C4
Öðákra S..............71 D3
Odda N................66 A1
Odden Færgehavn DK....70 C3
Odder DK..............70 B3
Odeceixe P............28 A2
Odeleite P............28 B2
Odemira P.............24 A4
Odense DK.............70 B3
Odenthal D............13 E1
Oderberg D............34 C3
Oderzo I..............44 B4
Odesa UA.............117 D2
Ödeshög S.............67 E3
Odiste EE.............73 D3
Odivelas P............24 B4

Odolanów PL...........93 E2
Odolo I...............43 E4
Odorheiu
  Secuiesc RO.........117 D2
Odra Wschodnia PL.....88 A3
Odry CZ...............41 F3
Odry PL...............89 E2
Odrzykoń PL...........99 D2
Odrzywół PL...........94 B3
Oebisfelde D..........33 F4
Oederan D.............39 F2
Oeiras P..............24 A3
Oelde D...............37 F1
Oelsnitz D............39 E2
Oettingen D...........39 D4
Oetz A................43 F2
Offenbach D...........13 F2
Offenburg D...........13 E4
Offida I..............48 B1
Offranville F.........11 F2
Ofir P................24 A4
Oggiono I.............43 D4
Oglaine LV............81 E1
Ogliastro Cilento I...49 D4
Ogonki PL.............90 C1
Ogošte SRB............59 E2
Ogre LV...............82 A1
Ogresgals LV..........82 A1
Ogrodniki PL..........91 E1
Ogrodzieniec PL.......98 A1
Ogulin HR.............54 B3
Ohanes E..............30 A3
Ohiró GR.............102 A1
Ohlstadt D............43 F2
Ohorn D...............39 F1
Ohrdruf D.............39 D2
Ohrid MK..............59 D4
Öhringen D............38 C4
Öhthia GR............104 B3
Ohthoniá GR..........106 A3
Ohtu EE...............72 A2
Oiartzun E............20 B3
Oidrema EE............72 A3
Oijärvi FIN...........65 D2
Oikarainen FIN........65 D1
Oirschot NL...........36 C1
Oisemont F............11 F2

Oisterwijk NL.........36 C1
Oisu EE...............72 C3
Õisu EE...............78 C1
Öja FIN...............68 C1
Ojaküla EE............73 D1
Ojakylä FIN...........65 D3
Ojasoo EE.............72 B2
Ojaäärse EE...........72 B3
Ojcowski Park
  Narodowy PL.........98 A2
Öje S.................67 D1
Öjebyn S..............64 C2
Ojos Negros E.........26 C1
Ojrzeń PL.............90 B3
Ojuelos E.............25 E4
Ojung S...............67 E1
Okainai LT............85 F1
Okehampton GB..........8 B4
Oker (Kreis Goslar) D..38 C1
Oknö S................71 E2
Okonek PL.............89 D2
Oksa PL...............94 B3
Oksbøl DK.............70 A3
Oksby DK..............70 A3
Øksfjord N............61 D1
Oksywie PL............89 F1
Okučani HR............55 D2
Okulovka RUS.........115 E1
Ólafsfjörður IS.......62 B1
Ólafsvík IS...........62 A1
Olaine LV.............81 F1
Olargues F............21 F2
Oława PL..............93 D3
Olazti/Olazagutia E...20 A3
Olbernhau D...........39 F2
Olbia I...............50 B1
Oldcastle /
  An Seanchaisleán IRL..3 D2
Oldebroek NL..........32 B4
Oldeide N.............62 A4
Olden N...............62 B4
Oldenburg (Oldb)
  (Kr. Oldenburg
  Oldb Stadt) D.......33 D3
Oldenburg i. Holstein (Kreis
  Ostholstein) D......33 F2
Oldenzaal NL..........32 C4
Olderdalen N..........60 C2
Oldervik N............60 C2

Oldham GB..............7 E4
Oldmeldrum GB..........5 D4
Oldsum D..............33 D1
Olecko PL.............91 D1
Oleggio I.............17 F3
Oleiros E.............18 B2
Oleiros P.............24 B2
Oleksandrija UA......117 F1
Ølen N................66 A2
Olesa de Montserrat E..21 E4
Oleśnica
  (Dolnośląskie) PL...93 E3
Oleśnica
  (Świętokrzyskie) PL..98 C1
Olesno (Opolskie) PL..93 F3
Oleszyce PL...........99 E2
Oletta F..............23 F3
Olette F..............21 E3
Olevs'k UA...........115 E4
Olgina P..............73 F2
Ølgod DK..............70 B3
Olhão P...............28 B3
Olhava FIN............65 D2
Oliana E..............21 E4
Olib HR...............54 B4
Olib (Otok) HR........54 B4
Oliena I..............50 B3
Oliete E..............27 D1
Olimbía GR...........104 C3
Olimbiáda GR.........102 A2
Olímbiáda GR.........101 E3
Ólimbos GR...........111 E3
Ólimbos (Óros) GR....101 E3
Olimbiáda GR.........102 A3
Olite E................20 B3
Oliva E................27 D4
Oliva de la Frontera E..24 C4
Oliva de Mérida E.....25 D3
Olivares de Júcar E...26 B2
Oliveira de Azeméis P..24 B1
Oliveira de Frades P..24 B1
Oliveira do Bairro P..24 B1
Oliveira do Douro P...18 A4
Oliveira do Hospital P..24 B1
Olivenza E............24 C3
Olivet F...............15 F1
Olivone CH............17 F2
Ölizha PL.............89 F1
Olkusz PL.............98 A2
Ollepa EE.............72 C3
Ollerton GB............9 D1

NANTES

Aiguillon (Q. d')..........BX 2
Anglais (Bd des)...........BV 4
Beaujoire (Bd de la).......CV 10
Belges (Bd des)............CV 12
Bocquerel (Bd H.)..........CV 14
Bouley Paty (Bd)...........BV 22
Cassin (Bd R.).............CV 34
Chapelle-sur-Erdre (Rte)...BV 39
Cholet (Bd Bâtonnier)......BX 42
Churchill (Bd W.)..........BX 43
Clemenceau (Pont G.).......CX 45
Coty (Bd R.)...............BX 55
Courbet (Bd Amiral)........CV 58
Dalby (Bd E.)..............CX 61
Dos-d'Ane (R.).............CX 68
Doulon (Bd des)............CV 70
Dreyfus
  (R. Commandant A.).......CV 71
Einstein (Bd A.)...........BV 75
Fraternité (Bd de la)......BX 84
Gabory (Bd E.).............CX 85
Gaulle (Bd Gén.-de).......CX 87
Jean XXIII (Bd)............BV 100
Jouhaux (Bd L.)............BX 102
Juin (Bd Mar.).............BX 103
Koenig (Bd Gén.)...........BX 107
Landreau (R. du)...........CV 108
Le Lasseur
  (Bd)....................BV 112
Lauriol (Bd G.)............CX 110
Liberté (Bd de la).........BX 115
Luther-King (Bd M.)........CV 118
Michelet (Bd)..............CV 127
Mollet (Bd G.).............CV 128
Monod (Bd du Prof.-J.).....CV 130
Orieux (Bd E.).............CV 133
Petite Baratte
  (R.).....................CV 141
Pirmil (Pont de)...........CX 145
Poilus (Bd des)............CV 147
Roch (Bd Gustave)..........CX 160
Romanet (Bd).............BX 163
St-Jacques (R.)............CX 169
St-Joseph (Rte de).........CV 171
St-Sébastien
  (Côte)...................CX 178
Sarrebrück (Bd de).........CX 186
Say (R. L.)................BV 186
Stalingrad (Bd de).........CV 190
Tertre (Bd du).............BV 192
Tortière (Pont de la)......CV 196
Victor-Hugo (Bd)...........CX 201
Viviani (R. René)..........CX 204

ORVAULT

Ferrière (Av. de la).......BV 80
Goupil (Av. A.)............BV 88
Mendès-France
  (Bd).....................BV 124
Rennes (Rte de)............BV 156

REZÉ

Gaulle (Bd Gén.-de).......CX 87

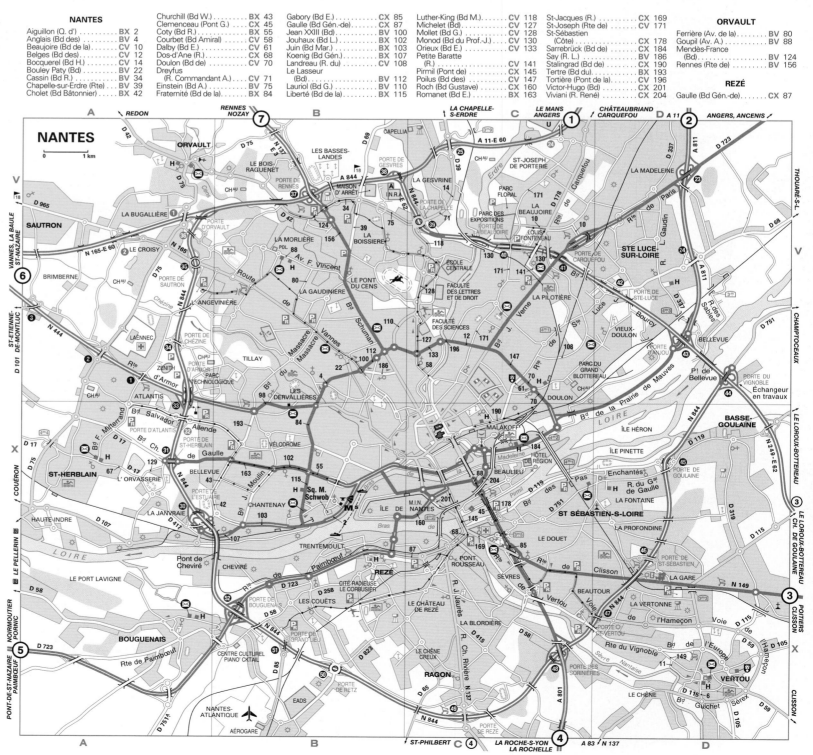

NANTES

NAPOLI

Augusto (Viale) . . . . AU 10
Capodichino (Calata) . . . . CT 16
Caravaggio
(V. Michelangelo Da). . . . . . AU 19

Casoria (Str. Prov.) . . . . CT 21
Cilea (V. Francesco). . . . . BU 26
Claudio (V.) . . . . AU 28
De Amicis (V. Tommaso) . . . . . . BT 41
De Pinedo (V.) . . . . CT 44
Di Vittorio (Pza) . . . . CT 45
Domiziana (V.) . . . . AU 46

Don Bosco (V.) . . . . CT 47
Europa (Cso) . . . . BU 52
Ferraris (V. Galileo) . . . . CTU 54
Garibaldi (Cso G.) . . . . DU 62
Gianturco (V. E.) . . . . CTU 64
Giulio Cesare (V.) . . . . AU 66
Imparato (V. F.) . . . . CTU 68

Jannelli (V. Gabriele) . . . . BT 69
Kennedy (Viale J. F.) . . . . AU 70
Maddalena (Viale U.) . . . . BU 71
Miraglia (V. Nicola) . . . . CT 79
Napoli Capodimonte (V.) . . . . . BT 92
Nicolini (V. Nicola) . . . . CT 95
Orazio (V.) . . . . BU 103

Piave (V.) . . . . AU 112
Pietravalle (V. M.) . . . . BT 114
Pigna (V.) . . . . BU 116
Ponti Rossi (V.) . . . . BT 122
Reggia di Portici

S. Giovanni a Teduccio
(Cso) . . . . CU 141
Taddeo da Sessa (V.) . . . . CT 157
Tasso (V. Torquato) . . . . BU 158
Tecchio (Piazzale V.) . . . . AU 160
Traccia a Poggioreale (V.). . . . . CT 164
Volta (V. A.) . . . . CU 173

Palazzo e Galleria di Capodimonte. . . . . BT M¹

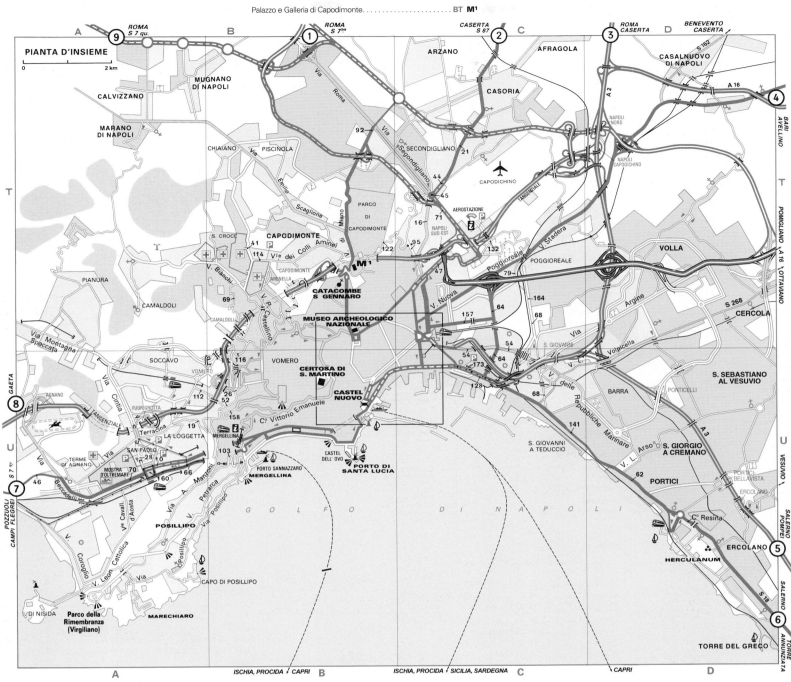

Olliergues F 16 B3
Ollioules F 22 C2
Olmedillo de Roa E 19 E4
Olmedo E 19 E4
Olmedo I 50 A3
Olmeto F 23 F4
Olocau del Rey E 27 D1
Olofström S 71 D3
Olombrada E 19 E4
Olomouc CZ 41 E3
Olonzac F 21 F2
Oloron-Ste-Marie F 20 C2
Olost E 21 E4
Olot E 21 F4
Olovo BIH 55 F3
Olpe D 13 E1
Olsberg D 37 F1
Olshammar S 67 E3
Olst NL 32 C4
Østykke DK 70 C3
Olszanica
(Podkarpackie) PL 99 E3
Olszanka
(Mazowieckie) PL 95 E1
Olszanka
(Opolskie) PL 93 E3
Olszówka PL 93 F1
Olsztyn (Śląskie) PL 94 A3
Olsztyn (Warmińsko-
Mazurskie) PL. 90 B2
Olsztynek PL 90 B2
Olszyna PL 92 B3
Oltedal N 66 A2
Olten CH 17 E1
Oltenia RO 117 E3
Olula del Río E 30 B3
Olustvere EE 72 C3
Olüti LV 83 E2
Ólvega E 20 A4
Olvera E 29 E3
Olza PL 97 E2
Omagh GB 3 D1
Omalí GR 101 D3
Omalós GR 109 D4
Omarska BIH 55 D3
Omedu EE 73 E2
Omegna I 17 F2
Omiš HR 58 A4
Omišalj HR 54 B3
Ommen NL 32 C4

Omoljica SRB 57 D2
Omorfohóri GR 101 E4
Ömossa FIN 68 C3
Oña E 19 F3
Oñati E 20 A2
Onciškiai LT 85 E3
Onda E 27 D2
Ondara E 27 D4
Ondarroa E 20 A2
Oneglia I 23 E1
Onesse-et-Laharie F 20 B1
Oneşti RO 117 E2
Onich GB 4 B4
Onkamo (Lappi) FIN 65 E1
Onkamo
(Pohjois-Karjala) FIN . . 69 F2
Ontaneda E 19 F2
Ontiñena E 20 C4
Ontinyent E 26 C4
Ontur E 26 C4
Onuškis
(Panevėžio) LT 82 C2
Onuškis (Vilniaus) LT 85 F3
Onzain F 15 E1
Oonurme EE 73 E2
Oost-Vlieland NL 32 B3
Oostburg NL 36 B2
Oostende B 12 A1
Oosterbeek NL 37 D1
Oosterend NL 32 B3
Oosterhout NL 36 C1
Oostkamp B 12 B1
Oostmalle B 36 C2
Öötla EE 72 C2
Ootmarsum NL 32 C4
Opalenica PL 92 C1
Opatija HR 54 A3
Opatovac HR 55 F2
Opatów (Śląskie) PL 93 F3
Opatów
(Świętokrzyskie) PL . . . 94 C3
Opatówek PL 93 E2
Opatowiec PL 98 C2
Opava CZ 41 F2
Opinogóra Górna PL 90 B3
Oplaget D 13 E1
Opočka RUS 115 D3
Opoczno PL 94 B3
Opole PL 97 E1

Opole Lubelskie PL 95 D3
Oporów PL 94 A1
Opovo SRB 56 C2
Oppach D 40 C1
Oppdal N 62 C4
Oppenau D 13 F4
Oppenheim D 13 F2
Opphaug N 62 C3
Oppido Lucano I 49 E4
Oppido Mamertina I 51 E4
Opuli LV 83 F2
Opuzen HR 58 A3
Ora / Auer I 43 F3
Oradea RO 116 C2
Oradour-sur-Glane F 15 E3
Oradour-sur-Vayres F 15 E3
Orahovac SRB 59 D3
Oraison F 22 C1
Orajärvi FIN 64 C1
Orange F 22 B1
Orani I 50 A3
Oranienbaum D 39 E1
Oranienburg D 34 B3
Oranmore IRL 2 B3
Orašac RO 58 B3
Orašac SRB 57 D3
Orašje BIH 55 E2
Orăştie RO 117 D2
Orava EE 79 E1
Oravais /
Oravainen FIN 68 C2
Oravikoski FIN 69 E2
Oravita RO 116 C3
Orba E 27 D4
Ørbæk DK 70 C3
Orbassano I 17 E4
Orbe CH 17 D2
Orbec F 11 E3
Orbetello I 47 D4
Orbey F 13 E4
Orce E 30 B2
Orcera E 26 A4
Orchies F 12 B1
Orchówek PL 95 F2
Orchowo PL 93 E1
Orcières F 17 D2
Orcival F 16 A3
Ordes E 18 A2
Ordizia E 20 A2

Orduña E 19 F2
Ordžonikidze UA 117 F1
Ore S 67 E1
Orea E 26 B2
Orebić HR 58 A3
Örebro S 67 E3
Orechovo-
Zujevo RUS 115 F2
Öregrund S 67 F2
Oreí GR 105 E1
Orellana de la Sierra E . . . 25 E3
Orellana la Vieja E 25 E3
Oréo GR 102 C1
Oreókastro GR 101 F2
Orestiáda GR 103 F1
Organí GR 103 D1
Organyà E 21 E4
Orgaz E 25 F2
Orgelet F 16 C2
Orgères-en-Beauce F 11 F4
Orgita EE 72 C2
Orgiva E 29 F3
Orgon F 22 B2
Orgosolo I 50 B3
Orhei MD 117 E2
Orhomenós GR 105 E2
Oria E 30 B3
Oria I 51 E1
Oricáin E 20 B3
Origny-Ste-Benoite F 12 B2
Orihuela E 30 C2
Orihuela
del Tremedal E 26 C2
Orimattila FIN 69 E4
Oriní GR 102 A1
Oriolo I 49 F4
Oripää FIN 68 C4
Orissaare EE 75 D2
Oristano I 50 A3
Orivesi FIN 69 D3
Orjahovo BG 117 D3
Ørje N 66 C2
Orkanger N 62 C3
Örkelljunga S 71 D3
Orlane SRB 59 D3
Orlat RO 117 D2
Orléans F 15 F1
Orlová CZ 41 F2
Orlovat SRB 56 C2
Orly F 12 A4

Orly PL 99 E2
Orménio GR 103 E1
Ormília GR 102 A3
Órmos GR 101 F3
Órmos Korthíou GR 106 C3
Órmos Panagías GR 102 A3
Órmos Prínou GR 102 B2
Ormož SLO 54 C1
Ormsjö S 64 A3
Ormskirk GB 7 D4
Ørnes N 60 A4
Ørnes N 66 B1
Orneta PL 90 B1
Ornós GR 106 C4
Örnsköldsvik S 68 B2
Or'ol RUS 115 F3
Orolik HR 55 F2
Orom SRB 55 F1
Oron-la-Ville CH 17 D2
Orońsko PL 94 C3
Oropa I 17 F3
Oropesa E 25 E2
Orosei I 50 B2
Orosháza H 116 C2
Orpesa / Oropesa
del Mar E 27 D2
Orpierre F 22 C1
Orpington GB 9 E3
Orreaga /
Roncesvalles E 20 B3
Orrefors S 71 E2
Orša BY 115 E3
Orsay F 12 A4
Orsières CH 17 E3
Orsogna I 48 C2
Orşova RO 116 C3
Ørsta N 62 B4
Ørsundsbro S 67 F2
Orta Nova I 49 E3
Orta S. Giulio I 17 F3
Orte I 47 D4
Orth A 45 E1
Orthez F 20 C2
Ortigueira E 18 B1
Ortisei / St Ulrich I 43 F3
Ortnevik N 66 A1
Orton GB 5 D3
Ortona I 48 C2
Ortrand D 39 F1

Örträsk S 64 B3
Oru EE 72 B2
Õru EE 79 D1
Orubica HR 55 D2
Orune I 50 B3
Orusco de Tajuña E 26 A2
Õruste EE 79 D1
Orvalho P 24 B2
Orvieto I 47 E4
Orvinio I 47 F4
Orzesze PL 97 F2
Orzinuovi I 46 C1
Orzyc PL 90 B3
Orzysz PL 90 C1
Os N 63 D4
Osa PL 89 F2
Osa de la Vega E 26 A3
Ošani LV 82 C2
Osby S 71 D2
Oschatz D 39 F1
Oschersleben D 34 A4
Oschiri I 50 A2
Ościłowo PL 90 B3
Osečina SRB 55 F3
Oseja de Sajambre E 19 E2
Osen N 63 D2
Ošenieki
(Jelgavas) LV 81 E1
Ošenieki (Saldus) LV 76 C3
Osera E 20 C4
Osie PL 89 E2
Osięciny PL 89 F3
Osieck PL 94 C2
Osieczna
(Pomorskie) PL 89 E2
Osieczna
(Wielkopolskie) PL . . . 93 D2
Osiecznica PL 92 B3
Osiek (Kujawsko-
Pomorskie) PL 90 A3
Osiek (Pomorskie) PL . . . 89 F2
Osiek
(Świętokrzyskie) PL . . 98 C1
Osielsko PL 89 E3
Osijek HR 55 E2
Osilo I 50 A2
Osimo I 47 F3
Osinja BIH 55 E3
Osipaonica SRB 57 D3
Osjaków PL 93 F3

Oškalni LV 77 F2
Oskarshamn S 71 E2
Oskarström S 71 D2
Oslo N 66 C2
Ösmo S 67 F3
Osnabrück D 33 D4
Ośno Lubuskie PL 92 B1
Osoblaha CZ 41 F2
Osoppo I 44 C3
Osor HR 54 B3
Osorno la Mayor E 19 E3
Osøyro N 66 A1
Osøyro RUS 115 D2
Ostrov (Karlovarský
kraj) CZ 40 B2
Ostrów PL 95 E2
Ostrów Lubelski PL 95 E2
Ostrów
Mazowiecka PL 91 D3
Ostrów
Wielkopolski PL 93 E2
Ostrówek
(Łódzkie) PL 93 F3
Ostrówek
(Lubelskie) PL 95 E2
Ostrowice PL 88 C3
Ostrowiec
Świętokrzyski PL 94 C3
Ostrowieckie
(Jezioro) PL 88 C3
Ostrowite (Kujawsko-
Pomorskie) PL 89 F3
Ostrowite
(Wielkopolskie) PL . . . 93 E1
Ostrožac (Bihać) BIH 54 C3
Ostrožac (Mostar) BIH . . . 55 E4
Ostrzeszów PL 93 E3
Ostuni I 49 F2
Osula EE 79 E2
Osuna E 29 E3
Oświęcim PL 97 F2
Oswestry GB 8 C1
Otanki LV 80 A1
Otanmäki FIN 65 E3
Otava FIN 69 E3
Otepää EE 79 D1
Oteren N 60 C2
Oteševo MK 59 E4
Othem S 67 F4
Othery GB 8 C3
Othoní (Nissi) GR 100 A3

Otívar E ... 29 F3
Otley GB ... 7 E4
Otmuchów PL ... 97 D1
Otmuchowskie
  (Jezioro) PL ... 97 D1
Otnes N ... 63 D4
Otočac HR ... 54 B3
Otok HR ... 55 F2
Otoka BIH ... 54 C3
Otranto I ... 51 F1
Otrokovice CZ ... 41 F3
Otsa EE ... 79 E2
Otta N ... 62 C4
Ottana I ... 50 A3
Ottaviano I ... 48 C4
Ottenschlag A ... 41 D4
Ottensheim A ... 44 C1
Otter Ferry GB ... 6 C1
Otterburn GB ... 7 E2
Otterlo NL ... 37 D1
Otterndorf D ... 33 E2
Otterøy N ... 63 D2
Ottersberg D ... 33 E3
Otterup DK ... 70 B3
Ottery St Mary GB ... 8 B4
Ottmarsheim F ... 17 E1
Ottnang A ... 44 C1
Ottobeuren D ... 43 E2
Ottobrunn D ... 43 F1
Ottsjö S ... 63 D3
Ottweiler D ... 13 E3
Otwock PL ... 94 C2

Oulunsalo FIN ... 65 D3
Oulx I ... 17 E4
Ôuna EE ... 73 D3
Oundle GB ... 9 E2
Ouranópoli GR ... 102 B3
Ourém P ... 24 B2
Ourense E ... 18 B3
Ourique P ... 24 B4
Ourol E ... 18 B1
Ourville-en-Caux F ... 11 E2
Oust F ... 21 D3
Outeiro de Rei E ... 18 B2
Outokumpu FIN ... 69 F2
Outomuro E ... 18 B3
Outwell GB ... 9 E1
Ouzouer-le-Marché F ... 15 F1
Ouzouer-sur-Loire F ... 16 A1
Ovada I ... 47 E1
Ovanåker S ... 67 E1
Ovar P ... 24 B1
Ovčar Banja SRB ... 56 C3
Overath D ... 13 E1
Øverbygd N ... 60 B1
Overhalla N ... 63 D2
Överhörnäs S ... 68 B2
Overijse B ... 12 C1
Överkalix S ... 64 C2
Övermark FIN ... 68 C2
Övertorneå S ... 64 C2
Överum S ... 67 E4
Oviedo E ... 19 D2
Ovindoli I ... 48 B2

Otyń PL ... 92 C2
Otziás GR ... 106 B3
Ouchy CH ... 17 D2
Oucques F ... 15 F1
Oud-Beijerland NL ... 36 C1
Ouddorp NL ... 36 B1
Oude Pekela NL ... 32 C3
Oudenaarde B ... 12 B1
Oudenbosch NL ... 36 C1
Oughterard /
  Uachtar Ard IRL ... 2 B2
Ouistreham F ... 11 E3
Oulainen FIN ... 65 D3
Oulchy-le-Château F ... 12 B3
Oulu (Uleåborg) FIN ... 65 D3

Øvre Årdal N ... 66 B1
Øvre Soppero S ... 61 D2
Øysang N ... 66 B3
Øystese N ... 66 A1
Oyten D ... 33 E3
Ozalj HR ... 54 B3
Ożarów PL ... 95 D3
Ożarowice PL ... 97 F1
Ożbalt SLO ... 54 B1
Ózd H ... 116 C2
Ozieri I ... 50 A3
Ozimek PL ... 97 E1
Ożkiniai
  (Panevėžio) LT ... 82 B3
Ożkiniai
  (Vilniaus) LT ... 86 C1

Ozolaine
  (Bauskas) LV ... 81 F2
Ozolaine
  (Daugavpils) LV ... 83 D3
Ozolaine
  (Limbažu) LV ... 78 B2
Ozolaine
  (Preilu) LV ... 83 E2
Ozolkalns LV ... 79 D3
Ozollejas LV ... 80 C1
Ozolmuiža LV ... 78 B2
Ozolnieki LV ... 77 E3
Ozorków PL ... 94 A2

Ozupine LV ... 83 F1

P

P"jatychatky UA ... 117 F1
Paakkila FIN ... 69 F2
Paakmenis LT ... 80 C3
Paalasmaa FIN ... 69 F1
Paalsys LT ... 85 E1
Paaluonys LT ... 85 E1
Päärdu EE ... 72 A3
Paasvere EE ... 73 D2
Paatsalu EE ... 75 D2

Paavola FIN ... 65 D3
Pažuoliai LT ... 86 B2
Pabaiskas LT ... 86 B1
Pabalve LT ... 81 D2
Pabare LT ... 86 B3
Pabaži (Saulkrasti) LV ... 77 F3
Pabaži (Sēja) LV ... 78 A3
Paberže
  (Kazimieravas) LT ... 86 B2
Paberže
  (Šalčininkai) LT ... 86 B3
Pabianice PL ... 94 A2
Pabiržė LT ... 81 F2
Pabrade LT ... 86 C2
Pabradume LT ... 80 C2
Pabutkalnis LT ... 81 D3

Pacanów PL ... 98 C1
Pâce (Bauskas) LV ... 81 F2
Pâce (Talsu) LV ... 76 C2
Paceco I ... 52 B3
Pačeriaukšte I LT ... 81 F2
Pachino I ... 53 E4
Paço de Sousa P ... 18 A4
Paços de Ferreira P ... 18 A4
Pacov CZ ... 41 D3
Pacy-sur-Eure F ... 11 F3
Pacyna PL ... 94 A1
Paczków PL ... 97 D1
Padainupys LT ... 85 E2
Padauguva LT ... 85 E1
Padej SRB ... 56 C1

Pađene HR ... 54 C4
Paderborn
  (Kreis Paderborn) D ... 37 F1
Paderne P ... 28 B2
Padew Narodowa PL ... 98 C1
Padiham GB ... 7 E4
Padina SRB ... 57 D2
Padinska Skela SRB ... 56 C2
Padise EE ... 72 A2
Padornelo P ... 18 C2
Padova I ... 44 B3
Padovinys LT ... 85 E2
Padrón E ... 18 A2
Padru I ... 50 B2
Padstow GB ... 8 A4
Padul E ... 29 D3
Padure (Kuldīgas) LV ... 76 C3
Padure (Liepājas) LV ... 76 B3
Padvares LT ... 86 C3
Padvariai LT ... 80 B2
Padvarionys
  (Medininkai) LT ... 86 C2
Padvarionys
  (Trakai) LT ... 86 B3
Pae (Harju) EE ... 72 A2
Pae (Rapla) EE ... 72 B2
Paeglesiai LT ... 81 D2
Paegli (Bauskas) LV ... 81 F2
Paegli (Liepājas) LV ... 80 B3
Paekna EE ... 72 B2
Paesana I ... 17 E4
Paestum I ... 49 D4
Paestum Antica I ... 49 D4
Paežeriai LT ... 85 E2
Paežeris LT ... 80 C3
Pag HR ... 54 B4
Pag (Otok) HR ... 54 B4
Paganico I ... 47 D4
Pagarde LT ... 80 C2
Pagari EE ... 73 D2
Pagegiai LT ... 84 B1
Pagermantis LT ... 80 C2
Pagerve LT ... 82 B2
Pagiai LT ... 81 D3
Pagirai (Kauno) LT ... 85 E3
Pagiriai (Utenos) LT ... 82 B3
Pagiriai (Vilniaus) LT ... 86 B2
Pagny-sur-Moselle F ... 13 D3
Pagóndas GR ... 105 F2
Pagóndas GR ... 107 E3
Pagoúria GR ... 102 C2
Pagramante LT ... 80 B2
Pagramantis LT ... 80 C3
Pagraužiai LT ... 85 D3
Pagrybis LT ... 80 C3
Pagryniai LT ... 80 B3
Páhi GR ... 105 F2
Pahiá Ámos GR ... 110 C4
Pahkla (Harju) EE ... 72 B2
Pähkla EE ... 74 C3
Pahtpää EE ... 79 E1
Pahuvere EE ... 78 C1
Paide EE ... 72 C3
Päidla EE ... 79 D1
Paignton GB ... 8 B4
Paikiškiai LT ... 85 D2
Paikuse EE ... 75 F3
Paimbœuf F ... 14 C1
Paimio FIN ... 68 C4
Paimpol F ... 10 B3
Painküla EE ... 73 D3
Painswick GB ... 8 C2
Päinurme EE ... 72 C3
Paisley GB ... 6 C1
Paistriečiai LT ... 81 F2
Paistrys LT ... 81 F3
Paistu EE ... 78 C1
Pajala S ... 64 C1
Pajęczno PL ... 93 F3
Pajevonys LT ... 85 D2
Pajieslys LT ... 85 E1
Pajiešmeniai LT ... 81 F2
Pajomantis LT ... 80 C3
Pajotijys LT ... 85 D1
Paju EE ... 79 D2
Pajuodupis LT ... 86 B3
Pajuostis LT ... 81 F3
Pajupea EE ... 72 B2
Pajūris (Reistrai) LT ... 80 C3
Pajūris (Taurage) LT ... 84 C1
Pajūris (Telšiu) LT ... 80 B3
Pajusi EE ... 72 C3
Pajusti EE ... 73 D2
Pakalne LT ... 80 A3
Pakalni LV ... 83 D2
Pakalniai LT ... 82 C3
Pakalniškes LT ... 86 A2
Pakalniškiai
  (Klaipedos) LT ... 80 B2
Pakalniškiai
  (Šiauliu) LT ... 81 E3
Pakalniškiai
  (Vilniaus) LT ... 86 B2
Pakape LT ... 81 D3
Pakarčemis LT ... 80 C3
Pakarkliai LT ... 81 E3
Pakene LT ... 86 C2
Paketuriai LT ... 82 B3
Pakevis LT ... 81 D3
Pakiršinys LT ... 81 E3
Pakość PL ... 89 E2
Pakosław PL ... 93 D2
Pakoštane HR ... 54 C4
Pakrac HR ... 55 D2
Pakriauniai LT ... 82 C2
Pakruojis LT ... 81 E2

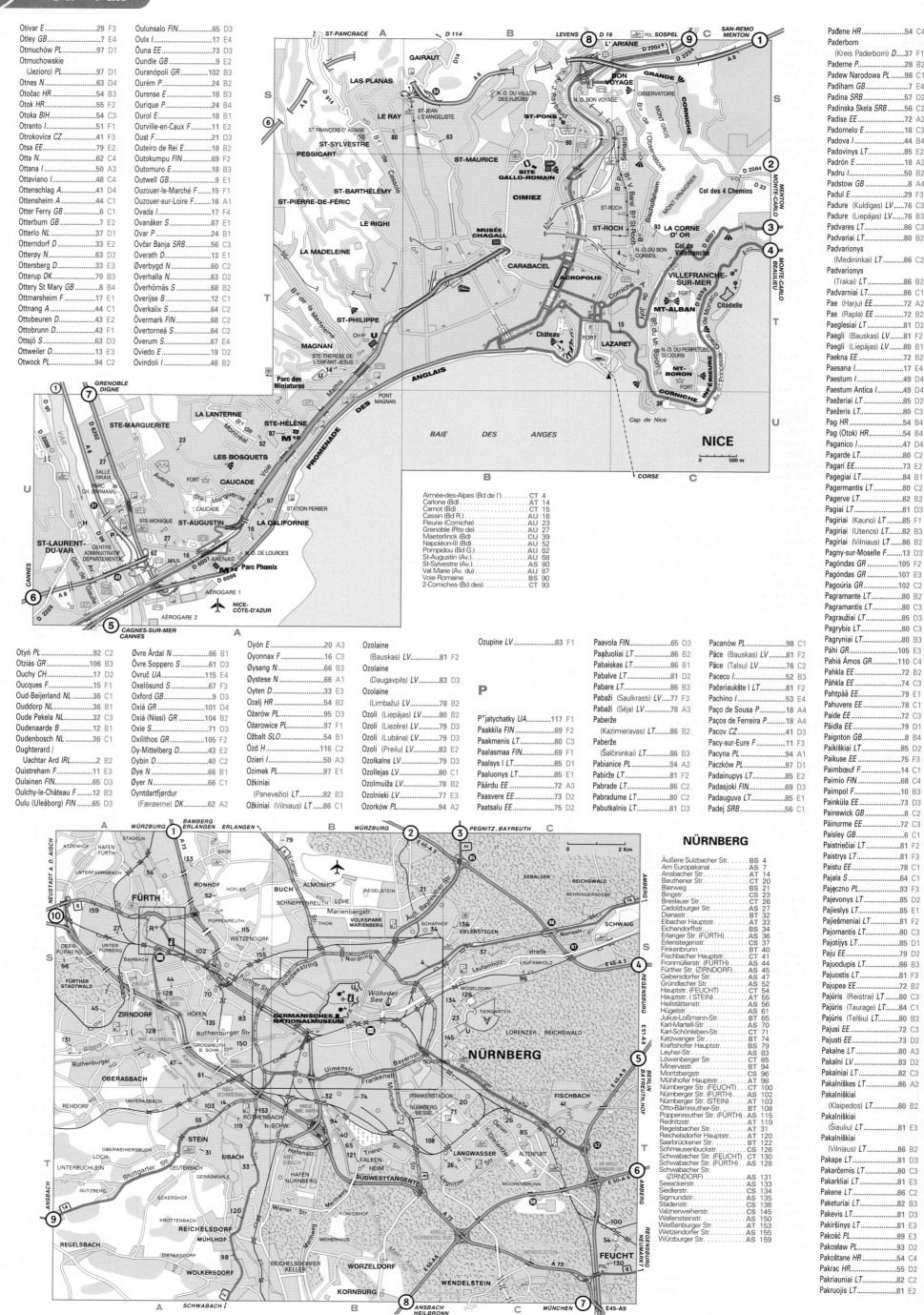

Paks H................116 B2
Pakšteliai LT............81 D2
Pakumulšiai LT..........81 D2
Pakuonis LT.............85 E2
Pal. Kávala GR.........102 B2
Pal. Krovili GR........103 D2
Pala EE.................73 E4
Palacios de la Sierra E...19 F4
Palacios de Sanabria E...18 C3
Palacios del Sil E......18 C2
Palade EE...............74 C1
Paládio EE.............102 C2
Paladru F...............16 C4
Palafrugell E...........21 F4
Palagía GR.............103 D2
Palagiano I.............49 F4
Palagonia I.............53 D2
Palagruža (Otoci) HR....54 A4
Palaia I................47 D3
Palaiseau F.............12 A4
Palamás GR.............101 E4
Palamós E...............21 F4
Palamuse EE.............73 D3
Palandio I.............105 D4
Palanga LT..............80 A2
Palas de Rei E..........18 B2
Palata I................49 D2
Palaítitsia GR.........101 E3
Palatna SRB.............57 F4
Palau I.................50 B2
Palavas-les-Flots F.....47 E2
Palazzo del Pero I......47 E3
Palazzo S. Gervasio I...49 E3
Palazzolo Acreide I.....53 E4
Palazzolo sull'Oglio I..43 E4
Palazzuolo sul Senio I..47 E2
Paldiski EE.............72 A2
Pale BIH................55 F4
Påle LV.................78 B2
Paleá Epídavros GR.....105 E4
Paleičiai LT............84 B1
Palékastro GR..........110 C4
Palena I................48 C2
Palencia E..............19 E4
Paleohóra GR...........105 E3
Paleohóra GR...........109 D4
Paleohóri GR...........100 C4
Paleohóri GR...........107 E1
Paleohóri
  (Arkadía) GR.........105 D4
Paleohóri (Árta) GR....101 D4
Paleohóri
  (Grevená) GR.........101 D3
Paleohóri
  (Tríkala) GR.........101 D4
Paleokastrítsa GR......100 A4
Paleókastro GR.........101 D3
Paleókastro GR.........104 C1
Paleókastro GR.........107 F3
Paleókastro
  (Halkidikí) GR.......102 A3
Paleókastro
  (Séres) GR...........102 A1
Paleokómi GR...........102 A2
Paleópirgos GR.........101 E4
Paleópirgos GR.........104 C2
Paleópoli GR...........103 D3
Paleópoli GR...........106 B3
Palermo I...............50 B4
Páleros GR.............104 B1
Palestrina I............48 B2
Palevenele LT...........82 B3
Palež BIH...............55 F3
Palgas LV...............76 C3
Páli GR................111 E1
Paliano I...............48 B3
Palić SRB...............55 F1
Palidoro I..............48 A3
Paliepiai LT............85 E1
Paliepis LT.............82 C2
Palinges F..............16 B2
Palinuro I..............50 C4
Palioúri GR............102 A4
Paliouriá GR...........101 D3
Paliseul B..............17 E2
Paliūnai LT.............85 D3
Paliūniškis LT..........81 F3
Palivere EE.............72 A2
Pålkäne FIN.............69 D2
Pålkem S................64 C2
Palluau F...............16 C4
Palma de Mallorca E.....31 E3
Palma del Río E.........29 E2
Palma
  di Montechiaro I......52 C4
Palmadula I.............50 A2
Palmanova I.............44 C4
Palmela P...............24 A3
Palmi I.................51 D4
Palmse EE...............72 C1
Palnosai LT.............81 D2
Palo del Colle I........49 F3
Palojoensuu FIN.........61 D1
Palokki FIN.............69 F2
Palomäki FIN............69 F1
Palomares
  del Campo E...........26 B2
Palomas E...............29 D3
Palombara Sabina I......47 F4
Palomene LT.............85 F2
Palonai LT..............81 F3
Palos de la Frontera E..28 C2
Pals E..................21 F4
Pålsboda S..............67 E3
Palsmane LV.............79 D2
Paltamo FIN.............65 E3

Paltaniemi FIN..........65 E3
Paluknys LT.............86 B2
Paluobiai LT............85 D2
Palupera EE.............79 D1
Paluzza I...............44 C3
Palvere EE..............72 C2
Pamažupiai LT...........81 F2
Pámfila GR.............107 E1
Pamhagen A..............45 F1
Pamieris LT.............85 F2
Pamiers F...............21 E2
Pamiškiai LT............86 C2
Pampilhosa P............24 B1
Pampilhosa da Serra P...24 B2
Pampliega E.............19 E3
Pamplona E..............20 B3
Pamporovo BG...........117 D4
Pamūša LV...............81 F2
Pamūšas Skola LV........81 F2
Pamuseliai LT...........85 F3
Pamūšis LT..............81 F2
Panagía GR.............102 C2
Panagía GR.............103 D3
Panagía GR.............100 C4
Panagía
  (Grevená) GR.........101 D3
Panagía (Tríkala) GR...101 D4
Panagjurište BG........117 D4
Panakatis LT............80 C3
Panara LT...............85 F3
Pancalieri I............17 E4
Pančevo SRB.............57 D2
Pancorbo E..............19 F3
Pandánassa GR..........108 B1
Pandeleimónas GR.......101 E4
Pandelys LT.............82 B2
Pandino I...............46 C1
Pandivere EE............73 D2
Pandrup DK..............70 B2
Panemunelis LT..........82 C3
Panemuninkai LT.........85 E3
Panemunis LT............82 B2
Paneriai LT.............86 B2
Panetólio GR...........104 C2
Panevėžiukas LT.........85 E1
Panevežys LT............81 F3
Panga (Lääne) EE........75 D2
Panga (Saare) EE........74 C2
Pangbourne GB............9 D2
Pankakoski FIN..........69 F1
Panki PL................93 F3
Pankow D................34 B4
Panočiai LT.............86 A3
Panórama GR............102 A1
Pánormos GR............101 F2
Pánormos GR............106 C4
Pánormos GR............109 E3
Panoteriai LT...........85 F1
Pansionäts LV...........80 C1
Päntäne FIN.............68 C2
Pantánassa LT...........81 E3
Pantelleria I...........52 A4
Paobelys LT.............85 F1
Paola I.................51 D2
Pápa H.................116 B2
Papádes GR.............105 E1
Papádos GR.............107 E1
Páparis GR.............105 D4
Papasidero I............51 D2
Pape LV.................80 A2
Papečiai LT.............85 E3
Papenburg
  (Kreis Emsland) D....33 D3
Papile LT...............81 D2
Papiliai LT.............82 B3
Papilys LT..............82 B2
Pápingo GR.............100 C3
Papiškes LT.............86 B3
Paplaka LV..............80 B1
Pappenheim D............39 D4
Paprotnia PL............95 D1
Papsaare EE.............72 A3
Papušynys LT............81 E3
Par. Arogis GR.........102 C2
Par. Avdiron GR........102 C2
Parabita I..............51 F1
Paracin SRB.............57 E3
Paracuellos
  de Jiloca E...........26 C1
Paradas E...............29 D3
Paradela P..............18 B4
Paradissiá GR.........104 C4
Parádissos GR..........102 C2
Paradyż PL..............94 B3
Parajes E...............18 B2
Parakálamos GR.........100 C4
Parákila GR............107 E1
Paralepe EE.............75 D2
Paralía GR.............101 F3
Paralía GR.............104 C3
Paralía GR.............108 B1
Paralía Akrátas GR.....105 D3
Paralía Kímis GR.......105 F2
Paralía Kotsikiás GR...105 E1
Paralía Sarándi GR.....105 E2
Paralía Skótinas GR....101 F3
Paralía Tiroú GR.......105 D4
Paralío Ástros GR......105 D4
Paralovo SRB............59 E3
Paramé F................10 C1
Paramithiá GR..........100 C4
Páramo del Sil E........18 C2

Parapésti GR...........102 B1
Parapótamos GR.........100 B4
Paray-le-Monial F.......16 B2
Parchim D...............34 A3
Parchowo PL.............89 E1
Parczew PL..............95 E2
Pardubice CZ............41 D2
Parečenai LT............85 E3
Paredes P...............18 A4
Paredes de Coura P......18 A3
Paredes de Nava E.......19 E3
Pareizgupis LT..........85 D1
Pareja E................26 B1
Parentis-en-Born F......20 B1
Párga GR...............100 A1
Pargas / Parainen FIN...68 C4
Päri EE.................78 C1
Parikkala FIN...........69 F3
Paris F.................12 A3
Párispea EE.............72 C1
Park Etnograficzny
  (skansen) PL..........90 B2
Parkalompolo S..........61 D3
Parkano FIN.............68 C3
Parkmali LV.............78 B2
Parksepa EE.............79 E1
Parla E.................25 F2
Parlavà E...............21 F4
Parłówko PL.............88 A2
Parma I.................46 C1
Parnassós (Óros) GR....105 D2
Parndorf A..............45 F1
Párnitha (Óros) GR.....105 F3
Párnjõe EE..............72 B3
Pärnu EE................72 A3
Pärnu-Jaagupi EE........72 A3
Parola FIN..............69 D2
Paromates
  Krušonys LT...........85 F2
Páros GR...............109 F1
Páros (Nissí) GR.......106 C4
Paroveja LT.............82 B2
Pärsama EE..............74 C2
Parsberg D..............39 E4
Parsdorf D..............43 F1
Parsęta PL..............88 C2
Pärsti EE...............72 C3
Partakko FIN............61 F2
Partanna I..............52 B3
Partenen A..............43 E3
Partenay F..............15 D2
Parthéni GR............107 E4
Partille S..............66 C4
Partínico I.............52 C3
Partizani SRB...........57 D3
Partizanske Vode SRB....56 C4
Partney GB...............9 E1
Partsi EE...............79 E1
Parudaminys LT..........86 B2
Parupe LT...............82 B2
Pārupe LV...............77 D3
Parysów PL..............95 D2
Pas-en-Artois F.........12 A2
Pasaia E................20 B2
Pasakiai LT.............81 E3
Pašaltuonys III LT......85 D1
Pašeimeniai LT..........85 D2
Pašerkšne LV............80 C2
Pašete LT...............85 F1
Pasewalk D..............34 C2
Pashalitsa GR..........105 D1
Pašiaušė LT.............81 D3
Pasiene (Pasine) LV.....83 F2
Pasikovci HR............55 D2
Pašile LT...............80 C3
Pečurice MNE............59 D3
Pašiliai (Utenos) LT....82 B3
Pašiliai (Vilniaus) LT..86 B2
Pasłęk PL...............90 A1
Pasłęka PL..............90 B2
Pašlūžmis LT............80 B3
Pašman FIN..............54 C4
Pašman (Otok) HR........54 C4
Passá-Limáni GR........107 D2
Passais F...............11 D4
Passás (Nissí) GR......107 E2
Passavás GR............108 B2
Passignano
  sul Trasimeno I.......47 E3
Pasta Māja LV...........78 B3
Pastališki LV...........81 E2
Pastavy BY.............115 D3
Pastende LV.............77 D3
Pastrana E..............26 A2
Pastrevýs LT............85 F2
Pašuliene LV............83 D3
Pašušvys LT.............81 E3
Pasvalys LT.............81 F2
Pašvitinys LT...........82 B3
Pasym PL................90 B2
Pašyšiai LT.............84 B1
Pásztó H...............116 C2
Patamošupiai LT.........85 D2
Patašine LT.............85 E2
Pataste EE..............73 E3
Patay F.................11 F4
Pateley Bridge GB........7 D3
Pateniemi FIN...........65 D3
Paterna de Rivera E.....29 D3
Paternion A.............44 C3
Paternò I...............53 D2
Paternopoli I...........49 D4
Patersdorf D............39 F4
Patika EE...............72 B2
Patillčiai LT...........85 D1
Patiópoulo GR..........104 B1

Patitíri GR............105 F1
Patküla EE..............78 C1
Pátmos GR..............107 E4
Pátmos (Nissí) GR......107 E4
Pątnów (Łódzkie) PL.....93 F3
Pątnów
  (Wielkopolskie) PL....93 F1
Pátra GR...............104 C2
Patreksfjörður IS.......62 A1
Peitz D.................34 C4
Péla GR................101 F2
Pelagiševo BIH..........55 E3
Pelaičiai LT............80 B3
Pelasgía GR............105 E1
Pelčí LV................76 C3
Pełczyce PL.............88 B3
Pełčči LV...............83 D2
Pelekános GR...........101 D3
Pélekas GR.............100 B4
Pelekonys LT............85 F2
Peleniškiai LT..........81 E2
Peletá GR..............108 B1
Pelhřimov CZ............41 D1
Pélia GR...............105 E1
Pelikapina LV...........77 D3
Pelilla LV..............76 B3
Pelkes LT...............85 F1
Pelkosenniemi FIN.......65 E1
Pellegrino Parmense I...46 C1
Pellegrue F.............15 D4
Pellesmäki FIN..........69 E2
Pellevoisin LT..........80 C2
Pello FIN...............64 C1
Pelplin PL..............89 E2
Peltes LV...............78 B3
Peltosalmi FIN..........69 E1
Peltovuoma FIN..........58 C2
Pélussin F..............16 C4
Pelutava LT.............85 E1
Pembroke / Penfro GB.....8 A2
Pembroke Dock /
  Doc Penfro GB.........8 A2
Penacova P..............24 B1
Peñafiel E..............19 E4
Penafiel P..............18 A4
Peñaflor E..............29 E2
Penalva do Castelo P....24 C1
Peñamacor P.............24 C2
Peñaranda
  de Bracamonte E.......25 E1
Peñaranda de Duero E....19 F4
Peñarroya-
  Pueblonuevo E.........25 E4
Peñas de San Pedro E....26 B4
Peñascosa E.............26 B4
Peñausende E............19 D4
Pendagií GR............104 C2
Pendálofo GR...........104 B2
Pendálofos GR..........101 D3
Pénde Vrisses GR.......101 F2
Pendéli GR.............105 F3
Pendeória GR...........105 D2
Peanía GR..............105 F3
Peć SRB.................59 D3
Pec pod Sněžkou CZ......41 D2
Peccia CH...............17 F2
Peccioli I..............47 D3
Pečenjevce SRB..........57 E4
Pećígrad BIH............54 C3
Pecínci SRB.............56 C2
Pecka SRB...............56 C3
Peckelsheim D...........37 F1
Pęcław PL...............92 C2
Pécs H................116 B3
Pęczniew PL.............93 F2
Pedaso I................48 B1
Dededze LV..............79 E2
Pedersker DK............71 E4
Pedersöre / Pedersören
  Kunta FIN............68 C1
Pédi GR................111 F1
Pedrafita
  do Cebreiro E.........18 C2
Pedrajas
  de San Esteban E......19 E4
Pedralba E..............26 C3
Pedralba
  de la Pradería E......18 C3
Pedras Salgadas P.......18 B4
Pedraza de la Sierra E..25 F1
Pedrera E...............29 E3
Pedro Abad E............25 E4
Pedro Bernardo E........25 E2
Pedro Muñoz E...........26 A3
Pedrógão P..............24 A2
Pedrógão P..............24 B4
Pedrógão Grande P.......24 B2
Pedrola E...............20 B4
Peebles GB..............7 D2
Peel GB..................3 C1
Peenemünde D............34 B2
Peetri (Harju) EE.......72 B2
Peetri (Järva) EE.......72 C2
Peetrimõisa EE..........78 C1
Pefkári GR.............102 B2
Pefkí GR...............105 E1
Péfkos GR..............100 C3
Pega E..................24 C1
Pegalajar E.............29 F2
Pegau D.................39 E1
Pegli I.................23 F1
Pegnitz D...............39 E3
Pego E..................27 D4
Pegognaga I.............47 D2
Pęgów PL................93 D3
Perdikáki GR...........104 B1

Peguera E...............31 E3
Pehčevo MK..............59 F3
Peine D.................33 F4
Peio I..................43 F3
Peíra-Cava F............23 D1
Peisiníki LT............83 D2
Peißenberg D............43 F2
Peiting D...............43 F2
Péla GR................101 F2
Pelagiševo BIH..........55 E3
Pelaičiai LT............80 B3
Pelasgía GR............105 E1
Pełczyce PL.............88 B3
Peri EE.................79 E1
Periana E...............29 F3
Périers F...............11 D3
Périgueux F.............15 E4
Periklía GR............101 E1
Perila EE...............72 B2
Perino I................46 C1
Periškiai LT............81 D3
Períssa GR.............109 F2
Perista GR.............104 C2
Peristerá GR...........101 F2
Peristéria
  (Tímvos) GR..........104 C4
Perithório GR..........102 A1
Perívlepto GR..........105 D1
Perívóli GR............101 D3
Perivólio GR...........104 C1
Perjasica HR............54 C1
Pérkoni LV..............78 C3
Perković HR.............55 D4
Perleberg D.............34 A3
Perlez SRB..............56 C2
Pērlīte LV..............83 D3
Perloja LT..............85 F3
Përmet AL.............100 B3
Perná / Pernaja FIN.....69 E4
Pernarava LT............85 E1
Pernarec CZ.............40 A3
Pernes-les-Fontaines F..22 C3
Pernik BG.............117 D4
Perniö FIN.............68 C3
Pernitz A...............45 E1
Péronne F...............12 A2
Perosa Argentina I......17 E4
Pérouges F..............16 C3
Perpignan F.............21 F3
Perrero I...............17 E4
Perreux F...............16 B3
Perros-Guirec F.........10 B3
Peršekininkai LT........85 E3
Persenbeug A............45 D1
Pershore GB.............9 E2
Persistéra (Nissí) GR..105 F1
Perstorp S..............71 D3
Perth GB.................7 D1
Pertisau A..............43 F2
Pertočа SLO.............54 C1
Pertoúli GR............101 D4
Pertteli FIN............69 D4
Pertuis F...............22 C2
Pertunmaa FIN...........69 E3
Pertusa E...............20 C4
Peručac Vrelo SRB.......56 C4
Perugia I...............47 E3
Perúnai LT..............86 B2
Perušić HR..............54 C2
Péruwelz B..............12 B1
Pervenchères F..........11 F4
Pervomajs'k UA.........117 F1
Perzów PL...............93 E3
Pesaro I................47 F2
Pescara I...............48 C2
Pescasseroli I..........48 C3
Peschici I..............49 D2
Peschiera del Garda I...47 D1
Pescia I................47 D2
Pescina I...............48 C3
Pescocostanzo I.........48 C3
Pescolanciano I.........48 C3
Pescopagano I...........49 D4
Pescorocchiano I........47 F4
Peshkopi AL............100 C4
Pesiökylä FIN...........65 E3
Peski LV................83 D3
Pesmes F................16 C1
Peso da Régua P.........18 B4
Pesočani MK.............59 E4
Pesoz E.................18 C1
Pessáni GR.............103 E1
Peštani MK..............59 E4
Pestovo RUS............115 F1
Pešu Ciems LV...........80 C3
Pešurići BIH............55 F4
Petačinci SRB...........57 F4
Petäjäskoski FIN........65 D2
Petäjävesi FIN..........69 D2
Petalax FIN.............68 C2
Petalidí GR............108 A1
Petalíi (Nissá) GR.....106 B3
Petaloúdes GR..........111 F4
Pétange L...............13 D3
Petás GR...............104 B1
Peteraičiai LT..........84 B1
Peterborough GB..........9 E2
Peterhead GB.............3 E2
Pēterlauki LV...........81 E1
Peterlee GB..............7 E3
Pēternieki LV...........81 F1
Petersfield GB...........9 D3
Petershagen D...........33 E4
Pēterupe LV.............77 D3
Pethelinós GR..........102 A2
Petilia Policastro I....51 E3

Perdikas GR............101 E2
Peréa (Péla) GR........101 E2
Peréa
  (Thessaloníki) GR....101 F2
Perejaslav-
  Chmel'nyc'kyj UA.....115 F4
Pereruela E.............19 D4
Pereslavl'-
  Zalesskij RUS........115 F1
Perg A..................45 D1
Pergine Valsugana I.....43 F4
Pergola I...............47 F3
Perho FIN...............69 D2
Peri EE.................79 E1
Periana E...............29 F3
Peribán GR............101 E1
Pēternieki LV...........81 F1
Petra (Monasterio de) E.26 B1
Petra I.................31 F3
Pétra GR...............107 D1
Pétra GR...............101 E3
Petralia Sottana I......53 D2
Petrálona GR...........101 F3
Petraná GR.............101 E3
Petravičiūnai LT........85 E1
Petrčane HR.............54 B4
Petreliai LT............80 B3
Petrer E................26 C4
Pétres GR..............101 D2
Petreto-Bicchisano F....23 E4
Petrič BG.............117 D4
Petrijevci HR...........55 E2
Petrina GR.............105 D4
Petrinja HR.............54 C2
Petrodvorec RUS........115 D1
Petrohóri GR...........104 C2
Petrohóri GR...........104 C2
Petróna GR.............104 C1
Petroşani RO...........117 D3
Petróšiai LT............85 E3
Petrotá GR.............103 E1
Petrothálassa GR.......105 E4
Petrotó GR.............104 C1
Petroússa GR...........102 B1
Petrovac (Bar) MNE......58 C3
Petrovac
  (Požarevac) SRB......57 D3
Petrovaradin SRB........55 F2
Petrovčić SRB...........56 C2
Petrovice
  (Příbram) CZ.........40 C3
Petrovka LV.............83 E2
Petrovo / Bosansko
  Petrovo Selo BIH.....55 E3
Petručaii LT............86 B2
Pettenbach A............44 C1
Pettigoe IRL.............2 C1
Petworth GB.............9 D3
Peuerbach A.............44 C1
Peura FIN...............65 D2
Pewsey GB................9 D3
Peyrat-le-Château F.....15 F3
Peyrehorade F...........20 B2
Peyriac-Minervois F.....21 F2
Peyrolles-
  en-Provence F........22 C2
Peyruis F...............22 C1
Pézenas F...............22 A2
Pezinok SK............116 B2
Pezoúla GR.............102 C2
Pfaffenhofen
  a. d. Ilm D..........43 F1
Pfäffikon CH............17 F1
Pfalzgrafenweiler D.....13 F4
Pfarrkirchen D..........44 B1
Pfeffenhausen D.........39 E4
Pforzheim D.............13 F3
Pfreimd D...............39 F3
Pfullendorf D...........43 D1
Pfullingen D............42 C1
Pfunds A................43 E3
Pfungstadt D............13 F2
Phalsbourg F............13 E3
Philippeville B.........12 C2
Philippsreut D..........40 C1
Piacenza I..............46 C1
Piadena I...............47 D2
Pian del Voglio I.......47 D2
Piana F.................23 E3
Piana degli Albanesi I..52 C3
Piancastagnaio I........47 E4
Piancavallo I...........44 B4
Piandelagotti I.........47 D2
Pianella I..............48 C2
Pianello I..............47 F3
Piano del Cansiglio I...44 B4
Pianoro I...............47 D2
Piansano I..............47 F4
Piaseczno
  (Mazowieckie) PL.....94 C2
Piaski (Lubelskie) PL...95 E3
Piaski (Pomorskie) PL...90 A1
Piaski (Warmińsko-
  Mazurskie) PL........90 C2
Piaski (Wielkopolskie) PL93 D2
Piastów PL..............94 C2
Piątek PL...............94 B2
Piątkowisko PL..........94 A2
Piątnica
  Poduchowna PL........91 D2
Piatra-Neamţ RO........117 D3
Piazza al Serchio I.....46 C2
Piazza Armerina I.......53 D3
Piazza Brembana I.......43 E4
Piazzola sul Brenta I...44 A4
Piber A.................45 D4
Pićan HR................54 A1
Picassent E.............26 C3
Picerno I...............49 E4
Pickering GB.............7 F3
Pico I..................27 D4
Pérdika (Ioánina) GR...100 C4
Pérdika
  (Thesprotía) GR......100 B4

Piecki PL...............90 C2
Piedicavallo I..........17 F3
Piedicroce F...........114 B3
Piediluco I.............47 F4
Piedimonte Matese I.....48 C3
Piedra
  (Monasterio de) E....26 B1
Piedrabuena E...........25 F3
Piedrafita de Babia E...18 C2
Piedralaves E...........25 E1
Piedras Albas E.........24 C2
Piedratajada E..........20 C4
Piedruja LV.............83 D3
Piekary Śląskie PL......97 F1
Piekoszów PL............94 B3
Pieksämäki FIN..........69 E2
Pielavesi FIN...........69 E1
Pielgrzymka
  (Dolnośląskie) PL....92 C3
Pielgrzymka
  (Podkarpackie) PL....98 C2
Pienava LV..............81 E1
Pieniężno PL............90 B1
Pienini (Pieni) LV......83 D2
Pieniny PL..............98 B3
Pienionys LT............82 B3
Piennes F...............13 D3
Pieńsk PL...............92 B3
Pienza I................47 E3
Piepaliai (Kauno) LT....85 E1
Piepaliai
  (Panevėžio) LT.......82 C2
Pierowall GB.............5 D1
Pierre-Buffière F.......15 F3
Pierre-de-Bresse F......16 C2
Pierrefitte-Nestalas F..20 C3
Pierrefitte-sur-Aire F..12 C3
Pierrefonds F...........12 A3
Pierrefontaine-
  les-Varans F.........17 D1
Pierrefort F............16 A4
Pierrelatte F...........22 B1
Pieskow D...............34 C4
Pieskowa Skała PL.......98 A2
Piešťany SK...........116 B2
Piešťuvenai LT..........85 F2
Pieszyce PL.............96 C1
Pietarlahti PL..........85 E3
Pietkowo PL.............91 E3
Pietra Ligure I.........23 F2
Pietralunga I...........47 E3
Pietraperzia I..........53 D3
Pietrasanta I...........46 C2
Pietrowice PL...........97 E2
Pieve del Cairo I.......17 F4
Pieve di Bono I.........43 E4
Pieve di Cadore I.......44 B3
Pieve di Soligo I.......44 B4
Pieve di Teco I.........23 E1
Pieve Santo Stefano I...47 E3
Pievenai LT.............80 C2
Pievepelago I...........47 D2
Pigádi GR.............105 E1
Pigés GR..............104 C1
Pigí GR...............104 C2
Pigna I.................23 E1
Pihlajaveden as FIN.....69 D2
Pihlajavesi (Keski-Suomen
  lääni) FIN...........69 D2
Pihlava FIN.............68 C3
Pihtipudas FIN..........69 D1
Pihtla EE...............74 C2
Piigandi EE.............79 E1
Piikkiö FIN.............68 C4
Piippola FIN............65 D3
Piira EE................73 D3
Piispajärvi FIN.........65 E3
Piissoo EE..............72 B2
Piistaoja EE............72 B4
Pikal'ovo RUS..........115 E1
Pikasilla EE............79 D1
Pikeliai (Šiauliu) LT...81 D3
Pikeliai (Telšiu) LT....80 C2
Pikeliškes LT...........86 B2
Pikérmi GR.............105 F3
Pikevere EE.............73 D3
Pikkjärve EE............73 D3
Pikknurme EE............73 D3
Piktuižiai LT...........81 D2
Piktupenai LT...........84 B1
Pikutiškes LT...........86 B2
Pikva EE................72 C2
Piła PL.................89 D3
Pilas E.................28 C3
Pilat-Plage F...........20 B1
Pilava Górna PL.........96 C1
Piłatki PL..............90 A2
Pilchowice PL...........97 F2
Pilcine LV..............83 F2
Pilda LV................83 E2
Piléa GR..............103 E2
Pilés GR..............111 E4
Pilés GR..............100 C2
Pili GR...............101 E2
Pilí GR...............105 F3
Pilikalnai LT...........81 D2
Pilio GR..............105 F3
Pilió (Óros) GR........101 F4
Pilioniai LT............81 E3
Pilis I LT..............85 D1
Pilis I LT..............85 D1
Piliškas LV............83 D2

PARIS

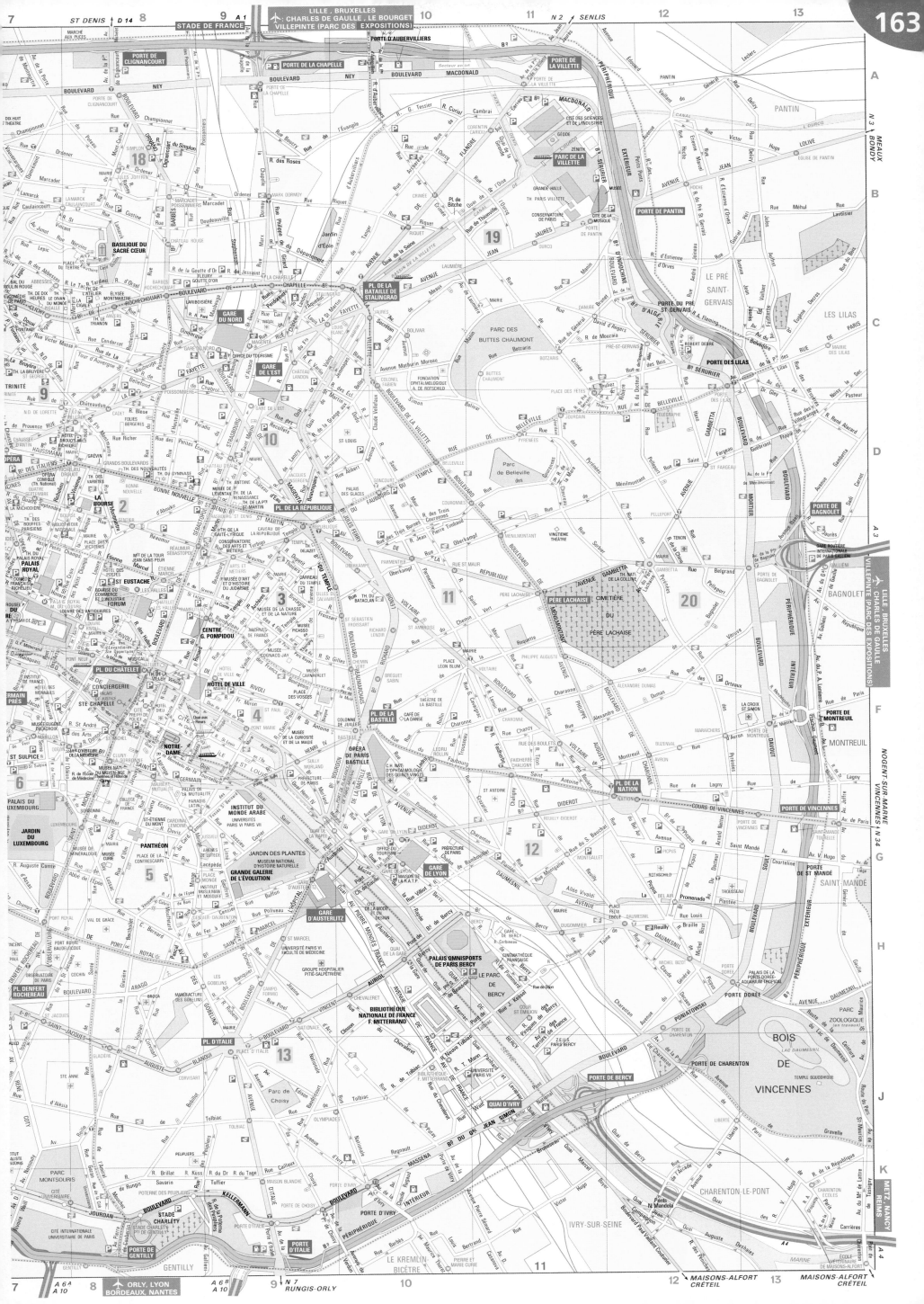

PARIS

Abbé-de-l'Épée (r. de l') G8
Abbé-Groult (r. de l') H5
Abbesses (r. des) C7
Aboukir (r. d') D8
Acclimatation (jardin d') C2
Alain (r.) H6
Albert-I}e}r (cours) E5
Alésia (r. d') J7
Alexander-Fleming (r.) C12
Alexandre-Dumas (r.) F12
Alexandre-III (pont) E6
Algérie (bd d') C12
Alibert (r.) D10
Alleray (r. d') H5
Alma (pont de l') E5
Alphonse-Daudet (r.) J7
Alsace (r. d') C9
Ambroise-Paré (r.) C8
Amélie (r.) F5
Amiral-Bruix (bd de l') D3
Amiral-de-Coligny (r. de l') E8
Amiral-Mouchez (r. de l') K8
Amsterdam (r. d') C7
Anatole-France (quai) E6
André-Citro'n (parc) G3
André-Citro'n (quai) G3
André-Rivoire (av.) K7
Aqueduc (r. de l') C9
Arago (bd) H8
Archereau (r.) B10
Archevêché (pont de l') F8
Archives (r. des) E9
Arcole (pont d') F8
Arcole (r. d') F8
Argenson (r. d') D6
Armaillé (r. d') C4
Artois (r. d') D5
Arts (pont des) F7
Assas (r. d') G7
Assomption (r. de l') F3
Auber (r.) D7
Aubervilliers (porte d') A10
Aubervilliers (r. d') A10
Auguste-Blanqui (bd) J8
Auguste-Comte (r.) G7
Augustin-Thierry (r.) D12
Aurelle-de-Paladines (bd d') C3
Austerlitz (pont d') G9
Austerlitz (quai d') H10
Auteuil (bd d') G1
Auteuil (r. d') G2
Auteuil-aux-Lacs (rte d') F1
Avron (r. d') F12
Babylone (r. de) F6
Bac (r. du) F7
Bagnolet (r. de) E12
Balard (r.) G3
Banque (r. de la) E8
Banquier (r. du) H9
Barbès (bd) B8
Bassano (r. de) D5
Bastille (bd de la) G10
Bastille (pl. de la) F10
Batignolles (bd des) C6
Batignolles (r. des) C6
Baudricourt (r.) J9
Beaubourg (r.) E9
Beaumarchais (bd) F10
Beaunier (r.) J7
Beaurepaire (r.) D9
Beauséjour (bd de) F3
Bel-Air (av. du) G12
Belgrand (r.) E12
Bellechasse (r. de) F6
Bellefond (r. de) C8
Belles-Feuilles (r. des) D3
Belleville (bd de) D11
Belleville (parc de) D11
Belleville (r. de) D11
Belloy (r. de) D4
Belvédère (av. du) C13
Benjamin-Franklin (r.) E4
Beno"t-Frachon (av.) F13
Bercy (bd de) H10
Bercy (le parc de) H11
Bercy (pont de) H10
Bercy (porte de) J11
Bercy (quai de) H11
Bercy (r. de) G9
Berri (r. de) D5
Berthier (bd) B5
Berthollet (r.) H8
Bessières (bd) A6
Bir-Hakeim (pont de) F4
Birague (r. de) F9
Bitche (pl. de) B10
Blanche (r.) C7
Bleue (r.) D8
Blomet (r.) G5
Bobillot (r.) J8
La Boétie (r.) D6
Bois (r. des) C12
Boissière (r.) E4
Boissy-d'Anglas (r.) D6
Bonaparte (r.) F7
Bonne-Nouvelle (bd de) D8
Bosquet (av.) F5
Botzaris (r.) C11
Boucry (r.) B9
Boulainvilliers (r. de) F3
Boulets (r. des) G11
Bourdon (bd) F10
La Bourdonnais (av. de) F5
Bourgogne (r. de) F6
Brancion (r.) H5
Branly (quai) E4
Bretagne (r. de) E9
Breteuil (av. de) F6
Brillat-Savarin (r.) K8
Brune (bd) J6
Bruneseau (r.) J11
La Bruyère (r.) C7
Buffon (r.) G9
Bugeaud (av.) D3
Buttes-Chaumont (parc des) C11
Cail (r.) C9
Caillaux (r.) K9
Cambacérès (r.) D6
Cambrai (r. de) A11
Cambronne (r.) G5
Capucines (bd des) D7
Capucines (r. des) D7
Cardinal-Lemoine (r. du) G8
Cardinet (r.) B6
Carnot (av.) D4
Carpeaux (r.) B7
Carrousel (pont du) E7
Castagnary (r.) H5
Castiglione (r. de) E7
Catalogne (pl. de) H6
Caulaincourt (r.) C7
Caumartin (r. de) D7
Ceinture-du-Lac-Daumesnil (rte de la) J12
Ceinture-du-Lac-Inférieur (chemin de) E2
Censier (r.) H9
Cévennes (r. des) G3
Chabrol (r. de) C9
Chaligny (r.) G11
Chalon (r. de) G10
Championnet (r.) A8
Champs-Élysées (av. des) D5
Change (pont au) F8
Chanzy (r.) F11
Chapelle (bd de la) C9
Chapelle (r. de la) B9
Chardon-Lagache (r.) G2
Charenton (r. de) G10
Charles-de-Gaulle (pl.) D4
Charles-de-Gaulle (pont) G10
Charonne (bd de) F12
Charonne (r. de) F11
Château (r. du) H6
Château-d'Eau (r. du) D9
Château-Landon (r. du) C9
Châteaudun (r. de) D8
Châtelet (pl. du) F8
Chaussée-d'Antin (r. de la) D7
Chemin-Vert (r. du) E10
Cherche-Midi (r. du) G6
Chevaleret (r. du) J10
Chine (r. de la) E12
Choisy (av. de) K9
Choisy (parc de) J9
Chomel (r.) F7
Cité (r. de la) F8
Cité-Universitaire (r. de la) K8
Claude-Bernard (r.) H8
Claude-Decaen (r.) H12
Claude-Farrère (r.) G1
Claude-Regaud (av.) K10
Claude-Terrasse (r.) H2
Claude-Vellefaux (av.) D10
Clichy (av. de) B7
Clichy (bd de) C7
Clichy (pl. de) C7
Clichy (r. de) C7
Clignancourt (r. de) B8
Clisson (r.) H10
Clo"tre-Notre-Dame (r. du) F8
Clovis (r.) G8
Commandant-Charcot (bd du) C1
Commandant-Guilbaud (r. du) G1
Commandant-René-Mouchotte (r. du) H6
Commerce (r. du) G4
Concorde (pl. de la) E6
Concorde (port de la) E6
Condorcet (r.) C8
Constantine (r. de) E6
Constantinople (r. de) C6
Conti (quai de) F8
Contrescarpe (pl. de la) G8
Convention (r. de la) G4
Copernic (r.) D4
Corbineau (r.) H11
Corentin-Cariou (av.) A11
Cortambert (r.) E3
Corvisart (r.) J8
Cotentin (r. du) H6
Cour-du-Maroc (parc de la) B9
Courcelles (bd de) C5
Courcelles (r. de) C5
Couronnes (r. des) D11
Courteline (av.) G13
Crimée (r. de) B10
Croix-des-Petits-Champs (r.) E8
Croix-Nivert (r. de la) G4
Crozatier (r.) G11
Curial (r.) A10
Custine (r.) B8
Cuvier (r.) G9
Daguerre (r.) H7
Damrémont (r.) B7
Danielle-Casanova (r.) E7
Danton (r.) F8
Dantzig (r. de) H5
Daumesnil (av.) H12
Dauphine (porte) D3
Dauphine (r.) F8
David-d'Angers (r.) C12
David-Weill (av.) K7
Davout (bd) F13
Debilly (passerelle) E4
Delcassé (av.) D6
Delessert (bd) F4
Denain (bd de) C9
Denfert-Rochereau (av.) H7
Denfert-Rochereau (pl.) H7
Départ (r. du) G6
Département (r. du) B9
Desnouettes (r.) H4
Diderot (bd) G11
Didot (r.) J6
Dijon (r. de) H11
Dr-Arnold-Netter (av. du) G12
Dr-Blanche (r. du) F2
Dr-Finlay (r. du) F4
Dr-Gley (av. du) C13
Dr-Potain (r. du) C12
Dr-Roux (r. du) G5
Dr-Tuffier (r. du) K9
Dorée (porte) H12
Douai (r. de) C7
Double (pont au) F8
Doudeauville (r.) B9
Duméril (r.) H9
Dunkerque (r. de) C8
Dupetit-Thouars (r.) E9
Dupleix (r.) F4
Duquesne (av.) F6
Duranton (r.) H4
Dutot (r.) H5
Éblé (r.) G6
Écluses-St-Martin (r. des) D10
École-de-Médecine (r. de l') F8
Écoles (r. des) G8
Edgar-Quinet (bd) H7
Édison (av.) J9
Émeriau (r.) F4
Émile-Augier (bd) E3
Émile-Zola (av.) G4
Entrepreneurs (r. des) G4
Épée-de-Bois (r. de l') G8
Ernest-Renan (r.) J4
Estrées (r. d') F5
États-Unis (pl. des) D4
Etex (r.) B7
Étienne-Marcel (r.) E8
Eugène-Varlin (r.) C9
Évangile (r. de l') B9
Exelmans (bd) G2
Eylau (av. d') E4
Fabert (r.) E5
Faidherbe (r.) F11
Faisanderie (r. de la) D3
Falguière (r.) G6
Faubourg-du-Temple (r. du) D10
Faubourg-Montmartre (r. du) D8
Faubourg-Poissonnière (r. du) C8
Faubourg-St-Antoine (r. du) G11
Faubourg-St-Denis (r. du) C9
Faubourg-St-Honoré (r. du) D5
Faubourg-St-Jacques (r. du) H7
Faubourg-St-Martin (r. du) D9
La Fayette (r.) C8
Fédération (r. de la) F4
Félix-Éboué (pl.) H12
Félix-Faure (av.) G4
Fer-à-Moulin (r. du) H9
Ferdinand-Buisson (av.) G1
Fêtes (pl. des) D11
Flandre (av. de) B10
Flandrin (bd) D3
Fleurs (quai aux) F8
Foch (av.) D4
La-Fontaine (r.) F3
Fossés-St-Bernard (r. des) G9
Four (r. du) F7
France (av. de) H10
François-Bonvin (r.) G5
François-I}e}r (r.) E5
François-Mauriac (quai) H10
François-Miron (r.) F9
François-Mitterrand (quai) E7
Francs-Bourgeois (r. des) F9
Franklin-D.-Roosevelt (av.) E5
Frémicourt (r.) G5
Frères-Morane (r. des) G4
Friedland (av. de) D5
Froidevaux (r.) H7
Froissart (r.) E9
Gabriel (av.) D6
Ga"té (r. de la) H6
Gambetta (av.) D12
Gare (quai de la) H10
Garibaldi (bd) G5
Garigliano (pont du) H2
Gassendi (r.) H7
Gaston-Tessier (r.) A10
Gay-Lussac (r.) G8
Gazan (r.) J8
Général-Brunet (r. du) C11
Général-Guillaumat (r. du) J4
Général-Jean-Simon (bd du) J11
Général-Leclerc (av. du) J7
Général-Lemonnier (av. du) E7
Général-Martial-Valin (bd du) H3
Général-Michel-Bizot (av. du) H12
Général-Sarrail (av. du) G1
Gentilly (porte de) K8
Geoffroy-St-Hilaire (r.) G9
George-Sand (r.) G2
George-V (av.) D5
Georges-Brassens (parc) J5
Georges-Lafenestre (av.) J5
Georges-Mandel (av.) E3
Georges-Pompidou (voie) G3
Gergovie (r. de) H6
Gilbert-Perroy (pl.) H6
Gironde (quai de la) B11
Glacière (r. de la) H8
Gobelins (av. des) H9
Godefroy-Cavaignac (r.) F11
Gordon-Bennett (av.) G1
Goutte-d'Or (r. de la) C9
Gouvion-St-Cyr (bd) C4
Grande-Armée (av. de la) D4
Grands-Augustins (quai des) F8
Grange-aux-Belles (r. de la) D10
Gravelle (av. de) J12
Grenelle (bd de) G5
Grenelle (pont de) F3
Grenelle (quai de) F3
Grenelle (r. de) F5
Grenier-St-Lazare (r. du) E9
Gros (r.) F3
Guébriant (r. de) D13
Guersant (r.) C4
Gustave-Eiffel (av.) F4
Guy-M(tm)quet (r.) B6
Guynemer (r.) G7
Halles (r. des) E8
Haussmann (bd) D6
Hauteville (r. d') D8
Havre (r. du) D7
Haxo (r.) D12
Henri-Chevreau (r.) D11
Henri-Heine (r.) F2
Henri-IV (bd) F9
Henri-IV (quai) G9
Henri-Martin (av.) E3
Henri-Ribière (r.) D12
Hippodrome (av. de l') F1
Hoche (av.) C5
H(tm)pital (bd de l') H9
H(tm)tel-de-Ville (quai de l') F9
Ibsen (av.) E13
Iéna (av. d') D4
Iéna (pont d') E4
Indochine (bd d') C12
Ingres (av.) F2
Inspecteur-Allès (r. de l') C12
Invalides (bd des) G6
Invalides (esplanade des) F6
Invalides (pont des) E5
Issy-les-Moulineaux (quai d') H2
Italie (av. d') K9
Italie (pl. d') J9
Italiens (bd des) D7
Ivry (av. d') J9
Ivry (quai d') J11
Jacob (r.) F7
Jacques-Baudry (r.) J5
Javel (r. de) G4
Jean-Baptiste-Berlier (r.) J11
Jean-Baptiste-Pigalle (r.) C7
Jean-Calvin (r.) G8
Jean-Jaurès (av.) B11
Jean-Moulin (av.) J6
Jean-Pierre-Timbaud (r.) E10
Jean-Zay (r.) H6
Jeanne-d'Arc (r.) H9
Jemmapes (quai de) C10
Jessaint (r. de) C9
La Jonquière (r. de) B6
Joseph-Bouvard (av.) F5
Joseph-de-Maistre (r.) B7
Joseph-Kessel (r.) H11
Jouffroy-d'Abbans (r.) C5
Jourdain (r. du) D11
Jourdan (bd) K8
Jules-Ferry (bd) E10
Julia-Bartet (r.) J5
Juliette-Dodu (r.) D10
Junot (av.) B7
Jussieu (r.) G9
Kellermann (bd) K9
Kléber (av.) D4
Küss (r.) K8
La Tour-d'Auvergne (r. de) C8
La Tour-Maubourg (bd de) E5
Lacépède (r.) G9
Lagny (r. de) G12
Lagrange (r.) F8
Lamarck (r.) B7
Lamballe (av. de) F3
Lancry (r. de) D9
Lannes (bd) D3
Laumière (av. de) C11
Lavandières-Ste-Opportune (r. des) F8
Leblanc (r.) H3
Lecourbe (r.) G5
Ledru-Rollin (av.) F10
Lefebvre (bd) J5
Legendre (r.) B6
Légion-Étrangère (r. de la) K6
Léon-Frapié (r.) D13
Léon-Frot (r.) F11
Léon-Gaumont (av.) F13
Léopold-Sédar-Senghor (pass) E7
Lepic (r.) B7
Leriche (r.) H4
Liège (r. de) C7
Lille (r. de) F7
Linné (r.) G9
Linois (r.) G3
Lisbonne (r. de) C6
Londres (r. de) C7
Longchamp (allée de) D2
Longchamp (r. de) E4
Louis-Blanc (r.) C9
Louis-Blériot (quai) G3
Louis-Braille (r.) H12
Louis-Philippe (pont) F9
Louise-Thuliez (r.) C12
Lourmel (r. de) G4
Louvre (quai du) F8
Louvre (r. du) E8
Lowendal (av. de) F5
Lucien-Descaves (av.) K7
Luxembourg (jardin du) G7
Lyon (r. de) G10
Mac-Mahon (av.) C4
Macdonald (bd) A11
Madeleine (bd de la) D7
Mademoiselle (r.) G5
Madrid (r. de) C6
Magenta (bd de) D9
Mahatma-Gandhi (av. du) D2
Maillot (bd) C3
Maillot (porte) C3
Maine (av. du) H6
Malakoff (av. de) D3
Malaquais (quai) F7
Malar (r.) E5
Malesherbes (bd) D6
Manin (r.) C11
Marcadet (r.) B7
Marceau (av.) D5
Marcel-Doret (av.) H2
Mare (r. de la) D11
Maréchal-Gallieni (av. du) E6
Marie (pont) F9
Marigny (av. de) D6
Martyrs (r. des) C8
Marx-Dormoy (r.) B9
Masséna (bd) K10
Mathurin-Moreau (av.) C10
Matignon (av.) D6
Maubeuge (r. de) C8
Maurice-Barrès (bd) C2
Mazarine (r.) F7
Mazas (voie) G10
Meaux (r. de) C10
Médicis (r. de) G8
Mégisserie (quai de la) F8
Mendelssohn (r.) F13
Ménilmontant (bd de) E11
Ménilmontant (r. de) D12
Messine (av. de) D6
Michel-Ange (r.) G2
Michel-le-Comte (r.) E9
Miollis (r.) G5
Mirabeau (pont) G3
Mirabeau (r.) G2
Miromesnil (r. de) D6
Mogador (r. de) D7
Molitor (porte) G1
Molitor (r.) G2
Monceau (parc) C5
Monceau (r. de) C6
Moncey (r.) C7
Monge (r.) G8
Mont-Cenis (r. du) B8
Montaigne (av.) E5
Montebello (quai de) F8
Montgallet (r.) G11
Montmartre (r.) D8
Montmorency (bd de) F2
Montorgueil (r.) E8
Montparnasse (bd du) G7
Montparnasse (r. du) G7
Montreuil (r. de) F12
Montsouris (parc) K7
Morillons (r. des) H5
Morland (bd) G9
Morland (pont) G9
Mortier (bd) D13
La Motte-Picquet (av. de) F5
Mouffetard (r.) H8
Mouton-Duvernet (r.) H7
Mouzaïa (r. de) C12
Mozart (av.) F2
Muette (porte de la) E2
Muette-à-Neuilly (rte de la) E2
Murat (bd) G1
Nansouty (r.) J7
Nation (pl. de la) G12
National (pont) J11
Nationale (r.) J9
Nations-Unies (av. des) E4
Neuf (pont) F8
Neuve-Tolbiac (r.) J10
New-York (av. de) E4
Ney (bd) A9
Niel (av.) C4
Norvins (r.) B8
Notre-Dame (pont) F8
N.-D.-de-Lorette (r.) C7
N.-D.-des-Champs (r.) G7
Nungesser-et-Coli (r.) G1
Oberkampf (r.) E10
Observatoire (av. de l') H7
Odéon (r. de l') F7
Oise (quai de l') B11
Olivier-de-Serres (r.) H4
Opéra (av. de l') D7
Ordener (r.) B9
Ornano (bd) B8
Orsay (quai d') E5
Orsel (r. d') C8
Orteaux (r. des) F12
Oudinot (r.) G6
Ourcq (r. de l') B11
Paix (r. de la) D7
Palais (bd du) F8
Panhard-et-Levassor (quai) J11
Pantin (porte de) B12
Paradis (r. de) D8
Parc (rte du) J12
Parc-Royal (r. du) F9
Parmentier (av.) E10
Pas-de-la-Mule (r. du) F10
Pascal (r.) H8
Passy (porte de) F2
Passy (r. de) F3
Pasteur (bd) G6
Patay (r. de) J10
Paul-Barruel (r.) H5
Paul-Doumer (av.) E3
Le Peletier (r.) D7
Pelleport (r.) E12
Pépinière (r. de la) D6
Percier (av.) D6
Perdonnet (r.) C9
Père-Lachaise (av. du) E12
Pereire (bd) B5
Pergolèse (r.) D4
Perle (r. de la) E9
Pershing (bd) C4
Petit-Pont F8
Petites-Écuries (r. des) D8
Petits-Champs (r. des) E7
Petits-Ponts (rte des) B12
Peupliers (r. des) J9
Philippe-Auguste (av.) F11
Philippe-de-Girard (r.) B9
Picpus (bd de) G12
Picpus (r. de) G12
Pierre-Charron (r.) D5
Pierre-de-Coubertin (av.) K8
Pierre-Demours (r.) C4
Pierre-Fontaine (r.) C7
Pierre-I}e}r-de-Serbie (av.) E4
Pierre-Larousse (r.) J6
Pierre-Mendès-France (av.) H10
Pinel (r.) H9
Pirogues-de-Bercy (r. des) H11
Plantes (jardin des) G9
Plantes (r. des) J6
Poissonnière (r.) D8
Poissonniers (r. des) B9
Poliveau (r.) H9
Pommard (r. de) H11
Pompe (r. de la) D3
Poniatowski (bd) H12
Pont-Neuf (r. du) E8
Ponthieu (r. de) D5
Port-Royal (bd de) H8
Portalis (r.) C6
Pte-Brancion (av. de la) J5
Pte-Brunet (av. de la) C12
Pte-d'Asnières (av. de la) B5
Pte-d'Aubervilliers (av. de la) A10
Pte-d'Auteuil (av. de la) G1
Pte-de-Bagnolet (av. de la) E13
Pte-de-Champerret (av. de la) B4
Pte-de-Charenton (av. de la) J12
Pte-de-Châtillon (av. de la) J6
Pte-de-Choisy (av. de la) K9
Pte-de-Clichy (av. de la) A5
Pte-de-Clignancourt (av. de la) A8
Pte-de-la-Chapelle (av. de la) A9
Pte-de-la-Plaine (av. de la) J4
Pte-de-la-Villette (av. de la) A11
Pte-de-Ménilmontant (av. de la) D13
Pte-de-Montmartre (av. de la) A7
Pte-de-Montreuil (av. de la) F13
Pte-de-Montrouge (av. de la) K6
Pte-de-Sèvres (av. de la) H3
Pte-de-St-Ouen (av. de la) A7
Pte-de-Vitry (av. de la) K10
Pte-des-Lilas (av. de la) C13
Pte-des-Poissonniers (av. de la) A8
Pte-des-Ternes (av. de la) C3
Pte-d'Issy (r. de la) H3
Pte-d'Italie (av. de la) K9
Pte-d'Ivry (av. de la) K10
Pte-d'Orléans (av. de la) K7
Pte-du-Pré-St-Gervais (av. de la) C12
Poteau (r. du) B8
Poterne-des-Peupliers (r. de la) K9
Pouchet (r.) A6
Poussin (r.) G2
Pré-St-Gervais (r. du) D11
Président-Kennedy (av. du) F3
Président-Wilson (av. du) E4
Professeur-André-Lemierre (av. du) F13
La Promenade Plantée G12
Prony (r. de) C5
Provence (r. de) D7
Prudhon (av.) E2
Pyramides (r. des) E7
Pyrénées (r. des) E12
Quatre-Fils (r. des) E9
Quatre-Septembre (r. du) D7
Raffet (r.) F2
Rambouillet (r. de) G10
Rambuteau (r.) E9
Ramey (r.) B8
Ranelagh (r. du) F3
Rapée (quai de la) G10
Rapha'l (av.) E2
Rapp (av.) E5
Raspail (bd) H7
Raymond-Losserand (r.) H6
Raymond-Poincaré (av.) E4
Raynouard (r.) F3
Réaumur (r.) E8
Récollets (r. des) D9
Regnault (r.) J10
Reille (av.) J8
Reims (bd de) B5
Reine (cours la) E6
Reine-Marguerite (allée de la) D1
Rémusat (r. de) G3
Renard (r. du) F8
René-Coty (av.) J7
Rennes (r. de) F7
République (av. de la) E10
République (pl. de la) E9
Reuilly (bd de) H12
Reuilly (r. de) G11
Richard-Lenoir (bd) E10
Richard-Lenoir (r.) F11
Richard-Wallace (bd) D1
Richelieu (r. de) D7
Richer (r.) D8
Richerand (av.) D9
Riquet (r.) B10
Rivoli (r. de) E8
Rochechouart (bd de) C8
Rochechouart (r. de) C8
Rocher (r. du) C6
Rome (r. de) C6
Roquette (r. de la) F10
Roses (r. des) B9
Royal (pont) E7
Royale (r.) D6
Rubens (r.) H9
Rungis (r. de) K8
Sablons (r. des) E3
St-Amand (r.) H5
St-André-des-Arts (r.) F8
St-Antoine (r.) F9
St-Bernard (quai) G9
St-Charles (r.) G3
St-Cloud (av. de) F1
St-Cloud (porte de) H1
St-Denis (bd) D9
St-Denis (r.) D8
St-Dominique (r.) E5
St-Éleuthère (r.) C8
Saint-Exupéry (quai) H2
St-Fargeau (r.) D12
St-Ferdinand (r.) C4
St-Florentin (r.) E6
St-Germain (bd) F8
St-Germain-des-Prés (pl.) F7
St-Gilles (r.) F10
St-Honoré (r.) E7
St-Jacques (bd) H7
St-Jacques (r.) G8
St-Lambert (r.) H4
St-Lazare (r.) D7
St-Louis (pont) F9
St-Louis-en-l'Île (r.) F9
St-Mandé (av. de) G12
St-Mandé (porte de) G13
St-Marcel (bd) H9
St-Martin (bd) D9
St-Martin (r.) E9
St-Maur (r.) D10
St-Maurice (av. de) J12
St-Michel (bd) G8
St-Michel (pont) F8
St-Michel (quai) F8
St-Ouen (av. de) B7
St-Paul (r.) F9
St-Pétersbourg (r. de) C6
St-Placide (r.) G7
Saint-Sa'ns (r.) F4
St-Sulpice (r.) F7
St-Vincent (r.) B8
Sts-Pères (r. des) F7
Santé (r. de la) H8
Sarrette (r.) J7
Saxe (av. de) G6
Scribe (r.) D7
Sébastopol (bd de) E8
Secrétan (av.) C10
Ségur (av. de) F5
Seine (quai de la) B10
Seine (r. de) F7
Sergent-Bauchat (r. du) G11
Sérurier (bd) C12
Sèvres (r. de) G6
Simon-Bolivar (av.) D10
Simone-de-Beauvoir (passerelle) H10
Singer (r.) F3
Solférino (passerelle) E7
Sorbier (r.) E11
Soufflot (r.) G8
Soult (bd) G13
Stéphane-Mallarmé (av.) B4
Stephenson (r.) B9
Strasbourg (bd de) D9
Suchet (bd) F2
Suffren (av. de) G5
Suisses (r. des) J6
Sully (ponts de) G9
Surène (r. de) D6
Suresnes (rte de) D2
Tage (r. du) K9
Taine (r.) H11
Tanger (r. de) B10
Tardieu (r.) C8
Temple (bd du) E9
Temple (r. du) E9
Ternes (av. des) C4
Terroirs-de-France (av. des) J11
Tertre (pl. du) B8
Théâtre (r. du) G4
Théophile-Gautier (av.) F3
Thionville (r. de) B11
Thomas-Mann (r.) J11
Thorigny (r. de) E9
Titon (r.) F11
Tocqueville (r. de) C6
Tolbiac (pont de) H11
Tolbiac (r. de) J9
Tombe-Issoire (r. de la) J7
Tour (r. de la) E3
Tournelle (pont de la) F9
Tournelle (quai de la) F9
Tournon (r. de) F7
Tourville (av. de) F5
Trocadéro et Onze-Novembre (pl. du) E4
Trois-Bornes (r. des) E10
Tronchet (r.) D7
Trousseau (r.) F10
Tuileries (jardin des) E7
Tuileries (quai des) E7
Turbigo (r. de) E9
Turenne (r. de) E9
Ulm (r. d') G8
Université (r. de l') E5
Valette (r.) G8
Valmy (quai de) C9
Van-Gogh (r.) G10
Vaneau (r.) F6
Vanves (porte de) J5
Varenne (r. de) F6
Vaugirard (bd de) G6
Vaugirard (r. de) G5
Vauquelin (r.) G8
Vauvenargues (r.) B7
Vend(tm)me (pl.) E7
Vercingétorix (r.) H6
Versailles (av. de) G2
Victor (bd) H3
Victor-Hugo (av.) D3
Victor-Massé (r.) C7
Victoria (av.) F8
Vieille-du-Temple (r.) E9
Vienne (r. de) C6
Vigée-Lebrun (r.) H5
Villars (av. de) F6
Villette (bd de la) D10
Villette (parc de la) B11
Villiers (av. de) C5
Villiot (r.) G10
Vincennes (cours de) G12
Vincennes (porte de) G13
Vincent-Auriol (bd) H10
Violet (r.) G4
Vitruve (r.) E12
Vivaldi (allée) G11
Vivienne (r.) D8
Volontaires (r. des) H5
Voltaire (bd) F11
Voltaire (quai) F7
Vosges (pl. des) F9
Vouillé (r. de) H5
Vulpian (r.) H8
Wagram (av. de) C5
Washington (r.) D5
Watt (r.) J11
Wilhem (r.) G2
Winston-Churchill (av.) E6
Yvonne-Le-Tac (r.) C8

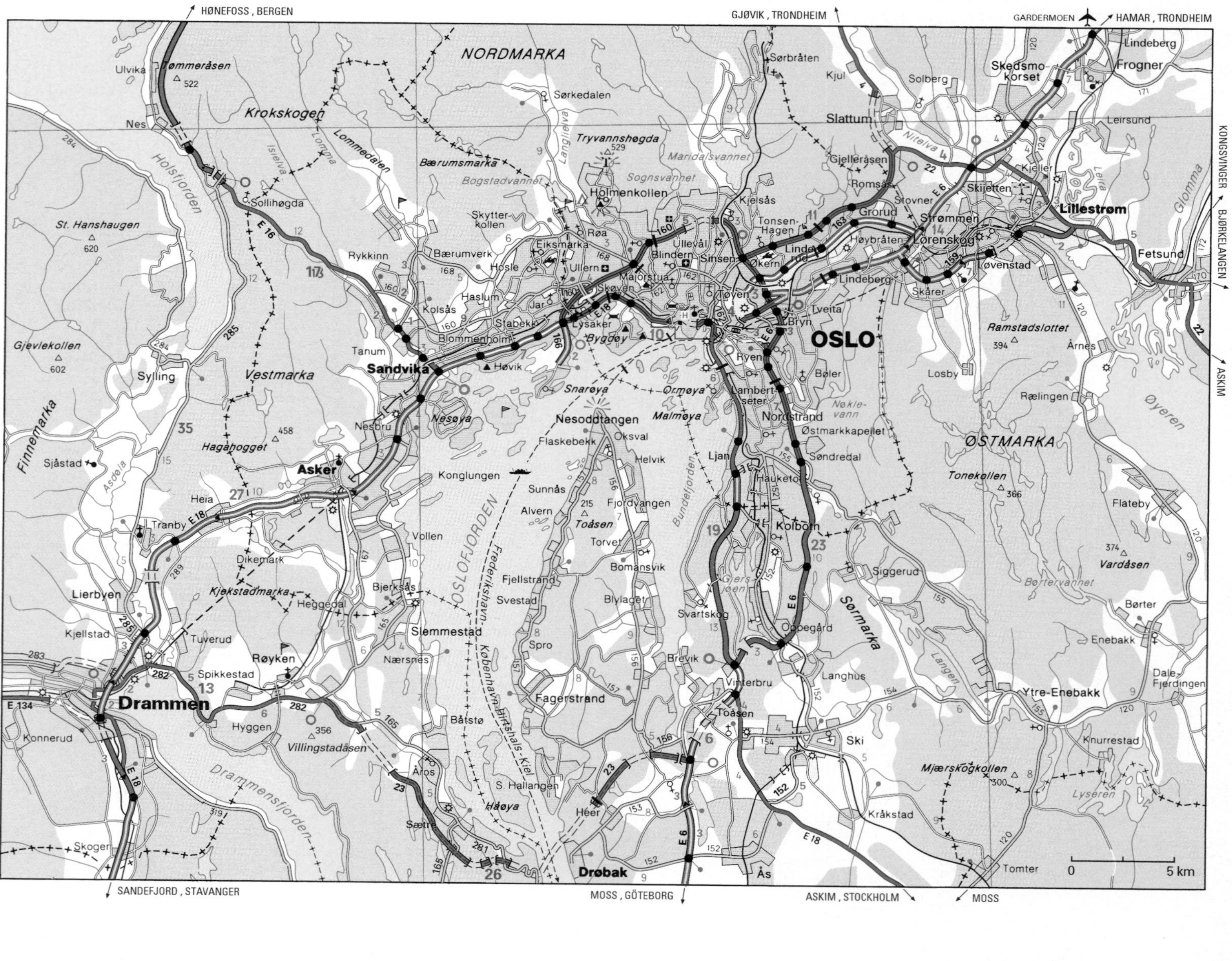

HØNEFOSS , BERGEN
GJØVIK , TRONDHEIM
GARDERMOEN
HAMAR , TRONDHEIM
KONGSVINGER
BJØRKELANGEN
ASKIM
KONGSBERG , HAUGESUND
SANDEFJORD , STAVANGER
MOSS , GÖTEBORG
ASKIM , STOCKHOLM
MOSS
NORDMARKA
Krokskogen
Vestmarka
ØSTMARKA
Sørmarka
OSLO
Sandvika
Asker
Drammen
Lillestrøm
Fetsund
Drøbak
Ski
Holmenkollen
Tryvannshøgda
Nesoddtangen
Slemmestad
Oslofjorden
Drammensfjorden
Holsfjorden
Finnemarka
Lindeberg
Frogner
Skedsmo-korset
Strømmen
Lørenskog
Ramstadslottet
Bærumsmarka
Sognsvann
Maridalsvannet
Bogstadvannet
Lysaker
Stabekk
Bygdøy
Nordstrand
Kolbotn
Ås
Vinterbro
Tomter
Hurum
Røyken
Spikkestad
Lierbyen
Konnerud
Villingstadåsen
Hyggen
Fagerstrand
Tanum
Sylling
Øyeren
0
5 km

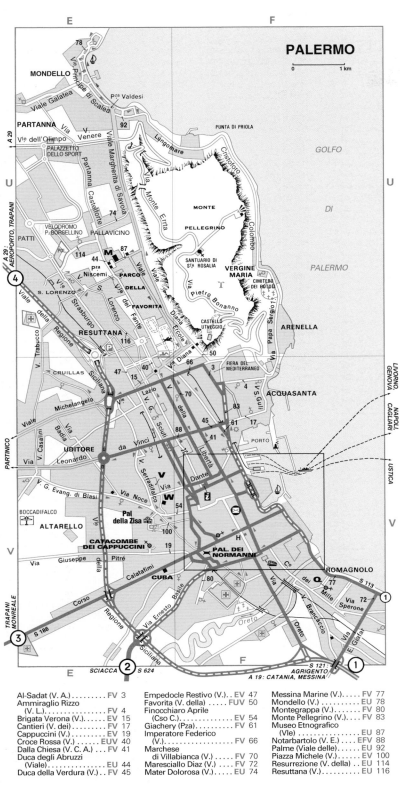

PALERMO
0   1 km

Al-Sadat (V. A.) . . . . FV 3
Ammiraglio Rizzo
  (V. L.). . . . . FV 4
Brigata Verona (V.). . . . . . . EV 15
Cantieri (V. dei) . . . . EV 17
Cappuccini (V.) . . . . EV 19
Croce Rossa (V.) . . . . EUV 40
Dalla Chiesa (V. C. A.) . . . FV 41
Duca degli Abruzzi
  (Viale) . . . . EU 44
Duca della Verdura (V.) . . . FV 45

Empedocle Restivo (V.) . . . EV 47
Favorita (V. della) . . . . . . FUV 50
Finocchiaro Aprile
  (Cso C.) . . . . EV 54
Giachery (Pza) . . . . FV 61
Imperatore Federico
  (Vle) . . . . FV 66
Marchese
  di Villabianca (V.) . . . . . EV 70
Maresciallo Diaz (V.) . . . . FV 72
Mater Dolorosa (V.) . . . . . EU 74

Messina Marine (V.) . . . . . FV 77
Mondello (V.) . . . . EU 78
Montegrappa (V.) . . . . FV 80
Monte Pellegrino (V.) . . . . FV 83
Museo Etnografico
  (V.) . . . . FV 66
Notarbartolo (V. E.) . . . . . EFV 88
Palme (Viale delle). . . . . . . EV 92
Piazza Michele (V.) . . . . . EV 100
Resurrezione (V. della) . . . EV 114
Resuttana (V.). . . . . EU 116

Plattling D............39 F4
Plau D............34 A3
Plaučiškes LT............86 C1
Plaučiškiai LT............81 E3
Plaue (Kreis Brandenburg) D............34 B4
Plauen D............39 E2
Plaušiniai LT............80 B2
Plav MNE............59 D3
Plavas LV............77 D3
Plavča HR............54 B3
Plavinas LV............82 C1
Plavna SRB............57 E3
Plavnica MNE............58 C3
Plavnik (Otok) HR............54 B2
Plavsk RUS............115 F2
Pleaux F............15 F4
Pleine-Fougères F............11 D4
Pleinfeld D............39 D4
Plélan-le-Grand F............10 C4
Plélan-le-Petit F............10 C4
Pléneuf-Val-André F............10 C4
Plentzia E............20 A2
Plépi GR............105 E4
Plešin SRB............59 D3
Plestin-les-Grèves F............10 C4
Pleszew PL............93 E2
Plettenberg D............37 E2
Pleumartin F............15 E2
Pleumeur-Bodou F............10 B3
Pleven BG............117 D3
Pleyben F............10 A4
Pliego E............30 C2
Plienciems LV............77 E3
Plieniškiai LT............85 D1
Plikiai (Kauno) LT............85 E1
Plikiai (Klaipedos) LT............80 B3
Plikiškiai LT............81 E2
Plitra GR............108 B1
Plitvička Jezera HR............54 C3
Plitvički Ljeskovac HR............54 C3
Pljevlja MNE............56 C4
Ploaghe I............50 A2
Ploče HR............55 E2
Plochingen D............43 D1
Plock PL............94 A1
Ploemeur F............14 A1
Ploërmel F............10 C4
Plœuc-sur-Lié F............10 C4
Ploiești RO............117 E3
Plokšciai (Klaipedos) LT............80 B2
Plokšciai (Marijampoles) LT............85 D1
Plomári GR............107 E4
Plombières-les-Bains F............13 E4
Plomin HR............54 A3
Plön D............33 F2
Plonéour-Lanvern F............10 A4
Płonia PL............88 A2
Ploski LV............83 F2
Ploskinia PL............90 A1
Ploty PL............88 B2
Ploubalay F............10 A4
Ploudalmézeau F............10 A4
Plouescat F............10 A3
Plougasnou F............10 B3
Plougastel-Daoulas F............10 B4
Plougonven F............10 B4
Plouguenast F............10 C4
Plouha F............10 B4
Plouigneau F............10 B4
Ploumanach F............10 B4
Plouzévédé F............10 A4
Plovdiv BG............117 D4
Plugawice PL............93 E3
Plumbridge GB............3 D1
Plümes LT............78 B2
Plunge LT............80 B2
Pluski PL............90 B2
Pl'ussa RUS............115 D1
Pluty PL............90 B1
Pluvigner F............14 B1
Plužine (Mostar) MNE............58 B2
Plužine (Žabljak) BIH............58 C1
Plymouth GB............8 B4
Plympton GB............8 B4
Plymstock GB............8 B4
Plzeň CZ............40 C2
Pniewy (Mazowieckie) PL............94 B2
Pniewy (Wielkopolskie) PL............92 C1
Pobiedziska PL............93 D1
Pobrđe SRB............57 D4
Pocaičiai LT............85 D1
Pocelonys LT............85 F3
Počep RUS............115 F3
Pociems LV............78 B2
Počinok RUS............115 E3
Počitelj BIH............58 A3
Pociūnai (Kauno) LT............85 E2
Pociūnai (Šiauliu) LT............81 E3
Pociūneliai LT............81 E3
Pocking D............45 D2
Poczesna PL............97 F1
Poda MNE............58 B3
Podareš MK............59 D2
Podbořany CZ............40 B2
Podčetrtek SLO............54 B2

Poddębice PL............93 F2
Poděbrady CZ............41 D2
Podedwórze PL............95 E2
Podegrodzie PL............98 B3
Podensac F............20 C1
Podersdorf am See A............45 F1
Podgajci Posavski HR............55 F2
Podgaje PL............89 D2
Podgarić HR............55 D2
Podgora HR............58 A2
Podgorač HR............55 E2
Podgorac SRB............57 E3
Podgorica MNE............58 C3
Podgórz PL............89 F3
Podgórzyn PL............92 C3
Podgrad SLO............54 A3
Podhum BIH............55 E3
Podjica HR............58 A4
Podkoren SLO............54 A1
Podkájas LV............77 F3
Podlugovi BIH............55 E3
Podnovlje BIH............55 E3
Podohóri GR............104 B1
Podogorá GR............102 B2
Podol'sk RUS............115 F2
Podpeč SLO............54 A2
Põdrangu EE............73 D2
Podrašnica BIH............55 D3
Podravski Kloštar HR............55 D2
Podromanija BIH............55 F4
Põdruse EE............73 D2
Podsreda SLO............54 B2
Podsused HR............54 C2
Podturen HR............54 C1
Podujevo SRB............59 E2
Podunavci SRB............57 D4
Poggibonsi I............47 D3
Poggio Imperiale I............49 D2
Poggio Mirteto I............47 F4
Poggio Renatico I............47 D1
Poggio Rusco I............47 D1
Pöggstall A............45 D1
Pogoniani GR............100 C3
Pogorzel PL............91 D1
Pogorzela PL............93 D2
Pogradec AL............116 C4
Pogwizdów PL............97 F2
Põhara EE............72 A3
Pohja / Pojo FIN............69 D4
Pohja-Lankila FIN............69 F3
Põhjaka EE............72 C3
Pohjaslahti (Häme) FIN............69 D2
Pohjaslahti (Lappi) FIN............65 D2
Pohorelice CZ............41 E4
Poiana Brașov RO............117 D2
Põikva EE............72 C3
Poio E............18 A3
Poirino I............17 E4
Poisson F............12 C4
Poissons F............15 E2
Poitiers F............15 E2
Poix-de-Picardie F............12 A2
Poix-Terron F............12 C2
Pojate SRB............57 E3
Poki LV............81 E1
Pokka FIN............61 E3
Poklečani BIH............55 E4
Pokój PL............93 E3
Pokrówka PL............95 F3
Pokupsko HR............54 C2
Pola de Allande E............18 C2
Pola de Laviana E............19 D2
Pola de Lena E............19 D2
Pola de Siero E............19 D2
Polače HR............58 A3
Polack BY............115 D3
Polakas LV............83 D1
Polán E............42 A2
Polana (Śląskie) PL............97 F2
Polanica-Zdrój PL............96 C1
Połanieć PL............98 C1
Polanów PL............89 D1
Polany PL............98 B3
Polbrenči LV............78 C1
Polčane SLO............54 B1
Polcenigo I............44 B3
Połczyn Zdrój PL............88 C2
Põlde E............78 C1
Põldeotsa EE............72 A3
Polegate GB............9 E4
Polekele LT............81 E3
Põlendmaa EE............72 A3
Polesella I............47 E1
Poleski Park Narodowy PL............95 E2
Polessk RUS............114 C3
Põlgaste EE............79 E1
Polhov Gradec SLO............54 A2
Policastro Bussentino I............50 C2
Police PL............88 A2
Polička CZ............41 E3
Poličnik HR............54 C4
Policoro I............49 F4
Policzna PL............95 D4
Polidéndri GR............105 F3
Polidrossos GR............105 E3
Poliegos (Nissi) GR............109 E1
Polignano a Mare I............49 F3
Poligny F............16 C2
Poligiros GR............102 A3
Polihnitos GR............107 D1
Polikárpi GR............101 E2
Polikástano GR............101 D3
Polikastro GR............101 E2
Polimilos GR............101 E3

Polinéri (Grevená) GR............101 D3
Poliníri (Trikala) GR............101 D4
Polióhni GR............103 D4
Polipótamo GR............101 D2
Polipótamos GR............106 B3
Poliraho GR............101 E3
Polirinía GR............108 C3
Políssito GR............102 C1
Polistena I............51 D4
Politiká GR............105 F3
Poljana SLO............54 B1
Poljana SRB............57 D3
Poljana Pakračka HR............55 D2
Polje BIH............55 E3
Poljica HR............58 A4
Poljice BIH............55 E3
Polkorona LV............83 E2
Polkowice PL............92 C2
Polla I............49 D4
PõllakFIN............69 F2
Põllküla EE............72 C2
Pöllau A............45 E2
Polle D............38 C1
Pollença E............31 E3
Pollfoss N............62 B4
Polli EE............78 C1
Pollos E............19 D4
Polmak N............61 F1
Polonne UA............117 C1
Polperro GB............8 A4
Polska Cerekiew PL............97 E2
Poltava UA............115 F4
Põltsamaa EE............72 C3
Põlva EE............79 E1
Polvijärvi FIN............69 F2
Polzela SLO............54 B1
Pomar E............20 C4
Pomarance I............47 D3
Pomarkku FIN............68 C3
Pombal P............24 B2
Pomezí CZ............40 C3
Pomezia I............48 C4
Pomiechówek PL............94 B1
Pomigliano d'Arco I............48 C4
Pommersfelden D............39 D3
Pomorie BG............117 E2
Pomorska (Zatoka) PL............88 A1
Pompei I............48 C4
Poncin F............16 C3
Pondoiráklia GR............101 E1
Pondokómi GR............101 D3
Ponferrada E............18 C3
Poniatowa PL............95 D3
Poniec PL............93 D2
Ponikovica SRB............56 C4
Ponkiškai LT............85 E3
Pons F............15 D3
Ponsacco I............47 D3
Pont-à-Marcq F............12 B1
Pont-à-Mousson F............13 D3
Pont-Audemer F............11 E3
Pont-Aven F............10 B4
Pont Canavese I............17 E3
Pont-Croix F............10 A4
Pont-d'Ain F............16 C3
Pont-de-Chéruy F............16 C3
Pont-de-Dore F............16 A3
Pont-de-l'Arche F............11 F3
Pont-de-Roide F............17 D1
Pont-de-Salars F............21 F1
Pont de Suert E............21 D3
Pont-de-Vaux F............16 C2
Pont-de-Veyle F............16 C3
Pont-d'Espagne F............20 C3
Pont-d'Ouilly F............11 D3
Pont-du-Château F............16 A3
Pont du Gard F............22 B1
Pont-en-Royans F............16 C4
Pont-l'Abbé F............10 A4
Pont-l'Évêque F............11 E3
Pont-Scorff F............14 A1
Pont-St-Esprit F............22 B1
Pont-St Martin I............17 E3
Pont-St-Vincent F............13 D4
Pont-Ste-Maxence F............12 A2
Pont-sur-Yonne F............12 B3
Pontacq F............20 C2
Pontailler-sur-Saône F............16 C1
Pontão P............24 B2
Pontardawe GB............8 C1
Pontarddulais GB............8 C1
Pontarion F............15 F3
Pontarlier F............17 D2
Pontassieve I............47 D2
Pontaubault F............11 D4
Pontaumur F............16 A3
Pontcharra F............17 D3
Pontchartrain F............12 A3
Pontchâteau F............14 C1
Ponte Arche I............43 F4
Ponte-Caldelas E............18 A3
Ponte da Barca P............18 A3
Ponte de Lima P............18 A3
Ponte de Sor P............24 B3
Ponte di Legno I............43 F3
Ponte di Piave I............44 B3
Ponte-Leccia F............23 F4
Ponte nelle Alpi I............44 B3
Ponte S. Pietro I............43 E4
Pontebba I............44 C3

Pontecagnano I............49 D4
Ponteceno I............46 C2
Ponteceso E............18 A2
Pontecorvo I............48 C3
Pontedecimo I............23 F2
Pontedera I............47 D3
Pontedeume E............18 B2
Pontefract GB............7 E4
Pontelandolfo I............49 D3
Pontevedra E............18 A3
Pontevico I............46 C1
Pontfaverger-Moronvilliers F............12 C3
Pontgibaud F............16 A3
Pontigny F............16 B1
Pontinia I............48 B3
Pontinvrea I............23 E1
Pontivy F............15 E1
Pontoise F............12 A2
Pontones E............26 A4
Pontoon IRL............2 B2
Pontorson F............11 D4
Pontremoli I............46 C2
Pontresina CH............43 E3
Pontrieux F............10 B3
Pontrilas GB............8 C2
Pontvallain F............15 E1
Pontypool / Pontypwl GB............8 A4
Pontypridd GB............8 B3
Poole GB............8 C4
Pootsi EE............75 E3
Popadić SRB............56 C3
Pope LV............76 C2
Poperinge B............12 A1
Popielów PL............93 E3
Popinci SRB............56 C2
Popoli I............48 C2
Popov Most BIH............55 F4
Popovac SRB............57 E3
Popovača HR............54 C2
Popovo BG............117 E3
Poppenhausen D............38 C2
Poppi I............47 E2
Poprad PL............97 F1
Poprad SK............116 C1
Poraj PL............97 F1
Porcari I............47 D2
Porchov RUS............115 D1
Porcuna E............29 F2
Pordenone I............44 B4
Poręba PL............98 A1
Poreč HR............54 A3
Porečje (Pareči) LV............83 F2
Pori (Björneborg) FIN............68 C3
Porijai I............81 F2
Porjus S............64 B2
Porkuni EE............73 D2
Porlock GB............8 B3
Pornainen FIN............69 E4
Pörnbach D............43 F1
Pornic F............14 C1
Pornichet F............14 B1
Poronin PL............98 B3
Póros (Kefaloniá) GR............104 B2
Póros (Lefkáda) GR............104 A2
Póros (Nissi) GR............105 E4
Porozina HR............54 A3
Pórpi GR............102 C2
Porrentruy CH............17 E1
Porretta Terme I............47 D2
Porriño E............18 A3
Porsgrunn N............66 B2
Port Askaig GB............6 B1
Port-Barcarès F............21 E4
Port Charlotte GB............6 B1
Port d'Alcúdia E............31 E3
Port d'Andratx E............31 E3
Port-de-Bouc F............22 B2
Port de Pollença E............31 E2
Port de Sóller / Puerto de Sóller E............31 E3
Port Ellen GB............6 B1
Port-en-Bessin F............11 D3
Port Erin GB............6 B2
Port-Eynon GB............8 B2
Port Glasgow GB............6 C1
Port-Joinville F............14 B2
Port-la-Nouvelle F............21 F4
Port-Leucate F............21 F3
Port-Louis F............14 A1
Port-Manech F............14 A1
Port-Navalo F............14 B1
Port of Ness GB............4 B1
Port-St-Louis-du-Rhône F............22 B2
Port St Mary GB............3 E2
Port-Ste-Marie F............21 D1
Port-sur-Saône F............17 D1
Port Talbot GB............8 B2
Port-Vendres F............21 F3
Port William GB............3 F1
Porta Westfalica D............33 D2
Portadown GB............3 D1
Portaferry GB............3 E1
Portalegre P............24 C2
Portalrubio E............26 C1
Portariá GR............101 E3
Portarlington / Cúil an tSúdaire IRL............6 A4
Portavogie GB............3 E1
Portbail F............10 C3
Portbou E............21 F3

Pilistvere EE............72 C3
Pilka EE............73 E3
Pilkuse EE............79 D1
Pille EE............79 E1
Pilori GR............101 D3
Pilos GR............108 A1
Pilsblidene LV............81 D1
Pilskalne (Aizkraukles) LV............82 B2
Pilskalne (Daugavpils) LV............83 D2
Pilskalns LV............79 E3
Pilskalns (Pilskolns) LV............83 E1
Pilsrundale LV............81 F2
Pilštanj SLO............54 B2
Pilsūdai LT............80 C3
Piltene LV............76 B3
Pilvingiai LT............85 E1
Pilviškiai LT............85 D2
Pilzno PL............98 C2
Piña de Campos E............19 E3
Pina de Ebro E............20 C4
Pińczów PL............98 B1
Pineda de la Sierra E............19 E3
Pineda de Mar E............21 E4
Pinerolo I............17 E4
Pines LV............77 D3
Pineto I............48 C2
Piney F............12 C4
pingeyri IS............62 A1
pingvellir IS............62 A2
Pinhal Novo P............24 A3
Pinhão P............18 B4
Pinheiro P............18 A4
Pinhel P............24 C1
Pinkafeld A............45 E2
Pinneberg D............33 E3
Pino F............23 F2
Pinofranqueado E............25 D3
Pinols F............16 A4
Pinos Puente E............29 F3
Pinoso / El Pinós E............26 C4
Pinsk BY............115 D4
Pinska EE............78 C1
Pintamo FIN............65 E2
Pinto E............25 F2

Pinzano al Tagliamento I............44 C3
Pinzolo I............43 F4
Piobbico I............47 F3
Piombino I............47 D4
Pione I............46 C2
Pionki PL............94 C2
Pionsat F............16 A3
Piotrków Kujawski PL............93 F1
Piotrków Pierwszy PL............95 E2
Piotrków Trybunalski PL............94 A3
Piove di Sacco I............47 E1
Piovene Rocchette I............43 F4
Pipéri (Nissi) GR............106 B1
Pipiki LV............76 B2
Pipriac F............14 C1
Pirãgi LV............81 F2
Piran SLO............54 A3
Pirčiupiai LT............86 B3
Pireás GR............105 F3
Pirgadikia GR............102 A3
Pirgetós GR............101 F4
Pirgi GR............102 B1
Pirgi GR............101 E2
Pirgi GR............100 B4
Pirgi GR............107 D2
Pirgos GR............101 F2
Pirgos GR............105 E2
Pirgos GR............107 E3
Pirgos GR............104 C3
Pirgos GR............109 F4
Pirgu EE............72 D2
Piriac-sur-Mer F............14 B1
Pirkkala FIN............69 D3
Pirmasens D............13 F3
Pirna D............39 F1
Pirok MK............59 E3
Pirot SRB............57 F4
Pirsógiani GR............100 C3
Pirttikoski FIN............65 E1
Pisa I............47 D2
Pisciotta I............50 C2
Pisek CZ............40 C3
Pisisaare EE............72 C3

Piski PL............91 D3
Piškorevci HR............55 E2
Pisogne I............43 E4
Pisses GR............106 B4
Pissódéri GR............101 D2
Pissónas GR............105 F2
Pissos F............20 C1
Pisticci I............49 F4
Pistoia I............47 D2
Pisz PL............91 D2
Piteå S............64 C3
Pitești RO............117 D3
Pithagório GR............107 F3
Pithio GR............103 E1
Pithio GR............101 E3
Pithiviers F............12 A4
Pitigliano I............47 E4
Pitlochry GB............4 C1
Pitomača HR............55 D2
Pitrags LV............76 C2
Pivka SLO............54 A2
Pivnica SRB............55 F2
Pivnice SRB............55 F2
Piwniczna Zdrój PL............98 C3
Pizarra E............29 E3
Pizzighettone I............46 C1
Pizzo I............51 D3
Pizzoli I............47 F4
Plabennec F............10 A4
Placis LV............78 B2
Plagiá GR............103 E1
Plagiá GR............101 F1
Plaisance F............20 C2
Plaka GR............103 D2
Plaka GR............103 D3
Plaka GR............105 E4
Plaka Litohórou GR............101 F3
Plakiás GR............109 E4
Plana BIH............58 B3
Planá CZ............40 B3
Plancoët F............10 C4
Plandište SRB............57 D2
Pláni LV............78 C2
Plánice CZ............40 B3

Planina SLO............54 A1
Planina SLO............54 B2
Planina SLO............54 A2
Planinica SRB............57 E3
Plános GR............104 B3
Plasencia E............25 D2
Plaška PL............91 D1
Plaški HR............54 B3
Plaskūnai LT............85 F2
Plasy CZ............40 B2
Platamona Lido I............50 A2
Platamónas GR............102 B2
Platamónas GR............101 F4
Platanákia GR............101 F1
Platanés GR............109 E4
Platania I............51 D3
Plataniá GR............102 B2
Plataniá GR............105 E1
Platánia GR............104 C4
Plataniás GR............109 D3
Platanistós GR............106 B3
Plátanos (Arkadía) GR............105 D4
Plátanos (Magnissía) GR............105 D1
Platariá GR............100 B4
Plateés GR............105 E3
Plateliai GR............80 B2
Platerów PL............95 E1
Platerówka PL............92 B3
Platiána GR............104 C4
Plátičevo SRB............56 C2
Platigiali GR............104 C2
Platikambos GR............101 F4
Platis Gialós GR............106 B4
Platis Gialós GR............109 E1
Platis Gialós (Kefaloniá) GR............104 A4
Platístomo GR............105 D1
Platja d'Aro E............21 F4
Platja de Sant Joan E............27 D4
Platja i Grau de Gandia E............27 D3
Platone LV............81 E1

Portel P.....24 B4
Portelo P.....18 C3
Pórtes (N. Égina) GR.....105 F3
Portezuelo E.....25 D2
Portglenone GB.....3 D1
Porthcawl GB.....8 B3
Porthmadog GB.....3 F3
Portici I.....48 C4
Portilla de la Reina E.....19 E4
Portillo E.....19 E4
Portimão P.....28 A2
Portimo FIN.....65 D2
Portinho da Arrábida P.....24 A3
Portishead GB.....8 C2
Portlaoise /
  Port Laoise IRL.....2 C3
Portman E.....30 C2
Portmarnock IRL.....3 D3
Portnacroish GB.....4 B2
Portnaguran GB.....4 A1
Portnahaven GB.....6 B1
Porto F.....23 F3
Porto P.....18 A4
Porto Alto P.....24 A3
Porto Azzurro I.....47 D4
Pórto Boúfalo GR.....105 F2
Pórto Carrás GR.....102 A3
Porto Ceresio I.....17 C3
Porto Cervo I.....50 B2
Porto Cesareo I.....51 F1
Porto Cristo E.....31 F3
Porto de Lagos P.....28 A2
Porto de Mós P.....24 A2
Porto do Barqueiro P.....18 B1
Porto do Son E.....18 A2
Porto Empedocle I.....52 C4
Porto Ercole I.....47 D4
Porto Garibaldi I.....47 E1
Portó Germenó GR.....105 E3
Pórto Kágio GR.....108 B2
Porto Pino I.....50 A4
Pórto Ráfti GR.....105 F3
Porto Recanati I.....48 B1
Porto Rotondo I.....50 B2
Porto S. Elpidio I.....48 B1
Porto S. Giorgio I.....48 B1
Porto Santo Stefano I.....47 D4
Porto Tolle I.....47 E1
Porto Torres I.....50 A2
Porto-Vecchio I.....23 F4
Portofino I.....23 F1
Portogruaro I.....44 B4
Portohéli GR.....105 E4
Pörtom FIN.....68 C2
Portomaggiore I.....47 E1
Portomarín E.....18 B3
Portomouro E.....18 A2
Portonovo E.....18 A3
Portopetro E.....31 F3

Portorož SLO.....54 A3
Portoscuso I.....50 A4
Portovenere I.....46 C2
Portpatrick GB.....3 E1
Portree GB.....4 B3
Portrush GB.....6 B2
Portsalon IRL.....6 A2
Pörtschach A.....44 C3
Portsmouth GB.....9 D4
Portstewart GB.....6 A2
Portugalete E.....19 F2
Portumna /
  Port Omna IRL.....2 C3
Poruba E.....41 F2
Porvoo / Borgå FIN.....69 E4
Porzuna E.....25 F3
Posada I.....50 B2
Posadas E.....29 E2
Poschiavo CH.....43 E4
Pošechonje-
  Volodarsk RUS.....115 F1
Posedarje HR.....54 C4
Positano I.....48 C4
Poškakaimis LT.....80 C3
Poškonys LT.....86 C3
Possidi GR.....102 A3
Possidónia GR.....106 C4
Posta I.....47 F4
Postira HR.....58 A4
Postojna SLO.....54 A2
Postomino PL.....89 D1
Póšupes LT.....81 E2
Posušje BIH.....58 A4
Poświętne
  (Łodzkie) PL.....94 B2
Poświętne
  (Mazowieckie) PL.....94 C1
Poświętne
  (Podlaskie) PL.....91 E3
Potamí GR.....102 B1
Potamiá GR.....108 B3
Potamiés GR.....109 F4
Potamós
  (N. Andikithira) GR.....108 C3
Potamós
  (N. Kithira) GR.....108 B2
Potamoúla GR.....104 C2
Potęgowo PL.....89 D1
Potenza I.....49 E4
Potenza Picena I.....48 B1
Potes E.....19 E2
Potigny F.....11 E3
Potoci BIH.....58 A2
Potok HR.....54 C2
Potorova LV.....83 F1
Potós GR.....102 B2
Potsdam D.....34 B4
Pottenstein A.....45 E1

Potters Bar GB.....9 E3
Pöttmes D.....43 F1
Potton GB.....9 E2
Potworów PL.....94 B2
Pouancé F.....14 C1
Pougues-les-Eaux F.....16 A2
Pouilly-en-Auxois F.....16 B1
Pouilly-sous-Charlieu F.....16 B3
Pouilly-sur-Loire F.....16 A1
Poúlithra GR.....105 E4
Poúnda GR.....109 F1
Pournári GR.....105 D1
Poussu FIN.....65 E2
Pouyastruc F.....20 C2
Pouzauges F.....15 D2
Považská Bystrica SK.....116 B1
Poveda de la Sierra E.....26 B3
Povilai LT.....80 A3
Povlja HR.....58 A4
Povljana HR.....54 B4
Powidz PL.....93 E1
Powodowo PL.....92 C2
Powroźnik PL.....98 C3
Poysdorf A.....41 E4
Poza de la Sal E.....19 F3
Požarane SRB.....59 E3
Požarevac SRB.....57 D2
Požarki PL.....90 C1
Požečiai LT.....85 E1
Požega SRB.....56 C4
Požega HR.....55 D2
Požerė LT.....80 C3
Požerūnai LT.....84 C1
Pozezdrze PL.....91 D1
Poznań PL.....93 D1
Prauthoy F.....16 C1
Pozo Alcón E.....30 A2
Pozo Cañada E.....26 B4
Pozo de Guadalajara E.....26 A3
Pozo Higuera E.....30 B3
Pozoblanco E.....25 E4
Pozohondo E.....26 C1
Pozondón E.....26 C1
Pozuelo E.....26 C1
Pozuelo de Calatrava E.....25 F3
Pozuelo de Zarzón E.....25 D2
Pozzallo I.....53 E4
Pozzuoli I.....48 C4
Pozzuolo del Friuli I.....44 C4
Pra-Loup F.....22 C1
Prabašćiškes LT.....86 C3
Prabuty PL.....89 F2
Prača BIH.....55 F4
Pradła PL.....98 A1

Prado del Rey E.....29 D3
Pradoluengo E.....19 F3
Præstø DK.....70 C4
Pragarele LT.....81 F3
Prägraten A.....44 B2
Praha CZ.....40 C2
Prahecq F.....15 D3
Praia a Mare I.....51 D2
Praia da Barra P.....24 B1
Praia da Rocha P.....28 A2
Praia da Tocha P.....24 A1
Praia da Vieira P.....24 A2
Praia de Mira P.....24 A1
Praia de Santa Cruz P.....24 A2
Prali I.....17 E4
Pralognan-la-Vanoise F.....17 D4
Prámanda GR.....100 C2
Pramedžiava LT.....85 D1
Prangio GR.....103 E1
Prangli EE.....79 E1
Pranjani SRB.....56 C3
Prapatnica HR.....58 A4
Prašćiūnai LT.....81 E3
Prassiá GR.....104 C1
Prassiés GR.....109 E4
Praszka PL.....93 F3
Prat del Comte E.....27 E1
Pratella I.....48 C3
Prati di Tivo I.....48 B2
Prato I.....47 D2
Prato I.....47 E4
Pratola Peligna I.....48 C2
Prats de Lluçanès E.....21 E4
Prats-de-Mollo-
  la-Preste F.....21 F3
Prauliai LT.....85 F1
Prauliena LV.....83 D1
Prauthoy F.....16 C1
Pravdinsk RUS.....114 C3
Pravia E.....19 D2
Pravienišķes I LT.....85 F2
Pravienišķes II LT.....85 F2
Pré-en-Pail F.....11 E4
Pré-St Didier I.....17 E3
Prebold SLO.....54 B2
Précy-sous-Thil F.....16 B1
Predappio I.....47 E2
Preddvor SLO.....54 A2
Predeal RO.....117 D1
Predejane SRB.....57 F4
Predel SLO.....54 A1
Predoi / Prettau I.....44 B2
Predošćica HR.....54 B3
Preetz D.....33 F2
Pregarten A.....44 C1
Preili LV.....83 D2
Prekaja BIH.....55 D4
Preko HR.....54 B3
Preljina SRB.....57 D3

Prelog HR.....54 C1
Preločšica HR.....54 C2
Přelouč CZ.....41 D2
Premantura HR.....54 A2
Prémery F.....16 A1
Premià de Mar E.....21 F4
Premilcuore I.....47 E2
Premnitz D.....34 B4
Prémuda HR.....54 B4
Premuda (Otok) HR.....54 B4
Prenzlau D.....34 C3
Přerov CZ.....41 F3
Prerow D.....34 A1
Preševo SRB.....59 E3
Presjeka MNE.....58 C2
Prešov SK.....116 C1
Préspa (Mikrí/Megáli
  Préspa) GR.....100 C2
Pressath D.....39 E3
Pressbaum A.....45 E1
Prestatyn GB.....3 F3
Presteigne GB.....8 C2
Prestfoss N.....66 B2
Přeštice CZ.....40 B3
Preston GB.....7 D4
Prestonpans GB.....7 D1
Prestwick GB.....6 C1
Pretoro I.....48 C2
Prettin D.....39 E1
Pretzsch D.....39 E1
Preuilly-sur-Claise F.....15 E2
Préveza GR.....104 B1
Prevršac HR.....54 C2
Prezid HR.....54 B2
Prezma LV.....83 E2
Prialgava LV.....81 D2
Pribini BIH.....55 E3
Priboj BIH.....55 F3
Priboj SRB.....56 C4
Příbor CZ.....41 F3
Příbram CZ.....40 C3
Priedaine LV.....76 C3
Priedāji LV.....78 B2
Priedes (Dobeles) LV.....81 A1
Priedes (Limbažu) LV.....78 B2
Priedes (Talsu) LV.....77 D3
Priedes
  (Valmieras) LV.....78 C2
Priednieki LV.....82 C1
Priedula LV.....81 D2
Priego E.....26 B3
Priego de Córdoba E.....29 F2
Priekule LV.....80 B3
Priekule LV.....80 B1
Priekuļi LV.....78 C3
Prien D.....44 B1
Prienai (Kauno) LT.....85 E2
Prienai (Vilniaus) LT.....86 C2
Prievidza SK.....116 B1
Priežmale LV.....83 E2

Priežu Sils LV.....83 D2
Prigradica HR.....58 A3
Prijeboj HR.....54 C3
Prijedor BIH.....55 D3
Prijepolje SRB.....56 C4
Prikuli LV.....83 D2
Prilep MK.....59 E4
Prilike SRB.....56 C4
Prillimäe EE.....78 B2
Priluka BIH.....55 D4
Primel-Trégastel F.....10 B3
Primišlje HR.....54 B3
Primolano I.....43 F4
Primorsk RUS.....115 D1
Primošten HR.....58 A4
Primstal D.....13 E2
Princetown GB.....8 B4
Prinés GR.....109 E4
Pringi EE.....72 B1
Prinkas LV.....77 F2
Prínos GR.....102 C2
Prisad MK.....59 E4
Prisoje BIH.....55 D4
Pritzerbe D.....34 B4
Pritzier D.....33 F3
Pritzwalk D.....34 A3
Privas F.....16 C4
Priverno I.....48 B3
Privlaka (Vukovar) HR.....55 F2
Privlaka (Zadar) HR.....54 B4
Prizren SRB.....59 D3
Prizzi I.....52 C3
Prnjavor BIH.....55 E3
Prnjavor SRB.....55 F3
Proaza E.....19 D2
Probište MK.....59 E4
Probstzella D.....39 D2
Prochowice PL.....92 C3
Procida I.....48 C4
Pročiūnai I LT.....81 E2
Pródromos GR.....105 D2
Proença-a-Nova P.....24 B2
Proevska Banja MK.....59 E3
Profitis Ilías GR.....111 F2
Profondeville B.....12 C2
Próhoma GR.....101 F2
Prokópi GR.....105 F2
Prokuplje SRB.....57 E4
Prolom SRB.....57 E4
Prómahi GR.....101 E2
Promahónas GR.....102 A1
Promíri GR.....105 E1
Promna PL.....94 C2
Pronsfeld D.....13 D2
Propriano F.....23 F4
Prositi PL.....90 B1
Proskinás GR.....105 E2
Prossedi I.....48 B3
Prossílio GR.....102 C1

Prossotsáni GR.....102 B1
Prostějov CZ.....41 E3
Prostki PL.....91 D2
Prószków PL.....97 E1
Proszowice PL.....98 B2
Próti GR.....102 B2
Próti (Nissí) GR.....108 A1
Protoklíssi GR.....103 E1
Prötzel D.....34 C3
Proussós GR.....104 C2
Provatónas GR.....103 E1
Provenchères-
  sur-Fave F.....13 E4
Provins F.....12 B4
Prozor BIH.....55 E4
Pruchnik PL.....99 E2
Prudhoe GB.....7 E3
Prudnik PL.....97 D2
Prüm D.....13 D2
Pruna E.....29 E3
Prunetta I.....47 D2
Prūsaliai LT.....80 B2
Prūseliai
  (Marijampoles) LT.....85 D1
Prūseliai
  (Panevežio) LT.....82 A3
Prusice PL.....93 D3
Pruszcz PL.....89 E2
Pruszcz Gdański PL.....89 F1
Pruszków PL.....94 B1
Pružany BY.....115 D4
Prvić (Otok) HR.....54 B3
Pryluky UA.....115 F4
Przasnysz PL.....90 C2
Przechlewo PL.....89 D2
Przecisznów PL.....98 A2
Przedbórz
  (Łodzkie) PL.....94 A3
Przedecz PL.....93 F1
Przelewice PL.....88 B3
Przemków PL.....92 C2
Przemyśl PL.....99 E2
Przerośl PL.....91 D1
Przesmyki PL.....95 E1
Przeworno PL.....97 C1
Przeworsk PL.....99 E2
Przewóz PL.....92 B2
Przezmark PL.....90 A2
Przodkowo PL.....89 E1
Przybiernów PL.....88 A2
Przygodzice PL.....93 E2
Przykona PL.....93 F2
Przyłęk
  (Mazowieckie) PL.....95 D3
Przyrów PL.....93 F3
Przystajń PL.....93 F3
Przysucha PL.....94 B3
Przytoczna PL.....88 B3
Przytuły PL.....91 D2
Przytyk PL.....94 C3

Przywidz PL.....89 E1
Przywory PL.....97 E1
Psača MK.....59 F3
Psahná GR.....105 F2
Psáka GR.....100 B3
Psará GR.....107 D2
Psará (Nissí) GR.....107 C3
Psarádes GR.....100 C2
Psári GR.....105 D3
Psári GR.....104 C4
Psáthi GR.....109 E1
Psathópirgos GR.....104 C2
Psathotópi GR.....104 C1
Psérimos (Nissí) GR.....111 E1
Psie Pole PL.....93 D3
Psihikó GR.....101 E4
Psihró GR.....109 F4
Psínthos GR.....111 F2
Pskov RUS.....115 D1
Pszczółki PL.....89 F1
Pszczyna PL.....97 F2
Pszów PL.....97 E2
Pteléa GR.....102 B1
Ptolemaïda GR.....101 D2
Ptuj SLO.....54 C1
Puchaczów PL.....95 D3
Puchberg
  am Schneeberg A.....45 E1
Pučišća HR.....58 A4
Puck PL.....89 E1
Puckeridge GB.....9 F2
Pückoriai LT.....80 B2
Puçol E.....27 D3
Pudasjärvi /
  Kurenalus FIN.....65 D2
Pūdinova LV.....83 E1
Pūdukolni LV.....83 E1
Puebla de Alcocer E.....25 E3
Puebla de Almenara E.....26 A3
Puebla de Beleña E.....26 A1
Puebla
  de Don Fadrique E.....30 B2
Puebla
  de Don Rodrigo E.....25 E3
Puebla de Guzmán E.....28 C2
Puebla de la Calzada E.....24 C3
Puebla de la Reina E.....25 D3
Puebla de Lillo E.....19 E3
Puebla de Obando E.....24 C3
Puebla de Sanabria E.....18 C3
Puebla de Trives E.....18 C3
Publica de Valverde E.....19 D3
Puente
  de Domingo Flórez E.....18 C3
Puente de Génave E.....26 A4
Puente de los Fierros E.....19 D2
Puente de Montañana E.....21 D4
Puente-Genil E.....29 F2
Puente la Reina E.....20 B3

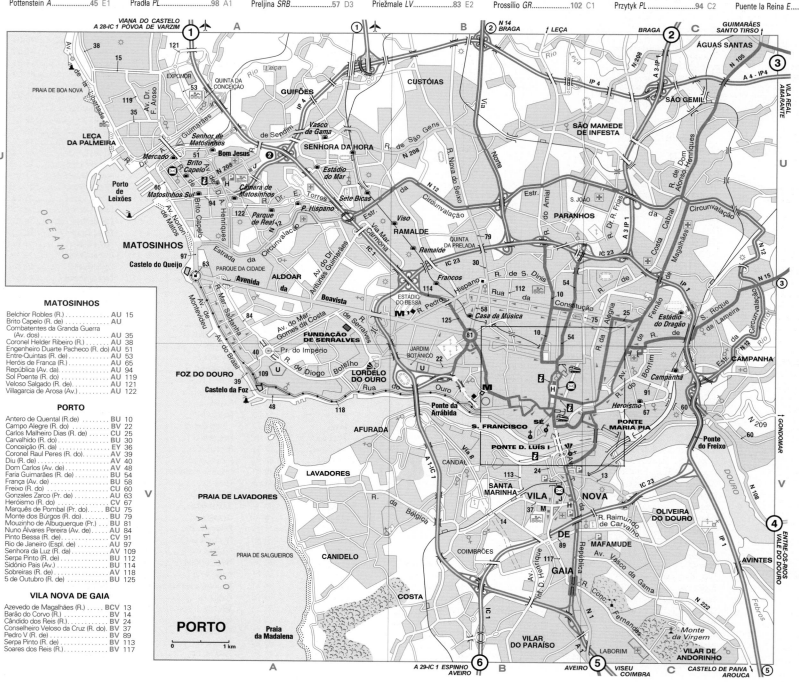

MATOSINHOS
Belchior Robles (R.)..........AU 15
Brito Capelo (R. de)..........AU
Combatentes da Granda Guerra
  (Av. dos)..........AU 35
Coronel Helder Ribeiro (R.)..........AU 38
Engenheiro Duarte Pacheco (R. do)..........AU 51
Entre-Quintas (R.)..........AU 53
Heróis de França (R.)..........AU 65
República (Av. da)..........AU 94
Sol Poente (R. de)..........AU 119
Veloso Salgado (R. de)..........AU 121
Villagarcia de Arosa (Av.)..........AU 122

PORTO
Antero de Quental (R.de)..........BU 10
Campo Alegre (R. do)..........BV 22
Carlos Malheiro Dias (R. de)..........CU 25
Carvalhido (R.)..........BU 30
Conceição (R. da)..........EY 36
Coronel Raul Peres (R. do)..........AV 39
Diu (R. de)..........AV 40
Dom Carlos (Av. de)..........AV 48
Faria Guimarães (R. de)..........BU 54
França (Av. de)..........BU 58
Freixo (R. do)..........CU 60
Gonzalez Zarco (Pr. de)..........AV 63
Heroísmo (R. do)..........CV 67
Marquês de Pombal (Pr. do)..........BCU 75
Monte dos Búrgos (R.)..........BU 79
Mouzinho de Albuquerque (Pr.)..........BU 81
Nuno Alvares Pereira (Av. de)..........BU 84
Pinto Bessa (R. de)..........CV 91
Rio de Janeiro (Espl. de)..........AV 97
Senhora da Luz (R. da)..........AV 109
Serpa Pinto (R. de)..........BU 112
Sidónio Pais (R. de)..........BU 114
Sobreiras (R. de)..........AV 118
5 de Outubro (R. de)..........BU 125

VILA NOVA DE GAIA
Azevedo de Magalhães (R.).....BV 13
Barão do Corvo (R.)..........BV 14
Cândido dos Reis (R.)..........BV 24
Conselheiro Veloso da Cruz (R. do).....BV 37
Pedro V (R. de)..........BV 89
Serpa Pinto (R. de)..........BV 113
Soares dos Reis (R.)..........BV 117

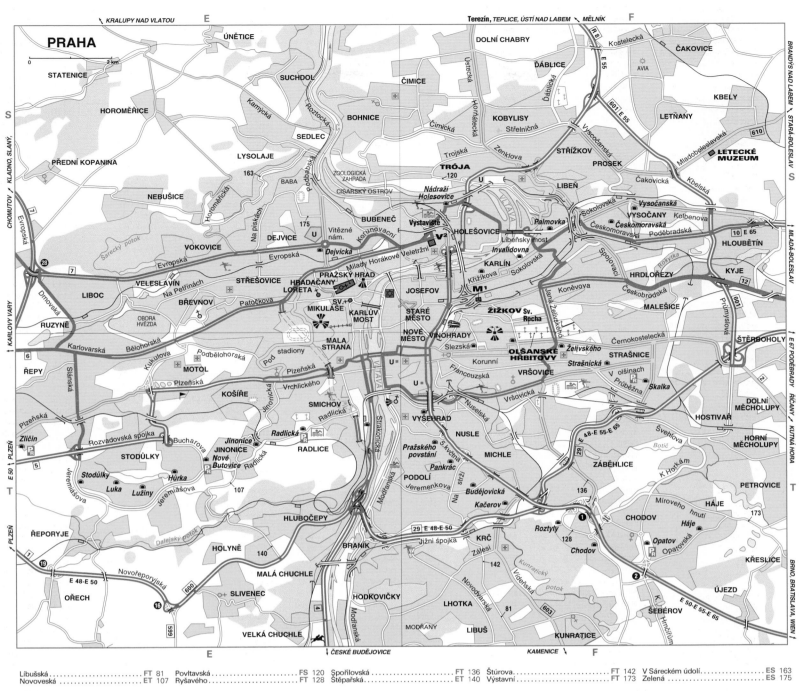

Libušská...............FT 81
Novoveská.............ET 107
Povltavská............FS 120
Ryšavého..............FT 128
Spořilovská...........FT 136
Štěpařská.............ET 140
Štúrova...............FT 142
Výstavní..............FT 173
V Sáreckém údolí......ES 163
Zelená................ES 175

Puente
　la Reina de Jaca E.....20 C3
Puente Viesgo E.....19 F2
Puentenansa E.....19 E2
Puerto Castilla E.....25 E2
Puerto de la Encina E.....29 E3
Puerto de Mazarrón E.....30 C2
Puerto
　de San Vicente E.....25 E1
Puerto Lápice E.....26 A3
Puerto Lumbreras E.....30 B2
Puerto Real E.....29 C3
Puerto Serrano E.....29 D3
Puertollano E.....25 F4
Puget-Théniers F.....23 D1
Pühajärve EE.....79 D1
Pühajõe EE.....73 F2
Puhja EE.....79 D1
Puhos FIN.....69 F2
Puhos (Oulu) FIN.....65 E2
Puiatu EE.....78 C1
Puig-reig E.....21 E4
Puiga EE.....79 E2
Puigcerdà E.....21 E3
Puikule LV.....78 E2
Puiseaux F.....12 A4
Puisserguier F.....21 F2
Pujols F.....15 D4
Puka EE.....79 D1
Pukë AL.....116 C4
Pukenieki LV.....76 A3
Pukiš BIH.....55 F3
Pukkila FIN.....69 E4
Puksti LV.....79 D3
Pula HR.....54 A3
Pula I.....50 A4
Puławy PL.....95 D2
Pulborough GB.....9 C4
Pulkau A.....41 D4
Pulkkila FIN.....65 D3
Pullans LV.....79 E2
Pulpi E.....30 B3
Pulsnitz D.....39 F1
Pulstakai LT.....86 B3
Pultusk PL.....90 C3
Pumpenai LT.....81 F2
Pumpuri LV.....80 C1
Punakülä EE.....78 C1
Pūnas LV.....77 F3
Punat HR.....54 B3
Punduri LV.....83 F2
Punia LT.....85 F2
Punkaharju FIN.....69 F2

Punkalaidun FIN.....68 C3
Punta Ala I.....47 D4
Punta Križa HR.....54 B3
Punta Umbría E.....28 C3
Puntuži I.....83 D1
Puodkaliai LT.....80 B2
Puodžiai LT.....81 F2
Puodžiūnai
　(Kyburiai) LT.....81 F2
Puodžiūnai
　(Pasvalys) LT.....81 F2
Puoke LT.....80 C2
Puokio FIN.....65 E3
Puolanka FIN.....65 E3
Puoriai LT.....86 B2
Pupiške LT.....86 C1
Pūpoli LV.....78 C2
Puponys LT.....82 B3
Purbach am
　Neusierdler See A.....45 E1
Purchena E.....30 B3
Purda PL.....90 B2
Pūre LV.....77 D3
Purgstall A.....45 D1
Purila EE.....72 B2
Purkersdorf A.....45 E1
Pürksi EE.....75 D1
Purku EE.....72 B3
Purmali LV.....80 B1
Purmerend NL.....32 B4
Purmsäti LV.....80 B1
Purtse EE.....73 E2
Purullena E.....30 A3
Purvenai LT.....80 C2
Purvini LV.....81 F1
Purviniške LT.....85 E2
Purvižkiai LT.....85 E1
Purvyne LT.....82 C3
Puša LV.....83 E2
Pušalotas LT.....81 F2
Pūšiliai LT.....81 D2
Puškin RUS.....115 D1
Puškoniai LT.....81 F2
Pušmucova LV.....83 F1
Pusne LT.....86 B1
Püspökladány H.....116 C2
Püssi EE.....73 E2
Pusta Kuznica PL.....97 F1
Pustinka LV.....83 E2
Pustoška RUS.....115 D2
Pusula FIN.....69 D4
Puszcza Mariańska PL.....94 C2
Puszczykowo PL.....93 D1
Putanges-
　Pont-Écrepin F.....11 E4

Putbus D.....34 B1
Putgarten D.....34 B1
Putignano I.....49 F3
Putkaste EE.....74 C2
Putlitz D.....34 A3
Putni LV.....81 F2
Puttelange-aux-Lacs F.....13 E3
Putten NL.....32 B4
Puttgarden D.....33 F1
Putyv'l UA.....115 F4
Puumala FIN.....69 F3
Püünsi EE.....72 B1
Puuri EE.....79 E1
Puurmani EE.....73 D3
Puusepa EE.....79 E2
Puy-Guillaume F.....16 A3
Puy-l'Évêque F.....21 D1
Puylaurens F.....21 E2
Puymirol F.....21 D1
Pužal LT.....80 C3
Puze LV.....76 C2
Pwllheli GB.....3
Pyhäjärvi FIN.....69 D1
Pyhäjoki FIN.....65 D3
Pyhäjoki FIN.....68 C3
Pyhältö FIN.....69 E3
Pyhäntä FIN.....65 E3
Pyhäntä FIN.....65 E3
Pyhäranta FIN.....68 C4
Pyhäsalmi FIN.....69 D1
Pyhäselkä FIN.....69 F2
Pyhtää / Pyttis FIN.....69 E4
Pyktiške LT.....80 B3
Pyla-sur-Mer F.....20 B1
Pylkönmäki FIN.....69 D2
Pypliai LT.....86 B1
Pyrjatyn UA.....115 F4
Pyry PL.....94 C2
Pyrzyce PL.....88 A3
Pyskowice PL.....97 F1
Pyzdry PL.....93 E2

Q

Quakenbrück D.....33 D4
Quarré-les-Tombes F.....16 B1
Quarteira P.....28 B3
Quarto d'Altino I.....44 B4
Quartu S. Elena I.....50 B4
Quatretonda E.....27 D4
Quedlinburg D.....39 D1
Queenborough GB.....9 F3

Queensferry GB.....8 C1
Queluz P.....24 A3
Queralbs E.....21 E3
Querfurt D.....39 D1
Quérigut F.....21 E3
Quero E.....26 A3
Quesada
　(Estación de) E.....30 A2
Questembert F.....14 B1
Quettehou F.....11 D2
Quiberon F.....14 B1
Quickborn D.....33 E2
Quiévrain B.....12 B2
Quigley's Point IRL.....6 A2
Quillan F.....21 E3
Quillebeuf-sur-Seine F.....11 D3
Quimper F.....10 A4
Quimperlé F.....10 B4
Quincinetto I.....43 F4
Quincoces de Yuso E.....19 F2
Quingey F.....17 D2
Quintana
　de la Serena E.....25 D3
Quintana del Puente E.....19 E3
Quintana-Martín
　Galíndez E.....19 F3
Quintana Redonda E.....20 A4
Quintanar
　de la Orden E.....26 A3
Quintanar
　de la Sierra E.....19 F4
Quintanar del Rey E.....26 B3
Quintanilha P.....18 C4
Quintanilla de Onésimo E.....19 E4
Quintin F.....10 B4
Quinto E.....20 C4
Quinzano d'Oglio I.....46 C1
Quiroga E.....18 B3
Quissac F.....22 A1

R

Raab A.....44 C1
Raabs an der Thaya A.....41 D4
Raadama EE.....79 E1
Raahe FIN.....65 D3
Raajärvi FIN.....65 D1
Rääkkylä FIN.....69 F3
Raalte NL.....32 C4
Raanujärvi FIN.....65 D1
Raasiku EE.....72 B2
Raate FIN.....65 F3

Raattama FIN.....61 E3
Rab HR.....54 B3
Rab (Otok) HR.....54 B3
Raba Wyżna PL.....98 B3
Rabac HR.....54 A3
Rábade E.....18 B2
Rabastens F.....21 E2
Rabastens-de-Bigorre F.....20 C2
Rabat M.....32 F4
Rabe HR.....99 E3
Rabe SRB.....56 C1
Rábida
　(Monasterio de la) E.....28 C2
Rabikiai LT.....81 F3
Rąbino PL.....88 C2
Rabivere EE.....72 B2
Rabka-Zdrój PL.....98 B3
Rabrovo MK.....59 F4
Rabrovo SRB.....57 D2
Rača
　(Kragujevac) SRB.....57 D3
Rača (Priština) SRB.....57 D4
Rača / Bosanska
　Rača BIH.....55 F2
Racconigi I.....17 E4
Rače SLO.....54 B1
Račeva LV.....83 F2
Rachanie PL.....99 F1
Rachiv UA.....117 D2
Raciąż (Kujawsko-
　Pomorskie) PL.....89 E2
Raciąż
　(Mazowieckie) PL.....90 B3
Raciborowice PL.....95 F3
Racibórz PL.....97 E2
Raciechowice PL.....98 B2
Račinovci HR.....55 F3
Račišće HR.....58 A3
Racławice PL.....98 B2
Račova LV.....83 F2
Raczki PL.....91 F1
Radailiai LT.....80 A3
Radalj SRB.....55 F3
Rădăuţi RO.....117 D2
Rade D.....33 E3
Råde N.....66 C2
Radeberg D.....39 F1
Radebeul D.....39 F1
Radeburg D.....39 F1
Radeče SLO.....54 B2
Radechiv UA.....117 D1
Radečnica PL.....99 F1
Radegunda SLO.....54 B1
Radeikiai LT.....82 C3
Radenci SLO.....54 C1

Radenthein A.....44 C3
Radevormwald D.....37 E2
Radicondoli I.....47 D3
Radimlja BIH.....58 B3
Radiovce MK.....59 E3
Radków
　(Dolnośląskie) PL.....96 C1
Radlin PL.....94 C3
Radlje ob Dravi SLO.....54 B1
Radljevo SRB.....56 C3
Radłów
　(Małopolskie) PL.....98 C2
Radłów (Opolskie) PL.....93 F3
Radnice CZ.....40 B3
Radolevo SRB.....56 C1
Radolfzell D.....17 F1
Radom PL.....94 C3
Radomice PL.....89 F3
Radomin PL.....89 F3
Radomsko PL.....94 A3
Radomyšl' UA.....115 E4
Radomyśl Wielki PL.....98 C2
Radopole LV.....83 E1
Radostowice PL.....97 F2
Radoszyce PL.....94 B3
Radotín CZ.....40 C3
Radovče MNE.....58 C3
Radovići MNE.....58 B3
Radoviš MK.....59 F3
Radovljica SLO.....54 A2
Radovnica SRB.....59 F3
Radruż PL.....99 F2
Radstadt A.....44 C2
Radstock GB.....8 C3
Raduša MNE.....59 E3
Radviliškis LT.....81 E3
Radvilonys LT.....85 E3
Radwanice
　(Dolnośląskie) PL.....92 C2
Radymno PL.....99 E2
Radzanów
　(Mazowieckie) PL.....94 C2
Radziejów PL.....89 F3
Radziejowice PL.....94 B2
Radzików PL.....91 D2
Radziwie PL.....90 B2
Radzymin PL.....94 C1
Radzyń Chełmiński PL.....89 F2
Radzyń Podlaski PL.....95 E2
Rae EE.....72 B2
Raesfeld D.....37 D1
Raffadali I.....52 C3
Rafina GR.....105 E3
Ragaciems LV.....77 D3

Rágama E.....25 E1
Ragana LT.....78 B3
Ragaz, Bad CH.....43 D3
Rageliai LT.....82 C3
Raglan GB.....8 C2
Ragozãi LT.....85 F1
Raguhn D.....39 E1
Ragūnai LT.....86 C2
Ragunda S.....68 A2
Ragusa I.....53 D4
Raguva LT.....81 F3
Raguvele LT.....81 F3
Raguviškiai LT.....80 B2
Rahačoū BY.....115 D3
Rahden D.....33 F4
Ráhes GR.....105 E1
Rahinge EE.....79 D1
Rahkla EE.....73 D2
Rahlstedt D.....33 F3
Rahóni GR.....102 C2
Rahumäe EE.....79 E1
Raibãmuiža LV.....80 B1
Raigaste EE.....79 D1
Raigla EE.....79 E1
Raikküla EE.....72 B2
Rain a. Lech D.....43 E1
Räisäla FIN.....65 E1
Raisio FIN.....68 C4
Raiskums LV.....78 B3
Raiste EE.....79 E1
Raitijärvi FIN.....61 D2
Raja (Jaskinia) PL.....94 B3
Raja Jooseppi FIN.....61 F3
Rajac SRB.....57 F3
Rajadell E.....21 E4
Rajamäki FIN.....69 D4
Rajgród PL.....91 E2
Rajince SRB.....59 E3
Rājumi LV.....81 F1
Raka SLO.....54 B2
Rakai LT.....85 F3

Raków PL.....98 C1
Rakšonys LT.....86 C2
Rakvere EE.....73 D2
Ralja SRB.....57 D3
Ram SRB.....57 D2
Ramacca I.....53 D3
Ramales
　de la Victoria E.....19 F2
Ramallosa E.....18 A2
Ramanava LT.....85 F2
Ramata LV.....78 B3
Rāmava LV.....77 F3
Ramberg N.....60 A3
Rambervillers F.....13 E4
Rambouillet F.....11 F4
Rambucourt F.....13 D3
Ramnoús GR.....105 E3
Ramoniškiai LT.....85 D2
Ramsau
　am Dachstein A.....44 C2
Ramsau
　b. Berchtesgaden D.....44 B2
Ramsele S.....68 A1
Ramsey GB.....3 F2
Ramsey GB.....9 E2
Ramsgate GB.....9 F3
Ramsi EE.....78 C1
Ramsjö S.....63 E4
Ramstein-
　Miesenbach D.....13 E3
Ramsund N.....60 B3
Ramučiai LT.....81 D3
Ramundberget S.....63 D4
Ramvik S.....68 A2
Ramygala LT.....81 F3
Ranalt A.....43 F3
Randaberg N.....66 A2
Randalstown GB.....3 D1
Randan F.....16 A3
Randanne F.....16 A3
Randazzo I.....50 C4
Randers DK.....70 B2
Randvere EE.....72 B1
Rånes S.....64 C2
Rangsdorf D.....34 B4
Rangu EE.....72 A2
Raniżów PL.....99 D2
Ranka LV.....79 D3
Ranki LV.....76 C3
Rankweil A.....43 D2
Rannakülä EE.....79 D1
Rannametsa EE.....75 E3
Rannamõisa EE.....72 B1
Rannapungerja EE.....73 E2
Rannu (Ida-Viru) EE.....73 E1

Rannu (Tartu) EE 79 D1
Ranovac SRB 57 E2
Rantasalmi FIN 69 F2
Rantsila FIN 65 D3
Ranua FIN 65 D2
Raon-l'Étape F 13 E4
Rapallo I 23 F1
Rapice PL 92 A2
Rapla EE 72 B2
Rapolano Terme I 47 E3
Rapolla I 49 E3
Rapperswil CH 17 F1
Rapsáni GR 101 E4
Raptópoulo GR 104 C4
Raša HR 54 A3
Räsälä FIN 69 E2
Rasbo S 67 F2
Rascafría E 25 F1
Raščiūnai LT 87 D1
Rasdorf D 38 C2
Raseiniai LT 81 D3
Rasina EE 79 E1
Raška SRB 57 D4
Rasno BIH 58 A2
Rasnupli LV 83 E1
Rasquera E 27 E1
Rastatt D 13 F3
Rastede D 33 D3
Rastenberg D 39 D1
Rastenfeld A 41 D4
Rastošnica BIH 55 F3
Rasueros E 25 E1
Raszków PL 93 E2
Raszyn PL 94 C1
Rätan S 63 E4
Rateče SLO 54 A1
Ratekau D 33 F2
Rates P 18 A4
Rathdowney IRL 2 C3
Rathdrum /
Ráth Droma IRL 3 E3
Rathenow D 34 B4
Rathfriland GB 3 D2
Rathkeale /
Ráth Caola IRL 2 B3
Rathmelton IRL 6 A2
Rathmore IRL 2 B4
Rathmullan IRL 6 A2
Rathnew IRL 3 D3
Ratingen D 37 E2
Ratkovac SRB 59 D3
Ratkovo SRB 57 D4
Ratnieki (Cēsu) LV 78 B3
Ratnieki (Talsu) LV 77 D3
Ratniki LV 83 F2
Ratten A 45 E1
Rattenberg A 43 F2
Rattersdorf-Liebing A 45 E1
Rattray GB 7 D1
Rättvik S 67 E4
Ratzeburg D 33 F2
Raubling D 44 B2
Raucourt-et-Flaba F 12 C2
Rauda
(Daugavpils) LV 83 D3
Rauda (Tukuma) LV 77 D3
Raudaskylä FIN 65 D3
Raudenai LT 81 D2
Raudondvaris
(Kauno) LT 85 E2
Raudondvaris
(Šiauliu) LT 81 D3
Raudondvaris
(Vilniaus) LT 86 B2
Raudone LT 85 D1
Raudonenai LT 85 D1
Raudoniai LT 80 B2
Raufarhöfn IS 62 B1
Raufoss N 66 C1
Rauha FIN 69 F3
Rauhamäki FIN 69 D3
Rauland N 66 B2
Rauma FIN 68 C3
Rauna LV 78 C3
Rauris A 44 B2
Rautalampi FIN 69 E2
Rautas S 60 C2
Rautavaara FIN 69 E1
Rautio FIN 65 D3
Rautjärvi FIN 69 F3
Räva LV 80 B1
Ravanjska HR 54 C4
Ravanusa I 53 D3
Ravello I 49 D4
Ravenna I 47 E2
Ravensbrück D 34 B3
Ravensburg D 43 D2
Ravila EE 72 B2
Ravna Dubrava SRB 59 F2
Ravna Gora HR 54 B3
Ravna Reka SRB 57 E3
Ravne na K. SLO 54 B1
Ravnje SRB 55 F2
Ravno BIH 58 B3
Ravno Bučje SRB 59 F2
Rawa Mazowiecka PL 94 B2
Rawicz PL 93 D2
Rawtenstall GB 7 E4
Rayleigh GB 9 F3
Rayol-Canadel-
sur-Mer F 22 C2
Räyrinki FIN 69 D1
Ražana SRB 56 C3
Ražanac HR 54 C4
Razboj BIH 55 E2
Razbojna SRB 57 D4
Raždaginja SRB 57 C4

Razgrad BG 117 E3
Ražiškiai LT 85 E2
Razlog BG 117 D4
Reading GB 9 D3
Réalmont F 21 E2
Rebais F 12 B3
Rębiechowo PL 89 E1
Rebordelo P 18 B4
Recanati I 48 B1
Recco I 23 F1
Recey-sur-Ource F 16 C1
Rechnitz A 45 E2
Rečica HR 54 C2
Recke D 33 D4
Recklinghausen D 37 E1
Recoaro Terme I 43 F4
Recuerda E 19 F4
Rečyca BY 115 E3
Reczno PL 94 A3
Reda PL 89 E1
Redange L 13 D2
Redcar GB 7 F3
Redditch GB 9 D2
Redhill GB 9 E3
Redon F 14 C1
Redondela E 18 A3
Redondo P 24 B3
Redruth GB 8 A4
Rędziny PL 94 A3
Reepham GB 9 F1
Rees D 37 D1
Reeth GB 7 E3
Refsnes N 60 B3
Reftele S 71 D2
Rega PL 88 C2
Regalbuto I 53 D3
Regen D 39 F4
Regensburg D 39 E4
Regenstauf D 39 E4
Reggello I 47 E2
Reggio di Calabria I 51 D4
Reggio nell' Emilia I 47 D1
Reggiolo I 47 D1
Reghin RO 117 D2
Regi LV 76 B3
Regimin PL 90 B3
Reguengos
de Monsaraz P 24 B4
Rehau D 39 E3
Rehburg-Loccum D 33 E4
Rehden D 33 D4
Rehna D 33 F3
Reichenau A 45 E1
Reichenau CH 43 D3
Reichenbach D 40 C1
Reichenbach D 39 E2
Reichertshofen D 43 F1
Reichshoffen F 13 E3
Reigate GB 9 E3
Reignier F 17 D3
Reiki LV 83 F1
Reillanne F 22 C1
Reims F 12 B3
Reinach CH 17 F1
Reinbek D 33 F3
Reinberg D 34 B2
Reine N 60 A3
Reinfeld D 33 F2
Reinheim D 13 F2
Reinli N 66 B1
Reinosa E 19 E2
Reischenhart D 44 B2
Reisjärvi FIN 69 D1
Reiss GB 5 D1
Reistrai LT 80 C3
Reit i. Winkl D 44 B2
Reitzenhain D 39 E2
Reizgiai LT 84 B1
Rejowiec PL 95 E3
Rejowiec Fabryczny PL 95 E3
Rekava LV 79 F3
Rekovac SRB 57 D3
Rekučiai LT 87 D1
Rekyva LT 81 E3
Remagen D 13 E1
Rémalard F 11 F4
Rembate LV 82 B1
Remeskylä FIN 69 E1
Remich L 13 D3
Remiremont F 13 E4
Remolinos E 20 B4
Remoulins F 22 B1
Rempstone GB 9 D1
Remscheid D 37 E2
Remte LV 81 D1
Rémuzat F 22 B1
Renavas LT 80 C2
Renazé F 14 C1
Rencēni LV 78 C2
Renchen D 13 F4
Renda LV 76 C3
Rendina GR 102 A2
Rendina GR 104 C1
Rendsburg D 33 E2
Renginio P 105 D2
Rengsdorf D 13 E1
Reni UA 117 E2
Renko FIN 69 D4
Renkum NL 37 D1
Rennebu N 62 C4

Rennerod D 13 F1
Rennes F 10 C4
Rennes-les-Bains F. 21 F3
Rennweg A 44 C2
Rensjön S 60 C3
Reńska Wieś PL 97 E2
Renwez F 12 C2
Reola EE 79 D1
Reopalu EE 72 C3
Repki PL 95 D1
Replot FIN 68 C2
Repojoki FIN 61 D2
Reposaari FIN 68 C3
Repubblica
di San Marino RSM 47 E2
Repvåg N 61 E1
Requena E 26 C3
Réquista F 21 F1
Rerik D 34 A2
Resanovci BIH 54 C4
Resavica SRB 57 E3
Resen MK 59 E4
Resende P 18 A4
Resita RO 116 C3
Resko PL 88 B2
Reškutenai LT 87 D1
Resmo S 71 E2
Resna MNE 58 C3
Resnik SRB 56 C2
Restelica SRB 59 D3
Restu EE 79 D1
Resuttano I 53 D3
Reszel PL 90 C1
Retford GB 9 D1
Rethem D 33 E4
Rethen (Leine) D 33 F4
Réthimno GR 109 E4
Retiers F 14 C1
Retla EE 72 C3
Retortillo de Soria E 26 A1
Retournac F 21 F2
Retuerta del Bullaque E 25 F3
Retz A 41 D4
Reuilly F 15 F2
Reus E 27 E1
Reusel NL 36 C2
Reutlingen D 43 D1
Reutte A 43 E2
Revel F 21 E2
Rēveli LV 79 D3
Revigny-sur-Ornain F. 12 C3
Revin F 12 C2
Řevničov CZ 40 B2
Revonlahti FIN 65 D3
Rewa PL 89 F1
Rewal PL 88 B1

Reyðarfjörður IS 62 C1
Reykhólar IS 62 A1
Reykholt IS 62 A1
Reykjahlið IS 62 B1
Reykjavík IS 62 A2
Rēzekne LV 83 E1
Režģaliai LT 84 C1
Režiai LT 86 B3
Rezzato I 43 E4
Rezzoaglio I 46 C2
Rgotina SRB 57 E3
Rhade D 37 F1
Rhade D 33 E3
Rhade D 37 D1
Rhayader / Rheaedr GB 3 F4
Rheda D 37 F1
Rhede D 37 D2
Rhede D 33 D3
Rheinbach D 13 E1
Rheinberg D 37 D1
Rheinböllen D 13 E2
Rheine D 33 D4
Rheinfelden CH 17 E1
Rheinfelden D 17 E1
Rheinhausen D 37 D1
Rheinsberg D 34 B3
Rhêmes-Notre Dame I 17 E3
Rhenen NL 36 C1
Rheydt D 37 D2
Rhinau F 13 F4
Rhinow D 34 B3
Rho I 46 B1
Rhondda GB 8 B3
Rhosneigr GB 3 F3
Rhossili GB 8 B3
Rhüden D 38 C1
Rhyl GB 3 F3
Rhynern D 37 E1
Rhynie GB 5 E3
Riaillé F 14 C1
Riákia GR 101 E3
Rial E 18 A3
Riaño E 19 E2
Rians F 22 C2
Rianxo E 18 A2
Riaza E 26 A1
Riba de Saelices E 26 B1
Riba de Santiuste E 26 B1
Ribadavia E 18 A3
Ribadelago E 18 C3
Ribadeo E 18 C1
Ribadesella E 19 E2
Ribarci SRB 59 F2
Ribariće SRB 59 D2
Ribarska Banja SRB 57 E4
Ribas de Campos E 19 E3
Ribčev Laz SLO 54 A2
Ribe DK 70 B3
Ribeauvillé F 13 E4

Ribécourt F 12 A3
Ribeira de Pena P 18 B4
Ribemont F 12 B2
Ribera I 52 C3
Ribera de Cardós E 21 D3
Ribera del Fresno E 25 D4
Ribérac F 15 E4
Ribes de Freser E 21 E3
Ribiers F 22 C1
Ribnica BIH 55 E3
Ribnica SLO 54 B2
Ribnica SLO 54 A2
Ribnica na P. SLO 54 B1
Ribnik HR 54 B2
Ribnița MD 117 E1
Ribnitz-Damgarten D 34 A2
Ribolla I 47 D3
Ríčany (Středočeský kraj) CZ 40 C3
Riccia I 49 D3
Riccione I 47 E2
Richelieu F 15 E2
Richmond GB 7 E3
Richmond-
upon-Thames GB 9 E3
Richtenberg D 34 B2
Ricieliai LT 85 E3
Rickling D 33 F2
Ricla E 20 B4
Ridaküla EE 73 D2
Ridalepa EE 72 A3
Ridica SRB 55 F1
Ridzene LV 78 C3
Riebini LV 83 E2
Riec-sur-Belon F 10 B3
Ried im Innkreis A 44 C1
Ried im Oberinntal A 43 E3
Riedenburg D 39 E4
Riedlingen D 43 D1
Riegel D 13 E4
Riegersburg A 45 E2
Riego de la Vega E 19 D3
Riesa D 39 F1
Rieše LT 86 B2
Riesi I 53 D3
Riestapurvs LV 79 E3
Riestedt D 39 D1
Rietavas LT 80 B3
Rietberg D 37 F1
Rieti I 47 F4
Rieumes F 21 E2
Rieupeyroux F 21 E1
Rieux F 21 D2
Riez F 22 C2
Riezlern A 43 E2
Rīga LV 77 F3
Rigáni GR 104 C2

Rígeo GR 105 D1
Rignac F 21 E1
Rignano Flaminio I 47 F4
Riguldi/Rickull EE 75 D1
Rihéa GR 108 C1
Riidaja EE 79 D4
Riihimäki FIN 69 D4
Riisipere EE 72 A2
Riistavesi FIN 69 E1
Rijeka BIH 55 F4
Rijeka HR 54 A3
Rijeka Crnojevica MNE 58 C3
Rijssen NL 32 C4
Rikava (Rikova) LV 83 E1
Riksgränsen S 60 C3
Rillo de Gallo E 26 C1
Rillo E 26 C1
Rimavská Sobota SK 116 C2
Rimeicāni LV 83 D2
Rimenai LT 85 F3
Rimini I 47 F2
Rimkai LT 85 F1
Rimkūnai LT 81 E2
Rimmi EE 79 D2
Rîmnicu Sărat RO 117 E2
Rîmnicu Vîlcea RO 117 D3
Rimnio GR 101 E3
Rimše LT 87 D1
Rimšėnai LT 87 D1
Rimske Toplice SLO 54 B2
Rimstavas LT 79 D3
Rincón de la Victoria E 29 F3
Rincón de Soto E 20 B3
Rindal N 62 C3
Ringaskiddy IRL 2 B4
Ringaudai LT 85 E2
Ringe DK 70 B3
Ringebu N 62 C4
Ringford GB 7 E4
Ríumar F 27 E1
Riva LV 76 B3
Riva del Garda I 43 F4
Rivarolo
Canavese I 17 E4
Rive-de-Gier F 16 C3
Rives F 16 C4
Rivesaltes F 21 F3
Rivio GR 104 B2
Rivisondoli I 48 C3
Rivne UA 115 D4
Rivolta d'Adda I 46 C1
Ríza GR 104 C2
Ríza F 104 C2
Rizário GR 101 E2
Rizia GR 103 E1
Rizoma GR 101 D4
Rizómilos GR 101 F4

Rizovoúni GR 101 E4
Rjánes N 62 A4
Rjukan N 66 B2
Roa de Duero E 19 E4
Roadside GB 5 D2
Roan N 62 C2
Roanne F 16 B3
Robbio I 17 F4
Röbel D 34 B3
Robertsfors S 64 B3
Robertville B 13 D1
Robežnieki LV 80 B1
Robežnieki
(Pustina) LV 83 F2
Robežsils LV 79 F3
Robič SLO 54 A2
Robledillo de Gata E 25 E2
Robledo E 27 D4
Robledo de
Chavela E 25 F1
Robres E 20 C4
Rocamadour F 15 E4
Rocca di Mezzo I 48 B2
Rocca di Papa I 48 B3
Rocca S. Casciano I 47 E2
Rocca Sinibalda I 47 F4
Roccadaspide I 49 D4
Roccalbegna I 51 D4
Roccalumera I 51 D4
Roccamonfina I 48 C3
Roccapalumba I 52 C3
Roccaraso I 48 C3
Roccastrada I 47 D3
Roccella Ionica I 51 E4
Rocchetta S. Antonio I 49 D3
Roceži LV 77 D3
Rochdale GB 7 E4
Rochechouart F 15 D3
Rochefort B 12 C2
Rochefort F 14 C3
Rochefort-en-Terre F 14 B1
Rochefort-Montagne F 16 A3
Rochefort-
sur-Nenon F 16 C1
Rochehaut B 12 C2
Rochemaure F 22 B1
Rocheservière F 14 C2
Rochester GB 9 E3
Rochlitz D 39 E1
Rociana del Condado E 28 C3
Rocinas LV 81 D1
Ročiškiai LT 84 C1
Rockenhausen D 13 F2
Rocroi F 12 C2
Ródão GR 100 B4
Roda de Isábena E 21 D3
Rodacherbrunn D 39 D2

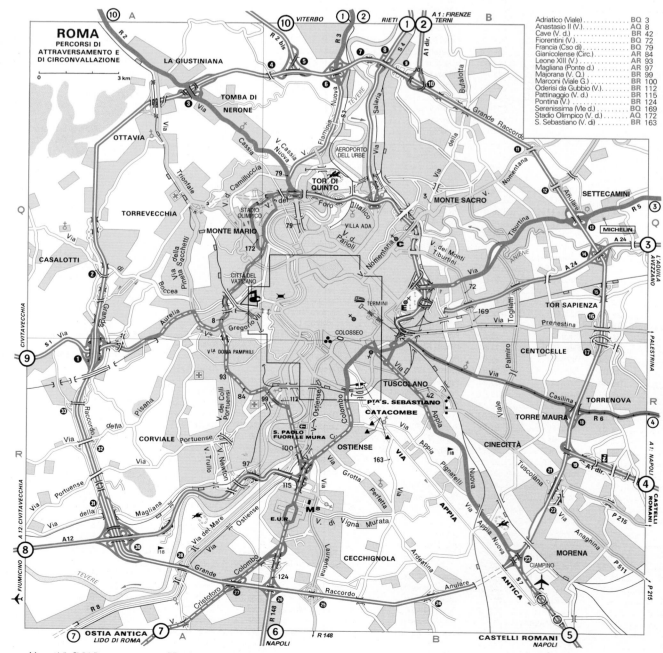

ROMA
PERCORSI DI ATTRAVERSAMENTO E DI CIRCONVALLAZIONE

Adriatico (Viale) . . . . BQ 3
Anastasio II (V.) . . . . AQ 8
Cave (V. d.) . . . . BR 42
Fiorentini (V.) . . . . BR 72
Francia (Cso di) . . . . BQ 79
Gianicolense (Circ.) . . . . . . AR 84
Leone XIII (V.) . . . . AR 93
Magliana (Ponte d.) . . . . . . AR 97
Majorana (V.) . . . . BR 99
Marconi (Viale G.) . . . . BR 100
Oderisi da Gubbio (V.) . . . . BR 112
Pattinaggio (V. d.) . . . . BR 115
Pontina (V.) . . . . BR 124
Serenissima (Vle d.) . . . . . BQ 169
Stadio Olimpico (V. d.) . . . . AQ 172
S. Sebastiano (V. di) . . . . . . BR 163

Museo della Civiltà Romana . . . . BR M⁸

Rodavgí GR ...104 B1
Rødberg N ...66 B1
Rødby DK ...70 C4
Rødbyhavn DK ...70 C4
Rødding DK ...70 B2
Rødding DK ...70 B3
Rödeby S ...71 E3
Rodeiro E ...18 B2
Rødekro DK ...70 B3
Rodel GB ...4 A3
Rodellar E ...20 C3
Roden NL ...32 C3
Rödenas E ...26 C1
Rödermark D ...13 F2
Rodewisch D ...39 E2
Rodez F ...21 E1
Rodi Garganico I ...49 E2
Rodiezmo E ...19 D2
Roding D ...39 E4
Roditis GR ...103 D1
Rododáfni GR ...104 C2
Rodohóri GR ...101 E2
Rodolívos GR ...102 B2
Rodön S ...63 E3
Rodópoli GR ...101 F1
Rodopós GR ...109 D3
Ródos GR ...111 F2
Ródos (Nissí) GR ...111 F2
Rodováni GR ...109 D4
Rodvattnet S ...68 A1
Roden N ...62 B3
Rødvig DK ...70 C4
Rodžia LT ...85 F3
Roela EE ...73 D2
Roermond NL ...13 D1
Roeselare B ...12 B1
Rogač HR ...58 A4
Rogača SRB ...57 D3
Rogačica (Užice) SRB ...56 C3
Rogačica (Vranje) SRB ...58 C2
Rogalin PL ...93 D1
Rogas (Kuldīgas) LV ...76 C3
Rogas (Saldus) LV ...80 C1
Rogaška Slatina SLO ...54 B1
Rogatec SLO ...54 B1
Rogatica BIH ...55 F4
Rogätz D ...34 A4
Roggendorf D ...33 F2
Roggiano Gravina I ...51 D2
Roggosen D ...40 C1
Rogliano F ...23 F2
Rogliano I ...51 D3
Rognan N ...60 B4
Rogoviki LV ...83 E2
Rogovka LV ...83 E1
Rogów PL ...94 A2
Rogowo (Rypin) PL ...90 A3
Rogowo (Żnin) PL ...89 E3
Rogoznica HR ...58 A4
Rogoznica PL ...92 C3
Rogoźno PL ...89 D3
Rogóźno (Kujawsko-Pomorskie) PL ...89 F2
Roguszyn PL ...95 D1
Rohan F ...10 C4
Rohatyn UA ...117 D1
Rohr D ...39 D2
Rohrbach im Oberösterreich A ...40 C4
Rohrbach-lès-Bitche F ...13 E3
Rohrbrunn D ...38 C3
Rohuküla EE ...75 D2
Rohuneeme EE ...72 B1
Roisel F ...12 B2
Roissy-en-France F ...12 A3
Roiu EE ...79 E1
Roja LV ...77 D2
Rojales E ...30 C2
Rojewo PL ...89 E3
Rokaiži LV ...80 B1
Rokasbirze LV ...80 B1
Rokiciny PL ...94 A2
Rokietnica (Podkarpackie) PL ...99 E2
Rokietnica (Wielkopolskie) PL ...93 D1
Rokiškis LT ...83 C2
Rokitno (Lubelskie) PL ...95 E1
Røkland N ...60 B4
Rokovci HR ...55 E2
Rokycany CZ ...40 B3
Røldal N ...66 A2
Rolfstorp S ...71 D2
Rolle CH ...17 D2
Roma I ...48 A3
Romagnano Sesia I ...17 F3
Roman RO ...117 E2
Romana I ...50 A3
Romangordo E ...25 D2
Romanija BIH ...55 F4
Romans-sur-Isère F ...16 C4
Romanshorn CH ...43 D2
Rombas F ...13 D3
Römhild D ...39 D2
Romilly-sur-Seine F ...12 B4
Romny UA ...115 F4
Romont CH ...17 E2
Romorantin-Lanthenay F ...15 F1
Romsey GB ...9 D3
Romučiai LT ...81 D2
Roncade I ...44 B4
Roncal/Erronkari E ...20 B3
Ronce-les-Bains F ...14 C3
Roncegno I ...43 F4
Ronchamp F ...17 D1
Ronchi dei Legionari I ...44 C4

Ronciglione I ...47 E4
Roncobilaccio I ...47 D2
Ronda E ...29 E3
Rønde DK ...70 C3
Rondissone I ...17 F4
Rönnäng S ...66 C3
Rønne DK ...71 E4
Ronneburg D ...39 E2
Ronneby S ...71 E3
Rønnede DK ...70 C3
Rönnöfors S ...63 E3
Ronse B ...12 B1
Roosendaal NL ...36 C1
Roosna EE ...72 C2
Roosna-Alliku EE ...72 C2
Rootsiküla EE ...75 D3
Ropaži LV ...78 A3
Ropczyce PL ...99 D2
Roperuelos del Páramo E ...19 D3
Ropinsalmi FIN ...61 D3
Ropotovo MK ...59 E4
Roquebilliere F ...23 D1
Roquebrun F ...21 F2
Roquebrune-Cap-Martin F ...23 D2
Roquecourbe F ...21 E2
Roquefort F ...20 C1
Roquefort-sur-Soulzon F ...21 F1
Roquemaure F ...22 B1
Roquesteron F ...23 D1
Roquetas de Mar E ...30 A4
Roquevaire F ...22 C2
Rore BIH ...55 D4
Røros N ...63 D4
Rørøs N ...63 D1
Rorschach CH ...43 D2
Rørvig DK ...70 C3
Rørvik (Nord-Trøndelag) N ...63 D3
Rørvik (Sør-Trøndelag) N ...62 C3
Roś (Jezioro) PL ...91 D2
Rosà I ...44 B4
Rosal de la Frontera E ...24 C4
Rosans F ...22 B1
Rosarno I ...51 D4
Rościszewo PL ...90 A3
Roscoff F ...10 A3
Roscommon / Ros Comáin IRL ...2 C2
Roscrea / Ros Cré IRL ...2 C2
Rose I ...51 D2
Rose MNE ...58 B3
Rosegg A ...44 A3
Rosendal N ...66 A1
Rosenheim D ...44 B1
Rosenthal D ...39 F2
Roses / Rosas E ...21 F3
Roseto degli Abruzzi I ...48 C2
Rosheim F ...13 E4
Rosice CZ ...41 E3
Rosières-en-Santerre F ...12 A2
Rosignano Marittimo I ...47 D3
Rosignano Solvay I ...47 D3
Roşiori de Vede RO ...117 D3
Roskilde DK ...70 C3
Rosko PL ...88 C3
Roslavl' RUS ...115 F3
Rosma EE ...79 E1
Rosmaninhal P ...24 C2
Rosme LV ...81 F1
Rosolina Mare I ...47 E1
Rosolini I ...53 E4
Rosoman MK ...59 F4
Rosporden F ...10 B4
Ross-on-Wye GB ...8 C2
Rossano I ...51 E2
Rosscarbery IRL ...2 B4
Roßdorf D ...13 F2
Rossell E ...27 D1

Rosses Point IRL ...2 C1
Roßhaupten D ...43 E2
Rossio ao Sul do Tejo P ...24 B2
Rosslare / Ros Láir IRL ...3 D4
Rosslare Harbour / Calafort Ros Láir IRL ...3 D4
Roßlau D ...39 E1
Rosslea GB ...3 D2
Rosson S ...68 A1
Rossosz PL ...95 E2
Roßwein D ...39 F1
Rosthwaite GB ...7 D3
Røstlandet N ...60 A4
Rostock D ...34 A2
Rostov RUS ...115 F1
Rostrenen F ...10 B4
Rostrevor GB ...3 E2
Røsvik N ...60 B4
Rosvik S ...68 C3
Rota E ...28 C3
Rotenburg D ...33 E3
Rotenburg D ...39 D3
Roth D ...39 D4
Rötha D ...39 E1
Röthenbach a. d. Pegnitz D ...39 D4
Rothenburg D ...40 C1
Rothenburg o. d. Tauber D ...38 C4
Rothéneuf F ...10 C4
Rotherham GB ...7 E4
Rothes GB ...5 D3
Rothesay GB ...6 C1
Rothwell GB ...9 D2
Rotinenai LT ...80 B1
Rotonda I ...51 D2
Rotondella I ...49 F4
Rott D ...43 F1
Rott a. Inn D ...43 F1

Rottach-Egern D ...43 F2
Rottenbach D ...39 D2
Rottenburg a. d. Laaber D ...39 E4
Rottenburg a. Neckar D ...43 D1
Rottenmann A ...45 D2
Rotterdam NL ...36 C1
Rotterdam NL ...36 C1
Rottne S ...71 E2
Rottneros S ...67 D2
Rottweil D ...13 F4
Rötz D ...39 E4
Roubaix F ...12 B1
Roudnice nad Labem CZ ...40 C2
Rouen F ...11 F3
Rouffach F ...13 E4
Rougé F ...14 C1
Rougemont F ...17 D1
Rougemont-le-Château F ...17 D1
Rouillac F ...15 D3
Roujan F ...21 F2
Roulans F ...17 D1
Roundstone IRL ...2
Roússa GR ...103 D1
Rovaniemi FIN ...65 D1
Rovato I ...43 E4
Rovereto I ...43 F4
Roverud N ...67 D2
Roves LV ...77 F3
Roviés GR ...105 E1
Rovigo I ...47 E1
Rovinj HR ...54 A3
Roviśče HR ...54 C2
Równia PL ...99 E3
Rožupe LV ...83 D2
Rowy PL ...89 D1
Royal Leamington Spa GB ...9 D2
Royal Tunbridge Wells GB ...9 E3
Royan F ...14 C3
Royat F ...16 A3
Roybon F ...16 C4
Royère-de-Vassivière F ...15 F3
Røyrvik N ...63 E2
Royston GB ...9 E2
Røyttä FIN ...65 D2
Rožaje MNE ...59 D2
Rožalimas LT ...81 E3
Różan PL ...90 C3
Rožanstvo SRB ...56 C4
Rozay-en-Brie F ...12 A4
Rozēni LV ...78 B1
Rozentova LV ...83 E2
Rozes LV ...78 C2
Rozites LV ...81 F1
Rožkalni LV ...82 B1
Rožmitál pod Třemšínem CZ ...40 C3
Rožňava SK ...116 C1
Rožnov pod Radhoštěm CZ ...41 F3
Rožnowskie (Jezioro) PL ...98 C2
Rozogi PL ...90 C2
Rozoy-sur-Serre F ...12 B2
Rozprza PL ...94 A3
Roztoczanski Park Narodowy PL ...99 E1
Roztocze PL ...95 E3
Roztoka PL ...92 C3
Roztoky (Praha-západ) CZ ...40 C2
Rozula LV ...78 B2
Rožupe LV ...83 D2
Rozvadov CZ ...40 A3
Rozwadów PL ...99 D1
Roźwienica PL ...99 E2

Rrogozhinë AL ...116 C4
Rtanj SRB ...57 E3
Ruabon GB ...8 C1
Ruba LV ...81 D2
Rubbestadneset N ...66 A2
Rubelninkai LT ...87 D1
Rubena E ...19 E3
Rubene LV ...78 B2
Rubeni LV ...82 C2
Rubi E ...21 E4
Rubí de Bracamonte E ...19 D4
Rubiães P ...18 A3
Rubielos de Mora E ...27 D2
Rubiera I ...47 D1
Rubikai LT ...80 C2
Rubuli LV ...83 F1
Rubuliai LT ...80 A2
Rucava LV ...80 A2
Ruciane-Nida PL ...90 C2
Ručiūnai LT ...85 F1
Rūda (Alytaus) LT ...85 F3
Rūda (Marijampoles) LT ...85 D2
Ruda Maleniecka PL ...94 B3
Ruda Śląska PL ...97 F2
Rūdaičiai LT ...80 A2
Rūdaičiai LT ...80 B3
Rudamina (Alytaus) LT ...85 E3
Rudamina (Vilniaus) LT ...86 B2
Rudare SRB ...57 E4
Rūdava LV ...83 F2
Rudbārži LV ...80 A1
Rude (Liepājas) LV ...80 A1
Rude (Talsu) LV ...77 D2
Rüdersdorf D ...35 D4
Rüdesheim a. Rhein D ...13 F2
Rudišķes LT ...86 B2
Rudiškiai LT ...81 E2
Rudka PL ...91 E3

Rudkøbing DK ...70 C4
Rudn'a RUS ...115 E2
Rudna (Dolnośląskie) PL ...92 C3
Rudna Glava SRB ...57 E3
Rudnia (Alytaus) LT ...85 F3
Rudnia (Vilniaus) LT ...86 C3
Rudnica (Novi Pazar) SRB ...57 D4
Rudnica (Pljevlja) MNE ...55 F4
Rudnik (Kragujevac) SRB ...57 D3
Rudnik (Peć) SRB ...59 D2
Rudnik n. Sanem (Podkarpackie) PL ...99 D1
Rudniki (Opolskie) PL ...93 D2
Rüdninkai LT ...86 B3
Rudno (Pomorskie) PL ...89 F2
Rudo BIH ...55 F4
Rudolphstein D ...39 E2
Rudolstadt D ...39 D2
Ruduši LV ...83 F1
Rudzāti LV ...83 D2
Rudžiai LT ...85 F1
Rudzica PL ...97 F2
Rudziniec PL ...97 F2
Rue F ...11 F2
Rueda E ...19 D4
Rueda de Jalón E ...20 B4
Ruelle-sur-Touvre F ...15 E3
Ruffec F ...15 D3
Ruffieux F ...17 D3
Rugāji LV ...79 E3
Rugby GB ...9 D2
Rugeley GB ...9 D1
Rügen D ...34 B1
Rugles F ...11 F3
Ruhla D ...38 C2
Ruhland D ...39 F1

Ruhnu EE ...77 E2
Ruhpolding D ...44 B2
Ruidera E ...26 A3
Ruidoms E ...27 E1
Rūjiena LV ...78 C1
Ruka FIN ...65 E1
Rukainiai LT ...86 C2
Rūki LV ...81 E1
Rukiškis LT ...82 B3
Rukla LT ...85 F1
Ruma SRB ...55 E4
Rumboci BIH ...55 E4
Rümene LV ...77 D3
Rumengol F ...10 A4
Rumenka SRB ...55 F2
Rumia PL ...89 E1
Rumigny F ...12 C2
Rumilly F ...17 D3
Rummu EE ...72 A2
Rumšiškes LT ...85 F2
Runcorn GB ...8 C1
Rundāni LV ...83 F2
Runde N ...62 A3
Rundvik S ...68 B1
Runni FIN ...69 E1
Runtuna S ...67 F3
Ruokojärvi FIN ...69 E4
Ruokolahti FIN ...69 F3
Ruokto S ...64 B1
Ruoms F ...22 A1
Ruotsinpyhtää / Strömfors FIN ...69 E4
Ruovesi FIN ...69 D3
Rupa HR ...54 A3
Rūpnieki LV ...78 C2
Ruponiai LT ...81 F2
Rupt-sur-Moselle F ...13 E4
Rusakalns LT ...86 B2
Ruse BG ...117 D1
Ruše SLO ...54 B1
Ruševo HR ...55 E2
Rush / An Ros IRL ...3 D2
Rushden GB ...9 E2
Rusiec PL ...93 F3
Rusinów PL ...94 B2
Rusiu Ragas LT ...85 F2
Ruski Krstur SRB ...55 F2
Rusko FIN ...68 C4
Rusko Selo SRB ...56 C1
Rusksele S ...64 B3
Ruskulova LV ...83 F1
Rusne LT ...84 B1
Rušona LV ...83 E2
Rusonys LT ...85 F2
Rüsselsheim D ...13 E2
Russenes N ...61 E1
Russi I ...47 E2
Russów PL ...93 E2
Rust A ...45 E1
Rustefjelbma N ...61 F1
Ruswil CH ...17 F1
Rute E ...29 F3
Rūteliai LT ...80 C3
Rüthen D ...37 F1
Ruthin / Rhuthun GB ...3 F3
Rūti CH ...17 F1
Rutigliano I ...49 F3
Rutka-Tartak PL ...91 E1
Rutki-Kossaki PL ...91 D1
Rutkiškiai LT ...85 D1
Rutledal N ...66 A3
Ruukki FIN ...65 D3
Ruuponsaari FIN ...69 D2
Ruurlo NL ...37 D1
Ruusa EE ...79 E1
Ruusmäe EE ...79 E2
Ruvo di Puglia I ...49 E3
Ruwer D ...13 E2
Ruynes-en-Margeride F ...16 A4
Ružomberok SK ...116 B1
Rõhu EE ...79 D1
Rõngu EE ...79 D1
Rõude EE ...72 A3
Rõuge EE ...79 E2
Rämsi EE ...79 D1
Räni EE ...79 D1
Räpina EE ...79 E1
Rätsepa EE ...72 B3
Rääbise EE ...73 D3
Röa EE ...72 C3
Ry DK ...70 C2
Rybczewice Drugie PL ...95 E3
Rybinsk RUS ...115 F1
Rybnik PL ...97 F2
Rybno (Mazowieckie) PL ...94 B1
Rybno (Warmińsko-Mazurskie) PL ...90 A2
Rychliki PL ...90 A2
Rychnov nad Kněžnou CZ ...41 D2
Rychtal PL ...93 E3
Rychwał PL ...93 E3
Rychwałd-Królewski PL ...89 F2
Ryczywół (Wielkopolskie) PL ...89 D3
Ryd S ...71 E3
Ryde GB ...9 D4
Rydułtowy PL ...97 E2
Rydzyna PL ...93 D3
Rye GB ...9 F4
Rygge N ...66 C2
Ryglice PL ...98 C2
Rykene N ...66 B3
Ryki PL ...95 D2
Ryl'sk RUS ...115 F4

Rymań PL ...88 B2
Rymanów PL ...99 D2
Rýmařov CZ ...41 E2
Rýmattylä FIN ...68 C4
Ryn PL ...90 C2
Rynia PL ...94 C1
Rypefjord N ...61 D1
Rypin PL ...90 A3
Rysjedalsvika N ...66 A1
Rysy PL ...98 B3
Ryttylä FIN ...69 D3
Rytwiany PL ...98 C1
Rząśnia PL ...93 F3
Rzeczenica PL ...89 D2
Rzeczniów PL ...94 C3
Rzeczyca (Łodzkie) PL ...94 B2
Rzekuń PL ...90 C3
Rzemień PL ...99 D2
Rzepedź PL ...99 D3
Rzepiennik Strzyżewski PL ...98 C2
Rzepin PL ...92 B1
Rzepińska (Puszcza) PL ...92 B1
Rzeszów PL ...99 D2
Ržev RUS ...115 F2
Rzezawa PL ...98 B2
Rzgów (Łodzkie) PL ...94 A2
Rzgów (Wielkopolskie) PL ...93 E2

S

's- Gravendeel NL ...36 C1
's- Heerenberg NL ...37 D1
's- Hertogenbosch NL ...36 C1
S. Karlovci SRB ...56 C2
Sa Calobra E ...31 E3
Sa Pobla E ...31 E3
Saadjärve EE ...73 D3
Sääksjärvi FIN ...69 D2
Saal a. d. Donau D ...39 E4
Saalbach A ...44 B2
Saales F ...13 E4
Saalfeld D ...39 D2
Saalfelden A ...44 B2
Saanen CH ...17 E2
Saarbrücken D ...13 E3
Saarburg D ...13 D2
Saarde EE ...75 F3
Sääre (Pärnu) EE ...75 F3
Sääre (Saare) EE ...74 B3
Saarenkylä FIN ...65 D1
Saarepeedi EE ...72 C3
Saari FIN ...69 F2
Saariharju FIN ...65 E2
Saarijärvi FIN ...69 D2
Saarikoski FIN ...61 D3
Saariselkä FIN ...61 D3
Saarlouis D ...13 E3
Saas Fee CH ...17 E3
Sääse EE ...73 D2
Saatse EE ...79 F2
Šabac SRB ...55 F3
Sabadell E ...21 E4
Sabaudia I ...48 B3
Sabero E ...26 C1
Sabile LV ...77 D3
Sabiñánigo E ...20 C3
Sabiote E ...26 A4
Sablé-sur-Sarthe F ...15 D1
Sables-d'Or-les-Pins F ...10 C4
Sabnie PL ...91 D3
Sabóia P ...28 A2
Sabres F ...20 C1
Sabrosa P ...18 B4
Sabugal P ...24 C1
Sacavém P ...24 A3
Sacedón E ...26 A2
Saceruela E ...25 F3
Sacile I ...44 B4
Sacramenia E ...19 E4
Sada E ...18 B2
Sádaba E ...20 B3
Sadala EE ...73 D3
Sadki PL ...89 D3
Sadlowo PL ...90 A3
Sadowie PL ...94 C3
Sadowne PL ...91 D3
Sadukülä EE ...73 D3
Sadūnai LT ...85 D3
Sadurki PL ...95 D3
Šadžiūnai LT ...85 D3
Sæbø N ...62 B4
Sæby DK ...70 C2
Saelices E ...26 A2
Sælvig DK ...70 C3
Sævråsvåg N ...66 A1
Safara P ...24 C4
Säffle S ...67 D2
Saffron Walden GB ...9 F2
Safonovo RUS ...115 F2
Sagard D ...34 B1
S'Agaró E ...21 F4
Sagéika GR ...104 C3
Sagiada GR ...100 C4
Sagres P ...28 A2
Sagunt / Sagunto E ...27 E4
Sagunto / Sagunt E ...27 D3
Sagvåg N ...66 A2
Saha EE ...72 B1
Sahagún E ...19 D3
Sahalahti FIN ...69 D3
Šahinovići BIH ...55 D3

Sahl DK ...70 B2
Sahloinen FIN ...69 D2
Saignelégier CH ...17 E1
Saija FIN ...65 E1
Saillagouse F ...21 E3
Saillans F ...16 C4
Saimaanranta FIN ...69 F3
Sains-du-Nord F ...12 B2
Sains-Richaumont F ...12 B2
Saint-Affrique F ...21 F1
Saint-Agnant F ...14 C3
Saint-Agrève F ...16 B4
Saint-Aignan F ...15 E1
Saint-Aignan-sur-Roë F ...14 C1
Saint-Alban-sur-Limagnole F ...16 A4
Saint Albans GB ...9 E3
Saint-Amand-en-Puisaye F ...16 A1
Saint-Amand-les-Eaux F ...12 B1
Saint-Amand-Longpré F ...15 E1
Saint-Amand-Montrond F ...16 A2
Saint-Amans F ...22 A1
Saint-Amans-des-Cots F ...21 F1
Saint-Amans-Soult F ...21 F2
Saint-Amant-Roche-Savine F ...16 B3
Saint-Amant-Tallende F ...16 A3
Saint-Amarin F ...13 E4
Saint-Ambroix F ...22 A1
Saint-Amé F ...13 E4
Saint-Amour F ...16 C2
Saint-André-de-Cubzac F ...15 D4
Saint-André-de-l'Eure F ...11 F3
Saint-André-de-Valborgne F ...22 A1
Saint-André-les-Alpes F ...22 C1
Saint Andrews GB ...7 D1
Saint-Anthème F ...16 B3
Saint-Antonin-Noble-Val F ...21 E1
Saint-Arnoult-en-Yvelines F ...12 A4
Saint Asaph GB ...3 F3
Saint-Astier F ...15 E4
Saint-Auban F ...23 D1
Saint-Aubin-d'Aubigné F ...11 D4
Saint-Aubin-du-Cormier F ...11 D4
Saint-Aubin-sur-Mer F ...11 E3
Saint-Aulaye F ...15 D4
Saint Austell GB ...8 B4
Saint-Avold F ...13 E3
Saint-Aygulf F ...23 D2
Saint-Béat F ...21 D3
Saint-Beauzély F ...21 F1
Saint-Benin-d'Azy F ...16 A2
Saint-Benoît-du-Sault F ...15 F2
Saint-Benoît-sur-Loire F ...15 F1
Saint-Bertrand-de-Comminges F ...21 D3
Saint-Blin F ...13 D4
Saint-Bonnet-de-Joux F ...16 B2
Saint-Bonnet-en-Champsaur F ...17 D4
Saint-Bonnet-le-Château F ...16 B4
Saint-Brevin-les-Pins F ...14 B1
Saint-Briac-sur-Mer F ...10 C4
Saint-Brice-en-Coglès F ...11 D4
Saint-Brieuc F ...10 C4
Saint-Calais F ...15 E1
Saint-CaSaint-le-Guildo F ...10 C4
Saint-Céré F ...15 F4
Saint-Cergue CH ...17 D2
Saint-Cernin F ...16 A3
Saint-Chamas F ...22 B2
Saint-Chamond F ...16 B4
Saint-Chély-d'Apcher F ...16 A4
Saint-Chély-d'Aubrac F ...21 F1
Saint-Chinian F ...21 F2
Saint-Ciers-sur-Gironde F ...15 D4
Saint-Cirq-Lapopie F ...21 E1
Saint-Clair-sur-l'Elle F ...11 D3
Saint-Clar F ...21 D2
Saint-Claud F ...15 E3
Saint-Claude F ...17 D2
Saint Clears / Sanclêr GB ...8 B2
Saint-Cyprien F ...15 E4
Saint-Cyprien-Plage F ...21 F3
Saint David's / Tyddewi GB ...8 A2
Saint-Denis F ...12 A3
Saint-Denis-d'Oléron F ...14 C3
Saint-Denis-d'Orques F ...15 D1
Saint-Didier-en-Velay F ...16 B4
Saint-Dié-des-Vosges F ...13 E4
Saint-Dier-d'Auvergne F ...16 A3
Saint-Dizier F ...12 C4

Saint-Donat-sur-l'Herbasse F ...16 C4
Saint-Éloy-les-Mines F ...16 A3
Saint-Émilion F ...15 D4
Saint-Étienne F ...16 B4
Saint-Étienne-Cantalès (Barrage de) F ...15 F4
Saint-Étienne-de-Baïgorry F ...20 B2
Saint-Étienne-de-Lugdarès F ...22 A1
Saint-Étienne-de-Montluc F ...14 C1
Saint-Étienne-de-Saint-Geoirs F ...16 C4
Saint-Étienne-de-Tinée F ...23 D1
Saint-Étienne-en-Dévoluy F ...17 D4
Saint-Étienne-les-Orgues F ...22 C1
Saint-Fargeau F ...16 A1
Saint-Félicien F ...16 B4
Saint-Firmin F ...17 D4
Saint-Florent F ...23 F3
Saint-Florent-le-Vieil F ...14 C1
Saint-Florent-sur-Cher F ...15 F2
Saint-Florentin F ...12 B4
Saint-Flour F ...16 A4
Saint-François-Longchamp F ...17
Saint-Fulgent F ...14 C2
Saint-Galmier F ...16 B3
Saint-Gaudens F ...21 D2
Saint-Gaultier F ...15 F2
Saint-Gene Saint-Malifaux F ...16 B4
Saint-Gengoux-le-National F ...16 C2
Saint-Geniez-d'Olt F ...21 F1
Saint-Genis-de-Saintonge F ...15 D4
Saint-Genis-Laval F ...16 C3
Saint-Genix-sur-Guiers F ...16 C3
Saint-Geoire-en-Valdaine F ...16 C4
Saint-Georges-de-Didonne F ...14 C3
Saint-Georges-en-Couzan F ...16 B3
Saint-Georges-sur-Loire F ...15 D1
Saint-Germain-de-Calberte F ...22 A1
Saint-Germain-des-Fossés F ...16 A3
Saint-Germain-du-Bois F ...16 C2
Saint-Germain-du-Plain F ...16 C2
Saint-Germain-du-Teil F ...21 F1
Saint-Germain-en-Laye F ...12 A3
Saint-Germain-Laval F ...16 B3
Saint-Germain-Lembron F ...16 A4
Saint-Germain-les-Belles F ...15 F3
Saint-Germain-l'Herm F ...16 B4
Saint-Gervais-d'Auvergne F ...16 A3
Saint-Gervais-les-Bains F ...17 D3
Saint-Gervais-les-Trois-Clochers F ...15 E2
Saint-Gervais-sur-Mare F ...21 F2
Saint-Géry F ...21 E1
Saint-Gildas-de-Rhuys F ...14 B1
Saint-Gildas-des-Bois F ...14 C1
Saint-Gilles F ...22 B2
Saint-Gilles-Croix-de-Vie F ...14 C2
Saint-Gingolph F ...17 D2
Saint-Girons F ...21 D3
Saint-Girons-Plage F ...20 B1
Saint-Gobain F ...12 B3
Saint-Guénolé F ...10 A4
Saint-Guilhem-le-Désert F ...22 A2
Saint-Haon-le-Châtel F ...16 B3
Saint-Helens GB ...7 D4
Saint-Herblain F ...14 C1
Saint-Hilaire F ...21 F2
Saint-Hilaire-de-Riez F ...14 C2
Saint-Hilaire-de-Villefranche F ...15 D3
Saint-Hilaire-des-Loges F ...15 D2
Saint-Hilaire-du-Harcouët F ...11 D4
Saint-Hippolyte F ...13 E3
Saint-Hippolyte-du-Fort F ...22 A1
Saint-Honoré-les-Bains F ...16 B2
Saint Hubert B ...12 C2
Saint-Imier CH ...17 E1
Saint-Ives GB ...9 E2
Saint-Ives GB ...8 A4

Saint-Jacques-de-la-Lande F ...10 C4
Saint-Jacut-de-la-Mer F ...10 C4
Saint-James F ...11 D4
Saint-Jean-Brévelay F ...14 B1
Saint-Jean-Cap-Ferrat F ...23 D2
Saint-Jean-d'Angély F ...15 D3
Saint-Jean-de-Bournay F ...16 C3
Saint-Jean-de-Daye F ...11 D3
Saint-Jean-de-Losne F ...16 C2
Saint-Jean-de-Luz F ...20 B2
Saint-Jean-de-Maurienne F ...17 D4
Saint-Jean-de-Monts F ...14 C2
Saint-Jean-du-Bruel F ...21 F1
Saint-Jean-du-Gard F ...22 A1
Saint-Jean-en-Royans F ...16 C4
Saint-Jean-Pied-de-Port F ...20 B2
Saint-Jeoire F ...17 D3
Saint-Jouin-de-Marnes F ...15 D2
Saint-Juéry F ...21 E1
Saint-Julien F ...16 C2
Saint-Julien-Chapteuil F ...16 B4
Saint-Julien-de-Vouvantes F ...14 C1
Saint-Julien-du-Sault F ...12 B4
Saint-Julien-en-Genevois F ...17 D3
Saint-Julien-l'Ars F ...15 E2
Saint-Junien F ...15 E3
Saint-JuSaint-en-Chaussée F ...12 A3
Saint-JuSaint-en-Chevalet F ...16 B3
Saint-Just GB ...8 A4
Saint-Just F ...20 C1
Saint-Justin F ...20 C1
Saint-Keverne GB ...8 A4
Saint-Lary-Soulan F ...21 D3
Saint-Laurent-de-Chamousset F ...16 B3
Saint-Laurent-de-la-Salanque F ...21 F3
Saint-Laurent-du-Pont F ...17 D4
Saint-Laurent-en-Grandvaux F ...17 D2
Saint-Laurent-les-Bains F ...22 A1
Saint-Laurent-Médoc F ...15 D4
Saint-Laurent-sur-Gorre F ...15 E3
Saint-Laurent-sur-Mer F ...11 D3
Saint-Laurent-sur-Sèvre F ...15 D2
Saint-Léger-sous-Beuvray F ...16 B2
Saint-Léonard-de-Noblat F ...15 F3
Saint-Lô F ...11 D3
Saint-Louis F ...13 F4
Saint-Loup-Lamairé F ...15 D2
Saint-Loup-sur-Semouse F ...17 D1
Saint-Luc CH ...17 E3
Saint-Lunaire F ...10 C4
Saint-Lys F ...21 D2
Saint-Macaire F ...20 C1
Saint-Maixent-l'École F ...15 D2
Saint-Malo F ...10 C4
Saint-Malo-de-la-Lande F ...11 D3
Saint-Mamet-la-Salvetat F ...15 F4
Saint-Mandrier-sur-Mer F ...22 C2
Saint-Marcellin F ...16 C4
Saint Margaret's Hope GB ...5 D2
Saint-Mars-la-Jaille F ...14 C1
Saint-Martin-d'Auxigny F ...16 A1
Saint-Martin-de-Belleville F ...17 D4
Saint-Martin-de-Crau F ...22 B2
Saint-Martin-de-Londres F ...22 A2
Saint-Martin-de-Ré F ...14 C3
Saint-Martin-de-Seignanx F ...20 B2
Saint-Martin-de-Valamas F ...16 B4
Saint-Martin-en-Bresse F ...16 C2
Saint-Martin-Vésubie F ...23 D1
Saint-Martory F ...21 D2
Saint-Mathieu F ...15 E3
Saint-Maurice CH ...17 E3
Saint-Mawes GB ...8 A4
Saint-Maximin-la-Sainte-Baume F ...22 C2
Saint-Médard-en-Jalles F ...15 D4
Saint-Méen-le-Grand F ...10 C4
Saint-Michel F ...12 B2
Saint-Michel-de-Maurienne F ...17 D4
Saint-Michel-en-Grève F ...10 B3
Saint-Michel-en-l'Herm F ...14 C2

Saint-Michel-Mont-Mercure F ...15 D2
Saint-Mihiel F ...13 D3
Saint-Monans GB ...7 D1
Saint-Nazaire F ...14 B1
Saint-Nectaire F ...16 A3
Saint-Neots GB ...9 E2
Saint-Nicolas-d'Aliermont F ...11 F2
Saint-Nicolas-de-la-Grave F ...21 D1
Saint-Nicolas-de-Port F ...13 D4
Saint-Nicolas-du-Pélem F ...10 B4
Saint-Omer F ...12 A1
Saint-Pair-sur-Mer F ...11 D3
Saint-Palais F ...20 B2
Saint-Palais-sur-Mer F ...14 C3
Saint-Pardoux-la-Rivière F ...15 E4
Saint-Paul F ...23 D2
Saint-Paul-Cap-de-Joux F ...21 E2
Saint-Paul-de-Fenouillet F ...21 F3
Saint-Paul-sur-Ubaye F ...23 D1
Saint-Paulien F ...16 B4
Saint-Pé-de-Bigorre F ...20 C2
Saint-Pée-sur-Nivelle F ...20 B2
Saint-Péray F ...16 C4
Saint-Père-en-Retz F ...14 C1
Saint-Philbert-de-Grand-Lieu F ...14 C2
Saint-Pierre-d'Albigny F ...17 D3
Saint-Pierre-de-Chartreuse F ...17 D4
Saint-Pierre-de-Chignac F ...15 E4
Saint-Pierre-d'Oléron F ...14 C3
Saint-Pierre-Église F ...11 D2
Saint-Pierre-le-Moûtier F ...16 A2
Saint-Pierre-Quiberon F ...14 B1
Saint-Pierre-sur-Dives F ...11 E3
Saint-Pois F ...11 D4
Saint-Pol-de-Léon F ...10 A3
Saint-Pol-sur-Ternoise F ...12 A2
Saint-Pons-de-Thomières F ...21 F2
Saint-Porchaire F ...15 D3
Saint-Pourçain-sur-Sioule F ...16 A3
Saint-Privat F ...15 F4
Saint-Quay-Portrieux F ...10 C4
Saint-Quentin F ...12 B2
Saint-Rambert-d'Albon F ...16 C4
Saint-Rambert-en-Bugey F ...16 C3
Saint-Raphaël F ...23 D2
Saint-Rémy-de-Provence F ...22 B2
Saint-Rémy-sur-Durolle F ...16 B3
Saint-Renan F ...10 A4
Saint-Riquier F ...12 A2
Saint-Romain-de-Colbosc F ...11 E3
Saint-Rome-de-Tarn F ...21 F1
Saint-Saëns F ...11 F2
Saint-Satur F ...16 A1
Saint-Saulge F ...16 A2
Saint-Sauveur-en-Puisaye F ...16 A1
Saint-Sauveur-le-Vicomte F ...11 D3
Saint-Sauveur-Lendelin F ...11 D3
Saint-Sauveur-sur-Tinée F ...23 D1
Saint-Savin F ...15 E2
Saint-Savin F ...15 D4
Saint-Savinien F ...15 D3
Saint-Seine-l'Abbaye F ...16 C1
Saint-Sernin-sur-Rance F ...21 F2
Saint-Servan-sur-Mer F ...10 C4
Saint-Sever F ...20 C2
Saint-Sever-Calvados F ...11 D3
Saint-Sulpice-les-Feuilles F ...15 F3
Saint-Symphorien F ...20 C1
Saint-Symphorien-de-Lay F ...16 B3
Saint-Symphorien-d'Ozon F ...16 C3
Saint-Symphorien-sur-Coise F ...16 B3
Saint-Thégonnec F ...10 B4
Saint-Trivier-de-Courtes F ...16 C2
Saint-Trivier-sur-Moignans F ...16 C3
Saint-Trojan-les-Bains F ...14 C3
Saint-Tropez F ...23 D2
Saint-VaaSaint-la-Hougue F ...11 D2
Saint-Valery-en-Caux F ...11 F2

Saint-Valery-sur-Somme F ...11 F2
Saint-Vallier F ...16 C4
Saint-Vallier-de-Thiey F ...23 D2
Saint-Varent F ...15 D2
Saint-Vaury F ...15 F3
Saint-Véran F ...17 E4
Saint Vincent I ...17 E3
Saint-Vincent-de-Tyrosse F ...20 B2
Saint-Vivien-de-Médoc F ...14 C4
Saint-Wandrille-Rançon F ...11 F3
Saint-Yorre F ...16 A3
Saint-Yrieix-la-Perche F ...15 E4
Sainte-Adresse F ...11 E3
Sainte-Anne-d'Auray F ...14 B1
Sainte-Croix CH ...17 D2
Sainte-Croix-du-Mont F ...20 C1
Sainte-Croix-Volvestre F ...21 D2
Sainte-Énimie F ...22 A1
Sainte-Foy-la-Grande F ...15 D4
Sainte-Foy-l'Argentière F ...16 B3
Sainte-Geneviève-sur-Argence F ...16 A4
Sainte-Hélène F ...14 C4
Sainte-Hermine F ...14 C2
Sainte-Livrade-sur-Lot F ...21 D1
Sainte-Lucie-de-Tallano F ...23 F4
Sainte-Marie-aux-Mines F ...13 E4
Sainte-Marie-Sicché F ...23 F4
Sainte-Maure-de-Touraine F ...15 E2
Sainte-Maxime F ...23 D2
Sainte-Menéhould F ...12 C3
Sainte-Mère-Église F ...11 D3
Sainte-Sévère-sur-Indre F ...15 F2
Sainte-Suzanne F ...11 E4
Sainte-Tulle F ...22 C2
Saintes F ...15 D3
Saintes-Maries-de-la-Mer F ...22 B2
Saintfield GB ...3 E1
Saissac F ...21 E2
Šajkaš SRB ...56 C2
Saka EE ...73 E2
Saka LV ...76 B3
Sakaline F ...84 C1
Šakarniai LT ...81 F2
Šakiai LT ...85 D2
Šakiai (Kauno) LT ...85 E2
Šakiai (Miestas) LT ...85 D2
Šakiai (Utenos) LT ...86 C1
Sakla EE ...74 C3
Sakskøbing DK ...70 C4
Sakstagals (Sakstagols) LV ...83 E1
Saku EE ...72 B2
Sakula SRB ...56 C2
Saky UA ...117 F2
Šākylä FIN ...68 C3
Šakyna LT ...81 D2
Sala LV ...82 C1
Sala S ...67 E2
Sala Consilina I ...49 E4
Salacgrīva LV ...78 C1
Salakas LT ...83 D3
Salamajärvi FIN ...69 D1
Salamanca E ...25 E1
Salamiestis LT ...82 B2
Salamína GR ...105 E3
Salamína (Nissí) GR ...105 E3
Salándi GR ...105 E4
Salantai LT ...80 B2
Salar E ...29 F3
Salardú E ...21 D3
Salas E ...18 C2
Salaš SRB ...57 D3
Salas de los Infantes E ...19 F4
Salaspils LV ...78 C2
Salbohed S ...67 E2
Salbris F ...15 F1
Šalčininkai LT ...86 B3
Salcombe GB ...8 B4
Salda EE ...79 E3
Saldaña E ...19 E3
Saldus LV ...80 C1
Saldutiškis LT ...86 C2
Sale I ...17 F4
Salem D ...43 D2
Salemi I ...52 B3
Salen GB ...4 B4
Salen (Argyll and Bute) GB ...4 B4
Salerno I ...49 D2
Salers F ...16 A4
Salgótarján H ...116 C2
Salgueiro do Campo P ...24 C2
Sali HR ...54 B4
Salice Terme I ...46 B1
Saliena (Salonāja) LV ...83 E3
Salies-de-Béarn F ...20 B2
Salies-du-Salat F ...21 D2
Salignac-Eyvigues F ...15 F4
Salihorsk BY ...115 D3
Salinas E ...19 D2

Salindres F ...22 A1
Sälinkää FIN ...69 D4
Salins-les-Bains F ...17 D2
Salisbury GB ...9 D3
Salkininkai LT ...86 B2
Salla EE ...73 D2
Salla FIN ...65 E1
Sallanches F ...17 D3
Sallent E ...21 E3
Sallent de Gállego E ...20 C3
Salles-Curan F ...21 F1
Salles-d'Aude F ...21 F2
Salme EE ...74 B3
Salmerón E ...26 B1
Salmini LV ...76 C3
Salmoral E ...25 E1
Salmünster D ...38 C3
Salnava (Salnova) LV ...83 F1
Salo FIN ...69 D4
Salò I ...43 E4
Salobreña E ...29 F3
Salociai LT ...81 F2
Salomenka LT ...87 D1
Salon-de-Provence F ...22 B2
Salonta RO ...116 C2
Salorino E ...24 C2
Salos (Alytaus) LT ...85 E3
Salos (Panevėžio) LT ...82 B3
Salou E ...27 E1
Salsbruket N ...63 D2
Salses-le-Château F ...21 F2
Salsomaggiore Terme I ...46 C1
Salsta S ...67 E2
Saltash GB ...8 B4
Saltburn-by-the-Sea GB ...7 D3
Saltcoats GB ...6 C2
Salto P ...18 B4
Saltoluokta S ...64 B1
Saltupi LV ...78 B4
Saltvik FIN ...68 B4
Saluggia I ...17 F4
Salutaguse EE ...72 B2
Saluzzo I ...17 E4
Salvacañete E ...26 C2
Salvagnac F ...21 E1
Salvan CH ...17 E3
Salvaterra de Magos P ...24 A3
Salvaterra de Miño E ...18 A3
Salvatierra / Agurain E ...20 A3
Salvatierra de los Barros E ...24 C4
Salviac F ...21 E1
Salzburg A ...44 B1
Salzgitter-Bad D ...33 F4
Salzhausen D ...33 F3
Salzkotten D ...37 F1
Salzwedel D ...34 A3
Sama de Langreo E ...19 D2
Šamac / Bosanski Šamac BIH ...55 E2
Samaniai LT ...82 C3
Samariás (Farángi) GR ...109 D4
Samarína GR ...100 C3
Samatan F ...21 D2
Sambatiki GR ...105 E4
Sambiase I ...51 D3
Sambir UA ...116 C1
Samboal E ...19 E4
Samborzec PL ...99 D3
Sambuca di Sicilia I ...52 C3
Samedan CH ...43 E3
Samer F ...9 F4
Sámi GR ...104 A2
Samikó GR ...104 C4
Sammati FIN ...69 D4
Sammichele di Bari I ...49 F3
Samnanger N ...66 A1
Samninkai LT ...85 F3
Samobor HR ...54 C2
Samodreža SRB ...59 E2
Samoëns F ...17 D3
Samoklęski Male PL ...89 E3
Samokov BG ...117 C2
Samos I ...18 B2
Sámos GR ...107 F3
Samoš SRB ...57 D2
Sámos (Nissi) GR ...107 E3
Samothráki GR ...103 D3
Samothráki (Nissí) GR ...103 D3
Samper de Calanda E ...27 D1
Sampeyre I ...23 F1
Samtens D ...34 B1
Samugheo I ...50 A3
Samur RUS ...120 C3
San Adrián E ...20 A3
San Agustín del Guadalix E ...26 A1
San Amaro E ...18 B3
San Andrés del Rabanedo E ...19 D3
San Bartolomé de la Torre E ...28 C2
San Bartolomé de las Abiertas E ...25 E3
San Bartolomeo in Galdo I ...49 D3
San Benedetto del Tronto I ...48 B3
San Benedetto in Alpe I ...47 E2
San Benedetto Po I ...43 D4
San Bernardino CH ...43 D3
San Bernardino (Passo del) CH ...43 D3
San Biagio Platani I ...52 C3
San Bonifacio I ...47 D1

San Candido / Innichen I 44 B3
San Carlos del Valle E 26 A4
San Casciano in Val di Pesa I 47 D3
San Cataldo I 51 F1
San Cataldo I 53 D3
San Cipirello I 52 C3
San Clemente E 26 B3
San Clemente a Casauria (Abbazia) I 48 C2
San Colombano al Lambro I 46 C1
San Cosme E 18 C1
San Cristóbal de Entreviñas E 19 D3
San Cristóbal de la Vega E 25 E1
San Damiano d'Asti I 17 F4
San Daniele del Friuli I 44 C3
San Daniele Po I 46 C1
San Demetrio Corone I 51 D2
San Donà di Piave I 44 B4
San Donaci I 51 F1
San Elia a Pianisi I 49 D3
San Elpidio a Mare I 48 B1
San Emiliano E 19 D2
San Esteban E 19 D2
San Esteban de Gormaz E 19 F4
San Esteban del Molar E 19 D4
San Esteban del Valle E 25 E2
San Eufemia Lamezia I 51 D3
San Fele I 49 D4
San Felice a Cancello I 48 C4
San Felice Circeo I 48 B3
San Felice sul Panaro I 47 D1
San Felices de los Gallegos E 25 D1
San Ferdinando di Puglia I 49 E3
San Fernando E 29 D3
San Fratello I 50 C4
San Gavino Monreale I 50 A4
San Gemini I 47 F4
San Giacomo / Sankt Jakob I 43 F3
San Gimignano I 47 D3
San Ginesio I 47 F3
San Giorgio Canavese I 17 F4
San Giorgio del Sannio I 49 D3
San Giorgio di Nogaro I 44 C4
San Giorgio Ionico I 49 F4
San Giorgio Piacentino I 46 C1
San Giovanni a Piro I 50 C2
San Giovanni di Sinis I 50 A3
San Giovanni in Fiore I 51 E3
San Giovanni in Persiceto I 47 D1
San Giovanni Lupatoto I 47 D1
San Giovanni Rotondo I 49 D3
San Giovanni Suergiu I 50 A4
San Giovanni Valdarno I 47 E3
San Giuliano Terme I 47 D3
San Giustino I 47 E3
San Ildefonso o la Granja E 25 F1
San Isidro E 30 B3
San Javier E 30 C2
San Jose E 30 B3
San Juan de los Terreros E 30 A4
San Juan del Olmo E 25 E1
San Juan del Puerto E 28 C2
San Lazzaro di Savena I 47 D2
San Leo I 47 E2
San Leonardo de Yagüe E 19 F4
San Leonardo in Passiria / Sankt Leonhard in Passeier I 43 F3
San Lorenzo de Calatrava E 25 F4
San Lorenzo de la Parrilla E 26 B2
San Lorenzo Nuovo I 47 E4
San Lucido I 51 D3
San Luis de Sabinillas E 29 E4
San Marcello I 47 F2
San Marcello Pistoiese I 47 D2
San Marco Argentano I 51 D2
San Marco dei Cavoti I 49 D3
San Marco in Lamis I 49 D3
San Martín de Castañeda E 18 C3
San Martín de la Vega E 26 A2
San Martín de Mondoñedo E 18 B1
San Martín de Montalbán E 25 F2

San Martín de Valdeiglesias E 25 F2
San Martino di Castrozza I 43 F3
San Mateo de Gállego E 20 C4
San Mauro Forte I 49 E4
San Michele all'Adige I 43 F4
San Miguel de Escalada E 19 D3
San Miguel del Arroyo E 19 E4
San Millán de la Cogolla E 20 A3
San Millán de Lara E 19 F3
San Miniato I 47 D3
San Nicolás del Puerto E 25 D4
San Nicoló I 47 E1
San Nicoló Gerrei I 50 B4
San Pancrazio Salentino I 51 F1
San Pedro E 26 B4
San Pedro de Alcántara E 29 E4
San Pedro de Latarce E 19 D4
San Pedro de Mérida E 25 D3
San Pedro del Arroyo E 25 E1
San Pedro del Pinatar E 30 C2
San Pedro Manrique E 20 A4
San Pellegrino Terme I 43 E4
San Piero a Sieve I 47 D2
San Pietro in Casale I 47 D1
San Pietro Vernotico I 51 F1
San Polo d'Enza I 46 C2
San Quirico d'Orcia I 47 E3
San Rafael E 25 F1
San Remo I 23 E1
San Roque E 18 A2
San Roque E 29 D4
San Rufo I 49 D4
San Sadurniño E 18 B1
San Salvador de Cantamuda E 19 E2
San Salvo I 48 C2
San Sebastiano Curone I 46 B1
San Severino Marche I 47 F3
San Severo I 49 D3
San Silvestre de Guzmán E 28 B2
San Sperate I 50 A4
San Telmo E 24 C4
San Valentino alla Muta / Sankt Valentin a. d. Haide I 43 E3
San Vicente de Alcántara E 24 C3
San Vicente de la Barquera E 19 E2
San Vigilio di Marebbe / Sankt Vigil I 44 B3
San Vincente de la Cabeza E 18 C4
San Vincenzo I 47 D3
San Vitero E 18 C4
San Vito I 50 B4
San Vito al Tagliamento I 44 B4
San Vito Chietino I 48 C2
San Vito dei Normanni I 51 E1
San Vito di Cadore I 44 B3
San Vito lo Capo I 50 A4
San Vito sullo Ionio I 51 E3
San Vittore del Lazio I 48 C3
Saná E 102 A3
Sanary-sur-Mer F 22 C2
Sancergues F 16 A1
Sancerre F 16 A1
Sanchidrián E 25 F1
Sancoins F 16 A2
Sancti Petri E 28 C4
Sancti-Spíritus E 25 D1
Sancy (Puy de) F 16 A3
Sand N 66 C1
Sand N 66 A2
Sandane N 62 B4
Sandanski BG 117 D4
Sandarne S 67 F1
Sandau D 34 A2
Sandbach GB 8 C1
Sande D 33 D3
Sande N 62 A4
Sande N 66 C2
Sande N 66 A2
Sandefjord N 66 C2
Sandeid N 66 A2
Sandgerði IS 62 A2
Sandla EE 74 C1
Sandnes N 66 A2
Sandness GB 5 F1
Sandnessjøen N 63 D1
Sandoméri GR 104 C3
Sandomierz PL 99 D1
Sandrigo I 43 F4
Šandrovac HR 55 D2
Sandstad N 62 C2
Sandur (Færøerne) DK 62 A3

Sandviken S 67 F1
Sandvikvåg N 66 A1
Sandwich GB 9 F2
Sandy GB 9 E2
Sangarcía E 25 F1
Sangaste EE 79 D1
Sangerhausen D 39 D1
Sangis S 64 C2
Sangrüda LT 85 D1
Sangüesa/Zangoza E 20 B3
Sanguinet F 20 C1
Saní GR 102 A3
Sanica BIH 55 D3
Sanitz D 34 A2
Sankt-Aegyd A 45 D1
Sankt-Andrä A 45 D2
Sankt-Andreasberg D 38 C1
Sankt-Anton am Arlberg A 43 E2
Sankt-Blasien D 17 E1
Sankt-Christophen A 45 D1
Sankt-Gallen A 45 D1
Sankt-Gallen CH 43 D2
Sankt-Gallenkirch A 43 E3
Sankt-Georgen D 13 F4
Sankt-Georgen am Längsee A 45 D2
Sankt-Georgen im Attergau A 44 C1
Sankt-Gilgen A 44 C1
Sankt-Goar D 13 E2
Sankt-Goarshausen D 13 E2
Sankt-Ingbert D 13 E3
Sankt-Jakob i. Rosental A 44 C3
Sankt-Johann im Pongau A 44 C2
Sankt-Johann in Tirol A 44 B2
Sankt-Lambrecht A 45 D2
Sankt-Leonhard a. Forst A 45 D1
Sankt-Leonhard im Pitztal A 43 F3
Sankt-Lorenzen im Lesachtal A 44 B3
Sankt-Margarethen D 33 E2
Sankt-Märgen D 13 F4
Sankt-Michael im Lungau A 44 C2
Sankt-Michael in Obersteiermark A 45 D2
Sankt-Michaelisdonn D 33 E2
Sankt Moritz CH 43 E3
Sankt Niklaus CH 17 E3
Sankt-Olof S 71 D3
Sankt-Oswald A 44 C3
Sankt-Paul im Lavanttal A 45 D3
Sankt-Peter in der Au Markt A 45 D1
Sankt-Peter-Ording D 33 D2
Sankt-Pölten A 45 D1
Sankt-Valentin A 45 D1
Sankt-Veit an der Glan A 45 D3
Sankt Vith B 13 D2
Sankt-Wendel D 13 E3
Sankt-Wolfgang im Salzkammergut A 44 C1
Sanlúcar de Barrameda E 28 C3
Sanlúcar de Guadiana E 28 B2
Sanlúcar la Mayor E 29 D2
Sanluri I 50 A4
Sannaicon HR 69 E4
Sannazzaro de' Burgondi I 17 F4
Sannicandro di Bari I 49 F3
Sannicandro Garganico I 49 D2
Sanniki PL 94 A1
Sanok PL 99 D3
Sanquhar GB 7 D2
Sansepolcro I 47 E3
Santa Agustí de Lluçanès E 21 E4
Sant Andreu de Llavaneres E 21 F4
Sant Antoni de Calonge E 21 F4
Sant Antoni de Portmany / San Antonio de Portmany E 31 D4
Sant Boi de Lluçanès E 21 E4
Sant Carles de la Ràpita E 27 E1
Sant Celoni E 21 F4
Sant Cugat del Vallès E 21 E4
Sant Esteve d'En Bas E 21 E4
Sant Feliu de Guíxols / San Feliú de Guixols E 21 F4
Sant Francesc E 31 D4
Sant Hilari Sacalm E 21 F4
Sant Hipòlit de Voltregà E 21 E4
Sant Joan d'Alacant E 27 D4
Sant Joan de Labritja E 31 D4
Sant Joan de les Abadesses E 21 E4

Sant Josep E 31 D4
Sant Llorenç de Morunys E 21 E4
Sant Lluís E 31 F3
Sant Mateu E 27 D2
Sant Miguel de Salinas E 30 C2
Sant Miguel E 31 D4
Sant Pau de Segúries E 21 E4
Sant Pol de Mar E 21 F4
Sant Quirze de Besora E 21 E4
Sant Quirze Safaja E 21 E4
Sant Ramon E 21 E4
Sant Sadurní d'Anoia E 21 E4
Sant Vicent del Raspeig E 27 D4
Santa Amalia E 25 D3
Santa Ana E 26 B4
Santa Bárbara E 27 E1
Santa Bárbara de Casa E 24 C4
Santa Catarina da Fonte do Bispo P 28 B2
Santa Caterina di Pittinuri I 50 A3
Santa Caterina Valfurva I 43 E3
Santa Caterina Villarmosa I 53 D3
Santa Cesarea Terme I 51 F1
Santa Clara-a-Velha P 28 A2
Santa Coloma de Farners E 21 F4
Santa Coloma de Queralt E 21 E4
Santa Colomba de Somoza E 18 C3
Santa Comba E 18 A2
Santa Comba Dão P 24 B1
Santa Comba de Rosas P 18 C4
Santa Cristina de Lena E 19 D2
Santa Cristina Valgardena / Sankt Christina in Gröden I 43 F3
Santa Croce di Magliano I 49 D3
Santa Cruz de Campezo E 20 A3
Santa Cruz de la Sierra E 25 D3
Santa Cruz de la Zarza E 26 A2
Santa Cruz de Moya E 26 C2
Santa Cruz de Mudela E 26 A4
Santa Cruz del Retamar E 25 F2
Santa Elena E 25 E4
Santa Eufemia E 25 E4
Santa Eugenia E 18 A2
Santa Eulália E 26 C2
Santa Eulália P 24 C3
Santa Eulalia de Oscos E 18 C2
Santa Eulària des Riu / Santa Eulalia del Río E 31 D4
Santa Fe E 29 F3
Santa Fiora I 47 E4
Santa Gertrude / St Gertraud I 43 F3
Santa Giusta I 50 A4
Santa Liestra y San Quílez E 21 D3
Santa Lucia del Mela I 51 D4
Santa Luzia P 24 A4
Santa Magdalena de Pulpis E 27 E1
Santa Margalida E 31 F3
Santa Margarida do Sado P 24 B4
Santa Margarida i els Monjós E 27 F1
Santa Margherita I 50 A4
Santa Margherita di Belice I 52 B3
Santa Margherita Ligure I 23 F1
Santa Maria Capua Vetere I 48 C3
Santa Maria da Feira P 18 A4
Santa María de Huerta E 26 B1
Santa María de Nieva E 30 B3
Santa María de Valverde E 19 D4
Santa María degli Angeli I 47 F3
Santa María del Campo E 19 E3
Santa María del Campo Rus E 26 B3
Santa María del Páramo E 19 D3
Santa Maria della Versa I 46 C1
Santa María la Real de Nieva E 25 F1

Santa María La Real de Oseira (Monasterio) E 18 B3
Santa Maria Maggiore I 17 F3
Santa Marina de Valdeón E 19 E2
Santa Marina del Rey E 19 D3
Santa Marinella I 48 A3
Santa Marta E 24 C3
Santa Marta de Penaguião P 18 B4
Santa Marta de Tormes E 25 E1
Santa Ninfa I 52 B3
Santa Olalla E 25 F2
Santa Olalla del Cala E 25 D4
Santa Pau E 21 F4
Santa Pola E 27 D4
Santa Ponça E 31 D3
Santa Severa I 48 A3
Santa Sofia I 47 D3
Santa Sofia d'Epiro I 51 D2
Santa Susanna E 21 F4
Santa Teresa di Riva I 51 D4
Santa Teresa Gallura I 50 A2
Santaella E 25 F3
Sant'Agata de' Goti I 48 C3
Sant'Agata di Militello I 50 C4
Sant'Agata di Puglia I 49 D3
Santana E 25 F4
Santana da Serra P 28 A2
Santander E 19 E2
Sant'Andrea Frius I 50 B4
Sant'Angelo dei Lombardi I 49 D4
Sant'Angelo in Vado I 47 E3
Sant'Angelo Lodigiano I 46 B1
Sant'Antioco I 50 A4
Sant'Antonio di Gallura I 50 A2
Santanyí E 31 F3
Sant'Apollinare in Classe I 47 E2
Santarcangelo di Romagna I 47 E2
Santarém P 24 A2
Santas Martas E 19 D3
Santeramo in Colle I 49 F3
Santhià I 17 F4
Santiago de Alcántara E 24 C2
Santiago de Compostela E 18 A2
Santiago de la Espada E 26 A4
Santiago de la Ribera E 30 C2
Santiago do Cacém P 24 A4
Santiago do Escoural P 24 B3
Santibáñez de Béjar E 25 E1
Santibáñez de la Peña E 19 D3
Santibáñez de la Sierra E 25 D1
Santibáñez de Vidriales E 18 C3
Santillana del Mar E 19 E2
Santiponce E 29 D2
Santisteban del Puerto E 26 A4
Santo Domingo de la Calzada E 19 F3
Santo Domingo de Silos E 19 F4
Santo Estêvão P 24 C1
Santo Estêvão P 24 A3
Santo-Pietro-di-Tenda F 23 F3
Santo Stefano d'Aveto I 46 C2
Santo Stefano di Cadore I 44 B3
Santo Stefano di Camastra I 50 C4
Santo Stefano Quisquina I 52 C3
Santo Stino di Livenza I 44 B4
Santo Tirso P 18 A4
Santo Tomé E 26 A4
Santok PL 88 B3
Santoña E 19 F2
Sant'Onofrio I 51 D3
Santu Lussurgiu I 50 A3
Santurtzi E 19 F2
Sanxenxo / Sangenjo E 18 A3
Sanza I 49 E4
São Bartolomeu de Messines P 28 A2
São Brás de Alportel P 28 B2
São Cristóvão P 24 B3
São Domingos P 24 A4
São Gregório P 18 A3
São Jacinto P 24 B1
São João da Madeira P 18 A4
São João da Pesqueira P 18 B4
São João de Tarouca P 18 B4
São João dos Caldeireiros P 28 B2

São José da Lamarosa P 24 B3
São Leonardo P 24 C4
São Manços P 24 B4
São Marcos da Serra P 28 A2
São Marcos do Campo P 24 B4
São Martinho das Amoreiras P 24 A4
São Martinho do Porto P 24 A2
São Matias P 24 B4
São Miguel de Machede P 24 B3
São Pedro da Torre P 18 A3
São Pedro de Moel P 24 A2
São Pedro do Sul P 24 B1
São Romão P 24 C1
São Teotónio P 28 A2
São Vicente da Beira P 24 C2
Saorge F 23 D1
Sapanca TR 117 F3
Sapataria P 24 A3
Sápes GR 103 D2
Sapiéndza (Nissí) GR 108 A1
Sappada I 44 B3
Sappee FIN 69 D3
Sapri I 51 D2
Saraiki LV 80 A1
Säräisniemi FIN 65 E3
Sarajärvi FIN 65 E2
Sarajevo BIH 55 E4
Sarakiní GR 101 E2
Sarakíniko GR 105 F2
Saramon F 21 D2
Sarandáporo GR 101 E2
Sarandë AL 100 B3
Sarapiniškes LT 85 F3
Saraválli GR 104 C3
Saray TR 117 E4
Sarbanovac SRB 57 E3
Sárbogárd H 116 B2
Sarcelles F 12 A3
Sardara I 50 A4
Sardinia GR 104 B1
Sardoal P 24 B2
S'Arenal E 31 E3
Sarentino / Sarntal I 43 F3
Sàrevere EE 72 C3
Sárgans CH 43 D3
Sari-d'Orcino F 23 F3
Sariá (Nissí) GR 111 D3
Sariai LT 86 C1
Sariñena E 20 C4
Šarkaičiai LT 85 D2
Sarkani (Cēsu) LV 78 C2
Sarkani (Madonas) LV 79 D3
Särkisalmi FIN 69 F3
Särkisalo / Finby FIN 68 C3
Sarma LV 81 F1
Sárna S 63 D4
Sarnaki PL 95 E1
Sarnano I 47 F3
Sarnen CH 17 F2
Sarnico I 43 D4
Sarno I 49 D4
Sarnów PL 97 F1
Sarnów (Mazowieckie) PL 97 F1
Sarnówka PL 93 D2
Sarny UA 115 D2
Särö S 66 C4
Sarón E 19 F2
Sarone I 44 B4
Saronída GR 105 F3
Saronno I 17 F4
Sárospatak H 116 C2
Sarpsborg N 66 C2
Sarracín E 19 F3
Sarral E 21 D4
Sarralbe F 13 E3
Sarre-Union E 13 E3
Sarrebourg F 13 E3
Sarreguemines F 13 E3
Sarria E 18 B2
Sarrión E 26 C2
Sarroch I 50 A4
Sars-Poteries F 12 B2
Sarsina I 47 E2
Sarstedt D 38 B1
Sarteano I 47 E3
Sartène F 23 F4
Sárti GR 102 B3
Sartilly F 11 D3
Sartininkai LT 84 B1
Saru EE 79 D1
Sarule I 50 A3
Sárvár H 116 B2
Sarvsjö S 63 D4
Sarzana I 46 C2
Sarzeau F 14 B1
Sarzedas P 24 B2
Sasa MK 59 F3
Sasnava LT 85 E1
Sassari I 50 A2
Sassello I 23 E2
Sassenage F 16 C4
Sassenberg D 37 E1
Sassenheim NL 36 C1
Sassetta I 47 D3
Sasso I 47 E4
Sasso Marconi I 47 D2

Sassoferrato I 47 F3
Sassoleone I 47 D2
Sassuolo I 47 D2
Sástago E 27 D1
Sátão P 24 C1
Šateikiai LT 80 B2
Säter S 67 E2
Šates LT 80 B2
Satiki LT 80 C2
Satiki LV 77 D3
Satillieu F 16 C4
Šātini LV 76 C3
Satkūnai (Kauno) LT 85 F1
Satkūnai (Panevežio) LT 82 B2
Satolas-et-Bonce F 16 C3
Šatorji PL 90 C1
Šatov CZ 41 E4
Satow D 34 A2
Sátres GR 102 C1
Satrup D 33 E1
Sattel CH 17 F1
Sattledt A 44 C1
Satu Mare RO 116 C2
Sauca E 26 B1
Sauda N 66 A2
Sauðárkrókur IS 62 A1
Saue EE 72 B2
Saulaine (Bauskas) LV 81 F2
Saulaine (Liepājas) LV 80 B1
Sauland N 66 B2
Saulgau D 43 D1
Saulieu F 16 B1
Saujon F 14 C3
Sauka LV 82 C2
Šaukenai LT 81 D3
Šaukotas I 81 E3
Saula EE 72 C2
Saulkrasti LV 77 F3
Sault F 22 B1
Saulx F 17 D1
Saulxures-sur-Moselotte F 13 E4
Saumur F 15 D1
Saundersfoot GB 8 A2
Sauris I 44 B3
Sausgalviai LT 84 B1
Sausininkai LT 85 E2
Sauve F 22 A1
Sauvere EE 74 C1
Sauveterre-de-Guyenne F 15 D4
Sauveterre-de-Béarn F 20 B2
Sauveterre-de-Rouergue F 21 F1
Sauvo FIN 68 C4
Sauxillanges F 16 B3
Sauze d'Oulx I 17 D4
Sauzé-Vaussais F 15 D3
Sauzon F 14 B1
Sava I 51 E1
Sāvaini LV 81 E1
Savala GR 73 E2
Savália GR 104 B3
Sävar S 68 B1
Saveikiai LT 81 D2
Savelli I 51 E2
Savenay F 14 C1
Saverdun F 21 E2
Saverne F 13 E3
Saverne I 44 B3
Säviena LV 83 D1
Savigliano I 17 D4
Savignac-les-Églises F 15 D3
Savignano Irpino I 49 D3
Savignano sul Rubicone I 47 E2
Savigny-sur-Braye F 15 E1
Savikosti EE 72 C3
Saviñán E 20 B4
Savines-le-Lac F 22 C1
Savino Selo SRB 55 F2
Savitaipale FIN 69 E2
Sävja S 67 F2
Šavnik MNE 58 C2
Savognin CH 43 D3
Savona I 23 E2
Savonlinna FIN 69 E2
Savonranta FIN 69 F2
Sävsjö S 67 D4
Savudrija HR 54 A3
Savukoski FIN 65 E1
Sawbridgeworth GB 9 E2
Sawin PL 95 E1
Sax E 27 D4
Saxmundham GB 9 F1
Saxnäs S 63 D2
Sayatón E 26 A2
Säynätsalo FIN 69 D2
Säyneinen FIN 69 E1

Scalby GB 7 F3
Scalea I 51 D2
Scalloway GB 5 F2
Scandiano I 47 D2
Scanno I 48 C3
Scansano I 47 E4
Scanzano Ionico I 49 E4
Scarborough GB 7 F3
Scardovari I 47 E1
Scarinish GB 4 A4
Scarriff / An Scairbh IRL 2 A3
Šćedro (Otok) HR 58 A4
Šćekino RUS 115 F2
Šćepan MNE 55 F4
Scey-sur-Saône-et-St-Albin F 17 D1
Schachendorf A 45 E2
Schaffhausen CH 17 F1
Schafstädt D 39 E1
Schagen NL 32 B4
Schaprode D 34 B1
Scharbeutz D 33 F2
Schärding A 44 C1
Scharnitz A 43 F2
Scheeßel D 33 E3
Scheggia I 47 F3
Scheibbs A 45 D1
Scheifling A 45 D2
Scheinfeld D 39 D3
Schenefeld D 33 E2
Schenefeld D 33 E3
Scherfede D 37 F1
Schermbeck D 37 E1
Scheßlitz D 39 D3
Scheveningen NL 36 B1
Schieder D 37 F1
Schierling D 44 C1
Schiermonnikoog NL 32 C3
Schiers CH 43 D3
Schifferstadt D 13 F3
Schildau D 39 F1
Schilpario I 43 E4
Schiltach D 13 F4
Schio I 43 F4
Schirmeck F 13 E3
Schirnding D 39 E3
Schkeuditz D 39 E1
Schköllen D 39 E2
Schladming A 44 C2
Schlagbrügge D 33 F2
Schlangenbad D 13 F2
Schleching D 44 B2
Schleiden D 13 D1
Schleiz D 39 E2
Schleswig D 33 E1
Schleusingen D 39 D2
Schlieben D 39 F1
Schliersee D 44 A2
Schlitz D 38 C2
Schlotheim D 39 D1
Schluchsee D 17 F1
Schlüchtern D 38 C2
Schlüsselfeld D 39 D3
Schlutup D 33 F2
Schmalkalden D 39 D2
Schmallenberg D 37 F2
Schmidmühlen D 39 E4
Schmilka D 40 C2
Schmölln D 39 E2
Schmölln D 35 E4
Schnackenburg D 34 A3
Schnaittenbach D 39 E4
Schneeberg D 39 E2
Schneverdingen D 33 E3
Schönau D 17 E1
Schönberg D 33 F2
Schönberg D 39 F4
Schönberg D 39 F4
Schönberg im Stubaital A 43 F3
Schönbrunn A 45 E1
Schönebeck D 34 A4
Schöneck D 39 E2
Schönecken D 13 D2
Schönewalde D 39 F1
Schongau D 43 E2
Schöningen D 33 F4
Schönmünzach D 13 F4
Schönsee D 39 E3
Schönthal D 39 F4
Schönwald i. Schwarzwald D 13 F4
Schönwalde D 33 F2
Schoonhoven NL 36 C1
Schopfheim D 17 E1
Schöppenstedt D 33 F4
Schoppernau A 43 E3
Schorndorf D 43 D1
Schortens D 33 D3
Schotten D 37 F2
Schramberg D 13 F4
Schrems A 41 D4
Schrobenhausen D 43 F1
Schröcken A 43 E3
Schrozberg D 38 C4
Schruns A 43 E3
Schüttorf D 32 C4
Schwaan D 34 A2
Schwabach D 39 D4
Schwäbisch-Gmünd D 43 D1
Schwäbisch-Hall D 38 C4
Schwabmünchen D 43 E1
Schwalenberg D 37 F1
Schwalmstadt-Treysa D 37 F2

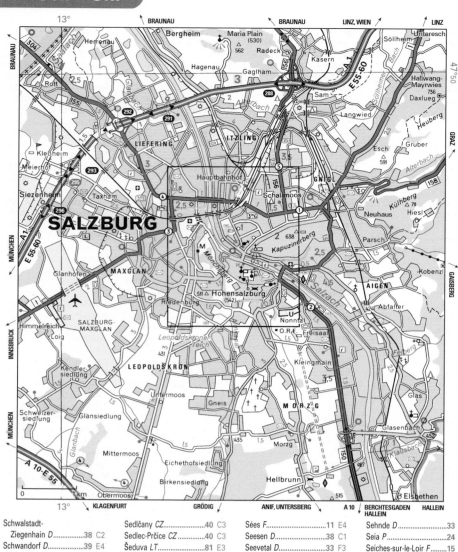

Schwalstadt-
Ziegenhain D..............38 C2
Schwandorf D..............39 E4
Schwanebeck D..............39 D1
Schwanenstadt A..............44 C1
Schwanewede D..............33 D3
Schwarmstedt D..............33 E4
Schwarza D..............39 D2
Schwarzach
   im Pongau A..............44 B2
Schwarzenbach
   a. d. Saale D..............39 E3
Schwarzenbek D..............33 F3
Schwarzenberg D..............39 E2
Schwarzenburg CH..............17 C2
Schwarzenfeld D..............39 E4
Schwarzheide D..............39 F1
Schwarzsee CH..............17 C2
Schwaz A..............43 F2
Schwechat A..............45 E1
Schwedt D..............34 C3
Schweich D..............13 E2
Schweinfurt D..............38 C2
Schweinitz D..............39 E1
Schwelm D..............37 E2
Schwendi D..............43 E1
Schwenningen
   (Villingen-) D..............13 F4
Schwerin D..............34 A2
Schwerte D..............37 E1
Schwetzingen D..............13 F3
Schwyz CH..............17 F1
Sciacca I..............52 C3
Scicli I..............53 D4
Scilla I..............51 D4
Scinawa PL..............92 C3
Scinawka Srednia PL..............96 C1
Scole GB..............9 F2
Sconser GB..............4 B3
Scopello I..............17 F3
Scordia I..............53 D3
Ščors UA..............115 F4
Scorzé I..............44 B4
Scourie GB..............4 A1
Scrabster GB..............5 D1
Ščučyn BY..............115 D3
Scunthorpe GB..............7 F4
Scuol / Schuls CH..............43 E3
Seaford GB..............9 E4
Seaham GB..............7 E3
Seaton GB..............8 C4
Seaton Delaval GB..............7 E2
Sebecevo SRB..............57 D4
Sebeş RO..............117 D2
Sebež RUS..............115 D2
Sebnitz D..............40 C1
Sečanj SRB..............57 D4
Sece LV..............82 C1
Secemin PL..............94 A3
Seckau A..............45 D2
Seclin F..............12 A1
Secondigny F..............15 D2
Seda D..............80 C2
Seda LV..............78 C2
Sedan F..............12 C2
Sedano E..............19 F3
Sedbergh GB..............7 E3
Šédere D..............83 D3
Séderon F..............22 C1
Sedgefield GB..............7 E3
Sedico I..............44 B4
Sedilo I..............50 A3
Sedini I..............50 A2
Sedlare SRB..............59 E3

Sedlčany CZ..............40 C3
Sedlec-Prčice CZ..............40 C3
Šeduva LV..............81 D3
Sędziejowice PL..............93 F2
Sędziszów
   Małopolski PL..............99 D2
Seebenau D..............33 F3
Seeboden A..............44 C3
Seebruck D..............44 B1
Seefeld in Tirol A..............43 F2
Seehaus A..............44 C1
Seehausen D..............34 A3
Seeheim-Jugenheim D..............13 F4
Seelisberg CH..............17 F2
Seelow D..............34 C4
Seen F..............24 C2
Sées F..............11 E4
Seesen D..............38 C1
Seevetal D..............33 F3
Seewalchen A..............44 C1
Seewiesen A..............45 D1
Sefkerin SRB..............56 C2
Segesta I..............52 B3
Segni I..............48 B3
Segonzac F..............15 D3
Segorbe E..............27 D2
Segovia E..............25 F1
Segré F..............15 D1
Segura F..............15 F4
Segura I..............21 D2
Segura de la Sierra E..............26 A4
Segura de León E..............24 C4
Segura de los Baños E..............26 C1
Šeja LV..............78 A3

Sėjas LV..............81 D1
Sejny PL..............91 E1
Sėkoulas GR..............104 C4
Sękowa PL..............98 C2
Selargius I..............50 B4
Selassía GR..............105 D3
Selb D..............39 E3
Selbekken N..............62 C3
Selbu N..............63 D3
Selby GB..............7 F4
Selce HR..............54 B3
Sele LT..............86 C1
Selema LT..............85 D2
Seleniai LT..............86 B2
Sélero GR..............102 C1
Sélestat F..............13 E4
Selevac SRB..............57 D3
Sélí GR..............101 E2
Selí GR..............109 E4
Sėli LV..............78 C3
Sėli LV..............79 D2
Selía GR..............109 E4
Selianítika GR..............104 C2
Seligenstadt D..............13 F2
Sėlija LV..............82 C1
Selínia GR..............105 F3
Selinunte I..............52 B3
Seliste EE..............75 E3
Selja EE..............72 B3
Seljametsa EE..............75 F3
Selje N..............62 A4
Seljord N..............66 B2
Selkirk GB..............7 D2
Sella Nevea I..............44 C3
Selles-sur-Cher F..............15 F1
Sellières F..............16 C2
Sellin D..............34 B1
Selm D..............37 E1
Selmsdorf D..............33 F2
Selna HR..............55 E2
Selommes F..............15 E1
Selongey F..............16 C1
Seløy N..............63 D1
Šėlpils LV..............82 C1
Selsey GB..............9 D4
Selters D..............13 F1
Seltz F..............13 F3
Selva I..............49 F3
Selva di Val Gardena /
   Wölkenstein in Gröden I..............43 F2
Selvino I..............43 E4
Semanova LV..............79 F3
Sème LT..............77 D3
Semeliškes LT..............85 F2
Semeljci BIH..............55 F2
Semič SLO..............54 B2
Semily CZ..............41 D2
Seminara I..............51 D4

Semizovac BIH..............55 E4
Semmering Kurort A..............45 E1
Semproniano I..............47 E4
Semur-en-Auxois F..............16 B1
Semur-en-Brionnais F..............16 B3
Sena E..............20 C4
Sénas F..............22 C2
Senas Tarpupis LT..............86 B2
Senden D..............43 E1
Sendim P..............18 C4
Senez F..............22 C1
Senftenberg D..............39 F1
Seniji Trakai LT..............86 B2
Senigallia I..............47 F2
Senise I..............49 E4
Senj HR..............54 B3
Senje SRB..............57 E3
Senlis F..............12 A3
Sennecey-le-Grand F..............16 C2
Sennen GB..............8 A4
Sennestadt D..............37 F1
Sennori I..............50 A2
Sennybridge GB..............8 C2
Senoji Radiške LT..............85 D3
Senonches F..............11 F4
Senones F..............13 E4
Senorbi I..............50 A4
Senožeče SLO..............54 A1
Sens F..............12 B4
Senta SRB..............55 F1
Sentilj SLO..............54 C1
Šentjernej SLO..............54 B2
Šentjur SLO..............54 B1
Sépeaux F..............16 A1
Šepeta LT..............82 B3
Šepetivka UA..............117 D1
Sepino I..............48 C3
Sępólno Krajeńskie PL..............89 D2
Sępopol PL..............90 C1
Sepúlveda E..............19 F4
Sequeros E..............25 D1
Seraing B..............13 D1
Serapiniške LT..............83 D3
Seravezza I..............46 C2
Serdokai LT..............85 D2
Seredžius LT..............85 E1
Seregno I..............43 D4
Sereikiai LT..............85 E3
Sėrene LV..............82 B1
Séres GR..............102 A8
Serfaus A..............43 E3
Serfopoúla
   (Nissi) GR..............106 B4
Sergijev Posad RUS..............115 F1
Seriate I..............43 E4
Šerići BIH..............55 E3
Šerifos GR..............106 B4
Šerifos (Nissi) GR..............106 B4
Séta LV..............105 F2
Šerikai LT..............80 C3

Šeršknenai LT..............80 C2
Sermaize-les-Bains F..............12 C3
Sermide I..............47 D1
Sermite LV..............80 B1
Šermūkši LV..............78 C3
Sernancelhe P..............24 C1
Serniki PL..............95 E2
Serock
   (Mazowieckie) PL..............94 C1
Serokomla PL..............95 D2
Serón E..............30 A3
Serón de Nágima E..............20 A4
Serós E..............21 E2
Serpa P..............24 B4
Serpuchov RUS..............115 F2
Serra E..............27 D2
Serra de Outes E..............18 A2
Serra S. Bruno I..............51 E3
Serracapriola I..............49 D2
Serrada I..............19 E4
Serradifalco I..............52 C3
Serradilla E..............25 D2
Serramanna I..............50 A4
Serravalle Scrivia I..............17 F4
Serres F..............22 C1
Serrières F..............16 C4
Sersale I..............51 E3
Sertã P..............24 B2
Sérvia GR..............101 E3
Servian F..............21 F2
Servigliano I..............48 B1
Sesa E..............20 C4
Seseña E..............25 F2
Sesimbra P..............24 A3
Sesklío (Nissi) GR..............111 F1
Sesma E..............20 A3
Sessa Aurunca I..............48 C3
Sesta Godano I..............23 F1
Šestanovac HR..............58 A2
Sestino I..............47 E2
Sesto / Sexten I..............44 B3
Sesto Calende I..............17 F3
Sesto Fiorentino I..............47 D2
Sesto S. Giovanni I..............46 B1
Šeštokai LT..............85 E3
Sestola I..............47 D2
Sestri Levante I..............23 F1
Sestriere I..............17 E4
Sestrunj HR..............54 B4
Sestrunj (Otok) HR..............54 B4
Sestu I..............50 A4
Šešuoleliai I LT..............86 B1
Šešuoleliai II LT..............86 B1
Šešuoliai LT..............86 B1
Sesvete HR..............54 C2
Séta GR..............105 F2
Šeta LT..............85 F1

Setcases E..............21 F3
Sète F..............22 A2
Setenil
   de las Bodegas E..............29 E3
Setermoen / Bardu N..............60 C3
Settebagni I..............47 F4
Settimo Torinese I..............17 E4
Settle GB..............7 E4
Setúbal P..............24 A3
Seui I..............50 B3
Seulo I..............50 B3
Seurre F..............16 C2
Sevastianá GR..............101 E3
Sevenoaks GB..............9 E3
Sever do Vouga P..............24 B1
Sévérac-le-Château F..............21 F1
Severenai LT..............80 C3
Seveso I..............43 D4
Sevilla E..............29 D3
Sevilleja de la Jara E..............25 E2
Sevlievo BG..............117 D4
Sevnica SLO..............54 B2
Sevojno SRB..............56 C4
Sévrier F..............17 D3
Sevsk RUS..............115 F3
Seyches F..............21 D1
Seyda D..............34 B4
Seyðisfjörður IS..............62 C1
Seyne F..............22 C1
Seyssel F..............17 D3
Sežana SLO..............54 A1
Sézanne F..............12 A3
Sézérac F..............17 D3
Sezimovo Ústí CZ..............40 C3
Sezze I..............48 B3
Sfáka GR..............110 C2
Sfakiá E..............109 D4
Sfaktiría (Nissi) GR..............108 A1
Sferracavallo I..............50 B4
Sfântu Gheorghe RO..............117 D2
Sforzacosta I..............47 F3
Shaftesbury GB..............8 C3
Shanklin GB..............9 D4
Shap GB..............7 D3
Sheerness GB..............9 E3
Sheffield GB..............9 D1
Shefford GB..............9 D1
Shēngjin AL..............116 C4
Shepshed GB..............9 D1
Shepton Mallet GB..............8 C3
Sherborne GB..............8 C3
Shercock IRL..............3 D2
Sheringham GB..............9 F1
Shiel Bridge GB..............4 B4
Shieldaig GB..............4 B3
Shijak AL..............116 C4
Shinás GR..............101 E2
Shiniás GR..............105 F3
Shínos GR..............104 C3

SEVILLA

Ada...............FR 3
Alameda de Hércules........FR 5
Alcade Juan Fernández........FR 8
América (Pl. de)...............FR 24
Antonio Bienvenida...............FR 28
Asunción...............FR 33
Borbolla (Av. de)...............FR 38
Capuchinos (Ronda)...............FR 45
Cardenal Ilundain...............FS 46
Carlos V (Av.de)...............FR 52
Castilla...............
Chapina (Puente)...............FR 59
Ciudad Jardín (Av.)...............FR 60
Cristóbal Colón (Pas. de)...............FR 72
Cruz del Campo (Av.)...............FR 80
Delicias (Pas. de las)...............FR 82
Diego Martínez Barrio...............FR 85
Doctor Fedriani...............FP 87
Don Fabrique...............FR 92
Eduardo Dato (Av.)...............FR 100
Éfeso...............FR 102
Enramadilla...............FR 107
Entarfia (Av.)...............FR 110
España (Pl. de)...............FR 114
Federico Mayo Gayarre...............FR 117
Felipe II...............FR 120
Francisco Buendía...............FR 125
Generalísimo (Puente del)...............FR 136
General Merry...............FR 132
El Greco (Av.)...............FR 139
Isabel II o de Triana (Puente)...............FR 145
López de Gomara...............ER 157
Luis de Morales...............FR 161
Manuel Fal Conde...............FS 165
Manuel Siurot (Av.)...............FS 167
Maqueda...............GR 170
María Auxiliadora...............FR 175
María Luisa (Av.)...............FR 175
Marqués de Luca de Tena...............FS 182
Marqués de Paradas (Av.)...............FR 185
Marqués de Pickman...............FR 187
Menéndez Pelayo...............FR 195
Miraflores (Av.)...............FR 198
Padre García Tejero (Av.)...............FS 212
Páez de Rivera...............FR 215
Pagés del Corro (Av.)...............FR 217
Pedro Gual Villalbi (Av.)...............FR 225
Pío XII (Ronda)...............FP 229
Quintillo (Camino)...............FR 244
Ramón de Carranza (Av.)...............FR 249
Ramón y Cajal (Av.)...............FR 247
Recaredo...............FR 252
República Argentina (Av.)...............ER 255
Resolana...............FR 257
Rubén Darío...............FR 265
Sánchez Pizjuán (Av.)...............FP 292
Santa Fé...............FR 295
San Fernando...............FR 267
San Francisco Javier (Av.)...............FR 270
San Juan de la Cruz (Av.)...............FR 275
San Juan de la Salle...............GR 282
San Juan de Ribera...............FR 282
San Luis...............FR 285
San Telmo (Puente de)...............FR 285
Tesalónica...............GR 305
Virgen de Luján...............FPR 322

Shinoússa (Nissí) GR....109 F1
Shipston-on-Stour GB....9 D2
Shizá (Nissí) GR....108 A1
Shkodër AL....116 C4
Sholári GR....102 A2
Shoreham GB....9 E4
Shrewsbury GB....8 C1
Shrewton GB....9 D3
Sianów PL....88 C1
Siátista GR....101 D3
Šiaudenai I LT....80 B3
Šiaudine
  (Marijampoles) LT....85 D1
Šiaudine (Šiauliu) LT....81 D2
Šiaudine (Vilniaus) LT....86 B2
Šiaudiniškiai LT....85 D2
Šiauduva LT....80 C3
Šiaulenai LT....81 E3
Šiauliai
  (Antanaičiai) LT....86 B2
Šiauliai
  (Bagaslaviškis) LT....86 B1
Šiauliai (Šiauliu) LT....81 E2
Šiauliškiai LT....85 E2
Sibari I....51 D2
Šibenik HR....54 C4
Šibinj HR....55 E2
Sibiu RO....117 D2
Sićevo SRB....57 E4
Sicienko PL....89 E3
Sicignano
  degli Alburni I....49 D4
Sick D....33 E3
Sićuraj HR....58 A3
Šid SRB....55 F2
Sidabravas LT....81 E3
Sidabrines LT....86 C1
Sidári GR....100 A4
Sideby FIN....68 C3
Sidensjö S....68 A2
Siderno I....51 E4
Sidgunda LV....78 B3
Sidiró GR....103 E1
Sidirókastro GR....102 A1
Sidirónero GR....102 B1
Sidmouth GB....8 B4
Sidrabini LV....82 C1
Sidrabnieki LV....81 E1
Siebenlehn D....39 F1
Sieciechów PL....95 D2
Siecino (Jezioro) PL....88 C2
Siedlce PL....95 D1
Siedlec
  (Wielkopolskie) PL....92 C2
Siedlisko
  (Lubuskie) PL....92 C2
Siedliszcze
  (Lubelskie) PL....95 E3
Siegburg D....13 E1
Siegen D....13 F1
Siegsdorf D....44 B1
Siekierczyn PL....92 B3
Sieksäte
  (Kalnmuiža) LV....80 C1
Siemianowice
  Śląskie PL....97 F2
Siemianowskie
  (Jezioro) PL....91 F3
Siemiatycze PL....95 E1
Siemień PL....95 E2
Siemkowice PL....93 F3
Siemyśl PL....88 B1
Siena I....47 D3
Sieniawa PL....99 E2
Šienlaukis LT....81 D3
Siennica PL....94 C2
Siennica Różana PL....95 F3
Sienno PL....94 C2
Sieppijärvi FIN....64 C1
Sieradz PL....93 F2
Sieraków PL....88 C3
Sierakowice
  (Pomorskie) PL....89 E1
Sierck-les-Bains F....13 D3
Sierentz F....17 E1
Sierninghofen A....44 C1
Sieroszewice PL....93 E2
Sierpc PL....90 A3
Sierpowo PL....89 D2
Sierra de Fuentes E....25 D3
Sierra de Yeguas E....29 E3
Sierra Nevada E....29 F3
Sierre CH....17 E2
Siersza PL....98 A2
Siesikai LT....85 F1
Siestrzeń PL....94 B2
Sievi FIN....69 D1
Sievin as FIN....69 D1
Siewierz PL....97 F3
Sífnos (Nissí) GR....109 E1
Sigaste EE....75 F3
Sigean F....21 F3
Sigerfjord N....60 B3
Siggjarvåg N....66 A2
Sighetu
  Marmaţiei RO....117 D2
Sighişoara RO....117 D2
Siglufjörður IS....62 B1
Sigmaringen D....43 D1
Signy-l'Abbaye F....12 C2
Sigri GR....107 D1
Sigtuna S....67 F2
Sigüenza E....26 B1
Sigulda LV....78 B3
Sihva EE....79 D1
Siikainen FIN....68 C3

Siikajoki FIN....65 D3
Siilinjärvi FIN....69 E1
Siimusti EE....73 D3
Sijarinska Banja SRB....59 E2
Sikaminiá GR....103 E4
Sikás S....63 E3
Sikí GR....105 E1
Sikiá GR....102 B3
Sikiá GR....108 B1
Sikinos GR....109 F1
Sikinos (Nissí) GR....109 F1
Sikióna GR....105 D3
Sikoráhi GR....103 D2
Sikoúrio GR....101 F4
Sikovuono FIN....61 E2
Sikrags LV....76 C2
Sikšni LV....80 B2
Sikšniai LT....85 D2
Šilai (Kauno) LT....85 F1
Šilai (Panevežio) LT....81 F3
Šilai (Tauragés) LT....80 C3
Šilajani LT....83 E2
Silaktis LV....79 E2
Šilale LT....80 C3
Silandro / Schlanders I....43 F3
Šilavotas LT....85 E2
Silba HR....54 B4
Silba (Otok) HR....54 B4
Šilbaš SRB....55 F2
Şile TR....117 F4
Šileikoniai LT....81 E3
Šilenai (Kuršenai) LT....81 D2
Šilenai (Šiauliu) LT....81 E3
Silene LV....83 E3
Siles E....26 A4
Šilgaliai (Šakiai) LT....85 D1
Šilgaliai (Slavikai) LT....85 D2
Šili (Aluksnes) LV....79 E2
Šili (Liepājas) LV....76 B3
Silini (Aluksnes) LV....79 E2
Silini (Ventspils) LV....76 B3
Simuna EE....73 D2
Siliqua I....50 A4
Silistra BG....117 D3
Silivri TR....117 F4
Siljan N....66 B2
Siljansnäs S....67 E1
Silkeborg DK....70 B3
Silla E....27 D3
Silla EE....75 F3
Sillamäe EE....73 F2
Sillé-le-Guillaume F....11 E4
Silleda E....18 A2
Sillian A....44 B3
Silloth GB....7 D3

Silmači LV....79 D3
Silmala LV....83 E2
Silnowo PL....88 C2
Šilo HR....54 B3
Sils E....21 F4
Sils Maria /
  Segl Maria CH....43 E3
Siltakylä FIN....69 E4
Šilukalns LV....83 E1
Šilute LT....80 B3
Šiluva LV....78 C2
Silva LV....78 C2
Silvalen N....63 D1
Silvaplana CH....43 E3
Silvares P....24 C2
Silves P....28 A2
Silvi Marina I....48 C2
Silz A....43 F2
Simancas E....19 E4
Simandra GR....102 A3
Šimanovci SRB....56 C2
Simaxis I....50 A3
Simbach D....44 B1
Simbach a. Inn D....44 B1
Šími GR....111 F1
Šími (Nissí) GR....111 F1
Šimići BIH....55 D3
Šimkaičiai LT....85 D1
Simlångsdalen S....71 D2
Širitovci HR....54 C4
Sirkka FIN....61 E3
Simmerath D....13 D1
Simmern (Hunsrück) D....13 E2
Simnas LT....85 E3
Simo FIN....65 D4
Simola FIN....69 F3
Šimoniai LT....81 F2
Simonsbath GB....8 B3
Simonswald D....13 F4
Šimonys LT....82 B3
Simópoulo GR....104 C3
Simrishamn S....71 D3
Šimuna EE....73 D2
Sinaia RO....117 D3
Sinalunga I....47 D3
Sinarádes GR....100 B4
Sinarcas E....26 C3
Sindelfingen D....43 D1
Sindi EE....72 B3
Síndos GR....101 F2
Sinettä FIN....61 E3
Sineu E....31 E3
Singen (Hohentwiel) D....17 F1
Siniküla EE....73 D3
Sinimäe EE....73 F2

Siniscola I....50 B3
Sinj HR....55 D4
Sinnicolau Mare RO....116 C2
Sinole LV....79 D3
Sinopoli I....51 D4
Sinsheim D....13 F3
Sint-Niklaas B....12 B1
Sint-Oedenrode NL....36 C1
Sint-Truiden B....12 C1
Sintautai LT....85 D2
Sintra P....24 A3
Sinzig D....13 E1
Siófok H....116 B2
Sion CH....17 E3
Sipa EE....72 B2
Šipan (Otok) HR....58 B3
Šipanska Luka HR....58 B3
Sipoli LV....78 B2
Sipoo / Sibbo FIN....69 D4
Šipovo BIH....55 D4
Sippola FIN....69 E3
Siprage BIH....55 D4
Sira N....66 A3
Siracusa I....53 E4
Siret RO....117 D2
Sirevåg N....66 A3
Sirig SRB....55 F2
Sirma N....61 E1
Sirmione I....43 E4
Sirna (Nissí) GR....111 D2
Široki Brijeg BIH....58 A2
Široko Polje HR....55 E2
Sirolo I....48 B1
Síros (Nissí) GR....106 C4
Siručiai LT....81 D3
Siruela E....25 E3
Sirutenai LT....82 C3
Sirutiškis LT....85 E1
Širvintos LT....86 B1
Sisak HR....54 C2
Šišan HR....54 A3
Sisante E....25 F3
Šišljavić HR....54 C2
Šiškiniai LT....86 C1
Sissa I....46 C1
Sissach CH....17 E1
Sisses GR....109 E3
Sissonne F....12 B3
Sisteron F....22 C1
Sistiana I....44 C4
Sistranda N....62 C3
Sitges E....27 F1

Sithonía GR....102 A3
Sitía GR....110 C4
Šitkūnai LT....85 E1
Sitno (Kujawsko-
  Pomorskie) PL....89 F3
Sittard NL....13 D1
Sittensen D....33 E1
Sittingbourne GB....9 F2
Šiūlenai LT....87 D1
Šiuliai LT....85 E2
Šiuntio / Sjundeå FIN....69 D4
Šiupyliai LT....81 D2
Siuro FIN....69 D3
Siurua FIN....65 D2
Siusi / Seis I....43 F3
Sivac SRB....55 F1
Šiviri GR....102 A3
Sivota GR....100 B4
Sivros GR....104 A2
Six-Fours-les-Plages F....22 C2
Siziano I....46 B1
Sizun F....10 A4
Sjenica SRB....56 C4
Sjenićak Lasinjski HR....54 C2
Sjøåsen N....63 D2
Sjöbo S....71 D3
Sjøholt N....62 B3
Sjötorp S....67 D3
Sjoutnäset S....63 E2
Sjøvegan / Salangen N....60 C3
Sjulsmark S....64 B3
Sjusjøen N....66 C1
Skaborai LT....80 C3
Skábu N....62 C4
Skačiai LT....81 D2
Skadovs'k UA....117 F2
Skælskør DK....70 C3
Skærbæk DK....70 B3
Skaftafell IS....62 B2
Skagastrond IS....62 A1
Skage N....63 D2
Skagen DK....70 C1
Skaidiškes LT....86 B2
Skaill GB....5
Skaista (Geibi) LV....83 E2
Skaistgirai LT....81 E2
Skaistgirys LT....81 E2
Skaistkalne LV....82 A2
Skafidiá GR....104 B3
Skakai LT....81 E2
Skála GR....105 E2
Skála GR....104 B2
Skála GR....108 B1
Skała PL....98 B2

Skála
  (Dodekánissa) GR....107 E4
Skála (Lésvos) GR....107 D1
Skála Eressoú GR....107 D1
Skála Kaliráhis GR....102 B2
Skála Oropoú GR....105 F2
Skála Potamiás GR....102 C2
Skála Rahoníou GR....102 C2
Skála Volissoú GR....107 D1
Skaland / Berg N....60 B2
Skalavik
  (Færøerne) DK....62 A3
Skalbes LV....77 F2
Skalbmierz PL....98 B2
Skålevik N....66 A4
Skalohóri GR....101 D3
Skalohóri GR....107 D1
Skaloti GR....102 B1
Skalupes LV....78 B3
Skamnéli GR....100 C3
Skandáli GR....103 D4
Skanderborg DK....70 B3
Skandzoúra
  (Nissí) GR....105 F1
Skånevik N....66 A2
Skangali LV....78 C2
Skåningsbukt N....60 C2
Skankalne LV....78 B2
Skänninge S....67 E3
Skanör-Falsterbo S....71 D3
Skąpe PL....92 B2
Skapiškis LT....82 B3
Skara S....67 D3
Skaramangás GR....105 F3
Skarberget N....60 B3
Skarda (Otok) HR....54 C4
Skåre S....67 D2
Skärfia GR....105 D1
Skärhamn S....66 C2
Skarnes N....66 C2
Skarplinge S....67 F2
Skarsvåg N....61 E1
Skarszewy PL....89 E1
Skärvången S....63 E3
Skaryszew PL....94 C3
Skarżysko-
  Kamienna PL....94 C3
Skattungbyn S....67 E1
Skatval N....63 D3
Skaudvile LT....80 C3
Skaulo N....62 C3
Skaun N....62 C3
Škaune LV....83 F2
Skawina PL....98 A2

Škėde (Liepajas) LV....80 A1
Škėde (Saldus) LV....76 C3
Skee S....66 C3
Skegness GB....9 E1
Skei N....62 B4
Skei (Sogn og
  Fjordane) N....62 C3
Skela SRB....56 C3
Skellefteå S....64 B3
Skelleftehamn S....64 B3
Skelmersdale GB....7 D4
Skemai LT....82 C1
Skemiai LT....81 E3
Skender Vakuf /
  Kneževo BIH....55 D3
Skepastó GR....102 A2
Skępe PL....89 F3
Skerries / Na Sceirí IRL....3 C3
Skersabaliai LT....93 F3
Ski N....66 C2
Skiáthos GR....105 F1
Skiáthos (Nissí) GR....105 F1
Skibbereen /
  An Sciobairín IRL....2 B4
Skibby DK....70 C3
Škibe LV....81 E1
Skibotn N....60 C2
Skidra GR....101 E2
Skiemonys LT....86 B1
Skien N....66 B2
Skierbieszów PL....95 F3
Skierniewice PL....94 B2
Škilbani LV....79 F3
Skillingaryd S....67 D4
Skilvioniai LT....81 E2
Skindzierz PL....91 E2
Skiniás GR....109 F4
Skinnarbu N....66 B2
Skinnskatteberg S....67 E2
Skipagurra N....61 F1
Skipton GB....7 D4
Skirmantiške LT....81 E3
Skíros GR....106 B1
Skíros (Nissí) GR....106 B1
Skíti GR....101 F4
Skive DK....70 D2
Skivjane SRB....59 D3
Skjeberg N....66 C2
Skjelvik N....60 A4
Skjern DK....70 B3
Skjersholmane N....66 A2
Skjerstad N....60 B4
Skjervøy N....60 C2

Skjønhaug N....66 C2
Sklavopoúla GR....108 C4
Škleriai LT....86 B2
Sklíthro GR....101 F4
Škloů BY....115 E3
Skočivir MK....59 F4
Skoczów PL....97 F2
Skodje N....62 B3
Škofja Loka SLO....54 A2
Škofljica SLO....54 B2
Skog S....68 A2
Skog N....67 F1
Skogar IS....62 A2
Skoghall S....67 D2
Skogstorp S....67 D2
Skoki PL....89 D3
Skokloster S....67 F2
Skollenborg N....66 B2
Skołyszyn PL....98 C3
Skomlin PL....93 F3
Skópelos GR....105 F1
Skópelos GR....107 E1
Skópelos (Nissí) GR....105 F1
Skopiá GR....105 D1
Skopje MK....59 E3
Skopós GR....101 D2
Skopun
  (Færøerne) DK....62 A3
Skórcz PL....89 F2
Skorenovac SRB....57 D2
Skoroszyce PL....97 D1
Skorovatn N....63 D2
Skorped S....63 F3
Skórzec PL....95 D2
Skorzęcin PL....93 E1
Skotína GR....101 F3
Skotterud N....67 D2
Skoulikariá GR....104 B1
Skoúra GR....108 B1
Skoúrta GR....105 F3
Skoutári GR....102 A2
Skoútari GR....108 B1
Skoutáros GR....107 D1
Skövde S....67 D3
Skrá GR....101 E1
Skrad HR....54 B3
Skradin HR....54 C4
Skreia N....66 C1
Skríni LV....83 F1
Skriveri LV....82 B2
Skroblis LT....80 B3
Skroderi LV....76 B3
Skrolsvik N....60 B3

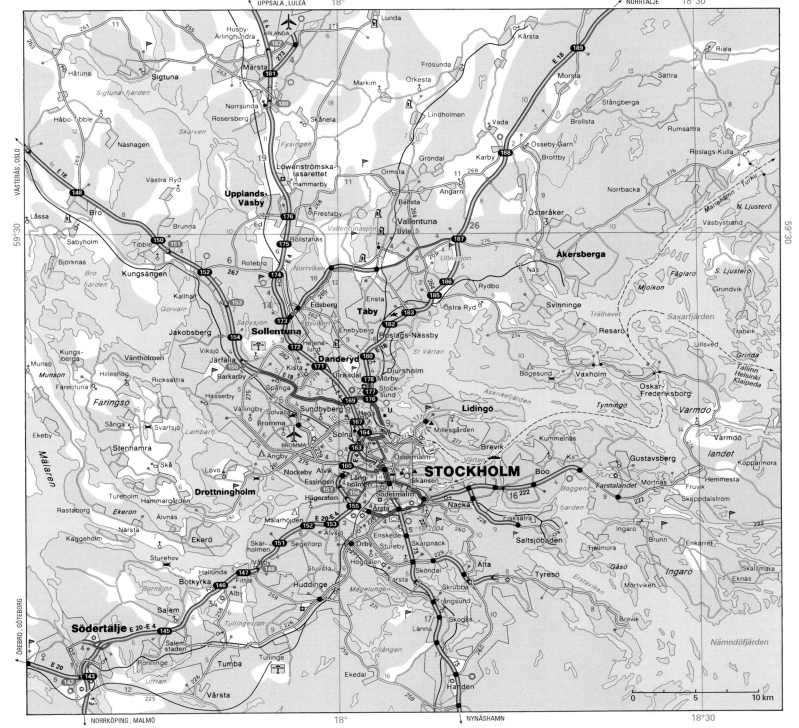

Skrudaliena LV 83 D3
Skrunda LV 80 C1
Skrydstrup DK 70 B3
Skrynupis LT 85 E2
Skrzyczne PL 97 F2
Skrzyszów PL 98 C2
Škuburi LV 80 A1
Skudeneshavn N 66 A2
Skudutiškis LT 86 C1
Skuige LT 85 E2
Skujaine LV 81 E1
Skujene LV 78 C3
Skujenieki LV 79 E3
Skujetniki LV 79 E3
Skujinas LV 83 D3
Skuki LV 78 C3
Skuki LV 83 F3
Skukiši LV 77 F3
Skull / Schull IRL 2 A4
Skulsk PL 93 F1
Skulte LV 77 F3
Skultuna S 67 E2
Skuodas LT 80 B2
Skuoliai LT 86 B1
Skurup S 71 D3
Skuteč CZ 41 D3
Skutskär S 67 F1
Skutvik N 60 B3
Skvyra UA 117 E1
Skwierzyna PL 88 B3
Skynimai (Merkine) LT 86 B3
Skynimai (Mostiškes) LT 86 C2
Slabadai LT 85 D2
Slagelse DK 70 C3
Slagnäs S 64 A2
Slakovac SRB 57 D2
Slampe LV 77 E3
Slânčev Brjag BG 117 E3
Slancy RUS 115 D1
Slane IRL 3 D2
Slangerup DK 70 C3
Slano HR 58 B3
Slaný CZ 40 C2
Šlapaberže LT 81 E3
Šlapaki LV 83 E3
Šlapanice CZ 41 E3
Slapy CZ 40 C2
Śląskie-Zdrój PL 92 C3
Slate LV 82 C2
Slatina BIH 55 D3
Slatina HR 55 D2
Slatina RO 117 D3
Slatina (Bor) SRB 57 E3
Slatina (Čačak) SRB 57 D4
Slatine HR 58 A4
Slatinski Drenovac HR 55 D2
Slaúharad BY 115 E3
Slav. Šamac HR 55 E2
Slavēkas LV 78 B3
Slavičín CZ 41 F3
Slavikai LT 85 D1
Slavinja SRB 57 F4
Slavinčiškis LT 82 B3
Slavinja SRB 57 F4
Slavkov u Brna CZ 41 E3
Slavkovica SRB 56 C3
Slavonice CZ 41 D4
Slavonski Brod HR 55 E2
Slavonski Kobaš HR 55 E2
Slavuta UA 117 D1
Sława (Lubuskie) PL 92 C2
Sławatycze PL 95 F2
Sławięcice PL 97 E1
Sławków PL 98 A2
Sławno (Łódzkie) PL 94 B3
Sławno (Zachodnio-pomorskie) PL 89 D1
Sławoborze PL 88 B2
Ślažaj LT 80 B3
Sleaford GB 9 E1
Šlečkai LT 80 C2
Slengiai LT 80 A3
Šlepečiai LT 82 C3
Slesin (Kujawsko-Pomorskie) PL 89 E3
Slesin (Wielkopolskie) PL 93 F1
Sliedrecht NL 36 C1
Sliema M 53 F4
Šlienava LT 85 F2
Sligachan (Loch) GB 4 B3
Sligo / Sligeach IRL 2 C1
Slikiai LT 85 F1
Šliktine LT 80 B2
Šlipinciems LV 77 D3
Slišane SRB 57 E4
Slite S 67 F4
Sliven BG 117 E2
Sliwice PL 89 E2
Sližiūnai LT 86 B3
Šljivovica SRB 56 C4
Slobozia RO 117 E3
Słomniki PL 98 B2
Słonim BY 115 D3
Słońsk PL 88 A3
Sloten NL 32 B4
Slough GB 9 E2
Sloup CZ 41 E3
Slovac SRB 56 C3
Slovenj Gradec SLO 54 B1
Slovenska Bistrica SLO 54 B1
Slovenske Konjice SLO 54 B1
Slovinci HR 55 D2

Słowiński Park Narodowy PL 89 D1
Słubice (Lubuskie) PL 92 A1
Słubice (Mazowieckie) PL 94 A1
Sluck BY 115 D3
Sluderno / Schluderns I 43 E3
Sluis NL 36 B2
Šluknov CZ 40 C1
Slunj HR 54 C3
Słup PL 92 C3
Słupca PL 93 E1
Słupia (Łódzkie) PL 94 B2
Słupia (Świętokrzyskie) PL 98 B1
Słupno PL 94 A1
Słupsk PL 89 D1
Smålands-stenar S 71 D2
Smalininkai LT 84 C1
Smalvos LT 85 E2
Smärde LV 77 E3
Smarhon' BY 115 D3
Smarje SLO 54 A2
Šmarjeske Toplice SLO 54 B2
Smarliūnai LT 85 E3
Šmartno SLO 54 B2
Smed. Palanka SRB 57 D3
Smedby S 71 E2
Smědeč CZ 40 C4
Smederevo SRB 57 D2
Smedjebacken S 67 E2
Smelteriai LV 83 D2
Smelyne LT 82 B3
Smętowo Graniczne PL 89 F2
Šmigáda GR 103 D1
Smigiel PL 93 D2
Smilčić HR 54 C4
Smilde NL 32 C4
Smilgiai (Daujenai) LT 81 F2
Smilgiai (Sujetai) LT 81 F3
Smilgudruvas LV 83 D2
Smilktini LV 78 C2
Smiltene LV 78 C2
Smojmirovo MK 59 F3
Smokovljani HR 58 A3
Smolensk RUS 115 E2
Smoljan BG 117 D4
Smolnica PL 88 A3
Smolnik PL 99 E3
Šmotišiai LT 85 E1
Smygehamn S 71 D3
Smyków PL 94 B3

Snaigupe LT 85 E3
Snaith GB 7 F4
Snåsa N 63 D2
Sneek NL 32 B4
Sneem IRL 2 A4
Šnepele LV 76 C3
Sniadowo PL 90 D1
Sniardwy (Jezioro) PL 90 C1
Sniežka CZ 92 C3
Snihurivka UA 117 F1
Snikere LV 81 D2
Snillfjord N 62 C3
Šniukščiai LT 82 A2
Šniukštai LT 82 C3
Šniūraičiai LT 81 E3
Šnjegotina Velika BIH 55 D3
Snotuli LV 83 F1
Soave I 43 F4
Sobĕslav CZ 40 C3
Sobienie-Jeziory PL 94 C2
Sobieszewo PL 89 F1
Sobieszów PL 92 B3
Sobolew PL 95 D2
Sobotka CZ 40 C2
Sobótka (Dolnośląskie) PL 93 D3
Sobra HR 58 A3
Sobrado dos Monxes E 18 B2
Sobral da Adiça P 24 C4
Sobral de Monte Agraço P 24 A3
Sobreira Formosa P 24 C2
Søby DK 70 B4
Sočanica SRB 57 D4
Soccia F 23 F3
Sochaczew PL 94 B1
Sochaux F 17 D1
Sochocin PL 90 B3
Socovos E 26 A4
Socuéllamos E 26 A3
Sodankylä FIN 65 D1
Sodeliai (Juodupe) LT 82 C2
Sodeliai (Prüseliai) LT 81 F3
Sodeliškiai LT 82 A2
Söderåkra S 71 E3
Söderbärke S 67 E2
Söderfors S 67 E1
Söderhamn S 67 E3
Söderköping S 67 E3
Södertälje S 67 E3
Sodražica SLO 54 B2
Sodupe E 19 F2
Soe EE 78 C1
Soest D 37 D2

Soest NL 36 C1
Soestdijk NL 36 C1
Soeva EE 72 A1
Sofádes GR 105 D1
Sofia BG 117 D4
Sofiero S 71 D3
Sofikó GR 105 E3
Sofó GR 101 E4
Sögel D 33 D4
Sogliano al Rubicone I 47 E2
Soglio CH 43 D4
Søgne N 66 A3
Soham GB 9 E2
Sohós GR 102 A2
Soignies B 12 B1
Soini FIN 69 D1
Soinlahti FIN 69 E1
Soissons F 12 B3
Sojamaa EE 73 D3
Sokna N 66 C2
Sokobanja SRB 57 E3
Sokolac BIH 55 E4
Sokolany PL 91 E2
Sokółka PL 91 E2
Sokolniki PL 93 F3
Sokolov CZ 40 A3
Sokołów Małopolski PL 99 D2
Sokołów Podlaski PL 95 D1
Sokoły PL 91 E3
Sola N 66 A2
Solana de los Barros E 24 C3
Solana del Pino E 25 F4
Solares E 19 F2
Solberg S 68 A1
Solčava SLO 54 B1
Sol'cy RUS 115 E1
Solda / Sulden I 43 E3
Sölden A 43 F3
Soldin EE 73 D2
Solec Kujawski PL 89 E3
Solec n. Wisłą PL 95 D3
Solenzara F 23 F4
Solesmes F 11 D3
Solesmes F 15 D1
Solevågen N 62 B4
Solf FIN 68 C2
Solferino I 46 C1
Solholmen N 62 B3
Solignac F 12 A3
Solignac-sur-Loire F 16 B4
Solihull GB 9 D1
Solin HR 58 A4
Solina PL 99 E3
Soline HR 55 D3
Solingen D 37 E2
Solinske (Jezioro) PL 99 E3
Šoliškes LT 85 F2

Söll A 44 B2
Sollana E 27 D3
Solleftea S 68 A2
Sollenau A 45 E1
Sollentuna S 67 F2
Sóller E 31 E3
Solleron S 67 E1
Søllested DK 70 C4
Solliès-Pont F 22 C2
Solnechnogorsk RUS 115 F2
Solofra I 49 D4
Solosancho E 25 E1
Solothurn CH 17 E1
Solre-le-Château F 12 B2
Solrød DK 70 C3
Solska (Puszcza) PL 99 E1
Solsona E 21 E4
Šolta (Otok) HR 58 A4
Soltau D 33 E3
Sölvesborg S 71 E3
Solvorn N 66 B1
Sombernon F 16 C1
Sombor SRB 55 F1
Someren NL 37 D2
Somero FIN 69 D4
Sömerpalu EE 79 E2
Sömeru EE 73 D2
Sômianka PL 90 C3
Sommarøy N 60 C1
Sommatino I 53 D3
Sommerda D 39 D2
Sommesous F 12 C4
Sommières F 22 A2
Somolinos E 26 A1
Somonino PL 89 E1
Sompa EE 73 E2
Sompolno PL 93 F1
Son Servera E 31 F3
Soncino I 46 C1
Søndeled N 66 B3
Sønder Felding DK 70 B3
Sønderborg DK 70 B4
Sønderby DK 70 B4
Sondershausen D 39 D1
Søndersø DK 70 B3
Sondori LV 83 F1
Sondrio I 43 E4
Songeons F 12 A3
Sonkajärvi FIN 69 E1
Sonneberg D 39 D2
Sonnewalde D 39 F1
Sonogno CH 17 F3
Sonsbeck D 37 D1
Sonseca E 25 F3
Sonta SRB 55 F1
Sonthofen D 43 E2

Sontra D 38 C2
Soodoma EE 79 E1
Soometsa EE 75 F3
Soomevere EE 72 C3
Soonurme EE 73 E2
Sooru EE 79 D2
Sopeira E 21 D3
Sopilja BIH 58 B2
Sopište MK 59 E3
Sopot PL 89 F1
Sopot SRB 57 D3
Sopotnica MK 59 D4
Sopron H 116 B2
Sør-Flatanger N 63 D2
Sora I 48 B3
Soragna I 46 C1
Söråker S 68 A2
Sorbas E 26 A4
Sore F 20 C1
Soresina I 46 C1
Sörforsa S 68 B3
Sorga D 38 C2
Sørgutvik N 63 D2
Sórgono I 50 A3
Sorgues F 22 B2
Soria E 20 A4
Soriano nel Cimino I 47 E4
Sørkjosen N 60 C2
Sorkwity PL 90 C2
Sorø DK 70 C3
Soroca MD 117 E1
Soroni GR 111 F2
Sørreisa N 60 C2
Sorrento I 48 C4
Sørrollnes N 60 B3
Sorsakoski FIN 69 E2
Sorsele S 64 A2
Sonda EE 73 E2
Sorso I 50 A2
Sort E 21 D3
Sortino I 53 E4
Sortland N 60 B3
Sôru EE 74 C2
Sorunda S 67 F2
Sørvær N 61 D1
Sørværøy N 60 A4
Sörvattnet S 63 D3
Sørvik N 60 B1
Sos del Rey Católico E 20 B3
Sosdvaris LT 81 E2
Soses E 21 D4

Sošno PL 89 E2
Sosnovyj Bor RUS 115 D1
Sosnowica PL 95 E2
Sosnowiec PL 97 F2
Sospel F 23 E2
Šoštanj SLO 54 B1
Sóstis GR 102 C1
Šostka UA 115 F3
Sota Seter N 62 B4
Sotillo de la Adrada E 25 E2
Sotin HR 55 F2
Sotira GR 101 E2
Sotkanlis LT 81 D3
Sotkamo FIN 65 E3
Soto de los Infantes E 18 C2
Soto de Luiña E 18 C2
Soto de Sajambre E 19 E2
Soto del Barco E 19 D2
Sotogrande E 29 D4
Sotopalacios E 19 F2
Sotrondio E 19 D2
Sottomarina I 47 E1
Sottrum D 33 E3
Sottunga FIN 68 C4
Sotuélamos E 26 A3
Souda GR 109 D3
Souesmes F 15 F1
Soufflenheim F 13 F3
Soufli GR 103 E1
Soúgia GR 109 D4
Sougné-Remouchamps B 13 D1
Souillac F 15 F4
Souilly F 13 D4
Soulac-sur-Mer F 14 C3
Soulaines-Dhuys F 12 C4
Soulinári GR 108 A1
Soulópoulo GR 100 C4
Soultz-Haut-Rhin F 42 B2
Soultz-sous-Forêts F 13 F3
Soúnio GR 105 F2
Soúnio (Akr.) GR 105 F2
Souppes-sur-Loing F 12 A4
Sourdeval F 11 D4
Soure F 24 B2
Sournia F 21 F3
Sourotí GR 101 F3
Sousceyrac F 15 F4
Sousel P 24 C3
Soustons F 20 B2
Soutelo E 18 A3
South Molton GB 8 C2
South Queensferry GB 7 D1
South Shields GB 7 E3
Southam GB 9 D2
Southampton GB 9 D4
Southborough GB 9 E3

Southend GB 6 B2
Southend-on-Sea GB 9 F3
Southport GB 7 D4
Southsea GB 9 D4
Southwell GB 9 D1
Southwold GB 9 F2
Souvála GR 105 F3
Souvigny F 16 A2
Sovata RO 117 D2
Sövdeborg S 71 D3
Soverato I 51 E3
Soveria Mannelli I 51 E3
Søvik N 62 B3
Sozopol BG 117 E4
Sp. Brnik SLO 54 A2
Spa B 13 D1
Spaichingen D 13 F4
Spaigiai LT 81 D2
Spakenburg NL 32 B4
Spalding GB 9 E1
Spalviškiai LT 82 B2
Spandau D 34 B4
Spanenai LT 85 F1
Spangenberg D 38 C2
Spåre (Cēsu) LV 78 B3
Spåre (Talsu) LV 76 C3
Sparlösa S 71 D1
Spárta GR 105 E2
Spárti GR 108 B1
Spárto GR 105 D3
Spáta GR 105 F2
Spatharéi GR 107 E3
Spean Bridge GB 4 B3
Spello I 47 E4
Spennymoor GB 7 E3
Sperhiáda GR 105 D1
Sperlonga I 48 B3
Spernia LT 85 F1
Spétses GR 105 E4
Spétses (Nissi) GR 105 E4
Spetsopoúla (Nissí) GR 105 E4
Speyer D 13 F3
Spezzano Albanese Terme I 51 E2
Spezzano della Sila I 51 E3
Spičiai LT 81 E3
Spiczyn PL 95 E3
Spiddal / An Spidéal IRL 2 B3
Spīdolas LV 83 E3
Spiekeroog D 33 D3
Spielfeld A 45 E4
Spiez CH 17 E2
Spijkenisse NL 36 B1
Spili GR 109 E4
Spiliá GR 101 F4

STRASBOURG AGGLOMÉRATION

0 ——— 2 km

BISCHHEIM
Marais (R. du) .... CS 121
Périgueux (Av. de) .... BS 159
Robertsau (R. de la) .... BS 179
Triage (R. du) .... BS 219

ECKBOLSHEIM
Gaulle (Av. du Gén.-de) .... BS 67
Wasselonne (Rte de) .... BS 237

HŒNHEIM
Fontaine (R. de la) .... BR 55
République (R. de la) .... BR 174

ILLKIRCH-GRAFFENSTADEN
Bürckel (Rte) .... BT 24
Ceinture (R. de la) .... BT 27
Faisanderie (R. de la) .... BT 91
Industrie (R. de l') .... BT 97
Kastler (R. Alfred) .... BT 118
Lixenbühl (R.) .... BT 115
Messmer (Av.) .... BT 138
Neuhof (Rte de) .... BT 144
Strasbourg (Rte de) .... BT 207
Vignes (R. des) .... BT 233

LINGOLSHEIM
Eckbolsheim (R. d') .... BS 44
Ostwald (R. d') .... BS 152
Près (R. des) .... BS 168

OBERHAUSBERGEN
Mittelhausbergen (Rte de) .... BS 139
Oberhausbergen (Rte de) .... BS 149

OSTWALD
Foch (R. du Maréchal) .... BT 50
Gelspolsheim (R. de) .... BT 73
Leclerc (R. du Gén.) .... BT 112
Vosges (R. des) .... BT 232
23-Novembre (R. du) .... BT 246

SCHILTIGHEIM
Bischwiller (Rte de) .... BS 18
Gaulle (Rte du Gén.-de) .... BS 70
Hausbergen (Rte de) .... BS 81
Mendès-France (Av. P.) .... BS 132
Pompiers (R. des) .... BS 164

STRASBOURG
Atenheim (Rte d') .... CT 8
Austerlitz (Pont d') .... BS 9
Bauerngrund (R. de) .... CT 15
Ganzau (R. de la) .... BT 66
Holtzheim (R. de) .... AS 88
Ill (R. de l') .... CS 96
Neuhof (Rte de) .... CT 144
Plaine des Bouchers (R. de la) .... BS 163
Polygone (Rte du) .... BS 165
Pont (R. du) .... CT 166
Ribeauvillé (R. de) .... CS 177
Romains (Rte des) .... BS 180
Schirmeck (Rte de) .... BS 198

WOLFISHEIM
Oberhausbergen (R. d') .... AS 148
Seigneurs (R. des) .... AS 204

Spilimbergo I....44 B3
Spilsby GB....9 E1
Spinalónga
(Hers.) GR....110 C4
Spinazzola I....49 E3
Spincourt F....13 D3
Špindlerův Mlýn CZ....41 D2
Spinni LV....76 C2
Špionica Donja BIH....55 E3
Špišić Bukovica HR....55 E1
Spišská Nová Ves SK....116 C1
Spital am Pyhrn A....44 C1
Spitami/Spithamn EE....75 D1
Spittal an der Drau A....44 C3
Spitz A....41 D4
Spjelkavik N....62 B3
Split HR....58 A4
Splügen CH....43 D3
Spodsbjerg DK....70 C4
Špogi (Spogi) LV....83 D2
Špola UA....117 F1
Spoleto I....47 F4
Sportnitz D....34 A4
Spotorno I....23 E1
Spremberg D....40 C1
Spresiano I....44 B4
Spříditis LV....78 C2
Sprikutova LV....83 F2
Springe D....33 E4
Sprogi (Oškalns) LV....82 B2
Sprungas LV....77 D3
Spunciems LV....77 E3
Spungēni LV....82 C1
Spuž MNE....58 C3
Spytkowice
(Małopolskie) PL....98 A2
Squillace I....51 E3
Squinzano I....51 F1
Srb HR....54 C4
Srbac BIH....55 D3
Srbica SRB....59 D2
Srbinje / Foca BIH....55 F4
Srbobran SRB....55 F2
Srđevići BIH....55 D4
Srebrenica BIH....55 F3
Srebrenik BIH....55 E3
Središče ob Dravi SLO....54 C1
Srednje BIH....55 E4
Sredska SRB....59 E3
Srem PL....93 D2
Srem. Kamenica SRB....55 F2
Sremska
Mitrovica SRB....55 F2
Sremska Rača SRB....55 F2
Šriubiškes LT....86 B2
Srnetica BIH....55 D3
Srnice Donje BIH....55 E3
Sroda Slaska PL....93 D3
Sroda Wielkopolska PL....93 D1
Srokowo PL....90 C1
Srpska Crnja SRB....56 C1
Srpska Kostajnica /
Bosanska
Kostajnica BIH....54 C3
Srpski Brod /
Bosanski Brod BIH....55 E2
Srpski Itebej SRB....56 C1
Srpski Miletić SRB....55 F1
Srpsko Sarajevo BIH....55 E4
Stabaunyčius LT....85 E1
Stabintiškes LT....85 F2
Stabulnieki
(Stabulnīki) LV....83 E2
Stacija Ventspils-2 LV....76 B2
Stačiūnai
(Panevežio) LT....81 F2
Stačiūnai (Šiauliu) LT....81 E2
Stade D....33 E3
Stádio GR....105 D4
Stadskanaal NL....32 C4
Stadt Wehlen D....39 F1
Stadthagen D....33 E4
Stadtilm D....39 D2
Stadtkyll D....13 D2
Stadtlohn D....37 E1
Stadtoldendorf D....38 C1
Stadtroda D....39 E2
Stadtsteinach D....39 D3
Staffanstorp S....71 D3
Staffelstein D....39 D3
Staffin GB....4 B3
Stafford GB....8 C1
Stágira GR....102 A2
Stahle D....38 C1
Stahovica SLO....54 A2
Staicele LV....78 B2
Staines GB....9 E3
Stainz A....45 D2
Stakai LT....86 C2
Štakeldanga LV....80 B1
Štaki LV....79 D3
Stakiai LT....85 D1
Stakliškes LT....85 F2
Stalać SRB....57 E4
Stalbe LV....78 B2
Štalcerji SLO....54 B2
Staldzene LV....76 B2
Stalgene LV....81 F1
Stalida GR....109 F4
Stalidzāni LV....83 D1
Stall A....44 B3
Stalowa Wola PL....99 D1
Stămeriena LV....79 E3
Stamford GB....9 E1
Stamnes N....66 A1
Stams A....43 F2
Stamsund N....60 A3

Stanelaui LT....80 C2
Stange N....66 C1
Stanin PL....95 D2
Staniśić SRB....55 F1
Stanišinci SRB....57 D4
Stanisławów PL....91 D3
Stánjel SLO....54 A2
Stankiškiai LT....80 A3
Staňkov CZ....40 B3
Stankovci HR....54 C4
Stanley GB....7 E3
Stanós GR....102 A2
Stános GR....104 B1
Stasylos LT....86 B3
Staszów PL....98 C1
Stathm. Angistis GR....102 B2
Stansstad CH....17 F2
Stansted
Mountfitchet GB....9 E2
Stapar SRB....55 F2
Stąporków PL....94 B3
Stará Błotnica PL....94 C2
Stará Boleslav CZ....40 C2
Stara Kamienica PL....92 B3
Stara Kiszewa PL....89 E2
Stara Kornica PL....95 E1
Stara Moravica SRB....55 F1
Stara Novalija HR....54 B4
Stara Pazova SRB....56 C2
Stara Wieś
(Mazowieckie) PL....95 D1
Stara Zagora BG....117 E4
Starachowice PL....94 C3
Staraja Russa RUS....115 C3
Staravina MK....59 F4
Starcza PL....97 F1
Stare Babice PL....94 C1
Stare Bogaczowice PL....92 C3
Stare Czarnowo PL....88 A2
Stare Iganie PL....95 D1
Stare Jabłonki PL....90 B2
Stare Kurowo PL....88 B3
Stare Pole PL....89 F1
Stare Sady PL....90 C2
Stargard
Szczeciński PL....88 B2
Stärheim D....62 A4
Stari LV....79 D3
Stari Bar MNE....58 C4
Stari Dojran MK....59 F4
Stari Gradac HR....55 D2
Stari Jankovci HR....55 F2
Stari Log SLO....54 B2
Stari Majdan BIH....55 D3
Stari Mikanovci HR....55 E2
Starica RUS....115 F2
Starigrad
(Hvar Otok) HR....58 A4
Starigrad (Senj) HR....54 B4
Starigrad Paklenica HR....54 C4
Starnberg D....43 F1
Staro Petrovo Selo HR....55 D2
Staro Slano BIH....58 B3
Starodub RUS....115 F3
Starogard Gdański PL....89 F2
Starożreby PL....90 B3

Stary Brus PL....95 E2
Stary Dzierzgoń PL....90 A2
Stary Dzikowiec PL....99 D2
Stary Gózd PL....94 C2
Stary Jarosław PL....88 C1
Stary Lubotyń PL....91 D3
Stary Sącz PL....98 B3
Starý Smokovec SK....116 C1
Stary Targ PL....89 F2
Stary Zamość PL....95 E3
Staškūniškis LT....86 B1
Staškūniškis LT....86 B1
Staßfurt D....39 D1
Stathelle N....64 C2
Statland N....63 D2
Stavanger N....64 A3
Staveley GB....9 D1
Stavelot B....13 D1
Stavenhagen
Reuterstadt D....34 B2
Stavenisse NL....36 B1
Stavern N....64 C2
Stavoren NL....32 B4
Stavrodrómi GR....104 C3
Stavrohóri GR....110 C4
Stavrós GR....102 A2
Stavrós GR....101 E2
Stavrós GR....104 A2
Stavrós GR....109 D3
Stavrós (Évia) GR....105 F2
Stavrós (Lárissa) GR....105 D1
Stavroúpoli GR....102 C1
Stavsjo N....66 C1
Stawiguda PL....90 B2
Stawiski PL....91 D2
Stawiszyn PL....93 D2
Štěchovice CZ....40 C3
Steckborn CH....17 F1
Steeg A....43 E2
Steenbergen NL....36 B1
Steenvoorde F....12 A1
Steenwijk NL....32 C4
Stefáni GR....104 B1
Stefáni GR....105 F3
Stefaniná GR....102 A2
Stefanodikio GR....101 F4
Stege DK....70 C4
Stegersbach A....45 E2
Stegna PL....89 F1
Steibis D....43 E2
Steigen N....60 B3
Steigra D....39 D2
Stein A....41 D4
Stein D....39 D4
Stein am Rhein CH....17 F1
Steinach A....43 F2
Steinach D....39 D2
Šteinalti LV....82 B1
Steinau a. d. Straße D....38 C3
Steinbach-
Hallenberg D....39 D2
Steine N....66 A1

Steinfeld A....44 C3
Steinfeld
(Oldenburg) D....33 D4
Steinfurt D....37 E1
Steingaden D....43 E2
Steinhausen D....43 D1
Steinheim D....37 F1
Steinheim D....43 E1
Steinkjer N....63 D2
Steinshamn N....62 B3
Steinsland N....66 A1
Stekene B....12 B1
Stelmuže LT....83 D3
Stelpe LV....81 F1
Stemnitsa GR....104 C4
Stemwede D....33 D4
Stenay F....12 C3
Stendal D....34 A4
Stende LV....77 D3
Stení GR....105 F2
Stenlille DK....70 C3
Stenløse DK....70 C3
Stenness GB....5 D2
Stenó GR....105 D4
Sténoma GR....104 C1
Stenudden S....64 A2
Stenungsund S....66 C3
Stepanci MK....59 E4
Stepi LV....79 D2
Stepnica PL....88 A2
Stepojevac SRB....56 C3
Steponkaimis LT....81 E3
Sterdyń-Osada PL....91 D3
Sterkrade D....37 E1
Stérna GR....103 E1
Stérna GR....102 B1
Stérna GR....105 D3
Sternberg D....34 A2
Šternberk CZ....41 E3
Stérnes GR....109 D3
Sterup D....34 B1
Stęszew PL....93 D1
Stevenage GB....9 E2
Stewarton GB....6 C2
Steyr A....44 C1
Steyrermühl A....44 C1
Stężyca
(Lubelskie) PL....95 D2
Stężyca
(Pomorskie) PL....89 E1
Stia I....47 E2
Stigliano I....50 C4
Stigtomta S....67 F3
Stiklestad N....63 D3
Stikli LV....76 C2
Štikoni LV....83 E2
Stilida GR....105 D1
Stilo I....51 E3
Stimfalía (L.) GR....105 D3
Štimlje SRB....59 E3
Stintino I....50 A2
Štip MK....59 F3
Stípnieki LV....81 F1
Stipsi GR....107 D1
Stira GR....106 B3
Stirling GB....7 D1

Stirniene LV....83 D1
Stirniškiai LT....85 D2
Štirovača HR....54 B3
Štitar SRB....55 F3
Štivan HR....54 B3
Štiveri LV....78 B3
Stjärnhov S....67 F3
Stjärnsund S....67 E3
Stjørdal N....63 D3
Stockach D....43 D2
Stockbridge GB....9 D3
Stockelsdorf D....33 F2
Stockerau A....41 E4
Stockholm S....67 F3
Stockport GB....7 E4
Stocksbridge GB....7 E4
Stockton-on-Tees GB....7 E3
Stoczek Łukowski PL....95 D2
Stod CZ....40 B3
Stöde S....68 A2
Stoke-on-Trent GB....8 C1
Stokke N....66 C1
Stokmarknes N....60 B3
Stolac BIH....58 B3
Stolberg D....39 F1
Stolberg D....13 D1
Stolerova LV....83 F2
Stolice SRB....55 F3
Stolin BY....115 D4
Stollberg D....39 E2
Stöllet S....67 D2
Stolno PL....89 F2
Stolpen D....39 F1
Stolzenau D....33 E4
Stómio GR....101 F4
Ston HR....58 A3
Stone GB....8 C1
Stonehaven GB....5 D4
Stonglandet N....60 B2
Stoniava LT....85 F2
Stopanja SRB....57 D4
Stopnica PL....98 C1
Storå S....67 E2
Stora Blåsjön S....63 E4
Stora Skedvi S....67 E1
Storby FIN....68 B4
Stordal N....62 B4
Store Heddinge DK....70 C3
Store Molvik N....61 F1
Storebø N....66 A1
Storebro S....67 E4
Støren N....62 C2
Storfors S....67 D2
Storforshei N....63 E1
Storkow D....34 C4
Stormi FIN....68 C3
Stornoway GB....4 B2
Storo I....43 E3
Storožynec' UA....117 D1
Storsjö S....63 D3
Storslett / Nordreisa N....60 C2
Storsteinen N....60 C2
Storsteinnes N....60 C2
Storuman S....64 A3
Storvik N....61 D1

Storvik S....67 E1
Stoszowice PL....96 C1
Stotel D....33 D3
Stoùbcy BY....115 D3
Stoúpa GR....108 A1
Stourbridge GB....8 C2
Stournaréika GR....101 D4
Stourport-on Severn GB....8 C2
Støvring DK....70 B2
Stow-on-the-Wold GB....9 D2
Stowmarket GB....9 F2
Strà I....44 B4
Strabane GB....6 A2
Strachosław PL....95 F3
Strachówka PL....94 C1
Stracin MK....59 F3
Stračiūnai LT....85 E3
Stradbally IRL....3 D3
Stradella I....46 B1
Stradi LV....79 E3
Stradsett GB....9 F1
Stradunia PL....97 E1
Straelen D....37 D1
Stragari SRB....57 D3
Stragute LT....84 C1
Strakonice CZ....40 C4
Stralsund D....34 B1
Stramberk CZ....41 F3
Strančice SLO....54 B1
Stranda N....62 B4
Strandbarm N....66 A1
Strandhill IRL....2 C1
Strangford GB....3 E2
Strängnäs S....67 F2
Stráni CZ....41 F3
Stranice SLO....54 B1
Stranorlar IRL....2 C1
Stranraer GB....3 E1
Strasbourg F....13 F4
Strasburg D....34 B2
Straßberg D....45 D2
Straßwalchen A....44 B1
Straszyn PL....89 F1
Stratford-
upon-Avon GB....9 D2
Strathaven GB....6 C2
Stratóni GR....102 A3
Stratoniki GR....102 A2
Strátos GR....104 B2
Stratton GB....8 A3
Straubing D....39 F4
Straulas I....34 C4
Straumen N....60 B4
Straumen
(Nord Trøndelag) N....63 D3
Straumen
(Nordland) N....60 A4
Straumsjøen N....60 A3
Straumsnes N....60 B4
Straupe LV....78 B2
Straupitz D....34 C4
Strausberg D....34 C4
Straußfurt D....39 D2
Strauti LV....80 A1
Strautini LV....79 E2
Strautmali LV....78 B3
Strawczyn PL....94 B3
Straža SLO....54 B2

Straža SRB....57 D2
Strazde LV....77 D3
Strážnice CZ....41 F4
Strážný CZ....40 C4
Streatley GB....9 D3
Street GB....8 C3
Strehaia RO....117 D3
Strehla D....39 F1
Streitberg D....39 D3
Strēlnieki
(Aizkraukles) LV....82 C1
Strēlnieki
(Bauskas) LV....81 F1
Strenči LV....78 C2
Strengberg A....45 D1
Stresa I....17 F3
Strezimirovci SRB....57 F4
Strezovce SRB....59 E2
Stříbro CZ....40 B3
Striki LV....80 B1
Strīķi LV....80 C1
Strimonikó GR....102 A2
Strmac HR....55 D2
Strmen HR....54 C2
Strmsten SRB....57 E3
Strobl A....44 C1
Strofádes (Nissiá) GR....104 B3
Strofiliá GR....105 E1
Strojkovce SRB....57 E4
Strokestown IRL....2 C2
Stromberg D....13 E2
Stromeferry GB....4 B3
Strömfors S....69 E4
Stromiec PL....94 C2
Stromness GB....5 D2
Strömsbruk S....68 A1
Strömsnasbruk S....71 D2
Strömstad S....66 C3
Strömsund S....63 E3
Strongoli I....51 E2
Stronie Śląskie PL....97 D3
Strontian GB....4 C4
Stropi LV....83 D3
Stroud GB....8 C2
Strövlés GR....109 D4
Struer DK....70 B2
Struga MK....59 E4
Struga PL....94 C1
Struge SLO....54 B2
Strumica MK....59 F4
Strumień PL....97 F2
Strūna LT....87 D1
Strunki LV....79 D3
Strupli LV....83 E1
Stružáni LV....83 E1
Stryj UA....117 D1
Stryjów PL....95 E3
Stryków PL....94 A2
Strykowo PL....93 D1
Stryn N....62 B4
Strzałkowo PL....93 E1
Strzegom PL....92 C3
Strzegowo PL....90 B3
Strzegów
(Opolskie) PL....97 D1
Strzelce (Łodzkie) PL....94 A1
Strzelce Krajeńskie PL....88 B3
Strzelce Opolskie PL....97 E1
Strzelce Wielkie PL....94 A3
Strzeleczki PL....97 E1
Strzelin PL....93 D3
Strzelno PL....89 E3
Strzybnica PL....97 F1
Strzyżewice PL....95 E3
Strzyżów
(Podkarpackie) PL....99 D3
Stubbekøbing DK....70 C4
Stubičke Toplice HR....54 C2
Štubik SRB....56 C3
Stubline SRB....56 C3
Stubno PL....99 E2
Stuburai LT....81 D1
Studena SRB....57 F4
Studenci HR....58 A4
Studenica SRB....57 D4
Studénka CZ....41 F2
Studzienna PL....97 E2
Stūgliai LT....82 C3
Stugun S....63 E3
Stühlingen D....17 F1
Stuhr D....33 E3
Stukmani LV....82 C1
Stulgiai LT....80 C3
Stultiškiai LT....81 F3
Stumbres LT....80 C3
Stumbriškis
(Pažasai) LT....81 F2
Stumbriškis
(Sodeliai) LT....81 F3
Stupari BIH....55 F3
Stupino RUS....115 F3
Stupnik HR....54 C2
Stupsk PL....90 B3
Stupurai LT....81 D1
Sturehov S....67 F3
Stūri LV....81 D1
Stūriši LV....77 D3
Sturminster Newton GB....8 C3
Stuttgart D....43 D1
Stykkishólmur IS....62 A1
Suances E....19 F2
Subačiškes LT....85 E2
Subačius LT....82 B3
Subate LV....82 C2
Subbiano I....47 E3
Subiaco I....48 B3
Subijana E....20 A3
Subkowy PL....89 F2
Subotica SRB....55 F1
Subotište SRB....56 C2
Suceava RO....117 D2
Sucevita RO....117 D2
Sucha Beskidzka PL....98 A2
Suchacz PL....90 A1
Suchań PL....88 B2
Suchedniów PL....94 C3
Suchiničí RUS....115 F2
Suchowola
(Podlaskie) PL....91 E2
Suchožebry PL....95 D1

STUTTGART

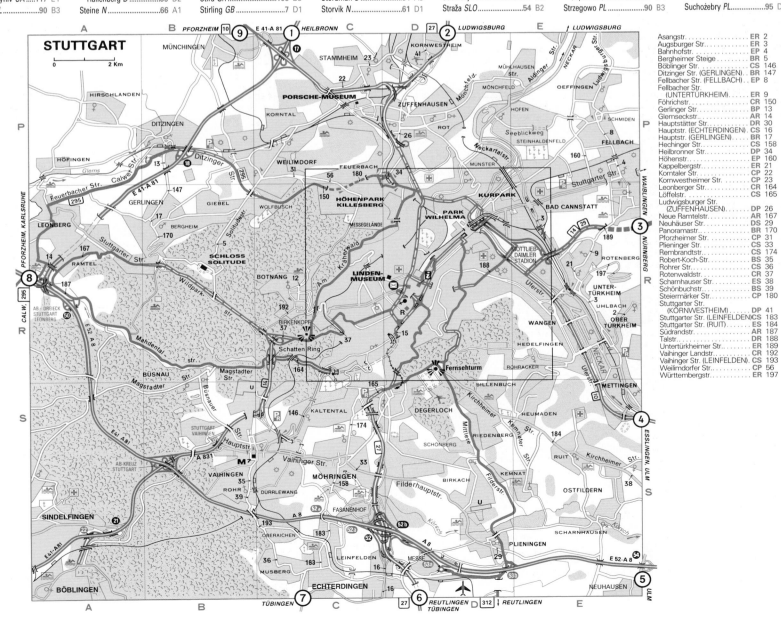

Asangstr. . . . . ER 2
Augsburger Str. . . . . ER 3
Bahnhofstr. . . . . EP 4
Bergheime Steige . . . . BR 5
Böblinger Str. . . . . CS 146
Ditzinger Str. (GERLINGEN) . BR 147
Fellbacher Str. (FELLBACH) . EP 8
Fellbacher Str.
(UNTERTÜRKHEIM) . . . . ER 9
Föhrichstr. . . . . CR 150
Gerlinger Str. . . . . BP 13
Glemseckstr. . . . . AR 14
Hauptstätter Str. . . . . DR 30
Hauptstr. (ECHTERDINGEN) . 16
Hauptstr. (GERLINGEN) . . . BR 17
Hechinger Str. . . . . DP 34
Heilbronner Str. . . . . EP 160
Höhenstr. . . . . CR 31
Kappelbergstr. . . . . CR 21
Korntaler Str. . . . . CP 22
Kornwestheimer Str. . . . . . CR 23
Leonberger Str. . . . . CR 164
Löffelstr. . . . . CR 165
Ludwigsburger Str.
(ZUFFENHAUSEN) . . . . . DP 26
Neue Ramtelstr. . . . . AR 167
Neuhäuser Str. . . . . DS 29
Panoramastr. . . . . BR 170
Pforzheimer Str. . . . . CP 31
Plieninger Str. . . . . CS 33
Rembrandtstr. . . . . CS 174
Robert-Koch-Str. . . . . BS 35
Rohrer Str. . . . . CS 36
Rotenwaldstr. . . . . CR 37
Scharnhauser Str. . . . . CS 180
Schönbuchstr. . . . . BS 39
Steiermärker Str. . . . . CP 180
Stuttgarter Str.
(KORNWESTHEIM) . . . . DP 41
Stuttgarter Str. (LEINFELDEN) CS 183
Stuttgarter Str. (RUIT) 184
Südrandstr. . . . . AR 187
Talstr. . . . . DR 188
Untertürkheimer Str. . . . . . ER 189
Vaihinger Landstr. . . . . CS 192
Vaihinger Str. (LEINFELDEN) CS 193
Weilimdorfer Str. . . . . CP 56
Württembergstr. . . . . ER 197

Süchteln D	37	D2
Suchy Las PL	93	D1
Sucina E	30	C2
Sudarbe LV	79	E3
Sudargas LT	84	C1
Sudbury GB	9	D1
Sudbury GB	9	F2
Suddesjaur S	64	B2
Sudeikiai LT	82	C3
Südenai LT	80	B2
Süderbrarup D	33	E1
Suderve LT	86	B2
Sudiste EE	78	C1
Sudoł PL	94	C3
Sudrabkalns LV	83	D2
Sudža RUS	115	F4
Sueca E	27	D3
Sueros de Cepeda E	19	D3
Suginčiai LT	86	C1
Suhl D	39	D2
Suho Polje BIH	55	F3
Suhopolje HR	55	D4
Šuica BIH	55	D4
Suigu EE	72	B3
Suinula FIN	69	D3
Suippes F	12	C3
Suislepa EE	78	C1
Sujainiai LT	81	D3
Sujetai LT	81	F3
Šuke LT	80	B2
Sukeva FIN	69	E3
Šukionys LT	81	E2
Šukionys LT	82	A2
Sukobin MNE	58	C4
Sukošan HR	54	C4
Sukovo SRB	57	F4
Sükuriai LT	85	E2
Šula MNE	58	C4
Sulbi EE	79	E1
Sulechów PL	92	C2
Sulęcin PL	92	B1
Sulęczyno PL	89	E2
Sulejów PL	94	A3
Sulejówek PL	94	A2
Sulejowski (Jezioro) PL	94	B3
Sulików PL	92	B3
Sulina RO	117	F2
Sulingen D	33	E4
Sulitjelma N	60	B4
Sulkava FIN	69	F3
Sułkowice PL	98	A2
Sully-sur-Loire F	15	F1
Sulmierzyce (Łódzkie) PL	94	A3
Sulmierzyce (Wielkopolskie) PL	93	E2
Sulmona I	48	C2
Sułoszowa PL	98	A1
Sułów (Lubelskie) PL	95	E3
Sultsi EE	78	C1
Sulustvere EE	73	D3
Sulz a. Neckar D	13	F4
Sulzbach (Saar) D	13	E3
Sulzbach a. d. Murr D	38	C4
Sulzbach-Rosenberg D	39	E3
Sulzemoos D	43	F1
Sumartin HR	58	B4
Sumba (Færøerne) DK	62	A3
Sümeg H	116	B2
Šumen BG	117	E3
Sumiainen FIN	69	E2
Sumiswald CH	27	F2
Šumperk CZ	41	E2
Šumskas LT	86	B1
Sumy UA	115	F4
Šunakojai LT	86	B1
Sunäkste LV	82	C1
Sünciems LV	80	B1
Sundankai LT	82	C1
Sunde N	66	A2
Sunde (Sør-Trøndelag) N	62	C3
Sunderland GB	7	E3
Sundern (Sauerland) D	37	E2
Sundom FIN	68	C2
Sundsvall S	68	A2
Suni I	50	A3
Suniši LV	78	B3
Sunja HR	54	C2
Sunnansjö S	62	C2
Sunndalsøra N	62	C3
Sunne S	63	E3
Sunne S	67	D2
Sunnemo S	67	D2
Šunskai LT	85	E2
Suntaži LV	78	B3
Suodenniemi FIN	68	C3
Suolahti FIN	69	D2
Suolijoki FIN	65	D2
Suomenlinna FIN	69	D4
Suomenniemi FIN	69	E3
Suomusjärvi FIN	69	D4
Suomussalmi FIN	65	E3
Suonenjoki FIN	69	E2
Suopelto FIN	69	E1
Suostas LT	82	B2
Super-Besse F	16	A4
Super Molina E	21	E4
Supetar HR	58	B4
Supetarska Draga HR	54	B3
Supino I	48	B3
Supraśl PL	91	E2
Supsi EE	78	C1
Surahammar S	67	E2
Suraż PL	91	E3
Suraž RUS	115	F3
Surbo I	51	F1
Surčin SRB	56	C2
Surdegis LT	82	B3
Surdulica SRB	59	F2
Surenenpass CH	17	F2
Surgères F	15	D3
Súria E	21	E4
Surju EE	75	F3
Surnadalsøra N	62	C3
Sursee CH	17	F1
Surviliškis LT	81	E1
Survilliers F	12	A3
Susa I	17	E4
Sušac (Otok) HR	58	A4
Susak HR	54	B4
Sušara SRB	57	D2
Susch CH	43	E3
Susek SRB	55	F2
Suševo MK	99	E1
Šuškova LV	83	F2
Sušice CZ	40	B1
Susuřeni LV	82	C1
Susurluk TR	117	F4
Susz PL	89	F2
Sutivan HR	58	B4
Šutai LT	86	C1
Sutinjske Toplice HR	54	C2
Sutjeska BIH	55	E4
Sutjeska SRB	57	D2
Sutkiai LT	85	D1
Sutlema EE	72	B2
Sutlepa EE	75	D1
Sutomore MNE	58	C3
Sutri I	47	E4
Sutri LV	83	D7
Sutterton GB	9	E1
Sutton GB	9	E2
Sutton Coldfield GB	9	D1
Sutton-in-Ashfield GB	9	D1
Sutvan HR	58	A3
Suure-Jaani EE	72	C3
Suurejõe EE	72	B3
Suuremõisa EE	74	C2
Suurküla EE	72	C1
Suurpea EE	72	C1
Suur-Rahula EE	74	C2
Suva Reka SRB	59	D3
Suvainiškis LT	82	B2
Suvenai LT	82	B2
Suviekas LT	83	D3
Suvodanja SRB	56	C3
Suvodol MK	59	E4
Suwałki PL	91	E1
Suži LV	77	F3
Sužionys LT	86	C2
Suzzara I	47	D1
Svanstein S	64	C1
Svanvik N	61	F1
Svappavaara S	64	B1
Svärdsjö S	67	E1
Svanvik N	64	C1
Svartå S	67	E3
Svartevatn N	66	A2
Svedala S	71	D3
Svedasai LT	82	B3
Svedriška E	83	D3
Sveg S	63	E4
Švekšna LT	80	B3
Svelbergis LV	79	D3
Svelgen N	62	A4
Svelvik N	62	C3
Švenčioneliai LT	86	C1
Švenčionys LT	87	D1
Svendborg DK	70	B4
Švendriai LT	81	D2
Svenljunga S	67	D4
Svensby N	60	C2
Svenstavik S	63	E4
Svente LV	83	D3
Sventes LV	83	D3
Šventežeris LT	85	E3
Šventininkai (Kauno) LT	85	F2
Šventininkai (Vilniaus) LT	86	B2
Šventragis LT	85	E2
Šventupe LT	86	B1
Šventybrastis LT	81	F3
Svetac (Otok) HR	58	A4
Svētciems LV	77	F2
Svēte LV	81	E1
Sveti Dorde (Manastir) MK	59	D4
Sveti Filip-Jakov HR	54	C4
Sveti Ivan Žabno HR	54	C2
Sveti Ivan Zelina HR	54	C2
Sveti Jovan Bigorski MK	59	D4
Sveti Juraj HR	54	B3
Sveti Naum MK	59	E4
Sveti Nikola MNE	58	C4
Sveti Nikole MK	59	F3
Sveti Petar na moru HR	54	C4
Sveti Rok HR	54	C4
Sveti Stefan MNE	58	C3
Svetlahorsk BY	115	E3
Svetlogorsk RUS	114	B3
Svetozar Miletić SRB	55	F1
Sviby GB	75	D1
Svidnik SK	116	C1
Svidžiai LT	82	B2
Sviesta Gārša LV	79	E2
Švihov CZ	40	B3
Svilajnac SRB	57	D3
Svilengrad BG	117	E4
Sviliai (Kauno) LT	85	E1
Sviliai (Panevežio) LT	82	B2
Svingvoll N	66	C1
Svinoy (Færøerne) DK	62	A3
Svinná MK	97	F2
Svinoujście PL	88	A2
Svirbūtes LT	81	D2
Svirnai II LT	86	B1
Svištov BG	117	D3
Svitavy CZ	41	E3
Svitavy CZ	116	B1
Svitene LV	81	E2
Svitlovods'k UA	117	F1
Svod SRB	57	F4
Svolvær N	60	A3
Svorkmo N	62	C3
Svoronáta GR	104	A3
Svorónos GR	101	E3
Syötekylä FIN	65	E2
Svrljig SRB	57	E4
Swadlincote GB	9	D1
Swaffham GB	9	F1
Swalmen NL	37	D2
Swanage GB	8	C4
Swanley GB	9	E3
Swanlinbar IRL	2	C3
Swansea / Abertawe GB	8	B2
Swarzędz PL	93	D1
Świątki PL	90	B2
Świątkowa Wielka PL	98	C3
Świbno PL	89	F1
Swidnica (Dolnośląskie) PL	92	C3
Swidnica (Lubuskie) PL	92	B2
Świdnik PL	95	E3
Świdwin PL	88	B2
Świebodzice PL	92	C3
Świebodzin PL	92	B1
Świecie PL	89	E2
Święciechowa PL	93	D2
Świekatowo PL	89	E2
Świeradów-Zdrój PL	92	B3
Świercze PL	90	B3
Świerczów PL	93	E3
Świerklaniec PL	97	F1
Świerklany Górne PL	97	F2
Świerzawa PL	92	C3
Świerzno PL	88	B2
Świeszyno (Zachodnio-pomorskie) PL	88	C1
Święta Katarzyna (Dolnośląskie) PL	93	D3
Świętniki PL	93	F2
Święta Lipka PL	90	C1
Świętochłowice PL	97	F2
Świętokrzyski Park Narodowy PL	94	C3
Świętokrzyskie (Góry) PL	94	B3
Szadek PL	93	F2
Szałas PL	94	B3
Swindon GB	9	D3
Swinford / Béal Atha na Muice IRL	2	B3
Swinice Warckie PL	93	F2
Swinna PL	97	F2
Świnoujście PL	88	A2
Swisłocz PL	91	F2
Swords / Sord IRL	3	D4
Syčovka RUS	115	F2
Syców PL	93	E3
Sykäräinen FIN	69	D1
Sykkylven N	62	B4
Syke D	33	E4
Sylt-Ost D	33	D1
Syltefjord N	61	F1
Synod Inn GB	3	F4
Syötekylä FIN	65	E2
Sypniewo (Mazowieckie) PL	90	B3
Sypniewo (Mazowieckie) PL	90	C3
Szydłów (Mazowieckie) PL	90	B3
Szydłowo (Wielkopolskie) PL	88	C3
Szymbark (Małopolskie) PL	98	C2
Szypliszki PL	91	E1
Szentendre H	116	B2
Szentes H	116	C2
Szepietewo PL	91	D3
Szerzyny PL	98	C2
Szigetvár H	116	B3
Szklarska Poręba PL	92	B3
Szlichtyngowa PL	92	C2
Szolnok H	116	C2
Szombathely H	116	B2
Szprotawa PL	92	B2
Sztabin PL	91	E1
Sztum PL	89	F2
Sztutowo PL	89	F1
Szubin PL	89	E3
Szudziałowo PL	91	F2
Szumowo PL	91	D3
Szydłów PL	98	C1
Szydłowiec PL	94	C3
Taggia I	23	E1

T

Taadikvere EE	72	C3
Taagepera EE	78	C1
Tääksi EE	72	C3
Taali EE	72	B3
Tabalenka LT	85	F3
Tabanovce MK	59	F3
Tábara E	19	D4
Tabariškes LT	86	C3
Tabasalu EE	72	B1
Taberg S	67	D4
Tabernas E	30	B3
Tabivere EE	73	D3
Taboada E	18	C2
Tábor CZ	40	C3
Tábua P	24	B1
Tabuaço P	18	C4
Tabuenca E	20	B4
Tachov CZ	40	A3
Tadaiki LV	80	B1
Tadaiku Skola LV	80	B1
Tadcaster GB	7	E4
Taebla EE	72	A2
Taevaskoja EE	79	D1
Tafalla E	20	B3
Tafjord N	62	B4
Tagadi EE	72	C2
Tagaküla EE	79	E1
Tagametsa EE	72	B2
Tagavere EE	74	C2
Taggia I	23	E1
Tagliacozzo I	47	F4
Taglio di Po I	47	E1
Tagula EE	79	D2
Tahal E	30	B3
Taheva EE	79	D2
Tahkuranna EE	75	E3
Tähkvere EE	73	D3
Taikse EE	72	C3
Tailfingen D	43	D1
Tain GB	4	C1
Tain-l'Hermitage F	16	C4
Taipadas P	24	A3
Taipalsaari FIN	65	E3
Taivalkoski FIN	65	E3
Taivassalo / Tövsala FIN	68	B3
Takniškiai LT	85	E3
Takovo SRB	57	D3
Taktikoúpoli GR	105	E4
Talačkoniai LT	81	F2
Tálanda GR	108	C3
Talarrubias E	25	E3
Talaván E	25	D3
Talavera de la Reina E	25	F3
Talavera la Real E	24	C3
Talayuela E	25	E2
Talayuelas E	26	C2
Taldom RUS	115	F1
Talgarth GB	8	C1
Tali EE	75	F3
Talla I	47	E3
Tallante E	30	C3
Tallard F	22	C1
Tällberg S	67	E1
Tallinn EE	72	B1
Talloires F	17	D3
Tallow IRL	2	C4
Talluskylä FIN	69	E2
Talmont-St-Hilaire F	14	C2
Tal'ne UA	117	F1
Talokiai LT	85	E3
Talsi LV	77	D3
Talvik N	61	D2
Tamames E	25	D1
Támara E	19	E3
Tamarinda E	31	F3
Tamarite de Litera E	21	D4
Tamási H	116	B2
Tåme S	64	C3
Tamme EE	72	B2
Tammela FIN	69	D4
Tammiku EE	73	E2
Tammiste (Pärnu) EE	72	B3
Tammiste (Tartu) EE	79	D1
Tammistu EE	73	D1
Tammneeme EE	72	B1
Tammuru EE	75	F3
Tampere FIN	69	D3
Tamsalu EE	73	D2
Tamsweg A	44	C2
Tamworth GB	9	D1
Tana N	61	F1
Tanágra GR	105	E3
Tänassilma EE	78	C1
Tandådalen S	67	D1
Tandragee GB	3	D3
Tandsbyn S	63	E4
Tandsjöborg S	63	E4
Tanganheira P	24	A4
Tangerhütte D	34	A4
Tangermünde D	34	A4
Tanhua FIN	61	F3
Taninges F	17	D3
Tanlay F	16	B1
Tann D	38	C2
Tännäs S	63	D4
Tänndalen S	63	D4
Tannheim A	43	E2
Tannila FIN	65	D3
Tanumshede S	66	C3
Tanvald CZ	41	D3
Taormina I	51	E4
Tapa EE	72	C2
Tapia de Casariego E	18	C1
Tapini LV	83	D3
Tapurla EE	72	C1
Tar HR	54	A2
Taracena E	26	A1
Tarancón E	26	A2
Taranto I	49	F4
Tarare F	16	B3
Taraš SRB	56	C2
Taraşča UA	117	F1
Tarascon E	26	A2
Tarascon-sur-Ariège F	21	F3
Tarazona E	20	B4
Tarazona de la Mancha E	26	A3
Tarbert GB	4	A3
Tarbert GB	6	C1
Tarbert IRL	2	B3
Tarbes F	20	C2
Tarbet GB	6	C1
Tarbja EE	72	C2
Tarcento I	44	C3
Tarčin BIH	55	E4
Tarczyn PL	94	C2
Tardets-Sorholus F	20	C2
Tardienta E	20	C4
Tärendö S	64	C1
Tärgale LV	76	B2
Targon F	15	D4
Targovište BG	117	E3
Târgu Mureș RO	117	D2

TORINO

Aeroporto (Strada dell')	GT 2
Agnelli (Cso G.)	FU 5
Agudio (V. T.)	HT 5
Bogino (V.)	GT 8
Borgaro (V.)	GU 9
Cebrosa (Str. d.)	HT 22
Cosenza (Cso)	FGU 29
De Sanctis (V. F.)	FT 30
Garibaldi (Cso)	GT 36
Grosseto (Cso)	GT 39
Lazio (Lungo Stura)	HT 41
Maroncelli (Cso P.)	GU 43
Potenza (Cso)	GT 58
Rebaudengo (P. Conti)	GT 59
Regio Parco (Cso)	HT 61
Sansovino (V. A.)	FGT 71
Savona (Cso)	GU 72
Sestriere (V.)	GU 74
Stampini (V. E.)	GT 78
Stradella (V.)	GT 79
S. M. Mazzarello (V.)	FT 68
Thovez (Viale E.)	GHT 80
Torino (Strada)	GU 81
Torino (Viale)	FU 82
Unità d'Italia (Cso)	GU 86
Vercelli (Cso)	HT 89
Voghera (Lungo Dora)	HT 92

Museo dell' Automobile Carlo Biscaretti di Ruffia .... GU M5

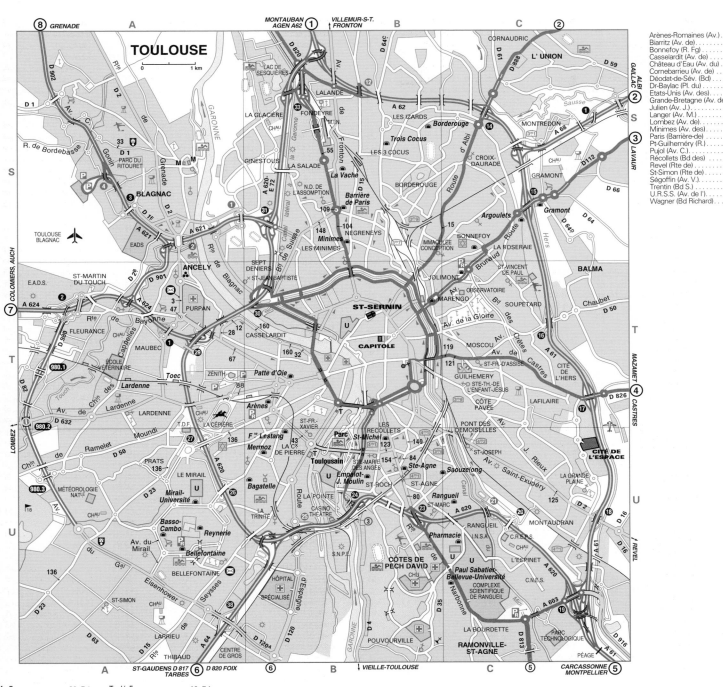

Arènes-Romaines (Av.) .... AT 3
Biarritz (Av. de) .... AT 12
Bonnefoy (R. Fg) .... CS 15
Casselardit (Av. de) .... AT 28
Château d'Eau (Av. du) .... BT 32
Cornebarrieu (Av. de) .... AS 33
Déodat-de-Sév. (Bd) .... AT 43
Dr-Baylac (Pl. du) .... AT 47
Etats-Unis (Av. des) .... BS 55
Grande-Bretagne (Av. de) .... AT 67
Julien (Av. J.) .... BU 80
Langer (Av. M.) .... BU 84
Lombez (Av.) .... AT 88
Minimes (Av. des) .... BS 104
Paris (Barrière-de) .... BS 109
Pt-Guilhemery (R.) .... CT 119
Pujol (Av. C.) .... CT 121
Récollets (Bd des) .... BU 123
Revel (Rte de) .... CU 125
St-Simon (Rte de) .... AU 136
Ségoffin (Av. V.) .... BU 140
Trentin (Bd S.) .... BS 148
U.R.S.S. (Av. de l') .... BU 154
Wagner (Bd Richard) .... BT 160

Teizininkai LT 85 E3
Tekeriš SRB 55 F3
Tekija SRB 57 E2
Tekirdağ TR 117 E4
Telakolni LV 83 F1
Telatyn PL 99 F1
Telavåg N 66 A1
Telč CZ 41 D3
Télendos (Nissi) GR 111 E1
Telese I 48 C3
Telford GB 8 C1
Telfs A 43 C1
Telgte D 37 E1
Tellingstedt D 33 C2
Telšiai LT 80 C2
Telti I 50 B2
Teltow D 34 B4
Témbi GR 101 F4
Tembleque E 26 A2
Temerin SRB 55 F2
Temmes FIN 65 D3
Tempio Pausania I 50 A2
Templemore /
  An Teampall Mór IRL 2 C3
Templin D 34 B3
Temse B 12 B1
Temska SRB 57 F4
Tenala / Tenhola FIN 69 D4
Tenbury Wells GB 8 C2
Tenby / Dinbych-
  y-pysgod GB 8 A2
Tence F 16 B4
Tende F 23 D1
Tendilla E 26 A1
Teneniai LT 80 B3
Tenja HR 55 E2
Tennes N 60 C2
Tensta S 67 C2
Tenterden GB 9 F3
Teolo I 47 D1
Teovo MK 59 E4
Tepasto FIN 61 E3
Tepelenë AL 100 B3
Teplá CZ 40 B3
Teplice CZ 40 B2
Teplice CZ 116 A1
Tepsa FIN 65 D1
Ter Apel NL 32 C4
Teramo I 48 B2
Terebovlja UA 117 D1
Terena P 24 C3
Teresin PL 94 B1
Terespol PL 95 F1
Tereszpol-Zaorenda PL 99 C1
Terezino Polje HR 55 D2
Tergnier F 12 B2
Terjärv FIN 68 C1
Terlizzi I 49 E3

Tarifa E 29 D4
Tarłów PL 95 D3
Tarm DK 70 B3
Tarmstedt D 33 E3
Tärnaby S 63 E1
Tarnawa Niżna PL 99 E3
Tarnawatka PL 99 F1
Tarnobrzeg PL 99 D1
Tarnogród PL 99 E1
Tarnos F 20 B2
Tarnów
  (Lubuskie) PL 88 B3
Tarnów
  (Małopolskie) PL 98 C2
Tarnów Opolski PL 97 E1
Tarnowiec PL 99 D2
Tarnówko PL 88 C3
Tarnowo Podgórne PL ...93 D1
Tarnowskie Góry PL 97 F1
Tarosai LT 85 D1
Tarp D 33 E1
Tarporley GB 8 C1
Tarprubežiai LT 85 D2
Tarpučiai I LT 85 D2
Tarquinia I 47 E4
Tarragona E 27 E1
Tarrasa / Terrassa E 21 E4
Tàrrega E 21 D4
Tårs DK 70 C4
Tarsia I 51 D2
Tartaki LV 83 E3
Tartaks LV 83 E3
Tartas F 20 C2
Tartu EE 79 D1
Tartupis LT 85 E2
Tarumaa EE 73 E2
Tarvasjoki FIN 68 C4
Tarvisio I 44 C3
Tarvydai LT 84 B1
Täsch CH 17 E3
Tåši LV 80 B1
Tåsjö S 64 A3
Tassin-la-Demi-Lune F ..16 C3
Tåstrup DK 70 C3
Tata H 116 B2
Tatabánya H 116 B2
Tatarbunary UA 117 F2
Tatkūnai LT 85 F1
Tatry PL 98 B3
Tau N 66 A2
Tauberbischofsheim D ..38 C4
Taubučiai LT 81 D3
Taucha D 39 E1
Taufkirchen D 43 F1
Taujankai LT 85 F1
Taujenai LT 86 B1
Taujūnai LT 87 D1

Taulé F 10 B4
Taunton GB 8 C3
Taunusstein-Neuhof D ..13 F2
Tauplitz A 44 C2
Taurage LT 84 C1
Tauragnai LT 82 C3
Taurene LV 78 C3
Taurianova I 51 D4
Taurini LV 77 F3
Taurkalne LV 82 B1
Taurupe LV 78 B3
Tauste E 20 B4
Tauves F 16 A3
Tavankut SRB 55 F1
Tavannes CH 17 E1
Tavarnelle Val
  di Pesa I 47 D3
Tavastila FIN 69 E4
Tavaux F 16 C2
Taverna I 51 E3
Tavernelle I 47 E3
Tavernes F 22 C2
Tavernes
  de la Valldigna E 27 D3
Tavira P 28 B3
Tavistock GB 8 B4
Tavşanlı TR 117 F4
Taxenbach A 44 B2
Taxiárhis GR 102 A3
Taxinloan GB 6 B2
Taynuilt GB 6 C1
Tayport GB 7 D1
Tazones E 19 D2
Tczew PL 89 F1
Tczów PL 94 C3
Teano I 48 C3
Teba E 29 E3
Tebay GB 7 D3
Téčeni LV 78 C1
Techendorf A 44 C3
Tecklenburg D 33 D4
Tecuci RO 117 D2
Teedla EE 79 D1
Teenuse EE 72 A3
Teeriranta FIN 65 E2
Teféli GR 109 F4
Tegéa GR 105 D4
Tegelen NL 37 D2
Teggiano I 49 E4
Teiberiai LT 85 D2
Teignmouth GB 8 B4
Teijo FIN 68 C4
Teisendorf D 44 B1
Teisko FIN 69 D3
Teixeiro E 18 B2
Teixoso P 24 C1
Teizai LT 85 E3

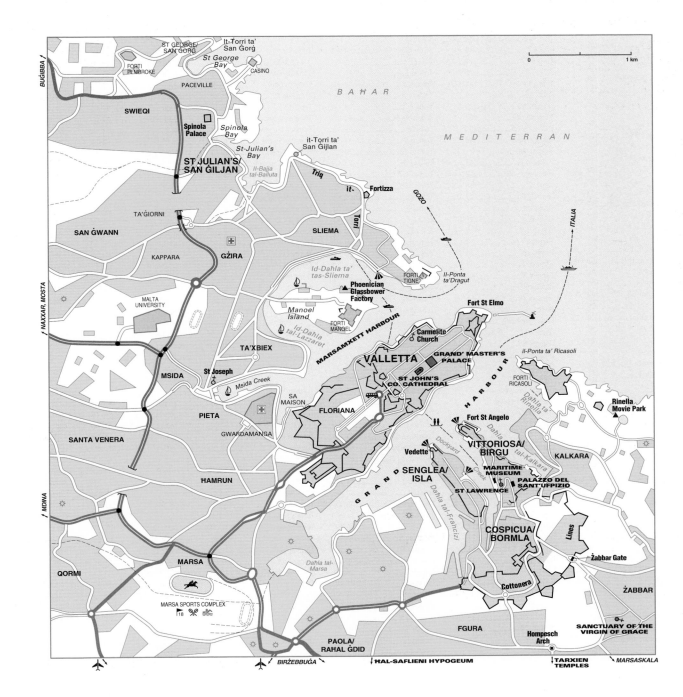

Termas de Monfortinho P....24 C2
Terme Luigiane I....51 D2
Termini Imerese I....52 C3
Terminillo I....47 F4
Termoli I....49 D2
Terneuzen NL....36 B2
Terni I....47 F4
Ternitz A....45 E1
Ternopil' UA....117 D1
Térovo GR....100 C4
Térpilos GR....101 F2
Terpní GR....102 A2
Terpsithéa GR....104 C2
Terracina I....48 B3
Terråk N....63 D2
Terralba I....51 D2
Terranova di Pollino I....51 D2
Terranuova Bracciolini I....47 E3
Terras de Bouro P....18 A4
Terrassa / Tarrasa E....21 E4
Terrasson-Lavilledieu F....15 E4
Terrenoire F....16 B4
Terriente E....26 C2
Teruel E....26 C2
Tervakoski FIN....69 D3
Tervete LV....81 E1
Tervo FIN....69 E2
Tervola FIN....65 D2
Tervuren B....12 C1
Terzaga E....26 B1
Tešanj BIH....55 E3
Teslić BIH....55 E3
Tessin D....34 A2
Tessy-sur-Vire F....11 D3
Tetbury GB....8 C3
Tetele LV....81 E1
Tetenai LT....86 B3
Teterow D....34 B2
Tetiiv UA....117 E1
Tetovo MK....59 E3
Tetrákomo GR....101 D4
Tettnang D....43 D2
Teuchern D....39 E1
Teufen CH....43 D2
Teulada I....50 A4
Teupitz D....34 C4
Teuva FIN....68 C2
Tewkesbury GB....8 C2
Tezze I....44 B4
Thale D....39 D1
Thalfang D....13 D2
Thalgau A....44 B1
Thalheim D....39 E1
Thalmässing D....39 D4
Thalwil CH....17 F1
Thame GB....9 D3
Thann F....17 E1
Thannhausen D....43 E1
Thaon-les-Vosges F....13 D4
Tharandt D....39 F1
Tharsis E....28 C2
Thássos GR....102 C2
Thássos (Nissi) GR....102 C2
Thèbes GR....105 E2
Themar D....39 D2
Thénezay F....15 D2
Thenon F....15 E4
Theológos GR....102 C2
Theológos GR....105 E2
Théoule-sur-Mer F....23 D2
Thermá GR....102 A2
Thérma GR....103 D3
Thérma GR....107 E4
Thérma Lefkádas GR....107 E4
Thérmi GR....101 F3
Thérmi GR....107 E1
Thermissía GR....105 E4
Thérmo GR....104 C2
Thermopiles GR....105 D2
Thérouanne F....12 A1
Thespiés GR....105 E2
Thesprotikó GR....104 B1
Thessaloniki GR....101 F2
Thetford GB....9 F2
Theux B....13 D1
Thèze F....20 C2

Thiaucourt-Regniéville F....13 D3
Thiberville F....11 E3
Thiéblemont-Farémont F....12 C4
Thiendorf D....39 F1
Thiene F....43 F4
Thiers F....16 B3
Thiesi I....50 A3
Thiessow D....34 B1
Thimariá GR....103 E2
Thímena GR....107 E4
Thímena (Nissi) GR....107 E4
Thionville F....13 D3
Thíra GR....109 F2
Thíra (Nissi) GR....109 F2
Thirassía (Nissi) GR....109 F2
Thirsk GB....7 E4
Thisted DK....70 B3
Thiviers F....15 E4
Thizy F....16 B3
Thoissey F....16 C3
Tholey D....13 E3
Thollon-les-Mémises F....17 D2
Tholó GR....104 C4
Tholopotámi GR....107 D3
Tholós GR....102 A2
Thomastown / Baile Mhic Andáin IRL....2 C4
Thônes F....17 D2
Thonon-les-Bains F....17 D2
Thorens-Glières F....17 D3
Thorikó GR....105 F3
Thorne GB....7 F4
Thornhill GB....3 F1
Thouarcé F....15 D1
Thouars F....15 D2
Thouría GR....108 A1
Thoúrio GR....103 E1
Thrapston GB....9 E2
Threshfield GB....7 E4
Thueyts F....22 A1
Thuin B....12 C2
Thuir F....21 F3
Thum D....39 F2
Thun CH....17 E2
Thüringen A....43 E2
Thurles / Durlas IRL....2 C3
Thursby GB....7 D2
Thurso GB....5 D2
Thury-Harcourt F....11 E3
Thusis CH....43 D3
Thyborøn DK....70 A2
Tibro S....67 D3
Tichvin RUS....115 E1
Tidö S....67 E2
Tiefenbronn D....13 F3
Tiefencastel CH....43 D3
Tiefensee D....34 C3
Tiegaži LV....78 B2
Tiel NL....36 C1
Tielt B....12 B1
Tienen B....12 C1
Tiengen D....17 F1
Tiercé F....15 D1
Tierga E....20 B4
Tierp S....67 F2
Tigharry GB....4 A3
Tighnabruaich GB....6 C1
Tignes F....17 E3
Tiheda EE....73 E3
Tihemetsa EE....75 F3
Tiheró GR....103 E2
Tihio GR....101 D2
Tiidu EE....79 D1
Tiistenjoki FIN....68 C2
Tijola E....30 B3
Tikaini LV....79 E3
Tikkakoski FIN....69 D2
Tikkala FIN....69 F2
Tilburg NL....36 C1
Tilbury GB....9 E3
Tilga EE....79 D1
Tilissos GR....109 F4
Tillberga S....67 F3
Tillières-sur-Avre F....11 F4
Tilly-sur-Seulles F....11 D3
Tilos (Nissi) GR....111 E2
Tilsi EE....79 E1
Tiltai LT....86 B3
Tilvikai LT....80 B3
Tilža (Tilža) LV....79 E3
Tilže (Šiauliu) LT....81 D2
Tilže (Utenos) LT....83 D3
Timbáki GR....109 E4
Tímbano GR....102 C2
Timfristós GR....104 C3
Timişoara RO....116 C3
Timmendorfer Strand D....33 F2
Timoleague IRL....2 B4
Timrå S....68 A2
Tinahely IRL....3 D3
Tinchebray F....11 D3
Tineo E....18 C2
Tingáki GR....111 E1
Tingere LV....78 C3
Tinglev DK....70 B4
Tingsryd S....71 E3
Tingvoll N....62 B3
Tinnikuru EE....78 C1
Tinnoset N....64 B2
Tinos GR....106 C4
Tinos (Nissi) GR....106 C4
Tiñosillos E....25 F1
Tintagel GB....8 A4
Tinténiac F....15 D1
Tinūži LV....77 F3
Tione di Trento I....43 F4
Tipasoja FIN....65 E2
Tipperary / Tiobraid Árann IRL....2 C4
Tipu EE....75 F3
Tiranë AL....116 C4
Tirano I....43 F4
Tiraspol MD....117 E2
Tireli LV....77 E3
Tîrgovişte RO....117 D3
Tîrgu Frumos RO....117 D3
Tîrgu Jiu RO....117 D3
Tîrgu-Neamţ RO....117 D2
Tîrgu Secuiesc RO....117 D2
Tîrig E....27 D2
Tîrintha GR....105 E4
Tiriolo I....51 F3
Tirkšliai LT....80 C2
Tirnavos GR....101 E4
Tirós GR....105 E4
Tírrenia I....46 C3
Tirschenreuth D....39 E3
Tîrstrup DK....70 C3
Tirza LV....79 D3

Tisaičiai LT....81 D3
Tiskadi (Ciskodi) LV....83 E2
Tiškai LT....80 C2
Tiskre EE....72 B1
Tisno HR....54 C4
Tišnov CZ....41 E3
Tisvildeleje DK....70 C3
Tiszafüred H....116 C2
Tiszavasvári H....116 C2
Titaguas E....26 C2
Titel SRB....56 C2
Titisee D....13 F4
Titkoniai LT....81 F2
Tito I....49 E4
Titoniai LT....81 F2
Titran N....62 C3
Tittmoning D....44 B1
Tivat MNE....58 B3
Tivenys E....27 E1
Tiverton GB....8 B3
Tivissa E....27 E1
Tivoli I....48 B3
Tjällmo S....67 E3
Tjeldstø N....66 A1
Tjentište BIH....55 F4
Tjøme N....66 C2
Tjong N....60 A4
Tjørnuvík (Færøerne) DK....62 A3
Tjøtta N....63 D1
Tkon HR....54 C4
Tłuchowo PL....90 A3
Tłumaczów PL....96 C1
Tłuszcz PL....94 C1
Tobarra E....26 B4
Tobercurry / Tobar an Choire IRL....2 B2
Tobermore GB....3 D1
Tobermory GB....6 B1
Toberonochy GB....6 B1
Tocha P....24 B1
Tocina E....29 D2
Todi I....47 F4
Todmorden GB....7 E4
Todorići BIH....55 D4
Todtmoos D....17 E1
Todtnau D....17 E1
Tódva EE....72 B2
Toft GB....5 F1
Tofte N....64 C1
Toftir (Færøerne) DK....62 A3
Toftlund DK....70 B3
Tohmajärvi FIN....69 F2
Toholampi FIN....69 D1
Tohvri EE....72 C3
Toijala FIN....69 D1
Tóikvere EE....73 D3
Toila EE....73 E2
Toivakka FIN....69 E2
Toivala FIN....69 E2
Tojšici BIH....55 F3
Tokaj H....116 C2
Tokarnia (Świętokrzyskie) PL....94 B3
Tüki EE....79 D1
Toledo E....25 F2
Tolentino I....47 F3
Tolfa I....47 E4
Tolga N....64 D4
Tolkmicko PL....90 A1
Tólla F....75 F3
Tollarp S....71 D3
Tølliste EE....79 D2
Tølløse DK....70 C3
Tolmezzo I....44 C3
Tolmin SLO....54 A2
Toló GR....105 E4
Tolosa E....20 A2
Tolosa F....24 B2
Tolox E....29 E3
Tolučiai LT....86 B1
Tolva FIN....65 E1
Tolve I....49 E4
Tomakaimis LT....82 C3
Tomar P....24 B2
Tomaševac SRB....56 C2
Tomašica BIH....55 D3
Tomaszów Lubelski PL....99 F1
Tomaszów Mazowiecki PL....94 B2
Tomaszowice PL....95 D3
Tombebœuf F....21 D1
Tome LV....82 A1
Tomelilla S....71 D3
Tomelloso E....26 A3
Tomice PL....98 A2
Tomično E....18 A3
Tomintoul GB....5 D4
Tomislavgrad BIH....55 D4
Tømmervåg N....62 B3
Tømra N....62 B3
Tona E....21 E4
Tonara I....50 A3
Tonbridge GB....9 E3
Tondela P....24 B1
Tønder DK....70 B4
Tongeren B....13 D1
Tongue GB....4 C2
Tonnay-Boutonne F....15 D3
Tonnay-Charente F....15 D3
Tonneins F....21 D1
Tonnerre F....16 B1
Tönning D....33 E2
Tønsberg N....66 C2
Tønstad N....66 A3
Toomja EE....72 B2
Tooste EE....79 F1

Tootsi EE....72 B3
Töpen D....39 E2
Topeno FIN....69 D4
Topla SLO....54 B1
Topli Dol SRB....57 F4
Toplița RO....117 D2
Topló GR....105 D4
Topola SRB....57 D3
Topolčani MK....59 E4
Toporčany SK....116 B2
Topólia GR....109 D3
Topólka PL....93 F1
Topolovnik SRB....57 D2
Topusko HR....54 C3
Torà E....21 E4
Torano Castello I....51 D2
Tóravere EE....79 D1
Torbole I....43 F4
Torcello I....44 B4
Torchiarolo I....51 F1
Torcy F....12 A3
Tordera E....21 F4
Tordesillas E....19 D4
Tordesilos E....26 C2
Tore I....4 C3
Töre S....64 C2
Töreboda S....67 D3
Törve EE....73 D3
Torella del Sannio I....48 C3
Toreno E....18 C3
Torgau D....39 E1
Torgelow D....34 C2
Torhout B....12 B1
Tori EE....72 B3
Türi EE....72 C3
Türi-Alliku EE....72 C3
Torigni-sur-Vire F....11 D3
Torija E....26 A1
Torino I....17 E4
Türisalu EE....72 A2
Torla E....20 C3
Torma EE....73 D3
Törma EE....73 D2
Törmänen FIN....61 F3
Törmänmäki FIN....65 E3
Tormos E....20 C4
Tornavacas E....25 E2
Tornimäe EE....75 D2
Tornio FIN....65 D2
Tornjoš SRB....55 F1
Toro E....19 D4
Törökszentmiklós H....116 C2
Toróni GR....102 A3
Toropec RUS....115 E2
Torpo N....66 B1
Torpoint GB....8 B4
Torpshammar S....68 A2
Torquay GB....8 B4
Torquemada E....19 E4
Torralba de Calatrava E....25 F3
Torrão P....24 B4
Torre Annunziata I....48 C4
Torre Beretti e Castellaro I....17 F4
Torre Canne I....49 F3
Torre de Dom Chama P....18 B4
Torre de Juan Abad E....26 A4
Torre de la Higuera E....29 D3
Torre de Moncorvo P....18 B4
Torre de' Passeri I....48 C2
Torre del Bierzo E....18 C3
Torre del Campo E....29 F2
Torre del Greco I....48 C4
Torre del Mar E....29 F3
Torre dell'Impiso I....50 A4
Torre Faro I....51 D4
Torre la Cárcel E....26 C1
Torre Orsaia I....49 E4
Torre Pacheco E....30 C2
Torre Pellice I....17 E4
Torrebaja E....26 C2
Torreblanca E....27 D2
Torrecaballeros E....25 F1
Torrecampo E....25 E4
Torrecilla en Cameros E....20 A3
Torrecillas de la Tiesa E....25 D2
Torredembarra E....27 F1
Torredonjimeno E....29 F2
Torregrossa E....21 D4
Torreira P....24 B1
Torrejón de Ardoz E....26 A2
Torrejón de la Calzada E....25 F2
Torrejón el Rubio E....25 D2
Torrejoncillo E....25 D2
Torrejoncillo del Rey E....26 B2
Torrelaguna E....26 A1
Torrelapaja E....20 A4
Torrelavega E....19 F2
Torrellano E....26 C4
Torrelobatón E....19 D4
Torrelodones E....25 F1
Torremaggiore I....49 D3
Torremegía E....25 D3
Torremocha E....25 D2
Torremolinos E....29 E3
Torrent E....27 D3
Torrente de Cinca E....21 D4
Torrenueva E....26 A4
Torreperogil E....26 A4
Torres del Río E....20 A3
Torres Novas P....24 B2
Torres Vedras P....24 A3

Torrevieja E....30 C2
Torri del Benaco I....43 F4
Torrin GB....4 B3
Torriglia I....46 B2
Torrijas E....26 C2
Torrijo E....20 A4
Torrijos E....25 F2
Tørring DK....70 B3
Torrita di Siena I....47 E3
Torroella de Montgrí E....21 F4
Torrox E....29 F3
Torsås S....71 E3
Torsby S....67 D2
Torshälla S....67 E2
Torshavn (Færøerne) DK....62 A3
Tórtoles de Esgueva E....19 E4
Tortoli I....50 B3
Tortona I....17 F4
Tortorici I....50 C4
Tortosa E....27 E1
Tortosendo P....24 C1
Toruń PL....89 F3
Torup S....71 D2
Tõrva EE....78 C1
Tõrve EE....79 D1
Tõrve EE....73 D3
Tõrvikbygd N....66 A1
Toržok RUS....115 F1
Torzym PL....92 B1
Tosbotn N....63 E1
Toscolano-Maderno I....43 E4
Tosno RUS....115 D1
Tossa de Mar E....21 F4
Tõstamaa EE....75 E3
Tostedt D....33 E3
Toszek PL....97 F1
Totana E....30 C2
Tôtes F....11 F2
Tøtlandsvik N....66 A2
Totnes GB....8 B4
Toucy F....16 A1
Toul F....13 D4
Toulon F....22 C2
Toulon-sur-Arroux F....16 B2
Toulouse F....21 E2
Toumbítsi GR....104 C3
Tourcoing F....12 B1
Tourlída GR....104 C2
Tournai B....12 B1
Tournan-en-Brie F....12 A4
Tournay F....21 D2
Tournon-d'Agenais F....21 D1
Tournon-St-Martin F....15 E2
Tournon-sur-Rhône F....16 C4
Tournus F....16 C2
Tourouvre F....11 E4
Tours F....15 E1
Toury F....12 A4
Tõusi EE....72 A3
Toužim CZ....40 B3
Tovariševo SRB....55 F2
Tovarnik HR....55 F2
Towcester GB....9 D2
Töysä FIN....69 D2
Tožas LV....78 B2
Trabanca E....18 C4
Trabazos E....18 C4
Traben-Trarbach D....13 E2
Trabia I....52 C3
Trąbki PL....98 B2
Trąbki Wielkie PL....89 F1
Trabotivište MK....59 F3
Tracino I....52 A4
Trafaria P....24 A3
Trafoi I....43 E3
Tragacete E....26 B2
Trahiá GR....105 E4
Trahíli GR....105 F2
Traiguera E....27 D2
Traisen A....45 D1
Traiskirchen A....45 E1
Traismauer A....41 D4
Trakai LT....86 B2
Trakiškiai (Kalvarija) LT....85 D2
Trakiškiai (Marijambole) LT....85 D2
Trakiškis LT....81 F3
Trakošćan HR....54 C1
Traksedis LT....80 C3
Tralee / Trá Li IRL....2 A4
Tramagal P....24 B2
Tramariglio I....50 A3
Tramatza I....50 A3
Tramonti di Sopra I....44 B3
Tramore / Trá Mhór IRL....2 C2
Tran BG....117 D4
Tranås S....67 D3
Trancoso P....24 C1
Tranebjerg DK....70 C3
Tranemo S....67 D4
Tranent GB....7 D1
Trani I....49 E3
Tranóvalto GR....101 E3
Transtrand S....67 D1
Trapani I....52 B3
Trapene LV....79 E3
Trápeza GR....105 D3
Trappstadt D....39 D3
Trasacco I....48 B3
Trassem D....13 D2
Traun A....44 C1
Traunkirchen A....44 C1
Traunreut D....44 B1
Traunstein D....44 B1

Traupis LT....82 B3
Travemünde D....33 F2
Travnik BIH....55 E4
Trawniki PL....95 E3
Trbovlje SLO....54 B2
Trbuk BIH....55 E3
Trbušani SRB....57 D3
Trebbin D....34 B4
Trébeurden F....10 B3
Trebinje BIH....58 B3
Trebisacce I....51 D2
Trebišnjica BIH....58 B3
Trebišov SK....116 C1
Trebnje SLO....54 B2
Tréboň CZ....40 C4
Tréboul F....10 A3
Trebsen D....39 E1
Trebujena E....29 D3
Trecastagni I....53 E3
Trecate I....17 F3
Treffort GB....8 C2
Treffurt D....38 C2
Tregaron GB....3 F4
Trégastel F....10 B3
Tregnago I....43 F4
Tregony GB....8 A4
Tréguier F....10 B3
Trehörningsjö S....68 B1
Treia I....47 F3
Treia D....33 E2
Treignac F....15 F3
Treimani EE....77 F1
Trekani LV....82 C1
Trelleborg DK....70 C3
Trelleborg S....71 D3
Tremestieri I....51 D4
Tremezzo I....43 D4
Tremp E....21 D3
Trenčín SK....116 B1
Trendelburg D....38 C1
Trenta SLO....54 A2
Trento I....43 F4
Trepča (Berane) MNE....58 C3
Trepča (Kosovska Mitrovica) SRB....59 D2
Trepuzzi I....51 F1
Trescore Balneario I....43 E4
Tresenda I....43 E4
Tresfjord N....62 B3
Tresjuncos E....26 A2
Treski EE....79 F1
Trešnjevica SRB....57 D3
Trespaderne E....19 F3
Třešť CZ....41 D3
Trets F....22 C2
Tretten N....66 C1
Treuchtlingen D....39 D4
Treuen D....39 E2
Treuenbrietzen D....34 B4
Treungen N....66 B2
Trevélez E....30 A3
Trèves F....22 A1
Trevi I....47 F3
Trévières F....11 D3
Treviglio I....46 C1
Trevignano Romano I....47 F4
Treviño E....20 A3
Treviso I....44 B4
Trévoux F....16 C3
Trezzo sull'Adda I....43 D4
Trgovište SRB....59 F3
Trhové Sviny CZ....40 C4
Tría Nissiá (Nissí) GR....111 D2
Triánda GR....111 F2
Triaucourt-en-Argonne F....12 C3
Tribanj Krušćica HR....54 C4
Triberg D....13 F4
Tribsees D....34 B2
Tricarico I....49 E4
Tricase I....51 F1
Tricesimo I....44 C3
Trichiana I....44 B4
Trie-sur-Baise F....21 D2
Trieben A....45 D2
Trier D....13 E2
Trieste I....44 C4
Trifili GR....103 E2
Trigóna GR....101 D4
Trigueros E....28 C2
Triigi (Lääne-Viru) EE....73 D2
Triigi (Saare) EE....74 C2
Trijueque E....26 A1
Trikala GR....105 D3
Trikala (Imathia) GR....101 E3
Trikala (Trikala) GR....101 D4
Trikáta LV....78 C2
Trikeri GR....105 E1
Trilj HR....55 D4
Trillevallen S....63 D3
Trillo E....26 B1
Trilofo GR....105 D1
Trim / Baile Átha Troim IRL....3 D2
Trindade P....18 B4
Třinec CZ....41 F2
Tring GB....9 E2
Trinità d'Agultu e Vignola I....50 A2
Trinitapoli I....49 E3
Trino I....17 F4
Triobiškiai LT....85 D2

Triora I....23 E1
Trípi GR....105 D4
Tripiti GR....102 B3
Tripiti GR....109 E4
Trípoli GR....105 D4
Triponzo I....47 F3
Tripótama GR....104 C3
Triptis D....39 E2
Tris Eklissíes GR....109 E4
Triškoniai LT....81 E2
Trittau D....33 F3
Trittenheim D....13 E2
Trivento I....48 C3
Trizina GR....105 E4
Trnava SK....116 B2
Trnova Poljana BIH....55 D4
Trnovo BIH....55 F4
Trnovo SLO....54 A2
Troarn F....11 E3
Trofa (perto de Felgueiras) P....18 A4
Trofa (perto de Santo Tirso) P....18 A4
Trofaiach A....45 D2
Trofors N....63 E1
Trogir HR....58 A4
Troia I....49 D3
Troina I....53 D3
Trois-Ponts B....13 D2
Troisdorf D....13 E1
Trojan BG....117 D4
Trojane SLO....54 B2
Trojanów PL....95 D2
Trollhättan S....66 C3
Tromsdalen N....60 C2
Tromsø N....60 C2
Trondheim N....62 C3
Tronö S....67 F1
Troo F....15 E1
Troon GB....6 C2
Trópea GR....104 C3
Tropea I....51 D3
Tropy Sztumskie PL....89 F2
Trosa S....67 F3
Troškås LV....83 D1
Troškūnai LT....82 B3
Trostberg D....44 B1
Trostjanec' UA....115 F4
Trouville-sur-Mer F....11 E3
Trowbridge GB....8 C3
Troyes F....12 B4
Trpanj HR....58 A3
Trpezi MNE....58 C3
Trpinja HR....55 F2
Trsa MNE....58 C2
Tršić SRB....58 A3
Trstenik HR....58 A3
Trstenik (Kruševac) SRB....59 D3
Trstenik (Priština) SRB....57 D4
Trsteno HR....58 A3
Trubčevsk RUS....115 F3
Trubia E....18 C3
Trubjela MNE....58 B3
Truchas E....18 C3
Truchtersheim F....13 E4
Trūdai LT....86 C1
Truikinai LT....80 B2
Trujillo E....25 D2
Trun F....11 E3
Truro GB....8 A4
Truskava LT....81 F3
Trutnov CZ....41 D2
Truva TR....117 E4
Trybsz PL....98 B3
Tryde S....71 D3
Tryńcza PL....99 E2
Tryškiai LT....80 C2
Tržac BIH....54 C3
Trzcianka (Wielkopolskie) PL....88 C3
Trzcianne PL....91 E2
Trzciel PL....92 C1
Trzcinica PL....93 E3
Trzcińsko-Zdrój PL....88 A3
Trzebiatów PL....88 B1
Trzebiechów (Lubuskie) PL....92 C2
Trzebiel PL....92 B2
Trzebielino PL....89 D1
Trzebieszów PL....95 E2
Trzebieszowice PL....96 C2
Trzebież PL....88 A2
Trzebinia PL....98 A1
Trzebnica PL....93 D3
Trzebownisko PL....99 E2
Trzemeszno PL....93 D1
Trześń (Świętokrzyskie) PL....99 D1

Tubilla del Agua E....19 F3
Túbines I LT....80 C3
Tübingen D....43 D1
Tubre / Taufers im Münstertal I....43 E3
Tučepi HR....58 A2
Tuchan F....21 F3
Tuchola PL....89 E2
Tucholski Park Narodowy PL....89 E2
Tuchomie PL....89 D1
Tuchów PL....98 C2
Tuczno (Zachodnio-pomorskie) PL....88 C2
Tudela E....20 B4
Tudela de Duero E....19 E4
Tudu EE....73 E2
Tudulinna EE....73 E2
Tuffé F....11 E4
Tuhalaane EE....78 C1
Tuheljske Toplice HR....54 C2
Tuhkakylä FIN....65 E3
Tui E....18 A3
Túja LV....77 F2
Tūjasmuiža LV....77 F2
Tukums LV....77 D3
Tula RUS....115 F2
Tulare SRB....59 E2
Tulcea RO....117 E2
Tul'čyn UA....117 E1
Tuliszków PL....93 F2
Tulla IRL....2 B3
Tullamore / Tulach Mhór IRL....2 C3
Tulle F....15 F4
Tullgarn S....67 F3
Tullins F....16 C4
Tulln A....41 E4
Tullow / An Tulach IRL....3 D3
Tulnikiai LT....80 C2
Tułowice (Mazowieckie) PL....94 B1
Tułowice (Opolskie) PL....97 E1
Tulpes LV....77 F3
Tulpiakiemis LT....85 F1
Tulppio FIN....61 F3
Tulsk IRL....2 C3
Tumba S....67 F3
Tume LV....77 D3
Tumšupe LV....78 A3
Tuohikotti FIN....69 E3
Tuoro sul Trasimeno I....47 E3
Tupadły PL....92 B2
Turaida LV....78 B2
Turaliči BIH....55 F3
Turawa PL....97 E1
Turawskie (Jezioro) PL....97 E1
Turba EE....72 A2
Turbe BIH....55 E4
Turbinava LT....86 B2
Turckheim F....13 E4
Turda RO....117 D2
Turégano E....25 F1
Turek PL....93 F2
Turenki FIN....69 D3
Turgeliai LT....86 C2
Turi I....49 F3
Turija BIH....55 F3
Turija SRB....55 F2
Turinge S....67 F3
Turís E....26 C3
Turja SRB....57 E2
Turjak SLO....54 B2
Türkheim D....43 E1
Turki LV....83 D1
Turku / Åbo FIN....69 C3
Turlava (Lipaiki) LV....76 B3
Turmantas LT....83 D3
Turmiel E....26 B1
Turnberry GB....6 C2
Turnhout B....36 C2
Türnitz A....45 D1
Turnov CZ....40 C2
Turnov CZ....116 A1
Turnu Măgurele RO....117 D3
Turobin PL....95 E3
Turośl (Podlaskie) PL....90 C2
Turowo (Warmińsko-Mazurskie) PL....91 E2
Turre E....30 B3
Turriers F....22 C1
Turriff GB....5 D3
Tursi I....49 E4
Tursučiai LT....85 D2
Turtola FIN....64 C1
Turturano I....51 F1
Turžėnai LT....85 F1
Tuscania I....47 E4
Tuse DK....70 C3
Tušilović HR....54 C2
Tusti EE....79 F1
Tuszów Narodowy PL....98 C1
Tuszyn PL....94 A2
Tutajev RUS....115 F1
Tutini LT....83 F1
Tutrakan BG....117 D3
Tuttlingen D....43 D2
Tuturano I....51 F1
Tutzing D....43 F1
Tuudi EE....75 E2
Tuula EE....72 A2
Tuulos FIN....69 D3
Tuupovaara FIN....69 F2
Tuusniemi FIN....69 F1
Tuusula FIN....69 D4

Tuxford GB 7 D4
Tuzi MNE 58 C3
Tuzla BIH 55 F3
Tvedestrand N 66 B3
Tver' RUS 115 F1
Tverai LT 80 C3
Tverečius LT 87 D1
Tvøroyri
(Færøerne) DK 62 A3
Twardogóra PL 93 E3
Twimberg A 45 D2
Twist D 32 C4
Twistringen D 33 E4
Tworóg PL 97 F1
Tychowo
(Białogard) PL 88 C2
Tychowo (Sławno) PL 89 D1
Tychy PL 97 F2
Tyczyn PL 99 D2
Tydal N 63 D3
Tyin N 66 B1
Tykocin PL 91 E2
Tyrawa PL 99 D3
Tylicz PL 98 C3
Tymbark PL 98 B2
Tyń PL 89 D1
Týn nad Vltavou CZ 40 C4
Tyndaris I 50 C4
Tyndrum GB 6 C1
Tynemouth GB 7 E3
Tyniec PL 98 A2
Tynkä FIN 65 D3
Tynset N 62 C4
Tyrawa Wołoska PL 99 E2
Tyresö S 67 F3
Tyringe S 71 D3
Tyristrand N 66 C2
Tyrnävä FIN 65 D3
Tyruliai LT 81 E3
Tysse N 66 A1
Tyssebotn N 66 A1
Tyssedal N 66 A1
Tyszowce PL 95 F3
Tytuvenai LT 81 D3
Tywa PL 88 A3
Tywyn GB 3 F4

U

Ub SRB 56 C3
Úbeda E 30 A2
Überlingen D 17 F1
Ubiške LT 80 C2
Ubiškes LT 85 F2
Ubja EE 73 D2
Ubľa SK 116 C1
Ubli HR 58 A3
Ubli MNE 58 C3
Ubrique E 29 D3
Uchanie PL 95 F3
Uchte D 33 E4
Uckange F 13 D3
Uckfield GB 9 E4
Uclés E 26 A2
Udbina HR 54 C3
Udbyhøj DK 70 B2
Uddevalla S 66 C3
Uddheden S 67 D2
Uden NL 37 D1
Uderna EE 79 D1
Udine I 44 C4
Udovo MK 59 F4
Ūdrija LT 85 E3
Udriku EE 73 D2
Ūdrinas LV 78 C2
Ūdruma EE 72 A3
Ūdrupe LV 79 D3
Udvar H 55 E1
Uebigau D 39 F1
Ueckermünde D 34 C2
Uelzen D 33 F3
Uetersen D 33 E3
Uetze D 33 F4
Uffenheim D 39 D4
Ugāle LV 76 C2
Ugao SRB 59 D2
Ugento I 51 F1
Ugíjar E 30 A3
Ugine F 17 D3
Uglič RUS 115 F1
Ugljan HR 54 B4
Ugljan (Otok) HR 54 B4
Ugljane HR 58 A4
Ugljevik BIH 55 F3
Ugrinovci SRB 57 D3
Ugunciems LV 77 D2
Uherské Hradiště CZ 41 F3
Uherský Brod CZ 41 F3
Uhingen D 43 D1
Uhlířské Janovice CZ 40 C3
Uhrsleben D 34 A4
Uhti EE 79 D1
Uhtna EE 73 D2
Uig GB 4 B3
Uimaharju FIN 69 F2
Uithoorn NL 36 C1
Uithuizen NL 32 C3
Ujazd (Łodzkie) PL 94 B2
Ujazd (Opolskie) PL 97 E1
Ujejsce PL 97 F1
Ujście PL 89 D3
Ukkola FIN 69 F2
Ukmerge LT 86 B1
Ukri LV 81 D2
Ulan-Majorat PL 95 D2
Ulanów PL 99 D1
Ulcinj MNE 58 C4
Ülde EE 72 C3
Ulefoss N 66 B2
Uleila del Campo E 30 B3
Ülejõe EE 72 C2
Ülensi EE 78 C1
Ülenurme EE 79 D1
Ulfborg DK 70 A2
Ulila EE 79 D1
Uljanik HR 55 D2
Uljanova LV 83 E1
Ul'janovka UA 117 E1
Uljma SRB 57 D2
Ullånger S 68 B2
Ullapool GB 4 B3
Ullared S 71 D2
Ullava FIN 68 C1
Ulldecona E 27 E2
Ulm (Donau) D 43 E1
Ulmen D 13 E2
Ulog BIH 55 E4
Ulricehamn S 67 D4
Ulrichsberg A 40 C4
Ulsberg N 62 C3
Ulsta GB 5 F1
Ulsteinvik N 62 A4
Ulverston GB 7 D3
Ulvi (Ida-Viru) EE 73 E3
Ulvi (Lääne-Viru) EE 73 D2
Ulvik N 66 A1
Ulvila FIN 68 C3
Ulvsjö S 67 D1
Umag HR 54 A3
Uman' UA 117 E1
Umbertide I 47 E3
Umbukta N 63 E1
Umbusi EE 73 D3
Umčari SRB 57 D3
Umeå S 68 B1
Umhausen A 43 F2
Umin Dol MK 59 E3
Umka SRB 56 C3
Umljanović HR 55 D4
Umurga LV 78 B2
Unametsa EE 78 C1
Unari FIN 65 D1
Uncastillo E 20 B3
Undersåker S 63 D3
Undredal N 66 A1
Uneča RUS 115 F3
Unešić HR 54 C4
Úněšov CZ 40 B3
Ungheni MD 117 E2
Ungilde E 18 C3
Ungurpils LV 78 B2
Unhais da Serra P 24 C1
Unhošť CZ 40 C3
Uničov CZ 41 E2
Uniejów PL 93 F2
Unije HR 54 A4
Uniküla (Ida-Viru) EE 73 E2
Uniküla (Tartu) EE 79 E1
Unisław PL 89 E3
Universitāte LV 77 F3
Unna D 37 E1
Unnaryd S 71 D2
Unquera E 19 E2
Unterach A 44 C1
Unterhaching D 43 F1
Unterschleißheim D 43 F1
Unterwasser CH 43 D2
Unterweißenbach A 41 D4
Uoginiai LT 82 B3
Uosininkai I LT 86 C2
Uosininkai II LT 86 C2
Uostadvaris LT 80 A3
Upa EE 74 C3
Upavon GB 9 D3
Upenieki
(Dobeles) LV 81 D1
Upenieki
(Kuldīgas) LV 76 C3
Upenieki
(Liepājas) LV 80 B1
Upenieki (Preilu) LV 83 D2
Upesgrīva LV 77 D2
Úpice CZ 41 D2
Upinniemi FIN 69 D4
Upīte LV 79 F3
Upītes LV 77 D2
Upmala LV 83 D2
Upmalas
(Carnikava) LV 77 F3
Upmalas
(Sidgunda) LV 78 B3
Upninkai LT 85 F1
Uppingham GB 9 E1
Upplands-Väsby S 67 F2
Uppsala S 67 F2
Upton-upon-Severn GB 8 C2
Upyna LT 80 C3
Upyte LT 81 F3
Uras I 50 A4
Urbania I 47 F2
Urbe I 23 E1
Urbino I 47 F2
Urda E 25 F3
Urdos F 20 C3
Urdzenieki LV 76 B3
Urdzinas LV 82 A1
Urepel F 20 B2
Urfahr A 44 C1
Urfeld D 43 F2
Urga LV 78 B2
Urge EE 72 B3
Uri I 50 A3
Uriage-les-Bains F 17 D4
Urissaare EE 75 F3
Urjala FIN 69 D3
Urk NL 32 B4
Urlingford IRL 2 C3
Urnäsch CH 43 D2
Urnežiai LT 85 E1
Uroševac SRB 59 E3
Urovica SRB 57 E2
Urshult S 71 E2
Urszulin PL 95 E2
Ururi I 49 D2
Urvaste EE 79 D1
Urvikiai LT 80 C2
Ury F 12 A4
Urzędów PL 95 D3
Urziceni RO 117 E3
Usagre E 25 D4
Ušća SRB 57 D4
Usedom D 34 C2
Usenai LT 84 B1
Ušēni LV 82 C1
Usingen D 13 F1
Usk / Brynbuga GB 8 C2
Uskoplje BIH 58 B3
Üsküdar TR 117 E4
Uslar D 38 C1
Usma LV 76 C3
Ussat F 21 E3
Ussé F 15 E1
Usseglio I 17 E4
Ussel F 15 F3
Usseln D 37 F2
Ussimäe EE 73 D2
Ustaoset N 66 B1
Ustaritz F 20 B2
Uster CH 17 F1
Ústí nad Labem CZ 40 B2
Ústí nad Labem CZ 116 A1
Ústí nad Orlicí CZ 41 E2
Ustibar BIH 56 C4
Ustikolina BIH 55 F4
Ustiprača BIH 55 F4
Ustka PL 89 D1
Ustroń PL 97 F2
Ustronie Morskie PL 88 B1
Ustrzyki Dolne PL 99 E3
Ustrzyki Górne PL 99 E3
Ust'užna RUS 115 F1
Ūta LT 86 C3
Utajärvi FIN 65 D3
Utåker N 66 A2
Utbjoa N 66 A2
Utebo E 20 B4
Utelle F 23 D1
Utena LT 82 C3
Utiel E 26 C3
Utne N 66 A1
Utrecht NL 36 C1
Utrera E 29 D3
Utrillas E 26 C1
Utsjoki FIN 61 E2
Uttendorf A 44 B1
Uttendorf A 44 B2
Utting D 43 F1
Uttoxeter GB 9 D1
Uudeküla EE 73 D2
Uue-Antsla EE 79 D2
Uuemõisa EE 75 D2
Uukuniemi FIN 69 F2
Uulu EE 75 F3
Uurainen FIN 69 D2
Uuri EE 72 C1
Uusikaupunki FIN 68 C4
Uusküla (Harju) EE 72 B1
Uusküla (Rapla) EE 72 B2
Uusna EE 78 C1
Uvac SRB 56 C4
Uvdal N 66 B1
Užava LV 76 B3
Užbaliai LT 85 D2
Uzdin SRB 56 C2
Uzdowo PL 90 B2
Uzel F 10 B4
Uzerche F 15 F4
Uzès F 22 A1
Užgirelis LT 85 F2
Užhorod UA 116 C1
Užice SRB 56 C4
Užini LV 81 E1
Užkapiai LT 85 F1
Užliekne LT 80 C2
Užliekniai LT 84 B1
Užlieknis LT 80 B2
Užpaliai LT 82 C3
Užpeliai LT 80 C3
Užpjauniai LT 85 D2
Užsieniai LT 81 D3
Užtakai LT 85 F2
Užtilte LT 82 C3
Užubaliai LT 85 E3
Užumiškiai LT 85 E1
Uzunköprü TR 117 E4
Užuperkasis LT 86 B3
Užupiai (Alytaus) LT 85 F3
Užupiai (Kauno) LT 85 F2
Užusaliai LT 85 F2
Užušiliai LT 82 B2
Uzvara LV 81 F2
Užventis LT 81 D3
Uzyn UA 115 E4

V

V. Jablanica SRB 59 D2
V. Prolog HR 58 A3
Vä S 71 D3
Vaabina EE 79 D2
Vaajakoski FIN 69 E2
Vääkiö FIN 65 E2
Vaala FIN 65 E3
Vaalajärvi FIN 65 D1
Vaalimaa FIN 69 F4
Vaals NL 13 D1
Väänä EE 72 A2
Väänä-Jõesuu EE 72 A1
Vaaraslahti FIN 69 E1
Vaasa / Vasa FIN 68 C2
Vaassen NL 32 B4
Väätsa EE 72 C2
Vabaliai LT 81 E3
Vabalninkas LT 82 B2
Vabole (Vabale) LV 83 D2
Vabre F 21 F2
Vác H 116 B2
Vacha D 38 C2
Vācpēteri LV 81 E1
Vacpils LV 83 E1
Vadakste LV 81 D2
Vadaktai LT 81 E3
Vadakteliai LT 81 F3
Väddö S 67 F2
Vadheim N 62 A4
Vado Ligure I 23 E1
Vadokliai LT 81 F3
Vadsø N 61 F1
Vadstena S 67 E3
Vaduz FL 43 D3
Vadžgirys LT 85 D1
Væggerløse DK 70 C4
Vaeküla EE 73 D2
Vaféika GR 102 C1
Vafiohóri GR 101 F2
Vågaholmen N 60 A4
Vågåmo N 62 C4
Vågan N 60 B4
Vägari EE 73 D3
Våge N 66 A1
Vägeva EE 73 D3
Vaggeryd S 67 D4
Vágia GR 105 E2
Vagioniá GR 109 F4
Vagnhärad S 67 F3
Vagos P 24 B1
Vagula EE 79 E2
Vagur (Færøerne) DK 62 A3
Vahakulmu EE 73 D2
Vähäkyrö FIN 68 C2
Vahastu EE 72 C2
Vahenurme EE 72 A3
Vahi EE 73 D3
Vahto FIN 68 C4
Vahuküla EE 73 D2
Váï GR 111 D4
Vaiano I 47 D2
Vaiatu EE 73 D3
Vaičiai LT 80 C3
Vaičlaukis LT 85 D2
Vaiculeva LV 83 F3
Vaida EE 72 B2
Vaidasoo EE 72 B2
Vaidava LV 78 B2
Vaidlonys LT 82 B3
Vaiges F 11 D4
Vaiguva LT 81 D3
Vaihingen a. d. Enz D 38 C4
Väike-Kamari EE 72 C3
Väike-Maarja EE 73 D2
Väike-Rakke EE 79 D1
Vailainiai LT 81 E3
Vailly-sur-Aisne F 12 B3
Vailly-sur-Sauldre F 16 A1
Vaimastvere EE 73 D3
Väimela EE 79 E1
Vainikai LT 85 E1
Vainikkala FIN 69 F3
Vainiūnai LT 81 E3
Vainiūniškis LT 82 B2
Vainode LV 80 B1
Vainodes Muiža LV 80 C1
Vainotiškiai LT 85 E1
Vainova LV 83 E2
Vainupea EE 73 D1
Vainutas LT 80 B3
Vaisaluokta S 64 A1
Vaišniūnai LT 87 D1
Vaison-la-Romaine F 22 B1
Vaiste EE 75 E3
Vaišvilčiai I LT 81 F3
Vaišvydava LT 85 E2
Vaitiekūnai LT 81 E3
Vaitkūnai LT 82 B3
Vaivadai LT 81 F3
Vaivadi LV 81 F1
Vaivadiškiai LT 85 F1
Vaivara EE 73 F2
Vaižgai LT 81 E3
Vaizgučiai LT 81 E2
Vajangu EE 73 D2
Vajasiškis LT 82 C3
Vaki EE 72 B3
Vaksdal N 66 A1
Val-de-Reuil F 11 F3
Val-d'Isère F 17 E3
Val-Thorens F 17 D4
Vålådalen S 63 D3
Valadares P 18 A4
Valai LT 86 B1
Valakeliai LT 81 F2
Valalta HR 54 A3
Valamen FIN 69 F2
Valandovo MK 59 F4
Valareña E 20 B4
Valašské Meziříčí CZ 41 F3
Valasti EE 72 C2
Valāta LV 80 B1
Valatkoniai LT 81 E3
Valavičiai LT 85 D2
Valax FIN 69 E4
Valbella CH 43 D3
Valberg F 23 D1
Vålberg S 67 D2
Valbiska HR 54 B3
Valbo S 67 F1
Valbondione I 43 E4
Valbonnais F 17 D4
Valčiūnai LT 86 B2
Valdagno I 43 F4
Valdahon F 17 D1
Valdaj RUS 115 E1
Valdaora / Olang I 44 B3
Valdecaballeros E 25 E3
Valdecabras E 26 B2
Valdecarros E 25 E1
Valdedíos E 19 D2
Valdefuentes E 25 D3
Valdeganga E 26 B3
Valdeki LV 77 D3
Valdelacasa de Tajo E 25 E2
Valdelinares E 27 D2
Valdemārpils LV 77 D2
Valdemarsvik S 67 E3
Valdemeca E 26 B2
Valdemorillo E 25 F1
Valdemoro E 26 A2
Valdenoceda E 19 F3
Valdepeñas E 26 A4
Valdepeñas de Jaén E 29 F2
Valderas E 19 D3
Valderiès F 21 E1
Valderrobres E 27 D1
Valdestillas E 19 E4
Valdeverdeja E 25 E2
Valdevimbre E 19 D3
Valdezcaray E 19 F3
Valdgale LV 77 D3
Valdieri I 23 D1
Valdobbiadene I 44 B4
Vale de Açor P 24 B4
Vale de Cambra P 24 B1
Vale de Estrela P 24 C1
Vale de Prazeres P 24 C2
Valeggio sul Mincio I 47 D1
Valença do Minho P 18 A3
Valençay F 15 F1
Valence F 16 C4
Valence-d'Agen F 21 D1
Valence-d'Albigeois F 21 F1
Valence-sur-Baïse F 21 D1
València E 27 D3
Valencia
de Alcántara E 24 C2
Valencia
de Don Juan E 19 D3
Valencia
de las Torres E 25 D4
Valencia del Ventoso E 24 C4
Valenciennes F 12 B2
Valenčiūnai LT 85 D1
Valensole F 22 C1
Valentano I 47 E4
Valentigney F 17 D1
Valenza I 17 F4
Våler (Hedmark) N 66 C1
Våler (Østfold) N 66 C2
Valeria E 26 B2
Valevåg N 66 A2
Valfabbrica I 47 F3
Valga EE 79 D2
Valgalciems LV 77 D2
Valgale LV 76 C3
Välgita EE 72 C3
Valgjärve EE 79 D1
Valgorge F 22 A1
Valgrisenche I 17 E3
Valgu EE 72 B3
Valguarnera I 53 D3
Valgunde LV 81 E1
Valguta EE 79 D1
Valhelhas P 24 C1
Valimítika GR 105 D2
Valingu EE 72 A2
Valíra GR 104 C4
Valjala EE 74 C3
Valjevo SRB 56 C3
Valjok N 61 E2
Valjunquera E 27 D1
Valka LV 78 C2
Valkeakoski FIN 69 D3
Valkeala FIN 69 E3
Valkenburg
aan de Geul NL 13 D1
Valkenswaard NL 36 C2
Valkininkai LT 86 B3
Valkla EE 72 C1
Valko FIN 69 E4
Vall d'Alba E 27 D2
Valladolid E 19 E4
Vallata I 49 D3
Vallbo S 63 D3
Valldal N 62 B4
Valldemossa E 31 E3
Valle LV 82 B1
Valle N 66 A2
Valle Castellana I 48 B2
Valle de Abdalajís E 29 E3
Valle de la Serena E 25 D3
Valle de los Caídos E 25 F1
Valle de Matamoros E 24 C4
Valle Mosso I 17 F3
Valleberga S 71 D3
Vallejera de Riofrío E 25 D1
Vallentuna S 67 F2
Valleraugue F 22 A1
Vallet F 14 C1
Valletta M 53 F4
Vallgrund FIN 68 C2
Vallø DK 70 C3
Vallo della Lucania I 49 D4
Valloire F 17 D4
Vallombrosa I 47 E3
Vallon-en-Sully F 16 A2
Vallon-Pont-d'Arc F 22 A1
Vallorbe CH 17 D2
Vallorcine F 17 E3
Vallouise F 17 D4
Valls E 27 E1
Vallsta S 67 E1
Valma EE 78 C1
Valmantiškiai LT 85 E1
Valmiera LV 78 C2
Valmojado E 25 F2
Valmont F 11 E2
Valmontone I 48 B3
Valmorel F 17 D3
Vālodzes LV 76 C3
Vālodzītes LV 79 F3
Valognes F 11 D3
Valongo P 18 A4
Valoria la Buena E 19 E4
Valøya N 63 D2
Valožyn BY 115 D3
Valpaços P 18 B4
Valpainiai LT 81 D3
Valpalmas E 20 B4
Valpovo HR 55 E2
Valprato Soana I 17 E3
Valras-Plage F 21 F2
Valréas F 22 B1
Vals-les-Bains F 22 A1
Valsamónero GR 109 E4
Valsavarenche I 17 E3
Valset N 62 C3
Valsjöbyn S 63 E3
Valtaiki LV 80 B1
Valtessiníko GR 104 C3
Valtierra E 20 B3
Valtimo FIN 69 F1
Váltos GR 103 E1
Valtotópi GR 102 A2
Valtournenche I 17 E3
Valtu EE 72 B2
Valun HR 54 B3
Väluste EE 78 C1
Valvasone I 44 B4
Valverde E 20 A4
Valverde de Júcar E 26 B2
Valverde de Leganés E 24 C3
Valverde del Camino E 28 C2
Valverde del Fresno E 24 C2
Våmb S 67 D3
Vamberk CZ 41 D2
Våmhus S 67 E1
Vamlingbo S 67 F4
Vammala FIN 68 C3
Vampula FIN 68 C3
Vamvakoú
(Lakonía) GR 105 D4
Vamvakoú
(Lárissa) GR 105 D1
Vana-Antsla EE 79 D2
Vanageliai LT 85 F2
Vanagi LV 78 C2
Vanagi (Vonogi) LV 83 D2
Vanagiai LT 80 B3
Vana-Kaiu EE 72 B2
Vana-Kariste EE 78 C1
Vana-Koiola EE 79 E1
Vana-Kuuste EE 79 E1
Vanamõisa EE 72 B2
Vana-Roosa EE 79 D2
Vanassaare EE 73 E3
Vana-Vastseliina EE 79 E2
Vana-Vigala EE 72 A3
Vana-Võidu EE 78 C1
Vandāni LV 83 D2
Vandellós E 27 E1
Vändra EE 72 B3
Vandzene LV 77 D2
Vandzenes
Vidusskola LV 77 D2
Vandžiogala LT 85 E1
Vāne LV 77 D3
Vänersborg S 66 C3
Vanga LV 76 B3
Vangaži LV 77 F3
Vangsvik N 60 C2
Vanha Vaasa FIN 68 C2
Vännäs S 68 B1
Vannavålen N 60 C2
Vannes F 14 B1
Vansbro S 67 D1
Vantaa / Vanda FIN 69 D4
Vanttauskoski FIN 65 D1
Vao (Järva) EE 72 C2
Vao (Lääne-Viru) EE 73 D2
Vaour F 21 E1
Vara EE 73 E3
Vara S 67 D3
Varades F 14 C1
Varaklāni LV 83 E1
Varallo I 17 F3
Varangerbotn N 61 F1
Varano de Melegari I 46 C1
Varavīksne LV 83 D3
Varaždin HR 54 C1
Varaždinske
Toplice HR 54 C1
Varazze I 23 E1
Varberg S 70 C2
Varbla EE 72 A3
Varbola EE 72 A2
Várda GR 104 B3
Varda SRB 56 C3
Varde DK 70 B3
Vardi EE 78 C1
Vardja (Harju) EE 72 B2
Vardja (Põlva) EE 79 E1
Vardja (Viljandi) EE 78 C1
Vårdö FIN 68 B4
Vardø N 61 F1
Varel D 33 D3
Vareleíi GR 106 B3
Varena LT 85 F3
Varengeville-sur-Mer F 11 F2
Varenna I 43 D4
Varennes-
en-Argonne F 12 C3
Varennes-sur-Allier F 16 A3
Varennes-
sur-Amance F 16 C1
Vareš BIH 55 E3
Varese I 17 F3
Varese Ligure I 23 F1
Vårgårda S 67 D3
Vargas E 19 F2
Varhaug N 66 A3
Vári GR 105 F3
Vári GR 106 C4
Varieba LV 77 D3
Varieši LV 82 C1
Variku EE 72 A2
Varilhes F 21 E3
Varimbómbi GR 105 F3
Varini (Jelgavas) LV 81 F1
Varini (Valkas) LV 79 D3
Váris GR 101 D3
Varja EE 73 E2
Varkalabiškes LT 86 C2
Varkales LT 85 F2
Varkali LV 80 C1
Varkaliai LT 80 B2
Varkaus FIN 69 E2
Várkiza GR 105 F3
Varkujai LT 82 C3
Varmahlíð IS 62 A1
Vārme LV 76 C3
Varmo I 44 C4
Varna BG 117 E3
Varna SRB 55 F3
Varnaičiai LT 80 C2
Värnamo S 71 D2
Vārnava LV 82 C2
Varnaviči LV 83 E3
Varnenai LT 85 E3
Varnhem S 67 D3
Varniai LT 80 C3
Varnikai LT 86 B2
Varnja EE 73 E3
Varnsdorf CZ 40 C1
Varnupiai LT 85 E2
Värö S 70 C2
Varoni LV 77 D3
Varoš Selo SRB 59 E3
Vārpa
(Sarkankrogs) LV 81 E1
Varpaisjärvi FIN 69 E1
Várpalota H 116 B2
Vārpas LV 81 F1
Varputenai LT 81 D3
Vars F 23 D1
Varsedžiai LT 80 C3
Värska EE 79 F1
Varstu EE 79 D2
Vartai (Alytaus) LT 85 E3
Vartai (Kauno) LT 85 E2
Vārtāja LV 80 B1
Vartholomió GR 104 B3
Vartius FIN 65 F3
Vartulenai LT 80 C3
Varvára GR 102 A2
Varvarin SRB 57 E3
Vārve LV 76 B2
Varzi I 46 B1
Varzy F 16 A1
Vasaknos LT 82 C3
Vasalemma EE 72 A2
Vasaraperä FIN 65 E2
Vásárosnamény H 116 C2
Vasavere EE 73 F2
Vašilenai LT 80 C3
Vaškai LT 81 F2
Vaski LV 77 D3
Vaskio FIN 68 C4
Vaskivesi FIN 69 D2
Vaskjala EE 72 B2
Vasknarva EE 73 F2
Vaslui RO 117 E2
Vassarás GR 105 D4
Vassés GR 104 C4
Vassieux-en-Vercors F 16 C4
Vassiliká GR 101 F3
Vassiliká GR 107 E1
Vassiliká GR 105 E1
Vassilikí GR 101 D4
Vassilikí GR 104 A2
Vassilikó GR 105 F2
Vassilikós GR 104 B3
Vassilís GR 105 D1
Vassy F 11 D3
Vasta EE 73 D1
Västanfjärd FIN 68 C4
Vastemõisa EE 72 C3
Västenbäck S 68 A2
Väster-Haninge S 67 F3
Västerås S 67 E2
Västervik S 67 E4
Vasto I 48 C2
Vastse-Kuuste EE 79 E1
Vastseliina EE 79 E2
Vasula EE 73 E3
Vašuokenai LT 82 B3
Vasyl'kiv UA 115 E4
Vatan F 15 F2
Väte S 67 F4
Vaterá GR 107 D1
Vateró GR 101 D3
Váthi GR 101 F1
Vathí GR 104 B2
Vathí GR 105 F2
Vathí GR 111 D1
Váthia GR 108 B2
Vathílakos GR 102 B1
Vathílakos GR 101 F2
Vathílakos GR 101 E3
Vathípetro GR 109 F4
Vathís GR 111 E1
Vatin SRB 57 D2
Vatla EE 75 D2
Vatne N 62 B3
Vatólakos GR 101 D3
Vatra Dornei RO 117 D2
Vattholma S 67 F2
Vaucouleurs F 13 D4
Vaŭkavysk BY 115 D3
Vauvert F 22 A2
Vauvillers F 42 A2
Vávdos GR 102 A3
Växjö S 71 E2
Våxtorp S 71 D3
Vayrac F 15 F4
V'az'ma RUS 115 F2
Veberöd S 71 D3
Vecate LV 78 B2
Vecauce LV 81 D1
Vecbebri LV 82 C1
Vecgaiki LV 77 D3
Vechta D 33 D4
Vecinos E 25 D1
Veckrape LV 82 B1
Vecmikeli LV 81 D1
Vecmuiža LV 77 F3
Vecpiebalga LV 78 C3
Vecpils (Dižlāni) LV 80 B1
Vecružina
(Vacružina) LV 83 E2
Vecsaikava LV 83 D1
Vecsalaca LV 77 F2
Vecsaule LV 81 F2
Vecsikeli LV 83 E3
Vecsīpoli LV 80 B2
Vecslabada
(Vacsloboda) LV 83 F2
Vecstāmeriena LV 79 E3
Vecstārasti LV 78 B2
Vecstropi LV 83 D3
Vecstrūžāni
(Strūžāni) LV 83 E1
Vecsvirlauka LV 81 E1
Vectilža (Vactilža) LV 79 E3
Vecumi (Vacumi) LV 79 F3
Vecumnieki LV 81 F1
Veczosna
(Vaczosna) LV 83 E2
Vēde LV 76 C2
Vedelago I 44 B4
Vedu EE 73 E3
Veelikse (Pärnu) EE 75 F3
Veelikse (Viljandi) EE 75 F3
Veendam NL 32 C3
Veenendaal NL 36 C1
Veere NL 36 B1
Vef Ozoli LV 77 F3
Vef-Pabaži LV 77 F3
Vega de Espinareda E 18 C2
Vega de Valcarce E 18 C3
Vegadeo E 18 C2
Vegarienza E 19 D2
Vegårshei N 66 B3
Vēgas LV 76 C3
Vegas del Condado E 19 D2
Vegesack D 33 E3
Veghel NL 36 C1
Vegi LV 76 C3
Veguellina
de Órbigo E 19 D3
Vehkalahti FIN 69 E4
Vehmaa FIN 68 C4
Vehmersalmi FIN 69 E2
Veidnesklubben N 61 E1
Veikkola FIN 69 D4
Veinge S 71 D2
Veiros P 24 C3
Veisiejai LT 85 E3
Veiveriai LT 85 E2
Veivirženai LT 80 B3
Vejen DK 70 B3
Vejer de la Frontera E 29 D4
Vejle DK 70 B3
Vejos LT 80 C3
Vel.-Kopanica HR 55 E2
Vel. Lašče SLO 54 B2
Vel. Trnovac SRB 59 E3
Vela Luka HR 58 A4
Velada E 25 E2
Velagići BIH 55 D3

VALÈNCIA

Alcade Reig............... BV 2
Ángel Guimerá............. AU 7
Burjassot (Av. de)........ AU 9
Campanar (Av.)............ AU 10
Cavanilles............... BU 14
Constitución (Av. de la).. BU 15
Doctor Peset Aleixandre (Av.) BU 20
Doctor Tomás Sala (Av. del) AU 21
Fernando el Católico (G. Vía) AU 26
Filipinas................ BV 29
Gaspar Aguilar (Av. de)... AV 31
General Avilés (Av.)...... AV 32
General Urrutia........... AV 36
Giorgeta (Av.)............ AV 37
Guadalaviar.............. AU 38
Hermanos Maristas (Av. de) BV 42
Ingeniero Manuel Soto (Av.) CV 43
José Soto Mico............ AV 46
Junta de Murs y Valls..... BV 44
Llano de la Zaidia........ BU 47
Maestro Rodrigo (Av.)..... AV 52
Mandingora (Av. de)....... AV 53
Manuel de Falla (Av.)..... AU 53
Menéndez Pidal (Av.)...... AU 58
Morenas (Camino).......... CV 60
Pechina (Paseo)........... AU 68
Pérez Galdós (Av. de)..... AV 69
Peris y Valero (Av. de)... BV 71
Pianista Martínez Carrasco
(Av. del)................. BV 72
Plata (Av. de la)......... BV 76
Primado Reig (Av.)........ BU 78
San José de Calasanz...... AU 82
San Vicente Mártir (Av.).. AU 84
Tirso de Molina (Av.)..... AU 92
9 de Octubre.............. AU 99

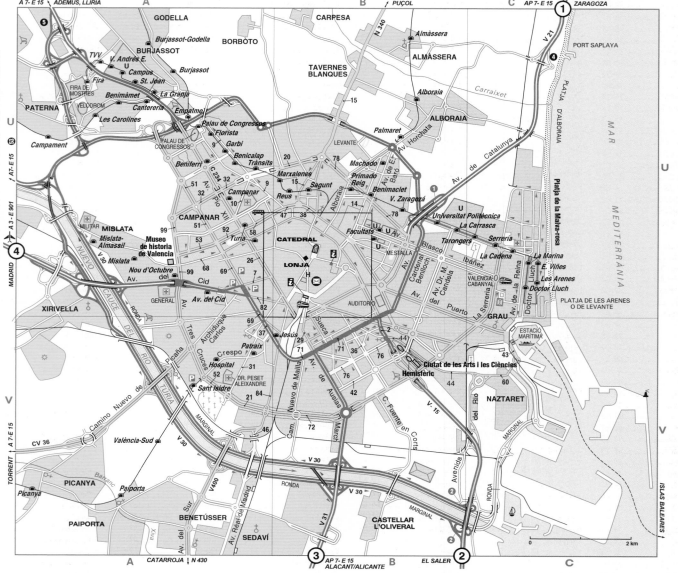

Velanídia GR 108 C2
Velayos E................25 F1
Velbert D................37 E2
Velburg D................39 E4
Velde N..................63 D2
Velden A.................44 C3
Velden D.................39 E3
Velden D.................44 B1
Veldhoven NL.............36 C2
Veldres LT...............81 E1
Veldze
(Rumbenieki) LV..........76 C3
Velēna LV................79 D3
Velenje SLO..............54 B1
Veles MK.................59 F3
Velešta MK...............59 E4
Velestíno GR............101 F4
Vélez Blanco E...........30 B2
Vélez de Benaudalla E....29 F3
Vélez Málaga E...........29 F3
Vélez Rubio E............30 B2
Veli Iž HR...............54 B4
Veli Lošinj HR...........54 B4
Veličani BIH.............58 B3
Veliés GR...............108 B1
Velika HR................55 D2
Velika Drenova SRB.......57 D4
Velika Gorica HR.........54 C2
Velika Jamnička HR.......54 C2
Velika Kladuša BIH.......54 C3
Velika Kruša SRB.........59 D3
Velika Mučna HR..........54 C1
Velika Plana
(Jagodina) SRB...........57 D3
Velika Plana
(Prokuplje) SRB..........57 E4
Veliki Bastaji HR........55 D2
Veliki Gaj SRB...........57 D2
Veliki Grđevac HR........55 D2
Veliki Izvor SRB.........57 E3
Veliki Popović SRB.......57 D3
Veliki Preslav BG.......117 E3
Veliki Radinci SRB.......57 F2
Veliki Raven HR..........54 C2
Veliki Zdenci HR.........55 D2
Velikije Luki RUS.......115 E2
Veliko Gradište SRB......57 D2
Veliko Orašje SRB........57 D3
Veliko Tārnovo BG.......117 E3
Velilla del Río
Carrión E................19 E3
Velimlje MNE.............58 B3
Vélines F................15 D4
Velingrad BG............117 D4
Veliučionys LT...........86 C2
Veliuona LT..............85 D1
Veliž RUS...............115 E2
Veljun HR................54 C3
Velká Bíteš CZ...........41 E3
Velká Bystřice CZ........41 E3
Velká nad Veličkou CZ....41 F4
Velké Meziříčí CZ........41 D3
Velkua FIN...............68 C4
Vellahn D................33 F3
Velletri I...............48 B3
Vellinge S...............71 D3

Velanídia GR............108 C2
Velopoúla (Nissí) GR....108 C1
Vélos GR................105 F2
Velpke D.................33 F4
Velten D.................34 B3
Veltsi EE................73 D2
Velvendós GR............101 E3
Velyka Lepetycha UA.....117 F1
Velžys LT................81 F3

Vembūtai LT..............80 C2
Vemdalen S...............63 E4
Vemdalsskalet S..........63 E4
Vemhån S.................63 E4
Véna GR.................103 D2
Venaco F.................23 F3
Venafro I................48 C3
Venarey-les-Laumes F.....16 B1

Venaria Reale I..........17 E4
Vence F..................23 D2
Venenvere EE.............73 D2
Venčiúnai LT.............85 F3
Venckai LT...............80 B3
Venda Nova P.............18 B4
Vendas Novas P...........24 B3
Vendeuvre-sur-Barse F....12 C4
Vendôme F................15 E1

Veneheitto FIN...........65 E3
Venevere EE..............73 D2
Venezia I................44 B4
Vengjaneset N............66 A1
Venialbo E...............19 D4
Venjan S.................67 D2
Venlo NL.................37 D2
Vennesla N...............66 A3

Vennesund N..............63 D2
Venosa I.................49 D3
Venray NL................37 D1
Venta LT.................81 D2
Venta LV.................76 C3
Venta Nueva E............18 C2
Ventas con Peña
Aguilera E...............25 F2

Ventas de Huelma E.......29 F3
Ventava LV...............76 B3
Vente LT.................80 A3
Ventimiglia I............23 D1
Ventnor GB................9 D4
Ventspils LV.............76 B2
Venturina I..............47 D3
Vepriai LT...............85 F1

Vera E...................30 B3
Vera N...................63 D3
Verbania I...............17 F3
Verberie F...............12 A3
Verbicaro I..............51 D2
Verbier CH...............17 E3
Verbūnai LT..............81 D2
Verbūškes LT.............86 C1
Verčane SRB..............57 D3
Vercel-Villedieu-
le-Camp F................17 D1
Vercelli I...............17 F4
Verchnjadzvinsk BY......115 D2
Verchn'odni-
provs'k UA..............117 E2
Verdalsøra N.............63 D3
Verden D.................33 E3
Verdikoússa GR..........101 E4
Verdini LV...............82 B2
Verdun F.................13 D3
Verdun-sur-Garonne F.....21 E2
Verdun-sur-le-Doubs F....16 C2
Verebiejai LT............85 E3
Vereduva LT..............85 D1
Vērgale LV...............80 B2
Vergato I................47 D2
Vergi EE.................73 D1
Vérgi GR................102 A2
Vergiate I...............17 F3
Vergio F.................23 F3
Vergt F..................15 E4
Véria GR................101 E4
Verijärve EE.............79 D3
Verilaske EE.............78 C1
Verín E..................18 B3
Veriora EE...............79 E1
Verioramôisa EE..........79 E1
Veriškes LT..............86 C2
Veriškiai LT.............81 E3
Verksnionys LT...........82 C3
Verl D...................37 F1
Vermand F................12 B2
Vermenton F..............16 B1
Vernet-les-Bains F.......21 E3
Verneuil-sur-Avre F......11 F4
Vernon F.................11 F3
Vernoux-en-Vivarais F....16 C3
Verny F..................13 D3
Veroli I.................48 B3
Verona I.................43 F4
Vērpēji LV...............77 D3
Verpena LT...............81 D2
Verpuleva LV.............79 E3
Verran N.................63 D3
Verrès I.................17 E3
Versailles F.............12 A3
Versmold D...............37 F1
Verstaminai LT...........85 E2
Verteillac F.............15 E4

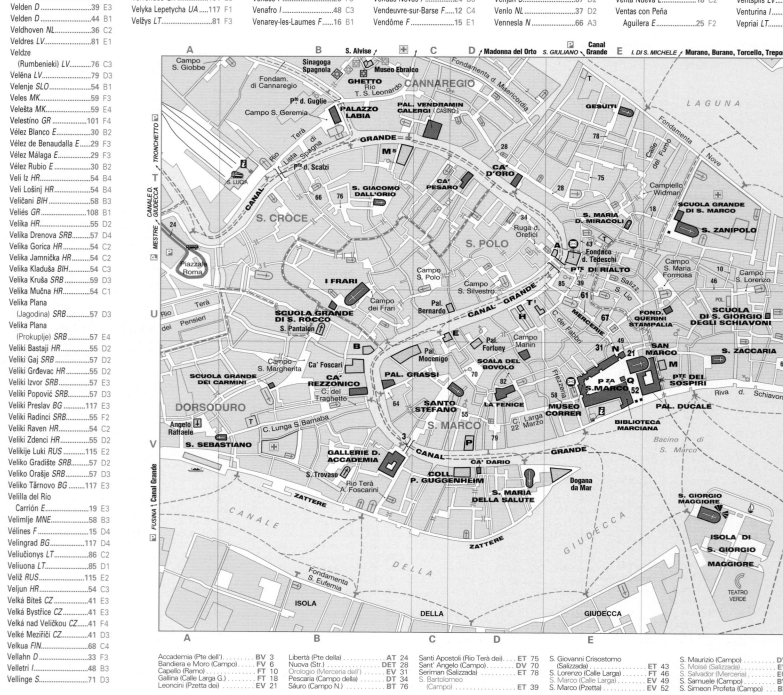

Accademia (Pte dell')....BV 3
Bandiera e Moro (Campo)...FV 6
Capello (Ramo)...........FV 10
Gallina (Calle Larga G.)..FT 18
Leoncini (Pzetta dei).....EV 21

Libertà (Pte della)......AT 24
Nuova (Str.).............DET 28
Orologio (Mercerie dell').EV 31
Pescaria (Campo della)...DT 34
Sáuro (Campo N.).........BT 76

Santi Apostoli (Rio Terà dei)..ET 75
Sant' Angelo (Campo).....DV 70
Seriman (Salizzada)......ET 78
S. Bartolomeo
(Campo)..................ET 39

S. Giovanni Crisostomo
(Salizzada)..............ET 43
S. Lorenzo (Calle Larga)..FT 46
S. Marco (Calle Larga)...EV 49
S. Marco (Pzetta)........EV 52
S. Simeone Profeta (Campo)..BT 66

S. Maurizio (Campo)......DV 55
S. Moisé (Salizzada).....DV 58
S. Salvador (Mercerie)...EU 61
S. Samuele (Campo).......BV 64
Verona (Calle Larga).....DV 82

S. Zulian (Mercerie).....EU 67
Traghetto
(Campo del)..............DV 79
2 Aprile (V.)............ET 85

Vertimai LT......84 C1
Vertus F......12 B3
Verucchio I......47 E2
Verviers B......13 D1
Vervins F......12 B2
Verzuolo I......17 E4
Verzy F......12 B3
Vesanto FIN......69 E2
Vescovato F......23 F3
Veselava LV......78 C3
Veselí nad Lužnicí CZ......40 C2
Veselí nad Moravou CZ......41 F3
Veselíba LV......82 C2
Vesilahti FIN......69 D3
Vesivehmaa FIN......69 E3
Vesjegonsk RUS......115 F1
Veskimäe EE......78 C1
Veskoniemi FIN......61 F2
Vesna LV......83 D2
Vesneri EE......73 E4
Vesoul F......17 D1
Vestby N......66 C2
Vestbygda N......66 A3
Vesterø Havn DK......70 C1
Vestertana N......61 E1
Vestiena LV......78 C3
Vestmanna (Færøerne) DK......62 A3
Vestnes N......62 B3
Vestone I......43 E4
Vestre jakobselv N......61 F1
Veszprém H......116 B2
Veteli FIN......69 D1
Vetiku EE......73 D2
Vetlanda S......67 E4
Vetralla I......47 E4
Vetriolo Terme I......43 F4
Vetschau D......34 C4
Veules-les-Roses F......11 F2
Veulettes-sur-Mer F......11 F2
Veurne B......12 A1
Vevey CH......17 D3
Vévi GR......101 D2
Veynes F......22 C1
Veyre-Monton F......16 A3
Veyrier-du-Lac F......17 D3
Vežaičiai LT......80 B3
Vezdemarbán E......19 D4
Vézelay F......16 B1
Vézelise F......13 D4
Vézénobres F......22 A1
Vézins-de-Lévézou F......21 F1
Vežionys LT......85 F2
Vezzani F......23 F3
Vezzano I......43 F4
Viadana I......47 F1
Viana E......20 A3
Viana do Alentejo P......24 B4
Viana do Bolo E......18 B3
Viana do Castelo P......18 A3
Vianden L......13 D2
Vianen NL......36 C1
Viareggio I......46 C2
Vias F......22 A2
Vibini LV......80 C1
Vibo Valentia I......51 D3
Viborg DK......70 B2
Vibraye F......11 F4
Vic E......21 E4
Vič SLO......54 B1
Vic-en-Bigorre F......20 C2
Vic-Fezensac F......21 D2
Vic-le-Comte F......16 A3
Vic-sur-Aisne F......12 B3
Vic-sur-Cère F......16 A4
Vicdessos F......21 E3
Vicebsk BY......115 E2
Vicenza I......43 F4
Vichy F......16 A3
Vico F......23 F3
Vico del Gargano I......49 D4
Vico Equense I......48 C4
Victoria M......53 F4
Vidaga P......79 D2
Vidago P......18 B4
Vidale LV......77 D2
Vidareidi DK......62 A2
Vidauban F......22 C2
Viddal N......62 B4
Videbæk DK......70 B3
Videm SLO......54 B2
Videniškiai LT......86 B1
Vidiáki GR......104 C3
Vidigueira P......24 B4
Vidin BG......117 D3
Vidiškes LT......87 D1
Vidiškiai LT......86 B1
Vidnava CZ......41 E2
Vidreres E......21 F4
Vidriži LV......78 B3
Vidsala LV......82 C2
Vidsel S......64 B2
Vidukle LT......81 D2
Vidutine LT......87 D2
Vidzeme LV......78 C3
Vidzgailai LT......85 D2
Viechtach D......39 F4
Viechtwang A......44 C1
Vieira de Leiria P......24 A2
Vieira do Minho P......18 A4
Vielha E......21 D3
Vielle-Aure F......21 D3
Vielmur-sur-Agout F......21 E2

Vielsalm B......13 D2
Vienenburg D......38 C1
Vieniba LV......77 D3
Vienne F......16 C3
Vieremä FIN......69 E1
Viernheim D......23 F1
Vierraden D......34 C3
Viersen D......37 D2
Viertiukšne LV......83 E2
Vierumäki FIN......69 E3
Vierzon F......15 F1
Viesatas (Viesati) LV......77 D3
Viešinteles LT......82 B3
Viesintos LT......82 B2
Vieste I......49 E2
Viesturi (Bauskas) LV......81 F1
Viesturi (Jelgavas) LV......81 E1
Viešvenai I LT......80 C2
Viešvile (Šiauliu) LT......81 E3
Viešvile (Tauragés) LT......84 C1
Vietalva LV......82 C1
Vietas S......64 A1
Vietri di Potenza I......49 D4
Vietri sul Mare I......49 D4
Vieux-Boucau-les-Bains F......20 B2
Vievis LV......86 B2
Vif F......16 C4
Víg DK......70 C3
Vigante LV......82 C1
Viganti (Lukna) LV......83 E2
Vigeland N......66 A3
Vigeois F......15 F4
Vigevano I......17 F4
Viggiano I......49 E4
Vígla GR......104 B1
Vignale Monferrato I......17 F4
Vignanello I......47 E4
Vigneulles-lès-Hattonchâtel F......13 D3
Vignola I......47 D2
Vignole Borbera I......17 F4
Vignory F......12 C4
Vigo E......18 A3
Vigo di Fassa I......43 F3
Vigone I......17 E4
Vigonza I......44 B4
Vigori LV......83 F2
Vihanti FIN......65 D3
Vihasoo EE......72 C1
Vihiers F......15 D1
Vihtavuori FIN......69 E2
Vihteljärvi FIN......68 C3

Vihti FIN......69 D4
Vihtra EE......72 B3
Vihula EE......73 D1
Viiala FIN......69 D3
Viiksimo FIN......65 F3
Viimsi EE......72 B1
Viinijärvi FIN......69 F2
Viinistu EE......72 C1
Viiratsi EE......78 C1
Viisu EE......72 C2
Viitasaari FIN......69 E2
Viitina EE......79 E2
Viitka EE......79 E2
Viitna EE......72 C1
Vijciems LV......78 C2
Vijeikiai LT......82 C3
Vik IS......62 B3
Vik N......66 B3
Vik (Nordland) N......63 D1
Vik (Sogn og Fjordane) N......66 A1
Vika S......67 E1
Vikaičiai LT......81 E3
Vikajärvi FIN......65 D1
Vikedal N......66 A2
Vikersund N......66 B2
Vikeså N......66 A3
Vikevåg N......66 A3
Viki LV......78 B2
Vikingstad S......67 E3
Vikoč BIH......55 F4
Vikou GR......100 C3
Vikran N......60 C2
Viksdalen N......62 A4
Viksjö S......68 A2
Viksna (Viksna) LV......79 E3
Viktarinas LT......85 D2
Vila Boim P......24 C3
Vila de Cruces E......18 B2
Vila de Rei P......24 B2
Vila do Bispo P......28 A2
Vila do Conde P......18 A4
Vila Fernando P......24 C3
Vila Flor P......18 B4
Vila Franca das Naves P......24 C1
Vila Franca de Xira P......24 A3
Vila Fresca de Azeitão P......24 A3
Vila Nova da Barquinha P......24 B2
Vila Nova de Cerveira P......18 A3
Vila Nova de Famalicão P......18 A4

Vila Nova de Foz Côa P......18 B4
Vila Nova de Gaia P......18 A4
Vila Nova de Milfontes P......24 A4
Vila Nova de Paiva P......24 C1
Vila Nova de Poiares P......24 B1
Vila Nova de Santo André P......24 A4
Vila Nova de São Bento P......24 B4
Vila Pouca de Aguiar P......18 B4
Vila Praia de Âncora P......18 A3
Vila-real E......27 D2
Vila Real P......18 B4
Vila Real de Santo António P......28 B2
Vila-rodona E......27 F1
Vila-seca E......27 F1
Vila Velha de Ródão P......24 C2
Vila Verde P......18 A4
Vila Verde de Ficalho P......24 C4
Vila Viçosa P......24 C3
Vilada E......21 E4
Viladrau E......21 F4
Vilafamés E......27 D2
Vilafranca del Penedès E......27 F1
Vilagarcía de Arousa E......18 A2
Vilaka LV......79 F3
Vilalba / Villalba E......18 B2
Vilaller E......21 D3
Vilallonga E......27 D4
Vilamarxant E......27 D3
Vilâni LV......83 E1
Vilanova E......18 B2
Vilanova d'Alcolea E......27 D2
Vilanova de Arosa E......18 A2
Vilanova de Sau E......21 F4
Vilanova i la Geltrú / Villanueva y Geltrú E......27 F1
Vilar de Barrio E......18 B3
Vilar Formoso P......24 C1
Vilcăni LV......83 E2
Vilce LV......81 E2
Vilches E......25 F4
Vildūnai LT......81 F2
Vileikiai (Klaipedos) LT......84 B1
Vileikiai (Vilniaus) LT......86 B1
Vileikiškiai LT......86 B2
Vilejka BY......115 D3

Vilgâle (Saldenieki) LV......76 C3
Vilhelmina S......64 A3
Vilia GR......105 E3
Vilina Vlas BIH......55 F4
Viliotes Užpelkis LT......80 C2
Viljakkala FIN......69 D3
Viljandi EE......78 C1
Viljete LV......77 D3
Vilkakrûgs LV......83 F2
Vilkaviškis LT......85 D2
Vilkenas I LT......80 B3
Vilkene LV......78 B2
Vilkija LT......85 E1
Vilkiškiai (Kauno) LT......81 D2
Vilkiškiai (Panevežio) LT......81 F3
Vilkupiai LT......85 D2
Vilkyškiai LT......84 C1
Villa EE......78 C1
Villa Adriana I......48 B3
Villa Bartolomea I......47 D1
Villa del Prado E......25 F2
Villa del Río E......25 F4
Villa Literno I......48 C4
Villa Minozzo I......47 D2
Villa Opicina I......44 C4
Villa Potenza I......47 E3
Villa S. Giovanni I......51 D4
Villa Santa Maria I......48 C2
Villa Santina I......44 B3
Villa Vomano I......48 B2
Villabassa / Niederdorf I......44 B3
Villablanca E......28 B3
Villablino E......18 C2
Villabona E......20 A2
Villabrágima E......19 D4
Villabuena del Puente E......19 D4
Villacañas E......26 A3
Villacarriedo E......19 F2
Villacarrillo E......26 A4
Villacastín E......25 F1
Villach A......44 C3
Villacidro I......50 A4
Villadangos del Páramo E......19 D3
Villadiego E......19 E3
Villadossola I......17 F3
Villaescusa de Haro E......26 A3
Villafáfila E......19 D4
Villaflores E......25 E1
Villafranca E......20 B3
Villafranca de los Barros E......25 D4

Villafranca de los Caballeros E......26 A3
Villafranca del Bierzo E......18 C3
Villafranca del Cid / Vilafranca E......27 D2
Villafranca di Verona I......47 D1
Villafranca in Lunigiana I......46 C2
Villafranca-Montes de Oca E......19 F3
Villafranca Piemonte I......17 E4
Villafranca Tirrena I......51 D4
Villafranco del Guadalquivir E......29 D3
Villafrati I......52 C3
Villafrechós E......19 D4
Villafruela E......19 E4
Villafuerte E......19 E4
Villager de Laciana E......18 C2
Villaggio Mancuso I......51 E3
Villahermosa E......26 A4
Villahoz E......19 F4
Villaines-la-Juhel F......11 E4
Villala FIN......69 F2
Villalba de Guardo E......19 E3
Villalba de la Sierra E......26 B2
Villalba de los Barros E......24 C4
Villalba del Rey E......26 B2
Villalcázar de Sirga E......19 E3
Villalgordo del Marquesado E......26 B3
Villalón de Campos E......19 D3
Villalpando E......19 D4
Villalpardo E......26 B3
Villaluenga E......20 A4
Villamañan E......19 D3
Villamanrique E......26 A4
Villamanrique de la Condesa E......28 C3
Villamanrique del Campo E......19 D4
Villamartín de Campos E......19 E4
Villamassargia I......50 A4
Villamayor E......20 C4
Villamayor de Campos E......19 D4
Villamayor de Santiago E......26 A2
Villandraut F......20 C1
Villandry F......15 E1
Villanova Monteleone I......50 A2
Villanubla E......19 E4

Villar de Domingo García E......26 B2
Villar de Peralonso E......25 D1
Villar del Arzobispo E......26 C3
Villar del Rey E......24 C3
Villarcayo E......19 F2
Villard-de-Lans F......16 C4
Villardeciervos E......18 C3
Villardefrades E......19 D4
Villarejo de Fuentes E......26 A2
Villarejo de Salvanés E......26 A2
Villarente E......19 D3
Villares de la Reina E......25 E1
Villares del Saz E......26 B2
Villargarcía del Llano E......26 B3
Villargordo del Cabriel E......26 C3
Villaricos E......30 B3
Villarino E......18 C4
Villaroya de los Pinares E......27 D2
Villarquemado E......19 E3
Villarrín de Campos E......19 D4
Villarrobledo E......26 A3
Villarroya E......20 A4
Villarroya de la Sierra E......20 B4
Villarrubia de los Ojos E......25 F3
Villarrubia de Santiago E......26 A2
Villarrubio E......26 A2
Villars-les-Dombes F......16 C3
Villars-sur-Ollon CH......17 E2
Villarta de San Juan E......26 A3
Villasalto I......50 B4
Villasana de Mena E......19 F2
Villasandino E......19 E3
Villasante de Montija E......19 F2
Villasarracino E......19 E3
Villaseco de los Reyes E......18 C4
Villasequilla E......25 F2
Villasimius I......50 B4
Villasor I......50 A4
Villatobas E......26 A2
Villatoya E......26 B3
Villava E......20 C3
Villaverde del Río E......29 D3
Villaviciosa E......19 D2
Villaviciosa de Córdoba E......25 E4
Villaviciosa de Odón E......25 F2

WARSZAWA

Armii Krajowej (al.)......DET 3
Bitwy Warszawskiej (ul.)......DU 4
Broniewskiego (ul.)......DET 7
Czecha (ul. Br.)......GU 9
Dolina Służewiecka (ul.)......EFV 12
Fieldorfa (ul. Gen. Emila)......GU 15
Hynka Franciszka (ul.)......DV 18
Marynarska (ul.)......EV 30
Niepodległości (al.)......EUV 34
Odyńca Antoniego (ul.)......EV 40
Płowiecka (ul.)......GU 43
Prymasa Tysiąclecia (al.)......DU 46
Puławska (ul.)......EUV 48
Rzymowskiego (ul. W.)......EV 49
Sikorskiego (al. Gen. W.)......FV 51
Starzyńskiego (ul. Stefana)......EFT 55
Widoczna (ul.)......GU 61
Wysockiego (ul. P.)......ET 63
Zwoleńska (ul.)......GV 67

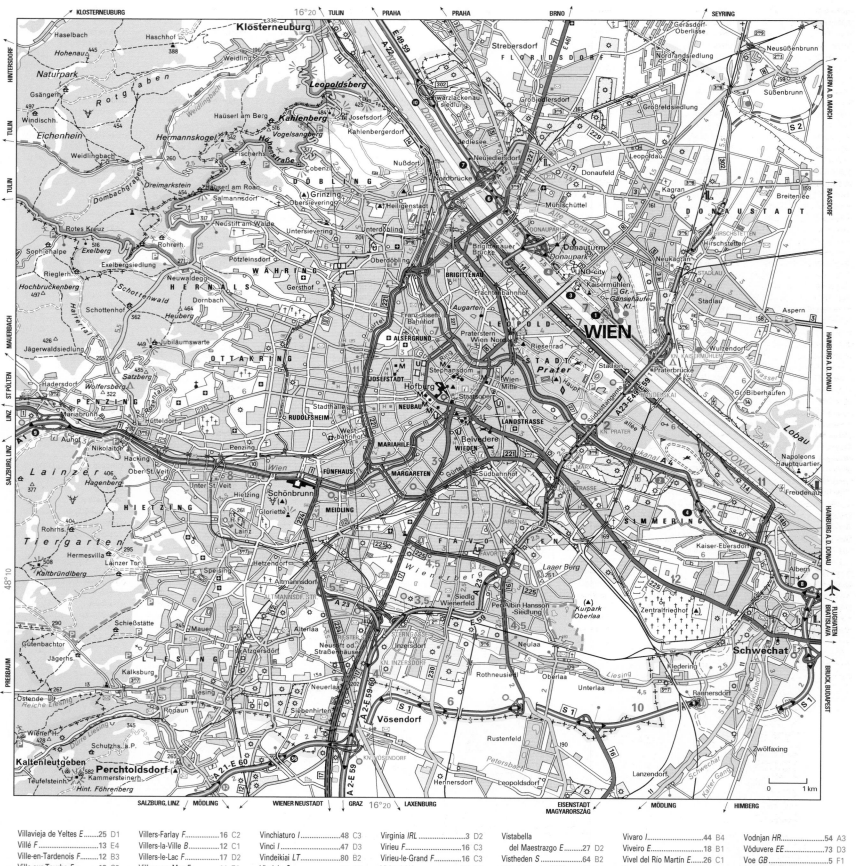

Völkermarkt A	45	D3
Völklingen D	13	E3
Volkmarsen D	37	F1
Volkovija MK	59	E4
Volmunster F	13	E3
Voločys'k UA	117	D1
Volodymyr-		
Volyns'kyj UA	115	D4
Volokolamsk RUS	115	F2
Volonne F	22	C1
Vólos GR	105	E3
Volpiano I	17	E4
Volta Mantovana I	47	D1
Volterra I	47	D3
Voltri I	23	F4
Volturara Appula I	49	D3
Volvic F	16	A3
Volx F	22	C1
Volyně CZ	40	C1
Vónitsa GR	104	C3
Vonnas F	16	C3
Võnnu EE	79	E1
Võõpste EE	79	E1
Võõpsu EE	79	F1
Voore EE	73	E3
Voorschoten NL	36	C1
Voorst NL	37	D1
Voorthuizen NL	36	C1
Vooru EE	78	C1
Voose EE	72	C2
Vopnafjörður IS	62	B1
Vörå / Vöyri FIN	68	C2
Vorau A	45	E2
Vorbuse EE	73	D3
Vorchdorf A	44	C1
Vorden NL	37	D1
Vordernberg A	45	D2
Vorderriß D	43	F2
Vordingborg DK	70	C4
Voreppe F	16	C4
Vorey F	16	B4
Vóri GR	109	E4
Vorískes LT	85	E1
Vorna FIN	65	D3
Voroneţ RO	117	D2
Vorsfelde D	33	F4
Võru EE	79	E1
Võrumõisa EE	79	E2
Vosbutai LT	85	E1
Vosgeliai LT	82	C3
Vosiliškis LT	81	E3
Vošiškes LT	85	E1
Vosiškiai LT	85	E1
Vosiūnai LT	87	E1
Voskoniai LT	81	E3
Voss N	66	A1
Võsu EE	73	D1
Võsupere EE	73	D1
Votice CZ	40	C3
Võtikvere EE	73	E3
Votonóssi GR	101	C4
Voúdia GR	109	E1
Vouhorina GR	101	D3
Vouillé F	15	D2
Voukoliés GR	109	C4
Voúla GR	105	E4
Vouliagméni GR	105	F3
Voúlpi GR	104	C3
Vouraïkós GR	105	D4
Vourgaréli (Árta) GR	101	D4
Vourkári GR	106	B4
Vourliótes GR	107	E3
Voúrvoura GR	105	D4
Vourvouroú GR	102	C3
Voutás GR	105	E1
Vouvant F	15	D2
Vouvray F	15	E1
Vouzela P	24	B1
Vouziers F	12	C3
Voves F	11	F4
Vovoússa GR	100	C3
Voz HR	54	B3
Vozarci MK	59	E4
Voznesens'k UA	117	F1
Vrå DK	70	B2
Vraca BG	117	D3
Vračev Gaj SRB	57	D2
Vračevšnica SRB	57	D3
Vrådal N	66	B2
Vraháti GR	105	E3
Vrahnéika GR	104	C3
Vrams-Gunnarstorp S	71	D3
Vrana N	67	—
Vranduk BIH	55	E4
Vranja HR	54	A3
Vranje SRB	59	E2
Vranjska Banja SRB	59	F2
Vransko SLO	54	B1
Vranštica MNE	58	C2
Vrasná GR	102	A3
Vrástama GR	102	A3
Vrataruca SRB	57	D3
Vratnica MK	59	E3
Vravróna GR	105	F3
Vražogrnac SRB	57	E3
Vrbanja HR	55	F2
Vrbas BIH	55	E4
Vrbas SRB	56	C2
Vrbaška BIH	55	D4
Vrbljani BIH	55	D4
Vrbnica SRB	59	D3
Vrbnik HR	54	B3
Vrbno pod		
Pradědem CZ	41	E2
Vrboska HR	58	A4
Vrbovec HR	54	C2
Vrbovsko HR	54	B3

Villavieja de Yeltes E	25	D1	Villers-Farlay F	16	C2	Vinchiaturo I	48	C3	Virginia IRL	3	D2
Villé F	13	E4	Villers-la-Ville B	12	C1	Vinci I	47	D3	Virieu F	16	C3
Ville-en-Tardenois F	12	B3	Villers-le-Lac F	17	D2	Vindeikiai LT	80	B2	Virieu-le-Grand F	16	C3
Ville-sur-Tourbe F	12	C3	Villers-sur-Mer F	11	E3	Vindeln S	64	B3	Virkêni LV	78	B1
Villebois-Lavalette F	15	E4	Villersexel F	17	D1	Vinderup DK	70	B2	Virkkala / Virkby FIN	69	D4
Villefagnan F	15	D3	Villerville F	11	E3	Vingåker S	67	E3	Virkkula FIN	65	E1
Villefort F	22	A1	Villetta Barrea I	48	C3	Vingelen N	62	C4	Virkšai LT	80	B2
Villefranche-			Villevere EE	72	C3	Vingininkai LT	80	C3	Virkščiai LT	86	B1
d'Albigeois F	21	F2	Villiers-St-Georges F	12	B4	Vinhais P	18	C4	Virmutjoki FIN	69	F3
Villefranche-			Villingen D	13	F4	Vinica MK	59	F3	Virolahti FIN	69	E4
de-Lauragais F	21	E2	Villoldo E	19	E3	Vinica SLO	54	B2	Virónia GR	102	A1
Villefranche-			Villora E	25	E1	Viničani MK	59	F4	Virovitica HR	55	D2
de-Lonchat F	15	D4	Villotta I	44	B4	Vinje N	66	B2	Virpazar MNE	58	C3
Villefranche-			Vilnius LT	86	B2	Vinkovci HR	55	E2	Virrat FIN	69	D2
de-Rouergue F	21	E1	Vil'nohirs'k UA	117	F1	Vinkšnenai			Virsbo S	67	E2
Villefranche-			Vilppula FIN	69	D2	(Panevėžio) LT	81	E3	Virserum S	71	E2
du-Périgord F	21	D1	Vilpulka LV	78	B1	Vinkšnenai			Virtasalmi FIN	69	E2
Villefranche-sur-Cher F	15	F1	Vilsbiburg D	44	B1	(Šiauliu) LT	81	E2	Virton B	13	D3
Villefranche-sur-Mer F	23	D2	Vilseck D	39	E3	Vinkšnininiai LT	82	B2	Virtsu EE	75	D2
Villefranche-			Vilshofen D	39	F4	Vinni EE	73	D2	Viru-Jaagupi EE	73	D1
sur-Saône F	16	C3	Vilūčiai LT	82	C3	Vinnycja UA	117	E1	Viru-Kabala EE	73	D2
Villel E	26	C2	Vilumi LV	81	E1	Vinstra N	62	C4	Viru-Nigula EE	73	D1
Villemur-sur-Tarn F	21	E2	Vilūnaičiai LT	81	E2	Vis (Otok) HR	58	A4	Vis HR	58	A4
Villena E	26	C4	Vilusi MNE	58	B3	Viñuelas E	26	A1	Visaginas LT	83	D3
Villenauxe-la-Grande F	12	B4	Viluste EE	79	E1	Vinuesa E	20	A4	Višakio Rūda LT	85	E1
Villeneuve F	21	E1	Vilvoorde B	12	C1	Vipava SLO	54	A2	Višby S	67	F4
Villeneuve-d'Ascq F	12	B1	Vilženi LV	78	B2	Vipe LV	83	D2	Visé B	13	D1
Villeneuve-de-Berg F	22	B1	Vimbas LV	81	D1	Vipiteno / Sterzing I	43	F3	Višegrad BIH	55	F4
Villeneuve-			Vimercate I	43	D4	Virbalai LT	80	B2	Viserba I	47	E2
de-Marsan F	20	C1	Vimianzo E	18	A2	Virbalis LT	85	D2	Viseu P	24	B1
Villeneuve-			Vimioso P	24	B3	Virbališkiai LT	82	B2	Viški (Viški) LV	83	E2
l'Archevêque F	12	B4	Vimmerby S	67	E2	Vircava LV	81	E1	Viskla EE	72	B2
Villeneuve-			Vimoutiers F	11	E3	Vire F	11	D3	Višnjagora SLO	54	B2
lès-Avignon F	22	B1	Vimpeli / Vindala FIN	69	D2	Vireši LV	79	D2	Višnjica SRB	57	D2
Villeneuve-sur-Lot F	21	D1	Vimperk CZ	40	C4	Vireux-Wallerand F	12	C2	Viso del Marqués E	25	F4
Villeneuve-			Vinac BIH	55	D4	Virga LV	80	B1	Visoko BIH	55	E4
sur-Yonne F	12	B4	Vinadio I	23	D1	Virgen A	44	B2	Visp CH	17	E2
Villeréal F	21	D1	Vinaixa E	21	F1	Virgen de la Cabeza			Víssani GR	100	C3
Villers-Bocage F	12	A2	Vinarós E	27	E1	(Santuario) E	25	F4	Visselhövede D	33	E3
Villers-Bocage F	11	D3	Vinça F	21	F3	Virga LV	80	B1	Vissenbjerg DK	70	B3
Villers-Bretonneux F	12	A2	Vinča SRB	57	D2				Vissiní GR	101	D2
Villers-Cotterêts F	12	B3							Visso I	47	F3
Villers-devant-Orval B	12	C2									

Vistabella			Vívaro I	44	B4	Vodnjan HR	54	A3
del Maestrazgo E	27	D2	Viveiro E	18	B1	Võduvere EE	73	D3
Vistheden S	64	B2	Vivel del Río Martín E	26	C1	Voe GB	5	F1
Vištyčio Laukas I LT	85	D2	Viver E	27	D2	Vogatsikó GR	101	D3
Vištytis LT	84	C2	Viverols F	16	B4	Vogelsdorf D	34	C4
Visusti EE	73	D3	Viveros E	26	A4	Voghera I	46	B1
Visuvesi FIN	69	D2	Viviers F	22	B1	Vogošća BIH	55	E4
Vitaby S	71	D3	Vivonne F	15	E2	Vohenstrauß D	39	E3
Vitala GR	105	F2	Vizille F	17	D4	Võhma (Saare) EE	74	C2
Vitanovac SRB	57	D4	Vižinada HR	54	A3	Võhma (Viljandi) EE	72	C3
Vitenai LT	85	E1	Vizitsa GR	105	E1	Võhmanõmme EE	73	D3
Viterbo I	47	E4	Vizovice CZ	41	F3	Vohnja EE	73	D2
Vitez BIH	55	E4	Vizzavona F	23	F3	Vöhringen D	43	E1
Viti EE	72	A1	Vizzini I	53	D3	Võibla EE	73	D3
Vitigudino E	25	D1	Vitina BIH	58	A2	Voïdu EE	75	F3
Vitina GR	105	D3	Vitina GR	59	E3	Voïka EE	79	D1
Vitini LV	81	D1	Vitkov CZ	41	F2	Voikka FIN	69	E3
Vitoli GR	104	C1	Vitkuški LV	82	C2	Voikoski FIN	69	E3
Vitolini LV	81	E1	Vitolište MK	59	F4	Voinić HR	54	C3
Vitomirica SRB	59	D3	Vitorchiano I	47	E4	Voiron F	16	C4
Vitoria-Gasteiz E	20	A3	Vitovlje BIH	55	D4	Võisiku EE	72	C3
Vitrey-sur-Mance F	16	C1	Vitré F	11	D4	Võiste EE	75	E3
Vitriola I	47	D2	Vittangi S	64	C1	Võistre EE	73	E3
Vitrupe LV	77	F2	Vittaux F	16	B1	Voiteur F	16	C2
Vitry-en-Artois F	12	A2	Vittel F	13	D4	Voitsberg A	45	D2
Vitry-le-François F	12	C4	Vittoria I	53	D4	Võivaku EE	72	C3
Vitsa GR	100	C3	Vittorio Veneto I	44	B4	Vojakkala FIN	65	D2
Vitsand S	67	D2	Vittsjö S	71	D3	Vojens DK	70	B3
Vittangi S	64	C1	Viù I	17	E4	Vojka SRB	56	C2
Vihó GR	104	A2				Vojnić HR	54	C3
Vlissingen NL	36	B2				Vojnik SLO	54	B1

̓rchlabí CZ	41	D2
̓rčin SRB	57	D2
̓rdnik SRB	55	F2
̓reden D	37	D1
̓rela SRB	59	D2
̓relo HR	54	C3
̓relo SRB	57	E4
̓reoci SRB	56	C3
̓resse-sur-Semois B	12	C2
̓résthena GR	105	D4
̓reta Kloster S	67	E3
̓rgorac HR	58	A2
̓rhnika SLO	54	A2
̓rhpolje BIH	55	D3
̓ria GR	101	E3
̓rissa GR	105	E1
̓risses GR	107	D1
̓risses GR	109	D4
̓rissiá GR	105	D1
̓rissoúla GR	104	B1
̓rlika HR	55	D4
̓rnjačka Banja SRB	57	D4
̓rnograč BIH	54	C3
̓rondádos GR	107	D2
̓rondamás GR	108	B1
̓ronderó GR	100	C4
̓rondissi GR	109	E4
̓rondoú GR	101	E3
̓rossina GR	100	C4
̓rouhás GR	110	C3
̓rpolje (Šibenik) HR	54	C4
̓rpolje (Slavonski Brod) HR	55	E2
̓ršac SRB	57	D2
̓ršani BIH	55	F3
̓rsar HR	54	A3
̓rsi HR	54	B4
̓rtoče BIH	54	C3
̓rutok MK	59	E4
̓setín CZ	41	F3
̓učitrn SRB	59	D2
̓učkovica SRB	57	D3
̓ukosavlje BIH	55	E3
̓ukovar HR	55	E3
̓uohijärvi FIN	69	E3
̓uokatti FIN	65	E3
̓uolijoki FIN	65	D3
̓uollerim S	64	B2
̓uonislahti FIN	69	F1
̓uoskojaure S	60	C2
̓uostimo FIN	65	E1
̓uotso FIN	61	F3
̓ydeikiai LT	80	B2
̓ydmantai LT	80	A2
̓ygreliai LT	85	D3
̓ylkove UA	117	E2
̓yškov CZ	41	E3
̓yšnij Voločok RUS	115	F1
̓yšniūnai LT	85	F2
̓ysoké Mýto CZ	41	D2
̓yšší Brod CZ	40	C4
̓ytogala LT	80	C3
̓yžuonos LT	82	C3

W

Vaalwijk NL	36	C1
Vaasmunster B	12	B1
Vabern D	38	C2
Vąbrzeźno PL	89	F3
Vąchock PL	94	C3
Vachow D	34	B4
Vächtersbach D	38	C3
Vadebridge GB	8	A4
Vädenswil CH	17	F1
Vadlew PL	94	A2
Vadowice PL	98	A2
Vaganiec PL	89	F3
Vagenfeld D	33	E4
Vageningen NL	37	D1
Vaging a. See D	44	B1
Vagrain A	44	C2
Vągrowiec PL	89	D2
Vahlstedt D	33	F2
Vaiblingen D	38	C4
Vaidhaus D	39	E3
Vaidhofen an der Thaya A	41	D4
Vaidhofen an der Ybbs A	45	D1
Vaidring A	44	B2
Vaischenfeld D	39	D3
Vaizenkirchen A	44	C1
Vakefield GB	7	E4
Valbrzych PL	96	C1
Valce PL	97	E1
Valchensee D	43	F2
Valchsee A	44	B2
Valcz PL	88	C3
Vald CH	17	F1
Vald-Michelbach D	13	F1
Valdbröl D	13	E1
Valdeck D	38	C2
Valdenbuch D	43	D1
Valdenburg D	39	E2
Valdfischbach-Burgalben D	13	E3
Valdheim D	39	F1
Valdkappel D	38	C2
Valdkirch D	13	F4
Valdkirchen D	39	F4
Valdkraiburg D	44	B1
Valdmünchen D	39	F4
Valdsassen D	39	E3

Waldshut D	17	F1
Walenstadt CH	43	D3
Walim PL	96	C1
Wallasey GB	7	D4
Walldorf D	13	F3
Walldürn D	38	C4
Wallenfels D	39	D3
Wallersdorf D	39	F4
Wallerstein D	38	C4
Wallingford GB	9	D3
Walls GB	5	F1
Walsall GB	9	D1
Walsrode D	33	E4
Walsum D	37	D1
Waltershausen D	39	D2
Walton-on-the-Naze GB	9	F2
Waltrop D	37	E1
Wambierzyce PL	96	C1
Wanderup D	32	C2
Wandlitz D	34	B3
Wandowo PL	89	F2
Wanfried D	38	C2
Wangen i. Allgäu D	43	E2
Wangenbourg F	13	E4
Wangerland-Hooksiel D	33	D3
Wangerooge D	33	D2
Wängi CH	17	F1
Wanna D	33	E3
Wanne-Eickel D	37	E1
Wanzleben D	34	A4
Warburg D	37	F1
Wardenburg D	33	D3
Ware GB	9	E2
Waregem B	12	B1
Wareham GB	8	C4
Waremme B	12	C1
Waren D	34	B2
Warendorf D	37	E1
Warin D	34	A2
Warka PL	94	C2
Warkworth GB	7	E2
Warlubie PL	89	F2
Warmensteinach D	39	D3
Warminster GB	8	C3
Warnemünde D	34	A2
Warnice (Zachodniopo-morskie) PL	88	A3
Warpuny PL	90	C2
Warrenpoint GB	3	D3
Warrington GB	7	D4
Warstein D	37	F1
Warszawa PL	94	C1
Warta PL	93	F2
Warta Bolesławiecka PL	92	B3
Warth A	43	E2
Wartha D	38	C4

Wartkowice PL	93	F2
Washington GB	7	E3
Wasilków PL	91	E2
Waśniów PL	94	C3
Wąsosz (Dolnośląskie) PL	93	D2
Wąsosz (Podlaskie) PL	91	D2
Wasselonne F	13	E4
Wassen CH	17	F2
Wassenaar NL	36	C1
Wassenberg D	13	D1
Wasseralfingen D	38	C4
Wasserbillig L	13	D3
Wasserburg a. Inn D	44	B1
Wassertrüdingen D	39	D4
Wassigny F	12	B2
Wassy F	12	C4
Wasungen D	38	C2
Watchet GB	8	B3
Waterford / Port Láirge IRL	2	C3
Waterloo B	12	C1
Waterville / An Coireán IRL	2	A4
Watford GB	9	E3
Wattens A	43	F2
Watton GB	9	F1
Wattwil CH	17	F1
Wawolnica PL	95	D3
Wawrzeńczyce PL	98	C2
Wawrzyszów PL	94	C3
Waxweiler D	13	D2
Wdzydze PL	89	E2
Wedel (Holstein) D	33	E3
Wedemark D	33	E4
Weener D	33	D3
Weert NL	37	D1
Weferlingen D	34	A4
Wegberg D	13	D1
Wegeleben D	39	D1
Weggis CH	17	F1
Węgierka PL	98	C1
Węgierska Górka PL	97	F3
Węgliniec PL	92	B3
Wegorzewo PL	90	C1
Węgorzyno PL	88	B2
Węgrów PL	95	D1
Wegscheid D	40	C4
Wehr D	17	F1
Weibersbrunn D	38	C4
Weichshofen D	39	F4
Weida D	39	E2
Weiden i. d. Oberpfalz D	39	E3
Weikersheim D	38	C4
Weil der Stadt D	43	D1

Weilburg D	13	F1
Weilheim a. d. Teck D	43	D1
Weilheim i. Oberbayern D	43	F2
Weimar D	39	D2
Weinfelden CH	17	F1
Weingarten D	43	D2
Weinheim D	13	F2
Weinsberg D	38	C4
Weismain D	39	D3
Weißbach NL	36	C1
Weißbach a. Lech A	43	E2
Weißenberg D	40	C1
Weißenborn D	43	F2
Weißenburg D	39	D4
Weißenfels D	39	E1
Weißenhorn D	43	E1
Weißenkirchen in der Wachau A	41	D4
Weißensee D	39	D2
Weißenstadt D	39	E3
Weißkirchen A	45	D2
Weißwasser D	40	C1
Weitra A	41	D4
Weiz A	45	E1
Wejherowo PL	89	E1
Weldon PL	9	E2
Wellin B	12	C2
Wellingborough GB	9	E2
Wellington GB	8	B3
Wellington Bridge IRL	3	D4
Wells GB	8	C3
Wells-next-the-Sea GB	9	F1
Wels A	44	C1
Welshpool / Trallwng GB	8	C1
Weltenburg D	39	E4
Welwyn Garden City GB	9	E2
Welzheim D	38	C4
Welzow D	39	F1
Wem GB	8	C1
Wemding D	39	D4
Wemyss Bay GB	6	C1
Wenden D	33	F4
Wengen CH	17	E2
Wenns A	43	E2
Werben D	34	A3
Werbkowice PL	95	F3
Werdau D	39	E2
Werder D	34	B4
Werdohl D	37	E2
Werfen A	44	B2
Werl D	37	E1
Werlte D	33	D4
Wermelskirchen D	13	E1
Wermsdorf D	39	E1
Wernberg-Köblitz D	39	E3
Werne D	37	E1
Werneck D	38	C3

Werneuchen D	34	C3
Wernigerode D	39	D1
Wertach D	43	E2
Wertheim D	38	C3
Werther D	37	F1
Wertingen D	43	E1
Wervik B	12	B1
Wesel D	37	D1
Wesenberg D	34	B3
Wesendorf D	33	F4
Wesoła (Mazowieckie) PL	94	C1
Wesselburen D	33	E2
Wessobrunn D	43	F2
West Auckland GB	7	E3
West Bridgford GB	9	D1
West Kilbride GB	6	C2
West Linton GB	7	D2
West Looe GB	8	A4
West Mersea GB	9	F2
West-Terschelling NL	32	B3
Westbury GB	8	C3
Westendorf A	44	B2
Westenholz D	33	E4
Westerburg D	13	F1
Westerholt D	33	D3
Westerland D	33	D1
Westerlo B	12	C1
Westernbödefeld D	37	F2
Westerstede D	33	D3
Westhofen D	13	F2
Westofen D	13	F2
Weston-super-Mare GB	8	C3
Westport / Cathair na Mart IRL	2	B2
Wetherby GB	7	E4
Wetlina PL	99	E3
Wetter (Ruhr) D	37	E1
Wetteren B	12	B1
Wettin D	39	E1
Wettringen D	33	D4
Wetwang GB	7	F4
Wetzikon CH	17	F1
Wetzlar D	13	F1
Wexford / Loch Garman IRL	3	D4
Weyer Markt A	45	D1
Weyhausen D	33	F4
Weyhill GB	9	D3
Weymouth GB	8	C4
Weyregg a. Attersee A	44	C1
Whaley Bridge GB	9	D1
Whitburn GB	7	D1
Whitby GB	7	F3
Whitchurch GB	8	C1
Whitebridge GB	4	C4
Whitehaven GB	7	D3
Whitehead GB	3	E1
Whiteness GB	5	F1
Whithorn GB	3	F1

Whitland GB	8	A2
Whitley Bay GB	7	E2
Whitstable GB	9	F3
Whittlesey GB	9	E2
Wiązów PL	93	D3
Wiązowna PL	94	C1
Wiązownica PL	99	E2
Wick GB	5	D2
Wickford GB	9	F3
Wicklow / Cill Mhantáin IRL	3	E1
Wicko PL	89	E1
Widawa PL	93	F3
Widnes GB	9	D1
Widuchowa PL	88	A3
Więcbork PL	89	D2
Więckowice PL	93	D1
Wiedenbrück D	37	F1
Wiefelstede D	33	D3
Wiehe D	39	D1
Wiek D	34	B1
Większyce PL	97	E2
Wielbark PL	90	C2
Wiele PL	89	D2
Wieleń PL	88	C2
Wielgie (Kujawsko-Pomorskie) PL	89	F3
Wielgowo PL	88	A2
Wielichowo PL	92	C2
Wieliczka PL	98	B2
Wielichowo PL	91	D1
Wielka Nieszawka PL	89	F3
Wielka Sowa PL	96	C1
Wielka Wieś PL	98	B2
Wielki Wełcz PL	89	F2
Wielkopolski Park Etnograficzny PL	93	E1
Wielkopolski Park Narodowy PL	93	D1
Wielopole Skrzyńskie PL	99	D2
Wielowieś (Śląskie) PL	97	F1
Wielowieś (Świętokrzyskie) PL	99	D1
Wieluń PL	93	F3
Wieniawa PL	94	C3
Wieprz (Małopolskie) PL	98	A2
Wieprza PL	89	D1
Wieruszów PL	93	E3
Wierzbica (Chełm) PL	95	F3
Wierzbica (Lublin) PL	95	D3
Wierzbica (Mazowieckie) PL	94	C3
Wierzbica Górna PL	93	E3

Wierzbięcin PL	88	B2
Wierzbinek PL	93	F1
Wierzchlas PL	93	F3
Wierzchosławice PL	98	C2
Wierzchowo (Zachodnio-pomorskie) PL	88	C2
Wies A	45	D2
Wiesau D	39	E3
Wiesbaden D	13	F2
Wieselburg A	45	D1
Wiesenburg D	34	B4
Wiesensteig D	43	D1
Wiesentheid D	39	D3
Wiesenttal D	39	D3
Wiesing A	43	F2
Wiesloch D	13	F3
Wiesmath A	45	E1
Wiesmoor D	33	D3
Wietrzychowice PL	98	C2
Wigan GB	7	D4
Wigierski Park Narodowy PL	91	E1
Wigry (Jezioro) PL	91	E1
Wigton GB	7	D3
Wigtown GB	3	F1
Wijewo PL	92	C2
Wijhe NL	32	C4
Wil CH	17	F1
Wilamowice PL	97	F2
Wilczęta PL	90	A1
Wilczy Szaniec PL	90	C1
Wilczyce PL	95	D3
Wilczyn PL	93	E1
Wildalpen A	45	D1
Wildbad i. Schwarzwald D	13	F3
Wildeck D	38	C2
Wildeck D	38	C2
Wildeshausen D	33	D4
Wildon A	45	E2
Wilferdsdorf A	41	E4
Wilga PL	94	C2
Wilhelmsburg A	45	D1
Wilhelmsburg D	33	D3
Wilhelmshaven D	33	D3
Wilhelmsburg D	33	D3
Wilhering A	44	C1
Wilkasy PL	90	C1
Wilkau-Haßlau D	39	E2
Wilkołaz Pierwszy PL	95	D3
Wilków (Opolskie) PL	93	E3
Wilkowice PL	97	F2
Willebroek B	12	C1
Willemstad NL	36	C1
Willingen D	37	F2
Williton GB	8	B3
Wilmslow GB	8	C1
Wilnsdorf D	13	F1
Wilsdruff D	39	F1
Wilster D	33	E2

Wilton GB	9	D3
Wiltz L	13	D2
Wimborne Minster GB	8	C4
Wimereux F	9	F4
Wincanton GB	8	C3
Winchcombe GB	9	D2
Winchelsea GB	9	F4
Winchester GB	9	D3
Windeck D	13	E1
Windermere GB	7	D3
Windischeschenbach D	39	E3
Windischgarsten A	44	C1
Windsbach D	39	D4
Windsor GB	9	E3
Winkleigh GB	8	B3
Winklern A	44	B3
Winnenden D	38	C4
Winnica PL	90	C3
Winnigstedt D	33	F4
Winniweiler D	13	E3
Winschoten NL	32	C3
Winsen D	33	F3
Winsen (Aller) D	33	F4
Winsford GB	8	C1
Wińsko PL	93	D2
Winsum GB	32	C3
Winterberg D	37	F2
Winterswijk NL	37	D1
Winterthur CH	17	F1
Wintzenheim F	13	E4
Wipperfürth D	13	E1
Wisbech GB	9	E1
Wischhafen D	33	E2
Wishaw GB	7	D1
Wiskitki PL	94	B2
Wisła PL	97	F2
Wiślana (Mierzeja) PL	89	F1
Wiślane (Żuławy) PL	89	F1
Wiślany (Zalew) PL	89	F1
Wiślica PL	98	B1
Wismar D	34	A2
Wiśniew PL	95	D2
Wiśniewo PL	90	B3
Wiśniowa (Małopolskie) PL	98	C2
Wiśniowa (Podkarpackie) PL	99	D2
Wissant F	9	F4
Wissembourg F	13	F3
Wissen D	13	E1
Wisznia Mała PL	93	D3
Wisznice PL	95	E2
Witham GB	9	F2
Withernsea GB	7	F4
Witkowo (Wielkopolskie) PL	93	E1
Witkowo (Zachodnio-pomorskie) PL	88	B2
Witney GB	9	D2

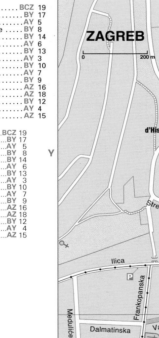

Augusta Šenoe	BCZ	19
Bakačeva	BY	17
Cirilometodska	AY	5
Felbingerove stube	BY	8
Frane Petrića	BY	14
Freudenreichova	BY	6
Habdelićeva	BY	13
Kapucinske stube	AY	3
Male stube	BY	10
Mletačka	AY	7
Mlinarske stube	BY	9
Perkovčeva	AZ	16
Runjaninova	AZ	18
Skalinska	AY	12
Vranicanijeva	AY	4
Vukotinovićeva	AZ	15

Augusta Šenoe	BCZ	19
Bakačeva	BY	17
Cirilometodska	AY	5
Felbingerove stube	BY	8
Frane Petrića	BY	14
Freudenreichova	AY	6
Habdelićeva	BY	13
Kapucinske stube	AY	3
Male stube	BY	10
Mletačka	AY	7
Mlinarske stube	BY	9
Perkovčeva	AZ	16
Runjaninova	AZ	18
Skalinska	BY	12
Vranicanijeva	AY	4
Vukotinovićeva	AZ	15

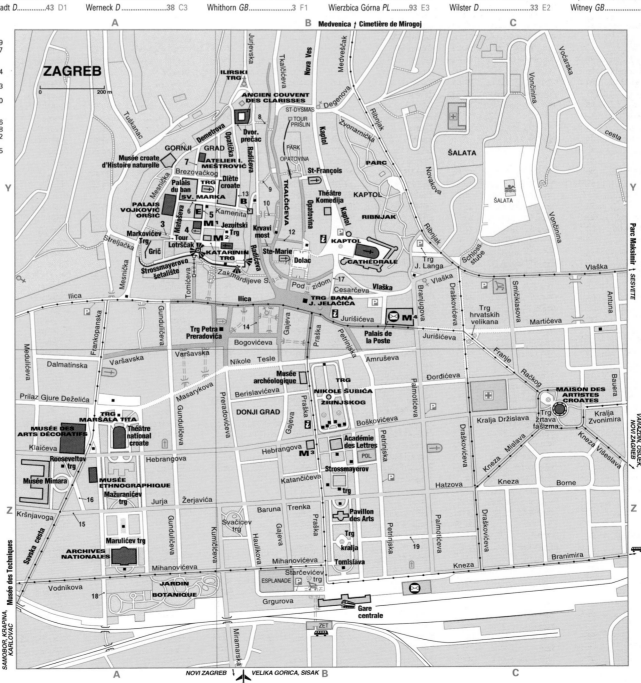

ZAGREB

Witnica (Lubuskie) PL...88 A3
Witonia PL...94 A2
Wittdün D...33 D1
Witten D...37 E1
Wittenberg D...39 E1
Wittenberge D...34 A3
Wittenburg D...33 F3
Wittichenau D...40 C1
Wittingen D...33 F4
Wittlich D...13 E2
Wittmund D...33 D3
Wittstock D...34 B3
Wiżajny PL...91 E1
Wizna PL...91 D3
Władysławów PL...93 F2
Władysławowo
 (Pomorskie) PL...89 E1
Wleń PL...92 C3
Włocławek PL...89 F3
Włodawa PL...95 F2
Włodowice PL...98 A1
Włoszakowice PL...92 C2
Włoszczowa PL...94 B3
Wöbbelin D...34 A3
Woburn GB...9 E2
Wodynie PL...95 D2
Wodzisław PL...98 B1
Wodzisław Śląski PL...97 F2
Woensdrecht NL...36 B2
Woerden NL...36 C1
Wœrth F...13 F4
Wohlen CH...17 F1
Woippy F...13 D3
Wojaszówka PL...99 D2
Wojciechów PL...95 D3
Wojcieszków PL...95 D2
Wojcieszów PL...92 C3
Wojnicz PL...98 C2
Wojsławice PL...95 F3
Woking GB...9 E3
Wokingham GB...9 D3
Wola PL...97 F2
Wola Jedlińska PL...94 A3
Wola Krzysztoporska PL...94 A3
Wola Prażmowska PL...94 C2
Wola Uhruska PL...95 F3
Wolanów PL...94 C3
Wolbrom PL...98 A1
Wołczyn PL...93 E3
Woldegk D...34 B2
Wolfach D...13 F4
Wolfegg D...43 D2
Wolfen D...39 E1
Wolfenbüttel D...33 F4
Wolfhagen D...37 F1
Wolfratshausen D...43 F1
Wolfsberg A...45 D2
Wolfsburg D...33 F4
Wolgast D...34 B2
Wolibórz PL...96 C1
Wolin PL...88 A2
Woliński Park
 Narodowy PL...88 A2
Wólka (Lubelskie) PL...95 E3
Wólka Mlądzka PL...94 C2
Wolkersdorf A...41 E4
Wöllersdorf A...45 E1
Wollersheim D...13 D1
Wollin D...34 B4
Wolmirstedt D...34 A4
Wolnzach D...43 F1
Wołomin PL...94 C1
Wołosate PL...99 E3
Wołów PL...93 D3
Wolsingham GB...7 E3
Wolsztyn PL...92 C2
Wolvega NL...32 B4
Wolverhampton GB...8 C1
Wolverton GB...9 D2
Wonieść (Jezioro) PL...93 D2
Woodbridge GB...9 F2
Woodhall Spa GB...9 E1
Woodstock GB...9 D2
Wooler GB...7 E2
Worb CH...17 E2
Worbis D...38 C1
Worcester GB...8 C2
Wörgl A...44 B2
Workington GB...3 F1
Worksop GB...9 D1
Workum NL...32 B4
Wörlitz D...39 E1
Wormerveer NL...32 B4
Wormhout F...12 A1
Worms D...13 F2
Wörrstadt D...13 F2
Wörth a. d. Donau D...39 E4
Wörth a. Main D...38 C3
Wörth a. Rhein D...13 F3
Worthing GB...9 E3
Woszczyce PL...97 F2
Woźławki PL...90 B1
Woźniki PL...98 A1
Wragby GB...9 E1
Wręczyca Wielka PL...93 F3
Wrexham /
 Wrecsam GB...8 C1
Wriezen D...34 C4
Wróblew PL...93 F2
Wrocław PL...93 D3
Wronki (Warmińsko-
 Mazurskie) PL...91 D1
Wronki
 (Wielkopolskie) PL...88 C3
Wroughton GB...9 D3
Września PL...93 E1

Wschowa PL...92 C2
Wsi Lubelskiej PL...95 E3
Wsi Radomskiej PL...94 C3
Wulfen D...37 E1
Wullowitz A...40 C4
Wünnenberg D...37 F1
Wünsdorf D...34 B4
Wunsiedel D...39 E3
Wunstorf D...33 E4
Wuppertal D...37 E2
Würzburg D...38 C3
Wurzen D...39 E1
Wusterhausen D...34 B3
Wustermark D...34 B4
Wustrow D...34 A3
Wustrow (Kreis Nordvor-
 pommern) D...34 A1
Wuustwezel B...36 C2
Wyczerpy Górne PL...94 A3
Wydminy PL...91 D1
Wyk a. Föhr D...33 D1
Wymondham GB...9 F2
Wyry PL...97 F2
Wyryki-Połód PL...95 F2
Wyrzysk PL...89 D3
Wyśmierzyce PL...94 C2
Wysoka
 (Wielkopolskie) PL...89 D3
Wysoka Kamieńska PL...88 A2
Wysokie
 (Lubelskie) PL...95 E3
Wysokie
 Mazowieckie PL...91 D3
Wysowa PL...98 C3
Wyszków
 (Mazowieckie) PL...90 C3
Wyszogród PL...94 B1

X

Xàbia / Jávea E...27 D4
Xanten D...37 D1
Xánthi GR...102 C1
Xàtiva E...27 D3
Xeresa E...27 D3
Xert E...27 D2
Xerta E...27 E1
Xertigny F...13 D4
Xifianí GR...101 E2
Xilagani GR...103 D2
Xiliki GR...105 D3
Xilókastro GR...105 D3
Xilopáriko GR...101 D4
Xilópoli GR...101 F2
Xilóskalo GR...109 D4
Xiniáda GR...105 D1
Xinó Neró GR...101 D2
Xinzo de Limia E...18 B3
Xirokámbi GR...108 B1
Xirókambos GR...107 F4
Xirolimni GR...101 D3
Xiropótamos GR...102 A2
Xixona E...27 D4
Xubia E...18 B1
Xunqueira de Ambía E...18 B3

Y

Yalova TR...117 F4
Yanguas E...20 A4
Yarmouth GB...9 D4
Ybbs an der Donau A...45 D1
Yebra E...26 A2
Yecla E...26 C4
Yenne F...17 D3
Yeovil GB...8 C3
Yepes E...26 A2
Yerville F...11 F2
Yesa E...26 B4
Yeste E...26 B4
Ylakiai LT...81 E3
Ylämaa FIN...69 F3
Ylämylly FIN...69 F2
Yläne FIN...68 C4
Yli-Ii FIN...65 D3
Yli-Kärppä FIN...65 D2
Yli-Muonio FIN...61 D3
Yli Nampa FIN...65 D1
Yli-Olhava FIN...65 D3
Ylihärmä FIN...68 C2
Ylikiiminki FIN...65 D3
Ylistaro FIN...68 C2
Ylitornio FIN...64 C2
Ylivieska FIN...65 D3
Ylläsjärvi FIN...61 E3
Ylöjärvi FIN...69 D3
York GB...7 F4
Youghal / Eochaill IRL...2 C4
Yoxford GB...9 F2
Ypäjä FIN...69 D4
Yport F...11 E2
Yppäri FIN...65 D3
Yssingeaux F...16 B4
Ystad S...71 D3
Ytterhogdal S...63 E4
Yttermalung S...67 D1
Yuncos E...26 A2
Yunquera E...29 E3
Yunquera
 de Henares E...26 A1
Yuste
 (Monasterio de) E...25 D2

Yverdon-les-Bains CH...17 D2
Yvetot F...11 F2
Yvoir B...12 C2
Yvoire F...17 D2
Yzeure F...16 A2

Z

Zaandam NL...32 B4
Zabaka LT...86 B2
Zabalj SRB...56 C2
Žabari SRB...57 D3
Żabia Wola
 (Mazowieckie) PL...94 B2
Zabičiūnai LT...82 C3
Zabierzów PL...98 A2
Ząbki PL...94 C1
Ząbkowice Śląskie PL...97 D1
Zablace HR...54 C4
Žabljak (Pljevlja) MNE...58 C2
Žabljak
 (Podgorica) MNE...58 C3
Zabłudów PL...91 E3
Żabno PL...98 C2
Zabok HR...54 C2
Zabór PL...92 C2
Zaborowo PL...93 D2
Zabrđe BIH...55 F3
Zábřeh CZ...41 E2
Ząbrowo PL...88 B1
Zabrze PL...97 F2
Zabrzeg HR...54 A2
Zadar HR...54 B4
Žadeikiai LT...80 C3
Žadeikoniai LT...81 E2
Žaduvenai LT...85 D2
Zadvarje HR...58 B3
Zadzim PL...93 F2
Žądžiūnai LT...81 E2
Zafarraya E...29 F3
Zafóra (Nissí) GR...111 D2
Zafra E...25 D4
Žaga SLO...54 A2
Zagań PL...92 B2
Žagare LT...81 E1
Žagarine LT...86 B3
Žagariškiai LT...81 E2
Zaglavak SRB...56 C4
Zagnańsk PL...94 B3
Zagorá GR...101 F4
Zagorje SLO...54 C2
Zagórów PL...93 E2
Zagórz PL...99 D3
Zagorzyce PL...99 D2
Zagreb HR...54 C2
Zagrodno PL...92 C3
Žagubica SRB...57 E3
Zagvozd HR...58 A2
Zahara
 de los Atunes E...29 D4
Zaháro GR...104 C4
Zahinos E...24 C4
Zahna D...34 B4
Záhony H...116 C2
Zaiceva LV...79 E2
Zaidin E...21 D4
Žaiginys LT...81 E3
Žaizdriai LT...86 B2
Zajas MK...59 E4
Zaječar SRB...57 E3
Žakainiai LT...80 B3
Zákinthos GR...104 A3
Zákinthos (Nissí) GR...104 A3
Zakliczyn PL...98 C2
Zaklików PL...95 D3
Zakopane PL...98 B3
Zakroczym PL...94 B1
Zákros GR...110 C4
Zakrzew
 (Mazowieckie) PL...94 C2
Zakrzewo (Kujawsko-
 Pomorskie) PL...89 F3
Zakrzewo
 (Wielkopolskie) PL...95 D3
Zakrzówek-Osada PL...95 D3
Zakumuiža LV...77 F3
Zalaegerszeg H...116 B2
Zalāji LV...79 D2
Zalamea
 de la Serena E...25 D4
Zalamea la Real E...28 C2
Zalasowa PL...98 C2
Zalău RO...117 D2
Zalavas LT...86 C2
Žalec SLO...54 B1
Zalenieki LV...81 E1
Zalesie
 (Lubelskie) PL...95 F2
Zalesie Śląskie PL...97 E1
Zalesje LV...83 F2
Zaleszany PL...95 D3
Zalewo PL...90 A2
Žalgiriai LT...80 B2
Zališčyky UA...117 D1
Žalīte LV...81 F1
Zalla E...19 F2
Zálongo GR...104 A1
Žalpiai (Klaipedos) LT...84 B1
Žalpiai (Šiauliu) LT...81 D3
Zaltbommel NL...36 C1
Zaltriškiai LT...84 C1
Zalumi LV...83 D2

Załuski PL...94 B1
Zalužnica HR...54 B3
Žalvariai LT...86 B1
Zalve LV...82 B2
Žamberk CZ...41 E2
Zambrana E...20 A3
Zambrów PL...91 D3
Zamora E...19 D4
Zamość PL...95 F3
Zandvoort NL...32 A4
Zanglivéri GR...102 A2
Zaniemyśl PL...93 D2
Zante LV...77 D3
Zaorejas E...26 B1
Zaostrog HR...58 A3
Zaovine Vežanja SRB...55 F4
Zapadnaja
 Dvina RUS...115 E2
Zapāni LV...83 F1
Zápio GR...101 E4
Zapponeta I...49 E3
Zaprešić HR...54 C2
Zapyškis LT...85 E2
Zaragoza E...20 B4
Zárakes GR...106 B2
Zarasai LT...83 D3
Zaratán E...19 E4
Zarautz E...20 C2
Zarcilla de Ramos E...30 B2
Žarenai (Šiauliu) LT...81 D3
Žarenai (Telšiu) LT...80 C3
Žarijos LT...85 E2
Żarki (Śląskie) PL...98 A1
Zárkos GR...101 E4
Żarnów PL...94 B3
Zarós GR...109 E4
Zaroúhla GR...105 D3
Żarów PL...92 C3
Zarrentin D...33 F3
Zarszyn PL...99 D2
Żary PL...92 B2
Zarza la Mayor E...24 C2
Zasa LV...82 C2
Žaškiv UA...117 E1
Žasliai LT...85 F2
Žatec CZ...40 B2
Zatišlje LV...79 F3
Zaton HR...54 C4
Zator PL...98 A2
Zaube LV...78 B3
Žaunieriškiai LT...85 E3
Zavala BIH...58 B3
Zavattarello I...46 B1
Zavidovići BIH...55 E3
Zavlaka SRB...55 F3
Zavodnje SLO...54 B1
Zawady
 (Podlaskie) PL...91 E3
Zawady (Śląskie) PL...93 F3
Zawadzkie PL...97 F1
Zawichost PL...95 D3
Zawidów PL...92 B3
Zawidz Kościelny PL...90 A3
Zawiercie PL...98 A1
Zawoja PL...98 A3
Zawonia PL...93 D3
Zawroty PL...90 A2
Žažina HR...54 C2
Zbaraž UA...117 D1
Zbąszyń PL...92 C1
Zbąszynek PL...92 C1
Zbiersk PL...93 E2
Zblewo PL...89 E2
Zbludowice PL...98 C1
Zbójna PL...91 D2
Zbójno PL...89 F3
Zbraslav (Praha) CZ...40 C3
Zbraslavice CZ...41 D3
Zbrosławice PL...97 F1
Zbuczyn-
 Poduchowny PL...95 D2
Žd'ár nad Sázavou CZ...41 D3
Zdenac HR...54 B3
Zdíce CZ...40 C3
Ždírec nad
 Doubravou CZ...41 D3
Zdrelac HR...54 C4
Ždrelo HR...57 D3
Zdunje MK...59 E3
Zduńska Wola PL...93 F2
Zduny (Łódzkie) PL...94 A2
Zduny
 (Wielkopolskie) PL...93 E2
Zdzieszowice PL...97 E1
Žeberiai (Šiauliu) LT...81 D3
Žeberiai (Telšiu) LT...80 C3
Žebertonys LT...85 F2
Zebreira E...24 C2
Zebrene LV...81 D1
Zebrzydowice PL...97 F2
Žednik SRB...55 F1
Zeebrugge B...36 B2
Zefiria GR...109 E2
Żegocina PL...98 B2
Žegra SRB...59 E3
Žegulja BIH...58 B3
Zehdenick D...34 B3
Žeimelis LT...81 E1
Žeimiai (Alytaus) LT...85 E3
Žeimiai (Kauno) LT...85 F1
Žeimiai (Šiauliu) LT...81 D3
Zeist NL...36 C1
Zeitz D...39 E2
Zejtun M...53 F4
Żelazków I...93 E2
Żelazno PL...96 C1

Żelazowa Wola PL...94 B1
Zele B...12 B1
Želechów PL...95 D2
Zelengora BIH...55 F4
Zelenika MNE...58 B3
Zelenogorsk RUS...115 D1
Železná Ruda CZ...40 B4
Železniki SLO...54 A2
Železnik SRB...56 C2
Železnogorsk RUS...115 F2
Zelgauska LV...79 D3
Zélio GR...105 E2
Željezno Polje BIH...55 E3
Žemaičiu Kalvarija LT...80 C2
Žemaičiu
 Naumiestis LT...80 B3
Žemaiteliai LT...86 C2
Žemaitkiemis
 (Alytaus) LT...85 E3
Žemaitkiemis
 (Klaipedos) LT...84 B1
Žemaitkiemis
 (Matiešionys) LT...85 E2
Žemaitkiemis
 (Tartupis) LT...85 E2
Žemaitkiemis
 (Vilniaus) LT...86 B1
Žemale LT...80 C2
Zembrzyce PL...98 A2
Zemgale
 (Demene) LV...83 D3
Zemgale (Ilūkste) LV...83 D2
Zemgale
 (Jelgavas) LV...81 E1
Zemīte LV...77 D3
Zemītes LV...79 D3
Zemkopibas
 Institūts LV...82 B1
Zemnieki LV...81 E1
Žemoji Panemune LT...85 E1
Zenica BIH...55 E4
Zentene LV...77 D3
Zerbst D...34 A4
Zeri I...23 D1
Žerków PL...93 E2
Zermatt CH...17 E3
Zernez CH...43 E3
Zerqan AL...116 C4
Zestoa E...20 A2
Zetel D...33 D3
Zeulenroda D...39 E2
Zeven D...33 E3
Zevenaar NL...37 D1
Zevgaráki GR...104 B2
Zevgolatió GR...104 C4
Zevio I...47 D1
Zg. Jezersko SLO...54 A1

Zgierz PL...94 A2
Zgorzelec PL...92 B3
Zibalai LT...86 B1
Žibavičiai LT...85 F2
Žibininkai LT...80 A2
Žiča SRB...57 D4
Zicavo F...23 F4
Židikai LT...80 C2
Židlochovice CZ...41 E3
Ziębice PL...97 D1
Ziedkalne LV...81 E1
Ziedonis LV...80 C1
Ziegenrück D...39 E2
Žiegždriai LT...85 F2
Zieleniec
 (Dolnośląskie) PL...96 C2
Zieleniewo PL...88 B3
Zielona Góra PL...92 B2
Zielonki PL...98 B2
Ziemelblāzma LV...77 F3
Ziemeli LV...81 F1
Ziemelnieki LV...76 C2
Ziemupe LV...76 A3
Zierikzee NL...36 B1
Ziersdorf A...41 E4
Zierzow D...34 A3
Ziesar D...34 B4
Žiežmariai LT...85 F2
Ziguri LV...79 F3
Zijemlje BIH...55 E4
Zilaiskalns LV...78 B2
Ziles (Dobeles) LV...81 E1
Ziles (Jelgavas) LV...81 E2
Žilina SK...116 B1
Žilinai LT...85 F3
Žilpamūšis LT...81 F1
Zilupe LV...83 F2
Žilviciai LT...81 E3
Zimnicea RO...117 D3
Zin'kiv UA...115 F1
Zindaičiai LT...85 D1
Zingst D...34 A1
Zinnowitz D...34 B2
Zinnwald D...39 E1
Žiobiškis LT...82 C2
Zirc H...116 B2
Zirchow D...34 C2
Žiri SLO...54 A2
Žirje (Otok) HR...58 A4
Zirl A...43 F2
Zirndorf D...39 D3
Zirni LV...81 D1
Ziros GR...110 C4
Zistersdorf A...41 E4
Zitkovac SRB...57 E4
Zitomislići BIH...55 E4
Žitorada SRB...57 E4
Zitsa GR...100 C4
Zittau D...40 C1
Zizdra RUS...115 F3
Zizonys LT...82 B2
Zjum SRB...59 D3

Zlatari SRB...57 D4
Zlaté Hory CZ...41 E2
Zlatica BG...117 D4
Zlatni Pjasaci BG...117 E3
Zlatni rat HR...58 A4
Zlatokop SRB...59 E2
Zławieś Wielka PL...89 E3
Žlebovi BIH...55 F4
Zlēkas LV...76 C3
Zletovo MK...59 F3
Zlín CZ...41 F3
Žlobin BY...115 D3
Złocieniec PL...88 C2
Złoczew PL...93 F3
Zlot SRB...57 E3
Złotniki Kujawskie PL...89 E3
Złotoria
 (Podlaskie) PL...91 E3
Złotoryja PL...92 C3
Złotów PL...89 D2
Złoty Stok PL...97 D1
Žlutice CZ...40 B2
Zmajevo SRB...55 F2
Žmerynka UA...117 E1
Żmigród PL...93 D2
Žminj HR...54 A2
Žmudź PL...95 F3
Znam"janka UA...117 F1
Žnin PL...89 E3
Znojmo CZ...41 E4
Znojno RUS...116 A1
Zöblitz D...39 F2
Zoetermeer NL...36 C1
Żółkiewka PL...95 E3
Zollikofen CH...17 E2
Žoločiv UA...117 D1
Zolotonoša UA...115 F4
Żołynia PL...99 D2
Zonguldak TR...117 F4
Zóni GR...103 E1
Zonianá GR...109 E4
Zonza F...23 F4
Zoodóhos Pigí GR...101 D3
Zoodóhos Pigí GR...105 D4
Żórawina PL...93 D3
Zörbig D...39 E1
Zorgi LV...81 F1
Zorita E...20 A2
Zorita E...25 D3
Žory PL...97 F2
Zoséni (Cēsu) LV...78 C3
Zoséni (Preilu) LV...83 D2
Zosna LV...83 E2
Zossen D...34 B4
Zostautai LT...85 E2
Zosuli LV...78 B3
Zoutkamp NL...32 C3
Zoutleeuw B...12 C1
Zoúzouli GR...101 D3
Žovkva UA...117 D1
Žovti Vody UA...117 F1
Zrin HR...54 C3
Zrze SRB...59 E3
Zschopau D...39 F2
Zubcov RUS...115 F2
Zubin Potoku SRB...59 D2
Žūbiškes LT...85 F2
Zubrzyca Górna PL...98 A3
Žuč SRB...59 D2
Zucaina E...27 D2
Zudar D...34 B2

Zuera E...20 C4
Zufre E...25 D4
Zug CH...17 F1
Zuidlaren NL...32 C3
Zújar E...30 A2
Zujūnai LT...86 B2
Žukai LT...84 C1
Žukaičiai LT...85 D1
Žukovka RUS...115 F3
Żuków (Zachodnio-
 pomorskie) PL...88 B3
Żukowice PL...92 C2
Żukowo PL...89 E1
Zukuli LV...83 E2
Žuljana HR...58 A3
Zülpich D...13 D1
Zumaia E...20 A2
Zumarraga E...20 A2
Zundert NL...36 C1
Zuoz CH...43 E3
Županja HR...55 E2
Žur SRB...59 D3
Žūras LV...76 B2
Žuravica HR...55 E2
Zürich CH...17 F1
Žuromin PL...90 A3
Zurrieq M...53 F4
Zürs A...43 E2
Zusmarshausen D...43 E1
Žut (Otok) HR...54 C4
Žuta Lokva HR...54 B3
Zutphen NL...37 D1
Žuvintai LT...85 E3
Žužemberk SLO...54 B2
Zvaigzne LV...81 F2
Zvečan SRB...59 D2
Zvejniekciems LV...77 F3
Zvejnieki LV...81 D1
Zvenyhorodka UA...117 F1
Žviguri LV...78 B2
Žvingiai LT...80 C3
Žvirblaičiai LT...80 B3
Žvirgždaičiai LT...85 E2
Žvirgždenai LT...85 F3
Zvirgzdene
 (Zviergzdine) LV...83 F1
Zvolen SK...116 B2
Zvonce SRB...57 F4
Zvornik BIH...55 F3
Žvyriai LT...85 E2
Zwardoń PL...97 F3
Zweibrücken D...13 E2
Zweisimmen CH...17 E2
Zwenkau D...39 E1
Zwettl A...41 D4
Zwettl an der Rodl A...40 C4
Zwickau D...39 F2
Zwiefalten D...43 D1
Zwierzyniec PL...99 E1
Zwiesel D...39 F4
Zwijndrecht NL...36 C1
Zwoleń PL...94 C3
Zwolle NL...32 C4
Zwönitz D...39 F2
Żychlin PL...94 A1
Žygaičiai LT...84 C1
Žygėnai LT...85 E1
Żyglin PL...98 A1
Żyrardów PL...94 B2
Žytkavičy BY...115 D3
Żytno PL...94 A3
Žytomyr UA...115 E4
Żywiec PL...97 F3

ZÜRICH